PC System Programming

by Michael Tischer

Abacus

A Data Becker Book

Printed in U.S.A.
10 9 8 7 6

Every effort has been made to ensure complete and accurate information concerning the material presented in this book. However, Abacus can neither guarantee nor be held legally responsible for any mistakes in printing or faulty instructions contained in this book. The authors always appreciate receiving notice of any errors or misprints.

This book contains trade names and trademarks of many companies and products. Any mention of these names or trademarks in this book are not intended to either convey endorsement or other associations with this book.

PC-DOS, IBM PC, XT, AT, PS/2, OS/2 and PC-BASIC are trademarks or registered trademarks of International Business Machines Corporation. Ventura Publisher is a trademark or registered trademark of Xerox Corporation. GEM and CP/M are trademarks or registered trademarks of Digital Research Corporation. Microsoft Works, Microsoft Quick C, Microsoft Windows, MS-DOS, XENIX and GW-BASIC are trademarks or registered trademarks of Microsoft Corporation. Lotus 1-2-3 is a trademark or registered trademark of Lotus Development Corporation. dBASE is a registered trademark of Ashton-Tate, Inc. Sidekick, Turbo C and Turbo Pascal are trademarks or registered trademarks of Borland International. UNIX is a registered trademark of Bell Laboratories. Mickey Mouse is a registered trademark of Walt Disney Corporation.

Library of Congress Cataloging-in-Publication Data
Tischer, Michael, 1953-
PC system programming for developers / Michael Tischer.
p. cm.
"A Data Becker book."
ISBN 1-55755-036-0
1. System programming (computer science) 2. Microcomputers-Programming.
I. Title
QA76.66.T57 1989 005.265--dc20 85-18350

Table of Contents

Chapter 1

Introduction

A few years ago, my computer was a small home computer. When I became interested in the IBM PC, I had to learn a lot of new things. I learned about MS-DOS and became familiar with 8088 assembly language. I soon reached a point where I started developing commercial PC programs in partnership with my friend Axel Sellemerten. All of this happened some time ago, but I still clearly remember sitting at my desk, looking through dozens of PC books and technical manuals, trying to find a critical piece of information.

These books and manuals were expensive and hard to find. Besides, none of them covered all aspects of the PC. Some books tell you about PC hardware or the BIOS or DOS. I could never find a book that dealt with the PC as a total system. No single book was able to provide me with a complete system overview.

This book is the result of my experience with all of these references. The three main areas of the PC (hardware, the BIOS and DOS) are combined in this book from a software developer's point of view. This book was written to serve as an instruction book as well as a reference manual. It is not, and was never intended to be, a book for the beginner. The book assumes that you're familiar with MS-DOS and are able to program in one of the four most popular PC programming languages (machine language, BASIC, Pascal or C).

Organization

The book is divided into five parts. Part 1 (Chapters 1-5) gives an introduction to the PC's internal components. Part 2 (Chapter 6) describes the Disk Operating System (DOS) and Part 3 (Chapter 7) describes the Basic Input Output System (BIOS). PC hardware that is not part of the central processor is discussed in Part 4 (Chapters 8-18). Part 5 (Chapter 19) describes the interaction between these components and the keyboard. The book concludes with a large reference section (Appendices) containing all functions of DOS and the BIOS, among other things.

To understand the content of this book, you must first know something about the different number systems used in computers. Readers unfamiliar with the binary and hexadecimal number systems should read Appendix G (Introduction to Number Systems) before continuing.

Chapters 2 through 5 contain descriptions of PC microprocessors and interrupts. If you're an experienced assembly language programmer you can skip these chapters, but you may learn something new by reading them anyway.

BASIC, Pascal and C programmers should read Chapters 2 and 3 and should work through the subsections in Chapter 4 devoted to your preferred language. Chapter 5 is devoted exclusively to assembly language programming and may be skipped.

Chapter 2

The PC's Brain

While working with the PC, many users have wondered about its ability to solve complex problems. Users often attribute these abilities to the software or operating system. The fact is, hardware is as important as the software.

Microprocessor

The *microprocessor* is the brain of the PC. It understands a limited number of machine language instructions and processes or executes programs in this machine language. These instructions are very simple and can't be compared to commands in *high level* languages such as BASIC, Pascal or C. Commands in these languages must be translated into a large number of machine language instructions that the PC's microprocessor can then execute. For example, displaying text with the BASIC PRINT statement requires the equivalent of several hundred machine language instructions.

Machine language instructions differ for each microprocessor used in different computers. When you hear someone talk about Z-80, 6502 or 8088 machine language, these terms refer to the microprocessor being programmed.

Intel's 80xx series

The PC has its own family of microprocessor chips, all designed by the Intel Corporation. The figure on the next page describes the Intel 80xx family tree. Your PC may contain an 8086, an 8088 (used in the PC/XT), an 80186, an 80286 (used in the AT) or even an 80386 microprocessor. The first generation of this group (the 8086) was developed in 1978. The successors of the 8086 were different from the original chip. The 8088 is actually a step backward since it has the same internal structure and instructions of the 8086, but is slower than the 8086. The reason is that the 8086 transfers 16 bits (2 bytes) between memory and the microprocessor at one time. The 8088 is slower since it transfers only 8 bits (1 byte) at one time.

Multiprocessing

The three other microprocessors of this family are improved versions of the 8086. The 80186 offers auxiliary functions. The 80286 has additional registers and extended addressing capabilities. The 80286's biggest advantages over its predecessors are its *multiprocessing* and *virtual memory* capabilities. Multiprocessing allows several programs to execute at the same time, such as compiling a program while using a word processor. This capability, which is based on the fast switching between the individual programs, can also be implemented through software (e.g., Microsoft Windows®), but working directly through the processor is more efficient.

Virtual memory

Virtual memory means that a program appears to use much more memory than is available in the computer's RAM. Portions of the programs or data which don't fit into memory are temporarily stored on the mass storage device (floppy or hard disk). The computer loads these sections into RAM as needed. The CPU and the operating system share the task of virtual memory management. Earlier versions of MS-DOS don't support the multiprocessing or virtual memory capabilities of the 80286, so most AT computers aren't working to their full potential.

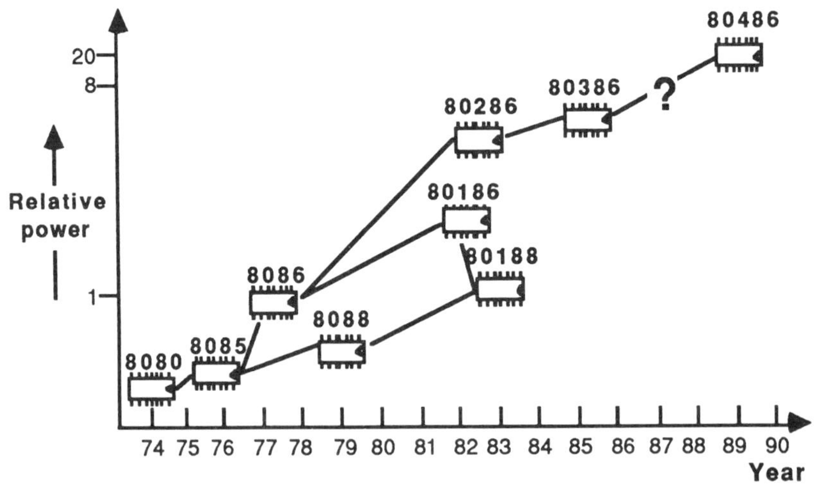

The Intel 80xx processor family

The 80386 represents current state of the art technology. It has a more extensive instruction set than the 80286, and offers additional memory protection features.

These processors are all *upwardly compatible* with software. This means that machine language programs developed for the 8086 can be executed on the other processors of this series. On the other hand, a program written for the 80386 may not run correctly on the 80286 or the 8088, because instructions available on the 80386 may not be available in the earlier processors.

Throughout this book the PC processor is designated as the 8088, even though your PC may use a different processor.

2.1 8088 Registers

Registers are memory locations within the processor itself, instead of in RAM. These registers can be accessed much faster than RAM. In addition, registers are specialized memory locations. The CPU performs arithmetic and logical operations using its registers.

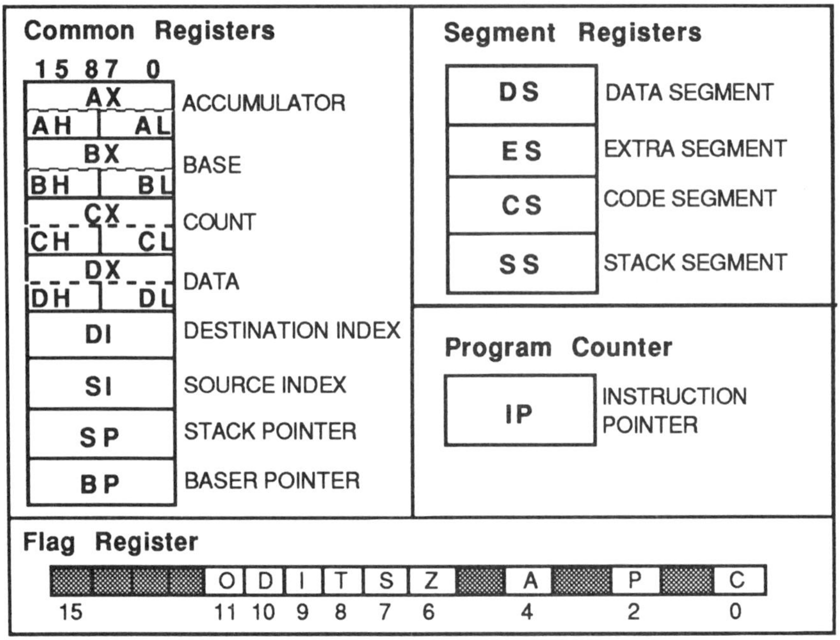

8088 registers

All registers are 16 bits (2 bytes) in size. If all 16 bits of a register contain a 1, this is the largest number that can be represented within 16 bits. This number is the decimal number 65535. Therefore, a register can contain any value from 0 to 65535.

Register groupings

As shown in the above figure, registers are divided into four groups: common registers, segment registers, the program counter and the flag register. The different register assignments are designed to duplicate the way in which a program processes data—which is the basic task of a microprocessor.

The disk operating system and the routines stored in ROM use the common registers a great deal, especially the AX, BX, CX and DX registers. The contents of these registers tell DOS what tasks it should perform and which data to use for execution.

These registers are affected mainly by mathematical (addition, subtraction, etc.) and input/output instructions. They are assigned a special position within the registers of the 8088 because they can be separated into two 8-bit (1-byte) registers. Each common register may be thought to consist of three registers: a single 16-bit register, or two smaller 8-bit registers.

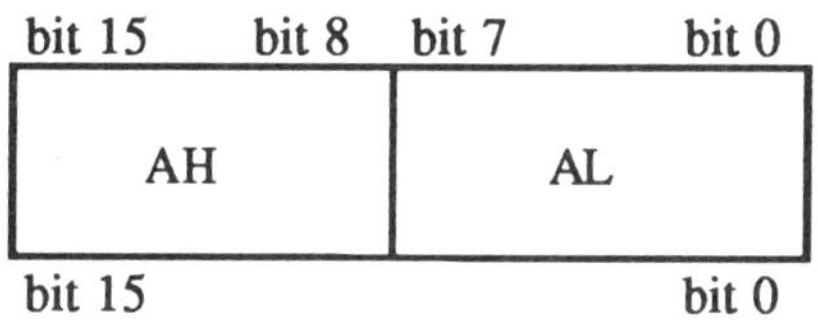

AX register

The registers have designators of H (high) and L (low). Thus the 16-bit AX register may be divided into an 8-bit AH and an 8-bit AL register. The H and the L register designators occur in such a way that the L register contains the lower 8 bits (bit 0 through 7) of the X register, and the H register the higher 8 bits (bits 8 through 15) of the X register. The AH register consists of bits 8-15 and the AL register of bits 0-7 of the AX register. However, the three registers cannot be considered independent of each other. For example, if bit 3 of the AH register is changed, then the value of bit 11 of the AX register also changes automatically. The values change in both the AH and the AX registers. The value of the AL register remains constant since it is made of bits 0-7 of the AX register (bit 11 of the AX register does not belong to it). This connection between the AX, the AH and the AL register is also valid for all other common registers and can be expressed mathematically.

You can determine the value of the X register from the values of the H and the L registers, and vice versa. To calculate the value of the X register, multiply the value of the H register by 256 and add the value of the L register.

Example: The value of the CH register is 10, the value of the CL register is 118. The value of the CX register results from CH*256+CL, which is 10*256+118 = 2678.

Specifying register CH or CL, you can read or write an 8-bit data item from or to any memory location. Specifying register CX, you can read or write a 16-bit data item from or to a memory location.

2.2 Segment and Offset Addressing

One of the design goals of the 8088 was to provide an instruction set that was superior to the earlier 8-bit microprocessors (6502, Z80, etc.). A second goal was to provide easy access to more than 64 kilobytes of memory. This goal was of special importance since increasing processor capabilities allow programmers to write more complex applications, which in turn require more memory. The designers of the 8088 increased the memory capacity or *address space* of the microprocessor by more than 16 times to one megabyte.

Address register

The number of memory locations which a processor can access depends on the width of the *address register*. Since every memory location is accessed by specifying a unique number or *address*, the maximum value contained in the address register determines the address space. Earlier microprocessors used a 16-bit address register enabling access to addresses from 0 to 65535. This corresponds to the 64K memory capacity of these processors.

To address one megabyte of memory the address register must be at least 20 bits wide. At the time the 8088 was developed, it was impossible to use a 20-bit address register, so the designers used an alternate way to achieve the 20-bit width: the contents of two different 16-bit numbers are used to form the 20-bit address.

Segment register

One of the numbers is contained in a *segment register*. The 8088 has four segment registers. The second number is contained in another register or in a memory location. To form a 20-bit number, the contents of the segment register are shifted left by 4 bits (thereby multiplying the value by 16) and the second number is added to the first.

Segment and offset addresses

These addresses are the *segment address* and the *offset address*. The segment address is formed by a segment register and indicates the start of a segment of memory. During the address formulation, the offset address is added to the segment address. The offset address indicates the number of the memory location within the segment whose beginning was defined by the segment register. Since the offset address can never be larger than 16 bits, a segment can be no larger than 65,535 bytes (64K).

Segmented address

The *segmented address* results from the combined segment and offset addresses. This segmented address specifies the exact number of the memory location which should be accessed. Unlike the segmented address, the segment and the offset addresses are *relative addresses* or *relative offsets*.

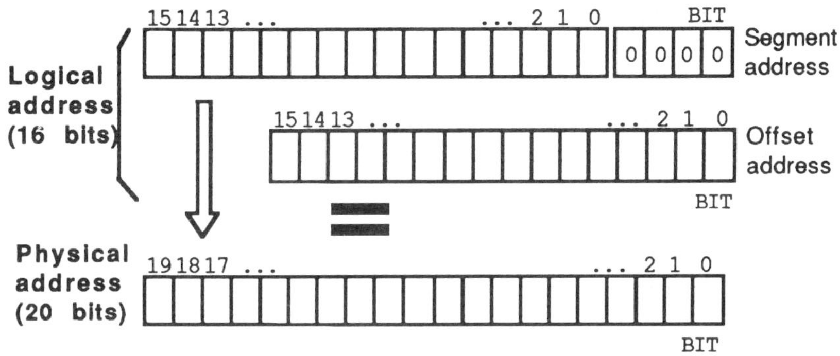

Memory structure using segment and offset addresses

A segment cannot start at every one of the million or so memory locations. Multiplying the segment register by 16 always produces a segment address that is divisible by 16. For example, it's not possible for a segment to begin at memory location 22.

Combining the segment and offset addresses requires special notation to indicate a memory location's address. This notation consists of the segment address in four-digit hexadecimal format, followed by a colon, and the offset address in four-digit hexadecimal format. For example, a memory location with a segment address of 2000H and an offset address of AF3H would appear in this notation as 2000:0AF3. Because of this notation, you can omit the H suffix from hexadecimal numbers.

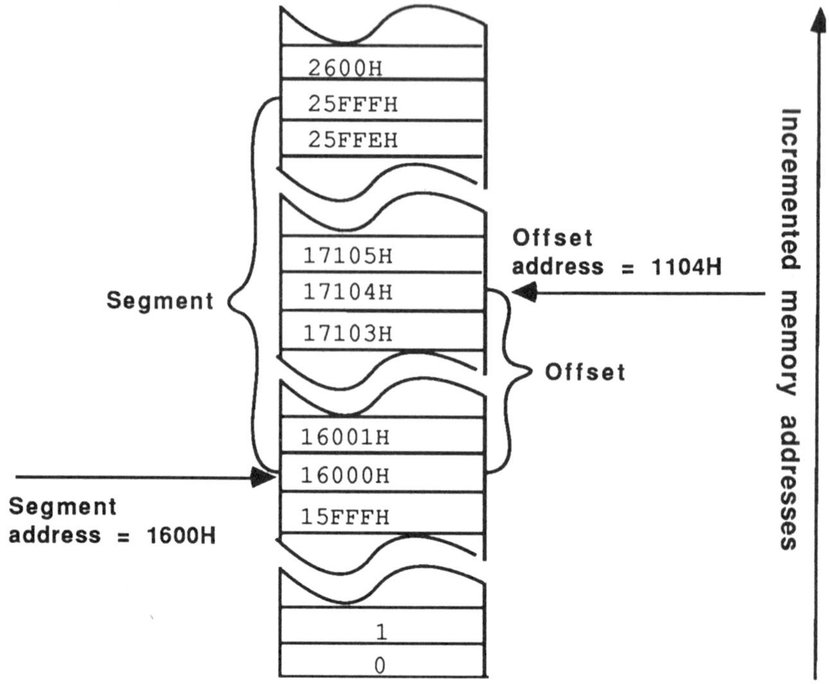

Segment and offset address

The 8088 has four segment registers, which have special roles in the execution of an assembly language program. There are four registers to accommodate the basic structure of any program. A program consists of a set of instructions (code). There are also variables and data items that are processed by the program. A structured program keeps the code and data separate from each other while they reside in memory. Assigning code and data their own segments conveniently separates them.

Each needs a segment address and a segment register. The CS (Code Segment) register uses the IP (Instruction Pointer) register as the offset address. The CS then determines the address at which the next assembly language instruction is located. The IP is also called the Program Counter. When the processor executes the current instruction, the IP register is automatically incremented to point to the next assembly language instruction. This ensures the execution of instructions in the correct order.

Like the CS register, the DS (Data Segment) register contains the segment address of the data which the program accesses (writing or reading data to or from memory). The offset address is added to the content of the DS register and may be contained in another register or may be contained as part of the current instruction.

The SS (Stack Segment) register specifies the starting address of the *stack*. The stack acts as temporary storage space by some assembly language programs. It allows fast storage and retrieval of data for various instructions. For example, when the CALL instruction is executed, the processor places the return address on the stack. The SS register and either the SP or BP registers form the address that is pushed onto the stack.

The last segment register is the ES (Extra Segment) register. It is used by some assembly language instructions to address more than 64K of data or to transfer data between two different segments of memory.

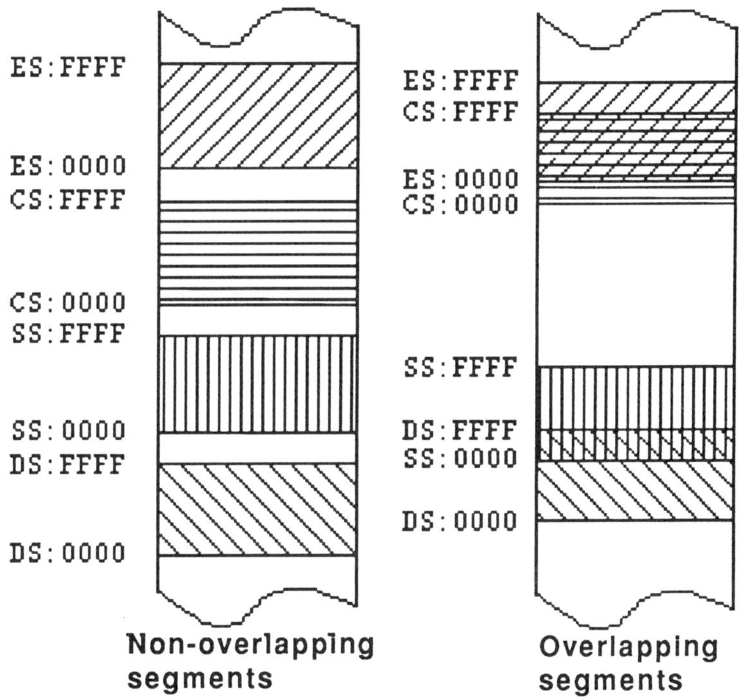

Overlapping and non-overlapping segments

As the figure above shows, two segment registers can specify areas of memory which overlap, or are completely different from one another. In many cases, a program doesn't require a full 64K segment for storing code or data. You can conserve memory by overlapping the segments. For example, you can store data immediately following the program code by setting the DS and CS registers accordingly.

The flag register is of special importance. Various bits in this register indicate or signal the special conditions which may occur during execution of an assembly language instruction. For example, if an arithmetic operation results in a negative number, the processor sets the S (sign) flag to 1 to indicate this change.

The C (carry) flag is set to 1 if the sum of two 8-bit numbers cannot be represented as an 8-bit number.

As the figure above shows, the processor doesn't use all 16 bits of this register. The unused bits normally contain the value 0.

This ends our short trip into the PC's brain. If you didn't quite follow some of these concepts, the sample application programs in the sections on the BIOS and DOS functions should help you understand.

2.3 The CPU Support Chips

The microprocessor is the computer's brain, and is probably the most intelligent component in a computer system. However, it cannot supervise all the computer's functions on its own. For this reason, other components called support chips perform many other tasks, leaving the processor to concentrate on its primary task of executing assembly language programs.

These support chips communicate with and control external peripherals such as a disk drive or the screen display.

Some of these support chips can be programmed using the assembly language instructions IN and OUT. Since the programming of most support chips is very complex, we recommend that you leave this up to DOS, unless you have a complete understanding of the structure and operation of these chips.

The following sections define the most important support chips in the PC.

2.3.1 The DMA Controller

This chip gets its name from the acronym DMA which stands for Direct Memory Access. This chip can directly write data to or read data from RAM. The DMA controller performs disk input/output operations, moving data from RAM to disk or from disk to RAM. This relieves the processor of this task and accelerates program execution.

2.3.2 The Interrupt Controller

Interrupts are signals from individual components of the system to get the CPU's attention and to initiate certain tasks. Several interrupts or requests for services from different system components can be outstanding at one time. These requests are initially handled by the interrupt controller, which passes them on to the CPU. It assigns priority to every interrupt request according to its source and passes the request with the highest priority to the CPU. The interrupt controller in the PC/XT can process up to 8 interrupt requests at the same time. ATs require more power, so they use two interconnected interrupt controllers which can process up to 15 interrupt requests simultaneously.

2.3.3 The Programmable Peripheral Interface

This chip provides a link between the CPU and the peripherals such as the keyboard or an audio speaker. However, it only operates as a mediator, addressed by the CPU for unit access and transmission of certain signals. You cannot bypass the PPI for direct communication between the CPU and peripherals.

2.3.4 The Clock

If the microprocessor is the brain of the computer, then the clock could be considered the heart of the computer. This heart beats several million times a second (about 14.3 megaHertz) and paces the microprocessor and the other chips in the system. Since almost none of the chips operate at such high frequencies, each support chip modifies the clock frequency to its own requirements.

2.3.5 The Timer

The timer chip can be used as a counter and timekeeper. This chip transmits constant electrical pulses from one of its output pins. The frequency of these pulses can be programmed as needed, and each output pin can have its own frequency. Each output pin leads to another component. One line goes to the audio speaker and another to the interrupt controller. The line to the interrupt controller triggers interrupt 8 at every pulse, which advances the timer count.

2.3.6 The Screen Controller

Unlike the chips discussed up until now, the CRT (Cathode Ray Tube) controller is separate from the main circuit board of the PC. You'll find this chip on the video board which is mounted in one of the computer's expansion slots. Even though there are many boards that differ widely in their capabilities (monochrome display, color display, etc.), all video boards are based on the 6845 CRT controller. It produces a display on the monitor connected to the computer. The controller has several internal registers which control the output of the display.

2.3.7 The Disk Controller

This chip is also usually located on an expansion board. It is addressed by the operating system and controls the functions of the disk drive. It moves the read/write head of the disk drive over the disk, reads data from the disk and writes data to the disk.

2.3.8 The Math Coprocessors (8087/80287/80387)

The 8088, 80286 and the 80386 are not capable of performing floating point arithmetic operations directly. There is a socket on the main circuit board of the PC for adding a special math coprocessor. The PC/XT uses the 8087, the AT the 80287 and the new 80386 uses the 80387 coprocessor.

While floating point arithmetic can be performed using software routines, a math coprocessor is up to 100 times faster. The 8087 and the 80287 can perform basic math functions such as addition, subtraction, multiplication and division, as well as the trigonometric functions sine, cosine, etc. They can also compute square roots of numbers.

In general, only a few application software packages support the math coprocessors.

2.4 The CPU and Memory

While the chips described up until now are intelligent system components, *memory* is a passive element. Data can be stored and later retrieved from memory. Each memory location is used to store one byte (8 bits) of data. Memory locations are identified by a unique address, starting from zero.

The support chips communicate with memory using a *bus* or path over which the electronic signals travel.

Address bus

The *address bus* carries the number of the memory location to be accessed. The signals on the bus represent a binary number whose value indicates the memory location for access. Since only those memory locations represented on the address bus can be accessed, the number which make up the bus lines determine the number of addressable memory locations.

The PC/XT has a 20-bit address bus and can address a maximum of 2^{20} (about 1 million) different memory locations. The AT has a 24-bit address bus and can address more than 16 million memory locations.

Data bus

Once the bus knows the address of the memory location to be accessed, data can be transferred between the individual chips and the memory location over the *data bus*. The number of lines in this circuit determine how many bits are transferred to or from memory simultaneously.

The PC/XT has 8 lines so it can transfer one byte at a time. However, since the 8088 is a 16-bit processor, 16-bit data must often be transferred. There aren't enough lines to transfer 16-bit data, so the system divides a 16-bit data item into two 8-bit numbers. These two 8-bit data bytes are transferred one after the other along the bus.

The 8086 and 80286 processors can transfer 16 bits simultaneously over their 16-bit-wide data buses. This is one reason why the AT executes programs faster than the 8088 processor. The 80386 processor can transfer 32 bits at a time.

Word storage

All members of the Intel 80xx processor family share the same method of storing words (16-bit data) in memory. The lower numbered memory location contains bits 0-7 (the low byte) and the higher numbered memory location contains bits 8-15 (the high byte). For example, if you store the word 3F87H starting at address 0000:0400, memory location 0000:0400 accepts the low byte 87H and memory location 0000:0401 accepts the high byte 3FH.

Two details were left out of the discussion of memory so far:

1.) The processor doesn't care if a memory address is located in a RAM chip or a ROM chip. The main difference between RAM and ROM lies in the fact that you can't write or store new data into ROM (hence its name: Read Only Memory).

2.) The addressable space of the microprocessor (1 megabyte) is allocated into 16 storage segments of 64K each. This is an almost universal division used on IBM PC/XTs and most compatible machines.

Block	Addresses	Description
15	F000:0000-F000:FFFF	BIOS ROM
14	E000:0000-E000:FFFF	ROM cartridge
13	D000:0000-D000:FFFF	ROM cartridge
12	C000:0000-C000:FFFF	additional BIOS ROM
11	B000:0000-B000:FFFF	video RAM
10	A000:0000-A000:FFFF	additional video RAM
9	9000:0000-9000:FFFF	RAM up to 640K
8	8000:0000-8000:FFFF	RAM up to 576K
7	7000:0000-7000:FFFF	RAM up to 512K
6	6000:0000-6000:FFFF	RAM up to 448K
5	5000:0000-5000:FFFF	RAM up to 384K
4	4000:0000-4000:FFFF	RAM up to 320K
3	3000:0000-3000:FFFF	RAM up to 256K
2	2000:0000-2000:FFFF	RAM up to 192K
1	1000:0000-1000:FFFF	RAM up to 128K
0	0000:0000-0000:FFFF	RAM up to 64K, CPU vector table, DOS & BIOS variables

Memory allocation

The first 10 memory segments are reserved for the main RAM memory, limiting maximum RAM to 640K. A computer's memory size may differ from one PC manufacturer to another but has at least 64K installed in segment 0. If you install additional RAM, its first memory address must immediately follow the last existing memory address, since no gaps may exist between individual RAM memory segments. Memory segment 0 has a special role since it contains important data and operating system routines.

Memory segment A follows the RAM memory. In this case, an EGA (Extended Graphics Adapter) is installed. This board uses the memory for the screen display in different graphic modes.

Memory segment B is reserved for a monochrome or color graphics board. They share the segment as screen memory. The monochrome board uses the lower 32K and the color board uses the upper 32K. Each board uses only as much memory as it needs for the screen display. The monochrome board uses 4K; the color board uses 16K because of the additional color capabilities.

The next memory segment contains ROM beginning at segment C. Some computers store the BIOS routines which aren't part of the original BIOS kernel at this location. For example, the XT uses these routines for hard disk support. Since this area isn't fully utilized, it is possible that BIOS routines supporting future hardware enhancements will also be placed in this memory range.

ROM cartridges

Segments D and E are reserved for *ROM cartridges*. These cartridges extend the computer with certain ROM routines. The PC has rarely used them and the area usually remains unused.

Segment F contains the actual BIOS routines, the system loader and the ROM BASIC available on many computers.

Chapter 3

Introduction to Interrupts

This chapter presents a view of interrupts, which are vitally important to the operation of the 8088 processor. An *interrupt* is a signal from a peripheral device or a request from a program to perform a specific service. When an interrupt occurs, the currently executing program is temporarily suspended and an *interrupt routine* begins execution to handle the condition that caused the interrupt.

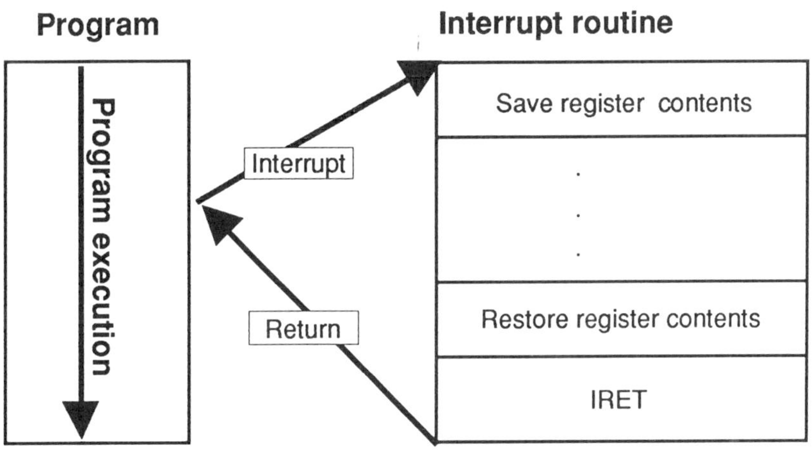

Program interrupt

When a program is suspended, the processor saves the contents of the CS and IP registers on the stack, and begins the interrupt routine. After the interrupt routine has completed its task, it issues the IRET (Interrupt RETurn) instruction which restores the contents of the CS and IP registers from the stack, thus resuming the program.

The interrupt routine saves and restores contents of the other registers before returning to the interrupted program.

3.1 The Structure of the Interrupt Vector Table

So far we've talked about a single interrupt and a single interrupt routine. In fact, the 8088 has 256 possible interrupts numbered from 0 to 255, not just one.

Each interrupt has an associated *interrupt routine* to handle the particular condition. To organize the 256 interrupts, the starting address of the corresponding interrupt routines are arranged in the *interrupt vector table.*

When an interrupt occurs, the processor automatically retrieves the starting address of the interrupt routine from the interrupt vector table.

The starting address of each interrupt routine is specified in the table in terms of the offset address and segment address. Both addresses are 16 bits (2 bytes) wide. Therefore each table entry occupies 4 bytes. The total length of the table is 256*4 or 1024 bytes (1K).

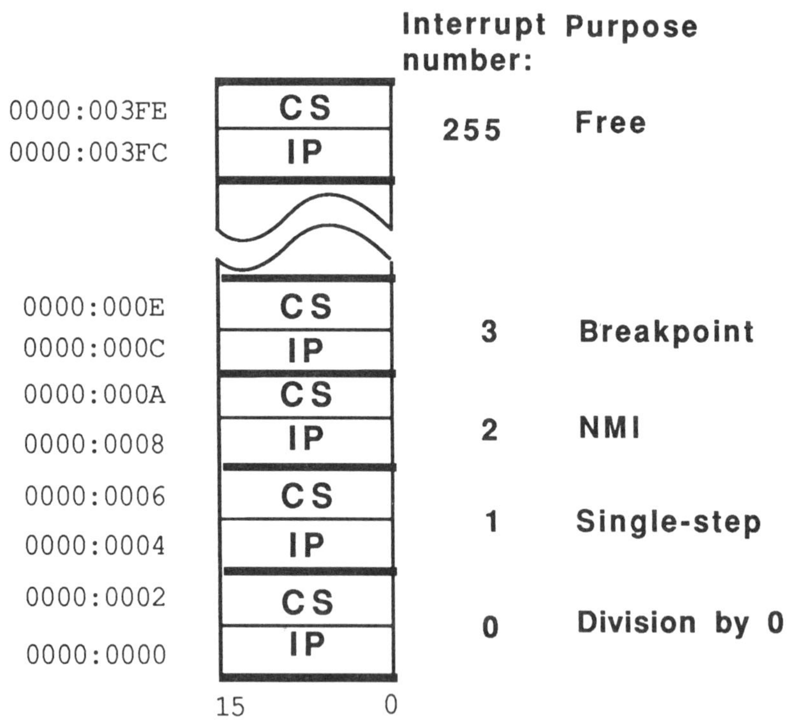

Interrupt vector table

The table itself is located in memory from 0H to 3FFH. Since the interrupt's number is the same as the table entry for the corresponding interrupt routine, the interrupt routine address for interrupt 0 is the zero table entry in locations 0H-3H.

Memory locations 4H—7H contain the address for the interrupt routine for interrupt 1, etc. The last interrupt, interrupt 255, occupies the end of the table at locations 3FCH—3FFH.

To calculate the starting address of an interrupt, simply multiply the interrupt number by four.

Advantages

An advantage of using the interrupt vector table is that it's easy to change an entry in the table to the starting address of a user-written interrupt routine. This makes a new interrupt routine available to any program which can invoke the routine simply by executing the corresponding interrupt instruction.

The next section explains the different types of interrupts and how they are used in the system.

3.2 Interrupt Types

Until now, we haven't talked about different types of interrupts. There are two major types of interrupts—hardware interrupts and software interrupts.

The figure below shows the different interrupt types.

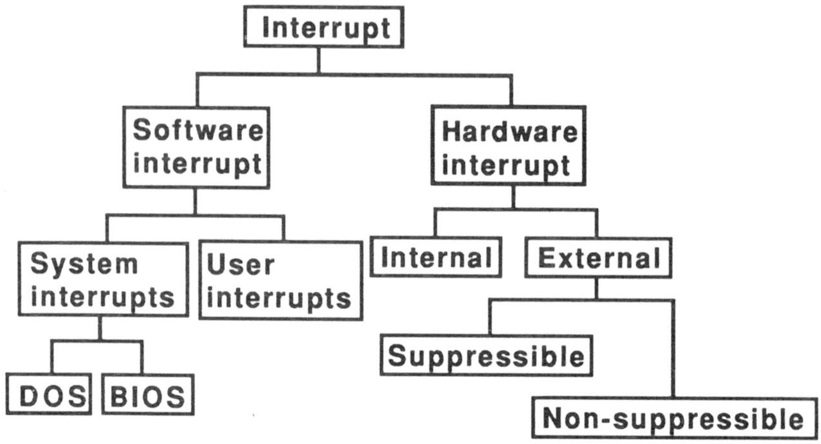

Interrupt types

3.2.1 Software Interrupts

A *software interrupt* is an interrupt called by the INT instruction in a machine language program. The INT instruction includes the number of the interrupt to be signalled. For example, the instruction to call interrupt 5, which sends a hardcopy of the current screen to the printer, appears as INT 5. The INT instruction allows you to call any one of the 256 interrupts.

Software interrupts make it possible to use many of the basic operating system services from either the assembler (or machine language) level or from many of the higher level languages which support interrupt processing.

3.2.2 Hardware Interrupts

A hardware device such as a disk drive or keyboard can trigger a *hardware interrupt.* This is a simple and efficient mechanism for handling events which require attention.

One example is the keyboard. When you press or release a key, interrupt 9 (the keyboard interrupt) is signalled. The standard DOS interrupt routine responds by placing the character value corresponding to the key that was pressed into the keyboard buffer following any value which may have been previously there. If the keyboard buffer is full, the routine generates a short beep. As in any other interrupt, the original program continues after the completion of the interrupt routine.

Maskable interrupts

This interrupt is designated as an external hardware interrupt, because it was triggered by an external device. For these interrupts, a distinction is also made between *maskable* and *non-maskable* interrupts. The keyboard interrupt just described belongs in the maskable interrupt category. You can mask (disable) this interrupt by using the assembler instruction STI (SeT Interrupt flag). If you mask interrupt 9H, the keyboard ignores any characters you type. To reverse this condition, use the CLI instruction (CLear Interrupt flag) to re-enable the interrupt.

Non-maskable interrupts

In contrast, a non-maskable interrupt cannot be disabled by the STI instruction. One example is interrupt 2. This interrupt indicates an error in the PC's memory. It displays a message on the screen that one or more of the RAM chips is defective and should be replaced.

The last interrupt type to be described is the internal hardware interrupt. The processors on the main circuit board of the PC trigger this interrupt. One example is interrupt 8 which is designated as a timer interrupt. The timer triggers this interrupt at a rate of 12.8 times per second. It also disables the disk drive motor if no disk access is in progress.

3.3 Interrupts at a Glance

The tables here show the significance which these interrupts occupy in the control and use of the PC. The next few chapters explain these interrupts in more detail.

Nr.	Vector	Purpose
00	000 - 003	CPU: Division by zero
01	004 - 007	CPU: Single step
02	008 - 00B	CPU: NMI (Error in RAM chip)
03	00C - 00F	CPU: Breakpoint
04	010 - 013	CPU: Numeric overflow
05	014 - 017	Hardcopy
06	018 - 01B	Unknown instruction (80286 only)
07	01D - 01F	reserved
08	020 - 023	IRQ0: Timer (Call 18.2 per/sec.)
09	024 - 027	IRQ1: Keyboard
0A	028 - 02B	IRQ2: Second 8259 (AT only)
0B	02C - 02F	IRQ3: Serial interface 2
0C	030 - 033	IRQ4: Serial interface 1
0D	034 - 037	IRQ5: Hard disk
0E	038 - 03B	IRQ6: Diskette
0F	03C - 03F	IRQ7: Printer
10	040 - 043	BIOS: Video functions
11	044 - 047	BIOS: Determine configuration
12	048 - 04B	BIOS: Determine RAM storage size
13	04C - 04F	BIOS: Diskette/hard disk functions
14	050 - 053	BIOS: Access to serial interface
15	054 - 057	BIOS: Cassette/enhanced functions
16	058 - 05B	BIOS: Keyboard sensing
17	05C - 05F	BIOS: Access to parallel printer
18	060 - 063	Call of ROM-BASIC
19	064 - 067	BIOS: System boot (ALT+CTRL+DEL)
1A	068 - 06B	BIOS: Read time/date
1B	06C - 06F	Break key not activated (not CTRL-C)
1C	070 - 073	called after every INT 08
1D	074 - 077	Address of the video parameter table
1E	078 - 07B	Address of the disk parameter table
1F	07C - 07F	Address of the character bit pattern
20	080 - 083	DOS: Terminate program
21	084 - 087	DOS: Call DOS function
22	088 - 08B	Address of DOS end of program routine
23	08C - 08F	Address of DOS CTRL-BREAK routine
24	090 - 093	Address of DOS error routine
25	094 - 097	DOS: Read diskette/hard disk
26	098 - 09B	DOS: Write diskette/hard disk
27	09C - 09F	DOS: End Prg., remain resident
28-	0A0 -	Reserved for various, non-
3F	- 0FF	documented DOS functions
40	100 - 103	BIOS: diskette functions
41	104 - 107	Address of hard disk table 1
42-	108 -	Reserved
45	- 117	
46	118 - 11B	Address of hard disk table 2
47-	11C -	can be used by application programs
49	- 127	for any purpose

Nr.	Vector	Purpose
4A	128 - 12B	Alarm time reached (AT only)
4B-	12C -	Can be used by application programs
67	- 19F	for any purpose
68-	1A0 -	Unused
6F	- 1BF	
70	1C0 - 1C3	IRQ08: Realtime clock (AT only)
71	1C4 - 1C7	IRQ09: (AT only)
72	1C8 - 1CB	IRQ10: (AT only)
73	1CC - 1CF	IRQ11: (AT only)
74	1D0 - 1D3	IRQ12: (AT only)
75	1D4 - 1D7	IRQ13: 80287 NMI (AT only)
76	1D8 - 1DB	IRQ14: Hard disk (AT only)
77	1DC - 1DF	IRQ15: (AT only)
78-	1E0 -	Unused
7F	- 1FF	
80-	200 -	Used by the BASIC
F0	- 3C3	interpreter
F1-	3C4 -	Unused
FF	- 3CF	

General overview—interrupts

Chapter 4

Using Interrupts from High Level Languages

The assembly language programmer can invoke an interrupt by loading the parameters required by the interrupt routine into designated registers and executing the INT instruction. Although these capabilities aren't available in all higher level languages, some languages such as Turbo Pascal®, Turbo C® and Microsoft C® have built-in functions, procedures or subroutines to call the interrupt.

A BASIC programmer can call an interrupt using a short assembly language program. You'll find an example of this in Section 4.1.

This chapter provides information on calling interrupts from Pascal, BASIC and C. Each describes how interrupts can be called in the particular language and the rules the programmer must observe. Each section concludes with a short demonstration program.

Read through the section devoted to the language with which you feel most comfortable. A comparison of the three sample programs could be interesting for those of you who wish to compare the similarities and differences in the three languages.

The programs are only examples. Experiment as much as you want–you won't damage your computer if you change them a little.

4.1 Interrupt Calls from BASIC

The two most commonly used BASIC interpreters are BASICA (from IBM) and GW-BASIC (from Microsoft). This book refers to GW-BASIC, since it can be used on IBM PCs as well as any compatible PC. The command sets of both are nearly identical.

GW-BASIC does not have a function for calling interrupts. However, the CALL command can be used to execute a machine language program. You can also use the CALL command to pass certain parameters to the called program. The called machine language program must be located in the 64K used by GW-BASIC for program statements and variable storage. Because of this, the interpreter must be told to reserve part of program memory for the machine language routine. Otherwise the program or variables may overwrite the machine language routine, causing a system crash. You can reserve memory directly when you call BASIC from the operating system. Enter the name GWBASIC followed by the /M: parameter. After the colon, enter the highest memory location you want used by BASIC. For example, since the sample program starts at memory location 60000, start the GW-BASIC interpreter as follows:

```
gwbasic /m:60000
```

This reserves the required memory space. Now you can place the machine language routine into memory by making it part of the current BASIC program and loading it into memory using a suitable subroutine. The current BASIC program must contain the following commands:

```
60000  '******************************************************************'
60010  '* initialize the routine for the interrupt call                  *'
60020  '*----------------------------------------------------------------*'
60030  '* Input: none                                                    *'
60040  '* Output: IA is the Start address of the Interrupt routine       *'
60050  '******************************************************************'
60060  '
60070  IA=60000!           'Start address of the routine in the BASIC segment
60080  DEF SEG             'set BASIC segment
60090  RESTORE 60130
60100  FOR I% = 0 TO 160 : READ X% : POKE IA+I%,X% : NEXT  'poke Routine
60110  RETURN                                              'back to caller
60120  '
60130  DATA  85,139,236, 30,  6,139,118, 30,139,  4,232,140,  0,139,118
60140  DATA  12,139, 60,139,118,  8,139,  4, 61,255,255,117,  2,140,216
60150  DATA 142,192,139,118, 28,138, 36,139,118, 26,138,  4,139,118, 24
60160  DATA 138, 60,139,118, 22,138, 28,139,118, 20,138, 44,139,118, 18
60170  DATA 138, 12,139,118, 16,138, 52,139,118, 14,138, 20,139,118, 10
60180  DATA 139, 52, 85,205, 33, 93, 86,156,139,118, 12,137, 60,139,118
60190  DATA  28,136, 36,139,118, 26,136,  4,139,118, 24,136, 60,139,118
60200  DATA  22,136, 28,139,118, 20,136, 44,139,118, 18,136, 12,139,118
60210  DATA  16,136, 52,139,118, 14,136, 20,139,118,  8,140,192,137,  4
60220  DATA  88,139,118,  6,137,  4, 88,139,118, 10,137,  4,  7, 31, 93
60230  DATA 202, 26,  0, 91, 46,136, 71, 66,233,108,255
```

The DATA statements contain the machine language routine which performs the interrupt call. The routine is READ and then POKEd into memory. To start this routine at another memory location, change the value in line 60070. Remember that the parameters used to start GW-BASIC must also be changed so that the routine cannot be overwritten by the variables of the program.

To use the machine language routine to call an interrupt, this subroutine must of course be called first. The first line of the user program should therefore be:

```
100 GOSUB 60000
```

The actual program which calls the interrupt function during its execution can be stored between line numbers 100 and 60000. The following program line demonstrates how this can be done:

```
200 CALL IA(INTNR%,AH%,AL%,BH%,BL%,CH%,CL%,DH%,DL%,DI%,SI%,ES%,FLAGS%)
```

The variables within parentheses are the variables passed to the assembly language program. All variables must pass true integer variables and not constants. The variable names mentioned above may be changed but their order must remain unchanged. Within your program they can have other names.

The first variable in this example, called INTNR%, is the number of the interrupt you want to call. Be careful to specify the exact interrupt number. Also, avoid passing a variable which has not been initialized. Otherwise, you may call the wrong interrupt, which could lead to a system crash. The variables following INTNR% are copied into the processor registers of the same names. If a register is not used by an interrupt routine, you can pass any integer variable in the corresponding register variable. The value of the ES register is treated differently. If the value of ES% is -1, the contents of the DS register is copied to the ES register.

Following the completion of the interrupt call, the values are returned in the designated register variables.

This technique works only with half registers (AH, AL, BH...). It may be necessary to transform these half registers into a whole register. This can be done as follows:

```
300  AX% = AH% * 256 + AL%
```

On the other hand, a whole register can be split into two half registers with the following commands:

```
410  AH% = INT(AX% / 256)
420  AL% = AX% AND 255
```

After calling interrupt functions, the carry flag in the flag register indicates if the called functions were executed correctly. In a BASIC program, it may be necessary to test the carry or zero flags. Since the content of the flag register is in the variable FLAGS% after the interrupt call, the status of individual flags can be inspected through this variable. This is possible with the following program statements:

```
200 IF FLAGS% AND 1=0 THEN PRINT "CARRY-FLAG OFF" ELSE
    PRINT "CARRY-FLAG SET"
210 IF FLAGS% AND 64=0 THEN PRINT "ZERO-FLAG OFF" ELSE
    PRINT "ZERO-FLAG SET"
```

Another problem with interrupt calling is passing variable addresses (e.g., character string output). BASIC stores this set of characters as a string. To determine the offset address of such a string (the segment address of all variables is constant), use the VARPTR function. The LO and HI byte of the offset address can be determined with the following two program lines:

```
300 LO=PEEK(VARPTR(STRING_NAME)+1)     'LO-Byte of the Offset address
310 HI=PEEK(VARPTR(STRING_NAME)+2)     'HI-Byte of the Offset address
```

Garbage collection

These addresses should be determined at the beginning of a BASIC program as well as immediately before each interrupt call, since BASIC frequently performs *garbage collection* (removing unused variables and junk data). Garbage collection frees up variable memory, rearranges remaining data in memory and changes addresses. If a string address is determined at the beginning of a program, it may change several times before the interrupt call is made.

Remember to include an end marker ("$" or a CHR$(0)) at the end of the string (BIOS and DOS functions expect one of these).

Note: Before copying this subroutine and trying it, we have a small suggestion. During your first attempts something will probably go wrong. This is perfectly normal, and you can even expect the computer to crash a couple of times. Save programs frequently...especially before running the program. This way, you won't have to type in the program again from the beginning.

Here is a short sample program which uses the subroutine described above to display text on the screen with function 9 of interrupt 21H.

```
100 '**********************************************************************'
110 '*                          I N T D O S B                             *'
120 '*--------------------------------------------------------------------*'
130 '*  Assignment     : outputs as an example of an Interrupt            *'
140 '*                   a String through a DOS function on               *'
150 '*                   the display screen                               *'
160 '*  Author         : MICHAEL TISCHER                                  *'
170 '*  developed      : 07/30/87                                         *'
180 '*  last Update    : 04/08/89                                         *'
190 '**********************************************************************'
200 '
210 CLS : KEY OFF
220 PRINT"NOTE: This program can only be started if the GWBASIC was "
230 PRINT"started from the DOS level with the command "
235 PRINT"<GWBASIC  /m:60000>."
240 PRINT : PRINT"If this is not the case, please input <s> for Stop."
250 PRINT"Otherwise press any key...";
260 A$ = INKEY$ : IF A$ = "s" THEN END
270 IF A$ = "" THEN 260
280 PRINT
290 GOSUB 60000                        'install function for interrupt call
```

```
300 T$ = CHR$(13) + CHR$(10) + "this text was output through "
305 T$ = T$ + "Function 9 of Interrupt 21H...$"
310 INR% = &H21                         'Number of interrupt to be called
320 FKT% = 9                            'Number of functions to be called
330 OFSLO% = PEEK(VARPTR(T$)+1)    'LO-Byte Offset address to the String
340 OFSHI% = PEEK(VARPTR(T$)+2)    'HI-Byte Offset address to the String
350 CALL IA(INR%,FKT%,Z%,Z%,Z%,Z%,Z%,OFSHI%,OFSLO%,Z%,Z%,Z%,Z%)
360 PRINT : PRINT : PRINT                    'output three blank lines
370 END
380 '
60000 '****************************************************************'
60010 '* initialize the routine for the interrupt call               *'
60020 '*--------------------------------------------------------------*'
60030 '* Input : none                                                 *'
60040 '* Output: IA is the Start address of the Interrupt routine     *'
60050 '****************************************************************'
60060 '
60070 IA=60000!        'Start address of the routine in the BASIC segment
60080 DEF SEG                                          'set BASIC segment
60090 RESTORE 60130
60100 FOR I% = 0 TO 160 : READ X% : POKE IA+I%,X% : NEXT 'poke Routine
60110 RETURN                                              'back to caller
60120 '
60130 DATA  85,139,236, 30,  6,139,118, 30,139,  4,232,140,  0,139,118
60140 DATA  12,139, 60,139,118,  8,139,  4, 61,255,255,117,  2,140,216
60150 DATA 142,192,139,118, 28,138, 36,139,118, 26,138,  4,139,118, 24
60160 DATA 138, 60,139,118, 22,138, 28,139,118, 20,138, 44,139,118, 18
60170 DATA 138, 12,139,118, 16,138, 52,139,118, 14,138, 20,139,118, 10
60180 DATA 139, 52, 85,205, 33, 93, 86,156,139,118, 12,137, 60,139,118
60190 DATA  28,136, 36,139,118, 26,136,  4,139,118, 24,136, 60,139,118
60200 DATA  22,136, 28,139,118, 20,136, 44,139,118, 18,136, 12,139,118
60210 DATA  16,136, 52,139,118, 14,136, 20,139,118,  8,140,192,137,  4
60220 DATA  88,139,118,  6,137,  4, 88,139,118, 10,137,  4,  7, 31, 93
60230 DATA 202, 26,  0, 91, 46,136, 71, 66,233,108,255
```

How it works

The program is composed of separate parts. Lines 210-290 call the subroutine to initialize the machine language function for the interrupt call. Then the individual variables for the interrupt call are loaded. T$ accepts the string to be output. CHR$(13) and CHR$(10) print a blank line before the output of the actual text. This text ends with the "$" character because the DOS function which outputs the string expects this character as an end marker (it will not display this character). INR% and FKT% contain the interrupt number and the function number to be called. Besides these two variables, the variables OFSLO% and OFSHI% contain the offset address of T$.

The CALL command (line 350) calls the interrupt. The first variable passed is INR% with the number of the interrupt to be called. Then follows FKT%, which transfers to the AH register before the interrupt call and informs interrupt 21H of the function number to be called. Several Z% variables follow. These act as dummy variables for all registers which have no special significance to the function which is called. The content of Z% is unimportant. The content of the register into which it is copied is irrelevant for the called function. After the Z% variables, which determine the contents of the AL, BH, BL, CH and CL registers, follow the variables OFSHI% and OFSLO%, which set the offset address of the string in the DX register. The remaining register contents are unimportant for the function call and are filled with Z%.

To permit the DOS function which is called to output the text, its offset and segment address must be known. This address is expected in the DS register and will be set automatically by GW-BASIC.

To conclude this section, here is the listing of the assembler program that we just used to call an interrupt.

```
;**********************************************************************
;*  BASINT.ASM:  This routine offers the capability of               *
;*  calling any interrupt from BASICA or                              *
;*  GWBASIC                                                           *
;*                                                                    *
;**------------------------------------------------------------------**
;*  Call:                                                             *
;* CALL ADR(INTNR%,AH%,AL%,BH%,BL%,CH%,CL%,DH%,DL%,DI%,SI%,ES%,FLAGS%) *
;**------------------------------------------------------------------**
;*  On passing control to the machine language program BASIC         *
;*  deposits the variables on the following positions of the stack   *
;*  INTNR% = SP+30  AH%    = SP+28   AL%    = SP+26   BH%    = SP+24   *
;*  BL%    = SP+22  CH%    = SP+20   CL%    = SP+18   DH%    = SP+16   *
;*  DL%    = SP+14  DI%    = SP+12   SI%    = SP+10   ES%    = SP+8    *
;*  FLAGS% = SP+6                                                     *
;**------------------------------------------------------------------**
;*  for ES the value -1 is passed, then ES is set to DS              *
;**********************************************************************!

code        segment

            assume cs:code,ds:code,es:code,ss:code

;-- the Routine for Interrupt call ----------------------------------

basint      proc far               ;GW expected during CALL far procedure

            push bp                ;GW base pointer saved
            mov  bp,sp             ;Send SP to BP
            push ds                ;GW dta segment stored
            push es                ;GW extra segment saved

            mov  si,[bp+30]        ;Get address of variable INTNR
            mov  ax,[si]           ;Move content of this variable to AX
            call set_intnr         ;Store interrupt number

ad_1        label near             ;Address for SET_INTNR

            mov  si,[bp+12]        ;Get address of DI% variables
            mov  di,[si]           ;Move content of variables to DI
            mov  si,[bp+8]         ;Get address of variable ES%
            mov  ax,[si]           ;Move content of variable to AX
            cmp  ax,-1             ;was -1 passed?
            jne  setes             ;No --> set ES

            mov  ax,ds             ;Set AX to DS and thereby ES = DS

setes:      mov  es,ax             ;transfer AX to ES
            mov  si,[bp+28]        ;Get address of variable AH%
            mov  ah,[si]           ;Move content of variable to AH
            mov  si,[bp+26]        ;Get address of variable AL%
            mov  al,[si]           ;Move content of variable to AL
            mov  si,[bp+24]        ;Get address of variable BH%
            mov  bh,[si]           ;Move content of variable to BH
            mov  si,[bp+22]        ;Get address of variable BL%
            mov  bl,[si]           ;Move content of variable to BL
            mov  si,[bp+20]        ;Get address of variable CH%
            mov  ch,[si]           ;Move content of variable to CH
            mov  si,[bp+18]        ;Get address of variable CL%
            mov  cl,[si]           ;Move content of variable to CL
```

```
        mov  si,[bp+16]          ;Get address of variable DH%
        mov  dh,[si]             ;Move content of variable to DH
        mov  si,[bp+14]          ;Get address of variable DL%
        mov  dl,[si]             ;Move content of variable to DL

        mov  si,[bp+10]          ;Get address of variable SI%
        mov  si,[si]             ;Move content of variable to SI
        push bp                  ;Store base pointer

ad_2    label near               ;Address for SET_INTNR

        int  21h                 ;Call interrupt

        pop  bp                  ;Replace base pointer
        push si                  ;Store SI
        pushf                    ;Store flag register

        mov  si,[bp+12]          ;Get address of variable DI%
        mov  [si],di             ;Move content of variable to DI
        mov  si,[bp+28]          ;Get address of variable AH%
        mov  [si],ah             ;Store AH in this variable
        mov  si,[bp+26]          ;Get address of variable AL%
        mov  [si],al             ;Store AL in this variable
        mov  si,[bp+24]          ;Get address of variable BH%
        mov  [si],bh             ;Store BH in this variable
        mov  si,[bp+22]          ;Get address of variable BL%
        mov  [si],bl             ;Store BL in this variable
        mov  si,[bp+20]          ;Get address of variable CH%
        mov  [si],ch             ;Store CH in this variable
        mov  si,[bp+18]          ;Get address of variable CL%
        mov  [si],cl             ;Store CL in this variable
        mov  si,[bp+16]          ;Get address of variable DH%
        mov  [si],dh             ;Store DH in this variable
        mov  si,[bp+14]          ;Get address of variable DL%
        mov  [si],dl             ;Store DL in this variable
        mov  si,[bp+8]           ;Get address of variable ES%
        mov  ax,es               ;transfer ES to AX
        mov  [si],ax             ;Store ES (AX) in this variable
        pop  ax                  ;Move flag register from stack to AX
        mov  si,[bp+6]           ;Get address of variable FLAGS%
        mov  [si],ax             ;Store FLAGs in this variable
        pop  ax                  ;Move DI register from stack to AX
        mov  si,[bp+10]          ;Get address of variable SI%
        mov  [si],ax             ;Store SI (AX) in this variable

        pop  es                  ;Get GW extra segment back
        pop  ds                  ;Get GW data segment back
        pop  bp                  ;Return GW base pointer

        ret  26                  ;Addresses of variables on the stack
                                 ;are no longer needed

basint  endp

;----------------------------------------------------------------------

set_intnr proc near              ;stores the interrupt number

        pop  bx
        mov  cs:[bx+ad_2-ad_1+1],al
        jmp  ad_1

set_intnr endp

;----------------------------------------------------------------------

code    ends
        end
```

Some brief notes on this program follow for those not familiar with the calling and linking of assembly language programs in GW-BASIC: The program first pushes the base pointer on the stack since it will be reset by the next instruction. During re-entry into GW-BASIC, the base pointer must have the value it had during the call of the routine. Then the base pointer is set to the value of the stack pointer for access to data on the stack. This is necessary for GW-BASIC to pass the BASIC variables named in the CALL command to the stack. In the next step, the DS and the ES registers are stored on the stack, because their content may change during execution of the routine and must be preserved for return to GW-BASIC.

Now the routine can read in the variables and set the various processor registers. It is important to note that the stack does not contain variable contents, but their addresses relative to the DS register. Because of this, the address of the variable must be loaded first and then the relative value of this address.

Which addresses contain the addresses of the individual variables stored on the stack can be determined from the header of the assembly language routine. First you must determine the number of the interrupt to be called. This value must be treated in a different manner than the other variables on the stack because it isn't passed in one of the processor registers, but is a part of the INT instruction which calls the interrupt. It is indicated as a byte following the code of the INT instruction (CDH).

To set the interrupt number, the number to be passed must be stored following the CDH code of the INT instruction. This creates a small problem since this routine can be POKEd by the BASIC program into any memory location. Because of this, the address of the INT instruction depends on the current starting address of the routine instead of remaining constant. The routine doesn't know where the INT instruction is located.

A small trick can be used to help here. The routine does not know where it is stored, but the processor knows the location of the INT instruction (it has to know, otherwise it couldn't execute the routine). The subroutine SET_INTR is called after the interrupt number is loaded into the AX register. The processor, as in any CALL instruction, stores the address where the program execution is to continue on the stack, before calling any subroutine. This is the instruction which precedes the label AD_1.

Subroutine SET_INTR gets the address of AD_1 from the stack. While the address of the INT instruction is still not known, the distance between AD_1 and the INT instruction remain constant, the address of the INT instruction can be calculated and the interrupt number can be stored following the instruction. The task ends and the routine returns to the main program (to the label AD_1).

The rest of the routine consists of repeating instructions which determine the contents of the different variables and pass them to the corresponding processor registers. The value for the ES register is given a special test: if it is equal to -1, the value of the DS register is copied to the ES register.

After all registers are loaded, the interrupt is called and the contents of the processor registers are transferred back to the corresponding BASIC variables. The last step is to restore the contents of all registers which had been saved on the stack. Finally control returns to GW-BASIC.

4.2 Interrupt Calls from Turbo Pascal

Calling interrupts from Turbo Pascal is very easy. Throughout this book we'll be using Turbo Pascal Version 4.0.

INTR

Turbo Pascal uses the INTR procedure. Since this parameter can accept any value between 0 and 255, all available interrupts can be called.

MSDOS

A special form of this INTR procedure is the MSDOS procedure. It is called in a manner similar to INTR:

```
MsDos( Regs:Registers );
```

The InterruptNumber parameter needed by Turbo Pascal Version 3.0 isn't required in this procedure since it always calls interrupt 21H, through which almost all operating system functions can be called.

In both procedures, the parameter register is a record type which holds the contents of the registers to be passed. These are copied into the registers before the interrupt call.

The DOS unit contains the parameters for the type called Registers:

```
type Registers = record
     case integer of
       0 : (AX, BX, CX, DX, BP, SI, DI, DS, ES, Flags : word);
       1 : (AL, AH, BL, BH, CL, CH, DL, DH : byte);
     end;
```

Once the DOS unit has been included in a Turbo Pascal source code, the var statement can be used to define the register variables under the name Regs:

```
var Regs : Registers;
```

Now Turbo Pascal can easily communicate with the following processor registers:

- `Regs.ax,`
- `Regs.bx,`
- `Regs.cx,`
- `Regs.ah, etc.`

You then pass the values to the registers through standard assignments. For example:

```
Register.ax := 254;
```

The same method is used with all other registers.

Unfortunately, the contents of the half registers AH, AL, BL, etc. can't be defined this way. In this case, a trick can be used by defining the half registers as normal integer or byte variables and then merging them together into a whole register.

In the case of the AX register, this could be done as follows:

```
var al,
    ah : integer;

Register.ax := ah shl 8 + al;
```

In this statement, the AX register is assigned value composed of the sum of the AH register multiplied by 256 (shifting a variable left by 8 places is equivalent to multiplying it by 256) and the AL register.

If you must do this repeatedly in a program, it would be useful to define a small function for this:

```
function WholeRegister(Lo, Hi : integer) : integer;

begin
  WholeRegister := Lo + Hi shl 8;
end;
```

Instead of the above, the following could be written:

```
Register.ax := WholeRegister(al, ah);
```

Before calling the interrupt, you must first specify the interrupt value in the register. The contents of all other registers are unimportant here. If the called interrupt returns values to the calling program through registers, they can be examined by looking at the individual components of the variable register.

Sometimes individual flags pass information from the interrupt to the calling program. In most cases, the Carry flag serves this purpose. If an error occurs during the execution of an interrupt, the flag is set.

To test for a set flag, the following Pascal statements are used. They return TRUE or FALSE as a result depending on whether the corresponding flag was set or not.

- `carry flag:   (register.flags and 1)`
- `zero flag:    (register.flags and 64)`
- `sign flag:    (register.flags and 128)`

Often the address of a variable (usually a text buffer) must be passed to an interrupt. In this case the Turbo functions Ofs and Seg are used to obtain the offset or segment addresses of a variable. The name of the variable whose address should be determined is passed to both functions as the argument:

```
ofs(variablename)
seg(variablename)
```

Turbo Pascal uses a different format than DOS and BIOS for string storage, especially for text buffers (mostly variables of type string).

These formats are illustrated below.

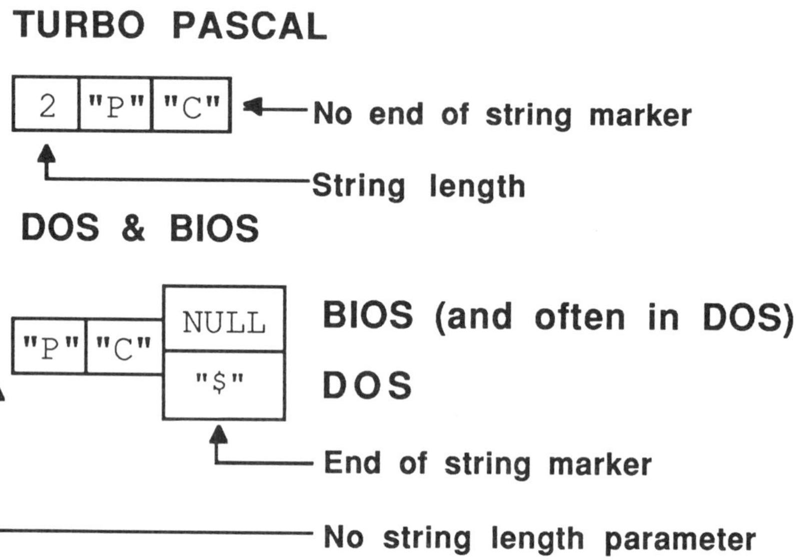

String storage - Turbo Pascal and BIOS-DOS

To convert a Turbo Pascal string into DOS or BIOS format, an end character (ASCII code 0) or the dollar sign "$" (ASCII code 36) is appended. Which of these two characters you should use for indicating the end of the string is described during the discussions of individual interrupts. Regardless of which format you use, the characters appear as in either of the following commands:

```
string := string+#0;
string := string+#36;
```

The address returned by the Ofs function plus 1 must be passed to the interrupt, otherwise the byte which indicates the length of the string is accepted by the interrupt as its first character.

Here is the sample program. Just like the example in Section 4.1, it displays text on the screen using function 9 of interrupt 21H:

```
{**********************************************************************}
{*                              I N T D O S                           *}
{*--------------------------------------------------------------------*}
{*    Task          : as an example this interrupt call outputs       *}
{*                    a string through a function of DOS on           *}
{*                    the display                                     *}
{*--------------------------------------------------------------------*}
{*    Author        : MICHAEL TISCHER                                 *}
{*    developed     : 07/30/87                                        *}
{*    last update   : 05/04/89                                        *}
{**********************************************************************}

program INTDOSP;
```

```
Uses Dos;

var Regs     : Registers;         { Register variables for interrupt call}
    Text     : string[128];                  { accepts the output text }

{*********************************************************************}
{*                          MAIN PROGRAM                            *}
{*********************************************************************}

begin

 Text := #13#10'this text was output with Function 9 of DOS-'+
         'Interrupt 21H ...'#13#10+'$';
 Regs.ah := $09;          { Function number 9 in the AH-Register }
 Regs.dx := Ofs(Text)+1;              { Offset address of the text }
 Regs.ds := Seg(Text);               { Segment address of the text }
 MsDos(Regs);                          { Call DOS-Interrupt 21(h) }
end.
```

The variable TEXT contains the text to be displayed. The sequence "#13#10" places the ASCII code 13, followed by ASCII code 10, at the beginning and the end of the text, creating a blank line before and after the text. The last character is the "$" character which indicates the last character of text to DOS.

The number of the function being called (9) is copied to the AH register. Since Turbo Pascal doesn't allow access to the AH register alone, the entire AX register must be addressed. The value 0 is loaded into the AL register, but any other value could be entered into this register since its content has no significance to the called function. As a last step, before calling interrupt 21H using the MSDOS procedure, the segment address of the string is placed in the DS register and the offset address in the DX register.

4.3 Interrupt Calls from C

The C language is the language of choice for most developers. Since it was originally designed for operating system development, C has provisions to include machine language routines, which is a benefit within the scope of this book.

The standard libraries of both the Microsoft C and Borland Turbo C compilers have a number of functions for calling interrupts.

The following functions are of interest to us in this book:

- `int86`
- `int86x`
- `intdos`
- `intdosx`
- `segread`

All functions and applicable data structures are declared in the DOS.H library file. A program which wants to access one of these functions must therefore link the file to the current program using the #include preprocessor command.

The three structures WORDREGS, BYTEREGS and SEGREGS pass register values. WORDREGS contains the whole registers AX, BX, CX, DX, SI, DI and the Carry flag. On the other hand, BYTEREGS contains the half registers AH, AL, BH, BL, CH, CL, DH and DL, while SEGREGS represents the segment registers DS, CS, SS and ES.

The BYTEREGS and the WORDREGS structures are joined in the union REGS which lets the programmer work selectively with either half or whole registers.

Using a variable of the type REGS (called register here for simplicity's sake) gives us the following:

```
union REGS register;
```

This allows access to individual registers:

- AX: `register.x.ax`
- BX: `register.x.bx` etc.
- AH: `register.h.ah`
- AL: `register.h.al`
- BH: `register.h.bh` etc.

The carry flag is represented by the variable register.x.cflag. If this variable is equal to 0, the carry flag remains unset. Any other value sets the carry flag.

In the case of the segment register a representative variable can be defined as follows:

```
struct SREGS SegRegister;
```

The individual components of the variables SegRegister.ds, SegRegister.es, etc., correspond to the equivalent processor registers.

The functions starting with the characters *int* all serve to call interrupts. The SEGREAD function reads the current contents of the segment register.

The functions that call interrupts use different register variables for input to the interrupt routine, and output from the interrupt routine. There is an advantage to this method over returning information to the same register variable in that the input information is not overwritten.

Since the individual functions pass only the address of the variable representing the register and not the variable itself, it is possible to combine the input and output registers into a single variable. In this case, the address of one variable is provided for the variable representing the input and the output registers (this method is used in the sample program at the end of this section).

Before calling the interrupt, the contents of the input variable are copied to the corresponding processor registers. Following the interrupt call their contents become the output variables.

All interrupt functions return the content of the AX register as a result code after the interrupt call.

Here are the details of the functions and their calls:

int86

The int86 function is called as follows:

```
int86(IntNumber, InRegister, OutRegister);
```

IntNumber is a variable or constant indicating the number of the interrupt to be called. InRegister and OutRegister contain the address of two (or one) variables of the REGS type. As the variable name suggests, InRegister contains the register contents before the interrupt call, and OutRegister contains the register contents after the interrupt call.

int86x

The int86x function differs from the int86 function in that it requires an additional argument of the SREGS type. Its contents are copied into the segment register before calling the interrupt, but are not copied back following the call to the interrupt routine.

The call of the function is as follows:

```
int86x(IntNumber, InRegister, OutRegister, SegRegister);
```

The intdos and the intdosx functions differ from the two functions described above, in that the number of the interrupt to the call is not passed. As the names suggest, they call DOS interrupt 21H through which most DOS functions can be accessed.

intdos

Only the addresses of the input and the output variables representing the processor registers are passed to the intdos function:

```
intdos(InRegister, OutRegister);
```

intdosx

The intdosx function, like the int86x function, has an additional parameter for the segment register. The function call is as follows:

```
intdosx(InRegister, OutRegister, SegRegister);
```

So far you've seen how to call an interrupt from C and how to set the registers. You also have to determine the address of a variable.

In C, you can easily determine the address of a variable. To do this, use the address operator &, which returns the offset address of any desired variable. Use the SEGREAD function mentioned above to determine the segment address of a variable. The address of a variable of the SREG type is passed to the function (using the address operator &) into which the content of the segment register can be copied.

If, for example, the address of the variable SegRegister is passed to the function and the variable was previously defined by the command:

```
union SREG SegRegister;
```

Then the variable SegRegister.ds contains the segment address of the variable SegRegister, after calling the SEGREAD function.

While C supports interrupt calls with numerous functions, the library of the Microsoft C compiler library does not have a function to return the contents of a memory location. Since such a function could be very valuable in some programs, the assembler program below contains the PEEKB and POKEB functions for inclusion in programs created with the Microsoft C compiler. PEEK returns the contents of a memory location (one byte), while the POKE function writes a one-byte value into a memory location.

Note: If you use the Borland Turbo C compiler, you won't need to use this program since the Turbo C library already contains the PEEK, PEEKB, POKE and POKEB functions. Because of this, linking the assembler program into the C example programs of this book is unnecessary. Additional information is presented in the header of each program.

If you are using the Microsoft C compiler, enter the following program with a text editor and save it under the name PEPO.ASM. It can then be assembled with:

```
masm pepo;
```

Here's the program:

```
;**********************************************************************;
;*                              P E P O                               *;
;*--------------------------------------------------------------------*;
;*    Task        : Makes the PEEKB and POKEB function available for *;
;*                  inclusion in a C program                          *;
;*--------------------------------------------------------------------*;
;*    Author      : MICHAEL TISCHER                                   *;
;*    developed   : 08/13/87                                          *;
;*    last Update : 04/08/89                                          *;
;*--------------------------------------------------------------------*;
;*    assemble    : MASM PEPO;                                        *;
;**********************************************************************;

IGROUP group _text                     ;Grouping of program segments
DGROUP group const,_bss,  _data        ;Grouping of data segments
       assume CS:IGROUP, DS:DGROUP, ES:DGROUP, SS:DGROUP

       public _PeekB                   ;Functions become accessible to
       public _PokeB                   ;other programs

CONST  segment word public 'CONST'     ;this segment accepts all constants
CONST  ends                            ;which are readable

_BSS   segment word public 'BSS'       ;this segment accepts all non-
_BSS   ends                            ;initialized static variables

_DATA  segment word public 'DATA'      ;all initialized global and
_DATA  ends                            ;static variables are stored in this
                                       ;segment

_TEXT  segment byte public 'CODE'      ;the Program segment

;-- PEEKB: read a byte from memory -----------------------------
;-- call of C: int = PeekB(int Segment, int Offset)

_PeekB    proc near

          push bp                      ;store BP on the stack
          mov  bp,sp                   ;transmit SP to BP
          push ds                      ;store data segment register
          mov  ax,[bp]+4               ;get first argument (Segment)
          mov  ds,ax                   ;set as data segment
          mov  bx,[bp]+6               ;get second argument (Offset)
          mov  al,[bx]                 ;read memory location
          xor  ah,ah                   ;HI-byte of INT to 0
          jmp  short fctend            ;terminate function

_PeekB    endp

;-- POKEB: write a byte into memory --------------------------
;-- Call C: PokeB(int Segment, int Offset, short int Wert)

_PokeB    proc near

          push bp                      ;store BP on the stack
          mov  bp,sp                   ;transmit SP to BP
```

```
        push ds                     ;store data segment register
        mov  ax,[bp]+4              ;Get first argument (Segment)
        mov  ds,ax                  ;Set as data segment
        mov  bx,[bp]+6              ;Get second argument (Offset)
        mov  al,[bp]+8              ;Get third argument (Value)
        mov  [bx],al                ;write into memory location
fctend: pop  ds                     ;Return data segment register
        mov  sp,bp                  ;Restore stack pointer
        pop  bp                     ;Get BP from stack
        ret                         ;Return to calling C program

_PokeB  endp

;----------------------------------------------------------------------

_text   ends                        ;End of the program segment
        end                         ;End of the assembler source
```

The example program below uses the two functions described above. This next program examines the model identification number or code of the PC and displays PC type on the screen using a DOS function:

```
/**********************************************************************/
/*                           I N T D O S                              */
/*--------------------------------------------------------------------*/
/*    Task          : an example of an interrupt call, outputs        */
/*                    a string through a DOS function on              */
/*                    the display screen                              */
/*--------------------------------------------------------------------*/
/*    Author        : MICHAEL TISCHER                                 */
/*    developed     : 08/30/87                                        */
/*    last update   : 04/08/89                                        */
/*--------------------------------------------------------------------*/
/*    (MICROSOFT C)                                                   */
/*    Creation      : MSC INTDOSC                                     */
/*                    LINK INTDOSC PEPO;                              */
/*    Call          : INTDOSC                                         */
/*--------------------------------------------------------------------*/
/*    (BORLAND TURBO C v2.0)                                          */
/*    Creation      : through the RUN command in the menu...or...     */
/*                    tcc -K intdosc                                  */
/*    Call          : intdosc                                         */
/**********************************************************************/

#include <dos.h>                       /* include header file         */
/* Microsoft C user must uncomment the following line                 */
/* extern short int peekb();           /* PEEKB must be linked to     */
/*                                        Microsoft C object code     */
/**********************************************************************/
/**                           MAIN PROGRAM                           **/
/**********************************************************************/

void main()

{
 static char AT[] = "\r\nthis computer is an AT\r\n$";
 static char XT[] = "\r\nthis computer is an XT\r\n$";
 static char PC[] = "\r\nthis computer is an PC\r\n$";

 union REGS Register;          /* Register variable for interrupt call */

 Register.h.ah = 9;            /* Function number for output of string */
 switch (peekb(0xF000, 0xFFFE))                 /* detect model of PC */
  {
   case 0xFE : Register.x.dx = (int) XT;         /* Address of XT text */
               break;
```

```
    case 0xFC : Register.x.dx = (int) AT;        /* Address of AT text */
                break;
    case 0xFF :
    default   : Register.x.dx = (int) PC;        /* Address of PC text */
   }
  intdos(&Register, &Register);              /*  Call DOS interrupt 21H */
}
```

The main function defines three CHAR pointers which point to the text for each PC type. Each of them starts and ends with an "\n" character. This creates a blank line before and after the text itself.

In the first instruction of the main program the AH register is loaded with the DOS function number for string output on the screen. Then the model identification byte is read from memory location F000:FFFE using the PEEKB function. Depending on the value read, the offset address of the accompanying text is transferred to the DX register where it is expected by the interrupt 21H function.

In addition to this offset address, the function also requires the segment address of the text in the DS register. Since the compiler automatically sets this register, you don't have to be concerned with the segment address. The last instruction of the program calls the INTDOS function which in turn calls interrupt 21H with the registers which were defined earlier.

The file header states how it can be executed: If you are using the Microsoft C computer, then it is important that you link the file with the previously assembled PEPO program so that the new program contains the PEEKB and POKEB functions. These can then be called from the C program.

The integrated environment of the Turbo C compiler requires a different procedure. Compiler options must be set to default values except for under "code generation." You must set "default char type" to "unsigned", then select Run from the menu. The options file appears on the disk under the filename INTBSPC.TC.

A small comment about using Borland Turbo C compiler. Several programs in this book include assembly language routines within the programs. Since Turbo C differentiates between upper and lowercase characters in function names, you may have problems compiling programs as entered from this book. To avoid this, select the OPTION command, then the LINKER command in the command line of Turbo C before creating a program. The lowest line in the window displays the option "Case sensitive link". Select OFF here to avoid difficulties with upper and lowercase letters.

Chapter 5

Using Interrupts from Assembly Language

Unlike programmers using any of the higher level languages, the assembly language programmer doesn't have to rely on complicated functions or procedures to call an interrupt. The MOV instruction loads the input parameters into the registers provided, and the INT instruction calls the interrupt.

Certain interrupts, or the functions hidden behind these interrupts, are called frequently in many programs. An example of this is interrupt 21H function 9, which displays text on the screen. You call it by placing function number 9 in the AH register and the offset address of the text you want displayed in the DX register. This process looks like this in assembly language:

```
mov  ah,9               ;load function number 9
mov  dx,offset Text     ;load offset address of text
int  21h                ;call DOS interrupt 21h
```

Even if you call the function very frequently, it doesn't pay to write a subroutine for it since the address of the text to be displayed must be passed. All that remains is to load the value 9 into the AH register and to call the interrupt. You'll find the three program lines described above included for every function call in a program in this chapter.

5.1 Using Assembler Macro Functions

An alternative to this method are *macros* which most assemblers support.

Macros

A macro is a "shorthand" way to write a series of assembly language instructions. It has a name and may have one or more parameters. During assembly, if the macro name is encountered, the series of instructions and parameters replace the macro.

Below is an example of defining and calling a macro using the Microsoft Assembler (MASM). See your assembler's reference manual for information on macro handling (and whether your assembler supports macros). Since this macro displays text, we've named the macro PRINT:

```
print macro string          ;Macro header with Name and Parameter

      mov  ah,9             ;load function 9
      mov  dx,offset string ;load offset address of the text
      int  21h              ;call DOS interrupt 21h

      endm                  ;the endm command terminates a macro
```

The first line declares the macro name (PRINT). In this case, the macro also has one parameter (string). The assembly language instructions follow in successive lines until the ENDM instruction terminates the macro.

Now you can use the macro to display text:

```
print Message
```

In this example, Message is the name of a variable containing the text to be displayed. In the macro declaration, string is a parameter. During assembly, string is replaced by Message and creates the following program lines:

```
mov  ah,9
mov  dx,offset Message
int  21h
```

5.2 A Sample Macro

The following program demonstrates the macro just described.

```
;**********************************************************************;
;*                              M A C R O                             *;
;*--------------------------------------------------------------------*;
;*    Task          : in this Program a Macro is used for output      *;
;*                    of a String with Function 9 of Interrupt 21H    *;
;*--------------------------------------------------------------------*;
;*    Author        : MICHAEL TISCHER                                 *;
;*    developed     : 08/30/87                                        *;
;*    last Update   : 04/08/89                                        *;
;*--------------------------------------------------------------------*;
;*    assembly      : MASM MACRO;                                     *;
;*                  : LINK MACRO;                                     *;
;*--------------------------------------------------------------------*;
;*    Call:         : MACRO                                           *;
;**********************************************************************;

;== Macro ==============================================================

Print     macro String              ;this is the macro

          mov ah,9                  ;load function number
          mov dx,offset String      ;load offset address of text
          int 21h                   ;call DOS interrupt

          endm                      ;End of macro

;== Constants ==========================================================

CR        equ 13                    ;ASCII-Code of carriage return
LF        equ 10                    ;ASCII-Code of linefeed
TEND      equ "$"                   ;End of a character string

;== Data ===============================================================

Data segment

Text      db CR,LF,"This is how MACROS are used",CR,LF,TEND

Data ends

;== stack ==============================================================

stack segment STACK

          dw 64 dup (?)

stack ends

;== Code ===============================================================

Program  segment

          assume CS:Program, DS: Data, SS:stack

Start     proc far              ;program starts here

          mov  ax,Data          ;set data segment register
          mov  ds,ax

          Print Text            ;Macro inserted here

          mov  ax,4C00h         ;Program terminated with call of a
          int  21h              ;DOS function with return of error-code 0
```

```
Start     endp                  ;End of procedure

;======================================================================

Program  ends
          end Start             ;begin with START
```

After you enter the source program, it can be assembled, linked and executed as indicated in the header.

Most of the lines in this listing have nothing to do with the actual program but are definitions and declarations for the assembler.

The macro and constants are defined in the first part of the program, which helps to make the listing more understandable to the reader. The definition of the data segment follows, where the string to be displayed is stored as a character string. It is preceded and followed by a carriage return and a linefeed to display a blank line before and after the actual text. The text ends with the character "$" (the DOS function used for text display always looks for this as the last character in a string).

Following the data segment is the stack segment, which controls the stack during program execution. Since the program is not very large, the stack can be fairly small. The last segment is the code segment which contains the program instructions. It consists of only five commands: The first two instructions initialize the program. They load the segment address of the data segment into the DS register to provide access to the text in this segment. Then the macro PRINT is called, and the text is passed to it.

The following instructions terminate the program by calling a DOS function.

Note: You may find it useful to group together certain macros into a file or library. When one of these macros will be used in a program, the library may be linked or included with the assembly language code.

Chapter 6

The Disk Operating System

The following chapter discusses the PC's operating system, which the PC loads from floppy diskette or hard disk. It is commonly referred to as PC-DOS, MS-DOS or just DOS.

What is DOS?

Most users only know the user interface of DOS, with which you run programs, format disks, etc. In the following sections, however, you'll view DOS from an angle you may not have known existed.

Beneath the surface of DOS many processes takes place. DOS uses a large number of different routines (called *functions*) to accomplish its tasks. These functions are available to the user as well as to DOS. The main focus is on how these functions can be used in practical applications.

This chapter includes a historical sketch of the development of DOS, highlighting its origins in the CP/M operating system. You'll learn the differences between transient and resident commands, COM and EXE files, and DOS file access.

The data structures which act as the connecting link between the different DOS functions will also be examined in this chapter. These data structures make mass storage devices such as floppy disks and a hard disk possible.

Finally, this chapter discusses each DOS function in detail, and includes a brief look at DOS Version 4.0.

6.1 A Short History of DOS

DOS appeared in 1980, at a time when 8-bit systems and CP/M 80 operating systems made up the majority of microcomputers. A few years before, Intel had designed the 8086 microprocessor, the first generation of 16-bit microprocessors.

In April 1980 the CP/M-86 operating system announced by Digital Research for use on the 8086 processor was unavailable. A programmer named Tim Paterson began developing a new operating system. This system is the ancestor of the current MS-DOS.

At this time a lot of software was available for CP/M-80 systems. The development of new software for an 8086 operating system would have required enormous expenses and effort. Paterson's goal was to allow easy conversion of existing software from CP/M-80 to the new operating system. He tried to include the functions and the most important data structures of the CP/M-80 operating system, while removing the weak points of CP/M-80. The finished product was an operating system that required only 6K of memory. Programs developed for CP/M-80 could also be converted with little effort to the 8086. The new system was named 86-DOS.

Meanwhile IBM was developing a 16-bit microcomputer. Microsoft offered to develop an operating system for it. Microsoft obtained a prototype of the new computer from IBM, bought the rights to Paterson's operating system, and made some enhancements to the software. Even though Paterson was participating in the project, the strict security provisions of IBM prevented him from seeing the machine for which he had developed an operating system. Despite this, the development work was concluded in August of 1981. The new operating system was released for the IBM PC under the name MS-DOS.

Many changes have been made to DOS since 1981. Because these changes are of great significance to the DOS programmer, this chapter contains a segment for each major version of DOS. Each segment lists changes from preceding versions with explanations. Many components of DOS are explained here, which will give you some idea of the complexity of an operating system.

Version 1.0

This version represented a compromise for Microsoft. They had relied heavily on CP/M-80 and needed to transfer existing programs quickly and easily. This can be seen in the fact that the file names (eight-character filename, three-character extension) was identical with CP/M-80. Also, the designation of the disk drives and the internal structure had many similarities to the successful 8-bit operating system.

During this time many improvements and enhancements of the hardware occurred, such as more RAM and faster disk drives. Microsoft decided to make DOS more hardware independent by removing the association between physical file length and logical file length.

In CP/M-80 every disk was divided into 128-byte units which could only be accessed as a whole. This is why you couldn't access individual bytes on the disk (this created a programming problem that shouldn't have existed in the first place). DOS solved this problem by making the logical and physical data length independent of one another. In addition, functions were implemented to permit reading or writing of more than one data set of a file on a disk. Treating the input and output *devices* like files achieved hardware independence. These input and output devices were assigned their own names:

```
CON     (Keyboard and Display)
PRN     (Printer)
AUX     (serial Interface)
```

If you used one of these three names instead of a filename to access a file with a DOS routine, then the computer addressed the corresponding device and not the disk drive. This also permitted redirecting input and output from the keyboard or screen to a file or other device.

Before this time, DOS only supported program files which loaded and executed from a fixed location in memory. This proved to be impractical, and so Version 1.0 introduced a new program file type. This new file type had a file extension of .EXE instead of .COM. An .EXE file could be stored and executed from almost any memory location.

Two changes were made to the *command processor*, the part of the operating system which accepts commands from the user and controls the execution of these commands. The first change was to store the command processor in a separate file named COMMAND.COM. This allowed programmers to develop a customized command processor and link it to the system.

The second change was to divide the command processor into a *resident* and a *transient* portion. This approach was taken because early PC systems contained only a small amount of memory. The resident portion was written to be as small as possible. Many DOS commands were stored on disk and loaded and run only when required, hence the name transient. Examples of transient commands are DISKCOPY and FORMAT.

A major innovation that took MS-DOS Version 1.0 beyond CP/M-80 was the introduction of the *FAT* (file allocation table) on disk. Every entry in this table corresponds to a data area of 512 bytes (called a *sector*) on the disk. The FAT indicates whether the sector is allocated to a file or is still available.

The FAT has special significance in connection with the directory entry which exists for every file type. Besides the filename and other information, it also indicates the number of an entry in the FAT which corresponds with the first sector of a file on the disk. This FAT entry points to another FAT entry which indicates the next sector which was allocated to the file. The other FAT entries on a disk perform the same task.

In conclusion two additional developments should be mentioned which make work with the PC easier for the user:

The introduction of *batch processing* offers the user the option of placing several DOS commands into one file. When you "run" this file (which has a file extension of .BAT), DOS executes the individual commands from this file as if you had entered the commands from the keyboard, thus saving the user time in entering frequently used groups of commands repeatedly.

The *current date and time* follows every filename. DOS includes this data to help the user determine the last time a file was modified.

When IBM introduced a new PC in 1982 which used both sides of a disk for data storage, Microsoft released DOS Version 1.1.

Version 2.0

IBM announced a new personal computer in March of 1983, called the PC XT, which in addition to the floppy disk drive also had a *hard disk* (also called a *fixed disk*). The enormous capacity of this hard disk (10 megabytes) allowed the user to store several hundred files on one unit, but created some problems for the operating system. The largest problem was that DOS could only handle one directory for each storage unit. It would be nearly impossible for the hard disk user to maintain hundreds of files in a single directory. Microsoft had two options to solve this problem: They could either borrow an idea from the CP/M-80 operating system, or from the UNIX operating system.

CP/M views a hard disk as several individual disk drives which share the total storage on the hard disk, each with only one directory.

UNIX uses a *hierarchical file system*, in which every storage unit has a root directory which can contain subdirectories as well as files. Every one of these subdirectories can have subdirectories within them. This creates a directory tree whose trunk is the root directory and whose branches are represented by the individual subdirectories.

Microsoft chose the hierarchical file system, which has since become a popular component of DOS. This was another step away from CP/M-80 toward an efficient 16-bit operating system. With the introduction of an hierarchical file system some major changes had to be made in the area of file control by DOS. Before this time, file access was conducted through a *file control block* or FCB.

This file control block had been introduced for compatibility with CP/M-80. The FCB contained important information about the name, size and location of a file on disk. This CP/M would not allow access to a file in another directory.

The DOS developers standardized file access through DOS functions. The access to a file occurs exclusively through the *file handles*. A handle is a numerical value passed to the program as soon as it opens a file through a DOS function. The FCBs were not eliminated, but the programmer no longer came in contact with them since DOS took over the control block manipulation.

An important innovation was the introduction of *installable device drivers*. They offer the programmer the capability of easily including different devices in DOS, such as an exotic hard disk, a mouse or a tape drive. Version 2.0 introduced the display device driver ANSI.SYS which gave the programmer flexibility in cursor positioning and color selection through DOS functions.

Version 2.0 added the option of formatting the individual tracks of a disk with nine sectors instead of eight. This increased the storage capacity of a single-sided disk from 160K to 180K, and the capacity of a double-sided disk from 320K to 360K.

Version 3.0

Version 3.0, like Version 2.0, was developed for a new PC, the IBM PC AT. It was released in August of 1984 and supported the 20 megabyte hard disk of the ATs as well as the high capacity 1.2 megabyte floppy disk drive. Many changes occurred in DOS's internal routines. They contributed to faster execution of certain operations, but are transparent to the programmer.

Version 4.0

DOS 4.0 appeared on the market in August 1988. Before this, Microsoft released a new multiprocessing operating system called OS/2. Before OS/2, multiprocessing was unknown to MS-DOS.

The user can easily see the changes to DOS 4.0 over earlier versions of DOS. In place of the line-oriented command line interpreter used by DOS versions 3.3 and earlier, DOS 4.0 has a Shell allowing user-defined menus, easy selection of applications, files and directories from both mouse and keyboard.

Most important are the unseen changes made to DOS, particularly in adapting the operating system to the new hardware standards on the market. As the operating system has grown in power, it has also grown in complexity and memory use. For example, earlier versions of DOS were limited to "only" 640K of RAM and a 32 megabyte hard disk. However, DOS 4.0 handles the Expanded Memory System (EMS) following the LIM standard, normal RAM capacity of up to 8 megabytes, and hard disks up to 2 gigabytes (2048 megabytes) capacity.

6.2 Internal Structure of DOS

Several major components comprise DOS, each with a certain task within the system. The three most important components are the DOS-BIOS, the DOS kernel and the command processor. Each appear in a separate file.

DOS-BIOS

DOS-BIOS is stored in a system file which appears under various names (IBMBIO.COM, IBMIO.SYS or IO.SYS). This file has the file attributes Hidden and Sys, which means this system file doesn't appear when the DIR command is entered. The DOS-BIOS contains the device drivers for the following units:

```
CON     (Keyboard and Display)
PRN     (Printer)
AUX     (Serial Interface)
CLOCK   (Clock)
Disk drives and/or hard disks which have the unit
designations A, B and C
```

If DOS wants to communicate with one of these, it accesses a device driver contained in this module, which in turn uses the routines of ROM-BIOS. The DOS-BIOS (i.e., the connection between individual device drivers and other hardware dependent routines) are the most hardware dependent components of the operating system, and vary from one computer to another.

Do not confuse the device drivers in this module with the installable device drivers. The DOS-BIOS device drivers cannot be changed by the user.

DOS kernel

The *DOS kernel* in the IBMDOS.COM or MSDOS.SYS file is normally invisible to the user. It contains file access routine handles, character input and output, and more. The routines operate independent of the hardware and use the device drivers of DOS-BIOS for keyboard, screen and disk access. The module can be used by different PCs without being limited to one machine. User programs can access these functions in the same manner as the ROM-BIOS functions: every function can be called with a software interrupt. The processor registers pass the function number and the parameters.

Command processor

Unlike the two modules described above, the command processor is contained in the file named COMMAND.COM. It displays the "A>" or "C>" prompt on the screen, accepts user input and controls input execution. Many users wrongly think that the command processor is actually the operating system. In reality it is only a special program which executes under DOS control.

The command processor, also called a *shell* in programmer's terminology, actually consists of three modules: A *resident portion*, a *transient portion* and the *initialization routine*.

The resident portion (the part that always stays in the computer's memory) contains various routines called *critical error handlers*. These allow the computer to react to different events, such as pressing the <Ctrl><C> or <Ctrl><Break> keys or errors during communication with external devices (e.g., disk drives and printers). The latter cause the message:

```
Abort, Retry, Ignore
or
Abort, Retry, Fail
```

The transient portion contains code for displaying the (A>) prompt, reading user input from the keyboard and executing the input. The name of this module is derived from the fact that the RAM memory where it is located is unprotected, and can be overwritten under certain circumstances. When a program ends, control returns to the resident portion of the command processor. It executes a checksum program to determine whether the transient portion was overwritten by the application program. If so, the resident portion reloads the transient portion.

The initialization portion loads during the booting process and initializes DOS. This part of the command processor will be examined in detail in the next chapter. When its job ends, it is no longer needed and the RAM memory it occupies can be overwritten by another program. The commands accepted by the transient portion of the command processor can be divided into three groups: internal commands, external commands and batch files.

Internal commands lie in the resident portion of the command processor. COPY, RENAME and DIR are internal commands.

External commands must be loaded into memory from diskette or hard disk as needed. FORMAT and CHKDSK are external commands.

After execution the command processor releases the memory used by these programs. This memory can then be used for other purposes.

Batch files

A batch file is a text file containing a series of DOS commands. When a batch file is started, a special interpreter in the transient portion of the command processor executes the batch file commands. Execution of batch file commands is the same as if the user entered them from the keyboard. An important batch file is the AUTOEXEC.BAT file which executes immediately after DOS is first loaded.

Like all commands of a batch file, these commands are checked for internal commands, external commands or calls to other batch files. If the first is true, the command executes immediately, since the code is already in memory (in the transient part of the command processor). If it is an external command or another batch file, the system searches the current directory for the command. If such a file doesn't exist in this directory, all directories specified in the PATH command are searched in sequence. During the search, only files with the .COM, .EXE or .BAT extensions are examined.

Since the command processor cannot search for all three extensions at the same time, it first searches for files with .COM extensions, then for .EXE files and finally for .BAT files. If the search is unsuccessful, the screen displays an error message and the system waits for new input.

6.3 Booting DOS

When a PC is turned on, the program contained in ROM begins executing. This ROM program is sometimes called the ROM-BIOS, POST (power-on self test), resident diagnostics or bootstrap ROM. It performs several tests on the hardware and memory and then starts to load the DOS.

First the PC checks for a disk in the floppy disk drive. If a disk exists in the floppy disk drive, the PC checks the disk for the *boot sector*. If a disk is not in the drive, the PC searches for a hard disk from which to boot DOS. If no hard disk exists, the PC displays an error message asking the user to insert a system disk.

The first sector on a bootable floppy disk or hard disk is called the boot sector. The program in the boot sector is read into memory and executes. First it checks for the presence of two files: IBMBIO.COM (sometimes called IO.SYS) and IBMDOS.COM (sometimes called MSDOS.SYS). A bootable floppy disk or hard disk must contain these two files or an error message is displayed. Next these program files are loaded into memory.

The program file IBMBIO.COM consists of two modules. The first contains the basic device drivers—keyboard, display and disk. The second contains the initialization sequence for DOS. When the IBMBIO.COM program executes it continues to initialize the system by moving the DOS kernal (loaded in the IBMDOS.COM program file) to the last available memory location.

The DOS kernal builds several important tables and data areas, and performs initialization procedures for individual device drivers which were loaded with the IBMBIO.COM program file.

Next, DOS searches the boot disk for a file named CONFIG.SYS. If found, the commands contained in the file are executed. These commands add device drivers to DOS, allocate disk buffers and file control blocks for DOS and initialize the standard input and output devices.

Lastly the command processor COMMAND.COM (or other shell specified in the CONFIG.SYS file) is loaded and control is passed to it. The booting process ends and the initialization routines remain as "garbage" data in memory until overwritten by another program.

6.4 COM and EXE Programs

DOS recognizes three types of "program" files: those with file extensions of BAT, COM and EXE.

This section describes the structure and functions of these last two program types.

One difference between COM and EXE program files is in the size limitation for each type of program. A COM program cannot exceed 64K in size. An EXE program can be as large as the memory capacity available to DOS.

In a COM program, the program code, data and stack are stored in one 64K partition. All of the segment registers are set at the start of the program and remain fixed for the duration of the program execution. They point to the start of the 64K memory segment. The contents of the ES register may be changed however, since it has no direct effect on program execution.

In an EXE program, the code, data and stack may be stored in different segments, and depending on program size, may be distributed over several segments.

While a COM program file is stored on disk as an image copy of RAM memory, an EXE program file is stored in a special format that will be described shortly.

EXEC

Both program types can be loaded and started using the DOS EXEC function. Any user can access this, but the command processor uses it for executing external commands. Before the EXEC function loads the program into memory, it reserves the RAM memory to hold the program. At the beginning of this memory the EXEC function stores a PSP (*program segment prefix*) data structure. The program is then loaded immediately following the PSP. The segment registers and the stack are initialized and the program is given control. Later, when the program ends, the memory is released based on the contents of the PSP.

Offset	Contents	Size
+ 00H	Interrupt 20H call	(2 bytes)
+ 02H	Segment address of memory allocated for a program	(1 word)
+ 04H	Reserved	(1 byte)
+ 05H	Interrupt 21H call	(5 bytes)
+ 0AH	Copy of interrupt vector 22H	(2 words)
+ 0EH	Copy of interrupt vector 23H	(2 words)
+ 12H	Copy of interrupt vector 24H	(2 words)
+ 16H	reserved	(22 bytes)
+ 2CH	Segment address of environment block	(1 word)
+ 2EH	reserved	(46 bytes)
+ 5CH	FCB 1	(16 bytes)
+ 6CH	FCB 2	(16 bytes)
+ 80H	Number of characters in command line	(1 byte)
+ 81H	Command line (ended by CR)	(127 bytes)

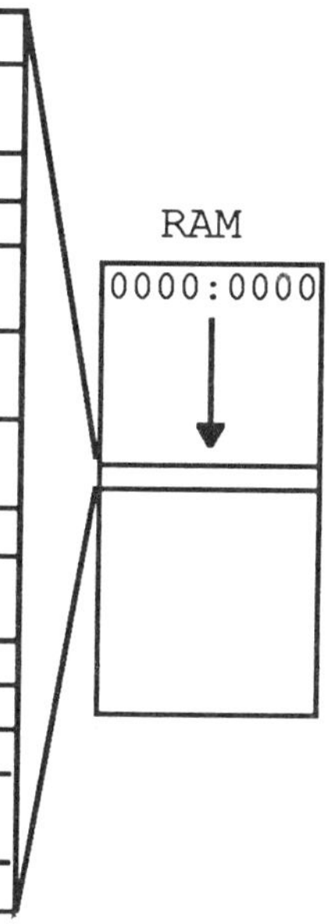

Structure of the PSP

The PSP itself is always 256 bytes long and contains information important for DOS and the program to be executed.

Memory location 00H of the PSP contains a DOS function call to terminate a program. This function releases program memory and returns control to the command processor or the calling program. Memory location 05H of the PSP contains a DOS function call to interrupt 21H. Neither of these are used by DOS, but are leftovers from the CP/M system.

Memory location 02H of the PSP contains the segment address to the end of the program. Memory location 0AH contains the previous contents of the program termination interrupt vector. Memory location 0EH contains the previous contents of the <Ctrl><C> or <Ctrl><Break> interrupt vector. Memory location 12H contains the previous contents of the critical error interrupt vector. For each of these memory locations, the program changes one of the corresponding vectors during execution; DOS can use the original vector in the event that it detects an error.

Location 2CH contains the segment address of the environment block. The environment block contains information such as the current search path and the directory in which the COMMAND.COM command processor is located on disk.

Memory locations 5CH through 6CH contain a *file control block*. This FCB is not often used by DOS since it does not support hierarchical files (paths) and is also left over from CP/M.

The string of parameters that are entered on the command line following the program name is called the *command tail*. The command tail is copied to the *parameter buffer* in the PSP beginning at memory location 81H and its length is stored at memory location 80H. Any redirection parameters are eliminated from the command tail as it is copied to the parameter buffer. The program can examine the parameters in the parameter buffer to direct its execution.

The parameter buffer is also used by DOS as a disk transfer area (DTA) for transmitting data between the disk drive and memory. Most DOS programs do not use the DTA contained in the PSP because it is another leftover from CP/M.

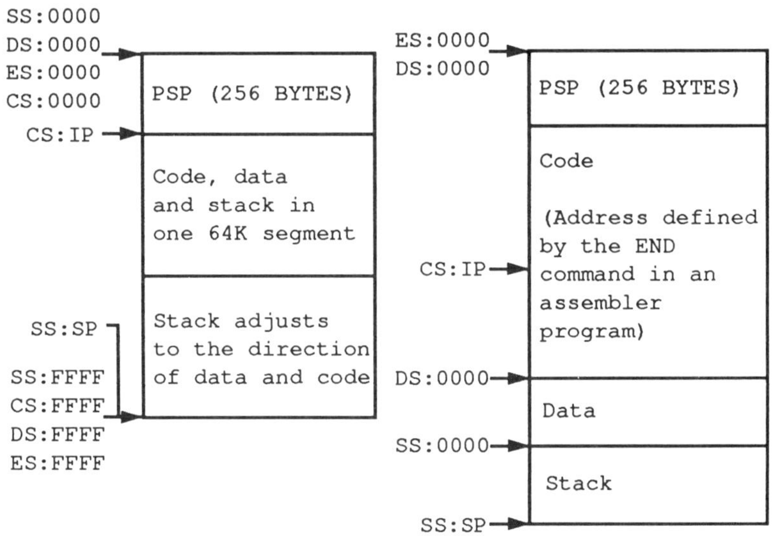

A comparison of COM and EXE programs in memory

6.4.1 COM Programs

COM program files are stored on disk as an image copy of memory. Because of this, no further processing is required during loading. Therefore COM programs load faster and start execution faster than EXE programs.

A COM program loads immediately following the PSP. Execution then begins at the first memory location following the PSP at offset 100H. For this reason, a COM program must begin with an executable instruction, even it if is only a jump instruction to the actual start of the program.

COM program memory limits

As described in the previous section, a COM program is limited to 64K (65,536 bytes) in length. The PSP (256 bytes) and at least 1 word (2 bytes) for the stack must be reserved from this total. Even though the length of the COM program can never exceed 64K, DOS reserves the entire available RAM for a program. Therefore DOS can allocate no further memory, and the COM program cannot call another program using the EXEC function. This limitation can be overcome by releasing the unused memory for other uses with a DOS function.

When control is turned over to the COM program, all segment registers point to the beginning of the PSP. Because of this, the beginning of the COM program (relative to the beginning of the PSP) is always at address 100H. The stack pointer points to the end of the 64K memory segment containing the COM program (usually FFFEH). During every subroutine call within the COM program, the stack is adjusted by 2 bytes in the direction towards the end of the program. The programmer is responsible for preventing the stack from growing and overwriting the program, which would cause it to crash.

There are several ways to end a COM program and return control to DOS or the calling program:

If the program runs under DOS Version 1.0, it can be terminated by calling interrupt 21H function 0, or by calling interrupt 20H. It can also be terminated by using the RET (RETurn) assembler instruction. When this instruction executes, the program continues at the address which is at the top of the stack. Since the EXEC function stored the value 0 at this location before turning control over to the COM program, program execution continues at location CS:0 (the start of the PSP). Recall that this location contains the call for interrupt 20H which terminates the program.

Programs that run on versions later than DOS Version 1.0, are terminated using interrupt 21H function 4CH. The terminating program can pass a numeric return code to the calling program. For example, a value of 0 may indicate that the program executed successfully, while a non-zero value indicates an error during execution.

Next we'll talk about a few of the details that the assembly language programmer will have to take care of in developing a COM program. Note that the high level language programmer is usually insulated from these details by the compiler or interpreter, so you may want to skip ahead.

A COM program is limited to a 64K size. The code and data for the program must be contained within a single segment and addressed through NEAR procedures. Therefore an assembly language program that is to become a COM program may not contain any FAR procedures.

Before calling a COM program, DOS reserves all available memory for the program even though it normally uses only one 64K segment and indicates this by setting memory location 2 in the PSP. Usually the program terminates and the memory is made available to DOS again.

In some circumstances you may want to write a program which is to remain resident after execution. But DOS thinks that there isn't any memory available. This prevents other programs from loading and executing.

In other circumstances you may want to execute another program from this COM program using the EXEC function. Again, since DOS thinks that memory is unavailable, it won't allow the new program to run.

Both of these problems can be circumvented by freeing up the unused memory.

There are two approaches in doing this: release only the memory outside of the 64K COM segment or release memory outside of the 64K COM segment plus any unused memory within the 64K COM segment. This creates more memory for other programs, but relocates the stack outside the protected COM segment memory, leaving it open to be overwritten by other programs. Because of this, the stack must be relocated to the end of the code segment before releasing the memory. The stack must have a certain limit in size (in most cases 512 bytes will be more than enough).

The following sample program can serve as an example for developing a COM program. A small (init) routine relocates the stack to the end of the code segment after the start of the program and releases all remaining memory. Even when this program loads another program, it remains resident. This routine can be useful to applications, and can be part of any COM program.

```
;testcom.asm
code      segment para 'CODE'      ;Definition of CODE-segments

          org 100h                 ;starts at Address 100H
                                   ;directly behind the PSP

          assume cs:code, ds:code, es:code, ss:code

                                   ;all  segments point to the CODE
                                   ;segment

start:    jmp  init                ;Call of the Initialization Routine

;== Data  ==============================================================

          ;-- Data, Buffers and ----------
          ;-- Variables can be stored here

;== Program ============================================================

prog      proc near                ;this Procedure is the actual
                                   ;Main program and is executed after
                                   ;the Initialization


          mov  ax,4C00h            ;Terminate Program through calling a
```

```
          int  21h              ;DOS function on error code 0

prog      endp                  ;End of the PROG procedure

;-- Initialization ---------------------------------------------------

init:     mov  ah,4Ah           ;Change Function number for memory size
          mov  bx,offset endp   ;Calculate number of paragraphs (16 byte
          mov  cl,4             ;each) available to the program
          shr  bx,cl
          inc  bx
          int  21h              ;Call function through DOS-Interrupt
          mov  sp,offset endp   ;Set new stack-Pointer
          jmp  prog

init_end label near

;== stack ============================================================


          dw (256-((init_end-init) shr 1)) dup (?)

                                ;the stack has 256 Words, but includes
                                ;the code of the INIT-Routine which
                                ;after its execution is no longer needed

endp      equ this byte         ;End of memory used by this
                                ;program

;== End ==============================================================

code      ends                  ;End of the CODE-segment
          end  start            ;End of the Assembler-Program. For
                                ;execution use START command
```

First you must assemble the source program using the assembler. In the following example, we are using the Microsoft assembler. Following assembly, you then link the object code using the LINK program. When you execute the LINK program, the following message appears:

```
Warning: no stack segment
```

You can disregard this message. If the program contains no errors, the LINK program creates an EXE file. Since you want a COM program and not an EXE program developed, you must run the EXE2BIN program as the last step. This converts EXE programs into COM programs. Here are the steps for preparing an assembly language program using the Microsoft assembler. The program to assemble is named TESTCOM.ASM.

```
masm testcom;
link testcom;
exe2bin testcom.exe testcom.com
```

If all steps were carried out correctly, the program TESTCOM.COM can be executed from DOS by simply typing TESTCOM.

6.4.2 EXE Programs

EXE programs have an advantage over COM programs because they are not limited to a maximum length of 64K for code, data and stack. The disadvantage of this is the greater complexity of these files. This means that in addition to the program itself, other information must be stored in an EXE file.

EXE vs. COM

EXE programs contain separate segments for code, data and stack which can be organized in any sequence. Unlike a COM program, an EXE program loads into memory from disk and undergoes processing by the EXEC function and then finally begins execution. This is necessary because of the limitations already described for COM programs.

EXE programs aren't limited to loading at a fixed memory location, but to any desired location in memory that's a multiple of 16. Since an EXE program can have several segments, this requires the use of FAR machine language instructions. For example, a main program can be in one segment and call a subroutine in another segment. The segment address must be provided for this FAR instruction in addition to the offset for the routine to be called. The problem is that the segment address may be different for every execution of the program.

COM files avoid this problem since the program size is limited to 64K, which makes the use of FAR commands unnecessary. EXE programs solve this problem in a more complex way: the LINK program places a data structure at the beginning of every EXE file which contains the addresses of all segments, among other things. It contains the addresses of all memory locations in which the segment address of a certain segment is stored during program execution.

If the EXEC function loads the EXE program, it knows the addresses where the various segments should be loaded. It can therefore enter these values into the memory locations at the beginning of the EXE file. Because of this, more time elapses between the initial program call and when the program actually begins execution than for a COM program. The EXE program also occupies more memory than a COM program. The following illustration shows the structure of the header for an EXE file.

EXE file header structure		
Address	Contents	Type
+00H	EXE program identifier (5A4Dh)	1 WORD
+02H	file length MOD 512	1 WORD
+04H	file length DIV 512	1 WORD
+06H	Number of segment addresses for passing	1 WORD
+08H	Head size in paragraphs	1 WORD
+0AH	Minimum no. of extra paragraphs needed	1 WORD
+0EH	Maximum no. of extra paragraphs needed	1 WORD
+10H	SP register contents on program start	1 WORD
+12H	Checksum based on EXE file header	1 WORD
+14H	IP register contents on program start	1 WORD
+16H	Start of code segment in EXE file	1 WORD
+18H	Relocation table address in EXE file	1 WORD
+1AH	Overlay number	1 WORD
+1CH	Buffer memory	1 WORD
+??H	Address of passing segment addresses (relocation table)	1 WORD
+??H	Program code, data and stack segment	1 WORD

EXE file header construction

After the segment references within the EXE program have been resolved to the current addresses, the EXEC function sets the DS and the ES segment register to the beginning of the PSP which also precedes all EXE programs in memory. Because of this, the EXE program can access the information contained in the PSP, such as the address of the environment block and the parameters contained in the command line (command tail). The stack address and the contents of the stack pointer are stored in the EXE file header and accessed from there. This also applies to the code segment address containing the first instructions of the program, and the program counter. After the values have been assigned, the program execution starts.

To ensure compatibility with future DOS versions, an EXE program should terminate by calling interrupt 21H function 4CH.

Of course, memory must be available for the EXE program. The EXE loader determines the total program size based on the size of the individual segments of the EXE program. Then it can allocate this amount of memory and some additional memory immediately following the EXE program. The first two fields of the EXE program file header contain the minimum and maximum size of memory required in *paragraphs* (1-6 bytes).

First, the EXE loader tries to reserve the maximum number of paragraphs. If this is not possible the loader tries to reserve the remaining memory which may be no smaller than the minimum number of paragraphs. These fields are determined by the compiler or assembler, not the linker. The minimum is 0 and the maximum allowed is FFFFH. This last number is unrealistic in most cases (it adds up to 1 megabyte) but reserves the entire memory for the EXE program.

This brings us back to the same problem as in COM programs. EXE files make poor resident programs, but an EXE program may need to call another program during execution. This is possible only by first releasing the additional reserved memory. The following program below contains a routine which reduces the reserved memory to a minimum.

The program uses separate code, data and stack segments. It can serve as a model for other EXE programs that you can write.

```
; testexe.asm
;== stack ==============================================================

stack     segment para stack       ;Definition of the stack-segment

          dw 256 dup (?)           ;the stack has 256 Words

stack     ends                     ;End of the stack-segment

;== Data ===============================================================

data      segment para 'DATA'      ;Definition of the Data-segment

          ;all data, buffers and variables can be stored here

data      ends                     ;End of the Data segment

;== Code ===============================================================

code      segment para 'CODE'      ;Definition of the CODE-segment

          assume cs:code, ds:data, ss:stack

                                   ;CS defines the Code, DS
                                   ;the Data and SS the stack
                                   ;segment

prog      proc far                 ;this procedure is the actual
                                   ;Main program and is executed after
                                   ;the program start

          mov  ax,data             ;Load segment address of the Data segment into
          mov  ds,ax               ;the DS-Register
          call setfree             ;release memory not needed

          ;store application program here  ----------------------

          mov  ax,4C00h            ;terminate with call of DOS function
          int  21h                 ;on return of error code 0
                                   ;terminate

prog      endp                     ;End of PROG Procedure

;-- SETFREE  : release memory storage not occupied  ----------------
;-- Inputt   : ES = Address of PSP
;-- Output   : none
;-- Register : AX, BX, CL and FLAGS are changed
;-- Info     : Since the stack-segment is always the last segment in an
;              EXE file, ES:0000 points to the beginning and SS:SP
;              to the end of the program in storage. Because of this the
;              length of the program can be calculated.
```

```
setfree   proc near

          mov  bx,ss               ;subtract the two segment addresses
          mov  ax,es               ;from each other. The result is the
          sub  bx,ax               ;number of paragraphs from PSP to
                                   ;the beginning of the stack
          mov  ax,sp               ;since the stackpointer is a the end
          mov  cl,4                ;of the stack segment, its content
          shr  ax,cl               ;gives the length of the stacks
          add  bx,ax               ;add to the present length
          inc  bx                  ;one more paragraph as a precaution
          mov  ah,4ah              ;pass new size to DOS
          int  21h

          ret                      ;back to calling program

setfree   endp

;== End ================================================================

code      ends                     ;End of the CODE-segment
          end  prog                ;End of the Assembler program.
                                   ;Start execution with the PROG procedure
```

To develop an EXE program, it must be assembled like a normal program with an assembler. Then it is linked with the LINK program. If the program contains no errors, the LINK program creates an EXE file.

Here are the individual steps for preparing an EXE program from the assembly language source named TESTEXE.ASM.

```
masm testexe;
link testexe;
```

If all these steps were executed correctly, the program TESTEXE.EXE can be started from the DOS level by typing TESTEXE.

6.5 Character Input and Output from DOS

When first learning a programming language, many beginners learn the basic input and output instructions of the language. In much the same way, programmers get their experience writing DOS accessible programming by using the functions for character input and output. For this reason, this book starts with these input and output functions instead of more complex functions. These input and output functions can address the keyboard, screen, printer and serial interface.

The functions can be divided into two types: those carried over from the CP/M operating system and those borrowed from the UNIX operating system. While the two types of functions can be intermixed, we recommend that you use one type of function throughout a program for the sake of consistency.

The UNIX type functions use a *handle* as an identifier to a device. Because of recent DOS trends to move closer to UNIX, you may want to give the handle functions precedence.

6.5.1 Handle Functions

The handle functions perform file access as well as character input to or output from a device. DOS recognizes the difference by examining the name assigned by the handle. If the handle is a device name, it addresses the device; otherwise it assumes that file access should occur. The device names are as follows:

```
CON     Keyboard and display
AUX     Serial Interface
PRN     Printer
NUL     Imaginary device (nothing happens on access)
```

Output and input go to and from the AUX, PRN and NUL devices. For the device CON, output is sent to the screen and input is read from the keyboard.

When DOS passes control to a program, five handles are available for access to individual devices. These handles have values from 0 to 4 and represent the following devices:

0	Standard input (CON)
1	Standard output (CON)
2	Standard output for error messages (CON)
3	Standard serial interface (AUX)
4	Standard printer (PRN)

Here is a short example to help demonstrate the use of this table:

Display error message

If a program wants to accept input from the user, the handle function 0 indicates this during the call since the standard input device is addressed. Handle 0 normally represents the keyboard, permitting user input from the user to the program. Since the user can redirect standard input, you can redirect input to originate from a file instead of the keyboard. This redirection remains hidden from the program.

Before discussing these devices, here are some functions used to access any device.

Function 40H of interrupt 21H sends data to a device. The function number (40H) is passed in the AH register and the handle is passed in the BX register. For example, to display an error message, the value 2 indicates the handle for displaying the error message (this device cannot be redirected, so handle 2 always addresses the console). The number of characters to be in the error message is passed in the CX register. The characters making up the message are stored sequentially in memory whose segment address is stored in the DS register and offset address in the DX register.

Following the call to the function, the carry flag signals any error. If there was no error, the carry flag is reset and the AX register contains the number of characters that were displayed. If the AX register contains the value 0, then there was no more space available on the storage medium for the message. If the carry flag is set, the error message was not sent and an error code is indicated in the AX register. An error code of 5 indicates that the device was not available. An error code of 6 indicates that the handle was not opened.

Function 3FH of interrupt 21H reads character data from a device and has many similarities to the previous function. Both functions have identical register usage. The function number is passed in the AX register and the handle in the BX register. The number of characters read is passed in the CX register and the memory address of the characters transferred are passed in the DS:DX register pair.

Following the call to the function, the carry flag also signals any error. Again, any error code is passed in the AX register. Error codes 5 and 6 have the same meaning as when using function 40H. If the carry flag is reset, then the function executed successfully. The AX register then contains the number of characters read into the buffer. A value of 0 in the AX register means that the data to be read should have come from a file, but that this file contains no more data.

As we already mentioned, it's possible to redirect the input or output when accessing DOS. For example, a program that normally expects input from the keyboard can be made to accept the input from a file. So, to avoid having input or output redirected, you can open a new handle to a specific device which insures that the transfer of data to or from the desired device takes place instead of to or from a redirected device.

Use function 3DH of interrupt 21H to open such a device.

The function number 3DH is passed in the AH register. The AL register contains 0 to enable reading from the device, 1 to enable writing to the device and 2 for both reading and writing to the device. The name of the device is placed in memory whose address is passed in the DS:DX register pair. So that the DOS can properly identify the device name, the names must be specified in uppercase characters. The last character of the string must be an end character (ASCII value 0).

Following the function calls the status is indicated by the carry flag. A reset flag means that the device was opened successfully and the handle number is passed back in the AX register. A set flag indicates an error and the AX register contains any error code.

The handle is closed using function 3EH of interrupt 21H. The function number is passed in the AH register and the handle number is passed in the BX register. The carry flag again indicates the status of the function call. A set carry flag indicates an error.

You can also close the predefined handles 0 through 4 using this function. But if you close handle 0 (the standard input device) you'll no longer be able to accept input from the keyboard.

Let's examine the special characteristics of each device.

Keyboard

The keyboard can perform only read operations. The results of the read operations depend on the mode in which the device was addressed. Here DOS differentiates between *raw* and *cooked*. In the *cooked mode* DOS checks every character sent to a device or received from a device to see if it is a special control character. If DOS finds a special control character, it performs a certain action in response to the character. In *raw mode* the individual characters are passed through unchecked and unmanipulated. DOS normally operates the device in cooked mode for character input and output. However, you can switch to raw mode within a program (see below).

The difference between cooked and raw mode can be best explained by an example of reading the keyboard. Assume that 30 characters are read from the keyboard in cooked mode. As you enter the characters DOS allows you to edit the input using several of the control keys. For example <Ctrl><C> and <Ctrl><Break> abort the input. <Ctrl><S> temporarily halts the program until another key is pressed. <Ctrl><P> directs subsequent data from the screen to the printer (until <Ctrl><P> is pressed again). <Backspace> removes the last character from the DOS buffer. If the <Enter> key is pressed, the first 30 characters (or all characters input up to now if there are less than 30) are copied from the DOS buffer into the input buffer of the program without the control characters.

In raw mode all characters entered (including control characters) are passed to the calling program without requiring the user to press the <Enter> key. After exactly

30 characters, control passes to the calling program, even if you pressed the <Enter> key as the second character of the input.

Screen

To display characters on the screen, handle 1 is usually addressed as the standard output device. Since this device can be redirected, output through this handle can pass to devices other than the screen. On the other hand, you cannot redirect the standard error output device (handle 2), so error messages that pass through this handle always appears on the screen. This handle is recommended for character display on the screen only.

The screen is normally addressed in cooked mode—every character displayed on the screen is tested for the <Ctrl><C> or the <Ctrl><Break> control characters. This test slows down the screen output, so sometimes changing to raw mode decreases program execution time.

Printer

Unlike the keyboard and screen, printer output cannot be redirected—at least not from the user level. An exception to this rule is redirecting output from a parallel printer to a serial printer. Characters ready to print can be sent to a buffer before they are sent to the printer. Handle 4 is used to address the standard printer. There are three standard printer devices LPT1, LPT2 and LPT3. Device PRN is synonymous with LPT1. When this handle is opened the device name is specified as one of the three: LPT1, LPT2 or LPT3.

Serial interface

Much of the information that applies to the printer also applies to the serial interface. For example, serial input and output cannot be redirected to another device (e.g., from a serial printer to a parallel printer). The programmer can use the predefined handle 3 for serial access, through which you can address the standard serial interface (AUX).

Handle 3 is used to address the standard serial device. The two are names COM1 and COM2. A PC can have multiple serial interfaces. Only the first two (COM1 and COM2) are supported by DOS. Since the system doesn't know exactly which interface to access during AUX device access, you should open a new handle for access to the specific device.

Errors during read operations in DOS mode are returned to the serial interface in cooked mode. The number returned to the AX register will not match the number of characters actually read. We recommend that you operate the serial interface in the raw mode, even if this mode ignores control characters such as <Ctrl><C> and EOF (end-of-file).

6.5.2 Traditional DOS Functions

The DOS functions for input and output aren't based on the handle oriented functions. If you use these functions you won't need to specify a handle, since each function pertains to a specific device.

Below are the various input and output devices and the way in which these functions work with them.

Keyboard

There are seven DOS functions for addressing the keyboard but they differ in many ways. For example, they respond differently to the <Ctrl> <Break> key. Some functions echo the characters on the screen; others don't.

You can use DOS functions 01H, 06H, 07H and 08H to read a single keyboard character. The function number is passed in the AH register. Following the call, the character is returned in the AL register.

For DOS function 01H, DOS waits for a keypress if the keyboard buffer is empty. When this happens, the character is echoed on the screen. If the keyboard buffer is not empty, a new character is fetched and returned to the calling program. DOS function 06H can be used for both character input and output. To input a character a value of FFH is loaded into the DL register. This function doesn't wait for a character to be input but returns immediately to the calling program. If the zero flag is set, a character was not read. If the zero flag is reset, a character was read and returned in the AL register. The character is not echoed on the screen.

DOS functions 07H and 08H are used to read the keyboard similar to function 1. Both either fetch a character from the keyboard buffer or wait for a character to be entered at the keyboard. Neither echo the character to the screen. They differ in that function 08H responds to <Ctrl><C> and function 07H does not.

By using function 0BH, a program can determine whether one or more characters are in the keyboard buffer before calling any functions that read characters. After calling this function, the AL register contains 0 if the keyboard buffer is empty, and FFH if the keyboard buffer is not empty.

DOS function 0CH is used to clear the keyboard buffer. After it is cleared, the function whose number was passed to function 0CH in the AL registered is automatically called.

DOS function 0AH is used to read a string of characters. Again this function number is passed in the AH register. In addition, the memory address of a buffer for the character string is passed in the DS:DX register pair. This buffer is used to hold the character string. The first byte of the buffer indicates the maximum number of characters that may be contained in the buffer.

When this function is called, DOS reads up to the maximum number of characters and stores them in the buffer starting at the third byte. It reads until either the maximum number of characters is entered or the <Enter> key is pressed. The actual number of characters is stored in the second byte of the buffer. Extended key codes which occupy two bytes each in the buffer may be entered. The first byte of the pair (ASCII value 0) signifies that an extended key code follows. This means, for example, that for a maximum buffer size of 10 bytes, only five extended characters may be entered.

The following table illustrates how the various functions respond to <Ctrl><C> or <Ctrl><Break>, and provides a quick overview of the individual functions for character input.

Fct.	Task	<Ctrl><C>	Echo
01H	Character input	yes	yes
06H	direct character input	no	no
07H	Character input	no	no
08H	Character input	yes	no
0AH	Character string input	yes	no
0BH	Read input-status	yes	no
0CH	Reset input-buffer then input	varies	varies

Screen output

There are three DOS functions for character output.

DOS function 02H outputs a single character to the screen or standard output device. The character is passed to the DL register.

DOS function 06H which is multi-purpose is also used to output a single character. The character is passed in the DL register. You can see that the character whose value is 255 cannot be output since this indicates that the function is to perform an input operation. Output using this function is faster than using function 02H since it doesn't test for the <Ctrl><C> or <Ctrl><Break> keys.

DOS function 09H is used for string output. Again, the function number is passed in the AH register. The address of the string is passed in the DS:DX register pair. The last character of the string is a dollar sign. In addition, the following control codes are recognized.

Code	Operation
7	"Bell", rings the bell on the PC
8	"Backspace", erases the preceding character and moves the cursor back by one character
10	"Line Feed", (LF) moves the cursor one line down
13	"Carriage Return", (CR) moves the cursor to the beginning of the current line

As with function 02H, this function also checks for <Ctrl><C> or <Ctrl><Break>.

Printer

DOS function 05H is used to output a single character to the printer. If the printer is busy, this function waits until it is ready before returning control to the calling program. During this time, it will respond to the <Ctrl><C> and <Ctrl><Break> keys.

The function number is passed in the AH register. The character to output is passed in the DL register. The status of the printer is not returned. Most programmers will elect to use the BIOS function instead of the DOS function for printer output since you can specify the exact printer device and determine the printer status using the BIOS version. See Section 7.12 for more detailed information.

Serial interface

There are two DOS functions for communicating using serial interface—one for input and one for output. Both functions respond to <Ctrl><C> and <Ctrl><Break>, but they don't return the status of the serial interface, nor do they recognize transmission errors.

DOS function 03H is used to input data from the serial interface. The character is returned in the AL register. Since the data is not buffered, the data can overrun the interface if the interface receives data faster than this function can handle it.

DOS function 04H is used to output data over the serial interface. The character to output is passed in the DL register. If the serial interface is not ready to accept the data, this function waits until it is free.

Again, most programmers prefer to use the BIOS equivalent functions (see Section 7.9) to perform serial data transmission because of their more complete data handling capabilities.

Demonstration programs

Earlier we mentioned that it was possible to switch a device from cooked mode to raw mode and back. The BASIC, Pascal and C programs that follow show you how to do this. They use the IOCTL functions which permit access to the DOS device drivers (see Section 6.11.7 for details on this routine). These are routines which serve as interfaces between the DOS input/output functions and the hardware. The IOCTL functions in these programs tell the CON device driver (responsible for the keyboard and the display) whether it should operate in the cooked mode or in the raw mode.

To demonstrate how differently characters respond in the two modes, the programs switch the CON driver into raw mode first. Then this driver displays a sample string several times. Unlike cooked mode, pressing <Ctrl><C> or <Ctrl><S> in raw mode has no effect on stopping program execution or text display.

After the program finishes displaying the sample string, the driver switches to the cooked mode. The sample string is displayed again several times. When you press <Ctrl><C> the program stops (Turbo Pascal version). For the BASIC and C versions, you can press <Ctrl><C> to stop the program, or press <Ctrl><S> to pause or continue the display.

Switching between the raw and the cooked mode does not take place directly through a function. First the *device attribute* of the driver is determined. This attribute contains certain information which identifies the driver and describes its method of operation. One bit in this word indicates if the driver operates in raw or cooked mode. The programs set or reset this bit, depending on the mode you want running the driver.

BASIC listing: RAWCOOK.BAS

```
100 '**********************************************************************'
110 '*                          R A W C O O K                             *'
120 '*--------------------------------------------------------------------*'
130 '*  Task        : make two subroutines available                      *'
140 '*                to switch the character driver into RAW- or         *'
150 '*                COOKED mode                                         *'
160 '*  Author      : MICHAEL TISCHER                                     *'
170 '*  developed   : 07/23/87                                            *'
180 '*  last Update : 04/08/89                                            *'
190 '**********************************************************************'
200 '
210 CLS : KEY OFF
220 PRINT"WARNING: This program can only be started if the GWBASIC was"
230 PRINT"started from DOS with the command <GWBASIC  /m:60000>."
240 PRINT : PRINT"If this is not the case, please input <s> for Stop."
250 PRINT"Otherwise press any key...";
260 A$ = INKEY$ : IF A$ = "s" THEN END
270 IF A$ = "" THEN 260
280 GOSUB 60000                        'Install function for interrupt call
290 CLS                                                       'erase display
300 HANDLE% = 0                   'handle is connected with console driver
310 PRINT"RAWCOOK (c) 1987 by Michael Tischer" : PRINT
320 PRINT"The Console driver (Keyboard and Display) is now in RAW-"
330 PRINT"Mode so that during input and output no control characters "
335 PRINT"are recognized."
340 PRINT"Because of this not even <CTRL> + <S> can stop the "
345 PRINT"following output."
350 PRINT"Try it ..." : PRINT
360 PRINT "Press any key to start output ..."
365 GOSUB 25000                                      'Clear keyboard buffer
370 A$ = INKEY$ : IF A$ = "" THEN 370                         'wait for a key
380 GOSUB 52000                        'Switch console driver into RAW mode
390 GOSUB 50000                                         'Output Test-String
400 CLS
410 PRINT"The Console driver (Keyboard and Display) is now in "
420 PRINT"COOKED mode. Control characters will be recognized during "
425 PRINT"input/output."
430 PRINT"The following output can be stopped with <CTRL> + <S>."
440 PRINT"Try it ..." : PRINT
```

```
450 PRINT "Press any key to start the output..."
455 GOSUB 25000                              'Clear the keyboard buffer
460 A$ = INKEY$ : IF A$ = "" THEN 460                     'wait for a key
470 GOSUB 51000              'change console driver to the COOKED mode
480 GOSUB 50000                                    'output Test-String
490 CLS
500 END
510 '
25000 A$ = INKEY$ : IF A$ = "" THEN RETURN   'Clear the keyboard buffer
25010 goto 25000
50000 '**************************************************************'
50010 '* outputs a Test-String on the Standard output device        *'
50020 '*------------------------------------------------------------*'
50030 '* Input : none                                               *'
50040 '* Output: none                                               *'
50050 '**************************************************************'
50060 '
50070 T$ = "Test.... "                             'Output Test-String
50080 FOR I = 1 TO 250                                      '250 times
50090 FCT% = &H40 : FCT1% = 0        'Write function number for handle
50100 INR% = &H21                            'Call DOS-Interrupt 21H
50110 ADRLO% = 9 : ADRHI% = 0          'output 9 characters at a time
50120 OFSLO% = PEEK(VARPTR(T$)+1)  'LO-byte of offset address of string
50130 OFSHI% = PEEK(VARPTR(T$)+2)     'HI-byte of offset address string
50140 HANDLO% = 1: HANDHI% = 0      'address the standard output device
50150 CALL IA(INR%,FCT%,FCT1%,HANDHI%,HANDLO%,ADRHI%,ADRLO%,OFSHI%,
      OFSLO%,Z%,Z%,Z%,Z%)
50160 NEXT                                                  'next run
50170 PRINT
50180 RETURN                                          'back to caller
50190 '
51000 '**************************************************************'
51010 '* change device driver to COOKED mode                        *'
51020 '*------------------------------------------------------------*'
51030 '* Input : HANDLE% = handle connected with the driver         *'
51040 '* Output: none                                               *'
51050 '**************************************************************'
51060 '
51070 GOSUB 53000                      'Get device attribute of driver
51080 ATTRIB% = ATTRIB% AND 223                      'Find COOKED-Bit
51090 GOSUB 54000                      'Set device attribute of driver
51100 RETURN                                          'back to caller
51110 '
52000 '**************************************************************'
52010 '* change device driver to RAW mode                           *'
52020 '*------------------------------------------------------------*'
52030 '* Input : HANDLE% = handle connected to the driver           *'
52040 '* Output: none                                               *'
52050 '**************************************************************'
52060 '
52070 GOSUB 53000                      'Get device attribute of driver
52080 ATTRIB% = ATTRIB% OR 32                            'Set RAW-Bit
52090 GOSUB 54000                      'Set device attribute of driver
52100 RETURN                                          'back to caller
52110 '
53000 '**************************************************************'
53010 '* Get device attribute of a driver                           *'
53020 '*------------------------------------------------------------*'
53030 '* Input : HANDLE% = handle connected with a driver           *'
53040 '* Output: ATTRIB% = Attribute of driver                      *'
53050 '* Info  : Z% used as Dummy-Variable                          *'
```

```
53060 '*         only Bits 0 to 7 of the device attribute           *'
53070 '*         determined                                         *'
53080 '**************************************************************'
53090 '
53100 FCT%=&H44                              'Function number for IOCTL
53110 FCT1%=0    'Read Function number for IOCTL: Read device attribute
53120 INR%=&H21                              'Call DOS-Interrupt 21H
53130 HANDHI% = INT(HANDLE%/256)               'HI-byte of the handle
53140 HANDLO% = HANDLE% AND 255                'LO-byte of the handle
53150 CALL IA(INR%,FCT%,FCT1%,HANDHI%,HANDLO%,Z%,Z%,Z%,ATTRIB%,Z%,Z%,Z%,Z%)
53160 RETURN                                            'back to caller
53170 '
54000 '**************************************************************'
54010 '* Set device attribute of a driver                           *'
54020 '*------------------------------------------------------------*'
54030 '* Input : HANDLE% = handle connected to a driver             *'
54040 '*         ATTRIB% = the attribute of the driver              *'
54050 '* Output: none                                               *'
54060 '* Info  : Z% used as Dummy-Variable                          *'
54070 '**************************************************************'
54080 '
54090 FCT%=&H44                              'Function number for IOCTL
54100 FCT1%=1          'Set function number for IOCTL: device attribute
54110 INR%=&H21                              'Call DOS-Interrupt 21(h)
54120 HANDHI% = INT(HANDLE%/256)               'HI-byte of the handle
54130 HANDLO% = HANDLE% AND 255                'LO-byte of the handle
54140 ATHI% = INT(ATTRIB%/256)              'HI-byte of the Attribute
54150 ATLO% = ATTRIB% AND 255               'LO-byte of the Attribute
54160 CALL IA(INR%,FCT%,FCT1%,HANDHI%,HANDLO%,Z%,Z%,ATHI%,ATLO%,Z%,Z%,Z%,Z%)
54170 RETURN                                            'back to caller
54180 '
60000 '**************************************************************'
60010 '* Initialize the Routine for Interrupt Call                  *'
60020 '*------------------------------------------------------------*'
60030 '* Input : none                                               *'
60040 '* Output: IA is the Start address of the Interrupt-Routine   *'
60050 '**************************************************************'
60060 '
60070 IA=60000!       'Start address of the routine in the BASIC-Segment
60080 DEF SEG                                        'Set BASIC-Segment
60090 RESTORE 60130
60100 FOR I% = 0 TO 160 : READ X% : POKE IA+I%,X% : NEXT  'Poke Routine
60110 RETURN                                            'back to caller
60120 '
60130 DATA  85,139,236, 30,  6,139,118, 30,139,  4,232,140,  0,139,118
60140 DATA  12,139, 60,139,118,  8,139,  4, 61,255,255,117,  2,140,216
60150 DATA 142,192,139,118, 28,138, 36,139,118, 26,138,  4,139,118, 24
60160 DATA 138, 60,139,118, 22,138, 28,139,118, 20,138, 44,139,118, 18
60170 DATA 138, 12,139,118, 16,138, 52,139,118, 14,138, 20,139,118, 10
60180 DATA 139, 52, 85,205, 33, 93, 86,156,139,118, 12,137, 60,139,118
60190 DATA  28,136, 36,139,118, 26,136,  4,139,118, 24,136, 60,139,118
60200 DATA  22,136, 28,139,118, 20,136, 44,139,118, 18,136, 12,139,118
60210 DATA  16,136, 52,139,118, 14,136, 20,139,118,  8,140,192,137,  4
60220 DATA  88,139,118,  6,137,  4, 88,139,118, 10,137,  4,  7, 31, 93
60230 DATA 202, 26,  0, 91, 46,136, 71, 66,233,108,255
```

Pascal listing: RAWCOOK.PAS

```
{**********************************************************************}
{*                              R A W C O O K                         *}
{*--------------------------------------------------------------------*}
{*    Task          :   provide two functions to switch               *}
{*                      a character device driver to the RAW-         *}
{*                      or the COOKED mode                            *}
{*--------------------------------------------------------------------*}
{*    Author          : MICHAEL TISCHER                               *}
{*    developed       : 08/16/87                                      *}
{*    last Update     : 05/11/89                                      *}
{**********************************************************************}

program RAWCOOKP;

Uses Crt, Dos;                                    { CRT and DOS units }

const STANDARDIN  = 0;     { handle 0 is connected with Standard input }
      STANDARDOUT = 1;    { handle 1 is connected with Standard output }

var Keys : char;                         { only needed for Demo program }

{**********************************************************************}
{* GETMODE: read attribute of device driver in                        *}
{* Input   : the handle passed must be connected to device addressed  *}
{* Output  : the device attribute                                     *}
{**********************************************************************}

function GetMode(Handle : integer) : integer;

var Regs : Registers;          { register-Variable for Interrupt call }

begin
 Regs.ah := $44;               { Function number for IOCTL: Get Mode }
 Regs.bx := Handle;
 MsDos( Regs );                            { Call DOS-Interrupt 21H    }
 GetMode := Regs.dx                          { Pass device attribute }
end;

{**********************************************************************}
{* SETRAW  : Change a character driver into RAW-Mode                  *}
{* Input   : the handle passed must be connected with                 *}
{*           addressed device                                         *}
{* Output  : none                                                     *}
{**********************************************************************}

procedure SetRaw(Handle : integer);

var Regs : Registers;          { register-Variable for Interrupt call }

begin
 Regs.ax := $4401;             { Function number for IOCTL: Set Mode }
 Regs.bx := Handle;
 Regs.dx := GetMode(Handle) and 255 or 32;     { new device attribute }
 MsDos( Regs );                            { Call DOS-Interrupt 21H    }
end;

{**********************************************************************}
{* SETCOOKED : Change a character driver into the COOKED-Mode         *}
{* Input     : the handle passed must be connected with the           *}
{*             device addressed                                       *}
{* Output    : none                                                   *}
{**********************************************************************}

procedure SetCooked(Handle : integer);

var Regs   : Registers;        { register-Variable for Interrupt call }
```

```
begin
 Regs.ax := $4401;          { Function number for IOCTL: Set Mode }
 Regs.bx := Handle;
 Regs.dx := GetMode(Handle) and 223;       { new device attribute }
 MsDos( Regs );                            { Call DOS-Interrupt 21H    }
end;

{*********************************************************************}
{* TESTOUTPUT : Output a Test-String 1000 times on the Standard      *}
{*              output device                                         *}
{* Input      : none                                                  *}
{* Output     : none                                                  *}
{*********************************************************************}

procedure TestOutput;

var Regs : Registers;           { register-Variable for Interrupt call }
    LoopCnt  : integer;                               { Loop variable }
    Test     : string[9];                  { The Test-String for output }

begin
 Test := 'Test.... ';
 Regs.bx := STANDARDOUT;        { output on the Standard output device }
 Regs.cx := 9;                                 { Number of characters }
 Regs.ds := Seg(Test);                  { Segment address of the text }
 Regs.dx := Ofs(Test)+1;                 { Offset address of the text }
 for LoopCnt := 1 to 1000 do
  begin
    Regs.ah := $40;                 { Write function number for handle }
    MsDos( Regs );                         { Call DOS-Interrupt 21H    }
   end;
  writeln;
end;

{*********************************************************************}
{*                            MAIN PROGRAM                            *}
{*********************************************************************}

begin
  ClrScr;                                              { Clear screen }
  writeln('RAWCOOK (c) 1987 by Michael Tischer'#13#10);
  writeln('The Console driver is now in RAW-Mode. Control keys such as <Ctrl><C>');
  writeln('are not recognized during output. Press a key to display a text on
'#13#10);
  writeln('the screen, and try stopping the display by pressing <Ctrl><C>');
  Keys := ReadKey;                                      { wait for key }
  SetRaw(STANDARDIN);                    { Console driver in RAW mode }
  TestOutput;                        { Output Test-String 1000 times }
  ClrScr;                                              { Clear Screen }
  while KeyPressed do
    Keys := ReadKey;                           { Empty keyboard buffer }
    writeln('The Console driver is now in COOKED mode. Control keys such as');
    writeln('<CTRL><C> are recognized during output');
    writeln('Press a key to start, then press <Ctrl><C> to stop the display');
  Keys := ReadKey;                                      { Wait for key }
  SetCooked(STANDARDIN);
  TestOutput;                        { Output Test-String 1000 times }
end.
```

C listing: RAWCOOK.C

```
/***********************************************************************/
/*                           R A W C O O K                             */
/*---------------------------------------------------------------------*/
/*    Task          : provides two functions for                       */
/*                    switching a character device driver into the RAW */
/*                    or into the COOKED mode                          */
/*---------------------------------------------------------------------*/
/*    Author        : MICHAEL TISCHER                                  */
/*    developed on  : 08/16/87                                         */
/*    last Update   : 04/08/89                                         */
/*---------------------------------------------------------------------*/
/*    (MICROSOFT C)                                                    */
/*    Creation      : MSC RAWCOOKC;                                    */
/*                    LINK RAWCOOKC;                                   */
/*    Call          : RAWCOOKC                                         */
/*---------------------------------------------------------------------*/
/*    (BORLAND TURBO C)                                                */
/*    Creation      : through command RUN in the menu                  */
/***********************************************************************/

#include <dos.h>                              /* include Header files */
#include <stdio.h>
#include <conio.h>

#define STANDARDIN 0        /* handle 0 is the Standard input device */
#define STANDARDOUT 1      /* handle 1 is the Standard output device */

/***********************************************************************/
/* GETMODE: read the attribute of an device driver                     */
/* Input  : the handle must be connected with the addressed device     */
/* Output : the device attribute                                       */
/***********************************************************************/

int GetMode(Handle)
int Handle;                         /* points to the character driver */

{
 union REGS Register;         /* register-Variable for Interrupt call */

 Register.x.ax = 0x4400;       /* Function number for IOCTL: Get Mode */
 Register.x.bx = Handle;
 intdos(&Register, &Register);            /* Call DOS-Interrupt 21H   */
 return(Register.x.dx);                     /* Pass device attribute  */
}

/***********************************************************************/
/* SETRAW : Change a character driver into RAW mode                    */
/* Input  : the handle passed must be connected with the addressed     */
/*          device                                                     */
/* Output : none                                                       */
/***********************************************************************/

int SetRaw(Handle)
int Handle;                         /* points to the character driver */

{
 union REGS Register;         /* register-Variable for Interrupt call */

 Register.x.ax = 0x4401;       /* Function number for IOCTL: Set Mode */
 Register.x.bx = Handle;
 Register.x.dx = GetMode(Handle) & 255 | 32; /* new device attribute */
 intdos(&Register, &Register);            /* Call DOS-Interrupt 21H   */
}
```

```
/***********************************************************************/
/* SETCOOKED: Changes a character driver into the COOKED mode         */
/* Input    : the handle passed must be connected with the device     */
/*            addressed                                                */
/* Output   : none                                                     */
/***********************************************************************/

int SetCooked(Handle)
int Handle;                          /* points to the character driver  */

{
 union REGS Register;        /* register-Variable for Interrupt call */

 Register.x.ax = 0x4401;      /* Function number for IOCTL: Set Mode */
 Register.x.bx = Handle;
 Register.x.dx = GetMode(Handle) & 223;      /* new device attribute */
 intdos(&Register, &Register);          /* Call DOS-Interrupt 21H    */
}

/***********************************************************************/
/* TESTOUTPUT: outputs a Test-String 1000 times on the Standard       */
/*             output device                                           */
/* Input     : none                                                    */
/* Output    : none                                                    */
/***********************************************************************/

void TestOutput()

{
 int i;                                              /* Loop Variable */
 static char Test[] = "Test.... ";              /* the text for output */

 printf("\n");
 for (i = 0; i < 1000; i++)                        /* output 1000 times */
  fputs(Test, stdout);      /* Output String on the Standard output. */
 printf("\n");
}

/***********************************************************************/
/**                              MAIN PROGRAM                         **/
/***********************************************************************/

void main()

{
 printf("\nRAWCOOK (c) 1987 by Michael Tischer\n\n");

 printf("The Console Driver (Keyboard, Display) is now in ");
 printf("RAW Mode.\nDuring the following output control characters,\n");
 printf("such as <CTRL-S> will not be recognized.\n");
 printf("Try it.\n\n");
 printf("Please press a key to start...");
 getch();                                            /* wait for key */
 SetRaw(STANDARDIN);                /* Console driver into RAW mode */
 TestOutput();
 while (kbhit())          /* in the meantime remove key codes from   */
  getch();                               /* keyboard buffer           */
 printf("\nThe console driver is now in COOKED mode. ");
 printf("Control keys such as\n<CTRL-S> are recognized during ");
 printf("output and answered accordingly!\n");
 printf("Please press a key to start ...");
 getch();                                            /* wait for key */
 SetCooked(STANDARDIN);          /* Console driver in the COOKED mode */
 TestOutput();
```

6.6 File Management in DOS

The DOS file management functions are among the most basic available to the programmer. These functions are used to:

- Create and delete files
- Open and close files
- Read from and write to files

Operating systems such as DOS provide the programmer with functions for file management. For example, DOS provides functions which return special file information or functions to rename a file. One peculiarity of DOS is that these functions exist in two forms because of the combined CP/M & UNIX compatibility. For every UNIX compatible file function, there is also a CP/M compatible file function.

FCB functions

The CP/M compatible functions are designated as FCB functions since they are based on a data structure called the FCB (File Control Block). DOS uses this data structure for information storage during file manipulation. The user must reserve space for the FCB within this program. The FCB permits access to the FCB functions which open, close, read from and write to files.

Since the FCB functions were developed for compatibility with CP/M's functions, and since CP/M has no hierarchical file system, FCB functions do not support paths. As a result, FCB functions can only access files which are in the current directory.

UNIX handle functions

The UNIX compatible handle functions don't have this problem. With these functions, a handle is used to identify the file to be accessed. The DOS stores information about each open file in an area that is separate from the program.

6.6.1 Handle Functions

It is easier for the programmer to access a file using the handle functions than to access a file using the FCB functions. The handle functions do not require a programmer to use a data structure for file access like the FCB functions do. In a manner similar to the functions of the UNIX operating system, file access is performed using a filename. The filename is passed as an ASCII string when the file is opened or first created. This must be performed before the first write or read operation to the file. In addition to the filename, it may contain a device designator, a pathname and a file extension. The ASCII string ends with the end character (ASCII code 0). After the file is opened, a numeric value called the handle is returned. Any further operations to this file are performed using this 16-bit handle. For a subsequent read or write operation, the handle and not the filename is passed to the appropriate function.

For each open file, DOS saves certain information pertaining to that file. If the FCB functions are used, DOS saves the information in the FCB table within the program's memory block. When the handle functions are used, the information is stored in an area outside of the program's memory block in a table that is maintained by the DOS. The number of open files is therefore limited by the amount of available table space. The amount of table space set aside by DOS is specified by the FILES parameter of the CONFIG.SYS file:

```
FILES = X
```

In DOS Version 3.0, this maximum is 255. If you change the maximum number of files in the CONFIG.SYS file, the change will not go into effect until the next time that DOS is booted.

FILES

While the FILES parameter specifies the maximum number of open files for the entire operating system, DOS limits the number of open files to 20 per program. Since five handles are assigned to standard devices such as the keyboard, monitor and line printer, only 15 handles are available for the program. For example, if a program opens three files, DOS assigns three available handles and reduces the number of additional handles available by three. If this program calls another program, the three files opened by the original program remain open. If the new program opens additional files, the remaining number of handles available is reduced even further.

In addition to the standard read and write functions, there is also a file positioning function. This lets you specify an exact location within the file for the next data access. Knowing both a record number and the length of each data record allows you to specify the position to access a particular data record:

```
position = record number * length of record
```

This function is not used during sequential file access since DOS sets the file pointer during opening or creation of a file to the first byte within the file. Each subsequent read or write operation moves the file pointer by the number of bytes read towards the end of the file so that the next file access starts where the previous one ended.

The following table summarizes the handle functions. For a more detailed description of these functions, see Appendix C.

Function No.	Operation
3CH	Create file
3DH	Open file
3EH	Close file
42H	Move file pointer/determine file size
43H	Read/Write file attribute
56H	Rename file
57H	Read/Write modifications & date/time of file

Here are a few general rules to follow when using these functions:

Functions which expect a filename or the address of a filename as an argument (e.g., Create File and Open File) expect the segment address of the name in the DS register and the offset address in the DX register. If the function successfully returns a handle, it is returned in the AX register.

Functions which expect a handle as an argument expect it in the DX register. After the call, the carry flag indicates if an error occurred during execution. If an error occurs, the carry flags is set and the error code is returned in the AX register.

Function 59H of DOS interrupt 21H returns very detailed information concerning errors which occur during disk operations. This function is available only in DOS Versions 3.0 and higher.

6.6.2 FCB Functions

As discussed earlier, DOS uses an FCB data structure for managing a file. The programmer can use this data structure to obtain information about a file or change information about a file. For this reason we shall examine the structure of an FCB before discussing the individual FCB functions.

The FCB is a 37-byte data structure which can be subdivided into different data fields. The following figure illustrates these fields.

Offset	Field	Size
+ 00H	Device name	(1 byte)
+ 01H	Filename	(8 bytes)
+ 09H	File mode	(3 bytes)
+ 0CH	Current block number	(1 word)
+ 0EH	Data record size	(1 word)
+ 10H	File size	(2 words)
+ 14H	Modification date	(1 word)
+ 16H	Modification time	(1 word)
+ 18H	Reserved	(8 bytes)
+ 20H	Current data record number	(1 byte)
+ 21H	Data record number for random access	(2 words)

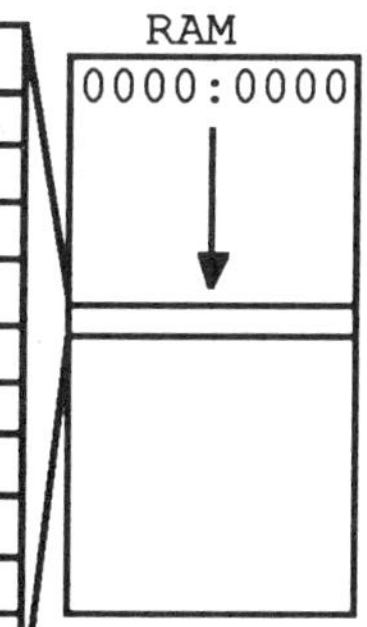

Structure of an FCB

Notice that the name of the file is found beginning at offsets 01H through 0BH of the FCB. The byte at offset 0 is the device indicator, 0 is the current drive, 1 drive A, 2 drive B, etc.

The filename which begins at offset 1 is an ASCII string. It may not contain a pathname since it's limited to 8 characters. For this reason, the FCB functions can access only files in the current directory. Filenames shorter than eight characters are padded with spaces (ASCII code 32). The file extension, if any, occupies the next three bytes of the FCB.

At offset 0CH of the FCB is the current number of the block for sequential file access. The two bytes at offset 0EH are the record size. The four bytes at offset 10H are the length of the file.

The date and time of the last modifications to the file are stored beginning at offset 14H of the FCB in encoded form.

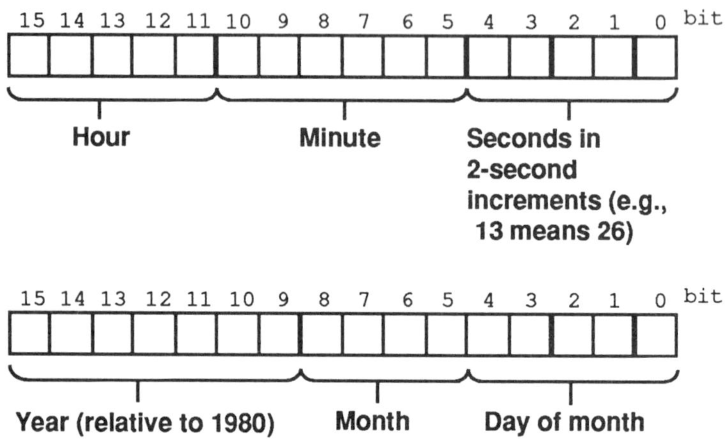

Format of time and date stamps in the FCB

An eight-byte data area follows and is reserved for DOS (no user modifications allowed). The use of this area varies from one version of DOS to another.

Following this reserved data area is the current record number which is used in connection with the current block number to simulate CP/M operations.

Random files

The last data field of the FCB is used for a type of access in which the data within the file may be retrieved or written in a non-sequential order. This field is four bytes long. If a record is equal to or larger than 64 bytes, only the first three bytes are used for indicating the current record number. All four bytes of this field are used for records smaller than 64 bytes.

Extended FCB

Besides a standard FCB, DOS also supports the extended FCB. Unlike normal FCBs, extended FCBs access files with special attributes, such as hidden files or system files. Furthermore, they permit access to volume names and subdirectories (this doesn't mean that you can access files in other directories besides the current directory).

An extended FCB is similar to a standard FCB, but it's seven bytes larger. These seven bytes are located at the beginning of the data structure. All subsequent fields are therefore displaced by seven bytes.

Offset	Field	Size
+ 00H	FF	(1 byte)
+ 01H	Reserved(0)	(5 bytes)
+ 06H	File attribute	(1 byte)
+ 07H	Device name	(1 byte)
+ 08H	Filename	(8 bytes)
+ 10H	File extension	(3 bytes)
+ 13H	Current block number	(1 word)
+ 15H	File record size	(1 word)
+ 17H	File size	(2 words)
+ 1BH	Modifications-date	(1 word)
+ 1DH	Modifications-time	(1 word)
+ 1FH	Reserved	(8 bytes)
+ 27H	Current data record number	(1 byte)
+ 28H	Data record number	(2 words)

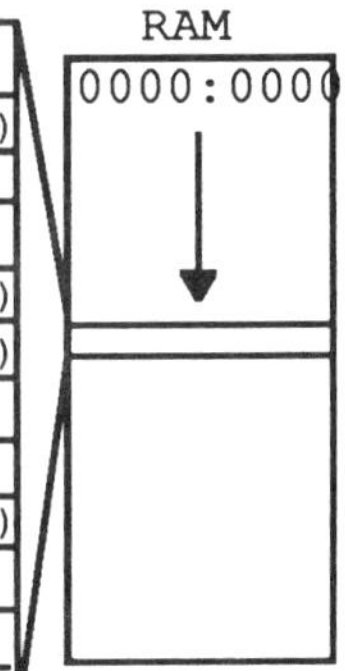

Structure of an extended FCB

The first byte of an extended FCB always contains the value 255 and identifies this as an extended FCB. Since this address contains the device number in a normal FCB and can therefore not contain the value 255, DOS can tell the difference between a normal and an extended FCB. The next five bytes are reserved exclusively for the use by DOS. They should not be changed. The seventh byte is a file attribute byte. See Section 6.1.2 for the details of the file attribute byte.

Now that you're familiar with the FCB structures, the next section focuses on using FCBs for accessing files.

FCB and file access

Before accessing a file, an FCB must be built in the program's memory area. The area can be reserved within the data segment of the program or by allocating additional memory using another DOS function (see Section 6.9).

Although it is possible to write the data directly into the FCB, it is better to use one of the appropriate DOS functions to do this.

For example, to set the filename in the FCB you can use DOS function 29H. The function number is passed in the AH register. The address of the FCB is passed in the ES:DI register pair. The address of the filename is passed in the DS:SI register pair. The filename is an ASCII string terminated by the end character (ASCII code 0). The AL register contains flags for converting the filename and are discussed in more detail in Appendix C.

Open FCB

After the FCB is properly formatted the file can be opened or created using a DOS function. When this happens DOS stores information about that file in the FCB such as the file size, date and time of file creation, etc. At this point the FCB is considered opened.

By default, the record length is set to 128 bytes when the FCB is opened. To override this record length, store the desired record length at offset 0EH of the FCB after it is opened. Otherwise the default length will be used.

DTA

For record lengths greater than 128 bytes, the record buffer also known as the DTA, or Disk Transfer Area must be moved to accommodate the longer record size. Normally, DOS builds the DTA in the PSP (Program Segment Prefix). Accessing the file using the default DTA for a record length greater than 128 bytes would overwrite some of the other fields in the PSP.

The most convenient way to select a new DTA is to reserve the space in the program's data segment. To change the address of the DTA use DOS function 1AH. The address of the new DTA is passed in the DS:DX register pair. DOS assumes that you have set aside an area large enough to accommodate your largest record length so you don't have to specify the new length.

File access

For sequential file access, processing begins at the first record in the file. DOS maintains a record pointer in the FCB to keep track of the current record within the file. Each time the file is accessed, DOS advances the pointer so that the second, third, fourth, etc record is processed in order.

For random file access, the records can be processed in any order. The position of each record relative to the beginning of the file determines its record number. This record number is then passed to DOS to access a specific record. The last field of the FCB is used to specify the record number to DOS.

It's also possible to change from sequential access mode to random access mode and vice versa since processing depends on a specific DOS function to access the file. In effect, there are two sets of independent functions, one for sequential access and one for random functions.

Following is a list of all of the FCB functions of DOS interrupt 21H. A more detailed description of the functions is found in Appendix C.

Function No.	Task
0FH	Open file
10H	Close file
13H	Delete file
14H	Sequential read
15H	Sequential write
16H	Create file
17H	Rename file

Function No.	Task
1AH	Set DTA address
21H	Random Read (of record)
22H	Random Write (of record)
23H	Determine file size
24H	Set record number for random access
27H	Random read (one or more records)
28H	Random write (one or more records)
29H	Enter filename into FCB

Some basic rules about these functions should be mentioned here:

Using the FCB functions, you can access several files, each with their own unique FCB. To tell DOS which file is to be accessed, pass the address of the file's FCB in the DS:DX register pair.

Most of the functions return an error code in the AL register or the value zero if the function was successfully completed. For functions which open, close, create or delete a file, a code of 255 is returned if an error occurs. The other functions return specific error codes. More detailed information about these errors can be determined by calling DOS function 59H but is available only in versions of DOS V3.0 or later.

Handles vs. FCBs

After the two groups of functions made available by DOS have been presented, the advantages and disadvantages of the individual functions should be discussed briefly. For those who want to convert a program from the CP/M or UNIX operating systems into DOS, the choice will be easy, but for those who want to develop a new program under DOS, this discussion can help in your deciding on which set of functions to use.

Handles

There are two main advantages to using handle functions. The first is the capability to access a file in any subdirectory of the disk. The second is that the handle functions are not limited to the number of FCBs which can be stored in a program's memory space.

There are a number of additional considerations. You can access the name of a disk drive only by using an FCB. When the FCB is opened, you can easily determine its file size and the date of the last modification. The handle functions automatically provide an area large enough to accommodate the records in the file.

As you can see there are arguments for and against using either the FCB functions or the handle functions. For future versions of DOS, the handle functions will play a more important role and the importance of the FCB functions will diminish. This is reason enough to use the handle functions for your new program development.

6.7 Accessing the DOS Directory

There are two groups of DOS functions for working with directories. The first group is used to manipulate the subdirectories and the second to search for files on the mass storage devices.

With DOS Version 2.0 came the introduction of subdirectories. A mass storage device could be logically divided into smaller subdirectories which could in turn be further subdivided. In effect this organization created a directory tree.

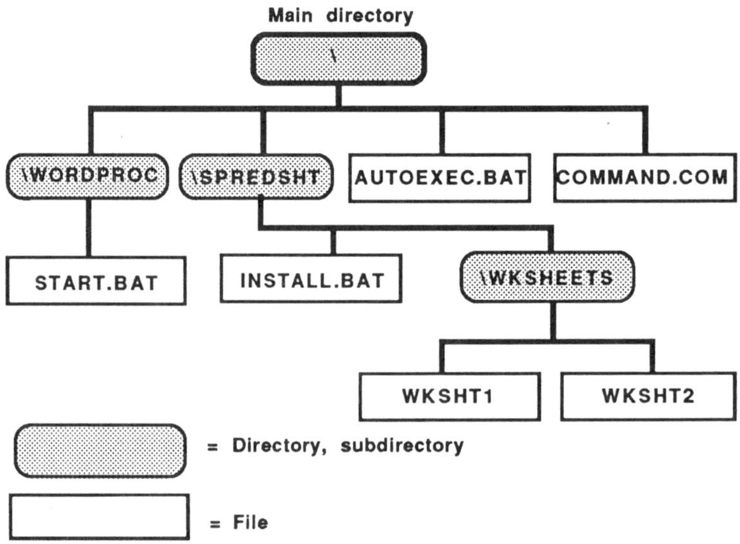

Directory tree

In this directory tree, the names and numbers of subdirectories are not static. Therefore there must be a way to add, change and delete entries on the tree. Other functions must be available to set the current directory so that a complete pathname is not required for all file accesses.

At the user level the MD, RD and CD commands can be used to make a directory, remove a directory and change a current directory. Internally, these commands are performed with functions 39H, 3AH and 3BH of DOS interrupt 21H.

All three functions use identical calling conventions.

The function number is passed in the AH register. The address of the path is passed in the DS:DX register pair. The path is a string and may be a complete path designation including a preceding drive letter followed by a colon (a device name) and terminated by ASCII code 0. If the device name is omitted, the current device is the default.

Following execution, the carry flag indicates the return code. If the carry flag is reset (0), then execution was successful. If the carry flag is set, then an error occurred and the error code is passed back in the AX register.

Function 39H creates or makes a new directory (Make Directory). The name for the new directory is specified as the last element in the path. An error will be returned by the functions if one or more of the directories specified in the path do not exist, if the new directory name already exists or if the maximum number of files in the root directory is exceeded.

Function 3AH deletes or removes a directory (Remove Directory). An error will be returned by the function if the target directory is not empty or the specified directory does not exist in the current path.

Function 3BH changes the current directory (Change Directory). An error is returned if the directories named in the path do not really exist.

Function 0EH sets the default disk drive. Besides the function number in the AH register, only the device code of the new current device must be passed in the DL register. Code 0 stands for the device A, 1 for B, 2 for C, etc.

Directory specification

Before specifying the current directory using function 3BH, it is sometimes necessary to find the current directory. DOS makes function 47H available to the programmer for this purpose. Since it can return the path of the current directory for any device, the device number must be passed to the function. If this is the current device, the value 0 must be passed in the DL register. For all other devices, the value 1 must be passed for drive A, 2 for B, 3 for C, etc.

Besides the device code, the function must also have the address of a 64-byte buffer within the user program. The DS register contains the segment and the SI register holds the offset address of this buffer. After the function call this buffer contains the path designation of the current directory, terminated with the end character (ASCII code 0). The path designation cannot be preceded by the device name or the \ character. If the current directory is the root directory, the buffer contains only the end character. If a device code unknown to DOS was passed during the function call, the carry flag is set and the AX register contains the error code 0FH.

Let's consider the functions for searching for one or more files in the current directory on the current device. Again the parallel between handle and FCB functions appears. Two function groups exist to search for files. The group of FCB functions has the disadvantage that they limit the search to files in the current directory of a certain device, while handle functions allow searching for files in any directories of any devices. The term "handle" functions doesn't really fit these functions since they are not addressed with a handle. This designation originated with the introduction of subdirectories (and therefore the handle functions) in DOS Version 2.0. Version 1.0 offered only the FCB functions.

6.7.1 Searching for Files using FCB Functions

This method of file search uses functions 11H and 12H. Using them you can search for files with a fixed name or files with a filename extension. Function 11H finds the first file in the current directory. Function 12H finds all other additional files. The FCBs play a significant role since they mediate between the calling program and the two functions. Let's see how we can search for files in a directory:

First the program must reserve space for two FCBs. This is done either by reserving memory in the data area of the program, or by requesting memory from DOS using function 48H. The programmer can use either normal or extended FCBs. Extended FCBs offer the advantage of being able to search for files with special attributes (system or hidden), volume names and subdirectories. The filename for which the search will be made is specified in one of the FCBs. DOS places the name of the file(s) that it finds in the other FCB. To differentiate between the two FCBs, they are designated with the names Search FCB and Found FCB.

The address of the Found FCB must be passed to DOS using function 1AH. The Found FCB becomes the new data transmission area (DTA) when this function call occurs. This area is important for these two functions as well as all other functions which transfer data between computer and disks. For this reason function 2FH should determine the address of the current DTA before activating the new DTA. When the file search ends, the DTA can be restored to its original state using function 1AH.

After the DTA is set to the Found FCB, the next step is to place the name of the file you are looking for into the Search FCB. For a more general search, the wildcards * and ? may be used. You can transfer the filename directly or transfer it using function 29H. If you want to search through all files, use the filename *.*. If an extended FCB is used, you may insert an additional value into the attribute field of the Search FCB to limit the search to files with certain attributes only (see Section 6.12 for more information on the various attributes).

This concludes the preliminary work. The file search can begin with the current directory. For this purpose, function 11H is called with the function number in the AH register, the segment address of the Search FCB in DS and the offset address in the DX register. If the system finds a file with the indicated name, the AL register contains the value 0 after the function call. If the filename wasn't found, the AL register contains a value of 255. The found filename and its attributes (if extended FCBs are used) can be read from the Found FCB. For additional searches, function 12H (not function 11H) is called. Function 12H's register contents during call and return are similar to function 11H. If it returns the value 255 in the AL register during one of the calls, the search has ended.

6.7.2 Searching for Files using Handle Functions

Working with handle functions is easier than working with the FCB functions. There are functions for searching for the first file (the 4EH function) and subsequent files (the 4FH function). Both functions return the information to the DTA. For this reason the DTA should be moved into an area accessible to the current program before calling either of these functions. This area must have at least 43 bytes available. As mentioned in connection with the FCB functions, the DTA should be restored to its original address after the search ends.

During the call of the 4EH function, the function number is passed in the AH register, the attribute in the CX register and the address of the file to be found in the DS:DX register pair. The filename is a series of ASCII characters, terminated with an end character (ASCII code 0). In addition to a device name, you may add a complete path designation and the wildcard characters * and ?. If a path is not specified, DOS assumes that the search should be made in the current directory of the indicated device. If a device is not specified, the search proceeds on the current device. After the function call, the carry flag indicates whether a file was found. If the file couldn't be found, the carry flag is set, and the AX register contains an error code. An error code of 2H is returned if the indicated path does not exist. If no file could be found, an error code of 12H is returned. If the carry flag is reset, the DTA contains the information about the file found. It has the following structure:

Address	Contents	Type
+00H	reserved for DOS	21 bytes
+15H	Attribute of file found	1 byte
+16H	Time of last modification	1 word
+18H	Date of last modification	1 word
+1AH	low word of file size	1 word
+1EH	high word of file size	12 bytes

Function 4FH executes any further searches. The function number is passed in the AH register, and no other parameters are required. The carry flag indicates if there are additional files in the current directory to which the search may be applicable.

Demonstration programs

The three programs below read directory entries and display them on the screen using one of the handle functions. You'll find the display more user friendly than the DOS DIR command: the files appear in a window, and the filename display stops as soon as the window is filled with filenames. This permits easy reading of filenames. By pressing any key, the program displays any additional pages of filenames.

All three programs are designed on the same basic principle: first the main program determines the search path. It contains the names of the directories in which the search should be made for the files, the names of the files and the device where the directory is located. This name can contain wildcards (* and ?) to search for several files at the same time. If the user does not indicate a search path, the program defaults to the search path "*.*". This displays all files in the current directory of the current device, as well as the hidden attribute files.

After the program determines the search path, a routine coordinates the loading and display of individual directory entries. First a routine creates the display window on the screen for individual entry output. Then a search proceeds for the first entry using DOS function 4EH. If an entry is found, the screen displays the entry. Function 4FH searches for all subsequent entries and displays them in the window.

The bottom line of the display window moves up one line with each new line displayed. Once the entire window fills with data, any further display of entries stops until the user presses a key. After all entries in the selected directory have been displayed, the number of files is displayed and the program ends.

BASIC listing: DIRB.BAS

```
100 '**********************************************************************'
110 '*                          D I R B                                   *'
120 '*--------------------------------------------------------------------*'
130 '*  Task        : display all files in a directory                   *'
140 '*                in a window on the display                          *'
160 '*  Author      : MICHAEL TISCHER                                     *'
170 '*  developed   : 07/23/87                                            *'
180 '*  last Update : 04/08/89                                            *'
190 '**********************************************************************'
200 '
210 CLS : KEY OFF
220 PRINT"WARNING: This program can be run only if GWBASIC was started"
225 PRINT" from the "
230 PRINT"DOS level with the <GWBASIC  /m:60000> command." : PRINT
240 PRINT"If this is not the case, please enter <s> for Stop."
250 PRINT : PRINT"Otherwise press any key ...";
260 A$ = INKEY$ : IF A$ = "s" THEN END
270 IF A$ = "" THEN 260
280 GOSUB 60000                    'Install function for calling interrupt
290 CLS
300 PRINT "DIR (c) 1987 by Michael Tischer"
310 PRINT
320 PRINT"Please input the search path for the file."
330 PRINT"Example: If all files with the extension .BAT in the Root"
340 PRINT"         directory of the disk in drive A should be displayed,"
350 PRINT"         then please input A:\*.BAT."
360 PRINT"With a blank input, all files in the current directory "
```

```
370 PRINT"are displayed." : PRINT
380 INPUT "Search Path: ",DIR$          'Input Search Path
390 IF DIR$ = "" THEN DIR$ = "*.*"      'search in current directory
400 ENTRY% = 14                         '14 Display entries in window
410 GOSUB 50000                         'Input Directory and output
420 END
430 '
50000 '*************************************************************'
50010 '* Input one Directory and display                           *'
50020 '*-----------------------------------------------------------*'
50030 '* Input:  DIR$    = the search path                         *'
50040 '*         ENTRY% = Number of entries in the window          *'
50050 '* Output: none                                              *'
50060 '*************************************************************'
50070 '
50080 DIM MONTH$[11]                          'accepts names of months
50090 RESTORE 50600
50100 FOR I% = 0 TO 11 : READ MONTH$[I%] : NEXT
50110 INR% = &H21                           'Call DOS-Interrupt 21H
50120 FCT% = &H2F                          'Get function number for DTA
50130 CALL IA(INR%,FCT%,Z%,OFSHI%,OFSLO%,Z%,Z%,Z%,Z%,Z%,Z%,DTASEG%,Z%)
50140 DTAOFS% = OFSLO% + OFSHI% * 256
50150 CLS
50160 OFFSET% = INT((20 - ENTRY%) / 2) + 1       'Start line of window
50170 LOCATE OFFSET%,14
50180 PRINT TAB(14)"┌────────────┬───────┬──────────┬──────────┬─────┐"
50190 PRINT TAB(14)"| Filename   | Size  |   Date   |   Time   |RHSVD|"
50200 PRINT TAB(14)"|────────────+───────+──────────+──────────+─────|"
50210 FOR I% = 1 TO ENTRY%            'output a line for every entry
50220 PRINT TAB(14)"|            |       |          |          |     |"
50230 NEXT                                      'output next line
50240 PRINT TAB(14)"└────────────┴───────┴──────────┴──────────┴─────┘"
50250 NUMWIND% = -1                        'Number of entries in window
50260 NUMFND% = 0                    'Number of entries found up to now
50270 ATTRIBUTE% = 255              'search for files with any Attribute
50280 GOSUB 51000                                'search for first entry
50290 IF NOT(FOUNDIT%) THEN 50500          'no entry found --> finished
50300 NUMFND% = NUMFND% + 1              'Increase number of entries found
50310 NUMWIND% = NUMWIND% + 1          'Increase number of entries in window
50320 IF NUMWIND% <> ENTRY% THEN 50410                     'window full?
50330 LOCATE OFFSET%+ENTRY%+4,14          'Set Cursor to line under window
50340 COLOR 0,7                     'switch on inverse character display
50350 PRINT"                 Please press any key                 ";
50360 A$ = INKEY$ : IF A$= "" THEN 50360                  'wait for a key
50370 LOCATE ,14                          'Cursor in line under window
50380 COLOR 7,0                         'switch on normal character color
50390 PRINT STRING$(51," ");
50400 NUMWIND% = -1           'the next entry is the first in the window
50410 NUMBER% = 1 : COLOUR% = 7
50420 ULR% = OFFSET% + 2 : LRR% = OFFSET%+ENTRY% + 1
50430 ULC% = 14 : LRC% = 62
50440 GOSUB 54000                                     'scroll window up
50450 LOCATE OFFSET%+ENTRY%+2,15           'Set Cursor to last window line
50460 PRINT "            |       |          |          |     "
50470 GOSUB 53000                                        'Output entry
50480 GOSUB 52000                                      'Get next entry
50490 IF FOUNDIT% THEN 50300           'continue if no entry is available
50500 LOCATE OFFSET%+ENTRY%+4,14           'Cursor in line under the window
50510 COLOR 0,7                     'switch on inverse character display
50520 PRINT STRING$(51," ");
50530 LOCATE ,14                             'Cursor in line under window
50540 IF NUMFND% = 0 THEN PRINT" no file found"; : GOTO 50570
50550 IF NUMFND% = 1 THEN PRINT" found one file"; : GOTO 50570
50560 PRINT NUMFND%;"files found";
50570 COLOR 7,0                         'switch on normal character color
50580 RETURN
50590 '
50600 DATA "JAN","FEB","MAR","APR","MAY","JUN","JUL","AUG","SEP"
50610 DATA "OCT","NOV","DEC"
```

```
50620 '
51000 '******************************************************************'
51010 '* Search for first entry in a Directory                          *'
51020 '*----------------------------------------------------------------*'
51030 '* Input:  DIR$        = Search path                              *'
51040 '*         ATTRIBUTE% = Attribute of file                         *'
51050 '* Output: FOUND_IT%   = -1 if entry found, otherwise 0           *'
51060 '* Info   : the Directory entry is entered into Variable DTA%     *'
51070 '*                                                                *'
51080 '*         Z% is a Dummy-Variable                                 *'
51090 '******************************************************************'
51100 '
51110 DIR$ = DIR$ + CHR$(0)          'Put End character on search path
51120 FCT% = &H4E              'Search function number for first entry
51130 INR% = &H21                          'Call DOS-Interrupt 21H
51140 ATLO% = ATTRIBUTE% AND 255                 'LO-Byte of Attribute
51150 ATHI% = INT(ATTRIBUTE% / 256)              'HI-Byte of Attribute
51160 OFSLO% = PEEK(VARPTR(DIR$)+1)          'LO-Byte of Offset address
51170 OFSHI% = PEEK(VARPTR(DIR$)+2)          'HI-Byte of Offset address
51180 CALL IA(INR%,FCT%,Z%,Z%,Z%,ATHI%,ATLO%,OFSHI%,OFSLO%,Z%,Z%,Z%,FLAGS%)
51190 FOUNDIT% = ((FLAGS% AND 1) = 0)                  'Test Carry-Flag
51200 RETURN                            'return to calling program
51210 '
52000 '******************************************************************'
52010 '* find next entry in Directory                                   *'
52020 '*----------------------------------------------------------------*'
52030 '* Input :  DIR$        = Search path                             *'
52040 '*          ATTRIBUTE% = Attribute of file                        *'
52050 '* Output:  FOUNDIT%   = -1 if file found, otherwise 0            *'
52060 '* Info  :  the Directory entry is read into Variable DTA%        *'
52070 '*                                                                *'
52080 '*          Z% is a Dummy-Variable                                *'
52090 '******************************************************************'
52100 '
52110 FCT% = &H4F                'Find function number for next entry
52120 INR% = &H21                          'Call DOS-Interrupt 21H
52130 CALL IA(INR%,FCT%,Z%,Z%,Z%,Z%,Z%,Z%,Z%,Z%,Z%,Z%,FLAGS%)
52140 FOUNDIT% = ((FLAGS% AND 1) = 0)                  'test Carry-Flag
52150 RETURN                               'back to calling program
52160 '
53000 '******************************************************************'
53010 '* Output a Directory entry from the DTA to the display          *'
53020 '*----------------------------------------------------------------*'
53030 '* Input:  OFFSET% = first line of the Directory window           *'
53040 '*         ENTRY%  = Number of entries in the Directory window    *'
53050 '*         DTAOFS% = Offset address of the DTA                    *'
53060 '*         MONTH$  = contains the names of months                 *'
53070 '* Output: none                                                   *'
53080 '******************************************************************'
53090 '
53100 DEF FNDTA(X) = PEEK(DTAOFS% + X)
53110 DEF SEG = DTASEG%                'Set Segment address of the DTA
53120 LOCATE OFFSET%+ENTRY%+2,15 'Output in the last line of the window
53130 I% = 30                      'Offset address in DTA for file names
53140 WHILE FNDTA(I%) <> 0       'the END character terminates the name
53150 PRINT CHR$(FNDTA(I%));       'output a character of the file name
53160 I% = I% + 1                                      'next character
53170 WEND                                                'End of Loop
53180 LOCATE OFFSET%+ENTRY%+2,28                'Set Cursor to column 28
53190 PRINT USING "#######"; FNDTA(26) + FNDTA(27) * 256! + FNDTA(28) *
      4096! + FNDTA(29) * 65536!;
53200 DATE = FNDTA(24) + FNDTA(25) * 256                       'Get Date
53210 LOCATE OFFSET%+ENTRY%+2,36                'Set Cursor to Column 36
53220 PRINT MONTH$[(INT(DATE / 32) AND 15) - 1];  'Output name of month
53230 PRINT"/";:PRINT USING "##";DATE AND 31;      'Output day of month
53240 PRINT USING "/####";INT(DATE / 512) + 1980;          'Output year
53250 LOCATE OFFSET%+ENTRY%+2,49                'Set Cursor to column 49
53260 FTIME = FNDTA(22) + FNDTA(23) * 256                      'Get time
53270 PRINT USING "##";INT(FTIME / 2048);                   'Output hour
53280 PRINT ":";
```

```
53290 PRINT USING "##";INT(FTIME / 32) AND 63;          'Output Minute
53300 LOCATE OFFSET%+ENTRY%+2,59                 'Set Cursor to column 59
53310 FOR I% = 0 TO 4               'test Bits 0 to 4 of file attribute
53320 IF (FNDTA(21) AND (2^I%)) <> 0 THEN PRINT"X"; ELSE PRINT" ";
53330 NEXT I%                                              'test next Bit
53340 DEF SEG : RETURN                           'back to calling program
53350 '
54000 '*****************************************************************'
54010 '* Scroll current display page up or erase                       *'
54020 '*---------------------------------------------------------------*'
54030 '* Input :  NUMBER% = how many lines scrolled                     *'
54040 '*          ULC%    = column upper left                          *'
54050 '*          ULR%    = line upper left                            *'
54060 '*          LRC%    = column lower right                         *'
54070 '*          LRR%    = line lower right                           *'
54080 '*          COLOR%  = color of erased line                       *'
54090 '* Output:  none                                                 *'
54100 '* Info  :  If 0 is given for NUMBER%, the screen area           *'
54110 '*          indicated is erased                                  *'
54120 '*          the Variable Z% is a Dummy                           *'
54130 '*****************************************************************'
54140 '
54150 FCT%=6                          'Function number for scrolling up
54160 INR%=&H10                       'Call BIOS-Video-Interrupt 16H
54170 CALL IA(INR%,FCT%,NUMBER%,COLOUR%,Z%,ULR%,ULC%,LRR%,LRC%,Z%,Z%,Z%,Z%)
54180 RETURN                                     'back to calling program
54190 '
60000 '*****************************************************************'
60010 '* Initialize Routine for Interrupt call                         *'
60020 '*---------------------------------------------------------------*'
60030 '* Input : none                                                  *'
60040 '* Output: IA is the Start address of the Interrupt-Routine      *'
60050 '*****************************************************************'
60060 '
60070 IA=60000!      'Start address of the Routine in the BASIC-Segment
60080 DEF SEG                                          'Set BASIC-Segment
60090 RESTORE 60130
60100 FOR I% = 0 TO 160 : READ X% : POKE IA+I%,X% : NEXT  'Poke Routine
60110 RETURN                                     'back to calling program
60120 '
60130 DATA  85,139,236, 30,  6,139,118, 30,139,  4,232,140,  0,139,118
60140 DATA  12,139, 60,139,118,  8,139,  4, 61,255,255,117,  2,140,216
60150 DATA 142,192,139,118, 28,138, 36,139,118, 26,138,  4,139,118, 24
60160 DATA 138, 60,139,118, 22,138, 28,139,118, 20,138, 44,139,118, 18
60170 DATA 138, 12,139,118, 16,138, 52,139,118, 14,138, 20,139,118, 10
60180 DATA 139, 52, 85,205, 33, 93, 86,156,139,118, 12,137, 60,139,118
60190 DATA  28,136, 36,139,118, 26,136,  4,139,118, 24,136, 60,139,118
60200 DATA  22,136, 28,139,118, 20,136, 44,139,118, 18,136, 12,139,118
60210 DATA  16,136, 52,139,118, 14,136, 20,139,118,  8,140,192,137,  4
60220 DATA  88,139,118,  6,137,  4, 88,139,118, 10,137,  4,  7, 31, 93
60230 DATA 202, 26,  0, 91, 46,136, 71, 66,233,108,255
```

One problem in the BASIC version of the directory listing occurs during the directory output. Functions 4EH and 4FH read the entry into the DTA. It would make more sense to move the DTA to a variable within the program (an integer array would be best) to make it easier for the routine which outputs the entry to access the data. BASIC's garbage collection feature makes this difficult. The integer array containing the DTA moves periodically in storage and the address of the DTA, stored internally in DOS, no longer corresponds with the address of this integer array.

For this reason, the DOS function 2FH determines the DTA address. As the entries are displayed, this address accesses the DTA to determine the file information.

Pascal listing: DIRP.PAS

```
{***********************************************************************}
{*                              D I R P                                *}
{*---------------------------------------------------------------------*}
{*    Task         : Display all files of any Directory,               *}
{*                   including Subdirectories and                      *}
{*                   Volume Names                                      *}
{*---------------------------------------------------------------------*}
{*    Author        : MICHAEL TISCHER                                  *}
{*    developed on  : 7.8.87                                           *}
{*    last Update   : 9.21.87                                          *}
{***********************************************************************}

program DIRP;


Uses                                                      {Turbo 4.0 Units}
  Crt,
  Dos;

const ENTRY = 14;                            { Number of entries visible }

type RegTyp     = record
                   ax, bx, cx, dx, bp,
                   di, si, ds, es, flags : integer;
  {! Turbo 4.0 owners should use the Registers type from the DOS unit.}
                  end;

     {** this is the format of a Directory entry *****}
     {** as returned by the functions 4EH and 4FH }
     DirBufTyp = record
                   Reservebuf : array [1..21] of char;
                   Attribut   : byte;
                   Ztime      : integer;
                   Zdate      : integer;
                   Datgrlo    : integer;
                   Datgrhi    : integer;
                   DatName    : array [1..13] of char
                  end;

     Path      = string[65];

var DirBuf  : DirBufTyp;                     { accepts a Directory entry }
    DatName : Path;                                  { Files to be found  }

{***********************************************************************}
{* GETFIRST: read in the first Directory entry                         *}
{* Input    : none                                                     *}
{* Output   : true or false, depending if an entry was found           *}
{*                                                                     *}
{* Info     : the entry is stored in Variable DIRBUF                   *}
{***********************************************************************}

function GetFirst(DateiName : Path;                  { files to be found }
                  Attribute : integer) : boolean;   { search Attribute }

var Register : regtyp;       { Register-Variable for call of Interrupt }

begin
  DateiName := DateiName + #0;             { terminate filename with NUL }
  Register.ax := $4E shl 8;        { Function number for search of first }
  Register.cx := Attribute; { Attribute, for which search is performed }
  Register.ds := seg(DateiName);             { Segment address of filename }
  Register.dx := succ(ofs(DateiName));      { Offset address of filename }
  msdos(Dos.Registers(Register));{ Call DOS Interrupt 21H (Turbo 4.0)}
     {NOTE:Turbo 3.0 users should change previous line to read msdos(Register);}
                                                   {  defined in DOS unit.}
  if (Register.flags and 1) = 0                         { Test Carry-Flag }
```

```
    then GetFirst := true                      { Equal to 0 : file found }
    else GetFirst := false;                             { no file found   }
end;

{*******************************************************************}
{* GETNEXT : read in the following Directory entry                *}
{* Input   : none                                                 *}
{* Output  : true or false, depending if another entry was found  *}
{*                                                                *}
{* Info    : this function can only be called after a successful  *}
{*          call of the function GETFIRST                         *}
{*          the entry is stored in the  Variable DIRBUF           *}
{*******************************************************************}

function GetNext : boolean;

var Register : regtyp;          { Register-Variable for interrupt call }

begin
  Register.ax := $4F shl 8;         { Function number for next search }
  msdos(Dos.Registers(Register));    { Call DOS Interrupt 21H V 4.0}
                   {NOTE: Turbo 3.0 users should change the previous}
                                    {line to read msdos(Register);}
  if (Register.flags and 1) = 0                      { Test Carry-Flag }
    then GetNext := true                  { Equal to 0 : File found }
    else GetNext := false;                { otherwise no file found }
end;

{*******************************************************************}
{* PRINTDATA: Output information on an entry                      *}
{* Input     : none                                               *}
{* Output    : none                                               *}
{* Info      : the information about the entry are taken by this  *}
{*             procedures from Variable DIRBUF                    *}
{*******************************************************************}

procedure PrintData;

var Counter    : byte;
    DataLenght1,                          { both Variables are used }
    DataLenght2 : real;                  { to calculate file length }
begin
  writeln;                    { the window is scrolled up by one line  }
  Counter := 1;        { begins with the first character of the name }
  while (DirBuf.DatName[Counter]<>#0) do          { repeat up to NUL }
   begin
    write(DirBuf.DatName[Counter]);      { output characters of name }
    Counter := succ(Counter)              { process next character }
   end;
  gotoxy(13, ENTRY);
  DataLenght1 := DirBuf.Datgrhi;             { determine file length }
  if DataLenght1 < 0 then DataLenght1 := 65536.0 + DataLenght1;
  DataLenght2 := DirBuf.Datgrlo;
  if DataLenght2 < 0 then DataLenght2 := 65536.0 + DataLenght2;
  write('|', DataLenght1 * 65536.0 + DataLenght2:7:0);
  gotoxy(21, ENTRY);
  write('|');
  case (DirBuf.Zdate shr 5 and 15) of              { determine month }
    1 : write ('Jan');
    2 : write ('Feb');
    3 : write ('Mar');
    4 : write ('Apr');
    5 : write ('May');
    6 : write ('Jun');
    7 : write ('Jul');
    8 : write ('Aug');
    9 : write ('Sep');
   10 : write ('Oct');
   11 : write ('Nov');
   12 : write ('Dec')
```

```
  end;
  write('/',DirBuf.Zdate and 31:2,'/');                    { determine day }
  write(DirBuf.Zdate shr 9 + 1980:4);                     { determine year }
  gotoxy(34, ENTRY);
  write('|', DirBuf.Ztime shr 11:2, ':');                 { determine hour }
  write(DirBuf.Ztime shr 5 and 63:3);                  { determine minutes }
  gotoxy(44, ENTRY);                             { evaluate file attribute }
  write('|');                                { separator to preceding field }
  if (DirBuf.Attribut and 1)<>0 then write('X')             { Read-only? }
                                else write(' ');
  if (DirBuf.Attribut and 2)<>0 then write('X')                { hidden? }
                                else write(' ');
  if (DirBuf.Attribut and 4)<>0 then write('X')                { system? }
                                else write(' ');
  if (DirBuf.Attribut and 8)<>0 then write('X')          { Volume-Label? }
                                else write(' ');
  if (DirBuf.Attribut and 16)<>0 then write('X')            { Directory? }
                                 else write(' ');
  write('║');                           { right border of window frame }
end;

{************************************************************************}
{* SETDTA  : set Address of DTA                                         *}
{* Input   : see above                                                  *}
{* Output  : none                                                       *}
{************************************************************************}

procedure SetDTA(Segment,                 { new Segment address of the DTA }
                 Offset  : integer);      { new Offset address of the DTA }

var Register : regtyp;   { Register-Variable for call of the Interrupt }

begin
  Register.ax := $1A shl 8;                 { Set Function number for DTA }
  Register.ds := Segment;              { Segment address into DS register }
  Register.dx := Offset;                { Offset address into DX register }
  msdos(Dos.Registers(Register));              { Call DOS-Interrupt 21H }
                    {NOTE: Turbo 3.0 users should change the previous}
                                      {line to read msdos(Register);}
end;

{************************************************************************}
{* BUILDSCREENDISPLAY: prepares the display for output of the           *}
{*                     Directory                                        *}
{* Input   : none                                                       *}
{* Output  : none                                                       *}
{************************************************************************}

procedure BuildScreenDisplay;

var Counter : integer;

begin
 clrscr;                                                { clear display }
 window(14,(20-ENTRY) shr 1+1,64,(20-ENTRY) shr 1 +5+ENTRY);
 gotoxy(1,1);                      { Cursor to left upper corner of window }
 write('┌─────────────┬────────┬──────────────┬─ ──────────┬─────┐');
 write('| Filename    | Size   |     Date     | Time       |RHSVD|');
 write('|─────────────┼────────┼──────────────┼────────────┼─────|');
 for Counter := 1 to ENTRY do
  write('|             |        |              |            |     |');
 write('└─────────────┴────────┴──────────────┴─ ──────────┴─────┘');
 window(15,(20-ENTRY) shr 1+4,66,(20-ENTRY) shr 1 +3+ENTRY);
 gotoxy(1, ENTRY);                 { Cursor to upper left corner of window }
end;

{************************************************************************}
{* DIR: controls the input and output of Directories                    *}
{* Input   : none                                                       *}
```

```
{* Output    : none                                                        *}
{**************************************************************************}

procedure Dir;

var NumEntries,                              { Total number of entries found }
    Numwind      : integer;                  { Number of entries in window }
    KeyPress     : char;                        { wait for key activation }
begin
 SetDTA(Seg(DirBuf), Ofs(DirBuf));                { DirBuf is the new DTA }
 clrscr;                                                  { clear display }
 writeln('DIR (c) 1987 by Michael Tischer'#13#10);
 writeln('Please indicate search path for files          ');
 writeln('Example: if all files with the extension .BAT in the root ');
 writeln('directory of the disk drive should be displayed please input ');
 writeln('       A:*.BAT.');
 writeln('       If no search path is indicated, all files in the current');
 writeln('       directory are displayed.'#13#10);

 write('Which files are to be displayed: ');
 readln(DatName);                                     { read in filenames }
 if DatName = '' then DatName := '*.*';             { search for all files }
 BuildScreenDisplay;                         { Construct display for output }
 Numwind := -1;                                     { no entry in window yet }
 NumEntries := 0;                                        { no entry found }
 if GetFirst(DatName, 255) then                   { search for first entry }
                                              { Attribute does not matter }
  repeat
   NumEntries := succ(NumEntries);                  { found another entry  }
   Numwind := succ(Numwind);                { one more entry into window }
   if Numwind = ENTRY then                              { window full ? }
    begin                                                          { Yes }
     window(14,(20-ENTRY) shr 1 +5+ENTRY,66,(20-ENTRY) shr 1 +6+ENTRY);
     gotoxy(1, 1);                          { Cursor to last line of window }
     textbackground(7);                                { white background }
     textcolor(0);                                     { black characters}
     write('                 Please press a key                  ');
     repeat until keypressed;                          { wait for key press }
     {read(kbd, KeyPress);}                                { read key code }
                                           { otherwise it remains in the buffer }
     gotoxy(1, 1);     { Cursor to the upper left corner of the window }
     textbackground(0);                                { black background }
     textcolor(15);                                    { white characters }
     write('                                                      ');
     window(15,(20-ENTRY) shr 1+4,65,(20-ENTRY) shr 1 +3+ENTRY);
     gotoxy(1, ENTRY);                        { return Cursor to old position }
     Numwind := 0;                              { start count with 0 again }
    end;
   PrintData;                                      { output data of entry }
  until not(GetNext);                          { does another entry exist ? }
  window(14,(20-ENTRY) shr 1 +5+ENTRY,65,(20-ENTRY) shr 1 +6+ENTRY);
  gotoxy(1, 1);            { Cursor to the upper left corner of window }
  textbackground(7);                                    { white background }
  textcolor(0);                                         { black characters }
  write('                                                      ');
  gotoxy(2, 1);
  case NumEntries of
   0 : write('no file found ');
   1 : write('found a file ');
   else write(NumEntries,' files found ')
  end;
 window(1, 1, 80, 25);                        { set whole display as window }
end;

{**************************************************************************}
{**                          MAIN PROGRAMM                               **}
{**************************************************************************}

begin
 Dir;                                        { Load Directory and display }
```

```
end.
```

In the above Pascal program and in the following C program, accessing the DTA is much easier than in the BASIC version of the same program. RECORD or STRUCT defines the structure of the directory entry into the DTA, and the programs implement a variable of this type. DOS function 1AH then transfers the DTA to this variable. All the information in a directory entry can be easily accessed. With Turbo Pascal, the display design is particularly easy. Turbo Pascal also has a procedure to define any display area as a window. However, the C language program uses the scroll function of the BIOS interrupt 10H to scroll the directory window one line upward.

C listing: DIRC.C

```
/***********************************************************************/
/*                              D I R C                                */
/*---------------------------------------------------------------------*/
/*    Task            : Displays all files in any Directory,           */
/*                      including Sub-Directories and volume names     */
/*                      on the screen.                                 */
/*---------------------------------------------------------------------*/
/*    Author          : MICHAEL TISCHER                                */
/*    developed on    : 08/15/87                                       */
/*    last Update     : 04/08/89                                       */
/*---------------------------------------------------------------------*/
/*    (MICROSOFT C)                                                    */
/*    Creation        : MSC DIRC;                                      */
/*                      LINK DIRC;                                     */
/*    Call            : DIRC                                           */
/*---------------------------------------------------------------------*/
/*    (BORLAND TURBO C)                                                */
/*    Creation        : With the RUN command in the command line       */
/*    Info              Arguments can be passed to the program with    */
/*                      the OPTION/ARGS command in the command line    */
/*                      of TURBO C                                     */
/*       or                                                            */
/*                                                                     */
/*    Creation         : TCC DIRC                                      */
/*    Call             : DIRC                                          */
/***********************************************************************/

#include <dos.h>                              /* include Header files */
#include <io.h>
#include <string.h>

#define FALSE 0                             /* Constants make reading of  */
#define TRUE 1                                    /* Program text easier  */
#define byte unsigned char
#define ENTRY 14   /* this many directory entries fit on the screen  */
#define EZ (20-ENTRY >> 1)          /* first line of Directory window  */
#define NRM 0x07              /* white characters on black background */
#define INV 0x70  /* black characters on white background (inverted) */

/*-- this is the format of a Directory entry returned by     --------*/
/*-- the functions 4EH and 4FH                                       */
struct DirStruct {
                  byte          Reservebuf[21];
                  byte          Attribute;
                  unsigned int  Ftime;
                  unsigned int  Fdate;
                  unsigned long Fsize;
                  char          Fname[13];
                 };
```

```
/***********************************************************************/
/* GETPAGE : gets the current display page                             */
/* Input   : none                                                      */
/* Output  : see above                                                 */
/***********************************************************************/

byte GETPAGE()

{
 union REGS Register;        /* Register-Variable for Interrupt call */

 Register.h.ah = 15;                              /* Function number */
 int86(0x10, &Register, &Register);             /* Call Interrupt 10H */
 return(Register.h.bh);                  /* Number of current display */
}

/***********************************************************************/
/* SCROLLUP: moves a display area one or more lines                    */
/*           upward or erases it                                       */
/* Input   : see above                                                 */
/* Output  : none                                                      */
/* Info    : if 0 is passed as number, the display area                */
/*           is filled with blanks                                     */
/***********************************************************************/

void ScrollUp(Number, Color, ColumnUL, LineUL, ColumnLR, LineLR)
int Number;                           /* Number of lines to be scrolled */
int Color;                            /* Color or attribute for blanks */
int ColumnUL;      /* Column in the upper left corner of display area */
int LineUL;          /* Line in the upper left corner of the display  */
int ColumnLR;/* Column in the lower right corner of the display area */
int LineLR;    /* Line in the lower right corner of the display area */

{
 union REGS Register;        /* Register-Variable for Interrupt call */

 Register.h.ah = 6;                               /* Function number */
 Register.h.al = Number;                          /* Number of lines */
 Register.h.bh = Color;                      /* Color of blank line(s) */
 Register.h.ch = LineUL;                 /* Coordinates of the scroll */
 Register.h.cl = ColumnUL;                          /* end or erase  */
 Register.h.dh = LineLR;                        /* Set display window */
 Register.h.dl = ColumnLR;
 int86(0x10, &Register, &Register);             /* Call Interrupt 10H */
}

/***********************************************************************/
/* SETPOS : sets the position of the cursor in current display page   */
/* Input  : see above                                                  */
/* Output : none                                                       */
/* Info   : the position of the blinking display cursor is changed    */
/*          by the call of this function only when the                 */
/*          display page indicated is the current display page         */
/*                                                                     */
/***********************************************************************/

void SetPos(Column, Line)
int Column;                                     /* new Cursor column */
int Line;                                         /* new Cursor line */

{
 union REGS Register;        /* Register-Variable for Interrupt call */

 Register.h.ah = 2;                               /* Function number */
 Register.h.bh = GETPAGE();                          /* Display page */
 Register.h.dh = Line;                               /* Display line */
 Register.h.dl = Column;                           /* Display column */
 int86(0x10, &Register, &Register);             /* Call Interrupt 10H */
}
```

```
/***********************************************************************/
/* GETPOS  : Get the position of the Cursor in current display page  */
/* Input   : none                                                     */
/* Output  : see below                                                */
/***********************************************************************/

void GetPos(Column, Line)
int *Column;                    /* Column where the Cursor is located */
int *Line;                        /* Line where the Cursor is located */

{
 union REGS Register;         /* Register-Variable for Interrupt call */

 Register.h.ah = 3;                                /* Function number */
 Register.h.bh = GETPAGE();                           /* Display page */
 int86(0x10, &Register, &Register);             /* Call Interrupt 10H */
 *Column = Register.h.dl;                /* Read result of the Function */
 *Line = Register.h.dh;                         /* from the Registers */
}

/***********************************************************************/
/* WRITECHAR: writes a character with an attribute to the current    */
/*            cursor position on the current display page             */
/* Input    : see below                                               */
/* Output   : none                                                    */
/***********************************************************************/

void WriteChar(Character, Color)
char Character;                              /* Character for output  */
int Color;                                  /* its Attribute or color */

{
 union REGS Register;         /* Register-Variable for Interrupt call */

 Register.h.ah = 9;                                /* Function number */
 Register.h.al = Character;                   /* character for output */
 Register.h.bh = GETPAGE();                           /* Display page */
 Register.h.bl = Color;               /* Color of character for output */
 Register.x.cx = 1;                     /* output character only once  */
 int86(0x10, &Register, &Register);             /* Call Interrupt 10H */
}

/***********************************************************************/
/* WT       : writes a character string with constant color starting  */
/*            at a specified position on the current display page.    */
/* Input    : see below                                               */
/* Output   : none                                                    */
/* Info     : Text is a Pointer to a character Vector, which contains */
/*            the text to be output and is terminated with a '\0'     */
/*            character.                                              */
/***********************************************************************/

void WT(Column, Line, Text, Color)
int Column;                           /* Display column for output  */
int Line;                               /* Display line for output  */
char *Text;                                     /* Text for output */
int Color;                           /* Color/Attribute of the Text */

{
 union REGS Register;         /* Register-Variable for Interrupt call */

 SetPos(Column, Line);                                  /* Set Cursor */
 while (*Text)                      /* Output Text up to '\0' character */
  {
   WriteChar(' ', Color);                          /* Indicate color */
   Register.h.ah = 14;                            /* Function number */
   Register.h.bh = GETPAGE();                        /* Display page */
   Register.h.al = *Text++;               /* of character to be output */
   int86(0x10, &Register, &Register);              /* Call Interrupt */
  }
```

```
}

/************************************************************************/
/* CLS     : Clear current display and set Cursor into upper left     */
/*           corner                                                     */
/* Input   : none                                                       */
/* Output  : none                                                       */
/************************************************************************/

void Cls()

{
 ScrollUp(0, NRM, 0, 0, 79, 24);                        /* Clear Screen */
 SetPos(0, 0);                                            /* Set Cursor */
}

/************************************************************************/
/* BUILDSCREENDISPLAY: prepares the display for the output of the      */
/*                     Directory.                                       */
/* Input             : none                                             */
/* Output            : none                                             */
/************************************************************************/

void BuildScreenDisplay()

{
 byte i;                                                /* Loop Counter */
 Cls();                                                 /* Clear Screen */
 WT(14,EZ,   "┌─────────────┬───────┬─────────────┬───────────┬─────┐",NOF);
 WT(14,EZ+1,"│ Filename    │ Size  │    Date     │  Time     │RHSVD│",NOF);
 WT(14,EZ+2,"├─────────────┼───────┼─────────────┼───────────┼─────┤",NOF);
 for (i = EZ+3; i < EZ+3+ENTRY; i++)
  WT(14,i, "│             │       │             │           │     │",NOF);
WT(14,EZ+ENTRY+3,"└─────────────┴───────┴─────────────┴───────────┴─────┘",
    NOF);
}

/************************************************************************/
/* PRINTDATA: Output information about an entry                        */
/* Input    : see below                                                 */
/* Output   : none                                                      */
/************************************************************************/

void PrintData(DirEntry, Line)
struct DirStruct *DirEntry;                        /* a Directory entry */
byte Line;                                     /* Display line of entry */

{
 byte i;                                                /* Loop Counter */
 static char *Month[] =      /* Vector with Pointer to name of month */
                         {
                          "JAN", "FEB", "MAR", "APR", "MAY", "JUN",
                          "JUL", "AUG", "SEP", "OCT", "NOV", "DEC"
                         };

 SetPos(15, Line);              /* Set Cursor position for file name */
 for (i=0; (*DirEntry).Fname[i] && i<15 ; printf("%c", (*DirEntry).Fname[i++]))
  ;
 SetPos(28, Line);              /* Set Cursor position for file size */
 printf("%7lu", (*DirEntry).Fsize);                 /* Output file size */
 SetPos(36, Line);                   /* Set Cursor position for Date */
 printf("%s-%2d-%4d", Month[((*DirEntry).Fdate >> 5 & 15) - 1],
         (*DirEntry).Fdate & 31, ((*DirEntry).Fdate >> 9) + 1980);
 SetPos(49, Line);                   /* Set Cursor position for Time */
 printf("%2d:%2d",(*DirEntry).Ftime >> 11,(*DirEntry).Ftime >> 5 & 63);
 SetPos(59, Line);              /* Set Cursor position for Attribute */
 for (i = 1; i <= 16; i <<= 1)
  if ((*DirEntry).Attribute & i) printf("X");
   else printf(" ");
```

```
}

/**********************************************************************/
/* GETNEXT : read the following Directory entry                      */
/* Input   : none                                                     */
/* Output  : TRUE, when an entry was found, otherwise FALSE           */
/* Info    : the entry is read into DTA rem                           */
/**********************************************************************/

byte GetNext()

{
 union REGS Register;       /* Register-Variable for Interrupt call  */

 Register.h.ah = 0x4F;   /* Function number for Search of next entry */
 intdos(&Register, &Register);                   /* Call DOS-Intr. 21H */
 return(!Register.x.cflag);             /* Carry-Flag = 0: file found */
}

/**********************************************************************/
/* GETFIRST : read the first Directory entry                          */
/* Input    : none                                                    */
/* Output   : TRUE, if entry was found, otherwise FALSE               */
/* Info     : Entry is read into the DTA                              */
/**********************************************************************/

byte GetFirst(Sname, Attribute)
char *Sname;                                       /* file to be found */
unsigned int Attribute;                        /* the Search Attribute */

{
 union REGS Register;        /* Register-Variable for Interrupt call */
 struct SREGS Segmente;                /* accepts Segment register */

 segread(&Segmente);          /* Read in content of Segment register */
 Register.h.ah = 0x4E;       /* Function number for search of first  */
 Register.x.cx = Attribute;   /* Attribute, for which search is made */
 Register.x.dx = (unsigned int) Sname;  /* Offset address search path*/
 intdosx(&Register, &Register, &Segmente);     /* Call DOS-Intr. 21H */
 return(!Register.x.cflag);            /* Carry-Flag = 0: file found */
}

/**********************************************************************/
/* SETDTA  : sets the DTA to a Variable in the Data Segment           */
/* Input   : see below                                                */
/* Output  : none                                                     */
/**********************************************************************/

void SetDTA(Offset)
unsigned int Offset;                /* new Offset address of the DTA */

{
 union REGS Register;        /* Register-Variable for Interrupt call */
 struct SREGS Segment;             /* accepts the Segment register */

 segread(&Segment);           /* Read in content of Segment register */
 Register.h.ah = 0x1A;                 /* Set Function number for DTA */
 Register.x.dx = Offset;           /* Offset address into DX-Register */
 intdosx(&Register, &Register, &Segment);       /* Call DOS-Intr. 21H */
}

/**********************************************************************/
/* DIR    : controls the input and output of Directories              */
/* Input  : see below                                                 */
/* Output : none                                                      */
/**********************************************************************/

void Dir(Sname, Attribute)
char *Sname;  /* Pointer to Character Vector, containing search path */
int Attribute;                        /* Attribute of file to be found  */
```

```
{
 int NumEntries,                        /* Total number of entries found  */
     Numwind;                            /* Number of entries in display  */
 struct DirStruct DirEntry;                         /* a Directory entry */

 SetDTA(&DirEntry);                              /* DIRENTRY is the new DTA */
 BuildScreenDisplay(); /* Construct display for new Directory output */

 Numwind = NumEntries = 0;        /* no entry displayed in the window  */
                                                    /* no entry found */
 if (GetFirst(Sname, Attribute))           /* search for first entry  */
  {
   do
    {
     PrintData(&DirEntry, EZ+ENTRY+2);                /* output entry  */
     if (++Numwind == ENTRY )                        /* Window full ? */
      {
       Numwind = 0;                                   /* fill a window  */
       WT(14, EZ+4+ENTRY,
          "                   Please press a key                  ",INV);
       getch();                                        /* wait for key */
       WT(14, EZ+4+ENTRY,
          "                                                       ",NRM);
      }
     ScrollUp(1, NRM, 15, EZ+3, 63, EZ+2+ENTRY);
     WT(15, EZ+2+ENTRY,
        "      |       |            |          |     ",NOF);
     ++NumEntries;
    }
   while (GetNext());
  }
 SetPos(14, EZ+4+ENTRY);
 switch (NumEntries)
  {
   case 0  : printf("no files found ");
             break;
   case 1  : printf("one file found ");
             break;
   default : printf("%d files found ", NumEntries);
  }
}

/***********************************************************************/
/**                            MAIN PROGRAM                          **/
/***********************************************************************/

void main(Number, Argument)
int Number;                            /* Number of Arguments + 1 passed */
char *Argument[];                    /* Vector with pointer to Arguments */
{
 switch (Number)                                /* react according to  */
  {                                                /* Arguments passed */
   case 1 : Dir("*.*", ~0);           /* Display all files in current  */
            break;                                      /* Directory */
   case 2 : Dir(Argument[1], ~0); /* Display all files in indicated  */
            break;                                      /* Directory */
   default : printf("Invalid number of Parameters\n");
  }
}
```

6.8 The EXEC Function

The EXEC function has been mentioned briefly several times before in relation to the command processor. We'll examine the EXEC function more fully here and describe its operation.

Parent/child

The EXEC function is one of the many DOS functions which can be called with interrupt 21H (function 4BH). Generally speaking, this function lets a *parent program* (main program) call a *child program* (secondary program). The child program is loaded from a mass storage device into memory and then executes. If this child program doesn't become resident, the memory occupied by the child is released following program execution. The child program can also call another program which works with the parent program. This creates a type of program chaining limited only by the amount of available RAM.

One example of the EXEC function is the command processor. Using the EXEC function, the command processor executes user-specified programs and becomes the parent program. Some programs (such as Microsoft Word®) permit the user to execute DOS commands from the main program using this function.

The parent program can pass parameters to the child program in the command line and can also pass parameters using the environment block. It can also transfer information to the child program within the PSP. Since the child program, like all executable programs, has a PSP preceding it, information can be entered into the two FCBs within this PSP and made accessible to the child program.

Child program

After transferring control to the child program, it can access all files and devices previously opened by the parent program (or one of the parent programs) with a handle function. This allows the child program to read information from a file or write information to a file whose handle is known (the child program doesn't need to know the filename). This is only possible if the handle was passed by the parent program in one of the three methods described, or if the child program refers to one of the five handles which are always open. These file accesses affect the file pointer. Since values are not reset, these file accesses become "visible" to the parent program when control returns to the parent program.

After execution of the child program, control returns to the parent program and execution continues. To pass information (e.g., an error that occurred during the execution of the child program), the child program can pass a numeric value at the end of its execution. This can be done using DOS function 4CH, which terminates a program and returns a code to the parent program.

The communication between parent and child program functions only if both programs agree on this return value. After control returns to the parent program, it can determine the code using function 4DH of interrupt 21H. To use function 4DH only the function number is passed in the AH register. The code passed by the child program is returned to the calling (parent) program in the AL register.

Ending the child program

In addition, the contents of the AH register indicate how the child program terminated. The value 0 indicates a normal termination, while 1 shows that the child program terminated when the user pressed <Control><C> or <Control><Break>. If an error during access to a mass storage device forced the child program to terminate, a code of 2 is passed in the AH register. Finally the value 3 indicates that the child program terminated from a call to function 31H, or interrupt 27H; the child program then becomes resident in memory.

As mentioned previously, the EXEC function can only load the child program if enough memory is available. While DOS can estimate the memory needed for EXE programs fairly accurately, it cannot do the same for COM programs. For COM programs DOS reserves all unused memory. Because of this, a COM program cannot call another program with the EXEC function, since DOS reserves no extra memory. The same is true for many EXE programs. If a call to a child program is necessary, the required memory space must be released from the calling program before calling the EXEC function (see Sections 6.4.1 and 6.4.2 for explanations on how this is done).

EXEC

If the EXEC function is called, the various parameters are loaded into the registers before calling interrupt 21H. Function number 4BH is passed in the AH register. A value of 0 or 3 is passed in the AL register. A value of 0 indicates that the EXEC function is to load and execute the program while a value of 3 indicates that the program is loaded as an overlay (without executing it). The address of the name of the program to be loaded or executed is passed in the DS:DX register pair. And the address of the *parameter block* is passed in the ES:BX register pair.

The program name is specified as an ASCII string and ended with a null character (ASCII code 0). The program name can include the device name and a complete path description. Its last element is the program name which, besides the name itself, must have the extension .COM or .EXE. If the device name or path designation are omitted, the system searches for the program in the current directory of the current device. Since the EXEC function cannot execute a batch file directly, the program name passed cannot contain the extension .BAT.

Batch child

If a batch file is to be executed, the COMMAND.COM (command processor) file must be invoked first. To indicate that a batch file should be executed, the parameter /c followed by the name of the batch file to be executed is included on the command line. Besides the ability to execute a batch file, calling the command processor with the /c parameter offers the option of calling any other program, and even internal DOS commands such as DIR.

Besides calling a program directly, it's possible to specify program names without file extensions during a command processor call. The command processor searches for an EXE file; then a COM file; and finally a BAT file. If none of these files exist in the current directory, it searches all directories specified in the PATH command. This chain of events is not followed during a direct program call without the addition of the command processor.

The directory which contains the command processor should be specified. If not specified, it will be loaded from the path indicated by the COMSPEC environment string of the SET command.

Parameter blocks

Parameters can be passed to the command processor in the parameter block following the program name. These parameters are identical to the parameters entered from the keyboard when the program is called. How these parameters affect the EXEC function will be seen shortly, but first take a look at the parameter block's structure when the AL register contains the value 0. This block's address is passed to the EXEC function in the register pair ES:BX.

1	0-1	Segment address of the environment block
2	2-3	Offset address of the command parameter
3	4-5	Segment address of the command parameter
4	6-7	Offset address of the first FCB
5	8-9	Segment address of the first FCB
6	10-11	Offset address of the second FCB
7	12-13	Segment address of the second FCB

Field 1 indicates the segment address of the child program's environment block. This block doesn't require an offset address since it always starts at a location divisible by 16, and therefore its offset address is always to 0.

Environment block

The command processor and other programs obtain information from the environment block. The environment block is a series of ASCII character strings. This information can include paths for file searches. Each string has the following syntax, terminated by a null character (ASCII code 0):

```
Name = Parameter
```

The individual strings follow each other sequentially (i.e., the null character of one string is immediately followed by the beginning character of the next string). The environment block ends with a null character. Any environment block has a maximum length of 32K.

The environment block can be changed or modified by the user using the DOS SET and PATH commands. Programs which remain resident after execution are unaffected by any changes made to the environment block through these two DOS commands once made resident.

If the parent program wants to pass information to the child program using the environment block, it can either construct a new environment block or supplement its own environment block with this information. In the first case, the segment address of the new environment block is specified in the first field of the parameter block. If the child program should have access to the environment block of the parent program, specify a value of 0 in this field. Before turning over control to the child program, the EXEC function stores the segment address of the environment block in the memory location at address 2CH of the child program's PSP.

If the child program is to use a new environment block, it should contain at least 3 strings which are normally part of the environment block of the parent program, and are important to the command processor:

```
COMSPEC = Parameter
PATH = Parameter
PROMPT = Parameter
```

If a child program modifies its environment block, the parent program's environment block remains unchanged after the child program completes its execution.

Fields 2 and 3 indicate the command parameters' address which is passed to the PSP of the program starting at address 80H. They must have the same structure in memory as expected by DOS in the PSP. The first byte indicates the number of command characters minus 1, then follows the command characters as normal ASCII codes. The command parameters terminate with a carriage return (ASCII code 13) which is not included in the character count. The first character in the string should be a space for compatibility with COMMAND.COM.

To call a batch program (called DO.BAT) using the command processor, the following command parameters must be specified as a string in memory:

```
        DB 10," /C DO.BAT",13
```

The EXEC function copies the command parameters in a controlled fashion into the PSP of the program to be executed. It removes all parameters which would redirect the input or output, since a redirection of the standard input/output can only be performed by the parent program. The child program can still use input/output redirection if the standard input/output handles have been redirected by the parent program (see Section 6.10 for more detailed information and an example of this process).

Fields 6, 7, 10 and 11 indicate two FCBs installed in the PSP at address 5CH or 6CH. If this is not required, specify -1 (FFFFH) in these two fields. If program execution requires it, enter the first two command parameters in the two FCBs with DOS function 29H. Before passing control to the child program, the EXEC function copies these two FCBs into the PSP of the child program.

Even though all registers and the parameter block now have the required values, the EXEC function cannot be called yet. Since it destroys the contents of all registers up to the CS and IP registers during execution, the contents of all registers must be placed on the stack before it is invoked. Then the contents of the SS and SP registers must be stored within the code segment. Only then can interrupt 21H function 4BH be called to activate the EXEC function. After the EXEC function ends, the carry flag signals if the function executed normally. Before program execution can continue, the value of the SS and SP registers must be restored, from the code segment. Then the contents of the other register can be restored again from the stack.

The EXEC function serves a different purpose when a value of 3 appears in the AL register. In this case, it loads a COM program or an EXE program into memory without executing. After the target program is loaded, control immediately returns to the calling program. In contrast with sub-function 0, the program loads to a memory address indicated by the calling program instead of loading to any non-specific location. Since no parameters are passed to the loaded program, the parameter block has a different structure during the call of sub-function 3 than during the call of sub-function 0:

Field	Byte	Purpose
1	0-1	Segment address where overlay is loaded
2	2-3	Relocation factor

Before the function is called, the segment address to which the program should be loaded is specified in the first field of the parameter block. If the calling program doesn't have enough memory available for loading the external program, it should request additional memory with one of the DOS memory management functions. The loaded program loads directly to the segment address indicated with the offset address 0 since no PSP precedes the program.

Relocation

The relocation factor adjusts the segment address of the called program. Since this factor applies only to EXE programs (COM programs cannot have specific segment assignments), the relocation factor for COM programs should always be equal to 0. The relocation factor for EXE programs should indicate the segment address where the program will be loaded to confirm to the program's segment assignments.

After the program is loaded, its routines are ready to be accessed. The routines of the loaded program should always be treated as subroutines; and therefore, called with the machine language CALL instruction. It must always be a FAR type instruction even though the loaded program may be located immediately following the calling program, but can never have the same segment address. The offset address for CALL is always 100H for a COM program, since execution always starts immediately following the PSP at address 100H. This creates a problem. Sub-function 3 prevents the PSP from loading. Therefore the code segment of the COM program starts at address 0, not at the offset address 100H (relative to the load segment). Since all jump instructions and accesses to data within the COM program are relative to address 100H and not address 0, you cannot execute a FAR CALL instruction with the address of the load segment as the segment address, and address 0 as the offset address. The segment address for the FAR CALL must indicate the address of the load segment minus 10H and the address 100H as the offset address.

If the COM program specifically acts as an overlay for another program, entry addresses other than address 100H are possible. In such a case, only the offset address for the FAR CALL instruction changes. The segment address must remain 10H smaller than the address of the load segment.

EXEC and memory

The problem is different for EXE programs. If they are loaded for execution using sub-function 0, the EXEC function sets the code segment and the instruction pointer to the instruction which was declared as the first instruction in the assembler source. This address, however, is unknown to the program which loaded the EXE program as an overlay. This can easily be remedied by placing the first executable instruction in the EXE program at the beginning of the EXE program. This makes its offset address 0. The EXE program source must not be in the normal sequence with the stack first. In this case, the code segment must be the first segment in the source to ensure that it begins the EXE program.

The FAR CALL uses the address of the load segment as the segment address, and address 0 as the offset address.

While BASIC, Pascal and C have commands or procedures to call a program from another program, assembly language routines must use DOS function 4BH. To help you further understand this function, here is an example program.

The framework of the EXE program listed in Section 6.4.2 acts as the basis for this program. The EXEPRG procedure performs the actual dirty work in this program. It calls the new program using function 4BH. Two strings which contain the name of the program to be called and the necessary parameters are passed to it. Both strings end with the null character (ASCII code 0). All variables required by EXEPRG for execution can be found in the code segment. This offers the advantage that the lines from the code segment only must be copied into one of the application programs to use this routine. After calling EXEPRG, the carry flag signals if an error occurred. If true (carry flag=1), the AX register contains the error code as returned by the EXEC function of DOS. If the called program executed correctly, the carry flag is reset (0) and the termination code of the called program, as returned by DOS function 4DH, is returned by the AX register.

Within this program, EXEPRG displays the current directory using the command processor. The command processor defaults to the current directory of the current device.

```
;**********************************************************************;
;*                             E X E C                                *;
;*--------------------------------------------------------------------*;
;*    Task         :   Calls a program with the help of the           *;
;*                     EXEC function of DOS. In this example          *;
;*                     program the content of the current             *;
;*                     Directory of the current device is displayed.  *;
;*--------------------------------------------------------------------*;
;*    Author         : MICHAEL TISCHER                                *;
;*    developed on   :  08/01/87                                      *;
;*    last Update    :  04/08/89                                      *;
;*--------------------------------------------------------------------*;
;*    assembly       : MASM EXEC;                                     *;
;*                     LINK EXEC;                                     *;
;*--------------------------------------------------------------------*;
;*    Call           : EXEC                                           *;
;**********************************************************************;

;== data ===============================================================

data      segment para 'DATA'      ;Definition of the data-segment

prgname   db "\command.com",0      ;Name of the program to be called
prgpara   db "/c dir",0            ;Parameters passed to program

data      ends                     ;end of data-segment

;== code ===============================================================

code      segment para 'CODE'      ;Definition of the CODE-segment

          assume cs:code, ds:data, ss:stack

exec      proc far

          mov  ax,data             ;Load segment address of the data segment
          mov  ds,ax               ;into the DS-register

          call setfree             ;release unused memory

          mov  dx,offset prgname   ;offset address of program name
          mov  si,offset prgpara   ;offset address of command line
          call exeprg              ;Call program

          mov  ax,4C00h            ;end program with call of a DOS function
          int  21h                 ;on return of error-code 0
exec      endp

;-- SETFREE: Release memory not used  ----------------
;-- Input    : ES = address of PSP
;-- Output   : none
;-- Register : AX, BX, CL and FLAGS are changed
;-- Info     : Since the stack-segment is always the last segment in an
;              EXE-file, ES:0000 points to the beginning and SS:SP
;              to the end of the program in memory. Through this the
;              length of the program can be calculated

setfree   proc near
```

```
          mov  bx,ss                ;first subtract the two segment addresses
          mov  ax,es                ;from each other. The result is
          sub  bx,ax                ;number of paragraphs from PSP
                                    ;to the beginning of the stack
          mov  ax,sp                ;since the stackpointer is at the end of
          mov  cl,4                 ;the stack segment, its content indicates
          shr  ax,cl                ;the length of the stack
          add  bx,ax                ;add to current length
          inc  bx                   ;as precaution add another paragraph

          mov  ah,4ah               ;pass new length to DOS
          int  21h

          ret                       ;back to caller

setfree   endp

;-- EXEPRG: call another program  -----------------------------
;-- Input    : DS:DX = address of the Program Name
;--            DS:SI = address of the Command Line
;-- Output   : carry flag = 1 : Error (AX = Error-code)
;-- Register : only AX and FLAGS are changed
;-- Info     : Program name and Command Line must be ASCII-String
;--            and terminated with ASCII-code 0

exeprg    proc near

          ;Transmit Command Line into own buffer  --
          ;and count characters                    --

          push bx                   ;Store all registers which are
          push cx                   ;destroyed by the call to the
          push dx                   ;DOS EXEC function
          push di
          push si
          push bp
          push ds
          push es

          mov  di,offset comline+1 ;address of chars in Command Line.
          push cs                   ;CS to stack
          pop  es                   ;back as ES
          xor  bl,bl                ;Set character count to 0
copypara: lodsb                     ;read a character
          or   al,al                ;is it a NUL-code (end)
          je   copyend              ;Yes --> copied enough
          stosb                     ;store in new buffer
          inc  bl                   ;increment character count
          cmp  bl,126               ;Maximum reached?
          jne  copypara             ;No --> continue

copyend:  mov  cs:comline,bl        ;store number of characters
          mov  byte ptr es:[di],13 ;finish command line

          mov  cs:merkss,ss         ;SS and SP must be stored in
          mov  cs:merksp,sp         ;variables in code segment

          mov  bx,offset parblock ;ES:BX points to parameter block
          mov  ax,4B00h             ;function number for EXEC function
          int  21h                  ;Call DOS-function

          cli                       ;Set interrupts for a moment from
          mov  ss,cs:merkss         ;stack segment and stackpointer to
          mov  sp,cs:merksp         ;their old values
          sti                       ;Switch interrupt on again

          pop  es                   ;Get all Registers from stack again
          pop  ds
          pop  bp
```

```
         pop  si
         pop  di
         pop  dx
         pop  cx
         pop  bx

         jc   exeend            ;Errors? YES --> end
         mov  ah,4dh            ;no errors, sense end-code of the
         int  21h               ;program which was executed

exeend:  ret                    ;back to caller

        ;-- Variables of this routine only addressable through CS --

merkss   dw (?)                 ;accepts SS during program call
merksp   dw (?)                 ;accepts SP during program call
parblock equ this word          ;Parameter block for EXEC function
         dw 0                   ;environment block
         dw offset comline      ;offset and segment address of
         dw seg code            ;modified Command Line
         dd 0                   ;no data in PSP #1
         dd 0                   ;no data in PSP #2

comline  db 128 dup (?)         ;accepts modified Command Line

exeprg   endp

;== stack ==========================================================

stack    segment para stack     ;Definition of the stack-segment

         dw 256 dup (?)         ;the stack has 256 Words

stack    ends                   ;End of the stack-segment

;== End ============================================================

code     ends                   ;End of the CODE-segment
         end  exec              ;for execution start with EXEC
```

6.9 Memory Allocation from DOS

DOS subdivides the maximum 640K of memory into roughly two areas. The first area is designated as the *operating system area*. It begins at memory location 0000:0000 and contains the interrupt vector table, some internal tables, buffers, variable memory and the operating system code. This code retains the resident portion of the command processor and the resident and installable device drivers. The size of this area varies with the version of DOS in use, the sizes of the device drivers installed, and other factors such as the number of disk buffers available.

The second area is designated as the *TPA* (Transient Program Area). It contains programs and their environment blocks for execution. The TPA starts after the end of the operating system area. Depending on the memory requirements of the individual programs, DOS assigns them different amounts of memory administered through a special data block preceding every memory range and connected with the data block of the next memory range. This also applies to memory not assigned to a program.

This data block, called a *memory control block* (or MCB) is a 16-byte block containing a variety of information. An MCB begins at one of the addresses divisible by 16, and controls memory allocation. DOS looks for the segment address of the allocated memory range, and is helped in this task through the MCB. The following table shows the structure of an MCB in memory:

Address	Contents	Type
+00H	ID ("Z"=last MCB, "M"=another MCB follows)	1 byte
+01H	Segment address of corresponding PSP	1 word
+03H	Number of paragraphs in allocated range	1 word
+05H	unused	11 bytes
+10H	Allocated memory range	x paragraphs

As the table above illustrates, the MCB contains three fields. The first field indicates whether any MCBs follow the current MCB under analysis. The letters "M" (more MCBs to follow) and "Z" (last MCB) are the initials of one of the creators of MS-DOS, Mark Zbikowski.

The second field specifies the segment address of the corresponding program's PSP. This only applies when memory allocation becomes a part of the environment of the program being handled, in which case the PSP is indicated by the contents of this field. In most cases, this field simply points to the memory range needed by the program.

The third field of the MCB specifies the size of the corresponding memory range in paragraphs. Next follows the memory range itself, then any further MCBs after that (provided that the first field contains an "M" ID letter). MCBs can be linked together to create a group, as shown in the figure below:

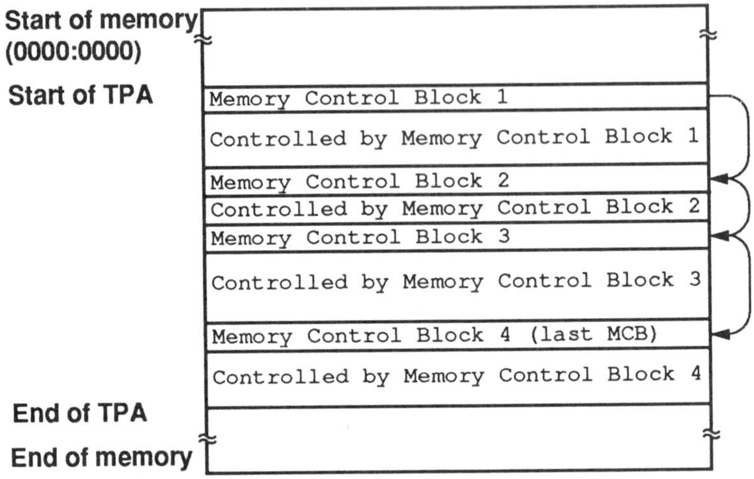

Memory allocation

If the DOS EXEC loader loads and executes a program, this function immediately requests two data areas through another DOS function. The first of these two areas stores the environment block, while the second accepts the current program and the program's PSP. The size of the area made available to a program is difficult to estimate from the EXEC loader. This is even more difficult for COM programs than for EXE programs since COM programs are copies of memory contents and have no information preceding them. DOS therefore defaults to the maximum and reserves the total available memory for a COM program.

This method worked well in the early days of DOS, but has created other problems. While only one program could exist in memory at a time in the early days of DOS, now it's common for one program to load and run a second program, or even make one of the programs permanently resident in memory. This can't be done if no memory exists, as would be the case after loading a COM program. This is why a COM program should always release the memory it no longer needs after it starts (see Section 6.4.1 for details on how this happens).

A COM program can only load when a memory range large enough to accommodate the COM program exists (plus 256 bytes for the PSP and at least 2 bytes for the stack). The COM program ensures that enough memory is available. Under the minimum conditions presented above, the program probably won't run without errors, since few programs can operate with only a 2-byte stack.

EXE program files have a set of information created by the linker. The EXEC loader can determine the amount of memory required for code segment, data and stack from this information. The start of the EXE program itself contains additional information about the amount of memory needed for the program. This amount defines an upper and lower limit of the additional memory, rather than a specific number of bytes. The EXEC loader tries to reserve the upper limit of memory if it can. If this is not possible, the EXEC loader uses the lower limit or reserves the remainder of memory. If the lower limit of memory cannot be allocated, the loading process aborts and control returns to the program which called the EXEC loader (in most cases, the command processor).

The same occurs after program execution when the EXEC loader releases the reserved memory space for further use, unless prevented by function 31H of interrupt 21H, called from the program.

Now that you know some of the theoretical aspects of DOS memory management, here are descriptions of the most important of these DOS functions. Functions 48H, 49H and 4AH are all called through interrupt 21H. The function number is passed in the AH register.

Function 48H allocates memory. The function number is passed in the AH register and the number of paragraphs to be reserved (16 bytes per paragraph) is passed in the BX register. If the requested number of paragraphs can be reserved, the function returns with the carry flag clear. The AX register indicates the segment address of the reserved memory. Therefore, it starts at address AX:0000. If the program required more memory than was available, the carry flag is set following the call to the function and the AX register contains an error code. The BX register contains the maximum memory available in paragraphs.

Function 49H performs the reverse of function 48H. This function releases memory previously reserved through function 48H. The segment address of the memory area to be released is passed in the ES register. This segment address was originally passed in the AX register when function 48H was called. Normally function 49H should execute without errors and the carry flag should be reset after the function call. If this is not the case, it could be caused by either a destroyed data block (placed ahead of a memory area by DOS), or a segment address passed in the ES register which doesn't match a reserved memory area.

A third function changes the size of memory area which had been previously reserved. The memory area can be either enlarged or reduced by using function 4AH. The segment address of the area to be modified is passed in the ES register. The BX register reserves the number of paragraphs (16-byte units) which the memory area should contain. The register contents following the call to the function are identical to those of function 48H.

Since calling DOS functions is relatively easy as far as memory management is concerned and no special tricks are required, the following program is dedicated to a different topic, which also relates to DOS memory management. We're talking about a program that pokes around the system and checks all allocated memory as well as its contents. The program is intelligent enough to differentiate between storage areas that contain the environment of a program, a PSP, or other information.

The assignment of this program is to go through the memory from MCB to MCB and examine the allocated storage areas. In order to move to the next MCB each time, it uses the third field within an MCB, which helps it point to the next MCB. This sets up a loop which will run until the last MCB is discovered, which will have the letter "Z" in its ID field.

But in order to move through the chain of MCBs, the address of the first link, that is the first MCB, must be known. DOS lists this within an internal structure called DIB (DOS Information Block), which is not normally accessible to application programs, i.e. this represents an undocumented DOS feature (see also Section 6.15). However, we can find out the address of this structure with the help of function 52H, which will output the address to the ES:BX register pair when called.

Curiously, this address points to the second field in the MCB rather than the first. But since it's the first field that contains the address of the first MCB, the information we're looking for is behind the pointer. Since the pointer on the first MCB consists of an offset address and a segment address, it is four bytes long and can therefore be found at the address ES:(BX-4). But be careful with the address statement, because it makes it seem as though all you have to do is subtract 4 from the contents of the BX register in order to get the effective address of the desired information in the ES:BX register pair. This will only be successful if the offset address in the BX register is greater than or equal to 4. But if it is less than 4, the consequences are disastrous, because this leaves a negative number. There is no such thing as a negative memory address. Let's use an example to make this clear:

If the value 0 is returned to the BX register as the offset address of the DIB, the subtraction would give the value 0FFFCH. With arithmetic operations, this is interpreted quite correctly as -4. However, during memory access, this will not point to the address -4, but rather right to 0FFFCH, and therefore to the end rather than the beginning of the accompanying segment. Of course, you won't find what you're looking for there.

The program will help you here, first of all by decrementing the delivered segment address by 1. This reduces the effective address, which you get by appending the segment address and the offset address, by 16. Finally, by adding 12 to the offset address, the effective address is reduced by only 4 and points to the desired memory location. The address of the first MCB can then be taken from this memory location without any problems.

The loop which runs through all MCBs and analyzes them begins with this address. First, some status information on the MCB and the memory it controls is given. This includes:

- the MCB number
- its address in memory

- the address of the memory it controls
- the contents of the ID field ("M" or "Z")
- the address of the accompanying PSP (independent of whether it even exists)
- the size of the accompanying storage area in paragraphs and bytes

Next, the contents of the storage area that belongs to it are examined. We get its address by incrementing the segment address of the MCB by 1. The first thing we'll determine is whether we're dealing with an environment block in this storage area. We'll know for sure if we find the string COMSPEC= at the beginning of the area. This string starts every environment block. If this string is found, the program proceeds as though this were indeed an environment block, and it lists the individual environment strings. In front of these, it lists the name of the program the environment block belongs to, which is located at the end of the environment block for DOS version 3.0 and higher.

If the storage area cannot be identified as an environment block, we could possibly be dealing with a PSP, and therefore a transient or resident program. The program will start from here if it finds the machine language command INT 20H (code 0CDH, 020H) in the first two positions of the memory range. This command starts every PSP.

If the program also does not run into this, it can't tell if the memory range contains program code, data, or whatever. In this case, the program will send the first 80 bytes of the storage area to the screen as a hex and ASCII dump, in order to give you a chance to figure it out for yourself.

After this, the user is prompted to strike any key. When the keystroke is received, the next MCB is examined, and the program will finally end when the last MCB has been handled.

The following programs in Pascal and C produce the MCB dump. A BASIC version could not be implemented here because this program works its way through the entire memory, and BASIC offers only the DEF, SEG and PEEK commands for this purpose. The use of these commands is too awkward in this case and would detract from the real task of the program.

Since both programs are very similar in terms of the logic, function calls, and variables used, they are described together in the following section.

Both access memory with FAR pointers, since the storage areas to be addressed are outside of their data segments. While Turbo Pascal automatically uses FAR pointers, C requires selection of the appropriate memory configuration through Compact, Huge, Large or with the help of Cast operations, each of which explicitly defines the task with a FAR pointer. This program goes the latter way, so that it may also be compiled in a memory configuration that works with NEAR pointers by default (Tiny, Small, Medium).

Converting separately retrieved offset and segment addresses to one FAR pointer presents a problem in both languages. This can be done in C with a macro, which is already defined in the Include file DOS.H in Turbo C, but is missing in Microsoft C. For this reason, the macro is defined within the C program, in case it hasn't been previously defined. In Pascal, the address conversions happen with the help of a small inline procedure, that enters both addresses directly into the memory locations that form the pointer.

Beyond these brief remarks, the listings should be able to speak for themselves, since they are fully documented.

Pascal listing: MEMP.PAS

```
{**********************************************************************}
{*                              M E M P                               *}
{*--------------------------------------------------------------------*}
{*    Description    : displays the memory blocks allocated by DOS.   *}
{*--------------------------------------------------------------------*}
{*    Author         : MICHAEL TISCHER                                *}
{*    developed on   : 08/22/1988                                     *}
{*    last update    : 08/22/1988                                     *}
{**********************************************************************}

program MEMP;

uses DOS, CRT;                          { bind in the DOS and CRT units }

type BytePtr = ^byte;                               { pointer to a byte }
     Range = array[0..1000] of byte;        { an area, anywhere in RAM }
     RngPtr  = ^Range;                               { pointer to an area }
     MCB     = record                           { a memory control block }
                 IdCode   : char;    { "M" = a block follows, "Z" = end }
                 PSP      : word;          { segment address of the PSP }
                 Distance : word;           { number of paragraphs - 1 }
               end;
     MCBPtr  = ^MCB;                                 { pointer to an MCB }
     MCBPtr2 = ^MCBPtr;                           { pointer to an MCBPtr }
     HexStr  = string[4];                { stores a four-digit hex string }

var  CvHStr  : HexStr;                { stores the converted hex string }

{**********************************************************************}
{* GetDosVer: determines the DOS version                              *}
{* Input   : none                                                     *}
{* Output  : the DOS version number (30 for DOS 3.0, 33 for 3.3 etc.) *}
{**********************************************************************}

function GetDosVer : byte;

var Regs : Registers;                 { stores the processor registers }


begin
  Regs.ah := $30;                    { function no. for "Get Dos Version" }
  MsDos( Regs );                              { call DOS interrupt $21 }
  GetDosVer := Regs.al * 10 + Regs.ah;            { get version number }
end;

{**********************************************************************}
{* MK_FP: creates a byte pointer out of the segment and offset        *}
{*        addresses passed.                                           *}
{* Input   : - Seg = segment to which the point should point          *}
{*           - Ofs = offset address to which the pointer should point *}
{* Output  : the pointer                                              *}
```

```
{* Info     : The pointer returned can be cast to any type pointer     *}
{**********************************************************************}

{$F+}               { This routine is intended for the FAR model and is  }
                    { also suited for binding into a unit.               }

function MK_FP( Seg, Ofs : word ) : BytePtr;

begin
  inline ( $8B / $46 / $08 /  { mov ax,[bp+8] (get segment address)     }
           $89 / $46 / $FE /  { mov [bp-2],ax (and put in pointer)      }
           $8B / $46 / $06 /  { mov ax,[bp+6] (get offset address)      }
           $89 / $46 / $FC ); { mov [bp-4],ax (and put in pointer)      }
end;

{$F-}                                     { NEAR routines possible again }

{**********************************************************************}
{* HexString: creates a 4-digit hex string out of the number passed   *}
{* Input    : - HexVal = the number to be converted                   *}
{* Output   : the hex string                                          *}
{**********************************************************************}

function HexString( HexVal : word ) : HexStr;

var Counter,                                          { loop counter }
    Nibble  : byte;                    { the lowest nibble of the word }

begin
  CvHStr := 'xxxx';                             { initialize the string }
  for Counter:=4 downto 1 do  { run through the 4 digits of the string }
    begin
      Nibble := HexVal and $000f;         { leave just the lower 4 bits }
      if ( Nibble > 9 ) then                     { convert to a letter? }
        CvHStr[ Counter ] := chr(Nibble - 10 + ord('A'))          { yes }
      else                                        { convert to a number }
        CvHStr[ Counter ] := chr(Nibble + ord('0'));
      HexVal := HexVal shr 4;           { shift HexVal 4 bits to the right }
    end;
  HexString := CvHStr;                       { return the created string }
end;

{**********************************************************************}
{* FirstMCB: Returns a pointer to the first MCB.                      *}
{* Input    : none                                                    *}
{* Output   : pointer to the firs MCB                                 *}
{**********************************************************************}

function FirstMCB : MCBPtr;

var Regs : Registers;                  { stores the processor registers }

begin
  Regs.ah := $52;           { ftn. no.: get address of the DOS info block }
  MsDos( Regs );                                 { call DOS interrupt $21 }

  {*-- ES:(BX-4) points to the first MCB, create pointer -------------*}

  FirstMCB := MCBPtr2( MK_FP( Regs.ES-1, Regs.BX+12 ) )^;
end;

{**********************************************************************}
{* Dump: outputs hex and ASCII dump of a memory block.                *}
{* Input    : - DPtr  = pointer to the memory block to be dumped      *}
{*            - Num   = number of lines to dump (16 bytes each)       *}
{* Output   : none                                                    *}
{**********************************************************************}

procedure Dump( DPtr : RngPtr; Num{Num} : byte);
```

```
type HBStr = string[2];                       { stores 2-digit hex numbers }

var  Offset,                                  { offset in the memory block }
     Z       : integer;                                     { loop Counter }
     HexStr  : HBStr;                  { stores a hex number for hex dump }

procedure HexByte( HByte : byte );

begin
  HexStr[1] := chr( (HByte shr 4) + ord('0') );             { first digit }
  if HexStr[1] > '9' then                            { convert to letters? }
    HexStr[1] := chr( ord(HexStr[1]) +  7 );                        { yes }
  HexStr[2] := chr( (HByte and 15) + ord('0') );           { second digit }
  if HexStr[2] > '9' then                            { convert to letters? }
    HexStr[2] := chr( ord(HexStr[2]) +  7 );                        { yes }
end;

begin
  HexStr := 'zz';                               { initialize the hex string }
  writeln;
  write('DUMP | 0123456789ABCDEF       00 01 02 03 04 05 06 07 08');
  writeln(' 09 0A 0B 0C 0D 0E 0F');
  write('-----+---------------------------------------------------------');
  writeln('--------------------------');
  Offset := 0;                    { start with the first byte in the block }
  while Num>0 do                          { run through the loop ANZ times }
    begin
      write(HexString(Offset), ' | ');
      for Z:=0 to 15 do                                 { process 15 bytes }
        if (Dptr^[Offset+Z] >= 32) then            { valid ASCII character? }
          write( chr(Dptr^[Offset+Z]) )            { yes, output character }
        else                                                            { no }
          write(' ');                  { output space instead of character }
      write('       ');                      { set cursor to the hex portion }
      for Z:=0 to 15 do                                 { process 15 bytes }
        begin
          HexByte( Dptr^[Offset+Z] );                 { convert byte to hex }
          write(HexStr, ' ');                          { output hex string }
        end;
      writeln;
      Offset := Offset + 16;                     { set offset in the next line }
      Dec( Num );                     { decrement number of remaining lines }
    end;
  writeln;
end;

{***********************************************************************}
{* TraceMCB: runs through the list of MCB's.                           *}
{* Input    : none                                                     *}
{* Output   : none                                                     *}
{***********************************************************************}

procedure TraceMCB;

const ComSpec : array[0..7] of char = 'COMSPEC=';

var  CurMCB{CurMCB}  : MCBPtr;
     Done     : boolean;
     Key      : char;
     NrMCB,                                      { number of current MCB }
     Z        : integer;                                    { loop counter }
     MemPtr   : RngPtr;
     DosVer   : byte;                                { DOS version number }

begin
  DosVer := GetDosVer;                                  { get DOS version }
  Done := false;
  NrMCB := 1;                                 { the first MCB is number 1 }
  CurMCB := FirstMCB;                      { get pointer to the first MCB }
  repeat                                          { follow the MCB chain }
```

```
if CurMCB^.IdCode = 'Z' then                          { last MCB reached? }
  Done := true;                                                    { yes }
writeln('MCB number      = ', NrMCB);
writeln('MCB address     = ', HexString(seg(CurMCB^)), ':',
                              HexString(ofs(CurMCB^)) );
writeln('Memory addr.    = ', HexString(succ(seg(CurMCB^))), ':',
                              HexString(ofs(CurMCB^)) );
writeln('ID              = ', CurMCB^.IdCode);
writeln('PSP address     = ', HexString(CurMCB^.PSP), ':0000');
writeln('Size            = ', CurMCB^.Distance, ' paragraphs ',
        '( ', longint(CurMCB^.Distance) shl 4, ' bytes )');
write('Contents        = ');

{*-- is it an environment? ----------------------------------------*}

Z := 0;                     { start the comparison at the first byte }
MemPtr := RngPtr(MK_FP(succ(Seg(CurMCB^)), 0));     { pointer in RAM }
while ( (Z<=7) and (ord(ComSpec[Z]) = MemPtr^[Z]) ) do
Inc(Z);                                { set Z to the nest character }
if Z>7 then                                  { was the string found? }
  begin                                { yes, this is an environment }
    writeln('environment');
    MemPtr := RngPtr(MK_FP(succ(Seg(CurMCB^)), 0));
    if DosVer>= 30 then                 { DOS Version 3.0 or higher? }
      begin                                  { yes, get program name }
        write('Program name  = ');
        Z := 0;                              { start with the first byte }
        while not( (MemPtr^[Z]=0) and (MemPtr^[Z+1]=0) ) do
          Inc( Z );                            { search for empty string }
        Z := Z + 4;               { set Z to the start of the prog name }
        if MemPtr^[Z]<>0 then            { is there a prog. name here? }
          begin
            repeat                        { run through the program name }
              write( chr(MemPtr^[Z]) );            { output characters }
              Inc( Z );                       { process the next character }
            until MemPtr^[Z]=0;                  { to the end of the string }
            writeln;
          end
        else                                  { program name not found }
         writeln('unknown');
      end;

    {*-- output the environment strings --------------------------*}

    writeln(#13,#10, 'Environment strings');
    Z := 0;      { start with the first byte in the allocated block }
    while MemPtr^[Z]<>0 do                  { repeat until empty string }
      begin
        write('       ');
        repeat                                       { output a string }
          write( chr(MemPtr^[Z]) );                  { print a character }
          Inc( Z );                          { process the next character }
        until MemPtr^[Z]=0;                      { to the end of the string }
        Inc( Z );                { set to the start of the next string }
        writeln;                                           { end line }
      end
  end
else                                                  { no envrionment }
  begin

    {*-- is it a PSP? ---------------------------------------------*}
    {*-- (starts with command INT 20 (code=$CD $20)) -------------*}

    MemPtr := RngPtr(MK_FP(succ(seg(CurMCB^)), 0));   { set pointer }
    if ( (MemPtr^[0]=$CD) and (MemPtr^[1]=$20) ) then
      begin                                           { it's a PSP }
        writeln('PSP (with program following)');
      end
    else                          { the command INT 20 was not found }
```

```
          begin
            writeln('unidentifiable (program or data)');
            Dump( MemPtr, 5);                 { dump the first 5x16 bytes }
          end;
      end;

    write('==========================================');
    writeln('=============== Press a key ===');
    if ( not Done ) then
     begin                               { set pointer to the next MCB }
       CurMCB := MCBPtr(MK_FP(seg(CurMCB^) + CurMCB^.Distance + 1, 0));
       Inc(NrMCB);                     { increment the number of the MCB }
       Key := ReadKey;
     end;
  until ( Done )               { repeat until the last MCB is processed }
end;

{***********************************************************************}
{**                            MAIN PROGRAM                           **}
{***********************************************************************}

begin
  ClrScr;                                           { clear the screen }
  TraceMCB;                                    { run through the MCBs }
end.
```

C listing: MEMC.C

```
/***********************************************************************/
/*                              M E M C                                */
/*---------------------------------------------------------------------*/
/*    Description    : Displays the memory blocks allocated by DOS     */
/*---------------------------------------------------------------------*/
/*    Author         : MICHAEL TISCHER                                 */
/*    developed on   : 08/23/1988                                      */
/*    last update    : 05/12/1989                                      */
/*---------------------------------------------------------------------*/
/*    (MICROSOFT C)                                                    */
/*    creation       : CL /AS /Zp memc.c                               */
/*    call           : MEMC                                            */
/*---------------------------------------------------------------------*/
/*    (BORLAND TURBO C)                                                */
/*    creation       : via the Compile-Make command                    */
/*                      (no project file)                              */
/***********************************************************************/

/*== Include files ====================================================*/

#include <dos.h>
#include <stdlib.h>

/*== Typedefs =========================================================*/

typedef unsigned char byte;                /* build ourselves a byte */
typedef unsigned segadr;                       /* a segment address */
typedef byte boolean;
typedef byte far *FB;                       /* FAR pointer to a byte */

/*== Constants ========================================================*/

#define TRUE  1                      /* needed for working with boolean */
#define FALSE 0

/*== Structures and unions ============================================*/

struct MCB {                              /* describes an MCB in memory */
            byte     id_code;       /* 'M' = a block follows, 'Z' = end */
            segadr   psp;                /* segment address of the PSP */
            unsigned distance;         /* number of paragraphs reserved */
```

```
        };

typedef struct MCB far *MCBPtr;            /* FAR pointer to an MCB */

/*== Macros ==================================================*/

#ifndef MK_FP                           /* was MK_FP defined already? */
#define MK_FP(seg, ofs) ((void far *) ((unsigned long) (seg)<<16|(ofs)))
#endif


/********************************************************************
*****
*  Function          : F I R S T _ M C B                            *
**------------------------------------------------------------------**
*  Description       : Returns a pointer to the first MCB.          *
*  Input parameters : none                                          *
*  Return value      : Pointer to the first MCB                     *
********************************************************************
****/

MCBPtr first_mcb()
{
 union REGS regs;                   /* stores the processor registers */
 struct SREGS sregs;                  /* stores the segment registers */

 regs.h.ah = 0x52;      /* ftn. no.: get address of the DOS info block */
 intdosx( &regs, &regs, &sregs );             /* call DOS interrupt 0x21 */

 /*-- ES:(BX-4) points to the firs MCB, create pointer ---------------*/

 return( *((MCBPtr far *) MK_FP( sregs.es-1, regs.x.bx+12 )) );
}

/**********************************************************************
*  Function          : D U M P                                        *
**------------------------------------------------------------------**
*  Description       : Outputs hex and ASCII dump of a memory range.  *
*  Input parameters : - bptr : pointer to a memory area               *
*                      - num  : number of dump lines (each 16 bytes)  *
*  Return value      : none                                           *
**********************************************************************/

void dump( FB bptr, byte num)
{
 FB lptr;                   /* running pointer for printing a dump line */
 unsigned offset;                 /* offset address relative to BPTR */
 byte i;                                             /* loop counter */

 printf("\nDUMP | 0123456789ABCDEF        00 01 02 03 04 05 06 07 08");
 printf(" 09 0A 0B 0C 0D 0E 0F\n");
 printf("-----+--------------------------------------------------------");
 printf("-----------------\n");

 for (offset=0;  num-- ; offset += 16, bptr += 16)
  {                                  /* run through the loop NUM times */
   printf("%04x | ", offset);
   for (lptr=bptr, i=16; i-- ; ++lptr)     /* print character as ASCII */
    printf("%c", (*lptr<32) ? ' ' : *lptr);
   printf("        ");
   for (lptr=bptr, i=16; i-- ; )          /* output character as hex */
    printf("%02X ", *lptr++);
   printf("\n");                           /* move to the next line */
  }
}


/**********************************************************************
*  Function          : T R A C E _ M C B                              *
**------------------------------------------------------------------**
```

```
*  Description      : Traces the chain of MCB's.                      *
*  Input parameters : none                                            *
*  Return value     : none                                            *
**********************************************************************/

void trace_mcb()
{
 static char fenv[] = {                    /* first environment string */
                      'C', 'O', 'M', 'S', 'P', 'E', 'C', '='
                     };

 MCBPtr cur_mcb;                          /* pointer to the current MCB */
 boolean done;                        /* TRUE if the last MCB was found */
 byte nr_mcb,                              /* number of the current MCB */
      i;                                               /* loop variable */
 FB lptr;                          /* running pointer in the environment */

 done = FALSE;                                      /* now we get going */
 nr_mcb = 1;                                /* the first MCB is number 1 */
 cur_mcb = first_mcb();                   /* get pointer to the first MCB */
 do                                      /* process the individual MCB's */
  {
   if ( cur_mcb->id_code == 'Z' )                   /* last MCB reached? */
    done = TRUE;                                                 /* yes */
   printf("MCB number      = %d\n", nr_mcb++);
   printf("MCB address     = %Fp\n", cur_mcb);
   printf("Memory addr.    = %Np:0000\n", FP_SEG(cur_mcb)+1);
   printf("ID              = %c\n", cur_mcb->id_code);
   printf("PSP address     = %Fp\n", (FB) MK_FP(cur_mcb->psp, 0) );
   printf("Size            = %u paragraphs ( %lu bytes )\n",
          cur_mcb->distance, (unsigned long) cur_mcb->distance << 4);
   printf("Contents        = ");

   /*-- is it an environment? -----------------------------------------*/

   for (i=0, lptr=(FB)cur_mcb+16;/* compare first ENV string with FENV */
        ( i<sizeof fenv ) && ( *(lptr++) == fenv[i++] ) ; )
    ;
   if ( i == sizeof fenv )                        /* was a string found? */
    {                                          /* yes, it's an environment */
     printf("environment\n");
     if ( _osmajor >= 3 )                       /* DOS version 3.0 or higher? */
      {                                         /* yes, get program name */
       printf("Program name   = ");
       for ( ; !(*(lptr++)==0 && *lptr==0) ; )
        ;                                          /* find last ENV string */
       if ( *(lptr += 3) )                  /* is there a program name here? */
        {                                                          /* yes */
         for ( ; *lptr ; )                  /* run through the program name */
          printf( "%c", *(lptr++) );              /* output a character */
        }
       else                                   /* no program name was found */
        printf("unknown");
       printf("\n");                                /* move to the next line */
      }

     /*-- output the environment strings ------------------------------*/

     printf("Environment strings\n");
     for (lptr=(FB) cur_mcb +16; *lptr ; ++lptr)
      {                                                 /* output a string */
       printf("            ");
       for ( ; *lptr ; )  /* run through the string to a NUL character */
        printf( "%c", *(lptr++) );                  /* output a character */
       printf("\n");                              /* move to the next line */
      }
    }
   else                                                  /* no envrionment */
    {
```

```
      /*- is it a PSP? -----------------------------------------------*/
      /*-- (introduced with the command INT 20 (Code=0xCD 0x20)) -------*/

      if (*((unsigned far *) MK_FP( cur_mcb->psp, 0 )) == 0x20cd)
       printf("PSP (with subsequent program)\n");              /* yes */
      else                        /* the command INT 0x20 was not found */
        {
         printf("unidentifiable (program or data)\n");
         dump( (FB) cur_mcb + 16, 5);       /* dump the first 5x16 bytes */
        }
     }

    printf("========================================");
    printf("=============== Please press a key   ===\n");
    if ( !done )                                     /* another MCB? */
     {                              /* yes, set pointer to the next MCB */
      cur_mcb = (MCBPtr)
                MK_FP( FP_SEG(cur_mcb) + cur_mcb->distance + 1, 0 );
      getch();                                         /* wait for a key */
     }
   }
  while ( !done );      /* repeat until the last MCB has been processed */
 }

/***********************************************************************/
/**                          MAIN PROGRAM                            **/
/***********************************************************************/

void main()

{
 printf("\nMEMC (c) 1988 by Michael Tischer\n\n");
 trace_mcb();                              /* trace the chain of MCB's */
}
```

6.10 DOS Filters

Filters are programs, routines or utilities which accept input and modify the data for output. Filters do the same on the operating system level: characters are passed to these filters as input, the filters modify the characters then send the modified characters as output. This manipulation takes many forms. Filters can sort data, replace certain data with other data, encode data or decode data.

DOS has three basic filters available:

FIND searches input for a specified set of characters

SORT arranges text or data in order

MORE formats text display

These filters perform simple redirection of standard input/output. They read characters from the standard input device, manipulate the characters as needed, then display them on the standard output device. The standard input device under DOS is the keyboard, and the standard output device is the monitor. DOS versions of 2.0 and higher allow the user to redirect the standard input/output to files. Therefore, a filter can read characters from the keyboard or from a file, depending on the standard input device selected. This is possible by using a filter in conjunction with one of the DOS handle functions for reading and writing. DOS offers five handles:

0	Standard input	CON (Keyboard)
1	Standard output	CON (Screen)
2	Standard error output	CON (Screen)
3	Standard serial interface	AUX
4	Standard printer	PRN

If the user calls a program from the DOS level, the < character redirects input and the > character redirects output. In the following example, the input comes from the file IN.TXT instead of the keyboard. The output is written to the file OUT.TXT instead of the screen:

```
sort <in.txt >out.txt
```

SORT

After the user enters the above command, DOS recognizes that a program named SORT should be called. Then it encounters the expression <IN.TXT which redirects the standard input. This occurs by assigning the handle 0 (standard input, which formerly pointed to the keyboard) to the file IN.TXT. The expression >OUT.TXT resets handle 1 to the OUT.TXT file instead of the screen. The affected handle is first closed, and then the redirected file is opened.

Once the command processor finishes with the command line it calls the SORT program using the EXEC function (DOS function 4BH). Since the program called with the EXEC function has all the handles of the calling program available, the SORT program can input/output characters to handles 0 and 1. Where the characters originate is unimportant to the program.

After the SORT program completes its work, it returns control to the command processor. The command processor resets the redirection and waits for further input from the user.

Pipes

The filter principle as supported by DOS becomes especially powerful through pipes. This expression comes from the idea of a pipeline used for transporting oil or gas. DOS pipes have a similar function: they carry characters from one program to another and permit the connection of various programs with each other.

When this happens, characters output from one program to the standard output device can be read by another program from the standard input device. As in the redirection of the standard input/output, the two programs do not notice the pipelines. The difference between the two procedures is that under redirection of the standard input/output devices, data can be redirected only to one device or file, while the use of pipes allows data transfer to another program.

Combined filters

Pipes allow the user to connect multiple filters. The pipe character | is inserted between the programs to be connected. An example should make this more understandable: A text file named DEMO.TXT is sorted and then displayed on the screen in page format. Even though this task appears to be very complicated at first, it can be performed easily using two DOS filters: SORT and MORE. SORT sorts the file and MORE displays the file on the screen in page format.

The question is, how can you tell the command processor to do these things? First SORT is used. This filter is told to sort the file DEMO.TXT. The redirection of standard input can be used as illustrated at the beginning of the chapter:

```
SORT <DEMO.TXT
```

After the user enters this command, SORT sorts the file DEMO.TXT then displays the file on the screen. This display would be much easier to read in page format. Formatted output can be implemented by redirecting the output from SORT to a file (for example TEMP.TXT) and displaying this file using the MORE command. The following sequence of commands do this:

```
SORT <DEMO.TXT >TEMP.TXT
MORE <TEMP.TXT
```

You can use a pipe to connect the SORT filter and the MORE filter, saving the user typing time. The following command line sends the output from SORT directly to MORE and immediately displays the sorted file in page format:

```
SORT <DEMO.TXT | MORE
```

Any number of filters can be connected using pipes. DOS always executes these pipelined filters from left to right. It sends the output from the first program as input to the second program, the second program's output as input to the third program, etc. The last program can again force the redirection of the output with the > character so that the final result of the whole program or filter chain travels to a file or other device instead of the screen.

Note: DOS cannot send data from one filter directly to another because it would have to execute both filters simultaneously, and the current version of DOS doesn't have multiprocessing capabilities. Instead, the following method is used. The input calls the first filter and redirects its output to a pipe file. After the first filter ends its processing, it calls the second filter but redirects its input to the pipe file to read in the output from the first filter. This principle applies to all filters. The pipe file is stored in the current working directory.

The word "dump" is a computer buzzword for a way to display the contents of a file in ASCII characters and/or hexadecimal numbers. The DUMP programs below performs this task as a filter. As the contents are displayed in ASCII format, DUMP differentiates between normal ASCII characters (letters, numbers, etc.) and control characters such as carriage return, linefeed, etc. These control characters are displayed in mnemonic form (e.g., <CR> for carriage return and <LF> for linefeed). This DUMP filter is fairly simple in structure, yet it can be very useful to quickly examine a file's contents.

The structure of the DUMP program is typical for a filter. Since DUMP displays a maximum of nine ASCII characters and/or hexadecimal codes per line, it asks for nine characters by using the read function from the standard input device. If not enough characters are available, it reads what characters are available. DUMP places these characters in a buffer, then converts the characters into ASCII characters and hex codes. This buffer will accept a complete line of 78 characters. When the buffer processing finishes, the filter uses the handle to write to the standard output device. This process is repeated until no more characters can be read from the standard input device.

The following programs are written in Pascal, C and assembly language. Note that there isn't a BASIC version. The reason is that BASIC, as an interpreted language, is unsuitable for developing a filter which can be called from the DOS level. A BASIC compiler would be required for this task.

Pascal listing: DUMPP.PAS

```
{***********************************************************************}
{*                              D U M P P                               *}
{*---------------------------------------------------------------------*}
{*    Task        : a Filter, which reads in characters from the      *}
{*                  Standard input device and outputs them             *}
{*                  as Hex and ASCII dump on                           *}
{*                  the Standard output device                         *}
{*---------------------------------------------------------------------*}
{*    Author        : MICHAEL TISCHER                                  *}
{*    developed on  : 08/08/87                                         *}
{*    last Update   : 05/04/89                                         *}
{*---------------------------------------------------------------------*}
{*    Info          : This program can only be called from the         *}
{*                    DOS level after compiling to an EXE file         *}
{*                    with TURBO                                       *}
{***********************************************************************}

program DUMP;

Uses Dos;                                              { Add DOS unit }

{$V-}                               { suppress length test on strings }

const NUL = 0;                          { ASCII-Code NUL-character     }
      BEL = 7;                          { ASCII-Code Bell character    }
      BS  = 8;                          { ASCII-Code Backspace         }
      TAB = 9;                          { ASCII-Code Tab               }
      LF  = 10;                         { ASCII-Code Linefeed          }
      CR  = 13;                         { ASCII-Code Carriage Return   }
      EOF = 26;                         { ASCII-Code End of File       }
      ESC = 27;                         { ASCII-Code Escape            }

type SZText = string[3];     { passes the name of a special character }
     DumpBf = array[1..80] of char;         { accepts the output Dump }

{***********************************************************************}
{* SZ     : writes the name of a control character into a Buffer      *}
{* Input  : see below                                                  *}
{* Output : none                                                       *}
{* Info   : after the call of this procedure the pointer               *}
{*          which was passed, points behind the last character of      *}
{*          the control character name in the Dump-Buffer              *}
{***********************************************************************}

procedure SZ(var Buffer  : DumpBf;                 { Text entered here }
                 Text    : SZText;               { Text to be entered }
             var Pointer : integer);          { addr. of text in buffer }

var Counter : integer;

begin
 Buffer[Pointer] := '<';                    { leads control character }
 for Counter := 1 to length(Text) do      { transfer Text to Buffer   }
  Buffer[Pointer + Counter] := Text[Counter];
 Buffer[Pointer + Counter + 1] := '>';      { terminates control char }
 Pointer := Pointer + Counter + 2;        { Pointer to next character }
end;

{***********************************************************************}
{* DODUMP : reads characters in and outputs them as Dump              *}
{* Input  : none                                                       *}
{* Output : none                                                       *}
{***********************************************************************}

procedure DoDump;
```

```
  Endc := false;                                        { not the End }
  repeat
   Regs.ah := $3F;                { Function number for reading handle }
   Regs.bx := 0;               { the Standard input device is handle 0 }
   Regs.cx := 9;                            { read in 9 characters }
   Regs.ds := seg(NewByte);             { Segment address of the buffer }
   Regs.dx := ofs(NewByte);              { Offset address of the buffer }
   MsDos( Regs );                           { Call DOS-Interrupt 21H    }
   if (Regs.ax = 0) then Endc := true;          { no character read? }
   if not(Endc) then
    begin                                                    { NO }
     for Counter := 1 to 30                { Fill buffer with blanks }
      do DumpBuf [Counter] := ' ';
     DumpBuf[31] := #219;       { Place Separator between Hex and ASCII }
     NextA := 32;                  { ASCII-characters follow separator }
     for Counter := 1 to Regs.ax do      { start processing characters }
      begin                                               { read in }
       HexChr := ord(NewByte[Counter]) shr 4 + 48;     { Hex top 4 bits }
       if (HexChr > 57) then HexChr := HexChr + 7;      { convert char }
       DumpBuf[Counter * 3 - 2] := chr(HexChr);        { store in buffer }
       HexChr := ord(NewByte[Counter]) and 15 + 48; { Hex bot. 4 bits }
       if (HexChr > 57) then HexChr := HexChr + 7;    { convert number }
       DumpBuf[Counter * 3 - 1] := chr(HexChr);        { store in buffer }
       case ord(NewByte[Counter]) of                  { test ASCII-Code }
        NUL : SZ(DumpBuf, 'NUL', NextA);              { NUL-character }
        BEL : SZ(DumpBuf, 'BEL', NextA);              { Bell character }
        BS  : SZ(DumpBuf, 'BS' , NextA);                 { Backspace }
        TAB : SZ(DumpBuf, 'TAB', NextA);                       { Tab }
        LF  : SZ(DumpBuf, 'LF' , NextA);                  { Linefeed }
        CR  : SZ(DumpBuf, 'CR' , NextA);           { Carriage Return }
        EOF : SZ(DumpBuf, 'EOF', NextA);               { End of File }
        ESC : SZ(DumpBuf, 'ESC', NextA);                    { Escape }
        else
         begin                                    { normal character }
          DumpBuf[NextA] := NewByte[Counter]; { Store ASCII-character }
          NextA := succ(NextA)        { Set pointer to next character }
         end
       end;
      end;
     DumpBuf[NextA] := #219;                       { Set End character }
     DumpBuf[NextA+1] := chr(CR); { Carriage-Return followed by Line- }
     DumpBuf[NextA+2] := chr(LF);               { feed to buffer end }
     Regs.ah := $40;              { Function number for writing handle }
     Regs.bx := 1;               { Standard output device is handle 1 }
     Regs.cx := NextA+2;                      { Number of characters }
     Regs.ds := seg(DumpBuf);           { Segment address of the buffer }
     Regs.dx := ofs(DumpBuf);            { Offset address of the buffer }
     MsDos( Regs );                         { Call DOS-Interrupt 21H    }
    end;
  until Endc;         { repeat until no more characters are available }
end;

{**********************************************************************}
{*                          MAIN PROGRAM                              *}
{**********************************************************************}

begin
  DoDump;                                             { Output Dump }
end.
```

C listing: DUMPC.C

```
/***********************************************************************/
/*                              D U M P C                              */
/*---------------------------------------------------------------------*/
/*    Task           : a Filter which reads in characters from the     */
/*                     Standard input and outputs them as              */
/*                     Hex and ASCII-Dump on                           */
/*                     the Standard output device                      */
/*---------------------------------------------------------------------*/
/*    Author         : MICHAEL TISCHER                                 */
/*    developed on   : 08/14/87                                        */
/*    last Update    : 04/08/89                                        */
/*---------------------------------------------------------------------*/
/*    (MICROSOFT C)                                                    */
/*    Creation       : MSC DUMPC;                                      */
/*                     LINK DUMPC;                                     */
/*    Call           : DUMPC [<Input] [>Output]                        */
/*---------------------------------------------------------------------*/
/*    (BORLAND TURBO C)                                                */
/*    Creation       : tcc dumpc                                       */
/*    Call           : DUMPC [<Input] [>Output]                        */
/***********************************************************************/

#include <stdio.h>                          /* include Header-files */
#include <dos.h>

#define byte unsigned char

#define NUL     0                          /* Code of NUL-character  */
#define BEL     7                          /* Code of Bell           */
#define BS      8                          /* Code of Backspace-key  */
#define TAB     9                          /* Code of Tab-key        */
#define LF      10                         /* Code of Linefeed       */
#define CR      13                         /* Code of Return-key     */
#define ESC     27                         /* Code of Escape-key     */

#define tohex(c) ( ((c)<10) ? ((c) | 48) : ((c) + 'A' - 10) )

/***********************************************************************/
/* GETSTDIN: reads a certain number of characters from the Standard */
/*           input device into a Buffer                               */
/* Input   : see below                                                */
/* Output  : Number of characters read                                */
/***********************************************************************/

unsigned int GetStdIn(Buffer, MaxChar)
char *Buffer;     /* Pointer in Character-Vector, which accepts data */
unsigned int MaxChar;         /* maximum of characters to be read in */

{
 union REGS Register;       /* Register-Variable for Interrupt-Call */
 struct SREGS Segment;              /* accepts the Segment register */

 segread(&Segment);             /* read content of Segment register */
 Register.h.ah = 0x3F;                      /* Function number for */
 Register.x.bx = 0;         /* the Standard input device is handle 0 */
 Register.x.cx = MaxChar;             /* Number of Bytes to be read */
 Register.x.dx = (unsigned int) Buffer; /* Offset address of Buffer */
 intdosx(&Register, &Register, &Segment);      /* Call Interrupt 21H */
 return(Register.x.ax);           /* Number of Bytes read to caller  */
}

/***********************************************************************/
/* STRAP  : Attach character to string                                */
/* Input  : see below                                                 */
/* Output : Pointer behind the last added character                   */
/***********************************************************************/
```

```
char *Strap(String, Textpointer)
char *String,                                   /* the source string */
     *Textpointer;          /* Pointer to the text to be attached */

{
 while (*Textpointer)                   /* repeat until '\0' detected */
  *String++ = *Textpointer++;                   /* transmit character */
 return(String);            /* Pass Pointer to calling function  */
}

/********************************************************************/
/* DODUMP : reads the characters in and outputs them as Dump        */
/* Input  : none                                                    */
/* Output : none                                                    */
/********************************************************************/

void DoDump()

{
 char NewByte[9],                      /*Accepts the characters read  */
      DumpBuf[80],                          /* accepts a line of DUMP */
      *NextAscii;    /* points to next ASCII-character in the buffer */
 byte i,                                              /* Loop counter */
      Readbytes;                           /* Number of bytes read in */

 DumpBuf[30] = 219;          /* Set separator between Hex and ASCII */
 while((Readbytes = GetStdIn(NewByte, 9)) != 0)
                             /* as long as characters are available */
  {
   for (i = 0; i < 30; DumpBuf[i++] = ' ');
                                           /* Fill buffer with spaces */
   NextAscii = &DumpBuf[31];          /* ASCII-characters start here */
   for (i = 0; i < Readbytes; i++)
                                  /* process all characters read in */
    {
     DumpBuf[i*3] = tohex((byte) NewByte[i] >> 4);
                                              /* convert Code in Hex */
     DumpBuf[i*3+1] = tohex((byte) NewByte[i] & 15);
     switch (NewByte[i])                        /* evaluate ASCII-Code */
      {
       case NUL : NextAscii = Strap(NextAscii, "<NUL>");
                  break;
       case BEL : NextAscii = Strap(NextAscii, "<BEL>");
                  break;
       case BS  : NextAscii = Strap(NextAscii, "<BS>");
                  break;
       case TAB : NextAscii = Strap(NextAscii, "<TAB>");
                  break;
       case LF  : NextAscii = Strap(NextAscii, "<LF>");
                  break;
       case CR  : NextAscii = Strap(NextAscii, "<CR>");
                  break;
       case ESC : NextAscii = Strap(NextAscii, "<ESC>");
                  break;
       case EOF : NextAscii = Strap(NextAscii, "<EOF>");
                  break;
       default  : *NextAscii++ = NewByte[i];
      }
    }
   *NextAscii = 219;       /* End character for ASCII representation */
   *(NextAscii+1) = '\r';        /* Carriage-Return to End of buffer */
   *(NextAscii+2) = '\0';           /* NUL converted to LF on output */
   puts(DumpBuf);          /* Write String on Standard output device */
  }
}

/********************************************************************/
/**                          MAIN PROGRAM                          **/
/********************************************************************/
```

```
void main()

{
 DoDump();                              /* Character input/output */
}
```

Assembler listing: DUMP.ASM

```
;**********************************************************************;
;*                              D U M P                               *;
;*--------------------------------------------------------------------*;
;*    Task : A Filter which reads characters from the Standard input *;
;*           and outputs them as Hex- and ASCII-Dump on               *;
;*           the Standard output device                               *;
;*--------------------------------------------------------------------*;
;*    Author          : MICHAEL TISCHER                               *;
;*    developed on    : 08/01/87                                      *;
;*    last Update     : 04/08/89                                      *;
;*--------------------------------------------------------------------*;
;*    assemble        : MASM DUMPA;                                   *;
;*                      LINK DUMPA;                                   *;
;*   (important)...     EXE2BIN DUMPA DUMP.COM                        *;
;*--------------------------------------------------------------------*;
;*    Call            : DUMP [<Input] [>Output]                       *;
;**********************************************************************;

;== Constants ==========================================================

     NUL    equ 0              ;ASCII-Code NUL-Character
     BEL    equ 7              ;ASCII-Code Bell
     BS     equ 8              ;ASCII-Code Backspace
     TAB    equ 9              ;ASCII-Code Tabulator
     LF     equ 10             ;ASCII-Code Linefeed
     CR     equ 13             ;ASCII-Code Carriage Return
     EOF    equ 26             ;ASCII-Code End of File
     ESC    equ 27             ;ASCII-Code Escape

;== Program starts here  ==============================

code      segment para 'CODE'     ;Definition of CODE-Segments

          org 100h

          assume cs:code, ds:code, es:code, ss:code

;-- Start routine ------------------------------------------------------

dump      label near

          ;-- Read in 9 Bytes from Standard input device --------------

          xor  bx,bx              ;Standard input has the handle 0
          mov  cx,9               ;read in 9 characters
          mov  dx,offset newbyte  ;Address of the buffer
          mov  ah,3Fh             ;Function code for handle reading
          int  21h                ;Call DOS-Function
          or   ax,ax              ;characters read in?
          jne  dodump             ;YES --> process line
          jmp  dumpend            ;NO --> DUMPEND

dodump:   mov  dx,ax              ;record number of characters read

          ;-- Fill output buffer with Spaces --------------------------

          mov  cx,15              ;15 Words (30 Bytes)
          mov  ax,2020h           ;ASCII-Code of " " to AH and AL
          mov  di,offset dumpbuf  ;the Address of the output buffer
          cld                     ;increment on String commands
          rep stosw               ;Fill buffer with Spaces
```

```
         ;-- Construct Output Buffer --------------------------------

         mov  cx,dx             ;Get number of characters read in
         mov  di,offset dumpbuf+31 ;Position Ascii-Codes in the buffer
         mov  bx,offset newbyte ;Pointer to input buffer
         mov  si,offset dumpbuf ;Position for Hex-Codes in Buffer

bytein:  mov  ah,[bx]           ;Read in Byte
         push si                ;store SI on the Stack
         mov  si,offset sotab   ;Address of special character table
         mov  dx,offset sotext-6 ;Address of special character text
sotest:  add  dx,6              ;next entry in special text
         lodsb                  ;Load code from special char table
         cmp  al,255            ;Reached end of table?
         je   noso              ;YES --> no special character
         cmp  ah,al             ;do codes agree?
         jne  sotest            ;NO --> test next table element

         ;-- Code was a special character ---------------------------

         push cx                ;Store Counter
         mov  si,dx             ;copy DX to SI
         lodsb                  ;read number of char control codes
         mov  cl,al             ;transfer number of characters to CL
         rep  movsb             ;copy designation into buffer
         pop  cx                ;get counter
         pop  si                ;return SI from Stack
         mov  al,ah             ;copy character to AL
         jmp  short hex         ;calculate Hex-Code

noso:    pop  si                ;return SI from Stack
         mov  al,ah             ;copy character to AL
         stosb                  ;store in buffer

hex:     mov  al,ah             ;Code of character to AL
         and  ah,1111b          ;mask upper 4 Bit in AH
         shr  al,1              ;shift AL right 4 Bits
         shr  al,1
         shr  al,1
         shr  al,1
         or   ax,3030h          ;convert AH and AL into ASCII-Codes
         cmp  al,"9"            ;is AL a letter ?
         jbe  nobal             ;NO --> no correction
         add  al,"A"-"1"-9      ;correct AL
nobal:   cmp  ah,"9"            ;is AH a letter ?
         jbe  hexout            ;NO --> no correction
         add  ah,"A"-"1"-9      ;correct AH
hexout:  mov  [si],ax           ;store Hex-Code in buffer
         add  si,3              ;point to next Position

         inc  bx                ;set pointer to next Byte
         loop bytein            ;process next Byte

         mov  al,219            ;set separator
         stosb

         mov  ax,LF shl 8 + CR  ;CR and LF terminate buffer
         stosw                  ;write in buffer

         ;-- Send Dump to the Standard output device ----------------

         mov  bx,1              ;Standard output is handle 1
         mov  cx,di             ;determine number of characters to be
         sub  cx,offset dumpbuf ;transmitted
         mov  dx,offset dumpbuf ;Address of buffer
         mov  ah,40h            ;Function code for handle
         int  21h               ;call DOS-function
         jmp  dump              ;read in next 9 Bytes
```

```
dumpend   label near

          mov  ax,4C00h            ;Function number for ending program
          int  21h                 ;end program with End code

;== Data =============================================================

newbyte   db 9 dup (?)             ;the 9 Bytes read in
dumpbuf   db 30 dup (?), 219       ;the output buffer
          db 49 dup (?)

sotab     db NUL,BEL,BS,TAB        ;Table of control characters
          db LF,CR,EOF,ESC
          db 255

sotext    equ this byte            ;Text of special characters
          db 5,"<NUL>"             ;NUL
          db 5,"<BEL>"             ;Bell
          db 4,"<BS> "             ;Backspace
          db 5,"<TAB>"             ;Tabulator
          db 4,"<LF> "             ;Linefeed
          db 4,"<CR> "             ;Carriage-Return
          db 5,"<EOF>"             ;End of File
          db 5,"<ESC>"             ;Escape

;== End ==============================================================

code      ends                     ;End of CODE-Segment
          end  dump
```

6.11 <Ctrl><Break> and Critical Error Interrupts

DOS offers two ways of stopping a program during execution. These situations occur when the user hits <Ctrl><Break> (<Ctrl><C>), or when a *critical error* occurs during access to an external device (i.e., printer, hard disk, disk drive, etc.). Although the key combination varies with the PC configuration, we'll use <Ctrl><Break> consistently in this section.

<Ctrl><Break>

Pressing <Ctrl><Break> to stop a program during execution can have some serious consequences. After the user presses this key combination, DOS abruptly takes control from the program without allowing the program to perform any "housekeeping" that may be needed. Files are not closed properly, diverted interrupt vectors are not reset, and allocated memory is not released. The final result can range from a loss of data to a system crash.

In order to prevent this, DOS calls interrupt 23H. This interrupt is also known as the <Ctrl><Break> interrupt. When a program is started, this interrupt points to a routine which brings about the end of the program. But a program is free to select a routine of its own, thus maintaining control of what occurs when the user presses <Ctrl><Break>.

However, the interrupt routine doesn't execute immediately. The break flag controls when the interrupt routine occurs. This flag can be set at the DOS prompt using the BREAK (ON/OFF) command from DOS, or with the help of DOS function 33H, sub-function 1. If the break flag is on, every time a function of DOS interrupt 21H is called, the keyboard buffer will be checked to see if either <Ctrl><Break> or <Ctrl><C> has been pressed. If the break flag is off, this check will be made only when calling the DOS functions that access the standard input and output devices.

If this test finds the appropriate key combination, the processor registers are loaded with the values contained in the DOS function to be executed. Only after this is interrupt 23H called.

If a program directs this interrupt to a routine of its own, there are several ways to react. For example, the program could open a window on the screen which asks if the user would like to end the program. It can also decide for itself whether or not the program should end.

Maintenance

If the program chooses to halt execution, some form of clean-up routine should follow. A routine of this type closes all open files, resets any changed interrupt pointers, and releases any allocated memory. After this, function 4CH can end the program without returning control to the interrupt 23H caller.

If <Ctrl><Break> is to be ignored, then the IRET assembly language instruction must return control to DOS. The program must then ensure that all processor registers contain the same values they had when interrupt 23H was invoked. Otherwise, the DOS function that was originally called cannot be completed without error.

Both ways of handling this situation will be demonstrated in an example at the end of this section.

Critical error interrupt

Unlike the <Ctrl><Break> interrupt, the critical error interrupt call is rarely a reaction to something the user does intentionally. It is usually a reaction to an error that occurs when accessing an external device, such as a printer, disk drive, or hard disk. While the user can correct the error in many cases (e.g., printer not turned on), other errors can be caused by hardware failures that require repairs (e.g., read error while accessing hard disk).

To make allowances for the various kinds of errors, the critical error interrupt (interrupt 24H) normally points to a DOS routine that displays the following or a similar message on the screen and waits for input from the user:

```
(A)bort (R)etry (I)gnore (F)ail
```

This clears the screen of the program currently under execution. In addition, this interrupt doesn't provide a "clean" program end. Like <Ctrl><Break>, the program is in a situation where files are not properly closed, allocated memory is not released, etc.

Installing an interrupt handler in a program to replace the DOS handler can help here, too. DOS enlists the help of a processor register to pass this handler various information when it is called. This helps the interrupt handler locate the source of the error. Bit 7 in the AH register indicates either a floppy or hard disk access error (bit 7 off), or some other error (bit 7 on). In addition, the BP:SI register pair points to the head of the device driver that was being called when the error appeared. A detailed error code is contained in the lower 8 bits of the DI register, and the contents of the upper 8 bits are undefined. This returns the following error codes:

Error Codes Passed to the Critical Error Handler

Code	Meaning
00h	Disk is write protected
01h	Access to an unknown device
02h	Drive not ready
03h	Unknown command
04h	CRC error
05h	Wrong data length
06h	Seek error
07h	Unknown device type
08h	Sector not found
09h	Printer out of paper
0Ah	Write error
0Bh	Read error
0Ch	General error

When called, the critical error handler can respond by opening a window on the screen that asks the user to decide to ignore the error, retry the access, or abort the program. The latter option can only instruct the interrupt to call DOS functions 01H to 0CH. This means that the program ends abruptly, similar to pressing <Ctrl><Break>. While it is true that calling other DOS functions within the handler causes no errors in itself, the return to DOS causes a system crash. Such handlers are also not allowed to end a program through the use of DOS function 4CH. Instead the handler must return to its caller with the help of the IRET command. With that, DOS expects a code in the AL register that will show it how to react to the error. It interprets the contents of the AL register as follows:

Output Codes of a Critical Error Handler

Code	Meaning
00h	Ignore the error
01h	Retry the operation
02h	End program with Interrupt 23h
03h	End function called with an
error	(DOS 3.0 up only)

The last output code in the above list represents the most sensible reaction to an error that can't be fixed by repeating the operation (as in the example where the printer needs to be turned on). The receipt of this code invokes the normal ending of the function call in which the error occurred. The function then sets the carry flag to signal the error. While this makes a "critical" error and a "normal" error indistinguishable to the program, it's possible to tell them apart by setting a flag within the critical error handler.

```
;**********************************************************************;
;*                          C E _ H A N D                             *;
;*--------------------------------------------------------------------*;
;*    Description     : Forms the basic structure of an assembler     *;
;*                      program, in which the DOS Ctrl-Break and      *;
;*                      Critical Error Interrupt are captured         *;
;*--------------------------------------------------------------------*;
;*    Author          : MICHAEL TISCHER                               *;
;*    developed on    : 9/5/1988                                      *;
;*    last update     : 4/8/1989                                      *;
```

```
;*    call           : CE_HAND                                    *;
;*                     (please leave the disk drive open so that a *;
;*                      Critical Error occurs.)                    *;
;*****************************************************************;
;== constants =====================================================

;== stack =========================================================
stack     segment para stack       ;definition of the stack segment
          dw 256 dup (?)           ;the stack is 256 words
stack     ends                     ;end of the stack segment
;== data ==========================================================
data      segment para 'DATA'      ;definition of the data segment
cr_err    db  0                    ;goes to 1, if a critical error occurs
                                   ;during access to a peripheral device
                                   ;(floppy, hard disk, or printer)
cr_typ    db  0                    ;error number of the critical error
cr_mes    db  "Critical error! (A)bort or (R)etry: $"
next_line db  13,10,"$"
end_mes   db  "Program ended normally.$"
brk_mes   db  "Program aborted.$"
dat_nam   db  "A:TEST.DAT",0       ;name of the test file
data      ends                     ;end of the data segment
;== code ==========================================================
code      segment para 'CODE'      ;definition of the CODE segment
          assume cs:code, ds:data, ss:stack
start     proc far
          ;-- install both Interrupt Handlers -------------------------
          push cs                  ;put CS on the stack
          pop  ds                  ;and return as DS
          mov  ax,2523h            ;fct.no.: set Ctrl-Break Handler
          mov  dx,offset cbreak    ;DS:DX now contains the address of H.
          int  21h                 ;call DOS Interrupt
          mov  al,24h              ;now set Interrupt 24h
          mov  dx,offset cerror    ;DS:DX contains the address of the new H.
          int  21h                 ;call DOS Interrupt
          mov  ax,data             ;load segment address of the data segment in
          mov  ds,ax               ;in the DS register
          ;-- you can add your program here  --------------------------
                                   ;
                                   ;
                                   ;
          ;-- for a demonstration, try to open a file  ----------------
          ;-- on the opened disk drive                 ----------------
dat_open: mov  ah,3dh              ;function number: open file
          mov  al,0                ;file mode: read only
          mov  dx,offset dat_nam   ;DS:DX = addresse of the filename
          int  21h                 ;call DOS Interrupt 21h
          jnc  exit                ;no error? NO --> END
          cmp  cr_err,0            ;critical error?
          je   exit                ;NO --> END
          call crit_err            ;a critical error occured
          jmp  dat_open            ;CRIT_ERR returns only if the operation
                                   ;should be retried
                                   ;(IGNORE is not possible)
          ;-- the handler must not be re-installed before the end ------
          ;-- of the program, since this is done by DOS          ------
exit:     mov  ah,9                ;function number: pass string
          mov  dx,offset end_mes   ;DS:DX = address of the message
          int  21h                 ;call DOS Interrupt
          mov  ax,4C00h            ;function no.: end program (ERRCODE=0)
          int  21h                 ;call DOS Interrupt and end the program
                                   ;with it
start     endp
;-- CRIT_ERR: called within the program after discovery of a  ----------
;--          critical error                                   ----------
crit_err  proc near
          ;-- output message and ask for user input  --------------------
ask:      mov  ah,9                ;function number: output string
          mov  dx,offset cr_mes    ;DS:DX = address of the message
          int  21h                 ;call DOS Interrupt
```

```
          mov  ah,1                 ;function number: input character
          int  21h                  ;call DOS Interrupt
          push ax                   ;note the input
          mov  ah,9                 ;function number: output string
          mov  dx,offset next_line;DS:DX = address of the message
          int  21h                  ;call DOS Interrupt
          ;-- interpret the user's input ------------------------------
          pop  ax                   ;retrieve the input
          cmp  al,"A"               ;abort?
          je   end_up               ;go to "clean-up" procedure
          cmp  al,"a"               ;abort?
          je   end_up               ;go to "clean-up" procedure
          cmp  al,"r"               ;retry?
          je   crend                ;go to end of procedure
          cmp  al,"R"               ;retry?
          jne  ask                  ;no, ask again
crend:    ret                       ;return to caller
crit_err  endp
;-- END_UP: executes a "clean" ending --------------------------------
end_up    proc near
          ;-- all opened files can be closed and the system memory  ----
          ;-- allocated by the program can be freed here             ----
                                    ;
                                    ;
                                    ;
          mov  ah,9                 ;function number: output string
          mov  dx,offset brk_mes    ;DS:DX = address of the message
          int  21h                  ;call DOS Interrupt
          mov  ax,4C00h             ;end the program normally with the
          int  21h                  ;4Ch function
end_up    endp
;-- CBREAK: the new Ctrl-Break Handler --------------------------------
cbreak    proc far
          ;-- all registers altered within this routine (excluding ----
          ;-- the Flag Register) have to be secured on the stack   ----
          push ds
          mov  ax,data              ;load the segment address of the
          mov  ds,ax                ;data segment in the DS-Register
          ;-- for example, you can open a window here in which the -----
          ;-- user is asked if he really wants to end the program  -----
                                    ;
                                    ;
                                    ;
          jmp  go_on                ;don't end program
          ;-- if the user decides to end the program, a routine with ---
          ;-- which the program can be ended can be started here     ---
          jmp   end_up              ;prepare termination of the program
          ;-- the program should not be aborted, continue normal  ------
          ;-- execution                                           ------
go_on:    pop  ds                   ;restore saved register
          iret                      ;back to DOS, where the interrupted
                                    ;function is continued normally
cbreak    endp
;-- CERROR: the new Critical Error Handler ----------------------------
cerror    proc far
          ;-- each of the registers (SS, SP, DX, ES, DX, CX und BX)  ----
          ;-- that was altered within this routine must be saved     ----
          ;-- on the stack                                           ----
          sti                       ;allow interrupts again
          push ds
```

```
          mov  ax,data           ;load segment address of the data segment
          mov  ds,ax             ;in the DS-Register
          mov  cr_err,1          ;point to critical error
          mov  ax,di             ;error number to AX
          mov  cr_typ,al         ;note error number
          mov  al,3              ;end function call with error
          pop  ds                ;fetch DS again
          iret
cerror    endp
;----------------------------------------------------------------------
code      ends                   ;end of the code segment
          end  start             ;start program execution with
                                 ;the START procedure
```

6.12 DOS Device Drivers

A device driver is the part of the operating system responsible for the control of, and the communication with, the hardware. It represents the lowest level of an operating system, and permits all other levels to work independent of hardware. When adapting an operating system to various computers, this is an advantage. The entire operating system doesn't have to be changed, only the various device drivers.

In earlier operating systems, device drivers resided in the operating system code. This meant that changes or upgrades of these routines to match new hardware were very difficult, if not impossible. DOS Version 2.0 introduced a flexible concept of device drivers. This makes it possible for the user to adapt even the most exotic PC clone to DOS.

Custom drivers

Since communication between DOS and a device driver is based on relatively simple function calls and data structures, the assembly language programmer can develop a device driver to adapt DOS to any device. Unfortunately, device drivers cannot be programmed in a higher level language.

When developing the code for a driver, the same rules are observed as for developing a COM program (no direct segment access). The difference is that a device driver starts at offset address 0H, and not at 100H. The end of this section explains the assembly language implementation in detail.

Drivers

During the DOS boot process, the drivers NUL, CON, AUX, PRN and the drivers for the disk drives and hard drive (if needed) are loaded and installed. They are arranged sequentially in memory and connected to each other. If the user wants to install his own driver, he has to inform DOS using the CONFIG.SYS file. This text file contains the information which DOS requires for configuring the system. Contents of the CONFIG.SYS file are read and evaluated during the boot process after linking the standard drivers. If DOS finds the DEVICE= command, it knows that a new driver should be included. The name of the driver and perhaps a device and path designation are indicated after the equal sign.

ANSI.SYS

The following command sequence includes the ANSI.SYS driver, which is supplied with DOS. This driver makes enhanced character output and keyboard functions available:

```
DEVICE=ANSI.SYS
```

The new driver is added to the chain immediately following the NUL device driver (the first driver in the chain). The ANSI.SYS driver replaces the default CON driver. To ensure that all function calls for monitor or keyboard communication operate through ANSI.SYS, the ANSI.SYS driver is placed first in the device group, and the CON driver is moved farther down the chain of devices. Since the operating system moves from link to link during the search, it finds the new CON driver (ANSI.SYS) first and uses it. Therefore, the system ignores the old CON driver as seen in the illustration below:

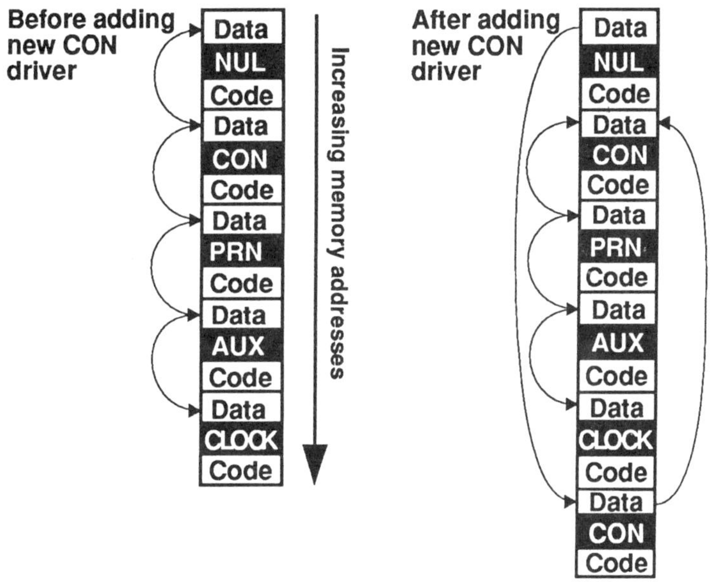

The driver chain

ASSIGN

Not all drivers can be replaced with new ones. The NUL driver is always the first driver in the chain. If you add a new NUL driver, the system ignores the new driver and continues accessing the original NUL driver. This also applies to the drivers for floppy disk drives and hard drives. The reason for this is that disk drives have drive specifiers instead of names such as CON (e.g., A:). A new disk drive can be added to the system, but since DOS may assign it the name D:, it may not be addressed by all programs which want to access device A:. This problem can be avoided by redirecting all device accesses using DOS's ASSIGN command. You can make the ASSIGN command part of the AUTOEXEC.BAT file. It executes after adding drivers and executing the CONFIG.SYS file. To redirect all accesses from drive A: (the first disk drive) to device D: (in this case, a new driver for a new disk drive), the AUTOEXEC.BAT file must contain the following command sequence:

```
ASSIGN A=D
```

The drivers for mass storage devices and the drivers such as PRN are handled differently. DOS has two kinds of device drivers:

- Character device drivers
- Block device drivers

Character device drivers communicate with the keyboard, screen, printer and other hardware on a character by character (byte by byte) basis. Block device drivers can transmit an entire series of characters during each function call (disks, hard disks, etc.). The two driver groups differ somewhat through the ways each supports different functions.

6.12.1 Character Device Drivers

Let's start with character device drivers because their structure is simpler than block device drivers. Character device drivers transmit one byte for every function call. They communicate with devices such as the keyboard, display, printer and modem. A device driver can service only one device. Therefore, individual drivers for keyboard, display, printer, etc., exist in DOS after booting.

Character devices can operate in either cooked mode or raw mode.

Cooked mode

In cooked mode, the device driver reads characters from the device and performs a test for certain control characters. DOS then passes the character to an internal buffer. DOS also checks to determine whether any <Enter>, <Ctrl><P>, <Ctrl><S> or <Ctrl><C> characters exist. If the system detects the <Enter> character, it ignores any further input from the device driver, even if the specified number of characters has not yet been read. Then the characters read are copied from the internal buffer to the buffer of the calling program. If characters are output in cooked mode, DOS tests for <Ctrl><C> or <Ctrl><Break>. If one of these combinations is detected, the currently running program stops. Pressing <Ctrl><S> temporarily stops the program until the user presses any other key. <Ctrl><P> redirects the output from the screen to the printer (PRN). Pressing <Ctrl><P> a second time redirects the output from the printer back to the screen.

Raw mode

In raw mode, the device driver reads all characters without testing. If a program wants to read in 10 characters, it reads exactly 10 characters, even if the user presses the <Enter> key as the second character of the string. Raw mode transmits the characters direct to the calling program's buffer, instead of using an internal DOS buffer. During character output, raw mode doesn't test for <Ctrl><C> or <Ctrl><Break>.

DOS function 44H of interrupt 21H defines the mode of the character device driver (see the end of this section for a detailed description of this interrupt).

6.12.2 Block Device Drivers

A block device driver normally communicates with mass storage devices such as floppy or hard disks, or high speed cassette tapes. For this reason, they simultaneously transmit a number of characters which are designated as a block. In some cases, a single call to a function transmits several blocks of data. The sizes of these blocks can differ from one mass storage device to another, as well as within one particular mass storage device.

How block device drivers work

Unlike character device drivers, a block device driver can control several devices at the same time. You can even divide one device into several logical units. For example, a 40 megabyte hard disk can be divided into two 20 megabyte hard disks with the names C and D. These logical devices have single-letter specifiers instead of device names or filenames. The device designation depends on its position in the chain of device drivers. If a device driver supports several logical devices, single letters can be used as specifiers in sequential order. This is why the example above lists two logical drives named C and D instead of C and F.

Every one of these devices must have a file allocation table (FAT) and a root directory. Block device drivers make no distinction between cooked and raw modes. They always read and write the exact number of blocks unless an error is detected.

Access

There are several ways to access a device driver. Character device drivers are accessed using the normal FCB or handle functions by simply indicating the name of a driver (e.g., CON: instead of a filename). A block device driver is accessed using the normal DOS functions (file, directory, etc.) by using the drive designator assigned by DOS during the boot process.

Functions 1H through CH of interrupt 21H invoke read and write operations in a device driver. Two other options exist for accessing device drivers. These will be discussed shortly.

6.12.3 Structure of a Device Driver

Even though the two types of device drivers differ in some important details, they do have similar structures. Each has a device header, a strategy routine and an interrupt routine (a different kind of interrupt from the ones you've read about up until now).

Device header

The device header appears at the beginning of each device driver and contains information needed by DOS for implementing the driver.

The first two fields are the link to the next driver (offset and segment address) in the chain of device drivers. The memory locations required for these link fields must be reserved by the programmer, but DOS fills in when the driver is installed in the system. The next field of the device header is the attribute word. The attribute word describes the device driver and tells DOS, among other things, if it is a block or character device driver.

Offset	Field	Size
+ 00H	Offset address of next driver	(1 word)
+ 02H	Segment address of next driver	(1 word)
+ 04H	Device attribute	(1 word)
+ 06H	Offset address of strategy routine	(1 word)
+ 08H	Offset address of interrupt routine	(1 word)
+ 0AH	Driver name from character driver or number of devices used by block driver	(8 bytes)

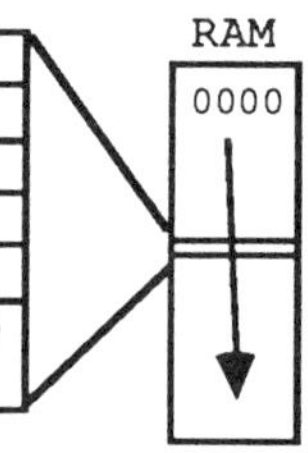

Device driver header

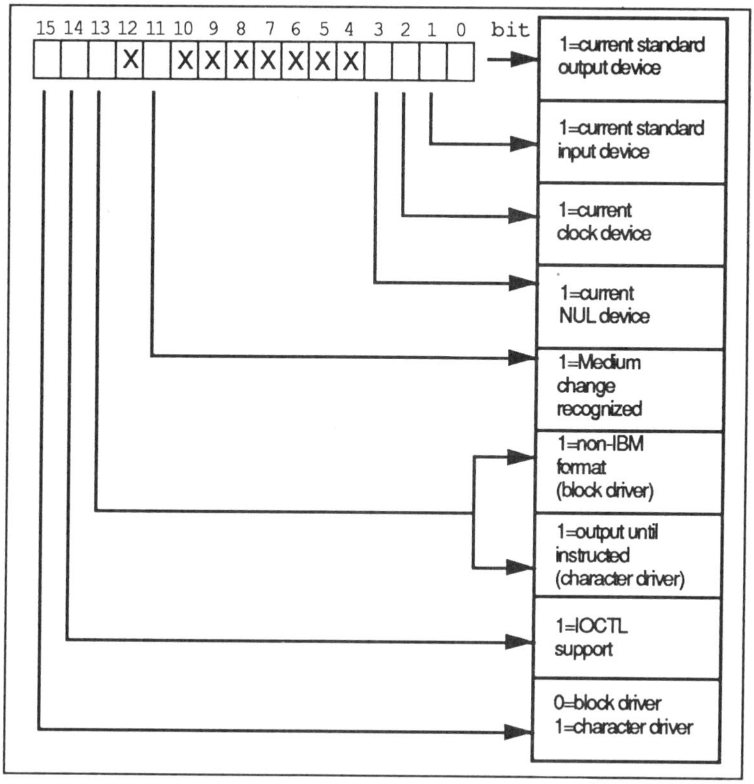

Structure of the device attribute

Only bits 11 through 15 are used by a block driver. The IOCTL bit tells DOS if this driver supports the IOCTL function of DOS. The end of this chapter and the descriptions of functions 3 and 12 describe this function in greater detail. Bit 11 first appears in DOS Version 3 and should be 0 in earlier versions. A block driver indicates whether a medium change is recognized on the device supported (e.g., a floppy disk drive). If the bit is set, the driver must support a few additional functions.

The next two fields contain the offset address of the strategy routine and interrupt routine. The last field contains the name of the device driver if it is a character device driver. If the name is less than eight characters in length, blank spaces (ASCII code 32) pad the remaining characters. If it is a block device driver, the first byte of this field contains the number of logical devices supported by the driver. The remaining seven bytes of this field remain unused and contain the value 0.

Strategy routine

DOS calls the strategy routine first to initialize the driver, then repeatedly before each subsequent I/O request from the driver's interrupt routine. The address of a data structure which contains information about the operation to be performed (the request header) is passed by DOS to the strategy routine in register pair ES:BX. The double word pointer to the data block is stored, and control immediately returns to DOS. DOS then calls the interrupt routine of the driver to perform the actual operation.

The request header, whose address is passed to the strategy routine, always contains at least 13 bytes and contains information which tells the driver how to perform the upcoming operation. Depending on the operations performed, further information can be added to the end of the request header which differs depending on the operation.

+ 00H	Data block length in bytes	(1 word)
+ 01H	Device number in communication	(1 word)
+ 02H	Command code	(1 word)
+ 05H	Reserved	(8 bytes)
+ 0DH	Media descriptor	(1 byte)
+ 0EH	Buffer offset address	(1 word)
+ 10H	Buffer segment address	(1 word)
+ 12H	Number	(1 word)
+ 14H	Starting sector	(8 bytes)

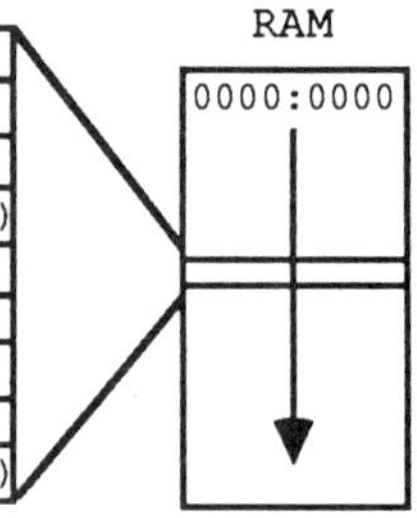

Structure of the request header

DOS calls the interrupt routine immediately after calling the strategy routine. Its first task is to save the processor registers that will have their contents changed by the various functions of the driver to the stack. Then it obtains the command code from field 3 of the request header and calls the appropriate command code routine. After executing the routine, it fills in the status field of the request header and restores the processor registers from the stack. As a last step it returns control to the calling DOS function.

Status field

The value of the status field specifies whether the function executed without error, or if an error occurred during execution. For this reason, every driver function must set the DONE bit (bit 8) in the status field. This DONE bit must be set even if the function is a dummy (non-performing) function.

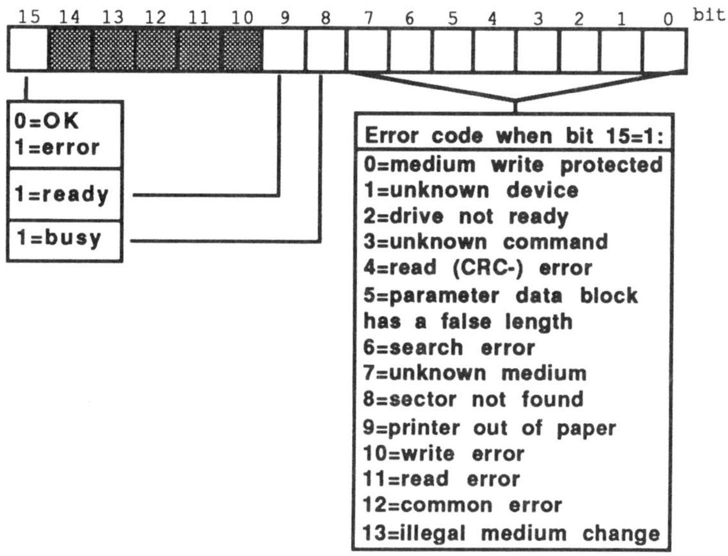

Status field error codes

6.12.4 Device Driver Functions

Under DOS Version 2, any installable device driver must support 13 functions, numbered from 0 to 12, even if their only action consists of setting the DONE flag in the status word. DOS Versions 3 and 4 include four additional functions which can be supported, but are not required. Some of these functions concern one of the two driver types, while others apply to both driver types (e.g., initialization). Unused functions must at least set the DONE flag of the status word. Let's look at the various functions in detail according to their function numbers.

Request header

Every function described here receives its arguments from the request header (whose address is passed by DOS to the strategy routine) and stores its "results" in the request header. For this reason, the offset address to the arguments, relative to the beginning of the request header, is passed to the specified function. These arguments are later transferred to variables. Besides this offset address, a flag indicates whether this information consists of a byte, word or *PTR*. The PTR data type represents a pointer to a buffer and consists of two adjacent words. The first word is the offset address of the buffer. The second word is the segment address of the buffer.

Function 0: Driver Initialization

DOS calls this function during the system boot procedure to initialize the device driver. This function can involve hardware initialization, setting various internal variables to their default values, or the redirection of interrupts. Since the entire operating system has not been completely initialized at this point, the initialization routine can only call functions 1 through 0CH and 30H of DOS interrupt 21H. These functions can be used to determine the DOS version number and to display a driver identification message on the screen. Even if the newly linked driver is a CON driver, the output to the display occurs through the old CON driver, because there are no new drivers linked into the system after completion of the initialization routine.

Initialization and the request header

The initialization routine can obtain two pieces of information from the request header. The first item is the memory address containing the text following the equal sign on the line in the CONFIG.SYS file that loaded the driver into the system.

A typical line in a CONFIG.SYS file can look like this:

```
DEVICE=ANSI.SYS
```

In this case, the device name is ANSI.SYS, which assigns the standard ANSI escape sequences for screen control to the PC. The memory address passed to the initialization routine points to the character following the equal sign (in this case, the A of ANSI.SYS). This makes it possible to store additional information following the name of the device driver. This information is ignored by DOS, but can be read by other routines.

Logical device designation

The second item is only available under DOS Version 3.0 and higher, and only if the driver is a block device driver. This is the letter designation of the first logical device of the driver. The value 0 stands for A, 1 for B, 2 for C, and so on.

The initialization routine must return four parameters to the calling DOS function. The first parameter is the status of the function, i.e., the indication of whether the function has executed correctly. For a block device driver, the number of logical devices supported must also be passed. This information could also be obtained from the device driver's header, but is ignored by DOS.

The next parameter that the device driver must pass to DOS is the highest memory address which it occupies or uses. This lets DOS know where the next device driver can be installed.

BPB

If the driver is a block device driver, the last argument passed must be the address of an array which contains an entry for every logical device. This array contains the addresses of BIOS parameter blocks (BPBs). The address is passed as two words, the first word contains the offset, and the second word contains the segment address of the array. The first two words within this table are the address for the first logical device supported. The next two words indicate the address for the second logical device, etc. The BPB, described in detail in Section 6.12, is a data block containing information which describes a logical device. If all or some of the logical devices have the same format, all entries in the BPB address table can point to a single BPB.

+ 00H	Bytes per sector	(1 word)
+ 02H	Sectors per cluster	(1 byte)
+ 03H	Reserved sectors (including boot sectors)	(1 word)
+ 05H	Number of FATs	(1 byte)
+ 06H	Maximum number of entries in root directory	(1 word)
+ 08H	Total number of sectors	(1 word)
+ 0AH	Media descriptor	(1 byte)
+ 0BH	Number of sectors per FAT	(1 word)

BIOS Parameter Block design

F8H	=	hard disk
F9H	=	5.25" diskette, double-sided, 15 sectors per track
FCH	=	5.25" diskette, single-sided, 9 sectors per track
FDH	=	5.25" diskette, double-sided, 9 sectors per track
FEH	=	5.25" diskette, single-sided, 8 sectors per track
FFH	=	5.25" diskette, double-sided, 8 sectors per track

Media descriptor byte

Calling parameters of function 0:	
Offset 2 (byte)	Function number (0)
Offset 18 (ptr)	Address of character that follows the equal sign after the DEVICE command in the CONFIG.SYS file
Offset 22 (byte)	Device number of the first device supported by the driver (0=A, 1=B...) (applies to block device drivers from DOS Version 3.0 up only)

Returned parameters of function 0:	
Offset 3 (word)	Status word
Offset 13 (byte)	Number of devices supported (block devices only)
Offset 14 (ptr)	Address of first available memory location following the driver
Offset 18 (ptr)	Address of array containing the addresses of BPB (block devices only)

Function 1: Media Check

This function is used only with a block device driver. A character device driver should merely set the DONE flag of the status word and exit. This function is used by DOS to determine whether the media (diskette) has changed. It is often used when examining a disk directory. If the disk medium was not changed since the last access, DOS still has this information in memory, otherwise DOS must reread the information from the media which delays the execution of the current task.

In some cases, as with floppy disks, the answer to the question is fairly complicated. For this reason DOS permits function 1 to answer not only with "yes" and "no", but also with "don't know." In any case, the answer affects further DOS activity.

If the media is unchanged, access to the media can take place immediately. If the media was changed, however, DOS closes all internal buffers related to the current logical device. This causes the loss of all data which should have been transmitted to the media. Then it calls function 2 of the current device driver, loads the FAT and the root directory. If the media check function answers with "don't know," the additional steps taken by DOS depend on the status of the internal buffers related to the current logical device. If these internal buffers are empty, DOS assumes that the media was changed and acts as if function 1 answered "yes." If the buffers contain data which should have been transmitted to the media, DOS assumes that the media is intact and writes the data. If the media was indeed changed, the data written to a changed media may damage the new diskette's file structure.

Since subsequent processing depends on the response from the media check function, the driver should handle the response carefully. Before enabling the mechanism used by the function to respond, the function examines the parameters passed to it. If the driver supports several logical devices, the first parameter is the number of devices. Next is a media descriptor code. This code contains information about the type of media last used in the current logical device. Only devices which can handle several different formats can use this task. For example, AT disk drives which can use both 360K and 1.2 megabyte diskette formats.

If the media check function determines that the medium in a device is non-removable (e.g., a fixed disk), it can always respond "not changed". If, on the other hand the device media can be changed (e.g., a disk), the correct response can only be determined by fairly complex procedures. If these procedures are not used, the response should be "don't know".

For the sake of completeness, here are the three procedures which provide fairly accurate results.

Since a device with changeable media has an opening and closing mechanism, the function should check to determine whether the media was removed. However, it cannot determine if the removed media is identical to the newly inserted medium.

If the media has a name, the function should read this name to determine whether the media was changed. This procedure only makes sense if every media has a unique name.

The disk drive procedure used by DOS hinges on the fact that changing medium takes some time. DOS assumes that even a user that can move fast needs about two seconds to remove a diskette from a drive and insert a new diskette in the same drive. If two consecutive diskette accesses occur less than two seconds apart, DOS assumes that no diskette change occurred.

A byte in the data block is used to indicate changes. The value -1 (FFH) means "changed", 0 means "don't know" and 1 means "not changed".

If the media was changed, the device driver signals a media change (bit 11 in the device attribute = 1), the address of a buffer must be passed to DOS Version 3 and newer, which contains the volume name of the previous media. This name must be stored there as an ASCII string and terminated with an end character (ASCII code 0).

Calling parameters of function 1:	
Offset 1 (byte)	Device number
Offset 2 (byte)	Function number (1)
Offset 13 (byte)	Media descriptor byte

Returned parameters of function 1:	
Offset 3 (word)	Status word
Offset 14 (byte)	Was media changed ? FFH = yes, 00H = don't know, 01H = no
Offset 15 (ptr)	Address of buffer containing the previous volume name (only if device indicates a media change)

Function 2: Build BIOS Parameter Block (BPB)

This function is used only by block device drivers. A character device driver should just set the DONE flag of the status word and exit. DOS calls this function when the media check function determines that the media was changed. This function returns a pointer to a new BPB for the media.

As you can see by the layout of the calling parameters, the device number media descriptor and a pointer to a buffer are passed to this function by DOS. If the device is a standard format (bit 13 of the device attribute =0), then the buffer contains the first sector of the FAT.

Calling parameters of function 2:	
Offset 1 (byte)	Device number
Offset 2 (byte)	Function number (2)
Offset 3 (byte)	Media descriptor byte
Offset 14 (ptr)	Address of a buffer containing the FAT (see above)

Returned parameters of function 2:	
Offset 3 (word)	Status word
Offset 18 (ptr)	Address of the BPB of addressed device

Function 3: I/O Control Read

This function passes control information from the character or block device driver to the application program. It can only be called through function 44H of interrupt 21H if the IOCTL bit in the device attribute word in the device driver header is set. Different parameters are passed to the function, depending on whether the driver is a character or a block device driver.

A character device driver is passed the number of characters to be transferred and the address of a buffer for the transfer of the data.

A block device driver is passed the device number, the media descriptor byte, the address of the buffer to be used for the data transfer, the pointer to the first sector to be read and the number of sectors to be read.

Calling parameters of function 3:	
Offset 1 (byte)	Device number (block devices only)
Offset 2 (byte)	Function number (3)
Offset 13 (byte)	Media descriptor byte (block devices only)
Offset 14 (ptr)	Address of buffer into which data should be transmitted
Offset 18 (word)	Number of sectors to be read (block device) or Number of characters to be read (character device)
Offset 20 (word)	First sector to be read (block devices only)

Returned parameters of function 3:	
Offset 3 (word)	Status word
Offset 18 (word)	Number of sectors read (block device) Number of characters read (character device)

Function 4: Read

This function reads data from the device to a buffer specified in the calling parameter. Should an error occur reading the data, the error status must be set. Additionally the function must report the number of sectors or bytes read successfully. Simply reporting an error is not good enough.

Calling parameters of function 4:	
Offset 1 (byte)	Device number (block device only)
Offset 2 (byte)	Function number (4)
Offset 13 (byte)	Media descriptor byte (block device only)
Offset 14 (ptr)	Address of buffer to which data should be read
Offset 18 (word)	Number of sectors to be read (block device) or Number of characters to be read (character device)
Offset 20 (word)	First sector to be read (block device only)

Returned parameters of function 4:	
Offset 3 (word)	Status word
Offset 18 (word)	Number of sectors read (block device) or Number of characters read (character device)
Offset 22 (ptr)	Pointer to volume ID on return of error 0FH (Version 3.0 and higher)

Function 5: Non-destructive Read

This function is used by a character device driver to test for unread characters in the input buffer. A block device should set the DONE flag of the status word and exit.

DOS tests for additional characters using this function. If more characters exist, the busy bit must be cleared (set to 0) and the next character passed to DOS. The character that is passed remains in the buffer so that a subsequent call to a read function will return this same character. If no additional characters exist, the busy bit must be set (set to 1).

Calling parameter of function 5:	
Offset 2 (byte)	Function number (5)

Returned parameters of function 5:	
Offset 3 (word)	Status word
Offset 13 (byte)	The character read

Function 6: Input Status

This function is used to determine if a character is waiting to be read from the input buffer of a character device. A block device driver should set the DONE flag of the status word and exit.

If a character is waiting to be read from the input buffer, the busy bit is cleared (set to 0). If a character is not in the input buffer, the busy bit is set (set to 1).

When a character is waiting to be read, the Input Status function (06H) resets the status word busy bit to 0 and returns the character to DOS. The character is not removed from the buffer and is therefore non-destructive. This function is equivalent to a one-character look ahead.

Calling parameter of function 6:	
Offset 2 (byte)	Function number (6)

Returned parameters of function 6:	
Offset 3 (word)	Status word: Characters already in buffer = 0; Read request to physical device = 1

Function 7: Flush Input Buffers

This function clears the internal input buffers of a character device driver. Any characters read but not yet passed to DOS are lost when this function is used. A block device driver should set the DONE flag of the status word and exit.

Calling parameter of function 7:	
Offset 2 (byte)	Function number (7)

Returned parameter of function 7:	
Offset 3 (word)	Status word

Function 8: Write

This function transfers characters from a buffer to the current device. If an error occurs during transmission, the status word is used to indicate this error. Both block and character devices use this function.

The parameters used for this function depend on whether the driver is for a character or block device. Both pass a buffer address from which a certain number of characters should be transferred. A character device driver is passed the number of bytes to be transferred in addition to this information.

A block driver is passed the number of sectors to transfer (not the number of characters), the number of the device to be addressed, its media descriptor and the address of the first sector on the medium.

Should an error occur writing the data, the error status must be set. Additionally the function must report the number of sectors or bytes written successfully. Simply reporting an error is not good enough.

Calling parameters of function 8:	
Offset 1 (byte)	Device number (block drivers only)
Offset 2 (byte)	Function number (8)
Offset 13 (byte)	Media descriptor of device addressed (block device only)
Offset 14 (ptr)	Address of the buffer containing data
Offset 18 (word)	Number of sectors to be written (block device) Number of characters to be written (character device)
Offset 20 (word)	first sector to be written (block device only)

Returned parameters of function 8:	
Offset 3 (word)	status word
Offset 18 (word)	Number of sectors written (block device) Number of characters written (character device)
Offset 22 (ptr)	Pointer to volume ID on return of error 0FH (Version 3.0 up)

Function 9: Write with Verify

This function is similar to function 8, but with the difference that the characters written are reread and verified.

Some devices, especially character devices such as a monitor or a printer, do not require verification since either no errors occur during transmission (monitor) or the data cannot be verified (printer).

Calling parameters of function 9:	
Offset 1 (byte)	Device number (block drivers only)
Offset 2 (byte)	Function number (9)
Offset 13 (byte)	Media descriptor of device addressed (block device only)
Offset 14 (ptr)	Address of the buffer containing data
Offset 18 (word)	Number of sectors to be written (block device) Number of characters to be written (character device)
Offset 20 (word)	First sector to be written (block device only)

Returned parameters of function 9:	
Offset 3 (word)	Status word
Offset 18 (word)	Number of sectors written (block device) Number of characters written (character device)
Offset 22 (ptr)	Pointer to volume ID on return of error 0FH (Version 3.0 up)

Function 10: Output Status

This function indicates whether the last write operation to a character device is completed or not. A block device should set the DONE flag in the status word and exit.

If the last write operation is complete then the busy bit of the status word is cleared; otherwise the busy bit is set to 1.

Calling parameter of function 10:	
Offset 2 (byte)	Function number (10)

Returned parameter of function 10:	
Offset 3 (word)	Status word: The busy bit is 1 if the last character output has not been completed

Function 11: Flush Output Buffers

This function completely clears the output buffer even if it contains characters waiting for output. A block device should set the DONE flag on the status word and exit.

Calling parameter of function 11:	
Offset 2 (byte)	Function number (11)

Returned parameter of function 11:	
Offset 3 (word)	Status word

Function 12: I/O Control Write

This function passes control information from the application program to the character or block device driver. It can only be called through function 44H of interrupt 21H provided the IOCTL bit in the device attribute word in the device driver header is set. Different parameters are passed to the function, depending on whether the driver is a character or a block device driver.

A character device driver is passed the number of characters to be written and the address of the buffer from which these characters are transferred.

A block device driver is passed the device number (in case the driver services logical devices), the media descriptor byte, the address of the buffer from which the data is to be written, the number of the first sector to be written and the number of sectors to be written.

A character device driver returns the number of bytes written. A block device driver returns the number of sectors written.

Calling parameters of function 12:	
Offset 1 (byte)	Device number (block device only)
Offset 2 (byte)	Function number (12)
Offset 13 (byte)	Media descriptor of addressed device (block device only)
Offset 14 (ptr)	Address of buffer from which data should be read
Offset 18 (word)	Number of sectors to be written (block device) Number of characters to be written (character device)
Offset 20 (word)	First sector to be written (block device only)

Returned parameters of function 12:	
Offset 3 (word)	Status word
Offset 18 (word)	Number of sectors written (block device) Number of characters written (character device)

The following four functions are supported by DOS version 3.0 and higher.

Function 13: Open

This function can be used only if the OCR (Open/Close/RM) bit in the device attribute word in the device driver header is set. Its task differs, depending whether it is a character or block driver.

A block driver uses this function every time a file is opened. This function determines how many open files exist on this device. Use this command carefully, since programs which access FCB function calls tend not to close open files. This problem can be avoided by assuming during every media change that no files remain open. For devices with non-changeable media (e.g., a hard disk) even this procedure may not help.

Within a character driver, this function can send an initialization string to the device before transmitting the data. This is an advantage when used for communication with the printer. The initialization string should not be included in the driver, but can be called, for example, with the IOCTL function of interrupt 21H, which calls function 12 of a driver to transmit it from an application program to the driver. The function can also be useful because it can prevent two processes (in a network or in multiprocessing) from both accessing the same device.

For the devices CON, PRN and AUX, this function is not called since they are always open.

Calling parameters of function 13:	
Offset 1 (byte)	Device number (block device only)
Offset 2 (byte)	Function number (13)

Returned parameter of function 13:	
Offset 3 (word)	Status word

Function 14: Device Close

This function is the opposite of function 13. This function can only be addressed if the OCR bit in the device attribute word of the device driver header is set. Its task differs, depending whether it is a character or block driver.

A block driver calls it after closing a file. This can be used to decrement a count of open files. Once all files on a device are closed the driver should flush the buffers on removable media devices, because it is likely that the user is about to remove the media.

A character driver can use this function to send some closing control information to a device after completing output. For a printer this could be a formfeed. As in function 13, the string could be transmitted from an application program using the IOCTL function.

Calling parameters of function 14:	
Offset 1 (byte)	Device number (block device only)
Offset 2 (byte)	Function number (14)

Returned parameter of function 14:	
Offset 3 (word)	Status word

Function 15: Removable Media

This function indicates if the media in a block device can be changed or not. This function is used only if the OCR bit in the device attribute word of the device driver is set. A character device driver should set the DONE flag in the status word and exit.

If the media can be removed, the busy bit is cleared; otherwise it is set to 1.

Calling parameters of function 15:	
Offset 1 (byte)	Device number (block device only)
Offset 2 (byte)	Function number (15)

Returned parameter of function 15:	
Offset 3 (word)	Status word: If the media can be removed, the busy bit must contain the value 0

Function 16: Output until Busy

This function transfers data from a buffer to an output device until the device is busy (i.e., can no longer accept more characters). As this function is supported by character devices, a block device driver should set the DONE flag on the status word and exit.

This function works particularly well with print spoolers, through which files can be sent to a printer as a background activity while a program executes in the foreground. It is possible that not all of the characters in the transfer request will be sent to a device during this function call. This is usually not an error, it could be the result of the device becoming busy. The function is passed the number of characters to be transmitted as well as the buffer address. If the output device indicates during transmission that it can no longer accept additional characters, it indicates the number of characters successfully transferred and returns control to the device driver.

Calling parameters of function 16:	
Offset 2 (byte)	Function number (16)
Offset 14 (ptr)	Address of buffer from which data should be read
Offset 18 (word)	Number of characters to be read

Returned parameters of function 16:	
Offset 3 (word)	Status word
Offset 18 (word)	Number of characters written

6.12.5 Clock Driver

The *clock driver* is a character device driver whose only function is to pass the date and time from DOS to an application. The clock driver can also have a different name, since DOS identifies it by the fact that bit 2 in the device attribute word of the device driver header is set to 1, instead of by name. Bit 15 must also be set since the clock driver is a character device driver. Functions 2AH to 2DH of DOS interrupt 21H read the date and time and call the driver. A clock driver must support only functions 4, 8 and 0 (initialization). During the call of function 4 (reading), the date and time pass from the driver to DOS. DOS can set a new date and time with function 8. Both functions have the time and date passed in a buffer of 6 bytes in length.

+ 00H	Number of days since Jan.1,1980	(1 word)
+ 02H	Minutes	(1 byte)
+ 03H	Hour	(1 byte)
+ 04H	Hundredths of seconds	(1 byte)
+ 05H	Seconds	(1 byte)

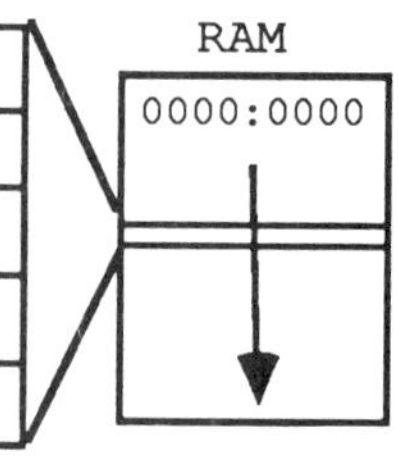

Passing date and time to a clock driver

The date format is unusual. Instead of passing the month, day and year separately, DOS passes the number of days elapsed since January 1, 1980 as a 16-bit number. A fairly complex formula converts this number into normal date format, taking leap years into account. The clock driver normally uses function 0 and 1 of the BIOS interrupt 1AH to read and set the time.

Clocks on AT models

AT and AT-compatible computers have a battery powered realtime clock. Functions 0 and 1 of interrupt 1AH use a software controlled time counter and not the battery powered realtime clock. When the computer is rebooted, the date and time previously set with driver function 8 is cleared. You can use the clock driver to access the realtime clock using functions 2 and 5 of interrupt 1AH instead of function 0 and 1.

6.12.6 Device Driver Calls from DOS

Now that you have some familiarity with the functions of the different device drivers, you can look toward developing your own personal device driver. Here are the steps which take place before and after calling a device driver function.

A chain of events begins when a DOS function which handles input and output is called using interrupt 21H. Calling one of these functions can in turn call a series of other functions and corresponding read and write operations.

Open

One example of this is when the Open function 3DH is called to open a file in a subdirectory. First of all, before it can be opened, DOS must find the file. This may require the searching of a set of directories instead of just reading in the FAT. During each access of interrupt 21H, DOS determines which of the available device drivers should be used to read or write characters. When this happens, DOS sets aside an area in memory to store the information required by the device driver.

For files, DOS must convert the number of records to be processed into logical sector numbers. DOS then calls the strategy routine of the device driver, to which it passes the address of the newly created data block (request header). Then the interrupt routine of the driver is called, which stores all registers. It isolates the function code of the requested function from the data block and starts to process the function.

If the addressed driver is a character device driver, the function only has to send the characters to the hardware or request the characters to be read.

Block devices

For a block device (e.g., a mass storage device such as a floppy or hard disk) the logical sector number must be converted into a physical address before a read or write access. The logical sector number is broken down into a head, track and physical sector number.

After the read or write operation ends, the driver function must place a result code in the status field of the request header to be returned to the calling DOS function. Next the contents of all registers are restored and control is returned to the calling DOS function, which, depending on the result of the driver function, sets or resets the carry flag and places any error code into the AX register. The interrupt function then returns control to the routine which called interrupt 21H.

6.12.7 Direct Device Driver Access: IOCTL

Here we discuss IOCTL in detail, since it offers an alternate method of communicating with the device driver. You can only use these functions if the IOCTL bit of the device attribute is set.

The IOCTL function itself is one of many functions addressable from DOS interrupt 21H. Its function number is 44H. Three groups of sub-functions are accessible:

- Device configuration
- Data transmission
- Driver status

The number of the desired sub-function is passed to the IOCTL function in the AL register. After the function call, the carry flag indicates whether the function executed correctly. A set carry flag indicates the occurrence of an error and the error code can be found in the AX register.

Character device driver status

The number of the desired sub-function is passed to the IOCTL function in the AL register. After the function call, the carry flag indicates whether the function executed correctly. A set carry flag indicates the occurrence of an error and the error code can be found in the AX register.

Sub-functions 6 and 7 can determine the status of a character device driver. Sub-function 6 can determine if the device is able to receive data. Sub-function 7 can determine if the device can send data. The handle of this device is passed in the BX register.

If the device is ready, both functions 6 and 7 return the value FFH in the AL register.

Sub-function 2 reads control data from the character device driver. The handle is passed in the BX register and the number of bytes to be read is passed in the CX register. In addition, the DS:DX register pair contain the address of the buffer into which the data will be read. If the carry flag is clear, then the function was successful and the AX register contains the number of characters read. If the carry flag is set, then there was an error and the AX register contains the error code.

Sub-function 3 writes control information from a buffer to the character device driver. Again, the handle is passed in the BX register, the number of bytes to be written in the CX register and the address of the buffer in the DS:DX register pair.

The return codes are the same as for sub-function 2. These two sub-functions are used to pass information between the application program and the device driver.

Block device driver status

Sub-functions 4 and 5 have the same task as sub-functions 2 and 3. However, they are used for block devices and not character devices. Instead of passing the handle in register BX, you pass the drive code (0=A, 1=B, etc.) in the BL register.

Sub-function 0 is used to get device information for a specified handle. The sub-function number is passed in the AL register and the handle in the BX register. The function returns the device information word in the DX register.

For block devices:

bits 8-15	=	reserved
bit 7	=	0 if a block device
bit 6	=	0 if file has been written
		1 if file has not been written
bits 0-5	=	drive code (0=A, B=1, etc.)

For character devices:

bit 15	=	reserved
bit 14	=	1 if device supports IOCTL sub-functions
		0 if device does not support IOCTL sub-functions
bits 8-13	=	reserved
bit 7	=	if a character device
bit 6	=	0 if end of file for input device
bit 5	=	0 if cooked mode
		1 if raw mode
bit 4	=	reserved
bit 3	=	1 if clock device
bit 2	=	1 if NUL device
bit 1	=	1 if standard output device
bit 0	=	1 if standard input device

Cooked and raw modes

Sub-function 1 is used to set device information for a specified handle. This sub-function is often used to set the standard input device from cooked mode to raw mode or back.

Two final interrupts are sometimes used by block device drivers. These two interrupts, 25H and 26H are used to read from and write to the disk drive. You can use these interrupts, for example, to process disks that were formatted using a "foreign" operating system.

The device number is passed in the AL register, the number of sectors to be transferred is passed in the CX register, the starting sector number to be transferred is passed in the DX register and the buffer is passed in the DS:BX register. The carry flag is clear if there was no errors. If the carry flag is set, then the error code is returned in the AX register.

6.12.8 Tips on Developing Device Drivers

Major headaches in developing a device driver occur because of problems that arise during the testing phases of a new driver. First, a device driver must load into a memory location assigned to it by DOS, at an address unknown to the programmer. Second, a newly developed CON driver can't be tested using the DEBUG program, since DEBUG uses this driver for character input and output.

We recommend that after you write the actual driver, you write a short test program that calls the individual functions in the same manner as DOS, but without having the driver installed as part of DOS. The advantages to this are that everything executes under user control, and the whole process can be corrected with a debugger. In any case, a new device driver (especially a block device driver) should only be linked into the system after it has been tested completely and has been proven to be error-free.

Note: When working with a hard disk, prepare a floppy system diskette before test booting the system from the hard disk with the new driver installed for the first time. If a small bug should exist in the new driver, and the initialization routine hangs up, the booting process will not end and DOS will be out of control. In such a case, the only remedy is to reset the system and boot with a DOS diskette in the floppy drive. Once DOS loads, you can then access the hard disk and remove the new driver.

6.12.9 Driver Examples

This section contains a sample device driver for each of the three different types of device drivers, to demonstrate the information you've read about so far.

The first program is a character driver which corresponds exactly to the format of a normal console driver. The second program is a block device driver which creates a 160K RAM disk. The final program is a DOS clock driver to support an AT computer realtime clock.

```
;**********************************************************************;
;*                           C O N D R V                             *;
;*-------------------------------------------------------------------*;
;*    Task          : This program represents a normal Console        *;
;*                    Driver (Keyboard and Display Monitor). It should *;
;*                    serve as a framework for a driver in the form of *;
;*                    an ANSI.SYS driver.                             *;
```

```
;*---------------------------------------------------------------------*;
;*    Author          : MICHAEL TISCHER                                 *;
;*    developed on    :  8.4.87                                         *;
;*    last Update     : 9.21.87                                         *;
;*---------------------------------------------------------------------*;
;*    assembly        : MASM CONDRV;                                    *;
;*                      LINK CONDRV;                                    *;
;*                      EXE2BIN CONDRV CONDRV.SYS                       *;
;*---------------------------------------------------------------------*;
;*    Call          : Copy into Root Directory, copy the command        *;
;*                    DEVICE=CONDRV.SYS into the file CONFIG.SYS        *;
;*                    and then boot the System.                         *;
;***********************************************************************;

code      segment

          assume cs:code,ds:code,es:code,ss:code

          org 0                     ;Program has no PSP therefore start
                                    ;at Offset address 0

;== Constants ==========================================================

cmd_fld   equ 2                     ;Offset command field in data block
status    equ 3                     ;Offset status field in data block
end_adr   equ 14                    ;Offset driver end-adr. in data block
num_db    equ 18                    ;Offset number in data block
b_adr     equ 14                    ;Offset buffer address in data block

KEY_SZ    equ 20                    ;Size of key board buffer
num_cmd   equ 16                    ;Subfunctions 0-16 are supported

;== Data ===============================================================

;-- Header of Device Driver -------------------------------------------

          dw -1,-1                  ;Connection to next driver
          dw 1010100000000011b      ;Driver attribute
          dw offset strat           ;Pointer to strategy routine
          dw offset intr            ;Pointer to interrupt routine
          db "CONDRV  "             ;new Console driver

;-- Jump Table for functions -------------------------

fkt_tab   dw offset init            ;Function  0: Initialization
          dw offset dummy           ;Function  1: Media Check
          dw offset dummy           ;Function  2: Create BPB
          dw offset no_sup          ;Function  3: I/O control read
          dw offset read            ;Function  4: Read
          dw offset read_b          ;Function  5: Non-dest. Read
          dw offset dummy           ;Function  6: Input-Status
          dw offset del_in_b        ;Function  7: Erase Input-Buffer
          dw offset write           ;Function  8: Write
          dw offset write           ;Function  9: Write & Verify
          dw offset dummy           ;Function 10: Output-Status
          dw offset dummy           ;Function 11: Erase Output-Buffer
          dw offset no_sup          ;Function 12: I/O control write
          dw offset dummy           ;Function 13: Open (starting at 3.0)
          dw offset dummy           ;Function 14: Close
          dw offset dummy           ;Function 15: changeable Medium
          dw offset write           ;Function 16: Output until Busy

db_ptr    dw (?),(?)                ;Address of data block passed

key_a     dw 0                      ;Pointer to next character in KEY_SZ
key_e     dw 0                      ;Pointer to last character in KEY_SZ
key_bu    db KEY_SZ dup (?)         ;internal Keyboard Buffer

;== Routines and functions of driver ================================
```

```
strat   proc far                ;Strategy routine

        mov  cs:db_ptr,bx       ;Store address of data block in the
        mov  cs:db_ptr+2,es     ;Variable DB_PTR

        ret                     ;back to caller

strat   endp

;----------------------------------------------------------------------

intr    proc far                ;Interrupt routine

        push ax                 ;Store registers on the stack
        push bx
        push cx
        push dx
        push di
        push si
        push bp
        push ds
        push es
        pushf                   ;store also the flag register

        push cs                 ;Set data segment register
        pop  ds                 ;Code is identical here with data

        les  di,dword ptr db_ptr;Address of data block to ES:DI
        mov  bl,es:[di+cmd_fld] ;Get command-code
        cmp  bl,num_cmd         ;is command-code permitted?
        jle  bc_ok              ;YES --> bc_ok

        mov  ax,8003h           ;Code for "unknown Command"
        jmp  short intr_end     ;back to caller

        ;-- Command-Code was o.k. --> Execute command ----------------

bc_ok:  shl  bl,1               ;Calculate pointer in jump table
        xor  bh,bh              ;erase BH
        call [fkt_tab+bx]       ;Call function
        les  di,dword ptr db_ptr;Address of the data block to ES:DI

        ;-- Execution of the function completed  --------------------

intr_end label near
        or   ax,0100h           ;Set finished-bit
        mov  es:[di+status],ax  ;store everything in the status field

        popf                    ;Restore flag register
        pop  es                 ;Restore other registers
        pop  ds
        pop  bp
        pop  si
        pop  di
        pop  dx
        pop  cx
        pop  bx
        pop  ax

        ret                     ;back to caller

intr    endp

;----------------------------------------------------------------------

dummy   proc near               ;This routine does nothing

        xor  ax,ax              ;Erase busy-bit
        ret                     ;back to caller
```

```
dummy    endp

;----------------------------------------------------------------------

no_sup   proc near               ;This routine called for all functions
                                 ;which should really not be called
         mov  ax,8003h           ;Error: Command not recognized
         ret                     ;back to caller

no_sup   endp

;----------------------------------------------------------------------

store_c  proc near               ;stores a character in the internal
                                 ;keyboard buffer
                                 ;Input: AL = character
                                 ;       BX = Position of the character

         mov  [bx+key_bu],al     ;store character in internal buffer
         inc  bl                 ;increment pointer to End
         cmp  bl,KEY_SZ          ;End of buffer reached ?
         jne  store_e            ;NO --> STORE_E

         xor  bl,bl              ;new end is the beginning of buffer

store_e: ret                     ;back to caller

store_c  endp

;----------------------------------------------------------------------

read    proc near                ;read a certain number of characters
                                 ;from the keyboard to a buffer

         mov  cx,es:[di+num_db]  ;read number of characters
         jcxz read_e             ;test if equal to 0
         les  di,es:[di+b_adr]   ;Address of character buffer to ES:DI
         cld                     ;on STOSB count up
         mov  si,key_a           ;Pointer to next character in KEY_SZ
         mov  bx,key_e           ;Pointer to last character in KEY_SZ

read_1: cmp  si,bx               ;other characters in keyboard buffer?
         jne  read_3             ;YES --> READ_3

read_2: xor  ah,ah               ;Function number for reading is 0
         int  16h                ;Call BIOS Keyboard-interrupt
         call store_c            ;Store characters in internal buffer
         cmp  al,0               ;test if extended code
         jne  read_3             ;no --> READ_3

         mov  al,ah              ;Extended Code is in AH
         call store_c            ;store
read_3: mov  al,[si+key_bu]      ;read character from keyboard buffer
         stosb                   ;transmit to buffer of calling funct.
         inc  si                 ;Increment pointer to next character
         cmp  si,KEY_SZ          ;End of buffer reached?
         jne  read_4             ;NO --> READ_4

         xor  si,si              ;next character is the first character
                                 ;in the keyboard buffer

read_4: loop read_1              ;repeat until all characters read
         mov  key_a,si           ;Store position of the next character
                                 ;in the key board buffer
         mov  byte ptr key_e,bl  ;Store position of the last character
                                 ;in the key board buffer

read_e: xor  ax,ax               ;everything o.k.
         ret                     ;back to caller
```

```
read    endp

;-----------------------------------------------------------------------

read_b  proc near                   ;read the next character from the
                                    ;key board but leave in the buffer

        mov  ah,1                   ;Function number for BIOS-interrupt
        int  16h                    ;call BIOS Keyboard-interrupt
        je   read_p1                ;no character present --> READ_P1

        mov  es:[di+13],al          ;store character in data block
        xor ax,ax                   ;everything o.k.
        ret                         ;back to caller

read_p1 label near

        mov  ax,0100h               ;Set busy-bit (no character)
        ret                         ;back to caller

read_b  endp

;-----------------------------------------------------------------------

del_in_b proc near                  ;erase input buffer

        mov  ah,1                   ;Still characters in the buffer?
        int  16h                    ;Call BIOS key board interrupt
        je   del_e                  ;no character in the buffer --> END

        xor  ah,ah                  ;Remove character from buffer
        int  16h                    ;Call BIOS key board interrupt
        jmp  short del_in_b         ;Test for additional characters

del_e:  xor ax,ax                   ;everything o.k.
        ret                         ;back to caller

del_in_b endp

;-----------------------------------------------------------------------

write proc near                     ;write a specified number of
                                    ;characters on the display screen

        mov  cx,es:[di+num_db]      ;Number of characters read
        jcxz write_e                ;test if equal to 0
        lds  si,es:[di+b_adr]       ;Address of character-buffer to DS:SI
        cld                         ;on LODSB increment count

        mov  ah,3                   ;read current display page
        int  16h                    ;Call BIOS Video-interrupt

        mov  ah,14                  ;Function number for BIOS interrupt

write_1:  lodsb                     ;read character to be output to AL
        int  10h                    ;call BIOS Video-interrupt
        loop write 1                ;repeat until all characters output

write_e:  xor ax,ax                 ;everything o.k.
        ret                         ;back to caller

write endp

;-----------------------------------------------------------------------

init    proc near                   ;Initialization routine

        mov  word ptr es:[di+end_adr],offset init  ;Set End-Address of
        mov  es:[di+end_adr+2],cs                  ;the driver
```

```
        xor  ax,ax              ;everything o.k.
        ret                     ;back to caller

init    endp

;=====================================================================

code    ends
        end
```

The header of this driver describes a character device driver which handles both the standard input device (keyboard) and the standard output device (monitor). After linking it into the system, setting the two bits in the device attribute calls this driver on all function calls previously handled by the CON driver. Like any other driver, this driver has a strategy routine and an interrupt routine. The former stores the address of the datablock in the variable DB_PTR.

The interrupt routine saves the contents of all registers which will be changed by it on the stack and gets the routine number to be called from the data block. It then checks whether CONDRV supports this function. If not, it jumps directly to the end of the interrupt routine and sets the proper error code in the status field of the request header which was passed to the routine. Then it restores the registers which were saved on the stack and returns control to the calling DOS function.

For any of the functions that are supported by the device driver, the offset address of a routine to handle a particular function is determined from the table labeled FKT_TAB. Notice that the routines named DUMMY and NO_SUP appear several times. DUMMY is for all functions which apply only to block device drives and therefore are not used in this driver. The DUMMY routine clears the AX register and sets the BUSY bit in the status word. The NO_SUP routine handles any functions which cannot be used since the drive attribute for CONDRV does not support these functions.

The STORE_C routine can be accessed from the lower level routines in this driver. Its purpose is to store a character in the internal keyboard buffer of the driver. The driver really shouldn't have this buffer available since BIOS (whose functions are used by the driver to read characters from the keyboard) also has such a buffer. The problem is that the BIOS always returns two characters when pressing a key with extended codes (cursor keys, function keys etc.). If the higher level functions of DOS only ask for one character at a time from CONDRV, the second character must not be lost. It should be stored in a buffer and delivered to DOS by the read function on the next call. This is STORE_C's task.

Reading characters

The next routine is the READ function. It obtains the number of characters to be read from the request header passed by DOS. If it is 0, the routine is terminated immediately. If not, then a loop starts which executes once for every character read. It first tests for characters still stored in the internal keyboard buffer. If so, a character is passed to the buffer of the calling function. If no additional character exists in the keyboard buffer, function 0 of the BIOS keyboard interrupt 16H inputs a character from the keyboard. This character is also passed to the internal keyboard buffer. If it's an extended keycode, it is divided into two characters. The next step removes a character from the internal keyboard buffer and passes the character to the buffer of the calling function. The process repeats until all characters requested have been passed to DOS. Then the routine ends.

The higher level DOS functions also call the function named READ_P. It tests whether a character was entered from the keyboard. If not, it sets the BUSY bit in the status field of the request header passed by DOS, and returns to the calling function. If a character was entered without having been read, the driver reads this character and passes it to the calling DOS function in the request header, and resets the busy bit. The character remains in the keyboard buffer, and on a subsequent call of the read function, it is again passed to DOS. To test the availability of a character, the READ_P function uses function 1 of the BIOS keyboard interrupt 16H.

The function DEL_IN_B also gets called by the higher level DOS functions. DEL_IN_B deletes the contents of the keyboard buffer. It removes characters from the buffer using function 0 of the BIOS keyboard interrupt until function 1 indicates that no more characters are available. This ends the function and it returns to the calling function after the busy bit is reset.

Writing characters

WRITE takes the number of characters from a buffer passed by DOS and displays the characters on the screen. This routine uses function 0EH of the BIOS video interrupt. Once all characters have been displayed, it sets the BUSY bit in the status field and ends the function. This function also executes when the higher level DOS functions call the Write and Verify functions.

Initialization

The last function, the initialization routine, is called first by DOS. Since CONDRV does not initialize variables and hardware, the routine simply enters the driver's ending address into the passed request header. The routine returns its own starting address since it will never be called again, and is the end of the chain of drivers.

In its current form the driver has little use, since it uses only those functions already available to the CON driver of DOS. It would be more practical if an enhanced driver like ANSI.SYS were developed, through which screen design could be more tightly controlled. For example, it's possible that such a driver would have complete windowing capability which could be accessed from any program, in any programming language.

The following block device driver creates a 160K RAM disk:

```
;**********************************************************************;
;*                         R A M D I S K                             *;
;*-------------------------------------------------------------------*;
;*    Task         : This Program is a Driver for a 160KB            *;
;*                   RAM-Disk.                                       *;
;*-------------------------------------------------------------------*;
;*    Author          : MICHAEL TISCHER                              *;
;*    developed onm   :  8.4.87                                      *;
;*    last Update     : 9.21.87                                      *;
;*-------------------------------------------------------------------*;
;*    assembly        : MASM RAMDISK;                                *;
;*                      LINK RAMDISK;                                *;
;*                      EXE2BIN RAMDISK RAMDISK.SYS                  *;
;*-------------------------------------------------------------------*;
;*    Call          : Copy into Root Directory, enter the command    *;
;*                    DEVICE=RAMDISK.SYS into  the CONFIG.SYS file  *;
;*                    and then boot the System.                      *;
;**********************************************************************;

code      segment

          assume cs:code,ds:code,es:code,ss:code

          org 0                     ;Program has no PSP therefore begin
                                    ;at the offset address 0

;== Constants ========================================================

cmd_fld    equ 2                    ;Offset command field in data block
status    equ 3                     ;Offset status field in data block
num_dev   equ 13                    ;Offset number of supported devices
changed   equ 14                    ;Offset medium changed?
end_adr   equ 14                    ;Offset driver end-aAdr. in data block
b_adr     equ 14                    ;Offset buffer address in data block
num_cmd   equ 16                    ;the functions 0-16 are supported
num_db    equ 18                    ;Offset number in data block
bpb_adr   equ 18                    ;Offset Address of BPB of the media
sector    equ 20                    ;Offset first sector number
dev_des   equ 22                    ;Offset device-description of RAM-Disk

;== Data  ============================================================

erst_b    equ this byte             ;this is the first byte of the driver

;-- Header of the Device-Driver --------------------------------------

          dw -1,-1                  ;Connection to next driver
          dw 0100100000000000b      ;Driver attribute
          dw offset strat           ;Pointer to strategy routine
          dw offset intr            ;Pointer to interrupt routine
          db 1                      ;a device is supported
          db 7 dup (0)              ;these bytes give the name

;-- Jump Table for the individual functions  -------------------------

fkt_tab   dw offset init            ;Function  0: Initialization
          dw offset med_test        ;Function  1: Media Test
          dw offset get_bpb         ;Function  2: created BPB
          dw offset read            ;function  3: direct reading
          dw offset read            ;Function  4: Read
          dw offset dummy           ;Function  5: Read, remain in Buffer
          dw offset dummy           ;Function  6: Input-Status
          dw offset dummy           ;Function  7: Erase Input-Buffer
          dw offset write           ;Function  8: Write
          dw offset write           ;Function  9: Write & Verification
          dw offset dummy           ;Function 10: Output-Status
          dw offset dummy           ;Function 11: Erase Output-Buffer
          dw offset write           ;Function 12: direct Write
          dw offset dummy           ;Function 13: Open (after DOS 3.0)
          dw offset dummy           ;Function 14: Close
```

```
        dw offset no_rem        ;Function 15: changeable Medium?
        dw offset write         ;Function 16: Output until Busy

db_ptr  dw (?),(?)              ;Address of the data block passed
rd_seg  dw (?)                  ;RD_SEG:0000 beginning of the RAM-Disk

bpb_ptr dw offset bpb,(?)       ;Accepts the address of the BPB

boot_sek db 3 dup (0)           ;normally a jump command to the boot
                                ;Routine is stored here
        db "MITI 1.0"           ;Name of creator & version number
bpb     dw 512                  ;512 bytes per sector
        db 1                    ;1 Sector per cluster
        dw 1                    ;1 reserved sector (boot-sector)
        db 1                    ;1 File-Allocation-Table (FAT)
        dw 64                   ;maximum 64 entries in root directory
        dw 320                  ;total of 320 sectors = 160 KB
        db 0FEh                 ;Media descriptor (1 Side with 40
                                ;Tracks of 8 sectors each)
        dw 1                    ;every FAT occupies one sector

        ;-- the Boot routine not included since a System can not-----
        ;-- be booted from a RAM-Disk

vol_name db "RAMDISK    "       ;the actual volume-name
        db 8                    ;Attribute, defines volume-name

;== Routines and functions of the Driver ==============================

strat   proc far                ;Strategy routine

        mov  cs:db_ptr,bx       ;Store address of the data block
        mov  cs:db_ptr+2,es     ;in the Variable DB_PTR

        ret                     ;back to caller

strat   endp

;----------------------------------------------------------------------

intr    proc far                ;Interrupt routine

        push ax                 ;Store registers on the stack
        push bx
        push cx
        push dx
        push di
        push si
        push bp
        push ds
        push es
        pushf                   ;also store flag register

        push cs                 ;Set data segment register
        pop  ds                 ;Code identical with data here

        les  di,dword ptr db_ptr;Address of data block to ES:DI
        mov  bl,es:[di+cmd_fld] ;Get command-code
        cmp  bl,num_cmd         ;is command-code permitted?
        jle  bc_ok              ;YES --> bc_ok

        mov  ax,8003h           ;Code for "unknown Command"
        jmp  short intr_end     ;back to caller

        ;-- Command-Code was o.k. --> Execute Command ----------------

bc_ok:  shl  bl,1               ;Calculate pointer in jump table
        xor  bh,bh              ;erase BH
        call [fkt_tab+bx]       ;Call function
```

```
        ;-- Execution of the function completed ---------------------

intr_end label near
        push cs                 ;Set data segment register
        pop  ds                 ;Code is identical with data here

        les  di,dword ptr db_ptr;Address of the data block to ES:DI
        or   ax,0100h           ;Set finished-bit
        mov  es:[di+status],ax  ;store everything in the status field

        popf                    ;Restore flag register
        pop  es                 ;restore other registers
        pop  ds
        pop  bp
        pop  si
        pop  di
        pop  dx
        pop  cx
        pop  bx
        pop  ax

        ret                     ;back to caller

intr    endp

;-----------------------------------------------------------------------

init    proc near               ;Initialization routine

        ;-- the following code is overwritten after the installation -
        ;-- by the RAM-Disk

        ;-- determine Device designation of the RAM-Disk ------------

        mov  ah,30h             ;Sense DOS Version with function 30(h)
        int  21h                ;of DOS-interrupt 21(h)
        cmp  al,3               ;is it Version 3 or higher ?
        jb   prinm              ;YES --> PRINM

        mov  al,es:[di+dev_des] ;Get device designation
        add  al,"A"             ;convert to letters
        mov  im_ger,al          ;store in installation message

prinm:  mov  dx,offset initm    ;Address of installation message
        mov  ah,9               ;output function number for string
        int  21h                ;Call DOS-interrupt

        ;-- Calculate Address of the first byte after the RAM-Disk --
        ;-- and set as End Address of the Driver

        mov  word ptr es:[di+end_adr],offset ramdisk+8000h
        mov  ax,cs                      ;Size of RAM-Disk is 32KB plus
        add  ax,2000h                   ;2 * 64KB
        mov  es:[di+end_adr+2],ax
        mov  byte ptr es:[di+num_dev],1              ;1 device supported
        mov  word ptr es:[di+bpb_adr],offset bpb_ptr ;Address of the
        mov  es:[di+bpb_adr+2],ds                    ;BPB-Pointer

        mov  ax,cs              ;Segment address of RAM-Disk beginning
        mov  bpb_ptr+2,ds       ;Segment address of BPB in BPB-Pointer
        mov  dx,offset ramdisk  ;calculate to offset address 0
        mov  cl,4               ;Divide offset address by 16 and thus
        shr  dx,cl              ;convert into segment address
        add  ax,dx              ;add the two segment addresses
        mov  rd_seg,ax          ;and store

        ;-- Create Boot-Sector ---------------------------------------

        mov  es,ax              ;transfer segment address to ES
        xor  di,di              ;Boots. begins with the 1. byte of RD
```

```
        mov  si,offset boot_sek ;Address of the boot-sector in memory
        mov  cx,15              ;only the first 15 words are used
        rep  movsw              ;copy boot-sector into RAM-Disk

        ;-- Create FAT -----------------------------------------

        mov  di,512             ;FAT begins with the byte 512 of RD
        mov  al,0FEh            ;Write media-descriptor into the first
        stosb                   ;byte of the FAT
        mov  ax,0FFFFH          ;Store code for bytes 2 and 3 of FAT
        stosw                   ;in FAT
        mov  cx,236             ;remaining 236 words occupied by FAT
        inc  ax                 ;Set AX to 0
        rep  stosw              ;Set all FAT-entries to unoccupied

        ;-- Create Root Directory with Volume-Name -------------

        mov  di,1024            ;Root Directory starts in 3rd Sector
        mov  si,offset vol_name ;Address of volume-name in memory
        mov  cx,6               ;the volume-name is 6 words long
        rep  movsw              ;Copy volume-name into RD

        mov  cx,1017            ;Fill the rest of the directories in
        xor  ax,ax              ;Sectors 2, 3, 4 and 5 with zeros
        rep  stosw

        xor  ax,ax              ;everything o.k.
        ret                     ;back to caller

init    endp

;--------------------------------------------------------------------

dummy   proc near               ;This Routine does nothing

        xor  ax,ax              ;Erase busy-bit
        ret                     ;back to caller

dummy   endp

;--------------------------------------------------------------------

med_test proc near              ;Media of RAM-Disk
                                ;cannot be changed

        mov  byte ptr es:[di+changed],1
        xor  ax,ax              ;Erase busy-bit
        ret                     ;back to caller

med_test endp

;--------------------------------------------------------------------

get_bpb proc near               ;Pass address of BPB to DOS

        mov  word ptr es:[di+bpb_adr],offset bpb
        mov  word ptr es:[di+bpb_adr+2],ds

        xor  ax,ax              ;Erase busy-bit
        ret                     ;back to caller

get_bpb endp

;--------------------------------------------------------------------

no_rem  proc near               ;Media of RAM-Disk cannot be changed
        mov  ax,20              ;Set busy-bit
        ret                     ;back to caller
```

```
no_rem   endp

;----------------------------------------------------------------------

write proc near

        xor  bp,bp              ;Transmission DOS --> RAM-Disk
        jmp  short move         ;Copy data

write endp

;----------------------------------------------------------------------

read    proc near

        mov  bp,1               ;Transmission RAM-Disk --> DOS

read    endp

;-- MOVE: Move a certain number of sectors between RD and DOS
;-- Input   : BP = 0 : transmit from DOS to RD (Write)
;--              1 : transmit from RD to DOS (Read)
;-- Output  : none
;-- Registers : AX, BX, CX, DX, SI, DI, ES, DS and FLAGS are changed
;-- Info      : Information required (number, first sector)
;--             is taken from the data block passed by DOS

move     proc near

         mov  bx,es:[di+num_db]  ;Number of sectors read
         mov  dx,es:[di+Sector]  ;Number of first sector
         les  di,es:[di+b_adr]   ;Address of buffer to ES:DI

move_1:  or   bx,bx             ;More sectors to read ?
         je   move_e            ;No more sectors --> END
         mov  ax,dx             ;Sector number to AX
         mov  cl,5              ;Calculate number of paragraphs
         shl  ax,cl             ;(Segment units) by Multiplication
         add  ax,cs:rd_seg      ;with 32, add to Segment start of RD
         mov  ds,ax             ;transmit to DS
         xor  si,si             ;Offset address is 0
         mov  ax,bx             ;Number of sectors to be read to AX
         cmp  ax,128            ;more than 128 sectors to read
         jbe  move_2            ;NO --> read all sectors
         mov  ax,128            ;YES --> read 128 sectors (64 KB)
move_2:  sub  bx,ax             ;subtract number of sectors read
         add  dx,ax             ;add to sectorsto be read next
         mov  ch,al             ;Number  sect. to be read * 256 words
         xor  cl,cl             ;Set Lo-byte of word-counter to 0
         or   bp,bp             ;Should be read ?
         jne  move_3            ;NO --> MOVE_3
         mov  ax,es             ;Store ES in AX
         push ds                ;Store DS on the stack
         pop  es                ;read ES
         mov  ds,ax             ;ES and DS are reversed now
         xchg si,di             ;exchange SI and DI
move_3:  rep  movsw             ;copy data into DOS-buffer
         or   bp,bp             ;read ?
         jne  move_1            ;NO --> maybe other sectors to copy
         mov  ax,es             ;Store ES in AX
         push ds                ;Store DS on the stack
         pop  es                ;read ES
         mov  ds,ax             ;ES and DS have been exchanged
         xchg si,di             ;exchange SI and DI again
         jmp  short move_1      ;additional sectors to copy

move_e:  xor  ax,ax             ;everything o.k.
         ret                    ;back to caller

move     endp
```

```
;-- RAM-Disk starts here ----------------------------

    if ($-erst_b) mod 16          ;must start on a memory address
      org ($-erst_b) + 16 - (($-erst_b) mod 16) ; divisible by 16
    endif

ramdisk  equ this byte

initm    db "**** 160 KB RAMDISK as Device"
im_ger   db "?"
         db ": installed (c) 1987 by MICHAEL TISCHER$",13,10,10

;----------------------------------------------------------------------

code     ends
         end
```

This driver is similar to the CONDRV driver. The biggest difference between the two lies in the functions which each supports.

Note: The initialization routine INIT here is more comprehensive than the CONDRV initialization routine, and remains in memory after the end of execution even though it is no longer needed. You'll see why this is so in the paragraph below entitled "The INIT routine".

First, this routine finds the DOS version number using function 30H. If the version number equals or is greater than 3, the request header passed by DOS contains the device designation of the RAM disk. The system reads the designation, changes it to a character and places the character into the installation message. DOS function 09H is used to display this message on the screen.

Next, the program computes the ending address of the RAM disk. Since the actual data area of the RAM disk starts immediately after the last routine of this driver, 160K is added to the program's ending address. Further, the address of a variable (BPB_PTR) containing the address of the BIOS parameter block is passed to DOS. This variable describes the RAM disk's format. In this case, it tells DOS that the RAM disk uses 512 bytes per sector. Each cluster is made up of one sector and only one reserved sector (the boot sector) exists. In addition, only one FAT exists. Additional information indicates that a maximum of 64 entries can be made in the root directory and that the RAM disk has 320 sectors available (160K of memory). The FAT occupies a single sector, and the media descriptor byte FEH designates a diskette with one side and 40 tracks of 8 sectors each.

These parameters are then placed into the request header of DOS and the segment address of the data area of the RAM disk is calculated (which the driver itself requires, DOS does not need this information).

The INIT routine

The RAM disk must now be formatted, to create a boot sector, FAT and a root directory. Since these data structures are in the first sectors of the RAM disk, a normal INIT routine (which releases its memory to DOS), would overwrite itself with these data structures and would crash the system. This is why the initialization routine is not at the end of the last routine of the driver, which would place it at the beginning of the RAM disk's data area.

The boot sector occupies the complete first sector of the RAM disk, but only the first 15 words are copied into it since DOS only needs these. The name "boot sector" is actually a misnomer here, since it's impossible to boot a system from a RAM disk.

The second sector of the RAM disk contains the FAT. The first two entries are the media descriptor byte and 0 in the entries that follow. These zeros indicate unoccupied clusters (an empty RAM disk).

The last data structure is the root directory. It contains no entries other than the volume name.

Remaining routines

This concludes the work of the initialization routine and returns the system to the calling function. The remaining driver routines are examined in order.

The DUMMY routine performs the same task as the routine of the same name in the CONDRV driver.

The MED_TEST routine is found only in block device drivers. This routine informs DOS whether or not the medium was changed.

The next routine, GET_BPB, simply passes the addresses of the variables which contain the address of the BPB of the RAM disk to DOS, as the initialization routine had already done.

NO_REM allows DOS to sense whether the medium (the RAM disk) can be changed. You cannot change a RAM disk, so the program sets the BUSY bit in the status field.

The two most important functions of the driver perform read and write operations. As in CONDRV, the program calls Write and Verify instead of the normal Write function, since no data error can occur during RAM access. The routine itself does very little; it loads the value 0 into the BP register and jumps to the MOVE routine. The READ routine performs in a similar manner, except that it loads a 1 into the BP register.

MOVE itself is an elementary routine for moving data. The BP register signals whether data is to move from the RAM disk to DOS or in the opposite direction. The routine receives all other data (the DOS buffer's address, the number of the sectors to be transferred and the first sector to be transferred) from the data block passed by DOS. See the comments in the MOVE routine for details of the procedure.

Changes

This RAM disk can of course be enhanced. If you have enough unused memory, you can extend the size of the RAM disk to 360K. AT owners could make the RAM disk resident beyond the 1 megabyte boundary. In this case, the data transfer between DOS and the RAM disk would use function 87H of interrupt 15H.

The clock driver

This final sample driver directly accesses the battery powered clock of an AT computer. It offers the advantage that when the two DOS commands DATE and TIME are used, the date and time are passed directly to the battery powered realtime clock. Reading the date and time reads the information directly from the memory locations of the realtime clock.

```
;**********************************************************************;
;*                            A T C L K                               *;
;*--------------------------------------------------------------------*;
;*    Task           : This program is a clock-driver which can be    *;
;*                     used by DOS for functions which access date    *;
;*                     and time on the battery powered clock          *;
;*                     of the AT.                                     *;
;*--------------------------------------------------------------------*;
;*    Author         : MICHAEL TISCHER                                *;
;*    developed on   : 8.4.87                                         *;
;*    last Update    : 9.21.87                                        *;
;*--------------------------------------------------------------------*;
;*    assembly       : MASM ATCLK;                                    *;
;*                     LINK ATCLK;                                    *;
;*                     EXE2BIN ATCLK ATCLK.SYS                        *;
;*--------------------------------------------------------------------*;
;*    Call          : Copy into root directory place the command      *;
;*                    DEVICE=ATCLK.SYS in the CONFIG.SYS file         *;
;*                    and then boot the system.                       *;
;**********************************************************************;

code     segment

         assume cs:code,ds:code,es:code,ss:code

         org 0                  ;Program has no PSP, therefore
                                ;beginning at offset address 0

;== Constants ==========================================================

cmd_fld  equ 2                  ;Offset command-field in data block
status   equ 3                  ;Offset status field in data block
end_adr  equ 14                 ;Offset driver end-adr. in data block
num_db   equ 18                 ;Offset number in data block
b_adr    equ 14                 ;Offset buffer-address in data block

;== Data ===============================================================

;-- Header of Device-Driver -------------------------------------------

         dw -1,-1               ;Connection to next driver
         dw 1000000000001000b   ;Driver attribute
         dw offset strat        ;Pointer to strategy routine
         dw offset intr         ;Pointer to interrupt routine
         db "$CLOCK "           ;new clock driver

db_ptr   dw (?),(?)             ;address of data block passed

mon_tab  db 31                  ;Table with number of days in
```

```
february db 28                  ;the months
         db 31,30,31,30,31,31,30,31,30,31

;== Routines and functions of the Driver ==============================

strat    proc far               ;Strategy routine

         mov  cs:db_ptr,bx      ;Record address of the data block in
         mov  cs:db_ptr+2,es    ;the variable DB_PTR

         ret                    ;back to caller

strat

;-----------------------------------------------------------------------

intr     proc far               ;interrupt routine

         push ax                ;Save registers on the stack
         push bx
         push cx
         push dx
         push di
         push si
         push bp
         push ds
         push es
         pushf                  ;Store the flag register

         cld                    ;increment for string commands

         push cs                ;Set data segment register
         pop  ds                ;Code is identical with data here

         les  di,dword ptr db_ptr;Address of data block to ES:DI
         mov  bl,es:[di+cmd_fld] ;Get command-code
         cmp  bl,4              ;Should Time/Date be read?
         je   ck_read           ;YES --> CK_READ
         cmp  bl,8              ;Should Time/Date be written?
         je   ck_write          ;YES --> CK_WRITE
         or   bl,bl             ;should the driver be initialized ?
         jne  unk_fkt           ;NO --> unknown function

         jmp  init              ;initialize driver

unk_fkt: mov  ax,8003h          ;Code for "unknown Command"

         ;-- Function Execution completed --------------------------

intr_end label near
         or   ax,0100h          ;Set finished-bit
         mov  es:[di+status],ax ;store everything in status field

         popf                   ;Restore flag register
         pop  es                ;Restore other registers
         pop  ds
         pop  bp
         pop  si
         pop  di
         pop  dx
         pop  cx
         pop  bx
         pop  ax

         ret                    ;back to caller

intr     endp

;-----------------------------------------------------------------------
```

```
ck_read proc near                   ;Read Time/Date from the clock

        mov  byte ptr es:[di+num_db],6 ;6 bytes are passed
        les  di,es:[di+b_adr]     ;ES:DI points to the DOS-buffer

        mov  ah,4                 ;Read function number for Date
        int  1Ah                  ;Call BIOS Time interrupt
        call date_ofs             ;Change Date after offset to 1.1.1980
        stosw                     ;store in buffer

        mov  ah,2                 ;Read function number for time
        int  1Ah                  ;Call BIOS Time interrupt
        mov  bl,ch                ;Store hour in BL
        call bcd_bin              ;convert minutes
        stosb                     ;Store in buffer
        mov  cl,bl                ;Hour to CL
        call bcd_bin              ;Convert hour
        stosb                     ;Store in buffer
        xor  al,al                ;Hundredth second is 0
        stosb                     ;Store in buffer
        mov  cl,dh                ;Seconds to CL
        call bcd_bin              ;Convert seconds
        stosb                     ;Store in buffer

        xor  ax,ax                ;everything o.k.
        jmp  short intr_end       ;back to caller

ck_read endp

;----------------------------------------------------------------------

ck_write   proc near              ;Write Time/Date into clock

        mov  byte ptr es:[di+num_db],6 ;6 bytes are read
        les  di,es:[di+b_adr]     ;ES:DI points to the DOS buffer

        mov  ax,es:[di]           ;Get number of days since 1.1.1980
        push ax                   ;store number
        call ofs_date             ;convert into a date
        mov  ch,19h               ;Year begins with 19..
        mov  ah,5                 ;Set function number for date
        int  1AH                  ;Call BIOS Time interrupt

        mov  al,es:[di+2]         ;Get minute from buffer
        call bin_bcd              ;convert to BCD
        mov  cl,al                ;bring to CL
        mov  al,es:[di+5]         ;Get seconds from buffer
        call bin_bcd              ;convert to BCD
        mov  dh,al                ;bring to DH
        mov  al,es:[di+3]         ;Get hours from buffer
        call bin_bcd              ;convert to BCD
        mov  ch,al                ;bring to CH
        xor  dl,dl                ;no summer time
        mov  ah,3                 ;Set function number for time
        int  1AH                  ;Call BIOS Time interrupt

        ;-- Calculate Day of the Week ------------------------------
        xor  dx,dx                ;HI-word for division
        pop  ax                   ;Get number of days from stack
        or   ax,ax                ;is number 0?
        je   nodiv                ;Yes --> bypass division
        xor  dx,dx                ;HI-word for division
        mov  cx,7                 ;week has seven days
        div  cx                   ;divide AX by 7
nodiv:  add  dl,3                 ;1.1.80 was a Tuesday (Day 3)
        cmp  dl,8                 ;is it a Sunday or Monday?
        jb   nosomo               ;NO --> no correction necessary
        sub  dl,cl                ;correct value
nosomo: mov  al,6                 ;Location 6 in RTC is day of week
        out  70h,al               ;Address to RTC-address register
```

```
        mov  al,dl              ;Day of the week to AL
        out  71h,al             ;Day of the week to RTC-data register

        xor  ax,ax              ;everything o.k.
        jmp  intr_end           ;back to caller

ck_write  endp

;-- OFS_DATE: Convert number of days since 1.1.1980 into date -------
;-- Input   : AX = Number of days since 1.1.1980
;-- Output   : CL = Year, DH = Month and DL = Day
;-- Registers : AX, BX, CX, DX, SI and FLAGS are changed
;-- Info      : For conversion of Offsets the Array MON_TAB
;--             is used

ofs_date proc near

        mov  cl,80              ;Year 1980
        mov  dh,01              ;January
ly:     mov  bx,365             ;Number of days in a normal year
        test cl,3               ;is year a leap year?
        jne  ly1                ;NO --> ly1
        inc  bl                 ;Leap Year has one day more
ly1:    cmp  ax,bx              ;another year passed?
        jb   mo                 ;NO --> Calculate months
        inc  cl                 ;YES --> Increment year
        sub  ax,bx              ;deduct number of days in this year
        jmp  short ly           ;calculate next year

mo:     mov  bl,28              ;Days in February in a normal year
        test cl,11b             ;is the year a leap year?
        jne  nolp2              ;NO --> nolp2
        inc  bl                 ;in leap year February has 29 days
nolp2: mov  february,bl         ;store number of days in February

        mov  si,offset mon_tab  ;Address of months table
        xor  bh,bh              ;every month has less than 256 days
mo1:    mov  bl,[si]            ;Get number of days in month
        cmp  ax,bx              ;another month passed?
        jb   day                ;NO --> calculate day
        sub  ax,bx              ;YES --> deduct day of the month
        inc  dh                 ;increment month
        inc  si                 ;SI to next month in the table
        jmp  short mo1          ;calculate next month

day:    inc  al                 ;the remainder  + 1 is the day
        call bin_bcd            ;Convert day to BCD
        mov  dl,al              ;transmit to DL
        mov  al,dh              ;transmit month to AL
        call bin_bcd            ;convert to BCD
        mov  dh,al              ;move to DH
        mov  al,cl              ;move year to AL
        call bin_bcd            ;convert to BCD
        mov  cl,al              ;move to CL

        ret                     ;back to caller

ofs_date endp

;-- BIN_BCD: Convert Binary-Number to BCD ----------------------------
;-- Input   : AL = Binary value
;-- Output   : AL = corresponding BCD-value
;-- Register : AX, CX and FLAGS are changed

bin_bcd  proc near

        xor  ah,ah              ;prepare 16 bit division
        mov  ch,10              ;work in decimal system
        div  ch                 ;divide AX by 10
        shl  al,1               ;Shift quotient left 4 places
```

```
         shl  al,1
         shl  al,1
         shl  al,1
         or   al,ah               ;OR remainder
         ret                      ;back to caller

bin_bcd  endp

;-- DATE_OFS: Convert Date in number of days since 1.1.1980 -----
;-- Input   : CL = Year, DH = Month and DL = Day
;-- Output  : AX = Number of days since 1.1.1980
;-- Register : AX, BX, CX, DX, SI and FLAGS are changed
;-- Info     : For conversion of date, the Array MON_TAB
;--            is used

date_ofs proc near

         call bcd_bin             ;Convert year to binary
         mov  bl,al               ;transmit to BL
         mov  cl,dh               ;transmit month to CL
         call bcd_bin             ;Convert Month to binary
         mov  dh,al               ;and transmit again to DH
         mov  cl,dl               ;transmit day to CL
         call bcd_bin             ;convert day to binary
         mov  dl,al               ;and again transmit to DL

         xor  ax,ax               ;0 days
         mov  ch,bl               ;store year
         dec  bl                  ;back one year
year:    cmp  bl,80               ;counted back to year 1980 ?
         jb   monat               ;YES --> convert month
         test bl,11b              ;is year a Leap year ?
         jne  nolpyr              ;NO --> NOLPYR
         inc  ax                  ;a leap year has one more day
nolpyr:  add  ax,365              ;add days of year
         dec  bl                  ;back one year
         jmp  short year          ;process next year

month:   mov  bl,28               ;Days in February in a normal year
         test ch,11b              ;is current year a Leap Year?
         jne  nolpyr1             ;NO --> NOLPYR1
         inc  bl                  ;in Leap Year February has 29 days
nolpyr1: mov  february,bl         ;store in Month table
         xor  ch,ch               ;every month has less than 256 days
         mov  bx,offset mon_tab   ;Address of month table
monat1:  dec  dh                  ;decrement number of months
         je   add_day             ;all month calculated --> TAG
         mov  cl,[bx]             ;Get number of days in month
         add  ax,cx               ;add to total-days
         inc  bx                  ;BX to next month in the table
         jmp  short monat1        ;calculate next month

add_day: add  ax,dx               ;add current day
         dec  ax                  ;deduct one day (1.1.80 = 0)
         ret                      ;back to caller

date_ofs  endp

;-- BCD_BIN: Convert BCD to Binary Number ----------------------------
;-- Input   : CL = BCD-Value
;-- Output  : AL = corresponding binary value
;-- Register : AX, CX and FLAGS are changed

bcd_bin  proc near                ;Convert BCD-value in CL to binary
                                  ;return in AL

         mov  al,cl               ;transmit value to AL
         shr  al,1                ;shift 4 places right
         shr  al,1
         shr  al,1
```

```
        shr  al,1
        xor  ah,ah              ;Set AH to 0
        mov  ch,10              ;process in decimal system
        mul  ch                 ;multiply AX by 10
        mov  ch,cl              ;transmit CL to CH
        and  ch,1111b           ;Set Hi-Nibble in CH to 0
        add  al,ch              ;add AL and CH
        ret                     ;back to caller

bcd_bin endp

;----------------------------------------------------------------------

init    proc near               ;Initialization routine

        ;-- the following code can be overwritten by DOS  ----------
        ;--  after installation of the clock

        mov  word ptr es:[di+end_adr],offset init  ;Set end address
        mov  es:[di+end_adr+2],cs                  ;of the driver

        mov  ah,9               ;Output installation message
        mov  dx,offset initm    ;Address of the text
        int  21h                ;Call DOS interrupt

        xor  ax,ax              ;everything o.k.
        jmp  intr_end           ;back to caller

initm   db 13,10,"**** ATCLK-Driver installed. (c) 1987 by"
        db " MICHAEL TISCHER",13,10,"$"

init    endp

;----------------------------------------------------------------------

code    ends
        end
```

The basic structure of this driver differs from the other drivers in that it calls the individual functions directly, not through a table of their addresses. Since it only supports functions 00H, 04H and 08H, it can test the function numbers passed by DOS directly. If any other function occurs, it signals an error. Besides the INIT routine, which only sets the ending address of the driver like CONDRV, the driver only has the Read Time and Date and Write Time and Date functions.

Time routine

The TIME routine is fairly simple. For reading the clock, the routine reads the time from the memory locations of the clock, converts the time from BCD to binary format and then passes the time to the DOS buffer. For setting the time, the reverse occurs: The routine reads the time from the DOS buffer, converts the code from binary to BCD format and writes the BCD code into the memory locations of the clock.

DOS uses the same format for indicating time as the clock: Hour, minute and seconds each comprise one byte.

Date routine

The DATE routine is more complicated. While the clock stores day, month and year as one byte each, date encoding by DOS is the number of days since January 1, 1980. This number must be converted into a date in the form of day, month and year as DOS writes the time and date. The reverse is true when you call the Read function: the clock date must be converted into the number of days. Let's look at how this is done.

The conversion routine starts with the year 1980. January 1, 1980 (called NUMDAYS from here on) is equal to the value 0. The routine tests whether this year is less than the current year. If so, it adds the number of days in this year to NUMDAYS, adding a day to compensate for each leap year. Then it increments the year and tests again for a smaller number than the current year. This loop repeats until it reaches the current year. The routine then computes the number of days in the current year's month of February, and enters this month into a table which contains the number of days for each month.

In the next step, for every month less than the current month, the routine adds the number of days in this month to NUMDAYS. Once it reaches the current month, only the current days of the month are added to NUMDAYS. The end result is transferred to the DOS buffer and the routine terminates.

Conversion to date format

Converting NUMDAYS into a date operates in reverse. The routine begins with the year 1980 and tests whether the number of days in this year is less than or equal to NUMDAYS. If this is the case, the year is incremented and the number of days in this year is subtracted from NUMDAYS. This loop is repeated until the number of days in a year is larger than NUMDAYS. The routine then computes the number of days in the current year's month of February, and enters this month into the table of the months.

January starts another loop which tests whether the number of days in the current month is less than or equal to NUMDAYS. If this is the case, the month increments and the routine subtracts the number of days from NUMDAYS. If the number of days in a month is larger than NUMDAYS, the loop ends. NUMDAYS must only be incremented enough to give the day of the month and complete the date.

The routine then converts the date to BCD format and enters the date in the memory locations of the clock.

6.12.10 CD-ROMs

Soon after their introduction into the audio world, the compact disk industry began approaching the PC market. A CD-ROM drive and a PC form an interesting combination. The compact disk medium itself is read-only, but 660 megabytes of data can be stored in the form of text, graphics, etc.

Many publications and references are currently available on CD-ROM, such as:

- Telephone directories
- Books in Print
- The Bible in various translations
- The English translation of Pravda

In addition, maps, photographic libraries, public domain program collections and medical databases are available in CD-ROM format. New titles are being published daily in this growing market.

Why CD-ROM?

The CD-ROM has a clear advantage over the printed medium. Once captured and digitized, information can be processed by a computer in whatever form the user needs. The possibilities appear to be limitless, considering how easy it is to read and compare information.

Another important consideration is the ease of access for many users. Load the driver software, press a key or two, and the information is on the screen and ready.

You can buy a PC-compatible CD-ROM player for $800 to $1,000 at the time of this writing. These players are available as either external or internal devices.

Interfacing

The PC's hardware can be easily interfaced to a CD-ROM player. The software may encounter some problems, however. This is understandable, since DOS was never intended to support these devices. This subsection shows how a CD-ROM drive, using the proper drivers and utility programs, can be accessed like a read-only floppy disk drive. This information may not be of immediate use to you. However, this data will give you a closer look into the world of the device driver and operating system organization.

This book mentioned earlier that the device drivers act as mediators between the disk operating system and the external devices such as monitor, printer, disk drives and hard disks. DOS differentiates between block device drivers and character device drivers. As a mass storage device capable of reading information in a block mode, a CD-ROM drive would normally be added to the rest of the system through a block driver. Here's where the problem begins: DOS makes a number of assumptions about block devices, and a CD-ROM drive cannot meet the criteria of these assumptions.

Memory limitations

In versions of DOS up to and including Version 3.3, the biggest obstacle to interfacing with a block driver was the 32 megabyte limit imposed on every volume designated as a block device. The second biggest obstacle is the lack of a file allocation table (FAT) on a CD-ROM. Instead of the FAT, the CD-ROM contains a form of data table into which the starting addresses of the various subdirectories and files are recorded. However, DOS still demands a FAT which it can at least read during driver initialization.

A character driver works better for implementing a CD-ROM driver, since DOS makes no assumptions about the structure of the devices connected through character drivers. Even character drivers are poorly suited for communication with a CD-ROM drive, since they transmit characters one at a time instead of in groups of characters. Another disadvantage is the need for a name (e.g., CON) instead of a device designation. DOS must first see the CD-ROM driver as a character driver to DOS to prevent read accesses to a non-existent FAT. The CONFIG.SYS file supplies the name of the device during the system booting process.

Configuring the CD-ROM

The manufacturer usually includes CD-ROM driver software with the CD-ROM drive package. A driver of this type usually has a name such as SONY.SYS or HITACHI.SYS, depending on the manufacturer.

The CONFIG.SYS sequence which installs this driver can look something like this:

```
DEVICE=HITACHI.SYS /D:CDR1
```

The device driver selects the name CDR1 as the name of the CD-ROM drive.

After executing the initialization routine from DOS, the CD-ROM is treated as a block driver which has been enhanced with a few special functions supporting CD-ROMs. However, DOS still views the CD-ROM player as a character driver: DOS cannot view the CD-ROM's directory, nor can it directly access the files on the CD-ROM.

Driver software extensions

To overcome this obstacle, many CD-ROM players come with a TSR (Terminate and Stay Resident) program named MSCDEX (Microsoft CD-ROM Extension) in addition to the device driver software (see Chapter 8 for information on TSR programs). This program must be called from within the AUTOEXEC.BAT file. The name of the CD driver can be passed to the program from the DOS prompt, as shown in the following example:

```
MSCDEX /D:CDR1
```

MSCDEX first opens this driver through the DOS OPEN function and provides it a device designation. DOS assumes that MSCDEX is a device on a remote network, as supported by DOS in Version 3.1.

MSCDEX brings us closer to the solution, since DOS handles network devices as files containing more than 32 megabytes. These devices are accessed through redirection, rather than direct access from DOS. The resident portion of MSCDEX interfaces to the redirector, and intercepts all calls to the redirector. If MSCDEX receives a call addressed to the CD-ROM drive, it adapts each instruction to a call applicable to the CD-ROM driver. This makes a perfect connection between DOS and the CD-ROM drive, while still allowing access to subdirectories and files at any time.

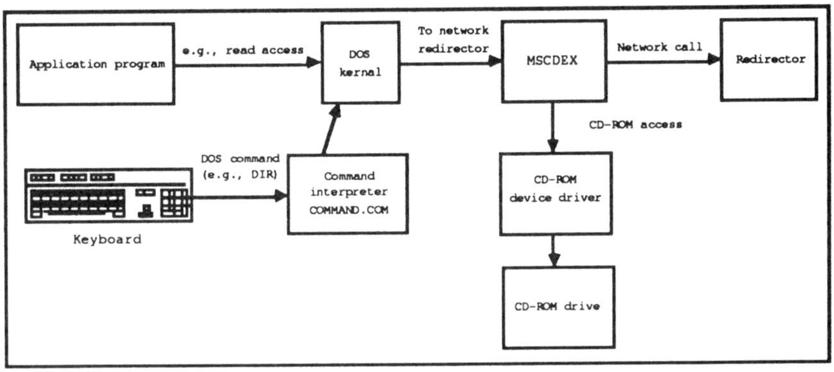

CD-ROM access through MSCDEX and its device driver

6.13 DOS Mass Storage

Many tasks performed by DOS are unseen by the user. This is why some users underestimate the complexity of DOS. For example, DOS requires many data structures for handling a mass storage device, and the user may not realize this. This section looks deeper into DOS and reveals the architecture and operation of these data structures.

From the user's viewpoint, DOS addresses mass storage devices as volumes where each individual volume has been assigned a letter. Floppy disk drives are identified by the letters A and B, while the letters C or D usually identify a hard disk. A mass storage device can have several volumes. This division into several volumes or partitions is very practical for hard disks. Partitions on a floppy diskette don't work as well due to the limited amount of storage space. A hard disk may be divided into additional partitions if UNIX (or XENIX) is used in addition to DOS. Each of the two operating systems then has its own volume which is also designated by its own letter.

Volume names

Each volume can be assigned a volume name when created, but this volume name is not a requirement. The DIR command lists volume names when they are available. Each volume has its own root directory, which can contain multiple subdirectories and files. These subdirectories and files can be maintained and manipulated by using one or more of the interrupt 21H functions.

Sectors

DOS subdivides each volume into a series of sectors. These sectors are organized sequentially. Each sector contains a specific number of bytes (usually 512) and is assigned a consecutive number beginning with sector 0. Since function calls with interrupt 21H are directed to files rather than individual sectors, DOS converts these file accesses into sector accesses. To do this, DOS uses directories and a data structure known as the FAT (file allocation table), which you read about earlier in this book. After the desired sector number has been determined, control is passed to the device driver which translates this sector number into a physical address. Mass storage devices such as floppy and hard disks are divided into individual tracks which contain a certain number of sectors. In addition to the physical sector number, the driver must also determine the number of the track and the number of the read head.

Sector number	
↓	Manufacturer's name, device driver, boot routine
	First file allocation table (FAT)
	One or more copies of FAT
	Root directory with volume names
	Data register for files and subdirectories

Mass storage device structure

As mentioned above, every volume is divided into various areas containing the various DOS data structures and individual files. Since the size of the individual areas can differ depending on the type of mass storage device (and the manufacturer), every volume contains a *boot sector*. The boot sector contains all the information required to access to the different areas and data structures. DOS creates this sector during disk formatting. Boot sectors always have the same structure and are always located in sector 0 so that DOS can find and interpret it properly.

The following illustration shows the layout of the boot sector.

Offset	Contents	Size	
00(h)	Jump command to boot routine (E9xxx or EBxx90)	(3 bytes)	
03(h)	Manufacturer's name and version number	(8 bytes)	
0B(h)	Bytes per sector	(1 word)	BPB
0D(h)	Sectors per cluster	(1 byte)	BPB
0E(h)	Number of reserved sectors	(1 word)	BPB
10(h)	Number of FATs	(1 byte)	BPB
11(h)	Number of entries in root directory	(1 word)	BPB
13(h)	Number of sectors in volume	(1 word)	BPB
15(h)	Media descriptor	(1 byte)	BPB
16(h)	Number of sectors per FAT	(1 word)	BPB
18(h)	Sectors per track	(1 word)	
1A(h)	Number of read/write heads		
1C(h)	Number of hidden sectors		
1E(h)-1FF(h)	**BOOT ROUTINE**		

Boot sector layout

Boot sector

The name boot sector comes from the fact that DOS boots (i.e., starts) from it. DOS is loaded and started from disk—it is not usually stored in permanent PC memory (ROM). After you turn the computer on, the BIOS takes over the system initialization and loads logical sector 0 of the floppy or hard disk into memory. Once it completes its work the BIOS starts execution at address 0.

The boot sector always contains an assembly language JUMP instruction at address 0. After execution the program continues at a location further into the boot sector. This instruction can be either a normal jump instruction or a "short jump." Since the field for this jump instruction is 3 bytes long, but a "short jump" only requires 2 bytes, a NOP (No Operation) instruction always follows the "short jump" to fill in the extra byte. This NOP does nothing. A series of fields follow which contain certain information about the organization of the media. The first field is 8 bytes long and contains the manufacturer's name, where this medium was formatted, as well as the DOS version number which performed the formatting. The next fields contain the physical format of the media (i.e., the number of bytes per sector, the number of sectors per track, etc.) and the size of the DOS data structures stored on the media. Since the BIOS and DOS-BIOS functions represent the lowest level of access to disk drives and hard disks, this area is also designated as the BIOS parameter block (BPB). Three additional fields, which can provide additional information to the device driver about the media, follow the BPB; these three fields aren't used directly by DOS.

Bootstrap

Next comes the *bootstrap* routine to which the jump instruction branches at the beginning of this boot sector. It handles the loading and starting of DOS through the individual system components (see Section 6.3).

Several reserved sectors may follow the boot sector. These reserved sectors can contain additional bootstrap code. The numbers of these sectors are recorded in the BPB in the field starting at address 0EH. It terminates the boot sector and a 1 in this field indicates that no additional reserved sectors follow the boot sector (this is the case for most PCs).

In order for DOS to add new files or enlarge existing files, it must know which sectors of the media are still available. This information is contained in a data structure called the FAT (file allocation table) which is immediately adjacent to the media's reserved area. Each entry in the FAT corresponds with a certain number of logically contiguous sectors, called *clusters*, on the media. Location 0DH of the boot sector specifies the number of sectors per cluster as part of the BIOS parameter table. Only multiples of 2 are legal values. On an XT hard disk this location contains the value 8 (8 consecutive sectors form a cluster). As the following table demonstrates, the number of sectors comprising a cluster depends on the storage medium.

Device	Sectors per cluster
Single sided disk drive	1
Double sided disk drive	2
AT hard disk	4
XT hard disk	8

The reason for joining several sectors into a cluster is derived from the logic used by DOS to write files to a media. It disassembles the file to fit the pieces into the sectors which are still available, instead of selecting adjoining sectors for file storage. This process slows file access since the read/write head must be repositioned after almost every read function. To avoid an excessive disassembly of the file, DOS gathers several sequential sectors on the media into a cluster. This ensures that at least the sectors of a cluster contain a portion of a file. If DOS didn't use clusters, a file of 24 sectors could be stored in many separate sectors, which would require the read/write head to be positioned a maximum of 24 times to read the entire file. The cluster principle saves a lot of time, since the file is stored in 6 clusters and the read/write head only has to be repositioned 6 times.

There is a problem however. Since a file is assigned at least one cluster, some storage space is wasted. Consider AUTOEXEC.BAT which is usually no longer than 150 bytes. Normally, a single sector could contain this file (and still waste almost 400 bytes), but AUTOEXEC.BAT occupies a cluster of 2048 bytes on an AT, which wastes more than 1.5K of hard disk space.

Now back to the file allocation table:

The size of individual entries in the FAT under DOS Versions 1 and 2 is 12 bits. For DOS Version 3 and later, the size of an entry in the FAT depends on the number of clusters: if a volume has more than 4,096 clusters, then each FAT entry is 16 bits; otherwise each FAT entry is 12 bits. The number of bits per FAT entry must be determined before file access. The information in the BIOS parameter block is used for this purpose. The total number of sectors in the volume can be found starting at location 13H. Divide this number by the number of sectors per cluster to obtain the number of clusters in the volume.

The first two entries of the FAT are reserved and have nothing to do with the cluster assignment. Depending on the sizes of the individual entries, 24 bits (3 bytes) or 32 bits (4 bytes) can be available. The first byte contains the media descriptor, while the value 255 fill in the other bytes. The media descriptor, which is also stored in address 15H of the BPB, indicates the device which the media uses (for example a diskette). The following codes are possible:

Code	Device
F8H	Hard disk
F9H	5.25" disk drive (AT only) 2 sides, 80 tracks, 15 sectors
FCH	5.25" disk drive 1 side, 40 tracks, 9 sectors
FDH	5.25" disk drive 2 sides, 40 tracks, 9 sectors
FEH	5.25" disk drive 1 side, 40 tracks, 8 sectors
FFH	5.25" disk drive 2 sides, 40 tracks, 8 sectors

This shows the various diskette formats which DOS supports in 5.25" diskettes.

Included in DOS version	1.00	1.10	2.00	2.00	3.00
Media descriptor	FE	FF	FC	FD	F9
Number of read/write heads	1	2	1	2	2
Number of tracks per head	40	40	40	40	80
Number of sectors per track	8	8	8	8	8
Number of bytes per sector	512	512	512	512	512
Number of sectors per cluster	1	2	1	2	1
Number of reserved sectors	1	1	1	1	1
Number of sectors per FAT	1	1	2	2	7
Number of FATs	2	2	2	2	2
Number of sectors in root directory	4	7	4	7	14
Number of entries in root directory	64	112	64	112	224
Total number of sectors	320	640	360	720	2400
Free sectors for data	313	620	351	708	2371
Number of clusters	313	315	351	354	2371
Total capacity	160K	320K	180K	360K	1.2Meg
Total file capacity	156.5K	315K	175.5K	354K	1.185Meg

DOS 5.25" diskette formats

You may have wondered why the individual entries of the FAT are 12 or 16 bits wide if all they do is indicate whether a cluster is occupied or not. This could have been done with one bit: The bit could contain 1 when the cluster is occupied and 0 if the cluster is available. The reason is that the entries in the FAT help mark the available clusters and identify the individual clusters containing a specific file. The directory entry of a file tells DOS which cluster holds the first data of a file. The number of this cluster corresponds to the number of the FAT entry belonging to it. In this entry is the number of the cluster containing the next sector of file data. As the following illustration shows, a chain forms in which the individual clusters assigned to a file can be located in the proper sequence.

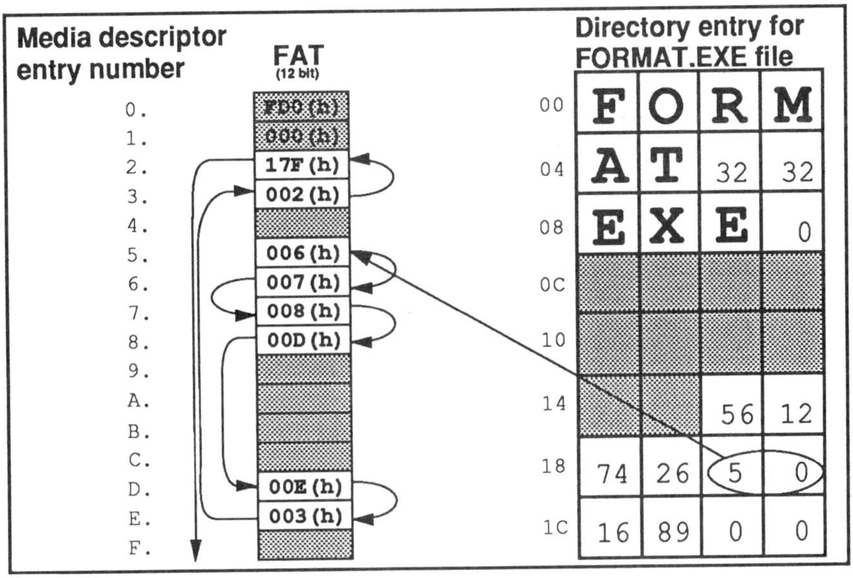

FAT entry and file clusters

The FAT entry which corresponds to the last cluster of a file must contain a special code which tells DOS that the file ends here. The following table shows the meanings of the various FAT entries.

Code	Meaning
(0)000H	Cluster is available
(F)FF0H - (F)FF6H	reserved cluster
(F)FF7H	Cluster damaged, not used
(F)FF8H - (F)FFFH	Last file cluster
(x)xxxH	Next file cluster

Note: The first hexadecimal number in parentheses refers to a FAT whose entries are 16 bits wide.

DOS is designed so that several identical copies of the FAT on the media may be kept. This offers the advantage that in case of damage to one FAT, it can be replaced with another, preventing data loss.

The DOS CHKDSK command tests the various FATs to see if they are identical.

Directory structure

Now let's look at the structure of a directory.

The root directory of a volume immediately follows the last copy of the FAT. This root directory (like all subdirectories) consists of 32-byte entries in which information can be stored about individual files, subdirectories and volume names. The maximum number of entries in the root directory, and therefore its size, is stored in the BPB starting at address 11H. The FORMAT command specifies both the size number and the BPB. Before considering individual fields of this data structure, here's a graphic overview of a directory entry:

+ 00H	Filename (blanks padded w/ spaces)	(8 bytes)
+ 08H	File extension (blanks padded w/ spaces)	(3 bytes)
+ 0BH	File attribute	(1 byte)
+ 0CH	Reserved	(10 bytes)
+ 16H	Time of last change	(1 word)
+ 18H	Date of last change	(1 word)
+ 1AH	First cluster of file	(1 word)
+ 1CH	File size	(2 words)

Directory entry layout

The first 8 bytes normally contain the name of the current file. If the filename is shorter than 8 characters, DOS fills the remaining characters with spaces (ASCII code 32). If the directory entry does not contain information on a file, but the file is used in another manner, the first byte of the filename (therefore the first byte of the directory entry) is identified by special code:

Code	Meaning
00H	Last directory entry
05H	First character of filename has ASCII code E5H
2EH	File applies to current directory
E5H	File deleted

The second field contains the three character filename extension. If the extension is less than three characters in length, DOS fills in the extra characters with blank spaces (ASCII code 32). The period between filename and extension is displayed by the DOS command DIR but is not kept in the directory; DIR displays it just to make the names between easier to read.

Next follows the one-byte attribute field. As shown in the following figure the individual bits of this field define certain attributes. The various attributes can be combined so that a file (as in the IBMBIOS.COM file) can have the attributes READ_ONLY, SYSTEM and HIDDEN.

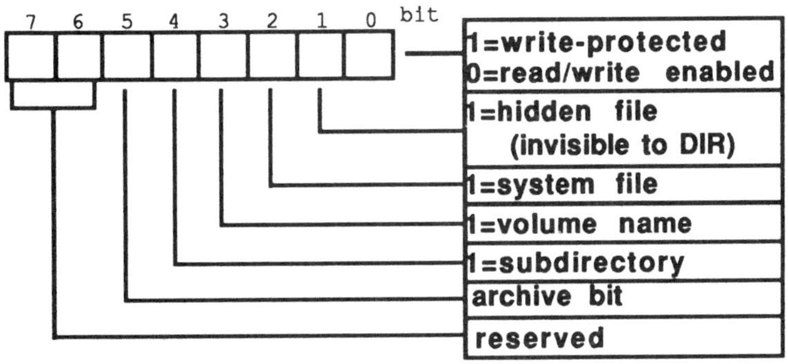

Attribute field in the directory

While the significance of bits 0 to 4 is easy to see, the significance of bit 5 needs additional explanation. The name *archive bit* comes from its use in making backup copies. Every time a file is created or modified, this bit is set to 1. If a program is used to backup this file, (for example the DOS BACKUP command), the archive bit is reset to 0. The next time the BACKUP command is used, it can determine from the archive bit whether this file has been modified since the last backup. If it still contains the value 0, the file doesn't have to be backed up again. If the archive bit contains a 1, the file was modified and should be backed up again.

The attributes volume name and subdirectory will be discussed in more detail below.

A reserved field which DOS requires for internal operations follows the attribute field.

The time and date fields indicate when the file was last created or modified. Both are stored as words (2 bytes), but have special and different formats.

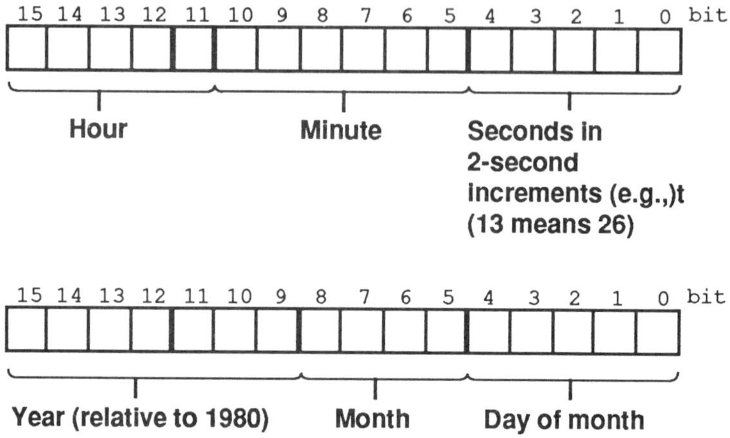

Time/date field formats in directory entry

The next field indicates the number of the cluster which contains the first data of the file. It also indicates the number of the FAT containing the number of the next cluster assigned to the file. This field forms the beginning of a chain through which all the clusters assigned to a file can be retrieved.

The file size in bytes is stored in 2 words with the lower word stored first. Using a small formula and the two words, the file size can be calculated as follows:

```
File size = word1 + word2 * 65,536
```

Subdirectory and volume name

Both subdirectory and volume name deserve special consideration. The volume name can only exist in the root directory and is indicated by bit 3 of the current directory entry's attribute field. The filename in a volume entry acts as the volume name; the DOS commands DIR, VOL and TREE can be used to display the volume name.

If bit 4 of the current directory's attribute field is set, then this entry is for a subdirectory. If in addition bit 1 in this field is set, the subdirectory can be addressed, but will not be displayed when you execute the DIR command. For these entries, the filename and extension field contain the subdirectory name; the date and time field contain the time of its creation. The file length field is always 0. The field which normally indicates the first cluster of the file now indicates the cluster which contains the directory entries of this subdirectory. They have the same 32-byte structure as the entries in the root directory. As in a normal file, the entry in the FAT, which corresponds with the subdirectory cluster, points to the next cluster of the subdirectory, as long as one cluster is enough for the directory of the subdirectory. This is not true of the root directory which extends through several sectors or clusters, which follow each other logically. Furthermore the individual clusters of the root directory cannot be connected through the FAT, because it only refers to the data area of the volume. This is the area which accepts files and subdirectories, but not the root directory.

The process described above reveals that DOS separates the individual files in a storage unit according to their directories. It doesn't store the files of one directory in one area, but scatters the files across the storage medium.

When a subdirectory is created, two files are created with the names '.' and '..' which can only be erased when you remove the entire subdirectory. The first of these two files points to the current subdirectory, and its cluster field contains the number of the first cluster of the current subdirectory. The second entry points to the parent directory, which in the directory tree is located ahead of the current directory. If the parent directory is the root directory, the cluster field contains the value 0. The path to the root directory can be traced back through this entry, since as every subdirectory searches for its parent directory it comes closer to the root directory.

Now back to our discussion of mass storage device structures. The file area follows the root directory just described. It occupies the remaining storage area of the mass storage device. It accepts the individual files and various subdirectories. For every cluster in this area there is an entry in the FAT corresponding to this cluster. If a file is enlarged, DOS reserves a cluster which is still available to store the additional data of the file. The FAT entry of the last cluster which formerly indicated the end of file is changed to point to the new cluster which in turn contains the new end character. In DOS Versions 1.0 and 2.0, unused clusters are searched for from the beginning. In DOS Versions 3.0 and up, a more sophisticated search is used to try to select an unused cluster in the vicinity of other clusters comprising the file. This reduces the access time to the file as much as possible. Conversely, when reducing file size or deleting a file, the FAT is updated to indicate that the unused clusters are again available. They can be used again when a new file is created or expanded.

6.14 Tips on Compatibility between Computers

This book discusses three methods of accessing PC hardware. On the one hand, you can access available DOS or BIOS functions. On the other hand, you have the option of developing new functions and routines for direct hardware control. While this offers no advantage in mass storage device and keyboard access, special routines for screen display are often much faster and more efficient than BIOS and DOS routines used to do the same job.

For compatibility, however, DOS functions win hands down. Those of you who want to develop programs which can run, without problems, on virtually any DOS computer, must observe some rules for DOS function calls. These rules also apply to future compatibility. To develop programs under the current DOS versions which should execute without problems under future versions of DOS, you should follow the suggestions made below.

- Use only DOS functions for screen and hardware access. Do not use BIOS or other hardware dependent functions.
- Display error messages on the standard error device (handle 2).
- Use Version 2 UNIX-compatible handle functions for file access. This ensures compatibility with future versions of DOS.
- If you use the old FCB functions for file or directory access (e.g., for special attributes), make sure no FCBs are opened which are already open, and no FCBs are closed which are already closed. This could cause problems in a network.
- Check the DOS version number at the beginning of the program and end the program with an error message if it cannot be executed under this version.
- Store as many constants as needed for program execution (e.g., the paths of programs and files to be loaded) within the environment block. Access these values from the environment block within the program.
- Release all memory not required by the program using the DOS functions (this is especially important when working with COM programs).
- If you need additional memory, request it by using the proper DOS functions.
- Use the available DOS functions for interrupt vectors; do not access interrupt vectors directly.
- To change the contents of various interrupt vectors within a program, first save the old contents and restore them before the end of the program.

- Call one of the DOS functions (31H or 4CH) before the end of the program to pass a value to the calling program to signal whether the program was executed correctly. Avoid using the other functions for ending a program (interrupt 20H and function 0 of interrupt 21H).

- Use function 59H of interrupt 21H (available in DOS Versions 3.0 and higher) to localize error sources.

In conclusion, here is an overview of the older DOS functions to avoid, and the new equivalent functions that can replace them.

Old		New		
00H	End program	4CH	End Process	
0FH	Open file	3DH	Open Handle	
10H	Close file	3EH	Close handle	
11H	Find first entry	4EH	Find first entry	
12H	Find next entry	4FH	Find next entry	
13H	Erase file	41H	Erase directory entry	
14H	Sequential read	3FH	Read (through handle)	
15H	Sequential write	40H	Write (through handle)	
16H	Created file	3CH	Created handle	or
		5AH	Created temporary file	or
		5BH	Created new file	
17H	Rename file	56H	Rename directory entry	
21H	Random access read	3FH	Read (through handle)	
22H	Random access write	40H	Write (through handle)	
23H	Sense file size	42H	Move file pointer	
24H	Set data set number	42H	Move file pointer	
26H	Create new PSP	4BH	Load and execute from file	
27H	Random access read	3FH	Read (through handle)	
28H	Random access write	40H	Write (through handle)	

If you follow all these suggestions, your programs will execute on other computers and under future DOS versions with little or no modifications.

6.15 Undocumented DOS Structures

DOS manages the operating storage media (RAM and mass storage) and programs which use multiple data structures. Some of these structures are thoroughly documented and have already been described in this book. These documented structures include:

- Program Segment Prefix (PSP), which precedes every program in memory
- File Control Blocks (FCBs), which control file access
- Memory Control Blocks (MCBs), which control RAM
- Structures in the header of a device driver
- Environment blocks, which contain information strings about every program in memory
- The many structures which DOS keeps in mass storage (boot sector, File Allocation Table [FAT], root directory, etc.)

In addition, there are a number of undocumented structures. Until quite recently, only a few people knew of the existence of these structures, since most technical manuals concerning DOS didn't describe them. The authors of many of these technical manuals felt that these structures weren't needed for programming, and that their coding would change in future versions of DOS. The fact is that certain kinds of programming do depend upon these structures, and that some applications couldn't be realized at all without them.

Floppy disk and hard disk management utilities make intensive use of the undocumented structures. If you examine the Norton Utilities® using a debugging application, you'd see how much this program accesses these structures.

A minor change in these structures took place between DOS Version 3.3 and Version 4.0, but this is the first change since the introduction of DOS Version 2.0 in 1983. Therefore, the chances are almost nil of finding altered coding in the undocumented structures of subsequent DOS versions.

Knowing about these structures can be practical data for programming some applications. This section lists our findings from viewing the Norton Utilities®.

The DOS Info Block (DIB) is the key to accessing the most important DOS structures. This block holds pointers to several DOS structures and to other information as well. The knowledge of its existence and construction is useful to a program only if its address in memory is known. This address is not in a fixed memory location, nor can it be obtained with any of the documented functions of DOS interrupt 21H. However, the undocumented function 52H can offer us some assistance in finding that address. Calling function 52H returns the address of the DOS Info Block to the ES:BX register pair.

As opposed to all other DOS functions that fetch pointers to a structure or data area, the contents of the ES:BX register pair point not to the first, but rather to the second field within the DIB after the function call.

DOS Info Block (DIB) structure		
Addr.	Contents	Type
-04H	Pointer to MCB	1 ptr
ES:BX	Pointer to first Drive Parameter Block (DPB)	1 ptr
+04H	Pointer to last DOS buffer	1 ptr
+08H	Pointer to clock driver ($CLOCK)	1 ptr
+0CH	Pointer to console driver (CON)	1 ptr
+10H	Maximum sector length (based on all connected mass storage devices)	1 word
+12H	Pointer to first DOS buffer	1 ptr
+16H	Pointer to path table	1 ptr
+1AH	Pointer to System File Table (SFT)	1 ptr
Length: 1EH (30) bytes		

The first field in the DIB contains a pointer to the Memory Control Block (MCB) of the first allocated memory area. You will find detailed information on this structure and what it does in Section 6.9 (Memory Allocation from DOS). The pointer in the second field of the DIB gives access to a wealth of information that could not be had in any other way. It points to the first Drive Parameter Block (DPB), a structure which DOS lays out for all mass storage devices (floppy disks, hard disks, tape drives, etc.).

Drive Parameter Block (DPB) structure		
Addr.	Contents	Type
+00H	Number or symbol for corresponding drive (0 = A, 1 = B, etc.)	1 byte
+01H	Sub-unit of device driver for drive	1 byte
+02H	Bytes per sector	1 word
+04H	Interleave factor	1 byte
+05H	Sectors per cluster	1 byte
+06H	Reserved sectors (for boot sector)	1 word
+08H	Number of File Allocation Tables (FATs)	1 byte
+09H	Number of entries in root directory	1 word
+0BH	First occupied sector	1 word
+0DH	Last occupied cluster	1 word
+0FH	Sectors per FAT	1 byte
+10H	First data sector	1 word
+12H	Pointer to header (correspond. device driver)	1 ptr
+16H	Media descriptor	1 byte
+17H	Used flag (0FFH=device not yet in use)	1 byte
+18H	Pointer to next DPB (xxxx:FFFF = last DPB)	1 ptr
Length: 1CH (28) bytes		

The first field of the DPB tells us to which device the block belongs. 0 stands for drive A, 1 for B, 2 for C, etc. The second field specifies the number of the subunit. To understand the meaning of this field, remember that access to the individual devices occurs through the device driver. DOS doesn't perform direct access to a disk drive or hard disk. This keeps DOS from having to deal with the physical characteristics of a mass storage device. Instead, DOS calls a device driver for this purpose, which acts as mediator between DOS and hardware.

Of course, not every device has a separate device driver, since one device driver can support many single devices. For example, the device driver built into DOS manages the floppy disk drives and the first available hard disk. DOS configures a DPB for each device, so a hard disk system would automatically have 3 DPBs available (a DPB is always configured for floppy drive B, even if only one floppy drive is actually available). Each device receives a number between 0 and the total number of devices minus 1, to help each driver to identify the devices it manages. This number is the one found in the subunit field.

The next field lists the number of bytes per sector. Under DOS this is almost always 512. After this comes the *interleave factor*, which gives the number of logical sectors displaced by physical sectors when the medium is formatted (more on this in Chapter 7). This value can be 1 for floppy disk drives, 6 for the XT hard disk and 3 for the AT hard disk. For floppy disk drives, this field can also have the value FEH if no access has been attempted to the disk in the drive. The value FEH means that the interleave factor is currently unknown.

There are a number of other fields related to these two which have already been named in connection with the management of mass storage devices through DOS (see Section 6.13). Among other things, they describe the status and the size of the structures DOS created to manage mass storage devices. A pointer to the header of the device driver lies within these fields. DOS uses this pointer when accessing the device. More information can be obtained with this pointer since, for example, the driver attribute is listed in the header of the device driver.

Following this field is the media descriptor to which the Used flag is connected. As long as no access to the device has occurred, this flag contains the value 0FFH. After the first access it changes to 0 and remains unchanged until a system reset.

The DPB ends with a pointer that establishes communication with the next DPB. Since every DPB defines its end with such a pointer, a kind of chain is created, through which all DPBs can be reached. To signal the end of the chain, the offset address of this pointer in the last DPB contains the value 0FFFFH. When a program needs the information within the DOS, there are many ways to find the address of the desired DPB. One method is to follow the chain described above by first finding out the address of the DIB. This gives you the pointer to the first DPB, from which you can follow the chain until you reach the DPB you want.

There's a better way, which isn't as susceptible to changes within the DIB, through two undocumented DOS functions. This involves the 1FH and 32H functions, which have been part of the DOS function repertoire since Version 2.0, although not documented by Microsoft. When called, both return a pointer to a DPB to the DS:BX register pair. While function 1FH always delivers a pointer to the DPB of the current disk drive, the address delivered by function 32H refers to the device whose number is passed to the function in the DL register at the time it's called. (0 represents the current drive, 1 is drive A, 2 drive B etc.). It's much more flexible than function 1FH.

Access to the various DPBs with the 1FH and 32H functions offers a further advantage, because it forces DOS to retrieve other information such as the interleave factor and the media descriptor byte, which is ascertained for the disk drive only after the first access. If you get to the DPB through the pointer in the DIB block, the various fields may not have been initialized, and could contain the wrong values.

Besides the pointer to the first DPB, the DIB contains the pointer to the first DOS buffer at address 12H. These DOS buffers store individual sectors, so that the sectors don't have to be repeatedly loaded from disk. The DOS buffers can be most effective when used for storing disk sectors that are frequently needed by the currently running program. Besides the FAT, these include the root directory and its subdirectories. The number of buffers can be defined by the user in the CONFIG.SYS file. If this number exceeds those needed for the FAT, root directory and subdirectories, normal sectors can also be temporarily stored here, in the hope that they are called to be loaded again in the near future, and can be taken directly from the buffer.

So that DOS can quickly check each buffer for the desired sector with every read operation, the individual sectors are linked together.

DOS buffer structure		
Addr.	Contents	Type
+00H	Pointer to next DOS buffer	1 ptr
+04H	Drive number (0 = A, 1 = B etc.)	1 byte
+05H	Flags	1 byte
+06H	Sector number	1 word
+08H	Reserved	2 bytes
+0AH	Contents of buffered sector	512 bytes
Length: 210H (528) bytes		

As with DPBs, this happens with the help of a pointer which appears at the start of every buffer. Also, the last buffer is reached when the offset address of the pointer contains the value 0FFFFH. After the field linking one buffer to the next comes the number of the drive where the buffered sector originates. The value would be 0 for drive A, 1 for B, 2 for C, etc. Besides the drive number, the identification of a sector requires a sector number. This is located beginning at position 06H in the DOS buffer. The last field in the buffer header stores a pointer to the corresponding DPB, so that DOS can get information on the device which loaded the buffered sector. Although this is the last field in the header of the DOS buffer, the buffered sector does not end immediately after this field. There are two more bytes which follow. The reason for this is that the DOS code is written in machine language, and when it comes to working with memory blocks, it is most efficient to have the buffered sector begin with an address that is divisible by 16.

The header of the DOS buffer is not the last place we run across the DPB. It turns up again in the path table, which starts at address 16H in the DIB. This contains the current path for each drive as well as a pointer to its DPB.

```
       0  1  2  3  4  5  6  7  8  9  A  B  C  D  E  F
0000: 41 3A 5C 43 41 43 48 45-00 00 00 00 00 00 00 00  A:\CACHE........
0010: 00 00 00 00 00 00 00 00-00 00 00 00 00 00 00 00  ................
0020: 00 00 00 00 00 00 00 00-00 00 00 00 00 00 00 00  ................
0030: 00 00 00 00 00 00 00 00-00 00 00 00 00 00 00 00  ................
0040: 00 00 00 00 40 20 74 80-02 27 03 FF FF FF FF 02  ....@ t..'......
0050: 00 42 3A 5C 00 00 00 00-00 00 00 00 00 00 00 00  .B:\............
0060: 00 00 00 00 00 00 00 00-00 00 00 00 00 00 00 00  ................
0070: 00 00 00 00 00 00 00 00-00 00 00 00 00 00 00 00  ................
0080: 00 00 00 00 00 00 00 00-00 00 00 00 00 00 00 00  ................
0090: 00 00 00 00 00 40 40 74-80 02 00 00 FF FF FF FF  .....@@t........
00A0: 02 00 43 3A 5C 54 43 5C-42 41 55 53 5C 41 53 4D  ..C:\TC\BAUS\ASM
00B0: 5C 48 45 52 43 4D 4F 4E-4F 00 00 00 00 00 00 00  \HERCMONO.......
00C0: 00 00 00 00 00 00 00 00-00 00 00 00 00 00 00 00  ................
00D0: 00 00 00 00 00 00 00 00-00 00 00 00 00 00 00 00  ................
00E0: 00 00 00 00 00 00 40 60-74 80 02 65 05 FF FF FF  ......@`t..e....
00F0: FF 02 00 44 3A 5C 4D 53-43 5C 42 49 4E 00 00 00  ...D:\MSC\BIN...
0100: 00 00 00 00 00 00 00 00-00 00 00 00 00 00 00 00  ................
0110: 00 00 00 00 00 00 00 00-00 00 00 00 00 00 00 00  ................
0120: 00 00 00 00 00 00 00 00-00 00 00 00 00 00 00 00  ................
0130: 00 00 00 00 00 00 00 40-00 00 80 0D 17 00 FF FF  .......@........
0140: FF FF 02 00
```

Memory dump of the path table contents

As long as the LASTDRIVE command is in the system's configuration file, the table will have entries for drives A through the one specified by LASTDRIVE. If this command is missing, however, the table will only have entries for each device supported by the installed device driver. If you change the entries in this table, you can divert one drive to another. The JOIN and SUBST DOS commands also take advantage of this by manipulating the path table entry of the drive to be diverted.

6.16 DOS 4.0

People were rather surprised when IBM introduced DOS 4.0 instead of DOS 3.4. The version number suggests vast improvements to this operating system. Version 4.0 does in fact have some features to offer which clearly set it apart from its predecessors:

- Full-screen system installation
- Graphic user interfaces for directory display, file selection and running programs
- Full mouse support
- Support of Extended Memory Specification (EMS) according to the LIM 4.0 specification for buffer storage
- Hard disk partition (volume) support and support for device capacity larger than 32 megabytes
- Improved file access through optimization of the system code

The introduction of these features mean changes in the operating system code. Although most of these changes will not affect most application programs, they may cause problems in programs that lie within the system, as well as programs developed without following rules of compatibility (see Section 6.14).

Compatibility problems

First of all, the support of hard disk partitions and files larger than 32 megabytes implies definite changes to the DOS file system. These changes don't affect programs that manipulate files only through the DOS interrupt 21H functions. However, many block device drivers and programs that access the DOS structures of the file system directly will have to be adapted to the new file system. This includes programs like the Norton Utilities®, PC Tools® and all the other utilities which perform tasks such as optimizing hard disks and restoring lost files. All of these will be of little or no use under DOS Version 4.0.

To give you a chance to adapt programs affected by these changes to DOS 4.0, the following pages give a description of changes to the file system (see Section 6.13 for a comprehensive look at the DOS file system).

In order to best visualize the changes to the file system, let's begin with a picture of its fundamental structure, which remains valid under Version 4.0. This fundamental structure can be divided into three layers, one on top of the other. These range from the logical partitioning of a mass storage device on the top layer to a purely physical system on the bottom layer. The top layer forms the function interface to user programs. This interface calls individual functions through interrupt 21H. No changes are allowed on this level in the switch to DOS 4.0 to ensure that all applications that use these functions will continue to run normally. File accesses from the first level are converted to device driver function calls on the second level. In order to locate each file (i.e., retrieve the sectors which must be accessed) this level uses various data structures which are kept in the storage medium. These include:

- The boot sector (including the BIOS parameter block [BPB])
- The root directory and its subdirectories
- The FAT and its duplicates

These functions cannot be changed as well, since one of the most important demands placed on the new DOS version is the ability to work with partitions that were created and formatted under previous versions. This is possible only if the structures listed above are not changed. This does not leave many ways to increase the capacity of a volume. Since the size of the FAT entry is limited to 16 bits, a volume can use no more than 65519 clusters. Therefore, an increase is possible only by using more sectors in a cluster.

When DOS 4.0 sets up new partitions, it assigns the following cluster sizes:

Partition and cluster sizes under DOS 4.0					
Max.partition size	128 meg	256 meg	512 meg	1028 meg	2048 meg
Cluster size	2 K	4 K	8 K	16 K	32 K
Secs. per cluster	4	8	16	32	64

While this procedure minimizes the changes on the second level of the file system, it also has a disadvantage: The bigger the partition, the more memory it wastes. Since the memory in a partition can only be allocated in clusters, some memory is always wasted when a cluster is not completely filled. This is true of files that are smaller than the cluster size. Memory space is also wasted in the last cluster of a larger file, since the size of a file is rarely an integral multiple of the cluster size.

Device driver level

The changes become most noticeable on the third level of the file system, called the device driver level. While character drivers remain unaffected by changes in the partition size, these changes have a great impact on block drivers that support partitions of more than 32 megabytes.

It's true that changes on this level could be kept to a minimum by increasing the sector size from 512 bytes, but this could lead to compatibility problems with partitions that were configured under previous versions of DOS. The only alternative was to increase the number of sectors per partition. But when a partition exceeds the 32-megabyte limit, the 16 bits, which up until now were used to store the logical sector number, are no longer enough. For this reason, DOS 4.0 has introduced a new type of block driver that supports partitions larger than 32 megabytes, and works with 32-bit sector numbers. DOS recognizes these drivers with the help of bit 1 in the device attribute. This bit carried a value of 0 in previous versions of DOS.

Starting with Version 4.0, DOS knows that it is dealing with a 32 bit driver if this bit is turned on. Increasing the sector number also changed the structure of the parameter data block, with which DOS passes information on the functions and parameters being called, to the device driver. Since a 16-bit field is no longer large enough for the sector number, DOS 4.0 adds a 32-bit field to the end of the block. This stores the sector number for a 32-bit driver as a dword (double word). As usual, the word with the smaller value is stored before that with the larger value. To indicate that the new field is in use, DOS also loads the value -1 (FFFFH) into the old field.

Structure of the extended parameter data block when calling a function of a 32-bit driver under DOS 4.0		
Addr.	Contents	Type
+00H	Length of data block in bytes	1 byte
+01H	Number of device being addressed	1 byte
+02H	Number of function being called	1 byte
+03H	Status word	1 word
+05H	Reserved	8 bytes
+0DH	Media descriptor	1 byte
+0EH	Address of parameter buffer	1 ptr
+12H	Number of sectors to process	1 word
+14H	Number of first sector for 16 bit drivers	1 word
+16H	Number of first sector for 32 bit drivers	1 dword
Length: 1AH (26) bytes		

The following driver functions are affected by the change to 32-bit sector numbers:

0	initialize driver
2	set BPB
3	direct read
4	read
8	write
9	write and encode
12	direct write

The structure of the BIOS parameter block (BPB), which the initialize driver function must pass to DOS, has also changed. This structure is also part of the boot sector of a DOS volume. It has been supplemented by two fields compared to the old BPB, and now looks like this:

Extended BIOS parameter block (BPB) structure under DOS 4.0		
Addr.	Contents	Type
+00H	Bytes per sector	1 word
+02H	Sectors per cluster	1 byte
+03H	Number of reserved sectors	1 word
+05H	Number of file allocation tables (FATs)	1 byte
+06H	Number of entries in root directory	1 word
+08H	Number of sectors in volume (partitions <= 32 MB only)	1 word
+0AH	Media descriptor	1 byte
+0BH	Number of sectors per FAT	1 word
+0DH	Sectors per spur	1 word
+0FH	Number of read/write heads	1 word
+11H	Distance of volume's first sector from first sector on medium (partitions <= 32 MB only)	1 word
+13H	Distance of first sector in volume from first sector on medium (partitions > 32 MB only)	1 dword
+17H	Number of sectors in volume (partitions > 32 MB only)	1 dword
Length: 1BH (27) bytes		

The two new fields in this extended BPB refer to the total number of sectors in the volume and the number of sectors between the first sector on the storage medium and the first sector of the volume. Even though these fields were already present in the old BPB, they were there only as 16-bit values, and had to be appended as 32-bit fields. To guarantee maximum compatibility with the drivers of previous DOS versions, DOS only needs to use the new BPB when the sector numbers cannot be represented as 16-bit values. This happens if the distance from the first sector on the storage medium to the first sector in the volume is greater than 32 megabytes.

The new BPB is installed while formatting a volume, but the old 16 bit fields are used to store the number of sectors and the distance from the first sector when the conditions mentioned above don't apply. Otherwise, the corresponding values are entered in the 32 bit fields and the 16 bit fields are assigned a value of 0.

Extending the logical sector number to 32 bits also caused a change in the way the 25H and 26H interrupt functions work. These functions represent the only way for an end-user program to directly access the individual sectors of a volume via DOS. If the number of the first sector to be processed was passed to the DX register of these interrupts by an earlier DOS version, direct sector access is only possible under Version 4.0 if the volume to be accessed is smaller than 32 megabytes. To access larger volumes in Version 4.0 and higher, the DS:BX register pair of these interrupts must receive a pointer to the data block pictured on the next page:

Structure of data block used in calling interrupts 25H and 26H under DOS 4.0		
Addr.	Contents	Type
+00H	Number of first sector	1 dword
+04H	Number of sectors	1 word
+06H	Pointer to buffer	1 ptr
Length: 0AH (10) bytes		

At the same time a value of -1 (FFFFH) must be passed to the CX register, so that DOS knows that the parameter transfer will not be following the old scheme. In conclusion, there is one more little innovation to mention. While this has no impact on program development under DOS 4.0, it does show that the 80386 has truly come of age. For example, 80386 PCs can use a particular trick to speed up file access and corresponding buffer and cache operations. DOS uses the capabilities of the 80386 very skillfully by running string instructions using bytes, words and dwords (double words). When copying and pushing memory blocks within the IO.SYS and MSDOS.SYS modules, the following code sequence is used to process the transcription in dwords:

```
MOV CX, NUMBER        ;load number of words to move
SHR CX, 1             ;cut number of words to move in half
DB  66h               ;dword prefix for string command
REP MOVSW             ;copy memory block
```

Since neither the 8088 nor the 80286 processors can perform dword operations, the SHR CX,1 and the DB 66H instructions are simply replaced with NOP instructions when installing the module, if the PC is equipped with a processor other than an 80386.

Chapter 7

The BIOS

BIOS is the abbreviation for Basic Input/Output System. The name indicates that the BIOS provides basic input and output routines for communicating between software and the hardware peripherals such as keyboard, screen and disk drive.

Why the BIOS is important

Since these routine calls are standardized, this saves the programmer the trouble of fitting programs to one particular PC hardware configuration. This means you can develop a program on one PC or compatible, and run it on another compatible PC without errors, even though neither the hardware nor the individual BIOS routines are completely compatible. This hardware independent concept contributed much to the popularity of the PC. It offers the computer manufacturers the ability to develop PCs which aren't quite identical to a true IBM PC, yet can run popular software.

About BIOS functions

BIOS functions occur through the individual routines contained in the *BIOS interrupts* 10H to 17H and 1AH. The processor registers, whose usage is also standardized, transfer data from the calling program to the interrupt and from the interrupt to the calling program.

Number	Meaning
10H	BIOS display function call
11H	Testing the configuration
12H	Testing RAM
13H	BIOS disk functions
14H	Functions for asynchronous communication
15H	Cassette functions
16H	Reading the keyboard

BIOS architecture

The BIOS itself is located in PC ROM, making it resident even after the computer has been turned off. It is stored very high in the processor's address space beginning at address F000:E000. It extends to address F000:FFFF, the last location addressable on the Intel 8088 microprocessor. The BIOS routines must create, store and modify variables, much like any other routine. Since this is impossible in the BIOS area itself, BIOS stores these variables in the lower part of memory starting at address 0040:0000.

This chapter begins with a description of the bootstrap, followed by descriptions of each BIOS function, call and application.

7.1 Booting the System

Section 6.3 described the booting process of DOS. The examination began at the point where the first sector of a diskette or hard disk loads into memory. From the time you switch on the computer to the booting process, a series of events occur. This section describes those interim events.

Initialization

Program execution in a computer based on the Intel 8088 (or one of its successors) starts after the computer is turned on at memory location F000:FFF0. This memory location is part of the ROM-BIOS and contains a jump command to a BIOS routine which takes over system initialization. The location of this routine may differ from one computer to another (actually from BIOS to BIOS) because the BIOS changes internally with each manufacturer. The task this routine performs remains identical for nearly all PCs, however.

System check

First the BIOS tests individual functions of the processor, its registers and some instructions. If an error occurs during this test, the system stops without displaying an error message (this is impossible with a defective processor). If the CPU passes the test, a checksum is computed from each of the ROM's contents and compared with the various ROMs to determine whether a defect exists there. Each chip on the main circuit board (such as the 8259 interrupt, the 8237 DMA controller, and the RAM chips) goes through tests and initialization.

Peripheral testing

After determining the functionality of the main circuit board, the computer tests the peripherals (keyboard, disk drive, etc.). In addition to these hardware related tasks, the BIOS variables and the interrupt vector table must be initialized.

The bootstrap loader

Note that no mention has been made of the operating system so far. It hasn't been loaded into the computer from diskette or hard disk yet. Interrupt 19H, known as the *bootstrap loader*, performs this task on startup or on system reset (when you press the <Alt><Ctrl><Delete> key combination). This routine tries to load some form of the basic operating system from a predetermined place on the diskette.

Reasons for failure

This bootstrap process may fail for a number of reasons:

- There is no disk in the disk drive.
- There is a disk in the drive, but the disk isn't bootable (the DOS files are not available on the diskette). If this occurs, the bootstrap routine

attempts to find the routine on the other disk drives connected to the PC, or on a predetermined location on an existing hard disk.

If the system still cannot find the bootable system disk, there are two other reasons that may be causing a problem:

- Some older systems switch to *ROM BASIC*. This is a small BASIC interpreter stored in PC ROM directly beneath the BIOS starting at memory location F000:6000. New PCs display a message on the screen requesting that the user insert a diskette containing the operating system into the drive.
- BIOS doesn't care what operating system it loads, so it may attempt to load a non-DOS operating system if one exists on the disk. This makes it possible to load other operating systems such as XENIX.

7.2 Determining BIOS Version

The previous section described memory location F000:FFF0 in conjunction with the system startup. Usually a 5-byte-long jump instruction can be found at this location. After this instruction, an additional 11 bytes are available (to F000:FFFF), which are normally used to store the release date of the BIOS version.

You can examine the contents of these memory locations to determine which BIOS version your PC uses. Call the DEBUG program from the DOS prompt:

```
debug
```

Enter the following line to display the bytes at the end of the ROM-BIOS:

```
d f000:fff0 l 10
```

The next line displays the contents of this memory location as a hexadecimal number; the characters to the right of the hex display are the corresponding ASCII codes. Day, month and year appear as two digits separated by "/" characters.

```
C>debug
-d f000:fff0 l 10
F000:FFF0  EA 5B E0 00 F0 30 32 2F-30 36 2F 38 36 00 FC 00   [...02/06/86...
-q
C>_
```

BIOS date display in DEBUG

7.3 Determining the PC Type

Usage of certain BIOS functions are more for model identification than for BIOS version identification. They indicate the type of PC in use. They also indicate when the BIOS has additional functions (e.g., AT BIOS is better equipped than the PC and XT BIOS). These extra functions essentially handle string output on the screen, realtime clock access (standard on the AT) and additional RAM beyond the 1 megabyte memory limit (also standard on the AT).

A program which calls these functions must first ensure that the computer in use is in fact an AT, and that the functions addressed are available. The programmer can use the model identification byte located in the last memory location of the ROM-BIOS at address F000:FFFE. This byte can contain the following codes:

```
252 or FCH:   AT

254 or FEH:   XT and portable PC

255 or FFH:   PC
```

Note: These values aren't entirely accurate. Many PC/XT compatibles indicate completely different values in the model identification byte. The following rule of thumb may be used: A model identification byte of 252 identifies an AT; any other number indicates a PC/XT.

Only IBM computers have guaranteed reliable model identification numbers at memory location F000:FFFE. This may not be the case for compatible computers. Use the DOS program DEBUG to obtain the model identification byte. Call DEBUG with

```
debug
```

Enter the following command sequence:

```
d f000:fffe l 1
```

The model identification appears as a hexadecimal number on the screen.

Access to the model identification byte from programs

The model identification can be obtained directly from a program. Here's a short assembler program to perform that task:

```
IDSeg segment at f000h
      org 0fffeh
      PcID db (?)
IDSeg ends
        .
        .
        .
      push ds                ;store data segment
      mov  ax,IDSeg
      mov  ds,ax             ;Set Data segment to BIOS
```

```
        cmp  PcID,252          ;test if AT-Code
        pop  ds                ;restore Data segment
        je   IstAT
           .
           ;Device is a PC/XT
           .
IstAT label near
           .
           .
           .
```

Higher level languages can also find the identification byte. The following BASIC program uses the PEEK statement for reading the model identification.

```
10 def seg = &hF000
20 if peek(&hFFFE) = 252 then print "AT" else print "PC/XT"
```

Turbo Pascal uses the mem array to read the model identification:

```
begin
  if mem[$F000 : $FFFE] = 252 then writeln('AT')
                             else writeln('PC/XT');
end;
```

How the model identification is used in a program will be demonstrated in the programs later in this chapter.

7.4 BIOS Screen Output Functions

The BIOS contains a series of routines which display data on the screen and maintain other display functions. In addition to the video mode, BIOS manages cursor positioning, text output and graphic display routines. Interrupt 10H calls all these routines. The processor registers transfer the data between the application program and the BIOS interrupt routine.

Under DOS versions 1.0 and 1.1, these BIOS routines were the only options for cursor positioning and color choice. DOS Versions 2.0 and up make these functions available under DOS as well.

More about compatibility

The BIOS routines execute faster than their corresponding DOS routines. Those concerned about compatibility and output device redirection may be better off using DOS routines. In any case, the application itself should dictate which routines will be used.

The BIOS routines, like the DOS routines, offer the programmer the advantage of independence from a particular video card (IBM monochrome, IBM color, Hercules, etc.), since they can be adapted to various cards. Because these cards have different features supported by BIOS, let's look at the capabilities of these cards before examining the routines of interrupt 10H. Programs demonstrating the function calls are listed in BASIC, Turbo Pascal, C and assembly language later in this chapter.

Monochrome display adapter

This card displays a page of 25 lines and 80 columns. Column 0 and line 0 are in the upper left hand corner of the display. The numbering continues to the right and down from column 0, line 0.

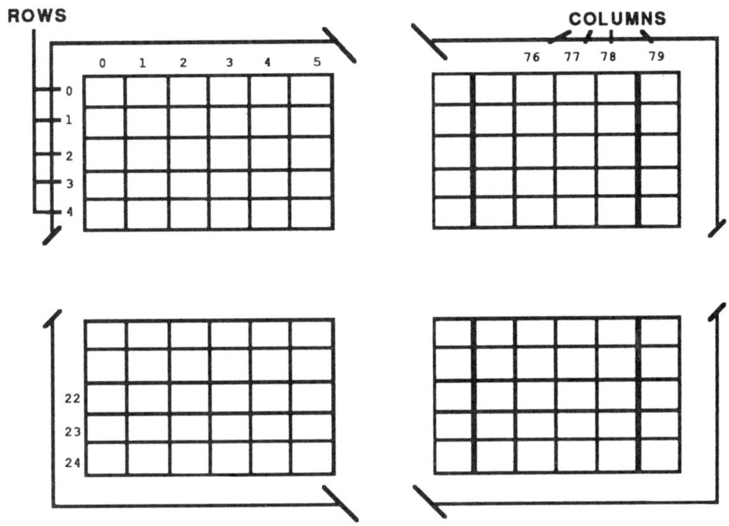

Line and column numbering—monochrome display

Each of the 2000 (80*25) positions on the screen is represented by a character from a set of 256 characters (IBM PC standard character set) and an attribute character, also called an *attribute byte*. Both characters require one byte apiece, so 2000*2 (4000 bytes) of video RAM must be available to display the entire screen. This video RAM exists on the video display card. Since video RAM is not part of the normal RAM, the starting address remains constant at address B000:0000 for the monochrome card.

While the PC systems have standard character sets for all the video cards described here, the attribute bytes change from card to card.

As the figure below shows, bits 0 to 2 and 4 to 6 of the attribute byte defines the foreground and background color of the displayed character.

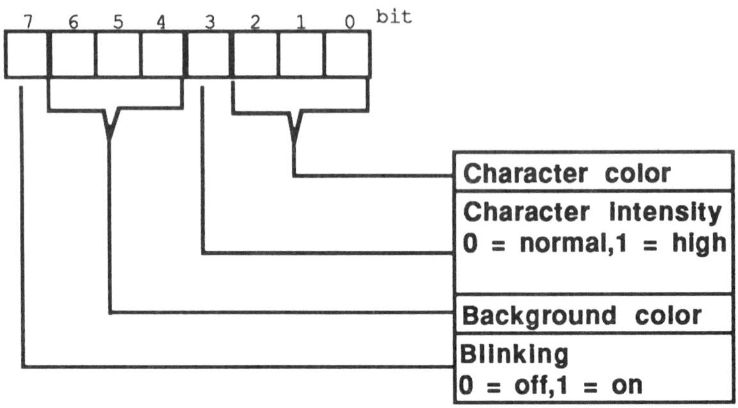

Attribute byte color structure—monochrome display adapter

Bit 3 of the attribute byte indicates the intensity of the foreground color. If it contains a 1, the character appears in high intensity. Bit 8 indicates whether the character on the screen should blink (a 1 in this bit causes the character to blink). While these bits can be set in any manner, only bit combinations which "look good" should be used for foreground and background color.

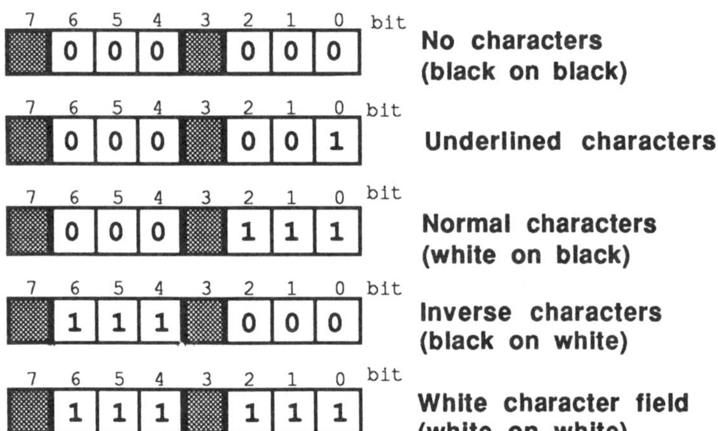

Colors and attribute byte—monochrome display adapter

Color graphics adapter (CGA)

This card offers text display of the IBM PC standard character set and various graphic modes. Text mode works with a resolution of either 80x25 or 40x25 characters. 40x25 resolution displays characters in double width. This mode allows the management of up to eight different video pages (80x25 mode allows up to four different pages). The line and column number assignment is similar to the monochrome display card.

CGA attribute bytes

The attribute byte used on this card mainly selects foreground and background colors of the characters. A total of 16 colors is available. The first eight of these may be used as background colors.

Binary	Dec.	Color
0000(b)	0	Black
0001(b)	1	Blue
0010(b)	2	Green
0011(b)	3	Turquoise
0100(b)	4	Red
0101(b)	5	Magenta
0110(b)	6	Brown (dark yellow on some monitors)
0111(b)	7	Light Gray (sometimes white)
1000(b)	8	Dark Gray (or black)
1001(b)	9	Light Blue
1010(b)	10	Light Green
1011(b)	11	Light Turquoise
1100(b)	12	Light Red
1101(b)	13	Light Magenta
1110(b)	14	Yellow (also light yellow)
1111(b)	15	White

As the figure below shows, bits 0 to 3 of the attribute bytes represent the foreground color, while bits 4 to 6 indicate the background color. Bit 7 means the same as in the monochrome display card: it decides whether the character should blink.

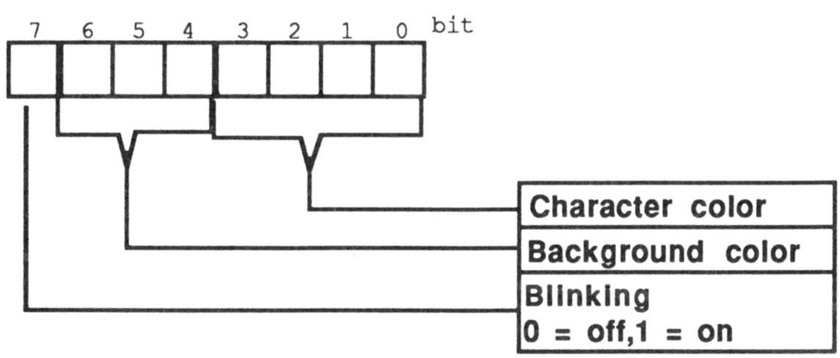

Attribute byte structure—color graphic adapter

This card can emulate a monochrome display card (see above) in which the attribute character has the same meaning as in the monochrome card, with the exception that no underlined characters can be produced.

Graphic modes and the CGA

Graphic modes can have either a resolution of 640x200 dots with 2 colors or 320x200 dots with 4 colors. In both modes the upper left corner of the screen has the coordinates 0/0.

No attribute byte exists in this mode since every dot on the display is either illuminated with a color or not, and not composed of standard characters from a character set. To display characters from the standard character set in this mode, they must be drawn on the screen with *pixels* (dots).

In 320x200 resolution, one of the 16 available colors can be defined as a background color. The foreground color must be one of three colors in a palette predetermined by the graphic card. Two palettes are normally available: One contains the colors cyan, magenta and white, while the other offers the colors green, red and yellow.

The video RAM of this card starts at location B800:0000 (unlike the monochrome display card which starts at B000:0000). This ensures that the video RAMs of the two cards do not overlap. They can be used in parallel with each displaying data on its own monitor.

Hercules graphic cards

The Hercules graphic card has the same text mode as the IBM monochrome display adapter, and can display two video pages of text at a time. A Hercules card also offers a graphic mode in which two video pages can be displayed with a resolution of 720x348 pixels. Unfortunately, the BIOS cannot access either the two video pages or the graphic mode. BIOS treats this card like a normal monochrome card, which can only display one text page of 80x25 characters.

Now that you have some general knowledge of graphic adapters, here are the functions called from interrupt 10H:

Decimal	Hex	Meaning
0	0H	Determine Video mode
1	1H	Define cursor size
2	2H	Determine cursor position
3	3H	Sense cursor position
4	4H	Read light pen
5	5H	Define current display page
6	6H	Scroll display up
7	7H	Scroll display down
8	8H	Read character / attribute at cursor position
9	9H	Write character / attribute at cursor position
10	AH	Write character at cursor position
11	BH	Determine color palette for graphic mode
12	CH	Set display point in graphic mode
13	DH	Sense display point in graphic mode

Decimal	Hex	Meaning
14	EH	Character output (like a terminal)
15	FH	Determine video mode
19	13H	Write character string (only available on AT)

As always, the processor registers pass the function arguments. Some common rules define which registers accept which arguments:

The AH register indicates the number of the function to be called with interrupt 10H. If character should be displayed, or a dot placed on the screen in graphic mode, its value passes to the AL register.

Hercules functions

If the function expects display coordinates for text mode, the X-coordinate (column) must be loaded into the DL and the Y-coordinate (line) into the DH register. In graphic mode the CX register accepts the X-coordinate and the DX register the Y-coordinate. The number of the display page (if required) should be contained in the BH register.

It is important for assembler programmers that the contents of the BX, CX, DX and the contents of the segment registers remain the same before *and after* the interrupt call. The contents of all other registers may change.

Function 0H: Set video mode

Before sending output to the screen, the video mode must be selected. The current video mode in use might not be the one you desire. Function 0 of interrupt 10H performs this task and also selects the active video card in case the PC has several video cards connected. For a call to this function through interrupt 10H, the AH register must contain function number 0 and the AL register must contain the number of the video mode to be activated. Of course only those video modes that are supported by the video card in the PC can be activated. The following numbers correspond to the various video modes (the video card supporting the mode is in parentheses):

0	40*25 character monochrome text display	(Color)
1	40*25 character color text display	(Color)
2	80*25 character monochrome text display	(Mono)
3	80*25 character color text display	(Color)
4	320*200 pixel graphics with 4 colors	(Color)
5	320*200 pixel graphics with 4 colors but shown monochrome	(Color)
6	640*200 pixel graphics with 2 colors	(Color)

The mode makes no difference on a monochrome card, since only one mode exists (80x25); this mode is constantly active. It uses the internal designation number of 7.

Function 0FH: Get video mode

The opposite of this function is function 0FH, which determines the current video mode. A value of 0FH in the AH register during a call to interrupt 10H executes this function. It returns the value of the video mode (refer to the table above) in the AL register. As mentioned above, a monochrome card always returns the value 7. Besides the video mode, the number of columns per display line in this mode (40 or 80) returns in the AH register and the current display page number in the BH register.

Function 02H: Set cursor position

After the video mode initialization, screen output can begin. Function 2 defines the cursor position. Calling this function places the blinking cursor in the desired location on the screen. This sets the starting position of character display. Prior to calling this function the AH register should be loaded with the function number (2), the DH register with the line location of the cursor, and the DL register with the column location of the cursor. The BH register holds the display page onto which the cursor should be positioned. Remember that every display page has its own cursor for positioning the text output, but only one active or blinking display cursor exists. This active cursor always appears on the currently displayed page. Function 2 moves the active cursor if the value in the BH register corresponds to the current screen page.

Function 03H: Read cursor position

The counterpart of this function is function 03H. It reads the current cursor position of a selected display page and returns the position to the calling program. At the call of this function the AL register must contain the function number (3) and the BH register the number of the display page whose cursor position is being read.

Monochrome display cards return a value of 0, since the card can only display one page (numbered 0). After the call of interrupt 10H the DH register contains the cursor position's line and the DL register the cursor position's column. In addition, two values are returned to the CH and CL registers which have special significance. They indicate the starting and ending raster scan (pixel) lines of the cursor. These lines are independent of the displayed page.

To understand this significance, it is important to know that every text mode character on color and monochrome cards have heights of 8 and 14 pixels per character, respectively. The programmer can choose at which of these pixel lines the blinking cursor begins and at which it stops.

These values must of course remain within the legal values of the individual video cards (i.e., 0 to 7 for a color card and 0 to 13 for a monochrome card), otherwise the blinking text cursor may disappear from the screen.

Function 01H: Define cursor size

While these values are read with the help of function 3, function 1 is used to set these values. The AH register loads with a 1, the CH register with the starting line of the cursor, and the CL register with the ending line of the cursor, before calling interrupt 10H. The starting line must be smaller than or equal to the ending line, or the cursor becomes invisible.

Function 05H: Set active display page

This book has frequently mentioned the *current display page* without telling how to activate this page. Function 05H of interrupt 10H performs this task. Place a value of 5 in the AH register and the number of the page you want activated (displayed on the monitor) in the AL register. The number of the page to activate depends on how many pages are available in the current video card and video mode. Since the monochrome video card offers only one display page, using this function with a monochrome card makes no sense at all. The following values are allowed for the color card's different video modes:

```
0 to 7 (40*25 character text display [Color-card])
0 to 3 (80*25 character text display [Color-Card])
```

After selecting the video mode and moving the cursor to the desired location on the screen, one or more characters are output on the screen in most cases. BIOS makes various functions available which have different abilities in providing character display on the screen. One difference between these functions is that they process *control codes* in various ways. These control codes are the ASCII codes 7, 8, 10 and 13. They represent the following:

7	Bell	produces a sound
8	Backspace	erases preceding character & moves cursor back one character position
10	Linefeed	moves cursor one line down
13	Carriage return	moves cursor to start of current line

Some functions view these codes as normal ASCII characters and execute them accordingly. Other functions see them as control codes. For example, code 7 produces a sound with some functions. The choice of which function to use depends on which control code processing is desired.

Text display in graphic mode

Text display functions can be used in both text and graphic modes. Text output in graphic mode creates different characters since the characters must be drawn on the screen from pixels. The PC uses ASCII codes to set the graphic pixels. While the character samples for the ASCII codes 0 to 127 are already stored in the ROM, the character patterns for the codes 128 to 255 must be read from a table in RAM. This table installs itself in RAM when you execute the DOS GRAFTABL command.

BIOS obtains the address of this table from the memory locations 0000:007C to 0000:007F, where the table's offset address lies in the lower two bytes and the table's segment address in the upper two bytes. These memory locations are inside the interrupt vector table but can be used for this purpose since interrupt 1FH (whose address normally appears there) remains unused.

Having this table stored in RAM makes it possible to define your own table, so that special characters which are not contained in the standard character set can be displayed on the screen. Since every character is comprised of 8 bytes, the first 8 bytes of the table are reserved for ASCII code 128, the next 8 for the code 129, etc. Each byte contains the bit pattern for one of the 8 lines which compose a character. Bit 0 represents the dot on the right border of the character matrix, bit 7 the dot on the left border. If you set a bit to 1, this illuminates the corresponding pixel on the screen.

Function 09H: Write character with attribute
Function 0AH: Write character

Functions 09H and 0AH are available for character output. Function 0AH displays the character in the color determined by the attribute corresponding to that particular screen position. Function 09H sets the color (attribute) of the character to be displayed. Neither function moves the cursor to the next screen position after character display. Character output resumes at the same location on the next function call. Function 02H must be called to move the cursor to the next screen position for displaying readable text.

Determining the function call

Both functions 09H and 0AH interpret the control codes described above as normal characters and display them accordingly. During the call of these functions the contents of the AH register depend on whether the user called function 09H and 0AH. The AL register accepts the ASCII code of the character to be displayed. The display page for character display can be found in the BH register. The CX register contains a number which indicates how many times the character should be displayed. Because of this, it's possible to display a character several times with just one interrupt call (this saves time and memory). If you want the character in the AL register displayed only once, a 1 must be stored in the CX register during the function call. Since function 09H also determines the color of the character to be output, the BL register passes the character color.

Function 0EH: Teletype mode

A serious disadvantage of these two functions is that the cursor's position does not advance after the function call. Function 0EH cures this problem. It acts like a terminal, hence its name—the TTY (Teletype output) routine. The cursor advances to the next screen position after a character is displayed. If the cursor reaches the end of the screen line, it moves to the beginning of the following line. If the cursor is in the last display screen position (line 24, column 79), the entire screen is scrolled one line upward and the top line of the screen disappears from the display area. In addition, the function clears line 24 and the cursor moves to the beginning of the line.

Another approach to control codes

Unlike functions 09H and 0AH, function 0EH treats control codes according to their functions, and not as normal ASCII codes. Like function 0AH, characters are displayed by function 0EH using the character color (attribute) already present at that screen location. This is valid for text mode only. In graphic mode, the foreground color must be passed in the BL register.

Prior to the function call, the AH register must be loaded with function number 0EH, the AL register loaded with the code of the character to be displayed and the BH register with the display page intended for character display.

Function 08H: Read character/attribute

While functions 09H, 0AH and 0EH display characters on the screen, function 08H makes it possible to read characters from the screen, i.e., to sense the character and attribute displayed. Before the call, the value 08 must be loaded into the AH register and the number of the display page from which the character should be loaded into the BH register. The display position from which the character should be read is the current cursor position in the display page indicated by the BH register.

In text mode the character code can be read directly from video RAM. However, graphic mode requires a comparison between the bit pattern at the current cursor position and every character's bit pattern in the character set.

After the function call, the AH register contains the attribute (color) and the AL register contains the ASCII code of the character read.

Function 06H: Scroll window up

Function 06H scrolls the screen up one or more lines, or clears sections of the screen by displaying spaces (ASCII code 32). These operations can only be performed on the current display page. To call this function, you must load the AH register with the function number (6). The AL register is loaded with the number of lines the display should be moved up. A 0 in this register instructs the function to fill the screen area with spaces instead of scrolling the screen. The BH register contains the color (attribute) for the blank line. The CH, CL, DH and DL registers define the display page window to be scrolled or cleared. The C register represents the upper left corner of the window, while the D register defines the lower right corner of the window. The following list illustrates the meaning of each register:

Reg	Meaning
CH	Line of the upper left corner of the window
CL	Column of the upper left corner of the window
DH	Line of the lower right corner of the window
DL	Column of the lower right corner of the window

Function 07H: Scroll window down

Function 07H scrolls the screen down one or more lines, or clears sections of the screen by displaying spaces (ASCII code 32). These operations can only be performed on the current display page. To call this function, you must load the AH register with the function number (7). The AL register is loaded with the number of lines the display should be moved down. A 0 in this register instructs the function to fill the screen area with spaces instead of scrolling the screen. The BH register contains the color (attribute) for the blank line. The CH, CL, DH and DL registers define the display page window to be scrolled or cleared. The C register represents the upper left corner of the window, while the D register defines the lower right corner of the window. The following list illustrates the meaning of each register:

Reg	Meaning
CH	Line of the upper left corner of the window
CL	Column of the upper left corner of the window
DH	Line of the lower right corner of the window
DL	Column of the lower right corner of the window

Graphic functions

The following are descriptions of the functions used in the different graphic modes. They can be used in connection with video cards capable of producing graphics.

Function 00H: Set video mode

Function 00H switches on one of the available graphic modes. The border color (or color palette) should then be selected for the 320x200 (or text) mode by loading function number 0AH in the AH register. The BH register dictates the use of the border color or the color palette. If during the function call the BH register contains a 0, the value in the BL register becomes the background and border color for the graphic mode. All 16 colors are available, so the BL register can contain a value between 0 and 15. This function remains valid for the text mode. However, only the border color can be set. The background color for each character is set individually by the top 4 bits of the color attribute, and therefore cannot be set for everything.

If the BH register contains a 1, the value in the BL register (0 or 1) selects the active color palette. The palettes contain the following colors:

0	Green, red, yellow
1	Cyan, magenta, white

Function 0BH: Set color palette

Once the graphic mode initializes and the colors are selected, graphic drawing can begin. Function 0BH writes graphic pixels at specified locations of the screen. The pixel coordinates to be addressed are passed in the CX and DX registers. The values in these registers depend on the graphic resolution of the current graphic mode. The CX register contains the X-coordinate (column coordinate) of the pixel, and the DX register the Y-coordinate (line coordinate) of the pixel. The function call must have the function number (0BH) passed in the AH register. The color value of the pixel to be manipulated is passed in the AL register. The Hercules card and the 640x200 mode of the color card permit the values 0 and 1 only. In the 320x200 mode of the color card, the values 0 to 3 are allowed for the 4 possible colors. The significance of these values depends on the active color palette. If a program enables palette 0, the values have the following significance:

0	Color selected for background with function 0BH
1	Green
2	Red
3	Yellow

An active palette 1 changes the values slightly:

0	Color selected for background with function 0BH
1	Cyan
2	Magenta
3	White

Function 0DH: Read pixel

Function 0DH is the equivalent of this function, which determines the color value of a pixel. Before the call, the value 0DH must be passed in the AH register, the X-coordinates of the pixel must be loaded into the CX register, and the Y-coordinates into the DX register. The pixel color is returned as a result in the AL register. This value corresponds to the rules described in function 0BH.

Function 13H: Write string

Interrupt 10H includes another function on AT computers. Function 13H displays strings of characters on the screen. During its call a series of arguments must be passed, in addition to passing the function number to the AH register. The BH register accepts the number of the display page on which the string should be displayed (not necessarily the current display page). The starting position of the character string on the display is in the DH (line) register and the DL register (column). The CX register contains the number of characters in the character string.

The AL register's contents define one of the four possible modes in which the character string can be displayed. The string format in modes 0 and 1 differ from string format in modes 2 and 3. Modes 2 and 3 place attribute bytes after every character in the string. In modes 0 and 1, the individual characters of the string follow one another in sequence. The attribute byte for all characters depends on the contents of the BL register. In modes 2 and 3, 2 bytes are stored in the string for every character displayed. For example, a character string of 4 characters requires 8 bytes of memory. The number of characters to be displayed (4 characters in this example) must be indicated in the CX register. Another difference between modes 0 and 2 and modes 1 and 3 is in display format. After the string display in modes 1 and 3, the cursor appears following the last character of the string. The next character displayed with one of the BIOS functions then appears at this position on the screen. The cursor position does not get updated in modes 0 and 2.

Demonstration programs

The following programs demonstrate the use of BIOS video interrupt functions available from higher level languages. In Pascal and C, you'll find that using BIOS display functions works much faster than the standard procedures and functions provided in these languages, which use the slower DOS functions. BASIC's use of BIOS screen functions is minimal, since these functions are even slower than the BASIC PRINT statement.

Advantage

Accessing BIOS video interrupt functions has an advantage over the use of onboard graphic commands in higher level languages: the BIOS functions can be accessed at any time.

Disadvantage

There is a serious disadvantage to using BIOS functions for screen output. The higher level language display commands can accept numerical variables, which are then converted to ASCII characters. These higher level commands can format the variables according to decimal places or a certain degree of precision, then display these variables. However, if numerical variables are to be displayed using the BIOS functions, they must first be converted into a character string which you must transfer to the BIOS output function. This procedure takes time.

All three programs are identical in function. Each fills the screen with continuous characters from the PC character set, then opens two windows in which two arrows move up and down. How this was done, and how it will actually appear on the screen, should become clear after you take a closer look at the program codes. The programs limit their access to one video page, due to incompatibility problems that could occur between monochrome and color cards. They also do not present subroutines, functions or procedures for calling the BIOS graphic functions.

Once you understand this section you should be able to easily add the missing functions and even write a short demo program of your own. Using BIOS video interrupt assures that the computer will not crash and that nothing major can go wrong.

BASIC listing: VIDEOB.BAS

```
100 '**********************************************************************'
110 '*                          V I D E O B                      BAS   *'
120 '*----------------------------------------------------------------*'
130 '*  Task          : Makes some Subroutines available for access    *'
140 '*                  to the Display using the BIOS-Video-Interrupt *'
150 '*                                                                 *'
160 '*  Author        : MICHAEL TISCHER                                *'
170 '*  developed on  : 07/18/87                                       *'
180 '*  last Update   : 05/14/89                                       *'
190 '**********************************************************************'
200 '
210 CLS : KEY OFF
220 PRINT"WARNING: This Program should only be started if GWBASIC was "
```

```
230 PRINT"started from the DOS level with <GWBASIC  /m:60000>. "
240 PRINT : PRINT"If this was not the case enter <s> for Stop."
250 PRINT"Otherwise press any key...";
260 A$ = INKEY$ : IF A$ = "s" THEN END
270 IF A$ = "" THEN 260
280 CLS
290 GOSUB 60000                    'Install function for interrupt call
300 PAGE%=0                      'Display page for the output is Page 0
310 COLRR%=7                        'light characters on dark background
320 FOR DISPROW%=1 TO 24                 'process all display lines
330   FOR DISPCOL%=0 TO 79              'process all display columns
340     CHARACTER$=CHR$((DISPCOL%+DISPROW%*80) AND 255)'continuous code
350     GOSUB 52000                             'Set cursor position
360     GOSUB 57000                               'Output character
370   NEXT                                           'next column
380 NEXT                                               'next line
390 VALUE%=0                                        'Erase Window
400 ULC%=5 : ULR%=8 : LRC%=19 : LLR%=22   'Coordinates of the 1. Window
410 GOSUB 55000                                     'Erase Window
420 ULC%=60 : ULR%=2 : LRC%=74 : LLR%=16  'Coordinates of the 2. Window
430 GOSUB 55000                                     'Erase Window
440 COLRR%=&H70          'dark letters on light background (inverse)
450 DISPCOL%=5 : DISPROW%=8             'Coordinates for Text output
460 T$="   Window 1   "                          'Text for output
470 GOSUB 58000                                    'Output Text
480 DISPCOL%=60 : DISPROW%=2            'Coordinates for text output
490 T$="   Window 2   "                          'Text for output
500 GOSUB 58000                                    'Output Text
510 DISPROW%=0 : DISPCOL%=0              'upper left Display corner
520 T$=STRING$(23," ")+"Arrow number__ is being drawn "+STRING$(23," ")
530 GOSUB 58000                                    'Output Text
540 COLRR%=&HF0      'dark chars on light background (inverse) blinking
550 DISPCOL%=24 : DISPROW%=12           'Coordinates for Text output
560 T$=" >>> PC SYSTEM PROGRAMMING <<< "          'Text for output
570 GOSUB 58000                                    'Output Text
580 VALUE%=1                                'always scroll one line
590 FOR ARROWS%=4 TO 0 STEP -1           'Output total of 10 Arrows
600 DISPCOL%=35: DISPROW%=0           'Position for number of Arrows
610 COLRR%=&H70        'dark characters on light background (inverse)
620 T$=STR$(ARROWS%)        'Convert number of Arrows into ASCII-String
630   GOSUB 58000                                  'Output Text
640   COLRR%=7                      'light characters on dark background
650   FOR COUNTL%=1 TO 8              'an Arrow consists of 8 Lines
660     DISPCOL%=5 : DISPROW%=9        'Coordinates in first Window
670     T$=STRING$(8-COUNTL%," ")+STRING$(2*COUNTL%-1,"*")+STRING$(8-COUNTL%," ")
680     GOSUB 58000                             'Output Arrow line
690     DISPCOL%=60 : DISPROW%=16      'Coordinates in second Window
700     GOSUB 58000                             'Output arrow line
710     ULC%=5 : ULR%=9 : LRC%=19: LLR%=22    'Coordinates of 1. Window
720     VALUE%=1                               'scroll one DISPROW
730     GOSUB 56000                            'Scroll Window down
740     ULC%=60 : ULR%=3 : LRC%=74: LLR%=16   'Coordinates of 2. Window
750     VALUE%=1                                 'Scroll one Line
760     GOSUB 55000                             'Scroll Window up
770   NEXT                                     'next Arrow Line
780 NEXT                                            'next Arrow
790 CLS
800 KEY ON
810 END
820 '
50000 '**************************************************************'
50010 '* Sense Video mode and other Parameters                      *'
50020 '*------------------------------------------------------------*'
50030 '* Input  : none                                              *'
50040 '* Output : VMODE%   = the current Video mode                 *'
50050 '*          PAGE%    = the current Display page               *'
50060 '*          DISPCOL% = the number of Columns per Line         *'
50070 '* Info   : the Variable Z% is used as Dummy                  *'
50080 '**************************************************************'
50090 '
```

```
50100 DISPCOL%=15                     'Get Function number for Video mode
50110 INR%=&H10                        'Call BIOS-Video-Interrupt 16(h)
50120 CALL IA(INR%,DISPCOL%,VMODE%,PAGE%,Z%,Z%,Z%,Z%,Z%,Z%,Z%,Z%,Z%)
50130 RETURN                                             'back to caller
50140 '
51000 '**************************************************************'
51010 '* Define appearance of blinking Text-Cursor                  *'
51020 '*------------------------------------------------------------*'
51030 '* Input : BEGLIN% = is the beginning Line of the Text-Cursor  *'
51040 '*         ENDL%   = is the End Line of the Text-Cursor        *'
51050 '* Output: none                                               *'
51060 '* Info  : the Variable Z% is used as Dummy                    *'
51070 '**************************************************************'
51080 '
51090 FKT%=1                'Set Function number for appearance of Cursor
51100 INR%=&H10                        'Call BIOS-Video-Interrupt 16(h)
51110 CALL IA(INR%,FKT%,Z%,Z%,Z%,BEGLIN%,ENDL%,Z%,Z%,Z%,Z%,Z%,Z%)
51120 RETURN                                             'back to caller
51130 '
52000 '**************************************************************'
52010 '* Set Cursor Position                                        *'
52020 '*------------------------------------------------------------*'
52030 '* Input  : PAGE%    = is the Number of the Display page       *'
52040 '*          DISPCOL% = is the new Column of the Cursor         *'
52050 '*          DISPROW% = is the new Row of the Cursor            *'
52060 '* Output : none                                              *'
52070 '* Info   : The position of the blinking Text-Cursor is only   *'
52080 '*          influenced by the call of this subroutine if the   *'
52090 '*          Display page indicated is the current Display page *'
52100 '*                                                            *'
52110 '*          the Variable Z% is used as Dummy                   *'
52120 '**************************************************************'
52130 '
52140 FKT%=2                     'Set Function number for Cursor position
52150 INR%=&H10                        'Call BIOS-Video-Interrupt 16(h)
52160 CALL IA(INR%,FKT%,Z%,PAGE%,Z%,Z%,Z%,DISPROW%,DISPCOL%,Z%,Z%,Z%,Z%)
52170 RETURN                                             'back to caller
52180 '
53000 '**************************************************************'
53010 '* Read Cursor Position and Beginning and End Row             *'
53020 '* of the blinking Text-Cursor                                *'
53030 '*------------------------------------------------------------*'
53040 '* Input : PAGE%    = is the Number of the Display page        *'
53050 '* Output: DISPCOL% = Column of the Cursor in the Display page *'
53060 '*         DISPROW% = Row of the Cursor in the Display page    *'
53070 '*         BEGLIN%  = beginning Line of the Text-Cursor        *'
53080 '*         ENDL%    = is the End Line of the Text-Cursor       *'
53090 '* Info  : the Variable Z% is used as Dummy                    *'
53100 '**************************************************************'
53110 FKT%=3                    'Read Function number for Cursor position
53120 INR%=&H10                        'Call BIOS-Video-Interrupt 16(h)
53130 CALL IA(INR%,FKT%,Z%,PAGE%,Z%,BEGLIN%,ENDL%,DISPROW%, DISPCOL%,Z%,Z%,Z%,Z%)
53140 RETURN                                             'back to caller
53150 '
54000 '**************************************************************'
54010 '* Set the current display page on the                        *'
54020 '* screen                                                     *'
54030 '*------------------------------------------------------------*'
54040 '* Input : PAGE% = is the Number of the Display page           *'
54050 '* Output: none                                               *'
54060 '* Info  : the Variable Z% is used as Dummy                    *'
54070 '**************************************************************'
54080 FKT%=5                        'Set Function number for Display page
54090 INR%=&H10                        'Call BIOS-Video-Interrupt 16(h)
54100 CALL IA(INR%,FKT%,PAGE%,Z%,Z%,Z%,Z%,Z%,Z%,Z%,Z%,Z%,Z%)
54110 RETURN                                             'back to caller
54120 '
55000 '**************************************************************'
55010 '* Scroll current Display page up or erase                    *'
55020 '*------------------------------------------------------------*'
```

```
55030 '* Input : VALUE%  = how many Lines to scroll                *'
55040 '*         ULC%    = Column upper left                       *'
55050 '*         ULR%    = Row upper left                          *'
55060 '*         LRC%    = Column lower right                      *'
55070 '*         LLR%    = Row lower right                         *'
55080 '*         COLRR%  = COLRR of erased Lines                   *'
55090 '* Output: none                                              *'
55100 '* Info  : If VALUE% 0 is indicated, the                     *'
55110 '*         Display area is erased                            *'
55120 '*         the Variable Z% is used as Dummy                  *'
55130 '*************************************************************'
55140 '
55150 FKT%=6                          'Function number for scrolling up
55160 INR%=&H10                        'Call BIOS-Video-Interrupt 16(h)
55170 CALL IA(INR%,FKT%,VALUE%,COLRR%,Z%,ULR%,ULC%,LLR%,LRC%, Z%,Z%,Z%,Z%)
55180 RETURN                                            'back to caller
55190 '
56000 '*************************************************************'
56010 '* Scroll current Display Page down or erase                 *'
56020 '*-----------------------------------------------------------*'
56030 '* Input : VALUE%  = how many Lines to scroll                *'
56040 '*         ULC%    = Column upper left                       *'
56050 '*         ULR%    = Row upper left                          *'
56060 '*         LRC%    = Column lower right                      *'
56070 '*         LLR%    = Row lower right                         *'
56080 '*         COLRR%  = COLRR of erased Lines                   *'
56090 '* Output: none                                              *'
56100 '* Info  : If VALUE% 0 is indicated, the                     *'
56110 '*         Display area is erased                            *'
56120 '*         The Variable Z% is used as Dummy                  *'
56130 '*************************************************************'
56140 '
56150 FKT%=7                        'Function number for scrolling down
56160 GOTO 55160                   'Call is identical with scrolling up
56170 '
57000 '*************************************************************'
57010 '* Write a character of a designated COLRR to the current     *'
57020 '* Cursor position in the designated Display Page            *'
57030 '*-----------------------------------------------------------*'
57040 '* Input : CHARACTER$ = the character for output             *'
57050 '*         COLRR%     = COLRR of the character for output    *'
57060 '*         PAGE%      = is the Number of the Display page    *'
57070 '* Output: none                                              *'
57080 '* Info  : the Variables ZL%, ZH% and ZE% are Dummies        *'
57090 '*************************************************************'
57100 '
57110 FKT%=9       'Output function numbers for character and Attribute
57120 INR%=&H10                        'Call BIOS-Video-Interrupt 16(h)
57130 ZL%=1                     'Output character only once (LO-Byte)
57140 ZH%=0                     'Output character only once (HI-Byte)
57150 ZE%=ASC(CHARACTER$)      'Get ASCII-Code of character to be output
57160 CALL IA(INR%,FKT%,ZE%,PAGE%,COLRR%,ZH%,ZL%,ZL%, ZL%,ZL%,ZL%,ZL%,ZL%)
57170 RETURN                                            'back to caller
57180 '
58000 '*************************************************************'
58010 '* Output a String starting at a certain Position within a   *'
58020 '* Display page with a constant Attribute                    *'
58030 '*-----------------------------------------------------------*'
58040 '* Input : T$        = the String for output                 *'
58050 '*         COLRR%    = COLRR of the String (Attribute)       *'
58060 '*         PAGE%     = is the number of the Display page     *'
58070 '*         DISPCOL% = Column - start of String               *'
58080 '*         DISPROW% = Row - start of String                  *'
58090 '* Output: none                                              *'
58100 '* Info  : the Variables ZC% and ZE% are Dummies             *'
58110 '*************************************************************'
58120 '
58130 GOSUB 52000                      'Set Cursor position for Output
58140 FOR ZC%=1 TO LEN(T$)   'process all chars or strings individually
58150   CHARACTER$=" "                              'output a blank first
```

```
58160   GOSUB 57000
58170   ZE%=ASC(MID$(T$,ZC%,1))        'Get a character from the String
58180   FKT%=14                    'Function number for Teletype-Output
58190   CALL IA(INR%,FKT%,ZE%,PAGE%,Z%,Z%,Z%,Z%,Z%,Z%,Z%,Z%,Z%)
58200 NEXT                                       'Output next character
58210 RETURN                                             'back to caller
58220 '
60000 '***************************************************************'
60010 '*  initialize the Routine for the Interrupt call              *'
60020 '*-------------------------------------------------------------*'
60030 '* Input : none                                                *'
60040 '* Output: IA is the Start address of the Interrupt-Routine    *'
60050 '***************************************************************'
60060 '
60070 IA=60000!        'Start address of the Routine in the BASIC-Segment
60080 DEF SEG                                       'Set BASIC Segment
60090 RESTORE 60130
60100 FOR I% = 0 TO 160 : READ X% : POKE IA+I%,X% : NEXT  'poke Routine
60110 RETURN                                             'back to caller
60120 '
60130 DATA   85,139,236, 30,  6,139,118, 30,139,  4,232,140,  0,139,118
60140 DATA   12,139, 60,139,118,  8,139,  4, 61,255,255,117,  2,140,216
60150 DATA  142,192,139,118, 28,138, 36,139,118, 26,138,  4,139,118, 24
60160 DATA  138, 60,139,118, 22,138, 28,139,118, 20,138, 44,139,118, 18
60170 DATA  138, 12,139,118, 16,138, 52,139,118, 14,138, 20,139,118, 10
60180 DATA  139, 52, 85,205, 33, 93, 86,156,139,118, 12,137, 60,139,118
60190 DATA   28,136, 36,139,118, 26,136,  4,139,118, 24,136, 60,139,118
60200 DATA   22,136, 28,139,118, 20,136, 44,139,118, 18,136, 12,139,118
60210 DATA   16,136, 52,139,118, 14,136, 20,139,118,  8,140,192,137,  4
60220 DATA   88,139,118,  6,137,  4, 88,139,118, 10,137,  4,  7, 31, 93
60230 DATA  202, 26,  0, 91, 46,136, 71, 66,233,108,255
```

The program can be divided into three parts. Lines 100 to 700 represent the demonstration program proper, which uses the subroutines in lines 50000 to 58220. These subroutines call a special function of the BIOS video interrupt and access the routine for interrupt calls as described earlier. The program DATA begins on line 60000.

See the header of each subroutine for the variables of each subroutine and what each variable does.

It should be noted that all subroutines receive and return numerical values as integer variables. Do not forget the percentage character after a variable. In certain cases a real variable of the same name can be initialized, but the subroutine expected an integer variable and the wrong parameters will be passed to the BIOS function.

Pascal and C implementations

The individual functions and procedures of the next two programs are fully documented and should be self-explanatory. The two programs resemble each other strongly, since the procedures, functions and variables have the same names.

Pascal listing: VIDEOP.PAS

```
{**********************************************************************}
{*                          V I D E O P                     PASCAL  *}
{*------------------------------------------------------------------*}
{*    Task          : makes functions available which are            *}
{*                    based on the BIOS-Video-Interrupt but are not  *}
{*                    provided by PASCAL                             *}
{*------------------------------------------------------------------*}
{*    Author         : MICHAEL TISCHER                                *}
{*    developed on   : 07/10/87                                       *}
{*    last Update    : 05/14/89                                       *}
{**********************************************************************}

program VIDEOP;


Uses Crt, Dos;                        { Adds DOS and CRT units to Turbo }

const NORMAL        = $07;          { Definition of character-attribute }
      BOLD          = $0f;          { in relation to a monochrome       }
      INVERS        = $70;          { Display card                      }
      UNDERLINE     = $01;
      BLINK         = $80;

type  TextTyp = string[80];

var  i,                            { Loop variable for the Main program }
     j,
     k,
     l       : integer;
     IString : string[2];                   { accepts number of Arrows }

{**********************************************************************}
{* GETVIDEOMODE: Read current Video mode and Parameters              *}
{* Input       : none                                                 *}
{* Output      : The Variables listed below get the values after the *}
{*               call of the Procedure                                *}
{**********************************************************************}

procedure GetVideoMode(var VideoMode,  { Number of current Video mode }
                           Number,       { Number of Columns per Line }
                           Page   : integer);  { current display page }

var Regs : Registers;         { Register-Variable for call of Interrupt }

begin
 Regs.ah := $0F;                                     { Function number }
 intr($10, Regs);                              { Call BIOS-Video-Interrupt }
 VideoMode := Regs.al;                         { Number of Video mode }
 Number := Regs.ah;                  { Number of characters per line }
 Page := Regs.bh;           { Number of the current display page }
end;

{**********************************************************************}
{* SETCURSORTYPE: defines the appearance of the blinking             *}
{*                Display cursor                                      *}
{* Input        : see below                                           *}
{* Output       : none                                                *}
{* Info         : for a monochrome display card the parameters        *}
{*                can be between 0 and 13, for a color display        *}
{*                card between 0 and 7                                *}
{**********************************************************************}

procedure SetCursorType(Beginline,      { Beginning line of the cursor }
                        Endl     : integer);  { End line of the cursor }

var Regs : Registers;        { Register variable for the interrupt call }
```

```
begin
 Regs.ah := 1;                                    { Function number }
 Regs.ch := Beginline;                            { Beginning and }
 Regs.cl := Endl;                                      { End line }
 intr($10, Regs);                      { Call BIOS-Video-Interrupt }
end;

{*******************************************************************}
{* SETCURSORPOS: defines the position of the cursor in the         *}
{*               display page output                               *}
{* Input        : see below                                        *}
{* Output       : none                                             *}
{* Info         : The position of the blinking display cursor changes *}
{*               only through the call of this procedure, if the   *}
{*               indicated display page is the current display page *}
{*******************************************************************}

procedure SetCursorPos(Page,          { display whose Cursor is set  }
                       Column,           { new Column of the Cursor }
                       Line   : integer);  { new Line of the Cursor }

var Regs : Registers;          { Register variable for the interrupt }

begin
 Regs.ah := 2;                                    { Function number }
 Regs.bh := Page;                                    { display page }
 Regs.dh := Line;                             { Display coordinates }
 Regs.dl := Column;
 intr($10, Regs);                      { Call BIOS-Video-Interrupt }
end;

{*******************************************************************}
{* GETCURSORPOS: senses the position of the cursor in a display    *}
{*               page and its start and end line                   *}
{* Input        : see below                                        *}
{* Output       : The variables listed below contain the values after *}
{*               the call of the procedure                         *}
{* Info         : the start and end line of the cursor is independent *}
{*               of the indicated display page                     *}
{*******************************************************************}

procedure GetCursorPos(Page : integer;            { the display page }
                       var Column,            { Column of the cursor }
                           Line,                { Line of the cursor }
                           Beginline,     { Start line of the cursor }
                           Endl   : integer); { End line of the cursor }

var Regs : Registers;          { Register variable for the interrupt }

begin
 Regs.ah := 3;                                    { Function number }
 Regs.bh := Page;                                    { Display page }
 intr($10, Regs);                      { Call BIOS-Video-Interrupt }
 Column := Regs.dl;                         { Result of the Function }
 Line := Regs.dh;                           { read from the Register }
 Beginline := Regs.ch;                        { and store in proper }
 Endl := Regs.cl;                                        { Variables }
end;

{*******************************************************************}
{* SETDISPLAYPAGE: set the display page                            *}
{*                 for output on the monitor                       *}
{* Input          : see below                                      *}
{* Output         : none                                           *}
{*******************************************************************}

procedure SetDisplayPage(Page : integer);     { the new display page }

var Regs : Registers;          { Register variable for the interrupt }
```

```
begin
 Regs.ah := 5;                       { Function number and display page }
 Regs.al := Page;                                        { Screen page }
 intr($10, Regs);                          { Call BIOS-Video-Interrupt }
end;

{**********************************************************************}
{* SCROLLUP: scrolls a display area by one or more                    *}
{*           lines up or erases it                                    *}
{* Input    : see below                                               *}
{* Output   : none                                                    *}
{* Info     : If Number 0 is passed, the display area                 *}
{*           is filled with blanks                                    *}
{**********************************************************************}

procedure ScrollUp(Number,              { Number of lines to be scrolled }
                   COLOR,       { Attribute for the blank lines created }
                   ColumnUL,     { Column in the upper left hand corner }
                   LineUL,              { line in the upper left corner }
                   ColumnLR,         { Column in the lower right corner }
                   LineLR : integer);{ line in the lower right corner }

var Regs : Registers;        { Register variable for calling Interrupt }

begin
 Regs.ah := 6;                          { Function number and number }
 Regs.al := Number;
 Regs.bh := COLOR;                          { Color of empty line(s) }
 Regs.ch := LineUL;                                     { Upper left }
 Regs.cl := ColumnUL;                                  { coordinates }
 Regs.dh := LineLR;                                    { Lower right }
 Regs.dl := ColumnLR;                                  { coordinates }
 Intr($10,Regs);                         { Call BIOS-Video-Interrupt }
end;

{**********************************************************************}
{* SCROLLDOWN: Scrolls a display area by one or more                  *}
{*             lines down or erases it                                *}
{* Input      : see below                                             *}
{* Output     : none                                                  *}
{* Info       : If Number 0 is passed, the display area               *}
{*             is filled with blanks                                  *}
{**********************************************************************}

procedure ScrollDown(Number,            { Number of lines to be scrolled }
                     COLOR, { Attribute for the blank line(s) created }
                     ColumnUL,         { Column in the upper left corner }
                     LineUL,             { line in the upper left corner }
                     ColumnLR,       { Column in the lower right corner }
                     LineLR : integer);  { Line in lower right corner }

var Regs : Registers;       { Register-Variable for call of Interrupt }

begin
 Regs.ah := 7;                          { Function number and number }
 Regs.al := Number;
 Regs.bh := COLOR;                          { Color of blank line(s) }
 Regs.ch := LineUL;                                     { upper left }
 Regs.cl := ColumnUL;                                  { coordinates }
 Regs.dh := LineLR;                                    { Lower right }
 Regs.dl := ColumnLR;                                  { coordinates }
 Intr($10, Regs);                        { Call BIOS-Video-Interrupt }
end;

{**********************************************************************}
{* GETCHAR: Read a character including Attribute from an indicated   *}
{*          position in a display page                                *}
{* Input  : see below                                                 *}
{* Output : see below                                                 *}
{**********************************************************************}
```

```
procedure GetChar(Page,                         { display page accessed  }
                  Column,                              { Display Column }
                  Line       : integer;                  { Display line }
                  var Character : char;                 { the character }
                  var COLOR   : integer);               { its Attribute }

var Regs : Registers;           { Register-Variable for the Interrupt }
    CurColumn,                              { current display Column }
    CurLine,                                  { current display line }
    CurPage,                                  { current display page }
    Dummy     : integer;      { stores Variables which are not needed  }

begin
 GetVideoMode(Dummy, Dummy, CurPage);     { sense current display page }
 GetCursorPos(CurPage, CurColumn, CurLine,       { Get cursor position }
             Dummy, Dummy);              { in the current display page }
 SetCursorPos(Page, Column, Line); { cursor on the position indicated }

 Regs.ah := 8;          { Get Function number for char. and Attribute }
 Regs.bh := Page;                                       { display page }
 Intr($10,Regs);                                { Invoke DOS registers }
 Character := chr(Regs.al);                   { ASCII-Code of character }
 COLOR := Regs.ah;                         { Attribute of the character }
  SetCursorPos(CurPage, CurColumn, CurLine);{ Set cursor old position }
end;

{*********************************************************************}
{* WRITECHAR: Writes a character with indicated color to the         *}
{*            current cursor position in the display page            *}
{*            indicated                                              *}
{* Input    : see below                                              *}
{* Output   : none                                                   *}
{* Info     : during the Output of characters, the control codes     *}
{*            such as Carriage-Return are treated as ASCII codes     *}
{*********************************************************************}

procedure WriteChar(Page    : integer;      { Display page for writing }
                    Character : char;   { ASCII-Code of the character }
                    COLOR   : integer);                  { its Attribute }

var Regs : Registers;           { Register variable for the interrupt }

begin
 Regs.ah := 9;
 Regs.al := ord(Character);       { Function number and character code }
 Regs.bh := Page;                                       { Display page }
 Regs.bl := COLOR;                                     { Display color }
 Regs.cx := 1;                             { output character only once }
 Intr($10,Regs);                            { Call BIOS-Video-Interrupt }
end;

{*********************************************************************}
{* WRITETEXT: Writes a String starting at an indicated position in   *}
{*            a display page.                                        *}
{* Input    : see below                                              *}
{* Output   : none                                                   *}
{* Info     : During output of characters the control characters     *}
{*            such as Carriage-Return are treated as such.           *}
{*            If writing continues beyond the End of the display,    *}
{*            will be scrolled up one line                           *}
{*********************************************************************}

procedure WriteText(Page,                      { Display page for output }
                    Column,          { Column, from which output starts }
                    Line,              { Line, from which output starts }
                    COLOR  : integer;        { Color for all characters }
                    Text   : TextTyp);                  { Text for output }

var Regs : Registers;      { Register variable for call of Interrupt }
```

```
    Counter  : integer;                                { Loop Counter }

begin
 SetCursorPos(Page, Column, Line);                       { Set cursor }

 for Counter := 1 to length(Text) do             { process characters }
  begin                                                 { in sequence }
   WriteChar(Page, ' ', COLOR);        { Color at the current position }
   Regs.ah := 14;
   Regs.al := ord(Text[Counter]);      { Function number and character }
   Regs.bh := Page;                                    { Display page }
   Intr($10,Regs);                         { Call BIOS-Video-Interrupt }
  end;
end;

{**********************************************************************}
{**                         MAIN PROGRAM                             **}
{**********************************************************************}

begin
 clrscr;                                              { Erase display }
 for i := 1 to 24 do                              { Perform line 1 to 24 }
  for j := 0 to 79 do                                 { do all Columns }
   begin
    SetCursorPos(0, j, i);                           { position cursor }
    WriteChar(0, chr(i*80+j and 255), NORMAL);    { Write a character }
   end;
 ScrollDown(0, NORMAL, 5, 8, 19, 22);                 { Erase Window 1 }
 WriteText(0, 5, 8, INVERS, '   Window 1    ');
 ScrollDown(0, NORMAL, 60, 2, 74, 16);                { Erase Window 2 }
 WriteText(0, 60, 2, INVERS, '   Window 2    ');
 WriteText(0, 24, 12, INVERS or BLINK, ' >>> PC SYSTEM PROGRAMMING <<< ');
 WriteText(0, 0, 0, INVERS, '                Still have to draw       '+
                           ' arrows on the screen                     ');
 for i := 49 downto 0 do                  { draw a total of 50 Arrows }
  begin
   str(i:2, IString);                     { convert i in ASCII-String }
   WriteText(0, 37, 0, INVERS, IString);
   j := 1;                         { every Arrow consists of 16 lines }
   while j <= 15 do
    begin
      k := 0;
      while k < j do                     { create a line of the Arrow }
       begin
        SetCursorPos(0, 12-(j shr 1)+k, 9);          { Arrow Window 1 }
        WriteChar(0, '*', BOLD);
        SetCursorPos(0, 67-(j shr 1)+k, 16);         { Arrow Window 2 }
        WriteChar(0, '*', BOLD);
        k := succ(k);
       end;
      ScrollDown(1, NORMAL, 5, 9, 19, 22);          { scroll Window 1 }
      ScrollUp(1, NORMAL, 60, 3, 74, 16);           { scroll Window 2 }
      for l := 0 to 8000 do                              { Wait Loop }
       ;
      j := j+2;
    end;
  end;
 clrscr;                                              { Erase display }
end.
```

C listing: VIDEOC.C

```
/***********************************************************************/
/*                              V I D E O C                            */
/*---------------------------------------------------------------------*/
/*    Task              : makes functions available which are not      */
/*                        available from the Library of MICROSOFT and  */
/*                        the TURBO C-Compilers                        */
/*---------------------------------------------------------------------*/
/*    Author            : MICHAEL TISCHER                              */
/*    developed on      : 08/13/87                                     */
/*    last Update       : 05/14/89                                     */
/*---------------------------------------------------------------------*/
/*    (MICROSOFT C)                                                    */
/*    Creation          : MSC VIDEOC;                                  */
/*                        LINK VIDEOC;                                 */
/*    Call              : VIDEOC                                       */
/*---------------------------------------------------------------------*/
/*    (BORLAND TURBO C)                                                */
/*    Creation          : through the RUN command on the menu bar      */
/***********************************************************************/

#include <dos.h>                              /* include Header-Files */
#include <io.h>

#define NORMAL          0x07  /* Definition of the character Attribute */
#define BOLD            0x0F          /* in relation to a monochrome */
#define INVERS          0x70                         /* Display card */
#define UNDERLINE       0x01
#define BLINK           0x80

/***********************************************************************/
/* GETVIDEOMODE: Read current Video mode and Parameters                */
/* Input        : none                                                 */
/* Output       : see below                                            */
/***********************************************************************/

void GetVideoMode(VideoMode, Number, Page)
int *VideoMode;                       /* the Number of the Video mode */
int *Number;                           /* Number of Columns per line */
int *Page;                         /* Number of current display page */

{
 union REGS Register;         /* Register variable for Interrupt-Call */

 Register.h.ah = 15;                              /* Function number */
 int86(0x10, &Register, &Register);           /* Call Interrupt 10(h) */
 *VideoMode = Register.h.al;                  /* Number of Video mode */
 *Number = Register.h.ah;            /* Number of Characters per line */
 *Page = Register.h.bh;            /* Number of current display page */
}

/***********************************************************************/
/* SETCURSORTYPE: defines the appearance of the blinking display       */
/*                cursor                                               */
/* Input         : see below                                           */
/* Output        : none                                                */
/* Info          : for a monochrome display card the parameters        */
/*                can be between 0 and 13. For a color                 */
/*                display card between 0 and 7                         */
/***********************************************************************/

void SetCursorType(Beginline, Endl)
int Beginline;                      /* Beginning line of the cursor */
int Endl;                                 /* End line of the cursor */

{
 union REGS Register;         /* Register variable for Interrupt-Call */
```

```
 Register.h.ah = 1;                                 /* Function number */
 Register.h.ch = Beginline;                    /* Beginning line of cursor */
 Register.h.cl = Endl;                              /* End line of cursor */
 int86(0x10, &Register, &Register);             /* Call Interrupt 10(h) */
}

/*********************************************************************/
/* SETCURSORPOS: defines the position of the cursor in the indicated */
/*               display page                                        */
/* Input       : see below                                           */
/* Output      : none                                                */
/* Info        : The position of the blinking display cursor changes */
/*               only if the call of this function refers to         */
/*               current display page                                */
/*********************************************************************/

void SetCursorPos(Page, Column, Line)
int Page;                 /* Display page where the cursor will be set */
int Column;                                      /* new cursor Column */
int Line;                                          /* new cursor line */

{
 union REGS Register;         /* Register variable for Interrupt-Call */

 Register.h.ah = 2;                                 /* Function number */
 Register.h.bh = Page;                                 /* Display page */
 Register.h.dh = Line;                                 /* Display line */
 Register.h.dl = Column;                             /* Display Column */
 int86(0x10, &Register, &Register);             /* Call Interrupt 10(h) */
}

/*********************************************************************/
/* GETCURSORPOS: Get the position of the cursor in a certain         */
/*               display page and its start and end line             */
/* Input       : none                                                */
/* Output      : see below                                           */
/*********************************************************************/

void GetCursorPos(Page, Column, Line, Beginline, Endl)
int Page;                                     /* Number of display page */
int *Column;                       /* Column, where the cursor is located */
int *Line;                           /* Line, where the cursor is located */
int *Beginline;                            /* Start line of the cursor */
int *Endl;                                   /* End line of the cursor */

{
 union REGS Register;         /* Register variable for Interrupt-Call */

 Register.h.ah = 3;                                 /* Function number */
 Register.h.bh = Page;                                 /* Display page */
 int86(0x10, &Register, &Register);             /* Call Interrupt 10(h) */
 *Column = Register.h.dl;                 /* Read result of the Function */
 *Line = Register.h.dh;                          /* from the Registers */
 *Beginline = Register.h.ch;                    /* and assign to proper */
 *Endl = Register.h.cl;                                     /* Variables */
}

/*********************************************************************/
/* SETDISPLAYPAGE: sets the display Page which is to be represented  */
/*                 on the display                                    */
/* Input         : see below                                         */
/* Output        : none                                              */
/*********************************************************************/

void SetDisplayPage(Page)
int Page;                   /* Number of the new current display page */

{
 union REGS Register;         /* Register variable for Interrupt call */
```

```
 Register.h.ah = 5;                              /* Function number */
 Register.h.al = Page;                              /* Display page */
 int86(0x10, &Register, &Register);          /* Call Interrupt 10(h) */
}

/**********************************************************************/
/* SCROLLUP: Scrolls a display area up one or several                 */
/*           lines or erases it                                       */
/* Input    : see below                                               */
/* Output   : none                                                    */
/* Info     : If 0 is passed as number, the display                   */
/*           area is filled with blanks                               */
/**********************************************************************/

void ScrollUp(Number, Color, ColumnUL, LineUL, ColumnLR, LineLR)
int Number;                           /* Number of lines to be scrolled */
int Color;                    /* Color or Attribute for the blank lines */
int ColumnUL;        /* Column in upper left corner of the display area */
int LineUL;            /* Line in upper left corner of the display area */
int ColumnLR;       /* Column in lower right corner of the display area */
int LineLR;           /* Line in lower right corner of the display area */

{
 union REGS Register;         /* Register variable for Interrupt call */

 Register.h.ah = 6;                              /* Function number */
 Register.h.al = Number;                         /* Number of lines */
 Register.h.bh = Color;                   /* Color of blank line(s) */
 Register.h.ch = LineUL;                  /* Set Coordinates of the */
 Register.h.cl = ColumnUL;         /* display Window to be scrolled */
 Register.h.dh = LineLR;                               /* or erased */
 Register.h.dl = ColumnLR;
 int86(0x10, &Register, &Register);          /* Call Interrupt 10(h) */
}

/**********************************************************************/
/* SCROLLDOWN: Scroll a display area by one or more                   */
/*             lines down or erase it                                 */
/* Input      : see below                                             */
/* Output     : none                                                  */
/* Info       : If 0 is passed as number, the display                 */
/*             area is filled with blanks                             */
/**********************************************************************/
void ScrollDown(Number, Color, ColumnUL, LineUL, ColumnLR, LineLR)
int Number;                           /* Number of lines to be scrolled */
int Color;                    /* Color or Attribute for the blank lines */
int ColumnUL;        /* Column in upper left corner of the display area */
int LineUL;            /* Line in upper left corner of the display area */
int ColumnLR;       /* Column in lower right corner of the display area */
int LineLR;           /* Line in lower right corner of the display area */

{
 union REGS Register;         /* Register variable for Interrupt call */

 Register.h.ah = 7;                              /* Function number */
 Register.h.al = Number;                         /* Number of lines */
 Register.h.bh = Color;                   /* Color of blank line(s) */
 Register.h.ch = LineUL;                 /* Set Coordinates for the */
 Register.h.cl = ColumnUL;                 /* display window to be */
 Register.h.dh = LineLR;                     /* scrolled or erased */
 Register.h.dl = ColumnLR;
 int86(0x10, &Register, &Register);          /* Call Interrupt 10(h) */
}

/**********************************************************************/
/* GETCHAR: Read from a designated display position                   */
/*          a character and its Attribute-Byte                        */
/* Input  : see below                                                 */
/* Output : see below                                                 */
/**********************************************************************/
```

```
void GetChar(Page, Column, Line, Character, Color)
int Page;     /* Display page from which the character is to be read */
int Column;                          /* Display column of the character */
int Line;                              /* Display line of the character */
char *Character;                       /* the character at this position */
int *Color;                              /* its Attribute-Byte (Color) */

{
 union REGS Register;          /* Register variable for Interrupt call */
 int Dummy;                    /* for Variables which are not required */
 int CurPage;                             /* the current display page */
 int CurLine;                             /* the current display line */
 int CurColumn;                         /* the current display Column */

 GetVideoMode(&Dummy, &Dummy, &CurPage); /* Get current display page */
 GetCursorPos(&CurPage, &CurColumn, &CurLine,  /* Get current cursor */
              &Dummy, &Dummy);                              /* position */
 SetCursorPos(Page, Column, Line);                        /* Set cursor */
 Register.h.ah = 8;                                  /* Function number */
 Register.h.bh = Page;                                  /* display page */
 int86(0x10, &Register, &Register);            /* Call Interrupt 10(h) */
 *Character = Register.h.al;       /* Read results from the Registers */
 *Color = Register.h.ah;                                  /* and assign */
 SetCursorPos(CurPage, CurColumn, CurLine);/* cursor to old position */
}

/***********************************************************************/
/* WRITECHAR: writes a character with an Attribute                     */
/*            at the current cursor position in the page indicated     */
/* Input    : see below                                                */
/* Output   : none                                                     */
/***********************************************************************/
void WriteChar(Page, Character, Color)
int Page;             /* The character appears in this display page */
char Character;                         /* the character to be output */
int Color;                                  /* its Attribute or Color */

{
 union REGS Register;          /* Register variable for Interrupt call */

 Register.h.ah = 9;                                  /* Function number */
 Register.h.al = Character;              /* the character to be output */
 Register.h.bh = Page;                                  /* display page */
 Register.h.bl = Color;           /* Color of character to be output */
 Register.x.cx = 1;                     /* output character only once */
 int86(0x10, &Register, &Register);            /* Call Interrupt 10(h) */
}

/***********************************************************************/
/* WRITETEXT: Writes a character string with constant color            */
/*            starting at a designated position within a display page*/
/* Input    : see below                                                */
/* Output   : none                                                     */
/* Info     : Text is a pointer to a character vector which contains */
/*            the text to be output and is terminated                  */
/*            with a '\0' character                                    */
/***********************************************************************/
void WriteText(Page, Column, Line, Color, Text)
int Page;             /* the Text is output in this display page */
int Column;                          /* display Column for Output */
int Line;                              /* display line for Output */
int Color;                         /* Color/Attribute of the Text */
char *Text;                                    /* Text for output */

{
 union REGS Register;          /* Register variable for Interrupt call */

 SetCursorPos(Page, Column, Line);                        /* Set cursor */
 while (*Text)                  /* Output Text up to '\0' character */
  {
```

```
    WriteChar(Page, ' ', Color);                  /* Color for characters */
    Register.h.ah = 14;                                /* Function number */
    Register.h.bh = Page;                                /* display page */
    Register.h.al = *Text++;               /* the character for output */
    int86(0x10, &Register, &Register);                  /* Call Interrupt */
  }
}

/**********************************************************************/
/* CLEARSCREEN: erase the 80*25 character Text display and set       */
/*              cursor into the upper left display corner             */
/* Input      : none                                                  */
/* Output     : none                                                  */
/**********************************************************************/
void ClearScreen()

{
 int CurPage;                                  /* current display page */
 int Dummy;                                          /* Dummy variable */

 ScrollUp(0, NORMAL, 0, 0, 79, 24);                     /* clear screen */
 GetVideoMode(&Dummy, &Dummy, &CurPage); /* Get current display page */
 SetCursorPos(CurPage, 0, 0);                             /* Set cursor */
}

/**********************************************************************/
/**                          MAIN PROGRAM                            **/
/**********************************************************************/
void main()

{
 int i, j, k, l;                                     /* Loop variables */
 char Arrows[3];          /* accepts number of Arrows as ASCII-String */

 ClearScreen();                                        /* Clear Screen */
 for (i = 1; i < 25; i++)                           /* process all lines */
  for (j = 0; j < 80; j++)                        /* process all Columns */
   {
    SetCursorPos(0, j, i);                           /* position cursor */
    WriteChar(0, i*80+j&255, NORMAL);               /* write characters */
   }
 ScrollDown(0, NORMAL, 5, 8, 19, 22);                 /* erase Window 1 */
 WriteText(0, 5, 8, INVERS, "   Window 1   ");
 ScrollDown(0, NORMAL, 60, 2, 74, 16);                /* erase Window 2 */
 WriteText(0, 60, 2, INVERS, "   Window 2   ");
 WriteText(0, 24, 12, INVERS | BLINK, " >>> PC SYSTEM PROGRAMMING <<< ");
 WriteText(0, 0, 0, INVERS, "                            There are    ");
 WriteText(0, 40, 0, INVERS,"arrows left to draw                     ");
 for (i = 49; i >= 0 ; i--)                           /* draw 50 Arrows */
  {
   sprintf(Arrows, "%2d", i);    /* Convert number of Arrows to ASCII */
   WriteText(0, 37, 0, INVERS, Arrows);                   /* and output */
   for (j = 1; j < 16; j+= 2)     /* every Arrow consists of 16 lines */
    {
     for (k = 0; k < j; k++)            /* create a line of the Arrow */
      {
       SetCursorPos(0, 12-(j>>1)+k, 9);               /* Arrow Window 1 */
       WriteChar(0, '*', BOLD);
       SetCursorPos(0, 67-(j>>1)+k, 16);              /* Arrow Window 2 */
       WriteChar(0, '*', BOLD);
      }
     ScrollDown(1, NORMAL, 5, 9, 19, 22);      /* Scroll Window 1 down */
     ScrollUp(1, NORMAL, 60, 3, 74, 16);         /* Scroll Window 2 up */
     for (l = 0; l < 4000 ; l++)                          /* Wait Loop */
      ;
    }
  }
 ClearScreen();                                        /* Clear Screen */
}
```

7.4.1 The EGA and VGA BIOS

The BIOS functions for screen output have been part of ROM-BIOS since the early days of the PC. Although they have proven themselves in thousands of applications, they don't work with the newer types of graphic cards. EGA and VGA cards are becoming more and more common in the PC market. Incompatibilities arise between hardware and software, because these cards have little in common with the CGA and MDA cards for which the original BIOS functions were intended.

To make EGA and VGA cards compatible with programs that use BIOS functions to do their screen output, the BIOS functions must first be adapted to the new hardware standards. The first option would be to replace the ROM-BIOS on the PC motherboard with new ROMs. This solution can create other problems, because no set standard currently exists for EGA or VGA. Unlike the CGA and MDA cards, where the IBM standard took over simply because there were no other alternatives, EGA and VGA manufacturers have yet to define a universal standard. Such a standard would have to apply to hardware, options and capabilities as offered by each manufacturer.

EGA/VGA ROM-BIOS

Since trying to adapt the ROM-BIOS included with the computer to every graphic card on the market is impractical, the manufacturers of these systems use the opposite approach. They package an independent ROM-BIOS with their video cards. There is a small ROM on the video card itself which contains the necessary screen output functions. When the system is booted, the BIOS detects this ROM expansion and allows it to redirect the BIOS video interrupt 16H to its own routines, replacing the old functions.

By using these routines, all of the programs which use BIOS functions for output can be executed without problems, but the enhanced capabilities of these video cards are not used. Since the ROM-BIOS on the motherboard is intended to work only with CGA and MDA cards, it supports only the capabilities of these cards. So the graphic card manufacturers extend the BIOS in these video cards by including new functions or upgrading old functions, so that the enhanced video capabilities can be used.

This section is dedicated to these functions. No real standard exists for these BIOS extensions, as mentioned previously. We could use this section to describe the video functions of the more important EGA and VGA cards (many different cards), but even with this information you still wouldn't be able to write programs which would be compatible with all of the video cards on the market. Writing a program for a specific video card makes sense only when you want the program to run with that card only.

EGA/VGA video modes

Instead, let's look at the lowest common denominator, the video modes and functions supported by virtually all EGA/VGA cards. If you stick to this "low-level" standard, you can be fairly sure that your programs will run properly with all EGA/VGA cards. The basis of this standard is the set of video modes supported by the original EGA card, introduced by IBM in 1985, or the original VGA card, introduced by IBM in 1987. All of the manufacturers of compatible cards have included similar functions in their own cards, and added their own features.

All EGA and VGA cards have flexibility in common, which allows them to emulate other video cards, as well as perform other tasks. The type of emulation depends on the monitor connected, since unlike other cards, EGA/VGA cards can by used with different types of monitors.

Monitors and EGA/VGA

If you connect a monochrome monitor to an EGA or a VGA card, it assumes the features of an MDA or Hercules graphic card. If you connect a color monitor to an EGA or a VGA, it emulates a normal CGA card. However, EGA/VGA cards run best when connected to a *multisync* monitor, which allows color displays at higher resolutions than Hercules or CGA. The standard resolutions (640x350 for EGA, 640x480 for VGA) can be displayed on a multisync monitor with no problem. However, multisync monitors also support the higher resolutions available on many EGA and VGA cards. Resolutions of 800x600 pixels and 1024x768 pixels, are common. These higher resolutions can be used only if the EGA/VGA card has enough RAM, since the extended graphics mode requires additional video RAM to handle the higher resolutions. The programmer doesn't have to worry much about this, because almost all EGA cards come with 256K RAM standard. Very few EGA cards come with a mere 64K and must be expanded to 256K. Most VGA cards come equipped with 256K of video RAM, as well as a special VGA BIOS. This special BIOS may require special drivers to operate in conjunction with graphical user interfaces such as GEM® or Microsoft Windows®.

In addition, to support the new graphic modes with higher resolutions, EGA cards offer a palette of 16 colors chosen from the 64 available colors. In text mode it is also possible to set the heights of individual characters, so that up to 43 lines can be displayed on the screen at once, instead of the normal 25 lines.

VGA features

The VGA card is even more powerful. In text mode, the VGA card can display 25 lines, 43 lines and even 50 lines of text. In addition, the VGA has even more colors available (262,144 colors, as opposed to the EGA's 64-color spectrum). Of course, these colors are only effective when displayed on a monitor that has a high enough resolution.

The rest of this section shows how these extended features can be used and how the original BIOS functions have changed.

As with the normal BIOS, all of the video modes in the EGA/VGA BIOS are set with the help of function 00H of the BIOS video interrupt. This function has not been changed since the old BIOS, but it has been extended. The number of the video mode to be set is passed in the AL register. The following codes are allowed:

EGA/VGA Card Video Modes				
Code	Mode	MONO	COLOR	EGA/VGA
00H	40x25 characters, 16 colors		■	■
01H	40x25 characters, 16 colors		■	■
02H	80x25 characters, 16 colors		■	■
03H	80x25 characters, 16 colors		■	■
04H	320x200 graphic pixels, 4 colors		■	■
05H	320x200 graphic pixels, 4 colors		■	■
06H	640x200 graphic pixels, 2 colors		■	■
07H	80x25 characters, monochrome	■		
0DH	320x200 graphic pixels, 16 colors			■
0EH	640x200 graphic pixels, 16 colors			■
0FH	640x350 graphic pixels, monochrome	■		
10H	640x350 graphic pixels,16 colors**			■
11H	640x480 graphic pixels, 2 colors			■*
12H	640x480 graphic pixels, 16 colors			■*
13H	230x200 graphic pixels, 256 colors			■*
* VGA only				
** EGA cards with 64K of added RAM can only display 4 colors				

EGA and VGA cards can suppress clearing the video RAM when switching to a new video mode. If you want to to do this, bit 7 of the AL register must be set in addition to video mode number when the function is called.

The codes listed above are also valid for the function 0FH, which is used to determine the current video mode.

Nothing much has changed in functions 01H to 0EH. Slight changes have been made to functions 01H and 03H, which define and read the design of the cursor. We will discuss these changes later. You can also get exact descriptions of these functions from the appendices, where all of the functions of the EGA/VGA BIOS are described.

Extended functions

After function 0FH, which also appeared in the old ROM-BIOS, we have three new EGA/VGA functions numbered 10H, 11H, and 12H. These new functions are dedicated to a specific task and have a number of sub-functions.

Function 10H

Function 10H comprises all of the sub-functions for using the color capabilities of the EGA/VGA cards. Before we describe these functions, we should first look at the way in which the EGA and VGA cards create colors.

Unlike the MDA and CGA cards, the two nibbles of the attribute byte of a character in text mode do not directly specify the color or attributes of the character in the EGA. They comprise an index to one of the 16 palette registers of the EGA card, which then contains the actual color. This makes it possible to set the desired colors individually, and allows color changes simply by changing the contents of the palette registers. The interpretation of the palette register contents, and the number of displayable colors, depend on the type of monitor used. The EGA card itself can generate 64 colors, but these can be displayed only on EGA or multisync monitors, since these monitors have the six color lines required ($2^6 = 64$). There are two lines available for each fundamental color (red, green, and blue), where the two lines control the intensity level of the color. These six lines correspond directly to the lower six bits of a palette register, as the following figure shows.

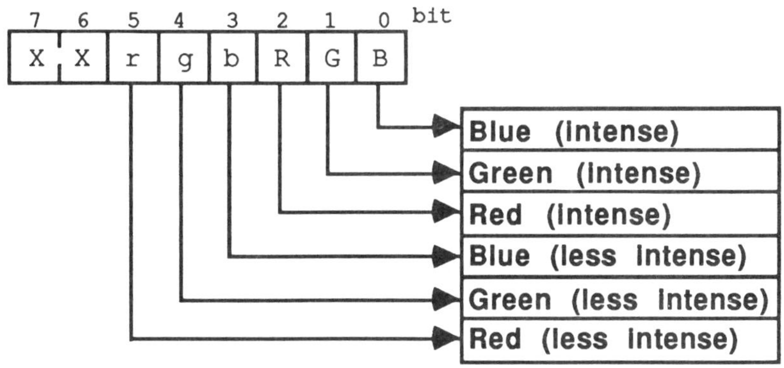

EGA palette registers when connected to EGA or multisync monitor

This color scheme is not available when a normal color monitor is connected. It has only four lines for the color representation, three of which are assigned the fundamental colors red, green, and blue. The fourth line simply allows the resulting color to be displayed at higher intensity. These limited possibilities affect the structure of the palette register, which clearly differs from the six-bit structure used when an EGA or multisync monitor is connected. A total of only 16 colors can be displayed in this mode.

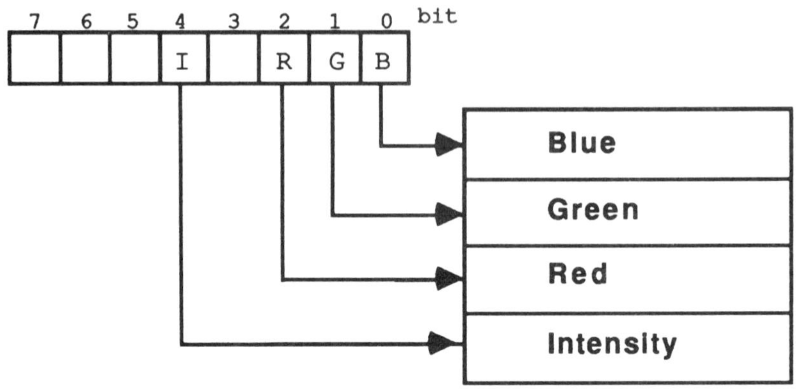

EGA palette registers when connected to a color monitor

The bits of a palette register take on a completely different meaning when the card is connected to a monochrome monitor. In this case the monitor cannot display different colors, and can only display bright, inverse, and underlined characters. When connected to such a monitor, the meanings of the individual bits correspond to those of the attribute byte of an MDA card, which we examined earlier in this chapter.

DAC color table

The VGA card also uses the most significant and least significant nibbles of the attribute byte as an index, pointing to one of 16 palette registers. Unlike the EGA card, which only contains the color code, this byte contains a value between 0 and 255. This number acts as a reference to the *DAC* (digital analog converter) *color table*. This table allows the VGA card to convert a digitally notated color code into an analog video signal. The DAC color table sees each color code as three six-bit values, with each value representing the degree of red, green and blue intensity in the color.

As the following figure shows, the color code layout in some registers plays a role which also involves the BIOS. Bit 7 of each value controls the grouping of the different registers in the DAC color table, thus controlling the mode control register of the video controller. If this bit contains a 0, the index in the DAC color table bases its palette register on the contents of bits 0 to 5, and the color select register on bits 2 and 3. The consequence is that the DAC color table is divided into four groups of 64 consecutive registers. The value in the palette register represents the index in this group, whereby the active group itself selects the color based on the contents of bits 2 and 3 of the color select register.

When bit 7 of the mode control register contains a 1, the DAC color table divides into 16 groups of 16 consecutive registers. The index of this table is based on bits 0-3 of the corresponding palette register, and bits 0-3 of the color select register.

These registers select the active color group from within the DAC color table, and the contents of the palette registers represent the index of this group.

You can use this form of coding for creating fast and easy color changes when characters on the screen must be changed rapidly. This involves storing different groups in the DAC color table which specify brighter or darker colors, and quickly incrementing the active color grouping through the color select register.

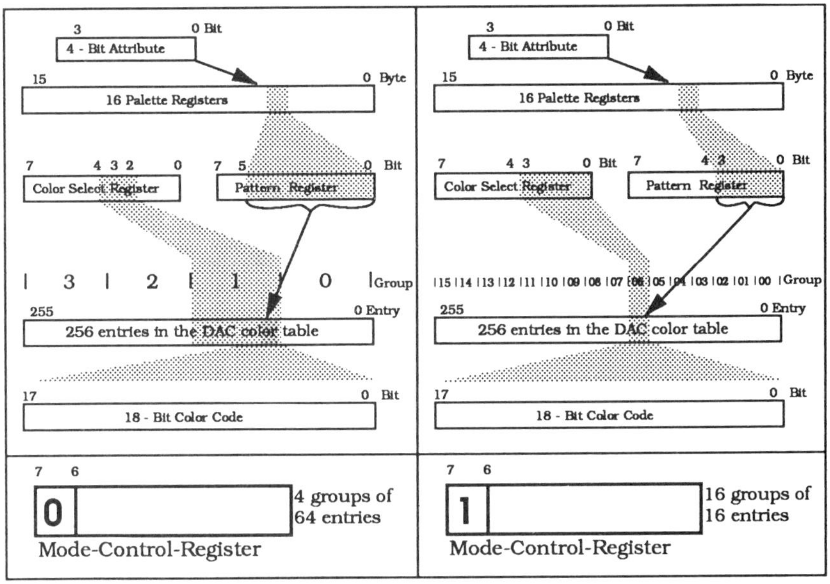

Color code layout of the VGA card

To perfectly emulate a CGA or an MDA card, the EGA/VGA BIOS sets the individual palette registers (or in the case of the VGA card, the DAC color registers) to the same color scheme used by a CGA or an MDA card when the corresponding mode is initialized. In the case of CGA emulation (EGA/VGA card and a CGA monitor), this means that palette register 0 contains the value 0, palette register 1 the value 1, etc. At the same time, the color select register of the VGA card must be set to the first of 16 palettes whose color codes correspond to those of a CGA card. This also applies to CGA modes 4 and 5 (320x200 pixels, four colors), which work with one of two color palettes which can be selected via function 0BH, sub-function 1. The EGA BIOS simply loads the corresponding colors into the lower three palette registers, depending on the palette selected.

There is normally no need to change the contents of the palette registers in this case, since no new colors can be displayed on the screen. Individual colors can easily be exchanged with each other.

Things are different when an EGA/VGA or multisync monitor is connected. The EGA/VGA BIOS loads values 0 to 15 into the 16 color registers when the text mode is initialized, but this does not exhaust the color options of the EGA card. To make full use of these options, sub-function 00H of function 10H can be used to load one of the 16 palette registers. In addition to the function number in the AH register and the sub-function number in AL, this function must also be passed the number of the palette (0 to 15) in BH and the new color value for this palette in the BL register. Since this function does not check the number of the register, it can also be used to change the contents of a 17th palette register (screen border and background color in the graphics mode), although it is better to use sub-function 01H of function 10H for this. Besides, it doesn't make much sense to set a background color in the text modes, because the text display takes up almost the entire screen with only two or three raster lines left over for the output of a border color. The contents of this palette register are ignored when a monochrome monitor is connected.

To call the function for accessing this palette register, the AH register must first be loaded with the function number 10H and the AL register with the sub-function number 01H. The BH register holds the border color, which is then loaded into palette register 16 when the function is called.

Sub-function 02H of function 10H is used when you want to load all of the palette registers at the same time, including the register for the border color. In addition to the function and sub-function numbers in AH and AL, respectively, the address of a table must be passed in the ES:DX register pair. This table contains the values for the 17 palette registers. When this function is executed, the contents of this table will be copied into the 17 palette registers and will cause all of the colors on the screen to change at once.

The last sub-function of function 10H (for EGA only) defines the meaning of a bit in the text modes. As with the CGA and MDA cards, this bit can also be used on the EGA card to emphasize a character by either displaying it on a bright background color or flashing it, if the bit is set. While the meaning of this bit can be changed only by directly programming the video hardware with CGA or MDA cards, the EGA/VGA BIOS can perform the same task using sub-function 03H of function 10H.

As with calling the other sub-functions, the function and sub-function numbers must be passed in registers AH and AL. The meaning of bit seven of the attribute byte is determined by the contents of the BL register. The value of zero in this register sets the bright background color, while the value one causes all characters on the screen, with bit seven of their attribute bytes set, to flash on and off.

The VGA card has additional functions available for accessing this table. These functions are all sub-functions of function 10H, and are only accessible from the VGA card.

The contents of a single DAC color register can be modified using sub-function 10H. Load the AL register with the sub-function number, the BX register with the number of the corresponding register (0-255) and the CH, CL and DH registers with the color code. Then call the function. To help correctly interpret the contents of this register, the DAC color table must be coded as an 18-bit value (6 bits for red, 6 bits for green and 6 bits for blue). The red components must be loaded into the DH register, the green components into the CH register, and the blue components into the DL register.

You must load the number of the register to be updated into the BX register. The registers receive the number of the DAC register to be updated when you call sub-function 15H.

Any number of DAC color registers can be loaded at a time using sub-function 12H. The number of the first DAC color register to be loaded is passed to the BX register, and the number of DAC color registers to be loaded is passed to the CX register. The new contents of the DAC color registers are loaded into a buffer (the address of this buffer is contained in the ES:DX register pair). Each DAC color register receives three consecutive bytes from this buffer. These three bytes specify the green components, the red components and the blue components of the color code.

Reading the DAC color table

Sub-function 17H reads the contents of a group of DAC color registers. The number of the first DAC color register to be read is passed to the BX register, and the number of registers is passed to the CX register. The contents of this register copies the VGA BIOS to a buffer, whose segment and offset address may be found in the ES.DX register pair. The structure is identical to that of sub-function 12H. Remember that the registers for each DAC color register consist of three bytes (not one), and to allocate a buffer of appropriate size.

Organizing the DAC color table

Sub-function 13H allows the organization of the DAC color table and the active color group, offering two of its own sub-functions. If the BL register contains the value 0, then the sub-function copies bit 0 of the BH register into bit 7 of the mode control register of the VGA controller. The organization of the DAC color table can then be broken down into 4 or 16 groups. However, if the BL register contains the value 1 when this sub-function is called, then the sub-function copies the contents of the BH register into the color select register, then selects the active color group.

The contents of both registers can be conveyed by calling sub-function 1AH. After calling this function, the content of bit 7 of the mode control register is passed to the BL register, and the contents of the color select register is passed to the BH register.

Gray scales

Sub-function 0BH converts the color codes within the DAC color table into gray scales. Pass the number of the first register to be converted into the BX register, and the number of registers to be converted to the CX register. The conversion results in a color value between 0 (black) and 1 (white), based on a red intensity of 30%, a green intensity of 59% and a blue intensity of 11%.

Palette registers

The VGA BIOS still has more sub-functions in function 10H for reading the palette registers. Sub-function 07H reads the contents of any palette register. When the function is passed and the number of the palette register is passed to the BL register, the number of the contents is returned in the BH register. This allows read access to the contents of the overscan register (the color border on palette register 16), but this access requires the use of sub-function 08H. Like sub-function 07H, the result is loaded into the BH register.

Sub-function 09H loads the contents of the entire palette table (i.e., all 16 palette registers and the overscan registers) into a 17-byte buffer. The segment address of this buffer is loaded into the ES register, and the offset address is loaded into the DX register.

Another feature of the EGA and VGA cards are their ability to work with a number of different fonts and font sizes. This feature allows the EGA/VGA cards to be used with different monitors, in different resolutions. Since the screen resolution is determined by the monitor hardware and cannot be changed, the video card must adapt to the monitor's resolution. Exceptions to the rule are the more versatile and expensive multisync monitors, which get their name from the ability to adapt themselves to different synchronizations (resolutions).

Of the different monitors which can be used in connection with an EGA or a VGA card, the color monitor, normally used in conjunction with a CGA card, has the poorest resolution. It only has a resolution of 640 pixels (horizontal direction) by 200 pixels (vertical direction). If you want to display 25 lines of 80 columns each on the screen, you will have to use a character matrix of 8 by 8 pixels so that all of the characters fit on the screen.

Even though the monochrome monitor cannot display different colors, it does offer a resolution of 720 by 350 pixels when used with an MDA or Hercules graphics card. The individual characters are displayed with a matrix of 9 by 14 pixels.

EGA and multisync monitors also have a vertical resolution of 350 pixels, but can only display 640 pixels horizontally. The resolution of individual characters is 8 x 14 pixels—only slightly less than that of the monochrome monitors. VGA cards and multisync monitors usually support a minimum vertical resolution of 480 pixels, but some units even support 600 raster lines. VGA cards often permit character matrices of 8x16 (text mode) and 9x16 pixels.

Character generators

In order to support the various resolutions, the EGA/VGA cards have their own character generators which can display characters in any height between one and 32 raster lines. The number of text lines per screen depends on the height of the displayed characters and the resolution of the monitor. To make the best use of this feature, the EGA/VGA cards get the bit patterns of the characters from a section of the video RAM instead of from ROM.

Function 11H

Normally the character generator is programmed automatically and the appropriate character set is loaded when a video mode is initialized, but it is possible for a program to control these features with function 11H. You might want to use this to display more than the usual 25 text lines on a monochrome, EGA, or multisync monitor. But even if you do want to use 25 lines, these functions offer the ability to redefine individual characters of the character set or to install an entirely new character set. This can be done with sub-function 00H. Like all of the sub-functions of function 11H, the value 11H must be passed in the AH register and the sub-function number must be passed in the AL register. A number of other parameters must also be passed in the other processor registers. The BH register stores the height of the individual characters. Since this function is intended for modifying individual characters of the current character set, you must load the height of these characters here. As mentioned above, the height of characters on monochrome, EGA, or multisync monitors is normally 14 lines (or with the VGA card, 16 lines on a VGA or multisync monitor), while on color monitors it is 8 lines. The BL register stores the number of the character table in which the character will be loaded. Theoretically a number 0 through 3 can be given here for one of the four different character tables, but you should restrict yourself to modifying character table 0, because it is the only table guaranteed to be accessible by EGA cards with less than 256K RAM. This character table is also the one into which the EGA BIOS loads the character definitions when the video mode is initialized with function 00H. Since you may not want to redefine the entire character set, the CX register holds the number of characters to be defined (maximum of 256). The number of the first character to be defined is placed in the DX register and may not exceed the value 255.

The character definitions themselves are stored in a buffer whose address is passed in the ES:BP register pair. The bit patterns of the individual characters are placed in this buffer such that the height of each character (BH register) also specifies the number of bytes per character in the buffer.

The individual characters are stored sequentially, so the total size of the buffer is the number of characters multiplied by the height of the characters. The eight bits of each byte reflect the status of the individual pixels in each raster line. If a bit is set, the pixel will appear at the corresponding position in the foreground color. If the bit is cleared, the pixel will appear in the background color. Note that the character matrix is actually eight pixels wide, even through the characters are displayed with a width of nine pixels on a monochrome screen. In this case the ninth bit is not taken from the character definition, the last bit on each line is simply duplicated.

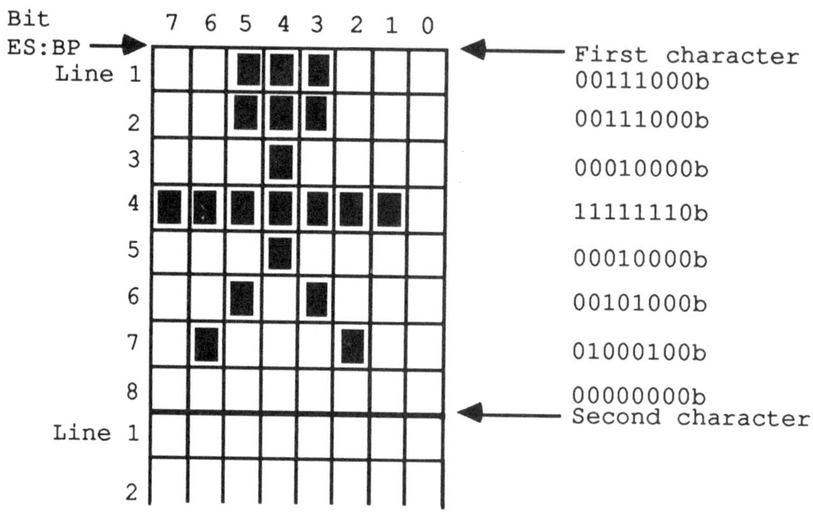

Buffer structure after calling function 11H, sub-function 00H

As long as characters with the appropriate ASCII codes are displayed on the screen, the changes will be noticeable immediately after this function is called.

While sub-function 00H can be used to load user-defined characters into the character set, sub-functions 01H and 02H are used to load the two ROM character sets contained on the EGA/VGA card. Sub-function 01H loads the entire 8x14 character set of the EGA/VGA card into one of the four character tables. Sub-function 02H loads the 8x8 CGA-compatible character set into one of the four character tables. In addition to the function and sub-function numbers, both functions are passed the number of the character table in which the character set is to be loaded in the BL register. If the character table involved is the one currently displayed on the screen, then the changes will be visible immediately after the function is called. Although these two functions load the character sets, they do not set the character generator to the height of the appropriate character set. For example, if you load the 8x8 character set into the current character table while the characters are being displayed in an 8x14 matrix, you will get a rather strange display. Raster lines one to eight will have the bit-map of the 8x8 character set while lines nine to 14 will have the remainder of the 8x14 set.

Sub-function 04H (available to VGA only) serves a similar purpose to sub-functions 01H, 02H and 03H. The difference is that calling sub-function 04H loads the 8x16 ROM character set into one of the four character tables.

If you want to work with several character sets in parallel, it is recommended that you load the individual character sets into their own character tables and then switch between the tables. Sub-function 03H is used to switch to a new character table. In addition to the function and sub-function numbers, it must be passed the number of the character table to be activated in the BL register.

Sub-functions 10H, 11H, and 12H are almost identical to sub-functions 00H, 01H, and 02H. They are also used for loading character sets, but they program the character generator at the same time. This has the result that the characters are displayed with the proper character height after the function is called. The number of text lines on the screen changes automatically.

Function 10H is used to load and activate user-defined character sets and is called exactly like function 00H. The number of text lines which are displayed after the call to the function results from the vertical resolution of the monitor divided by the height of the individual characters. If this division is not even and there is a remainder, the remaining lines will be divided equally between the top and bottom borders of the screen. Partial text lines are not displayed.

Sub-functions 11H and 12H load and activate entire character sets. If the 8x14 character set is loaded with sub-function 11H and a monochrome, EGA, or multisync monitor is being used, 25 lines (EGA) or 28 lines (VGA) will be displayed on the screen. If this is done while a color monitor is connected, which has a vertical resolution of only 200 lines, only 14 lines will be displayed on the screen.

These changes must also be taken into account when calling function 12H, which loads and activates the 8x8 character set. The usual 25 lines will be visible on a color monitor, while on the other monitors the screen will consist of 43 text lines (EGA) or 50 text lines (VGA).

VGA BIOS has an additional sub-function. When sub-function 14H is called, it loads and activates the 8x16 ROM character set. Only 25 lines of text will appear on the screen.

Regardless of the number of text lines which result from calling one of these functions, the EGA BIOS ensures that the traditional BIOS functions for screen output (function numbers 00H to 0FH) will still work properly. Even if the screen contains 43 lines, you can call the functions for character output, scrolling the screen, and access the lines outside of the usual 25-line boundary. However, you should avoid using multiple screen pages and just use page 0, or you may run into problems with the BIOS versions of various manufacturers.

Cursor emulation

Certain EGA cards can have problems with the mechanism called cursor emulation. This involves converting the starting and ending lines of the cursor when the height of the character matrix is changed. For example, if the character height decreases from 14 to 8 lines, then the cursor will be invisible if it was in the range of raster lines from 9 to 14. To prevent this, the BIOS converts the starting and ending lines to the new matrix height. This mechanism must be disabled at the beginning of a program. Unfortunately, no function for doing this exists in the EGA BIOS; the only way to disable it is to clear a flag in one of the BIOS variables (bit 0 in the byte at address 0040:0087). The programs at the end of this section demonstrate this in practice. The VGA BIOS does possess such a function, as we'll see shortly.

Function 12H

All of the functions described so far can only be used in conjunction with an EGA card or a VGA card. To determine if an EGA/VGA card is installed, the EGA/VGA BIOS offers function 12H, which is not available in the normal ROM-BIOS. It is called with the function number in AH and the value 10H in the BL register. If this value is still in the BL register after the call, you can assume that no EGA/VGA card is available and the normal ROM-BIOS was called, which does not support this function. A different value shows that an EGA or a VGA card is available. In this case the BH, BL, and CL registers contain configuration information about the installed EGA/VGA card.

The value in BH specifies the video mode that will be activated after the system is booted. Since another mode may have been enabled in the meantime, this information is of little use. The value in the CL register, which tells you what kind of monitor the card is driving, is much more useful. The following values are returned for the individual monitor types:

0BH	monochrome monitor
09H	high-resolution (EGA/VGA or multisync) monitor
08H	color monitor

The contents of the BL register are also useful. They specify the amount of RAM installed in the EGA card. The following codes can appear:

0	64K	1	128K
2	192K	3	256K

This distinction is important if you want to work with multiple character tables or with the high-resolution graphics modes of the EGA/VGA card. For example, graphics mode number 10H, which offers a resolution of 640x350 pixels, can be used only if the EGA/VGA card has at least 128K of RAM. The number of character tables available also depends on the size of the RAM. This can be determined by the incrementing by 1 the number returned in the BL register.

Function 1AH

Function 1AH, sub-function 00H informs the user of whether an EGA card or a VGA card is installed. This function is only available to VGA cards. You must pass the function number to the AH register and place the value 00H in the AL register. This determines whether a VGA card is installed. If the value 00H remains unchanged, there is no VGA card available, while a returned value of 1AH indicates a VGA card. The contents of the BL register indicate the active video mode:

Code	Meaning
00H	No video card
01H	MDA card / monochrome monitor
02H	CGA card / color monitor
03H	Reserved
04H	EGA card / high-res monitor
05H	EGA card / monochrome monitor
06H	Reserved
07H	VGA card / analog monochrome monitor
08H	VGA card / analog color monitor

Function 12H, sub-function 20H can be used to install an alternate hardcopy routine. This can be used when the screen is displaying more or fewer than 25 lines. Since the normal hardcopy routine of the BIOS assumes that there are 25 lines on the screen, it always prints exactly 25 lines, which may omit some lines from the hardcopy. The alternate hardcopy of the EGA/VGA BIOS always accounts for the actual number of lines displayed on the screen, and is therefore preferable to the normal hardcopy routine. It is installed by calling the BIOS video interrupt 10H, whereby the value 12H is passed in the AH register and the value 20H must be in the BL register.

The VGA BIOS includes six other sub-functions of function 12H, exclusively for control of the VGA card. Sub-function 30H helps determine the number of raster lines available (not text lines) when a VGA is operating with a VGA or multisync monitor. In CGA mode this becomes only 200 lines instead of 400. The sub-function number must be loaded into the BL register. The VGA BIOS interprets the number it finds in the AL register as the number of raster lines. A value of 0 in the AL register indicates 200, the value 1 indicates 350 and the value 2 indicates 400 raster lines.

Working in conjunction with color selection as mentioned above, so that EGA and VGA cards can load their palettes or DAC registers, the color spectrum of a CGA card can be emulated. Sub-function 31H enables or disables this emulation in the VGA card after calling function 00H (video mode selection). Calling this sub-function signaled by the value 0 in the AL register activates green light, while a value of 1 tells the VGA BIOS to avoid loading the corresponding register.

Automatic gray scaling

Sub-function 33H specifies the status of automatic gray scale summing. This summing instructs BIOS accesses to the DAC color table to automatically convert color values into gray scales. The contents of the AL register indicate this status: A value of 0 indicates conversion enabled, while a value of 1 indicates no conversion.

Function 12H, sub-function 34H controls the suppression of cursor emulation. A value of 0 in the AL register enables cursor emulation, while a value of 1 suppresses this emulation.

Function 13H

We will mention one last function of the EGA/VGA BIOS. It is not exactly new, since it was already in the AT ROM-BIOS, but it was not in the PC or XT BIOS. This is function 13H, which displays a string on the screen. There are four different output modes available, which differ in how the string is passed to the BIOS and whether or not the cursor will be placed at the end of the string when the output is done. Also, the functions differ in whether all the characters in the string will be given a constant color or provided with individual attributes. In the first case, the buffer, the address of which is passed in the ES:BP register pair, need only contain the ASCII codes of the characters to be printed. The color for all of the characters is taken from the BL register. In the second case, the attribute byte for each character follows its ASCII code in the buffer.

The contents of the AL register determine which mode will be used:

0 = One color for all of the characters. The cursor position does not change.

1 = One color for all of the characters. The cursor will be placed after the last character of the string.

2 = The buffer contains the individual attributes. The cursor position does not change.

3 = The buffer contains the individual attributes. The cursor will be placed after the last character of the string.

The number of the screen page on which the string is to appear can be specified in the BH register, but this should always be the current page. Otherwise problems will arise with printing control characters (carriage return, linefeed, etc.). The CX register holds the length of the string. This refers to the number of characters to be printed (attributes must not be counted in modes 2 and 3). The output position is passed to function 13H in registers DH (line) and DL (column). And, finally, we shouldn't forget the function number in the AH register.

Demonstration programs

After so many register assignments, function numbers, and the like, it helps to be able to see some example programs to put the information into perspective. Many of the functions we discussed are found in the programs listed below. Not all of them are called by the actual main program but are included to show you how it's done.

The programs have two main tasks. First, they show you how to work with and program the color palettes. Second, and even more important, these programs show you what possibilities are offered by defining your own character sets. Here this is used to display a small graphic in text mode. This could be used when you want to display a personal or company logo on the screen, but the characters needed are not found in the ASCII character set. In the example program, this is demonstrated by displaying the text "PC Internals Michael Tischer" on the screen in large, fancy lettering while in text mode. This message was first drawn with a graphics program and then converted to a kind of virtual raster. This corresponds in density to the character matrix of 8x14 pixels in the text mode when an EGA monitor is connected. With the help of this raster we discovered that four rows of 30 characters each, for a total of 120 characters, were required to display this graphic in text mode. The next step was to convert the bit-map of this graphic so that it could be loaded into one of the character tables with the help of sub-function 00H of function 11H. Each eight consecutive pixels were combined into a byte and then 14 of these eight-bit units in a column were combined together. The results are the initialized arrays in the program listing.

Once these data are created, the most time-consuming part of the whole procedure is done, since all we have to do is call the appropriate function in order to load the characters into the character table so we are able to display them on the screen. This proved to be something of a problem in C because none of the functions for interrupt calls allowed a value to be assigned to the BP register, which is where the offset address of the character buffer must be passed. We had to write a small assembly language routine which just loads the parameters passed to it into the required registers and then calls the BIOS video interrupt.

Inside the example program the bit patterns for the graphic are loaded into the character definitions for the ASCII codes 128 to 248 with the help of this function. The new characters replace the foreign characters and the border characters, but the standard ASCII characters like letters and numbers are retained. You can load the bit patterns in other parts of the character set as well, if you wish.

One routine in the program which is not executed is called SetLine and allows the number of text lines on the screen to be set (25 or 43). If you use this function to put the screen in 43 line mode, you first make certain arrangements regarding screen output. Both Pascal and C send their output to the screen using DOS functions when printf or writeln is called. Turbo Pascal allows direct access to the video RAM under certain conditions, but this doesn't change the problem. Here it depends on whether or not an extended screen driver (ANSI.SYS) is installed. If such a driver is not installed, the DOS will use BIOS function 0EH of interrupt 16H, which also handles screen scrolling. Since this function is part of the EGA BIOS, it will properly recognize that the screen consists of 43 lines and will not scroll it until the 44th line is reached. Things are different with most ANSI.SYS drivers, which perform scrolling themselves. Since many of them assume a 25-line screen, they will scroll until the 26th line is reached and the remaining lines will be wasted.

To avoid such problems, the two output routines in the example programs offer the ability to output strings directly to the video RAM and avoid the DOS functions.

Pascal listing: EGAP.PAS

```
{$V-}                                    { don't check length of strings }

{*********************************************************************}
{*                            E G A P                                *}
{*-------------------------------------------------------------------*}
{*    Description     : demonstrates the use of the functions of the *}
{*                      EGA/VGA BIOS.                                *}
{*-------------------------------------------------------------------*}
{*    Author          : MICHAEL TISCHER                              *}
{*    developed on    : 08/30/1988                                   *}
{*    last update     : 06/07/1989                                   *}
{*********************************************************************}

program EGAVGAP;

Uses Dos, CRT;                           { bind in the DOS and CRT units }
type BytePtr = ^byte;                                { pointer to a byte }

     VElb = record              { describes a screen position as 2 bytes }

              Character : char;                         { the   ASCII code }
              Attribute : byte;                          { the attribute }
              end;
     VRam  = array[0..4000] of VelB;            { describes the video RAM }
     string8 = string[80];                   { output string for PrintAt }

const VIDEO_INT = $10;                           { BIOS video interrupt }
      LINE25    = 25;                                 { 25 line screen }
      LINE43    = 43;                                 { 43 line screen }
      MOMO      = 0;                         { constants for GetMonTyp }
      COLOR     = 1;
      EGA       = 2;
      Font : array[1..120, 1..14] of byte = (
      (  0,  0,255, 62, 28, 28, 28, 28, 28, 28, 28, 28, 28, 31),    { E }
      (  0,  0,252,  7,  1,  1,  1,  1,  1,  1,  1,  1,  7,252),    { A }
      (  0,  0,  0,  0,129,195,195,199,199,206,206,142, 14, 14),    { C }
      (  0,  0, 62,193,128,128,  0,  0,  0,  0,  0,  0,  0,  0),    { H }
      (  0,  0, 16,144,112, 48, 48, 16, 16,  0,  0,  0,  0,  0),    {   }
      (  0,  0,  0,  0,  0,  0,  0,  0,  0,  0,  0,  0,  0,  0),    { L }
      (  0,  0,  3,  0,  0,  0,  0,  0,  0,  0,  0,  0,  0,  0),    { I }
      (  0,  0,254,248,112,112,112,112,112,112,112,112,112,112),    { N }
      (  0,  0,  0,  0,  0,  0,  0,  0,  0,252, 61, 30, 30, 28),    { E }
      (  0,  0,  0,  0,  0,  0,  0,  0,  0,248,  6,  7,  3,  3),    {   }
      (  0,  0,  0,  0,  0,  0,  0,  0,  0,  7,  0,  0,  0,128),    { C }
      (  0,  0, 32, 96,224,224,224,224,224,254,224,224,224,224),    { O }
      (  0,  0,  0,  0,  0,  0,  0,  0,  0,  1,  6, 12, 28, 24),    { N }
      (  0,  0,  0,  0,  0,  0,  0,  0,  0,240, 28,  6,  7,  7),    { T }
      (  0,  0,  0,  0,  0,  0,  0,  0,  0, 63, 15,  7,  7,  7),    { A }
```

```
( 0,  0,  0,  0,  0,  0,  0,  0,  0, 30, 39, 71,135,128),    { I }
( 0,  0,  0,  0,  0,  0,  0,  0,  0,126, 30, 15, 15, 14),    { N }
( 0,  0,  0,  0,  0,  0,  0,  0,  0,124,131,  3,  1,  1),    { S }
( 0,  0,  0,  0,  0,  0,  0,  0,  0,  0,  0,129,131,195),    {   }
( 0,  0,  0,  0,  0,  0,  0,  0,  0,  0, 62,193,128,  0),    { T }
( 0,  0,  0,  0,  0,  0,  0,  0,  0,  0,  0,192,224,224),    { H }
( 0,  0,248,120, 56, 56, 56, 56, 56, 56, 56, 56, 56, 56),    { E }
( 0,  0,  0,  0,  0,  0,  0,  0,  0, 31, 48, 48, 48, 48),    {   }
( 0,  0,  0,  0,  0,  0,  0,  0,  0,196, 52, 12,  4,  4),    { B }
( 0,  0,  0,  0,  0,  0,  0,  0,  0,  0,  0,  0,  0,  0),    { I }
( 0,  0,  0,  0,  0,  0,  0,  0,  0,  0,  0,  0,  0,  0),    { T }
( 0,  0,  0,  0,  0,  0,  0,  0,  0,  0,  0,  0,  0,  0),    {   }
( 0,  0,  0,  0,  0,  0,  0,  0,  0,  0,  0,  0,  0,  0),    { P }
( 0,  0,  0,  0,  0,  0,  0,  0,  0,  0,  0,  0,  0,  0),    { A }
( 0,  0,  0,  0,  0,  0,  0,  0,  0,  0,  0,  0,  0,  0),    { T }
( 28, 28, 28, 28, 28, 28, 28, 28, 62,255,  0,  0,  0,  0),   { T }
( 0,  0,  0,  0,  0,  0,  0,  0,  0,128,  0,  0,  0,  0),    { E }
( 14, 14, 14,  7,  7,  3,  3,  1,  0,  0,  0,  0,  0,  0),   { R }
( 0,  0,  0,  0,  0,  0,128,128,193, 62,  0,  0,  0,  0),    { N }
( 0,  0,  0,  0, 16, 16, 32, 64,128,  0,  0,  0,  0,  0),    {   }
( 0,  0,  0,  0,  0,  0,  0,  0,  0,  0,  0,  0,  0,  0),    { O }
( 0,  0,  0,  0,  0,  0,  0,  0,  0,  3,  0,  0,  0,  0),    { F }
(112,112,112,112,112,112,112,112,248,254,  0,  0,  0,  0),   {   }
( 28, 28, 28, 28, 28, 28, 28, 28, 62,255,  0,  0,  0,  0),   { A }
(  3,  3,  3,  3,  3,  3,  3,  3,  7,159,  0,  0,  0,  0),   {   }
(128,128,128,128,128,128,128,128,192,240,  0,  0,  0,  0),   { C }
(224,224,224,224,224,224, 96,112, 49, 30,  0,  0,  0,  0),   { H }
( 56, 63, 56, 56, 56, 24, 92, 76,134,  1,  0,  0,  0,  0),   { A }
(  7,255,  0,  0,  0,  0,  1,  2, 12,240,  0,  0,  0,  0),   { R }
(  7,  7,  7,  7,  7,  7,  7,  7, 15, 63,  0,  0,  0,  0),   { A }
( 0,  0,  0,  0,  0,  0,  0,  0,128,224,  0,  0,  0,  0),    { C }
( 14, 14, 14, 14, 14, 14, 14, 14, 31,127,  0,  0,  0,  0),   { T }
(  1,  1,  1,  1,  1,  1,  1,  1,  3,207,  0,  0,  0,  0),   { E }
(192,192,192,193,193,195,195,193,225,248,  0,  0,  0,  0),   { R }
( 0,  7,120,192,192,128,128,192,195,124,  0,  0,  0,  0),    {   }
(224,224,224,224,224,224,224,240,112, 29,  0,  0,  0,  0),   { I }
( 56, 56, 56, 56, 56, 56, 56, 56,124,255,  0,  0,  0,  0),   { N }
( 31, 31, 31,  0,  0, 64, 96, 96,112, 71,  0,  0,  0,  0),   {   }
( 0,224,248,252, 28, 12,  4, 12, 24,224,  0,  0,  0,  0),    { T }
( 0,  0,  0,  0,  0,  0,  0,  0,  0,  0,  0,  0,  0,  0),    { H }
( 0,  0,  0,  0,  0,  0,  0,  0,  0,  0,  0,  0,  0,  0),    { E }
( 0,  0,  0,  0,  0,  0,  0,  0,  0,  0,  0,  0,  0,  0),    {   }
( 0,  0,  0,  0,  0,  0,  0,  0,  0,  0,  0,  0,  0,  0),    { A }
( 0,  0,  0,  0,  0,  0,  0,  0,  0,  0,  0,  0,  0,  0),    { S }
( 0,  0,  0,  0,  0,  0,  0,  0,  0,  0,  0,  0,  0,  0),    { C }
( 0,  0,252, 60, 30, 30, 30, 23, 23, 23, 19, 19, 19, 17),    { I }
( 0,  0,  0,  0,  0,  0,  0,  1,  1,  1,130,130,130,196),    { I }
( 0,  0,126,120,240,240,240,112,112,112,112,112,112,112),    {   }
( 0,  0, 28, 28, 28,  0,  0,  0,  0,252, 60, 28, 28, 28),    { C }
( 0,  0,  0,  0,  0,  0,  0,  0,  0,  1,  6, 12, 28, 24),    { H }
( 0,  0,  0,  0,  0,  0,  0,  0,  0,240, 12,  2,  7,  7),    { A }
( 0,  0, 63, 15,  7,  7,  7,  7,  7,  7,  7,  7,  7,  7),    { R }
( 0,  0,  0,  0,  0,  0,  0,  0,  0, 62, 65,129,128,  0),    { A }
( 0,  0,  0,  0,  0,  0,  0,  0,  0,  0,128,192,192,224),    { C }
( 0,  0,  0,  0,  0,  0,  0,  0,  0, 63, 64,224,224,224),    { T }
( 0,  0,  0,  0,  0,  0,  0,  0,  0,  0,192, 96,112,112),    { E }
( 0,  0,  0,  0,  0,  0,  0,  0,  0,  7, 24, 48,112, 96),    { R }
( 0,  0,  0,  0,  0,  0,  0,  0,  0,192,112, 24, 28, 28),    {   }
( 0,  0,252, 60, 28, 28, 28, 28, 28, 28, 28, 28, 28, 28),    { S }
( 0,  0,  0,  0,  0,  0,  0,  0,  0,  0,  0,  0,  0,  0),    { E }
( 0,  0,  0,  0,  0,  0,  0,  0,  0,  0,  0,  0,  0,  0),    { T }
( 0,  0, 63, 56, 48, 48, 32, 32, 32,  0,  0,  0,  0,  0),    {   }
( 0,  0,255,112,112,112,112,112,112,112,112,112,112,112),    { O }
( 0,  0,225,225, 97, 32, 32, 32, 32, 15,  3,  1,  1,  1),    { F }
( 0,  0,192,192,192,  0,  0,  0,  0,192,193,195,195,195),    {   }
( 0,  0,  0,  0,  0,  0,  0,  0,  0,252,  3,  0,  0,  0),    { T }
( 0,  0,  0,  0,  0,  0,  0,  0,  0, 64, 65,195, 71, 70),    { H }
( 0,  0,  0,  0,  0,  0,  0,  0,  0,124,131,  0,  1,  1),    { E }
( 0,  0, 15,  3,  1,  1,  1,  1,  1,  1,  1,129,193,193),    {   }
( 0,  0,192,192,192,192,192,192,192,207,208,224,224,192),    { I }
```

```
( 0,  0,  0,  0,  0,  0,  0,  0,  0,128, 96,112, 48, 56),   { B }
( 0,  0,  0,  0,  0,  0,  0,  0,  0,  3, 12, 24, 56, 48),   { M }
( 0,  0,  0,  0,  0,  0,  0,  0,  0,224, 56, 12, 14, 14),   { - }
( 0,  0,  0,  0,  0,  0,  0,  0,  0,126, 30, 14, 15, 15),   { P }
( 0,  0,  0,  0,  0,  0,  0,  0,  0, 60, 78,142, 14,  0),   { C }
( 17, 17, 16, 16, 16, 16, 16, 16, 48,254,  0,  0,  0,  0),
(196,196,232,232,232,112,112, 80, 32, 35,  0,  0,  0,  0),
(112,112,112,112,112,112,112,112,248,254,  0,  0,  0,  0),
( 28, 28, 28, 28, 28, 28, 28, 28, 62,255,  0,  0,  0,  0),
( 56, 56, 56, 56, 56, 24, 28, 12,  6,129,  0,  0,  0,  0),
(  7,  0,  0,  0,  0,  0,  1,  2, 12,240,  0,  0,  0,  0),
(  7,  7,  7,  7,  7,  7,  7,  7, 15, 63,  0,  0,  0,  0),
(  0,  0,  0,  0,  0,  0,  0,  0,129,231,  0,  0,  0,  0),
(224,224,224,224,224,225,225,224,240,252,  0,  0,  0,  0),
(  0,  3, 60,224,224,192,192,224,225, 62,  0,  0,  0,  0),
(112,240,112,112,112,112,112,120,184, 14,  0,  0,  0,  0),
(224,255,224,224,224, 96,112, 48, 24,  7,  0,  0,  0,  0),
( 28,252,  0,  0,  0,  0,  4,  8, 48,192,  0,  0,  0,  0),
( 28, 28, 28, 28, 28, 28, 28, 28, 62,255,  0,  0,  0,  0),
(  0,  0,  0,  0,  0,  0,  0,  0,  0,128,  0,  0,  0,  0),
(  0,  0,  0,  0,  0,  0,  0,  0,  0,  0,  0,  0,  0,  0),
(  0,  0,  0,  0,  0,  0,  0,  0,  0,  3,  0,  0,  0,  0),
(112,112,112,112,112,112,112,112,248,254,  0,  0,  0,  0),
(  1,  1,  1,  1,  1,  1,  1,  1,  3, 15,  0,  0,  0,  0),
(193,193,192,192,192,194,195,195,227,250,  0,  0,  0,  0),
(240,254,255, 15,  1,  0,  0,  0,129,126,  0,  0,  0,  0),
( 14, 14,142,206,206,198, 71,195,129,  0,  0,  0,  0,  0),
(  1,  0,  0,  0,  0,  0,  0,  0,131,124,  0,  0,  0,  0),
(193,  1,  1,  1,  1,  1, 65,129,  3, 15,  0,  0,  0,  0),
(192,192,192,192,192,192,192,192,224,249,  0,  0,  0,  0),
( 56, 56, 56, 56, 56, 56, 56, 56,124,255,  0,  0,  0,  0),
(112,127,112,112,112, 48, 56, 24, 12,  3,  0,  0,  0,  0),
( 14,254,  0,  0,  0,  0,  2,  4, 24,224,  0,  0,  0,  0),
( 14, 14, 14, 14, 14, 14, 14, 14, 31,127,  0,  0,  0,  0),
(  0,  0,  0,  0,  0,  0,  0,  0,  0,192,  0,  0,  0,  0));

var   VLine{VLine},                  { stores the current cursor position }
      VColumn{VColumn},
      NumLine{NumLine} : byte;             { number of screen lines }
      Mono    : boolean;              { TRUE, if monochrome monitor }

{**********************************************************************}
{* CEmul: Switches the cursor emulation of the EGA card on or off.    *}
{* Input    : - DOIT = TRUE : Cursor emulation on.                   *}
{*                     FALSE: Cursor emulation off.                   *}
{* Output   : the current cursor column                               *}
{**********************************************************************}

procedure CEmul( DoIt : boolean );

var VioInfoByte : byte absolute $0040:$0087;          { BIOS info byte }

begin
  if DoIt then                                    { turn emulation on? }
    VioInfoByte := VioInfoByte or 1                   { yes, set bit 0 }
  else                                                          { NO }
    VioInfoByte := VioInfoByte and 254                { mask out bit 0 }
end;

{**********************************************************************}
{* GetCS: Returns the current output column.                          *}
{* Input    : none                                                    *}
{* Output   : the current cursor column                               *}
{**********************************************************************}

function GetCS : byte;

begin
  GetCS := VColumn;                     { get column from global variable }
end;
```

```
{***********************************************************************}
{* GetCZ: Return the current output line.                             *}
{* Input   : none                                                      *}
{* Output  : the current output line                                   *}
{***********************************************************************}

function GetCZ : byte;

begin
  GetCZ := VLine;                        { get line from global variable }
end;

{***********************************************************************}
{* CharDef: Defines the bit pattern of an individual character.       *}
{* Input   : - ASCII   = ASCII code of the first char to be defined    *}
{*           - TABLE   = number of the character table ( 0 bis 3 )     *}
{*           - MATRIX  = number of lines in the character matrix       *}
{*           - NUMBER  = number of characters to be defined            *}
{*           - BUFPTR  = pointer to the buffer with the character      *}
{* Output  : none                                                      *}
{***********************************************************************}

procedure CharDef( Ascii, Table, Matrix, Number : byte;
                   BufPtr : BytePtr );

var Regs : Registers;         { processor registers for interrupt call }

begin
  Regs.ax := $1100;          { ftn. no.: character generator, subftn. 0 }
  Regs.bh := Matrix;                      { line height of the matrix }
  Regs.bl := Table;                  { number of the character table }
  Regs.cx := Number;            { number of the character to be defined }
  Regs.dx := Ascii;                  { first character to be defined }
  Regs.bp := Ofs( BufPtr^ );          { offset address of the buffer }
  Regs.es := Seg( BufPtr^ );          {segment address of the buffer }
  intr(VIDEO_INT, Regs);                  { call BIOS video interrupt }
end;

{***********************************************************************}
{* GetMonTyp: Determines the type of monitor attached.                 *}
{* Input   : none                                                      *}
{* Output  : the monitor type: MOMO  = monochrome monitor              *}
{                              COLOR = color monitor                   *}
{*                             EGA   = EGA or Multisync monitor        *}
{***********************************************************************}

function GetMonTyp : byte;

var Regs : Registers;         { processor registers for interrupt call }

begin
  Regs.ah := $12;                      { ftn. no.: get configuration }
  Regs.bl := $10;                                { subfunction number }
  intr(VIDEO_INT, Regs);                 { call BIOS video interrupt }
  case Regs.cl of                      { CL contains the monitor type}
    $0B : GetMonTyp := MOMO;                     { monochrome monitor }
    $08 : GetMonTyp := COLOR;                         { color monitor }
    $09 : GetMonTyp := EGA;                             { EGA monitor }
  end;
end;

{***********************************************************************}
{* SetCur : Sets the blinking cursor and the internal output position *}
{* Input   : - COLUMN = output column   ( 0 .. 79 )                    *}
{*           - LINE   = output line     ( 1 .. n )                     *}
{* Output  : none                                                      *}
{***********************************************************************}

procedure SetCur( Column, Line : byte );
```

```
var Regs : Registers;          { processor registers for interrupt call }

begin
  Regs.ah := $2;                          { ftn. no.: set cursor position }
  Regs.bh := 0;                                            { screen page 0 }
  Regs.dh := Line;                                       { set coordinate }
  Regs.dl := Column;
  intr(VIDEO_INT, Regs);                      { call BIOS video interrupt }
  VLine := Line;               { save coordinates in internal variables }
  VColumn := Column;
end;

{**********************************************************************}
{* SetCol : Defines the contents of one of the 16 color registers in  *}
{*          the EGA card.                                             *}
{* Input  : - REGNR = number of the color register                   *}
{*           - COLOR = color value (0 to 63)                          *}
{* Output  : none                                                     *}
{**********************************************************************}

procedure SetCol(regnr, color : byte);

var Regs : Registers;          { processor registers for interrupt call }

begin
  Regs.ah := $10;                      { ftn. no.: set colors/attributes }
  Regs.al := 0;                                            { subfunction 0 }
  Regs.bl := regnr;                         { set number of the register }
  Regs.bh := color and 63;    { set color value (mask out bits 6 and 7) }
  intr(VIDEO_INT, Regs);                      { call BIOS video interrupt }
end;

{**********************************************************************}
{* SetBorder : Defines the border color.                              *}
{* Input   : - COLOR = color value (0 to 63)                          *}
{* Output  : none                                                     *}
{**********************************************************************}

procedure SetBorder(color : byte);

var Regs : Registers;          { processor registers for interrupt call }

begin
  Regs.ah := $10;                       { ftn. no.: set colors attributes }
  Regs.al := 1;                                            { subfunction 0 }
  Regs.bh := color and 63;    { set color value (mask out bits 6 and 7) }
  intr(VIDEO_INT, Regs);                      { call BIOS video interrupt }
end;

{**********************************************************************}
{* SetLines : Sets the number of lines.                               *}
{* Input    : Sub-function of function 11H:                           *}
{*            $11 : 8x4 character set                                 *}
{*            $12 : 8x8 character set                                 *}
{*            $14 : 8x16 character set                                *}
{* Output   : none                                                    *}
{**********************************************************************}

procedure SetLines( Lines : byte);

var Regs : Registers;          { processor registers for interrupt call }

begin
  Regs.ah := $11;                       { ftn. no.: character generator }
  Regs.al :=  Lines;                          { sub-function of fnc. 11h }
  Regs.bl := 0;                                { use character table 0 }
  intr(VIDEO_INT, Regs);                      { call BIOS video interrupt }
end;
```

```
{***********************************************************************}
{* IsEga: Determines if an EGA card is installed and handles the      *}
{*        initialization of the global variables.                     *}
{* Input   : none                                                      *}
{* Output  : TRUE, if an EGA card is installed, else FALSE.            *}
{***********************************************************************}

function IsEga : boolean;

var Regs : Registers;         { processor registers for interrupt call }

begin
  Regs.ah := $12;                  { ftn. no.: get video configuration }
  Regs.bl := $10;                                { subfunction number }
  intr(VIDEO_INT, Regs);                     { call BIOS video interrupt }
  if Regs.bl <> $10  then                  { is it an EGA or VGA card? }
    begin                                                       { yes }
      {*- create pointer to VRAM depending on the monitor connected  -*}
      Mono := Regs.bh = 1;           { connected to monochrome monitor? }
      IsEga := TRUE;                       { an EGA card was discovered }
    end
  else
    IsEga := FALSE;                             { no EGA card discovered }
end;

{***********************************************************************}
{* IsVga: Determines whether a VGA card is installed, and initializes *}
{*        the global variables.                                        *}
{* Input   : none                                                      *}
{* Output  : TRUE if a VGA card is installed, otherwise FALSE.         *}
{* Info    : Use this function BEFORE calling the ISEGA in your own    *}
{*           application, since the TRUE for some EGAs also applies    *}
{*           to this routine as well.                                  *}
{***********************************************************************}

function IsVga : boolean;

var Regs : Registers;     { processor register for the interrupt call }

begin
  Regs.ah := $1A;              { function no.: Determine video system }
  Regs.al := $00;
  intr(VIDEO_INT, Regs);                     { Call BIOS video interrupt }
  if ( Regs.al = $1A ) and (( Regs.bl = 7 ) or ( Regs.bl = 8 )) then
    begin                               { VGA card installed and active }
      Mono  := FALSE;
      IsVga := TRUE;                   { definitely a VGA card on board }
    end
  else
    IsVga := FALSE;                              { no VGA card connected }
end;

{***********************************************************************}
{* PrintAt: Outputs a string at the give screen position with a       *}
{*          certain attribute.                                         *}
{* Input  :  - COLUMN = output column  ( 0 .. 79 )                     *}
{*           - LINE   = output line    ( 0 .. NUMLINE-1 )              *}
{*           - COLOR  = attribute for the characters to be printed     *}
{*           - OUSTR  = the string to be printed                       *}
{* Output : none                                                       *}
{***********************************************************************}

procedure PrintAt( Column, Line, Color :
byte; OutStr : string8);

var ColorRAM : VRam absolute $B800:0000;      { describes physical VRAM }
    MonoRAM  : VRam absolute $B000:0000;      { describes physical VRAM }
    Index    : word;                          { index into the VRAM array }
    Stren,                              { length of the string to be printed }
    i        : byte;                       { running pointer to the string }
```

```
begin
  Stren := length( OutStr );                    { get length of the string }
  Index := Line * 80 + Column;                    { set index in the array }
     if Mono then
        begin                                                       { yes }
          for i:=1 to Stren do                    { run through the string }
            begin
              MonoRAM[ Index ].Character := OutStr[i]; { set character }
              MonoRAM[ Index ].Attribute := Color;          { set color }
              inc( Index );                         { increment the index }
            end;
        end
      else                                     { output to the color screen }
        begin
          for i:=1 to Stren do                    { run through the string }
            begin
              ColorRAM[ Index ].Character := OutStr[i];{ set character }
              ColorRAM[ Index ].Attribute := Color;         { set color }
              inc( Index );                         { increment the index }
            end;
        end;
  {*-- calculate new cursor position ---------------------------------*}
  SetCur((VColumn + VLine * 80 + Stren) mod 80,
         (VColumn + VLine * 80 + Stren) div 80);
end;

{***********************************************************************}
{* Blinking : Defines the meaning of bit 7 in the attribute of a       *}
{*            character in the text modes.                             *}
{* Input    : - DoBlink = TRUE : blinking                              *}
{*                        FALSE: intense background color              *}
{* Output   : none                                                     *}
{***********************************************************************}

procedure Blinking( DoBlink : boolean );

var Regs : Registers;          { processor registers for interrupt call }

begin
  Regs.ah := $10;                        { ftn. no.: set colors/attributes }
  Regs.al := $3;                                     { subfunction number }
  if DoBlink then                                           { blinking? }
    Regs.bl := 1                                { yes, BL = 1 : blinking }
  else                                                            { no }
    Regs.bl := 0;               { yes, BL = 0 : intense background color }
  intr(VIDEO_INT, Regs);                        { call BIOS video interrupt }
end;


{***********************************************************************}
{* Cls: Clears the screen, causing the video mode to be reset.          *}
{*      The palette registers will also be filled with the default      *}
{*      values and the character set will be reset.                     *}
{* Input    : none                                                      *}
{* Output   : none                                                      *}
{***********************************************************************}

procedure Cls;

var Regs : Registers;          { processor registers for interrupt call }

begin
  Regs.ah := $0;                               { ftn. no.: set video mode }
  if Mono then                         { connected to monochrome monitor }
    Regs.al := 7                                { yes, 80x25 text display }
  else                                               { no, color monitor }
    Regs.al := 3;                     { yes, 80x25 character text display }
  intr(VIDEO_INT, Regs);                        { call BIOS video interrupt }
end;
```

```
{***********************************************************************}
{* EgaVga : Demonstrates how to use the functions of the EGA/VGA BIOS.*}
{* Input  : TRUE if VGA card installed, otherwise FALSE               *}
{* Output : none                                                      *}
{***********************************************************************}

procedure EgaVga (VGA : boolean);

var i, j, k : word;                                    { loop counter }
    OutStr  : string8;                           { logo output string }
    Regs    : Registers;  { processor register for the interrupt call }

begin
  {*-- Add EGA/VGA hardcopy routine *}
  Regs.ah := $12;                           { alternate select function }
  Regs.bl := $20;                          { sub-function: install rtne }
  intr(VIDEO_INT,Regs);                                { call interrupt }
  {*-- prepare screen layout -----------------------------------------*}
  SetCur(0,0);
  Cls;                                                { clear the screen }
  Blinking( FALSE );             { light background instead of blinking }

  if ( VGA ) then      { Check compatibility in case characters must be }
    begin              { redefined, and the characters must be changed  }
      Regs.ah := $12;  { into 350-line mode (changed back into EGA      }
      Regs.bl := $30;  { mode).                                         }
      Regs.al := 1;
      intr(VIDEO_INT, Regs);                { call BIOS video interrupt }

      SetLines( $11 );                     { activate 8x14 character set }
    end;

  CharDef(128, 0, 14, 120, BytePtr(@font));          { define character }

  for i:=1 to 250 do                        { run through the loop 500 times }
    begin                                 { write color bars to the video RAM }
      PrintAt(GetCs, GetCZ, ((i mod 14) + 1) shl 4, '     ');
      if i <> 250 then                                  { last color bar? }
        PrintAt(GetCs, GetCZ, 0, '   ');                             { no }
    end;
  for i:=10 to 15 do                                 { make room for logo }
    PrinTat(22, i, 0, '
                                                      ');
  k := 128;                                     { first character in logo }
  for i:=0 to 3 do                          { the logo consists of 4 lines }
    begin
      OutStr := '';                                     { empty the string }
      for j:=1 to 30 do               { each line consists of 30 characters }
        begin
          OutStr := OutStr + chr( k ); { append the char to the string }
          inc( k );                                         { increment K }
        end;
      PrintAt(24, i+11, 15, OutStr);                   { output the string  }
    end;
  PrintAt(1, 1, 15, ' The most important characters are   ');
  PrintAt(1, 2, 15, ' still present in spite of the logo! ');
  Printat(1, 3, 15, '                                     ');
  Printat(1, 4, 15, ' !"#$%&''()*+-./0123456789:;<=>?@ ');
  Printat(1, 5, 15, ' ABCDEFGHIJKLMNOPQRSTUVXXYZ[\]^_ ');
  Printat(1, 6, 15, ' `abcdefghijklmnopqrstuvxyz{|}~  ');
  Printat(33, 21, 15, '                                        ');
  Printat(33, 22, 15, '     press any key to end the program.   ');
  Printat(33, 23, 15, '                                        ');
  SetCur(34, 22);
  {*-- change the colors in the color bars --------------------------*}
  i := 0;                          { start value for the color registers }
  while ( not KeyPressed ) do           { repeat until key is pressed }
    begin
      inc( i );     { increment the color value for the first register }
        for j:=1 to 14 do              { run through registers 1 to 14 }
```

```
        SetCol(j, i+j and 63);     { write color value in the register }
      end;

  if ( VGA ) then             { Switch VGA card back into 400-line mode }
    begin
      Regs.ah := $12;
      Regs.bl := $30;
      Regs.al := 2;
      intr(VIDEO_INT, Regs);              { call BIOS video interrupt }

      SetLines( $14 );                { activate 8x16 character set }
    end;

  Cls;                                             { clear screen }
end;

{*********************************************************************}
{**                          MAIN PROGRAM                           **}
{*********************************************************************}

begin
  if IsVga then                               { VGA card installed? }
    EgaVga( true )                                 { YES, run demo }
  else
    begin
      if IsEga then                           { EGA card installed? }
        begin                                                { YES }
          if ( GetMonTyp = EGA ) then       { EGA monitor attached? }
            EgaVga( false )                          { YES, run demo }
          else                                   { NO, wrong monitor }
            begin
              writeln('This program only works with an EGA ');
              writeln('card or VGA card, and a monitor     ');
              writeln('supported by one of these cards.    ');
            end;
        end
      else
        writeln( 'No EGA or VGA card installed...'+
                 ' Program aborted.' );
    end;
end.
```

C listing: EGAVGAC.C

```
/*********************************************************************/
/*                           E G A V G A C                           */
/*-------------------------------------------------------------------*/
/*    Task            : Demonstration using the functions available  */
/*                      in the EGA-/VGA-BIOS                         */
/*-------------------------------------------------------------------*/
/*    Author          : MICHAEL TISCHER                              */
/*    Developed on    : 08/30/1988                                   */
/*    Last update     : 05/02/1989                                   */
/*-------------------------------------------------------------------*/
/*    (MICROSOFT C)                                                  */
/*    Creation        : CL /AS /c EGAVGAC.C                          */
/*                      LINK EGAVGAC EGAVGACA;                       */
/*    Call            : EGAC                                         */
/*-------------------------------------------------------------------*/
/*    (BORLAND TURBO C)                                              */
/*    Creation        : Make a project file containing the following: */
/*                        EGAVGAC                                    */
/*                        EGAVGACA.OBJ                               */
/*                      Before compiling, select the Options menu    */
/*                      and the Compiler option - make sure that the */
/*                      Small model is active                        */
/*                      Select the Linker option - make sure that the */
/*                      Case-sensitive link is set to Off            */
/*                      The program will compile with one warning... */
```

```
/*                       this is okay, it will run correctly            */
/************************************************************************/

/*== Add include files ==============================================*/

#include <dos.h>
#include <stdlib.h>
#include <string.h>
#include <stdarg.h>
#include <bios.h>

/*== Typedefs ========================================================*/

typedef unsigned char BYTE;                          /* Create a byte */
typedef unsigned int WORD;
typedef BYTE BOOL;                            /* like BOOLEAN in Pascal */
typedef struct velb far * VP;    /* VP = FAR pointer to the video RAM */

/*== Function definition from the assembler module ===================*/

extern void chardef( BYTE ascii, BYTE table, BYTE lines,
                     BYTE amount, BYTE far * buf );

/*== Structures ======================================================*/

struct velb {          /* Describes a two-byte position on the screen */
            BYTE ascii_code,                           /* ASCII code */
                 attribute;                /* Corresponding attribute */
            };

/*== Macros ==========================================================*/

/*-- MK_FP creates a FAR pointer to an object out of a ---------------*/
/*-- segment address and an offset address ---------------------------*/

#ifndef MK_FP                              /* MK_FP not defined yet? */
#define MK_FP(seg, ofs) ((void far *) ((unsigned long) (seg)<<16|(ofs)))
#endif

#define VOFS(x,y)  ( 80 * ( y ) + ( x ) )   /* Offsetpos. in video RAM */
#define VPOS(x,y)  (VP) ( vptr + VOFS( x, y ) )      /* Pointer in VRAM */
#define GETCZ()    (vline)            /* Returns the current cursor line */
#define GETCS()    (vcolumn)        /* Returns the current cursor column */

/*== Constants =======================================================*/

#define TRUE  ( 1 == 1 )          /* Constants for working with BOOL */
#define FALSE ( 1 == 0 )

#define VIDEO_INT 0x10                         /* BIOS video interrupt */

#define MONO  0                            /* Monitor types for GETMON */
#define COLOR 1
#define EGA   2

#define PAUSE 100

/*== Global variables ================================================*/

VP vptr;              /* Pointer to the first character in video RAM */
BYTE vline,                   /* States the current cursor position */
     vcolumn;
BOOL mono;               /* TRUE if a monochrome monitor is connected */

/************************************************************************
*  Function        : C E M U L                                        *
**--------------------------------------------------------------------**
*  Task            : Enables/disables cursor emulation on the         *
*                    EGA card.                                        *
*  Input parameters : - DOIT = TRUE : Emulation on                    *
```

```
*                              FALSE: Emulation off                     *
*  Return values     : None                                             *
************************************************************************/

void cemul( BOOL doit )

{
 /*-- Definition of video info byte at offset address 0x87 within ----*/
 /*-- the BIOS variable segment --------------------------------------*/

 #define VIO_INFO_BYTE ((BYTE far *) MK_FP(0x40, 0x87))

 if ( doit )                             /* Cursor emulation enabled? */
  *VIO_INFO_BYTE |= 1;                               /* YES, set bit 0 */
 else                                                         /* NO, */
  *VIO_INFO_BYTE &= 254;                              /* clear bit 0 */
}

/***********************************************************************
*  Function          : G E T M O N                                      *
**--------------------------------------------------------------------**
*  Task              : Determines the type of monitor connected.        *
*  Input parameters : None                                              *
*  Return values     : Monitor type                                     *
*                        MONO = monochrome monitor                      *
*                        COLOR= Color monitor                           *
*                        EGA  = EGA or multisync monitor                *
************************************************************************/

BYTE getmon()
 {
  union REGS regs;           /* Processor register for interrupt call */

  regs.h.ah = 0x12;       /* Function number: Determine configuration */
  regs.h.bl = 0x10;                            /* Sub-function number */
  int86(VIDEO_INT, &regs, &regs);          /* Call BIOS video interrupt */
  if ( regs.h.cl == 0x0B )                   /* Monochrome monitor? */
   return( MONO );                                             /* YES */
  if ( regs.h.cl == 0x08 )                        /* color monitor? */
   return( COLOR );                                            /* YES */
  else                                             /* NO, must be EGA */
   return( EGA );
 }

/***********************************************************************
*  Function          : S E T C U R                                      *
**--------------------------------------------------------------------**
*  Task              : Sets the screen cursor and the internal          *
*                      position of the output.                          *
*  Input parameters : - COLUMN    = the cursor column                   *
*                      - LINE      = the cursor line                     *
*  Return values     : None                                             *
************************************************************************/

void setcur(BYTE column, BYTE line)
 {
  union REGS regs;           /* Processor register for interrupt call */

  regs.h.ah = 2;                                   /* Function number */
  regs.h.bh = 0;                                /* Use video page zero */
  regs.h.dh = vline = line;   /* Use global variables for coordinates */
  regs.h.dl = vcolumn = column;
  int86(VIDEO_INT, &regs, &regs);          /* Call BIOS video interrupt */
 }

/***********************************************************************
*  Function          : S E T C O L                                      *
**--------------------------------------------------------------------**
*  Task              : Defines the contents of one of the 16 EGA        *
*                      color registers.                                 *
```

```
*  Input parameters : - REGNR = Color register number                 *
*                     - COLOR = Color value (0-15)                     *
*  Return values    : None                                             *
**********************************************************************/

void setcol(BYTE regnr, BYTE color)

{
 union REGS regs;          /* Processor register for the interrupt call */

 regs.h.ah = 0x10;                /* Function no.: Set color/attribute */
 regs.h.al = 0;                                    /* Sub-function 0 */
 regs.h.bl = regnr;                           /* Set register number */
 regs.h.bh = color & 63;          /* Set color number ( Bits 6 and 7 ) */
 int86(VIDEO_INT, &regs, &regs);       /* Call BIOS video interrupt */
}

/**********************************************************************
*  Function          : S E T B O R D E R                               *
**-------------------------------------------------------------------**
*  Task              : Sets the border color.                          *
*  Input  parameters: - COLOR = Color value (0-15)                     *
*  Return values      : None                                           *
**********************************************************************/

void setborder( BYTE color )

{
 union REGS regs;          /* Processor register for the interrupt call */

 regs.h.ah = 0x10;                /* Function no.: Set color/attribute */
 regs.h.al = 1;                                    /* Sub-function 1 */
 regs.h.bh = color & 15;                          /* Set color value */
 int86(VIDEO_INT, &regs, &regs);          /* Call BIOS video interrupt */
}

/**********************************************************************
*  Function          : S E T L I N E S                                 *
**-------------------------------------------------------------------**
*  Task              : Determines the number of lines.                 *
*  Input  parameters: - Sub-function no. for calling function 11H      *
*                       0x11 : 8*14 character set                      *
*                       0x12 : 8*8  character set                      *
*                       0x14 : 8*16 character set (VGA only)           *
*  Return values      : None                                           *
**********************************************************************/

void setlines( BYTE lines )

{
 union REGS regs;          /* Processor register for the interrupt call */

 regs.h.ah = 0x11;              /* Function no.: Character generator */
 regs.h.al = lines;                             /* Sub-function no. */
 regs.h.bl = 0;                         /* Use character table 0 */
 int86(VIDEO_INT, &regs, &regs);          /* Call BIOS video interrupt */
}

/**********************************************************************
*  Function          : I S _ E G A                                     *
**-------------------------------------------------------------------**
*  Task              : Determines whether an EGA card is installed.    *
*  Input  parameters: None                                             *
*  Return values       TRUE when an EGA or VGA card is installed, and  *
*                      false in any other case                         *
**********************************************************************/

BOOL is_ega()
 {
  union REGS regs;         /* Processor register for the interrupt call */
```

```
  regs.h.ah = 0x12; /* Function number: Determine video configuration */
  regs.h.bl = 0x10;                             /* Sub-function number */
  int86(VIDEO_INT, &regs, &regs);         /* Call BIOS video interrupt */
  if ( regs.h.bl != 0x10 )                /* Is it an EGA or VGA card? */
   /*-- Set pointer in video RAM for attached monitor ----------------*/
   vptr = (VP) MK_FP( (mono = regs.h.bh) ? 0xb000 : 0xb800, 0);
  return( regs.h.bl != 0x10 );            /* BL != 0x10 --> EGA or VGA */
 }

/**********************************************************************
* Function          : I S _ V G A                                     *
**------------------------------------------------------------------**
* Task              : Determines whether a VGA card is installed.     *
* Input  parameters: None                                             *
* Return values     : TRUE when a VGA card is installed;              *
*                     FALSE in any other case.                        *
* Info              : This function should be called before the       *
*                     is_ega function, because the parameters in the  *
*                     is_ega function also apply to VGA cards (i.e.,  *
*                     TRUE will be returned to is_ega for a VGA card. *
*                     Call is_vga first in your own applications,     *
*                     then call is_ega.                               *
**********************************************************************/

BOOL is_vga()
 {
  union REGS regs;          /* Processor register for the interrupt call */

  regs.h.ah = 0x1A;      /* Function no.: Determine video configuration */
  regs.h.al = 0x00;                             /* Sub-function number */
  int86(VIDEO_INT, &regs, &regs);          /* Call BIOS video interrupt */
  if ( regs.h.al == 0x1A && ( regs.h.bl==7 || regs.h.bl==8 ) )
   {                           /* VGA card connected to VGA monitor? */
    mono = FALSE;
    vptr = (VP) MK_FP( 0xb800, 0 );          /* Set pointer in video RAM */
    return TRUE;
   }
  return FALSE;                              /* No VGA card installed */
 }

/**********************************************************************
* Function          : P R I N T A T                                   *
**------------------------------------------------------------------**
* Task              : Displays a string on the screen.                *
*                                                                     *
* Input  parameters: - COLUMN   = Display column.                     *
*                    - LINE     = Display line.                       *
*                    - CHCOLOR  = Character attribute.                *
*                    - STRING   = Pointer to string.                  *
* Return values     : None                                            *
* Information       : - This function does not recognize format specs *
*                       as supplied by PRINTF.                        *
*                     - When the function reaches the end of the      *
*                       screen, the screen will not scroll up.        *
**********************************************************************/

void printat(BYTE column, BYTE line, BYTE chcolor, char * string)

 {
  register VP lptr;                    /* Floating pointer to video RAM */
  register BYTE i;                 /* points to the number of characters */
  unsigned newofs;                        /* Computes new coordinates */

  lptr = VPOS(column, line);               /* Set pointer in video RAM */
  for (i=0 ; *string ; ++lptr, ++i)                  /* execute string */
   {
    lptr->ascii_code = *(string++);          /* Character in video RAM */
    lptr->attribute = chcolor;              /* Set character attribute */
   }
```

```
  /*-- Compute new cursor coordinates --------------------------------*/

  vcolumn = (newofs = ((unsigned) line * 80 + column + i)) % 80;
  vline = newofs / 80;
 }

/***********************************************************************
*  Function         : P R I N T F A T                                  *
**------------------------------------------------------------------**
*  Task             : Displays a string on the screen (like PRINTF),   *
*                     writing the string directly to video RAM.        *
*  Input  parameters: - COLUMN = Display column.                       *
*                     - LINE   = Display line.                         *
*                     - CHCOLOR= Character color.                      *
*                     - STRING = Pointer to the string.                *
*                     - ...    = Additional arguments as needed.       *
*  Return values      : None                                           *
*  Information      : - When the end of the screen is reached, the     *
*                       screen will not scroll up.                     *
*                   : -  string can use the normal format specifier    *
*                       group as used with PRINTF.                     *
**********************************************************************/

void printfat(BYTE column, BYTE line, BYTE chcolor, char * string,...)

 {
  va_list parameter;     /* Take parameter list for VA_... Macros from */
  char output[255];                /* the formatted, displayed string */

  va_start(parameter, string);/* Get parameters in PARAMETER variable */
  vsprintf(output, string, parameter);             /* Convert string */
  printat(column, line, chcolor, output);           /* Display string */
 }

/***********************************************************************
*  Function         : B L I N K I N G                                  *
**------------------------------------------------------------------**
*  Task             : Defines the meaning of bit 7 of the attribute    *
*                     byte of a character in text mode.                *
*  Input  parameters: DOBLINK = TRUE  : Blink.                         *
*                               FALSE : Light background color.        *
*  Return values      : none                                           *
**********************************************************************/

void blinking( BOOL doblink )
 {
  union REGS regs;        /* Processor register for the interrupt call */

  regs.h.ah = 0x10;             /* Function no.: Set color/attribute */
  regs.h.al = 0x3;                             /* Sub-function number */
  regs.h.bl = doblink ? 1 : 0;                   /* BL = 1 : blinking */
  int86(VIDEO_INT, &regs, &regs);         /* Call BIOS video interrupt */
 }

/***********************************************************************
*  Function         : C L S                                            *
**------------------------------------------------------------------**
*  Task             : Clears the screen and resets the video mode.     *
*                     This reset includes the palette registers, as    *
*                     well as the character set in use.                *
*  Input  parameters: none                                             *
*  Return values    : none                                             *
**********************************************************************/

void cls()
 {
  union REGS regs;        /* Processor register for the interrupt call */

  regs.h.ah = 0x0;                   /* Function no.: Set video mode */
  regs.h.al = ( mono ) ? 7 : 3;            /* 80x25-char text mode */
```

```
  int86(VIDEO_INT, &regs, &regs);        /* Call BIOS video interrupt */
 }

/***********************************************************************
*  Function         : N O K E Y                                        *
**--------------------------------------------------------------------**
*  Task             : Tests for a depressed key.                       *
*  Input  parameters: none                                             *
*  Return values    : TRUE if a key is depressed, otherwise            *
*                     FALSE.                                           *
***********************************************************************/

BOOL nokey()

{
#ifdef __TURBOC__                               /* Using TURBO C to compile?  */
 return( bioskey( 1 ) == 0 );                 /* YES, read keyboard from BIOS */
#else                                     /* Using Microsoft C to compile... */
 return( _bios_keybrd( _KEYBRD_READY ) == 0 );         /* Read from BIOS */
#endif
}

/***********************************************************************
*  Function         : E G A V G A                                      *
**--------------------------------------------------------------------**
*  Task             : Demonstrates the application of EGA/VGA BIOS     *
*                     functions                                        *
*  Input  parameters: VGA : TRUE when working with VGA card            *
*                           FALSE in any other case                    *
*  Return values    : none                                             *
***********************************************************************/

void egavga( BOOL VGA )
 {
  static BYTE font[120][14] = {        /* Character definition for logo */
   {  0,  0,255, 62, 28, 28, 28, 28, 28, 28, 28, 28, 28, 31},    /* T */
   {  0,  0,252,  7,  1,  1,  1,  1,  1,  1,  1,  1,  7,252},    /* h */
   {  0,  0,  0,  0,129,195,195,199,199,206,206,142, 14, 14},    /* e */
   {  0,  0, 62,193,128,128,  0,  0,  0,  0,  0,  0,  0,  0},    /* s */
   {  0,  0, 16,144,112, 48, 48, 16, 16,  0,  0,  0,  0,  0},    /* e */
   {  0,  0,  0,  0,  0,  0,  0,  0,  0,  0,  0,  0,  0,  0},    /*   */
   {  0,  0,  3,  0,  0,. 0,  0,  0,  0,  0,  0,  0,  0,  0},    /* l */
   {  0,  0,254,248,112,112,112,112,112,112,112,112,112,112},    /* i */
   {  0,  0,  0,  0,  0,  0,  0,  0,  0,252, 61, 30, 30, 28},    /* n */
   {  0,  0,  0,  0,  0,  0,  0,  0,  0,248,  6,  7,  3,  3},    /* e */
   {  0,  0,  0,  0,  0,  0,  0,  0,  0,  7,  0,  0,  0,128},    /* s */
   {  0,  0, 32, 96,224,224,224,224,224,254,224,224,224,224},    /*   */
   {  0,  0,  0,  0,  0,  0,  0,  0,  0,  1,  6, 12, 28, 24},    /* c */
   {  0,  0,  0,  0,  0,  0,  0,  0,  0,240, 28,  6,  7,  7},    /* o */
   {  0,  0,  0,  0,  0,  0,  0,  0,  0, 63, 15,  7,  7,  7},    /* n */
   {  0,  0,  0,  0,  0,  0,  0,  0,  0, 30, 39, 71,135,128},    /* t */
   {  0,  0,  0,  0,  0,  0,  0,  0,  0,126, 30, 15, 15, 14},    /* a */
   {  0,  0,  0,  0,  0,  0,  0,  0,  0,124,131,  3,  1,  1},    /* i */
   {  0,  0,  0,  0,  0,  0,  0,  0,  0,  0,  0,129,131,195},    /* n */
   {  0,  0,  0,  0,  0,  0,  0,  0,  0,  0, 62,193,128,  0},    /*   */
   {  0,  0,  0,  0,  0,  0,  0,  0,  0,  0,  0,192,224,224},    /* t */
   {  0,  0,248,120, 56, 56, 56, 56, 56, 56, 56, 56, 56, 56},    /* h */
   {  0,  0,  0,  0,  0,  0,  0,  0,  0, 31, 48, 48, 48, 48},    /* e */
   {  0,  0,  0,  0,  0,  0,  0,  0,  0,196, 52, 12,  4,  4},    /*   */
   {  0,  0,  0,  0,  0,  0,  0,  0,  0,  0,  0,  0,  0,  0},    /* b */
   {  0,  0,  0,  0,  0,  0,  0,  0,  0,  0,  0,  0,  0,  0},    /* i */
   {  0,  0,  0,  0,  0,  0,  0,  0,  0,  0,  0,  0,  0,  0},    /* t */
   {  0,  0,  0,  0,  0,  0,  0,  0,  0,  0,  0,  0,  0,  0},    /*   */
   {  0,  0,  0,  0,  0,  0,  0,  0,  0,  0,  0,  0,  0,  0},    /* p */
   {  0,  0,  0,  0,  0,  0,  0,  0,  0,  0,  0,  0,  0,  0},    /* a */
   { 28, 28, 28, 28, 28, 28, 28, 28, 62,255,  0,  0,  0,  0},    /* t */
   {  0,  0,  0,  0,  0,  0,  0,  0,  0,128,  0,  0,  0,  0},    /* t */
   { 14, 14, 14,  7,  7,  3,  3,  1,  0,  0,  0,  0,  0,  0},    /* e */
   {  0,  0,  0,  0,  0,  0,128,128,193, 62,  0,  0,  0,  0},    /* r */
   {  0,  0,  0,  0, 16, 16, 32, 64,128,  0,  0,  0,  0,  0},    /* n */
```

```
{  0,  0,  0,  0,  0,  0,  0,  0,  0,  0,  0,  0,  0,  0},     /* s */
{  0,  0,  0,  0,  0,  0,  0,  0,  0,  3,  0,  0,  0,  0},     /*   */
{112,112,112,112,112,112,112,112,248,254,  0,  0,  0,  0},     /* f */
{ 28, 28, 28, 28, 28, 28, 28, 28, 62,255,  0,  0,  0,  0},     /* o */
{  3,  3,  3,  3,  3,  3,  3,  3,  7,159,  0,  0,  0,  0},     /* r */
{128,128,128,128,128,128,128,128,192,240,  0,  0,  0,  0},     /*   */
{224,224,224,224,224,224, 96,112, 49, 30,  0,  0,  0,  0},     /* t */
{ 56, 63, 56, 56, 56, 24, 92, 76,134,  1,  0,  0,  0,  0},     /* h */
{  7,255,  0,  0,  0,  0,  1,  2, 12,240,  0,  0,  0,  0},     /* e */
{  7,  7,  7,  7,  7,  7,  7,  7, 15, 63,  0,  0,  0,  0},     /*   */
{  0,  0,  0,  0,  0,  0,  0,  0,128,224,  0,  0,  0,  0},     /* c */
{ 14, 14, 14, 14, 14, 14, 14, 14, 31,127,  0,  0,  0,  0},     /* h */
{  1,  1,  1,  1,  1,  1,  1,  1,  3,207,  0,  0,  0,  0},     /* a */
{192,192,192,193,193,195,195,193,225,248,  0,  0,  0,  0},     /* r */
{  0,  7,120,192,192,128,128,192,195,124,  0,  0,  0,  0},     /* a */
{224,224,224,224,224,224,224,240,112, 29,  0,  0,  0,  0},     /* c */
{ 56, 56, 56, 56, 56, 56, 56, 56,124,255,  0,  0,  0,  0},     /* t */
{ 31, 31, 31,  0,  0, 64, 96, 96,112, 71,  0,  0,  0,  0},     /* e */
{  0,224,248,252, 28, 12,  4, 12, 24,224,  0,  0,  0,  0},     /* r */
{  0,  0,  0,  0,  0,  0,  0,  0,  0,  0,  0,  0,  0,  0},     /* s */
{  0,  0,  0,  0,  0,  0,  0,  0,  0,  0,  0,  0,  0,  0},     /*   */
{  0,  0,  0,  0,  0,  0,  0,  0,  0,  0,  0,  0,  0,  0},     /* n */
{  0,  0,  0,  0,  0,  0,  0,  0,  0,  0,  0,  0,  0,  0},     /* e */
{  0,  0,  0,  0,  0,  0,  0,  0,  0,  0,  0,  0,  0,  0},     /* e */
{  0,  0,  0,  0,  0,  0,  0,  0,  0,  0,  0,  0,  0,  0},     /* d */
{  0,  0,252, 60, 30, 30, 30, 23, 23, 23, 19, 19, 19, 17},     /* e */
{  0,  0,  0,  0,  0,  0,  0,  1,  1,  1,130,130,130,196},     /* d */
{  0,  0,126,120,240,240,240,112,112,112,112,112,112,112},     /*   */
{  0,  0, 28, 28, 28,  0,  0,  0,  0,252, 60, 28, 28, 28},     /* i */
{  0,  0,  0,  0,  0,  0,  0,  0,  0,  1,  6, 12, 28, 24},     /* n */
{  0,  0,  0,  0,  0,  0,  0,  0,  0,240, 12,  2,  7,  7},     /*   */
{  0,  0, 63, 15,  7,  7,  7,  7,  7,  7,  7,  7,  7,  7},     /* t */
{  0,  0,  0,  0,  0,  0,  0,  0,  0, 62, 65,129,128,  0},     /* h */
{  0,  0,  0,  0,  0,  0,  0,  0,  0,  0,128,192,192,224},     /* e */
{  0,  0,  0,  0,  0,  0,  0,  0,  0, 63, 64,224,224,224},     /*   */
{  0,  0,  0,  0,  0,  0,  0,  0,  0,  0,192, 96,112,112},     /* l */
{  0,  0,  0,  0,  0,  0,  0,  0,  0,  7, 24, 48,112, 96},     /* o */
{  0,  0,  0,  0,  0,  0,  0,  0,  0,192,112, 24, 28, 28},     /* g */
{  0,  0,252, 60, 28, 28, 28, 28, 28, 28, 28, 28, 28, 28},     /* o */
{  0,  0,  0,  0,  0,  0,  0,  0,  0,  0,  0,  0,  0,  0},     /*   */
{  0,  0,  0,  0,  0,  0,  0,  0,  0,  0,  0,  0,  0,  0},     /* a */
{  0,  0, 63, 56, 48, 48, 32, 32, 32,  0,  0,  0,  0,  0},     /* t */
{  0,  0,255,112,112,112,112,112,112,112,112,112,112,112},     /*   */
{  0,  0,225,225, 97, 32, 32, 32, 32, 15,  3,  1,  1,  1},     /* t */
{  0,  0,192,192,192,  0,  0,  0,  0,192,193,195,195,195},     /* h */
{  0,  0,  0,  0,  0,  0,  0,  0,  0,252,  3,  0,  0,  0},     /* e */
{  0,  0,  0,  0,  0,  0,  0,  0,  0, 64, 65,195, 71, 70},     /*   */
{  0,  0,  0,  0,  0,  0,  0,  0,  0,124,131,  0,  1,  1},     /* c */
{  0,  0, 15,  3,  1,  1,  1,  1,  1,  1,  1,129,193,193},     /* e */
{  0,  0,192,192,192,192,192,192,192,207,208,224,224,192},     /* n */
{  0,  0,  0,  0,  0,  0,  0,  0,  0,128, 96,112, 48, 56},     /* t */
{  0,  0,  0,  0,  0,  0,  0,  0,  0,  3, 12, 24, 56, 48},     /* e */
{  0,  0,  0,  0,  0,  0,  0,  0,  0,224, 56, 12, 14, 14},     /* r */
{  0,  0,  0,  0,  0,  0,  0,  0,  0,126, 30, 14, 15, 15},     /*   */
{  0,  0,  0,  0,  0,  0,  0,  0,  0, 60, 78,142, 14,  0},     /* o */
{ 17, 17, 16, 16, 16, 16, 16, 16, 48,254,  0,  0,  0,  0},     /* f */
{196,196,232,232,232,112,112, 80, 32, 35,  0,  0,  0,  0},     /*   */
{112,112,112,112,112,112,112,112,248,254,  0,  0,  0,  0},     /* t */
{ 28, 28, 28, 28, 28, 28, 28, 28, 62,255,  0,  0,  0,  0},     /* h */
{ 56, 56, 56, 56, 56, 24, 28, 12,  6,129,  0,  0,  0,  0},     /* e */
{  7,  0,  0,  0,  0,  0,  1,  2, 12,240,  0,  0,  0,  0},     /*   */
{  7,  7,  7,  7,  7,  7,  7,  7, 15, 63,  0,  0,  0,  0},     /* s */
{  0,  0,  0,  0,  0,  0,  0,  0,129,231,  0,  0,  0,  0},     /* c */
{224,224,224,224,224,225,225,224,240,252,  0,  0,  0,  0},     /* r */
{  0,  3, 60,224,224,192,192,224,225, 62,  0,  0,  0,  0},     /* e */
{112,240,112,112,112,112,112,120,184, 14,  0,  0,  0,  0},     /* e */
{224,255,224,224,224, 96,112, 48, 24,  7,  0,  0,  0,  0},     /* n */
{ 28,252,  0,  0,  0,  0,  4,  8, 48,192,  0,  0,  0,  0},     /*   */
{ 28, 28, 28, 28, 28, 28, 28, 28, 62,255,  0,  0,  0,  0},
{  0,  0,  0,  0,  0,  0,  0,  0,  0,128,  0,  0,  0,  0},
```

```
{  0,  0,  0,  0,  0,  0,  0,  0,  0,  0,  0,  0,  0,  0},
{  0,  0,  0,  0,  0,  0,  0,  0,  0,  3,  0,  0,  0,  0},
{112,112,112,112,112,112,112,112,248,254,  0,  0,  0,  0},
{  1,  1,  1,  1,  1,  1,  1,  1,  3, 15,  0,  0,  0,  0},
{193,193,192,192,192,194,195,195,227,250,  0,  0,  0,  0},
{240,254,255, 15,  1,  0,  0,  0,129,126,  0,  0,  0,  0},
{ 14, 14,142,206,206,198, 71,195,129,  0,  0,  0,  0,  0},
{  1,  0,  0,  0,  0,  0,  0,  0,131,124,  0,  0,  0,  0},
{193,  1,  1,  1,  1,  1, 65,129,  3, 15,  0,  0,  0,  0},
{192,192,192,192,192,192,192,192,224,249,  0,  0,  0,  0},
{ 56, 56, 56, 56, 56, 56, 56, 56,124,255,  0,  0,  0,  0},
{112,127,112,112,112, 48, 56, 24, 12,  3,  0,  0,  0,  0},
{ 14,254,  0,  0,  0,  0,  2,  4, 24,224,  0,  0,  0,  0},
{ 14, 14, 14, 14, 14, 14, 14, 14, 31,127,  0,  0,  0,  0},
{  0,  0,  0,  0,  0,  0,  0,  0,  0,192,  0,  0,  0,  0}
};

union REGS regs;        /* Processor register for the interrupt call */
unsigned i, j, k;                                     /* Loop counter */
double delay;                               /* Loop counter for PAUSE */

/*-- Prepare screen ------------------------------------------------*/

cls();                                               /* Clears screen */
blinking( FALSE );     /* Light background color instead of blinking */
setcur(0, 0);                      /* Move cursor to upper left corner */

/*-- Install EGA and VGA hardcopy routine --------------------------*/
regs.h.ah = 0x12;                  /* Function no.: Alternate Select */
regs.h.bl = 0x20;      /* Sub-funct. 0x20 = Install hardcopy routine */
int86(VIDEO_INT, &regs, &regs);          /* Call BIOS video interrupt */

if ( VGA )                                 /* Check for compatibility */
 {                                     /* and check custom characters */
  regs.h.ah = 0x12;                      /* VGA card in 350-line mode */
  regs.h.bl = 0x30;                                 /* Toggle EGA card */
  regs.h.al = 1;
  int86(VIDEO_INT, &regs, &regs);        /* Call BIOS video interrupt */

  setlines( 0x11 );                      /* Enable 8x14 character set */
 }

chardef(128, 0, 14, 120, (BYTE far *) font);   /* Define characters */

for (i=0; i<250; ++i)                      /* Execute loop 250 times */
 {                                    /* Write color blocks to video RAM */
  printfat(GETCS(), GETCZ(), ((i % 14) + 1) << 4, "     ");
  printfat(GETCS(), GETCZ(), 0, "   ");
 }
for (i=10; i<16; ++i)                      /* Allocate space for logo */
 printat(22, i, 0, "                                  ");
for (k=128, i=0; i<4; ++i)              /* The logo consists of ASCII */
 {                                              /* characters 128-248 */
  for (j=0; j<30; ++j)
   printfat(j+24, i+11, 15, "%c", k++);
 }
printat(1, 1, 15, "The most important characters are");
printat(1, 2, 15, "still present despite the logo!  ");
printat(1, 3, 15, "                                 ");
printat(1, 4, 15, " !\"#$%&'()*+-./0123456789:;<=>?@ ");
printat(1, 5, 15, " ABCDEFGHIJKLMNOPQRSTUVXXYZ[\\]^_ ");
printat(1, 6, 15, " `abcdefghijklmnopqrstuvxyz{|}~  ");
printat(33, 21, 15, "                                     ");
printat(33, 22, 15, " Press any key to end the program.   ");
printat(33, 23, 15, "                                     ");
setcur( 34, 22);

/*-- Change colors in the color blocks -----------------------------*/

i = 0;                           /* Starting value for color register */
```

```
   while ( nokey() )              /* Repeat until the user presses a key */
    {
     for ( delay=0.0; delay < PAUSE; ++delay )
      ;
     ++i;              /* Increment color value for the first register */
     for (j=1; j<15; ++j)              /* Go through registers 1 to 14 */
      {
       setcol(j, i+j & 63);           /* Write color value in register */
       if ( !nokey() )                                /* Key pressed? */
        break;                 /* YES --> Stop loop before restarting */
      }
    }

   if ( VGA )                                  /* Go into 400 line mode */
    {                          /* Enable VGA card                      */
     regs.h.ah = 0x12;
     regs.h.bl = 0x30;
     regs.h.al = 2;
     int86(VIDEO_INT, &regs, &regs);      /* Call BIOS video interrupt */

     setlines( 0x14 );                    /* Enable 8*16 character set */
    }

   cls();                                             /* Clear screen */
  }

/***********************************************************************/
/**                           MAIN PROGRAM                            **/
/***********************************************************************/

void main()
{
 if ( is_vga() )                   /* Is there a VGA card installed? */
   egavga( TRUE );                                           /* YES */
 else                                   /* No VGA installed - go on */
  {
   if ( is_ega() )                 /* Is there an EGA card installed? */
    {                                                         /* YES */
     if ( getmon() == EGA )    /* Is there an EGA monitor connected? */
      egavga( FALSE );                           /* YES, start demo */
     else
      {                                            /* wrong monitor */
       printf("This program functions only with an\n");
       printf("EGA monitor.                        \n");
      }
    }
   else                          /* If no EGA or VGA card connected  */
    printf( "ATTENTION! There is neither an EGA nor a "
            " VGA card installed.\n" );
  }
}
```

Assembler listing: EGAVGACA.ASM

```
;***********************************************************************;
;*                          E G A V G A C A                            *;
;*---------------------------------------------------------------------*;
;*    Task            : Generates a functions for custom designing     *;
;*                      characters.                                    *;
;*---------------------------------------------------------------------*;
;*    Author          : MICHAEL TISCHER                                *;
;*    Developed on    : 09/25/1988                                     *;
;*    Last update     : 06/07/1988                                     *;
;*---------------------------------------------------------------------*;
;*    Assembly        : MASM EGAVGACA;                                 *;
;*                      ... Link with a C program whose memory model   *;
;*                          has been set to SMALL                      *;
;***********************************************************************;
```

```
;== Segment declarations for the C program ============================

IGROUP group _text                 ;Addition to program segment
DGROUP group const,_bss,  _data    ;Addition to data segment
       assume CS:IGROUP, DS:DGROUP, ES:DGROUP, SS:DGROUP

CONST  segment word public 'CONST';This segment includes all read-only
CONST  ends                        ;constants

_BSS   segment word public 'BSS'  ;This segment includes all un-initial-
_BSS   ends                        ;ized static variables

_DATA  segment word public 'DATA' ;This segment includes all initialized
                                   ;global and static variables
_DATA  ends

;== Program ===========================================================

_TEXT  segment byte public 'CODE' ;Program segment

public     _chardef

;----------------------------------------------------------------------
;-- CHARDEF: Defines the appearance of a character --------------------
;-- Call from C : void chardef( BYTE ascii, BYTE table, BYTE lines,
;--                            BYTE amount, BYTE far * buf);
;-- Return value: none

_chardef   proc near

sframe     struc                   ;Stack access structure
bptr       dw ?                    ;Take BP
ret_adr    dw ?                    ;Return address of calling program
ascii      dw ?                    ;ASCII code of character
table      dw ?                    ;Number of character table
lines      dw ?                     ;Character matrix height
amount     dw ?                    ;Number of characters to be defined
bufptr     dd ?                    ;FAR pointer to buffer
sframe     ends                    ;End of structure

frame      equ [ bp - bptr ]       ;Addresses elements of structure

           push bp                 ;Push BP onto stack
           mov  bp,sp              ;Transfer SP to BP


           mov  ax,1100h           ;Function no. 11H, sub-funct. 0
           mov  bh,byte ptr frame.lines   ;Character matrix height
           mov  bl,byte ptr frame.table    ;Number of character table
           mov  cl,byte ptr frame.amount   ;Number of characters
           xor  ch,ch
           mov  dl,byte ptr frame.ascii    ;Get ASCII code of character
           xor  dh,dh
           les  bp,frame.bufptr    ;Buffer address to ES:BP
           int  10h                ;Call EGA BIOS video interrupt

           pop  bp                 ;Pop BP off of stack
           ret                     ;Return to C program

_chardef   endp

;----------------------------------------------------------------------

_text      ends                    ;End of code segment
           end                     ;End of program
```

7.5 Determining System Configuration using BIOS

Some programs (e.g., copy programs) must determine how many disk drives are connected to the PC, or how much RAM exists on the main circuit board or motherboard. This information can be obtained with the help of BIOS interrupt 11H.

The content of individual registers is not important during the call of this interrupt, since neither the function number nor another argument must be passed.

The configuration, which is determined during the system booting process, is returned in the AX register. The individual bits of this register contain the following information:

Bit(s)	Meaning
0	Equal to 1 if 1 or more disk drives are available
1	Unused
2 & 3	RAM memory on the main circuit board
	00 = 16K
	01 = 32K
	10 = 48K
	11 = 64K
4 & 5	Video mode during system boot
	00: unused
	01: 40*25 characters - color card
	02: 80*25 characters - color card
	03: 80*25 characters - mono card
6 & 7	Indicates number of disk drives in system if bit 0 is 1
	00 = 1 disk drive
	01 = 2 disk drives
	10 = 3 disk drives
	11 = 4 disk drives
8	Equal to 0 when DMA chip is available
9 - 11	Number of RS-232 cards attached
12	Equal to 1 if joystick attached
13	Unused
14 & 15	indicates the number of printers

While this bit assignment is the same for the PC and the XT, it differs from the configuration word returned by the AT. To interpret the content of the AX register correctly, you must know the model of the computer being tested.

Bit	Meaning
00	Equal to 1 if 1 or more disk drives are available
01	Equal to 1 if system has a math coprocessor
02-03	Unused
04-05	Video mode during system boot
	00: Unused
	01: 40*25 characters - color card
	02: 80*25 characters - color card
	03: 80*25 characters - mono card
06-07	Indicates number of disk drives in system if bit 0 is 1
	00 = 1 disk drive
	01 = 2 disk drives
	10 = 3 disk drives
	11 = 4 disk drives
08	Unused
09-11	Number of RS-232 cards attached
12-13	Unused
14-15	indicates the number of printers

Do not use this function to sense the current video mode, since it only indicates the video mode switched on during system booting. Function 15H of interrupt 10H provides the number of the current video mode.

7.6 Determining Available RAM using the BIOS

While interrupt 11H only returns the amount of RAM on the main circuit board, interrupt 12H obtains the amount of RAM available in the entire system. The total amount of RAM from the main circuit board and any memory expansion cards are returned. The DIP switch settings on the memory boards determine the amount of memory reported available on the PC and XT. The interrupt routines derive the amount of RAM on an AT by reading one of the 64 memory locations on the battery powered realtime clock.

Memory limits

This method determines RAM below the 1 megabyte limit only. The 8088's addressing capability limits memory to 1 megabyte, so the PC and XT can report on the entire memory available. The AT's 80286 processor can manage up to 16 megabytes of memory. However, interrupt 12H cannot report on any RAM beyond 1 megabyte.

The memory size returned is passed in the AX register as a multiple of 1K (1024 bytes, not 1000 bytes). For example, if the AX register contains 256, you have 256K of RAM available in your PC.

Demonstration programs

The three program listings in this section are practical examples of the interrupts described in the preceding section. The three programs, which were written in BASIC, Pascal and C, are identical in their basic design.

They test the model identification byte in memory location F000:FFFE to determine whether the computer is a PC, XT or AT. The equipment designation appears on the screen. This model identification acts as the basis for identifying the processor type as well. The program assumes that an AT has an 80286 and all other PCs have an 8088 processor. During the next step in the programs, interrupt 12H determines the amount of RAM on the circuit board and returns that amount. As mentioned above, the AT can have additional RAM memory beyond the 1 megabyte limit. Each program tests for that additional RAM if the equipment designation indicates an AT. The programs use function 88H of interrupt 15H (see Appendix B for detailed documentation). For the moment, all you need to know is that this function passes the amount, in multiples of 1K, of RAM above the 1 megabyte limit to the AX register.

After displaying this information, interrupt 11H determines the equipment configuration. The last task of the program consists of filtering out the information encoded in the bits of the configuration word and displaying it on the screen.

To keep the program from becoming too long, the programs limit themselves to the identical bits of the configuration words in the PC, XT and AT. For example, the programs skip the AT information concerning the availability of a math coprocessor.

You may want to rewrite this program so that it displays all the information contained in the configuration word according to computer type.

The comments in each listing should answer any questions you may have about program flow.

BASIC listing: CONFIGB.BAS

```
100 '******************************************************************'
110 '*                         C O N F I G B                          *'
120 '*----------------------------------------------------------------*'
130 '*  Task        : Displays the Configuration of the PC            *'
140 '*                                                                *'
150 '*  Author         : MICHAEL TISCHER                              *'
160 '*  developed on   : 7.20.87                                      *'
170 '*  last Update    : 9.21.87                                      *'
180 '******************************************************************'
190 '
200 CLS : KEY OFF
210 PRINT"WARNING: This program should only be started if the GWBASIC "
220 PRINT"was started from the DOS level with <GWBASIC  /m:60000>."
230 PRINT : PRINT"If this was not the case, then input <s> for Stop."
240 PRINT"Else press any key ...";
250 A$ = INKEY$ : IF A$ = "s" THEN END
260 IF A$ = "" THEN 250
270 GOSUB 60000              'Install Function for interrupt Call
280 CLS                      'Clear Screen
290 DEF SEG = &HF000         'BIOS-Segment
300 PRINT "CONFIG (c) 1987 by Michael Tischer"
310 PRINT
320 PRINT "Configuration of Your PC"
330 PRINT "-------------------------------------------------------------"
340 PRINT "PC-Type                                : "; 'determine PC type
350 IF PEEK(&HFFFE) = &HFF THEN PRINT "PC" : GOTO 390
360 IF PEEK(&HFFFE) = &HFE THEN PRINT "XT" : GOTO 390
370 IF PEEK(&HFFFE) = &HFC THEN PRINT "AT" : GOTO 390
380 PRINT "unknown"
390 PRINT "Processor                              : 80";
400 IF PEEK(&HFFFE) = &HFC THEN PRINT "286" ELSE PRINT "88"
410 INR% = &H12                           'BIOS-interrupt reads RAM size
420 DEF SEG                               'Set BASIC-Segment again
430 CALL IA(INR%,RAMHI%,RAMLO%,Z%,Z%,Z%,Z%,Z%,Z%,Z%,Z%,Z%,Z%)
440 PRINT "RAM-Memory (Main Circuit Board) :";RAMHI%*256+RAMLO%;"KB"
450 DEF SEG = &HF000                      'BIOS-Segment
460 IF PEEK(&HFFFE) <> &HFC THEN 520      'branch if not AT
470 DEF SEG                               'set BASIC-Segment again
480 INR% = &H15                           'Call Cassette interrupt
490 RAMHI% = &H88               'Function for reading of HI-RAM size
500 CALL IA(INR%,RAMHI%,RAMLO%,Z%,Z%,Z%,Z%,Z%,Z%,Z%,Z%,Z%,Z%)
510 PRINT "Additional RAM-Memory              :";RAMHI%*256+RAMLO%;"KB beyond 1 MB"
520 DEF SEG                     'Set BASIC-Segment again
525 INR% = &H11                 'BIOS-interrupt reads Configuration
530 CALL IA(INR%,CONFHI%,CONFLO%,Z%,Z%,Z%,Z%,Z%,Z%,Z%,Z%,Z%,Z%)
540 PRINT "Video mode after Start             : ";
550 IF CONFLO% AND 48 = 0 THEN PRINT"undefined" : GOTO 590
560 IF CONFLO% AND 48 = 16 THEN PRINT"40*25 Character, Color-Card" : GOTO 590
570 IF CONFLO% AND 48 = 32 THEN PRINT"80*25 Character, Color Card" : GOTO 590
580 PRINT"80*25 Character, Mono-Card"
590 PRINT"Disk drives                        :";INT(CONFLO%/64)+1
600 PRINT"RS232 cards                        :";INT(CONFHI%/2) AND 3
610 PRINT"Printer cards                      :";INT(CONFHI%/64)
620 PRINT
```

```
630 END
640 '
60000 '***************************************************************'
60010 '* Initialize the Routine for interrupt-Call                  *'
60020 '*-----------------------------------------------------------*'
60030 '* Input: none                                                *'
60040 '* Output: IA  the Start address of the interrupt-Routine     *'
60050 '***************************************************************'
60060 '
60070 IA=60000!         'Start address of the Routine in the BASIC-Segment
60080 DEF SEG           'Set BASIC-Segment
60090 RESTORE 60130
60100 FOR I% = 0 TO 160 : READ X% : POKE IA+I%,X% : NEXT  'Poke Routine
60110 RETURN                                            'back to Caller
60120 '
60130 DATA  85,139,236, 30,  6,139,118, 30,139,  4,232,140,  0,139,118
60140 DATA  12,139, 60,139,118,  8,139,  4, 61,255,255,117,  2,140,216
60150 DATA 142,192,139,118, 28,138, 36,139,118, 26,138,  4,139,118, 24
60160 DATA 138, 60,139,118, 22,138, 28,139,118, 20,138, 44,139,118, 18
60170 DATA 138, 12,139,118, 16,138, 52,139,118, 14,138, 20,139,118, 10
60180 DATA 139, 52, 85,205, 33, 93, 86,156,139,118, 12,137, 60,139,118
60190 DATA  28,136, 36,139,118, 26,136,  4,139,118, 24,136, 60,139,118
60200 DATA  22,136, 28,139,118, 20,136, 44,139,118, 18,136, 12,139,118
60210 DATA  16,136, 52,139,118, 14,136, 20,139,118,  8,140,192,137,  4
60220 DATA  88,139,118,  6,137,  4, 88,139,118, 10,137,  4,  7, 31, 93
60230 DATA 202, 26,  0, 91, 46,136, 71, 66,233,108,255
```

Pascal listing: CONFIGP.PAS

```
{*********************************************************************}
{*                          C O N F I G P                   PASCAL  *}
{*-------------------------------------------------------------------*}
{*    Task         : Outputs the Configuration of the PC on the      *}
{*                   Display Screen                                   *}
{*-------------------------------------------------------------------*}
{*    Author         : MICHAEL TISCHER                                *}
{*    developed on   : 7/7/87                                         *}
{*    last Update    : 5/18/89                                        *}
{*********************************************************************}

program CONFIGP;


Uses Crt, Dos;                                      { Add DOS and Crt }

{*********************************************************************}
{* PRINTCONFIG: Display PC's configuration                           *}
{* Input  : none                                                     *}
{* Output : none                                                     *}
{* Info    : The configuration output depends on the PC type         *}
{*********************************************************************}

procedure PrintConfig;

var AT   : boolean;                               { is the PC an AT? }
    Regs : Registers;            { Register variable for interrupt call }

begin
 clrscr;                                              { Clear screen }
 if mem[$F000:$FFFE] = $FC then AT := true           { test if AT or }
                          else AT := false;             { PC or XT }
 writeln('Configuration of this PC');
 writeln('-----------------------------------------------------');
 write('PC-Type                   : ');
 case mem[$F000:$FFFE] of                       { Read PC type again }
  $FF : writeln('PC');                                { $FF is a PC }
  $FE : writeln('XT');                               { $FE is an XT }
  $FC : writeln('AT')                                { $FC is an AT }
  else writeln('Unknown');
```

```
 end;
 write('Processor                : INTEL ');
 if AT then writeln('80286')                     { the AT has an 80286, }
       else writeln('8088');          { PC and XT have an 8088 processor }
 intr($12, Regs);
 writeln('RAM-Memory              : ',Regs.ax,' KB');
 if AT then                                          { is the PC an AT? }
  begin                                                          { YES }
   Regs.ah := $88;         { Function number for additional RAM size }
   Intr($15, Regs);                    { Call BIOS cassette interrupt }
   writeln('additional RAM    : ',Regs.ax,' KB beyond 1 MB');
  end;
Intr($11, Regs);                    { Call BIOS configuration interrupt}
 write('Video mode after start : ');
 case Regs.al and 48 of                          { Determine video mode }
   0 : writeln('undefined');
  16 : writeln('40x25 character color card');
  32 : writeln('80x25 character color card');
  48 : writeln('80x25 character mono card')
 end;
 writeln('Disk  drives            : ', succ(Regs.al shr 6 and 3));
 writeln('RS-232  cards           : ', Regs.ah shr 1 and 3);
 writeln('Printer cards           : ', Regs.ah shr 6)
end;

{**********************************************************************}
{*                          MAIN PROGRAM                              *}
{**********************************************************************}

begin
 PrintConfig;                                  { Display configuration }
end.
```

C listing: CONFIGC.C

```
/**********************************************************************/
/*                           C O N F I G C                            */
/*--------------------------------------------------------------------*/
/*    Task          : Outputs the configuration of the PC on the      */
/*                    Display Screen                                  */
/*--------------------------------------------------------------------*/
/*    Author          : MICHAEL TISCHER                               */
/*    developed on    : 8.13.87                                       */
/*    last Update     : 9.21.87                                       */
/*--------------------------------------------------------------------*/
/*    (MICROSOFT C)                                                   */
/*    Creation      : MSC CONFIGC                                     */
/*                    LINK CONFIGC PEPO;                              */
/*    Call          : CONFIGC                                         */
/*--------------------------------------------------------------------*/
/*    (BORLAND TURBO C)                                               */
/*    Creation      : With the RUN command in the Command Line        */
/**********************************************************************/

#include <dos.h>                            /* Include Header-Files */
#include <io.h>

extern short int PeekB();         /* PEEKB linked  with MicroSoft C */

#define FALSE 0                         /* Constants make reading the  */
#define TRUE 1                                  /* Program text easier */

/**********************************************************************/
/* CLS: Clear Screen and Cursor to upper left corner                  */
/* Input : none                                                       */
/* Output : none                                                      */
/**********************************************************************/

void Cls()
```

```
{
 union REGS Register;          /* Register-Variable for interrupt-Call */

 Register.h.ah = 6;                  /* Function number for Scroll-UP */
 Register.h.al = 0;                                  /* 0 for clear  */
 Register.h.bh = 7;          /* white characters on black background */
 Register.x.cx = 0;                       /* left upper screen corner  */
 Register.h.dh = 24;                     /* Coordinates of the lower */
 Register.h.dl = 79;                        /* right screen corner   */
 int86(0x10, &Register, &Register);     /* Call BIOS-Video-interrupt */

 Register.h.ah = 2;        /* Set Function number for Cursor position */
 Register.h.bh = 0;                                 /* Screen page 0 */
 Register.x.dx = 0;      /* Coordinates of upper left screen corner  */
 int86(0x10, &Register, &Register);     /* Call BIOS-Video-interrupt */
}

/*********************************************************************/
/* PRINTCONFIG: Output the PC Configuration                          */
/* Input  : none                                                     */
/* Output : none                                                     */
/* Info     : the configuration output  dependent on the PC-Type     */
/*********************************************************************/

void PrintConfig()

{
 union REGS Register;          /* Register-Variable for interrupt-Call */
 short int AT;                                  /*  the PC and AT? */

 Cls();                                             /* Clear Screen */
 if (PeekB(0xF000, 0xFFFE) == 0xFC) AT = TRUE;  /* Determine if the  */
  else AT = FALSE;                              /* PC  and AT        */
 printf("CONFIG (c) 1987 by Michael Tischer\n\n");
 printf("Configuration of this PC\n");
 printf("----------------------------------------------------------\n");
 printf("PC-Type                   : ");
 switch(PeekB(0xF000, 0xFFFE))             /* Determine PC-Type again */
  {
   case 0xFF : printf("PC\n");                  /* 0xFF  a normal PC */
               break;
   case 0xFE : printf("XT\n");                        /* 0xFE  an XT */
               break;
   case 0xFC : printf("AT\n");                        /* 0xFC  an AT */
               break;
   default   : printf("Unknown\n");                  /* Code unknown */
               break;
  }
 printf("Processor                 : INTEL 80");
 if (AT) printf("286\n");                      /* the AT has an 80286, */
  else printf("88\n");             /* PC and XT have an 8088 Processor */
 printf("RAM-Memory                : ");
 int86(0x12, &Register, &Register);                  /* Get RAM size  */
 printf("%d KB\n",Register.x.ax);                      /* and output */
 if (AT)                                           /*  the PC an AT? */
  {                                                          /* YES */
   Register.h.ah = 0x88;        /* Function number for additional RAM */
   int86(0x15, &Register, &Register);                 /* Get RAM size */
   printf("additional RAM          : %d KB beyond 1MB\n", Register.x.ax);
  }
 int86(0x11, &Register, &Register);  /* BIOS-Configuration-interrupt */
 printf("Video mode after Start  : ");
 switch(Register.x.ax & 48)
  {
   case  0 : printf("undefined\n");
             break;
   case 16 : printf("40*25 Character Color-Card\n");
             break;
   case 32 : printf("80*25 Character Color-Card\n");
```

```
            break;
   case 48 : printf("80*25 Character Mono-Card\n");
            break;
  }
 printf("Disk drives              : %d\n", (Register.x.ax >> 6 & 3) + 1);
 printf("RS232-Card               : %d\n", Register.x.ax >> 9 & 0x03);
 printf("Printer-Card             : %d\n\n", Register.x.ax >> 14);
}

/***********************************************************************/
/**                          MAIN PROGRAM                             **/
/***********************************************************************/

void main()

{
 PrintConfig();                          /* Output the Configuration */
}
```

7.7 Accessing the Floppy Disk from the BIOS

A cassette recorder was the primary form of mass storage in the early days of personal computing. However, floppy drives soon became the standard. PCs can control a maximum of four disk drives, numbered 0 to 3. DOS designates the first two units as drive A and drive B.

Early disk-based PC systems used only one side of disks for data storage. DOS Versions 1.1 and later store data on both sides of the disk.

Disk structure

Each side of a disk consists of 40 tracks of 9 sectors each. Each sector has a capacity of 512 bytes. The tracks are numbered from 0 to 39. Track 0 is located on the outer edge and track 39 on the inner edge of the disk. The two disk sides have designations of side 0 (front) and side 1 (back). This disk has a total storage capacity of 360K.

The disk drives included with AT computers have 80 tracks with 15 sectors instead of 40 tracks with 9 sectors. An AT floppy drive can store up to 1.2 megabytes of data per disk. Systems with a 1.2 megabyte drive can read both 1.2 meg disks as well as 360K disks.

Note: While it's possible to write 360K formatted disks using an AT type 1.2 megabyte drive, the resulting disks are not always readable by a standard PC/XT 360K drive.

The following shows the structure of a disk:

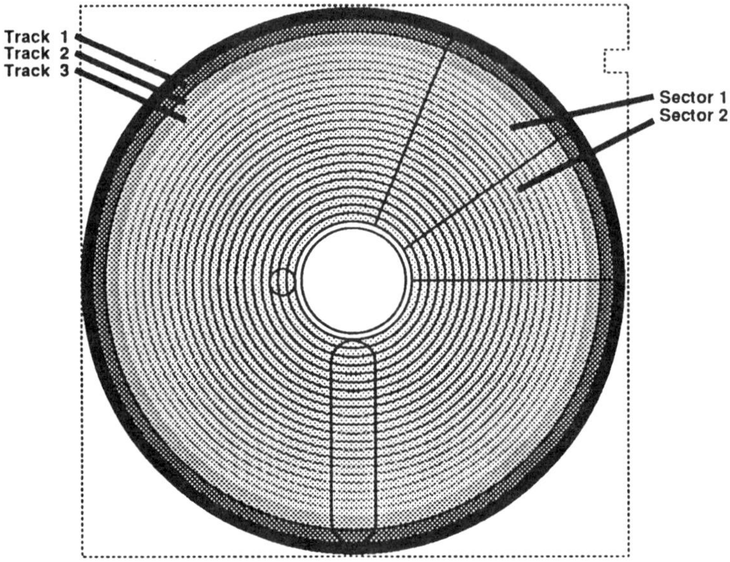

Structure of a disk

This structure is based on DOS specifications. It's possible to program the disk controller directly or use the various BIOS functions to alter the disk structure. Some methods of copy protection take advantage of this capability to arrange the data on the disk in such a way that DOS cannot use the data directly.

The methods of transferring data to or from the disk are identical. First the read/write head moves to the proper track. Since the disk moves constantly, the sector to be processed eventually passes by the head, allowing data transfer.

BIOS makes some functions available for disk access at the lowest level. BIOS thinks of *DASD* (Direct Access Storage Device) rather than disk drives.

A total of six BIOS disk functions can be accessed by calling interrupt 13H and passing the function number to the AH register.

Function 0: Reset disk

Function 0 resets the disk drive. The reset always executes automatically during system start, but should also occur when an error occurs during the call of one of these six functions. Before the interrupt call, function number 0 must be loaded into the AH register. After the execution of the function the error status is returned in the AH register. A value which indicates the type of error if any, is returned in the AH register after all 6 functions.

If a program calls the reset function without the disk drive previously reporting an error, error code 1 (function number not permitted) may be returned in certain cases, even though no error occurred. For this reason, the function should be called only after an error, and not after every disk operation.

Function 1: Status

Function 1 senses disk status without disk access. If it returns a value of 0 as a result, no error occurred. Another value represents one of the following error codes:

01H	Function number not permitted
02H	Address-marking not found
03H	Write attempt on write protected disk
04H	Sector address not found
06H	disk changed
08H	DMA-Overrun
09H	Data transmission beyond segment border
10H	Read error
20H	Disk controller error
40H	Track not found
80H	Time-Out error, drive does not respond

If one of these errors appear, the disk operation just completed has been repeated several times following a reset. Most of the time the repeated operation succeeds without an error. If not, the current program in memory should react to the error condition in a suitable manner and display an error message.

Working with the functions presented here, a time-out error can occur frequently after a read operation. It usually occurs because of the speed decrease required to read the disk: The old speed cannot be resumed immediately after reading.

Function 2: Read

Function 2 reads disk data. The BIOS must know the location from which you want disk data read. This information is passed in the DL, DH, CL and CH registers:

DL	Drive number (0 to 3)
DH	Disk side (always 0 for single sided disks) 0 = Front side 1 = Back side
CL	First sector to be read (1 to 9/1 to 15)
CH	Track containing sector to be read

Up to 9 sectors (PC/XT disk drives) or 15 sectors (AT disk drives) can be read using one function call. The AL register specifies this number of sectors. Since disk drives usually store data belonging together in sequential sectors, this enables fast data access (e.g., 9 x 512 bytes = 4.5K in one disk revolution).

The address of a buffer in memory must be passed in registers ES and BX since the data transfer area has no fixed location in RAM in which it can reside. The ES register accepts the segment address of the buffer and the BX register accepts the offset address.

The function returns the error status to the AH register, and the number of sectors read in the AL register. In addition to the AH register, a set carry flag (carry flag = 1) signals the occurrence of an error.

Function 3: Write

Function 3 allows write access to the disk. It accepts arguments similar to those used in function 2 above:

DL	Number of the drive (0 to 3)
DH	Disk side (always 0 for single sided disks) 0 = Front side 1 = Back side
CL	First sector to be written (1 to 9/1 to 15)
CH	Track in which the sector to be written is located

The value in the AL register indicates the number of sectors to be written, while the ES and BX registers indicate the address of the memory area from which the data should be read. The function passes the error status in the AH register, and the number of sectors written in the AL register. The carry flag has the same meaning as in function 2.

Function 4: Verify disk

Function 4 tests whether data is transferred properly to and from the disk. The BIOS bases correct data transmission on a *cyclical redundancy check* (CRC) value, instead of just comparing data in memory with data on disk. Using a CRC involves summing the value of each individual byte in a sector with a specific formula. Since most disk drives work well and have exceptional reliability, most programmers ignore this function. DOS only uses this function to test data that was transmitted to a disk in response to an active VERIFY ON flag.

The register setup is similar to functions 2 and 3 (see above), with the difference that the AH register must contain 4. Since the function doesn't need a buffer address, this function does not use the BX and the ES registers.

Note: This function only works properly on a PC or an XT: ATs may return incorrect results.

Function 5: Format

The last function of interrupt 13H allows the user to format part of a disk. Disk formatting (e.g., with the DOS command FORMAT) is a requirement since disks used by the PC are soft-sectored. This means that software, not hardware, determines the positioning of the sectors and tracks on the disk. The operating system must install the tracks and sectors on the disk using this function. Sectors don't have to contain 512 bytes. This BIOS function lets you format 128, 256, 512 or 1,024 bytes per sector. However, you must format a complete track.

The function number (5) must be passed in the AH register. The AL register is loaded with the number of sectors to format the track with. This number can be less than the DOS default values of 9 or 15. The number of the track to be formatted is passed in the CH register. This track number must be a value from 0 to 39 (PC/XT) or from 0 to 79 (AT). The number of the disk drive is passed in the DL register and the disk's side in the DH register.

Besides this information, the format function also requires a field containing formatting characteristics, which is also needed by the functions for reading, writing and verifying a sector. The address of this field is passed in the ES and BX registers. The segment address is loaded in the ES register and the offset address in the BX register.

This table contains an entry consisting of four bytes for every sector to be formatted:

Byte 1	Track to be formatted
Byte 2	Disk side (always 0 for single sided disks) 0 = Front side 1 = Back side
Byte 3	Number of sector
Byte 4	Number of bytes in this sector 0 = 128 bytes 1 = 256 bytes 2 = 512 bytes 3 = 1024 bytes

Even though the function already possesses the number of the track to be formatted and the disk side, these items appear here again for reasons of safety. The sectors are placed into this table sequentially, which assigns the first sector the logical number 1 and the second sector the logical number 7.

While the logical and physical numbers of the sectors usually agree in a disk drive, it makes sense in a hard disk to change the logical number of a sector instead of its physical number. The hard disk of the XT reduces access time for individual sectors by displacing the logical sectors by six in relation to the physical sectors.

Also the number of bytes which a sector can accommodate does not have to be uniform, since each sector may be defined in the table. With this and other parameters of the table, copy protection can be developed based on formatting. Format-based copy protection cannot be processed by the operating system.

In addition to information such as the disk drive and sector number passed to the BIOS functions during a call, the BIOS also requires a series of other items to enable some disk operations. These parameters are passed in the device parameter table. Such a table exists in the ROM BIOS, but you can install your own in RAM. The address of the new device parameter table must be placed into memory locations 0000:0078 to 0000:007B. These memory locations should contain the address of interrupt 1EH (the PC doesn't use this interrupt).

DOS also offers the option of providing a unique device parameter table which changes some values of this table from the BIOS default, accelerating access to the disk drives.

The table itself consists of 11 bytes. The first two bytes transfer directly to the disk controller. They indicate the step time and the DMA mode. The step time is the maximum time period in which the read/write head of the disk drive can move from one track to another.

The second byte indicates the time the disk drive motor can continue to run after a disk operation. It defaults to 2 seconds since it assumes that this is the maximum amount of time between consecutive disk accesses. Disk access speed is quicker if the disk motor has already achieved operational speed and does not have to be brought up to speed again. The value in this memory location is based on the 18 unit per second system clock, so a value of 18 represents running time of about one second.

The value in byte 3 indicates the number of bytes per sector for a write or read operation. It corresponds to the values for formatting a sector, so it normally contains the value 3 (512 bytes per sector). If you want to write or read sectors with other sector sizes, the proper value must be entered into this memory location.

Byte 4 gives the maximum number of sectors per track. The PC/XT disk drive defaults to the value 9 in this location, while the AT defaults to the value 15 decimal.

Byte 5 of the table contains a value that represents the amount of empty space between the end of a sector and the start of the following sector. This space relates to the time BIOS must allow to elapse until the next sector appears under the read/write head (not units of length). The value for this memory location defaults to 42.

Byte 6 determines the data transfer length, which has no influence on data transmission in most cases.

Since formatting of a disk occurs through the magnetization of certain areas, the sizes of the non-magnetic spaces between sectors must be determined. Byte 7 records this, and these spaces must be larger than the space between sectors in byte 5 so that the beginning of a sector can be recognized properly.

Byte 8 accepts the ASCII code of the character which fills a sector during formatting. The BIOS defaults to the division character V (ASCII code 246).

After the read/write head moves from one track to another it requires a rest period to let the vibrations connected with the movement fade away. Then it can properly perform any disk accesses which follow.

This rest period given in byte 9 of the table defaults to multiples of 1 millisecond. While the BIOS grants 25 milliseconds of rest, DOS only permits 15 milliseconds.

The last entry of the table in byte 10 gives the time duration during which the disk motor achieves operating speed. The value in this memory location defaults to multiples of 1/8 second. Even here DOS requires more from the read/write head than BIOS. It provides only a 1/4 second waiting period, as opposed to 1/2 second for BIOS.

High density disk drives

Part of the introduction of the AT included high density 1.2 megabyte disk drives. To ensure compatibility with earlier disk drives, they are capable of reading and writing 320/360K disks despite the increase to the higher capacity of 1.2 megabytes. They can also recognize a change of the disk media. For support of this new capability, AT BIOS contains three new disk functions which are called through interrupt 13H like previous functions.

The first of these new functions determines the drive type in use. During the function call, in addition to function number 15H, the number of the drive (0 or 1, 2 reserved for the hard disk) must be passed in the DL register. The function returns the type of the drive in the AH register:

AH = 0	no drive available
AH = 1	disk drive does not detect disk change
AH = 2	disk drive does detect disk change
AH = 3	Hard disk

If the drive detects a disk change it can be sensed with the help of function 16H. After calling this function by passing the value 16H to the AH register and the number of the drive (0 or 1), the function returns a number to the AH register which tells whether the disk was changed since the last disk access. If this register contains the value 6, the disk was changed. The value 0 indicates that no change took place.

The last new function, function 17H, must be called before calling the formatting function (function number 5) on PC/AT or PS/2 machines to tell the controller how it should format the disk. It should format the disk in either the 320/360K or the 1.2 megabyte format. Besides the function number in the AH register and the drive number in the DL register, a code must be passed to the AL register indicating not only the format type, but also the type of disk drive in use. This code has the following meaning:

1	format to 320/360K on a 320/360K-drive
2	format to 320/360K on a 1.2 megabyte-drive
3	format to 1.2 MByte on a 1.2 megabyte-drive

Demonstration programs

The disk monitor in this section combines all the functions you have read about so far. The monitor versions, written in BASIC, Pascal and C, all have the same basic structure. Let's examine this structure before looking at the individual programs.

The beginning of each program initializes variables, configures the screen and resets the disk drives. Next the input loop executes; this loop is the center point of the program. It displays the program prompt DISKMON> and then waits for user input. After the user enters input and presses the <Return> key, the program ensures that this input calls an executable command. If the input is illegal, the program displays an error message and returns to the program prompt. Legal input calls the subroutine, function or procedure requested.

All three programs support the Help, Format, Get, Fill, Constants and End commands. The Fill command fills a sector with one character. The End command terminates the program. There is no Write command in the monitor's command set. This is because the amount of coding required to create a window for editing the 512 bytes of a sector would have made the program listings too long.

All disk access commands ask for the track and perhaps the sector number of the disk, but not the disk drive number or the disk side number. The program defaults to disk drive 0 (drive A:) and disk side 0. The Constants command lets you change these defaults so you can access another disk drive or disk side. This command also specifies the format parameter needed for an AT (i.e., what disk format should be used).

Like all other user input, the program transfers this input to the BIOS instead of the program itself. This disk monitor checks the BIOS's reaction to the input. The BIOS returns an error message in response to illogical or false input. Every disk monitor command which accesses the disk drive reads the error status of the disk drive after command execution. An error message then appears on the screen as needed.

Let's take a close look at the monitor commands:

? Entering a question mark (?) at the program prompt displays a list of the available commands.

Get This overview includes a Get command which reads and displays a sector of the disk. An internal buffer stores the contents of this sector after input and displays the contents on the screen. Certain control characters such as carriage returns or linefeed are shown as character strings instead of as ASCII codes. For example, <CR> appears instead of an actual a carriage return, and <LF> appears instead of a linefeed. While reading a sector the program assumes that the sector has the standard format of 512 bytes.

Format The Format command formats the selected sector in a 512-byte format. Remember that a 360K disk can have a maximum of 9 sectors per track and a 1.2 megabyte disk can have a maximum of 15 sectors per track. You can assign fewer sectors, but you must specify at least one sector.

Reset The Reset command resets the disk drives. It also can be called by various commands when the disk drive reports an error. If it's called by the user before an error occurs, this can cause an error message. Most disk error messages cannot cause damage to the drive.

BASIC listing: DISKMONB.BAS

```
100 '******************************************************************'
110 '*                      D I S K M O N B                          *'
120 '*----------------------------------------------------------------*'
130 '*  Task           : Diskmon is a small Diskette monitor based   *'
140 '*                   on the BIOS-Interrupt 13(h)                  *'
150 '*  Author         : MICHAEL TISCHER                              *'
160 '*  developed on   : 07/24/87                                     *'
170 '*  last Update    : 05/20/89                                     *'
180 '******************************************************************'
190 '
200 CLS : KEY OFF
210 PRINT "WARNING: This Program should only be started if GWBASIC was"
220 PRINT "started from the DOS level with <GWBASIC  /m:60000>."
230 PRINT : PRINT"If this was not the case, please input <s> for Stop."
240 PRINT "Else press any key ...";
250 A$ = INKEY$ : IF A$ = "s" THEN END
260 IF A$ = "" THEN 250
270 DIM SECTOR%[255]               'Stores Sectors to be read or written
280 DIM FD%[29]              'Formatting data (maximum 0-29 = 30 Words)
290 GOSUB 60000                            'Initialize Interrupt-Routine
300 CLS                                                    'Clear Screen
310 KEY OFF                                'Turn off Function key assignment
320 COLOR 0,7              'dark characters on light background (invers)
330 PRINT" DISKMON (c) 1987 by Michael Tischer                ? = Help "
340 COLOR 7,0                          'light characters on dark background
350 VIEW PRINT 2 TO 24                         'Lines 2 to 24 form a window
360 DR% = 0                                          'access unit 0 (A) first
370 SIDE% = 0                                'access the first Diskette side
380 FTYP% = 3                                '1.2 MB Diskettes in 1.2 MB drive
390 DEF SEG = &HF000                                   'Set BIOS-Segment
400 IF PEEK(&HFFFE) = &HFC THEN AT% = - 1 ELSE AT% = 0      'test if AT
410 DEF SEG                                        'Set BIOS-Segment again
420 GOSUB 50000                                            'Execute Reset
430 GOSUB 51000                        'Output Error message if necessary
440 INPUT"DISK-MON>",E$                                'User input prompt
450 IF E$ = "" THEN 440             'no input  --> repeat input prompt
460 IF E$ = "?" THEN GOSUB 53000 : GOTO 440           'Display Help-Text
470 IF E$ = "r" THEN GOTO 420                                     'Reset
480 IF E$ = "s" THEN GOSUB 54000 : GOTO 430               'fill a Sector
490 IF E$ = "f" THEN GOSUB 55000 : GOTO 430               'format a Track
500 IF E$ = "g" THEN GOSUB 56000 : GOTO 430   'Read Sector and display
510 IF E$ = "c" THEN GOSUB 57000 : GOTO 440             'Input Constants
520 IF E$ = "e" THEN VIEW PRINT 1 TO 24: CLS : END          'End Program
530 PRINT"unknown Command!" : GOTO 440
540 '
50000 '****************************************************************'
50010 '* Execute Reset of all Disk drives                             *'
50020 '*--------------------------------------------------------------*'
50030 '* Input : none                                                 *'
50040 '* Output: DST% = the Diskette-Status                           *'
50050 '* Info  : Z% is a Dummy-Variable                               *'
```

```
50060 '****************************************************************'
50070 '
50080 DST% = 0                                'Function number for Reset
50090 INR% = &H13                     'Call BIOS-Diskette-Interrupt 13(h)
50100 CALL IA(INR%,DST%,Z%,Z%,Z%,Z%,Z%,Z%,Z%,Z%,Z%,Z%,Z%)
50110 RETURN                                             'back to caller
50120 '
51000 '****************************************************************'
51010 '* Output Error Message based on the Diskette-Status            *'
51020 '*--------------------------------------------------------------*'
51030 '* Input : DST% = Status of the last Diskette operation          *'
51040 '* Output: none                                                 *'
51050 '****************************************************************'
51060 '
51070 IF DST% = 0 THEN RETURN                     '0 = everything o.k.
51080 PRINT "ERROR: ";
51090 IF DST% = &H1 THEN PRINT"Function number not allowed " : GOTO 50000
51100 IF DST% = &H2 THEN PRINT"Address-Marking not found" : GOTO 50000
51110 IF DST% = &H3 THEN PRINT"Write attempt on protected Disk" : GOTO 50000
51120 IF DST% = &H4 THEN PRINT"Sector not found" : GOTO 50000
51130 IF DST% = &H6 THEN PRINT"Diskette changed" : GOTO 50000
51140 IF DST% = &H8 THEN PRINT"DMA Overrun" : GOTO 50000
51150 IF DST% = &H9 THEN PRINT"Data transmission beyond segment border" : GOTO 50000
51160 IF DST% = &H10 THEN PRINT"Read Error" : GOTO 50000
51170 IF DST% = &H20 THEN PRINT"Error of Disk-Controller" : GOTO 50000
51180 IF DST% = &H40 THEN PRINT"Track not found" : GOTO 50000
51190 IF DST% = &H80 THEN PRINT"Time Out Error" : GOTO 50000
51200 PRINT"Error ";DST%;" unknown" : GOTO 50000
51210 '
53000 '****************************************************************'
53010 '* Display Help-Text on the screen                              *'
53020 '*--------------------------------------------------------------*'
53030 '* Input : none                                                 *'
53040 '* Output: none                                                 *'
53050 '****************************************************************'
53060 '
53070 PRINT
53080 PRINT"C O M M A N D   O V E R V I E W"
53090 PRINT"--------------------------------"
53100 PRINT"e = End"
53110 PRINT"g = Get (Read)"
53120 PRINT"s = Sector fill"
53130 PRINT"r = Reset"
53140 PRINT"f = Format"
53150 PRINT"c = Constants"
53160 PRINT"? = Help"
53170 PRINT
53180 RETURN                                             'back to caller
53190 '
54000 '****************************************************************'
54010 '* Fill a Sector                                                *'
54020 '*--------------------------------------------------------------*'
54030 '* Input : DR%   = the Number of the unit addressed             *'
54040 '*         SIDE% = the number of the Disk side addressed        *'
54050 '* Output: DST%  = the Diskette status                          *'
54060 '* Info  : Z% is a Dummy-Variable                               *'
54070 '****************************************************************'
54080 '
54090 INPUT "Track  : ",TRACK%    'Track in which the Sector is located
54100 INPUT "Sector : ",SECTOR%                  'Sector to be filled
54110 INPUT "Character: ",Z$                       'Fill Character
54120 IF Z$ = "" THEN Z$ = CHR$(0)
54130 FOR I% = 0 TO 511 : POKE VARPTR(SECTOR%[0])+I%,ASC(Z$) : NEXT
54140 DST% = 3                           'Function number for writing
54150 INR% = &H13                    'Call BIOS-Diskette-Interrupt 13(h)
54160 NUM% = 1                                     'Number of Sectors
54170 OFSLO% = 0 : OFSHI% = 0                   'initialize Variables
54180 SEG% = -1                                   'Use BASIC DS for ES
54190 NUM% = 1                          'Number of Sectors to be read
54200 OFSLO% = VARPTR(SECTOR%[0]) AND 255   'LO & HI-Byte of the Offset
```

```
54210 OFSHI% = INT(VARPTR(SECTOR%[0]) / 256)'address of Var SECTOR%[0]
54220 CALL IA(INR%,DST%,NUM%,OFSHI%,OFSLO%,TRACK%,SECTOR%,SIDE%,DR%, Z%,Z%,SEG%,Z%)
54230 RETURN                                              'back to caller
54240 '
55000 '***************************************************************'
55010 '* Format a Track                                              *'
55020 '*-------------------------------------------------------------*'
55030 '* Input : DR%   = the number of the unit                      *'
55040 '*         SIDE% = the number of the disk side                 *'
55050 '*         FTYP% = Type of Disk drive                          *'
55060 '*         AT%   = -1 if computer is an AT, otherwise 0        *'
55070 '* Output: DST%  = the Diskette status                         *'
55080 '* Info  : Z% is a  Dummy-Variable                             *'
55090 '***************************************************************'
55100 '
55110 IF NOT(AT%) THEN 55150         'if not AT, then no format fitting
55120 FKT% = &H17                    'Set Function number for DASD Type
55130 INR% = &H13                   'Call BIOS-Diskette-Interrupt 13(h)
55140 CALL IA(INR%,FKT%,FTYP%,Z%,Z%,Z%,Z%,Z%,DR%,Z%,Z%,Z%,Z%)
55150 INPUT "Track   : ",TRACK%        'Number of Track to be formatted
55160 INPUT "Number Sectors: ",NUM%  'Number of Sectors to be installed
55170 IF NUM% > 15 THEN 55160   'maximum of 15 Sectors can be installed
55180 FOR I% = 0 TO NUM%-1                 'one entry for every Sector
55190 POKE VARPTR(FD%[0])+I%*4,TRACK%            'Enter number of Track
55200 POKE VARPTR(FD%[0])+I%*4+1,SIDE%            'Enter number of side
55210 POKE VARPTR(FD%[0])+I%*4+2,I%+1              'Enter Sector number
55220 POKE VARPTR(FD%[0])+I%*4+3,2        'Format Sector with 512 Bytes
55230 NEXT                               'Process Entry for next Sector
55240 DST% = 5                          'Function number for Formatting
55250 INR% = &H13                   'Call BIOS-Diskette-Interrupt 13(h)
55260 OFSLO% = 0 : OFSHI% = 0                    'initialize Variables
55270 SEG% = -1                                  'Use BASIC DS for ES
55280 OFSLO% = VARPTR(FD%[0]) AND 255         'LO and HI-Byte of Offset
55290 OFSHI% = INT(VARPTR(FD%[0]) / 256)       'address of Var. FD%[0]
55300 CALL IA(INR%,DST%,NUM%,OFSHI%,OFSLO%,TRACK%,Z%,SIDE%,DR%, Z%,Z%,SEG%,Z%)
55310 RETURN                                              'back to caller
55320 '
56000 '***************************************************************'
56010 '* read a Sector and display                                   *'
56020 '*-------------------------------------------------------------*'
56030 '* Input : DR%   = the Number of the drive to be accessed      *'
56040 '*         SIDE% = the number of the Diskette side             *'
56050 '* Output: DST%  = the Diskette status                         *'
56060 '* Info  : Z% is a Dummy-Variable                              *'
56070 '***************************************************************'
56080 '
56090 INPUT "Track  : ",TRACK%    'Track in which the Sector is located
56100 INPUT "Sector: ",SECTOR%                 'the Sector to be filled
56110 DST% = 2                             'Function number for reading
56120 INR% = &H13                   'Call BIOS-Diskette-Interrupt 13(h)
56130 NUM% = 1                                           'Read a Sector
56140 OFSLO% = 0 : OFSHI% = 0                        'Create Variables
56150 SEG% = -1                                   'Use BASIC DS for ES
56160 OFSLO% = VARPTR(SECTOR%[0]) AND 255     'LO and HI-Byte of Offset
56170 OFSHI% = INT(VARPTR(SECTOR%[0]) / 256)'addr of the Var SECTOR%[0]
56180 CALL IA(INR%,DST%,NUM%,OFSHI%,OFSLO%,TRACK%,SECTOR%,SIDE%,DR%, Z%,Z%,SEG%,Z%)
56190 IF DST% <> 0 THEN RETURN             'on error do not output data
56200 PRINT STRING$(80,"-");
56210 FOR I% = 0 TO 511           'process all Bytes of the Sector read
56220 Z% = PEEK(VARPTR(SECTOR%[0]) + I%)     'get a Byte from the Sector
56230 IF Z% = 0 THEN PRINT "<NUL>"; : GOTO 56350
56240 IF Z% = 7 THEN PRINT "<BEL>"; : GOTO 56350
56250 IF (Z% = 8) OR (Z% = 29) THEN PRINT "<BS>"; : GOTO 56350
56260 IF Z% = 9 THEN PRINT "<TAB>"; : GOTO 56350
56270 IF Z% = 10 THEN PRINT "<LF>"; : GOTO 56350
56280 IF Z% = 11 THEN PRINT "<HOM>"; : GOTO 56350
56290 IF Z% = 12 THEN PRINT "<FF>"; : GOTO 56350
56300 IF Z% = 13 THEN PRINT "<CR>"; : GOTO 56350
56310 IF Z% = 27 THEN PRINT "<ESC>"; : GOTO 56350
56320 IF Z% = 30 THEN PRINT "<CUP>"; : GOTO 56350
```

```
56330 IF Z% = 31 THEN PRINT "<CDN>"; : GOTO 56350
56340 PRINT CHR$(Z%);                    'output Byte as ASCII character
56350 NEXT                                           'output next Byte
56360 PRINT
56370 PRINT STRING$(80,"-");
56380 RETURN                                          'back to caller
56390 '
57000 '*****************************************************************'
57010 '* Input Constants (Unit number, Diskette side, etc.)            *'
57020 '*---------------------------------------------------------------*'
57030 '* Input : AT%    = -1 if computer is an AT, else 0              *'
57040 '* Output: DR%    = Number of unit to be accessed                *'
57050 '*         SIDE%  = Number of disk. side                         *'
57060 '*         FTYP%  = Type of Disk drive                           *'
57070 '*****************************************************************'
57080 '
57090 INPUT "Unit-Number (0-3)    : ",DR%
57100 INPUT "Diskette side (0 or 1): ",SIDE%
57110 IF NOT(AT%) THEN RETURN              'Diskette format only for AT
57120 PRINT"Formatting Parameter:"
57130 PRINT"  1 = 320/360 KB diskette in 320/360 KB Drive"
57140 PRINT"  2 = 320/360 KB diskette in 1.2 MB Drive"
57150 INPUT"  3 = 1.2 MB diskette in 1.2 MB Drive -- Please input: ",FTYP%
57160 RETURN                                          'back to caller
57170 '
60000 '*****************************************************************'
60010 '* initialize the Routine for Interrupt call                     *'
60020 '*---------------------------------------------------------------*'
60030 '* Input : none                                                  *'
60040 '* Output: IA is the Start address of the Interrupt-Routine      *'
60050 '*****************************************************************'
60060 '
60070 IA=60000!       'Start address of the Routine in the BASIC-Segment
60080 DEF SEG                                      'Set BASIC-Segment
60090 RESTORE 60130
60100 FOR I% = 0 TO 160 : READ X% : POKE IA+I%,X% : NEXT  'Poke Routine
60110 RETURN                                          'back to caller
60120 '
60130 DATA  85,139,236, 30,  6,139,118, 30,139,  4,232,140,  0,139,118
60140 DATA  12,139, 60,139,118,  8,139,  4, 61,255,255,117,  2,140,216
60150 DATA 142,192,139,118, 28,138, 36,139,118, 26,138,  4,139,118, 24
60160 DATA 138, 60,139,118, 22,138, 28,139,118, 20,138, 44,139,118, 18
60170 DATA 138, 12,139,118, 16,138, 52,139,118, 14,138, 20,139,118, 10
60180 DATA 139, 52, 85,205, 33, 93, 86,156,139,118, 12,137, 60,139,118
60190 DATA  28,136, 36,139,118, 26,136,  4,139,118, 24,136, 60,139,118
60200 DATA  22,136, 28,139,118, 20,136, 44,139,118, 18,136, 12,139,118
60210 DATA  16,136, 52,139,118, 14,136, 20,139,118,  8,140,192,137,  4
60220 DATA  88,139,118,  6,137,  4, 88,139,118, 10,137,  4,  7, 31, 93
60230 DATA 202, 26,  0, 91, 46,136, 71, 66,233,108,255
```

Structurally this program resembles the other BASIC programs which have been presented. The main program with the input loop is in lines 300 to 540. Then follow the individual commands of DISKMON which exist as subroutines between lines 50000 and 57170. The subroutine for initializing the interrupt call starts at line 60000 (the program uses this interrupt frequently).

The use of a BASIC variable as a buffer for the reading and writing of data is somewhat complicated in this program. The program dimensions an integer array with elements from 0 to 255. Since every element in this array requires 2 bytes (for integer), the program allocates 512 bytes for a buffer. The problem arises from the BASIC interpreter's garbage collection routine. When it removes data, which is no longer needed, from the variable storage area, it also moves the data buffer. The address of this buffer which was supposed to be passed to BIOS is no longer valid. Other data are now stored there.

During a write operation this wouldn't be very bad, since only false data would be written to the disk. During a read operation this could lead to a crash of the BASIC interpreter, since variable memory could be destroyed. To prevent this, establish the address of the buffer variable immediately before the BIOS function call. Also, make sure that the variables which accept this address are constantly available. For this reason DISKMON initializes the two variables with 0 before storing the buffer address in them. This offset address must receive the segment address of the current BIOS function in the ES register. Since the BASIC data segment contains the buffer address, the contents of the Data segment register DS must be passed to ES. This is done by passing the value -1 for ES which causes the interrupt function to copy the contents of the DS registers to ES.

Pascal listing: DISKMONP.PAS

```
{***********************************************************************}
{*                          D I S K M O N P                            *}
{*---------------------------------------------------------------------*}
{*    Task           : DISKMON is a small disk monitor based on        *}
{*                     the functions of the BIOS diskette              *}
{*                     interrupt 13(h)                                 *}
{*---------------------------------------------------------------------*}
{*    Author         : MICHAEL TISCHER                                 *}
{*    developed on   : 7/9/87                                          *}
{*    last update    : 5/19/89                                         *}
{***********************************************************************}

program DISKMON;

Uses Crt, Dos;                              { adds Crt and Dos features }

type BufferTyp = array [1..1] of char;
     FormatTyp = record           { BIOS requires this information for •}
                  Track,                             { every sector of  }
                  Side,                         { a track to be formatted }
                  Sector,
                  Length  : byte;
                end;

var ErrCode      : byte;        { Error status after diskette operation }
    Command      : string[1];              { Command input by the user  }
    FTyp,                       { Diskette type for formatting function }
    DriveNum,                                { Number of current drive }
    Side        : integer;      { Number of the current diskette side }
    Dummy        : integer;                            { Dummy variable }
    AT           : boolean;                      { is the computer an AT? }

{***********************************************************************}
{* RESETDISK: Reset for all attached disk drives                       *}
{* Input     : none                                                    *}
{* Output    : error status                                            *}
{***********************************************************************}

function ResetDisk : integer;

var Regs : Registers;             { Register variable for interrupt call }

begin
 Regs.ah := 0;                          { Function number for reset is 0 }
```

```
 intr($13, Regs);                            { Call BIOS disk interrupt }
 ResetDisk := Regs.ah;                              { Read error status }
end;

{**********************************************************************}
{* GETDISKSTATUS: reads the error status                              *}
{* Input : none                                                       *}
{* Output : the error status                                          *}
{**********************************************************************}

function GetDiskStatus : integer;

var Regs : Registers;          { Register variable for interrupt call }

begin
 Regs.ah := 1;                 { Function number for error status is 1 }
 intr($13, Regs);                            { Call BIOS disk interrupt }
 GetDiskStatus := Regs.ah;                          { Read error status }
end;

{**********************************************************************}
{* READSECTORS: read a certain number of sectors                      *}
{* Input : see below                                                  *}
{* Output : error status                                              *}
{**********************************************************************}

function ReadSectors(DriveNum,                  { Disk drive for reading  }
                     Side,              { Side or read/write head number }
                     Track,                          { track to be read  }
                     Sector,                  { The first sector to be read }
                     Number,                { Number of sectors to be read  }
                     SegAdr,                { Segment address of the buffer }
                     OfsAdr : integer; { Offset address of the buffer }
                     var NumRead : integer) : integer;

var Regs : Registers;          { Register variable for interrupt call }

begin
 Regs.ah := 2;                    { Function number for reading is 2 }
 Regs.al := Number;               { Set number of sectors for reading }
 Regs.dh := Side;                                   { Set side number }
 Regs.dl := DriveNum;                              { Set drive number }
 Regs.ch := Track;                                 { Set track number }
 Regs.cl := Sector;                               { Set sector number }
 Regs.es := SegAdr;                              { Set buffer address }
 Regs.bx := OfsAdr;
 intr($13, Regs);                            { Call BIOS disk interrupt }
 NumRead := Regs.al;                          { Number of sectors read  }
 ReadSectors := Regs.ah;                            { Read error status }
end;

{**********************************************************************}
{* WRITESECTORS: Write a certain number of sectors                    *}
{* Input  : see below                                                 *}
{* Output : error status                                              *}
{**********************************************************************}

function WriteSectors(DriveNum,                          { Disk drive  }
                      Side,                    { Side or read/write head }
                      Track,                        { Track to be written  }
                      Sector,                 { First sector to be written }
                      Number,            { Number of sectors to be written  }
                      SegAdr,               { Segment address of the buffer }
                      OfsAdr : integer;{ Offset address of the buffer }
                      var NumWritten : integer) : integer;

var Regs : Registers;          { Register variable for interrupt call }

begin
 Regs.ah := 3;                    { Function number for writing is 3 }
```

```
 Regs.al := Number;                  { Set number of sectors to be read }
 Regs.dh := Side;                                   { Set side number }
 Regs.dl := DriveNum;                              { Set drive number  }
 Regs.ch := Track;                                 { Set track number }
 Regs.cl := Sector;                               { Set sector number }
 Regs.es := SegAdr;                              { Set buffer address }
 Regs.bx := OfsAdr;
 intr($13, Regs);                           { Call BIOS disk interrupt }
 NumWritten := Regs.al;                   { Number of sectors written  }
 WriteSectors := Regs.ah;                          { Read error status }
end;

{**********************************************************************}
{* SETDASD: must be called for an AT before formatting to indicate   *}
{*          if it should be formatted with 360 KB                     *}
{*          or with 1.2 MB                                            *}
{* Input : see below                                                  *}
{* Output : none                                                      *}
{**********************************************************************}

procedure SetDasd(DiskFormat : integer);

var Regs : Registers;          { Register variable for interrupt call }

begin
 Regs.ah := $17;                                   { Function number }
 Regs.al := DiskFormat;                                     { Format }
 Regs.dl := DriveNum;                                 { Drive number }
 intr($13, Regs);                           { Call BIOS disk interrupt }
end;

{**********************************************************************}
{* FORMATTRACK:  formats a track                                      *}
{* Input : see below                                                  *}
{* Output : the error status                                          *}
{**********************************************************************}

function FormatTrack(DriveNum,                { Number of the disk drive }
                     Side,                    { the side or head number  }
                     Track,                       { Track to be formatted }
                     Number,          { Number of sectors in this track  }
                     Bytes    :  integer) :  integer;

var Regs : Registers;          { Register variable for interrupt call }
    DataField : array [1..15] of FormatTyp;     { maximum 15 sectors }
    LoopCnt   : integer;                              { Loop counter }

begin
 for LoopCnt := 1 to Number do              { Create sector descriptor }
  begin
   DataField[LoopCnt].Track    := Track;         { Number of the track }
   DataField[LoopCnt].Side   := Side;                 { Diskette side }
   DataField[LoopCnt].Sector := LoopCnt;        { Number of the sector }
   DataField[LoopCnt].Length := Bytes;{ Number of bytes in the sector }
  end;
 Regs.ah := 5;
 Regs.al := Number;                        { Function number, Number }
 Regs.es := seg(DataField[1]);          { Address of the data field in }
 Regs.bx := ofs(DataField[1]);                { registers ES and BX }
 Regs.dh := Side;                                      { Side number }
 Regs.dl := DriveNum;                                   { Drive unit }
 Regs.ch := Track;                                { Set track number }
 intr($13, Regs);                           { Call BIOS disk interrupt }
 FormatTrack := Regs.ah;                         { Read error status }
end;

{**********************************************************************}
{* WRITEERROR: Output error message according to error value         *}
{* Input : the error number                                           *}
{* Output : none                                                      *}
```

```
{**********************************************************************}

procedure WriteError(ErrorNumber : integer);

begin
 case ErrorNumber of
  $00 : ;                                      { 0 means no error  }
  $01 : writeln('ERROR: Invalid function number');
  $02 : writeln('ERROR: Address marking not found');
  $03 : writeln('ERROR: Write attempt on protected disk');
  $04 : writeln('ERROR: Sector not found');
  $06 : writeln('ERROR: Diskette changed');
  $08 : writeln('ERROR: DMA overrun');
  $09 : writeln('ERROR: Data transmission beyond segment border');
  $10 : writeln('ERROR: Read error');
  $20 : writeln('ERROR: Disk controller error');
  $40 : writeln('ERROR: Track not found');
  $80 : writeln('ERROR: Time out error');
  else  writeln('ERROR: Error ',ErrorNumber,' unknown');
 end;
 if (ErrorNumber <> 0) then ErrorNumber:=ResetDisk; { Reset performed }
end;

{**********************************************************************}
{* CONSTANTS:  Input of the two constants and                         *}
{*             diskette side or head number, as well as diskette      *}
{*             type for AT                                            *}
{* Input : none                                                       *}
{* Output : none                                                      *}
{**********************************************************************}

procedure Constants;

begin
 write('Unit-Number (0-3)    : ');
 readln(DriveNum);                             { Read unit number }
 write('Diskette side (0 or 1): ');
 readln(Side);                                 { Read head number }
 if AT then                                         { only for AT }
  begin
   writeln('Format-Parameter:');
   writeln('  1 = 320/360-KB-Diskette in 320/360-KB drive');
   writeln('  2 = 320/360-KB-Diskette in 1.2-MB drive');
   write('  3 = 1.2-MB-Diskette in 1.2-MB-drive -- Please input: '),
   readln(FTyp)
  end;
end;

{**********************************************************************}
{* HELP: Display help text on the screen                              *}
{* Input : none                                                       *}
{* Output : none                                                      *}
{**********************************************************************}

procedure Help;

begin
 writeln(#13#10'C O M M A N D   O V E R V I E W');
 writeln('-------------------------------');
 writeln('e = End');
 writeln('g = Get (Read)');
 writeln('s = Sector fill');
 writeln('r = Reset');
 writeln('f = Format');
 writeln('c = Constants');
 writeln('? = Help'#13#10);
end;

{**********************************************************************}
{* READSEC: Read a diskette sector and display it on the screen      *}
```

```
{* Input : none                                                         *}
{* Output : none                                                        *}
{***********************************************************************}

procedure READSEC;

var DataBuffer : array [1..512] of char;       { the characters read }
    Track,                               { the track from which to read }
    Sector : integer;                                 { Sector to be read }

begin
 write('Track : ');
 readln(Track);                              { Read track from keyboard }
 write('Sector: ');
 readln(Sector);                        { Read sector from the keyboard }
 ErrCode := ReadSectors(DriveNum, Side, Track, Sector, 1,
                        seg(DataBuffer), ofs(DataBuffer), Dummy);
 if (ErrCode = 0) then                { Error occurred during reading? }
  begin
   write('----------------------------------------'+
         '---------------------------------------');
   for Dummy:=1 to 512 do                    { output the 512 characters }
    begin
     case DataBuffer[Dummy] of
      #00 : write('<NUL>');    { treat control characters separately }
      #07 : write('<BEL>');
      #08 : write('<BS>');
      #09 : write('<TAB>');
      #10 : write('<LF>');
      #13 : write('<CR>');
      #27 : write('<ESC>');
      else  write(DataBuffer[Dummy]);    { output normal character }
     end;
    end;
   write(#13#10'----------------------------------------'+
               '---------------------------------------');
  end
  else WriteError(ErrCode);                        { output error message }
end;

{***********************************************************************}
{* FORMATIT:    format a certain number of sectors of a               *}
{*              track with 512 bytes each                              *}
{* Input : none                                                         *}
{* Output : none                                                        *}
{***********************************************************************}

procedure FormatIt;

var Track,                                        { Track to be formatted  }
    Sector : integer;                                { Number of sectors }

begin
  write('Track : ');
  readln(Track);                { Read number of tracks from keyboard }
  write('Sector: ');
  readln(Sector);          { Read number of sectors from the keyboard  }
  if AT then SetDasd(FTyp);                 { if AT then diskette type }
  WriteError(FormatTrack(DriveNum, Side, Track, Sector, 2));
end;

{***********************************************************************}
{* FILLSECTOR: Fill a sector with a character                          *}
{* Input : none                                                         *}
{* Output : none                                                        *}
{***********************************************************************}

procedure FillSector;

var DataBuffer : array [1..512] of char;  { Content of sector to fill }
```

```
    LoopCnt,                                            { Loop counter }
    Track,                          { Track in which the sector is located  }
    Sector : integer;                       { Number of sector to be filled }
    FillChar : char;                                { the fill character }

begin
 write('Track    : ');
 readln(Track);                              { Read track from keyboard }
 write('Sector   : ');
 readln(Sector);                            { Read sector from keyboard  }
 write('Character: ');
 readln(FillChar);           { Read the fill character from the keyboard }
 for LoopCnt := 1 to 512 do
  DataBuffer[LoopCnt] := FillChar;       { Fill buffer with characters }
 WriteError(WriteSectors(DriveNum, Side, Track, Sector, 1,
                         seg(DataBuffer), ofs(DataBuffer), Dummy));
end;

{***********************************************************************}
{**                            MAIN PROGRAM                          **}
{***********************************************************************}

begin
 clrscr;                                                { Clear screen }
 textbackground(7);                                { light background }
 textcolor(0);                                      { dark characters }
 writeln(' DISKMON: (c) 1987 by Michael Tischer    '+        { Headline }
                                        ? = Help ');
 textbackground(0);                                  { dark background }
 textcolor(7);                                            { light text }
 window(1, 2, 80, 25);     { only first line does not belong to window }
 DriveNum := 0;                           { Indicate unit 0 as constant  }
 Side := 0;                                         { Side 0 as constant }
 FTyp := 3;                             { 1.2 MB diskette in 1.2 MB unit }
 if mem[$F000:$FFFE] = $FC then AT := true                { test if AT or }
                             else AT := false;               { PC or XT }
 WriteError(ResetDisk);                                  { perform Reset }
 repeat
  repeat
   write('DISKMON>');                                    { output prompt }
   readln(Command);                          { Read command from keyboard }
  until (Command <> '');
  case (Command [1]) of
  '?'  : Help;                                     {? display help text }
  'r'  : WriteError(ResetDisk);                        {r perform reset }
  's'  : FillSector;                                   {s fill a sector }
  'f'  : FormatIt;                                    {f format a track }
  'g'  : READSEC;                                      {g read a sector }
  'c': Constants;                                  {c input constants }
 else if Command <> 'e' then writeln('unknown command');
  end;
 until (Command = 'e');                                 {e end program }
end.
```

The DISKMON in Pascal and the following version in C strongly resemble each other. Both have the input loop inside the main program and the individual commands placed in procedures or functions outside the main program. Unlike the BASIC version of DISKMON, a difference exists between the DISKMON commands and the BIOS function call. They are stored in separate program sections. This has the advantage that the BIOS function calls can be easily transferred as stand alone modules to other programs.

Problems with addressing the data buffer don't exist in C or in Pascal as they do in BASIC. The buffer is a local variable.

There are two small differences between the C and Pascal versions. They are in the screen display and the administration of constants for unit number, disk side, etc. While the Pascal version defines these as global variables, the C version defines them as local variables within the main() program area.

C doesn't allow easy window definition for performing tasks. This is why the C version of DISKMON doesn't use the first screen line as a status line to output a copyright notice and call the Help command.

C listing: DISKMONC.C

```
/***********************************************************************/
/*                          D I S K M O N C                            */
/*---------------------------------------------------------------------*/
/*    Task          : DISKMON is a short disk monitor program,         */
/*                    using BIOS interrupt 13(h) functions             */
/*---------------------------------------------------------------------*/
/*    Author        : MICHAEL TISCHER                                  */
/*    Developed on  : 08/15/1987                                       */
/*    last update   : 06/08/1989                                       */
/*---------------------------------------------------------------------*/
/*    (MICROSOFT C)                                                    */
/*    Creation      : CL /AS DISKMONC.C                                */
/*    Call          : DISKMONC                                         */
/*---------------------------------------------------------------------*/
/*    (BORLAND TURBO C)                                                */
/*    Creation      : Make sure Case-sensitive link is OFF before      */
/*                    compiling & linking                              */
/*                    Select Compile/Make or RUN (no project file)     */
/***********************************************************************/

/*== Add include files ==============================================*/

#include <dos.h>
#include <stdio.h>
#include <ctype.h>

/*== Typedefs =======================================================*/

typedef unsigned char byte;                           /* Create a byte */

/*== Constants ======================================================*/

#define FALSE 0                   /* Constants to make reading the    */
#define TRUE 1                    /* source code easier               */

#define NUL     0                                    /* null character */
#define BEL     7                               /* bell character code */
#define BS      8                          /* backspace character code */
#define TAB     9                                /* tab character code */
#define LF      10                          /* linefeed character code */
#define CR      13                                  /* Return key code */
#define EF      26                                 /* End of file code */
#define ESC     27                                      /* Escape code */

/*== Macros =========================================================*/

#ifndef MK_FP                                 /* MK_FP still undefined? */
#define MK_FP(s,o) ((void far *) (((unsigned long)(s) << 16) | (o)))
#define peekb(a,b) (*((byte far *) MK_FP((a),(b))))
#endif

/*-- The following macros state the offset and segment addresses of --*/
/*-- any pointer ------------------------------------------------------*/
```

```
#define GETSEG(p) ((unsigned)(((unsigned long) ((void far *) p)) >> 16))
#define GETOFS(p) ((unsigned) ((void far *) p))

/* -- Function declarations -------------------------------------------*/

byte DRead( byte, byte, byte, byte, byte, byte far * );
byte DWrite( byte, byte, byte, byte, byte, byte far * );

/*== Structures ======================================================*/

struct FormatDes {                  /* Describes format of a sector */
                  byte Track,
                       Side,
                       Sector,            /* logical sector number */
                       Length;
                 };

/**********************************************************************/
/* RESETDISK: Reset  all drives connected to system                   */
/* Input      : none                                                  */
/* Output     : error status                                          */
/**********************************************************************/

byte ResetDisk()

{
 union REGS Register;         /* Register variable for interrupt call */

 Register.h.ah = 0;                 /* Function number for reset = 0 */
 Register.h.dl = 0;                             /* Reset disk drives */
 int86(0x13, &Register, &Register);        /* Call BIOS disk interrupt */
/* printf("Result: %d\n", Register.h.ah); */
 return(Register.h.ah);                          /* Return error status */
}

/**********************************************************************/
/* WDS: Display status of the last disk operation                     */
/* Input      : see below                                             */
/* Output     : TRUE if no error, otherwise FALSE                     */
/**********************************************************************/

byte WDS(Status)
byte Status;                                         /* Disk status */

{
 if (Status)                                     /* Error occurred? */
  {                                                         /* YES */
   printf("ERROR: ");
   switch (Status)                            /* Display error msg */
    {
     case 0x01 : printf("Function number not permitted\n");
                 break;
     case 0x02 : printf("Address marking not found\n");
                 break;
     case 0x03 : printf("Disk is write-protected\n");
                 break;
     case 0x04 : printf("Sector not found\n");
                 break;
     case 0x06 : printf("Disk changed\n");
                 break;
     case 0x08 : printf("DMA overflow\n");
                 break;
     case 0x09 : printf("Data transfer past segment limit\n");
                 break;
     case 0x10 : printf("Read error\n");
                 break;
     case 0x20 : printf("Disk controller error\n");
                 break;
     case 0x40 : printf("Track not found\n");
                 break;
```

```
    case 0x80 : printf("Time Out error\n");
                break;
    case 0xff : printf("Illegal parameter\n");
                break;
    default   : printf("Error %d unknown\n", Status);
   }
  ResetDisk();                              /* Execute reset on error */
 }
 return(!Status);
}

/*********************************************************************/
/* DREAD: Read specified sector from disk                            */
/* Input     : see below                                             */
/* Output    : error status                                          */
/*********************************************************************/

byte DRead(Drive, Side, Track, Sector, Number,  Buffer)
byte Drive,                                         /* Drive number */
     Side,                 /* Disk side or read-write head number */
     Track,                                         /* Track number */
     Sector,                              /* First sector to be read */
     Number,                      /* Number of sectors to be written */
     far * Buffer;                    /* FAR pointer to a byte vector */

{
 union REGS Register;         /* Register variable for interrupt call */
 struct SREGS SRegs;                /* Variables for segment register */

 Register.h.ah = 2;                    /* Function no. for read is 2 */
 Register.h.al = Number;                    /* Number in AL register */
 Register.h.dh = Side;                        /* Side in DH register */
 Register.h.dl = Drive;                        /* Drive number in DL */
 Register.h.ch = Track;                      /* Track in CH register */
 Register.h.cl = Sector;                    /* Sector in CL register */
 Register.x.bx = GETOFS ( Buffer );       /* Offset address of buffer */
 SRegs.es = GETSEG( Buffer );            /* Segment address of buffer */
 int86x(0x13, &Register, &Register, &SRegs);
 return(Register.h.ah);                          /* Return error status */
}

/*********************************************************************/
/* DWRITE: Write to the specified number of sectors                  */
/* Input     : see below                                             */
/* Output    : error status                                          */
/*********************************************************************/

byte DWrite(Drive, Side, Track, Sector, Number,  Buffer)
byte Drive,                            /* Number of drive to be accessed */
     Side,              /* Disk side or number of read-write head */
     Track,                                         /* Track number */
     Sector,                           /* First sector to be written */
     Number,                                   /* Number of sectors */
     far * Buffer;                    /* FAR pointer to a byte vector */

{
 union REGS Register;         /* Register variable for interrupt call */
 struct SREGS SRegs;                      /* Segment register variables */

 Register.h.ah = 3;                   /* Function no. for write is 3 */
 Register.h.al = Number;                    /* Number in AL register */
 Register.h.dh = Side;                        /* Side in DH register */
 Register.h.dl = Drive;                        /* Drive number in DL */
 Register.h.ch = Track;                      /* Track in CH register */
 Register.h.cl = Sector;                    /* Sector in CL register */
 Register.x.bx = GETOFS( Buffer );        /* Offset address of buffer */
 SRegs.es = GETSEG( Buffer );            /* Segment address of buffer */
 int86x(0x13, &Register, &Register, &SRegs);   /* BIOS disk int. call */
 return(Register.h.ah);                          /* Return error status */
}
```

```
/************************************************************************/
/* FORMAT: format a track                                               */
/* Input     : see below                                                */
/* Output    : error status                                             */
/* Info      : BYTES parameter gives the number of bytes in the for-   */
/*             matted sector. The following codes are allowed:         */
/*                             0 = 128 bytes, 1 =  256 bytes           */
/*                             2 = 512 bytes, 3 = 1024 bytes           */
/************************************************************************/

byte Format(Drive, Side, Track, Number, Bytes)
byte Drive,
     Side,                                       /* Side/head number */
     Track,                                   /* Track to be formatted */
     Number,                        /* Number of sectors in this track */
     Bytes;                              /* Number of bytes per sector */

{
 union REGS Register;         /* Register variable for interrupt call */
 struct SREGS SRegs;                    /* Segment register variables */
 struct FormatDes Formate[15];               /* Maximum of 15 sectors */
 byte i;                                              /* Loop counter */

 if (Number <= 15)                                 /* Is number o.k.? */
  {
   for (i = 0; i < Number; i++)                /* Set sector descriptor */
    {
     Formate[i].Track = Track;                         /* Track number */
     Formate[i].Side = Side;                              /* Disk side */
     Formate[i].Sector = i+1;                /* Sector increments by 1 */
     Formate[i].Length = Bytes;           /* Number of bytes in sector */
    }
   Register.h.ah = 5;                 /* Function number for formatting */
   Register.h.al = Number;                            /* Number in AL */
   Register.h.dh = Side;                          /* Side number in DH */
   Register.h.dl = Drive;                              /* Drive in DL */
   Register.h.ch = Track;                        /* Track number in CH */
   Register.x.bx = GETOFS ( Formate );          /* Offset addr. of table */
   SRegs.es=GETSEG( Formate );             /* Segment address of buffer */
   int86x(0x13, &Register, &Register, &SRegs); /* Call BIOS disk intr.*/
   return(Register.h.ah);                       /* Return error status */
  }
 else return(0xFF);                              /* Illegal parameters */
}

/************************************************************************/
/* CONSTANTS : Change drive number, disk side and disk type            */
/*             (PC/XT or AT)                                           */
/* Input     : see below                                               */
/* Output    : none                                                    */
/************************************************************************/

void Constants(Drive, Side, FTyp, AT)
byte *Drive,                               /* Pointer to drive variable */
     *Side,                                 /* Pointer to side variable */
     FTyp,                                          /* Disk drive type */
     AT;                                 /* TRUE if computer is an AT */

{
 printf("Drive number (0-3): ");
 scanf("%d", &Drive);                              /* Read drive number */
 printf("Disk side (0 or 1): ");
 scanf("%d", &Side);                                /* Read head number */
 if (AT)                                            /* Used only by ATs */
  {
   printf("Format parameter:\n");
   printf("  1 = 320/360K diskette in 320/360K drive\n");
   printf("  2 = 320/360K diskette in 1.2MB drive\n");
   printf("  3 = 1.2MB diskette in 1.2MB drive - please enter choice: ");
```

```
   scanf("%d", &FTyp);
  }
}

/****************************************************************************/
/* HELP: Display help screen                                                */
/* Input     : none                                                         */
/* Output    : none                                                         */
/****************************************************************************/

void Help()

{
 printf("\nDISKMON (c) 1987 by Michael Tischer\n\n");
 printf("C O M M A N D   O V E R V I E W\n");
 printf("--------------------------------\n");
 printf("[E/e] = End\n");
 printf("[G/g] = Get (read)\n");
 printf("[S/s] = Fill a sector\n");
 printf("[R/r] = Reset\n");
 printf("[F/f] = Format\n");
 printf("[C/c] = Constants\n");
 printf("[?]   = Help\n\n");
}

/****************************************************************************/
/* GET  : Read a disk sector and display it on the screen                   */
/* Input     : none                                                         */
/* Output    : none                                                         */
/****************************************************************************/

void ReadSector(Drive, Side)
byte Drive;      /* Drive number */
byte Side;                                       /* Disk side number */

{
 byte Buffer[512];                       /* Contents of filled sector */
 int  i,                                                /* Loop counter */
      Track,                         /* Track in which filled sector lies */
      Sector;                          /* Number of sector to be filled */

 printf("Track : ");
 scanf("%d", &Track);              /* Read track number from keyboard */
 printf("Sector: ");
 scanf("%d", &Sector);                            /* Read sector number */
 if (WDS(DRead(Drive, Side, Track, Sector, 1, Buffer)))
  {
   printf("----------------------------------------");
   printf("----------------------------------------");
   for (i = 0; i < 512; i++)      /* Display characters read from disk */
    switch (Buffer[i])                         /* ASCII code conversion */
     {
      case NUL : printf("<NUL>");
                 break;
      case BEL : printf("<BEL>");
                 break;
      case BS  : printf("<BS>");
                 break;
      case TAB : printf("<TAB>");
                 break;
      case LF  : printf("<LF>");
                 break;
      case CR  : printf("<CR>");
                 break;
      case ESC : printf("<ESC>");
                 break;
      case EF : printf("<EOF>");
                 break;
      default  : printf("%c", Buffer[i]);
     }
```

```
    printf("\n----------------------------------------");
    printf("----------------------------------------\n");
  }
}

/**********************************************************************/
/* FORMAT:    Format a specified number of sectors in a track with    */
/*            512 bytes                                               */
/* Input      : none                                                  */
/* Output     : none                                                  */
/**********************************************************************/

void FormatIt(Drive, Side, AT, FTyp)
byte Drive,       /* Drive number */
     Side,                                     /* Disk side number */
     AT,                               /* TRUE if computer is an AT */
     FTyp;                                      /* Disk drive type */

{
 int  Track,                               /* Track to be formatted */
      Number;                   /* Number of sectors to be formatted */

 printf("Track          : ");
 scanf("%d", &Track);            /* Read track number from keyboard */
 printf("No. of sectors : ");
 scanf("%d", &Number);                   /* Read number of sectors */
 if (AT)                                    /* Is computer an AT? */
  {
   union REGS Register;       /* Register variable for interrupt call */

   Register.h.ah = 0x17;           /* Function no. for set DASD-Type */
   Register.h.al = FTyp;
   Register.h.dl = Drive;
   int86(0x13, &Register, &Register);     /* Call BIOS disk interrupt */
  }
 WDS(Format(Drive, Side, Track, Number, 2, AT, FTyp));
}

/**********************************************************************/
/* FILL   : Fill a sector with a character                            */
/* Input      : see below                                             */
/* Output     : none                                                  */
/**********************************************************************/

void FillIt(Drive, Side)
byte Drive;                                         /* Drive number */
byte Side;                                      /* Disk side number */

{
 byte Buffer[512];               /* Contents of sector to be filled */
 int  i,                                            /* Loop counter */
      Track,                       /* Track in which the sector lies */
      Sector;                       /* Number of sector to be filled */
 char Character;                                  /* Fill character */


 printf("Track        : ");
 scanf("%d", &Track);            /* Read track number from keyboard */
 printf("Sector       : ");
 scanf("%d", &Sector);          /* Read sector number from keyboard */
 printf("Fill char.   : ");
 scanf("\r%c", &Character);     /* Read fill character from keyboard */
 for (i = 0; i < 512; Buffer[i++] = Character)
  ;
 WDS(DWrite(Drive, Side, Track, Sector, 1, (byte far *) Buffer));
}

/**********************************************************************/
/**                          MAIN PROGRAM                            **/
/**********************************************************************/
```

```
void main()

{
 int  Drive,                                          /* Drive */
      Side,                                       /* Disk side */
      FTyp;                         /* Disk and disk drive format */
 byte AT;                          /* Computer type (AT or PC/XT) */
 char Entry;                                 /* Accept user input */

 Drive = Side = 0;                  /* Default of drive 0, side 0 */
 FTyp = 3;                /* 1.2-MB diskette in 1.2-MB disk drive */

 /*-- Read PC type from location in ROM-BIOS -------------------------*/

 AT = (((byte) peekb(0xF000, 0xFFFE)) == 0xFC) ? TRUE : FALSE;
 printf("\n\nDISKMON (c) 1987 By Michael Tischer\n\n");
 WDS(ResetDisk());                          /* Execute reset first */
 do
  {
   printf("? = Help> ");                          /* Display prompt */
   scanf("\r %1c", &Entry);                       /* Get user input */
   switch(Entry = toupper(Entry))                /* Execute command */
    {
     case '?' : Help();                       /* Display help screen */
                break;
     case 'R' : WDS(ResetDisk());                     /* Execute reset */
                break;
     case 'S' : FillIt(Drive, Side);                  /* Fill a sector */
                break;
     case 'F' : FormatIt(Drive, Side, AT, FTyp);
                break;
     case 'G' : ReadSector(Drive, Side);               /* Read sectors */
                break;
     case 'C' : Constants(&Drive, &Side, &FTyp, AT);
                break;
     default  : if (Entry != 'E') printf("Unknown command\n");
    }
  }
 while (Entry != 'E');                 /* "E" or "e" ends program */
}
```

7.8 Accessing the Hard Disk from the BIOS

The original XT models included 10 megabyte hard disks. Hard disk drives are now the mass storage device of choice on PCs, with the floppy disk running a close second. However, the two devices have many features in common.

Like the floppy disk, a hard disk consists of magnetized plates, also called disks, which can store data as magnetic impulses. Unlike the floppy disk, a hard disk contains several of these disks. The plates in a hard disk can store data on both sides, and therefore must have a read/write head above and below each disk for reading and writing data.

Hard disk format

Hard disk formatting is similar to that of a floppy disk: Each disk is divided into tracks which have sectors within them. A *cylinder* consists of all sectors which can be accessed without moving the read/write heads. In other words, the heads remain stationary within one cylinder while the disk moves beneath them. Moving the heads to another set of tracks accesses another cylinder. Every cylinder contains the same number of sectors, which in turn contain a constant number of bytes.

Partitions

The hard disk has another division beyond track, sector and cylinder levels: *Partitions* allow you to configure parts of a hard disk for different operating systems. Although you can format a disk according to one operating system and use that operating system exclusively, hard disks allow you to store several operating systems at once. You can allocate the number of cylinders needed for each operating system when formatting a hard disk. The first sector of the hard disk contains the information about this memory allocation. This information includes data about the beginning of each partition and its size, as well as which operating system lies in this partition (e.g., DOS has code 1). It also records which operating system is active and which operating system should be started during the system boot.

XT and AT models can control hard disks capable of storing 10 megabytes, 20 megabytes, 40 megabytes and more. Both hard disks have 2 disks (4 sides) (numbered 0 through 3) and accept 17 sectors per cylinder of 512 bytes each. The difference in capacity lies only in the number of cylinders. The XT hard disk has 306 cylinders numbered from 0 to 305 on each side of its disk medium; the AT has 615 cylinders numbered from 0 to 614 on each side of its disk medium. The XT hard disk has a minimum capacity of 10.16 megabytes and the AT hard disk a minimum capacity of 20.41 megabyte.

Note: Exercise extreme caution when using the BIOS hard disk access functions. Unlike a disk drive which you can test out with an unused disk, you can't do the same with a hard disk. Careless use of the Write or Formatting function could lead to irretrievable data loss. If you plan to try these functions, back up the entire hard disk before you try these functions.

BIOS accesses the hard disk through interrupt 13H—the same interrupt used for floppy disk access. The individual functions are identical for hard disk and floppy disk drives, but hard disk control is very different from floppy disk drive control. BIOS uses different modules for controlling the hard disk and disk drives. When you call interrupt 13H, it accesses the hard disk routine first. This routine tests whether the hard disk or floppy disk drive should be addressed, based on the device number in the DL register. If the hard disk is involved, it calls the proper routine in the hard disk module. On the other hand, if the floppy disk drive should be addressed, another module must be called by calling interrupt 40H, which points to the old disk interrupt 13H.

All hard disk functions share the condition that after the function call they use the carry flag to signify whether they could perform their task or if an error occurred. If this is the case, the carry flag sets and an error code passes to the AH register. The individual codes have the following meanings:

01H	Addressed unavailable function or drive
02H	Address marking not found
04H	Sector not found
05H	Error during controller reset
07H	Error during controller initialization
09H	DMA transmission error: Segment border crossed
0AH	Sector defective
10H	Read error
11H	Read error corrected with ECC
20H	Controller defect
40H	Search operation failed
80H	Drive does not respond (Time out)
AAH	Drive not ready
CCH	Write error

When any one of these errors occur except error 01, execute a reset and try calling the function again. Most of the time the error won't recur.

More about errors

If error 11H occurs during the read function, the data read in may not actually be defective. This error indicates that a read error occurred, but that it could be corrected with the help of the ECC (Error Correction Code) algorithm. This procedure is similar to the CRC (Cyclic Redundancy Check) process used in the disk drives. A complicated mathematical formula adds the individual bytes of a sector. The result of the process goes to the disk in the form of a sector plus four bytes. If a read error occurs, it can be corrected within certain limits with the help of the stored ECC results.

The use of processor registers for data transmission becomes another parallel between the hard disk and floppy disk functions. The function number passes to the AH register. If the program requires the number of the hard disk to be addressed, it always passes to the DL register. The value 80H always stands for the first hard disk, and 81H for the second hard disk. The number of the read/write head (and indirectly of the disk addressed) passes to the DH register. The CH register accepts the cylinder number. Remember that a 10 megabyte hard disk has more than 306 cylinders. Since this 8-bit register can only address 256 cylinders at a time, this register alone isn't enough to indicate the cylinder number.

For this reason bits 6 and 7 of the CL register help indicate the cylinder number. They form bits 8 and 9 of the cylinder number, permitting an addressable range of 1,024 cylinders (0-1,023). Bits 0 to 5 of the CL register provide the number of the sector to address (they are numbered from 1 to 17 in each cylinder). If you attempt to access several sectors at a time, the numbers of these sections pass to the AL register. During read/write operations a buffer address must be indicated from which data can be read or to which data can be transferred. In such a case, the ES register passes the segment address and the BX register the offset address of this buffer.

Function 00H: Reset

Function 0H resets the controller without the need of any other parameters. After an error occurs, this function should always be called before the next data access. The information from the hard disk on which the execution of the reset is based passes to the DL register.

Function 01H: Status

Function 01H reads the hard disk drive status (this status is indicated after every hard disk operation). The number of the drive whose status should be read must be stored in the DL register.

Function 02H: Read sector

Function 02H reads one or more sectors. A single call of this function can read up to 128 sectors. This limitation occurs because the hard disk controller transfers data directly into RAM through the DMA. The DMA chip can only transfer a maximum of 64K at a time, in one memory segment at a time. For this reason, it is important that the complete buffer whose address passes to ES:BX fits into the 64K starting with the segment address in ES. Otherwise the DMA chip may report an error.

This function initially reads all sectors in numerical order within the cylinder indicated, using the read/write head indicated. Once the function reads the last sector of a cylinder, and additional sectors should be read, reading continues with the first sector of the same cylinder, but using a different read/write head. After the function accesses the last read/write head and additional sectors still remain, the read process continues in the first sector of the following cylinder on the first read/write head.

Function 03: Write sector

Function 03H writes one or more sectors. A single call of this function can write data in up to 128 sectors. This limitation is also caused by the DMA (see function 02H above).

This function initially writes all sectors in numerical order within the cylinder indicated, using the read/write head indicated. Once the function writes to the last sector of a cylinder, and additional sectors should be written, writing continues with the first sector of the same cylinder, but using a different read/write head. After the function reaches the last read/write head and additional sectors still remain, the write process continues in the first sector of the following cylinder on the first read/write head.

Function 04H: Verify

Function 04H verifies the different sectors of a cylinder. No comparison occurs between the data on the disk and the data in memory (no buffer address needed in ES:BX). ECC numbers verify whether the bytes stored return the same results after processing through the ECC algorithm. The AL register indicates the number of sectors to be verified.

Function 05H: Format

Function 05H formats the hard disk. Before a hard disk can be accessed it must be formatted. Similar to the function used for formatting a disk, this function must know the read/write head and cylinder number. In addition, it must pass the address of the buffer to the register pair ES:BX. This buffer must be 512 bytes long, even if the function only accesses the first 34 bytes. It contains two bytes for each of the 17 sectors to be formatted. The first byte indicates whether the sector is in good condition. Assuming that every sector is in good condition, the value 0 is entered into this byte. The second byte accepts the logical number which should be assigned to the current sector. BIOS takes information from the first two bytes in the table about the first physical sector of the cylinder. Bytes 3 and 4 supply information about the second physical cylinder. Once the physical series has already been determined, the logical sequence of the sectors can be set through 2 bytes of a sector indication in this table.

The numbers differ between a logical sector and its respective physical sector. This shift in logical sectors, called *sector interleaving*, help optimize access time on a hard disk.

The average hard disk rotates at 60 revolutions per second. This means that the next physical sector appears under the read/write head every thousandth of a second. The hard disk controller is incapable of transferring the 512 bytes of the sector previously read into the PC's memory. For this reason, the logical sectors shift in relation to the physical sectors, so that the next logical sector only appears under the read/write head after the hard disk controller completes the transmission of the last sector.

The interleave factor, i.e., the number of sectors by which the logical sectors shift in relation to the physical sectors, depends on the relationship between the speed at which the hard disk revolves, and the processing speed of the hard disk controller. For example, if the interleave factor is 6, this means that for every sector read, a "jump" of 5 sectors takes place before the next logical sector follows. The closer this factor comes to 1 (in which case the physical and logical sectors are identical), the faster the hard disk and the closer the transmission speed comes to the physical limit.

While XT hard disks operate with an interleave factor of 1:6, AT hard disks are twice as fast, with an interleave factor of 1:3. The effects of the interleave factor and the relationship between logical and physical sectors can be seen in the following table:

AT: physical logical sector	XT: physical sector	logical sector	sector
1	1	1	1
2	7	2	4
3	13	3	7
4	2	4	10
5	8	5	13
6	14	6	16
7	3	7	2
8	9	8	5
9	15	9	8
10	4	10	11
11	10	11	14
12	16	12	17
13	5	13	3
14	11	14	6
15	17	15	9
16	6	16	12
17	12	17	15

During a function call, BIOS enters a value into the first byte of a sector marker which tells the calling program whether or not the sector is OK. The value 0 means OK, and the value 128 means a magnetization error occurred. Besides the registers mentioned above, the AL register accepts the number of sectors to be processed. Since the cylinders of the AT and XT hard disks have 17-sector formats, the AL register should contain the value 17 during the call of this function.

Function 08H: Check disk specs

Function 08H, passing the number of the hard disk in the DL register, checks hard disk specifications. This is important for examining hard disks with unusual formats.

After the function call the DL register contains the number of attached hard disks. This number can be 0, 1 or 2. In addition, the DH register contains the number of read/write heads. Since the read/write head count always starts at 0, a value of 7 means that 8 heads are available. The CL register (bits 0-7 of the cylinder number) and the upper two bits of the CH register (bits 8 and 9 of the cylinder number) indicate the number of cylinders. The counting here also starts at 0. The last information is found in the lower 6 bits of the CH register. It shows the number of sectors per cylinder, where the counting begins at 1 (an exception to the rule, since the other counts in this function begin with 0).

When a user interfaces a foreign hard disk to a PC, the BIOS must know the characteristics of this hard disk to perform correct access. For this reason it uses interrupt 41H for hard disk 0 and the interrupt 46H for hard disk 1 as pointers to a table. This table has a format prescribed by BIOS and describes the attached hard disk drive. BIOS stores a whole series of tables so that BIOS can adjust itself properly during the system boot from the booting hard disk drive.

Note: If the hard disk is already in the PC and functions properly, do not attempt to access the hard disk description table, since the hard disk could be damaged.

A table must be constructed in RAM for foreign hard disk interfacing, and interrupt vectors 41H or 46H must point to this table. In addition, function 9 must configure BIOS to use this table. The number 9 declares the function. The number of the drive (80H or 81H) is loaded into the DL register. You may never have to use this complicated function: Most hard disk manufacturers include a configuration program which performs the same task. Check the documentation which came with the hard disk for the parameters needed for the hard disk description table.

Function 0AH: read ECC
Function 0BH: Write ECC

Functions 0AH and 0BH are additional read/write functions. They differ from functions 2 and 3 in that they read and write the four ECC bytes at the end of each sector in addition to the 512 bytes of data. Because of this, every sector has 516 bytes instead of 512 bytes, and only 127 sectors can be read or written at one time, instead of 128 as in functions 2 and 3.

Function 0BH: Recalibrate

Function 0BH recalibrates one of two hard disks. It also returns the error status, passing the error number to the DL register.

Function 10H: Check ready status

Function 10H tests whether or not the hard disk whose number is in the DL register is currently prepared to execute commands. If the carry flag is set on the return of this function, the hard disk isn't ready. An error code passes to the AH register.

Function 14H: Self test

Function 14H forces the controller to perform an internal self test. If the controller is OK, it returns with a reset carry flag.

Function 15H: Check drive type

Function 15H determines the type of drive. The number of the drive (80H or 81H) passes to the DL register. If the drive is unavailable, it returns the value 0 in the AH register after the function call. If the AH register contains a value of 1 or 2, the device indicated is a floppy disk drive. The value 3 indicates a hard disk. If this is the case, the CX and DX registers contain the number of sectors on this hard disk. The two registers form a 32-bit number (the CX register contains the upper 16 bits, and the DX register the lower 16 bits).

Note: We chose not to include demonstration programs in this section, because accessing a hard disk without proper knowledge can have serious consequences. While floppy disk drive access can be practiced with an unused or empty disk without worrying about damage, you only get one hard disk with a PC. One small mistake during access could destroy all data on a hard disk.

Avoid hard disk access using BIOS functions unless absolutely necessary. Leave these tasks to DOS functions as much as possible.

7.9 Accessing the Serial Port from the BIOS

Computers in every part of the world communicate with each other and exchange data. Most of the time these computers use normal telephone lines for this communication. Phone lines only permit slow data transfer, but allow users to communicate from almost anywhere on the planet. Data transfers serially (i.e., one bit at a time), while the sender and receiver maintain similar *transfer protocols* (parameters for data transfer).

Serial card

Since basic PC configurations aren't equipped for this type of data transmission, data transfer is only possible when the user adds an *asynchronous communication port* (IBM's catch phrase for an *RS-232 card*, or *serial interface card*).

This type of card enables data transfer between two computers direct through a cable or through phone lines. Both the sender and receiver require a *modem* to communicate using the latter method. Modems convert computer signals into acoustical signals which can then be transmitted over telephone lines.

In addition to hardware, data communication requires software which controls the RS-232 card. BIOS offers this software in four functions called by interrupt 14H. Before discussing these functions in detail, let's examine data transfer protocol.

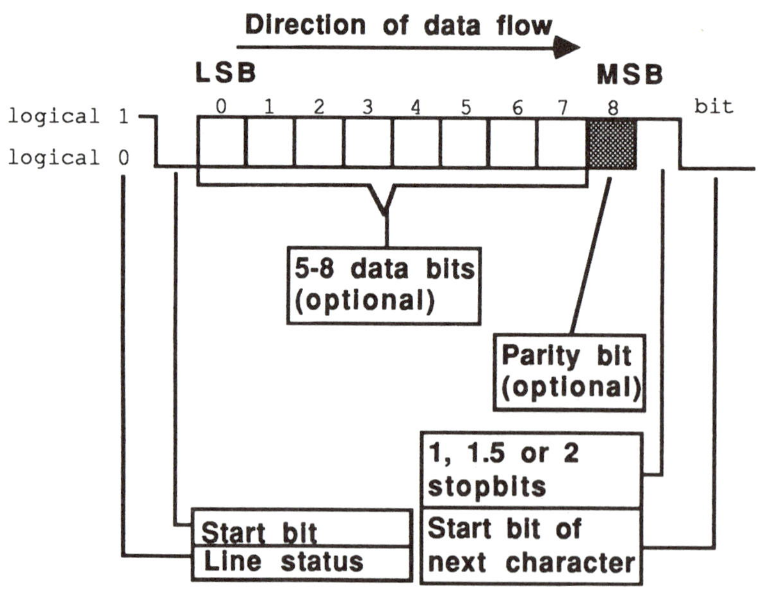

Asynchronous transmission protocol

Word length

As the figure above shows, only the two line states, 0 and 1 (also called high and low) are important. The line remains high if no data transmission takes place. If the line's state changes to low, the receiver knows that data is being transmitted. Between 5 and 8 bits transfer over the line, depending on the *word length*. Unfortunately the BIOS functions only support a word length of 7 or 8 bits. If the line is low during data transmission, this means that the bit to be sent is 0. High signals a set bit. The least significant bit is transferred first, and the most significant bit of the character to be transmitted is transferred last.

Parity

The character can be followed by a *parity bit* which permits error detection during data transmission. Parity can be even or odd. For even parity, the parity bit augments the data word to be transmitted, so that an even number of bits results. For example, if the data word to be transmitted contains three bits set to 1, the parity bit becomes 1 so that the number of 1 bits increments to four, making an even number. If the data word contained an even number of 1 bits, the parity bit would be zero. For odd parity the parity bit is set in such a manner that the total number of 1 bits is odd.

Stop bits

The *stop bits* signal the end of the transmission of data. Data transmission protocol permits 1, 1.5 and 2 stop bits. Some users are confused about the option of working with 1.5 stop bits, since some believe that you can't divide a bit. The explanation for this paradox comes from the data transmission protocol.

Baud rate

Old standards dictate that data transfers at a rate of 300 *baud* (about 300 bits per second), and one stop bit. The signal for a 1 bit and the signal for a 0 bit are both *events*. Binary bits when transmitted in an analog environment such as phone lines may not be identical with baud rates. Since stop bits always have the value 1, the line would be high for 1/300 second. If instead you keep the line high for 1/200 second, 1.5 bits are transmitted. The line remains high until a new character transfers and sets the line transmitting the start bit to low.

Some interfaces work with negative logic. In such a case the conditions for 0 and 1 in the illustration above must be reversed. This doesn't change the basic principle of serial transmission.

Protocol settings

Data transmission only works if the sender and receiver both match various protocol parameters. First the *baud rate* (the number of bits transmitted per second) must be set. The standard baud rates for data exchange over voice telephone lines are 300, 1200 and 2400 baud. These baud rates depend on the capabilities of the modem in use. For a dedicated (data only) telephone line or for direct data transmission through a cable, speeds up to 9600 baud are possible. Up to 80 bytes per second or 4800 bytes per minute can be transmitted at 9600 baud.

The *word length* depends on the data being transmitted. If the data consists of normal ASCII characters, a 7-bit word is enough, since the ASCII character set has only 128 characters. If the data encompasses the complete PC set of 256 characters, 8-bit words are more practical.

Next the necessity of a *parity check* should be determined, and whether even or odd parity should be used. In most cases parity checking is recommended, since phone lines do not always transmit all data correctly. The parity selected is unimportant, as long as both sender and receiver select the same parity.

The number of *stop bits* must be defined. One stop bit transmits successive characters faster than a setting of two stop bits. On the other hand, two stop bits increase the reliability of transmission.

Sample protocol

The following illustration shows a sample transmission of an "A" character with a protocol of 8 data bits, odd parity and one stop bit. Positive logic and a 300 baud transmission rate are assumed. Since the ASCII code of the "A" character is 65 (01000001(b)) and therefore contains only two 1 bits, the parity bit changes to 1 to set the number of 1 bits to an odd number.

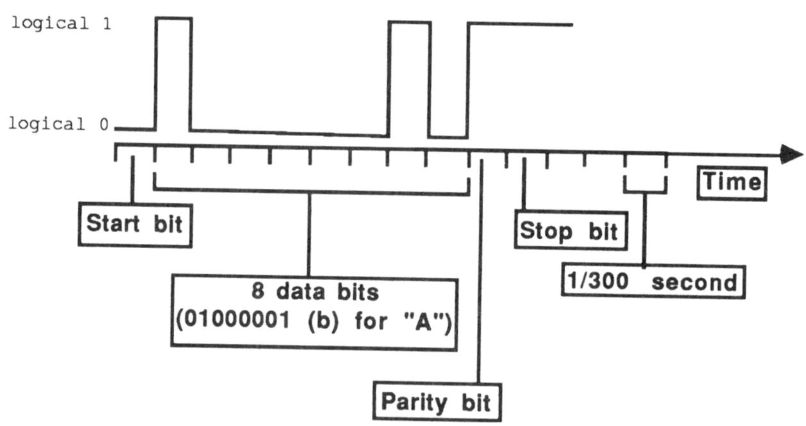

Transmitting A character: 8-bit word length, 1 stop bit, odd parity and 300 baud

UART

The brain of an RS-232 card is the UART (Universal Asynchronous Receiver Transmitter). You should be familiar with the design and capabilities of this processor, so that you can properly adapt programs to the error messages returned by the different BIOS functions.

Transfer registers

A character transmitted on a data line passes first to a register designated as a *transfer holding register*. It remains there until processing ends on the character preceding it. Then the character moves to the *transfer shift register* from where the UART transmits the character bit by bit over the data line. Depending on the configuration, parity and stop bits implement the stream of data. When the BIOS function passes the status of the data lines to the AH register, bits 5 and 6 indicate whether these two registers are empty.

Receiver registers

The *receiver shift register* accepts received data, then transmits the data to the *receiver data register* where the UART removes the parity and stop bits. If a previously received character is still in the data register, bit 1 of the line status sets to 1 to avoid overwriting. Bit 0 indicates that a character was received. If while processing the character, the UART discovers that a parity error occurred during the transmission, it sets bit 2 of the line status. If a breakdown occurs in the agreed-upon protocol (number of parity and stop bits), the action sets bit 3. The UART always sets bit 4 if the data line remains longer in low (0) status than required for the transmission of a character. Bit 7 signals a *time out* error. This occurs occasionally when the communication between the RS-232 card and the modem isn't working properly.

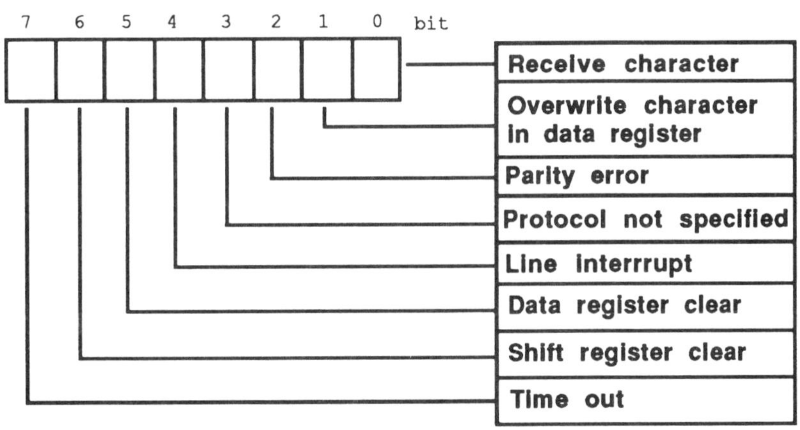

Line status

Function 0: Passing protocol

Before data can be transmitted or received, the UART must be informed of the number of stop bits, etc. Function 0 of interrupt 14H serves this purpose. The function number (0) enters the AH register, and the protocol passes to the AL register. The bits of the AL register indicate the various parameters:

Bits	Protocol
bit 0,1	Word length 10(b) - 7 bits 11(b) - 8 bits
bit 2	Number of Stop bits 0 - 1 Stop bit 1 - 2 Stop bits
bit 3,4	Parity check 00(b) - none 01(b) - odd 10(b) - even
bit 5 -7	Baud rate 000 - 110 Baud 001 - 150 Baud 010 - 300 Baud 011 - 600 Baud 100 - 1200 Baud 101 - 2400 Baud 110 - 4800 Baud 111 - 9600 Baud

After initialization the function loads the line status into the AH register.

Function 1: Transmit character

Function 1 transmits characters. During its call, the AH register must contain 1 and the AL register must contain the character to be transmitted. If the character was transmitted, bit 7 of the AH register changes to 0 after the function call. A 1 signals that the character could not be transmitted. The remaining bits correspond to the line status.

Function 2: Receive character

Function 2 receives characters. After calling this function the AL register contains the character received. AH contains the value 0 if no error occurred, otherwise the value corresponds to the line status.

Function 3: Line/modem status

Function 3 senses and returns the modem status and line status. It returns the line status in the AH register and the modem status in the AL register:

Bit 0	Modem ready to send status change
Bit 1	Modem on status change
Bit 2	Telephone ringing status change
Bit 3	Connection to receiver status change
Bit 4	Modem ready to send
Bit 5	Modem on
Bit 6	Telephone ringing
Bit 7	Connection to receiver modem

Bits 4 to 7 represent a duplication of bits 0 to 3. Bits 0 to 3 indicate whether the contents of bits 4 to 7 have changed since the last reading of the modem status. If this is the case, the corresponding bit contains the value 1. For example, if bit 2 contains the value 1, this means that the content of bit 6 has changed since the last reading. In reality it means that the phone just started to ring or has stopped ringing, depending on the previous value of bit 6.

7.10 The Cassette Interrupt

The cassette interrupt (interrupt 15H) is a leftover from the days when PCs used cassette recorders exclusively as data storage devices. This interrupt provided four functions (numbered 0 through 3) for enabling and disabling the cassette recorder motor, reading from and writing to magnetic tape. As the PC gained ground in the business world, the disk drive became popular. Consequently, the cassette drive's popularity faded.

The four cassette interrupt functions remain part of the PC's ROM-BIOS. The XT has no cassette recorder interface. In addition, the XT's cassette interrupt consists of a short routine which sets the carry flag and stores an error code in the AH register to tell the program that the function called is unavailable.

The AT and the cassette interrupt

The cassette interrupt returned with the introduction of the AT. New functions can be called which have nothing to do with cassette recorder control. The following describes these functions, available only on AT models.

Among other things, the interrupt makes two functions available based on the time measurement of the onboard AT realtime clock. The first of these is function 83H. It is useful in situations where the CPU is engaged in a time consuming task (e.g., computing a complicated formula), but other duties must be performed at the same time (e.g., checking the keyboard to determine if the user wants to terminate the operation).

Function 83H: Time flag

Function 83H calls the address of a flag (a byte in the user program) in which the highest level bit is set after a certain time period has elapsed. Within an executing program this flag can be tested after certain amounts of time. Only two assembly language instructions are necessary for this, so the testing requires little time. Function number 83H passes information to the AH register. The segment address of the flag is loaded into the ES register and the offset address into the BX register. The time that should elapse until the flag is set is passed to the CX and DX registers. Both registers form a 32-bit number which indicates the number of microseconds to wait (1 second = 1,000,000 microseconds).

The CX register represents the upper 16 bits of this number. To calculate the total time, the contents of the CX register must be multiplied by 65,536 and the DX register must then be added to the total. If the waiting period is known in microseconds, the value for the CX and the DX register can be calculated:

```
CX = int(Waiting period /65,536)
DX = Waiting period mod 65,536
```

This function can only be called if the previous call of this function has ended (the time indicated has elapsed). If this is not the case, the function returns immediately with the carry flag set.

Function 86H: Wait for end time

The second time function, function 86H, differs from function 83H in that it waits until the time indicated has elapsed. For this reason the function number must pass to the AH register, and the waiting time to the CX and DX registers during the function call. To convert the waiting time into two values for the CX and DX registers, the formula above can be used. This function can only be called if function 83H was not called previously, and if the time period set during its call has not yet elapsed. In such a case, the function returns immediately with a set carry flag to the calling program.

Extended memory

The AT accepts more than 640K of memory. This additional memory (called *extended*) begins at 1 megabyte and cannot be accessed in *real mode*, in which the 80286 processor operates as an 8086 processor. Function 88H determines the availability and size of this memory. Placing a value of 88H in the AH register returns the size of RAM beyond the 1 megabyte boundary (excluding RAM from 0 to 640K) in 1K increments in the AX register.

Function 87H: Move memory block

Function 87H moves blocks of memory within the total memory space. This means that blocks of memory can be moved from the area below the 1 megabyte limit to the area above the 1 megabyte limit, and the other way around. The function should not be used for the latter, since its call is complicated and has other disadvantages. To access memory beyond the 1 megabyte barrier, the processor must be switched into *protected mode* (full 80286 mode). Function 87H requires very comprehensive information, since the 80286 processor is more difficult to program in protected mode than in real mode (8086 emulation under DOS). See the end of this section for a program which demonstrates the use of function 87H.

The function number 87H must first be passed to the AH register, then the number of the words to be moved (words only—not bytes) must be passed to the CX register. A maximum value of 8000H corresponds to a maximum value of 64K.

Global Descriptor Table

The ES:SI register pair receive the address of the GDT (Global Descriptor Table), which must be installed in the user program. The GDT describes the individual memory segments of the 80286 in protected mode. The segments in protected mode are exempt from the limitations made in real mode. While segments can only start at memory locations divisible by 16 in real mode, protected mode segments may start at any memory location. Furthermore, protected mode segments may be any size from 1 byte to 64K.

Another protected mode innovation is the access code defined for every segment. It indicates whether the segment described is a data segment or a code segment (only code segments can be executed). The access code also contains information on access priority, and whether access is even permitted. Every segment descriptor consists of 8 bytes apiece. Function 87H expects during its call that six segment descriptors have been prepared in the GDT (i.e., memory space reserved for them). The figure below illustrates which segment descriptors are involved, as well as the construction of a segment descriptor.

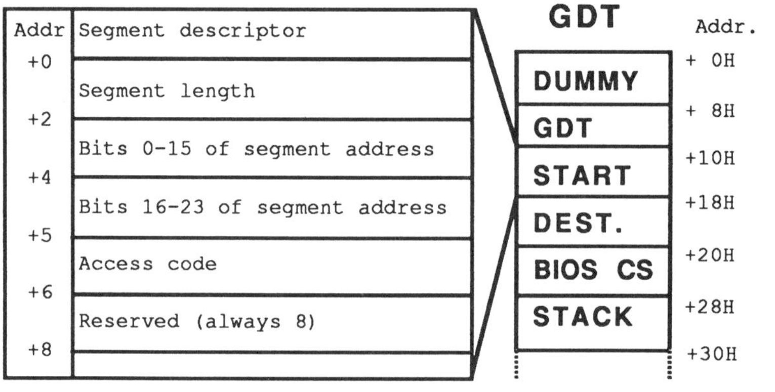

Segment descriptor structure as seen by function 87H

Only the segment descriptors designated as start and destination are of interest here, since the BIOS functions fill out the other descriptors. The first describes the segment from which the data are taken. The destination descriptor describes the segment into which the data are copied. The length of both segments can be 0FFFFH (64K decimal), even if fewer bytes (or words) copy over in the process. If a lower value is indicated, do not allow the number of bytes (number of words multiplied by 2) to be copied to exceed this amount. Otherwise the processor notices an access across a segment boundary during copying, which triggers an error. The address of the two memory areas must be converted to a (physical) 24-bit address. The lower 16 bits of this address enter the second field of the segment descriptor and the upper 8 bits enter the third field. As access code 92H can be used, which signals the processor that the described segment is a data segment with the highest priority; that the segment exists in memory; and that the segment can be written. The last field of the descriptor exists for reasons of compatibility with the 80386 processor, and should always contain the value 0.

While the address of the user program's buffer stays fixed, the address beyond the 1 megabyte boundary to which data should be copied can be freely selected (subject to RAM availability). The following table shows the addresses of the various 1K blocks beyond the 1 megabyte border as 24-bit addresses.

0 K	= 100000H	124 K	= 11F000H
1 K	= 100400H	125 K	= 11F400H
2 K	= 100800H	126 K	= 11F800H
3 K	= 100C00H	127 K	= 11FC00H
4 K	= 101000H	128 K	= 120000H
5 K	= 101400H	129 K	= 120400H
6 K	= 100800H	130 K	= 120800H
7 K	= 100C00H	131 K	= 120C00H
8 K	= 102000H	132 K	= 121000H
9 K	= 102400H	133 K	= 121400H
60 K	= 10F000H	252 K	= 13F000H
61 K	= 10F400H	253 K	= 13F400H
62 K	= 10F800H	254 K	= 13F800H
63 K	= 10FC00H	255 K	= 13FC00H
64 K	= 110000H	256 K	= 140000H
65 K	= 110400H	257 K	= 140400H
66 K	= 110800H	258 K	= 140800H
67 K	= 110C00H	259 K	= 140C00H
68 K	= 111000H	260 K	= 141000H
69 K	= 111400H	261 K	= 141400H

After the function call the carry flag indicates the success of the function call. If the carry flag sets, an error occurred. The value in the AH register indicates the cause of the error:

AH = 0	No error (carry flag reset)
AH = 1	RAM parity error
AH = 2	GDT defective at function call
AH = 3	protected mode could not be initialized properly

A disadvantage of this function is that while the processor is in protected mode, all interrupts must be suppressed. The reason is the fact that during the protected mode, BIOS interrupts (e.g., timer or keyboard) can be called, but these routines were developed for operation in real mode only. These interrupts may not work properly in protected mode. The disadvantage can be clearly seen when you call the timer. Since its interrupts are suppressed, protected mode performs no time measurement, and time remains frozen for a moment. If programs call function 87H frequently, the clock may run slow by 20 or 30 seconds in one day. The clock can be reset easily to the proper time with software, so software can bypass most of the disadvantages.

Function 89H: Protected mode

Function 89H switches the AT into protected mode. Only someone developing his own operating system may have any interest in this function. Any system capable of multiprocessing must run in protected mode. This function goes far beyond the scope of this book. See the AT technical manual for more information.

Function 84H: Joystick reader

Function 84H reads two joysticks connected to the AT. Two sub-functions operate within this function: Both return a set carry flag if the adaptor to which the joysticks should be connected doesn't exist.

The first sub-function executes by passing the function number to the AH register and the value 0 to the DX register. It returns the status of the joystick fire buttons in bits 4 to 7 of the AL register.

The second sub-function executes by passing the function number to the AH register and the value 1 to the DX register. It returns current joystick positions using X- and Y-coordinates. The X-coordinate for the first joystick can be found in the AX, and the Y-coordinate in the BX register. For the second joystick, the CX register contains the X-coordinate and the DX register the Y-coordinate.

Function 85H: Read SysReq key

The <System Request> key on the AT keyboard triggers an interrupt without producing a character code. It cannot be tested with the BIOS keyboard reading functions. Function 85H reads the keyboard for the <System Request> key. Passing the function number to the AH register executes the function. The current BIOS version doesn't implement this function within the cassette interrupt. Usually the <System Request> key does nothing when the user presses it. However, a machine language routine can assign a special application to the <System Request> key. This program must only "deflect" interrupt 15H to its own routine. If it's called by a user program or by the system, a user routine executes instead of the cassette interrupt. It can test whether the AH register contains the function number 85H. If this is not the case, it calls the old cassette interrupt. If the AH register contains this function number, the user routine performs the desired action.

The content of the AL register is also important to this user routine because it indicates whether the user pressed or released the <System Request> key. 0 means activated, 1 released.

Demonstration programs

Of all the functions made available by this interrupt, the most interesting is probably function 88H. It permits the owners of ATs with memory beyond the 1 meg limit to use memory that is inaccessible to DOS. The programs presented in this section demonstrate easy calls to function 87H within user programs. To illustrate the function call, each one of these programs copies the current video RAM contents directly beyond the 1 megabyte memory border. It then erases the video RAM and restores it again. The core of these programs is always the routine which calls function 88H of interrupt 15H. It constructs a GDT for this, enters the addresss of the start and destination area, as well as the GDT. First it converts the two addresses (passed as segment and offset addresses) into a 24-bit-wide address. This routine must be constructed first in assembly language for the higher level languages, then integrated into the higher level language programs. You'll see how this is done in the documentation of the individual listings. To avoid detailed comparison of the various assembler programs for linking into the move function, the difference lies almost exclusively in the area of the variable passing. Otherwise the programs are almost identical.

BASIC listing: MOVE.BAS

```
100 '*******************************************************************'
110 '*                               M O V E                           *'
120 '*-----------------------------------------------------------------*'
130 '* Task         : uses the Routine for moving a storage area       *'
140 '*                to store the Video-RAM                           *'
150 '* Author       : MICHAEL TISCHER                                  *'
160 '* developed on : 7.22.87                                          *'
170 '* last Update  : 9.21.87                                          *'
180 '*******************************************************************'
190 '
200 CLS   : KEY OFF
210 PRINT"WARNING: This program can only be started if the GWBASIC "
220 PRINT"was started from the DOS level with <GWBASIC  /m:60000>"
230 PRINT : PRINT"If this is not the case, input an <s> to Stop "
240 PRINT"Else, press any key...";
250 A$ = INKEY$ : IF A$ = "s" THEN END
260 IF A$ = "" THEN 250
270 CLS                                      'Clear Screen
280 PRINT"MOVE (c) 1987 by Michael Tischer" : PRINT
290 PRINT"This Program uses Function 87(h) of Interrupt 15(h) to copy blocks "
300 PRINT"of memory between the 'normal' RAM and the RAM beyond the "
310 PRINT"1-Megabyte border."
320 DEF SEG = &HF000                         'Set BIOS-segment
330 IF PEEK(&HFFFE) = &HFC THEN 380          'test if AT
340 PRINT"Since this unit is not an AT, but a PC or "
350 PRINT"XT, and they do not have memory the 1-MB limit, "
360 PRINT"this program can not be executed! Sorry..."
370 END                                      'Terminate Program (PC or XT)
380 PRINT"The Program will first copy the current display immediately beyond the "
390 PRINT"1 MB border and thens clear the screen. If you then press a key, "
400 PRINT"the old screen content is restored."
410 PRINT : PRINT"Please activate a key to start the program...";
420 A$ = INKEY$ : IF A$ = "" THEN 420        'wait for key
430 STARTS% = VIDEOS% : STARTO% = 0 'Start-area is Video-RAM:0000
440 GOSUB 60000                     'install Function for Interrupt call
450 GOSUB 61000                     'install Function for copying memory
460 GOSUB 50000                     'get current Video mode
470 IF VMODE% = 7 THEN VIDEOS% = &HB000 ELSE VIDEOS% = &HB800
480 STARTO% = 0 : STARTS% = VIDEOS% 'Start address  is the Video-RAM
```

```
490 DESTS% = 0 : DESTO% = 0         'destination area is 10000:0000
500 DIRECTION% = 1                  'copy from below to above 1 MB
510 SIZE% = 2000                    'the size of the Video-RAM is 200 Words
520 GOSUB 51000                     'move memory
530 CLS                             'clear screen
540 PRINT"Please activate a key  ..."
550 A$ = INKEY$ : IF A$ = "" THEN 550  'wait for key
560 STARTS% = 0 : STARTO% = 0          'Start area is 10000:0000
570 DESTS% = VIDEOS% : DESTO% = 0      'Destination area is Video-RAM:0000
580 DIRECTION% = 2                     'copy from above to below 1 MB
590 GOSUB 51000                        'move memory
600 LOCATE 15,1                        'Set Cursor to column 1 of line 15
610 END
620 '
50000 '**************************************************************'
50010 '* Sense current Video Mode                                   *'
50020 '*------------------------------------------------------------*'
50030 '* Input:   none                                              *'
50040 '* Output:  VMODE% = the current Video mode                   *'
50050 '* Info    : the Variable Z% is used as Dummy                 *'
50060 '**************************************************************'
50070 Z%=15                          'get Function number for Video mode
50080 INR%=&H10                      'call BIOS-Video-Interrupt 16(h)
50090 CALL IA(INR%,Z%,VMODE%,PAGE%,Z%,Z%,Z%,Z%,Z%,Z%,Z%,Z%,Z%)
50100 RETURN                         'back to caller
50110 '
51000 '**************************************************************'
51010 '* move a memory area                                         *'
51020 '*------------------------------------------------------------*'
51030 '* Input: STARTS% = segment address of the Start area         *'
51040 '*        STARTO% = Offset address of the Start area          *'
51050 '*        DESTS%  = segment address of the destination area   *'
51060 '*        DESTO%  = Offset address of the destination area    *'
51070 '*        SIZE%   = Number of words to be moved               *'
51080 '*   DIRECTION%   = Direction in which to move                *'
51090 '*           data:                                            *'
51100 '*              0 = from below 1 MB --> to below 1 MB         *'
51110 '*              1 = from below 1 MB --> beyond 1 MB           *'
51120 '*              2 = from above 1 MB --> below 1 MB            *'
51130 '*              3 = from beyond 1 MB --> beyond 1 MB          *'
51140 '* Output: none                                               *'
51150 '**************************************************************'
51160 CALL MOVE(STARTS%,STARTO%,DESTS%,DESTO%,SIZE%,DIRECTION%)
51170 RETURN                                 'back to caller
51180 '
60000 '**************************************************************'
60010 '* initialize the Routine for Interrupt call                  *'
60020 '*------------------------------------------------------------*'
60030 '* Input: none                                                *'
60040 '* Output: IA is the Start address of the Interrupt-Routine   *'
60050 '**************************************************************'
60060 '
60070 IA=60000!          'Start address of the Routine in the BASIC-segment
60080 DEF SEG            'Set BASIC-segment
60090 RESTORE 60130
60100 FOR I% = 0 TO 160 : READ X% : POKE IA+I%,X% : NEXT 'poke Routine
60110 RETURN             'back to caller
60120 '
60130 DATA  85,139,236, 30,  6,139,118, 30,139,  4,232,140,  0,139,118
60140 DATA  12,139, 60,139,118,  8,139,  4, 61,255,255,117,  2,140,216
60150 DATA 142,192,139,118, 28,138, 36,139,118, 26,138,  4,139,118, 24
60160 DATA 138, 60,139,118, 22,138, 28,139,118, 20,138, 44,139,118, 18
60170 DATA 138, 12,139,118, 16,138, 52,139,118, 14,138,2 0,139,118, 10
60180 DATA 139, 52, 85,205, 33, 93, 86,156,139,118, 12,137, 60,139,118
60190 DATA  28,136, 36,139,118, 26,136,  4,139,118, 24,136, 60,139,118
60200 DATA  22,136, 28,139,118, 20,136, 44,139,118, 18,136, 12,139,118
60210 DATA  16,136, 52,139,118, 14,136, 20,139,118,  8,140,192,137,  4
60220 DATA  88,139,118,  6,137,  4, 88,139,118, 10,137,  4,  7, 31, 93
60230 DATA 202, 26,  0, 91, 46,136, 71, 66,233,108,255
60240 '
```

```
61000 '*****************************************************************'
61010 '* Initialize Routine for moving of mremory areas.               *'
61020 '*---------------------------------------------------------------*'
61030 '* Input: none                                                   *'
61040 '* Output: MOVE is the Start address of the Routine              *'
61050 '*****************************************************************'
61060 '
61070 DEF SEG                          'Set BASIC segment
61080 MOVE=61000!                      'Start address of the Routine
61090 RESTORE 61130
61100 FOR I% = 0 TO 140: READ BYTE% : POKE MOVE+I%,BYTE% : NEXT
61110 RETURN                           'back to caller
61120 '
61130 DATA 232,115,  0,  0,  0,  0,  0,  0,  0,  0,  0,  0,  0,  0,  0
61140 DATA   0,  0,  0,  0,255,255,  0,  0, 16,146,  0,  0,255,255,  0
61150 DATA   0,  0,146,  0,  0,  0,  0,  0,  0,  0,  0,  0,  0,  0,  0
61160 DATA   0,  0,  0,  0,  0,  0, 85,139,236,139,126,  6,138, 45,139
61170 DATA 126, 12,139,  5,139,126, 10,139, 29,246,197,  1,232, 46,  0
61180 DATA 136, 84, 28,137  68, 26,139,126, 16,139,  5,139,126, 14,139
61190 DATA  29,246,197,  2,232, 24,  0,136, 84, 20,137, 68, 18,180,135
61200 DATA 139,126,  8,139, 13,205, 21,139,229, 93,202, 12,  0, 94,235
61210 DATA 186,138,212,177,  4,210,234,117,  3,128,202, 16,211,224,  3
61220 DATA 195,115,  2,254,194,195
```

The DATA statements integrated the interrupt call routine and the memory movement routine into BASIC. They contain the machine language command codes, read and POKEd into the BASIC section starting at address 61000. This address is also stored in the MOVE variable so that the program can be called from the CALL command in line 51160. For those of you who have mastered assembly language, here is the program listing from which the DATA lines of the MOVE function were derived.

Assembler listing: MOVEBA.ASM

```
;**********************************************************************;
;*                              M O V E B A                          *;
;*-------------------------------------------------------------------*;
;*    Task   : Makes the functions for moving of                      *;
;*             memory blocks beyond the 1MB memory limit              *;
;*             available in BASIC for linking                         *;
;*-------------------------------------------------------------------*;
;*    Author          : MICHAEL TISCHER                               *;
;*    developed on    : 8.22.87                                       *;
;*    last Update     : 9.21.87                                       *;
;*-------------------------------------------------------------------*;
;*    Info: the Code is fully relocatable so that the                 *;
;*          Routine can be poked to any place within the              *;
;*          BASIC segment                                             *;
;*-------------------------------------------------------------------*;
;*    assembly  : MASM MOVEBA;                                        *;
;*                LINK MOVEBA;                                        *;
;*                EXE2BIN MOVEBA MOVEBA.COM                           *;
;**********************************************************************;

code      segment

          assume cs:code,ds:code,es:code,ss:code

;-- MOVE: Copy storage blocks beyond the 1MB limit --------------------
;-- Call from BASIC: CALL ADR(Sourcesegment, StartOffset, Destsegment,
;--                           DestOffset, Size, Direction);
;-- Info  : - after the call Variables are in the following
;--                    Positions on the Stack:
;--                      Startsegment = SP + 16
;--                      StartOffset  = SP + 14
```

```
;--                     Destsegment  = SP + 12
;--                     DestOffset   = SP + 10
;--                     Size         = SP + 8
;--                     Direction    = SP + 6
;--         - for Direction the following Codes are accepted
;--                 0 = from below 1 MB --> to below 1 MB
;--                 1 = from below 1 MB --> to over 1 MB
;--                 2 = from above 1 MB  --> to below 1 MB
;--                 3 = from above 1 MB  --> to above 1 MB
;--                 - the number concerns words not
;--               bytes, and can not be larger than 8000(h)

move      proc far            ;GW expects during CALL Far-Procedure

          call get_adr        ;the Address of the Routine

;-- The Global Descriptor Table ---------------------------------------
GDT       equ this word

          dw 4 dup (?)        ;segment Descriptors for Dummy-segment
          dw 4 dup (?)

      ;-- segment Descriptors of the Source-Area -----------------------
          dw Offffh          ;segment length = 64 KB
sa_lo     dw (?)             ;Lo-Word of the 24 bit-Address
sa_hi     db 010h            ;Hi-Byte of the 24 bit-Address
          db 10010010b       ;Data segment in memory with
                             ;highest priority, Writeable
          dw 00000h          ;Compatibility Word for 80386

      ;-- segment Descriptors of the Destination-Area ------------------
          dw Offffh          ;segment length = 64 KB
da_lo     dw (?)             ;Lo-Word of the 24 bit-Address
da_hi     db (?)             ;Hi-Byte of the 24 bit-Address
          db 10010010b       ;Data segment in memory with
                             ;highest priority, Writeable
          dw 00000h          ;Compatibility Word for 80386

          dw 4 dup (?)       ;segment Descriptors BIOS-Code-segment
          dw 4 dup (?)       ;segment Descriptors Stack-segment

;-- the Code of the MOVE-Routine --------------------------------------

movel:    push bp             ;store GW Basepointer
          mov  bp,sp          ;move SP to BP

          mov  di,[bp+6]      ;get Address of the direction Variable
          mov  ch,[di]        ;move direction to CH
          mov  di,[bp+12]     ;get Address of Destsegment-Variable
          mov  ax,[di]        ;move destination segment address to AX
          mov  di,[bp+10]     ;get address of DestOffset-Variable
          mov  bx,[di]        ;move destination Offset address to BX
          test ch,1           ;Destination beyond 1 MB?
          call calc_adr       ;form 24 bit Address

          mov  [si+da_hi-gdt],dl   ;store result
          mov  [si+da_lo-gdt],ax

          mov  di,[bp+16]        ;get address of the Startsegment-Variable
          mov  ax,[di]           ;move Source segment address to mov
          mov  di,[bp+14]        ;get Address of StartOffset-Variable
          mov  bx,[di]           ;Source Offset address to BX
          test ch,2              ;is Source beyond 1 MB?
          call calc_adr          ;form 24 bit Address
          mov  [si+sa_hi-gdt],dl ;store result
          mov  [si+sa_lo-gdt],ax
          mov  ah,087h           ;Parameter for the Function call
          mov  di,[bp+8]         ;get Address of the Size-Variables
          mov  cx,[di]           ;get number of words
          int  15h               ;call RAM-displacement function
```

```
          mov  sp,bp              ;restore Stackpointer
          pop  bp                 ;return BP from the Stack
          ret  12                 ;Addresses of the Variables on the Stack
                                  ;are no longer required

Move      endp

;-- GET_ADR:   returns the Offset address of the GDT ------------------
;-- Input   :  none
;-- Output   : SI = Offset address of the GDT
;-- Register : SI is changed

get_adr   proc near

          pop  si             ;get Address of GDT from Stack
          jmp  short move1    ;jump to actual Routine

get_adr   endp

;-- CALC_ADR:  calculates the 24 bit (physical) Address ---------------
;-- Input     : AX:BX = Buffer address to be converted
;--             Zero Flag = 1 : Buffer address beyond 1 MB
;-- Output    : DL = HI-Byte of Buffer address  (bit 16-23)
;--           : BX = Lo-Word of Buffer address (bit 0-15)
;-- Register : AX, BX, DL, CL and FLAGS are changed

calc_adr  proc near

          mov  dl,ah        ;Hi-Byte of the segment address to DL
          mov  cl,4         ;move Hi-Nibble of the segment
          shr  dl,cl        ;address to the Lo-Nibble
          jne  under_1mb    ;test if beyond 1 MB

          or   dl,010h      ;is beyond 1 MB

under_1mb:shl  ax,cl        ;segment address times 16
          add  ax,bx        ;add Offset address
          jnc  no_more      ;test if excess

          inc  dl           ;yes

no_more: ret                ;back to caller

calc_adr  endp

;======================================================================

code      ends
          end
```

The INLINE command, not DATA statements, integrate the MOVE routine into the following Pascal program.

Pascal listing: MOVEP.PAS

```
{**********************************************************************}
{*                              M O V E P                             *}
{*--------------------------------------------------------------------*}
{*    Task      : With the help of a procedure, Data are              *}
{*                copied in RAM below and above 1 MB                  *}
{*--------------------------------------------------------------------*}
{*    Author          : MICHAEL TISCHER                               *}
{*    developed on    :  8/8/87                                       *}
{*    last Update     : 6/8/89                                        *}
{*--------------------------------------------------------------------*}
{*    Info         : This program runs only on ATs and                *}
{*                   only if RAM beyond 1 MB                          *}
```

```
{*                  is available                                        *}
{**********************************************************************}

program MOVEP;


Uses Crt, Dos;                                 {add Crt and Dos units}

var Keypress : char;

{**********************************************************************}
{* GETPAGE: returns the segment address of the current display page   *}
{* Input  :  none                                                      *}
{* Output : the segment address of the current display page            *}
{**********************************************************************}

function GetPage : Longint;

var Regs : Registers;         {Processor registers for interrupt calls}

begin
 Regs.ah := 15;                                  { Function number }
 intr($10, Regs);                       { Call BIOS video interrupt }
 if Regs.al = 7 then GetPage := $B000            { Monochrome card }
                else GetPage := $B800;                { Color card }
end;

{************************************************************************}
{* MOVE:    moves memory areas                                          *}
{* Input :  see below                                                   *}
{* Output : none                                                        *}
{* Info: Direction:           0 = from below 1 MB--> to below 1 MB      *}
{*                            1 = from below 1 MB--> to above 1 MB      *}
{*                            2 = from above 1 MB--> to below 1 MB      *}
{*                            3 = from above 1 MB--> to above 1 MB      *}
{*               Addresses above the 1MB boundary are given relative    *}
{*               to this value                                          *}
{************************************************************************}

{$F+}
procedure HiMove(StartSeg,          { Segment address of the start buffer }
          StartOfs,                  { Offset address of the start buffer }
          DestSeg,                 { Segment address of destination buffer }
          DestOfs,                  { Offset address of destination buffer }
          Size,                            { Number of words to be copied }
          Direction : integer);              { Direction in which to copy }
begin
 inline(
       $8B/$7E/$10/$8B/$76/$0E/$8B/$46/$0C/$8E/$C0/$8B/$5E/$0A/
       $8B/$46/$08/$8B/$4E/$06/$8A/$E9/$55/$E8/$5E/$00/$00/$00/
       $00/$00/$00/$00/$00/$00/$00/$00/$00/$00/$00/$00/$00/$00/
       $FF/$FF/$00/$00/$10/$92/$00/$00/$FF/$FF/$00/$00/$00/$92/
       $00/$00/$00/$00/$00/$00/$00/$00/$00/$00/$00/$00/$00/$00/
       $00/$00/$00/$00/$50/$8C/$C0/$F6/$C5/$01/$E8/$28/$00/$2E/
       $88/$56/$1C/$2E/$89/$46/$1A/$8B/$C7/$8B/$DE/$F6/$C5/$02/
       $E8/$16/$00/$2E/$88/$56/$14/$2E/$89/$46/$12/$B4/$87/$0E/
       $07/$59/$8B/$F5/$CD/$15/$EB/$17/$5D/$EB/$CF/$8A/$D4/$B1/
       $04/$D2/$EA/$75/$03/$80/$CA/$10/$D3/$E0/$03/$C3/$73/$02/
       $FE/$C2/$C3/$5D
      );
end;

{**********************************************************************}
{*                          MAIN PROGRAM                              *}
{**********************************************************************}

begin
  clrscr;                                          { Clear Screen }
  writeln('MOVEP (c) 1987 by Michael Tischer');
  writeln(#13#10'This Program uses Function 87(h) of  '+
```

```
        'Interrupt 15(h) to move blocks of storage ');
  writeln('between the "normal" RAM and the RAM beyond the 1 Mega-'+
          'Byte storage boundary');
  if mem[$F000:$FFFE] <> $FC then          { test if computer is an AT }
   begin
    writeln('Since this computer is not an AT, '+
            'but a PC or');
    writeln('an XT, and these can not have storage '+
            'beyond the 1 MB boundary,');
    writeln('this program can not execute on your PC! ');
    writeln('Sorry....');
   end
  else
   begin
   writeln('First this display page is moved immediately '+
           'beyond the 1 MB storage ');
    writeln('boundary. The screen is then cleared. '+
            'After a key has been activated, ');
    writeln('the old display page is restored.');
    writeln(''#13#10'Please activate a key now to '+
            'start the program...');
    repeat until keypressed;                       { Wait for a key }
    Keypress := ReadKey;                                 { Read key }
    HiMove(GetPage,$0000,$0000,$0000,$2000,$1);    { Copy video RAM }
    clrscr;                                          { Clear screen }
    writeln('Please press a key ...');
    Keypress:= ReadKey;                                  { Read key }
    HiMove($0000,$0000,GetPage,$0000,$2000,$2);  { Restore video RAM }
    gotoxy(1,15);
    writeln('That`s All!');
   end;
end.
```

For the Pascal programmers interested in assembly language, the assembler listing of the MOVE function appears here.

Assembler listing: MOVEPA.ASM

```
;**********************************************************************;
;*                            M O V E P A                             *;
;*--------------------------------------------------------------------*;
;*    Task  : copies Data between the RAM below 1 MB and              *;
;*            above 1 MB                                              *;
;*            CAUTION! This is the Version for linking                *;
;*                     in a Pascal Program with INLINE-               *;
;*                     commands                                       *;
;*--------------------------------------------------------------------*;
;*    Author        : MICHAEL TISCHER                                 *;
;*    developed on :  6.8.87                                          *;
;*    last Update  :  6.8.89                                          *;
;*--------------------------------------------------------------------*;
;*    assembly      : MASM MOVEPA;                                    *;
;*                    LINK MOVEPA;                                    *;
;*                    convert to INLINEs and add to Turbo Pascal      *;
;**********************************************************************;

;== Code-segment =====================================================

code    segment para 'CODE'  ;Definition of the CODE-segment

          org 100h           ;it begins at Address 100(h)
                             ;directly behind the PSP

          assume cs:code, ds:code, es:code, ss:code

;== Program ==========================================================

;--Call:  HiMoves(StartSeg,
```

```
;--              StartOfs,
;--              DestSeg,
;--              DestOfs,
;--              NumWords,
;--              Direction : word);
;-- This routine is designed as a FAR call model

movepa   proc near

sframe   struc              ;Access structure on stack
bptr     dw ?               ;Taken by BP
ret_adr  dd ?               ;Return address (FAR)
directn  dw ?               ;Copy direction
numwords dw ?               ;Number of Words being copied
destofs  dw ?               ;Destination buffer's offset address
destseg  dw ?               ;Destination buffer's segment address
startofs dw ?               ;Starting buffer's offset address
startseg dw ?               ;Starting buffer's segment address
sframe   ends               ;End of structure

frame    equ [ bp - bptr ]  ;For stack addressing

         push bp            ;Store BP on the Stack
         mov  bp,sp         ;Move SP to BP

         mov  di,frame.startseg ;Get source segment from stack
         mov  si,frame.startofs ;Get source offset from stack
         mov  ax,frame.destseg  ;Get destination segment from stack
         mov  es,ax             ;and move to ES
         mov  bx,frame.destseg  ;Get destination offset from stack
         mov  ax,frame.numwords ;Get numwords from stack
         mov  cx,frame.directn  ;Get direction from stack
         mov  ch,cl             ;and send to CH
         push bp                ;Mark BP
         call getgdt            ;Determine address of GDT

;-- Variables and Data of the MOVE-Function ---------------------------

GDT      equ this word

    ;-- THIS IS THE GDT (GLOBAL DESCRIPTOR TABLE) ---------------------
         dw 4 dup (?)     ;segment Desc. for Dummy-segment
         ;-- this segment Descriptor describes the GDT itself --------
         dw 4 dup (?)
         ;-- segment Descriptor of the Source-Area -------------------
         dw 0ffffh          ;segment length  = 64 KB
sa_lo    dw (?)             ;Lo-Word of the 24 bit-Address
sa_hi    db 010h            ;Hi-Byte of the 24 bit-Address
         db 10010010b       ;Data segment in storage with
                            ;highest Priority, Writeable
         dw 00000h          ;Compatibility Word for 80386
         ;-- segment Descriptor of the Destination-Area --------------
         dw 0ffffh          ;segment length = 64 KB
da_lo    dw (?)             ;Lo-Word of the 24 bit-Address
da_hi    db (?)             ;Hi-Byte of the 24 bit-Address
         db 10010010b       ;Data segment in storage with
            ;highest Priority, Writeable
         dw 00000h          ;Compatibility Word for 80386
         ;-- this segment Descriptor describes the BIOS-Code-segment
         dw 4 dup (?)
         ;-- this segment Descriptor describes the Stacksegment ------
         dw 4 dup (?)
         ;-- END OF THE GDT ------------------------------------------

;-- MOVE: Moves Data between memory above and below 1 MB --------------
;-- Input : DI:SI = Source address (if above 1 MB as Offset to 1 MB)
;-- ES:BX = Dest. address (if above 1 MB as Offset to 1 MB)
;--          CH    = move ... from --> to
;--               00b = from below 1 MB --> to below 1 MB
;--               01b = from below 1 MB --> to above 1 MB
```

```
;--                10b = from above 1 MB  --> to below 1 MB
;--                11b = from above 1 MB  --> to above 1 MB
;--                AX  = Number of words to be moved (max. 08000h)
;-- Output  : Carry-Flag = 1 : Error
;-- Register : AX, BX, DL, CL, SI, ES and FLAG are changed
;-- Info : This function should not be used to move RAM below the
;             1-MB boundary
move:     push ax             ;Store number of words on the Stack
          mov  ax,es          ;Destination segment address to AX
          test ch,1           ;is destination above 1 MB?
          call calc_adr       ;form 24 bit Address
          mov  cs:[bp+28],dl  ;store result
          mov  cs:[bp+26],ax
          mov  ax,di          ;Source segment address to AX
          mov  bx,si          ;Source Offset address to BX
          test ch,2           ;is Source above 1 MB?
          call calc_adr       ;form 24 bit Address
          mov  cs:[bp+20],dl  ;store result
          mov  cs:[bp+18],ax
          mov  ah,087h        ;load Parameter for function call
          push cs
          pop  es             ;set ES to CS
          pop  cx             ;Get number of Words from Stack
          mov  si,bp          ;load Offset address of GDT
          int  15h            ;call RAM moving function
          jmp short ende      ;back to Turbo


movepa   endp

;-- GETGDT: Get Address of the GDT and jump to MOVE -------------------
;-- Input   : none
;-- Output   : CS:BP = Address of the GDT
;-- Register : only BP is changed
;-- Info : this Routine can only be used in the environment
;--          of this Program

getgdt    proc near

          pop  bp             ;Get Address of GDT from the Stack
          jmp  short move     ;Jump to MOVE-Routine

getgdt    endp

;-- CALC_ADR: calculates 24 bit (physical) Address --------------------
;-- Input     : AX:BX = Buffer address to be converted
;--             Zero Flag = 1 : Buffer address beyond 1 MB
;-- Output : DL = HI-Byte of the Buffer address (bit 16-23)
;--          : BX = Lo-Word of the Buffer address (bit 0-15)
;-- Register : AX, BX, DL, CL and FLAGS are changed

calc_adr  proc near

          mov  dl,ah       ;Hi-Byte of segment address to DL
          mov  cl,4        ;shift Hi-Nibble of segment
          shr  dl,cl       ;address into Lo-Nibble
          jne  under_1mb   ;test if above 1 MB

          or   dl,010h     ;is above 1 MB

under_1mb:shl  ax,cl       ;segment address times 16
          add  ax,bx       ;add Offset address to it
          jnc  no_more     ;test if overflow

          inc  dl          ;yes

no_more: ret               ;back to caller

calc_adr  endp
```

```
ende      label near      ;Code stops here
          pop bp          ;Restore BP from atack


;== End ================================================================

code      ends            ;End of the CODE segment
          end  movepa     ;End of the assembler program
```

The C program differs from the BASIC and Pascal programs in that the MOVE function is also present as an assembler routine, but excluded from the C program listing. First the MOVE assembler program assembles, then the C program is compiled. You then merge the two programs using the linker. For this reason the listing of the C program follows with the source listing of the corresponding assembler function.

C listing: MOVEC.C

```
/**********************************************************************/
/*                           M O V E C                                */
/*--------------------------------------------------------------------*/
/* Task: integrates an Assembler-Routine in C, which can              */
/*       move memory blocks beyond the 1 MB boundary                  */
/*--------------------------------------------------------------------*/
/*    Author        : MICHAEL TISCHER                                 */
/*    developed on  : 8.13.87                                         */
/*    last Update   : 9.21.87                                         */
/*--------------------------------------------------------------------*/
/*    (MICROSOFT C)                                                   */
/*    Creation      : MSC MOVEC;                                      */
/*                    LINK MOVEC MOVECA PEPO;                         */
/*    Call          : MOVEC                                           */
/*--------------------------------------------------------------------*/
/*    (BORLAND TURBO C)                                               */
/* Creation: with Project-File with the following content:            */
/*               movec                                                */
/*               moveca.obj                                           */
/**********************************************************************/

#include <dos.h>                          /* include Header-Files */
#include <io.h>
#include <conio.h>

extern void AdMove();                    /* ADMOVE must be linked */
extern int PeekB();                       /* PEEKB must be linked */

/**********************************************************************/
/* GETPAGE; returns the Address of the current display page          */
/* Input :  none                                                      */
/* Output : see below                                                 */
/**********************************************************************/

unsigned int GetPAge()

{
 union REGS Register;         /* Register-Variable for Interrupt call */

 Register.h.ah = 15;        /* Function number to get Video parameter */
 int86(0x10, &Register, &Register);          /* Call Interrupt 10(h) */
 return((Register.h.al == 7) ? 0xB000 : 0xB800);
}

/**********************************************************************/
/* CLS    : Clear Screen                                              */
/* Input  : none                                                      */
/* Output : none                                                      */
```

```
/*************************************************************************/

void Cls()

{
 union REGS Register;          /* Register-Variable for Interrupt call */

 Register.h.ah = 6;                  /* Function number for Scroll-UP */
 Register.h.al = 0;                                 /* 0 is for clear */
 Register.h.bh = 7;          /* white characters on black background */
 Register.x.cx = 0;                        /* upper left display corner */
 Register.h.dh = 24;                      /* Coordinates of the lower */
 Register.h.dl = 79;                            /* right display corner */
 int86(0x10, &Register, &Register);     /* Call BIOS-Video-Interrupt */
}

/*************************************************************************/
/**                           MAIN PROGRAM                             **/
/*************************************************************************/

void main()

{
 printf("\nMOVE (c) 1987 by Michael Tischer\n\n");
 printf("This Program uses the Function 87(h) of Interrupt 15(h)");
 printf(" to move memory blocks\nbetween the \"normal\" RAM and the ");
 printf("RAM beyond the 1 Mega-Byte storage limit.\n");
 if (PeekB(0xF000, 0xFFFE) != 0xFC)                    /* test if AT */
  {
 printf("Since this PC is not an AT, but a ");
 printf("PC or XT\nand this PC can not have RAM ");
 printf("beyond the 1 MB storage limit, ");
 printf("this program can not be executed! Sorry...\n\n");
  }
 else
  {
   printf("After starting the program by pressing a key ");
   printf("the current display\n content is ");
   printf("copied directly beyond the 1 MB-limit\n ");
   printf("and then the display is cleared. If another key is ");
   printf("\npressed ,the old display is again  ");
   printf("restored.\n\nPlease press a key to ");
   printf("start the Program ...");
   getch();                                        /* wait for a key */

   /*-- Copy current Video Rrm beyond 1 MB --------------------------*/
   AdMove(GetPage(), 0x0000, 0x0000, 0x0000, 0x2000, 1);

   Cls();                                           /* Clear Screen */
   printf("\nPlease press a key ...");
   getch();                                             /* get a key */

   /*-- Restore Video-RAM ------------------------------------------*/
   AdMove(0x0000, 0x0000, GetPage(), 0x0000, 0x2000, 2);
   printf("\n\nThat's It!\n");
  }
}
```

Assembler listing: MOVECA.ASM

```
;***********************************************************************;
;*                             M O V E C A                             *;
;*---------------------------------------------------------------------*;
;*    Task    : Makes the Functions for moving of                       *;
;*              Storage blocks beyond the 1MB memory limit             *;
;*              available for inclusion in C                           *;
;*---------------------------------------------------------------------*;
;*    Author        : MICHAEL TISCHER                                  *;
```

```
;*    developed on : 8.13.87                                          *;
;*    last Update  : 9.21.87                                          *;
;*--------------------------------------------------------------------*;
;*    assembly     : MASM MOVECA;                                     *;
;**********************************************************************;

IGROUP group _text                  ;Grouping of Program-segments
DGROUP group const,_bss,  _data     ;Grouping of Data-segments
       assume CS:IGROUP, DS:DGROUP, ES:DGROUP, SS:DGROUP

       public _AdMove ;Functions become accessible to other
                                    ;programs

CONST  segment word public 'CONST'  ;this segment accepts all
CONST  ends                         ;readable Constants

_BSS   segment word public 'BSS'    ;this segment accepts not all
_BSS   ends                         ;initialized static Variables

_DATA  segment word public 'DATA'   ;all initialized global and
                                    ;static Variables are stored in this
                                    ;segment

GDT       equ this word             ;the Global Descriptor Table

          dw 4 dup (?)              ;segment Desc. for Dummy-segment
          dw 4 dup (?)

       ;-- segment Descriptors of the Source-Area ---------------------
          dw 0ffffh         ;segment length = 64 KB
sa_lo     dw (?)            ;Lo-Word of the 24 bit-Address
sa_hi     db 010h           ;Hi-Byte of the 24 bit-Address
          db 10010010b      ;Data segment in storage with
                            ;highest Priority, Writeable
          dw 00000h         ;Compatibility word for 80386

      ;-- segment Descriptors of the Destination-Area -----------------
          dw 0ffffh         ;segment length = 64 KB
da_lo     dw (?)            ;Lo-Word of the 24-bit-Address
da_hi     db (?)            ;Hi-Byte of the 24-bit-Address
          db 10010010b      ;Data segment in storage with
                            ;highest Priority, Writeable
          dw 00000h         ;Compatibility word for 80386

          dw 4 dup (?)      ;segment Desc. BIOS-Code-segment
          dw 4 dup (?)      ;segment Descriptors Stack-segment

_DATA  ends

_TEXT  segment byte public 'CODE' ;the Program segment

;- ADMOVE: Copy Storage Blocks beyond the 1MB limit -------------------
;- Call of C: AdMove(Startsegment, StartOffset, Destsegment,
;--                    DestOffset, Size, Direction);
;-- Info : - for DIRECTION the following Codes are accepted:
;--                0 = from below 1 MB --> to below 1 MB
;--                1 = from below 1 MB --> to above 1 MB
;--                2 = from above 1 MB  --> to below 1 MB
;--                3 = from above 1 MB  --> to above 1 MB
;--              - the number relates to words, not Bytes
;--                and can not be larger than 8000(h)
;--              - for moving of RAM below the 1-MB border
;--                the Functions MOVEDATA or MEMCPY should
;--                be called

_AdMove   proc near

          push bp                   ;store BP on the Stack
          mov  bp,sp                ;move SP to BP
          push si                   ;C expects unchanged SI
```

```
        mov  ch,[bp+14]            ;move Direction to CH
        mov  ax,[bp+8]             ;Destination segment address to AX
        mov  bx,[bp+10]            ;Destination Offset address to BX
        test ch,1                  ;is Destination beyond 1 MB?
        call calc_adr              ;form 24 bit Address
        mov  da_hi,dl              ;store result
        mov  da_lo,ax
        mov  ax,[bp+4]             ;Source segment address to AX
        mov  bx,[bp+6]             ;Source Offset address to BX
        test ch,2                  ;is Source beyond 1 MB?
        call calc_adr              ;form 24 bit Address
        mov  sa_hi,dl              ;store result
        mov  sa_lo,ax
        mov  ah,087h               ;Parameter for the Function call
        push ds                    ;load
        pop  es                    ;st ES to DS
        mov  cx,[bp+12]            ;get number of Words
        mov  si,offset DGROUP:GDT  ;load Offset address of GDT
        int  15h                   ;call RAM moving functions

        pop  si                    ;restore old SI from Stack
        mov  sp,bp                 ;restore Stackpointer
        pop  bp                    ;get BP from Stack
        ret                        ;Return to calling C-Program

_AdMove  endp

;-- CALC_ADR: calculates 24 bit (physical) Address --------------------
;-- Input  : AX:BX = Buffer address to be converted
;--           Zero Flag = 1 : Buffer address beyond 1 MB
;-- Output : DL = HI-Byte of the Buffer address (bit 16-23)
;--        : BX = Lo-Word of the Buffer address (bit 0-15)
;-- Register : AX, BX, DL, CL and FLAGS are changed

calc_adr  proc near

        mov  dl,ah                 ;Hi-Byte of segment address to DL
        mov  cl,4                  ;move Hi-Nibble of segment address
        shr  dl,cl                 ;into the Lo-Nibble
        jne  under_1mb             ;test if beyond 1 MB

        or   dl,010h               ;beyond 1 MB

under_1mb:shl  ax,cl               ;segment address times 16
        add  ax,bx                 ;add Offset address
        jnc  no_more               ;test if overflow

        inc  dl                    ;yes

no_more: ret                       ;back to caller

calc_adr  endp

;---------------------------------------------------------------------

_text    ends                      ;End of the Program-segment
         end                       ;End of the Assembler-Source
```

Here is the assembler program. No additional program code is required for integrating the MOVE function because it is built-in.

Assembler listing: MOVEA.ASM

```
;**********************************************************************;
;*                              M O V E A                             *;
;*--------------------------------------------------------------------*;
;*    Task    : copies data between RAM below 1 MB and                *;
;*              above 1 MB                                            *;
;*--------------------------------------------------------------------*;
;*    Author        : MICHAEL TISCHER                                 *;
;*    developed on  :  6.8.87                                         *;
;*    last Update   : 9.21.87                                         *;
;*--------------------------------------------------------------------*;
;*    assembly      : MASM MOVEA;                                     *;
;*                    LINK MOVEA;                                     *;
;*                    EXE2BIN MOVEA MOVEA.COM                         *;
;*--------------------------------------------------------------------*;
;*    Call          : MOVEA                                           *;
;**********************************************************************;

;== BIOS-segment ======================================================

bios      segment at 0F000h      ;used for Addressing of the
                                 ;Device-Codes

          org 0FFFEh             ;Address of the Device-Codes in BIOS
gercode   equ this byte

bios      ends                   ;End of the BIOS-segments

;== Code-segment ======================================================

code    segment para 'CODE'      ;Definition of the CODE-segment

          org 100h               ;it begins at Address 100(h)
                                 ;directly after the PSP

          assume cs:code, ds:code, es:bios, ss:code

;== Program ===========================================================

movea     proc near

      ;-- Output Initiation Message -----------------------------------

     mov  dx,offset initm         ;Offset address of the Init message
     mov  ah,9                    ;output Function number for String
          int  21h                ;Call DOS-Interrupt

          mov  ax,0F000h          ;segment address of BIOS
          mov  es,ax              ;to ES
          cmp  es:gercode,0FCh    ;is the device an AT
          je   isat    ;YES --> continue to execute Program

       ;-- Device is PC or XT, Program doesn't run --------------------

      mov  dx,offset sorrym       ;Offset address of Text
      jmp  short pcxt             ;Output message and terminate program

          ;-- User must activate a key to start the program

isat:     mov  dx,offset dom      ;Offset address of the Text
          mov  ah,9               ;output function number for String
          int  21h                ;call DOS-Interrupt

          xor  ah,ah              ;read a character from the keyboard
```

```
          int  16h              ;call BIOS-Keyboard-Interrupt

          ;-- Move Video-RAM to 1 MB ----------------------------------

          call getvseg          ;Get segment address of Video-RAM
          mov  di,ax            ;and move to DI
          xor  si,si            ;copy starting at Offset address 0

          xor  bx,bx            ;copy after 1MB + 0000:0000
          mov  es,bx
          mov  ch,1             ;from below 1 MB to above 1 MB
          mov  ax,2000          ;move 2000
          call move             ;Words
          jc   fehler           ;on error terminate

          ;-- Fill Video-RAM with characters --------------------------

          call getvseg          ;Get segment address of the Video-RAM
          mov  es,ax            ;and move to ES
          xor  di,di            ;start at Offset address 0
          mov  cx,2000          ;fill the complete Video-RAM with
          mov  ax,87FEh         ;blinking Block-Character
          rep  stosw

          ;-- User must activate a key --------------------------------

          mov  dx,offset userm  ;Offset address of the Text
          mov  ah,9             ;output function number for String
          int  21h              ;call DOS-Interrupt

          xor  ah,ah            ;read a character from the keyboard
          int  16h              ;call BIOS-Keyboard-Interrupt

          ;-- Restore Video-RAM again ---------------------------------

          xor  di,di            ;restore 1 MB + 0000:0000
          xor  si,si
          xor  bx,bx
          mov  ch,10b           ;from beyond 1 MB to below 1 MB
          mov  ax,2000          ;move 2000
          call move             ;Words
          jc   fehler           ;terminate on error

          mov  ax,4C00h         ;terminate Program with call of a DOS
          int  21h              ;function on return of Error-Code 0

error:    mov  dx,offset errm   ;Offset address of  error message
pcxt:     mov  ah,9             ;output function number for String
          int  21h              ;call DOS-Interrupt
          mov  ax,4C01h         ;terminate Program with call of a DOS
          int  21h              ;function on return of Error-Code 1

movea     endp

;-- GETVSEG  : returns the segment address of the Video-RAM -
;-- Input    : none
;-- Output   : AX = segment address of the Video-RAM
;-- Register : AX, BH and FLAGS are changed

getvseg   proc near

          mov  ah,0FH           ;get function number for Video
          int  10h              ;call BIOS-Video-Interrupt
          cmp  al,7             ;is a Mono-Card installed?
          jne  colvideo         ;NO --> Color-Card

          mov  ax,0B000h        ;segment addr. of the mono Video-RAM
          ret                   ;back to caller

colvideo: mov  ax,0B800h        ;segment addr. of color Video-RAM
```

```
         ret               ;back to caller

getvseg  endp

;-- MOVE: Moves Data between Storage above and below 1 MB -
;-- Input : DI:SI = Sourceaddress (if above 1 MB as Offset to 1 MB)
;--   ES:BX = Dest address (if above 1 MB as Offset to 1 MB)
;--   CH    = move ... from --> to
;--              00b = from below 1 MB --> to below 1 MB
;--              01b = from below 1 MB --> to above 1 MB
;--              10b = from above 1 MB  --> to below 1 MB
;--              11b = from above 1 MB  --> to above 1 MB
;--   AX    = Number of words to be moved  (max. 08000h)
;-- Output  : Carry-Flag = 1 : Error
;-- Register : AX, BX, DL, CL, SI, ES and FLAG are changed
;-- Info     : this function should not be used for moving
;--            from RAM below the 1 MB limit

move     proc near

         push ax                ;record number of Words on the Stack
         mov  ax,es             ;Destination segment address to AX
         test ch,1              ;is Destination above 1 MB?
         call calc_adr          ;form 24 bit Address
         mov  da_hi,dl          ;store result
         mov  da_lo,ax
         mov  ax,di             ;Source segment address to AX
         mov  bx,si             ;Source Offset address to BX
         test ch,2              ;is Source above 1 MB?
         call calc_adr          ;form 24 bit Address
         mov  sa_hi,dl          ;store result
         mov  sa_lo,ax
         mov  ah,087h           ;Parameter for the Function call
         push ds                ;load
         pop  es                ;set ES to DS
         pop  cx                ;read number of Words from Stack
         mov  si,offset GDT     ;load Offset address of GDT
         int  15h               ;call RAM move function
         ret                    ;back to caller

;-- Variables and Data of the MOVE-Function ---------------------------

GDT      equ this word

         ;-- THIS IS THE GDT (GLOBAL DESCRIPTOR TABLE) ---------------
         dw 4 dup (?)                ;segment Descs. for Dummy-segment
         ;-- this segment Descriptor describes the GDT itself --------
         dw 4 dup (?)
         ;-- segment Descriptor of the Source-Area -------------------
         dw 0ffffh                   ;segment length = 64 KB
sa_lo    dw (?)                      ;Lo-Word of the 24 bit-Address
sa_hi    db 010h                     ;Hi-Byte of the 24 bit-Address
         db 10010010b                ;Data segment in storage with
                                     ;highest Priority, Writeable
         dw 00000h                   ;Compatibility Word for 80386
         ;-- segment Descriptor of the Destination-Area --------------
         dw 0ffffh                   ;segment length = 64 KB
da_lo    dw (?)                      ;Lo-Word of the 24 bit-Address
da_hi    db (?)                      ;Hi-Byte of the 24 bit-Address
         db 10010010b                ;Data segment in storage with
                                     ;highest Priority, Writeable
         dw 00000h                   ;Compatibility Word for 80386
         ;-- this segment Descriptor describes the BIOS-Code-segment
         dw 4 dup (?)
         ;-- this segment Descriptor describes the Stack segment -----
         dw 4 dup (?)
         ;-- END OF THE GDT ------------------------------------------

move     endp
```

```
;-- CALC_ADR : calculates 24 bit (physical) Address -------------------
;-- Input    : AX:BX = Buffer address to be converted
;--            Zero Flag = 1 : Buffer address above 1 MB
;-- Output   : DL = HI-Byte of the Buffer address (bit 16-23)
;--          : BX = Lo-Word of the Buffer address (bit 0-15)
;-- Register : AX, BX, DL, CL and FLAGS are changed

calc_adr  proc near

          mov  dl,ah              ;Hi-Byte of the segment address to DL
          mov  cl,4               ;Hi-Nibble of the segment address
          shr  dl,cl              ;shifted to Lo-Nibble
          jne  under_1mb          ;test if above 1 MB

          or   dl,010h            ;lies above 1 MB

under_1mb:shl  ax,cl              ;segment address times 16
          add  ax,bx              ;add Offset address
          jnc  no_more            ;test for overflow

          inc  dl                 ;yes

no_more: ret                      ;back to caller

calc_adr  endp

;== Data  ==============================================================

initm     db 13,10,"MOVE (c) 1987 by Michael Tischer",13,10,13,10
          db "This Program uses the Function 87(h) of Interrupt "
          db "15(h) to copy memory blocks",13,10,"between 'normal' "
          db "RAM and RAM above the 1-Megabyte boundary".",13,10,"$"

dom       db "The Program copies first the current display "
          db "content directly",13,10,"after the 1-MB-boundary and "
          db "the fills the screen with characters.",13,10
          db "After a key has been activated, the old "
          db "display content ",13,10,"is restored and the Pro"
          db "gram terminated.",13,10,"Please press a key, to "
          db "start the Program ...$"

sorrym    db "Since this computer is not an AT, "
          db "but a PC or",13,10,"XT, and these "
          db "PCs can not have storage beyond the 1-MB limit,"
          db 13,10,"this program can not be started! "
          db "Sorry...",13,10,"$"

userm     db 13,10,"                        Please press a  "
          db "key $"

errm      db "WARNING ! Error on access to RAM above 1 MB"
          db 13,10,"$"

;== End ================================================================

code      ends                    ;End of the CODE-segment
          end movea               ;End of the Assembler-Program.
```

7.11 Accessing the Keyboard from the BIOS

Interrupt 16H provides three functions to read the keyboard and keyboard status. The BIOS keyboard functions are very limited: No BIOS functions exist for removing characters from the keyboard buffer or renaming keys. DOS functions can perform these operations.

BIOS-proof keys

Some key combinations cannot be read by BIOS as key codes because they execute commands. Activating the <PrtSc> or <Print> key calls BIOS interrupt 5H. This starts a routine which sends the current screen display to a printer, producing a hardcopy.

The <Ctrl><Num Lock> keys stop the complete system until the user presses another key. The keyboard buffer ignores the <Ctrl><Num Lock> keys and the subsequently pressed key, so programs cannot read these keys.

Pressing the <Ctrl><Break> key combination calls interrupt 1BH. Normally the current program stops and returns to DOS. To prevent this, this interrupt can be directed to a routine within the application program which continues program execution if the routine consists of an IRET assembly language instruction only.

ATs and a few advanced PC/XTs have the <Sys Req> key. Its activation calls interrupt 15H by passing the value 8500H to the AX register. When the user releases the key, the AX register then receives the value 8501H. The value 85H in the AH register represents the function number of interrupt 15H. After starting the system, function 85H of the BIOS interrupt 15H consists only of an IRET instruction; pressing the <Sys Req> key has no visible result.

Control codes

Most people know that any ASCII code can be entered from the keyboard using the <Alt> key and the keys of the numeric keypad. Few users know about character entry with the help of the <Ctrl> key. When used in connection with other keys, this key can enter ASCII codes smaller than code number 32. The following figure shows which keys can be accessed.

Dec	Symbol	Keystrokes
0	(Nul)	Ctrl 2
1	☺	Ctrl A
2	☻	Ctrl B
3	♥	Ctrl C
4	♦	Ctrl D
5	♣	Ctrl E
6	♠	Ctrl F
7	• BEL	Ctrl G
8	◘ BS	Ctrl H, Backspace, Shift-Backspace
9	○ TAB	Ctrl I
10	◙ LE	Ctrl J, Ctrl
11	♂	Ctrl K
12	♀ FF	Ctrl L
13	♪ CR	Ctrl M, ↵, Shift ↵
14	♫	Ctrl N
15	☼	Ctrl O
16	►	Ctrl P
17	◄	Ctrl Q
18	↕	Ctrl R
19	‼	Ctrl S
20	¶	Ctrl T
21	§	Ctrl U
22	▬	Ctrl V
23	↨	Ctrl W
24	↑	Ctrl X
25	↓	Ctrl Y
26	→ EOF	Ctrl Z
27	← ESC	Ctrl [, Esc, Shift-Esc, Ctrl-Esc
28	∟	Ctrl \
29	↔	Ctrl]
30	▲	Ctrl 6
31	▼	Ctrl -
32	Space	Space, Shift-Space, Ctrl-Space, Alt-Space

Character input with the <Ctrl> key

Function 0: Read keyboard

Interrupt 16H normally receives a call when a program expects user input of one or more characters. If a character was already entered before the function call, the keyboard buffer empties this character and passes it to the calling program. If there is no character in the keyboard buffer, function 0 waits until a character has been input and then returns to the calling program. The caller can determine the character or activate a key from the contents of the AL and the AH registers.

ASCII

If the AL register contains a value other than 0, it contains the ASCII code of the character. The AH register contains the scan code of the active key. The code in the AL register corresponds to the ASCII codes for character output on the screen. Some differences occur in the control keys:

Code	Key(s)
8	<Backspace>
9	<Tab>
10	<Ctrl><Return>
13	<Return>
27	<Esc>

Scan codes

The scan code in the AH register indicates the number of the active key, where the keys on the keyboard are numbered starting with 0. Since PC, XT and AT keyboards differ, this is unimportant for most programs. Scan codes of the various keyboards can be found in the Appendices of this book.

Extended key codes

If the AL register contains the value 0 after the call, the AH register indicates an extended keyboard code. The difference between the ASCII code and the extended keyboard code lies in the fact that certain keys (e.g., the cursor keys) cannot fit within the PC's 256-character set. The following table provides an overview of extended keyboard codes:

Code(s)	Key(s)
15	<Shift><Tab>
16-25	<Alt><Q>,<W>,<E>,<R>,<T>,<Y>,<U>,<I>,<O>,<P>
30-38	<Alt><A>,<S>,<D>,<F>,<G>,<H>,<J>,<K>,<L>
44-50	<Alt><Z>,<X>,<C>,<V>,<B>,<N>,<M>
59-68	<F1>-<F10>
71	<Home>
72	<Cursor Up>
73	<Page Up>
75	<Cursor Left>
77	<Cursor Right>

Code(s)	Key(s)
79	<End>
80	<Cursor Down>
81	<Page Down>
82	<Insert>
83	<Delete>
84-93	<Shift><F1>-<F10>
94-103	<Ctrl><F1>-<F10>
104-113	<Alt><F1>-<F10>
115	<Ctrl><Cursor Left>
116	<Ctrl><Cursor Right>
117	<Ctrl><End>
118	<Ctrl><Page Down>
119	<Ctrl><Home>
120-131	<Alt><1>,<2>,<3>,<4>,<5>,<6>,<7>,<8>,<9>,<0>
132	<Ctrl><Page Up>

Key combinations not contained in this table cannot be sensed using the BIOS keyboard functions, since they don't generate keyboard codes.

Function 1: Read keyboard

Function 1 also reads the keyboard. Unlike function 0, function 1 leaves the preceding character in the keyboard buffer. Repeated calls of function 1 or function 0 read the keyboard again. Place the value 1 in the AH register to call function 1. In contrast to function 0, function 1 immediately informs the calling program with the zero flag after the function call if a character is available or not. If the zero flag equals 1, no character was available. If the zero flag resets, the AL and the AH registers contain information about the activated key. As in function 0, the AL register contains the value 0 if the user activated an extended key, and a value unequal to 0 if the user pressed a "normal" key. The AH register contains the scan code of normal keys; extended keys place their codes in the AH register.

Function 2: Read control keys

Function 2 has a completely different task. It reads the status of certain control keys and conditions (e.g., <Insert>). Place the number 2 in the AH register to call the function. The keyboard status can be found in the AL register after the function call.

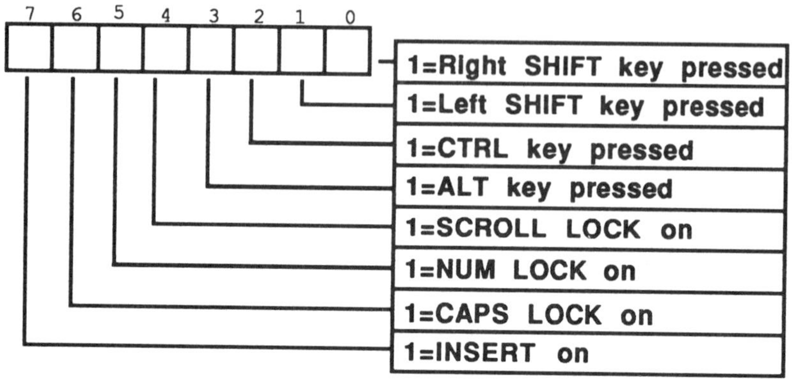

Keyboard status byte

Demonstration programs

The following programs demonstrate the various functions of BIOS keyboard interrupts as presented here. The four programs can be divided into two groups. The first three programs are written in the higher level languages used throughout this book. They call the various functions of BIOS keyboard interrupts for their own uses. The fourth program is an assembler program. It modifies the BIOS keyboard interrupt functions and processing, and acts as a resident program which can be accessed at a keypress.

Checking key status

All three higher level programs make a subroutine or a function available for reading characters from the keyboard. This alone is nothing special, since these languages have their own instructions that serve the same purposes. The important feature of the function is that it accepts other jobs in addition to the original task of reading characters. It displays the status of the keyboard functions <Insert>, <Caps Lock> and <Num Lock> in the upper right hand corner of the screen. This is especially useful for XT and PC owners, since most keyboards don't indicate the key status. AT keyboards and some XT keyboards provide light emitting diodes (LED) which indicate the status of these keys. You never really know if the <Insert> or <Caps Lock> mode is on or not.

Each program begins with a routine which reads the status of the keyboard functions through function 2 of BIOS keyboard interrupt 16H. Since the program only uses the <Insert>, <Caps Lock> and <Num Lock> modes, the program only views the three highest level bits in the keyboard status byte. Based on this status byte, a flag initializes for every keyboard function, which indicates the status of one of these functions or modes within the program. It is reversed when compared with the current mode. For example, if the <Insert> mode is switched off, the flag applying to it changes to OFF. An explanation of this follows below.

Calling the interrupt function

After initializing the internal flags, the actual routine for keyboard reading can be called. It also uses function 2 of the BIOS keyboard interrupt to read the keyboard function status. It then compares the current status of each individual function with the previous status stored in a flag. During its first call after the initialization routine, it determines if the status of all three functions has changed since its previous status. The change in status causes the routine to display the new status on the screen.

This explains the reason for the flag reversal in the initialization routine. It allows display of the keyboard function status on the screen during the first call of the keyboard routine, and not after it changed by pressing a key.

Now the routine can proceed to its actual task and read the keyboard. It uses function 1 of the BIOS keyboard interrupt to detect whether a key is available in the keyboard buffer of BIOS. If this is not the case, the program jumps to the beginning of the routine and reads the keyboard function status again. This creates a loop which runs until a keypress occurs. This loop ensures that any status change is documented immediately on the screen.

Reading the keys

If a character appears in the BIOS keyboard buffer the loop terminates and BIOS keyboard interrupt function 2 reads the key. The last step of this routine tests for an extended key code. If this is the case, the program adds 256 to the code to signal the calling routine that an extended keyboard code was received. Then control returns to the calling routine.

This routine reads characters from the keyboard and displays them on the screen. This process repeats until the user presses a certain key. If the user presses the <Num Lock>, <Caps Lock> or <Insert> key, the screen immediately displays the result.

A centralized keyboard routine as presented here can be used in other programs for additional tasks. For example, with the help of this routine a macro conversion can change one key into a string of characters. Another application could display help text on the screen when the user presses a certain key. Lotus 1-2-3® and dBASE® use this method for displaying help screens.

Note: A small problem occurs with keyboard flag output. Since displaying keyboard flags on the screen changes the cursor's position, subsequent screen output from the program occurs at different locations than expected. These can disturb the screen display. To prevent this, the keyboard routine must determine the current cursor position before the keyboard flag display. Then the routine must restore the cursor position to its old value after displaying keyboard status. The problem of color is very similar. Here the flag output assumes a certain color and the old color must be restored after the output. The problem is that none of the three languages has a command to determine the current color. In Pascal programs for keyboard reading, only a special procedure can set the color by recording the colors in a variable and setting it with a command. With these variables the keyboard routine restores the current color after display of the individual flags.

BASIC listing: KEYB.BAS

```
100 '*****************************************************************'
110 '*                          K E Y B                              *'
120 '*---------------------------------------------------------------*'
130 '*  Task           : makes a subroutine available which          *'
140 '*                   reads a character from the keyboard. The    *'
150 '*                   status of the control keys                  *'
160 '*                   (INSERT, CAPS, NUM) are displayed           *'
170 '*                   on the screen                               *'
180 '*  Author         : MICHAEL TISCHER                             *'
190 '*  developed on   : 7.22.87                                     *'
200 '*  last Update    : 9.21.87                                     *'
210 '*****************************************************************'
220 '
230 CLS : KEY OFF
240 PRINT"WARNING: This Program can only be started if GWBASIC was "
250 PRINT"started from the DOS level with <GWBASIC  /m:60000>."
260 PRINT : PRINT"If this is not the case, please input <s> for Stop."
270 PRINT"Else press any key...";
280 A$ = INKEY$ : IF A$ = "s" THEN END
290 IF A$ = "" THEN 280
300 GOSUB 60000               'install function for Interrupt call
310 CLS                                        'Clear Screen
320 PRINT"TAST (c) 1987 by Michael Tischer" : PRINT
330 PRINT"You can input some characters and change the status of the NUM,"
340 PRINT"CAPS and INSERT mode, where every change is documented in "
350 PRINT"the upper right corner of the display."
360 PRINT"The input of <RETURN> terminates the Program..." : PRINT
370 PRINT"Your Input: ";
380 GOSUB 50000                'initialize keyboard-Flags
390 GOSUB 51000                'read a character
400 IF LEN(Z$) = 2 THEN 390    'on extended Code do nothing
410 PRINT Z$;                  'output characters
420 IF ASC(Z$) <> 13 THEN 390  'on RETURN terminate
430 PRINT
440 END
450 '
50000 '**************************************************************'
50010 '* initialize keyboard-Flags                                   *'
50020 '*------------------------------------------------------------*'
50030 '* Input: none                                                 *'
50040 '* Output: none                                                *'
50050 '* Info   : the Variable Z% is used as a Dummy                 *'
50060 '*          the Status of the keyboard Flags is stored in      *'
50070 '*          variables INSERT%, CAPS% and NUM%                  *'
50080 '**************************************************************'
50090 '
50100 FKT%=2                   'get function number for keyboard status
50110 INR%=&H16                'call BIOS-keyboard-Interrupt 16(h)
50120 CALL IA(INR%,FKT%,FLAGS%,Z%,Z%,Z%,Z%,Z%,Z%,Z%,Z%,Z%,Z%)
50130 IF FLAGS% AND 128 THEN INSERT% = 0 ELSE INSERT% = -1
50140 IF FLAGS% AND 64 THEN CAPS% = 0 ELSE CAPS% = -1
50150 IF FLAGS% AND 32 THEN NUM% = 0 ELSE NUM% = -1
50160 RETURN                   'back to caller
50170 '
51000 '******************************************************************'
```

```
51010 '* get a character from the keyboard and maybe output         *'
51020 '* Flag-Status                                                *'
51030 '*-----------------------------------------------------------*'
51040 '* Input: none                                                *'
51050 '* Output: Z$ = the character read                            *'
51060 '* Info   : the Variable Z% is used as Dummy                  *'
51070 '*          if Z$ is two character long, an extended          *'
51080 '*          keyboard code was input. The first character of the*'
51090 '*          string is in such a case the NUL-character,        *'
51100 '*          and the second character indicates the Code of the *'
51110 '*          extended key                                      *'
51120 '*************************************************************'
51130 '
51140 FKT%=2                  'get function number for keyboard status
51150 INR%=&H16               'call BIOS-keyboard-Interrupt 16(h)
51160 CALL IA(INR%,FKT%,FLAGS%,Z%,Z%,Z%,Z%,Z%,Z%,Z%,Z%,Z%,Z%)
51170 IF INSERT% = ((FLAGS% AND 128) = 128) THEN 51230
51180 INSERT% = NOT INSERT%   'Insert-Status has changed
51190 COLMN% = 75             'Column for Insert-Text
51200 FLAG% = INSERT%         'Status of Insert-Flags
51210 FTEXT$ = "INSERT"       'Flag-Text
51220 GOSUB 52000             'output Flag-Text
51230 IF CAPS% = ((FLAGS% AND 64) = 64) THEN 51290
51240 CAPS% = NOT CAPS%       'Caps-Status has changed
51250 COLMN% = 69             'Column for Caps-Text
51260 FLAG% = CAPS%           'Status of Caps-Flag
51270 FTEXT$ = " CAPS "       'Flag-Text
51280 GOSUB 52000             'output Flag-Text
51290 IF NUM% = ((FLAGS% AND 32) = 32) THEN 51350
51300 NUM% = NOT NUM%         'Num-Status has changed
51310 COLMN% = 66             'Column for Num-Text
51320 FLAG% = NUM%            'Status of Num-Flag
51330 FTEXT$ = "NUM"          'Flag-Text
51340 GOSUB 52000             'output Flag-Text
51350 FKT%=1                  'test function number for characters
51360 INR%=&H16               'call BIOS-keyboard-Interrupt 16(h)
51370 CALL IA(INR%,FKT%,Z%,Z%,Z%,Z%,Z%,Z%,Z%,Z%,Z%,Z%,FLAGREG%)
51380 IF (FLAGREG% AND 64) = 64 THEN 51140'no key --> get Flags
51390 Z$ = INKEY$
51400 RETURN                  'back to caller
51410 '
52000 '*************************************************************'
52010 '* Set Cursor Position                                        *'
52020 '*-----------------------------------------------------------*'
52030 '* Input: FLAG%   = Status of Flags either on or off          *'
52040 '*        FTEXT$  = Flag-Text                                 *'
52050 '*        COLMN%  = is the new column for Cursor              *'
52060 '*        CLINE%  = is the new line for Cursor                *'
52070 '* Output: none                                               *'
52080 '* Info   : the Variable Z% is used as a Dummy                *'
52090 '*************************************************************'
52100 '
52110 CURCLINE% = CSRLIN-1               'record current Cursor line
52120 CURCOLMN% = POS(0)-1               'record current Cursor column
52130 LOCATE 1,COLMN%                    'Cursor position for Flag-Text
52140 IF FLAG% THEN COLOR 0,7 ELSE COLOR 0,0
52150 PRINT FTEXT$
52160 LOCATE CURCLINE%+1,CURCOLMN%+1     'set old Cursor position
52170 FKT%=2                  'set function number for Cursor position
52180 INR%=&H10               'call BIOS-Video-Interrupt 10(h)
52190 SEITE% = 0              'set Cursor in display page 0
52200 CALL IA(INR%,FKT%,Z%,SEITE%,Z%,Z%,Z%,CURCLINE%, CURCOLMN%,Z%,Z%,Z%,Z%)
52210 COLOR 7,0
52220 RETURN                  'back to caller
52230 '
60000 '*************************************************************'
60010 '* initialize the Routine for Interrupt-call                  *'
60020 '*-----------------------------------------------------------*'
60030 '* Input: none                                                *'
60040 '* Output: IA is the Start address of the Interrupt-Routine    *'
```

```
60050 '******************************************************************'
60060 '
60070 IA=60000!        'Start address of the Routine in the BASIC-Segment
60080 DEF SEG          'set BASIC-Segment
60090 RESTORE 60130
60100 FOR I% = 0 TO 160 : READ X% : POKE IA+I%,X% : NEXT  'poke Routine
60110 RETURN           'back to caller
60120 '
60130 DATA  85,139,236, 30,  6,139,118, 30,139,  4,232,140,  0,139,118
60140 DATA  12,139, 60,139,118,  8,139,  4, 61,255,255,117,  2,140,216
60150 DATA 142,192,139,118, 28,138, 36,139,118, 26,138,  4,139,118, 24
60160 DATA 138, 60,139,118, 22,138, 28,139,118, 20,138, 44,139,118, 18
60170 DATA 138, 12,139,118, 16,138, 52,139,118, 14,138, 20,139,118, 10
60180 DATA 139, 52, 85,205, 33, 93, 86,156,139,118, 12,137, 60,139,118
60190 DATA  28,136, 36,139,118, 26,136,  4,139,118, 24,136, 60,139,118
60200 DATA  22,136, 28,139,118, 20,136, 44,139,118, 18,136, 12,139,118
60210 DATA  16,136, 52,139,118, 14,136, 20,139,118,  8,140,192,137,  4
60220 DATA  88,139,118,  6,137,  4, 88,139,118, 10,137,  4,  7, 31, 93
60230 DATA 202, 26,  0, 91, 46,136, 71, 66,233,108,255
```

Pascal listing: KEYP.PAS

```
{*******************************************************************}
{*                              K E Y P                            *}
{*-----------------------------------------------------------------*}
{*    Task             : makes a function available for reading a  *}
{*                       character from the keyboard and outputting *}
{*                       the Status of the control keys (INSERT,    *}
{*                       CAPS, NUM) on the display.                 *}
{*-----------------------------------------------------------------*}
{*    Author           : MICHAEL TISCHER                           *}
{*    developed on     :  07/08/87                                 *}
{*    last Update      :  06/10/89                                 *}
{*******************************************************************}

program KEYP;


Uses  Crt,Dos;                              { Add Crt, Dos units }

{$V-}                              { Suppresses string length check }

type FlagText = string[6];         { used for passing the Flag-Name }


const FZ       = 1;              { Line in which the Flags are output }
      FS       = 65;             { Column from which Flags are output }
      FlagFore = 0;                      { Foreground color of Flags }
      FlagBck  = 7;                      { Background color of Flags }

       {** BIOS keyboard status bits **********************************}
       SCRL = 16;                                   { ScrollLock bit }
       NUML = 32;                                      { NumLock bit }
       CAPL = 64;                                     { CapsLock bit }
       INS = 128;                                        { Insert bit}
       {** Codes of some keys as presented by GETKEY *****************}
      BEL     = 7;                        { Code for bell character }
      BS      = 8;                   { Code for Backspace character }
      TAB     = 9;                          { Code for Tab character }
      LF      = 10;                             { Code for Linefeed }
      CR      = 13;                               { Code for Return }
      ESC     = 27;                     { Code for Escape character }
      F1      = 315;                              { Code for F1 key }
      F2      = 316;                              { Code for F2 key }
      F3      = 317;                              { Code for F3 key }
      F4      = 318;                              { Code for F4 key }
      F5      = 319;                              { Code for F5 key }
      F6      = 320;                              { Code for F6 key }
      F7      = 321;                              { Code for F7 key }
```

```
      F8      = 322;                          { Code for F8 key }
      F9      = 323;                          { Code for F9 key }
      F10     = 324;                         { Code for F10 key }
      CUP     = 328;                       { Code for Cursor up }
      CLEFT   = 331;                     { Code for Cursor left  }
      CRIGHT  = 333;                     { Code for Cursor right }
      CDOWN   = 328;                      { Code for Cursor down }

var Insert,                              { Status of INSERT flag }
    Num,                                    { Status of NUM flag }
    Caps     : boolean;                    { Status of CAPS flag }
    ForeColor,                         { current foreground color }
    BckColor,                          { current background color }
    key     : integer;                          { Code of key read }

{*******************************************************************}
{* NEGFLAG: negate Flag and output Text                            *}
{* Input : s.u.                                                    *}
{* Output : the new Status of the Flags (true = on, false = off)   *}
{*******************************************************************}

function NegFlag(Flag     : boolean;     { the last Status of the Flags }
                 FlagReg,       { current Status of the Flag (0 = off) }
                 Column,           { Column for the name of the Flags }
                 Cline    : integer;  { Line for the Names of the Flags }
                 Text     : FlagText) : boolean;     { Name of the Flags }

var CurCline,                                      { current Line }
    CurColumn : integer;                          { current Column }

begin
 if (Flag and (FlagReg = 0)) or                      { test if Status }
    (not(Flag) and (FlagReg <> 0)) then    { of the Flags has changed }
  begin                                                       { YES }
   CurCline := WhereY;                          { record current Line }
   CurColumn := WhereX;                       { record current Column }
   gotoxy(Column, Cline);           { Cursor to Position for Flag-Name }
   if FlagReg = 0 then                              { is Flag reset? }
    begin                                                     { YES }
     NegFlag := false;            { Result of the function : Flag off }
     textcolor(0);                        { Foreground color is black }
     textbackground(0);                   { Background color is black }
    end
   else
    begin                                            { Flag is now on }
     NegFlag:=true;                { Result of the function : flag on }
     textcolor(FlagFore);              { Foreground color is FLAGFORE}
     textbackground(FlagBck)           { Background color is FLAGBCK }
    end;
   write(Text);                             { Output name of the flag }
   gotoxy(CurColumn, CurCline);         { restore old cursor position }
   textcolor(ForeColor);               { restore old foreground color }
   textbackground(BckColor)            { restore old background color }
  end
  else
   NegFlag := Flag                    { Status of flags has not changed }
end;

{*******************************************************************}
{* GETKEY: Read a character and output the flag status             *}
{* Input : none                                                    *}
{* Output : Code of the key < 256 : normal key                     *}
{*                          >= 256 : extended key                  *}
{*******************************************************************}

function Getkey : integer;

var Regs : Registers;           { Register variable for interrupt call }
    keyRec :  boolean;            { indicates if key already received }
```

```
begin
 keyRec := false;                                     { no key received }
 repeat
  Regs.ah := $2;           { read function number for keyboard status }
  intr($16, Regs);                    { call BIOS keyboard interrupt }

  {** Adjust flags to new status **********************************}
  Insert := NegFlag(Insert, Regs.al and INS, FS+9, FZ, 'INSERT');
  Caps := NegFlag(Caps, Regs.al and CAPL, FS+3, FZ, ' CAPS ');
  Num := NegFlag(Num, Regs.al and NUML, FS, FZ, 'NUM');
  Regs.ah := $1;             { function number for character ready? }
  intr($16, Regs);                    { call BIOS keyboard interrupt }
  if (Regs.flags and FZero = 0) then
   begin
    KeyRec := true;
    Regs.ah := 0;
    intr($16, Regs);
    if (Regs.al = 0)                            { is zero flag set ? }
     then Getkey := Regs.ah or $100                          { YES }
     else Getkey := Regs.al;                                  { NO }
   end;
 until keyRec;                       { repeat until a key is received }
end;

{**********************************************************************}
{* INIKEY: initialize keyboard flags                                  *}
{* Input : none                                                       *}
{* Output : none                                                      *}
{* Info    : the keyboard flags are inverted from the current         *}
{*           status. This outputs their current                       *}
{*           status during the next call of the GETKEY function.      *}
{**********************************************************************}

procedure Inikey;

var Regs : Registers;          { Register variable for interrupt call }

begin
 Regs.ah := $2;            { Read function number for keyboard status }
 intr($16, Regs);                     { call BIOS keyboard interrupt }
 if (Regs.al and INS <> 0) then Insert := false        { INSERT flag  }
                           else Insert := true;                { set }
 if (Regs.al and CAPL <> 0) then Caps   := false         { CAPS flag }
                            else Caps   := true;               { set }
 if (Regs.al and NUML <> 0) then Num    := false          { NUM flag }
                            else Num    := true                { set }
end;

{**********************************************************************}
{* SCOLOR: sets foreground and background colors for display          *}
{* Input : see below                                                  *}
{* Output : none                                                      *}
{* Var.    : the color is stored in the global variables FORECOLOR    *}
{*           and BCKCOLOR                                             *}
{* Info    : this procedure must be called for setting the color      *}
{*           so that after the output of the keyboard flag status,    *}
{*           the current text color can be restored                   *}
{*           since in TURBO no functions exist for sensing            *}
{*           this color                                               *}
{**********************************************************************}

procedure Scolor(Foreground, Background : integer);

begin
 ForeColor := Foreground;                  { Record foreground color }
 BckColor := Background;                   { Record background color }
 textcolor(Foreground);                       { Set foreground color }
 textbackground(Background)                   { Set background color }
end;
```

```
{*********************************************************************}
{*                        MAIN PROGRAM                               *}
{*********************************************************************}

begin
 Inikey;                                { Initialize keyboard flags }
 Scolor(7,0);                            { Color is white on black }
 clrscr;                                            { Clear screen }
 writeln(#13#10'KEYP (c) 1987 by Michael Tischer');
 writeln(#13#10'A few characters can be input now and switch '+
        'INSERT-, CAPS- or NUM-');
 writeln('mode on or off. The status of the three '+
        'modes is always displayed in');
 writeln('the upper right corner of the screen.');
 writeln('Pressing the <RETURN> or the <F1>-key terminates the '+
        'program...');
 write(#13#10'Your Input: ');
 repeat                                               { Input loop }
  key := Getkey;                                         { Get key }
  if (key < 256) then write(chr(key))          { Output (if normal) }
 until (key = 13) or (key = F1);           { Repeat until F1 or CR }
 writeln;
end.
```

C listing: KEYC.C

```
/*********************************************************************/
/*                               K E Y C                             */
/*-------------------------------------------------------------------*/
/*    Task           : provides a function for reading a            */
/*                     character from the keyboard and to output    */
/*                     the Status of the control keys (INSERT,      */
/*                     CAPS, NUM) on the display.                   */
/*-------------------------------------------------------------------*/
/*    Author         : MICHAEL TISCHER                               */
/*    developed on   : 8/13/87                                       */
/*    last update    : 6/09/89                                       */
/*-------------------------------------------------------------------*/
/*    (MICROSOFT C)                                                  */
/*    Creation       : MSC TASTC;                                    */
/*                     LINK TASTC;                                   */
/*    Call           : TASTC                                         */
/*-------------------------------------------------------------------*/
/*    (BORLAND TURBO C)                                              */
/*    Creation      : Make sure that Case-sensitive link is OFF in   */
/*                    the Options menu/Linker option                 */
/*                    Select RUN menu                                */
/*********************************************************************/

#include <dos.h>                             /* include Header-Files */
#include <io.h>
#include <bios.h>

/*== Type definitions ===============================================*/

typedef unsigned char byte;                         /* Create a byte */

/*== Constants ======================================================*/

/*-- Bit layout in BIOS keyboard status -----------------------------*/

#define SCRL 16                                    /* ScrollLock bit */
#define NUML 32                                       /* NumLock bit */
#define CAPL 64                                      /* CapsLock bit */
#define INS 128                                        /* Insert bit */

#define FALSE 0                      /* Constants make reading of the */
#define TRUE 1                      /* Program text easier           */
```

```
#define FZ        0        /* Line in which the Flags should be output  */
#define FS        65          /* Column, in which Flags will be output */
#define FlagColour 0x70            /* black characters on white ground */

/*-- Codes of some keys as returned by GETKEY() ---------------------*/
#define BEL       7                            /* Bell character code */
#define BS        8                             /* Backspace key code */
#define TAB       9                                   /* Tab key code */
#define LF        10                                 /* Linefeed code */
#define CR        13                               /* Return key code */
#define ESC       27                               /* Escape key code */
#define F1        315                                  /* F1 key code */
#define F2        316                                  /* F2 key code */
#define F3        317                                  /* F3 key code */
#define F4        318                                  /* F4 key code */
#define F5        319                                  /* F5 key code */
#define F6        320                                  /* F6 key code */
#define F7        321                                  /* F7 key code */
#define F8        322                                  /* F8 key code */
#define F9        323                                  /* F9 key code */
#define F10       324                                 /* F10 key code */
#define CUP       328                               /* Cursor up code */
#define CLEFT     331                             /* Cursor left code */
#define CRIGHT    333                            /* Cursor right code */
#define CDOWN     328                                  /* Cursor down */

/*-- global Variables -----------------------------------------------*/

byte Insert,                               /* Status of INSERT flag */
     Num,                                     /* Status of NUM flag */
     Caps;                                   /* Status of CAPS flag */

/********************************************************************/
/* GETPAGE: get the current display page                            */
/* Input  : none                                                    */
/* Output : see below                                               */
/********************************************************************/

byte GETPAGE()

{
 union REGS Register;         /* Register variable for interrupt call */

 Register.h.ah = 15;                              /* function number */
 int86(0x10, &Register, &Register);          /* call interrupt 10(h) */
 return(Register.h.bh);            /* Number of current display page */
}

/********************************************************************/
/* SETPOS: sets the position of cursor in current display page      */
/* Input  : see below                                               */
/* Output : none                                                    */
/* Info   : the position of the blinking cursor changes             */
/*          with the call of this function only if                  */
/*          display page indicated is the current display page      */
/********************************************************************/

void SetPos(byte Column, byte Line)

{
 union REGS Register;         /* Register-Variable for Interrupt call */

 Register.h.ah = 2;                               /* function number */
 Register.h.bh = GETPAGE();                          /* Display Page */
 Register.h.dh = Line;                               /* Display Line */
 Register.h.dl = Column;                           /* Display Column */
 int86(0x10, &Register, &Register);          /* call Interrupt 10(h) */
}

/********************************************************************/
```

```
/* GETPOS: Gets the Position of Cursor in the current Display Page    */
/* Input : none                                                        */
/* Output : see below                                                  */
/**********************************************************************/

void GetPos(byte * CurColumn, byte * CurLine)

{
 union REGS Register;        /* Register variable for interrupt call */

 Register.h.ah = 3;                              /* function number */
 Register.h.bh = GETPAGE();                         /* Display page */
  int86(0x10, &Register, &Register);        /* call Interrupt 10(h) */
 *CurColumn = Register.h.dl;              /* Result of the function */
 *CurLine = Register.h.dh;                /* Read from the register */
}

/**********************************************************************/
/* WRITECHAR: writes a character with an Attribute to                 */
/*            the current cursor position in current display page     */
/* Input : see below                                                   */
/* Output : none                                                       */
/**********************************************************************/

void WriteChar(char Zcharacter, byte Colour)

{
 union REGS Register;        /* Register variable for interrupt call */

 Register.h.ah = 9;                              /* function number */
 Register.h.bh = GETPAGE();                         /* Display Page */
 Register.h.al = Zcharacter;           /* the character for output */
 Register.h.bl = Colour;         /* Color of character to be output */
 Register.x.cx = 1;                 /* output character only once  */
 int86(0x10, &Register, &Register);         /* call Interrupt 10(h) */
}

/**********************************************************************/
/* WRITETEXT: write a character chain with constant color             */
/*            starting at a certain location in the current           */
/*            Display Page                                             */
/* Input : see below                                                   */
/* Output : none                                                       */
/* Info    : Text is a Pointer to a character-Vector which            */
/*           contains the Text to be output and is terminated with    */
/*            a '\0' character.                                        */
/**********************************************************************/

void WriteText(byte Column, byte Line, char *Text, byte Colour)

{
 union REGS InRegister,
           OutRegister;      /* Register variable for interrupt call */

 SetPos(Column, Line);                                /* set Cursor */
 InRegister.h.ah = 14;                           /* function number */
 InRegister.h.bh = GetPage( );                      /* Display Page */
 while (*Text)                 /* output Text until '\0' character */
  {
   WriteChar(' ', Colour);          /* Indicate color for character  */
   InRegister.h.al = *Text++;            /* the character for output */
   int86(0x10, &InRegister, &OutRegister);         /* call Interrupt */
  }
}

/**********************************************************************/
/* CLS: erase current Display Page                                     */
/* Input : none                                                        */
/* Output : none                                                       */
/**********************************************************************/
```

```
void Cls()

{
 union REGS Register;        /* Register variable for interrupt call */

 Register.h.ah = 6;                   /* function number for scroll up */
 Register.h.al = 0;                              /* 0 stand for clear */
 Register.h.bh = 7;              /* white letters on black background */
 Register.x.cx = 0;                        /* upper left display corner  */
 Register.h.dh = 24;                      /* Coordinates of the lower  */
 Register.h.dl = 79;                           /* right display corner */
 int86(0x10, &Register, &Register);      /* call BIOS-Video-Interrupt */
}

/**********************************************************************/
/* NEGFLAG: negate Flag and output Text                               */
/* Input : see below                                                  */
/* Output : the new Status of Flags (TRUE = on, FALSE = off)          */
/**********************************************************************/

byte NegFlag(byte Flag, unsigned int FlagReg,
             byte Column, byte Line, char * Text)


{
byte CurLine,                                         /* current Line */
     CurColumn,                                     /* current Column */
     Colour;                                /* for Output of Flag-Text */

 if (!(Flag == (FlagReg != 0)))                   /* did Flag change? */
  {                                                            /* YES */
   GetPos(&CurColumn, &CurLine);       /* get current Cursor position */
   WriteText(Column, Line, Text, (Flag) ? 0 : FlagColour);
   SetPos(CurColumn, CurLine);             /* set old Cursor position */
   return(Flag ^1);                        /* reverse Bit 1 of Flags  */
  }
 else return(Flag);                     /* everything remains the same */
}

/**********************************************************************/
/* KEYREADY: Tests for a character from the keyboard                  */
/* Input:  none                                                       */
/* Output: TRUE if a key is pressed, otherwise FALSE                  */
/**********************************************************************/

int KeyReady()

{
#ifdef __TURBOC__

  struct REGPACK Register;

  Register.r_ax = 1 << 8;
  intr(0x16, &Register);
  return(! (Register.r_flags & 64) );

#else

  return( bios keybrd( KEYBRD READY ) );

#endif
}

/**********************************************************************/
/* GETKEY: Read a character and Output Flag-Status                    */
/* Input : none                                                       */
/* Output : Code of key read  < 256 : normal key                      */
/*                           >= 256 : extended ke y                   */
/**********************************************************************/
```

```
unsigned int GetKey()

{
 union REGS Register;       /* Register  Variable for Interrupt call */

 do
 {
 Register.h.ah = 2;       /* read function number for keyboard status */
 int86(0x16, &Register, &Register);   /* call BIOS keyboard interrupt*/
 Insert = NegFlag(Insert, Register.h.al & INS, FS+9, FZ, "INSERT");
 Caps = NegFlag(Caps, Register.h.al & CAPL, FS+3, FZ, " CAPS ");
 Num = NegFlag(Num, Register.h.al & NUML, FS, FZ, "NUM");
 }
 while ( !KeyReady() );
 Register.h.ah = 0;                  /* read function number for key */
 int86(0x16, &Register, &Register);    /*call BIOS-keyboard-Interrupt*/
 return((Register.h.al) ? Register.h.al : Register.h.ah | 256);
}

/*********************************************************************/
/* INIKEY: initialize keyboard-Flags                                 */
/* Input : none                                                      */
/* Output : none                                                     */
/* Info    : the keyboard-Flags are reversed compared with the       */
/*           current status. This makes it possible that their       */
/*           current Status is output on the next call of the        */
/*           GETKEY-function.                                        */
/*********************************************************************/

void Inikey()

{
 union REGS Register;        /* Register variable for interrupt call */

 Register.h.ah = 2;       /* read function number for keyboard status */
 int86(0x16, &Register, &Register);   /* call BIOS-keyboard-Interrupt*/
 Insert = (Register.h.al & INS) ? FALSE : TRUE ;  /* reverse the     */
 Caps = (Register.h.al & CAPL) ? FALSE : TRUE ;   /* current content */
 Num = (Register.h.al & NUML) ? FALSE : TRUE ;
}

/*********************************************************************/
/**                          MAIN PROGRAM                           **/
/*********************************************************************/

void main()

{
 unsigned int key;

 Cls();                                            /* Clear Screen */
 SetPos(0,0);                 /* Cursor to left upper screen corner */
 printf("KEY (c) 1987 by Michael Tischer\n\n");
 printf("You can input some characters and at the same time change ");
 printf("INSERT-, CAPS-\nor NUM-status. Every change ");
 printf("is displayed in the upper right corner of the screen.\n");
 printf("\n<RETURN> or <F1> terminates the Input...\n\n");
 printf("Your Input: ");
 Inikey();                           /* initialize keyboard-Flags */
 do
 {
   if ((key = Getkey()) < 256)                         /* read key */
    printf("%c", (char) key);                /* output (if normal) */
  }
 while (!(key == CR || key == F1));         /* repeat until F1 or CR */
 printf("\n");
}
```

A resident interrupt driver

The next assembler program is a *resident* interrupt driver. Once a resident program is installed in memory, other programs or data cannot overwrite it. Another reason for the name resident lies in the program's ability to point to an interrupt in its own routine. Instead of DOS, BIOS or another interrupt routine called up to now, the program calls its own interrupt driver routine. Before examining how this is done, the assembler program should be explained.

The SHOWCLK program displays the current time on the screen every time the user presses a certain key after installing it. This occurs until another key is depressed. The key which causes the time to be displayed must be passed to the program in the command line during its call. For example, entering the following at the DOS prompt invokes the program and tells the program to display the time when the user presses the <F10> key on the XT, or the <F8> key on the AT keyboard. When the key is pressed, the time appears on the screen at line 1 starting at column 40:

```
showclk 68 /l1 /c40
```

The following removes the SHOWCLK program from memory (note the lack of parameters):

```
showclk
```

The only stipulation is that the actuating key must be one that generates an extended key code (e.g., a cursor key or function key). The program sets the default clock position to the upper right corner of the screen. This can be changed by passing parameters in the command line during the program call. Another facet of the program is its ability to re-install itself during a new call, if the user desires.

```
;***********************************************************************;
;*                            S H O W C L K                            *;
;*---------------------------------------------------------------------*;
;*    Task           : Outputs the time on the display after pressing*;
;*                     a key which generates an extended key code    *;
;*                     stops when another key is pressed             *;
;*---------------------------------------------------------------------*;
;*    Author         : MICHAEL TISCHER                                *;
;*    developed on   :  8/1/87                                        *;
;*    last Update    : 9/21/87                                        *;
;*---------------------------------------------------------------------*;
;*    assembly       : MASM SHOWCLK                                   *;
;*                     LINK SHOWCLK                                   *;
;*                     EXE2BIN SHOWCLK SHOWCLK.COM                    *;
;*---------------------------------------------------------------------*;
;*    Call         : SHOWCLK [Key-code] [/lLine] [/cColumn]           *;
;***********************************************************************;

;== Constants =========================================================

      TAB    equ 9
      LF     equ 10
      CR     equ 13

;== here starts the actual Program ==============================
```

```
code       segment para 'CODE'     ;Definition of the CODE-Segment

           org 100h

           assume cs:code, ds:code, es:code, ss:code

start:     jmp  showinit           ;Call of the Initialization-Routine

;== Data (remain in memory) ========================================

alterint  equ this dword          ;old interrupt vector 16(h)
intaltofs dw (?)                  ;Offset address interrupt vector 16(h)
intaltseg dw (?)                  ;Segment address interrupt vector 16(h)

extkey    db (1)                  ;extended keyboard-code, on which
keycode   db (?)                  ;the program is called

linepos   equ this word
column    db 75                   ;Line and column in which the time
line      db 0                    ;is output

buffer    dw 5 dup (?)            ;stores the characters from the clock

;== this is the new kyboard-interrupt (remains in memory) ==========

newint     proc far

           jmp  short newi_1

           db "MT"                 ;Identification of the program

newi_1:    or   ah,ah              ;read character (Function 0)?
           je   newi_2             ;YES --> get character and test
           jmp  aint               ;NO --> call old interrupt

newi_2:    pushf                   ;for smulation of an interrupt call
           call cs:[alterint]      ;call old interrupt
           cmp  ax,cs:word ptr extkey ;was it the specified key?
           je   showtime           ;YES --> display clock
           jmp  aiend              ;NO --> back

           ;-- the specified key was activated ----------------------

showtime:  pushf                   ;all registers which are changed
           push ax                 ; must be stored
           push bx
           push cx
           push dx
           push di
           push si
           push es
           push ds

           cld                     ;on sring commands count up
           mov  ah,15              ;read current display page
           int  10h                ;call BIOS video-interrupt
           mov  ah,3               ;read current cursor position
           int  10h                ;call BIOS video-interrupt
           push dx                 ;store on the stack
           push cs                 ;Code-sgment to the stack
           pop  ds                 ;return as DS
           mov  dx,linepos         ;set cursor position
           mov  ah,2               ;for the time
           int  10h                ;call BIOS video-interrupt
           push cs                 ;Code-segment to the stack
           pop  es                 ;return as ES
           mov  cx,5               ;read 5 characters
           mov  di,offset buffer   ;Address of the character-buffer
getz:      mov  ah,8               ;read 1 character
           int  10h                ;call BIOS video-interrupt
```

```
        stosw                   ;store character in the buffer
        inc  dl                 ;next display column
        mov  ah,2               ;set cursor position
        int  10h                ;call BIOS video-interrupt
        loop getz               ;get next character
        mov  dx,linepos         ;set cursor position
        mov  ah,2               ;for the time
        int  10h                ;call BIOS video-interrupt
        mov  ah,2CH             ;get time from DOS
        int  21h                ;call DOS-interrupt
        mov  bl,70h             ;color of clock: inverted
        push cx                 ;record minutes
        mov  al,ch              ;change hours to ASCII
        call bia                ;and output
        mov  al,":"             ;output colon
        call prz
        pop  ax                 ;get minutes
             ;function number for character output
        xchg bl,ah              ;exchange AH and BL
        int  10h                ;call BIOS video-interrupt
        inc  dl                 ;next column
        mov  ah,2               ;set cursor position
        int  10h                ;call BIOS video-interrupt
        dec  di                 ;output another character ?
        jne  storz              ;YES --> STORZ
        pop  dx                 ;get old cursor position
        mov  ah,2               ;and set again
        int  10h                ;call BIOS video-interrupt

        pop  ds                 ;restore all stored registers
        pop  es
        pop  si
        pop  di
        pop  dx
        pop  cx
        pop  bx
        pop  ax
        popf
        xor   ah,ah
        jmp   newi_2

aint:   pushf                   ;simulate interrupt-routine
        call cs:[alterint]      ;call next keyboard-routine
aiend:  ret  2                  ;flag-register

newint  endp

;-- BIA: change binary to ASCII and output -------------------------
;-- Input  : AL = the number to be converted
;-- Output : none
;-- Register : CX, AX, DL and FLAGS are changed

bia     proc near

        mov  cl,10              ;we work in the decimal system
        xor  ah,ah              ;prepare 16 bit division
        div  cl                 ;divide AX by CL
        or   ax,3030h           ;change result to ASCII
        push ax                 ;store number
        call prz                ;output character and advance cursor
        pop  ax                 ;read number
        mov  al,ah              ;move character to AL
        call prz                ;output character and advance cursor
        ret                     ;back to caller

bia     endp

;-- PRZ: output character and increment cursor position ------------
;-- Input    : BH = Display page for Output
;--            AL = the character for output
```

```
;--           BL = Attribute (color) of the character
;-- Output   : none
;-- Register : CX, AH, DL and FLAGS are changed

prz       proc near

          mov  ah,9              ;function number for character output
          mov  cx,1              ;output character only once
          int  10h               ;call BIOS video-interrupt
          mov  ah,3              ;read current cursor position
          int  10h               ;call BIOS video-interrupt
          inc  dl                ;increment cursor column
          mov  ah,2              ;set
          int  10h               ;call BIOS video-interrupt
          ret                    ;back to caller

prz       endp

instend   equ this byte          ;if SHOWCLK installed, memory can be
                                 ;released starting at this location

;== Data (can be overwritten by DOS) ========================

badp      db "Invalid Parameter",CR,LF,"$"
installm  db "SHOWCLK (c) 1987 by Michael Tischer",13,10,13,10
          db "SHOWCLK was installed and can be deactivated ",13,10
          db "with a new call  ",13,10
          db "(but without Parameters)",CR,LF,"$"

deactivm  db "SHOWCLK was deactivated",CR,LF,"$"
allinm    db "SHOWCLK is already installed",CR,LF,"$"
noinstm   db "no SHOWCLK installed",CR,LF,"$"

partab    dw 63 dup (?)          ;Address of command line parameter

;== program (can be overwritten by DOS) ======================

deactivate label near             ;turn SHOWCLK off

          mov  ax,3516h          ;get content of interrupt vector 16
          int  21h               ;call DOS-Function
          cmp  word ptr es:[bx+2],"TM" ;test if SHOWCLK-program
          jne  noinst            ;SHOWCLK not  installed --> End

          mov  dx,es:intaltofs   ;Offset address of interrupt 16(h)
          mov  ax,es:intaltseg   ;Segment address of interrupt 16(h)
          mov  ds,ax             ;to DS
          mov  ax,2516h          ;reset content of
          int  21h               ;interrupt vector 16(h) old routine

          mov  ah,49h            ;release storage
          int  21h               ;of old SHOWCL again

          push cs                ;store CS on the Stack
          pop  ds                ;restore DS

entfe:    mov  dx,offset deactivm ;Message: program removed
          xor  al,al             ;program performed correctly
          jmp  showend           ;to end of program

noinst:   mov  dx,offset noinstm  ;Error-Message: no SHOWCLK installed
          jmp  short noinerr     ;output Error-Message and terminate

;-- Start and Initialization-Routine --------------------------------

showinit  proc near

          cld                    ;on String commands count up
          mov  di,offset partab  ;Address of Parameter-Table
```

```
          call parmtest            ;count Parameter/determine Address
          or   dl,dl               ;if no Parameter indicated
          je   deactivate          ;YES --> remove last SHOWCL

          ;evaluate Parameter ----------------------------------------

          mov  bx,offset partab    ;Address of the Parameter-Table
paraout:  mov  si,[bx]             ;get Address of a Parameter
          lodsw                    ;get first two chars of parameter
          and  ah,11011111b        ;lower case letters --> upper case
          cmp  ax,"L/"             ;is it line indication ?
          je   getline             ;YES --> GETLINE
          cmp  ax,"C/"             ;is it column indication?
          je   getcolumn           ;YES --> GETCOLUMN

          ;-- Parameter must be Key code ------------------------

          cmp  extkey,0            ;Key code discovered?
          je   badpara             ;YES --> Error

          push bx                  ;save Pointer in PARTAB
          push dx                  ;save remaining number of Parameters
          sub  si,2                ;set SI to beginning of number
          call asciibin            ;convert Code to binary
          pop  dx                  ;get remaining number of Parameters
          pop  bx                  ;get Pointer in PARTAB

          jc   badpara             ;no number found  --> Error
          or   ah,ah               ;number larger than 255?
          jne  badpara             ;YES --> wrong number
          mov  keycode,al          ;number o.k. record it
          mov  extkey,0            ;announce Key code discovery

nextpara: add  bx,2                ;Address of the next PARTAB-Element
          dec  dl                  ;decrease Parameter counter
          jne  paraout             ;last Parameter? NO --> continue
          jmp  short install       ;Parameter o.k. --> install program

getline:  mov  di,offset line      ;Address of Line-Variable
          mov  dh,24               ;Maximum value for Line
          jmp  pareval             ;evaluate Parameter

getcolumn:mov  di,offset column    ;Address of the Column-Variable
          mov  dh,75               ;Maximum value for column

pareval:  push bx                  ;store Pointer in PARTAB
          push dx                  ;store remaining number of Parameters
          call asciibin            ;convert Code to binary
          pop  dx                  ;get remaining number of Parameters
          pop  bx                  ;get Pointer in PARTAB

          jc   badpara             ;no number found --> Error
          or   ah,ah               ;Number larger than 255?
          jne  badpara             ;YES --> wrong number
          cmp  al,dh               ;Number larger than permitted?
          ja   badpara             ;YES --> wrong number
          mov  [di],al             ;Number o.k. therefore store
          jmp  short nextpara      ;evaluate next prameter

allinst:  mov  dx,offset allinm    ;Error-Message: already installed
          jmp  short noinerr       ;output Error-Message and terminate

badpara:  mov  dx,offset badp      ;Error-Message: invalid parameter
noinerr:  mov  al,1                ;Error-Code
          jmp  showend             ;terminate program

install:  cmp  extkey,0            ;Key-code discovered?
          jne  badpara             ;NO --> Error
          mov  ax,3516h            ;get content of interrupt vector 16
          int  21h                 ;call DOS-function
```

```
          cmp  word ptr es:[bx+2],"TM" ;test if already installed
          je   allinst              ;YES --> Error

          mov  intaltseg,es         ;segment and offset address of the
          mov  intaltofs,bx         ;stored-interrupt vector 16(h)

          mov  dx,offset newint     ;Offset address new interrupt routine
          mov  ax,2516h             ;change content interrupt vector 16
          int  21h                  ;to user routine

          mov  dx,offset installm ;Message: program installed
          mov  ah,9                 ;output function number for string
          int  21h                  ;call DOS-function

          ;-- only the PSP, the new interrupt-Routine and the ----------
          ;-- Data must remain resident.

          mov  dx,offset instend  ;calculate number of paragraphs
          mov  cl,4                 ; (each 16 Bytes) at the disposal
          shr  dx,cl                ; of the program
          inc  dx
          mov  ax,3100h             ;terminate program with End-Code 0
          int  21h                  ;remain resident

showend:  mov  ah,9                 ;output string
          int  21h                  ;call DOS-function
          mov  ah,4Ch               ;function number for program
          int  21h                  ;terminate program with End-Code

showinit  endp                      ;End of PROG-procedure

;-- ASCIIBIN: convert ASCII number to binary (max. 16 Bit) ------------
;-- Input    : DS:SI = Address of Number as ASCII-string
;-- Output   : AX = the converted Number
;--            Carry-Flag = 1 : Number too large
;-- Register : AX, BX, CX, SI and FLAGS are changed
;-- Info     : the ASCII-string must be ended with Code 0

asciibin  proc near

          xor  bh,bh                ;Hi-Byte of every position
          mov  cx,10                ;we use decimal system
          xor  ax,ax                ;preliminary result
nx_num:   mov  bl,[si]              ;get next number
          or   bl,bl                ;NUL-Code (End)?
          je   ab_ende              ;YES --> number converted
          cmp  bl,"0"               ;test if number
          jb   ab_ret               ;NO --> Error
          cmp  bl,"9"               ;test if number
          ja   ab_err               ;NO --> Error
          mul  cx                   ;preliminary Number * 10
          jc   ab_ret               ;Number > 65535 --> Error
          and  bl,1111b             ;convert number to binary
          add  ax,bx                ;add to preliminary Number
          inc  si                   ;process next number
          jmp  short nx_num

ab_ende:  clc                       ;no Error
          ret                       ;back to caller

ab_err:   stc                       ;Error
ab_ret:   ret                       ;back to caller

asciibin  endp

;-- PARMTEST: capture Parameter in the Command Line -----------------
;-- Input    : DS:0000 = Address of PSP
;-- Output   : DL = number of parameters found
;-- Register : AX, CX, DX, SI and FLAGS are changed
```

```
;-- Info     : Address of every parameter is stored in Array-PARTAB as
;--             Offset address to DS. In addition behind every
;--             parameter an ASCII-Code 0 is stored.

parmtest  proc near

          cld                        ;on string commands count up
          xor  dx,dx                 ;number of parameters found
          mov  si,80h                ;address where number of characters
                                     ;of the command line is stored in PSP
          mov  cl,byte ptr [si]      ;get number of character
          or   cl,cl                 ;have parameters been passed?
          je   parmtend              ;NO --> End

          inc  si                    ;SI points to start of command line
          xor  ch,ch                 ;in CX is the number of characters
getez:    lodsb                      ;move next character to AL
          cmp  al," "                ;is it a space ?
          je   space                 ;YES --> SPACE
          cmp  al,TAB                ;is it a Tab-character?
          je   space                 ;YES --> SPACE

          ;-- no Space or Tabulator --------------------------

          or   dh,dh                 ;was last character space ?
          jne  nextz                 ;NO --> process next character

          inc  dl                    ;increment number parameters found
          not  dh                    ;indicates no " " or TAB
          mov  ax,si                 ;calculate address of
          dec  ax                    ;parameter
          stosw                      ;store in parameter-Table

nextz:    loop getez                 ;get next character
          mov  byte ptr [si],0       ;NUL-character as parameter-End

parmtend: ret                        ;back to caller

space:    or   dh,dh                 ;was last character space character?
          je   nextz                 ;YES --> process next character

          ;-- found next parameter -----------------------------

          xor  dh,dh                 ;this character was a space
          mov  byte ptr [si-1],0     ;NUL-character as parameter-End
          jmp  short nextz           ;process next character

parmtest  endp

;== End ==============================================================

code      ends                       ;End of CODE-Segment
          end  start
```

Program flow

The file header describes the DOS call of the program. As mentioned above, there are two basic options for the call: If you call the program without parameters in the command line, it tries to remove any previously installed SHOWCLK. If you call the program with parameters, SHOWCLK installs itself. The first parameter must be the scan code which the user wants to trigger the clock display. The line and column parameters indicate the clock display area on the screen. If these two parameters are missing, the clock appears in the upper right hand corner of the screen.

The constant definition follows the file header to ease your reading of the listing.

The code segment definition follows, which accepts the program code and the data. The ORG 100H instruction, which places the beginning of the program at address 100H, indicates that SHOWCLK is a COM program. A COM program is a good choice for a resident interrupt driver because of the compactness of having data, code and stack in one segment.

The label START shows the first executable instruction of the program. It jumps first to the installation routine of SHOWCLK which has the name SHOWINIT.

This routine loads the address of a table and calls the procedure PARMTEST. It counts the number of arguments passed in the command line and stores the starting addresses of the individual parameters into the passed table. After this procedure ends, SHOWINIT tests whether parameters were passed in the command line. If this is not the case, it jumps to DEACTIVATE which removes the old SHOWCLK from memory.

Assuming that arguments were passed to SHOWCLK in the command line, SHOWINIT now reads the passed parameters and tests them for accuracy. If it finds a correct key code, this code passes to the KEYCODE variable. If the indication of a line or column is found, it's tested for an acceptable value. If YES, it moves to the COLUMN or LINE variable. If an error and unknown parameter or an illegal coordinate occurs during the argument checking, the program ends with an error code. If the parameters evaluated are correct, a jump goes to the label INSTALL. A test searches for a keyboard code. If no keyboard code exists, the program ends with an error message. If it's available, the program first tests if SHOWCLK is already installed.

DOS function 35H determines the address of the BIOS keyboard interrupt (the interrupt pointing to a user routine). It returns the segment address of the interrupt routine in ES, and the offset address in the BX register. If SHOWCLK was already installed, an interrupt routine must be located at this address which is constructed exactly like the interrupt routine which is installed, since SHOWCLK always installs the same interrupt routine.

The routine starts with a 2-byte jump instruction to the routine itself. An identification code follows, consisting of two ASCII characters, which can be the initials of the author. In this case the initials are MT. INSTALL tests the address of the interrupt routine plus 2 for the ASCII codes of the initials MT. The test is not for MT, but for TM, since the low byte is always stored before the high byte. If the code exists, SHOWCLK is already installed and the program terminates with an error message. If INSTALL finds another bit pattern, it means that no previous version of SHOWCLK existed. INSTALL can then proceed with installation.

Installing SHOWCLK

First INSTALL stores the address of the old interrupt routine in the INTALTOFS and INTALTSEG variables. Next the interrupt 16H points through DOS function 25H to the NEWINT routine. The new interrupt routine of interrupt 16H is called if a program wants to call one of the three functions of this interrupt. A message tells the user that the program is now installed, and the DOS prompt returns. It's important that DOS not release the memory occupied by SHOWCLK for other programs. This could result in another program overwriting the new interrupt routine, and a system crash during the call of interrupt 16H. To prevent this, the program terminates with a DOS function which makes a portion of this program resident and prevents overwriting by other programs. Function 31H must be informed how many 16-byte paragraphs must be protected, starting from the beginning of the PSP.

Protecting memory

Once installed, the new interrupt routine must stay protected from changes that other registers could make to it. At the same time, SHOWCLK's installation routine must remain unprotected. SHOWCLK places the interrupt routine before the installation routine. Only the number of bytes between the beginning of the PSP and the last byte of the interrupt routine, converted into paragraphs, must be passed to function 32H. The new interrupt routine cannot be overwritten.

This interrupt routine must also contain variables. They are stored between the program start instruction and the interrupt routine code proper. This ensures that the variables remain resident in memory. At the beginning of the interrupt routine (NEWINT) is a jump instruction followed by the identification code. When a program calls interrupt 16H, a jump occurs directly to label NEWI_1. NEWI_1 tests for whether the function number passed to interrupt 16H in the AH register is 0. This is the only function applicable to this program, since the function reads characters from the keyboard buffer. If you called one of the two other functions, the program calls the old interrupt 16H and passes control to the calling program. If function 0 is called, it reads a character from the keyboard with the old keyboard interrupt. The program then compares this character with the key indicated when the program call occurred. If this is not the case, control returns to the calling program. If it was the indicated key, preparations begin to display the time on the screen.

Stack activity

First the contents of all registers which change during the course of the program are stored on the stack so they can be restored to the calling program. Then the five characters of the display in the position where the time appears are read from the screen and stored. DOS function 2CH reads the time and converts it to an ASCII string for display. After the time appears on the screen, the old keyboard interrupt waits for a keypress. When this occurs, the characters formerly located where the time appears return to their old positions. The registers return from the stack and the program jumps to the beginning of the routine to read in a key, display the time again, or pass the key to the calling program.

Deactivating SHOWCLK

The last component to be examined is the program routine called when SHOWCLK is removed from memory. The installation routine calls it if no parameter was passed in the command line and begins with the DEACTIVATE label. The routine tests for whether SHOWCLK is already installed. If this isn't the case, it cannot be removed, and the program terminates with an error message. If SHOWCLK was already installed, the keyboard interrupt must point to the old interrupt routine. The memory containing the old SHOWCLK routine must be released.

The problem is that the new SHOWCLK, which should remove the SHOWCLK already in memory, doesn't know the address of the old interrupt routine of interrupt 16H. It's stored in the old SHOWCLK in the variables INTALTOFS and INTALTSEG. The two variables are in completely different programs, but there is a simple method of reading these variables. The old SHOWCLK lies in a different memory segment from the new SHOWCLK, but the offset addresses of the variables and routines in both programs are identical. Since you know the segment address of the old SHOWCLK (the segment address of the interrupt routine), the contents of the variables INTALTOFS and INTALTSEG can be read from the old SHOWCLK and the interrupt 16H can again point to the original interrupt routine. Memory can be released again through the segment address of the old SHOWCLK routine with the help of DOS function 49H. This concludes the task of DECACTIVATE and the program can terminate after displaying a message.

Examine the listing step by step and read the comments carefully. This is important, because the program can serve as a basic framework for any resident interrupt driver. We'll discuss another form of resident program (the TSR program) in Chapter 8.

7.12 Accessing the Printer from the BIOS

BIOS offers three functions, called by interrupt 17H, for communicating with one or more printers interfaced to the PC. These functions have an advantage over the DOS printer output functions: They can specify the printer to which the output should go. The printer's number (0, 1 or 2) must be loaded into the DX register during the function call. After each of the three function calls, the printer status passes to the AH register. Each bit in this status byte provides information about the printer's task, whether it still has paper, etc.

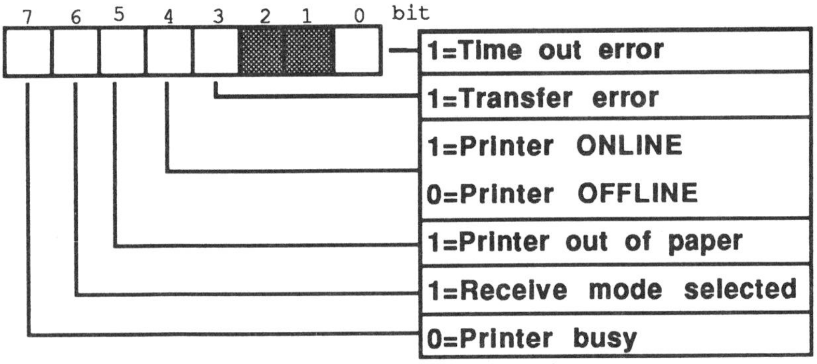

Printer status byte

Time out

A time out error occurs when BIOS tries to send data for a certain amount of time to the printer, but the printer refuses the data and returns a busy message (bit 7 becomes 0). The number of tries BIOS makes before signaling a time out error depends on the contents of address 0040:0078 in RAM. ROM uses this address for storing variables. The value 20 which BIOS enters into these memory locations during the system boot is different from the repeat factor of 20. The value in these memory locations must be multiplied first by 4, then by 65,536. A value of 20 actually refers to 5 million attempts. This number is relative since the loop which checks the printer has only a few assembly language instructions processed very quickly by the CPU. This results in a waiting period of only a few seconds before the BIOS reports a time out error. If working with the BIOS routine seems to create more time out errors than usual, try increasing the value in the memory locations mentioned above so that BIOS makes more attempts. This may help communication between BIOS and the printer.

Various printer conditions can change a series of bits in the status byte. An ON LINE (ready to print) printer sets bits 7 and 4. If the printer switches to OFF LINE (e.g., for page advance) then bit 7 and bit 4 reset and bit 3 sets, indicating a transmission error.

The program must decide whether new data should be sent to the printer, whether printer output should end or further steps should be taken.

Function 0: Send character

Function 0 transmits a character to the printer. Load the function number into the AH register and the ASCII code of the character you want sent into the AL register. After the function call the AH register contains the status byte. If the character transmission/printing failed, the AH register contains the value 1.

Function 1: Initialize printer

The second function initializes the printer ports. You should always execute this function before sending data to the printer for the first time. Load the function number 1 into the AH register; no other arguments are required.

Function 2: Read printer status

Function 2 loads the status byte into the AH register. As mentioned above, the status byte tells you the current status of the printer. Load the function number 2 into the AH register; no other arguments are required.

Demonstration programs

The programs listed in this section use the BIOS printer interrupt in the same way as the programs listed earlier to demonstrate the BIOS keyboard interrupt. The three higher level language programs listed here send strings to a printer using the BIOS printer interrupt. The fourth program is an assembly language routine which adapts the BIOS printer interrupt to its own routine.

The three higher level language programs are similar in organization and are divided into five sections. One section is the main program. The other four sections call the various functions of the BIOS printer interrupt. These sections include a routine for initializing a specific printer interface, a routine for character or string output and a routine which displays an error message on the screen if needed. The main program initializes printer interface 0, then prints a test string on the printer connected to this interface. If an error occurs during one of these two operations, an error message is displayed on the monitor. This message can be delayed if no printer is attached to the PC, since BIOS continues addressing the printer, and gives up after a few attempts. If nothing happens for some time, don't panic. The program will eventually report its error status.

BASIC listing: PRINTB.BAS

```
100 '********************************************************************'
110 '*                          P R I N T B                             *'
120 '*------------------------------------------------------------------*'
130 '*  Task          : makes a subroutine available for sending        *'
140 '*                  strings to a printer and                        *'
150 '*                  registering errors during the output to the     *'
160 '*                  printer                                         *'
170 '*  Author        : MICHAEL TISCHER                                 *'
180 '*  developed on  : 7/22/87                                         *'
190 '*  last Update   : 9/21/87                                         *'
200 '********************************************************************'
210 '
220 CLS : KEY OFF
230 PRINT"WARNING: This program should be started only if GWBASIC was "
240 PRINT"started from the DOS level with <GWBASIC  /m:60000>."
250 PRINT : PRINT"If this is not the case, please input <s> for Stop."
260 PRINT"Otherwise press any key...";
270 A$ = INKEY$ : IF A$ = "s" THEN END
280 IF A$ = "" THEN 270
290 GOSUB 60000              'install Function for Interrupt-Call
300 CLS                      'Clear Screen
310 PRINT"PRINT (c) 1987 by Michael Tischer" : PRINT
320 PRINT"If a parallel printer is interfaced to your PC, the "
330 PRINT"following text should appear on it immediately:" : PRINT
340 PRINT"a test of the printer routines..." : PRINT
350 PRINT"If not, an error message will be output." : PRINT
360 PRINTER% = 0             'address the first Printer on the PC
370 GOSUB 50000              'initialize Printer
380 GOSUB 53000              'output message
390 T$ = "a test of the printer routines..."+CHR$(13)+CHR$(10)
400 GOSUB 51000              'output String on the Printer
410 GOSUB 53000              'output Message
420 PRINT
430 END
440 '
50000 '******************************************************************'
50010 '* initialize one of the Printer interfaces                       *'
50020 '*----------------------------------------------------------------*'
50030 '* Input: PRINTER% = the Number of the Printer to be addressed *'
50040 '* Output: DS% is the Status of the Printer                       *'
50050 '* Info   : the Variable Z% is used as Dummy                      *'
50060 '******************************************************************'
50070 '
50080 PRTHI% = 0             'Hi-Byte of the Printer number
50090 FKT%=2                 'initialize Function number for Interface
50100 INR%=&H17              'call BIOS-Printer-Interrupt 17(h)
50110 CALL IA(INR%,FKT%,Z%,Z%,Z%,Z%,Z%,PRTHI%,PRINTER%,Z%,Z%,Z%,Z%)
50120 DS% = FKT% AND &H21    'store Printer status in DS%
50130 RETURN                 'back to Caller
50140 '
51000 '******************************************************************'
51010 '* send a String to one of the Printers                           *'
51020 '*----------------------------------------------------------------*'
51030 '* Input: T$       = the String to be output                      *'
51040 '*          PRINTER% = the Number of the Printer                  *'
51050 '* Output: the Variable DS% contains the Printer status           *'
51060 '******************************************************************'
51070 '
51080 FOR I = 1 TO LEN(T$)   'process all characters of the string
51090 Z$ = MID$(T$,I,1)      'isolate one character from the string
51100 GOSUB 52000            'output character on the printer
51110 IF DS%<>0 THEN I = LEN(T$)     'on error terminate output
51120 NEXT I                 'process next character
51130 RETURN                 'back to Caller
51140 '
52000 '******************************************************************'
52010 '* send a Character to one of the Printers                        *'
```

```
52020 '*-------------------------------------------------------------*'
52030 '* Input: Z$       = the Character to be output                *'
52040 '*           PRINTER% = the Number of the Printer              *'
52050 '* Output: the Variable DS% contains Printer status (0=o.k.)   *'
52060 '* Info    : the Variable Z% is used as a Dummy                *'
52070 '***************************************************************'
52080 '
52090 CHARACTER% = ASC(Z$)    'the ASCII-Code of the Character
52100 FKT%=0                  'print Function number for Character
52110 INR%=&H17               'call BIOS-Printer-Interrupt 17(h)
52120 CALL IA(INR%,FKT%,CHARACTER%,Z%,Z%,Z%,Z%, PRTHI%,PRINTER%,Z%,Z%,Z%,Z%)
52130 DS% = FKT% AND &H21     'record Printer status in DS%
52140 RETURN                  'back to Caller
52150 '
53000 '***************************************************************'
53010 '* Output an error-message on the basis of the Printer-Status  *'
53020 '*-------------------------------------------------------------*'
53030 '* Input: DS% = the Printer status                             *'
53040 '* Output: none                                                *'
53050 '* Info    : if the Printer status is  o.k., no output         *'
53060 '***************************************************************'
53070 '
53080 IF DS% = 0 THEN RETURN 'everything o.k. --> back to Caller
53090 PRINT"Error on access to Printer: ";
53100 IF (DS% AND 1) <> 0 THEN PRINT"Time-Out-Error" : RETURN
53110 IF (DS% AND 8) <> 0 THEN PRINT"I/O Error" : RETURN
53120 IF (DS% AND 32) <> 0 THEN PRINT"no more paper " : RETURN
53130 PRINT"Error type unknown" : RETURN
53140 '
60000 '***************************************************************'
60010 '* initialize the Routine for Interrupt-Call                   *'
60020 '*-------------------------------------------------------------*'
60030 '* Input: none                                                 *'
60040 '* Output: IA is the Start address of the Interrupt-Routine    *'
60050 '***************************************************************'
60060 '
60070 IA=60000!        'Start address of the Routine in the BASIC-Segment
60080 DEF SEG          'set BASIC-Segment
60090 RESTORE 60130
60100 FOR I% = 0 TO 160 : READ X% : POKE IA+I%,X% : NEXT  'poke Routine
60110 RETURN           'back to Caller
60120 '
60130 DATA  85,139,236, 30,  6,139,118, 30,139,  4,232,140,  0,139,118
60140 DATA  12,139, 60,139,118,  8,139,  4, 61,255,255,117,  2,140,216
60150 DATA 142,192,139,118, 28,138, 36,139,118, 26,138,  4,139,118, 24
60160 DATA 138, 60,139,118, 22,138, 28,139,118, 20,138, 44,139,118, 18
60170 DATA 138, 12,139,118, 16,138, 52,139,118, 14,138, 20,139,118, 10
60180 DATA 139, 52, 85,205, 33, 93, 86,156,139,118, 12,137, 60,139,118
60190 DATA  28,136, 36,139,118, 26,136,  4,139,118, 24,136, 60,139,118
60200 DATA  22,136, 28,139,118, 20,136, 44,139,118, 18,136, 12,139,118
60210 DATA  16,136, 52,139,118, 14,136, 20,139,118,  8,140,192,137,  4
60220 DATA  88,139,118,  6,137,  4, 88,139,118, 10,137,  4,  7, 31, 93
60230 DATA 202, 26,  0, 91, 46,136, 71, 66,233,108,255
```

Pascal listing: PRINTP.PAS

```
{**********************************************************************}
{*                              P R I N T P                          *}
{*--------------------------------------------------------------------*}
{*    Task        : Makes a function available for sending           *}
{*                    strings to a printer and registers             *}
{*                    errors during the output to the printer        *}
{*--------------------------------------------------------------------*}
{*    Author        : MICHAEL TISCHER                                *}
{*    developed on  :  7/9/87                                        *}
{*    last Update   : 6/09/89                                        *}
{**********************************************************************}

program PRINTPP;

Uses Crt, Dos;                                  { Add Crt and Dos units }

{$V-}                                         { Don't test string length }

type Output = string[255];

var PrintError : byte;                             { Printer error code }

{**********************************************************************}
{* PRINTCHARACTER: sends a character to the printer                  *}
{* Input  : see below                                                *}
{* Output  : TRUE  if an error occurred, else FALSE                  *}
{* Info    : if an error is discovered, the status of the printer is *}
{*           stored in the global variable PRINTERROR                *}
{**********************************************************************}

function PrintCharacter(Character : char;     { Character to be output }
                      Printer : integer) : boolean;  { Nr. of Printer }

var Regs : Registers;           { Register variable for interrupt call }

begin
 Regs.ah := 0;
 Regs.al := ord(Character);     { Function number & code of character }
 Regs.dx := Printer;                                 { Printer number }
 intr($17, Regs);                       { Call BIOS printer interrupt }
 if (Regs.ah and $21) <> 0 then                 { Did an error occur? }
  begin                                                         { YES }
   PrintCharacter := false;                           { Display error }
   PrintError := Regs.ah;                         { Record error code }
  end
 else PrintCharacter := true                               { No error }
end;

{**********************************************************************}
{* PRINTSTRING: sends a string to the selected printer               *}
{* Input  : see below                                                *}
{* Output  : TRUE  if no error occurred, else FALSE                  *}
{**********************************************************************}

function PrintString(Text    : Output;       { the string to be output }
                   Printer : integer) : boolean;{ Number of printer }

var Counter : integer;                                 { loop counter }
    Ok      : boolean;          { Result of the PRINTCHARACTER function }

begin
 Counter := 1;           { begin with the first character in the string }
 repeat
  Ok := PrintCharacter(Text[Counter], Printer);   { Print a character }
  Counter := succ(Counter)                   { Process next character }
 until not(Ok) or (Counter > length(Text));       { Terminate on error }
 PrintString := Ok;                         { Set result of the function }
```

```
end;

{***********************************************************************}
{* INITPRINTER: initializes the printer interface                      *}
{* Input : see below                                                    *}
{* Output : true, if no error occurred, otherwise false                *}
{* Info    : if an Error is detected, the Status of the Printer is      *}
{*           stored in the global Variable PRINTERROR                   *}
{***********************************************************************}

function InitPrinter(Printer : integer) : boolean;   { Printer number }

var Regs : Registers;         { Register variables for interrupt call }

begin
 Regs.ah := $2;                              { Function number for Init }
 Regs.dx := Printer;                                   { Printer number }
 intr($17, Regs);                          { Call BIOS printer interrupt }
 if (Regs.ah and $21) <> 0 then                    { Did an error occur ? }
  begin                                                           { YES }
   InitPrinter := false;                                 { Display error }
   PrintError := Regs.ah;                            { Record error code }
  end
 else InitPrinter := true                                     { No error }
end;

{***********************************************************************}
{* PRINTERROR: outputs error message                                    *}
{* Input : none                                                         *}
{* Output : none                                                        *}
{* Info    : the error message is displayed according to the content *}
{*           of the variable                                            *}
{*           PRINTERROR                                                 *}
{***********************************************************************}

procedure PrinterError;

begin
 write('Error during printer access: ');
 if PrintError and 1 <> 0                              { Time out error? }
  then writeln('Time-Out Error')                                  { YES }
  else if PrintError and 8 <> 0                             { I/O error? }
   then writeln('I/O Error')                                      { YES }
    else if PrintError and 32 <> 0                    { No more paper ? }
     then writeln('out of paper')                                 { YES }
     else writeln('Error unknown');
end;

{***********************************************************************}
{*                            MAIN PROGRAM                              *}
{***********************************************************************}

begin
 clrscr;                                                  { Clear screen }
 writeln('PRINT (c) 1987 by Michael Tischer');
 writeln(#13#10'If a printer is interfaced to the parallel interface '+
         '0 of the PC, ');
 writeln('the following text should now appear on this '+
         'printer:');
 writeln(#13#10'a test of the printer routines...'#13#10);
 writeln('Otherwise the program will display an error message !');
 writeln;
 if InitPrinter(0) then              { Initialize printer interface 0 }
  begin
   if PrintString('a test of the printer routines...'#13#10, 0)
    then writeln('all o.k.')
    else PrinterError                            { display error message }
  end                                             { Initialization error }
 else PrinterError;                              { display error message }
end.
```

C listing: PRINTC.C

```
/**********************************************************************/
/*                          P R I N T C                               */
/*--------------------------------------------------------------------*/
/*    Task        : Makes a function available for sending a         */
/*                  string to a printer. If any errors occur         */
/*                  during printing, the program will display        */
/*                  errors on the screen                             */
/*--------------------------------------------------------------------*/
/*    Author        : MICHAEL TISCHER                                 */
/*    developed on  : 8/13/87                                         */
/*    last update   : 6/09/89                                         */
/*--------------------------------------------------------------------*/
/*    (MICROSOFT C)                                                   */
/*    Creation      : MSC PRINTC                                      */
/*                    LINK PRINTC;                                    */
/*    Call          : PRINTC                                          */
/*--------------------------------------------------------------------*/
/*    (BORLAND TURBO C)                                               */
/*    Creation      : with the RUN command in the command line        */
/**********************************************************************/

#include <dos.h>                            /* include header files */
#include <io.h>

/*== Type definitions ===============================================*/

typedef unsigned char byte;                         /* Create a byte */
#define FALSE 0                   /* Constants make reading of the  */
#define TRUE 1                    /* program text easier            */

/**********************************************************************/
/* PRINTERROR: displays error message                                */
/* Input : 0 stands for o.k., else error code                        */
/* Output : TRUE  if no error is displayed, else FALSE               */
/**********************************************************************/

byte PrintError(Status)
int Status;                                        /* Printer status */

{
 if (Status)                              /* Did an error occur ? */
  {                                                        /* YES */
   printf("Error during printer access:");
   if (Status & 1)                              /* Time-Out Error? */
    printf("Time-Out Error\n");                            /* YES */
     else if (Status & 8)                           /* I/O error? */
      printf("I/O error\n");                               /* YES */
       else if (Status & 32)                    /* No more paper ? */
        printf("no more paper\n");                         /* YES */
         else printf("Error unknown\n");
   return(FALSE);
  }
 else return(TRUE);                              /* Error detected */
}

/**********************************************************************/
/* PRINTCHARACTER: sends a character to the printer                  */
/* Input : see below                                                  */
/* Output : FALSE if no error occurred, else                         */
/*          error number                                              */
/**********************************************************************/

byte PrintCharacter(Character, Printer)
char Character;                           /* The character for output */
unsigned int Printer;           /* Number of the designated printer */

{
```

```
 union REGS Register;      /* Register variables for interrupt call */

 Register.h.ah = 0;       /* Function number for character printing */
 Register.h.al = Character;                      /* Character code */
 Register.x.dx = Printer;                        /* Printer number */
 int86(0x17, &Register, &Register);  /* call BIOS printer interrupt */
 return(Register.h.ah & 0x29);             /* Leave only error bits */
}

/********************************************************************/
/* PRINTSTRING: sends a string to the selected printer              */
/* Input  : see below                                               */
/* Output : FALSE, if no error occurred, else                       */
/*          error number                                            */
/********************************************************************/

byte PrintString(Text, Printer)
char *Text;              /* String to be output (character vector) */
unsigned int Printer;                       /* Number of the printer */

{
 byte Status;                                  /* The printer status */

 Status = FALSE;                   /* Initialize if string is empty */

 /* Output string until end is reached or error occurs during output*/
 while (*Text && !(Status = PrintCharacter(*Text++, Printer)))
  ;
 return(Status);
}

/********************************************************************/
/* INITPRINTER: initialize the printer interface                    */
/* Input  : see below                                               */
/* Output : FALSE if no error occurred, else                        */
/*          error number                                            */
/********************************************************************/

byte InitPrinter(Printer)
int Printer;                 /* Printer interface to be initialized */

{
 union REGS Register;      /* Register variables for interrupt call */

 Register.h.ah = 2;                      /* Function number for Init */
 Register.x.dx = Printer ;               /* Printer/interface number */
 int86(0x17, &Register, &Register);  /* Call BIOS printer interrupt */
 return(Register.h.ah & 0x29);             /* Leave only error bits */
}

/********************************************************************/
/**                         MAIN PROGRAM                           **/
/********************************************************************/

void main()

{
 printf("\nPRINT (c) 1987 by Michael Tischer\n\n");
 printf("If a parallel printer is interfaced to this PC\n");
 printf(" the following text should appear soon:\n\n");
 printf("a test of the printer routines...\n\notherwise ");
 printf("an error message is displayed on the monitor screen.\n\n");
 if (PrintError(InitPrinter(0)))
  PrintError(PrintString("a test of the printer routines...\r\n"),0);

}
```

The assembly language program listed below is a resident interrupt driver. It can help the user whose printer runs a character set other than the PC standard. This is true of some Epson printers, whose foreign characters are different from the PC ASCII character set. The program converts these characters before sending them to the printer by turning the BIOS printer interrupt to its own routine, which is called every time the BIOS printer interrupt is called.

It tests for whether or not function 0 (character output to a printer) should be called, because only this function changes. If not, the call passes to the old printer interrupt.

If a character should be output, the interrupt looks into a table, with the name CODETAB, for the character. This table consists of 2-byte entries. The first (low) byte contains the new code of the character to be converted. The second (high) byte contains the old character code. The table ends with a byte containing the value 0.

The routine checks the second byte of a table entry if it is identical to the character to be printed. If the character cannot be found in the table, it passes unchanged through the old printer interrupt for output. If the character exists in the table, it is replaced by the first byte of the current entry, then sent for output using the old printer interrupt.

This program has a similar structure to the resident keyboard interrupt driver presented in Section 7.11. The main difference between the two programs lies in the command line, because PRUM (the program listed here) doesn't pass any parameters. It tests for an existing pre-installed version of itself when it is called. If no installed PRUM routine exists, it installs itself. Otherwise the installed version loads from disk or hard disk.

This program can transmit output to the printer using the BIOS printer interrupt as well as DOS.

Assembler listing: PRUM.ASM

```
;**********************************************************************;
;*                              P R U M                               *;
;*--------------------------------------------------------------------*;
;*    Task          :  Points the BIOS printer interrupt to its own   *;
;*                      Routine and makes it possible for example     *;
;*                      to convert IBM-ASCII to EPSON.                *;
;*                      The program is deactivated again on the       *;
;*                      second call and removed from memory.          *;
;*--------------------------------------------------------------------*;
;*    Author         : MICHAEL TISCHER                                *;
;*    developed on   :  8/2/87                                        *;
;*    last update    :  6/09/89                                       *;
;*--------------------------------------------------------------------*;
;*    assembly       : MASM PRUM;                                     *;
;*                     LINK PRUM;                                     *;
;*                     EXE2BIN PRUM PRUM.COM                          *;
;*--------------------------------------------------------------------*;
;*    Call           : PRUM                                           *;
;**********************************************************************;

;== Actual program starts here ================================
```

```
code      segment para 'CODE'     ;Definition of the CODE segment

          org 100h

          assume cs:code, ds:code, es:code, ss:code

start:    jmp prumini             ;the first executable command

;== Data (remain in memory) ========================================

alterint  equu this dword        ;Old interrupt vector 17(h)
intaltofs dw (?)                 ;Offset address Interrupt vector 17(h)
intaltseg dw (?)                 ;Segment address Interrupt vector 17(h)

          ;-- The following table contains the new  -----------
          ;-- code followed by the old code -------------------

codetab   db   64, 21             ; ¶  --------- > '@'
          db  125,129             ; 'ü' ----------> '}'
          db  123,132             ; 'ä' ----------> '{'
          db   91,142             ; 'Ä' ----------> '['
          db  124,148             ; 'ö' ----------> '|'
          db   92,153             ; 'Ö' ----------> '\'
          db   93,154             ; 'Ü' ----------> ']'
          db  126,225             ; 'ß' ----------> '~'
          db  0                   ;End of the table

;== this is the new printer interrupt (remains in memory) ===========

newpri    proc far

          jmp  short newpri_1

          db "CW"                 ;Identification of the program

newpri_1: or   ah,ah              ;print character (function 0)?
          jne  aint               ;NO --> ;address of the code table
          mov  bl,al              ;store code in BL
testcode: lodsw                   ;load old (AH) and new code (AL)
          or   al,al              ;Reached end of table ?
          je   notfound           ;YES --> Code not found
          cmp  ah,bl              ;Is it the code for conversion
          jne  testcode           ;NO --> continue to search table
          jmp  short nreset      ;it was a code for conversion

notfound: mov  al,bl              ;move old code to AL again
nreset:   xor  ah,ah              ;set function number 0 again
          pop  ds                 ;restore registers
          pop  si
          pop  bx
          popf

aint:     jmp  cs:[alterint]      ;to old printer routine

newpri    endp

instend   equ this byte           ;up to this mem location everything must
                                  ;remain resident

;== Data (can be overwritten by DOS) =======================

installm  db 13,10,"PRUM (c) 1987 by Michael Tischer",13,10,13,10
          db "PRUM was installed and can be deactivated with ",13,10
          db "a new call",13,10,"$"

removeit  db "PRUM was deactivated$",13,10

;== Program (can be overwritten by DOS) ======================
;-- Start and Initialization Routine ----------------------------------
```

```
prumini   label near

          mov  ax,3517h           ;get content of interrupt vector 17(h)
          int  21h                ;call DOS function
          cmp  word ptr es:[bx+2],"WC" ;test if PRUM program
          jne  install            ;SHOWCL not installed --> INSTALL

          ;-- PRUM was deactivated ------------------------------------

          mov  dx,es:intaltofs    ;Offset address of interrupt 17(h)
          mov  ax,es:intaltseg    ;Segment address of interrupt 17(h)
          mov  ds,ax              ;to DS
          mov  ax,2517h           ;deflect content of the interrupt
          int  21h                ;vector 17(h) to old routine

          mov  ah,49h             ;release storage of old PRUM
          int  21h                ;again

          push cs                 ;store CS on stack
          pop  ds                 ;restore DS

          mov  dx,offset removeit ;Message: Program removed
          mov  ah,9               ;write function number for atring
          int  21h                ;call DOS function

          mov  ax,4C00h           ;terminate program
          int  21h                ;call function program termination

          ;-- install PRUM ------------------------------------

install   label near

          mov  ax,3517h           ;get content of interrupt vector 17
          int  21h                ;call DOS function
          mov  intaltseg,es       ;save segment- and offset address
          mov  intaltofs,bx       ; of the interrupt vector 17(h)

          mov  dx,offset newpri   ;Offset address new interrupt routine
          mov  ax,2517h           ;deflect content of interrupt
          int  21h                ; vector 17 to user routine

          mov  dx,offset installm ;Message: Program installed
          mov  ah,9               ;output function number for string
          int  21h                ;call DOS function

          ;-- only the PSP, the new interrupt routine and the ---------
          ;-- data pertaining to it must remain resident.    ----------

          mov  dx,offset instend  ;calculate the number of
          mov  cl,4               ;paragraphs (each 16 bytes) available
          shr  dx,cl              ; to the program
          inc  dx
          mov  ax,3100h           ;end program with end code 0 (o.k)
          int  21h                ;but remain resident

;== End ==============================================================

code      ends                    ;End of the CODE segment
          end  start
```

7.13 Reading the Date and Time from the BIOS

The various time functions of the ROM-BIOS can be addressed through BIOS interrupt 1AH. The PC and XT each have two time/date functions. The AT has eight time/date functions available to the user.

Realtime clock

The enhanced functions included in the AT operate in conjunction with the AT's battery powered realtime clock (RTC). The realtime clock continues keeping time even when the AT is switched off. This clock's method of timekeeping is quite different from PC and XT time. PC and XT models measure time using timer interrupt 8H, which the system calls about 18.2 times per second. Timer interrupt 8H remains independent of the CPU's clock frequency. The AT ROM-BIOS maintains control of this interrupt, but only for maintaining software compatibility with the PC and XT. The AT BIOS receives the current time from the realtime clock accessing the CPU.

Function 00H: Get clock

Function number 00H gets the current clock time. You can call this function by passing the number (0) to the AH register. The function loads the time into the CX and DX registers. These two registers combine to form a 32-bit counter value (CX contains the most significant 16 bits, while DX contains the least significant 16 bits). The BIOS timer increments this value by 1 each time interrupt 8H is called (18.2 times per second). The total value is the result of multiplying the contents of CX register by 65,536 and adding the contents of the DX register. Dividing this value by 18.2 returns the number of seconds elapsed, which can then be converted into minutes and hours.

The AT interprets time differently from the PC and XT. The PC/XT BIOS sets this counter to 0 during the system booting process. The value returned is the time passed since the computer was switched on (not the actual time). To obtain the time, the current time must be converted to the value corresponding to the counter, then passed to the BIOS (more on this later). The AT doesn't require this time value conversion since BIOS reads the actual time from the realtime clock during the system boot. It converts this time into a suitable timer value and saves it. Reading the counter with the help of function 0 on the AT thus provides the current time.

Besides this counter, a value the AL register indicates whether or not 24 hours have passed since the last reading. If the AL register contains a value other than 0, 24 hours have passed. This value does not indicate how many 24-hour periods have elapsed since the last reading.

If the conversion of time values into clock time is too complicated, function 2CH of DOS interrupt 21H can be used. This function simply reads and converts the current time using function 0 of interrupt 1AH (see Chapter 18 of this book for more information about function 2CH of DOS interrupt 1AH).

Function 01H: Set clock

Function number 01H sets the current clock time. You can call this function by loading the number 1 into the AH register, the most significant 16 bits of the counter into the CX register and the least significant 16 bits into the DX register. These two registers combine to form a 32-bit time value. If the conversion of the current time into a timer value is too complicated, function 2DH of DOS interrupt 21H can be used instead (see Chapter 18 of this book for more information about function 2DH of DOS interrupt 21H).

The next six functions are available only on the AT. If you attempt to call these functions on a PC or an XT, nothing will happen (use the model identification program described in Section 7.3 to check for AT hardware).

All six functions use BCD format for time and date indications. In this format, two characters are coded per byte, where the higher number is coded in the higher nibble and the lower number in the lower nibble. All six functions use the carry flag following a return from the function call. If the carry flag is set, this indicates that the realtime clock is malfunctioning (e.g., dead battery). The called function could not be executed properly.

Function 02H: Get current time

Function 02H reads the realtime clock time. You can call the function by loading the function number (2) into the AH register. The current time is returned with the hour in the CH register, minutes in the CL register and the seconds in the DH register.

Function 03H: Set current time

Function 03H sets the time on the realtime clock. You can call the function by loading the function number (3) into the AH register, the hour into the CH register, minutes into the CL register and seconds into the DH register. The DL register indicates whether the "daylight savings time" option is desired. A 1 in the DL register selects daylight savings time, while 0 maintains standard time.

Function 04H: Get current date

Functions 4 and 5 read and set the date stored in the realtime clock. Both functions use the century, the year, the month and the day as arguments. The day of the week (also administered by the realtime clock) does not apply to these functions. If you want to read the day of the week, direct access must be made to the realtime clock (see Chapter 10 for instructions on direct access).

Function 04H gets the current date from the realtime clock. You can call this function by loading the function number (4) into the AH register. The CH register contains the first two numbers of the year (the century). The CL register contains the last two numbers of the year (e.g., 88). The month is returned in the DH register, and the day of the month in the DL register.

Function 05H: Set current date

Function 05H sets the current date in the realtime clock. You can call this function by loading the function number (5) into the AH register, either 19 or 20 into the CH register, the last two numbers of the year into the CL register (e.g., 89 decimal), the month into the DH register, and the day of the month into the DL register.

Function 06H: Set alarm time

Function 06H allows the user to set an alarm. Since only the hour, minute and second can be indicated, the alarm time applies only to the current day. When the clock reaches the alarm time, the realtime clock calls a BIOS routine which in turn calls interrupt 4AH. A user routine can be installed under this interrupt to simulate the sound of an alarm clock (you can program the routine to make other sounds). During the system initialization interrupt 4AH moves to a routine which contains only the IRET assembly language instruction. The IRET instruction forces the CPU to terminate the interrupt so that arriving at alarm time doesn't result in any action visible to the user. You can call this function by loading the function number (6) into the AH register, the alarm hour into the CH register, the alarm minute into the CL register and the alarm second into the DH register.

Function 07H: Reset alarm time

Only one alarm time can be set. If this function is called while another alarm time is set, or has not yet been reached, the carry flag is set after the function call. A new alarm time doesn't replace the old alarm time; the old time must be deleted first. You can call this function by loading the function number (7) into the AH register; no other parameters are required. This call clears the last alarm time so that a new alarm time can be programmed.

7.14 BIOS Variables

The preceding sections described different BIOS interrupts and their functions. These functions require a segment of memory for storing variables and data. For this reason, the BIOS reserves the area of memory between addresses 0040:000 and 0050:0000 for storing internal variables. The contents of most of these variables can be read using some BIOS functions, or by using direct access. Sometimes direct access is the easiest method of the two, but it increases the odds of a program not executing properly on certain PCs. Since the BIOS can vary from PC to PC, different BIOS versions may use individual memory locations within this area in different ways. When working with "standard issue" PCs and compatibles (e.g., IBM, Tandon, etc.), you can assume that the memory assignment provided here remains constant between machines.

The following list describes the individual variables, their purposes and addresses. The address indicated is the offset address of segment address 0040H. For example, a variable with the offset address 10H has the address 0040:0010 or 10H.

00H—07H

During the booting process, a BIOS routine determines the configuration of its PC. It determines, among other things, the number of installed serial (RS-232) interfaces. These interface numbers are stored as four words in memory locations 0040:0000 to 0040:0007. Each one of these words represents one of the four cards that can be installed for asynchronous data transmission. First the low byte is stored, followed by the high byte. Since few PCs have four serial cards at their disposal, the words which represent a missing card contain the value 0.

08H—0FH

During the booting process, a BIOS routine determines the configuration of its PC. It determines, among other things, the number of installed parallel interfaces. These card numbers are stored as four words in memory locations 0040:0008 to 0040:000F. Each one of these words stands for one of the four cards that can be installed for parallel data transmission. First the low byte is stored, followed by the high byte. Since few PCs have four parallel cards at their disposal, the words which represent a missing card contain the value 0.

10H—11H

This word represents the hardware configuration of the PC as called through BIOS interrupt 11H. Similar to the above two words, this configuration is determined during the booting process. The purposes of individual bits of this word are standardized for the PC and the XT, but can differ in some other computers.

12H

This byte provides storage for information gathered during the system self-test, executed during the booting process and after a warm start. BIOS routines also use this byte for recognizing active keys. It has no practical use for the programmer.

13H—14H

This word indicates the RAM capacity of the system in kilobytes. This information is also gathered during the booting process, and can be read using BIOS interrupt 12H.

15H—16H

These two bytes test the hardware during the booting process. They have no further use after each hardware test.

17H

This is called the *keyboard status byte* because it contains the status of the keyboard and different keys. Function 02H of BIOS keyboard interrupt 16H reads this byte. Accessing this byte allows the user to toggle the <Insert> or <Caps Lock> key on or off. The upper four bits of this byte may be changed by the user; the lower four bits must remain undisturbed.

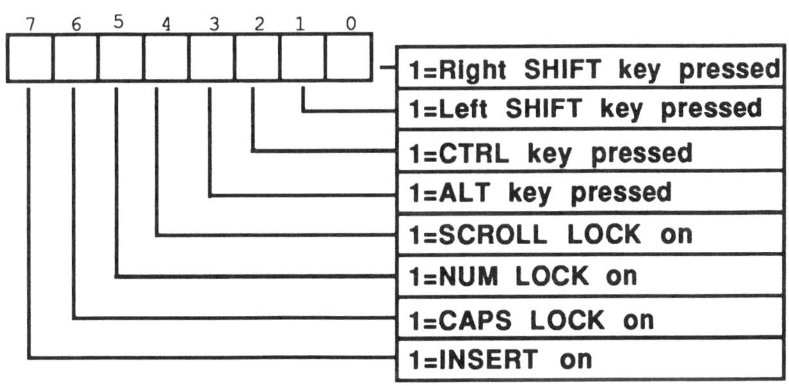

Keyboard status byte

18H

This byte is similar to byte 17H above, with the difference that this byte indicates the active status of the <SysReq> and <Break> keys.

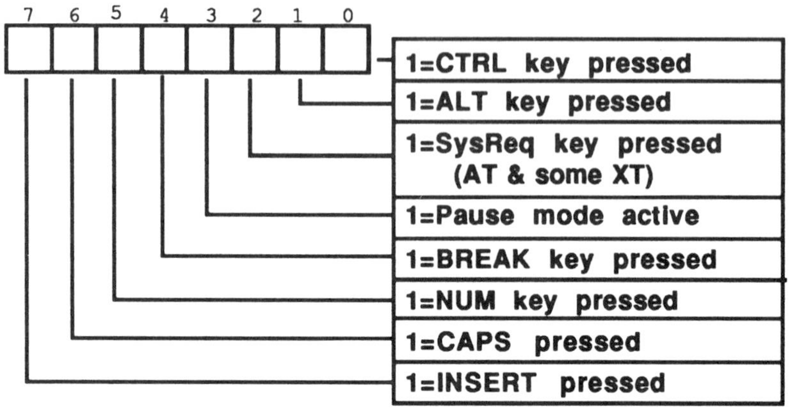

Extended keyboard status byte

19H

This byte currently serves no purpose; it will be used for status in a proposed extended keyboard once that keyboard appears on the market.

1AH-1BH

This word contains the address of the next character to be read in the keyboard buffer (see also 1EH—3DH below).

1CH—1DH

This word contains the address of the last character in the keyboard buffer (see also 1EH—3DH below).

1EH—3DH

This area of memory contains the actual keyboard buffer. Since every character stored in the keyboard buffer requires 2 bytes, its 32-byte capacity offers space for a maximum of 16 characters. For a normal ASCII character, the buffer stores the ASCII code and then the character's *scan code*. The scan code is the number of the activated key which generated the ASCII character. If the character in the keyboard buffer uses an extended code (e.g., a cursor key), then the first byte contains the value 0 and the second byte contains the extended key code.

The computer constantly reads characters from the keyboard buffer. If the buffer is not full, characters can be added. The address of the next character to be read from the keyboard buffer is stored in the word at memory location 0040:001AH. When a character is read, the character moves by 2 bytes toward the end of the buffer in memory. When a character was read from the last memory location of the buffer, this pointer resets to the beginning of the buffer.

The same is true of the pointer in memory location 0040:001C, which indicates the end of the keyboard buffer. If you add a new character, it is stored in the keyboard buffer at the location indicated by this pointer. Then the pointer is incremented by 2 to move toward the end of the buffer. If a new character is stored at the last memory location of the buffer, this pointer resets to the beginning of the buffer.

The relationship between the start and end pointers tells something about the buffer's status. Two conditions are of special interest. The first is the condition when both pointers contain the same address (no characters are currently available in the keyboard buffer). The other condition is when a character should be appended to the end of the keyboard buffer, but adding 2 to the end pointer would point it to the start pointer. This means that the keyboard buffer is full, i.e., no additional characters can be accepted.

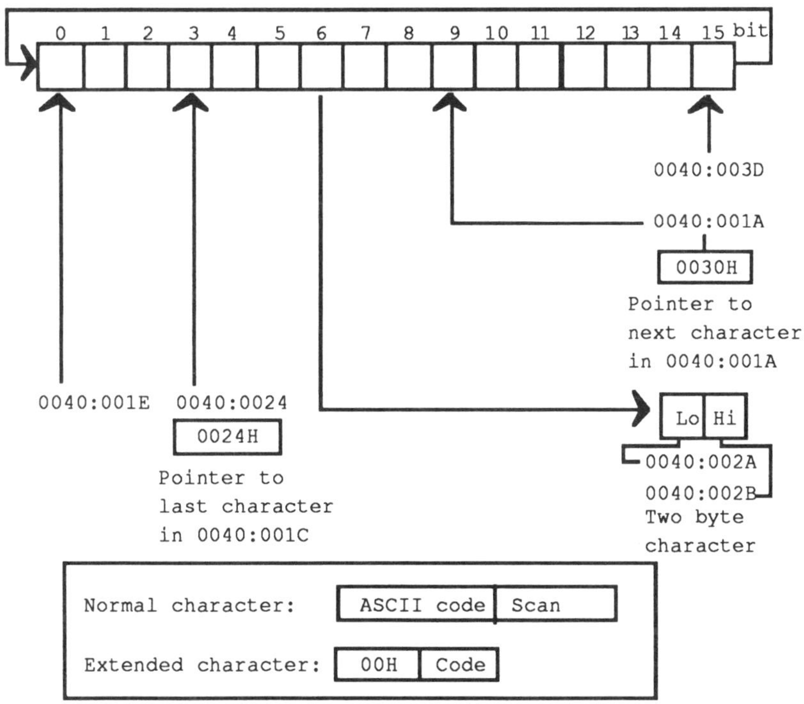

Keyboard buffer with start and end pointers

3EH

The lowest four bits correspond to the number of installed PC disk drives (you are allowed a maximum of four drives). These bytes also indicate whether the connected drives must be calibrated. This is mostly the case after an error occurs during read, write or search access. When an error occurs, the corresponding bit in this byte is set to 0.

3FH

The four lower bits of this byte indicate whether the current disk drive motor is in motion. A 1 in the corresponding bit indicates this. In addition, bit 7 is always set when write access is in progress.

40H

This byte contains a numerical value which indicates the time period until a disk drive motor switches off. Since BIOS can only access one disk drive at a time, this value refers to the drive last accessed. Following access to this drive, BIOS places the value 37 into this register. During every timer interrupt (which occurs about 18.2 times per second), the value in this byte is decremented by 1. When it finally reaches 0, the disk motor is turned off. This takes place after about two seconds.

41H

This byte contains the status of the last disk access. When the byte contains the value 0, the last disk operation was performed in an orderly manner. Another value signals that an error code was transmitted by the disk controller.

42H—48H

These seven bytes indicate the status of the NEC disk controller. They also indicate hard disk controller status on hard disk systems.

49H

This byte contains the current display mode as reported by the BIOS. This is the same value indicated when the user activates a display mode through function 0 of the BIOS video interrupt 10H.

4AH

This word contains the number of text columns per display line in the current display mode.

4CH

This word contains the number of bytes required for the display of a screen page in the current display mode, as reported by the BIOS. In the 80x25-character text mode, this is 4,000 bytes.

4EH—4FH

This word contains the address of the current screen page now on the monitor, relative to the beginning of video card RAM. The video RAM of the color card starts at B800:0000 for the first screen page, and at B800:1000 for the second screen page in 80x25-character text mode. This variable usually contains the value 1000H.

50H—5FH

These 16 bytes contain the current cursor position for each screen page. BIOS can control a maximum of 8 screen pages. BIOS reserves two bytes for each screen page. The low byte indicates the screen column, which can have values ranging from 0 to 39 (in 40-column mode) or from 0 to 79 (in 80-column mode). The high byte indicates the screen line, which can have values ranging from 0 to 24. If you change the values in this table, the immediate position of the blinking cursor remains unchanged, but the change will become noticeable the next time you enter characters into the corresponding display page.

You can use these bytes for positioning the cursor, but we don't recommend this method.

60H

This byte contains the starting line of the blinking cursor, which can have values ranging from 0 to 7 (color graphic card) or from 0 to 14 (monochrome graphic card). Changing the contents of this byte doesn't change the cursor's appearance, since it must first be transmitted by BIOS to the video controller.

61H

This byte contains the ending line of the blinking cursor, which can have values ranging from 0 to 7 (color graphic card) or from 0 to 14 (monochrome graphic card). Changing the contents of this byte doesn't change the cursor's appearance, since it must first be transmitted by BIOS to the video controller.

62H

This byte contains the number of the currently displayed screen page.

63H—64H

This word contains the video card port. If a PC contains several video cards, the value stored will be the address of the currently active video card.

65H

The contents of a video controller card's mode selector dictates the current display mode. The current value is stored in this memory location.

66H

A color card in medium-resolution graphic mode can display 320x200 pixels in four different colors. Three of these colors originate from one of the two color palettes. This byte contains the currently active color palette (either 0 or 1).

67H—6BH

The early PC BIOS versions could use a cassette recorder for data storage. Those early versions of BIOS used these five bytes for cassette access when storing data. XT and AT models, which do not have this interface, use these memory locations in connection with RAM expansion.

6CH—6FH

These four bytes act as a 32-bit counter for both BIOS and DOS. The counter is incremented by 1 on each of the 18.2 timer interrupts per second. This permits time measurement and time display. The value of this counter can be read and set with BIOS interrupt 1AH. If 24 hours have elapsed, it resets to 0 and counts up from there.

70H

This byte contains a 0 when the timer routine is between 0 and 24 hours. Byte 70H changes to 1 when the time counter routine exceeds its 24-hour limit. For every subsequent 24-hour count, this byte remains at 1.

If the BIOS timer interrupt 1AH is used to set the time, this byte resets to 0.

71H

This byte indicates whether or not a keyboard interrupt occurs after the user presses <Ctrl><C> or <Ctrl><Break>. If bit 7 of this byte contains the value 1, a keyboard interrupt has occurred.

72H—73H

During the booting process, a reset command is sent to the keyboard Controller. For the duration of this reset, the word at this location assumes the value 1234H.

XT BIOS variables

The hardware configurations of the XT permit the introduction of additional variables. The following is a list of BIOS variables found in the XT and AT.

74H—77H

These four bytes are used only by hard disk systems for hard disk control.

78H—7BH

Each of these four bytes returns the status of one of the four printer ports.

7CH—7FH

Each of these four bytes returns the status of one of the four asynchronous communication (RS-232) ports.

80H—81H

This word contains the beginning of the keyboard buffer as the offset address to the segment address 0040. Since the keyboard buffer normally starts at address 0040:001E, this memory location usually contains the value 1EH.

82H—83H

This word contains the end of the keyboard buffer as the offset address to the segment address 0040. Since the keyboard buffer normally ends at address 0040:003E, this memory location usually contains the value 3EH.

AT BIOS variables

The advanced features of the AT require even more BIOS variables. Here is a list of the BIOS variables found only on AT models.

88H

This byte contains the last data transmission speed of the disk drive or hard disk.

8CH—96H

This memory range contains variables necessary during disk/hard disk access.

97H

This byte reserves a keyboard flag which shows the status of the AT keyboard's LED (light-emitting diode).

98H—A0H

This memory range accepts variables from the battery-powered realtime clock.

All members of the PC family (PC, XT and AT) have a variable in memory location 0050:0000. This variable works in conjunction with the hardcopy routine (interrupt 5) to prevent printer output during the printing of another hardcopy. The hardcopy routine tests for whether this flag has a value of 0. If so, and no hardcopy is being printed, the flag changes to 1. The BIOS can check this variable to see whether a printout is in process. After a successful printout, this flag resets to 0 to allow additional printing. If an error was detected during printer access, this flag is set to the value 255 and the printing procedure aborts.

Chapter 8

Terminate and Stay Resident Programs

Since its birth, DOS has been criticized for its inability to handle multitasking (running more than one program at a time). Even though OS/2 is capable of multitasking, it runs only on ATs or 80386-based computers. But TSR (Terminate and Stay Resident) programs can bring some of the advantages of multitasking into the world of DOS machines. This type of program moves into the "background" once it is started, and becomes active when the user presses a particular key combination. The SideKick® program produced by Borland International made TSR programs very popular.

Running a TSR program isn't multitasking in the true sense of the word, since only one program is actually running at any given time. However, with the touch of a key, the user can immediately access such useful tools as a calculator, calendar, or note pad. In addition to these applications, macro generators, screen layout utilities and text editors can also be found in TSR form.

Many TSR programs can even interact with the programs that they interrupt, and transfer data between the TSR and the interrupted program. One example of this would be a TSR appointment book that inserts a page from its calendar in a file loaded into a currently running word processor.

Although many different applications can be implemented with TSR programs, TSR programs have two things in common:

- all use the same basic method of operation
- all are built on similar programming concepts

This chapter examines these two items, and demonstrates simple implementations of TSR programs.

Before we begin, we should point out that this involves very complex programming. Comprehending this material requires a certain level of understanding about how things work within the system. This is especially true of TSR programs, since by their very definition they all but ignore the single-task nature of DOS, in which one program has access to all of the system resources (RAM, screen, disk, etc.). A TSR program must contend with many other elements of the system such as the BIOS, DOS, the interrupted program, and even other TSR programs. Managing this is a difficult but rewarding task, and can only be realized in assembly language. Of the available PC languages, only assembly language offers the ability to work at the lowest system level, the interrupt level. But although it has this capability, assembly language is as flexible as high level languages for writing TSR applications such as calculators or note pads. Because of this we'll list two assembly language programs in this chapter which will allow you to "convert" Turbo Pascal, Turbo C, and Microsoft C programs into TSR programs.

Activating TSR programs

Let's start by looking at how a TSR program is activated. To make our TSR program come to the foreground immediately after we press a certain key combination (called the *hotkey*), we must install some sort of activiation mechanism tied to the keyboard. We can use interrupts 09H and 16H, two system keyboard calls. Interrupt 16H is the BIOS keyboard interrupt, which programs use to read characters and keyboard status. If we use this interrupt, then our TSR program can only be activated when the main program is using interrupt 16H for keyboard input.

It would be better to use interrupt 09H, which is called by the processor whenever a key is pressed or released. We can redirect this interrupt to our own routine, which can check to see if the TSR program should be activated or not. Before it does this, the routine should call the old interrupt 09H handler. There are two reasons for this. The first has to do with the task of interrupt 09H, which informs the system that the keyboard needs the system's attention in order to transfer information about a key event. Therefore, interrupt 09H normally points to a routine within the ROM BIOS which accepts and evaluates information from the keyboard. Specifically, it receives the code from the keyboard, converts it to an ASCII code, and then places this code in the BIOS's keyboard buffer. Since our TSR program neither wants nor is able to handle this job, we must call the original routine, or keyboard input will be impossible.

The second reason has to do with the fact that it is possible that other TSR programs were installed before ours, which have redirected interrupt 09H to their own routines. Since our program is in front of these programs in the interrupt handler chain, their interrupt routines will not be called automatically if we do not call the old interrupt handler. The result would be that we could no longer activate these TSR programs. The end result is that when a TSR program is called via a redirected interrupt routine, it should always call the old interrupt handler before or after its own interrupt processing.

The call must not be made with the INT assembly language instruction, since this would just recall our own interrupt handler. This would lead to an infinite loop in most cases, a stack overflow and an eventual system crash. To avoid this we must save the address of the old interrupt handler when the TSR program is installed. We can then call the old interrupt handler with this stored address with the help of a FAR CALL instruction. To simulate calling this handler through the INT instruction, we must first place the contents of the flag register on the stack with the PUSHF instruction before the CALL.

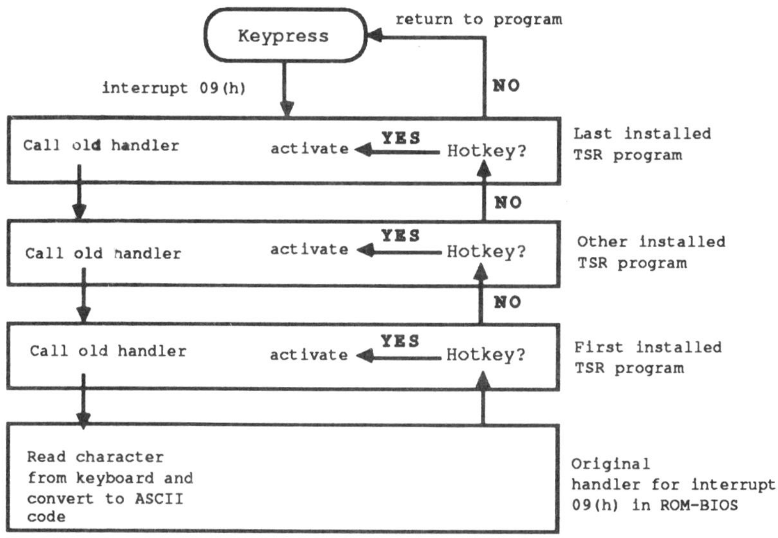

Reading keys for TSR programs using interrupt 09H

After the return from the interrupt handler, we can check to see if the hotkey was pressed to activate the TSR. The BIOS keyboard flag at address 17H in the BIOS variable segment (segment address 0040H) indicates the status of the following keys:

- right <Shift> key
- left <Shift> key
- <Ctrl> key
- <Alt> key
- <Num> key
- <Scroll Lock> key

- <CapsLock> key
- <SysReq> key (AT keyboard only)

If the appropriate keys are pressed, the user is trying to activate the TSR program. We can only do this if certain conditions are met, all of which come down to the fact that the DOS is not re-entrant.

DOS

Since the TSR program can be activated from the keyboard at any time, regardless of the other processes in the system, it could conceivably interrupt a call to a DOS function. This may not lead to problems as long as the TSR program returns to the interrupted DOS function properly. The problem occurs when the TSR itself tries to call DOS functions, which is hard to avoid when programming in a high level language. Here we see the problem of re-entry. This refers to the ability of a system to allow multiple programs to call and execute its code at the same time. DOS is not re-entrant, however, since it is a single-task system and assumes that DOS functions will be called in sequence, and not in parallel.

Calling a DOS function from within a TSR program while another function is executing leads to problems because the processor register SS:SP is loaded with the address of one of three DOS stacks when interrupt 21H is called. Which of the three stacks is used depends on the function group to which the DOS function belongs, and cannot be determined by the caller. While the DOS function is being executed, it places temporary data on this stack as well as the return address to the calling program. If the execution of the function is then interrupted by the activation of a TSR program which then calls a DOS function, DOS will again load register pair SS:SP with the starting address of an internal stack. If it is the same stack that the interrupt function was using, each access to the stack will destroy the data of the other function call. The DOS function called by the TSR program will be executed properly, but the problem will occur when the TSR program ends and control returns to the interrupted DOS function. Since the contents of the stack have been changed in the meantime by other DOS calls, the DOS function will probably crash the system.

Bypassing re-entry

There are two ways to get around these re-entry problems: Avoid calling DOS functions, or allow the TSR program to be activated only if no DOS functions are being executed. We have already ruled out the first option, so we must use the second. DOS helps us here by providing the INDOS flag, which is normally only used inside DOS but which is very useful to us as well. It is a counter which counts the nesting depth of DOS calls. If it contains the value 0, no DOS functions are currently being executed. The value 1 indicates the current execution of a DOS function. Under certain conditions this counter can also contain larger values, such as when one DOS function calls another DOS function, which is allowed only in special cases.

Since there is no DOS function to read the value of this flag, we have to read the contents directly from memory. The address does not change after the system is booted, so we can get the address when the TSR is installed and save it in a variable. DOS function 34H returns the address of the INDOS flag in register pair ES:BX.

This flag is read in the interrupt handler for interrupt 09H since it checks to see if the hotkey was pressed, and allows the TSR program to be activated only if the INDOS flag contains the value 0. This is not the whole solution to the problem, however. It coordinates the activation of the TSR program with DOS function calls of the transient program being executed in the foreground, but it does not allow the TSR program to be called from the DOS user interface. Since the DOS command processor (COMMAND.COM) uses some DOS functions for printing the prompt and accepting input from the user, the INDOS flag always contains the value 1. In this special case we can interrupt the executing DOS function, but we must make sure that the INDOS flag contains the value 1, because a DOS function can be called from transient program or from the DOS command processor.

There is a solution for this problem too. It involves the fact that the DOS is in a kind of a wait state when it is waiting for input from the user in the command processor. To avoid wasting any valuable processor time, it periodically calls interrupt 28H, which is responsible for short term activation of background processes like the print spooler (DOS PRINT command) and other tasks. If this interrupt is called, it is relatively safe to interrupt DOS and call the TSR program.

To use this procedure, a new handler for interrupt 28H is installed when the TSR program is installed. It first calls the old handler for this interrupt and then checks to see if the hotkey has been pressed. If this has occurred, the TSR program can be activated, even if the INDOS flag is not 0.

One more restriction must still be added—we cannot allow the TSR program to be activated, even using the handler for interrupt 09H, if time-critical actions are being performed in the system.

Time-critical actions

These are actions which, for various reasons, cannot be interrupted because they must complete execution in a relatively short time. In the PC this includes accesses to the floppy and hard disk, which at the lowest levels are controlled by BIOS interrupt 13H. If an access to these devices is not completed by a certain time it can cause serious system disruptions. A dramatic example is if the TSR program performs an access to these devices before another access, which is initiated by the interrupted program, has finished. Even if this doesn't crash the system, it will lead to loss of data.

We can avoid this by installing a new interrupt handler for BIOS interrupt 13H. When this handler is called, it sets an internal flag which shows that the BIOS disk interrupt is currently active. Then it calls the old interrupt handler which performs the access to the floppy or hard disk. When it returns to the TSR handler, the flag is cleared, signalling the end of BIOS disk activity.

To prevent this interrupt handler from being interrupted, the other TSR interrupt handlers all monitor this flag and will activate the TSR program only if the flag indicates that the BIOS disk interrupt is not active.

Recursion

One last condition placed on the activation of a TSR program is that recursive activations are prohibited. Since the hotkey can still be pressed after the TSR program has been activated, we must prevent the TSR program from being reactivated before it is finished. We can simply add another flag which is checked before the TSR is activated. The TSR program sets this flag when it begins and clears it again just before it ends. If an interrupt handler determines that this flag is set, it will simply ignore the hotkey.

Once all of these conditions have been satisfied, we can activate the TSR program.

Context switch

The process of activating a TSR program is called a *context switch*. The program context or environment is all the information needed for operating the program. This includes such things as the contents of the processor registers, important operating system information, and the memory occupied by the program. We don't have to worry about the program memory in our context switch, however, since our TSR program is already marked as resident, meaning that the operating system will not give the memory it occupies to other programs.

The processor registers, especially the segment registers, must be loaded with the values which the TSR program expects. These are saved in internal variables when the TSR program is installed. Since the contents of these and other registers will be changed by the TSR program, the contents of the registers must be saved because they belong to the context of the interrupted program and must be restored when it is resumed.

The same applies for context dependent operating system information, which for DOS includes just the PSP (Program Segment Prefix) of the program and the DTA (Disk Transfer Area). The addresses of both structures must be determined and saved when the TSR program is installed, so that they can be reset when context is changed to the TSR program. Also, we must not forget to save the addresses of the PSP and DTA of the interrupted program before the context change to the TSR program. There are DOS functions for setting and reading the address of the DTA (DOS functions 1AH and 2FH), but there are no corresponding documented functions for the PSP. DOS Version 3.0 includes function 62H, which returns the address of the current PSP, but has no function for setting the address. Undocumented functions for doing both exist in DOS 2.0: function 50H (set PSP address) and 51H (get PSP address). Both of these are used in our TSR demonstration program.

One final task is required of the TSR code. When the TSR program is activated using interrupt 28H, an active DOS function is interrupted—one whose stack must not be disturbed. Generally we should take the top 64 words from the current stack and place them on the stack of the TSR program. This completes the context change to the TSR program, which means that the TSR program can now be started.

At the moment, the TSR program can be viewed as a completely normal program which can call arbitrary DOS and BIOS functions. The only competitor left in the system is the foreground program. The TSR must ensure that it leaves both the foreground program and its screen undisturbed.

Saving the screen context

The tasks were exclusively handled in assembly language. However, the C or Pascal program comprising the TSR program itself can save the screen context. This screen context includes the current video mode, the cursor position and the screen's contents. The contents of the color registers and other registers on the video card must also be saved, if any of these values are changed by the TSR program.

As described in Section 7.4, the video mode can easily be determined with function 00H of BIOS video interrupt 16H. If the screen is in text mode (modes 0, 1, 2, 3, and 7), the TSR program must save the first 4000 bytes of video RAM. The video BIOS can be used for this (see Section 7.4), or you can access the video RAM directly (see Chapter 10).

Saving the video mode becomes very complicated if a graphics mode is active, since the video RAM for EGA and VGA cards can be as large as 256K in some modes. If the TSR program interrupted a transient program, it may not be possible to allocate a large enough buffer to handle both programs.

This is why many TSR programs will not activate themselves from within graphics mode, and can only be used in text mode. Since PCs mostly use text mode, this doesn't present a big problem. GEM® and Microsoft Windows®, which operate only in graphics mode, are exceptions. Since these programs usually support some mechanism for parallel execution of calculators, note pads, etc., TSR programs can prove less useful under these systems.

The assembler interface

We now have enough information to understand the operation of the two assembly language interfaces. The two programs are based on the principles we have outlined here; the differences between them reflect the different syntaxes of compiled C and

Pascal programs. We will first concentrate on the common points of the two programs.

Both programs assume that the TSR program was installed by the first call from the DOS level, and will be reinstalled on each new call. It is important to remember one general rule: a TSR program can be reinstalled only if no other TSR programs have been installed in the meantime. The LIFO (Last In, First Out) principle applies here, so the only way a TSR program can be reinstalled is if it was the last one to be installed, and if the corresponding interrupt vectors point to its interrupt handlers. If another TSR program was installed following it, the interrupt vectors point to its handlers.

To support this mechanism, the assembly language interface offers the high-level program three routines with which install and later reinstall the TSR program. To decide whether the program should be installed or reinstalled, the first function should be called to see if the TSR program is already installed. This routine is passed an identification string, which will play an important role later when the program is installed. The routine looks for this ID string within the handler for interrupt 09H. If it finds the string, the TSR program is already installed and can be reinstalled.

If the ID string is not discovered, the TSR program has not been installed, or another TSR program redirected the interrupt 09H vector in the meantime. The TSR program can then be installed with the help of the installation routine. This routine must receive the ID string used to detect whether the program has already been installed, the address of the high level routine which will be called when the TSR program is activated, and the hotkey value. The hotkey value is the bit pattern in the BIOS keyboard flag which will activate the TSR program and can be defined within the high level language program with the help of predefined constants.

The initialization routine first saves the addresses of the interrupt handlers for interrupts 09H, 13H and 28H. Then the data for the context of the high level program are read and saved in variables within the code segment, so that they are available for the interrupt handler and for activation of the TSR program. In the next step, the new interrupt handlers for interrupts 09H, 13H, and 28H are installed. Finally, the number of paragraphs after the end of the program which are to remain resident must be calculated. Here the C and Pascal interfaces differ from each other. Information about this calculation can be found in the individual descriptions of the interfaces.

The actual installation is now over and the program is terminated as resident. Notice that the installation routine does not return to the high level language program, so all initialization such as memory allocation or variable initialization must be performed before the call to this routine.

If the test function of the assembly language module determines that the program is already installed, it can be reinstalled with the help of another function. This function is passed the address of a routine in the high level language program which will perform a "cleanup" of the program. This process includes releasing allocated memory and other tasks. If no such routine is to be called, the assembly language routine must be passed the value -1. Since the "cleanup" function is in the TSR program, and not in the program which is performing the reinstallation, a context switch is necessary. Unlike activation of the TSR program and the corresponding interruption of the foreground program, this is from the program which is doing the reinstallation to the already installed TSR program. The reinstallation returns the redirected interrupt handlers to their old routines and releases the memory allocated by the TSR program.

In addition to these three functions which are called from the high level language program, the assembler module contains some routines which may not be called by high level language programs. These include the interrupt handlers for interrupts 09H, 13H, and 28H as well as a routine which accomplishes the context switch to and from the TSR program.

The high level language programs

The following programs in C and Pascal demonstrate the assembly language routines. They first check to see if the program is already installed or not. On a new installation, a TSR routine is installed. You can activate the TSR by pressing both <Shift> keys. It stores the screen contents, then displays a message and asks the user to press a key. After this is done, the old screen contents are copied back and the execution of the interrupted program continues.

On a reinstallation, the assembly language reinstallation program calls a cleanup function in the TSR program. It prints the number of activations of the TSR program, which is set to zero when the TSR program is installed and incremented on each activation. This makes it clear that the cleanup function is actually executed in the installed TSR program and not in the program which performs the reinstallation.

TSR development

There are some procedures you should follow when developing TSR programs, that apply to the special characteristics of these programs. First, the program should be developed as a completely normal program, compiled and executed from the DOS user interface, or an interactive environment. To prepare for conversion to a TSR program, you can write an initialization routine and the actual TSR routine which will be called when the hotkey is pressed. Unlike the TSR version, you can call these routines in the main procedure/function of the program, allowing activation independent of any hotkeys. You should completely develop and test the program in this manner. Once it works correctly, you can convert it to a TSR program.

The conversion to a TSR program is relatively simple, and involves linking in the assembly language module to the program and calling the corresponding functions. You can see how this is done in detail in the two example programs.

After linking the assembly language routines and converting the program to an EXE file, it should be started only from DOS. Do not start it from within an interactive environment like Turbo Pascal or Turbo C.

The C implementation

Since TSR programs should use as little memory as possible, the assembly language interface was developed to be linked with the smallest C memory model (the small model). In both Microsoft and Turbo C compilers, the program code and data are placed in two separate segments, each of which may be no larger than 64K. The data includes global and static data as well as the stack and the heap. As the following figures show, Turbo C and Microsoft C use different memory organization, despite their similarities. While in Turbo C the stack is placed behind the heap and moves from the end of the data segment to the end of the heap, the stack is between the global data and the heap in Microsoft C.

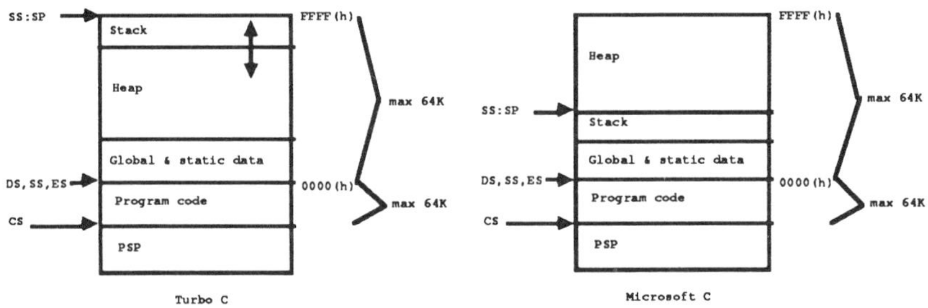

Structure of a small model program (Turbo C/Microsoft C)

If this organization had no effect on the assembly language interface, we would be ready to allocate the entire 64K of the data segment resident in memory in addition to the program code. Since this would mean a significant waste of memory, and TSR programs should use as little memory as possible, the assembly language should mark as resident only the part of the data segment which is actually required.

The size of this memory area depends on the size of the data (or objects) which will be allocated on the heap by the functions calloc() and malloc(). You must guess this size and pass it to the initialization routine so that the end of the required memory in the data segment can be calculated.

This mechanism allows you to use the heap functions normally within the TSR program. Unfortunately, this applies only to the Turbo C compiler. Microsoft C uses an allocation algorithm which assumes that all of the memory to the end of the data segment is available, so allocating heap storage should be avoided within a

TSR program compiled with Microsoft C. You should allocate the buffers and variables required when the TSR program is initialized or place the required objects in global variables. The example C program allocates the two buffers it needs in the main() function and then places the addresses of the buffers in global variables.

There is something else you should be aware of when using Turbo C. Since the stack grows from the end of the 64K data segment to the heap, it finds itself outside the program when parts of the data segment are released again, and this in an area of memory which DOS may give to other programs. To avoid problems with this, the assembly language interface places the stack immediately after the heap, giving it 512 bytes of space. This should suffice for most applications, but may lead to problems if you use large objects (such as arrays) as local variables or pass them to other functions via the stack. In this case you should enlarge the stack by setting the constant TC_STACK in the assembly language interface to a larger value.

The different treatment of the stack is the reason that the initialization routine in the assembly language interface must be told what compiler the TSR program will be compiled with. In practice you don't have to worry about this since it is handled within the C program with the help of constants defined with conditional preprocessor statements.

The TSR initialization routine TSR_INIT must be called with the following parameters (in the specified order):

- Compiler type (0 = Microsoft C, 1 = Turbo C)
- Pointer to the C TSR function
- Hotkey (mask for reading the BIOS keyboard flag)
- Number of bytes to keep free on the heap
- Pointer to an identification string

The initialization routine uses the information about the compiler type and the number of bytes which must be available on the stack to calculate the number of paragraphs which must remain resident in memory. The C library function SBRK is called from the assembly language routine to determine the offset address of the current end of heap. The number of bytes which must be reserved for the heap is added to this address. With Turbo C we also add the size of the stack, which is appended to the heap and must also stay resident. The result of this addition is the offset address of the last byte in memory relative to the start of the data segment.

This address is converted to paragraphs by shifting it four places to the right, dividing it by 16. The result is the number of paragraphs which must remain resident in the data segment. In addition, there are the paragraphs from the PSP and the code segment. They can be calculated by subtracting the segment address of the data segment (which is also the ending address of the code segment) and the segment address of the PSP. Since both Turbo C and Microsoft C store the segment address of the PSP in a global variable called _PSP, it can be read by the assembly language routine and included in the subtraction. The program is then ended by a call to DOS function 31H, which keeps the specified number of paragraphs (passed in the DX register) resident. The TSR program is installed.

If a cleanup program is to be called when the program is reinstalled with the UNINST function, the UNINST function must be passed a pointer to this function. In C this is done simply by using the name of the function to be called as a parameter.

If no such function is to be called, the argument -1 must be passed. Since this is not a valid function pointer, it must be preceded by the following cast operator:

```
(void (*)(void)) -1
```

There is a symbol, NO_END_FTN, defined with this expression in the C program which you can use in the call to UNINST.

You can get additional information from the following listing. It will make a good basis for developing your own TSR programs.

C listing: TSRC.C

```
/**********************************************************************/
/*                              T S R C                               */
/*--------------------------------------------------------------------*/
/*    Description    : C module which is turned into a TSR program    */
/*                     with the help of an assembly language routine. */
/*--------------------------------------------------------------------*/
/*    Author         : MICHAEL TISCHER                                */
/*    developed on   : 08/15/1988                                     */
/*    last update    : 08/19/1988                                     */
/*--------------------------------------------------------------------*/
/*    (MICROSOFT C)                                                   */
/*    creation       : CL /AS /c TSRC.C                               */
/*                     LINK TSRC TSRCA;                               */
/*    call           : TSRC                                           */
/*--------------------------------------------------------------------*/
/*    (BORLAND TURBO C)                                               */
/*    creation       : Create project file with the following        */
/*                     contents:                                      */
/*                     TSRC                                           */
/*                     TSRCA.OBJ                                      */
/*                     Before compiling, set Options menu / linker    */
/*                     option / Case sensitive link to OFF            */
/**********************************************************************/

/*== Include files ===================================================*/

#include <stdlib.h>
#include <dos.h>

/*== Typedefs ========================================================*/

typedef unsigned char BYTE;                    /* build ourselves a byte */
typedef unsigned int WORD;
typedef BYTE BOOL;                             /* like BOOLEAN in Pascal */
```

```
typedef union vel far * VP;      /* VP is a FAR pointer into the VRAM */

/*== Macros ===================================================*/

#ifndef MK_FP                          /* was MK_FP already defined? */
#define MK_FP(seg, ofs) ((void far *) ((unsigned long) (seg)<<16|(ofs)))
#endif
#define VOFS(x,y) ( 80 * ( y ) + ( x ) )
#define VPOS(x,y) (VP) ( vptr + VOFS( x, y ) )

/*== Structures and unions ====================================*/

struct velb {              /* describes a screen position as two bytes */
            BYTE character,                        /* the ASCII code */
                 attribute;                /* corresponding attribute */
           };

struct velw {               /* describes a screen position as one word */
            WORD contents;    /* stores ASCII character and attribute */
           };

union vel {                             /* describes a screen position */
          struct velb h;
          struct velw x;
         };

/*== Link the functions from the assembly module =====================*/

extern int is_inst( char * id_string );
extern void uninst( void (*fkt)(void) );
extern int tsr_init(BOOL TC, void (*fkt)(void), unsigned hotkey,
                    unsigned heap, char * id_string);

/*== Constants ===================================================*/

#ifdef __TURBOC__                    /* are we compiling with TURBO-C? */
  #define TC TRUE                                              /* yes */
#else                                    /* we are using Microsoft C */
  #define TC FALSE
#endif

/*-- codes of the individual control keys for building the hotkey mask */

#define RSHIFT      1                        /* right SHIFT key pressed */
#define LSHIFT      2                         /* left SHIFT key pressed */
#define CTRL        4                              /* CTRL key pressed */
#define ALT         8                               /* ALT key pressed */
#define SCRL_AN    16                               /* Scroll Lock ON */
#define NUML_AN    32                                  /* Num Lock ON */
#define CAPL_AN    64                                 /* Caps Lock ON */
#define INS_AN    128                                    /* Insert ON */
#define SCR_LOCK  4096                          /* Scroll Lock pressed */
#define NUM_LOCK  8192                             /* Num Lock pressed */
#define CAP_LOCK 16384                            /* Caps Lock pressed */
#define INSERT   32768                           /* INSERT key pressed */
#define NOF      0x07                                 /* normal color */
#define INV      0x70                                /* inverse color */
#define HNOF     0x0f                          /* bright normal color */
#define HINV     0xf0                         /* bright inverse color */

#define HEAP_FREE 1024                     /* leave 1K space on the heap */

#define TRUE  1                        /* constants for working with BOOL */
#define FALSE 0

#define NO_END_FTN ((void (*)(void)) -1)     /* don't call an end ftn. */

/*== Global variables ============================================*/

char id_string[] = "MiTi";                    /* identification string */
```

```
VP vptr;                 /* pointer to the first character in video RAM */
unsigned atimes = 0;        /* number of activations of the TSR program */
union vel * scrbuf;       /* pointer to the buffer with screen contents */
char * blank_line;                          /* pointer to a blank line */

/***********************************************************************
*  Function          : D I S P _ I N I T                               *
**-------------------------------------------------------------------**
*  Description       : Determines the base address of the video RAM.   *
*  Input parameters  : none                                            *
*  Return value      : none                                            *
***********************************************************************/

void disp_init(void)
 {
  union REGS regs;             /* processor regs for the interrupt call */

  regs.h.ah = 15;              /* function number: determing video mode */
  int86(0x10, &regs, &regs);           /* call the BIOS video interrupt */

  /* calculate base addr of the video RAM according to the video mode */

  vptr = (VP) MK_FP((regs.h.al == 7) ? 0xb000 : 0xb800, 0);
 }

/***********************************************************************
*  Function          : D I S P _ P R I N T                             *
**-------------------------------------------------------------------**
*  Description       : Output a string to the screen.                  *
*  Input parameters  : - COLUMN    = the output column                 *
*                      - LINE      = the output line                   *
*                      - COLOR     = attribute for the characters      *
*                      - STRING    = pointer to the string             *
*  Return value      : none                                            *
***********************************************************************/

void disp_print(BYTE column, BYTE line, BYTE
color, char * string)
 {
  register VP lptr;     /* running pointer for accessing the video RAM */

  lptr = VPOS(column, line);             /* set pointer to the video RAM */
  for ( ; *string ; ++lptr)                   /* run through the string */
   {
    lptr->h.character = *(string++); /* write char into the video RAM */
    lptr->h.attribute = color;      /* set attribute for the character */
   }
 }

/***********************************************************************
*  Function          : S A V E _ S C R E N                             *
**-------------------------------------------------------------------**
*  Description       : Saves the screen contents in a buffer.          *
*  Input parameters  : - SPTR     = pointer to the buffer in which the *
*                                   screen will be saved.              *
*  Return value      : none                                            *
*  Info              : It is assumed that the buffer is large enough to *
*                      hold the screen contents.                       *
***********************************************************************/

void save_screen( union vel * sptr )
 {
  register VP lptr;     /* running pointer for accessing the video RAM */
  unsigned i;                                        /* loop counter */
  lptr = VPOS(0, 0);                   /* set pointer in the video RAM */

  for (i=0; i<2000; i++)      /* run through the 2000 screen positions */
   (sptr++)->x.contents = (lptr++)->x.contents; /* save char. & attr. */
 }
```

```
/*************************************************************************
*  Function          : R E S T O R E _ S C R E E N                      *
**-------------------------------------------------------------------**
*  Description       : Copies the contents of a buffer into the video   *
*                      RAM.                                             *
*  Input parameters : - SPTR     = pointer to the buffer in which the  *
*                                  screen contents are located         *
*  Return value      : none                                             *
*************************************************************************/

void restore_screen( union vel * sptr )
 {
  register VP lptr;              /* pointer for accessing the video RAM */
  unsigned i;                                            /* loop counter */
  lptr = VPOS(0, 0);                  /* set pointer to the video RAM */

  for (i=0; i<2000; i++)      /* run through the 2000 screen positions */
   (lptr++)->x.contents = (sptr++)->x.contents; /* restore char.&attr.*/
 }

/*************************************************************************
*  Function          : E N D F T N                                      *
**-------------------------------------------------------------------**
*  Description       : Called when the TSR program is reinstalled.      *
*  Input parameters : none                                              *
*  Return value      : none                                             *
*************************************************************************/

void endftn( void )
{
 /*-- release the allocated buffers ----------------------------------*/

 free( blank_line );                   /* release the allocated buffer */
 free( (void *) scrbuf );                          /* release the buffer */

 printf("The TSR program was activated %u times.\n", atimes);
}

/*************************************************************************
*  Function          : T S R                                            *
**-------------------------------------------------------------------**
*  Description       : Called by the assembler routine when the hotkey  *
*                      is pressed.                                      *
*  Input parameters : none                                              *
*  Return value      : none                                             *
*************************************************************************/

void tsr( void )
{
 BYTE i;                                                 /* loop counter */

 ++atimes;                          /* increment the number of activations */
 disp_init();                        /* determine address of the video RAM */
 save_screen( scrbuf );                /* save the current screen contents */
 for (i=0; i<25; i++)                  /* run through the 25 screen lines */
  disp_print(0, i, INV, blank_line);                       /* clear the line */
 disp_print(22, 11, INV, "TSRC  -  (c) 1988 by MICHAEL TISCHER");
 disp_print(28, 13, INV, "Please press a key ...");
 getch();                                               /* wait for a key */
 restore_screen( scrbuf );                      /* copy the old screen back */
}

/*************************************************************************/
/**                          MAIN PROGRAM                              **/
/*************************************************************************/

void main()
{
 printf("TSRC  -  (c) 1988 by MICHAEL TISCHER\n\n");
 if ( is_inst( id_string ) )     /* is the program already installed? */
```

```
  { /* yes */
   printf("TSRC was already installed--now disabling.\n");
   uninst( endftn );               /* reinstall prg., call ftn. ENDFKT */

   /*-- if no end function is to be called, the call is: -------------*/
   /*-- uninst( NO_END_FTN );                            -------------*/
  }
 else                    /* no, the program has not been installed yet */
  {
   /*-- with MSC the heap buffers must be allocated now --------------*/

   scrbuf = (union vel *) malloc(80 * 25 * sizeof(union vel));
   blank_line = (char *) sbrk( 80 + 1 );          /* allocate buffer */
   *(blank_line + 80 ) = '\0';             /* terminate buffer with NUL */
   memset(blank_line, ' ', 80);          /* fill the buffer with spaces */

   printf("TSRC now enabled - Start: <LSHIFT> + <RSHIFT>\n");
   tsr_init(TC, tsr, RSHIFT | LSHIFT, HEAP_FREE, id_string);
  }
}
```

Assembler listing: TSRCA.ASM

```
;***********************************************************************;
;*                              T S R C A                              *;
;*---------------------------------------------------------------------*;
;*    Description    : represents the assembler interface to a         *;
;*                      C program which can be activated by a hotkey   *;
;*                      as a TSR program.                              *;
;*---------------------------------------------------------------------*;
;*    Author         : MICHAEL TISCHER                                 *;
;*    developed on   : 08/10/1988                                      *;
;*    last update    : 05/26/1989                                      *;
;*---------------------------------------------------------------------*;
;*    to assemble    : MASM TSRCA;                                     *;
;*                      ... combine with C program                     *;
;***********************************************************************;

IGROUP group _text                ;combination of program segments
DGROUP group const,_bss,  _data   ;combination of data segments
       assume CS:IGROUP, DS:DGROUP, ES:DGROUP, SS:DGROUP

CONST  segment word public 'CONST';this segment holds all read-only
CONST  ends                       ;constants

_BSS   segment word public 'BSS'  ;this segment stores all uninitialized
_BSS   ends                       ;static variables

_DATA  segment word public 'DATA' ;all initialized and global static
                                  ;variables are stored in this
                                  ;segment

extrn  __psp : word               ;segment addr of the PSP of the C prg

_DATA  ends

;== Constants ==========================================================

MAX_ID_LEN equ 16                 ;maximum length of the ID string
TC_STACK   equ 512                ;512 bytes are reserved for the stack
                                  ;with TURBO-C

;== Program ============================================================

_TEXT  segment byte public 'CODE' ;the program segment

;-- Reference to external (C) functions --------------------------------

extrn      _sbrk:near             ;returns end address of the heap
```

```
;-- Public declarations of internal functions --------------------------

public      _tsr_init              ;allows call from C program
public      _is_inst
public      _uninst


;-- Variables for the interrupt handler --------------------------------
;-- (only accessible via the code segment) -----------------------------

id_buf      db (MAX_ID_LEN + 1) dup (0)  ;buffer for the ID string
ce_ptr      equ this dword         ;points to the routine CALL_END
ce_ofs      dw offset call_end     ;in the already-installed TSR program
ce_seg      dw ?

;-- Variables needed for activation of the C program -------------------

c_ss        dw 0                   ;C stack segment
c_sp        dw 0                   ;C stack pointer
c_ds        dw 0                   ;C data segment
c_es        dw 0                   ;C extra segment

c_dta_ofs   dw 0                   ;DTA address of the C program
c_dta_seg   dw 0

c_psp       dw 0                   ;segment addr of the PSP of the C prg
break_adr   dw 0                   ;break address of the heap
fkt_adr     dw 0                   ;address of the C TSR function

;-- Variables for testing for the hotkey -------------------------------

key_mask    dw 0                   ;hotkey mark for BIOS keyboard flag
recur       db 0                   ;prevents recursive TSR calls
in_bios     db 0                   ;shows activity of the BIOS disk
                                   ;interrupt

daptr       equ this dword         ;pointer to the DOS Indos flag
daptr_ofs   dw 0                   ;offset address
daptr_seg   dw 0                   ;segment address

;-- The following variables store the old addresses of the interrupt ---
;-- handler, which will be replaced by the new interrupt handler     ---

int9_ptr    equ this dword         ;old interrupt vector 9h
int9_ofs    dw 0                   ;offset address of the old handler
int9_seg    dw 0                   ;segment address of the old handler

int13_ptr   equ this dword         ;old interrupt vector 13h
int13_ofs   dw 0                   ;offset address of the old handler
int13_seg   dw 0                   ;segment address of the old handler

int28_ptr   equ this dword         ;old interrupt vbector 28h
int28_ofs   dw 0                   ;offset address of the old handler
int28_seg   dw 0                   ;segment address of the old handler

;-- Variables which store the information of the interrupted -----------
;-- program.                                                 -----------

u_dta_ofs   dw 0                   ;DTA address of interrupted program
u_dta_seg   dw 0

u_psp       dw 0                   ;segment addr of the PSP of int. prg.

uprg_ss     dw 0                   ;SS and SP of the interrupted prg.
uprg_sp     dw 0

;-----------------------------------------------------------------------
;-- TSR_INIT: ends the C program and makes the new interrupt -----------
;--           interrupt handler active
```

```
;-- Call from C: void tsr_init( bool TC,
;--                              void (fkt *)(void),
;--                              int key_mask,
;--                              unsigned heap_byte,
;--                              char * id_string );

_tsr_init  proc    near

sframe0    struc                    ;structure for accessing the stack
bp0        dw ?                     ;stores BP
ret_adr0   dw ?                     ;return address
tc0        dw ?                     ;compiler (1 = TURBO-C, 0 = MSC )
fktptr0    dw ?                     ;pointer to C TSR function
keymask0   dw ?                     ;mask for hotkey
heap0      dw ?                     ;heap bytes required
idptr0     dw ?                     ;pointer to the ID string
sframe0    ends                     ;end of the structure

frame      equ [ bp - bp0 ]

           push bp                  ;store BP on the stack
           mov  bp,sp               ;move SP to BP

           ;-- save the C segment registers ----------------------------

           mov  cs:c_ss,ss          ;store the registers in the
           mov  cs:c_sp,sp          ;corresponding variables
           mov  cs:c_es,es
           mov  cs:c_ds,ds

           ;-- copy the ID string into the internal buffer ------------

           mov  si,frame.idptr0     ;DS:SI now points to the string
           push cs                  ;move CS to the stack
           pop  es                  ;and restore as ES
           mov  di,offset id_buf    ;ES:DI now points to ID_BUF
           mov  cx,MAX_ID_LEN       ;copy maxmimum of MAX_ID_LEN chars
ti0:       lodsb                    ;get character from string
           stosb                    ;and place in internal buffer
           or   al,al               ;test for end of string
           loopne ti0               ;continue if char!=0 and CX!=0

           ;-- store the parameters passed ----------------------------

           mov  ax,frame.fktptr0    ;get pointer to the C TSR function
           mov  cs:fkt_adr,ax       ;and save
           mov  ax,frame.keymask0   ;get mask for hotkey
           mov  cs:key_mask,ax      ;and save


           ;-- determine DTA address of the C program -----------------

           mov  ah,2fh              ;ftn. no.: get DTA address
           int  21h                 ;call DOS interrupt
           mov  cs:c_dta_ofs,bx     ;store address in the corresponding
           mov  cs:c_dta_seg,es     ;variables

           ;-- determine address of the INDOS flag --------------------

           mov  ah,34h              ;ftn. no.: get addr of the INDOS flag
           int  21h                 ;call DOS interrupt
           mov  cs:daptr_ofs,bx     ;save address in the corresponding
           mov  cs:daptr_seg,es     ;variables

           ;-- get the addresses of the interrupt handler  ------------

           mov  ax,3509h            ;get interrupt vector 9h
           int  21h                 ;call DOS interrupt
           mov  cs:int9_ofs,bx      ;save address of the handler in the
           mov  cs:int9_seg,es      ;appropriate variable
```

```
          mov  ax,3513h          ;get interrupt vector 13h
          int  21h               ;call DOS interrupt
          mov  cs:int13_ofs,bx   ;store address of the handler in the
          mov  cs:int13_seg,es   ;corresponding variables

          mov  ax,3528h          ;get interrupt vector 28h
          int  21h               ;call DOS interrupt
          mov  cs:int28_ofs,bx   ;store address of the handler in the
          mov  cs:int28_seg,es   ;corresponding variables

          ;-- install the new interrupt handlers ---------------------

          push ds                ;save data segment
          mov  ax,cs             ;CS to AX and then load into DS
          mov  ds,ax

          mov  ax,2509h          ;ftn. no.: set interrupt 9h
          mov  dx,offset int09   ;DS:DX stores the addr of the handler
          int  21h               ;call DOS interrupt

          mov  ax,2513h          ;ftn. no.: set interrupt 13h
          mov  dx,offset int13   ;DS:DX stores the addr of the handler
          int  21h               ;call DOS interrupt

          mov  ax,2528h          ;ftn. no.: set interrupt 28h
          mov  dx,offset int28   ;DS:DX stores the addr of the handler
          int  21h               ;call DOS interrupt

          pop  ds                ;restore DS from stack

          ;-- calculatre number of paragraphs which must remain -------
          ;-- in memory.                                         -------

          xor  ax,ax             ;determine current break address
          push ax                ;as argument for SBRK on the stack
          call _sbrk             ;call C function SBRK
                                 ;AX contains the end addr of the heap
          pop  cx                ;get argument from stack again
          add  ax,frame.heap0    ;add required heap memory

          ;-- With TURBO-C the stack is found behind the heap and -----
          ;-- begins with the end of the segment. It must thus
          ;-- be moved near the heap.

          cmp  byte ptr frame.tc0,0  ;using TURBO-C?
          je   msc               ;no, MSC

          add  ax,TC_STACK-1     ;calculate new stack pointer for TC
          mov  cs:c_sp,ax        ;and store
          inc  ax                ;set break address

          ;-- Calculate number of paragraphs which must remain --------
          ;-- resident in memory.

msc:      mov  dx,ax             ;get break address into DX
          add  dx,15             ;avoid loss through integer division
          mov  cl,4              ;shift 4 times to the right and then
          shr  dx,cl             ;divide by 16
          mov  ax,ds             ;move AX to DS
          mov  bx,__psp          ;get segment address of the PSP
          mov  cs:c_psp,bx       ;save in a variable
          sub  ax,bx             ;subtract DS from PSP
          add  dx,ax             ;and add to the number of paragraphs
          mov  ax,3100h          ;ftn. no.: end resident program
          int  21h               ;call DOS interrupt and end program

_tsr_init endp

;-------------------------------------------------------------------
```

```
;-- IS_INST: determines if the program is already installed ------------
;-- Call from C : int ist_inst( char * id_string );
;-- Return value: 1, if the program was already installed, else 0

_is_inst   proc    near

sframe1    struc                    ;structure for accessing the stack
bp1        dw ?                     ;hold BP
ret_adr1   dw ?                     ;return address
idptr1     dw ?                     ;pointer to the ID string
sframe1    ends                     ;end of the structure
frame      equ [ bp - bp1 ]

           push bp                  ;save BP on the stack
           mov  bp,sp               ;move SP to BP
           push di                  ;save DI on the stack
           push si                  ;save SI on the stack
           push es                  ;save ES on the stack

           ;-- determine segment address of the current int 9 handler --

           mov  ax,3509h            ;get interrupt vector 9h
           int  21h                 ;DOS interrupt puts seg addr in ES
           mov  di,offset id_buf    ;ES:DI points to installed ID_BUF
           mov  si,frame.idptr1     ;DS:SI points to the ID_STRING passed

           mov  cx,0                ;return code: not installed
isi0:      lodsb                    ;load character from the string
           cmp  al,es:[di]          ;compare to other string
           jne  not_inst            ;not equal --> NOT_INST
           inc  di                  ;increment pointer in String2
           or   al,al               ;end of string reached?
           jne  isi0                ;no, keep comparing --> ISI0

           mov  cl,1                ;yes --> the program is installed

not_inst:  mov  ax,cx               ;get return code from ax
           pop  es                  ;restore saved registers from stack
           pop  si
           pop  di
           pop  bp
           ret                      ;back to the caller

_is_inst   endp                     ;end of the procedure

;-----------------------------------------------------------------------
;-- CALL_END: calls the end function on reinstallation of the TSR ------
;--          program.
;-- Input    : DI = offset address of the routine to be called
;-- Info     : This function is not intended to be called by a C program.

call_end   proc far

           call di                  ;call the end function
           ret                      ;back to the caller

call_end   endp

;-----------------------------------------------------------------------
;-- UNINST: reinstalls the TSR program and releases the allocated ------
;--         memory again.
;-- Call from C : void uninst( void (endfkt *) ( void ) );
;-- Info        : if the value -1 (0xffff) is passed as the pointer to
;--               the end function, no end function will be called.
;-- Note        : This function should be called only when a prior call
;--               to IS_INST() has returned the value 1.

_uninst    proc    near

sframe2    struc                    ;structure for accessing the stack
```

```
bp2         dw ?                  ;stores BP
ret_adr2    dw ?                  ;return address
ftnptr2     dw ?                  ;pointer to the end function
sframe2     ends                  ;end of the structure

frame       equ [ bp - bp2 ]

            assume  es:IGROUP     ;allow access to the CS variables
                                  ;via ES

            push bp               ;save BP on the stack
            mov  bp,sp            ;move SP to BP
            push di               ;store DI on the stack
            push si               ;store SI on the stack
            push ds               ;store DS on the stack
            push es               ;store ES on the stack

            ;-- determine the seg addr of the current int 9 handler ---
            mov  ax,3509h         ;get interrupt vector 9h
            int  21h              ;DOS interrupt puts seg addr in ES

            mov  di,frame.ftnptr2 ;get address of the end function
            cmp  di,0ffffh        ;no end function called?
            je   no_endftn        ;NO ---> NO_ENDFTN

            ;-- Perform context switch to C program and execute -------
            ;-- the specified end funtion

            mov  cs:ce_seg,es     ;save ES in jump vector

            mov  cs:uprg_ss,ss    ;save current stack segment and
            mov  cs:uprg_sp,sp    ;stack pointer

            cli                   ;allow no more interrupts
            mov  ss,es:c_ss       ;activate the stack of the TSR
            mov  sp,es:c_sp       ;program
            sti                   ;allow interrupts again

            push es               ;save ES on the stack
            mov  ah,2fh           ;ftn. no.: get DTA address
            int  21h              ;call DOS interrupt
            mov  cs:u_dta_ofs,bx  ;save address of the DTA of the
            mov  cs:u_dta_seg,es  ;interrupted program
            pop  es               ;get ES back from the stack

            mov  ah,50h           ;ftn. no.: set address of the PSP
            mov  bx,es:c_psp      ;get seg addr of the PSP of the C prg
            int  21h              ;call DOS interrupt

            push ds               ;save ES and DS on the stack
            push es

            mov  ah,1ah           ;ftn. no.: set DTA address
            mov  dx,es:c_dta_ofs  ;get offset address of the new DTA
            mov  ds,es:c_dta_seg  ;and segment address of the new DTA
            int  21h              ;call DOS interrupt

            mov  ds,es:c_ds       ;set segment register for the
            mov  es,es:c_es       ;C program
            call cs:[ce_ptr]      ;call the function

            ;-- perform context change to the interrupt program -------

            mov  ah,1ah           ;ftn. no.: set DTA address
            mov  dx,cs:u_dta_ofs  ;load offset and segment address of
            mov  ds,cs:u_dta_seg  ;the interrupted program
            int  21h              ;call DOS interrupt

            pop  es               ;seg addr of the TSR prog from stack
            pop  ds               ;restore DS from stack
```

```
          mov  ah,50h            ;ftn. no.: set address of the PSP
          mov  bx,__psp          ;load seg addr of the PSP
          int  21h               ;call DOS interrupt

          cli                    ;don't allow interrupts
          mov  ss,cs:uprg_ss     ;restore stack pointer and stack
          mov  sp,cs:uprg_sp     ;segment
          sti                    ;allow interrupts again

          ;-- reinstall the interrupt handler of the TSR --------------
          ;-- program                                     --------------

no_endftn: cli                   ;don't allow interrupts
          mov  ax,2509h          ;ftn. no.: set handler for int 9
          mov  ds,es:int9_seg    ;segment address of the old handler
          mov  dx,es:int9_ofs    ;offset address of the old handler
          int  21h               ;install the old handler again

          mov  ax,2513h          ;ftn. no.: set handler for int 13
          mov  ds,es:int13_seg   ;segment address of the old handler
          mov  dx,es:int13_ofs   ;offset address of the old handler
          int  21h               ;reinstall the old handler

          mov  ax,2528h          ;ftn. no.: set handler for int 28
          mov  ds,es:int28_seg   ;segment address of the old handler
          mov  dx,es:int28_ofs   ;offset address of the old handler
          int  21h               ;reinstall the old handler

          sti                    ;allow interrupts again

          mov  es,es:c_psp       ;seg addr of the PSP of the TSR prg
          mov  cx,es             ;save in CX
          mov  es,es:[ 02ch ]    ;get seg addr of environment from PSP
          mov  ah,49h            ;ftn. no.: release allocated memory
          int  21h               ;call DOS interrupt

          mov  es,cx             ;restore ES from CX
          mov  ah,49h            ;ftn. no.: release allocated memoru
          int  21h               ;call DOS interrupt

          pop  es                ;get the saved registers back from
          pop  ds                ;the stack
          pop  si
          pop  di

          pop  bp
          ret                    ;back to the called

          assume es:DGROUP       ;combine ES with DGROUP again

_uninst   endp                   ;end of the procedure

;----------------------------------------------------------------------
;-- The new interrupt routine follows ---------------------------------
;----------------------------------------------------------------------

;-- The new interrupt 09h handler -------------------------------------

int09     proc far

          pushf                  ;simulate the call of the old handler
          call cs:int9_ptr       ;via the INT 9h instruction

          cli                    ;suppress interrupts
          cmp  cs:recur,0        ;is the TSR prog already active?
          jne  ik_end            ;YES: back to the called of int 9

          ;-- test to see if the BIOS disk int is being executed now

          cmp  cs:in_bios,0      ;BIOS disk interrupt active?
```

```
           jne  ik_end           ;yes --> back to the caller

           ;-- BIOS disk interrupt not active, test for hotkey --------

           push ax               ;save ES and AX on the stack
           push es
           xor  ax,ax            ;set ES to the lowest memory segment
           mov  es,ax
           mov  ax,word ptr es:[417h] ;get BIOS keyboard flag
           and  ax,cs:key_mask   ;mask out the non-hotkey bits
           cmp  ax,cs:key_mask   ;are only the hotkey bits left?
           pop  es               ;get ES and AX
           pop  ax
           jne  ik_end           ;hotkey discovered? no --> back

           ;-- the hotkey was pressed, test to see if DOS is active ---

           push ds               ;save DS and BX on the stack
           push bx
           lds  bx,cs:daptr      ;DS:BX now point to the INDOS flag
           cmp  byte ptr [bx],0  ;DOS function active?
           pop  bx               ;restore BX and DS from the stack
           pop  ds
           jne  ik_end           ;DOS function active --> IK_END

           ;-- DOS is not active, activatr TSR program ----------------

           call  start_tsr       ;start the TSR program
ik_end:    iret                  ;back to the interrupted program

int09      endp
;-- the new interrupt 13h handler --------------------------------------

int13      proc far

           mov  cs:in_bios,1     ;set flag and show that the BIOS disk
                                 ;interrupt is active
           pushf                 ;call the old interrupt handler
           call cs:int13_ptr     ;simulate via int 13h
           mov  cs:in_bios, 0    ;BIOS disk interrupt no longer active

           ret  2                ;back to the caller, but don't remove
                                 ;the flag reg from the stack first
int13      endp

;-- the new interrupt 28h handler -------------------------------------

int28      proc far

           pushf                 ;simulate calling the old interrupt
           call cs:int28_ptr     ;handler via int 28h

           cli                   ;suppress further interrupts
           cmp  cs:recur,0       ;is the TSR program already active?
           je   id01             ;NO ---> ID01
id_end:    iret                  ;YES  ---> back to the caller

           ;-- the TSR program is not yet active ---------------------

id01:      cmp  cs:in_bios, 0    ;BIOS disk interrupt active?
           jne  id_end           ;YES --> back to the caller

           ;-- BIOS disk interrupt not active, test for hotkey --------

           push ax               ;save ES and AX on the stack
           push es
           xor  ax,ax            ;st ES to the lowest memory segment
           mov  es,ax
           mov  ax,word ptr es:[417h] ;get BIOS keyboard flag
           and  ax,cs:key_mask   ;mask out the non-hotkey bits
```

```
        cmp  ax,cs:key_mask     ;are only the hotkey bits left?
        pop  es                 ;restore ES and AX
        pop  ax
        jne  ik_end             ;hotkey discovered? NO --> back

        call  start_tsr         ;start the TSR program
        iret                    ;back to the interrupted program

int28   endp

;-- START_TSR: activate the TSR program ------------------------------

start_tsr proc near

        mov  cs:recur,1         ;set TSR recursion flag


        ;-- perform context change to the C program -----------------

        mov  cs:uprg_ss,ss      ;save current stack segment and
        mov  cs:uprg_sp,sp      ;stack pointer

        mov  ss,cs:c_ss         ;activate the C program's stack
        mov  sp,cs:c_sp

        push ax                 ;save the processor registers on the
        push bx                 ;C stack
        push cx
        push dx
        push bp
        push si
        push di
        push ds
        push es

        ;-- save 64 words from the DOS stack ------------------------

        mov  cx,64              ;loop counter
        mov  ds,cs:uprg_ss      ;set DS:SI to the end of the DOS stack
        mov  si,cs:uprg_sp

tsrsl:  push word ptr [si]      ;save word from the DOS stack to the
        inc  si                 ;C stack and set SI to the next
        inc  si                 ;stack word
        loop tsrsl              ;process all 64 words

        mov  ah,51h             ;ftn. no.: determine address of PSP
        int  21h                ;call DOS interrupt
        mov  cs:u_psp,bx        ;save segment address of the PSP

        mov  ah,2fh             ;ftn. no.: get DTA address
        int  21h                ;call DOS interrupt
        mov  cs:u_dta_ofs,bx    ;store address of the DTA of the
        mov  cs:u_dta_seg,es    ;interrupted program

        mov  ah,50h             ;ftn. no.: set address of the PSP
        mov  bx,cs:c_psp        ;get seg addr of the PSP of the C prg
        int  21h                ;call DOS interrupt

        mov  ah,1ah             ;ftn. no.: set DTA address
        mov  dx,cs:c_dta_ofs    ;get offset address of the new DTA
        mov  ds,cs:c_dta_seg    ;and the segment address of new DTA
        int  21h                ;call DOS interrupt

        mov  ds,cs:c_ds         ;set segment register for the C
        mov  es,cs:c_es         ;program

        sti                     ;allow interrupts again
        call cs:fkt_adr         ;call the start function of the C prg.
        cli                     ;disable interrupts
```

```
        ;-- perform context change to the interrupted program -------

        mov  ah,1ah            ;ftn. no.: set DTA address
        mov  dx,cs:u_dta_ofs   ;load offset and segment addresses
        mov  ds,cs:u_dta_seg   ;of the DTA of the interrupted program
        int  21h               ;call DOS interrupt

        mov  ah,50h            ;ftn. no.: set address of the PSP
        mov  bx,cs:u_psp       ;seg addr PSP of the interrupted prg.
        int  21h               ;call DOS interrupt

        ;-- restore DOS stack again -------------------------------

        mov  cx,64             ;loop counter
        mov  ds,cs:uprg_ss     ;load DS:SI with the end address of
        mov  si,cs:uprg_sp     ;the DOS stack
        add  si,128            ;set SI to the start of the DOS stack
tsrs2:  dec  si                ;SI to the previous stack word
        dec  si
        pop  word ptr [si]     ;get word from the C stack to DOS stack
        loop tsrs2             ;process all 64 words

        pop  es                ;restore the saved registers from the
        pop  ds                ;C stack
        pop  di
        pop  si
        pop  bp
        pop  dx
        pop  cx
        pop  bx
        pop  ax

        mov  ss,cs:uprg_ss     ;reset stack pointer and stack segment
        mov  sp,cs:uprg_sp     ;of the interrupted program

        mov  cs:recur,0        ;reset TSR recursion flag
        ret                    ;back to the caller

start_tsr  endp

;------------------------------------------------------------------

_text      ends                ;end of the code segment
           end                 ;end of the program
```

Turbo Pascal offers only one memory model, unlike the various C compilers. The organization of this model is well suited to TSR programs.

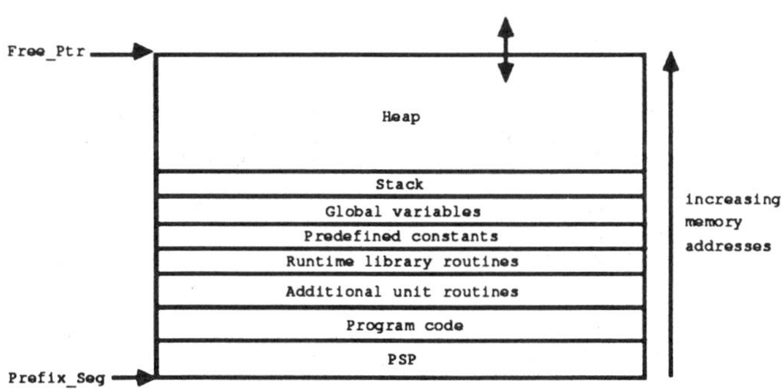

Memory layout of a Pascal program under Turbo Pascal 4.0

The figure above shows that the program code and the required routines from the various units and the runtime library follow the PSP. After these are the predefined constants, the global data, and the stack segment. While the size of these program components are set at compilation and cannot be changed after the program is loaded into memory, this doesn't apply to the size of the heap, which follows the stack segment. When new objects are created with the NEW command, the heap grows toward the end of memory.

Turbo Pascal offers the significant advantage over C compilers of being able to set the maximum size of the heap, as well as the stack size, with a compiler directive inside the source code. This is the $M directive, which must be passed the following parameters:

```
{$M stack size, minimum heap size, maximum heap size}
```

All specifications are in bytes, so the directive

```
{$M 2048, 0, 5000}
```

results in a 2K stack and a maximum 5000-byte heap. If no such directive is found in a program, the heap is not limited and it can grow to the end of main memory. This would have catastrophic results for a TSR program, however, since the entire memory would have to be reserved for the TSR program and there would be no memory left for additional programs. But with the $M directive placed at the beginning of the program, we can set the maximum size of the program in memory and the number of paragraphs which must remain resident after the program is terminated.

Turbo Pascal also allows the number of paragraphs to be reserved to be calculated from the Pascal program, eliminating the complicated calculation in the assembly language interface. In a C program, important data needed for this calculation (segment addresses of the PSP and data segment, and size of the heap) are available only at the assembly language level, but Turbo Pascal places this information in normal variables, which are available to a Pascal program in the form of pointers. For our purposes, we need the starting address of the PSP and the end of the heap, since they mark the start and end of the TSR program in memory.

The figure shows that the segment address of the PSP is found in the variable PrefixSeg; while the end of the heap is determined with the help of the pointer variable FreePtr. This variable does not point directly to the end of the heap, but the segment portion of this pointer contains the end address of the heap minus $1000. This information is used within the TSR program in the ResPara procedure, which calculates the number of paragraphs to remain resident after the installation of the TSR.

In addition to this information, the initialization routine TsrInit in the assembly language module must be passed the following information (in the specified order):

- Address of the Pascal TSR function
- Hotkey (mask for reading the BIOS keyboard flag)
- Number of paragraphs to be reserved
- Identification string

The Pascal TSR function, the address of which is passed as the first parameter to TsrInit, must be a procedure within the main program and may not be contained in a unit. Moreover, it may not be converted to a FAR procedure with the $F+ compiler directive, since the assembly language interface assumes that it is a NEAR procedure. The address of the procedure is determined with the help of the function OFS and passed to TsrInit, since Turbo Pascal would otherwise place both the offset address and the segment address on the stack.

The same applies to passing the address of a "cleanup" procedure to the function UnInst, which reinstalls the TSR program. If such an address is passed, the corresponding procedure within the installed TSR program will be called before the reinstallation. If the value $FFFF is passed as the address of this procedure, this tells the assembly language function that no "cleanup" procedure is to be called. To improve the readability of the listing, the constant NO_END_FTN is defined in the constant definitions at the start of the listing. NO_END_FTN is given the value $FFFF and should be used when calling the assembly language function UnInst.

The following listing can answer any additional questions you may have, and will make a good starting point for your own TSR programs.

Pascal listing: TSRP.PAS

```
{**********************************************************************}
{*                               T S R P                              *}
{*--------------------------------------------------------------------*}
{*    Description    : creates a TSR program with the help of an      *}
{*                     assembly language module.                      *}
{*--------------------------------------------------------------------*}
{*    Author         : MICHAEL TISCHER                                *}
{*    developed on   : 08/18/1988                                     *}
{*    last update    : 05/26/1989                                     *}
{**********************************************************************}

program TSRP;

uses DOS, CRT;                         { bind in the DOS and CRT units  }

{$M 2048, 0, 5120}        { 2KB for the stack and max. 5KB for the heap }
{$L tsrpa}                              { bind in the assembler module }

const LSHIFT =     1;                                 { left SHIFT key }
      RSHIFT =     2;                                { right SHIFT key }
      CTRL   =     4;                                       { CTRL key }
```

```
      ALT    =     8;                                      { ALT key }
      SYSREQ =  1024;                 { SYS REQ key (ST keyboard only) }
      BREAK  =  4096;                                    { BREAK key }
      NUM    =  8192;                                      { NUM key }
      CAPS   = 16384;                                     { CAPS key }
      INSERT = 32768;                                   { INSERT key }

      NO_END_FTN = $FFFF;                { don't call an end function }

type IdsType = string[ 16 ];      { describes the identification string }
     VBuf    = array[1..25, 1..80] of word;      { describes the screen }
     VPtr    = ^VBuf;                    { pointer to a screen buffer }

var IdString : IdsType;             { the ID string for the TSR program }
    MBuf     : VBuf absolute $B000:0000;    { the monochrome video RAM }
    CBuf     : Vbuf absolute $B800:0000;         { the color video RAM }
    VioPtr   : VPtr;                        { pointer to the video RAM }

{** Declaration of the external functions in the assembly module ******}

procedure TsrInit( PrcPtr   : word;      { offset addr of the TSR proc }
                   KeyMask  : word;            { the hotkey (see CONST) }
                   ResPara  : word;   { number of para. to be reserved }
                   IdString : IdsType ) ; external ;     { the ID string }

function IsInst( IdString : IdsType ) : boolean ; external ;

procedure UnInst( PrcPtr : word ); external;   { reinstall TSR program }


var ATimes : integer;                      { number of TSR activations }

{**********************************************************************}
{* DispInit: creates a pointer to the video RAM                        *}
{* Input  : none                                                        *}
{* Output : none                                                        *}
{**********************************************************************}

procedure DispInit;

var Regs: Registers;                  { stores the processor registers }

begin
  Regs.ah := $0f;             { function no. 15 = read the video mode }
  Intr($10, Regs);                     { call the BIOS video interrupt }
  if Regs.al=7 then                           { monochrome video card? }
    VioPtr := @MBuf     { yes, set pointer to the monochrome video RAM }
  else                                 { it's an EGA, VGA, or CGA card }
    VioPtr := @CBuf;                  { set pointer to color video RAM }
end;

{**********************************************************************}
{* SaveScreen: saves the screen contents in a buffer                   *}
{* Input  : SPTR : pointer to a buffer in which the screen contents    *}
{*                 will be saved                                       *}
{* Output : none                                                        *}
{**********************************************************************}

procedure SaveScreen( SPtr : VPtr );

var line,                                          { the current line }
    column : byte;                               { the current column }

begin
  for line:=1 to 25 do              { run through the 25 screen lines }
    for column:=1 to 80 do        { run through the 80 screen columns }
      SPtr^[line, column] := VioPtr^[line, column];   { save ch.&attr. }

end;
```

```
{***********************************************************************}
{* RestoreScreen: copies the contents of a buffer into the video RAM  *}
{* Input  : BPTR : pointer to the buffer whose contents are to be      *}
{*                 copied into the video RAM                           *}
{* Output : none                                                       *}
{***********************************************************************}

procedure RestoreScreen( BPtr : VPtr );

var line,                                          { the current line }
    column : byte;                               { the current column }

begin
  for line:=1 to 25 do               { run through the 25 screen lines }
    for column:=1 to 80 do         { run through the 80 screen columns }
      VioPtr^[line, column] := BPtr^[line, column];  { get ch. & attr. }
end;

{***********************************************************************}
{* ResPara: calculates the number of paragraphs which must be          *}
{*          allocated for the program                                  *}
{* Input  : none                                                       *}
{* Output : the number of paragraphs to be reserved                    *}
{***********************************************************************}

function ResPara : word;

begin
  ResPara := Seg(FreePtr^)+$1000-PrefixSeg;     { number of paragraphs }
end;

{***********************************************************************}
{* EndProc: Called by the assembler module when the TSR program is     *}
{*          reinstalled                                                *}
{* Input  : none                                                       *}
{* Output : none                                                       *}
{* Info   : This procedure must be in the main program and may not     *}
{*          be turned into a FAR procedure by the $F+ compiler         *}
{*          directive.                                                 *}
{***********************************************************************}

{$F-}                                        { don't make a FAR procedure }

procedure EndProc;

begin
  TextBackground( Black );                         { dark background }
  TextColor( LightGray );                               { light text }
  writeln('The TSR program was called ', ATimes, ' times.');
end;

{***********************************************************************}
{* Tsr: This procedure is called by the assembler module after the     *}
{*      hotkey is pressed.                                             *}
{* Input  : none                                                       *}
{* Output : none                                                       *}
{* Info   : This procedure must be in the main program and may not     *}
{*          be turned into a FAR procedure by the $F+ compiler         *}
{*          directive.                                                 *}
{***********************************************************************}

{$F-}                                        { don't make a FAR procedure }

procedure Tsr;

var BufPtr : VPtr;           { stores pointer to the allocated blocks }
    Column,                                { the current screen column }
    Line  : byte;                            { the current screen line }
    Key   : char;
```

```
begin
  inc( ATimes );                              { increment call counter }
  DispInit;                          { determine address of the video RAM }
  GetMem(BufPtr, SizeOf(VBuf) );                      { allocate buffer }
  SaveScreen( BufPtr );                       { save the screen contents }
  Line := WhereY;                              { get current screen line }
  Column := WhereX;                          { get current screen column }
  TextBackground( LightGray );                       { light background }
  TextColor( Black );                                     { dark text }
  ClrScr;                                     { clear the whole screen }
  GotoXY(22, 12);
  write('TSRP  -  (c) 1988 by MICHAEL TISCHER');
  GotoXY(30, 14);
  write('Please press a key...');
  Key := ReadKey;                                      { wait for a key }
  RestoreScreen( BufPtr );           { copy the old screen contents back }
  FreeMem( BufPtr, SizeOf(VBuf) );           { release allocated buffer }
  GotoXY( Column, Line );             { cursor back to original position }
end;

{***********************************************************************}
{**                           MAIN PROGRAM                            **}
{***********************************************************************}

begin
  writeln('TSRP  -  (c) 1988 by MICHAEL TISCHER');
  IdString := 'TROTZKY';
  if ( IsInst( IdString ) ) then          { program already installed? }
    begin                                                       { YES }
      writeln('The TSR program now disabled.');
      UnInst( Ofs( EndProc ) );                    { remove the program }

      {** if no end function is to be called, the call is: ************
       ** UnInst( NO_END_FTN );                              ************}
    end
  else                                 { the program is not installed yet }
    begin
      ATimes := 0;                 { the program was not activated yet }
      writeln('TSR program now enabled.  Start: <LSHIFT> + ',
              '<RSHIFT>');
      TsrInit( Ofs(Tsr), LSHIFT or RSHIFT, ResPara, IdString );
    end;
end.
```

Assembler listing: TSRPA.ASM

```
;***********************************************************************;
;*                              T S R P A                              *;
;*---------------------------------------------------------------------*;
;*    Description     : This is the assembler interface to a Turbo      *;
;*                      Pascal 4.0 program which can be activated       *;
;*                      via a hotkey.                                   *;
;*---------------------------------------------------------------------*;
;*    Author          : MICHAEL TISCHER                                 *;
;*    developed on    : 08/12/1988                                      *;
;*    last update     : 08/18/1988                                      *;
;*---------------------------------------------------------------------*;
;*    Info            : The module must be in a program and may not     *;
;*                      be bound into a UNIT.                           *;
;*---------------------------------------------------------------------*;
;*    to assemble     : MASM TSRPA;                                     *;
;*                      ... combine with a Turbo Pascal program         *;
;***********************************************************************;

DATA   segment word public        ;Turbo data segment

DATA       ends                   ;end of the data segment
```

```
;== Constants ==========================================================

MAX_ID_LEN equ 16                    ;maximum length of the ID string

;== Program ============================================================

CODE       segment byte public    ;the Turbo code segment

           assume cs:CODE, ds:DATA, es:CODE

;-- Public declarations of internal functions -------------------------

public     tsrinit                   ;allows access by the Turbo program
public     isinst
public     uninst

;-- Variables for the interrupt handler -------------------------------
;-- (accessible only via the code segment -----------------------------

id_buf     db (MAX_ID_LEN + 1) dup (0)  ;buffer for the ID string
ce_ptr     equ this dword            ;points to the routine CALL_END in the
ce_ofs     dw offset call_end        ;already-installed TSR program
ce_seg     dw ?

;-- Variables neded for activation of the Turbo program --------------

t_ss       dw 0                      ;Turbo stack segment
t_sp       dw 0                      ;Turbo stack pointer
t_ds       dw 0                      ;Turbo data segment
t_es       dw 0                      ;Turbo extra segment

t_dta_ofs  dw 0                      ;DTA address of the Turbo program
t_dta_seg  dw 0

t_psp      dw 0                      ;seg addr of the PSP of the Turbo prg.
prc_adr    dw 0                      ;address of the Turbo TSR procedure

;-- Variables for testing for the hotkey -----------------------------

key_mask   dw 0                      ;hotkey mask for BIOS keyboard flag
recur      db 0                      ;prevents recursive TSR calls
in_bios    db 0                      ;shows activity of the BIOS disk
                                     ;interrupt

daptr      equ this dword            ;pointer to the DOS INDOS flag
daptr_ofs  dw 0                      ;offset address
daptr_seg  dw 0                      ;segment address

;-- The following variables store the old addresses of the interrupt ---
;-- handlers which will be replaced by new interrupt handlers        ---

int9_ptr   equ this dword            ;old interrupt vector 9h
int9_ofs   dw 0                      ;offset address of the old handler
int9_seg   dw 0                      ;segment address of the old handler

int13_ptr  equ this dword            ;old interrupt vector 13h
int13_ofs  dw 0                      ;offset address of the old handler
int13_seg  dw 0                      ;segment address of the old handler

int28_ptr  equ this dword            ;old interrupt handler 28h
int28_ofs  dw 0                      ;offset address of the old handler
int28_seg  dw 0                      ;segment address of the old handler

;-- Variables for storing information about the interrupted ------------
;-- program                                                  ------------

u_dta_ofs  dw 0                      ;DTA address of interrupted program
u_dta_seg  dw 0

u_psp      dw 0                      ;seg addr of the PSP of the int. prg.
```

```
uprg_ss     dw 0                ;SS and SP of the interrupted prg.
uprg_sp     dw 0

;-----------------------------------------------------------------
;-- TSRINIT: ends the Turbo program and activates the new interrupt ----
;--          handler
;-- Call from Turbo: procedure TsrInit( PrzPtr   : word;
;--                                     KeyMask  : word;
;--                                     ResPara  : word;
;--                                     IdString : string[16] );

tsrinit     proc    near

sframe0     struc               ;structure for accessing the stack
bp0         dw ?                ;stores BP
ret_adr0    dw ?                ;return address
idptr0      dd ?                ;pointer to the ID string
respara0    dw ?                ;number of paragraphs to be reserved
keymask0    dw ?                ;mask for hotkey
prcptr0     dw ?                ;pointer to the Turbo TSR procedure
sframe0     ends                ;end of the structure

frame       equ [ bp - bp0 ]

            push bp             ;save BP on the stack
            mov  bp,sp          ;move SP to BP
            push es             ;save ES on the stack
            ;-- save the Turbo segment registers -----------------------

            mov  cs:t_ss,ss     ;save the registers in the appropriate
            mov  cs:t_sp,sp     ;variables
            mov  cs:t_es,es
            mov  cs:t_ds,ds

            ;-- copy the ID string into the internal buffer -------------

            push ds              ;save DS on the stack
            lds  si,frame.idptr0 ;DS:SI now points to the string
            push cs              ;put CS on the stack
            pop  es              ;and restore as ES
            mov  di,offset id_buf ;ES:DI now points to ID_BUF
            xor  ch,ch           ;clear high byte of the counter
            mov  cl,[si]         ;get length of the string
            inc  cl              ;copy the length byte too
            rep  movsb           ;copy the entire string
            pop  ds              ;restore DS

            ;-- determine PSP of the Turbo program ----------------------

            mov  bx,cs          ;transfer CS to BX
            sub  bx,10h         ;10h paragraphs = subtract 256 bytes
            mov  cs:t_psp,bx    ;save segment address

            ;-- save the parameters passed ------------------------------

            mov  ax,frame.prcptr0 ;get pointer to the TSR procedure
            mov  cs:prc_adr,ax   ;and save
            mov  ax,frame.keymask0 ;get mask for the hotkey
            mov  cs:key_mask,ax  ;and save

            ;-- determine DTA address of the Turbo program --------------

            mov  ah,2fh          ;ftn. no.: get DTA address
            int  21h             ;call DOS interrupt
            mov  cs:t_dta_ofs,bx ;store address in the appropriate
            mov  cs:t_dta_seg,es ;variables

            ;-- determine the address of the INDOS flag -----------------
```

```
          mov  ah,34h            ;ftn. no.: get adr of the INDOS flag
          int  21h               ;call DOS interrupt
          mov  cs:daptr_ofs,bx   ;save address in the appropriate
          mov  cs:daptr_seg,es   ;variables

          ;-- get the addresses of the interrupt handlers to change ---

          mov  ax,3509h          ;get interrupt vector 9h
          int  21h               ;call DOS interrupt
          mov  cs:int9_ofs,bx    ;save address of the handler in the
          mov  cs:int9_seg,es    ;appropriate variables

          mov  ax,3513h          ;get interrupt vector 13h
          int  21h               ;call DOS interrupt
          mov  cs:int13_ofs,bx   ;save address of the handler in the
          mov  cs:int13_seg,es   ;appropriate variables

          mov  ax,3528h          ;get interrupt vector 28h
          int  21h               ;call DOS interrupt
          mov  cs:int28_ofs,bx   ;save addres of the handler in the
          mov  cs:int28_seg,es   ;appropriate variables

          ;-- install the new interupt handlers ----------------------

          push ds                ;save data segment
          mov  ax,cs             ;CS to AX and then load into DS
          mov  ds,ax

          mov  ax,2509h          ;ftn. no.: set interrupt 9h
          mov  dx,offset int09   ;DS:DX stores the addr of the handler
          int  21h               ;call DOS interrupt

          mov  ax,2513h          ;ftn. no.: set interrupt 13h
          mov  dx,offset int13   ;DS:DX stores the addr of the handler
          int  21h               ;call DOS interrupt

          mov  ax,2528h          ;ftn. no.: set interrupt 28h
          mov  dx,offset int28   ;DS:DX stores the addr of the handler
          int  21h               ;call DOS interrupt

          pop  ds                ;get DS back from the stack

          ;-- End resident program ------------------------------------

          mov  ax,3100h          ;ftn. no.: end resident program
          mov  dx,frame.respara0 ;get number of reserved paragraphs
          int  21h               ;call DOS interrupt and thus end
                                 ;the program

tsrinit  endp

;-----------------------------------------------------------------------
;-- ISINST: Determines if the program is already installed -------------
;-- Call from Turbo: function IsInst( IdString : IdsType ) : boolean;
;-- Return value: 1, if the program was already installed,
;--                else 0

isinst     proc    near

sframe1    struc                       ;structure for accessing the stack
bp1        dw ?                        ;stores BP
ret_adr1   dw ?                        ;return address
idptr1     dd ?                        ;pointer to the ID string
sframe1    ends                        ;end of the structure

frame      equ [ bp - bp1 ]

           push bp                     ;save BP on the stack
           mov  bp,sp                  ;transfer Sp to BP
           push ds                     ;save DS on the stack
```

```
          ;-- determine segment address of the current int 9 handler --

          mov  ax,3509h          ;get interrupt vbector 9h
          int  21h               ;DOS interrupt gets seg addr in ES
          mov  di,offset id_buf  ;ES:DI points to the installed ID_BUF
          lds  si,frame.idptr1   ;DS:SI points to the ID_STRING passed

          xor  dl,dl             ;return code: not installed
          mov  cl,[si]           ;get length of the string
          mov  ch,dl             ;high byte of the counter to 0
isi0:     lodsb                  ;load character from string
          cmp  al,es:[di]        ;compare with other string
          jne  not_inst          ;not equal --> NOT_INST
          inc  di                ;increment pointer to string 2
          loop isi0              ;compare the next characters

          mov  dl,1              ;the strings are identical

not_inst: mov  al,dl             ;put return code in AL
          pop  ds                ;get DS back from stack
          pop  bp                ;get BP back from stack
          ret  4                 ;back to the caller

isinst    endp                   ;end of the procedure

;-----------------------------------------------------------------------
;-- CALL_END: calls the end function when the TSR is reinstalled -------
;-- Input  : DI = offset address of the routine to be called
;-- Info   : This function is not intended to be called by a Turbo
;--          program

call_end  proc far

          call di                ;call the end function
          ret                    ;back to the caller

call_end  endp

;-----------------------------------------------------------------------
;-- UNINST: removes the TSR program and releases the allocated ---------
;--         memory.
;-- Call from Turbo : procedure UnInst( EndPtr : word ); external;
;-- Info          :      If the value $FFFF is passed as the address,
;--                      then no end function will be called.
;-- Note         : This function should be called only if a previous
;--                call to IS_INST() returned a value of 1.

uninst    proc   near

sframe2   struc                  ;structure for accessing the stack
bp2       dw ?                   ;stores BP
ret_adr2  dw ?                   ;return address
prcptr2   dw ?                   ;pointer to the end procedure
sframe2   ends                   ;end of the structure

frame     equ [ bp - bp2 ]


          push bp                ;save BP on the stack
          mov  bp,sp             ;transfer SP to BP
          push ds                ;save DS on the stack

          ;-- determine seg addr of the current int 9h handler ---
          mov  ax,3509h          ;get interrupt vector 9h
          int  21h               ;DOS interrupt puts seg addr in ES

          mov  di,frame.prcptr2  ;get address of the end procedure
          cmp  di,0ffffh         ;no end procedure called?
          je   no_endprc         ;NO ---> NO_ENDPRC
```

```
          ;-- Perform context change to the Turbo program and ------
          ;-- execute the specified end procedure

          mov  cs:ce_seg,es      ;save ES in the jump vector

          mov  cs:uprg_ss,ss     ;save current stack segment and stack
          mov  cs:uprg_sp,sp     ;pointer

          cli                    ;disable interrupts
          mov  ss,es:t_ss        ;activate the stack of the TSR
          mov  sp,es:t_sp        ;program

          push es                ;save ES on the stack
          mov  ah,2fh            ;ftn. no.: get DTA address
          int  21h               ;call DOS interrupt
          mov  cs:u_dta_ofs,bx   ;save DTA address of the interrupted
          mov  cs:u_dta_seg,es   ;program
          pop  es                ;get ES from the stack

          mov  ah,50h            ;ftn. no.: set address of the PSP
          mov  bx,es:t_psp       ;get segment address of the PSP
          int  21h               ;call DOS interrupt

          push ds                ;save ES and DS on the stack
          push es

          mov  ah,1ah            ;ftn. no.: set DTA address
          mov  dx,es:t_dta_ofs   ;get offset address and segment
          mov  ds,es:t_dta_seg   ;address of the new DTA
          int  21h               ;call DOS interrupt

          mov  ds,es:t_ds        ;set segment register for the Turbo
          mov  es,es:t_es        ;program

          call cs:[ce_ptr]       ;call the end procedure

          ;-- context change to the Turbo program --------------------

          mov  ah,1ah            ;ftn. no.: set DTA address
          mov  dx,cs:u_dta_ofs   ;load offset and segment addresses
          mov  ds,cs:u_dta_seg   ;of the DTA of the interrupted program
          int  21h               ;call DOS interrupt

          pop  es                ;restore seg addr of the Turbo program
          pop  ds                ;from the stack

          mov  ah,50h            ;ftn. no.: set address of the PSP
          mov  bx,cs             ;put CS in BX
          sub  bx,10h            ;calculate segment address of the PSP
          int  21h               ;call DOS interrupt

          cli                    ;disable interrupts
          mov  ss,cs:uprg_ss     ;restore stack pointer and stack
          mov  sp,cs:uprg_sp     ;segment
          sti                    ;allow interrupts again

          ;-- reinstall the interrupt handler of the TSR --------------
          ;-- program again                              --------------

no_endprc: cli                   ;disable interrupts
          mov  ax,2509h          ;ftn. no.: set handler for int 9
          mov  ds,es:int9_seg    ;segment address of the old handler
          mov  dx,es:int9_ofs    ;offset address of the old handler
          int  21h               ;reinstall the old handler

          mov  ax,2513h          ;ftn. no.: set handler for int 13
          mov  ds,es:int13_seg   ;segment address of the old handler
          mov  dx,es:int13_ofs   ;offset address of the old handler
          int  21h               ;reinstall the old handler
```

```
        mov  ax,2528h          ;ftn. no. set handler for int 28
        mov  ds,es:int28_seg   ;segment address of the old handler
        mov  dx,es:int28_ofs   ;offset address of the old handler
        int  21h               ;reinstall the old handler

        sti                    ;allow interrupts again

        mov  es,es:t_psp       ;save seg addr of the PSP of the
        mov  cx,es             ;Turbo program in CX
        mov  es,es:[ 02ch ]    ;get seg addr of environ from PSP
        mov  ah,49h            ;ftn. no.: release allocated memory
        int  21h               ;call DOS interrupt
        mov  es,cx             ;restore ES from CX
        mov  ah,49h            ;ftn. no.: release allocated memory
        int  21h               ;call DOS interrupt

        pop  ds                ;restore DS and BP from stack
        pop  bp
        ret  2                 ;return to the caller

uninst  endp                   ;end of the procedure

;----------------------------------------------------------------------
;-- The new interrupt handlers follow ---------------------------------
;----------------------------------------------------------------------

;-- the new interrupt 09h handler -------------------------------------

int09   proc far

        pushf                  ;simulate calling the handler via the
        call cs:int9_ptr       ;INT 9h instruction

        cli                    ;suppress interrupts
        cmp  cs:recur,0        ;is the TSR program already active?
        jne  ik_end            ;Yes, back to the caller of int 9

        ;-- test to see if the BIOS disk int is being executed

        cmp  cs:in_bios,0      ;BIOS disk interrupt active?
        jne  ik_end            ;YES --> abck to caller

        ;-- BIOS disk interrupt is not active, test for hotkey -----

        push ax                ;save ES and AX on the stack
        push es
        xor  ax,ax             ;set ES to the lowest memory segment
        mov  es,ax
        mov  ax,word ptr es:[417h] ;get BIOS keyboard flag
        and  ax,cs:key_mask    ;mask out the non-hotkey bits
        cmp  ax,cs:key_mask    ;are only the hotkey bits left?
        pop  es                ;restore ES and AX
        pop  ax
        jne  ik_end            ;hotkey discovered? NO --> return

        ;-- the hotkey was pressed, test to see if DOS is active ---

        push ds                ;save DS and BX on the stack
        push bx
        lds  bx,cs:daptr       ;DS:BX now point to the INDOS flag
        cmp  byte ptr [bx],0   ;DOS function active?
        pop  bx                ;get BX and DS from the stack
        pop  ds
        jne  ik_end            ;DOS function active --> IK_END

        ;-- DOS is not active, activate TSR program ----------------


        call  start_tsr        ;start the TSR program
```

```
ik_end:   iret                    ;back to the interrupted program

int09     endp

;-- the new interrupt 13h handler ------------------------------------

int13     proc far

          mov  cs:in_bios,1       ;set flag and show that the BIOS disk
                                  ;interrupt is active
          pushf                   ;simulate calling the old interrupt
          call cs:int13_ptr       ;handler via int 13h
          mov  cs:in_bios, 0      ;BIOS disk interrupt no longer active

          ret  2                  ;back to the caller, but don't get
                                  ;the flag reg from the stack first
int13     endp

;-- the new interrupt 28h handler ------------------------------------

int28     proc far

          pushf                   ;simulate calling the old interrupt
          call cs:int28_ptr       ;handler via int 28h

          cli                     ;suppress further interrupts
          cmp  cs:recur,0         ;is the TSR program already active?
          je   id01               ;NO ---> ID01
id_end:   iret                    ;YES  ---> back to the caller

          ;-- the TSR program is not yet active ---------------------

id01:     cmp  cs:in_bios, 0      ;is BIOS disk interrupt active?
          jne  id_end             ;YES --> back to the caller

          ;-- BIOS disk interrupt not active, test for hotkey -------

          push ax                 ;save ES and AX on the stack
          push es
          xor  ax,ax              ;set ES to the lowest memory segment
          mov  es,ax
          mov  ax,word ptr es:[417h] ;get BIOS keyboard flag
          and  ax,cs:key_mask     ;mask out the non-hotkey bits
          cmp  ax,cs:key_mask     ;are only the hotkey bits left?
          pop  es                 ;restore ES and AX
          pop  ax
          jne  ik_end             ;hotkey discovered? NO --> return

          call  start_tsr         ;start the TSR program
          iret                    ;back to the interrupted program

int28     endp


;-- START_TSR: activate the TSR program -------------------------------
start_tsr proc near

          mov  cs:recur,1         ;set the TSR recursion flag

          ;-- perform context change to the TSR program --------------

          mov  cs:uprg_ss,ss      ;save current stack segment and
          mov  cs:uprg_sp,sp      ;stack pointer

          mov  ss,cs:t_ss         ;activate the stack of the
          mov  sp,cs:t_sp         ;Turbo program

          push ax                 ;save the processor registers on the
          push bx                 ;turbo stack
          push cx
```

```
            push dx
            push bp
            push si
            push di
            push ds
            push es

            ;-- save 64 words from the DOS stack ----------------------

            mov  cx,64              ;loop counter
            mov  ds,cs:uprg_ss      ;set DS:SI to the end of the DOS stack
            mov  si,cs:uprg_sp

tsrs1:      push word ptr [si]      ;save word from the DOS stack on the
            inc  si                 ;C stack and set SI to the next word
            inc  si
            loop tsrs1              ;process all 64 words

            mov  ah,51h             ;ftn. no.: get addr of the PSP
            int  21h                ;call DOS interrupt
            mov  cs:u_psp,bx        ;save seg addr of the PSP

            mov  ah,2fh             ;ftn. no.: get DTA address
            int  21h                ;call DOS interrupt
            mov  cs:u_dta_ofs,bx    ;save address of the DTA of the
            mov  cs:u_dta_seg,es    ;interrupted program

            mov  ah,50h             ;ftn. no.: set address of the PSP
            mov  bx,cs:t_psp        ;get seg addr of the Turbo prg PSP
            int  21h                ;call DOS interrupt

            mov  ah,1ah             ;ftn. no.: set DTA address
            mov  dx,cs:t_dta_ofs    ;get offset address of the new DTA
            mov  ds,cs:t_dta_seg    ;and segment address of the new DTA
            int  21h                ;call DOS interrupt

            mov  ds,cs:t_ds         ;set segment register for the
            mov  es,cs:t_es         ;Turbo program

            sti                     ;allow interrupts again

            call cs:prc_adr         ;call the start function
            cli                     ;disable interrupts

            ;-- perform context change to the interrupted program ------

            mov  ah,1ah             ;ftn. no.: set DTA address
            mov  dx,cs:u_dta_ofs    ;load offset and segment addresses
            mov  ds,cs:u_dta_seg    ;of the interrupted program's DTA
            int  21h                ;call DOS interrupt

            mov  ah,50h             ;ftn. no.: set address of the PSP
            mov  bx,cs:u_psp        ;seg addr of the interrupted prg's PSP
            int  21h                ;call DOS interrupt

            ;-- restore DOS stack again --------------------------------

            mov  cx,64              ;loop counter
            mov  ds,cs:uprg_ss      ;load DS:SI with the end address of
            mov  si,cs:uprg_sp      ;the DOS stack
            add  si,128             ;set SI to the start of the DOS stack
tsrs2:      dec  si                 ;Si to the previous stack word
            dec  si
            pop  word ptr [si]      ;words from Turbo stack to DOS stack
            loop tsrs2              ;process all 64 words

            pop  es                 ;restore the saved registers from the
            pop  ds                 ;Turbo stack
            pop  di
            pop  si
```

```
          pop  bp
          pop  dx
          pop  cx
          pop  bx
          pop  ax

          mov  ss,cs:uprg_ss    ;set stack pointer and segment
          mov  sp,cs:uprg_sp    ;of the interrupted program

          mov  cs:recur,0       ;resset TSR recursion flag
          ret                   ;back to the caller

start_tsr endp

;----------------------------------------------------------

CODE      ends                  ;end of the code segment
          end                   ;end of the program
```

Chapter 9

Sound on the PC

Every PC has a built in speaker which beeps when some errors occur, or when the keyboard buffer is full. The speaker can also generate other sounds. This chapter demonstrates sound generation through software.

How the PC generates sound

Tones occur when the cone of a speaker *oscillates* (moves back and forth). A single oscillation creates a click instead of a musical sound. If a group of oscillations sounds in rapid succession, a tone occurs. The *pitch* (the note value) of a tone depends on the number of *cycles* (oscillations) that occur per second. The pitch of a tone in cycles per second is measured in Hertz. For example, if the speaker oscillates at a rate of 440 times per second, it generates a tone with a frequency of 440 Hertz. Certain pitches have specific note names assigned to them, such as A440 (the note that sounds at 440 Hertz). The following table shows the pitches and frequencies of tones generated by the PC. This range covers 8 octaves (almost the range of a full piano keyboard):

Octave	0		1		2		3	
	C	16.35	C	32.70	C	65.41	C	130.81
	C#	17.32	C#	34.65	C#	69.30	C#	138.59
	D	18.35	D	36.71	D	73.42	D	146.83
	D#	19.45	D#	38.89	D#	77.78	D#	155.56
	E	20.60	E	41.20	E	82.41	E	164.81
	F	21.83	F	43.65	F	87.31	F	174.61
	F#	23.12	F#	46.25	F#	92.50	F#	185.00
	G	24.50	G	49.00	G	98.00	G	196.00
	G#	25.96	G#	51.91	G#	103.83	G#	207.65
	A	27.50	A	55.00	A	110.00	A	220.00
	A#	29.14	A#	58.27	A#	116.54	A#	233.08
	B	30.87	B	61.74	B	123.47	B	246.94

Octave	4		5		6		7	
	C	261.63	C	523.25	C	1046.50	C	2093.00
	C#	277.18	C#	554.37	C#	1108.74	C#	2217.46
	D	293.66	D	587.33	D	1174.66	D	2349.32
	D#	311.13	D#	622.25	D#	1244.51	D#	2489.02
	E	329.63	E	659.26	E	1328.51	E	2637.02
	F	349.23	F	698.46	F	1396.91	F	2793.83
	F#	369.99	F#	739.99	F#	1479.98	F#	2959.96
	G	392.00	G	783.99	G	1567.98	G	3135.96
	G#	415.30	G#	830.61	G#	1661.22	G#	3322.44
	A	440.00	A	880.00	A	1760.00	A	3520.00
	A#	466.16	A#	923.33	A#	1864.66	A#	3729.31
	B	493.88	B	987.77	B	1975.53	B	3951.07

The speaker in the PC can generate frequencies from 1 Hertz up to more than 1,000,000 Hertz. However, most human ears are only capable of hearing frequencies between 20 and 20,000 Hertz. In addition, PC speakers don't reproduce music very well since they play some tones louder than others. Since the speaker has no volume control, this effect cannot be changed.

A sound program should oscillate the speaker according to the frequency of the tones desired. Here is a rough outline of a possible sound generation program:

- Invoke the instruction to move the cone forward, then undo the instruction (move the cone back to its original position). Repeat these steps in a loop so that it occurs as many times per second as required by the frequency of the tone being generated.

The above procedure has several disadvantages:

- The execution speed of individual instructions depends on the processing speed of the computer.
- This program must be adjusted to the processing speed of individual computers.
- The tone becomes distorted when the tone production loop ends.

8253 timer

Every PC uses one particular chip for tone generation: The 8253 programmable timer, which actually maintains control of the internal clock. The 8253 can perform both timing and sound thanks to its ability to enable a certain action at a certain point in time. It senses timing from oscillations it receives from the PC's 8284 oscillator, which generates 1,193,180 impulses per second. The 8253 can then be instructed how many of these impulses it should wait before triggering a certain action. In the case of tone generation, this action consists of sending an impulse to the speaker. Before executing this action, the chip must be programmed for the particular frequency it should generate. The frequency must be converted from cycles per second into the number of oscillations coming from the oscillator. This is done with the help of the following formula:

```
counter = 1,193,180 / frequency
```

The result of this formula, the variable counter, passes to the chip. As the formula demonstrates, the result for a high frequency is relatively low, and the result for a low frequency is relatively high. This makes sense, since it tells the 8253 chip how many of the 1,193,180 cycles per second it must wait until it can send another signal to the speaker. The lower the value, the more often it sends a signal to move the speaker cone back and forth, causing a higher tone.

Ports and PC sound

Communication between the CPU and the 8253 occurs through ports. First the value 182 is sent to port 43H. This instructs the 8253 that it should start generating a signal as soon as the interval between individual signals has been passed. This interval is the value which was calculated with the formula above. Since the 8253 stores this value internally as a 16-bit number (a value between 0 and 65,535), it limits the range of tones generated to frequencies between 18 and 1,193,180 Hertz. This number must be transmitted to port 42H. Since this is an 8-bit port, the 16 bits of this number cannot be transmitted simultaneously. First the least significant eight bits are transmitted, then the most significant eight bits are transmitted.

Now the second step occurs—the 8253 signal is sent to the speaker. The speaker access occurs through port 61H, which is connected to a programmable peripheral chip. The two lowest bits of this port must be set to 1 to transmit the 8253 signal to the speaker. Since the remaining six bits are used for other purposes, they cannot be changed. For this reason, the contents of port 61H must be read, the lowest two bits must be set to 1 (an OR combination with 3) and the resulting value must be returned to port 61H. A tone sounds, which ends only when the bits just set to 1 are reset again to 0.

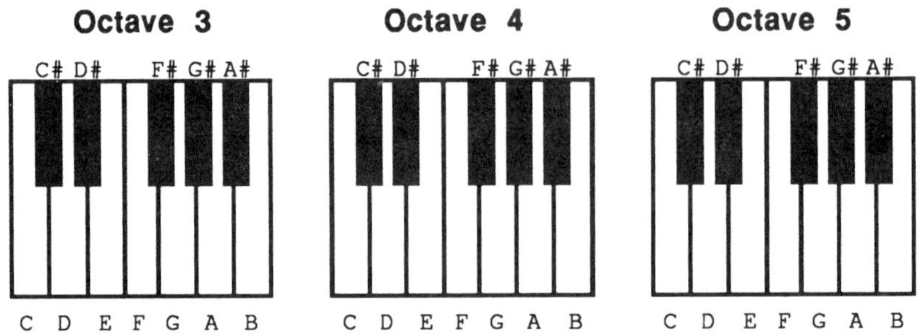

Octave 3		Octave 4		Octave 5	
C = 9121	F#= 6449	C = 4560	F#= 3224	C = 2280	F#= 1612
C#= 8609	G = 6087	C#= 4304	G = 3043	C#= 2152	G = 1521
D = 8126	G#= 5746	D = 4063	G#= 2873	D = 2031	G#= 1436
D#= 7670	A = 5423	D#= 3834	A = 2711	D#= 1917	A = 1355
E = 7239	A#= 5119	E = 3619	A#= 2559	E = 1809	A#= 1292
F = 6833	B = 4831	F = 3416	B = 2415	F = 1715	B = 1207

Keyboard setup and timer frequencies

Demonstration programs

GW-BASIC and Turbo Pascal have resident sound commands. The machine language programmer and C programmer must create their own sound applications.

Demonstration programs follow for both these languages. They can be added to your own C or assembly language programs.

How they work

Both programs produce tones for specific time periods. This is done with the help of the timer interrupt 1CH which is called by the timer interrupt 8H 18.2 times per second. When the tone generation routine executes, it receives the frequency of the tone and the tone's *duration* (length). The duration is measured in 18ths of a second, so the value 18 corresponds to a second and the value 9 corresponds to a half-second. This value is stored in a variable.

Immediately before activating the tone output, the interrupt routine of interrupt 1CH turns to a user-defined routine. This routine, called 18.2 times per second, decrements the tone duration in the variable during every call. When it reaches the value, the tone duration ends and the tone must be switched off. The routine allocates a variable to notify the actual sound routine of this end. The sound routine recognizes this immediately, since it has been in a constant wait loop since switching on the tone. All this loop does is monitor the contents of this variable. After recognizing the end of the tone, it stops the sound output and returns the timer interrupt to its old routine.

The sound routine requires the number assigned to this tone, rather than the frequency itself. This number is related to the table containing the frequencies of octaves 3 to 5. The value 0 stands for C of the third octave, 1 stands for C-sharp, 2 for D, 3 for D-sharp, etc.

Note: Both the C program and assembly language program demonstrate the sound routine by playing a scale over the course of two octaves, with each note sounding for a half a second each. The machine language demo program and sound routine are stored in one file. The C versions of these programs are split into two source code files. The C demo program contains the sound function call only, and the machine language program which creates the sound must be linked to the demonstration program.

Assembler listing: SOUNDA.ASM

```
;**********************************************************************;
;*                            S O U N D A                            *;
;*-------------------------------------------------------------------*;
;*    Task           : Plays a scale between octaves 3 and 5 of the  *;
;*                     PC's musical range. This routine can be used  *;
;*                     for other applications                        *;
;*-------------------------------------------------------------------*;
;*    Author         : MICHAEL TISCHER                               *;
;*    Developed on   : 08/06/1987                                    *;
;*    Last update    : 05/26/89                                      *;
;*-------------------------------------------------------------------*;
;*    Assembly       : MASM SOUNDA;                                  *;
;*                     LINK SOUNDA;                                  *;
;*                     EXE2BIN SOUNDA SOUNDA.COM                     *;
;*-------------------------------------------------------------------*;
;*    Call from DOS  : SOUNDA                                        *;
;**********************************************************************;

code      segment para 'CODE'     ;Definition of CODE segments

          org 100h                ;Starts at address 100H
                                  ;directly following PSP

          assume cs:code, ds:code, es:code, ss:code

;== Program ============================================================

sound     proc near

          ;-- Display message -------------------------------------------

          mov  ah,9               ;Function number for displaying string
          mov  dx,offset initm    ;String's offset address
          int  21h                ;Call DOS interrupt 21H

          ;-- Play scale ------------------------------------------------

          xor  bl,bl              ;Start at C of octave 3
          mov  dl,9               ;for duration of 1/2 second
nextune:  call play_tune          ;Play note
          inc  bl                 ;Next note
          cmp  bl,36              ;All notes in this octave played?
          jne  nextune            ;NO --> Play next note

          ;-- Display end message ---------------------------------------

          mov  ah,9               ;Function number for string display
```

```
          mov  dx,offset endmes    ;String's offset address
          int  21h                 ;Call DOS interrupt 21H

          mov  ax,4C00h            ;Program ends when call to a DOS
          int  21h                 ;function results in an error code
                                   ;of 0

sound     endp

;== Main program data ===============================================

initm     db 13,10,"SOUND (c) 1987 by Michael Tischer",13,10,13,10
          db "Your PC should now be playing a chromatic scale in the"
          db "3rd and 5th      ",13,10,"octaves of its range, if   "
          db "your PC speaker works.",13,10,"$"

endmes    db 13,10,"End",13,10,"$"

;-- PLAY_TUNE: Play a note -------------------------------------------
;-- Input    : BL = Note number (relative to C of the 3rd octave)
;--            DL = Duration of note in 1/18 second increments
;-- Output   : none
;-- Register : AX, CX, ES and FLAGS are changed
;-- Info     : Immediately after the tones, control returns to the
;--            calling routine

play_tune proc near

          push dx                  ;Push DX and BX onto the stack
          push bx

          ;-- Adapt timer interrupt to user program ---------------------
          push dx                  ;Push DX and BX onto stack
          push bx
          mov  ax,351ch            ;Get address of time interrupt
          int  21h                 ;Call DOS interrupt
          mov  old_time,bx         ;Offset address of old interrupt
          mov  old_time+2,es       ;and note segment address

          mov  dx,offset sound_ti  ;Offset address of new timer routine
          mov  ax,251ch            ;Set new timer routine
          int  21h                 ;Call DOS interrupt
          pop  bx                  ;Pop BX and DX off of stack
          pop  dx

          mov  al,182              ;Prepare to play note
          out  43h,al              ;Send value to time command register
          xor  bh,bh               ;BH for addressing note table  = 0
          shl  bx,1                ;Double note number (fr. word table)
          mov  ax,[note+bx]       ;Get tone value
          out  42h,al              ;LO-byte on timer counter register
          mov  al,ah               ;Transfer HI-byte to AL
          out  42h,al              ;and to timer counter register
          in   al,61h              ;Read speaker control bit
          or   al,11b              ;Lowest two bits enable speaker
          mov  s_ende,1            ;Note still has to be played
          mov  s_counter,dl        ;Play note for duration
          out  61h,al              ;Disable speaker

play:     cmp  s_ende,0            ;Note finished?
          jne  play                ;N) --> Wait

          in   al,61h              ;Read speaker control bit
          and  al,11111100b        ;Clear lowest two bits
          out  61h,al              ;Disable speaker

          ;-- Reactivate old timer interrupt --------------------------

          mov cx,ds                ;Note DS
          mov ax,251ch             ;Set function no. for intrrpt vector
```

```
        lds dx,dword ptr old_time ;Load old address into DS:DX
        int 21h                   ;Call DOS interrupt
        mov ds,cx                 ;Return DS

        pop  bx                   ;Pop BX and DX off of stack
        pop  dx
        ret                       ;Return to calling program

play_tune endp

;-- new timer interrupt -------------------------------------------------

sound_ti  proc far                ;Call 18 times per second

          dec  cs:s_counter       ;Decrement counter
          jne  st_ende            ;If still >0, end
          mov  cs:s_ende,0        ;Signal note end
st_ende:  jmp  dword ptr cs:[old_time] ;Goto old timer interrupt

sound_ti  endp

;== Variable set needed by the routines ================================

old_time  dw (?),(?)              ;Address of old timer interrupt
s_counter db (?)                  ;counter for note duration in 1/18
                                  ;second increments
s_ende    db (?)                  ;Displays whether note already played
note     dw 9121,8609,8126,7670  ;Note values for octave 3
          dw 7239,6833,6449,6087
          dw 5746,5423,5119,4831
          dw 4560,4304,4063,3834  ;Note values for octave 4
          dw 3619,3416,3224,3043
          dw 2873,2711,2559,2415
          dw 2280,2152,2031,1917  ;Note values for octave 5
          dw 1809,1715,1612,1521
          dw 1436,1355,1292,1207

;== End =================================================================

code      ends                    ;End of CODE segment
          end  sound              ;End of the Assembler-Program
```

Here's the C program to call the sound function and the assembly language listing of the C sound function.

C listing: SOUNDC.C

```
/***********************************************************************/
/*                            S O U N D C                              */
/*---------------------------------------------------------------------*/
/*    Task           : Plays a scale between octaves 3 and 5 of the    */
/*                     PC musical range, using an assembler function   */
/*---------------------------------------------------------------------*/
/*    Author         : MICHAEL TISCHER                                 */
/*    Developed on   : 08/15/1987                                      */
/*    Last update    : 05/26/1989                                      */
/*---------------------------------------------------------------------*/
/*    (MICROSOFT C)                                                    */
/*    Creation       : CL /AS SOUNDC.C                                 */
/*                     LINK SOUNDC SOUNDCA;                            */
/*    Call           : SOUNDC                                          */
/*---------------------------------------------------------------------*/
/*    (BORLAND TURBO C)                                                */
/*    Creation       : Create a project file listing the following:    */
/*                     soundc                                          */
/*                     soundca.obj                                     */
/*    Options        : Before compiling and linking, select the        */
/*                     Options menu and Linker option. Under the       */
```

```
/*                     Linker options menu, make sure that the        */
/*                     Case sensitive link option is set to Off       */
/**********************************************************************/

/*== Function declaration from the assembler module ==================*/

extern void Sound();          /* Add the external assembler routine  */

/**********************************************************************/
/**                          MAIN  PROGRAM                          **/
/**********************************************************************/

void main()

{
 int Note;

 printf("\nSOUND (c) 1987 by Michael Tischer\n\n");
 printf("Your PC should now be playing a musical scale in the 3rd & ");
 printf(" 5th octaves of\nits range. If you aren't hearing the notes");
 printf(" your PC's speaker may be damaged.\n\n");

 for (Note = 0; Note < 35; Sound(Note++, 9))    /* Play a note once each */
  ;                                           /* 1/2 second            */
 printf("End\n");
}
```

Assembler listing: SOUNDCA.ASM

```
;**********************************************************************;
;*                           S O U N D C A                            *;
;*--------------------------------------------------------------------*;
;*    Task            : Creates a function suitable for inclusion in  *;
;*                      C codes, which enables C to play notes in the *;
;*                      3rd, 4th and 5th PC musical octave            *;
;*--------------------------------------------------------------------*;
;*    Author          : MICHAEL TISCHER                               *;
;*    Developed on    : 08/15/1987                                    *;
;*    Last update     : 05/26/1989                                    *;
;*--------------------------------------------------------------------*;
;*    assembly        : MASM SOUNDCA;                                 *;
;**********************************************************************;

IGROUP group _text                 ;Merging of program segment
DGROUP group const,_bss,  _data    ;Merging of data segment
       assume CS:IGROUP, DS:DGROUP, ES:DGROUP, SS:DGROUP

       public _Sound               ;Make function public (accessible to
                                   ;other programs)

CONST  segment word public 'CONST';This segment denotes all read-only
CONST  ends                        ;constants

_BSS   segment word public 'BSS'  ;This segment denotes all static, non-
_BSS   ends                        ;initialized variables

_DATA  segment word public 'DATA' ;This segment contains all initialized
                                   ;global and static varibles

old_time  dw (?),(?)               ;Address of old timer interrupt
s_counter db (?)                   ;Counts duration of notes in
                                   ;1/18 second increments

s_endit     db (?)                  ;Indicates whether note already played
tones       dw 9121,8609,8126,7670 ;Note values for octave 3
            dw 7239,6833,6449,6087
            dw 5746,5423,5119,4831
            dw 4560,4304,4063,3834 ;Note values for octave 4
            dw 3619,3416,3224,3043
```

```
          dw 2873,2711,2559,2415
          dw 2280,2152,2031,1917  ;Note values for octave 5
          dw 1809,1715,1612,1521
          dw 1436,1355,1292,1207

_DATA  ends

;== Program ========================================================

_TEXT  segment byte public 'CODE' ;Program msegment

;-- SOUND: Plays a note ---------------------------------------------
;-- Call from C : Sound((int) Note, (int) Duration);
;-- Output      : none
;-- Info        : Note is the number of the note relative to 3rd octave
;--               C
;--               Duration=duration of the note in 1/18-sec. increments

_Sound    proc near

          push bp                 ;Push BP onto stack
          mov  bp,sp              ;Transfer SP to BP

          ;-- Modify timer interrupt for user application -------------
          mov  word ptr cs:setds+1,ds ;Store DS for new timer interrupt
          mov  ax,351ch           ;Get timer interrupt's address
          int  21h                ;Call DOS interrupt
          mov  old_time,bx        ;Note offset address and segment
          mov  old_time+2,es      ;address of old interrupt
          mov  word ptr cs:stjump+1,bx ;Save for new timer interrupt
          mov  word ptr cs:stjump+3,es ;
          mov  bx,ds              ;Place DS in BX
          push cs                 ;Push CS onto stack
          pop  ds                 ;and pop off DS
          mov  dx,offset sound_ti ;Offset address of new timer routine
          mov  ax,251ch           ;Set new timer routine
          int  21h                ;Call DOS interrupt
          mov  ds,bx              ;Restore DS

          mov  al,182             ;Get ready to generate tone
          out  43h,al             ;Send value to timer command register

          mov  bx,[bp+4]          ;Get note
          xor  bh,bh              ;BH for addressing of note table = 0
          shl  bx,1               ;Divide note number (for word table)
          mov  ax,[tones+bx]      ;Get note value
          out  42h,al             ;Pass low byte to timer counter register
          mov  al,ah              ;Pass high byte to AL
          out  42h,al             ;and to timer counter register
          in   al,61h             ;Read speaker control bit
          or   al,11b             ;Two lowest bits activate speaker
          mov  s_endit,1           ;Still have to play note
          mov  dl,[bp+6]          ;Get note duration
          mov  s_counter,dl       ;and store it
          out  61h,al             ;Turn on speaker

play:     cmp  s_endit,0           ;Note ended?
          jne  play               ;NO --> wait

          in   al,61h             ;Read speaker control bit
          and  al,11111100b       ;Clear two lowest bits to
          out  61h,al             ;disable speaker

          ;-- re-activate original timer interrupt --------------------
          mov cx,ds               ;Note DS
          mov ax,251ch            ;Set function no. for interrupt vector
          lds dx,dword ptr old_time ;Load old address into DS:DX
          int 21h                 ;Call DOS interrupt
          mov ds,cx               ;Return DS
```

```
         mov  sp,bp              ;Restore stack pointer
         pop  bp                 ;Pop BP off of stack
         ret                     ;Return to calling program

_Sound   endp

;-- new timer interrupt ----------------------------------------------

sound_ti  proc far               ;Call this 18 times per second

         push ax                 ;Push AX and DS onto stack
         push ds
setds:   mov  ax,0000h           ;Transfer C to DS
         mov  ds,ax
         dec  s_counter          ;Decrememt time counter
         jne  st_endit           ;If still unequal to 0 then end
         mov  s_endit,0          ;Signal end of note duration
st_endit: pop  ds                ;Pop value off of DS (reset to old value)
         pop  ax                 ;Get AX from stack again

stjump:  db   0EAh,0,0,0,0       ;FAR-JUMP to old timer interrupt

sound_ti  endp

;== Ende ============================================================

_text    ends                    ;End of program segment
         end                     ;End of assembler source
```

Chapter 10

Accessing and Programming the Video Cards

This chapter explains methods of programming the most popular video cards on the PC market. Even though the video cards mentioned here differ in their capabilities, they are all based on the same basic principle. High level languages such as BASIC, Pascal or C often have their own specific keywords and commands for controlling screen display. However, many of these commands merely call BIOS or DOS functions, which are both slow and inflexible in execution.

Direct access

Direct access to the video card is the alternative. Applications from Lotus 1-2-3® to dBASE® use direct video access coding, to guarantee both speed and that element of extra control over the video display. The main disadvantage: Programming in assembly language is required, since the communication here occurs at the system level. This chapter examines the programming needed for the best known video cards on the market:

- Monochrome Display Adapter (MDA), also called a *monochrome card*
- Color Graphics Adapter (CGA), also called a *color card*
- Hercules Graphic Card (HGC)
- Enhanced Graphic Adapter (EGA)
- Video Graphics Array (VGA)

Most of the graphic cards on the market are compatible with one of the cards mentioned in this chapter, and the descriptions stated here should apply to those cards.

Video Graphics Array (VGA)

This also applies to the newest generation of video cards, the VGA card. Designed in conjunction with the IBM PS/2 system, the VGA card is now available to the general public as an add-on card. This chapter demonstrates some general features of the EGA and VGA, as well as a few programming techniques.

What's needed

Before a video card can display a character or graphic pixel on a monitor screen or *CRT* (cathode ray tube), the card must know the following:

- which character or graphic pixel to display
- The color of the character or pixel
- The location on the screen at which it should be displayed.

PC video cards include RAM which collects information about every CRT screen pixel or screen location. This RAM memory is called *video RAM* and interfaces with the PC's RAM, allowing direct access from the microprocessor.

Speed

Rapid screen changes are important in word processing programs and other PC applications. For example, if you are paging through a word processing document at high speed, a 25-line, 80-column screen requires the transmission of 2,000 characters through the video card at one time. Fast data transfer is even more important for high-resolution graphics. For example, the 200x640-pixel IBM Color Graphics Adapter transmits 128,000 pixels of graphic information at a time.

Display modes

Each type of video card can have more than one display mode. Text and graphics display may be very different from one another. The monitor cannot distinguish between the two modes; it just processes the graphic information sent by the video card (or *video controller*). For the programmer and the video card, the modes require completely different programming techniques.

Graphic mode and text mode

Graphic mode stores the color of a screen pixel in one or more bits, then transmits the contents of video RAM more or less directly to the screen. Text mode uses a different method. The ASCII code of a character is stored in video RAM for each screen location. When the video controller displays the screen, it obtains the character pattern of the ASCII code from the ROM chip on the video card, then converts the code into a character matrix of pixels. This pattern then passes to the monitor and appears on the screen.

PC text mode uses the 256-character extended character set (see Appendix I). Since these characters are numbered sequentially from 0 to 255, one byte is enough for each screen position to display the character at the proper position.

Attribute bytes

Every screen position has an *attribute byte* which indicates the color or display attribute of the character (underlined, blinking, inverse video, etc.). This means that two bytes are needed for each position on the screen. Therefore, a total of 4000 bytes are required for a 25-line, 80-column screen. This appears to be a lot of memory at first glance, but is fairly small when compared to the memory requirements for bit-mapped graphic screen. In graphic mode, each dot is represented by one or more bits. A resolution of 640x200 pixels requires 128,000 bits (16K).

Another advantage of text mode is the simplicity in exchanging one character for another on the screen. The bit-map mode has its own advantages. Besides graphic displays, text can be displayed as individual dots whose pattern is derived from a character table in RAM installed by the user. This means that the user can design his own fonts (character sets).

10.1 Anatomy of a Video Card

The figure below shows the individual hardware components of a video card. The starting point for creating the picture is always the video RAM. This video RAM contains information about the characters to be displayed, and their display attributes (color, style, etc.).

Getting to the screen

The character generator first accesses video RAM, reading the characters one by one, and uses a character pattern table to construct the bit-map that will later form the character on the screen. The attribute controller also gets information about the display attributes (color, underlining, reverse, etc.) of the character from the video RAM. Both modules prepare this information and send it to the signal controller, which converts it to appropriate signals to be sent to the monitor. The signal controller itself is controlled by the CRT controller, which is the central point of video card operations. Besides the monitor and the video RAM, this CRT controller is one of the most important components of a video system. We will examine all these components in greater detail.

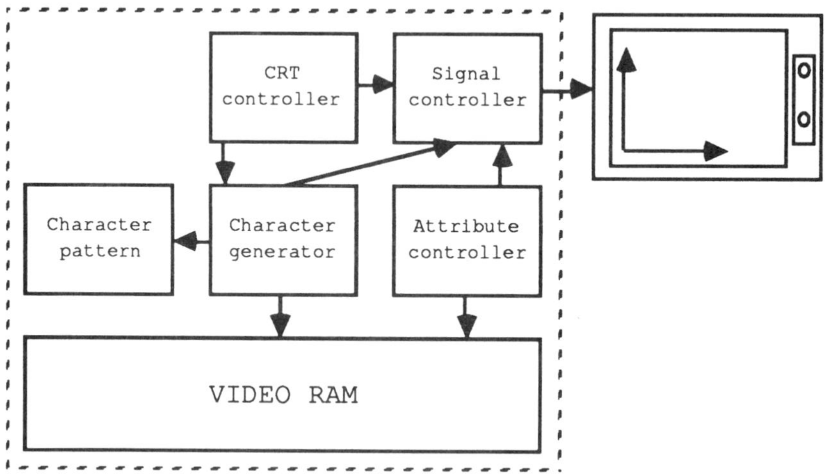

Block diagram of a video card

The monitor

The monitor is the device on which the video data is displayed. Unlike the video card, the monitor is a "dumb" device. This means it has no memory and cannot be programmed. All monitors used with PCs are *raster-scan devices*, in which the picture is made up of many small dots arranged in a rectangular pattern or raster.

When forming the picture, the electron beam of the picture tube touches each individual dot and illuminates it if it is supposed to be visible on the screen. This is done by switching on the electron beam as it passes over this dot, causing a phosphor particle on the picture tube to light up.

Color monitors

While monochrome monitors need only one electron beam to create a picture, color monitors use three beams which scan the screen simultaneously. Here a screen pixel consists of three phosphor particles in the basic colors of light: red, green, and blue. Each color has a matching electron beam. Any color in the spectrum can be created by combining these three colors and varying their intensities.

But since an ionized phosphor particle emits light for only a very brief period of time, the entire screen must be scanned many times per second to create the illusion of a stationary picture. PC monitors perform this task between 50 and 70 times per second. This repeated re-scanning is called the *refresh rate*. One rule of thumb for this rate: The faster the refresh rate, the better quality the picture.

Each new screen image begins in the upper left corner of the screen. From there the electron beam moves to the right along the first raster line. When it reaches the end of this line, the electron beam moves back to the start of the next line down, similar to pressing the <Return> key on a typewriter. The electron beam then scans the second raster line, at the end of which it moves to the start of the next raster line, and so on. Once it reaches the bottom of the screen, the electron beam returns to the upper left corner of the screen and the process starts over again. The illustration below shows the path of the electron beam.

Remember that the movement of the electron beam is controlled by the video card, not by the monitor itself.

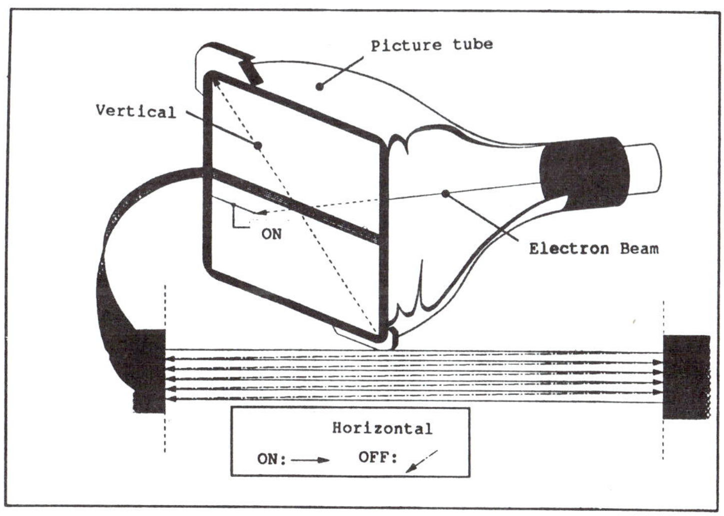

Electron beam scan movement

The resolution of the monitor naturally controls the number of raster lines and columns which the electron beam scans when creating a display. Thus, a monitor which has only 200 raster lines of 640 raster columns each clearly cannot handle the high resolutions of an EGA card at 640x350 pixels. The four monitor types used with a PC generally have the following resolutions:

Resolutions of different monitors		
Monitor	Vertical	Horizontal
Monochrome	350	720
Color	200	640
EGA	350	640
Multisync	varies, up to 600	varies, up to 800

The CRT controller

The CRT Controller or CRTC is the heart of a video card. It controls the operation of the video card and generates the signals the monitor needs to create the picture. Its tasks also include controlling light pens, generating the cursor and controlling the video RAM.

To inform the monitor of the next raster line, the CRTC sends a display enable signal at the start of each line, which activates the electron beam. While the beam moves from left to right over each raster column of the line, the CRTC controls the individual signals for the electron beam(s) so that the pixels appear on the screen as desired. At the end of the line, the CRTC disables the display enable signal so that the electron beam's return to the next raster line doesn't make a visible line on the screen. The electron beam is directed to the left edge of the following raster line by the output of a horizontal synchronization signal. The display enable signal is again enabled at the start of the next raster line, and the generation of the next line begins.

Overscan

Since the time that the electron beam needs to return to the start of the next line is less than the time the CRTC needs to get and prepare new information from the video RAM, there is a short pause. But the electron beam cannot be stopped, so we get something called *overscan*, which is visible as the left and right borders of the actual screen contents. Although this is an undesirable side effect in one sense, it is useful because it prevents the edges of the screen contents from being hidden by the edge of the monitor. If the electron beam is enabled while it is traveling over this border, a color screen border can be created.

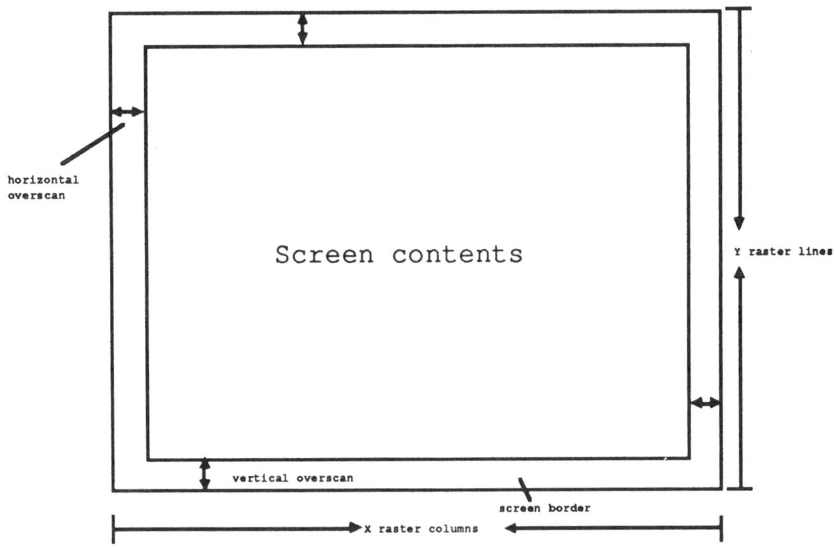

Rasters and overscan on a screen

Once the electron beam reaches the end of the last raster line, the display enable signal is disabled, and a vertical synchronization signal is sent. The electron beam returns to the upper left corner of the screen. Again the display enable signal is re-enabled and scanning again begins.

Pause and overscan

As with the horizontal electron beam return, a pause results which is displayed in the form of overscan, creating a vertical screen border.

Signal timing

The timing of individual signals varies from video mode to video mode. For this reason, the CRTC has a number of registers which describe the signal outputs and their timing. The structure of these registers and how they are programmed will be discussed in the remainder of this section. Many of these registers come from the registers of the 6845 video controller from Motorola. This controller is used in the MDA, CGA, and Hercules graphics cards. The EGA and VGA cards use a special VLSI (very large scale integration) chip as a CRTC, and its registers are somewhat more complicated. The techniques described here are intended as general descriptions for all video cards.

Registers of the 6845 video controller from Motorola		
Reg.	Meaning	Access
00H	Total horizontal character	Write
01H	Display horizontal character	Write
02H	Horizontal synchronization signal after ...char	Write
03H	Duration of horizontal synchronization signal in char.	Write
04H	Total vertical character	Write
05H	Adjust vertical character	Write
06H	Display vertical character	Write
07H	Vertical synchronization signal after ...char	Write
08H	Interlace mode	Write
09H	Number of scan lines per screen line	Write
0AH	Starting line of screen cursor	Write
0BH	Ending line of screen cursor	Write

These registers, like all of the other registers on the video card, are accessed via I/O ports with the assembly language instructions IN and OUT. The registers of the CRTC are accessed through a special address register, rather than directly from the address space of the processor. The number of the desired CRTC register is written to the port corresponding to this address register. Then the contents of this register can be read into a special data register with the IN assembly language instruction. If a value is to be written to the addressed register, it must be transferred to the data register with the OUT instruction. Then the CRTC automatically places it in the desired register. These two registers are actually found at successive port addresses, but these addresses vary from video card to video card.

We will include tables throughout the chapter to describe the contents of individual CRTC registers under the various video modes. Here's an example which shows how the contents of these registers are calculated and how the individual registers are related to each other. If you try some of these calculations with your calculator or PC, you will notice that some of them do not work out evenly. But since the registers of the CRTC hold only integer values, they will be rounded up or down.

The basis for the various calculations are the bandwidth and the horizontal and vertical scan rates of a monitor.

Bandwidth and scan rates of different video cards				
Video system rate	Resolution	Bandwidth	Vert. scan rate	Horiz. scan
MDA		720 x 350	16.257 MHz 50 Hz *	18.43 KHz*
CGA		640 x 200	14.318 MHz 60 Hz	15.75 KHz
HGC		640 x 200	14.318 MHz 50 Hz	18.43 KHz
EGA		640 x 350	16.257 MHz 60 Hz	21.85 KHz
		640 x 200	14.318 MHz 60 Hz	15.75 KHz
		720 x 350	16.257 MHz 50 Hz	18.43 KHz
(*MHz=Megahertz, KHz=Kilohertz, Hz=Hertz				

The bandwidths in the figure above specify the number of points which the electron beam scans per second, and is therefore also called the point or dot rate. The vertical scan rate specifies the number of screen refreshes per second, while the horizontal scan rate refers to the number of raster lines which the electron beam scans per second.

Starting with these values, let's practice calculating the individual CRTC register values for the 80x25 character text mode on a CGA card.

Dividing the bandwidth by the horizontal scan rate we get the number of pixels (screen dots) per raster line.

```
        Bandwidth                  14.318 MHz
  +     Horizontal scan rate       15.570 KHz
---------------------------------------------
        Pixels per line          919
```

Since the CRTC registers generally refer to the number of characters rather than pixels, this value must be converted to the number of characters per line. This is done by dividing the number of pixels per line by the width of the character matrix. On the CGA card this is eight pixels.

```
        Pixels per line          919
  ÷     Pixels per character       8
--------------------------------------------
        Characters per line      114
```

This value, decremented by one, is placed in the first register of the CRTC and specifies the total number of characters per line. In the second register we load the number of characters that will actually be displayed per line. The 80x25 character text mode usually offers 80 characters.

The difference between the total and the number of characters actually displayed per line is the number of characters which can be displayed between the horizontal return and the overscan. The difference in this case is 34 characters.

The duration of the horizontal beam return must be entered in the fourth register of the CRTC. This register stores the number of characters which could be displayed during this time, rather than the actual time duration. The monitor specifications define this instead of the video card itself. As a rule this number is between 5% and 15% of the total number of characters per line. A color monitor uses exactly ten characters.

This leaves 24 characters for the overscan (the horizontal screen border). The third CRTC register specifies how these characters are divided between the left and right screen borders. This register specifies the number of character positions which will be scanned before the horizontal beam return occurs. The BIOS specifies the value 90 here, or after ten characters have been displayed for the screen borders. The remaining 14 characters are placed at the start of the next line and form the left screen border.

The calculations for the vertical data, the number of vertical lines, the position of the vertical synchronization signal, etc., follow a similar scheme. The first calculation is the number of raster lines per screen. This results from the division of the number of lines displayed per second by the number of screen refreshes per second:

```
        Pixels per line          919
   +    Pixels per character       8
   --------------------------------------------
        Characters per line      114

        Horizontal scan rate      15.750 KHz
   +    Screen refreshes          60      Hz
   ---------------------------------------------
        Raster lines             262
```

Since the characters in CGA text mode are eight pixels high by eight pixels wide, we again divide by eight to get the number of text lines per screen:

```
        Raster lines             262
   +    Pixels per character       8
   --------------------------------------------
        Lines per screen          32
```

This result must be decremented by one and then loaded into the fifth register of the CRTC. The number of displayed lines is loaded into the seventh register. Since seven fewer lines are displayed than are actually available, these extra lines are used for the vertical beam return and overscan, whereby the vertical beam return begins after the 28th line.

The character height must be decremented by one and loaded into CRTC register nine. The decrement results is 7 in this example. This value also determines the range for the values loaded into register ten and eleven. They specify the first and last raster lines of the screen cursor. The cursor position is determined by the contents of registers 14 and 15. They refer to the distance of the character from the upper left corner of the screen, instead of line and column. This value is calculated by multiplying the cursor line by the number of columns per line and then adding the cursor column. The high byte of the result must be loaded into register 14 and the low byte in register 15.

The video RAM area

The contents of registers 12 and 13 determine the area of video RAM displayed on the screen. To understand these registers, we first need to know something about the way video RAM is organized.

The third component of the video system determines what will eventually be displayed on the screen. In text mode, the video RAM contains the ASCII codes of the characters to be displayed and their attributes. While the organization of video RAM in this mode is identical for all of the video cards discussed here, the organization for graphic mode varies from card to card. The description of each card discusses the way video RAM organizes graphic modes (more on this later).

As the illustration below shows, each screen position occupies two bytes in video RAM. The ASCII code of the character to be displayed is placed in the first of these two bytes, the one with the even address. By using eight bits per character code, a maximum of 256 different characters can be displayed.

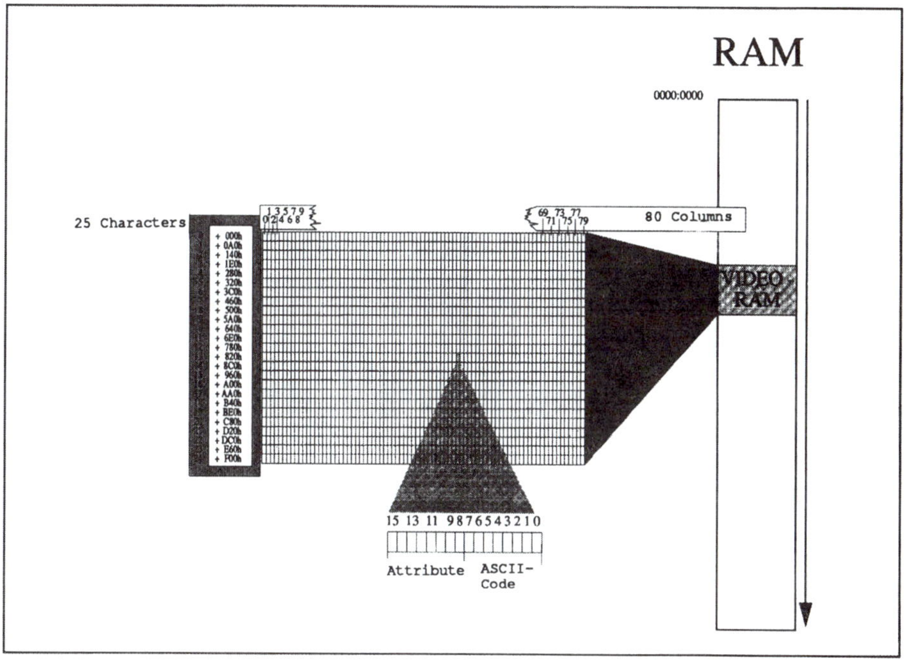

Normal text mode structure in video RAM

After the ASCII code, and always at an odd offset address, follows the attribute byte, which defines the appearance of the character on the screen. The attribute controller divides it into two nibbles, whereby the upper nibble (bits four to seven) describes the character background, and the lower nibble (bits zero to three) describes the character foreground. This results in two values between zero and fifteen which are interpreted depending on the type of monitor attached. With a color monitor (and a CGA or EGA card) both values select one of 16 possible colors. Each character on the screen can thus have its own foreground and background colors.

A monochrome monitor cannot display colors, regardless of the adapter. Here the attribute controls whether the character is displayed at high or low intensity, inverse, or underlined.

Character organization in video RAM

To access video RAM, you must know how the individual characters are organized within this memory. This organization is similar to character display on the screen.

The first character on the screen (the character in the upper left corner) is also the first character in video RAM, located at offset position 0000H. The next character to the right is located at offset position 0002H. All 80 characters of the first screen line follow in this manner. Since each screen character takes two bytes of memory, each line occupies 160 bytes of RAM. The first character of the second screen line follows the last character of the first line, and so on.

Finding character locations in video RAM

You can easily find the starting address of a line within video RAM by multiplying the line number (starting with zero) by 160. To get from the beginning of the line to a character within the line, the distance of the character from the start of the line must be added to this value. Since each character takes two bytes, this is done simply by multiplying the column number (also starting at zero) by two. Adding both products together yields the offset position of the character in the video RAM. These calculations can be combined into a single formula:

```
Offset_position(row, column) = row * 160 + column * 2
```

Note: Since only 40 characters per line are displayed in 40-column video modes, the factor 80 must replace the original 160.

The RAM memory of the video card is integrated into the normal RAM of the PC system, so you can use normal memory access commands to access video RAM. You must know the segment address of video RAM, which is used together with the formula above to find the offset position. Section 10.7 shows how this can be done easily in assembly language, BASIC, Pascal, and C.

Now that we have discussed the most important similarities between the four video cards, the following four sections describe the capabilities of these cards. In addition, these sections explain how these capabilities can be used for optimal screen output.

10.2 The IBM Monochrome Card

The IBM Monochrome Display Adapter, or MDA, is probably the oldest of the video cards. This card is based on the Motorola 6845 video controller, which is an intelligent peripheral chip. The 6845 controller constructs a display by generating the proper signals for the monitor from video RAM.

This card is excellent for text display. This is achieved with a 9x14 character matrix, which permits high-resolution character display. The format of this matrix is unusual since a character generator containing the bit pattern of each character can only produce characters 8 pixels wide. Characters from the IBM character set may not connect with each other (e.g., using box characters to draw a box). A circuit on the graphics card sidesteps this disadvantage by copying the eighth pixel of the line into the ninth pixel for any characters whose ASCII codes are between B0H and DFH. This allows the horizontal box drawing characters to connect.

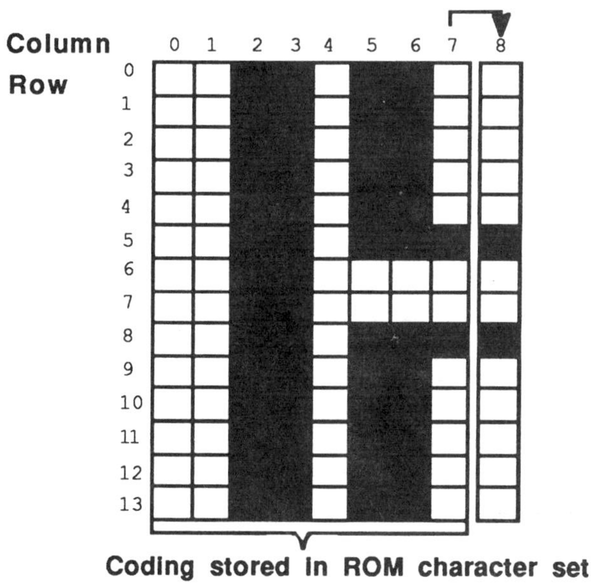

Monochrome display adapter—9x14 character matrix

The character generator requires one byte for each screen line: one bit per pixel, eight bits per line. Each character requires 14 bytes. The complete character set has a memory requirement of almost 4K, stored in a ROM chip on the card. For some reason the card has an 8K ROM, leaving the second bank of 4K unused.

Video RAM on the MDA

The video RAM of the card starts at address B000:0000 and extends over 4K (4,096 bytes). Since the screen display only has space for 2,000 characters and requires only 4,000 bytes of memory for those characters, the unused 96 bytes at the end of video RAM are available for other applications.

The following figure shows the meanings of the different values representing the attribute byte:

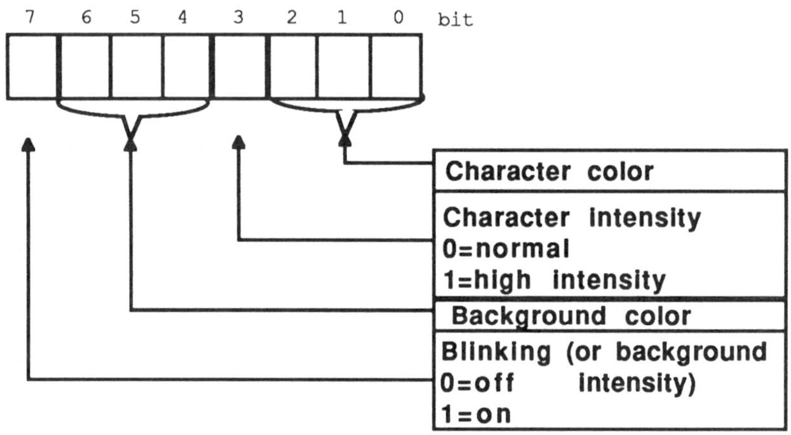

Attribute byte values—IBM monochrome display adapter

Any combination of bits can be loaded into this byte. However, the MDA only accepts the following combinations:

7	6	5	4	3	2	1	0	
?	0	0	0	?	0	0	0	No character (black on black)
?	0	0	0	?	0	0	1	underlined character (white on black)
?	0	0	0	?	1	1	1	White character on black
?	1	1	1	?	0	0	0	Black character on white (inverse)
?	1	1	1	?	1	1	1	No character (white on white)

Byte combinations—IBM monochrome display adapter

Besides these bit combinations, bits 3 and 7 of the attribute byte can be set or unset. Bit 3 defines the intensity of the foreground display. When this bit is set, the characters appear in higher intensity. Bit 7's purpose varies with the contents of the control registers (more on this later). For now, all you need to know is that bit 7 can either enable blinking characters, or enable an intensity matching the background color.

Monochrome cards have two more registers available: the control register and the status register.

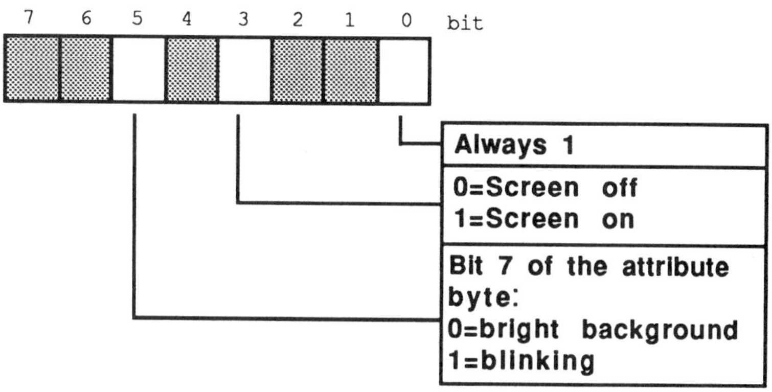

Control register

MDA control register

The control register located at port 3B8H controls the monochrome display adapter's different functions. As the figure below shows, only bits 0, 3 and 5 are of importance. Bit 0 controls the resolution on the card. Although the card only supports one resolution (80x25 characters), this bit must be set to 1 during system initialization. Otherwise the computer goes into an infinite wait loop. Bit 3 controls the creation of a visible display on the monitor. If bit 3 is set to 0, the screen is black and the blinking cursor disappears. If bit 3 is set to 1, the display returns to the screen. Bit 5 has a similar function: If bit 7 in the attribute byte of the character is set to 1, it enables blinking characters. If bit 7 contains the value 0, the character appears, unblinking, in front of a light background color. This means that bit 7 of the attribute byte acts as an intensity bit for the background. This register can only be written. This makes it impossible for a program to determine whether the display is turned on or off. The normal value for this register is 29H, meaning that all three relevant bits default to 1.

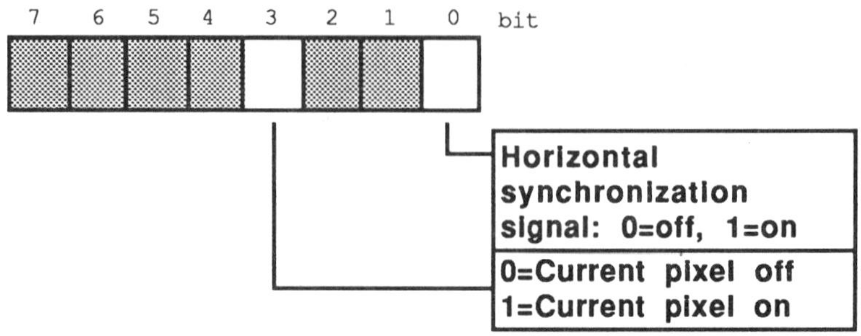

Status registers (3BAH)

MDA status register

Only bits 0 and 3 are used in the status register; all the other bits must contain the value 1. Unlike the control register, programs can read this register, but register contents cannot be changed by program code.

Horizontal synchronization

Bit 0 indicates if a horizontal synchronization signal is being sent to the display screen. The video card sends this signal after creating a screen line (not to be confused with a text line, which consists of 14 screen lines) on the screen. This signal informs the electron gun, which "draws" the picture on the screen, that it should return to the left border of the current screen line. In this case the bit has the value 1. Bit 3 contains the value of the pixel where the electron beam is currently located. A 1 signals that the pixel is visible on the screen and 0 means that the screen remains black at this location.

MDA internal registers

Besides the two registers directly connected to the hardware of the monochrome display adapter, the 6845 video processor contains a series of internal registers. These 18 registers are open to user access through the 6845 index register and data register. The index register is connected to port address 3B4H, the data register at port address 3B5H. You can only write to the 6845 registers—you cannot read data from them.

When you enter a value into one of the 18 registers, the number of the register (0-17) passes first into the index register. Then the value which is transmitted to the register passes into the data register. The 6845 then transmits the indicated value to the proper register. Most of these 18 registers should not be modified, since they contain important data about the screen structure (e.g., synchronization signals) and incorrect values in these registers can damage the monitor. The following table shows the meanings of the individual registers and the values which ensure a correct display.

Registers of the CRTC register in 80x25 text mode on the Monochrome Display Adapter (MDA)		
Reg.	Meaning	Content
00H	Total horizontal character	97
01H	Display horizontal character	80
02H	Horizontal synchronization signal after ...char	82
03H	Duration of horizontal synchronization signal in char.	15
04H	Total vertical character	25
05H	Adjust vertical character	6
06H	Display vertical character	25
07H	Vertical synchronization signal after ...char	25
08H	Interlace mode	2
09H	Number of scan lines per screen line	13
0AH	Starting line of blinking screen cursor	11
0BH	Ending line of blinking screen cursor	12
0CH	Starting address of displayed screen page (low byte)	0
0DH	Starting address of displayed screen page (high byte)	0
0EH	Character address of blinking screen cursor (high byte)	0
0FH	Character address of blinking screen cursor (low byte)	0
10H	Light pen position (high byte)	*
11H	Light pen position (low byte)	*
	*not available on MDA	

The following program makes full use of the monochrome display adapter's capabilities. It was written in assembly language. The individual routines are fully documented and require no additional explanation. The demonstration program built into the listing shows practical application of the individual routines.

Assembler listing: VMONO.ASM

```
;***********************************************************************;
;*                            V M O N O                                *;
;*---------------------------------------------------------------------*;
;*    Task            : makes some elementary functions available for *;
;*                      access to the monochrome display screen       *;
;*---------------------------------------------------------------------*;
;*    Info            : all functions subdivide the screen            *;
;*                      into columns 0 to 79 and lines 0 to 24        *;
;*---------------------------------------------------------------------*;
;*    Author          : MICHAEL TISCHER                               *;
;*    Developed on    : 8/11/87                                       *;
;*    Last Update     : 6/14/89                                       *;
;*---------------------------------------------------------------------*;
;*    assembly        : MASM VMONO;                                   *;
;*                      LINK VMONO;                                   *;
;*---------------------------------------------------------------------*;
;*    Call            : VMONO                                         *;
;***********************************************************************;

;== Constants =======================================================

CONTROL_REG  = 03B8h              ;Control register port address
ADDRESS_6845 = 04B4h              ;6845 address register
DATA_6845    = 03B5h              ;6845 data register
VIO_SEG      = 0B000h             ;Segment address of video RAM
CUR_START    = 10                 ;Register # CRTC: Starting cursor line
CUR_END      = 11                 ;Register # CRTC: Ending cursor line
CURPOS_HI    = 14                 ;Register # CRTC: Cursor pos. hi byte
CURPOS_LO    = 15                 ;Register # CRTC: Cursor pos. lo byte

DELAY        = 20000              ;Counter for delay loop
```

```
;== Stack ==========================================================

stack     segment para stack        ;Definition of stack segment

          dw 256 dup (?)            ;256-word stack

stack     ends                      ;End of stack segment

;== Data ===========================================================

data    segment para 'DATA'       ;Define data segment

;== the Data for the Demo-Program ==================================

str1    db "a" ,0
str2    db " >PC SYSTEM PROGRAMMING< ",0
str3    db "   window 1   ",0
str4    db "   window 2   ",0
str5    db "              the program is stopped by "
        db " pressing a Key....               ",0

initm   db 13,10,"VMONO (c) 1987 by Michael Tischer",13,10,13,10
        db "This demonstration program only runs with "
        db " a monochrome",13,10,"display card. If your PC "
        db "has another type of display card,",13,10
        db "please enter <s> to stop the "
        db " program.",13,10,"Otherwise press any "
        db "key to start ",13,10
        db "the program ...",13,10,"$"

;== Data ===========================================================

linen     dw  0*160,1*160,2*160 ;Start addresses of the lines as
          dw  3*160,4*160,5*160 ;offset addresses in the video RAM
          dw  6*160,7*160,8*160
          dw  9*160,10*160,11*160,12*160,13*160,14*160,15*160,16*160
          dw 17*160,18*160,19*160,20*160,21*160,22*160,23*160,24*160

data      ends                     ;End of data segment

;== Code ================================================

code      segment para 'CODE'      ;Definition of the CODE segment

          assume cs:code, ds:data, es:data, ss:stack

;== this is the Demo-Program =====================================

demo      proc far

          mov ax,data              ;Get segment address of data segment
          mov ds,ax                ;and load into DS
          mov es,ax                ;as well as ES

          ;-- Display initial msg./wait for input ----------------

          mov  ah,9                ;String output function
          mov  dx,offset initm     ;Address of initial message
          int  21h                 ;Call DOS interrupt 21H

          xor  ah,ah               ;Get function number for key
          int  16h                 ;Call BIOS keyboard interrupt
          cmp  al,"s"              ;was <s> entered?
          je   ende                ;YES --> end program
          cmp  al,"S"              ;was <S> entered?
          jne  startdemo           ;NO --> start demo

ende:     mov  ax,4c00h            ;Function number for program end
          int  21h                 ;Call DOS interrupt 21H
```

```
startdemo label near
        mov  cx,0d00h           ;Enable full cursor
        call cdef
        call cls                ;Clear screen

        ;-- Fill screen with ASCII characters -------------

        xor  di,di              ;Start in upper left corner
        mov  si,offset str1     ;Offset address of string1
        mov  cx,2000            ;2,000 characters fit on the screen
        mov  al,07h             ;white letters on black background
demo1:  call print              ;Display string
        inc  str1               ;Increment character in test string
        jne  demo2              ;NUL code suppressed
        inc  str1
demo2:  loop demo1              ;Repeat output

        ;-- Create window 1 and window 2 ----------

        mov  bx,0508h           ;Upper left corner of window 1
        mov  dx,1316h           ;Lower right corner of window 1
        mov  ah,07h             ;White letters, black background
        call clear              ;Clear window 1
        mov  bx,3C02h           ;Upper left corner of window 2
        mov  dx,4A10h           ;Lower right corner window 2
        call clear              ;Clear window 2
        mov  bx,0508h           ;Upper left corner of window 1
        call calo               ;Convert to offset address
        mov  si,offset str3     ;Offset address string 3
        mov  ah,70h             ;Black characters, white background
        call print              ;Display string 3
        mov  bx,3C02h           ;Upper left corner of window 2
        call calo               ;Convert to offset address
        mov  si,offset str4     ;Offset address string 4
        call print              ;Display string 4
        xor  di,di              ;Upper left display corner
        mov  si,offset str5     ;Offset address string 5
        call print              ;Display string 5

        ;-- Display program logo ------------------------------

        mov  bx,1E0Ch           ;Column 30, line 12
        call calo               ;Convert offset address
        mov  si,offset str2     ;Offset address string 2
        mov  ah,0F0h            ;Inverse blinking
        call print              ;Display string 2

        ;-- Fill window with arrows ---------------------------

        xor  ch,ch              ;Hi-byte of the counter to 0
arrow:  mov  bl,1               ;Asterisk
arrow0: push bx                 ;Push BX on the stack
        mov  di,offset str3     ;Draw arrow line in string 3
        mov  cl,15              ;Total of 15 characters in a line
        sub  cl,bl              ;Calculate number of spaces
        shr  cl,1               ;Divide by 2 (for left half)
        or   cl,cl              ;No blanks ?
        je   arrow1             ;YES --> ARROW1
        mov  al," "
        rep  stosb              ;Draw blanks in string 3
arrow1: mov  cl,bl              ;Number of asterisks in counter
        mov  al,"*"
        rep  stosb              ;Draw stars in string 3
        mov  cl,15              ;Total of 15 characters in a line
        sub  cl,bl              ;Calculate number of blanks
        shr  cl,1               ;Divide by 2 (for right half)
        or   cl,cl              ;No blanks?
        je   arrow2             ;YES --> ARROW2
        mov  al," "
```

```
        rep  stosb              ;Draw blanks in string 3
arrow2: mov  bx,0509h           ;below the first line of window 1
        call calo               ;Convert to offset address
        mov  si,offset str3     ;Offset address string 3
        mov  ah,07h             ;White characters, black background
        call print              ;Display string 3
        mov  bx,3C10h           ;into the lowest line of window 2
        call calo               ;Convert offset address
        call print              ;Display string 3

        ;-- Brief pause ----------------------------------------

        mov  cx,DELAY           ;Loop counter
waitlp: loop waitlp             ;Count loop to 0

        ;-- Scroll window 1 line down -------------------------

        mov  bx,0509h           ;Upper left corner of window 1
        mov  dx,1316h           ;Lower right corner window 1
        mov  cl,1               ;Scroll down
        call scrolldn           ;one line

        ;-- Scroll window 2 one line up ------------------------

        mov  bx,3C03h           ;Upper left corner window 2
        mov  dx,4A10h           ;Lower right corner window 2
        call scrollup           ;Scroll up

        ;-- Was a key pressed? (end program) -------------------

        mov  ah,1               ;Function number for testing key
        int  16h                ;Call BIOS keyboard interrupt
        jne  end_it             ;Keypress -> goto end of program

        ;-- NO, display next arrow ----------------------------

        pop  bx                 ;Pop BX from stack again
        add  bl,2               ;2 more stars in next line
        cmp  bl,17              ;Reached 17 ?
        jne  arrow0             ;NO --> next arrow
        jmp  arrow              ;No key --> next arrow

        ;-- Get ready to end program

end_it: xor  ah,ah              ;Get function number for key
        int  16h                ;Call BIOS-keyboard-interrupt
        mov  cx,0D0Ch           ;Restore normal cursor
        call cdef
        call cls                ;Clear screen
        jmp  ende               ;Go to end of program

demo    endp

;== Functions ===============================================

;-- SOFF: switches the display off  -----------------------
;-- Input    : none
;-- Output   : none
;-- register : AX and DX are changed

SOFF    proc near

        mov  dx,CONTROL_REG     ;Address of display control register
        in   al,dx              ;read its content
        and  al,11110111b       ;bit 3 = 0: display off
        out  dx,al              ;set new value (display off)

        ret                     ;back to caller

SOFF    endp
```

```
;-- SON: switches the display on -------------------------
;-- Input    : none
;-- Output   : none
;-- register : AX and DX are changed

SON       proc near

          mov  dx,CONTROL_REG     ;Address of display control register
          in   al,dx              ;Read its content
          or   al,8               ;Bit 3 = 1: display on
          out  dx,al              ;Set new value (display on)
          ret                     ;Back to caller

SON       endp

;-- CDEF: sets the start and end line of the cursor -------------
;-- Input   : CL = Start line
;--           CH = End line
;-- Output  : none
;-- register : AX and DX are changed
cdef      proc near

          mov  al,CUR_START       ;Register 10: start line
          mov  ah,cl              ;Start line to AH
          call setvk              ;Transmit to video controller
          mov  al,CUR_END         ;Register 11: end line
          mov  ah,ch              ;End line to AH
          jmp  short setvk        ;Transmit to video controller

cdef      endp

;-- SETBLINK: sets the blinking display cursor --------------------
;-- Input    : DI = offset address of the cursor
;-- Output   : none
;-- register : BX, AX and DX are changed

setblink  proc near

          mov  bx,di              ;Transmit offset to BX
          mov  al,CURPOS_HI       ;Register 15:Hi-byte of cursor offset
          mov  ah,bh              ;HI-byte of the offset
          call setvk              ;Transmit to video controller
          mov  al,CURPOS_LO       ;Register 15:Lo-byte of cursor offset
          mov  ah,bl              ;Lo-byte of the offset

          ;-- SETVK is called automatically ------------------------

setblink  endp

;-SETVK: sets a byte in one of the registers of the video controller --
;-- Input    :  AL = number of the register
;--             AH = new content of the register
;-- Output   :  none
;-- register : DX and AL are changed

setvk     proc near

          mov  dx,ADDRESS_6845    ;Address of the index register
          out  dx,al              ;Send number of the register
          jmp  short $+2          ;Small I/O pause
          inc  dx                 ;Address of the index register
          mov  al,ah              ;Content to AL
          out  dx,al              ;Set new content
          ret                     ;Back to caller

setvk     endp

;-- GETVK: reads a byte from one register of the video controllers -
;-- Input     : AL = number of the register
```

```
;-- Output   : AL = content of the register
;-- register : DX and AL are changed

getvk     proc near

          mov  dx,ADDRESS_6845      ;Address of the index register
          out  dx,al                ;Send number of the register
          jmp short $+2
          inc  dx                   ;Address of the index register
          in   al,dx                ;Read content to AL
          ret                       ;Back to caller

getvk     endp

;-- SCROLLUP: scrolls a window up by N lines ----------------
;-- Input   :   BL = line upper left
;--             BH = column upper left
;--             DL = line lower right
;--             DH = column lower right
;--             CL = number of lines to scroll
;-- Output   : none
;-- register : only FLAGS are changed
;-- Info     : the display lines released are erased

scrollup  proc near

          cld                       ;Increment on string instructions

          push ax                   ;Push all changed registers on the
          push bx                   ;stack
          push di                   ;In this case the sequence
          push si                   ;must be observed!

          push bx                   ;These three registers are restored
          push cx                   ;from the stack before ending
          push dx
          sub  dl,bl                ;Calculate the number of lines
          inc  dl
          sub  dl,cl                ;Deduct number of lines scrolled
          sub  dh,bh                ;Calculate number of columns
          inc  dh
          call calo                 ;Convert upper left in offset
          mov  si,di                ;Record Address in SI
          add  bl,cl                ;First line in scrolled window
          call calo                 ;Convert first line to offset
          xchg si,di                ;Exchange SI and DI
          push ds                   ;Store segment register on
          push es                   ;the stack
          mov  ax,VIO_SEG           ;Segment address of the video RAM
          mov  ds,ax                ;to DS
          mov  es,ax                ;and ES
supl:     mov  ax,di                ;Record DI in AX
          mov  bx,si                ;Record SI in BX
          mov  cl,dh                ;Number of column in counter
          rep movsw                 ;Move a line
          mov  di,ax                ;Restore DI from AX
          mov  si,bx                ;Restore SI from BX
          add  di,160               ;Set next line
          add  si,160
          dec  dl                   ;Processed all lines ?
          jne  supl                 ;NO --> move another line
          pop  es                   ;Get segment register from
          pop  ds                   ;stack
          pop  dx                   ;Get lower right corner
          pop  cx                   ;Read number of lines
          pop  bx                   ;Get upper left corner
          mov  bl,dl                ;Lower line to BL
          sub  bl,cl                ;Deduct number of lines
          inc  bl
          mov  ah,07h               ;Color : black on white
```

```
         call clear             ;Erase lines freed

         pop  si                ;CX and DX have already
         pop  di                ;been read
         pop  bx
         pop  ax

         ret                    ;Back to caller

scrollup endp

;-- SCROLLDN: scrolls a window down N lines ---------------
;-- Input  :  BL = line upper left
;--           BH = column upper left
;--           DL = line lower right
;--           DH = column lower right
;--           CL = number of lines to scroll
;-- Output   : none
;-- register : only FLAGS are changed
;-- Info     : display lines released are erased

scrolldn proc near

         cld                    ;Increment on string instructions

         push ax                ;Store all changed registers on the
         push bx                ;stack
         push di                ;In this case the sequence
         push si                ;must be observed !

         push bx                ;These three registers are returned
         push cx                ;from the stack before the end
         push dx                ;of the routine

         sub  dh,bh             ;Calculate the number of the column
         inc  dh
         mov  al,bl             ;Record line upper left in AL
         mov  bl,dl             ;Line upper right to line upper left
         call calo              ;Convert upper left into offset
         mov  si,di             ;Record address in SI
         sub  bl,cl             ;Deduct number of lines to scroll
         call calo              ;Convert upper left in offset
         xchg si,di             ;Exchange SI and DI
         sub  dl,al             ;Calculate number of lines
         inc  dl                ;Deduct number
         sub  dl,cl             ;of lines to be scrolled
         push ds                ;Push segment register onto stack
         push es
         mov  ax,VIO_SEG        ;Segment address of video RAM
         mov  ds,ax             ;to DS
         mov  es,ax             ;and ES
sdn1:    mov  ax,di             ;Move DI to AX
         mov  bx,si             ;Move SI to BX
         mov  cl,dh             ;Number column in counter
         rep movsw              ;Scroll one line
         mov  di,ax             ;Get DI from AX
         mov  si,bx             ;Restore SI from BX
         sub  di,160            ;Set next line
         sub  si,160
         dec  dl                ;All lines processed ?
         jne  sdn1              ;NO --> scroll another line
         pop  es                ;Get segment register from
         pop  ds                ;stack
         pop  dx                ;Return lower right corner
         pop  cx                ;Return number of lines
         pop  bx                ;Return upper left corner
         mov  dl,bl             ;Upper line to DL
         add  dl,cl             ;Add number of lines
         dec  dl
         mov  ah,07h            ;Color : black on white
```

```
         call clear              ;Erase lines which were released

         pop  si                 ;CX and DX are
         pop  di                 ; already returned
         pop  bx
         pop  ax

         ret                     ;Back to caller

scrolldn endp

;-- CLS: Clear the complete screen ------------------------------
;-- Input   : none
;-- Output   : none
;-- register : only FLAGS are changed

cls      proc near

         mov  ah,07h             ;Color is white on black
         xor  bx,bx              ;Upper left is (0/0)
         mov  dx,4F18h           ;Lower right is (79/24)

         ;-- Execute Clear -----------------------------------------

cls      endp

;-- CLEAR: fills a designated display with space characters ----
;-- Input   : AH = Attribute/color
;--              BL = line upper left
;--              BH = column upper left
;--              DL = line lower right
;--              DH = column lower right
;-- Output   : none
;-- register : only FLAGS are changed

clear    proc near

         cld                     ;Increment on string instructions
         push cx                 ;Store all registes which
         push dx                 ;are changed on the stack
         push si
         push di
         push es
         sub  dl,bl              ;Calculate number of lines
         inc  dl
         sub  dh,bh              ;Calculate number of columns
         inc  dh
         call calo               ;Offset address of upper left corner
         mov  cx,VIO_SEG         ;Segment address of the video RAM
         mov  es,cx              ;to ES
         xor  ch,ch              ;Hi-bytes of the counter to 0
         mov  al," "             ;Space character
clear1:  mov  si,di              ;Move DI to SI
         mov  cl,dh              ;Number of column in counter
         rep stosw               ;Store space character
         mov  di,si              ;Restore DI from SI
         add  di,160             ;Set in next line
         dec  dl                 ;All lines processed ?
         jne  clear1             ;NO --> erase another line

         pop  es                 ;Restore registers from
         pop  di                 ;stack
         pop  si
         pop  dx
         pop  cx
         ret                     ;Back to caller

clear    endp

;-- PRINT: outputs a string on the Display --------------------
```

```
;-- Input     : AH = Attribute/color
;--             DI = offset address of the first character
;--             SI = offset address of the string to DS
;-- Output    : DI points behind the last character output
;-- register  : AL, DI and FLAGS are changed
;-- Info      : the string must be terminated with a NUL-character.
;--             other control characters are not recognized

print     proc near

          cld                        ;Increment on string instructions
          push si                    ;Store SI, DX and ES on the stack
          push es
          push dx
          mov  dx,VIO_SEG            ;Segment address of the video RAM
          mov  es,dx                 ;First to DX and then to ES
          jmp  print1                ;YES --> Output finished

print0:   stosw                      ;Store attribute and color in V-RAM
print1:   lodsb                      ;Get next character from the string
          or   al,al                 ;Is it NUL
          jne  print0                ;NO --> output

printe:   pop  dx                    ;Get SI, DX and ES back from stack
          pop  es
          pop  si
          ret                        ;Back to caller

print     endp

;- CALO: converts line and column into offset address ----------------
;-- Input     : BL = line
;--             BH = column
;-- Output    : DI = the offset address
;-- Registers: DI and FLAGS are changed

calo      proc near

          push ax                    ;Store AX on the stack
          push bx                    ;Store BX on the stack

          shl  bx,1                  ;Column and line times 2
          mov  al,bh                 ;Column to AL
          xor  bh,bh                 ;Get Hi-byte
          mov  di,[linen+bx]         ;Offset address of the line
          xor  ah,ah                 ;HI-byte for column offset
          add  di,ax                 ;Add line- and column offset

          pop  bx                    ;Get BX from stack again
          pop  ax                    ;Get AX from stack again
          ret                        ;Back to caller

calo      endp

;== End ====================================================

code      ends                       ;End of the CODE segment
          end  demo                  ;Start program execution w/ demo
```

10.3 The Hercules Graphic Card

The Hercules display adapter displays text in both text mode and graphics mode, with a graphic resolution of 720x348 pixels. This card contains enough RAM for two display pages. Each display page is 32K, so video RAM can accept a 4K text page and a graphic page. The first display page extends from address B000:0000 to B000:7FFF. The second screen page goes from B000:8000 to B000:FFFF.

Hercules video RAM

The Hercules card's video RAM in text mode has the same cursor character and port addresses as the IBM monochrome display adapter. With the graphic capabilities, only a few bits in the status and control register are different from the monochrome card. An additional configuration register can be addressed from 3BFH. You can write to this register only. Only bits 0 and 1 are of interest to the programmer. The former indicates whether the graphic mode can be switched on (1) or not (0). Bit 1 determines whether the second display page can be used. Bit 1 contains the value 1 if the second page is usable.

To avoid conflicts with other video cards (especially color cards), both bits are set to 0 at the start of the system so that neither graphic mode nor the second display page are accessible at first. Application programs must configure the Hercules display adapter through the configuration register if the programs require graphic mode or the second screen page.

The control register of the Hercules graphic card has some differences from that of the MDA discussed in the preceding section.

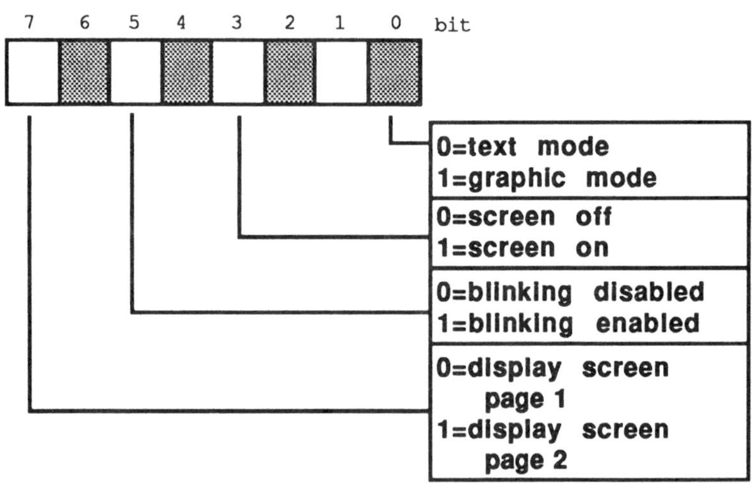

The Hercules control register (3B8H)

Unlike the IBM monochrome display adapter, bit 0 is unused and doesn't have to be set to 1 during the system boot. Bit 1 determines text or graphic mode: a 0 in bit 1 enables text mode, while a 1 in bit 1 enables graphic mode. As you shall see in the following examples, changing these bits isn't enough to switch between text and graphic modes. The internal registers of the 6845 must be reset as well. During this process, the screen display must be switched off to prevent the 6845 from creating garbage during its reprogramming.

The Hercules card has a seventh bit in this register. Its contents determine which of the two screen pages appear on the monitor screen. If this bit is 0, the first screen page appears; a 1 calls the second screen page on the screen. Independent of each other, the user can write to or read from either page at any time. You can only write to this register; attempts to read this register return the value FFH. Because of this, it is impossible to switch off the display simply by reading the contents of the status register and erasing bit 3, regardless of the display mode and the screen page selected.

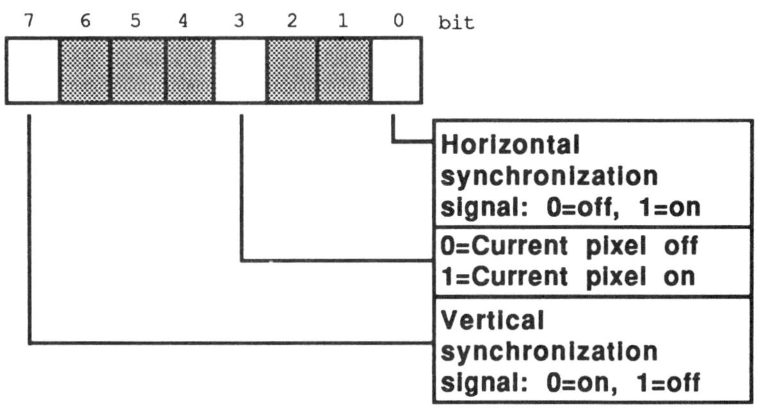

Hercules status register (3BAH)

Only the significance of bit 7 makes this register different from the IBM monochrome card. It's always set to 0 when the 6845 sends a vertical synchronization signal to the display. This signal is always sent when the last screen line has been constructed. The electron beam, which constructs the display, then jumps to the first line of the screen to start constructing a new screen.

Since the Hercules card uses the same processor as the IBM card, the internal registers of the 6845 and their meaning are identical to the IBM card. The index register and data register are also located at the same address. The following values must be assigned to the various registers in the text and graphic modes respectively:

No.	Meaning	Text	Graphic
0	Horizontal character seeded	97	53
1	Horizontal character displayed	80	45
2	Horiz. synchronization signal after...character	82	46
3	Horiz. synchronization signal width	15	7
4	Vertical character seeded	25	91
5	Vertical character justified	6	2
6	Vertical character displayed	25	87
7	Vert. synchronization signal after...character	25	87
8	Interlace mode	2	2
9	Number of ccan-lines per line	13	3
10	Starting line of blinking cursor	11	0
11	Ending line of the blinking cursors	12	0
12	High byte of screen page starting address	0	0
13	Low byte of screen page starting address	0	0
14	High byte of blinking cursor char. address	0	0
15	Low byte of blinking cursor char. address	0	0
16	Reserved		
17	Reserved		

As mentioned earlier, the Hercules card in graphic mode provides 348x720 resolution. Every pixel on the screen corresponds to one bit in the video RAM. If the corresponding bit contains the value 1, the dot is visible on the display, otherwise it remains dark. The following figure shows the construction of the video RAM in the graphic mode.

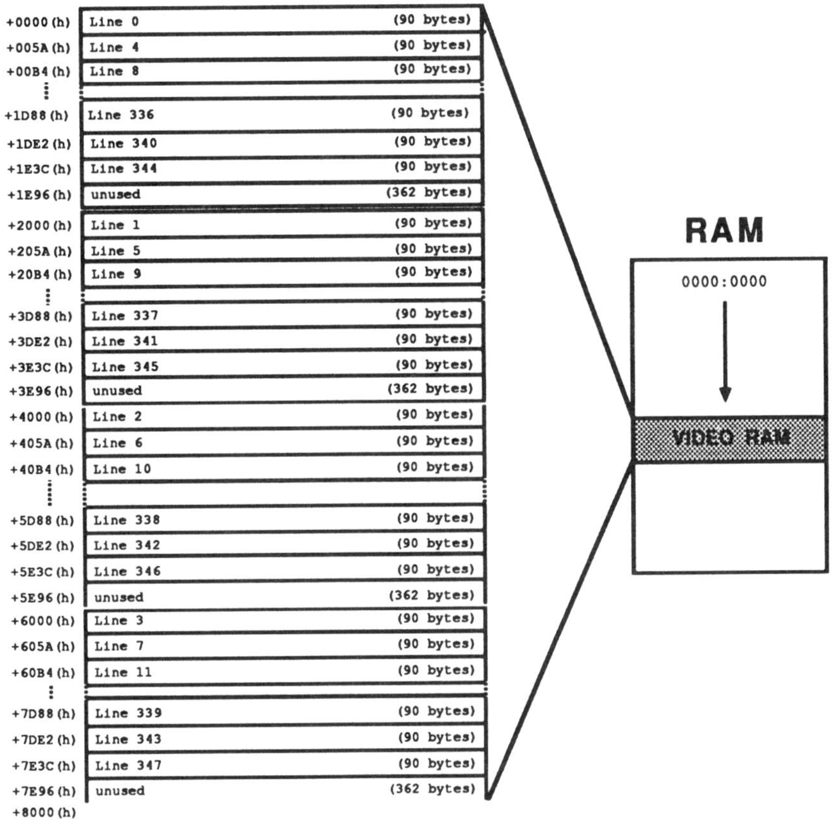

Video RAM and the screen under construction

The bit patterns of the individual lines in the video RAM aren't arranged sequentially, as you might have assumed. The 32K of video RAM is divided into four 8K blocks. The first block contains the bit pattern for any lines divisible by 4 (0, 4, 8, 12, etc.). The second block contains the bit patterns for lines 1, 5, 9, 13 etc. The third block contains the bit patterns for lines 2, 6, 10, 14, etc., while the last block contains lines 3, 7, 11, 15 etc. When the 6845 generates a display, it obtains information for screen line zero from the first data block, screen line one from the second data block, etc. After it has obtained the contents of the third screen line from the fourth data block, it accesses the first data block again for the structure of the fourth line. Each line requires 90 bytes within the individual data blocks—every pixel requires a bit, and 720 pixels divided by 8 bits (per byte) equals 90. The first 90 bytes in the first memory area provide the bit pattern for screen line zero, and the 90 bytes following provide the bit pattern for the fourth screen line. The zero byte of one of these 90-byte sets represents the first eight columns of a screen line (columns 0-8). The first byte represents columns 8-15, etc. Within one of these bytes, bit 7 corresponds to the left screen pixel and bit 0 corresponds to the right screen pixel.

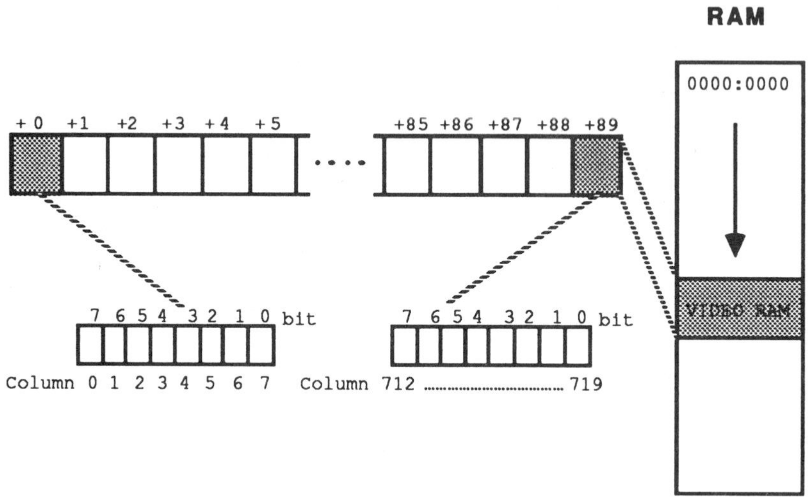

Relationship between 90-line bytes and screen display

If the screen pixels of a line (0 to 719) and the screen pixels of a column (0 to 347) are sequentially numbered, an equation indicates the address of the bytes relative to the beginning of the screen page. This address contains the information for a pixel with the coordinates X/Y.

To determine the bit within the byte which represents the pixel, the following formula can be used:

```
Address = 2000H * (Y mod 4) + 90 * int(Y/4) + int(X/8)
```

The following program demonstrates the abilities of the Hercules display adapter. The individual routines within this program have some differences from the routines shown in the monochrome display adapter demo program from the previous section. The routines here enable access to both screen pages, and support the Hercules graphic mode.

Assembler listing: VHERC.ASM

```
;**********************************************************************;
;*                            V H E R C                               *;
;*--------------------------------------------------------------------*;
;*    Task          : makes a basic function available for            *;
;*                    access to the HERCULES GRAPHICS CARD            *;
;*--------------------------------------------------------------------*;
;*    Info          : all functions partition the screen display      *;
;*                    into columns  0-79 and lines 0-24 (text mode)   *;
;*                    & columns 0-719 and lines 0-347 (graphic mode)  *;
;*--------------------------------------------------------------------*;
;*    Author        : MICHAEL TISCHER                                 *;
;*    developed on  : 8/11/87                                         *;
```

```
;*    last update      : 6/15/89                                        *;
;*----------------------------------------------------------------------*;
;*    assembly         : MASM VHERC;                                    *;
;*                       LINK VHERC;                                    *;
;*----------------------------------------------------------------------*;
;*    call             : VHERC                                          *;
;************************************************************************;

;== Constants ===========================================================

CONTROL_REG   = 03B8h                  ;Control register port address
ADDRESS_6845  = 03B4h                  ;6845 address register
DATA_6845     = 03B5h                  ;6845 data register
CONFIG_REG    = 03BFh                  ;Configuration register
VIO_SEG       = 0B000h                 ;Video RAM segment address
CUR_START     = 10                     ;Reg. # for CRTC: Start cursor line
CUR_END       = 11                     ;Reg. # for CRTC: End cursor line
CURPOS_HI     = 14                     ;Reg. # for CRTC: Cursor pos hi byte
CURPOS_LO     = 15                     ;Reg. # for CRTC: Cursor pos lo byte

DELAY         = 20000                  ;Count for delay loop

;== Macros ==============================================

setmode    macro modus              ;Set control register

           mov  dx,CONTROL_REG      ;Screen control register address
           mov  al,modus            ;Put new mode in AL register
           out  dx,al               ;Send mode to control register

           endm

setvk      macro                    ;Write value to CRTC registers
                                    ;Input: AL = register number
                                    ;       AH = Value for register

           mov  dx,ADDRESS_6845     ;Index register address
           out  dx,ax               ;Display register number and new value

           endm

;== Stack ===============================================

stack      segment para stack       ;Definition of stack segment

           dw 256 dup (?)           ;Stack is 256 words in size

stack      ends                     ;End of stack segment

;== Data ==================================================

data       segment para 'DATA'      ;Define data segment

;== Data needed for demo program ==========================

initm      db 13,10,"VHERC (c) 1987 by Michael Tischer",13,10,13,10
           db "This demonstration program runs only with "
           db " a HERCULES",13,10,"graphics card. If your PC "
           db "has another type of display card, ",13,10
           db "please input an >s< to stop the "
           db " program.",13,10,"Otherwise please press any "
           db "key to start the ",13,10
           db "program ...",13,10,"$"

str1       db 1,17,16,2,7,0
str2       db 2,16,17,1,7,0

domes      db 13,10
           db "This program creates a short graphic demo ",13,10
           db "and a text demo. Pressing a key during the",13,10
```

```
        db "demo ends the program.",13,10
        db "Press a key to start the program...",13,10,"$"

;== Table of line offset addresses ========================

lines   dw  0*160,1*160,2*160 ;Beginning addresses of the lines as
        dw  3*160,4*160,5*160 ;offset addresses in video RAM
        dw  6*160,7*160,8*160
        dw  9*160,10*160,11*160,12*160,13*160,14*160,15*160,16*160
        dw 17*160,18*160,19*160,20*160,21*160,22*160,23*160,24*160

grafikt db 35h, 2Dh, 2Eh, 07h, 5Bh, 02h  ;Register values for the
        db 57h, 57h, 02h, 03h, 00h, 00h  ;graphic mode

textt   db 61h, 50h, 52h, 0Fh, 19h, 06h  ;Register values for the
        db 19h, 19h, 02h, 0Dh, 0Bh, 0ch  ;text mode

data    ends                  ;End of data segment

;== Code segment ==========================================

code    segment para 'CODE'     ;Definition of the code segment

        org 100h

        assume cs:code, ds:data, es:data, ss:stack

;== this is only the Demo-Program =============================

demo    proc far

        mov  ax,data            ;Get segment address of data segment
        mov  ds,ax              ;Load into DS
        mov  es,ax              ;and ES

        ;-- Opening msg., wait for input --------------------

        mov  ah,9               ;Output function number for string
        mov  dx,offset initm    ;address of the message
        int  21h                ;Call DOS interrupt

        xor  ah,ah              ;Get function number for key
        int  16h                ;Call BIOS keyboard interrupt
        cmp  al,"s"             ;Was <s> entered?
        je   ende               ;YES--> End program
        cmp  al,"S"             ;Was <S> entered?
        jne  startdemo          ;NO --> Start demo

ende:   mov  ax,4C00h           ;Function number - end program
        int  21h                ;Call DOS interrupt 21H

startdemo label near
        mov  ah,9               ;Output function number for string
        mov  dx,offset domes    ;address of the message
        int  21h                ;Call DOS interrupt

        xor  ah,ah              ;Get function number for key
        int  16h                ;Call BIOS keyboard interrupt

        ;-- Initialize graphic mode -------------------------

        mov  al,11b             ;Graphic and page 2 possible
        call config             ;Configure
        xor  bp,bp              ;Access display page 0
        call grafik             ;Switch to graphic mode
        xor  al,al
        call cgr                ;Erase graphic page 0
        xor  bx,bx              ;Begin in the upper left
        xor  dx,dx              ;Display corner
        mov  ax,347             ;Vertical pixels
```

```
        mov  cx,719            ;Horizontal pixels
gr1:    push cx                ;Push horizontal pixels on stack
        mov  cx,ax             ;Vertical pixels in counter
        push ax                ;Push vertical pixels on stack
gr2:    call spix              ;Set pixel
        inc  dx                ;Increment line
        loop gr2               ;Draw line
        pop  ax                ;Get vert. pixels from stack
        sub  ax,3              ;next line 3 pixels less
        pop  cx                ;Get horiz. pixels from stack
        push cx                ;Store horizontal pixels
        push ax                ;Push vertical pixels on stack
gr3:    call spix              ;Set pixel
        inc  bx                ;Increment column
        loop gr3               ;Draw line
        pop  ax                ;Get vertical pixels from stack
        pop  cx                ;Get horizontal pixels from stack
        sub  cx,6              ;Next line 6 pixels less
        push cx                ;Record horizontal pixels
        mov  cx,ax             ;Vertical pixels in counter
        push ax                ;Note vertical pixels on stack
gr4:    call spix              ;Set pixel
        dec  dx                ;Decrement line
        loop gr4               ;Draw line
        pop  ax                ;Get vertical pixels from stack
        sub  ax,3              ;Next line 3 pixels less
        pop  cx                ;Get horizontal pixels from stack
        push cx                ;Record horizontal pixels
        push ax                ;Record vertical pixels on stack
gr5:    call spix              ;Set pixel
        dec  bx                ;Increment column
        loop gr5               ;Draw line
        pop  ax                ;Get vertical pixels from stack
        pop  cx                ;Get horizontal pixels from stack
        sub  cx,6              ;Next line 6 pixels less
        cmp  ax,5              ;Is the vertical line longer than 5
        ja   gr1               ;YES --> continue

        xor  ah,ah             ;Wait for function nr. for key
        int  16h               ;Call BIOS keyboard interrupt

        ;-- Initialize text mode ------------------------------

        call text              ;Switch on text mode
        mov  cx,0d00h          ;Switch on full cursor
        call cdef
        call cls               ;Clear screen

        ;-- Display strings in display page 0 ------------------

        xor  bx,bx             ;Start in upper left display corner
        call calo              ;Convert to offset address
        mov  si,offset str1    ;Offset address of string1
        mov  cx,16*25          ;The string is 5 characters long
demo1:  call print             ;Output string
        loop demo1

        ;-- Display strings in display page 1 ------------------

        inc  bp                ;Process display page 1
        xor  bx,bx             ;Start in the upper left corner
        call calo              ;Convert to offset address
        mov  si,offset str2    ;Offset address of string1
        mov  cx,16*25          ;string is 5 characters long
demo2:  call print             ;Output string
        loop demo2

demo3:  setmode 10001000b      ;Display text page 1

        ;-- short Pause -------------------------------------------
```

```
          mov  cx,DELAY          ;Load counter
pause:    loop pause             ;Count to 65,536

          setmode 00001000b      ;Display page 0

          ;-- short pause -----------------------------------------------
          mov  cx,DELAY          ;Load counter
pause1:   loop pause1            ;Count to 65,536

          mov  ah,1              ;Test function nr. for key
          int  16h               ;Call BIOS-keyboard-Interrupt
          je   demo3             ;No key --> continue

          xor  ah,ah             ;Get function number for key
          int  16h               ;Call BIOS-keyboard-Interrupt

          mov  bp,0              ;Display page 1
          call cls               ;Clear screen
          mov  cx,0D0ch          ;Restore normal cursor
          call cdef
          call cls               ;Clear screen
          jmp  ende              ;End program

demo      endp

;== The actual functions follow  ===========================

;-- CONFIG: configures the HERCULES card -----------------------------
;-- Input     : AL : bit 0 = 0 : Only text presentation possible
;--                          1 : also graphic presentation possible
;--                  bit 1 = 0 : RAM for display page 2 off
;--                          1 : RAM for display page 2 on
;-- Output    : none
;-- Register : AX and DX are changed

config    proc near

          mov  dx,CONFIG_REG     ;Address of configuration register
          out  dx,al             ;Set new value
          ret                    ;Back to caller

config    endp

;-- TEXT: switches the text presentation on ---------------------------
;-- Input    : none
;-- Output    : none
;-- Register : AX and DX are changed

text      proc near

          mov  si,offset textt   ;Offset address of the register-table
          mov  bl,00100000b      ;Display page 0,text mode,blinking
          jmp  short vcprog      ;Program video-controller again

text      endp

;-- GRAFIK: switches on the graphic mode ------- ----------------------
;-- Input    : none
;-- Output    : none
;-- Register : AX and DX are changed

grafik    proc near

          mov  si,offset grafikt ;Offset address of the register-table
          mov  bl,00000010b      ;Display page 0, graphic mode

grafik    endp

;-- VCPROG: programs the video controller -----------------------------
;-- Input   :    SI = address of a register-table
```

```
;--            BL = value for display-control-register
;-- Output   : none
;-- register : AX, SI, BH, DX and FLAGS are changed

vcprog    proc near

          setmode bl              ;Bit 3 = 0: display aus

          mov  cx,12              ;12 registers are set
          xor  bh,bh              ;Start with register 0
vcp1:     lodsb                   ;Get register value from the table
          mov  ah,al              ;Register value to AH
          mov  al,bh              ;Number of the register to AL
          setvk                   ;Transmit value to the controller
          inc  bh                 ;Address next register
          loop vcp1               ;Set additional registers

          or   bl,8               ;Bit 3 = 1: display on
          setmode bl              ;Set new mode
          ret                     ;Back to caller

vcprog    endp

;-- cDEF: sets the start and end line of the cursor--------------------
;-- Input    : cL = start line
;--            cH = end line
;-- Output   : none
;-- register : AX and DX are changed

cdef      proc near

          mov  al,CUR_START       ;Register 10: start line
          mov  ah,cl              ;Start line to AH
          setvk                   ;Transmit to video-controller
          mov  al,CUR_END         ;Register 11: Endline
          mov  ah,ch              ;End line to AH
          setvk                   ;Transmit to video-controller
          ret

cdef      endp

;-- SETBLINK : sets the blinking display cursor -----------------------
;-- Input    : DI = offset address of the cursor
;-- Output   : none
;-- register : BX, AX and DX are changed

setblink  proc near

          mov  bx,di              ;Transmit offset to BX
          mov  al,CURPOS_HI       ;Register 15:Hi Byte of cursor offset
          mov  ah,bh              ;HI byte of the offset
          setvk                   ;Transmit to video-controller
          mov  al,CURPOS_LO       ;Register 15:Lo-Byte of cursor offset
          mov  ah,bl              ;Lo byte of the offset
          setvk                   ;Transmit to CRTC
          ret

setblink  endp

;-- GETVK    : reads a byte from one register of the video-controller -
;-- Input    : AL = number of the register
;-- Output   : AL = content of the register
;-- register : DX and AL are changed

getvk     proc near

          mov  dx,ADDRESS_6845    ;Address of the index register
          out  dx,al              ;Send number of the register
          jmp $+2                 ;Short io pause
          inc  dx                 ;Address of the index register
```

```
        in   al,dx              ;Read content to AL
        ret                     ;Back to caller

getvk   endp

;-- SCROLLUp: scrolls a window by N lines upward ----------------------
;-- Input  :    BL = line upper left
;--             BH = column upper left
;--             DL = line lower right
;--             DH = column lower right
;--             CL = number of the lines to be scrolled
;--          :  BP = number of the display page (0 or 1)
;-- Output   :  none
;-- register :  only FLAGS are changed
;-- Info     :  the display lines released are erased

scrollup proc near

        cld                     ;Increment for string instructions
        push ax                 ;Store all changed registers
        push bx                 ;on the stack
        push di                 ;In this case the sequence
        push si                 ;must be followed !

        push bx                 ;These three registers are returned
        push cx                 ;from the stack before
        push dx                 ;the end of the routine
        sub  dl,bl              ;Calculate number of lines
        inc  dl                 ;Deduct number
        sub  dl,cl              ;of lines to be scrolled
        sub  dh,bh              ;Calculate number of columns
        inc  dh
        call calo               ;Convert upper left in offset
        mov  si,di              ;Note address in SI
        add  bl,cl              ;First line in scrolled window
        call calo               ;Convert first line in offset
        xchg si,di              ;Exchange SI and DI
        push ds                 ;Store segment register
        push es                 ;on the stack
        mov  ax,VIO_SEG         ;Segment address of the video RAM
        mov  ds,ax              ;to DS
        mov  es,ax              ;and ES
supl:   mov  ax,di              ;Note DI in AX
        mov  bx,si              ;Note SI in BX
        mov  cl,dh              ;Number of columns in counter
        rep movsw               ;Move a line
        mov  di,ax              ;Restore DI from AX
        mov  si,bx              ;Restore SI from BX
        add  di,160             ;Set next line
        add  si,160
        dec  dl                 ;Processed all lines ?
        jne  supl               ;NO --> move another line
        pop  es                 ;Get segment register from
        pop  ds                 ;stack
        pop  dx                 ;Get lower right corner
        pop  cx                 ;Get number of lines
        pop  bx                 ;Get upper left corner
        mov  bl,dl              ;Lower line to BL
        sub  bl,cl              ;Deduct number of lines
        inc  bl
        mov  ah,07h             ;Color : black on white
        call clear              ;Erase liberated lines

        pop  si                 ;CX and DX have been brought back
        pop  di                 ;already
        pop  bx
        pop  ax

        ret                     ;Back to caller
```

```
scrollup  endp

;-- SCROLLDN: scroll a Window by N lines upwards ----------------------
;-- Input    : BL = line upper left
;--            BH = column upper left
;--            DL = line lower right
;--            DH = column lower right
;--            CL = number of the lines to be scrolled
;--          : BP = number of the display page (0 or 1)
;-- Output   : none
;-- register : only FLAGS are changed
;-- Info     : released lines are deleted

scrolldn  proc near

          cld                       ;Increment on string instructions

          push ax                   ;Secure all changed registers on the
          push bx                   ;stack
          push di                   ;In this case the sequence must
          push si                   ;be followed!

          push bx                   ;These three registers are
          push cx                   ;returned from the stack before the
          push dx                   ;end of the routine

          sub  dh,bh                ;Calculate number of columns
          inc  dh
          mov  al,bl                ;Record line upper left in AL
          mov  bl,dl                ;Line lower right top lower left
          call calo                 ;Convert upper left in offset
          mov  si,di                ;Note address in SI
          sub  bl,cl                ;Deduct number of chars to scroll
          call calo                 ;Convert upper left in offset
          xchg si,di                ;Exchange SI and DI
          sub  dl,al                ;Calculate number of lines
          inc  dl
          sub  dl,cl                ;Deduct number of lines to scroll
          push ds                   ;Store segment register on the
          push es                   ;stack
          mov  ax,VIO_SEG           ;Segment address of the video RAM
          mov  ds,ax                ;to DS
          mov  es,ax                ;and ES
sdn1:     mov  ax,di                ;Record DI in AX
          mov  bx,si                ;Record SI in BX
          mov  cl,dh                ;Number of columns in counter
          rep movsw                 ;Move a line
          mov  di,ax                ;Restore DI from AX
          mov  si,bx                ;Restore SI from BX
          sub  di,160               ;Set next line
          sub  si,160
          dec  dl                   ;All lines processed ?
          jne  sdn1                 ;NO --> move another line
          pop  es                   ;Get segment register from
          pop  ds                   ;stack
          pop  dx                   ;Get lower right corner
          pop  cx                   ;Get number of lines
          pop  bx                   ;Get upper left corner
          mov  dl,bl                ;Upper line to DL
          add  dl,cl                ;Add number of lines
          dec  dl
          mov  ah,07h               ;Color : black on white
          call clear                ;Erase liberated lines

          pop  si                   ;CX and DX have already
          pop  di                   ;been read
          pop  bx
          pop  ax

          ret                       ;Back to caller
```

```
scrolldn  endp

;-- cLS: clear the whole screen ----------------------------------------
;-- Input    : BP = number of the display page (0 or 1)
;-- Output   : none
;-- register : only FLAGS are changed

cls       proc near

          mov  ah,07h             ;Color is white on black
          xor  bx,bx              ;Upper left is (0/0)
          mov  dx,4F18h           ;Lower right is (79/24)

          ;-- perform clear ----------------------------------------

cls       endp

;-- CLEAR: fills a designated display area with space character -------
;-- Input    : AH = Attribute/color
;--            BL = line upper left
;--            BH = column upper left
;--            DL = line lower right
;--            DH = column lower right
;--            BP = number of the display page (0 or 1)
;-- Output   : none
;-- register : only FLAGS are changed

clear     proc near

          cld                     ;Increment on string instructions
          push cx                 ;Secure all changed
          push dx                 ;registers on the stack
          push si
          push di
          push es
          sub  dl,bl              ;Calculate number of lines
          inc  dl
          sub  dh,bh              ;Calculate number of columns
          inc  dh
          call calo               ;Offset address of upper left corner
          mov  cx,VIO_SEG         ;Segment address of the video RAM
          mov  es,cx              ;to ES
          xor  ch,ch              ;Hi byte of the counter to 0
          mov  al," "             ;Space character
clearl:   mov  si,di              ;Note DI in SI
          mov  cl,dh              ;Number of columns in counter
          rep stosw               ;Store space character
          mov  di,si              ;Restore DI from SI
          add  di,160             ;Set next line
          dec  dl                 ;All lines processed ?
          jne  clearl             ;NO --> erase another line

          pop  es                 ;Get secured registers
          pop  di                 ;from the stack
          pop  si
          pop  dx
          pop  cx
          ret                     ;Back to caller

clear     endp

;-- PRINT: outputs a string on the display ---------------------------
;-- Input    : AH = attribute/color
;--            DI = offset address of the first character
;--            SI = offset address of the strings to DS
;--            BP = number of the display page (0 or 1)
;-- Output   : DI points behind the last character to be output
;-- register : AL, DI and FLAGS are changed
;-- Info     : the string must ne terminated with NUL-character.
```

```
;--          other control characters are not recognized

print     proc near

          cld                      ;Increment on string instructions
          push si                  ;SI, DX and ES to the stack
          push es
          push dx
          mov  dx,VIO_SEG          ;First segment address of video RAM
          mov  es,dx               ;to DX and then to ES
          jmp  print1              ;Get first character from string
print0:   stosw                    ;Store attribute and color in V-RAM
print1:   lodsb                    ;Get next character from the string
          or   al,al               ;Is it NUL
          jne  print0              ;NO --> output

printe:   pop  dx                  ;Get SI, DX and ES from stack again
          pop  es
          pop  si
          ret                      ;Back to caller

print     endp

;-- cALO: converts line and column into offset address ----------------
;-- Input    : BL = line
;--            BH = column
;--            Bp = number of the display page (0 or 1)
;-- Output   : DI = offset address
;-- register : DI and FLAGS are changed

calo      proc near

          push ax                  ;Record AX on the stack
          push bx                  ;Record BX on the stack

          shl  bx,1                ;Column and line times 2
          mov  al,bh               ;Column to AL
          xor  bh,bh               ;Hi byte
          mov  di,[lines+bx]       ;Get offset address of the line
          xor  ah,ah               ;Hi byte for column offset
          add  di,ax               ;Add lines- and column offset
          or   bp,bp               ;Display page 0?
          je   caloe               ;YES --> address ok

          add  di,8000h            ;Add 32 KB for display page 1

caloe:    pop  bx                  ;Get BX from stack again
          pop  ax                  ;Get AX from the stack again
          ret                      ;Back to caller

calo      endp

;-- CGR: clear the complete graphic screen ----------------------------
;-- Input    : BP = number of the display page (0 or 1)
;--            AL = 00H : erase all pixels
;--                 FFH : set all pixels
;-- Output   : none
;-- register : AH, BX, cX, DI and FLAGS are changed

cgr       proc near

          push es                  ;Record ES on the stack
          cbw                      ;Expand AL to AH
          xor  di,di               ;Offset address in video RAM
          mov  bx,VIO_SEG          ;Segment address display page 0
          or   bp,bp               ;Erase page 1?
          je   cgr1                ;NO --> erase page 0

          add  bx,0800h            ;Segment address display page 1
```

```
cgrl:     mov  es,bx              ;Segment address to segment register
          mov  cx,4000h           ;A page is 16K-words
          rep stosw               ;Fill page
          pop  es                 ;Get ES from stack
          ret                     ;Back to caller

cgr       endp

;-- SPIX: sets a pixel in the graphic display ---------------------------
;-- Input    : BP = number of the display page (0 or 1)
;--            BX = column  (0 to 719)
;--            DX = line   (0 to 347)
;-- Output   : none
;-- register : AX, DI and FLAGS are changed

spix      proc near

          push es                 ;Store ES on the stack
          push bx                 ;Store BX on the stack
          push cx                 ;Store cX on the stack
          push dx                 ;Store DX on the stack

          xor  di,di              ;Offset address in video RAM
          mov  cx,VIO_SEG         ;Segment address display page 0
          or   bp,bp              ;Access page 1 ?
          je   spix1              ;NO --> access page 0

          mov  cx,0800h           ;Segment address display page 1

spix1:    mov  es,cx              ;Segment address in segment register
          mov  ax,dx              ;Move line to AX
          shr  ax,1               ;Shift line right 2 times
          shr  ax,1               ;This divides by four
          mov  cl,90              ;The factor is 90
          mul  cl                 ;Multiply line by 90
          and  dx,11b             ;AND all bits except for  0 and 1
          mov  cl,3               ;3 shifts
          ror  dx,cl              ;Rotate right  (* 2000H)
          mov  di,bx              ;Column to DI
          mov  cl,3               ;3 shifts
          shr  di,cl              ;divide by 8
          add  di,ax              ;+ 90 * int(line/4)
          add  di,dx              ;+ 2000H * (line mod 4)
          mov  cl,7               ;Maximum of 7 moves
          and  bx,7               ;Column mod 8
          sub  cl,bl              ;7 - column mod 8
          mov  ah,1               ;Determine bit value of the pixels
          shl  ah,cl
          mov  al,es:[di]         ;Get 8 pixels
          or   al,ah              ;Set pixel
          mov  es:[di],al         ;Write 8 pixels ;

          pop  dx                 ;Get DX from stack
          pop  cx                 ;Get cX from stack
          pop  bx                 ;Get BX from stack
          pop  es                 ;Get ES from stack
          ret                     ;Back to caller

spix      endp

;== End ===============================================================

code      ends                    ;End of the code segment
          end  demo
```

10.4 The IBM Color Card

The IBM Color/Graphics Adapter (CGA) supports two text modes and three different graphic modes. Like the other two cards, the CGA is based on a 6845 video processor and is equipped with 16K of video RAM which begins at address B800:0000.

Text modes

Besides the normal text mode of 25 lines and 80 columns, the CGA also has a text mode consisting of 25 lines and 40 columns. This 40-column mode displays characters twice as wide as normal 80-column mode. CGA characters are displayed in an 8x8 matrix, which results in a less distinct display than monochrome display adapter text. The CGA's video RAM assignment is almost identical to that of the monochrome card. The attribute byte is different from that of the monochrome display adapter.

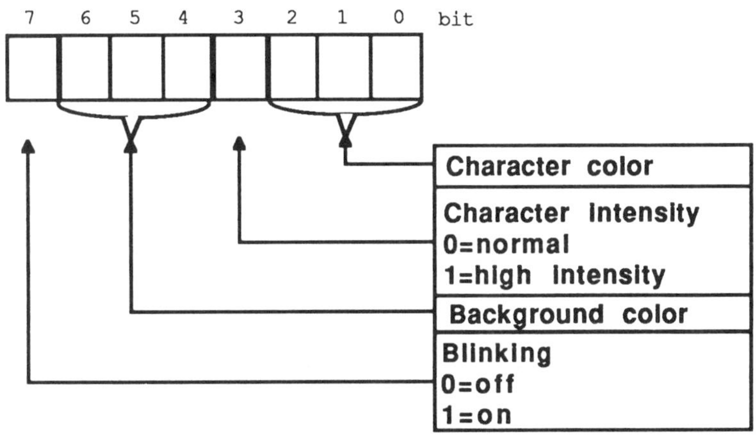

Color/Graphics Adapter attribute byte

The lower four bits of the attribute byte indicate one of the 16 available colors. The meanings of the upper four bits depend on whether blinking is active. If it is active, bits 4 to 6 indicate the background color (taken from one of the first eight colors of the color palette), while bit 7 determines whether or not the characters blink. If blinking is disabled, bits 4 to 7 indicate the background color (taken from one of the 16 available colors).

Decimal	Hexadecimal	Binary	Color
0	0	0000	Black
1	1	0001	Blue
2	2	0010	Green
3	3	0011	Cyan
4	4	0100	Red
5	5	0101	Magenta
6	6	0110	Brown
7	7	0111	Light gray
8	8	1000	Dark gray
9	9	1001	Light blue
10	A	1010	Light green
11	B	1011	Light cyan
12	C	1100	Light red
13	D	1101	Light magenta
14	E	1110	Yellow
15	F	1111	White

Color/Graphics Adapter color palette

Each 80x25 text page requires 4,000 bytes of video RAM. 16K allows a total of four text pages. The first display page starts at address B800:0000, the second at B800:1000, the third at B800:2000 and the last at B800:3000. The 40x25 mode allows storage of eight display pages, because each display page only requires 2,000 bytes in this mode. The first display page starts at address B800:0000, the second at B800:0800, the third at B800:1000, etc.

Graphic modes

The CGA supports three different graphic modes, of which only two are usually used. The *color-suppressed* mode displays 160x100 pixels with 16 colors. The 6845 supports this resolution, but the rest of the hardware doesn't offer color-suppressed mode support. The remaining two graphic modes have resolutions of 320x200 and 640x200 respectively. The 320x200 resolution permits four-color graphics, while 640x200 resolution only allows two colors.

320x200 resolution

The CGA uses up all 16K of its video RAM for displaying a graphic in 320x200 resolution with four colors. This limits the user to one graphic page at a time. Of the four colors permitted, the background can be selected from the 16 available colors. The other three colors originate from one of the two user-selected color palettes, which contain three colors each.

Palette 1:	Color 1: Cyan	Palette 2:	Color 1: Green
	Color 2: Violet		Color 2: Red
	Color 3: White		Color 3: Yellow

Since a total of four colors are available, each screen pixel requires two bits. Four bits can represent the color numbers (0 to 3). The following values correspond to the various colors:

0 00(b) = freely selectable background color
1 01(b) = color 1 of the selected palette
2 10(b) = color 2 of the selected palette
3 11(b) = color 3 of the selected palette

The video RAM assignment in this mode is similar to that of the Hercules card during graphic display. The individual graphic lines are stored in two different blocks of memory. The first block, which begins at address B800:0000, contains the even lines (0, 2, 4...); the second block, which begins at B800:2000, contains odd lines (1,3,5).

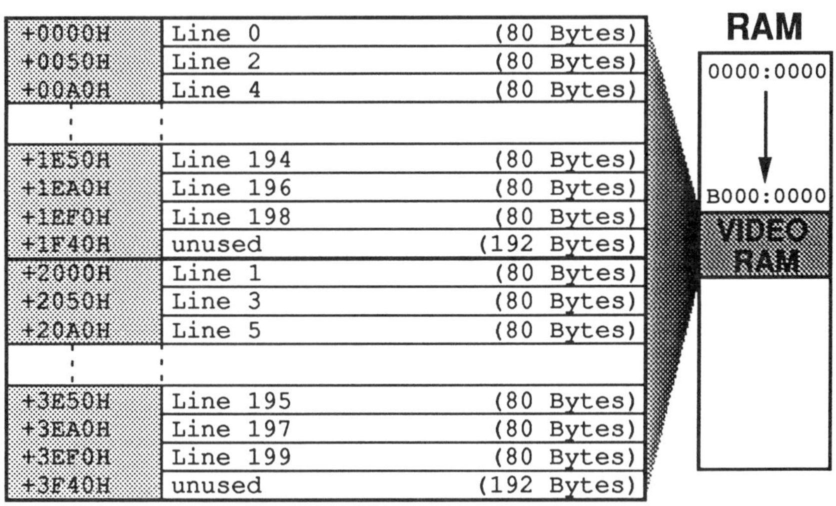

Video RAM assignment in graphic mode (blocking)

Each graphic line within the two blocks requires 80 bytes, since the 320 pixels in a line are coded into four pixels to a byte. The first byte in a graphic line (an 80-byte series) corresponds to the first four dots of the graphic on the screen. Bits 7 and 8 contain the color information for the leftmost pixel, while bits 0 and 1 contain the color information for the rightmost pixel of the byte.

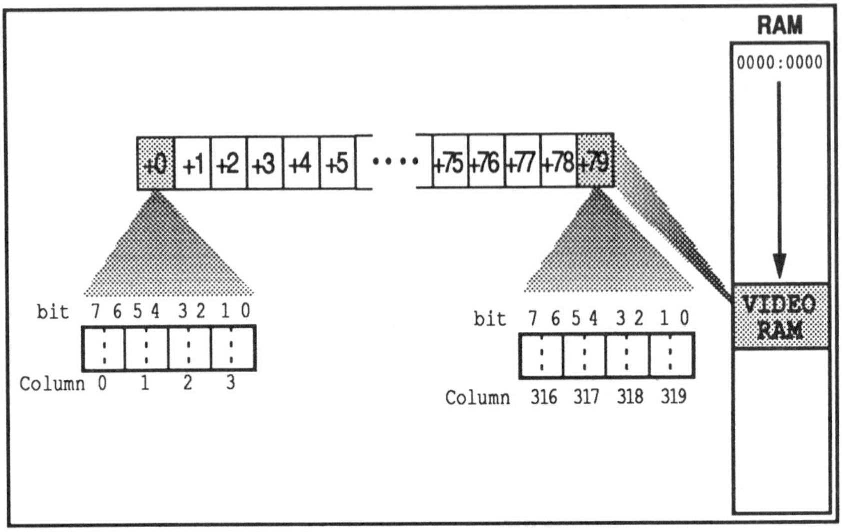

Graphic line coding in 320x200 resolution

A formula can be derived with the help of this information to determine the byte in video RAM, similar to the Hercules card. This byte is relative to the starting address of the screen page, which contains the color information for a pixel. The screen column (0—319) is designated as X and the screen line (0—199) as Y:

```
Address = 2000H * (Y mod 2) + 80 * int(Y/2) + int(X/4)
```

To determine the number of the two bits within this byte which represents the pixel, use the following formula:

```
Bit number = 6 - 2 * (X mod 4)
```

For example, if this formula returns 4, this means that the color information for the dot is coded into bits 4 and 5.

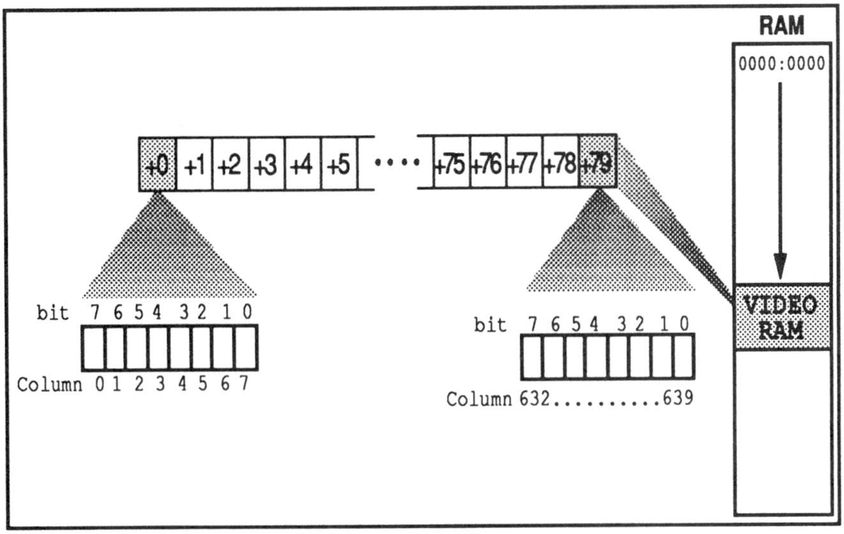

Graphic line coding in 640x200 resolution

640x200 resolution

High-resolution mode with a resolution of 640x200 dots only allows the use of two colors. The video RAM assignment in this mode is similar to 320x200 mode. Each line displays twice as many pixels, with one bit encoding the line instead of 2 bits. Because of this, one screen line requires 880 bytes. Therefore the formulas for access to a screen pixel are similar.

```
Address = 2000H * (Y mod 2) + 80 * int(Y/2) + int(X/8)

Bit number = 7 - (X mod 8)
```

CGA registers

The CGA has a mode selection register at address 3D8H which is comparable with the control register of the monochrome display adapter. You can write to this register but not read it.

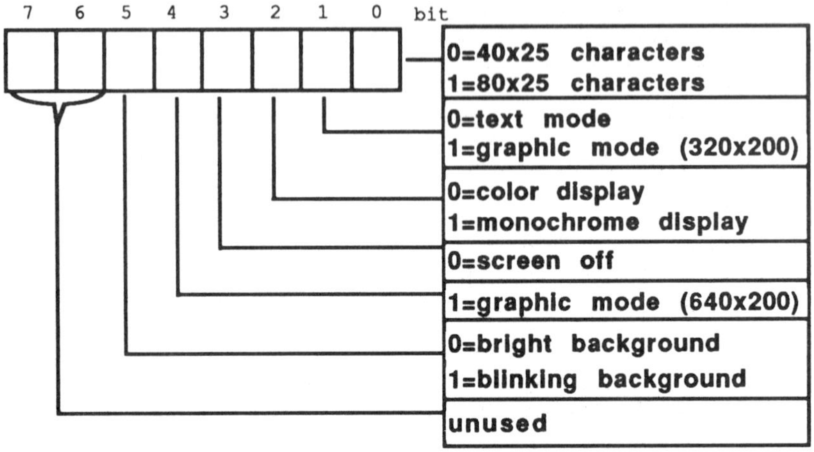

Mode selection register

Bit layout

Bit 0 of this register determines the text mode display of 80 or 40 columns per line. A 1 in bit 0 displays 80 columns, while a 0 in bit 0 displays 40 columns.

The status of bit 1 switches the CGA from text mode to the 320x200 bit-mapped graphic mode. A 1 in this register selects graphic mode, while a 0 selects text mode.

Bit 2 should be of interest to any users who want to operate their CGA with a monochrome monitor. If this bit contains the value 1, the 6845 suppresses the color signal, displaying monochrome mode only.

Bit 3 is responsible for creating screens. If it contains the value 0, the screen remains black. This suppression is useful when changing between display modes; it prevents sudden signals from reaching the monitor which could cause damage.

Bit 4 enables and disables 640x200 bitmapped graphic mode. A 1 in bit 4 enables this mode, while a 0 disables it.

Bit 5 has the same significance as in the monochrome card. If it contains a 0, blinking stops and bit 7 returns one of the 16 available background colors. This bit contains a default value of 1, which causes blinking characters.

The various text or graphic modes and the color or monochrome display can be selected in these modes with this register. Bits 0, 1, 2 and 4 are used for this. The following table shows how these bits must be programmed to obtain certain modes:

Bit 4	Bit 2	Bit 1	Bit 0	Result
0	1	0	0	40x25 text monochrome
0	0	0	0	40x25 text color
0	1	0	1	80x25 text monochrome
0	0	0	1	80x25 text color
0	1	1	0	320x200 graphic monochrome
0	0	1	0	320x200 graphic color
1	1	1	0	640x200 graphic monochrome

The CGA also has a status register similar to the status register in the monochrome display adapter. The following figure shows the construction of this register, which can be found at address 3DAH. It is a read-only register.

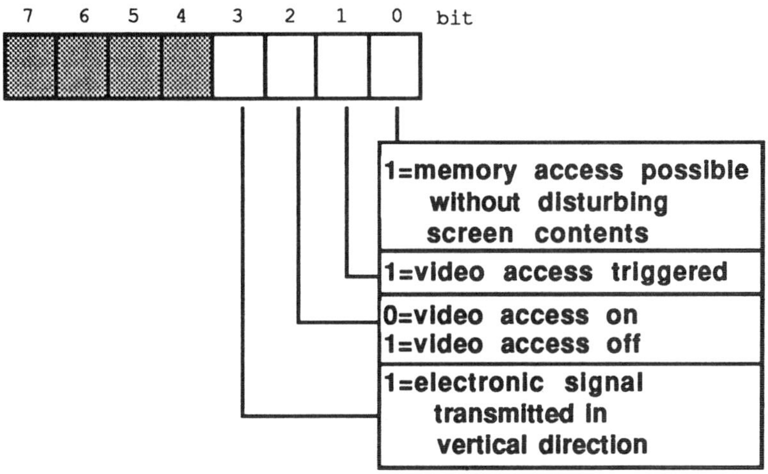

Status register structure

Bit 0 of this register always contains the value 1 when the 6845 sends a horizontal synchronization signal to the monitor. This signal is transmitted when the creation of a line ends and the CRT's electron beam reaches the end of the screen line. The electron beam then jumps back to the left corner of the screen line. The bit gets its significance from the condition that the CGA doesn't always allow data reading or writing within video RAM.

Flickering and the CGA

This problem occurs because the 6845 must continuously access video RAM to read its contents for screen display. If a program tries to transmit data to video RAM, problems can arise when the 6845 accesses video RAM at the same time. The result of this memory collision is an occasional flickering on the screen.

To avoid this problem, you should only access video RAM when the 6845 is not accessing it. This only occurs when a horizontal synchronization signal travels to the screen, because it requires a moment of time until the electron beam has carried out this instruction. For this reason, the status register must be read before every video RAM access on a CGA. This process must be repeated until bit 0 contains the value 1. When this happens, a maximum of two bytes can then be transmitted to video RAM.

Demonstration program

The program at the end of this section demonstrates how this process functions. This delay in video RAM access doesn't occur with monochrome cards because they are equipped with special hardware logic and fast RAM chips. This is also true of most of the newer model color cards. Before waiting for the horizontal synchronization signal, which results in an enormous delay of the display output, the user should try direct access to video RAM to test his color card's reaction time.

If many accesses to video RAM occur within a short period of time (e.g., scrolling the screen), the electron beam doesn't respond fast enough. The screen should be switched off using bit 3 of the mode selection register. This prevents the 6845 from accessing video RAM, permitting unlimited user access to video RAM. When data transfer ends, the screen can be switched on again. BIOS uses this method during scrolling, which results in the flickering "silent movie effect."

Color selection register

The color selection register is located at address 3D9H. This register is write-only (cannot be read).

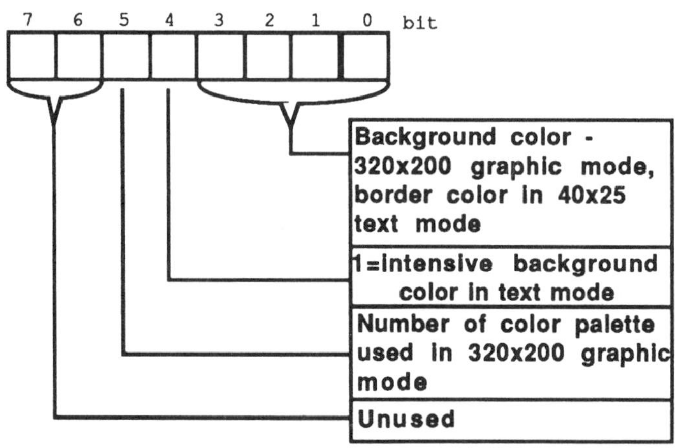

Color selection register

The meanings of individual bits in this register depend on the display mode. Text mode uses the lowest four bits for assigning the background color from the 16 available colors. In 320x200 graphic mode, these four bits indicate the color of all pixels represented by the bit combination 00(b) (background color).

Bit 5 selects the color palette for 320x200 mode. If this bit contains the value 1, the first color palette (cyan, violet, white) is selected. A value of 0 selects the second color palette (green, yellow, red).

Internal registers

The 18 internal registers of the 6845 on this card are accessed exactly like the monochrome card. The only difference is that the index and the data register are located at 3D4H and 3D5H. The following table shows the contents which the register must have for various display modes.

No.	Meaning	Text1	Text2	Graphics
0	Horiz. characters seeded	56	113	56
1	Horiz. characters displayed	40	80	40
2	Horiz. synchronization signal to .... Characters	45	90	45
3	Horiz. synchronization signal in characters	10	10	10
4	Vert. characters seeded	31	31	127
5	Vert. characters justified	6	6	6
6	Vert. characters displayed	25	25	100
7	Vert. synchronization signal to ... characters	28	28	112
8	Interlace mode	2	2	2
9	Number of scan-lines per line	7	7	1
10	Starting line of blinking cursor	6	6	6
11	Ending line of blinking cursor	7	7	7
12	Display page starting address (high byte)	0	0	0
13	Display page starting address (low byte)	0	0	0
14	Cusrsor character address (high byte)	0	0	0
15	Cursor character address (low byte)	0	0	0
16	Reserved			
17	Reserved			

These registers are of interest to the user since they define the position and appearance of the cursor on the screen. Section 10.1 described programming these registers. The CGA adds registers 12 and 13. They indicate the start of the video page which must be displayed on the screen, as offset of the beginning of the 16K RAM on the card (B800:0000), divided by 2. Register 12 contains the most significant 8 bits of this offset, while register 13 contains the least significant 8 bits. Normally both registers contain the value 0, displaying the first screen page (beginning at the address B800:0000) on the screen. For display of the first screen page, which begins at location B800:1000 in the 80x25 text mode, the value 1000H divided by 2 (800H) must be entered in both registers.

The last of the three programs in this chapter accesses the color/graphics adapter. The only significant difference between the two preceding programs lies in the fact that the video controller can synchronize video RAM access and screen construction. This is necessary on all video cards where direct access to video RAM causes a flickering on the screen. The WAIT constant, defined directly after the program header, switches synchronization on or off. Its contents decide during the assembly of the program, whether to assemble the program lines for synchronization listed in the source listing. These lines would slow down the screen considerably, and should only be included if it is absolutely necessary.

Assembler listing: VCOL.ASM

```
;**********************************************************************;
;*                              V C O L                              *;
;*------------          ----------------------------------------------*;
;*    Task           : Makes some basic functions available for       *;
;*                     access to the Color Graphics Adapter (CGA)     *;
;*-------------------------------------------------------------------*;
;*    Info           : All functions subdivide the screen             *;
;*                     into  columns 0 to 79 and lines 0 to 24        *;
;*                     in text mode and into  columns 0 to 719 and    *;
;*                     the lines 0 to 347 in graphic mode.            *;
;*                     the 40 column text mode is not supported !     *;
;*                     A high resolution graphic screen should appear*;
;*                     first, followed by a text screen. If the high *;
;*                     res screen doesn't appear, try running the     *;
;*                     program a few times in succession.             *;
;*-------------------------------------------------------------------*;
;*    Author         : MICHAEL TISCHER                                *;
;*    Developed on   : 8/13/87                                        *;
;*    Last update    : 6/16/89                                        *;
;*-------------------------------------------------------------------*;
;*    assembly       : MASM VCOL (program will assemble with one      *;
;*                              warning - it WILL link & run)         *;
;*                     LINK VCOL;                                     *;
;*-------------------------------------------------------------------*;
;*    Call           : VCOL                                           *;
;**********************************************************************;

;== Constants =========================================================

CONTROL_REG   = 03D8h              ;Control register port address
CCHOICE_REG   = 03D9h              ;Color select register port address
ADDRESS_6845 = 03D4h               ;6845 address register
DATA_6845     = 03D5h              ;6845 data register
VIO_SEG       = 0B800h             ;Video RAM segment address
CUR_START     = 10                 ;Reg # for CRTC: Cursor start line
CUR_END       = 11                 ;Reg # for CTRC: Cursor end line
CURPG_HI      = 12                 ;Page address (high byte)
CURPG_LO      = 13                 ;Page address (low byte)
CURPOS_HI     = 14                 ;Reg # for CRTC: Cursor pos high byte
CURPOS_LO     = 15                 ;Reg # for CRTC: Cursor pos low byte
DELAY         = 20000              ;Counter for delay loop

;== Macros ============================================================

;-- SETMODE : Macro for configuring screen control register ---------

setmode   macro modus

          mov  dx,CONTROL_REG      ;Address of the display control register
          mov  al,modus            ;New mode into the AL register
          out  dx,al               ;Send mode to control register

          endm

;-- WAITRET: waits until display is completed ------------------------

waitret   macro
local     wrl                      ;Local label

          mov  dx,3DAh             ;Address of the display status register
wrl:      in   al,dx               ;Get content
```

```
local   wrl                         ;Local label

        mov  dx,3DAh                ;Address of the display status register
wrl:    in   al,dx                  ;Get content
        test al,8                   ;Vertical retrace?
        je   wrl                    ;NO --> wait

        endm

;== Stack =============================================================

stack   segment para stack          ;Definition of stack segment

        dw 256 dup (?)              ;256-word stack

stack   ends                        ;End of stack segment

;== Data ==============================================================

data    segment para 'DATA'         ;Definition of data segment

;== Data required for demo program ====================================

initm   db 13,10
        db "VCOL (c) 1988,1989 by Michael Tischer "
        db 13,10,13,10
        db "This demo program only runs with a Color/Graphics",13,10
        db "Adapter ( CGA ).  If your PC uses another type of",13,10
        db "video card press the <s> key to stop the program.",13,10
        db "Press any other key to start the program...",13,10,"$"

strl    db 1,0

;== Table of offset addresses of line beginnings ======================
lines   dw  0*160, 1*160, 2*160 ;start addresses of the lines as
        dw  3*160, 4*160, 5*160 ;offset addresses in the video RAM
        dw  6*160, 7*160, 8*160
        dw  9*160,10*160,11*160,12*160,13*160,14*160,15*160,16*160
        dw 17*160,18*160,19*160,20*160,21*160,22*160,23*160,24*160

graphict  db 38h, 28h, 2Dh, 0Ah, 7Fh, 06h  ;register values for the
          db 64h, 70h, 02h, 01h, 06h, 07h  ;graphic-modes

textt     db 71h, 50h, 5Ah, 0Ah, 1Fh, 06h  ;register-values for the
          db 19h, 1Ch, 02h, 07h, 06h, 07h  ;graphic-modes

wait      db 0                      ;TRUE (<>0) when caller uses the
                                    ;/F switch

data      ends                      ;End of data segment

;== Code ==============================================================

code      segment para 'CODE'       ;Definition of the CODE segment

          assume cs:code, ds:data, es:data, ss:stack

;== This is only the Demo-Program =====================================

demo      proc far

          ;-- Look for /F from DOS prompt ------------------------

          mov  cl,ds:128            ;Get number of bytes from prompt
          or   cl,cl                ;No parameters given?
          je   switchl              ;NO --> Ignore
          mov  bx,129               ;BX points to first byte in prompt
          mov  ch,bh                ;Set loop high byte to 0

switch:   cmp  [bx],"F/"            ;Switch in this position?
```

```
            je   switch1              ;YES --> Switch found
            cmp  [bx],"f/"            ;Switch in this position?
            je   switch1              ;YES --> Switch found
            inc  bl                   ;Set BX to next character
            loop switch               ;Check next character

switch1:    mov  ax,data              ;Get segment addr. of data segment
            mov  ds,ax                ;and load into DS
            mov  es,ax                ;and ES

            mov  wait,cl              ;Set WAIT flag

            ;-- Display init message and wait for input -------------

            mov  ah,9                 ;Function number for string display
            mov  dx,offset initm      ;Address of intial message
            int  21h                  ;Call DOS interrupt 21H

            xor  ah,ah                ;Function number: get key
            int  16h                  ;Call BIOS keyboard interrupt
            cmp  al,"s"               ;<s> key pressed?
            je   ende                 ;YES --> End program
            cmp  al,"S"               ;<S> key pressed?
            jne  startdemo            ;NO --> Start demo

ende:       mov  ax,4C00h             ;Function number: End program
            int  21h                  ;Call DOS interrupt 21H

startdemo label near
            call grafhi               ;switch on 320*200 pixel graphic
            xor  al,al
            call cgr                  ;Clear graphic display

            xor  bx,bx                ;Column 0
            xor  dx,dx                ;Line 0
            mov  ax,199               ;Pixels-vertical
            mov  cx,639               ;Pixels-horizontal
gr1:        push cx                   ;Record horizontal pixels
            mov  cx,ax                ;Vertical pixels to counter
            push ax                   ;Record vertical pixels on the stack
            mov  al,1
gr2:        call pixhi                ;Set pixel
            inc  dx                   ;Increment line
            loop gr2                  ;Draw line
            pop  ax                   ;Get vertical pixels from the stack
            sub  ax,3                 ;Next line 3 pixels less
            pop  cx                   ;Get horizontal pixels from the stack
            push cx                   ;Record horizontal pixels
            push ax                   ;Record vertical pixels on the stack
            mov  al,1
gr3:        call pixhi                ;Set pixel
            inc  bx                   ;Increment column
            loop gr3                  ;Draw line
            pop  ax                   ;Get vertical pixels from stack
            pop  cx                   ;Get horizontal pixels from stack
            sub  cx,6                 ;Next line 6 pixels less
            push cx                   ;Record horizontal pixels
            mov  cx,ax                ;Vertical pixels to counter
            push ax                   ;Record vertical pixels on the stack
            mov  al,1
gr4:        call pixhi                ;Set pixel
            dec  dx                   ;Decrement line
            loop gr4                  ;Draw line
            pop  ax                   ;Get vertical pixels from stack
            sub  ax,3                 ;Next line 3 pixels less
            pop  cx                   ;Get horizontal pixels from stack
            push cx                   ;Record horizontal pixels
            push ax                   ;Record vertical pixels on the stack
            mov  al,1
gr5:        call pixhi                ;Set pixel
```

```
          dec  bx               ;Increment column
          loop gr5              ;Draw line
          pop  ax               ;Get vertical pixels from the stack
          pop  cx               ;Get horizontal pixels from the stack
          sub  cx,6             ;Next line 6 pixels less
          cmp  ax,5             ;Is the vertical line longer than 5
          ja   gr1              ;YES--> continue

          xor  ah,ah            ;Wait for function number of key wait
          int  16h              ;Call BIOS keyboard interrupt

          call text             ;Switch on 80x25 character text mode
          xor  bp,bp            ;Process screen page 0 first
demo1:    mov  al,30h           ;ASCII code "0"
          or   ax,bp            ;Convert page number to ASCII
          mov  str1,al          ;Store in string
          call setcol           ;Set color
          call setpage          ;Activate screen page in BP
          call cls              ;Clear screen page
          xor  bx,bx            ;Begin in the upper left
          call calo             ;Screen corner with output
          mov  cx,2000          ;A page contains 2,000 characters
          xor  ah,ah            ;Start with color code 0
          mov  si,offset str1   ;Offset address of string 1
demo2:    inc  ah               ;Increment color value
          call print            ;Output string 1
          loop demo2            ;Repeat until screen is full

          xor  ah,ah            ;Wait for key
          int  16h              ;Call BIOS-Keyboard-Interrupt
          inc  bp               ;Increment page number
          cmp  bp,4             ;All 4 pages processed ?
          jne  demo1            ;NO --> then next page

          xor  bp,bp            ;Activate page 0 again
          call setpage
          jmp  ende
demo      endp                  ;Goto program end

;== The actual functions follow ===========================

;-- TEXT: switches the text display on --------------------------------
;-- Input    : none
;-- Output   : none
;-- Register : AX, SI, BH, DX and FLAGS are changed

text      proc near

          mov  si,offset textt  ;Offset address of the register-table
          mov  bl,00100001b     ;80x25 text mode,blinking
          jmp  short vcprog     ;Program video controller again

text      endp

;-- GRAFHI: switches the 640*200 pixel graphic mode on ------------------
;-- Input    : none
;-- Output   : none
;-- Register : AX, SI, BH, DX and FLAGS are changed

grafhi    proc near

          mov  bl,00010010b      ;Graphic mode with 640*200 pixels
          jmp  short graphic     ;Program video controller again

grafhi    endp

;-- GRAFLO: switches the 320*200 pixel graphic mode on ------------------
;-- Input    : none
;-- Output   : none
;-- Register : AX, SI, BH, DX and FLAGS are changed
```

```
graflo    proc near

          mov  bl,00100010b        ;Graphic mode with 320*200 pixels
graphic:   mov  si,offset graphict ;Offset address of the register table

graflo    endp

;-- VCPROG: programs the video controller ----------------------------
;-- Input    : SI = Address of a register table
;--             BL = Value for display control register
;-- Output   : none
;-- Register : AX, SI, BH, DX and FLAGS are changed

vcprog    proc near

          setmode bl               ;Bit 3 = 0: screen off

          mov  cx,12               ;12 registers are set
          xor  bh,bh               ;Start with register 0
vcp1:     lodsb                    ;Get register value from table
          mov  ah,al               ;Register value to AH
          mov  al,bh               ;Number of the register to AL
          call setvk               ;Transmit value to controller
          inc  bh                  ;Address next register
          loop vcp1                ;Set additional registers

          or   bl,8                ;Bit 3 = 1: screen on
          setmode bl               ;Set new mode
          ret                      ;Back to caller

vcprog    endp

;-- SETCOL   : Sets the color of the display frame and Background -----
;-- Input    : AL = color value
;-- Output   : none
;-- register : AX and DX are changed
;-- Info     : in text mode the lowest 4 bits indicate the frame color
;--             in graphic mode the lowest 4 bits indicate the frame
;--             and background color, bit 5 selects the color palette

setcol    proc near

          mov  dx,CCHOICE_REG      ;Address of the color selection register
          out  dx,al               ;Output color value
          ret                      ;Back to caller

setcol    endp

;-- CDEF    : sets the start  and end line of the cursor -------------
;-- Input   : CL = start line
;--            CH = end line
;-- Output   : none
;-- register : AX and DX are changed

cdef      proc near

          mov  al,CUR_START        ;Register 10: start line
          mov  ah,cl               ;Start line to AH
          call setvk               ;Transmit to video controller
          mov  al,CUR_END          ;Register 11: end line
          mov  ah,ch               ;End line to AH
          jmp  short setvk         ;Transmit to video controller

cdef      endp

;-- SETPAGE  : sets the screen page ---------------------------------
;-- Input    : BP = Number of the screen page (0 to 3)
;-- Output   : none
;-- register : BX, AX, CX and DX are changed
```

```
;-- Info     : in the Graphic modes the first screen page has the
;--            number 0, the second the number 2

setpage    proc near

         mov  bx,bp                ;Screen page to BX
         mov  cl,5                 ;Multiply by 2,048
         ror  bx,cl
         mov  al,CURPG_HI          ;Register 12: Hi byte page address
         mov  ah,bh                ;Hi byte of the screen page to AH
         call setvk                ;Transmit to video controller
         mov  al,CURPG_LO          ;Register 13: Lo byte page address
         mov  ah,bl                ;Lo byte of the screen page to AH
         jmp  short setvk          ;Transmit to video controller

setpage    endp

;-- SETBLINK : sets the blinking cursor ------------------------------
;-- Input    : DI = Offset address of the cursor
;-- Output   : none
;-- register : BX, AX and DX are changed

setblink  proc near

         mov  bx,di              ;Move offset to BX
         mov  al,CURPOS_HI       ;Hi byte of the cursor offset
         mov  ah,bh              ;HI byte of the offset
         call setvk              ;Transmit to video controller
         mov  al,CURPOS_LO       ;Lo byte of the cursor offset
         mov  ah,bl              ;Lo byte of the offset

         ;-- SETVK is called automatically --------------------------

setblink  endp

;-- SETVK    : sets a byte in one register of the video controller ----
;-- Input    : AL = Number of the register
;--            AH = new content of the register
;-- Output   : none
;-- register : DX and AL are changed

setvk     proc near

         mov  dx,ADDRESS_6845      ;Address of the index register
         out  dx,al                ;Send number of the register
         jmp  short $+2            ;Short I/O pause
         inc  dx                   ;Address of the index register
         mov  al,ah                ;Content to AL
         out  dx,al                ;Set new content
         ret                       ;Back to caller

setvk     endp

;-- GETVK    : gets a byte from one register of the video controller -
;-- Input    : AL = Number of the register
;-- Output   : AL = Contents of register
;-- register : DX and AL are changed

getvk     proc near

         mov  dx,ADDRESS_6845      ;Address of the index register
         out  dx,al                ;Send number of the register
         inc  dx                   ;Index register address
         jmp  short $+2            ;Short io pause
         in   al,dx                ;Set new contents
         ret                       ;Back to caller

getvk     endp

;-- SCROLLUP: scrolls a window N lines upward ------------------------
```

```
;-- Input    : BL = line upper left
;--            BH = column upper left
;--            DL = line below right
;--            DH = column below right
;--            CL = Number of lines, to be scrolled
;--          : BP = Number of the screen page (0 to 3)
;-- Output   : none
;-- register : only FLAGS are changed
;-- Info     : the display lines liberated are cleared

scrollup  proc near

          cld                         ;On string commands count up

          push ax                     ;All changed registers to the
          push bx                     ;Secure stack
          push di                     ;In this case the sequence
          push si                     ;must be observed !

          push bx                     ;These three registers are returned
          push cx                     ;before the end of the routine
          push dx                     ;From the stack
          sub  dl,bl                  ;Calculate the number of lines
          inc  dl
          sub  dl,cl                  ;Subtract number of lines to be scrolled
          sub  bh,dh                  ;Calculate number of columns
          inc  dh
          call calo                   ;Convert upper left in offset
          mov  si,di                  ;Record address in SI
          add  bl,cl                  ;First line in scrolled window
          call calo                   ;Convert first line in offset
          xchg si,di                  ;Exchange SI and DI

          cmp  wait,0                 ;Flicker suppressed?
          je   sup0                   ;NO --> SUP0

          waitret                     ;YES -->Wait for retrace
          setmode 00100101b           ;Disable screen

sup0:     push ds                     ;Store segment register
          push es                     ;On the stack
          mov  ax,VIO_SEG             ;Segment address of the video RAM
          mov  ds,ax                  ;To DS
          mov  es,ax                  ;And ES

sup1:     mov  ax,di                  ;Record DI in AX
          mov  bx,si                  ;Record SI in BX
          mov  cl,dh                  ;Number of columns in counter
          rep movsw                   ;Move a line
          mov  di,ax                  ;Restore DI from AX
          mov  si,bx                  ;Restore SI from BX
          add  di,160                 ;Set next line
          add  si,160
          dec  dl                     ;processed all lines ?
          jne  sup1                   ;NO --> move another line

          pop  es                     ;Get segment register from
          pop  ds                     ;Stack

          cmp  wait,0                 ;Flickering suppressed?
          je   sup2                   ;NO --> SUP2

          setmode 00101101b           ;YES --> Enable screen

sup2:     pop  dx                     ;Get lower right corner back
          pop  cx                     ;Return number of lines
          pop  bx                     ;Return upper left corner
          mov  bl,dl                  ;Lower line to BL
          sub  bl,cl                  ;Subtract number of lines
          inc  bl
```

```
        mov  ah,07h             ;Color : black on white
        call clear              ;Clear lines

        pop  si                 ;CX and DX have already been
        pop  di                 ;Restored
        pop  bx
        pop  ax

        ret                     ;Back to caller

scrollup  endp

;-- SCROLLDN: scrolls a window N lines down ---------------------------
;-- Input    : BL = line upper left
;--            BH = column upper left
;--            DL = line below right
;--            DH = column below right
;--            CL = number of lines to be scrolled
;--          : BP = number of the screen page (0 to 3)
;-- Output   : none
;-- register : only FLAGS are changed
;-- Info     : the display lines liberated are cleared

scrolldn  proc near

        cld                     ;On string commands count up

        push ax                 ;Record all changed registers
        push bx                 ;On the stack
        push di                 ;In this case the sequence
        push si                 ;Must be observed !

        push bx                 ;These three registers are returned
        push cx                 ;From the stack before the end
        push dx                 ;Of the routine

        sub  dh,bh              ;Calculate the number of columns
        inc  dh
        mov  al,bl              ;Record line upper left in AL
        mov  bl,dl              ;Line below right to line below left
        call calo               ;Convert upper left in offset
        mov  si,di              ;Record address in SI
        sub  bl,cl              ;Subtract number of characters to scroll
        call calo               ;Convert upper left in offset
        xchg si,di              ;Exchange SI and DI
        sub  dl,al              ;Calculate number of lines
        inc  dl
        sub  dl,cl              ;Subtract number of lines to be scrolled

        cmp  wait,0             ;Flicker suppressed?
        je   sdn0               ;NO --> SDN0

        waitret                 ;YES --> Wait for retrace
        setmode 00100101b       ;Disable screen

sdn0:   push ds                 ;Store segment register on the
        push es                 ;Stack
        mov  ax,VIO_SEG         ;Segment address of the video RAM
        mov  ds,ax              ;To DS
        mov  es,ax              ;and ES

sdn1:   mov  ax,di              ;Record DI in AX
        mov  bx,si              ;Record SI in BX
        mov  cl,dh              ;Number of columns in counter
        rep movsw               ;Move a line
        mov  di,ax              ;Restore DI from AX
        mov  si,bx              ;Restore SI from BX
        sub  di,160             ;Set into next line
        sub  si,160
        dec  dl                 ;processed all lines ?
```

```
          jne  sdn1                  ;NO --> move another line

          pop  es                    ;Return segment register from
          pop  ds                    ;Stack

          cmp  wait,0                ;Flicker suppressed?
          je   sdn2                  ;NO --> SDN2

          setmode 00101101b          ;YES --> Enable screen


sdn2:     pop  dx                    ;Get lower right corner
          pop  cx                    ;Return number of lines
          pop  bx                    ;Return upper left corner
          mov  dl,bl                 ;upper line to DL
          add  dl,cl                 ;Add number of lines
          dec  dl
          mov  ah,07h                ;Color : black on white
          call clear                 ;Erase liberated lines

          pop  si                    ;CX and DX have already been
          pop  di                    ;Returned
          pop  bx
          pop  ax

          ret                        ;Back to caller

scrolldn  endp

;-- CLS: Clear the screen completely ----------------------------------
;-- Input  : BP = number of the screen page (0 or 1)
;-- Output  : none
;-- register : only FLAGS are changed

cls       proc near

          mov  ah,07h                ;Color is white on black
          xor  bx,bx                 ;upper left is (0/0)
          mov  dx,4F18h              ;Lower right is (79/24)

          ;-- Execute Clear -------------------------------------------

cls       endp

;-- CLEAR: fills a designated display area with space characters ------
;-- Input     : AH = attribute/color
;--             BL = line upper left
;--             BH = column upper left
;--             DL = line below right
;--             DH = column below right
;--             BP = number of the screen page (0 to 3)
;-- Output    : none
;-- register : only FLAGS are changed

clear     proc near

          cld                        ;On string commands count up
          push cx                    ;Store all register which are
          push dx                    ;Changed on the stack
          push si
          push di
          push es
          sub  dl,bl                 ;Calculate number of lines
          inc  dl
          sub  dh,bh                 ;Calculate number of columns
          inc  dh
          call calo                  ;Offset address of the upper left corner
          mov  cx,VIO_SEG            ;Segment address of the video RAM
          mov  es,cx                 ;To ES
          xor  ch,ch                 ;Hi bytes of the counter to 0
```

```
        mov  al," "             ;Space character

        cmp  wait,0             ;Flickering suppressed?
        je   clear1             ;NO --> CLEAR1

        push dx                 ;Store DX on the stack
        waitret                 ;Retrace wait
        setmode 00100101b       ;Switch screen off
        pop  dx                 ;Return DX from the stack

clear1: mov  si,di              ;Record DI in SI
        mov  cl,dh              ;Number columns in counter
        rep stosw               ;Store space character
        mov  di,si              ;Return DI from SI
        add  di,160             ;Set in next line
        dec  dl                 ;All lines processed ?
        jne  clear1             ;NO --> erase another line

        cmp  wait,0             ;Flicker suppressed?
        je   clear2             ;NO --> CLEAR2

        setmode 00101101b       ;Enable screen

clear2: pop  es                 ;Get registers from
        pop  di                 ;Stack again
        pop  si
        pop  dx
        pop  cx
        ret                     ;Back to caller

clear   endp

;-- PRINT: outputs a string on the screen -----------------------------
;-- Input   :  AH = attribute/color
;--             DI = offset address of the first character
;--             SI = offset address of the strings to DS
;--             BP = number of the screen page (0 to 3)
;-- Output   : DI points behind the last character output
;-- register : AL, DI and FLAGS are changed
;-- Info     : the string must be terminated by a NUL-character.
;--             other control characters are not recognized

print   proc near

        cld                     ;On string commands count up
        push si                 ;Store SI, DX and ES on the stack
        push es
        push cx
        push dx
        mov  dx,VIO_SEG         ;Segment address of the video RAM
        mov  cl,wait            ;Get WAIT flag
        mov  es,dx              ;First to DX and then to ES

        jmp  short print3       ;Get character and display it

print1  label near

        or   cl,cl              ;Flicker suppressed?
        je   print2             ;NO --> PRINT2

        push ax                 ;Record characters and color
        mov  dx,3DAh            ;Address of the display-status-register
hr1:    in   al,dx              ;Get content
        test al,1               ;Horizontal retrace?
        jne  hr1                ;NO --> wait
        cli                     ;permit no further interrupts
hr2:    in   al,dx              ;Get content
        test al,1               ;Horizontal retrace?
        je   hr2                ;YES --> wait
        pop  ax                 ;Restore characters and color
```

```
         sti                    ;Do not suppress Interrupts any more

print2:  stosw                  ;Store attribute and color in V-RAM
print3:  lodsb                  ;Get next character from the string
         or   al,al             ;Is it NUL
         jne  print1            ;NO --> output

printe:  pop  dx                ;Get SI, DX, CX and ES from stack
         pop  cx
         pop  es
         pop  si
         ret                    ;Back to caller

print    endp

;-- CALO: Converts line and column into offset address ----------------
;-- Input    : BL = line
;--            BH = column
;--            BP = number of the screen page (0 to 3)
;-- Output   : DI = the offset address
;-- register : DI and FLAGS are changed

calo     proc near

         push ax                ;Secure AX on the stack
         push bx                ;Secure BX on the stack

         shl  bx,1              ;Column and line times 2
         mov  al,bh             ;Column to AL
         xor  bh,bh             ;Hi byte
         mov  di,[lines+bx]     ;Get offset address of the line
         xor  ah,ah             ;HI byte for column offset
         add  di,ax             ;Add line and column offset
         mov  bx,bp             ;Screen page to BX
         mov  cl,4              ;Multiply by 4,096
         ror  bx,cl
         add  di,bx             ;Add beginning of screen page to offset
         pop  bx                ;Restore BX from stack
         pop  ax                ;Restore AX from stack
         ret                    ;Back to caller

calo     endp

;-- CGR: Erase the complete Graphic display ---------------------------
;-- Input    : AL = 00H : erase all pixels
;--                 FFH : set all pixels
;-- Output   : none
;-- register : AH, BX, CX, DI and FLAGS are changed
;-- Info     : this Function erases the Graphic display in both
;--            Graphic modes

cgr      proc near

         push es                ;Store ES on the stack
         cbw                    ;Expand AL to AH
         xor  di,di             ;Offset address in video RAM
         mov  bx,VIO_SEG        ;Segment address screen page
         mov  es,bx             ;Segment address into segment register
         mov  cx,2000h          ;One page is 8KB words
         rep stosw              ;Fill page
         pop  es                ;Return ES from stack
         ret                    ;Back to caller

cgr      endp

;-- PIXLO: sets a pixel in the 320*200 pixel graphic mode -----------------
;-- Input   :  BP = number of the screen page (0 or 1)
;--            BX = column  (0 to 319)
;--            DX = line    (0 to 199)
;--            AL = color of the pixels (0 to 3)
```

```
;-- Output   : none
;-- register : AX, DI and FLAGS are changed

pixlo     proc near

          push ax                 ;Secure AX on the stack
          push bx                 ;Note BX on the stack
          push cx                 ;Store CX on the stack
          mov  cl,7
          mov  ah,bl              ;Transmit column to AH
          and  ah,11b             ;Column mod 4
          shl  ah,1               ;Column * 2
          sub  cl,ah              ;7 - 2 * (column mod 4)
          mov  ah,11              ;Bit value
          shl  ax,cl              ;Move to pixel position
          not  ah                 ;Reverse AH
          shr  bx,1               ;Divide BX by 4 by shifting
          shr  bx,1               ;Right twice
          jmp  short spix         ;Set pixel

pixlo     endp

;-- PIXHI: sets a pixel in the 640*200 pixel graphic mode -----------------
;-- Input  :   BP = number of the screen page (0 or 1)
;--            BX = column (0 to 639)
;--            DX = line   (0 to 199)
;--            AL = color of the pixels (0 or 1)
;-- Output   : none
;-- register : AX, DI and FLAGS are changed

pixhi     proc near

          push ax                 ;Store AX on the stack
          push bx                 ;Note BX on the stack
          push cx                 ;Note CX on the stack
          mov  cl,7
          mov  ah,bl              ;Transmit column to AH
          and  ah,111b            ;Column mod 8
          sub  cl,ah              ;7 - column mod 8
          mov  ah,1               ;Bit value
          shl  ax,cl              ;Move pixel position
          not  ah                 ;Reverse AH
          mov  cl,3               ;3 shifts
          shr  bx,cl              ;Divide BX by 8

          ;-- set pixel ------------------------------------------------

pixhi          endp

;-- SPIX: sets a pixel in the graphic display ---------------------------
;-- Input    : BX = column offset
;--            DX = line   (0 to 199)
;--            AH = Value to cancel old Bits
;--            AL = new Bit value
;-- Output   : none
;-- register : AX, DI and FLAGS are changed

spix      proc near

          push es                 ;Secure ES on the stack
          push dx                 ;Secure DX on the stack
          push ax                 ;Secure AX on the stack

          xor  di,di              ;Offset address in video RAM
          mov  cx,VIO_SEG         ;Segment address screen page
          mov  es,cx              ;Segment address into segment register
          mov  ax,dx              ;Move line to AX
          shr  ax,1               ;Divide line by 2
          mov  cl,80              ;The factor is 90
          mul  cl                 ;Multiply line by 80
```

```
        and  dx,1              ;Line mod 2
        mov  cl,3              ;3 shifts
        ror  dx,cl             ;Rotate right (* 2000H)
        mov  di,ax             ;80 * int(line/2)
        add  di,dx             ;+ 2000H * (line mod 4)
        add  di,bx             ;Add column offset
        pop  ax                ;Return AX from stack
        mov  bl,es:[di]        ;Get pixel
        and  bl,ah             ;Erase Bits
        or   bl,al             ;Add pixel
        mov  es:[di],bl        ;write pixel back

        pop  dx                ;Return DX from stack
        pop  es                ;Return ES from stack
        pop  cx                ;Return CX from stack
        pop  bx                ;Return BX from stack
        pop  ax                ;Return AX from stack

        ret                    ;Back to caller

spix    endp

;== end ================================================================

code    ends                   ;End of the code segment
        end  demo
```

10.5 EGA and VGA Cards

The EGA and VGA cards far exceed their predecessors in both graphics and in text display capabilities. Other computers have had EGA and VGA capabilities for some time (e.g., work stations, CAD/CAM applications), but these video cards are now at prices where many home systems will soon have them.

The range of power of this new generation of video cards can be seen in their very sharp resolutions and their ability to display almost any number of lines on the screen. The EGA and VGA cards' greatest feature lies in their ability to emulate other video cards.

These capabilities come with a price—more complicated hardware and programming are required. One result of this is that the features of an EGA card or a VGA card can no longer be realized with the traditional PC video controller (the Motorola 6845). Instead, most EGA and VGA cards contain a VLSI chip developed especially for use on an EGA card. At the heart of this component is a video controller that controls the video signal generation. Its basic task is similar to that of the 6845, but its registers differ from those of the 6845, both in number and interaction between registers. Comparing the 6845 and VSLI is like comparing BASIC and assembly language, where the increase of power is in proportion to the degree of language complexity.

We recommend that you avoid programming the hardware registers directly unless you absolutely must do so. Many tasks can be delegated to the BIOS without wasting much time. Not only will this keep your program code more compact and easier to read, it will greatly improve the compatibility of your code with other video cards. Among the tasks which the various functions of the BIOS video interrupt can perform are:

- Initialization of the video mode
- Selection of the display page
- Cursor positioning
- Defining the starting and ending line of the cursor
- Palette and border color selection
- Setting the size of the character matrix, and thereby the number of text lines which can be displayed on the screen
- Loading user-defined character sets
- Reading configuration data

Detailed information about traditional BIOS video functions and the new functions of the EGA/VGA BIOS can be found in Sections 7.4.

If you need speed and maximum control over the screen, you should still perform time-critical actions (e.g., manipulating video RAM) "by hand."

EGA/VGA and text mode

There is no difference between the EGA and MDA or CGA card in text mode. The video RAM and attribute byte are organized the same way for the EGA card as for the other two cards—even the location of the video RAM is the same. But since an EGA card can emulate either a CGA card or an MDA card, depending on the monitor to which it is connected, you should first determine what kind monitor is in use. From this the EGA can determine which of the two systems to emulate (routines presented in Section 10.7 show how this is done). The type of card being emulated determines where the video RAM can be found in memory, how the bits of the character attribute byte are interpreted, and how many screen pages are available.

Remember that the EGA or VGA card does not contain a 6845 CRTC, despite the fact that it can perfectly emulate its video predecessors. This means that the status and control registers of the MDA and CGA cards are unavailable. However, since the settings that are normally made with these registers can also be performed with the BIOS, we don't really need these registers. You should also remember that there are no restrictions to accessing the video RAM of an EGA card or a VGA card when it is in CGA emulation. It is unnecessary to synchronize screen access with the activity of the CRTC by reading the status register.

The parallels between the organization of the video RAM in the CGA and MDA cards also apply when the text mode is switched to 43 lines (which is impossible in CGA emulation). As with any other number of displayed lines, this does not change the basic structure of the video RAM at all. It is larger, but the formulas for calculating the offset position of a character and its attribute byte within the video RAM are still valid.

The VGA card is capable of 25, 43 and even 50 lines in text mode, depending on the monitor in use.

These parallels also apply to the graphics modes already available to the CGA card. The position of the video RAM and its structure are identical to the those of the CGA card.

EGA/VGA and graphic modes

The EGA card offers the following new graphics modes:

- 320x200 pixels, 16 colors (BIOS code: 0DH)
- 640x200 pixels, 16 colors (BIOS code: 0EH)
- 640x350 pixels, 2 colors (BIOS code: 0FH)

- 640x350 pixels, 16 colors (BIOS code: 10H)

The VGA card offers the following graphic modes:

- 640x480 pixels, 2 colors (BIOS code: 11H)
- 640x480 pixels, 16 colors (BIOS code: 12H)
- 320x200 pixels, 256 colors (BIOS code: 13H)

Some EGA cards have even more modes with higher resolution or more colors, but these modes are not part of the EGA standard and are supported by only a few programs.

It is somewhat difficult to talk about a "standard", because almost every manufacturer has their own modes. Let's look at the lowest common denominator—the modes which practically all EGA/VGA cards support. These are the modes supported by the original EGA card, the IBM EGA.

These video modes, in which the video RAM can occupy more than 100K, show a structure quite different from those used by the MDA, CGA and Hercules cards. The maximum of 256K of RAM is divided into four *bitplanes* which are arranged in a kind of a three-dimensional organization. From the processor's point of view these bitplanes reside between segment addresses A000H and B000H.

Each bitplane contains one bit for each individual pixel. If you place the bitplanes on top of each other, each pixel is represented by a total of four bits, which together make up the color value of the pixel. Bitplane zero contains bit zero of the color value of each pixel, bitplane one contains bit one, and so on. This limits the number of displayable colors to 16, since four bits (or bitplanes) can represent 2^4, or 16 different numbers.

The color value obtained from combining individual bitplanes does not correspond directly to a color. It is actually used as an index into one of the 16 palette registers of the EGA card, each of which designates a particular color. Since the EGA card can display a total of 64 different colors, the palette registers allow you to select 16 of these colors to be displayed on the screen simultaneously. The individual palette registers can be loaded with the help of the extended EGA BIOS functions, as described in Section 7.4.

The structure of each bitplane corresponds to the organization of the pixels on the screen, and parallels that of video RAM in text mode. Since each pixel occupies one bit in the bitplane, eight consecutive pixels are combined into a byte. The pixels on each line are placed left to right in successive memory locations. The length of each line can be determined using the formula:

```
horizontal_resolution / 8
```

Since the individual screen lines follow each other in sequence starting from the top of the screen, the starting address of each line is obtained by multiplying the line number by this value. The byte within this line which contains the desired pixel is calculated by dividing the column number by eight (bits per byte). Adding this to the starting address of the line gives us the following formula, which calculates the offset address of the byte containing the coordinates (X, Y):

```
Y * (horizontal_resolution / 8) + X / 8
```

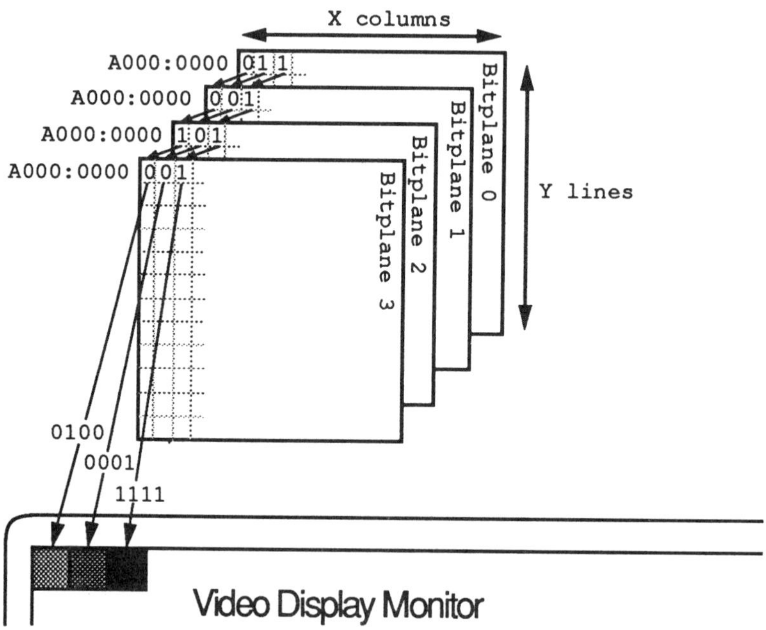

Bitplane arrangement on EGA card

The bit number at which the pixel is located in this byte results from the remainder of the division of the column number by eight:

```
7 - (column_number MOD 8)
```

These two formulas can be used to localize a pixel within a bitplane and implement graphics primitives.

However, the bitplanes cannot be accessed individually because they all lie at the identical segment address. The EGA card has four latch registers, each of which contains a complete byte from one of the four bitplanes. When the CPU performs a read access from the EGA video RAM at segment address A000H, one byte is first read from each of the four bitplanes at the specified offset address and loaded into the four latch registers. This applies to instructions which access memory directly, such as MOV or LODS, as well as all instructions in which a byte from the video RAM appears as an operand. This can be the case with arithmetic instructions (ADD, SUB, OR, AND, etc.) and comparison instructions (CMP, CMPS).

The process is similar for writing bytes to the video RAM. In this situation the contents of the four latch registers are written back to the four bitplanes.

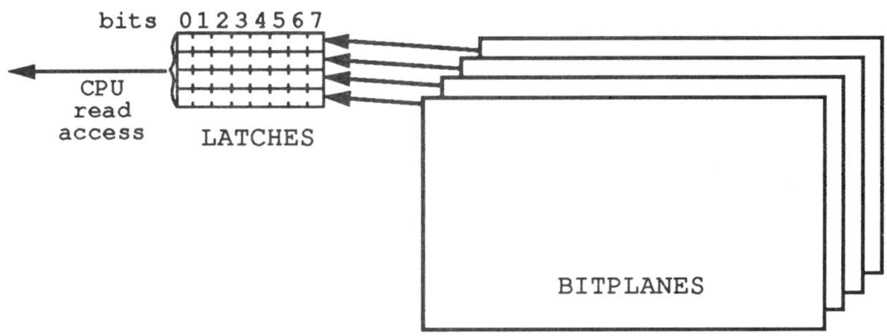

Video RAM access—loading the four latch registers

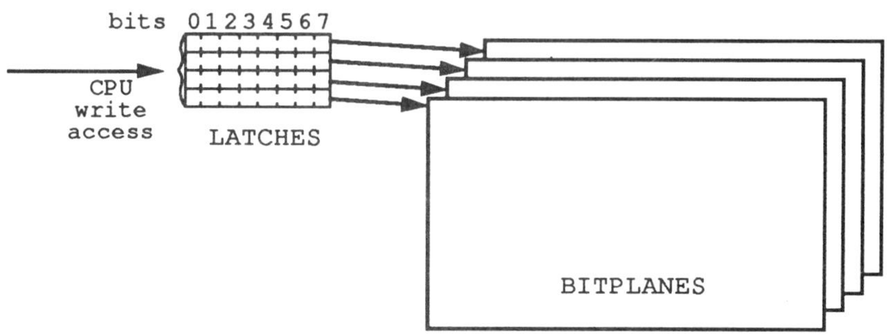

Video RAM access—writing the four latch registers

Since the latch registers are not directly accessible to the processor, we must alternate conversion between eight and 32 bits when reading and writing the video RAM. When reading, 32 bits from the latch registers must be compressed into one byte, while the eight bits from the CPU when writing must be divided among the 32 bits of the latch registers. The nine graphic controller registers in the EGA card perform this conversion.

EGA graphic controller registers and their default values		
Register	Meaning	Default
00H	Set / Reset	00H
01H	Enable Set / Reset	00H
02H	Color Compare	00H
03H	Function Select	00H
04H	Read Map Select	00H
05H	Mode	00H
06H	Miscellaneous	varies
07H	Color Don't Care	0FH
08H	Bit Mask	FFH

Access to these registers is similar to CRTC register access on the Hercules graphics card. Here too there is an address register at port address 3DEH, into which we must first load the number of the register in the graphics controller that we want to access. The value for this register can then be written to the data register located at address 3CFH, immediately after the address register. These ports do not have to be accessed separately: A 16-bit OUT instruction to the address register performs the access in one move. The AX register, which will be sent to this port, must contain the register number in the low-order byte (AL), and the value for this register in the high-order byte (AH). Although values can be loaded into the graphics controller registers in this manner, it is not possible to read data from the EGA card.

The contents of register number five, the mode register, are responsible for the behavior of the video RAM. This register controls the current read and write modes and thereby the manner in which the data from the latch registers is combined with the other registers in the graphics controller and the CPU data.

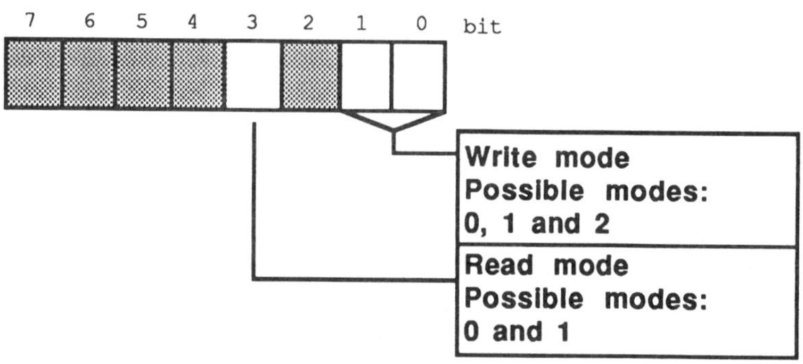

Mode register structure in EGA card graphics controller

There are a total of two different read modes and three write modes.

Read mode 0

Read mode 0 is the simpler of the two read modes. As usual, a read access in this mode first loads the specified byte from the four bitplanes into the four latch registers. Then the contents of the latch register specified by the lower two bits of the read map select register (register four) are transferred to the CPU.

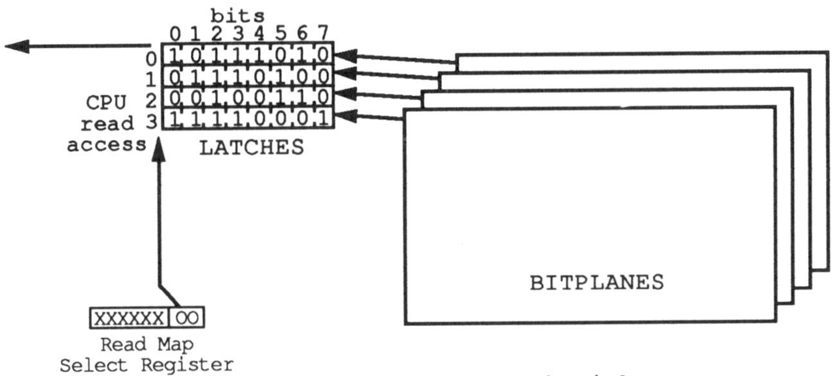

Video RAM read access in read mode 0

The following sequence of assembly language instructions first sets read mode 0, then writes the value 2 into the Read Map Select register, and finally reads a byte from offset address 0003H in the video RAM. As a result, the AL register contains the bit values for the pixels with coordinates (24, 0) to (31, 0) from bitplane 2.

```
mov dx,3CEh          ;port address of the graphics cont. addr. reg.
mov ax,0005h         ;write read mode 0 in the mode register
out dx,ax
mov ax,0204h         ;write the value 2 (plane number) in the
out dx,ax            ;read map select register
mov ax,0A000h        ;segment address of the video RAM
mov ds,ax            ;to DS
mov si,0003h         ;offset address into the video RAM
lodsb                ;read byte from plane 2
```

Read mode 1

Read mode 1 specifies which of the eight pixels in the specified byte of video RAM is set to a certain color. This is determined by the individual bits in the read byte which correspond to the one of the eight pixels from the specified byte in the video RAM. If a pixel has the specified color (appropriate bit map), then the corresponding bit will be 1, else 0. The bit pattern of the color to be compared must be loaded into the lower four bits of the Color Compare register. The lower four bits of the Color Don't Care register show which bitplanes will be taken into consideration in the comparison. The value 1 includes the given plane in the comparison, while the value 0 excludes it.

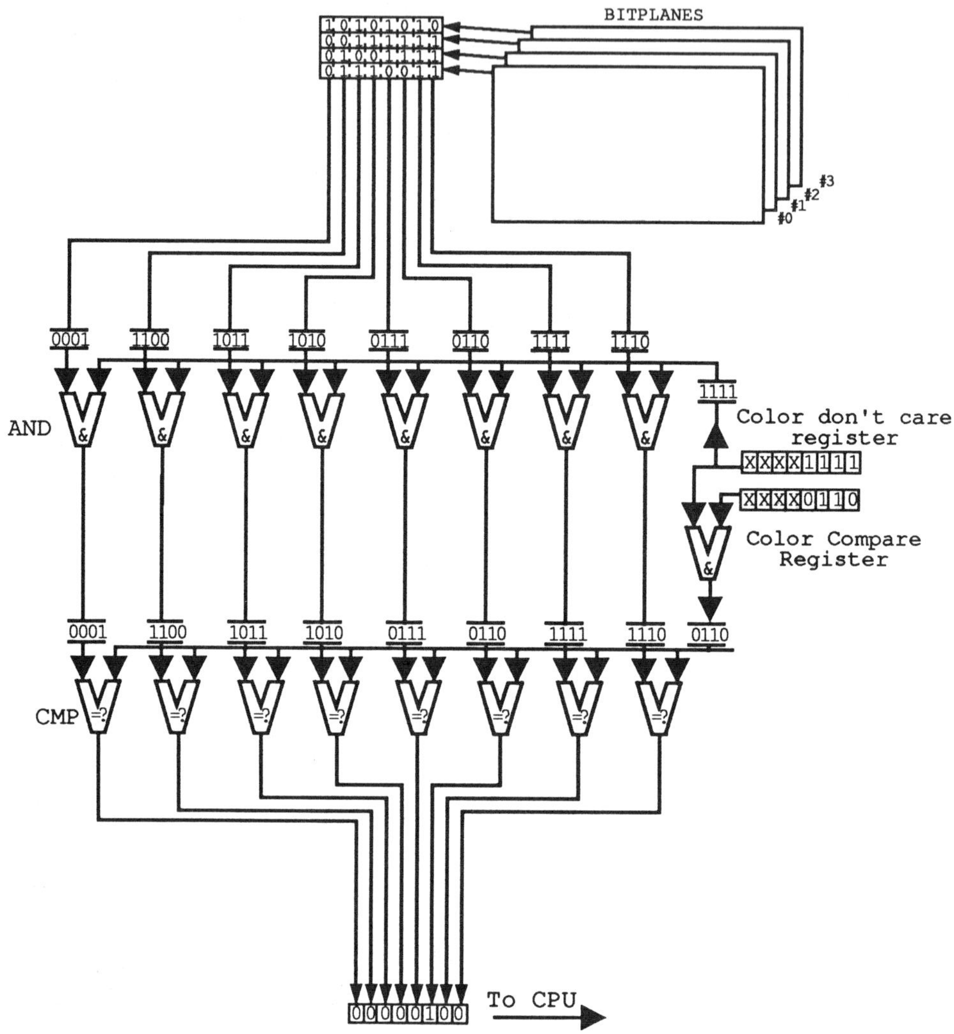

Video RAM read access in read mode 1

The following program sequence determines which of the pixels between coordinates (0, 0) and (7, 0) have color value five. First, read mode 1 is set by the Mode register. Then the color value to be tested (five) is loaded into the Color Compare register. We must also load the Color Don't Care register with the value 1111b so that all four bitplanes will be included in the comparison. However, this is the default value and we have not loaded any other value into this register, so we can skip this step. After programming the registers of the graphics controller, we load the segment and offset addresses of the pixels to be compared into the DS and SI registers. Then the read is executed from the video RAM.

```
mov dx,3CEh             ;port address of the graphics cont. addr. reg.
mov ax,0805h            ;write read mode 1 into the mode register
out dx,ax
mov ax,0502h            ;write color value 15 into the
out dx,ax               ;Color Compare register
mov ax,0A000h           ;segment address of the video RAM
mov ds,ax               ;to DS
xor si,si               ;load offset address 0
lodsb                   ;read and compare pixels,
                        ;return result in AL
```

Write mode 0

Writing to the video RAM in write mode 0 results in a number of operations, all of which depend on the contents of several registers. The contents of the Bit Mask register determine whether the value of a bit in the four latch registers will be written unchanged to the found bitplanes or whether it will first be modified. The individual bits in the Bit Mask register correspond to the individual bits in the four latch registers. If a bit in the Bit Mask register is 0, the corresponding bits in the latch registers will be written to the bitplanes unchanged. If this bit is 1, a modification will take place, dependent on the contents of the Function Select register. As the following figure shows, the bits can be replaced or modified with the logical operations AND, OR, and XOR.

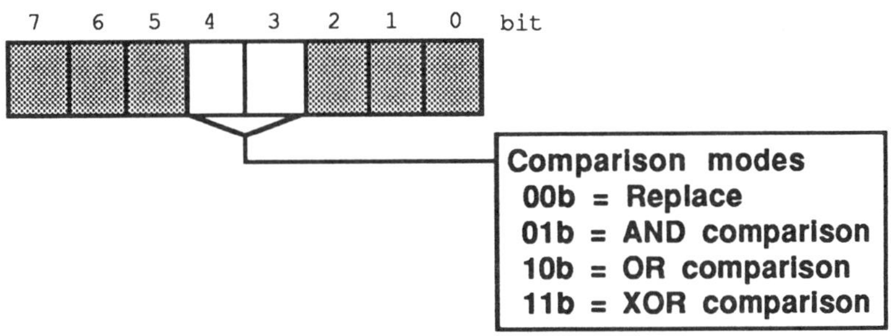

Function Select Register structure in EGA card graphics controller

The contents of the Enable Set/Reset register determines from where the other operand in these operations will come. If the lower four bits contain the value 1, the other operand will come from the lower four bits of the Set/Reset register. Each of these bits is then combined with the bits from the latch registers as described by the contents of the Function Select register. All of the bits to be modified from latch register 0 will then be operated on with bit 0 of the Set/Reset register. In the same manner, all of the bits to be modified from latch registers 1, 2, and 3 are combined with bits 1, 2, and 3 of the Set/Reset register, respectively. The byte which is actually written to the graphics controller becomes irrelevant at this point—the write access is reduced to a trigger, which cannot have any direct influence on the contents of the latch register (and therefore the bitplanes).

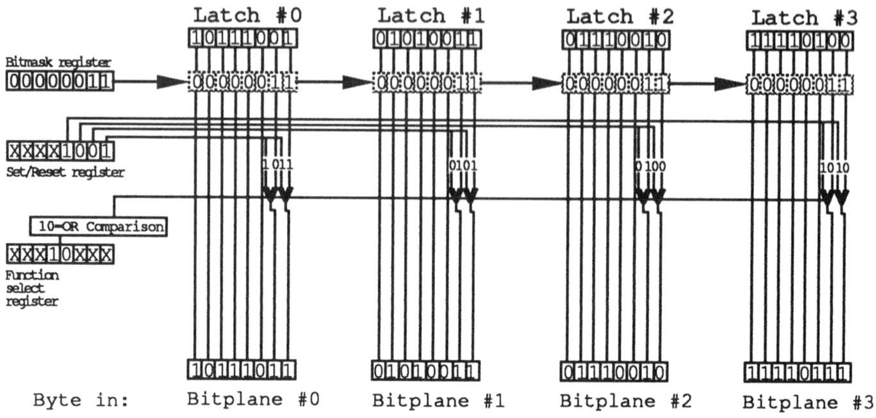

Write access to video RAM (write mode 0) when Enable Set/Reset register contains a value of 00001111(b)

The following assembly language fragment assigns the pixels at coordinates (5, 0) and (7, 0), found at offset address 0000H in the video RAM, the color 1011(b).

Since we don't want to change the color of the other pixels, the contents of the byte are first read into the latch register with a read access to the video RAM. It is not important which read mode is active because the byte transmitted to the CPU is irrelevant; all we are interested in is loading the latch register. Since only bits 0 (coordinates (7, 0)) and 2 (coordinates (5, 0)) will be changed, we load the value 00000101b (05h) into the bitmask register. In the Function Select register we write the value 0 because we want to replace bits 0 and 2 with a new bit combination. We write the color we want to give to the two bits (1011b = 0Bh) in the Set/Reset register. We must also write the value 1111(b) (0FH) to the Enable Set/Reset register of the graphics controller so that the color value will be taken from the Set/Reset register. We can then execute the write access to video RAM.

```
mov ax,0A000h          ;segment address of the video RAM
mov ds,ax              ;to DS
xor bx,bx              ;load offset address 0
mov al,[bx]            ;load byte 0 in the latch register
mov dx,3CEh            ;port address of the graphic cont. addr. reg.
mov ax,0005h           ;read mode 0, write more 0
out dx,ax              ;write in the mode register
mov al,03h             ;write 0 in the Function Select register
out dx,ax
mov ax,0508h           ;write bit mask in the bitmask register
out dx,ax
mov ax,0B00h           ;write new color value in the Set/Reset register
out dx,ax
mov ax,0F01h           ;write 1111b in the Enable Set/Reset register
out dx,ax
mov [bx],al            ;trigger latch register
```

Things are different when the Enable Set/Reset register contains the value zero. In this case all of the bits to be modified from the four latch registers are combined with the CPU byte latch by latch. Here again the type of operation performed depends on the contents of the Function Select register. For example, if the OR operation is selected and bits 1, 2, 4, and 6 are to be modified, than these bits of all four latch registers will be individually ORed with bits 1, 2, 4, and 6 in the CPU byte.

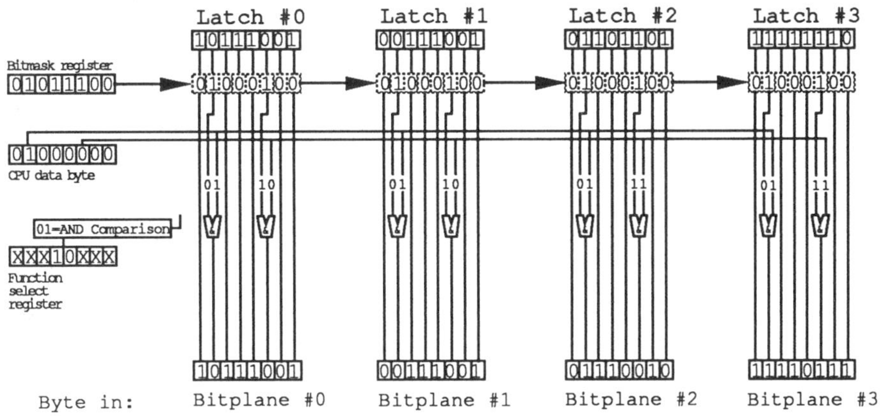

Write mode 1

Write mode 1 is quite simple compared to the complex operations of write mode 0. The contents of the registers and the CPU byte are irrelevant because the contents of the four latch registers are loaded unchanged into the specified offset address within the four bitplanes. This is useful for copying the color values of eight successive pixels to eight other pixels, for instance. The byte containing the eight pixels can be read under one of the read modes, placing it in the latch registers. Then a write access can be made to the byte in video RAM to which you want to copy the color values. The graphics controller will automatically copy the contents of the latch registers to the specified position within the four bitplanes.

To write these color values to other locations, you can use additional write accesses. No more read accesses are necessary, since the latch registers already contain the appropriate values and their contents are not changed by the write access.

Write mode 2

Write mode 2 resembles a combinátion of the various modes of write mode 0. As in write mode 0, the bitmask register determines which bits will be taken directly from the latch registers and which will be modified. The manner in which these bits are manipulated is again determined by the mode selected in the Function Select register. The lower four bits of the CPU byte will be combined with the latch registers, independent of the Enable Set/Reset register. Bit zero of the CPU byte is combined with all bits in latch register zero which are to be modified. The same applies for CPU bits 1, 2, and 3, which are combined with the bits of latch registers 1, 2, and 3, respectively.

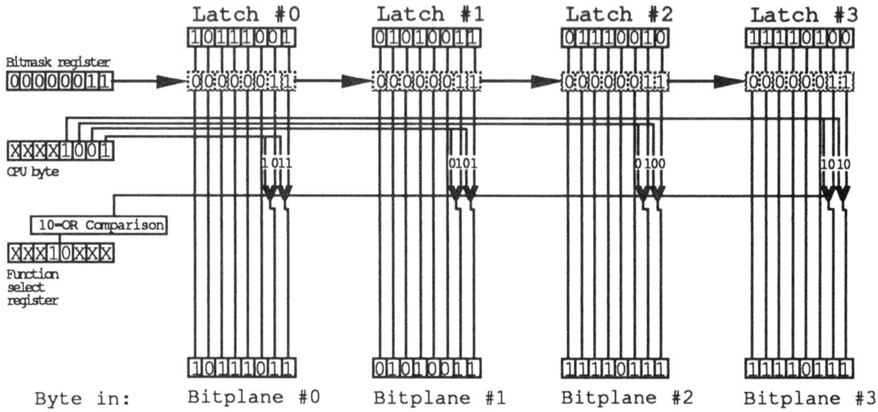

Write access to video RAM in write mode 2

This mode is good for setting the colors of individual pixels, as we demonstrated in the example in write mode 0. In contrast to write mode 0, the assembly-language fragment is somewhat shorter because neither the Enable Set/Reset nor the Set/Reset register has to be programmed. Here is the same example using write mode 2:

```
mov ax,0A000h        ;segment address of the video RAM
mov ds,ax            ;in DS
xor bx,bx            ;load offset address 0
mov al,[bx]          ;load byte 0 in the latch registers
mov dx,3CEh          ;port address of the graphics cont. addr. reg.
mov ax,0205h         ;read mode 0, write mode 2
out dx,ax            ;write into the mode register
mov ax,0003h         ;write REPLACE mode (0) in the Function
out dx,ax            ;Select register
mov ax,0508h         ;write the bit mask to the bitmask register
out dx,ax
mov al,0Bh           ;new color value in AL
mov [bx],al          ;and from there to the video RAM and
                     ;into the latch regs and bitplanes
```

Demonstration program

The following program demonstrates the following basic graphics routines:

- Calculating the position of a pixel within the video RAM
- Setting the color of a pixel
- Reading the color of a pixel
- Filling the entire video RAM with a color

If you have followed this section closely, especially the material on the read and write modes, you won't have any problems following the logic of the various functions. Since it contains detailed documentation, we won't say anything more about it.

It should be noted that the program is intended for demonstration purposes only. You can develop it further if you want to make a graphics library out of these functions. For example, the function PIXPTR loads the segment address of the video RAM into the ES register for calculating the position of a pixel within the video RAM each time it is called. This can be eliminated by loading this address into the register once at the beginning of the program and leaving it there, as long as the other functions do not change this register.

The graphics controller register programming can also be improved. Here the various registers are reloaded with the ROM-BIOS default values after the function has completed. This can be eliminated as long as you do not use the BIOS functions for character output (in the graphics mode) or the functions for setting and testing points within the module or program. If you avoid these calls, then these registers can be reset to their default values once at the end of the program instead of at the end of each routine.

Assembler listing: VEGA.ASM

```
;**********************************************************************;
;*                              V E G A                               *;
;*--------------------------------------------------------------------*;
;*     Task            : Creates elementary functions for accessing the *;
;*                       graphic modes on an EGA/VGA card             *;
;*--------------------------------------------------------------------*;
;*     Author          : MICHAEL TISCHER                              *;
;*     Developed on    :  10/3/1988                                   *;
;*     Last update     :  6/19/1989                                   *;
;*--------------------------------------------------------------------*;
;*     Assembly        : MASM VEGA;                                   *;
;*                       LINK VEGA;                                   *;
;*--------------------------------------------------------------------*;
;*     Call            : VEGA                                         *;
;**********************************************************************;

;== Constants =========================================================

VIO_SEG      = 0A000h              ;Segment address of video RAM
                                   ;in graphic mode
LINE_LEN     = 80                  ;Every graphi line in EGA/VGA graphic
                                   ;modes require 80 bytes
BITMASK_REG  = 8                   ;Bitmask register
MODE_REG     = 5                   ;Mode register
FUNCSEL_REG  = 3                   ;Function select register
MAPSEL_REG   = 4                   ;Map-Select register
ENABLE_REG   = 1                   ;Enable Set/Reset register
SETRES_REG   = 0                   ;Set/Reset register
GRAPH_CONT   = 3CEh                ;Port addressd of graphic controller
OP_MODE      = 0                   ;Comparison operator mode:
                                   ;   00h = Replace
                                   ;   08h = AND comparison
                                   ;   10h = OR comparison
                                   ;   18h = EXCLUSIVE OR comparison

GR_640_350   = 10h                 ;BIOS code for 640x350-pixel
```

```
                                        ;16-color graphic mode
TX_80_25      = 03h                     ;BIOS code for 80*25-char.
                                        ;text mode

;== Stack =================================================================

stack       segment para stack          ;Definition of stack segment

            dw 256 dup (?)              ;256-word stack

stack       ends                        ;End of stack segment

;== Data ==================================================================

data        segment para 'DATA'         ;Definition of data segment

;== Data for the demo program =============================================

initm    db 13,10
           db "VEGA (c) 1988 by Michael Tischer"
       db 13,10,13,10
       db "This demonstration program operates only with an EGA/",13,10
           db "card and a hi-res monitor. If your PC doesn't have this",13,10
           db "configuration, please press the <s> key to abort the",13,10
           db "program.",13,10
       db "Press any other key to start the program.",13,10,"$"

data        ends                        ;End of data segment

;== Code ==================================================================

code        segment para 'CODE'         ;Definition of code segment

            assume cs:code, ds:data, es:data, ss:stack

;== Demo program ==========================================================

demo        proc far

            mov  ax,data                ;Get segment addr. from data segment
            mov  ds,ax                  ;and load into DS
            mov  es,ax                  ;and ES

            ;-- Display opening message and wait for input ---------------

            mov  ah,9                   ;Function number for string display
            mov  dx,offset initm        ;Message address
            int  21h                    ;Call DOS interrupt

            xor  ah,ah                  ;Get function number for key
            int  16h                    ;Call BIOS keyboard interrupt
            cmp  al,"s"                 ;Was <s> entered?
            je   ende                   ;YES --> End program
            cmp  al,"S"                 ;Was <S> entered?
            jne  startdemo              ;NO --> Start demo

ende:       mov  ax,4C00h               ;Function no. for end program
            int  21h                    ;Call DOS interrupt 21H

            ;-- Initialize graphic mode ----------------------------------

startdemo label near

            mov  ax,GR_640_350          ;Initialize 64x350-pixel
            int  10h                    ;16-color graphic mode
```

```
        mov  ch,000100001b        ;Color: Blue
        mov  ax,350               ;Number of raster lines: 350
        call fillscr              ;Fill screen

        ;-- The program displays two squares on the screens (the     --
        ;-- second is really a copy of the first) until the user     --
        ;-- presses a key to end the program                         --

        xor  ch,ch                ;Set color to 0
d1:     mov  ax,100               ;Starting line of first square

        inc  ch                   ;Increment color
        and  ch,15                ;AND bits 4 and 7

d2:     mov  bx,245               ;Starting column of first square
d3:     call setpix               ;Set pixel
        push cx                   ;Save color
        call getpix               ;Get pixel color
        push ax                   ;Push coordinates onto stack
        push bx
        add  bx,100               ;Compute position of second
        add  ax,100               ;square
        call setpix               ;Set pixel of copy
        pop  bx                   ;Return coordinates of first square
        pop  ax
        pop  cx                   ;Get color
        inc  bx                   ;Increment column
        cmp  bx,295               ;Reached the last column?
        jne  d3                   ;NO --> Set next pixel

        inc  ax                   ;YES, Increment line
        cmp  ax,150               ;Reached the last line?
        jne  d2                   ;NO --> Work with next line

        mov  ah,1                 ;Read keyboard
        int  16h                  ;Call BIOS keyboard interrupt
        je   d1                   ;No key pressed --> Continue

        mov  ax,TX_80_25          ;80x25 text mode
        int  10h                  ;Initialization
        jmp  short ende           ;End programm

demo    endp

;== Functions used in the demo program =================================

;-- PIXPTR: Computes the address of a pixel within video RAM for the   -
;--         new EGA/VGA graphic modes
;-- Input    : AX    = Graphic line
;--            BX    = Graphic column
;-- Output   : ES:BX = Pointer to the byte in video RAM containing pixel
;--            CL    = Number of right shifts for the byte
;--                  = Number of byte shifts in ES:BX needed to isolate
;--                    the pixel
;--            AH    = Bitmask for combining with all other pixels
;-- Registers: ES, AX, BX and CL are changed

pixptr  proc near

        push dx                   ;Push DX onto stack

        mov  cl,bl                ;Save low byte of graphic column
        mov  dx,LINE_LEN          ;Number of bytes per line to DX
        mul  dx                   ;AX = graphic line * LINE_LEN
        shr  bx,1                 ;Shift graphic column three places to
        shr  bx,1                 ;the right, divide by 8
```

```
          shr  bx,1
          add  bx,ax              ;Add line offset

          mov  ax,VIO_SEG         ;Load segment address of video RAM
          mov  es,ax              ;into ES

          and  cl,7               ;And bits 4 - 7 of graphic column
          xor  cl,7               ;Turn bits 0 - 3 then
                                  ;subtract 7 - CL
          mov  ah,1               ;After shift, bit 0 should be
                                  ;left alone

          pop  dx                 ;Pop DX off of stack
          ret                     ;Back to caller

pixptr    endp

;-- SETPIX: Sets a graphic pixel in the new EGA/VGA graphic modes ------
;-- Input    : AX    = graphic line
;--            BX    = graphic column
;--            CH    = pixel color
;-- Output   : none
;-- Registers: ES, DX and CL are changed

setpix    proc near

          push ax                 ;Push coordinates onto
          push bx                 ;the stack

          call pixptr             ;Computer pointer to the pixel

          mov  dx,GRAPH_CONT      ;Load port addr. of graphic controller

          ;-- Set bit position in bitmask register --------------------

          shl  ah,cl              ;Mask for bit to be changed
          mov  al,BITMASK_REG     ;Move bitmask register from AL
          out  dx,ax              ;Write to register

          ;-- Set read mode 0 and write mode 2 -- ---------------------

          mov  ax,MODE_REG + (2 shl 8) ;Reg. no. and ,mode value
          out  dx,ax              ;Write in the register

          ;-- Define comparison mode between preceding latch -----------
          ;-- contents, and CPU byte                         -----------

          mov  ax,FUNCSEL_REG + (OP_MODE shl 8) ;Write register number
          out  dx,ax              ;and comparison operator

          ;-- Pixel control ------------------------------------------

          mov  al,es:[bx]         ;Load latches
          mov  es:[bx],ch         ;Move color into bitplanes

          ;-- Set altered registers to their default (BIOS) ------------
          ;-- status                                        ------------

          mov  ax,BITMASK_REG + (0FFh shl 8) ;Set old bitmask
          out  dx,ax              ;Write in the register
          mov  ax,MODE_REG        ;Write old value for for mode register
          out  dx,ax              ;into register
          mov  ah,FUNCSEL_REG     ;Write old value for function select
          out  dx,ax              ;register into register
```

```
        pop  bx                 ;Pop coordinates off of stack
        pop  ax                 ;
        ret                     ;Back to caller

setpix  endp

;-- GETPIX: Places a pixel's color in one of the new EGA/VGA -----------
;--         graphic modes
;-- Input    : AX    = graphic line
;--            BX    = graphic column
;-- Output   : CH    = graphic pixel color
;-- Registers: ES, DX , CX and DI are changed

getpix  proc near

        push ax                 ;Push coordinates onto
        push bx                 ;the stack

        call pixptr             ;Computer pointer to pixel
        mov  ch,ah              ;Move bitmask to CH
        shl  ch,cl              ;Shift bitmask by bit positions

        mov  di,bx              ;Move video RAM offset to DI
        xor  bl,bl              ;Color value will be computed in BL

        mov  dx,GRAPH_CONT      ;Load graphic controller port address
        mov  ax,MAPSEL_REG + (3 shl 8) ;Access bitplane #3

        ;-- Go through each of the four bitplanes --------------------

gpl:    out  dx,ax              ;Activate bitplane #AH only
        mov  bh,es:[di]         ;Get byte from the bitplane
        and  bh,ch              ;Omit uninteresting bits
        neg  bh                 ;Bit 7 = 1, when a pixel is set
        rol  bx,1               ;Shift bit 7 from BH to Bit 1 in BL

        dec  ah                 ;Decrement bitplane number
        jge  gpl                ;Not  -1 yet? --> next bitplane

        ;-- The map select register must not be reset, since        --
        ;-- the EGA- and VGA-BIOS default to a value of 0            --

        mov  ch,bl              ;Get color from CH
        pop  bx                 ;Pop coordinates off
        pop  ax                 ;of stack
        ret                     ;Back to caller

getpix  endp

;-- FILLSCR: Sets all screen pixels to one color ------ ----------------
;-- Input    : AX    = number of graphic lines on the screen
;--            CH    = pixel color
;-- Output   : none
;-- Registers: ES, AX, CX, DI, DX and BL are changed

fillscr proc near

        mov  dx,GRAPH_CONT      ;Load graphic controller port address
        mov  al,SETRES_REG      ;Numbmer of Set-/Reset registers
        mov  ah,ch              ;Move bit combination to AL
        out  dx,ax              ;Write to the register

        mov  ax,ENABLE_REG + (0Fh shl 8) ;Write 0FH in the
        out  dx,ax              ;Enable Set-/Reset register

        mov  bx,LINE_LEN / 2    ;Length of a graphic line / 2 into BX
        mul  bx                 ;Multiply by number of graphic lines
        mov  cx,ax              ;Move to CX as repeat counter
        xor  di,di              ;Address first byte in video RAM
        mov  ax,VIO_SEG         ;Segment address of video RAM
```

```
        mov  es,ax              ;Load into ES
        cld                     ;Increment on string instructions
        rep  stosw              ;Fill video RAM

        ;-- Return old contents of Enable Set-/Reset register    -----

        mov  dx,GRAPH_CONT      ;Load graphic controller port address
        mov  ax,ENABLE_REG      ;Write 00H in Enable Set-/
        out  dx,ax              ;Reset register

        ret                     ;Back to caller

fillscr endp

;== End ============================================================

code    ends                    ;End of code segment
        end  demo               ;Start program execution with DEMO
```

10.6 Determining the Type of Video Card

Whenever you want to access video card hardware or use a BIOS function which is only available in special versions of the BIOS, you should first ensure that the card in question is actually installed in the system. If your program doesn't make such a test, then the result may not be what you wanted to appear on the screen.

It is especially important for an application program to recognize the type of video card installed, if your program is supposed to work the same on all types of cards while still directly accessing video hardware. The output routines need this information to make optimum use of the special properties of the given card.

Remember that the PC can have both a monochrome video card (MDA, HGC or EGA with a monochrome monitor) and a color video card (EGA, VGA, or CGA) installed, although only one of the two cards may be active at one time.

Combinations allowable for PC video cards					
	VGA	EGA	HGC	CGA	MDA
VGA			■		■
EGA			■	■	■
HGC	■	■		■	
CGA		■	■		■
MDA	■	■		■	

We need to find out what video cards are installed. There are no BIOS or DOS functions for doing this, nor are there any variables we can read. We have to write an assembly language routine which checks the existence of different video cards. We can refer to the documentation for the various cards, since most manufacturers include some procedure for determining if their card is in use. It is important to keep the test specific (i.e., it does not return a positive result if a certain type of video card is not installed). This presents problems for EGA and VGA cards, which can emulate CGA or MDA cards with the appropriate monitor, and are difficult to distinguish from true CGA or MDA cards.

All of the tests described here are found at the end of this section in the form of two assembly language programs intended for use with C and Pascal programs. The functions place the type of video card installed and the type of monitor connected to it into an array to which the function is passed a pointer. If two video cards are installed, their order in the array indicates which one is active.

The following cards can be detected by the assembly language routine:

- MDA cards
- CGA cards
- HGC cards

- EGA cards
- VGA cards

Since the assembly language routine checks selectively for the existence of a certain video card, there is a separate subroutine for each type of video card. It bears the name of the video card for which it tests. These routines have names like TEST_EGA, TEST_VGA, etc. The tests could be called sequentially, but certain tests can be excluded if we know they would return a negative result. This is case for the CGA test, for example, if an EGA or VGA card has already been detected and is connected to a high-resolution color monitor. A CGA card cannot be installed alongside such a card, so there is no point in testing for it.

There is a flag for each test which determines whether or not the test will be performed. Before the first test, the VGA test, all of the flags are set to 1 so that all of the tests will be performed in order. During the testing, certain flags can be set to 0 for reasons mentioned above, and the corresponding tests will not be made.

VGA test

The tests begin with the VGA test. It is very easy because there is a special function in the VGA BIOS, sub-function 00H of function 1AH, which returns precisely the information that the assembly language routine needs. The information is available only if a VGA card and hence a VGA BIOS is installed. This is the case if the value 1AH is found in the AL register after the call. If the test routine encounters a different value there, the VGA test will be terminated and the other tests will be performed. This indicates that a VGA card is not installed.

After this function is called, the BL register contains a special device code for the active video card and the BH register contains a code for the inactive card. The following codes can occur:

Code	Meaning
00H	No video card
01H	MDA card/monochrome monitor
02H	CGA card/color monitor
03H	Reserved
04H	EGA card/high-resolution monitor
05H	EGA card/monochrome monitor
06H	Reserved
07H	VGA card/analog monochrome monitor
08H	VGA card/analog color monitor

These codes are separated into values for the video card and the monitor connected to it, and loaded into the array whose address is passed to the assembly language routine. Since this routine already has information about both video cards, the following tests do not have to be performed. The routine executes the monochrome test, however, if the functions discover a monochrome card, since it cannot distinguish between an MDA and HGC card.

EGA test

After the VGA test comes the EGA test, which it performed only if the VGA test was unsuccessful, and thus the EGA flag was not cleared. It uses a function which is found only in the EGA BIOS: sub-function 10H of function 12H. If no EGA card is installed and this function is not available, the value 10H will still be found in the BL register after the function call. In this case the EGA test ends.

If an EGA card is installed, the CL register will contain the settings of the DIP switches on the EGA card after the call. These switches indicate what type of monitor is connected. They are converted to the monitor codes the assembly language routine uses and placed in the array along with the code for the EGA card. The CGA or monochrome test flag is cleared depending on the type of monitor connected. The EGA routine ends.

CGA test

If the CGA flag has not been cleared by the previous tests, the CGA test follows the EGA test. As with the monochrome test, there are no special BIOS functions which can be used and we have to check for the presence of the appropriate hardware. In both routines this is done by calling the routine TEST_6845, which tests to see if the 6845 video controller found on these cards is at the specified port address. On a CGA card this is port address 3D4H, which is passed to the routine TEST_6845.

The only way to test the existence of the CRTC at a given port address is to write some value (other than 0) to one of the CRTC registers and then read it back immediately. If the value read matches the value written, then the CRTC and thus the video card are present. But before writing a value into a CRTC register, we should stop to consider that these registers have a major impact on the construction of the video signals and careless access to them can not only thoroughly confuse the CRTC, it can even harm the monitor. Registers 0 to 9 are out of the question for this test, leaving us with registers 10 to 15, all of which have an effect on the screen contents. The best we can do is registers 10 and 11, which control the starting and ending lines of the cursor.

The assembly language routine first reads the contents of register 10 before it loads any value into this register. After a short pause so that the CRTC can react to the output, the contents of this register are read back. Before the value read is compared to the original value, the old value is first written back into the register so that the test disturbs the screen as little as possible. If the comparison is positive, then a CRTC is present and so is the video card (CGA in this case). The CGA routine responds by loading the code for a color monitor into the array, since this is the only type of monitor which can be used with a CGA card.

Monochrome test

The last test is the monochrome test, which also checks for the existence of a CRTC, this time at port address 3B4H. If it finds a CRTC there, then a monochrome card is installed and we have to figure out if it is an MDA or HGC hard. The status registers of the two cards, at port address 3BAH, are used to determine this. While bit 7 of this register has no significance on the MDA card and its value is thus undefined, it contains a 1 on an HGC card whenever the electron beam is returning across the screen. Since this is not permanent and occurs only at intervals of about two milliseconds, the contents of this bit constantly alternates between 0 and 1.

Hercules

The test routine first reads the contents of this register and masks out bits 0 to 6. The resulting value is used in a maximum of 32768 loop passes, where the value is read again and compared with the original value. If the value changes, meaning that the state of bit 7 changes, then an HGC card is probably installed. If this bit does not change over the course of 32768 loop passes, then an MDA card is in use.

Here again we place the appropriate code for the video card in the array. The monitor code is also set to monochrome, since this is the only monitor which can be connected to an MDA or HGC card.

Primary and secondary video systems

The tests are now over. Now we have to figure out which card is active (primary) and which is inactive (secondary). If the outcome of the VGA test was positive, we can skip this because the VGA BIOS routine determines the active card automatically.

In other cases we can determine the active video card from the current video mode, which can be read with the help of function 0FH of the BIOS video interrupt. If the value seven is returned, then the 80x25 text mode of the monochrome card is active. All of the other modes indicate that a CGA, EGA, or VGA card is active. This information is used to exchange the order of the two entries in the array if it does not match the actual situation.

The assembly language routine returns control to the calling program.

Here we include C and Pascal programs which call the function GetVIOS from the assembly language module, and demonstrate how GetVIOS works.

C listing: VIOSC.C

```
/***********************************************************************/
/*                              V I O S C                              */
/*---------------------------------------------------------------------*/
/*    Task            : Determines the type of video card and monitor  */
/*                      installed in the system.                       */
/*---------------------------------------------------------------------*/
/*    Author          : MICHAEL TISCHER                                */
/*    Developed on    : 10/02/1988                                     */
/*    Last update     : 06/20/1988                                     */
/*---------------------------------------------------------------------*/
/*    (MICROSOFT C)                                                    */
/*    Creation        : CL /AS /c VIOSC.C                              */
/*                      LINK VIOSC VIOSCA                              */
/*    Call            : VIOSC                                          */
/*---------------------------------------------------------------------*/
/*    (BORLAND TURBO C)                                                */
/*    Creation        : Create project file made of the following:     */
/*                      VIOSC                                          */
/*                      VIOSCA.OBJ                                     */
/*    Info            : Some cards may return errors or "unknown"      */
/***********************************************************************/

/*== Declarations of external functions ================================*/

extern void get_vios( struct vios * );

/*== Type defs ========================================================*/

typedef unsigned char BYTE;                           /* Create a byte */

/*== Structures =======================================================*/

struct vios {          /* Describes video card and attached monitor */
             BYTE vcard,
                  monitor;
            };

/*== Constants ========================================================*/

/*-- Constants for the video card ------------------------------------*/

#define NO_VIOS    0                                  /* No video card */
#define VGA        1                                       /* VGA card */
#define EGA        2                                       /* EGA card */
#define MDA        3                      /* Monochrome Display Adapter */
#define HGC        4                        /* Hercules Graphics Card */
#define CGA        5                        /* Color Graphics Adapter */

/*-- Constants for monitor type --------------------------------------*/

#define NO_MON     0                                     /* No monitor */
#define MONO       1                             /* Monochrome monitor */
#define COLOR      2                                  /* Color monitor */
#define EGA_HIRES  3                     /* High-res/multisync monitor */
#define ANLG_MONO  4                      /* Analog monochrome monitor */
#define ANLG_COLOR 5                           /* Analog color monitor */

/***********************************************************************/
/**                           MAIN  PROGRAM                           **/
/***********************************************************************/

void main()

{
 static char *vcnames[] = {          /* Pointer to the video card name */
                          "VGA",
                          "EGA",
```

```
                               "MDA",
                               "HGC",
                               "CGA"
                              };

  static char *monnames[] = {    /* Pointer to the monitor type's name */
                               "monochrome monitor",
                               "color monitor",
                               "high-res/multisync monitor",
                               "analog monochrome monitor",
                               "analog color monitor"
                              };

  struct vios vsys[2];                          /* Vector for GET_VIOS */

  get_vios( vsys );                          /* Determine video system */
  printf("\nVIOSC (c) 1988 by Michael Tischer\n\n");
  printf("Primary Video System:   %s card/ %s\n",
         vcnames[vsys[0].vcard-1], monnames[vsys[0].monitor-1]);
  if ( vsys[1].vcard != NO_VIOS )  /* Is there secondary video system? */
    printf("Secondary Video System: %s card/ %s\n",
           vcnames[vsys[1].vcard-1], monnames[vsys[1].monitor-1]);
}
```

Assembler listing: VIOSCA.ASM

```
;**********************************************************************;
;*                           V I O S C A                              *;
;*--------------------------------------------------------------------*;
;*    Task            : Creates a function for determining video      *;
;*                      adapter and monitor type, when linked with    *;
;*                      a C program.                                  *;
;*--------------------------------------------------------------------*;
;*    Author          : MICHAEL TISCHER                               *;
;*    Developed on    : 10/02/1988                                    *;
;*    Last update     : 06/20/1989                                    *;
;*--------------------------------------------------------------------*;
;*    Assembly        : MASM VIOSCA;                                  *;
;*                      ... link to a C program                       *;
;**********************************************************************;

;== Constants for VIOS structure ========================================

                                  ;Video card constants
NO_VIOS     = 0                   ;No video card
VGA         = 1                   ;VGA card
EGA         = 2                   ;EGA card
MDA         = 3                   ;Monochrome Display Adapter
HGC         = 4                   ;Hercules Graphics Card
CGA         = 5                   ;Color Graphics Adapter

                                  ;Monitor constants
NO_MON      = 0                   ;No monitor
MONO        = 1                   ;Monochrome monitor
COLOR       = 2                   ;Color monitor
EGA_HIRES   = 3                   ;High-resolution or multisync monitor
ANLG_MONO   = 4                   ;Analog monochrome monitor
ANLG_COLOR  = 5                   ;Analog color monitor

;== Segment declarations for the C program ==============================

IGROUP group _text                ;Addition to program segment
DGROUP group const,_bss,  _data   ;Addition to data segment
       assume CS:IGROUP, DS:DGROUP, ES:DGROUP, SS:DGROUP

CONST  segment word public 'CONST';This segment includes all read-only
CONST  ends                       ;constants

_BSS   segment word public 'BSS'  ;This segment includes all
```

```
_BSS   ends                          ;un-initialized static variables

_DATA  segment word public 'DATA' ;Data segment

vios_tab   equ this byte

           ;-- Conversion table for return values of function 1AH, ---
           ;-- sub-function 00H of the VGA-BIOS                      ---

           db NO_VIOS, NO_MON     ;No video card
           db MDA    , MONO       ;MDA card and monochrome monitor
           db CGA    , COLOR      ;CGA card and color monitor
           db ?      , ?          ;Code 3 unused
           db EGA    , EGA_HIRES  ;EGA card and hi-res monitor
           db EGA    , MONO       ;EGA card and monochrome monitor
           db ?      , ?          ;Code 6 unused
           db VGA    , ANLG_MONO  ;VGA card and analog mono monitor
           db VGA    , ANLG_COLOR ;VGA card and analog color monitor

ega_dips   equ this byte

           ;-- Conversion table for EGA card DIP switch settings -------

           db COLOR, EGA_HIRES, MONO
           db COLOR, EGA_HIRES, MONO

_DATA  ends

;== Program ============================================================

_TEXT  segment byte public 'CODE' ;Program segment

public     _get_vios

;-----------------------------------------------------------------------
;-- GET_VIOS: Determines types of installed video cards ----------------
;-- Call from C : void get_vios( struct vios *vp );
;-- Declaration : struct vios { BYTE vcard, monitor; };
;-- Return value: none
;-- Info        : This example uses function in SMALL memory model

_get_vios  proc near

sframe     struc                  ;Stack access structure
cga_possi  db ?                   ;Local variable
ega_possi  db ?                   ;Local variable
mono_possi db ?                   ;Local variable
bptr       dw ?                   ;Take BP
ret_adr    dw ?                   ;Return address to caller
vp         dw ?                   ;Pointer to first VIOS structure
sframe     ends                   ;End of structure

frame      equ [ bp - cga_possi ] ;Address elements of the structure

           push bp                ;Push BP onto stack
           sub  sp,3              ;Allocate space for local variables
           mov  bp,sp             ;Transfer SP to BP
           push di                ;Push DI onto stack

           mov  frame.cga_possi,1 ;Could be CGA
           mov  frame.ega_possi,1 ;Could be EGA
           mov  frame.mono_possi,1;Could be MDA or HGC

           mov  di,frame.vp       ;Get offset address of structure
           mov  word ptr [di],NO_VIOS    ;Still no video
           mov  word ptr [di+2],NO_VIOS  ;system found

           call test_vga          ;Test for VGA card
           cmp  frame.ega_possi,0 ;EGA card still possible?
           je   gvl               ;NO --> Test for CGA
```

```
            call test_ega         ;Test for EGA card
gv1:        cmp  frame.cga_possi,0 ;CGA card still possible
            je   gv2              ;NO --> Test for MDA/HGC

            call test_cga         ;Test for CGA card
gv2:        cmp  frame.mono_possi,0;MDA or HGC card still possibleh?
            je   gv3              ;NO --> End tests

            call test_mono        ;Test for MDA/HGC cards

            ;-- Determine active video card ----------------------------

gv3:        cmp  byte ptr [di],VGA ;VGA card active?
            je   gvi_end          ;YES, active card already determined
            cmp  byte ptr [di+2],VGA ;VGA card as secondary system?
            je   gvi_end          ;YES, active card already determined

            mov  ah,0Fh           ;Determine active video mode using the
            int  10h              ;BIOS video interrupt

            and  al,7             ;Only modes 0-7 are of interest
            cmp  al,7             ;Monochrome card active?
            jne  gv4              ;NO, in CGA  or EGA mode

            ;-- MDA, HGC, or EGA card (mono) is active ------------------

            cmp  byte ptr [di+1],MONO ;Mono monitor in first structure?
            je   gvi_end          ;YES, Sequence o.k.
            jmp  short switch     ;NO, Change sequence

            ;-- CGA or EGA card currently active -----------------------

gv4:        cmp  byte ptr [di+1],MONO ;Mono monitor in first structure?
            jne  gvi_end          ;NO, Sequence o.k.

switch:     mov  ax,[di]          ;Get contents of first structure
            xchg ax,[di+2]        ;Exchange with second structure
            mov  [di],ax

gvi_end:    pop  di               ;Get DI from stack
            add  sp,3             ;Get local variables from stack
            pop  bp               ;Get BP from stack
            ret                   ;Return to C program

_get_vios   endp

;----------------------------------------------------------------------
;-- TEST_VGA: Determines whether a VGA card is installed

test_vga    proc near

            mov  ax,1a00h         ;Function 1AH, sub-function 00H
            int  10h              ;calls VGA-BIOS
            cmp  al,1ah           ;Is this function supported?
            jne  tvga_end         ;NO --> End routine

            ;-- If function is supported, BH contains the active video --
            ;-- system code; BH contains the inactive video sys. code  --

            mov  cx,bx            ;Move result to CX
            xor  bh,bh            ;Set BH to 0
            or   ch,ch            ;Just one video system?
            je   tvga_1           ;YES --> Convey first system's code

            ;-- Convert code of second system --------------------------

            mov  bl,ch            ;Move second system code to BL
            add  bl,bl            ;Add offset to table
            mov  ax,offset DGROUP:vios_tab[bx] ;Get code from table and
```

```
          mov  [di+2],ax          ;place in caller's structure
          mov  bl,cl              ;Move first system's codes to BL

          ;-- Convert code of first system ---------------------------

tvga_1:   add  bl,bl              ;Add offset to table
          mov  ax,offset DGROUP:vios_tab[bx] ;Get code from table and
          mov  [di],ax            ;place in caller's structure

          mov  frame.cga_possi,0 ;CGA test failed
          mov  frame.ega_possi,0 ;EGA test failed
          mov  frame.mono_possi,0 ;MONO still needs testing

          mov  bx,di              ;Address of active structure
          cmp  byte ptr [bx],MDA ;Monochrome system available?
          je   do_tmono           ;YES --> Execute MDA/HGC test

          add  bx,2               ;Address of inactive structure
          cmp  byte ptr [bx],MDA ;Monochrome system available?
          jne  tvga_end           ;NO --> End routine

do_tmono: mov  word ptr [bx],0   ;Pretend that this system
                                  ;is still unavailable
          mov  frame.mono_possi,1;Execute monochrome test

tvga_end: ret                     ;Back to caller

test_vga  endp

;----------------------------------------------------------------------
;-- TEST_EGA: Determines whether an EGA card is installed

test_ega  proc near

          mov  ah,12h             ;Function 12H
          mov  bl,10h             ;Sub-function 10H
          int  10h                ;Call EGA-BIOS
          cmp  bl,10h             ;Is the function supported?
          je   tega_end           ;NO --> End routine

          ;-- When this function is supported, CL contains the EGA ----
          ;-- card's DIP switch settings                            ----

          mov  al,cl              ;Move DIP switch settings to AL
          shr  al,1               ;Shift one position to the right
          mov  bx,offset DGROUP:ega_dips ;Offset address of table
          xlat                    ;Move element AL from table to AL
          mov  ah,al              ;Move monitor type to AH
          mov  al,EGA             ;It's an EGA card
          call found_it           ;Move data to vector

          cmp  ah,MONO            ;Connected to monochrome monitor?
          je   is_mono            ;YES --> not MDA or HGC

          mov  frame.cga_possi,0 ;Cannot be a CGA card
          jmp  short tega_end    ;End routine

is_mono:  mov  frame.mono_possi,0;If EGA card is connected to a mono
                                  ;monitor, it can be installed as
                                  ;either an HGC or MDA

tega_end: ret                     ;Back to callerr

test_ega  endp

;----------------------------------------------------------------------
;-- TEST_CGA: Determines whether a CGA card is installed

test_cga  proc near
```

```
          mov  dx,3D4h            ;CGA tests port addr. of CRTC addr.
          call test_6845          ;reg., to see if 6845 is installed
          jc   tega_end           ;NO --> End test

          mov  al,CGA             ;YES --> CGA is installed
          mov  ah,COLOR           ;CGA has color monitor attached
          jmp  found_it           ;Transfer data to vector

test_cga  endp

;---------------------------------------------------------------------
;-- TEST_MONO: Checks for the existence of an MDA or HGC card

test_mono proc near

          mov  dx,3B4h            ;Check port address of CRTC addr. reg.
          call test_6845          ;with MONO to see if there's a 6845
                                  ;installed
          jc   tega_end           ;NO --> End test

          ;-- If there is a monochrome video card installed, the ------
          ;-- following determines whether it's an MDA or an HGC ------

          mov  dl,0BAh            ;Read MONO status port using 3BAH
          in   al,dx              ;
          and  al,80h             ;Check bit 7 only and
          mov  ah,al              ;move to AH

          ;-- If contents of bit 7 change during one of the following -
          ;-- readings, the card is handled as an HGC                 -

          mov  cx,8000h           ;Maximum of 32768 loop executionse
test_hgc: in   al,dx              ;Read status port
          and  al,80h             ;Check bit 7 only
          cmp  al,ah              ;Contents changed?
          jne  is_hgc             ;Bit 7 = 1 --> HGC
          loop test_hgc           ;Continue loop

          mov  al,MDA             ;Bit 7 <> 1 --> MDA
          jmp  set_mono           ;Set parameters

is_hgc:   mov  al,HGC             ;Bit 7 = 1 --> ist HGC
set_mono: mov  ah,MONO            ;MDA/HGC on mono monitor
          jmp  found_it           ;Set parameters

test_mono endp

;---------------------------------------------------------------------
;-- TEST_6845: Sets carry flag if no 6845 exists in port address of DX

test_6845 proc near

          mov  al,0Ah             ;Register 10
          out  dx,al              ;Register number of CRTC address reg.
          inc  dx                 ;DX now in CRTC data register

          in   al,dx              ;Get contents of register 10
          mov  ah,al              ;and move to AH

          mov  al,4Fh             ;Any value
          out  dx,al              ;Write to register 10

          mov  cx,100             ;Short delay loop--gives 6845 time
wait:     loop wait               ;to react

          in   al,dx              ;Read contents of register 10
          xchg al,ah              ;Exchange AH and AL
          out  dx,al              ;Send old valuen

          cmp  ah,4Fh             ;Written value read?
```

```
            je   t6845_end          ;YES --> End test

            stc                     ;NO --> Set carry flag

t6845_end:  ret                     ;Back from caller

test_6845   endp

;----------------------------------------------------------------------
;-- FOUND_IT: Transfers video card type to AL and monitor type to  -----
;--          AH in the video vector                                -----

found_it    proc near

            mov bx,di               ;Address of active structure
            cmp word ptr [bx],0     ;Video system already onboard?
            je  set_data            ;NO --> Data in active structure

            add bx,2                ;YES, Address of inactive structure

set_data:   mov [bx],ax             ;Place data in structure
            ret                     ;Back to caller

found_it    endp

;----------------------------------------------------------------------

_text       ends                    ;End of code segment
            end                     ;End of program
```

Pascal listing: VIOSP.PAS

```
{*********************************************************************}
{*                              V I O S P                            *}
{*-------------------------------------------------------------------*}
{*    Task             : Returns the type of video card installed.   *}
{*-------------------------------------------------------------------*}
{*    Author           : MICHAEL TISCHER                             *}
{*    Developed on     :  10/02/1988                                 *}
{*    Last update      :  06/19/1989                                 *}
{*-------------------------------------------------------------------*}
{*    Info             : Some of the values given here may not coincide *}
{*                       with some video cards (e.g., some CGA cards *}
{*                       may return "Unknown card").                 *}
{*********************************************************************}

program VIOSP;


{$L c:\masm\viospa}                              { Link assembler module }
                                        { Change path to suit your DOS needs }
const NO_VIOS     = 0;                                     { No video card }
      VGA         = 1;                                        { VGA card }
      EGA         = 2;                                        { EGA card }
      MDA         = 3;                        { Monochrome Display Adapter }
      HGC         = 4;                            { Hercules Graphics Card }
      CGA         = 5;                            { Color Graphics Adapter }

      NO_MON      = 0;                                        { No monitor }
      MONO        = 1;                                { Monochrome monitor }
      COLOR       = 2;                                     { Color monitor }
      EGA_HIRES   = 3;                           { High-resolution monitor }
      ANLG_MONO   = 4;                         { Monochrome analog monitor }
      ANLG_COLOR  = 5;                              { Color analog monitor }

type Vios = record            { Describes video card and attached monitor }
              VCard,
              Monitor : byte;
             end;
```

```
    ViosPtr = ^Vios;                    { Pointer to a VIOS structure }

procedure GetVios( vp : ViosPtr ) ; external ;

var VidSys : array[1..2] of Vios;  { Array containing video structures }

{*********************************************************************}
{* PrintSys: Gives information about a video system                  *}
{* Input    : - VCARD: Code number of the video card                 *}
{*            - MON  : Code number of the attached monitor           *}
{* Output   : none                                                   *}
{*********************************************************************}

procedure PrintSys( VCard, Mon : byte );

begin
  write(' ');
  case VCard of
    NO_VIOS : write('Unknown');                   { For "other" code }
    VGA : write('VGA');
    EGA : write('EGA');
    MDA : write('MDA');
    CGA : write('CGA');
    HGC : write('HGC');
  end;
  write(' card/ ');
  case Mon of
    NO_MON : write('unknown monitor');          { For "other" monitors }
    MONO        : writeln('monochrome monitor');
    COLOR       : writeln('color monitor');
    EGA_HIRES   : writeln('high-resolution monitor');
    ANLG_MONO   : writeln('monochrome analog monitor');
    ANLG_COLOR  : writeln('color analog monitor');
  end;
end;

{*********************************************************************}
{**                           MAIN  PROGRAM                         **}
{*********************************************************************}

begin
  GetVios( @VidSys );                       { Check installed video card }
  writeln('VIOSP  -  (c) 1988 by MICHAEL TISCHER');
  write('Primary video system: ');
  PrintSys( VidSys[1].VCard, VidSys[1].Monitor );
  writeln(#13#10);
  if VidSys[2].VCard <> NO_VIOS then  { Second video system installed? }
    begin                                                        { YES }
      write('Secondary video system:');
      PrintSys( VidSys[2].VCard, VidSys[2].Monitor );
      writeln(#13#10);
    end;
end.
```

Assembler listing: VIOSPA.ASM

```
;*********************************************************************;
;*                            V I O S P A                            *;
;*-------------------------------------------------------------------*;
;*    Task            : Creates a function for determining the type  *;
;*                      of video card installed on a system. This    *;
;*                      routine must be assembled into an OBJ file,  *;
;*                      then linked to a Turbo Pascal (4.0) program. *;
;*-------------------------------------------------------------------*;
;*    Author          : MICHAEL TISCHER                              *;
;*    Developed on    : 10/02/1988                                   *;
;*    Last update     : 06/19/1989                                   *;
;*-------------------------------------------------------------------*;
;*    assembly        : MASM VIOSPA;                                 *;
```

```
;*                    ... Link to a Turbo Pascal program           *;
;*                        using the {$L VIOSPA} compiler directive *;
;*******************************************************************;

;== Constants for the VIOS structure ===============================

                                   ;Video card constants
NO_VIOS     = 0                    ;No video card/unrecognized card
VGA         = 1                    ;VGA card
EGA         = 2                    ;EGA card
MDA         = 3                    ;Monochrome Display Adapter
HGC         = 4                    ;Hercules Graphics Card
CGA         = 5                    ;Color Graphics Adapter

                                   ;Monitor constants
NO_MON      = 0                    ;No monitor/unrecognized code
MONO        = 1                    ;Monochrome monitor
COLOR       = 2                    ;Color Monitor
EGA_HIRES   = 3                    ;High-resolution/multisync monitor
ANLG_MONO   = 4                    ;Monochrome analog monitor
ANLG_COLOR  = 5                    ;Analog color monitor

;== Data segment ===================================================

DATA   segment word public         ;Turbo data segment

DATA   ends

;== Code segment ===================================================

CODE       segment byte public     ;Turbo code segment

           assume cs:CODE, ds:DATA

public     getvios

;-- Initialized global variables must be placed in the code segment ----

vios_tab   equ this word

           ;-- Conversion table for supplying return values of VGA  ----
           ;-- BIOS function 1A(h), sub-function 00(h)              ----

           db NO_VIOS, NO_MON      ;No video card
           db MDA    , MONO        ;MDA card/monochrome monitor
           db CGA    , COLOR       ;CGA card/color monitor
           db ?      , ?           ;Code 3 unused
           db EGA    , EGA_HIRES   ;EGA card/hi-res monitor
           db EGA    , MONO        ;EGA card/monochrome monitor
           db ?      , ?           ;Code 6 unused
           db VGA    , ANLG_MONO   ;VGA card/analog mono monitor
           db VGA    , ANLG_COLOR  ;VGA card/analog color monitor

ega_dips   equ this byte

           ;-- Conversion table for EGA card DIP switches -----

           db COLOR, EGA_HIRES, MONO
           db COLOR, EGA_HIRES, MONO

;-------------------------------------------------------------------
;-- GETVIOS: Determines type(s) of installed video card(s) ---------
;-- Pascal call : GetVios ( vp : ViosPtr ); external;
;-- Declaration : Type Vios = record VCard, Monitor: byte;
;-- Return Value: None

getvios  proc near

sframe     struc                   ;Stack access structure
cga_possi  db ?                    ;local variables
```

```
ega_possi  db ?                    ;local variables
mono_possi db ?                    ;local variables
bptr       dw ?                    ;BPTR
ret_adr    dw ?                    ;Return address of calling program
vp         dd ?                    ;Pointer to first VIOS structure
sframe     ends                    ;End of structure

frame      equ [ bp - cga_possi ] ;Address elements of structure

           push bp                 ;Push BP onto stack
           sub  sp,3               ;Allocate memory for local variables
           mov  bp,sp              ;Transfer SP to BP

           mov  frame.cga_possi,1 ;Is it a CGA?
           mov  frame.ega_possi,1 ;Is it an EGA?
           mov  frame.mono_possi,1;Is it an MDA or HGC?

           mov  di,word ptr frame.vp     ;Get offset addr. of structure
           mov  word ptr [di],NO_VIOS    ;No video system or unknown
           mov  word ptr [di+2],NO_VIOS  ;system found

           call test_vga           ;Test for VGA card
           cmp  frame.ega_possi,0 ;Or is it an EGA card?
           je   gv1                ;NO -->Go to CGA test

           call test_ega           ;Test for EGA card
gv1:       cmp  frame.cga_possi,0 ;Or is it a CGA card?
           je   gv2                ;NO --> Go to MDA/HGC test

           call test_cga           ;Test for CGA card
gv2:       cmp  frame.mono_possi,0;Or is it an MDA or HGC card?
           je   gv3                ;NO --> End tests

           call test_mono          ;Test for MDA/HGC card

           ;-- Determine video configuration ---------------------------

gv3:       cmp  byte ptr [di],VGA ;VGA card?
           je   gvi_end            ;YES --> Active card already indicated
           cmp  byte ptr [di+2],VGA;VGA card part of secondary system?
           je   gvi_end            ;YES --> Active card already indicated

           mov  ah,0Fh             ;Determine video mode using BIOS video
           int  10h                ;interrupt

           and  al,7               ;Only modes 0-7 are of interest
           cmp  al,7               ;Mono card active?
           jne  gv4                ;NO --> CGA or EGA mode

           ;-- MDA, HGC or EGA card (mono) currently active ------------

           cmp  byte ptr [di+1],MONO ;Mono monitor in first structure?
           je   gvi_end            ;YES, Sequence o.k.
           jmp  short switch       ;NO, Switch sequence

           ;-- CGA or EGA card currently active ------------------------

gv4:       cmp  byte ptr [di+1],MONO ;Mono monitor in first structure?
           jne  gvi_end            ;NO -->Sequence o.k.

switch:    mov  ax,[di]            ;Get contents of first structure
           xchg ax,[di+2]          ;Switch with second structure
           mov  [di],ax

gvi_end:   add  sp,3               ;Add local variables from stack
           pop  bp                 ;Pop BP off of stack
           ret  4                  ;Clear variables off of stack;
                                   ;Return to Turbo
getvios    endp
```

```
;-----------------------------------------------------------------------
;-- TEST_VGA: Determines whether a VGA card is installed

test_vga   proc near

           mov  ax,1a00h          ;Function 1A(h), sub-function 00(h)
           int  10h               ;Call VGA-BIOS
           cmp  al,1ah            ;Function supported?
           jne  tvga_end          ;NO --> End routine

           ;-- If function is supported, BL contains the code of the ---
           ;-- active video system, while BH contains the code of    ---
           ;-- the inactive video system                             ---

           mov  cx,bx             ;Move result in CX
           xor  bh,bh             ;Set BH to 0
           or   ch,ch             ;Only one video system?
           je   tvga_1            ;YES --> Display first system's code

           ;-- Convert code of second system ---------------------------

           mov  bl,ch             ;Move second system's code to BL
           add  bl,bl             ;Add offset to table
           mov  ax,vios_tab[bx]   ;Get code from table and move into
           mov  [di+2],ax         ;caller's structure
           mov  bl,cl             ;Move first system's code into BL

           ;-- Convert code of second system ---------------------------

tvga_1:    add  bl,bl             ;Add offset to table
           mov  ax,vios_tab[bx]   ;Get code from table
           mov  [di],ax           ;and move into caller's structure

           mov  frame.cga_possi,0 ;CGA test fail?
           mov  frame.ega_possi,0 ;CGA test fail?
           mov  frame.mono_possi,0 ;Test for mono

           mov  bx,di             ;Address of active structure
           cmp  byte ptr [bx],MDA ;Monochrome system online?
           je   do_tmono          ;YES --> Execute MDA/HGC test

           add  bx,2              ;Address of inactive structure
           cmp  byte ptr [bx],MDA ;Monochrome system online?
           jne  tvga_end          ;NO --> End routine

do_tmono:  mov  word ptr [bx],0   ;Emulate if this system
                                  ;isn't available
           mov  frame.mono_possi,1;Execute monochrome test

tvga_end:  ret                    ;Return to caller

test_vga   endp

;-----------------------------------------------------------------------
;-- TEST_EGA: Determine whether an EGA card is installed

test_ega   proc near

           mov  ah,12h            ;Function 12(h)
           mov  bl,10h            ;Sub-function 10(h)
           int  10h               ;Call EGA-BIOS
           cmp  bl,10h            ;Is this function supported?
           je   tega_end          ;NO --> End routine

           ;-- If the function IS supported, CL contains the        ----
           ;-- EGA card DIP switch settings                          ----

           mov  bl,cl             ;Move DIP switches to BL
           shr  bl,1              ;Shift one position to the right
           xor  bh,bh             ;Index high byte to 0
```

```
          mov  ah,ega_dips[bx]    ;Get element from table
          mov  al,EGA             ;Is it an EGA card?
          call found_it           ;Transfer data to the vector

          cmp  ah,MONO            ;Mono monitor connected?
          je   is_mono            ;YES --> Not MDA or HGC

          mov  frame.cga_possi,0 ;No CGA card possible
          jmp  short tega_end     ;End routine

is_mono:  mov  frame.mono_possi,0;EGA can either emulate MDA or HGC,
                                  ;if mono monitor is attached

tega_end: ret                     ;Back to caller

test_ega  endp

;----------------------------------------------------------------------
;-- TEST_CGA: Determines whether a CGA card is installed

test_cga  proc near

          mov  dx,3D4h            ;Port addr. of CGA's CRTC addr. reg.
          call test_6845          ;Test for installed 6845 CRTC
          jc   tega_end           ;NO --> End test

          mov  al,CGA             ;YES, CGA installed
          mov  ah,COLOR           ;CGA uses color monitor
          jmp  found_it           ;Transfer data to vector

test_cga  endp

;----------------------------------------------------------------------
;-- TEST_MONO: Checks for MDA or HGC card

test_mono proc near

          mov  dx,3B4h            ;Port addr. of MONO's CRTC addr. reg.
          call test_6845          ;Test for installed 6845 CRTC
          jc   tega_end           ;NO --> End test

          ;-- Monochrome video card installed                    ------
          ;--
          mov  dl,0BAh            ;MONO status port at 3BA(h)
          in   al,dx              ;Read status port
          and  al,80h             ;Separate bit 7 and
          mov  ah,al              ;move to AH

          ;-- If the contents of bit 7 in the status port change   ----
          ;-- during the following readings, it is handled as an   ----
          ;-- HGC                                                  ----

          mov  cx,8000h           ;maximum 32768 loop executions
test_hgc: in   al,dx              ;Read status port
          and  al,80h             ;Isolate bit 7
          cmp  al,ah              ;Contents changed?
          jne  is_hgc             ;Bit 7 = 1 --> HGC
          loop test_hgc           ;Continue

          mov  al,MDA             ;Bit 7 <> 1 --> MDA
          jmp  set_mono           ;Set parameters

is_hgc:   mov  al,HGC             ;Bit 7 = 1 --> HGC
set_mono: mov  ah,MONO            ;MDA and HGC set as mono screen
          jmp  found_it           ;Set parameters

test_mono endp

;----------------------------------------------------------------------
;-- TEST_6845: Returns set carry flag if 6845 doesn't lie in the
```

```
;--           port address in DX

test_6845  proc near

           mov  al,0Ah           ;Register 10
           out  dx,al            ;Register number in CRTC address reg.
           inc  dx               ;DX now in CRTC data register

           in   al,dx            ;Get contents of register 10
           mov  ah,al            ;and move to AH

           mov  al,4Fh           ;Any value
           out  dx,al            ;Write to register 10

           mov  cx,100           ;Short wait loop to which
wait:      loop wait             ;6845 can react

           in   al,dx            ;Read contents of register 10
           xchg al,ah            ;Exchange Ah and AL
           out  dx,al            ;Send value

           cmp  ah,4Fh           ;Written value been read?
           je   t6845_end        ;YES --> End test

           stc                   ;NO --> Set carry flag

t6845_end: ret                   ;Back to caller

test_6845  endp

;----------------------------------------------------------------------
;-- FOUND_IT: Transfers type of video card to AL and type of       -----
;--           monitor in AH in the video vector                    -----

found_it   proc near

           mov bx,di             ;Address of active structure
           cmp word ptr [bx],0   ;Video system already  onboard?
           je  set_data          ;NO --> Data in  active structure

           add bx,2              ;YES --> Address of inactive structure

set_data:  mov [bx],ax           ;Place data in structure
           ret                   ;Back to caller

found_it   endp

;----------------------------------------------------------------------

code       ends                  ;End of code segment
           end                   ;End of program
```

10.7 Accessing Video RAM from High Level Languages

The beginning of this chapter mentioned the option of video RAM access from high level languages. This would allow the developer to write screen output routines for high level languages that would execute faster than output commands available to the languages, BIOS functions, or DOS functions. This option would be particularly attractive if it meant that we could write these routines without assembly language programming.

The demonstration programs below implement direct video RAM access routines which display a string on the screen. Althrough there are some major differences between the three programs as a result of the differences between the respective languages (BASIC, Pascal and C), all three programs contain the same elements.

Initialization

Each program includes an initialization routine which determines the segment address of the video RAM. The routine has a variable which contains the address of the CRTC address register. There is a direct relationship between the video RAM and this address register: just as this register is always at port address 3B4H, the video RAM on a monochrome card is always found at segment address B000H. This combination also applies to color cards, where the address register is at port address 3D4H and the video RAM is at segment address B800H. If we know the port address of the CRTC address register, we can determine the segment address of the video RAM. Once we have determined this address, we can place it in a global variable and execute the initialization routine.

Output

All three programs have an output routine which uses the segment address we determined above. Each time the routine displays something, it determines the starting address of the video page currently displayed on the screen. This ensures that the output appears on the visible screen, and not on an undisplayed video page. We can find this from the CRT_START BIOS variable. This variable is located at address 0040:004E, and specifies the offset address of the displayed video page relative to the video page found at offset address 0000H.

After this address is determined, we can access the video RAM. The method used in the program depends on the given programming language. Let's look at each program in more detail.

The C implementation

From a programming point of view, this is the cleanest of the three implementations because the video RAM can be treated as a normal variable in C. We first define the structure VELB, which describes the ASCII/attribute pair as it appears in the video RAM. We create a new data type, VP, to act as a pointer to this structure. It is important that this pointer be of type FAR because these structures are in the video RAM and therefore outside the C data segment. Smaller memory models in C require the declaration of this pointer as a FAR pointer.

The global variable VPTR is initialized to be a pointer to the first ASCII/attribute pair in page 0 of the video RAM. This occurs in the INIT_DPRINT routine. It is used within the DPRINT function (the function used for display) as the basis for addressing the characters within the video RAM.

The DPRINT function loads the LPTR pointer with the address of the screen output position passed to the routine. LPTR is first loaded with the contents of the global variable VPTR, and then with the offset address of the active video page, as found in the CRT_START BIOS variable. LPTR must be cast as a BYTE pointer because the contents of the BIOS variable refers to bytes, and not to VELB structures. If the cast operator were missing, the C compiler would generate code which would first multiply the contents of the BIOS variable by the length of the VELB structure before adding it, resulting in the wrong value.

We can now add the display position to this pointer. The output position is passed to DPRINT as row and column coordinates. The video RAM is treated as an array of 2000 components, each of which is a VELB structure. Since we have computed the base address of the array in LPTR, all we need is to index into it. We multiply the row coordinate by 80 (columns per line) and then add the column coordinate. Finally we have a pointer to the output position in video RAM, which we can treat like any other C pointer.

Each time through, the loop increments the pointer to the next VELB structure. We write the ASCII code of the character and the color passed to DPRINT to the specified address. This repeats until the program reaches the end of the string.

C listing: DVIC.C

```
/**********************************************************************/
/*                              D V I C                               */
/*--------------------------------------------------------------------*/
/*    Task           : Demonstrates direct access to video RAM.       */
/*--------------------------------------------------------------------*/
/*    Author         : MICHAEL TISCHER                                */
/*    Developed on   : 10/01/1988                                     */
/*    Last update    : 06/21/1989                                     */
/*--------------------------------------------------------------------*/
/*    (MICROSOFT C)                                                   */
/*    Creation       : CL /AS DVIC.C                                  */
/*    Call           : DVIC                                           */
/*--------------------------------------------------------------------*/
/*    (BORLAND TURBO C)                                               */
/*    Creation       : RUN menu command (no project file needed)      */
/**********************************************************************/

/*== Include files ===================================================*/

#include <dos.h>
#include <stdlib.h>
#include <string.h>
#include <stdarg.h>
#include <bios.h>
```

```
/*== Type definitions ==============================================*/

typedef unsigned char BYTE;                        /* Create a byte */
typedef struct velb far * VP;         /* VP = FAR pointer in video RAM */
typedef BYTE BOOL;                      /* similar to BOOLEAN in Pascal */

/*== Structures ===================================================*/

struct velb {           /* Describes a 2-byte position on the screen */
             BYTE character,                          /* ASCII code */
                  attribute;                 /* Character attribute */
            };

/*== Macros =======================================================*/

/*-- MK_FP creates a FAR pointer to an object from a segment   -------*/
/*-- address and offset address                                -------*/

#ifndef MK_FP                                  /* MK_FP not defined yet? */
#define MK_FP(seg, ofs) ((void far *) ((unsigned long) (seg)<<16|(ofs)))
#endif

#define COLOR(VG, HG) ((VG << 3) + HG)

/*== Constants ====================================================*/

#define TRUE  1                         /* Constants for use with BOOL */
#define FALSE 0

/*-- The following constants return pointers to variables from the ---*/
/*-- BIOS variable segment at segment address 0x40                  ---*/

#define CRT_START ((unsigned far *) MK_FP(0x40, 0x4E))
#define ADDR_6845 ((unsigned far *) MK_FP(0x40, 0x63))

#define NORMAL       0x07          /* Character attribute definition */
#define BRIGHT       0x0f          /*  Based on monochrome video card*/
#define INVERSE      0x70
#define UNDERSCORED  0x01
#define BLINKING     0x80

#define BLACK        0x00         /* Color attributes for color card */
#define BLUE         0x01
#define GREEN        0x02
#define COBALTBLUE   0x03
#define RED          0x04
#define VIOLET       0x05
#define BROWN        0x06
#define LIGHTGRAY    0x07
#define DARKGRAY     0x01
#define LIGHTBLUE    0x09
#define LIGHTGREEN   0x0A
#define LIGHTCOBALT  0x0B
#define LIGHTRED     0x0C
#define LIGHTVIOLET  0x0D
#define YELLOW       0x0E
#define WHITE        0x0F

/*== Global variables =============================================*/

VP vptr;                    /* Pointer to first character in video RAM */

/*********************************************************************
*  Function          : D P R I N T                                    *
**------------------------------------------------------------------**
*  Task              : Writes a string directly to video RAM          *
*                                                                     *
*  Input parameters : - COLUMN   = Output column                      *
*                     - LINES    = Output row                         *
*                     - COLOR    = Character attribute                *
```

```
*                       - STRING    = Pointer to string                  *
*  Return value        : None                                            *
**************************************************************************/

void dprint(BYTE column, BYTE lines, BYTE color, char * string)

{
 register VP lptr;                    /* Floating pointer in video RAM */
 register BYTE i;                    /* Points to number of characters */

 /*-- Set pointer to output position in video RAM --------------------*/
 lptr = (VP) ((BYTE far *) vptr + *CRT_START) + lines * 80 + column;
 for (i=0 ; *string ; ++lptr, ++i)                /* Execute string */
  {
   lptr->character = *(string++);           /* Character in video RAM */
   lptr->attribute = color;                /* Set character attribute */
  }
}

/*************************************************************************
*  Function            : I N I T _ D P R I N T                           *
**---------------------------------------------------------------------**
*  Task                : Determines video RAM segment address for DPRINT *
*  Input parameters    : None                                            *
*  Return value        : None                                            *
*  Info                : Allocates segment address of video RAM in VPTR  *
*                        global variable                                 *
**************************************************************************/

void init_dprint()

{
 vptr = (VP) MK_FP( (*ADDR_6845 == 0x3B4) ? 0xB000 : 0xB800, 0 );
}

/*************************************************************************
*  Function            : C L S                                           *
**---------------------------------------------------------------------**
*  Task                : Clears the screen with the help of DPRINT       *
*                                                                        *
*  Input parameters    : - COLOR    = Character attribute                *
*  Return value        : None                                            *
**************************************************************************/

void cls( BYTE color )

{
 static char blankline[81] =
  { ' ',' ',' ',' ',' ',' ',' ',' ',' ',' ',' ',' ',' ',' ',' ',
    ' ',' ',' ',' ',' ',' ',' ',' ',' ',' ',' ',' ',' ',' ',' ',
    ' ',' ',' ',' ',' ',' ',' ',' ',' ',' ',' ',' ',' ',' ',' ',
    ' ',' ',' ',' ',' ',' ',' ',' ',' ',' ',' ',' ',' ',' ',' ',
    ' ',' ',' ',' ',' ',' ',' ',' ',' ',' ',' ',' ',' ',' ',' ',
    ' ',' ',' ',' ',' ','\0'
  };

 register BYTE i;                                    /* Loop counter */

 for (i=0; i<24; ++i)                           /* Execute each line */
  dprint(0, i, color, blankline);               /* Display blank line */
}

/*************************************************************************
*  Function            : N O K E Y                                       *
**---------------------------------------------------------------------**
*  Task                : Tests for a keypress                            *
*  Input parameters    : None                                            *
*  Return value        : TRUE if a key is pressed, otherwise FALSE       *
**************************************************************************/
```

```
BOOL nokey()

{
#ifdef __TURBOC__                         /* Compiling this with TURBO C? */
 return( bioskey( 1 ) == 0 );             /* YES, read keyboard from BIOS */
#else                                              /* Using Microsoft C */
 return( _bios_keybrd( _KEYBRD_READY ) == 0 );        /* Read from BIOS */
#endif
}

/**********************************************************************/
/**                            MAIN  PROGRAM                        **/
/**********************************************************************/

void main()
{
 BYTE firstcol,                 /* Color of first square on the screen */
      color,                                /* Color of current square */
      column,                               /* Current output position */
      lines;

 init_dprint();              /* Determine segment address of video RAM */
 cls( COLOR(BLACK, GREEN) );                             /* Clear screen */
 dprint(22, 0, WHITE, "DVIC  - (c) 1988 by Michael Tischer");
 firstcol = BLACK  ;                                 /* Start with black */
 while( nokey() )               /* Repeat until the user presses a key */
  {
   if (++firstcol > WHITE)                         /* Reached last color? */
    firstcol = BLUE;                             /* YES, continue with blue */
   color = firstcol;                       /* Set first color on the screen */

   /*-- Fill screen with squares -------------------------------------*/

   for ( column=0; column < 80; column += 4)
    for (lines=1; lines < 24; lines += 2)
      {
      dprint( column, lines,   color, "████");/* Block characters can */
      dprint( column, lines+1, color, "████");/* be created by press- */
      color = ++color & 15;                   /* ing <Alt><2><1><9>    */
      }
  }
}
```

The Pascal implementation

By using the keyword ABSOLUTE or by linking in a small assembly language routine it would also be possible to treat the video RAM as a normal variable in Turbo Pascal. But there's an easier way.

Turbo Pascal offers the arrays MEMW and MEM for accessing memory which is outside of the data segment of the Turbo Pascal program. The array MEM consists of bytes and the array MEMW of words. The two arrays don't actually exist and are just mapped to the address space, but that doesn't affect their usefulness.

We can write values into the array as well as read from it. This is done with the following statement:

```
MEMW[ segment address : offset address ] := expression
```

or

```
variable := MEMW[ segment address : offset address ]
```

The MEM array might be easier to use for this particular application since we will be alternating between ASCII characters and a constant attribute. However, the output procedure DPrint uses the MEMW array instead, because 16-bit accesses are performed faster than two successive 8-bit accesses on 16-bit machines.

When accessing the MEMW array, DPrint takes the segment address of the video RAM from the variable VSeg, which is initialized at the start of the program in the procedure InitDPrint. As described before, this is done by examining the BIOS variable which contains the port address of the CRTC address register. This and the other BIOS variables are declared using the ABSOLUTE keyword, allowing them to be used in the program like any other global variables.

The offset within the MEMW array is computed from the starting address of the screen page. The coordinates are passed to DPrint, in which the row coordinate is multiplied by 160 and the column coordinate by two. When running through the string to be printed, the memory offset is incremented by two on each pass, moving it one ASCII/attribute pair to the right.

Pascal listing: DVIP.P

```
{**********************************************************************}
{*                              D V I P                               *}
{*--------------------------------------------------------------------*}
{*    Task             : Demonstrates direct access to video RAM from *}
{*                       Turbo Pascal                                 *}
{*--------------------------------------------------------------------*}
{*    Author           : MICHAEL TISCHER                              *}
{*    Developed on     : 10/02/1987                                   *}
{*    Last update      : 06/20/1989                                   *}
{**********************************************************************}

program DVIP;

Uses Crt, Dos;                                { Use CRT and DOS units }

const NORMAL        = $07;              { Define character attributes in }
      LIGHT         = $0f;              { conjunction with monochrome    }
      INVERSE       = $70;              { video card                     }
      UNDERSCORED   = $01;
      BLINKING      = $80;

      BLACK         = $00;             { Color attributes for color card }
      BLUE          = $01;
      GREEN         = $02;
      COBALTBLUE    = $03;
      RED           = $04;
      VIOLET        = $05;
      BROWN         = $06;
      LIGHTGRAY     = $07;
      DARKGRAY      = $01;
      LIGHTBLUE     = $09;
      LIGHTGREEN    = $0A;
      LIGHTCOBALT   = $0B;
      LIGHTRED      = $0C;
      LIGHTVIOLET   = $0D;
      YELLOW        = $0E;
      WHITE         = $0F;

type TextTyp = string[80];

var VSeg : word;                         { Segment address of video RAM }
```

```
{***********************************************************************}
{* InitDPrint: Determines segment address of video RAM for DPrint     *}
{* Input   : none                                                      *}
{* Output  : none                                                      *}
{***********************************************************************}

procedure InitDPrint;

var CRTC_PORT : word absolute $0040:0063;  { Variable in BIOS var.seg. }

begin
  if CRTC_PORT = $3B4 then                  { Monochrome card connected? }
    VSeg := $B000                          { YES, video RAM at B000:0000 }
  else                                      { NO, must be a color card }
    VSeg := $B800;                            { Video RAM at B800:0000 }
end;

{***********************************************************************}
{* DPrint: Writes a string direct into video RAM                       *}
{* Input    : - COLUMN: Output column                                  *}
{*            - LINES : Output line                                    *}
{*            - COLOR : Color (attribute) for individual characters    *}
{*            - STROUT: String to be displayed                         *}
{* Output   : none                                                     *}
{***********************************************************************}

procedure DPrint( Column, Lines, Color : byte; StrOut : TextTyp);

var PAGE_OFS : word absolute $0040:$004E;  { Variable in BIOS var.seg. }
    Offset   : word;             { Pointer to current output position }
    i, j     : byte;                                   { Loop counter }
    Attribute : word;                         { Attribute for output }

begin
  Offset := Lines * 160 + Column * 2 + PAGE_OFS;
  Attribute := Color shl 8;   { High byte for word access to video RAM }
  i := length( StrOut );                      { Determine string length }
  for j:=1 to i do                                   { Execute string }
    begin          { Put character & attribute directly into video RAM }
      memw[VSeg:Offset] := Attribute or ord( StrOut[j] );
      Offset := Offset + 2;  { Set offset to next ASCII/attribute pair }
    end;
end;


{***********************************************************************}
{* Demo: Demonstrates application of DPrint                            *}
{* Input    : none                                                     *}
{* Output   : none                                                     *}
{***********************************************************************}

procedure demo;

var Column,                                  { Current output position }
    Lines,
    Color    : integer;

begin
  TextBackGround( BLACK );                      { Turn background black }
  ClrScr;                                                { Clear screen }
  DPrint( 22, 0, WHITE, 'DVIP  - (c) 1988 by Michael Tischer');
  Randomize;                           { Enable random number generator }
  while not KeyPressed do             { Repeat until user presses a key }
    begin
      Column := Random( 76 );                   { Select column, row and  }
      Lines := Random( 22 ) + 1;                { color at random         }
      Color := Random( 14 ) + 1;
      DPrint( Column, Lines,   Color, '[[[[');{ Block character can be }
```

```
      DPrint( Column, Lines+1, Color, '[[[[');{ created by pressing    }
    end;                                      {<Alt><2><1><9>          }
  ClrScr;                                              { Clear screen }
end;

{***********************************************************************}
{**                          MAIN  PROGRAM                           **}
{***********************************************************************}

begin
  InitDPrint;                         { Initialize output using DPrint }
  Demo;                                           { Demonstrate DPrint }
end.
```

The BASIC implementation

This version doesn't really fulfill its goal, since it is slower than the already slow PRINT command. But we have included it for the sake of completeness, and because it is a good example of how you can access the entire address space of the 8088 from within BASIC.

The commands DEF SEG, PEEK, and POKE are the heart of memory access in BASIC. DEF SEG sets the segment address of the "current" 64K segment. PEEK and POKE can then be used to read and write bytes from or to this segment. This technique is used in the initialization routine at line number 50000, which first defines the BIOS variable segment as the current segment. From there two PEEK commands read the port address of the CRTC address register and the variable VR is loaded with the segment address of the video RAM.

This address is used in the output routine at line number 51000 in combination with the DEF SEG command, which defines the video RAM as the current segment. But first we calculate the offset address in the video RAM by reading the start address of the current screen page from the BIOS variable area and then adding the offset address of the output position within the video RAM. As in the Pascal version, this is calculated by adding the product of the row coordinate (variable CLINE%) by 160 and the column coordinate (COLUMN%) by 2.

BASIC listing: DVIB.B

```
100 '*******************************************************************'
110 '*                              D V I B                            *'
120 '*-----------------------------------------------------------------*'
130 '*  Task           : Demonstrates direct access to video RAM       *'
150 '*  Author         : MICHAEL TISCHER                                *'
160 '*  Developed on   : 10/01/1988                                     *'
170 '*  Last update    : 06/21/1989                                     *'
180 '*******************************************************************'
190 '
200 CLS : KEY OFF
210 GOSUB 50000                      'Determine segment address of video RAM
220 COLUMN%=22 : CLINE%=0 : COL% = 15
230 T$ = "DIVB - (c) 1988 by MICHAEL TISCHER" : GOSUB 51000
240 FCOL% = 0 : T$ = "[[[["            'Define string and starting color
250 A$ = INKEY$ : IF A$<>"" THEN 400    'Repeat until user presses a key
260 FCOL% = FCOL% + 1                            'Increment starting color
270 IF FCOL% > 15 THEN FCOL% = 1              'When FCOL%=16 make FCOL%=1
280 COL% = FCOL%                              'Set color for first square
290 FOR COLUMN%=0 TO 76 STEP 4                  'Execute for each column
300   FOR Z%=1 TO 24 STEP 2                        'Execute for each line
```

```
310     CLINE% = Z% : GOSUB 51000          'Display first line of square
320     CLINE% = Z%+1 : GOSUB 51000              'Display second line
330     COL% = COL% + 1 AND 15                         'Set next color
340   NEXT
350 NEXT
360 GOTO 250
370 '
400 CLS                                                   'Clear screen
410 END
460 '
50000 '**************************************************************'
50010 '* Determine segment address of video RAM                     *'
50020 '*------------------------------------------------------------*'
50030 '* Input  : none                                               *'
50040 '* Output : VR is the segment address of video RAM             *'
50050 '**************************************************************'
50060 '
50070 DEF SEG = &H40              'Segment address of BIOS variable range
50080 VR = PEEK(&H63) + PEEK(&H64) * 256                  'Get CRTC port
50090 IF VR = &H3B4 THEN VR = &HB000 ELSE VR = &HB800
50100 RETURN                                             'Back to caller
50120 '
51000 '**************************************************************'
51010 '* Write string direct into video RAM                          *'
51020 '*------------------------------------------------------------*'
51030 '* Input  : - COLUMN% = the output column                       *'
51040 '*          - CLINE%  = the output line                         *'
51050 '*          - COL%    = string color                            *'
51060 '*          - T$      = the string to be displayed              *'
51070 '* Output : none                                               *'
51080 '**************************************************************'
51090 '
51100 DEF SEG = &H40              'Segment address of BIOS variable range
51110 OF% = PEEK(&H4E) + PEEK(&H4F) * 256     'Starting address of page
51120 OF% = OF% + COLUMN% * 2 + CLINE% * 160  'Offset of first character
51130 DEF SEG = VR                   'Set segment address of video RAM
51140 FOR I%=1 TO LEN(T$)                                'Execute string
51150   POKE OF%, ASC(MID$(T$,I%,1))              'ASCII code in video RAM
51160   POKE OF%+1, COL%                              'Color in video RAM
51170   OF% = OF% + 2                     'Set offset to next character
51180 NEXT
51190 RETURN                                             'Back to caller
51200 '
```

Chapter 11

Accessing and Programming the AT Realtime Clock

The AT has a battery operated realtime clock on the main circuit board. The clock is part of the Motorola MC-146818 processor. This processor also contains 64 bytes of battery backup RAM. This RAM accepts clock data and system configuration data. It can be accessed through port addresses 70H to 7FH. However, only ports 70H and 71H are of interest to the user.

Realtime clock registers

As the following table shows, the clock has thirteen memory registers of interest:

Register	Meaning
0	Current second
1	Alarm second
2	Current minute
3	Alarm minute
4	Current hour
5	Alarm hour
6	Day of the week
7	Number of day
8	Month
9	Year
10	Clock status register A
11	Clock status register B
12	Clock status register C
13	Clock status register D

Every time field (second, minute, hour) has a similar alarm field. These alarm fields allow the programmer to set the clock to trigger an interrupt at a particular time of the current day (more on this later).

Weekday

The day of the week provides the number of the current weekday: The value 1 represents Sunday, the value 2 stands for Monday, 3 for Tuesday, etc.

Year

The year is counted relative to the century (the system assumes 1900). The value 87 in this field represents the year 1987.

The four status registers allow user programming of the clock.

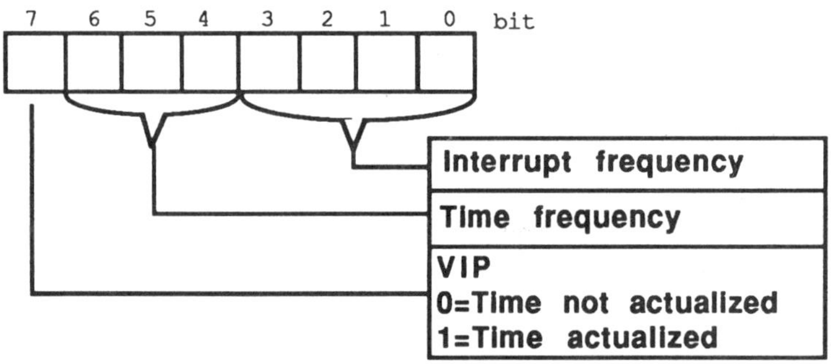

Status register A of the clock

The ROM-BIOS set the two lower fields of these registers during the system boot. The interrupt frequency field has a default value of 0110(b). This value results in an interrupt frequency of 1024 interrupts per second (an interrupt every 976,562 microseconds).

The contents of the time frequency field is 010(b). This field triggers a time frequency of 32,768 kiloHertz.

Bit 7 of the status register is of interest to the programmer in conjunction with these two fields. It indicates whether a second has just elapsed, and increments the time fields (seconds, minutes, hour). If a second hasn't elapsed, this bit contains a 1. This bit is interesting because you can only read the individual time fields when the time is not being updated. Otherwise a minute could pass and the second counter reset to 0 before the minute counter could be incremented. This could cause a time jump from 13:59:59 to 13:59:00, then the correct display of 14:00:01 one second later.

Accessing status register A

Since status register A is a part of the 64-byte RAM, you can access it like any other memory location. First you load the number of the memory location to be accessed into the AL register (in this case, the value 10). Then you pass this value to port 70H using the OUT instruction. The chip recognizes that an access to one of its memory locations occurred. Either an OUT instruction then writes to port 71H or an IN instruction reads the memory contents from port 71H.

The following instructions read or write a memory location in the realtime clock:

```
READ:                           WRITE:
mov    al,Memory_location       mov    al,Memory_location
out    70h,al                   out    70h,al
in     al,71h                   mov    al,New_contents
                                out    71h,al
```

Status register B

Some clock settings can be programmed through status register B. Bit 0 of status register B controls daylight savings time status. When this bit is set to 1, it indicates that daylight savings time is in effect. A value of 0 (the default value for this bit) shows that standard time is in effect.

Bit 1 decides whether the clock should operate in 12-hour or 24-hour mode. In 12-hour mode it switches after every 12 hours (midnight and noon) to 1 o'clock again. The 24-hour mode switches to 1 o'clock after 24 hours. 24-hour mode is active when you boot the system.

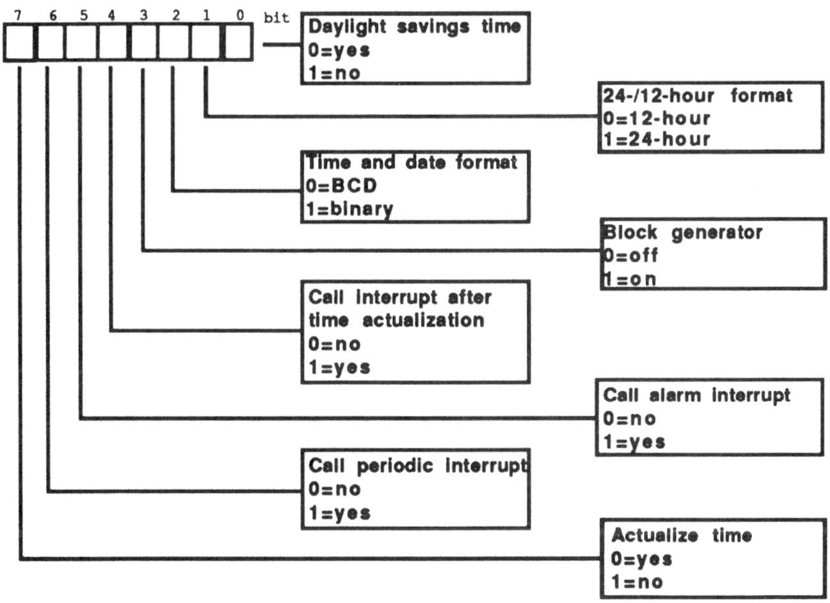

Clock status register B

Bit 2 defines the format in which the time and date fields are stored. If this bit contains a 1, the various dates are stored in binary notation. The year (19)87 is coded as 01010111(b) in BCD format, which is switched on by the value 0 in bit 2. Two numbers are stored in every byte. The higher half is stored in the most significant four bits and the lower half in the least significant four bits.

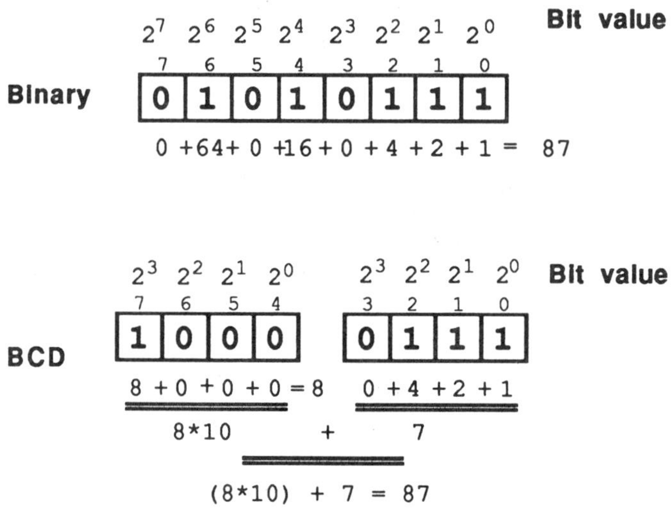

The number 87 in binary and in BCD (Binary Coded Decimal) format

Normally this bit contains a 0 and the numbers are stored in BCD format.

Note: BIOS assumes BCD representation when performing the date function with interrupt 1AH. Application programs which call these functions and obtain the information in binary format instead of the expected BCD may crash. The same applies to the 12-hour/24-hour time measurement, although a change to the 12-hour cycle wouldn't result in as serious consequences as the change in the date.

Bit 4 determines whether an interrupt should be called after the time (and date) update. This bit must contain a 1 if an interrupt should be called. The system suppresses this interrupt by setting this bit to 0 during the booting process.

Bit 5 can trigger an alarm. The clock reads the alarm time from locations 1, 3 and 5 (seconds, minutes and hours) of clock RAM. When the alarm time is reached, an interrupt executes when bit 5 is set to 1. The system suppresses this interrupt when it sets bit 5 to 0 during the booting process.

Bit 6 controls periodic interrupt calls when it is set to 1. The frequency of the interrupt calls depends on the interrupt frequency coded into bits 0-3 of status register A. Since the default value on bootup is a frequency of 1,024 kiloHertz, the interrupt triggers every 967,562 microseconds. Since bit 6 is set to 0 at the system start, an application program must set it to 1 before periodic interrupt calls can execute.

Bit 7 controls the periodic updating of the time and date, once every second. This bit is set to 0 when you boot the system so that the time constantly increments. Before entering a new date and time in the various memory locations, this bit should be first set to 1 to prevent the clock from changing the time immediately. Once you have entered all the data necessary, this bit can be reset and the time can continue updating.

Calling the correct interrupt

We've used the phrase "calling the interrupt" many times in this section, without really telling you which interrupt should be called. Even though there are several reasons for the clock to call an interrupt (alarm time, periodic interrupts, etc.), interrupt 70H is the interrupt consistently called. This interrupt contains a BIOS routine which controls the two time functions in interrupt 15H, among other things.

The routine uses status register C of the clock to determine the reason for the call. Only bits 4, 5 and 6 of this register are of interest to us here. They correspond to the bits in status register B. For example, when you trigger the alarm interrupt (which can only occur if bit 5 in status register B was set) then bit 5 in status register C is also set to indicate that the alarm time has been reached.

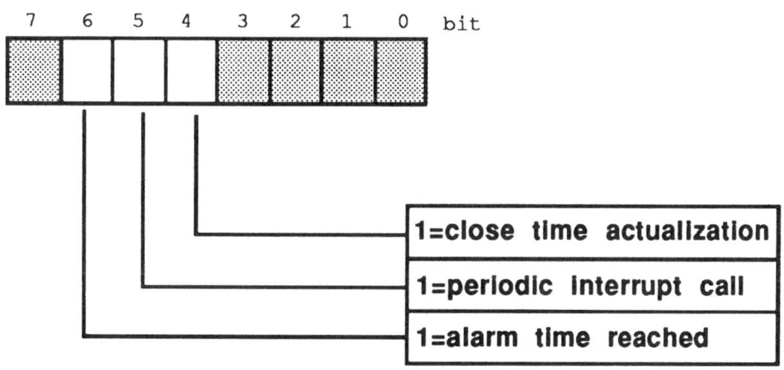

Status register C

The first task of the routine which intercepts interrupt 70H is to read status register C. The routine then determines the reason for the interrupt call and reacts accordingly.

Status register D

Status register D only has one bit of interest: bit 7. It indicates the status of the battery which maintains the storage of data, even when the PC's power supply is turned off. If this bit has the value 0, you should replace the battery because the present battery is dead or near death.

Some configuration information follows status register D.

Byte	Meaning
14	Diagnostic byte
15	Status on termination of the system
16	Disk description
17	reserved
18	Hard Disk description
19	reserved
20	Configuration
21	Low byte of the main memory in kilobytes
22	High byte of the main memory in kilobytes
23	Low byte of the additional memory in kilobytes
24	High byte of the additional memory in kilobytes
25-45	reserved
46	High byte of the checksum for memory locations 16-32
47	Low byte of the checksum for memory locations 16-32
48	Low byte of the additional memory in kilobytes
49	High byte of the additional memory in kilobytes
50	the first two numbers of the century as BCD number
51	Boot information
52-63	reserved

Diagnostic byte (address 14)

Bit	Meaning
0-2	reserved
3	0 = Hard disk and controller o.k. 1 = Hard disk not present or not functional
4	0 = Memory size in memory locations 21-24 1 = other memory size determined during booting
5	0 = Configuration in memory location 20 o.k. 1 = another configuration found during booting
6	0 = Checksum in memory location 46 and 47 o.k. 1 = Checksum in memory location 46 and 47 is false
7	0 = Battery is o.k. 1 = Battery dead or almost dead

Disk description (address 16)

bit	meaning
0-3	Type of second installed drive (DOS designation: B)
	0000(b) = no second disk drive
	0001(b) = 320/360K drive
	0010(b) = 1.2 megabyte drive
4-7	Type of first installed drive (DOS designation: A)
	0000(b) = no disk drive
	0001(b) = 320/360K drive

Note: If you program the clock for generating time-dependent interrupts, and you point interrupt vector 70H to a user routine, remember that if the user routine's end doesn't return to the BIOS, you must send an EOI instruction to the AT's two interrupt controllers, since interrupt 70H is a hardware interrupt triggered by one of these controllers.

Demonstration programs

The three programs listed below show how you can access the realtime clock from BASIC, Pascal or C. Three routines in particular perform most of the functions. The first routine reads a value from one of the clock's memory locations. The second routine places a value there. The third routine checks whether the clock is operating in binary mode or BCD mode, then reads a memory location in the clock, converting the contents of this location from BCD into binary if necessary. This routine is important for access to all memory locations containing information on date and time which could be coded in BCD or in binary format.

The main program checks the battery on the clock. If there's power in the battery, the program calls two routines which read the contents of the memory locations for the current date and current time from the clock, among other things. This data appears on the screen.

The main program doesn't access the routine for description of memory locations. It should be easy to convert the program so that the routine for the description of memory locations writes to the clock instead of reading date and time. This is just a suggestion; feel free to experiment.

BASIC listing: RTC.BAS

```
100 '*****************************************************************'
110 '*                             R T C                             *'
120 '*---------------------------------------------------------------*'
130 '*  Task             : makes two Subroutines available           *'
140 '*                     for reading and writing data              *'
150 '*                     from the RTC of the AT                    *'
160 '*  Author           : MICHAEL TISCHER                           *'
170 '*  developed on     : 7.24.87                                   *'
180 '*  last Update      : 9.21.87                                   *'
190 '*****************************************************************'
200 '
210 CLS                                      'Clear Screen
230 PRINT"RTC (c) 1987 by Michael Tischer" : PRINT
```

```
240 PRINT"Information from the battery buffered real time clock "
250 PRINT"======================================================"
260 PRINT
270 ADR% = 14 : GOSUB 50000              'read diagnostic-byte from the RTC
280 IF (CON% AND 128) =  0 THEN 310      'bit 8 = 1 --> battery o.k.
290 PRINT"        WARNING! The battery of the clock is low!"
300 END
310 ADR% = 11 : GOSUB 50000              'read status-register B of the RTC
320 PRINT"- the clock is operated in ";(CON% AND 2) * 6 + 12;"hour-mode "
330 PRINT"- the time: ";
340 ADR% = 4 : GOSUB 52000        'read the hour and convert to decimal
350 PRINT USING "##:";CON%;
360 ADR% = 2 : GOSUB 52000        'read the minutes and convert to decimal
370 PRINT USING "##:";CON%;
380 ADR% = 0 : GOSUB 52000        'read the seconds and convert to decimal
390 PRINT USING "##";CON%
400 PRINT"- the date: ";
410 ADR% = 6 : GOSUB 52000        'read day of week and convert to decimal
420 RESTORE 540
430 FOR I% = 1 TO CON% : READ DAY$ : NEXT       'read name of the day
440 PRINT DAY$;", the ";
450 ADR% = 7 : GOSUB 52000       'read day of month and convert to decimal
460 PRINT USING "##.";CON%;
470 ADR% = 8 : GOSUB 52000       'read month and convert to decimal
480 PRINT USING "##.";CON%;
490 ADR% = 9 : GOSUB 52000       'read year and convert to decimal
500 PRINT USING "####";CON%+1900
510 PRINT
520 END
530 '
540 DATA "Sunday","Monday","Tuesday","Wednesday"
550 DATA "Thursday","Friday","Saturday"
560 '
50000 '**************************************************************'
50010 '* read the content of a memory location of the RTC           *'
50020 '*------------------------------------------------------------*'
50030 '* Input:  ADR% = the number of the memory location (0 to 63)  *'
50040 '* Output: CON% = the content of this storage location        *'
50050 '**************************************************************'
50060 '
50070 OUT &H70,ADR%     'number of memory location to RTC-address-register
50080 CON% = INP(&H71)  'read Content from RTC-data-register
50090 RETURN            'back to caller
50100 '
51000 '**************************************************************'
51010 '* write a memory location in the RTC                          *'
51020 '*------------------------------------------------------------*'
51030 '* Input:   ADR% = the number of the memory location (0 to 63) *'
51040 '*          CON% = the new content of this memory location     *'
51050 '* Output: none                                                *'
51060 '**************************************************************'
51070 '
51080 OUT &H70,ADR%    'number of memory location to RTC-address-register
51090 OUT &H71,CON%    'write new content into RTC-data-register
51100 RETURN           'back to the caller
51110 '
52000 '**************************************************************'
52010 '* read the content of a date or time memory location          *'
52020 '* from the RTC and convert to decimal                         *'
52030 '*------------------------------------------------------------*'
52040 '* Input : ADR% = the number of the memory location (0 to 63)  *'
52050 '* Output: CON% = the new content of this memory location      *'
52060 '* Info  : ADR% is changed by this subroutine                  *'
52070 '**************************************************************'
52080 '
52090 GOSUB 50000           'read content of the memory location
52100 BCD% = CON%          'record content of the memory location
52110 ADR% = 11            'Address of the Status registers B of the RTC
52120 GOSUB 50000          'read its content
52130 IF (CON% AND 2) = 0 THEN 52150              'test if BCD-mode
```

```
52140 BCD% = (BCD% AND 15) + INT(BCD% / 16) * 10    'convert BCD to decimal
52150 CON% = BCD%                                   'set return value
52160 RETURN                                        'back to caller
```

Pascal listing: RTC.PAS

```
{**********************************************************************}
{*                                R T C                               *}
{*--------------------------------------------------------------------*}
{*    Task           : makes two Functions available for reading and  *}
{*                     writing data in the RTC                        *}
{*--------------------------------------------------------------------*}
{*    Author         : MICHAEL TISCHER                                *}
{*    developed on   : 7.10.87                                        *}
{*    last Update    : 9.21.87                                        *}
{**********************************************************************}

program RTCP;


Uses                                                  {Turbo 4.0 only}
  Crt;

const RTCAdrPort   = $70;              { Address-Register of the RTC }
      RTCDtaPort   = $71;                 { Data-Register of the RTC }

      SECONDS      =  0;  { Addresses of some memory locations of RTC }
      MINUTE       =  2;
      HOUR         =  4;
      DAYOFWEEK    =  6;
      DAY          =  7;
      MONTH        =  8;
      YEAR         =  9;
      STATUSA      = 10;
      STATUSB      = 11;
      STATUSC      = 12;
      STATUSD      = 13;
      DIAGNOSIS    = 14;
      YEARHUNDRED  = 50;

{**********************************************************************}
{* RTCREAD: reads the content of a memory location of the RTC         *}
{* Input  : the address of the memory location in the RTC             *}
{* Output : the content of this memory location                       *}
{* Info   : if the Address is outside the permitted area              *}
{*          (0 to 63), the value -1 is returned                       *}
{**********************************************************************}

function RTCRead(Address : integer) : integer;

begin
 if (Address < 0) or (Address > 63)          { is the Address o.k.? }
  then RTCRead := -1                                         { NO! }
  else
   begin
    port[RTCAdrPort] := Address;          { transmit Address to the RTC }
    RTCRead := port[RTCDtaPort]                    { read its Content }
   end
end;

{**********************************************************************}
{* RTCDT  : read a memory location for date or time from the          *}
{*          RTC and convert the result into a binary value            *}
{*          if the RTC works in BCD-Format                            *}
{* Input  : the address of the memory location in the RTC             *}
{* Output : the content of this memory location as binary value       *}
{* Info   : if the address is outside the permitted area (0 - 63)     *}
{*          the value  -1 is returned                                 *}
```

```
{***********************************************************************}

function RTCDT(Address : integer) : integer;

var Value : integer;           { for memory of a value which was read }

begin
 if (RTCRead(STATUSB) and 2 = 0)               { BCD- or Binary-Mode? }
  then RTCDT := RTCRead(Address)                     { is Binary-Mode }
  else                                                  { is BCD-Mode }
   begin
    Value := RTCRead(Address);    { get Content of the memory location }
    RTCDT := (Value shr 4) * 10 + Value and 15{ convert BCD to binary }
   end
end;

{***********************************************************************}
{* RTCWRITE: write a value into one of the memory locations of RTC    *}
{* Input    : see below                                                *}
{* Output   : none                                                     *}
{* Info     : the address can be between 0 to 63                       *}
{***********************************************************************}

procedure RTCWrite(Address : integer;   { the address of the location }
                   Content  : byte);                { the new content }

begin
 port[RTCAdrPort] := Address;          { transmit address to the RTC }
 port[RTCDtaPort] := Content                       { write new value }
end;

{***********************************************************************}
{*                           MAIN PROGRAM                              *}
{***********************************************************************}

begin
 clrscr;                                               { Clear Screen }
 writeln('RTC (c) 1987 by Michael Tischer'#13#10);
 writeln('Information from the real time clock ');
 writeln('==================================================='#13#10);
 if RTCRead(Diagnosis) and 128 = 0 then         { is the Battery o.k.? }
  begin                                          { the Battery is o.k. }
  writeln('-the clock is being operated in ', (RTCRead(STATUSB) and 2)*6+12,
          ' hour-mode');
   writeln('- the time: ', RTCDT(HOUR), ':', RTCDT(MINUTE):2,
          ':', RTCDT(SECONDS):2);
   write('- the date: ');
   case RTCDT(DAYOFWEEK) of                      { Read Day of the Week }
    1 : write('Sunday');
    2 : write('Monday');
    3 : write('Tuesday');
    4 : write('Wednesday');
    5 : write('Thursday');
    6 : write('Friday');
    7 : write('Saturday')
   end;
  writeln(', the ',RTCDT(DAY), '.', RTCDT(MONTH), '.',
          RTCDT(YEARHUNDRED), RTCDT(YEAR));
  end
 else                          { the Battery of the RTC is exhausted! }
  write('       WARNING! The Battery of the clock is low!')
end.
```

C listing: RTC.C

```
/***********************************************************************/
/*                              R T C                                  */
/*-------------------------------------------------------------------*/
/*    Task           : provides two Functions for reading and writing */
/*                     Data in the Real Time clock                   */
/*-------------------------------------------------------------------*/
/*    Author         : MICHAEL TISCHER                               */
/*    developed on   : 8.15.87                                       */
/*    last Update    : 9.21.87                                       */
/*-------------------------------------------------------------------*/
/*    (MICROSOFT C)                                                  */
/*    Creation       : MSC RTCC;                                     */
/*                     LINK RTCC;                                    */
/*    Call           : RTCC                                          */
/*-------------------------------------------------------------------*/
/*    (BORLAND TURBO C)                                              */
/*    Creation       : Through the RUN command in the command line   */
/***********************************************************************/

#include <dos.h>                              /* Include header-files */
#include <conio.h>

#define byte unsigned char

#define RTCAdrPort  0x70               /* address-register of the RTC */
#define RTCDtaPort  0x71                  /* data-register of the RTC */

#define SECONDS      0  /* addresses of some memory locations of RTC */
#define MINUTE       2
#define HOUR         4
#define DAYOFWEEK    6
#define DAY          7
#define MONTH        8
#define YEAR         9
#define STATUSA     10
#define STATUSB     11
#define STATUSC     12
#define STATUSD     13
#define DIAGNOSE    14
#define YEARHUNDRED 50

/***********************************************************************/
/* RTCREAD: reads the content of a memory location of the RTC        */
/* Input  : the address of the memory location in the RTC            */
/* Output : the Content of this memory location                      */
/***********************************************************************/

byte RTCRead(Address)
byte Address;                          /* the memory location of the RTC */

{
 outp(RTCAdrPort, Address);              /* transmit address to the RTC */
 return(inp(RTCDtaPort));        /* read content and transmit to caller */
}

/***********************************************************************/
/* RTCDT  : reads date or time from one of the memory locations      */
/*          and converts the result into a Binary value              */
/*          if the clock works in BCD-Format                         */
/* Input  : the address of the memory location in the RTC            */
/* Output : the content of this memory location as Binary Value      */
/* Info    :if the address is outside the permitted area             */
/*          (0 to 63) the Value -1 is returned                       */
/***********************************************************************/

byte RTCDt(Address)
byte Address;                          /* the memory location in the RTC */
```

```
{
 if (RTCRead(STATUSB) & 2)                      /* BCD- or binary mode? */
  return((RTCRead(Address) >> 4) * 10 + (RTCRead(Address) & 15));
 else return(RTCRead(Address));                         /* is binary mode */
}

/**********************************************************************/
/* RTCWRITE: write a value into one of the memory locations of RTC   */
/* Input    : see below                                               */
/* Output   : none                                                    */
/* Info     : the address must be between 0 to 63                     */
/**********************************************************************/

void RTCWrite(Address, Content)
byte Address;                        /* address of the memory location */

{
 outp(RTCAdrPort, Address);          /* transmit address to the RTC */
 outp(RTCDtaPort, Content);                       /* write new value */
}

/**********************************************************************/
/**                           MAIN PROGRAM                          **/
/**********************************************************************/

void main()

{
 static char *Weekdays[] =                  /* Names of the weekdays */
                             {
"Sunday","Monday","Tuesday","Wednesday","Thursday","Friday","Saturday"
                             };

 printf("\nRTC (c) 1987 by Michael Tischer\n\n");
 printf("Information from the real time clock\n");
 printf("====================================================\n\n");
 if (!(RTCRead(DIAGNOSE) & 128))              /* is the Battery o.k.? */
  {                                            /* the Battery is o.k. */
   printf("- The clock is operated in %d hour mode \n",
          (RTCRead(STATUSB) & 2)*6+12);
   printf("- the time: %2d:%2d:%2d\n",
          RTCDt(HOUR), RTCDt(MINUTE), RTCDt(SECONDS));
   printf("- the date: ");
   printf("%s, der %d.%d.%d%d\n", Weekdays[RTCDt(DAYOFWEEK)-1],
          RTCDt(DAY), RTCDt(MONTH), RTCDt(YEARHUNDRED), RTCDt(YEAR));

  }
 else printf("       WARNING! The battery of the clock is low!\n");
}
```

Chapter 12

Keyboard Programming

The keyboard is an independent unit in the PC system, and has its own microprocessor and memory. The processor informs the system when a key is pressed or released. It does this by sending the system something called a *scan code* when a key is pressed or released. In both cases the key is indicated by a code which depends on the position of the key. These scan codes have nothing to do with the ASCII or extended keyboard codes to which the system later converts the keypresses.

Communication with the system is performed over two bidirectional lines using a synchronous serial communications protocol. In addition to the actual data line used to transfer the individual bits, the clock line synchronizes the periodic transmission of signals. Transfers are made in one-byte increments, whereby a stop bit is transmitted first (with the value 0), followed by the eight data bits, beginning with the least significant bit. A parity bit, calculated using odd parity, follows the eighth data bit. The transfer of a byte then concludes with a stop bit, which forms the eleventh bit of the transfer. At both ends of the communications line (i.e., in the PC and in the keyboard itself) are devices which convert the signals on the data line to bytes and back again.

Although all types of PCs use this form of communication, we must distinguish between PC/XT and AT models. These systems use different processors as keyboard controllers. The Intel 8048 used in the keyboards of PCs and XTs is a relatively "dumb" device, which can only send the scan codes to the system. However, the 8042 processor used in AT and 80386 keyboards can do much more. Here the communication between the system and the keyboard becomes relatively complex, and the system can even control parts of the keyboard.

The heart of this communication at the keyboard end is represented by a status register and input and output buffers. The buffers transfer:

- Keyboard codes which correspond to pressing or releasing a key
- Data which the system requests from the keyboard

These buffers can be accessed at port 60H on the AT.

The input buffer can be written at port 60H as well as port 64H. The port which is used depends on the type of information to be transferred. If the system wants to send a command code to the keyboard, it must be sent to port 60H, while the corresponding data byte is sent to port 64H. Both end up in the keyboard input buffer, but a flag in the status register indicates whether a command byte (port 64H) or a data byte (port 60H) is involved.

In addition to this flag, bits 0 and 1 of the keyboard status register are especially important for communication with the keyboard. Bit 0 indicates the status of the output buffer. If this bit is 1, then the output buffer of the keyboard contains information which has not yet been read from port 60H. Reading from this port will automatically set this bit back to 0, indicating that there is no longer a character in the output buffer.

Bit 1 of the status register is always set whenever the system has placed a character in the input buffer, before this character is processed by the keyboard. Nothing should be written to the keyboard input buffer unless this bit is equal to 0, signalling that the input buffer is empty.

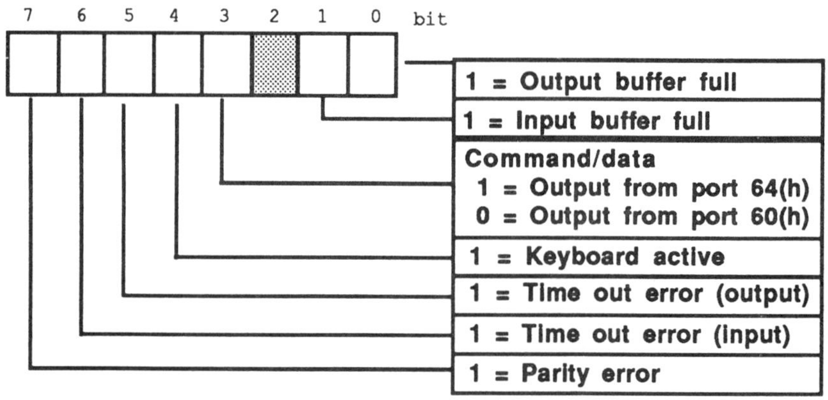

AT keyboard controller status registers

Of the various commands that a system can send to the keyboard, two are of interest for applications programs because they also play a roll outside a keyboard interrupt handler. The first of these commands sets the typematic or repeat rate of the keyboard. This is the number of make codes per second which the keyboard will send to the system when a key is pressed and held down. It can be between two and 30 codes per second. To prevent the keys from repeating unintentionally, this repeat function does not begin until after a certain delay. This delay time can be set by the user and is encoded in binary as follows:

Coding for AT keyboard delay rate	
Code	Delay rate
00(b)	1/4-second
01(b)	1/2-second
10(b)	1/4-second
11(b)	1 second

The keyboard will observe these times with a tolerance of ±20%.

The repeat rate, also called the *typematic* rate by IBM, is also encoded in binary. The following table shows the relationship between the repeat (typematic) rate and the number of repetitions per second.

Typematic rate codes for the AT keyboard							
Code	RPS*	Code	RPS	Code	RPS	Code	RPS
11111(b)	2.0	10111(b)	4.0	01111(b)	8.0	00111(b)	16.0
11110(b)	2.1	10110(b)	4.3	01110(b)	8.6	00110(b)	17.1
11101(b)	2.3	10101(b)	4.6	01101(b)	9.2	00101(b)	18.5
11100(b)	2.5	10100(b)	5.0	01100(b)	10.0	00100(b)	20.0
11011(b)	2.7	10011(b)	5.5	01011(b)	10.9	00011(b)	21.8
11010(b)	3.0	10010(b)	6.0	01010(b)	12.0	00010(b)	24.0
11001(b)	3.3	10001(b)	6.7	01001(b)	13.3	00001(b)	26.7
11000(b)	3.7	10000(b)	7.5	01000(b)	15.0	00000(b)	30.0
*Repetitions per second							

This relationship may seem somewhat arbitrary at first, but it does follow a mathematical formula. The binary value of bits 0, 1, and 2 of the repeat rate form variable A, and the binary value of bits 3 and 4 form variable B:

$$(8 + A) * 2^{B} * 0.00417 * 1/\text{second}$$

The delay and repeat rate values are combined into a byte by placing the five bits of the repeat rate in front of the delay value. However, we can't just send this value straight to the keyboard. We must first send the appropriate command code (34H) and then the repeat parameters. Both bytes must be sent to port 60H, but we cannot just send them with an OUT instruction. We have to use a transmission protocol which includes reading the keyboard status, and which also accounts for the possibility that the transfer might not work the first time. Since we have to do this for both bytes, we should write a subroutine to do it. The structure of this subroutine is shown in the following flowchart.

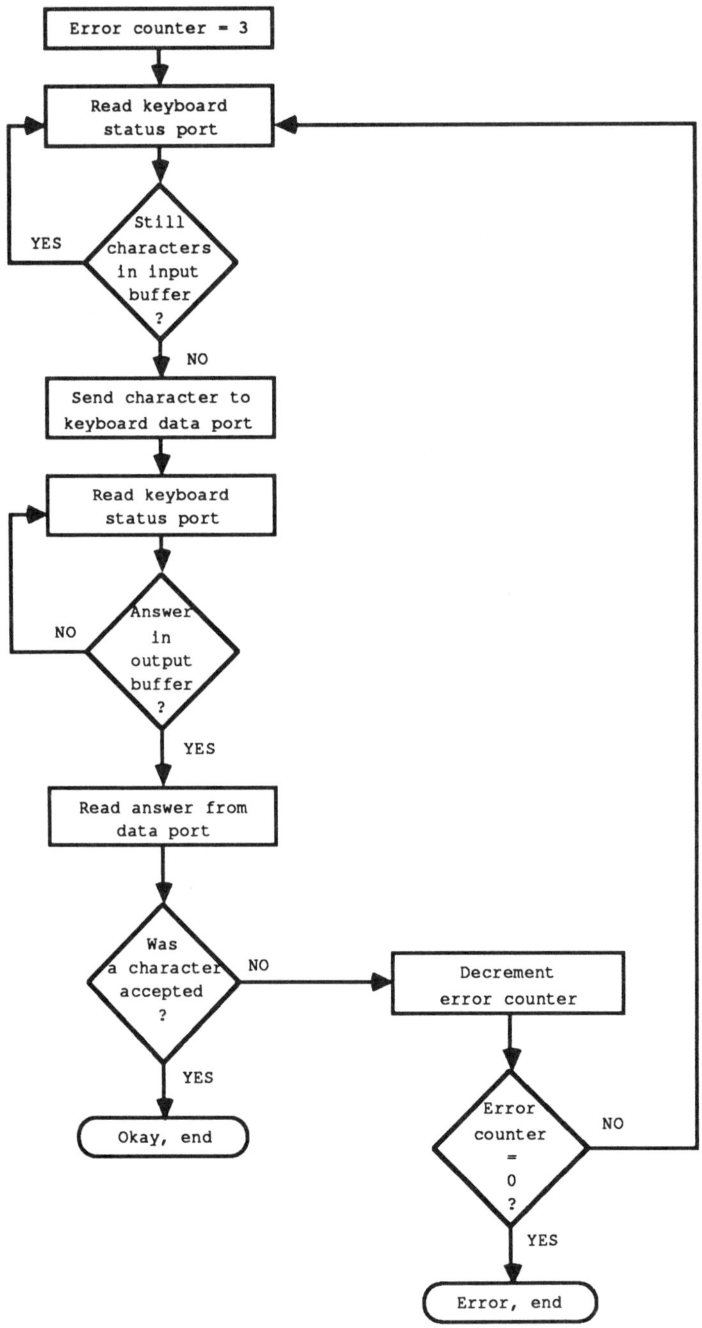

Program flowchart—byte transfer via keyboard

We first load an error counter which allows the routine to try to send the byte three times before an error is returned. Then the keyboard status port is read in a loop until bit 0 is cleared and the input buffer of the keyboard is empty. Then we can send the character to port 60H. To make sure that the character got there all right (a parity error might have occurred, for example), the keyboard sends back a reply code. This has been received when bit 1 of the keyboard status port is set.

This register is again read from port 64H in a loop until this condition is met. Now we can read the reply to our transmission from the keyboard data port. If it is the code 0FAH, which stands for "acknowledge," the transmission was successful. Any other code indicates an error, which tells the subroutine to decrement the error counter and repeat the whole process, provided the counter has not reached zero. In this case the subroutine ends and signals an error to the caller.

Demonstration programs

To give you an example of how this works, the following pages contain programs in BASIC, Pascal, and C which you can use to set the key repeat parameters on your keyboard. The heart of these programs is an assembly language routine which sends the parameters to the keyboard. Within this routine is the subroutine we just discussed, which is first called to send the Set Typematic instruction to the keyboard. Another call is used to send the parameters themselves.

In the Pascal and C versions, the key repeat rate and the delay values are specified as separate parameters following the program name entered at the DOS prompt. Naturally this is not possible in GW-BASIC, so the two parameters are read within the program with the INPUT command.

We also included the listing of the assembly routines for the various programs. The BASIC and Pascal programs include these with DATA or INLINE statements; the linker links these statements to the C version of the program.

To see the effect of the key repeat rate, first try setting the smallest repeat rate (0) and then the highest rate (30). Try pressing and holding a key at each of these settings to see the results.

BASIC listing: TYPMB.BAS

```
100 '**********************************************************************'
110 '*                              T Y P M B                             *'
120 '*--------------------------------------------------------------------*'
130 '*  Description     : Sets the key repeat rate of the AT keyboard.  *'
150 '*  Author          : MICHAEL TISCHER                                *'
160 '*  developed on    : 09/08/1988                                     *'
170 '*  last update     : 09/08/1988                                     *'
180 '**********************************************************************'
190 '
200 CLS : KEY OFF
210 PRINT "Note: This program may be run only if GWBASIC has been started";
220 PRINT "from the DOS level"
230 PRINT "with the command  <GWBASIC /m:60000> and the computer is an AT."
260 PRINT : PRINT"If this is not the case, then please enter <s> for Stop."
280 PRINT "Otherwise press any other key...";
```

```
290 A$ = INKEY$ : IF A$ = "s" THEN END
300 IF A$ = "" THEN 290
310 CLS                                                    'clear screen
320 GOSUB 60000                                 'install assembler routine
330 PRINT "TYPMB - (c) 1988 by MICHAEL TISCHER"
340 PRINT "Sets the repeat rate of the AT keyboard." : PRINT
350 INPUT "Delay before repeat (0=minimum, 3=maximum) ";V%
360 IF V%<0 OR V%>3 THEN 350
370 INPUT "Key repeat rate (30=minimum, 0=maximum) ";W%
380 IF W%<0 OR W%>30 THEN 370
390 TYPRATE% = V% * 32 +  W%
400 CALL TR(TYPRATE%, OK%)                        'set key repeat rate
410 IF NOT OK% THEN 440
420 PRINT "The key repeat rate has been set."
430 END
440 PRINT "Error accessing the keyboard controller."
450 END
460 '
60000 '****************************************************************'
60010 '* Install the routine for setting the key repeat rate.         *'
60020 '*--------------------------------------------------------------*'
60030 '* Input : none                                                 *'
60040 '* Output: TR is the start address of the assembler routine     *'
60050 '* Calling the routine: CALL TR(TYPRATE%, OK%)                  *'
60060 '****************************************************************'
60070 '
60080 TR=60000!          'start addr of the routine in the BASIC segment
60090 DEF SEG                                        'set BASIC segment
60100 RESTORE 60140
60110 FOR I% = 0 TO 71 : READ X% : POKE TR+I%,X% : NEXT    'poke routine
60120 RETURN                                        'back to the caller
60130 '
60140 DATA  85,139,236, 51,210,180,243,250,232, 23,  0,117, 11,139, 94
60150 DATA   8,138, 39,232, 13,  0,117,  1, 74,251,139, 94,  6,137, 23
60160 DATA  93,202,  4,  0, 81, 83,179,  3, 51,201,228,100,168,  2,224
60170 DATA 250,138,196,230, 96,228,100,168,  1,225,250,228, 96, 60,250
60180 DATA 116,  7,254,203,117,230,128,203,  1, 91, 89,195
```

Assembler listing: TYPMBA.ASM

```
;**********************************************************************;
;*                              T Y P M B A                           *;
;*--------------------------------------------------------------------*;
;*    Description     : Assembler routine for use with a GWBASIC      *;
;*                      program, which sets the key repeat rate of the *;
;*                      AT keyboard.                                  *;
;*--------------------------------------------------------------------*;
;*    Author          : MICHAEL TISCHER                               *;
;*    developed on    : 27.08.1988                                    *;
;*    last update     : 27.08.1988                                    *;
;*--------------------------------------------------------------------*;
;*    to assemble     : MASM TYPMBA;                                  *;
;*                      LINK TYPMBA                                   *;
;*                      EXE2BIN TYPMBA TYPMBA.BIN                     *;
;*                      ... convert to DATA statements and insert in  *;
;*                          a BASIC program                           *;
;**********************************************************************;

;== Constants =========================================================

KB_STATUS_P   equu 64h             ;status port of the keyboard
KB_DATA_P     equ 60h              ;keyboard data port

OB_FULL       equ 1                ;Bit 0 in the keyboard status port
                                   ;one character in the output buffer
IB_FULL       equ 2                ;Bit 1 in the keyboard status port
                                   ;one character in the input buffer

ACK_SIGNAL    equ 0fah             ;keyboard acknowledge signal
```

```
SET_TYPEM      equ 0f3h            ;set-key-repeat code

MAX_TRY        equ 3               ;number of retries

;== Program code ==========================================================

code        segment para 'CODE'   ;definition of the CODE segment

            org  100h

            assume cs:code, ds:code, ss:code, es:code

;-------------------------------------------------------------------------
;-- SET_TYPM: Determines the key repeat rate to be sent to the  --------
;--           keyboard controller
;-- Call     : CALL Adresse(TYPRATE%, OK%)
;-- Info     : If the key repeat rate can be set, the value will be
;--            placed in TYPRATE, else 0

set_typm    proc far               ;GW expects FAR procedures

sframe      struc                  ;structure for accessing the stack
bptr        dw ?                   ;stores BP
ret_adr     dd ?                   ;return address to the caller
                                   ;(FAR address)
ok_adr      dw ?                   ;address of the OK variable
tr_adr      dw ?                   ;address of the var with the rep rate
sframe      ends                   ;end of the structure

frame       equ [ bp - bptr ]      ;addresses the elements of the structure

            push bp                ;save BP on the stack
            mov  bp,sp             ;transfer SP to BP

            xor  dx,dx             ;assume transfer failed
            mov  ah,SET_TYPEM      ;set command code for key rep rate
            cli                    ;disable interrupts
            call send_kb           ;send to the controller
            jne  error             ;error? yes --> Error

            mov  bx,frame.tr_adr   ;get address of the TYPRATE variable
            mov  ah,[bx]           ;get key repeat rate
            call send_kb           ;send to the controller
            jne  error             ;error? yes --> Error

            dec  dx                ;everything OK, return -1

error:      sti                    ;allow interrupts again
            mov  bx,frame.ok_adr   ;get address of the OK variable
            mov  [bx],dx           ;put error static there
            pop  bp                ;get BP back from stack
            ret  4                 ;back to GW-BASIC and remove the
                                   ;variables from the stack
set_typm    endp

;-------------------------------------------------------------------------
;-- SEND_KB: send a byte to the keyboard controller --------------------
;-- Input    : AH = the byte to be sent
;-- Output   : zero flag: 0=error, 1=OK
;-- Registers: AX and the flag register are used
;-- Info     : this routine is intended for use only within this
;--            module

send_kb     proc near

            push cx                ;save all registers used in this
            push bx                ;routine on the stack

            mov  bl,MAX_TRY        ;maximum of MAX_TRY retries
```

```
          ;-- wait until the controller is ready to receive data -------

skb_1:    xor  cx,cx             ;maximum of 65536 loop passes
skb_2:    in   al,KB_STATUS_P    ;read contents of the status port
          test al,IB_FULL        ;still a character in the input buffer?
          loopne skb_2           ;yes --> SKB_2

          ;-- send character to the controller -------------------------

          mov  al,ah             ;get character in AL
          out  KB_DATA_P,al      ;send character to the data port
skb_3:    in   al,KB_STATUS_P    ;read contents of the status port
          test al,OB_FULL        ;answer in the output buffer?
          loope skb_3            ;no --> SKB_3

          ;-- get reply from controller and evaluate -------------------

          in   al,KB_DATA_P      ;read reply from data port
          cmp  al,ACK_SIGNAL     ;was the character accepted?
          je   skb_end           ;YES --> everything OK

          ;-- the character was not accepted ---------------------------

          dec  bl                ;decrement error counter
          jne  skb_2             ;retries left?
                                 ;YES --> SKB_2

          or   bl,1              ;NO, set zero flag to 0, indicating
                                 ;an error

skb_end:  pop  bx                ;restore the registers from the stack
          pop  cx
          ret                    ;back to the caller

send_kb   endp

;== Ende ===============================================================

code      ends                   ;end of the code segment
          end  set_typm
```

Pascal listing: TYPMP.PAS

```
{**********************************************************************}
{*                             T Y P M P                              *}
{*--------------------------------------------------------------------*}
{*    Description    : Sets the key repeat rate of the AT keyboard.   *}
{*--------------------------------------------------------------------*}
{*    Author         : MICHAEL TISCHER                                *}
{*    developed on   : 08/27/1988                                     *}
{*    last update    : 08/27/1988                                     *}
{**********************************************************************}

program TYPMP;

{**********************************************************************}
{* SetTypm: Sends the key repeat rate to the keyboard controller      *}
{* Input  : RATE : the repeat rate to be set                          *}
{* Output : TRUE, if the value was set, FALSE if an error occurred    *}
{*          accessing the controller                                  *}
{* Info   : This function can be bound into a UNIT                    *}
{**********************************************************************}

{$F+}                         { this function uses the FAR call model }

function SetTypm( Rate : byte ) : boolean;

begin
 inline(
```

```
        $32/$D2/$B4/$F3/$FA/$E8/$13/$00/$75/$0A/$8A/$66/$06/$E8/
        $0B/$00/$75/$02/$FE/$C2/$FB/$88/$56/$FF/$EB/$27/$90/$51/
        $53/$B3/$03/$33/$C9/$E4/$64/$A8/$02/$E0/$FA/$8A/$C4/$E6/
        $60/$E4/$64/$A8/$01/$E1/$FA/$E4/$60/$3C/$FA/$74/$07/$FE/
        $CB/$75/$E6/$80/$CB/$01/$5E/$59/$C3
       );
end;

{$F-}

{**********************************************************************}
{**                          MAIN PROGRAM                            **}
{**********************************************************************}

var  Delay,                                          { stores the delay }
     Speed,                                { stores the key repeat rate }
     Fpos1,
     FPos2  : integer;             { error position in string conversion }
     ParErr : boolean;                     { error in parameter passing }

begin
  writeln(#13#10,'TYPMP  -  (c) 1988 by MICHAEL TISCHER');
  ParErr := true;                          { assume error in parameters }
  if ParamCount = 2 then                  { were 2 parameters passed? }
    begin                                                        { YES }
      val(ParamStr(1), Delay, FPos1);     { first parameter to integer }
      val(ParamStr(2), Speed, FPos2);    { second parameter to integer }
      if ((FPos1=0) and (FPos2=0)) then          { error in conversion? }
        if ((Delay < 4) and (Speed <32)) then           { no, value OK? }
          ParErr := false;               { yes, then parameters are OK }
    end;
  if ( ParErr ) then                            { are parameters OK? }
    begin                                                         { no }
      writeln(Call  : TYPMP       delay     key_repeat_rate');
      writeln('                        ',#30,'              ',#30);
      writeln('                        |              |');
{*  Vertical line can be created using <Alt><179>;                     *}
      writeln('     ┌─────────────┴───┐ ┌───────┴───────────┐');
{*  Upper left corner can be created using <Alt><218>;                  *}
{*  Horizontal line can be created using <Alt><196>;                    *}
{*  Brace pointing 'up' can be created using <Alt><193>;                *}
{*  Upper right corner can be created using <Alt><191>                  *}
      writeln('     | 0 : 1/4 second    | | 0 : 30.0 rep./s. |');
{*  Vertical line can be created using <Alt><179>;                     *}
      writeln('     | 1 : 1/2 second    | | 1 : 26.7 rep./s. |');
      writeln('     | 2 : 3/4 second    | | 2 : 24.0 rep./s. |');
      writeln('     | 3 : 1 second      | | 3 : 21.8 rep./s. |');
      writeln('     ├───────────────────┤ |         .          |');
{*  Left brace can be created using <Alt><195>;                         *}
{*  Horizontal line can be created using <Alt><196>;                    *}
{*  Right brace can be created using <Alt><180>;                        *}
      writeln('     |all values    q20% | |        .         |');
      writeln('     └───────────────────┘ |        .          |');
{*  Lower left corner can be created using <Alt><192>;                  *}
{*  Horizontal line can be created using <Alt><196>;                    *}
{*  Lower right corner can be created using <Alt><217>;                 *}
      writeln('                           |28 :  2.5 rep./s. |');
{*  Vertical line can be created using <Alt><179>;                     *}
      writeln('                           |29 :  2.3 rep./s. |');
      writeln('                           |30 :  2.1 rep./s. |');
      writeln('                           |31 :  2.0 rep./s. |');
      writeln('                           └──────────────────┘');
{*  Lower left corner can be created using <Alt><192>;                  *}
{*  Horizontal line can be created using <Alt><196>;                    *}
{*  Lower right corner can be created using <Alt><217>;                  *}
    end
```

```
  else                                         { the parameters are OK }
  begin
    if (SetTypm( (Delay shl 5) + Speed )) then   { set key repeat rate }
      writeln('The keboard repeat rate was set.')
    else
      writeln('ERROR accessing the keyboard controller.');
  end;
end.
```

Assembler listing: TYPMPA.ASM

```
;**********************************************************************;
;*                              T Y P M P A                           *;
;*--------------------------------------------------------------------*;
;*    Description     : Assembler routine for use with a Turbo Pascal   *;
;*                      program, which sets the key repeat rate of the *;
;*                      AT keyboard.                                  *;
;*--------------------------------------------------------------------*;
;*    Author          : MICHAEL TISCHER                               *;
;*    developed on    : 27.08.1988                                    *;
;*    last update     : 27.08.1988                                    *;
;*--------------------------------------------------------------------*;
;*    to assemble     : MASM TYPMPA;                                  *;
;*                      LINK TYPMPA                                   *;
;*                      EXE2BIN TYPMPA TYPMPA.BIN                     *;
;*                      ... convert to INLINE statements *;
;**********************************************************************;

;== Constants =========================================================

KB_STATUS_P    equ 64h              ;status port of the keyboard
KB_DATA_P       equ 60h              ;keyboard data port

OB_FULL        equ 1                ;Bit 0 in the keyboard status port
                                    ;one character in the output buffer
IB_FULL        equ 2                ;Bit 1 in the keyboard status port
                                    ;one character in the input buffer

ACK_SIGNAL     equ 0fah             ;keyboard acknowledge signal
SET_TYPEM      equ 0f3h             ;set-key-repeat code

MAX_TRY        equ 3                ;number of retries

;== Program code ======================================================

code      segment para 'CODE'       ;definition of the CODE segment

          org  100h

          assume cs:code, ds:code, ss:code, es:code

;----------------------------------------------------------------------
;-- SET_TYPM:  Determines the key repeat rate to be sent to the --------
;--           keyboard controller
;-- Info     : Set up as a NEAR call

set_typm   proc near                ;GW expects FAR procedures

sframe0     struc                    ;structure for accessing the stack
bp0        dw ?                     ;stores BP
ret_adr0   dd ?                     ;return address to the caller
                                    ;(FAR address)
trate0      dw ?                     ;address of the var with the rep rate
sframe0    ends                     ;end of the structure

frame      equ [ bp - bp0 ]        ;addresses the elements of the structure

                                    ;The following instructions are executed by Turbo
;           push bp                  ;save BP on the stack
```

```
;            mov  bp,sp              ;transfer SP to BP

             xor  dl,dl              ;assume transfer failed
             mov  ah,SET_TYPEM       ;set command code for key rep rate
             cli                     ;disable interrupts
             call send_kb            ;send to the controller
             jne  error              ;error? yes --> Error

             mov  ah,byte ptr frame.trate0  ;get address of the TYPRATE variable
             call send_kb            ;send to the controller
             jne  error              ;error? yes --> Error

             inc  dl                 ;everything OK, return TRUE

error:       sti                     ;allow interrupts again
             mov  [bp-1],dl            ;put error static there
             pop  bp                 ;get BP back from stack
             jmp ende                  ;back to Turbo Pascal
set_typm     endp

;----------------------------------------------------------------------
;-- SEND_KB: send a byte to the keyboard controller --------------------
;-- Input    : AH = the byte to be sent
;-- Output   : zero flag: 0=error, 1=OK
;-- Registers: AX and the flag register are used
;-- Info     : this routine is intended for use only within this
;--            module

send_kb   proc near

          push cx                    ;save all registers used in this
          push bx                    ;routine on the stack

          mov  bl,MAX_TRY            ;maximum of MAX_TRY retries

          ;-- wait until the controller is ready to receive data -------

skb_1:    xor  cx,cx                 ;maximum of 65536 loop passes
skb_2:    in   al,KB_STATUS_P        ;read contents of the status port
          test al,IB_FULL            ;still a character in the input buffer?
          loopne skb_2               ;yes --> SKB_2

          ;-- send character to the controller -------------------------

          mov  al,ah                 ;get character in AL
          out  KB_DATA_P,al          ;send character to the data port
skb_3:    in   al,KB_STATUS_P        ;read contents of the status port
          test al,OB_FULL            ;answer in the output buffer?
          loope skb_3                ;no --> SKB_3

          ;-- get reply from controller and evaluate -------------------

          in   al,KB_DATA_P          ;read reply from data port
          cmp  al,ACK_SIGNAL         ;was the character accepted?
          je   skb_end               ;YES --> everything OK

          ;-- the character was not accepted ---------------------------

          dec  bl                    ;decrement error counter
          jne  skb_2                 ;retries left?
                                     ;YES --> SKB_2

          or   bl,1                  ;NO, set zero flag to 0, indicating
                                     ;an error

skb_end:  pop  bx                    ;restore the registers from the stack
          pop  cx
          ret                        ;back to the caller

send_kb   endp
```

```
;-----------------------------------------------------------
ende            label near
;== End ============================================================

code       ends                        ;end of the code segment
           end  set_typm
```

C listing: TYPMC.C

```
/*********************************************************************/
/*                            T Y P M C                              */
/*-------------------------------------------------------------------*/
/*    Description    : Sets the key repeat rate on the AT keyboard   */
/*                     according to the preferences of the user.     */
/*-------------------------------------------------------------------*/
/*    Author         : MICHAEL TISCHER                               */
/*    developed on   : 08/28/1988                                    */
/*    last update    : 08/28/1988                                    */
/*-------------------------------------------------------------------*/
/*    (MICROSOFT C)                                                  */
/*    creation       : CL /AS /c TYPMC.C                             */
/*                     LINK TYPMC TYPMCA;                            */
/*    call           : TYPMC                                         */
/*-------------------------------------------------------------------*/
/*    (BORLAND TURBO C)                                              */
/*    creation      :  via project file with following contents:      */
/*                     TYPMC                                         */
/*                     TYPMCA.OBJ                                    */
/*********************************************************************/

/*== Include files ==================================================*/

#include <stdlib.h>

/*== Typedefs =======================================================*/

typedef unsigned char byte;                  /* build ourselves a byte */
typedef byte bool;                            /* always TRUE or FALSE */

/*== Constants =====================================================*/

#define TRUE  1                        /* needed for working with BOOL */
#define FALSE 0

/*== Declaration of external functions in the assembler module =======*/

extern bool set_typm( byte trate );       /* sets the key repeat rate */

/*********************************************************************/
/**                          MAIN PROGRAM                           **/
/*********************************************************************/

void main(int argc, char *argv[] )
{
 int delay,                              /* stores the specified delay */
     speed;                        /* stores the specified repeat rate */

 printf("\nTYPMC  -  (c) 1988 by MICHAEL TISCHER\n");
 if (argc!=3 || ( (delay = atoi(argv[1]))<0 || delay>3 ) ||
               ( (speed = atoi(argv[2]))<0 || speed>31 ))
  {        /* illegal parameters were passed */
   printf("call: TYPMC          delay      key_repeat_rate\n");
   printf("                      \x1e               \x1e\n");
   printf("                      |               |\n");
/*  Vertical line can be created using <Alt><179>;                   */
   printf("     ┌──────────────┴───┐ ┌───────┴───────────┐'\n");
/*  Upper left corner can be created using <Alt><218>;                */
```

```
/*  Horizontal line can be created using <Alt><196>;                 */
/*  Brace pointing 'up' can be created using <Alt><193>;             */
/*  Upper right corner can be created using <Alt><191>               */
  printf("     | 0 : 1/4 second     | | 0 : 30.0 rep./s. |\n");
/*  Vertical line can be created using <Alt><179>;                */
  printf("     | 1 : 1/2 second     | | 1 : 26.7 rep./s. |\n");
  printf("     | 2 : 3/4 second     | | 2 : 24.0 rep./s. |\n");
  printf("     | 3 : 1 second       | | 3 : 21.8 rep./s. |\n");
  printf("    {-----------------------{ |       .        |\n");
/*  Left brace can be created using <Alt><195>;                      */
/*  Horizontal line can be created using <Alt><196>;                 */
/*  Right brace can be created using <Alt><180>;                     */
  printf("     |all values   q20% | |       .        |\n");
  printf("     L--------------------J |       .        |\n");
/*  Lower left corner can be created using <Alt><192>;               */
/*  Horizontal line can be created using <Alt><196>;                 */
/*  Lower right corner can be created using <Alt><217>;              */
  printf("                           | 28 :  2.5 rep./s. |\n");
/*  Vertical line can be created using <Alt><179>;                */
  printf("                           | 29 :  2.3 rep./s. |\n");
  printf("                           | 30 :  2.1 rep./s. |\n");
  printf("                           | 31 :  2.0 rep./s. |\n");
  printf("                           L-------------------J\n");
/*  Lower left corner can be created using <Alt><192>;               */
/*  Horizontal line can be created using <Alt><196>;                 */
/*  Lower right corner can be created using <Alt><217>;              */
 }
else                                     /* the parametes are OK */
 {
  if (set_typm( (delay << 5) + speed ))          /* set repeat rate */
   printf("The keyboard repeat rate was set.\n");
  else
   printf("ERROR accessing the keyboard controller.\n");
 }
}
```

Assembler listing: TYPMCA.ASM

```
;**********************************************************************;
;*                              T Y P M C A                           *;
;*--------------------------------------------------------------------*;
;*    Description     : Assembler routine for setting the key repeat  *;
;*                      rate on an AT keyboard. For linking with a    *;
;*                      C program.                                    *;
;*--------------------------------------------------------------------*;
;*    Author          : MICHAEL TISCHER                               *;
;*    developed on    : 08/27/1988                                    *;
;*    last update     : 08/27/1988                                    *;
;*--------------------------------------------------------------------*;
;*    to assembler    : MASM TYPMCA;                                 *;
;*                      ... link with a C program                     *;
;**********************************************************************;

;== Constants ==========================================================

KB_STATUS_P   equ 64h             ;keyboard status port
KB_DATA_P      equ 60h             ;keyboard data port

OB_FULL       equ 1               ;bit 0 in keyboard status port
                                  ;a character in the output buffer
IB_FULL       equ 2               ;bit 1 in the keyboard status port
                                  ;a character in the input buffer

ACK_SIGNAL    equ 0fah            ;keyboard acknowledge signal
SET_TYPEM     equ 0f3h            ;set-repeat-rate code
```

```
MAX_TRY       equu 3              ;number of retries allowed

;== Segment declarations for the C program ============================

IGROUP group _text                ;combination of the program segments
DGROUP group const,_bss,  _data   ;combination of the data segments
       assume CS:IGROUP, DS:DGROUP, ES:DGROUP, SS:DGROUP

CONST  segment word public 'CONST';this segment stores all of the
CONST  ends                       ;read-only constants

_BSS   segment word public 'BSS'  ;this segment stores all of the
_BSS   ends                       ;uninitialized static variables

_DATA  segment word public 'DATA' ;all initialized global and static
                                  ;variables are stored in this segment
_DATA  ends

;== Program ============================================================

_TEXT  segment byte public 'CODE' ;the program segment

public      _set_typm

;-----------------------------------------------------------------------
;-- SET_TYPM: sends the key repeat rate to the keyboard controller -----
;-- Call from C : bool set_typem( byte trate );
;-- Return value: TRUE, if the repeat rate was set
;--               FALSE, if an error occurred

_set_typm  proc near

sframe0    struc                  ;structure for accessing the stack
bp0        dw ?                   ;stores BP
ret_adr0   dw ?                   ;return address to caller
trate0     dw ?                   ;repeat rate to be set
sframe0    ends                   ;end of the structure

frame      equ [ bp - bp0 ]       ;addresses the elements of the structure

           push bp                ;save BP on the stack
           mov  bp,sp             ;transfer SP to BP

           xor  dx,dx             ;assume transfer fails
           mov  ah,SET_TYPEM      ;set command code for rep rate
           cli                    ;disable interrupts
           call send_kb           ;send to the controller
           jne  error             ;error? YES --> Error

           mov  ah,byte ptr frame.trate0 ;get key repeat rate
           call send_kb           ;send to the controller
           jne  error             ;error? YES --> Error

           inc  dl                ;everything OK, return TRUE

error:     sti                    ;allow interrupts again
           mov  ax,dx             ;return value to AX
           pop  bp                ;get BP back from stack
           ret                    ;back to the C program

_set_typm  endp

;-----------------------------------------------------------------------
;-- SEND_KB: send a byte to the keyboard controller --------------------
;-- Input    : AH = the byte to be sent
;-- Output   : zero flag: 0=error, 1=OK
;-- Registers: AX and the flag register are changed
;-- Info     : This routine is to be called only within the module

send_kb   proc near
```

```
        push cx                 ;save all registers which are changed
        push bx                 ;in this routine on the stack

        mov  bl,MAX_TRY         ;maximum of MAX_TRY retries

        ;-- wait until the controller is ready to receive data ------

skb_1:  xor  cx,cx              ;maximum of 65536 loop passes
skb_2:  in   al,KB_STATUS_P     ;read contents of status port
        test al,IB_FULL         ;still a char in the input buffer?
        loopne skb_2            ;YES --> SKB_2

        ;-- send character to the controller -------------------------

        mov  al,ah              ;get character in AL
        out  KB_DATA_P,al       ;send character to the data port
skb_3:  in   al,KB_STATUS_P     ;read contents of the status port
        test al,OB_FULL         ;reply in output buffer?
        loope skb_3             ;NO --> SKB_3

        ;-- get and evaluate relpy from controller -------------------

        in   al,KB_DATA_P       ;read reply from data port
        cmp  al,ACK_SIGNAL      ;was the character accepted?
        je   skb_end            ;YES --> everything OK

        ;-- the character was not accepted ---------------------------

        dec  bl                 ;decrement error counter
        jne  skb_2              ;still retries left?
                                ;YES --> SKB_2

        or   bl,1               ;NO, set zero flag to 0 to indicate
                                ;the error

skb_end: pop bx                 ;restore the registers from the stack
        pop  cx
        ret                     ;return to caller

send_kb endp

;-----------------------------------------------------------------------

_text     ends                  ;end of the code segment
          end                   ;end of the program
```

We can use this same method to turn the LEDs on the AT keyboard on and off. The corresponding instruction code is number 0EDH, and is called the Set/Reset Mode Indicators instruction.

After this command code has been successfully transmitted, the keyboard waits for a byte which reflects the status of the three LEDs. One bit in this byte stands for one of the three LEDs, which is turned on when the corresponding bit is set.

Bit #	LED
0	Scroll Lock
1	Num Lock
2	Caps Lock
Bits 3-7	unused

Setting and resetting these bits make sense only when the keyboard mode which they indicate is enabled or disabled.

These modes are managed in the BIOS, not the keyboard. For example, the keyboard doesn't automatically convert all of the letters to uppercase in Caps Lock mode. The keyboard can only associate a key with a virtual key number, rather than a specific character. This key number is then converted to an ASCII or extended keyboard code by the BIOS. Naturally this also applies to the Caps Lock key, which simply sends a scan code to the computer when it is pressed. The BIOS assigns the Caps Lock function to this key by setting an internal flag which marks this mode as active, then sends the Set/Reset Mode Indicators instruction to the keyboard to light the appropriate LED.

Although these keyboard modes are normally enabled and disabled by the user pressing the corresponding keys, it may be useful to set a mode from within a program. This is the case for keyboards which have separate cursor keys and a numerical keypad, for example. Since most keyboards can only enter numbers when Num Lock mode is on, it makes sense to set this mode automatically when the system is started.

To do this we just set the appropriate BIOS flag and then turn on the corresponding LED on the keyboard to inform the user that this mode has been activated.

In practice, a program just has to set the appropriate BIOS mode, since the BIOS automatically controls the keyboard LEDs. Whenever one of the functions of the BIOS keyboard interrupt is called, the BIOS checks to see if the status of the LEDs matches the keyboard status, as indicated in an internal variable. If a discrepancy arises, the BIOS automatically sets the LEDs to the status given in the keyboard status flag.

Since the position of this flag in the BIOS variable segment and the meaning of the individual bits is completely documented (see also Section 7.14), we can easily change these modes.

The following programs in BASIC, Pascal, and C offer routines which can enable or disable the individual modes. It should be noted that although PCs and XTs have corresponding LEDs, these programs will not work or change the modes without changing the status of the LEDs on a PC or XT keyboard. This is because these keyboards are equipped with an 8048 processor, which does not offer the ability to manage the LEDs. The fact that these LEDs do turn on and off according to the modes has nothing to do with the BIOS, and is handled directly by the keyboard.

BASIC listing: LEDB.BAS

```
100 '*******************************************************************'
110 '*                              L E D B                             *'
120 '*-----------------------------------------------------------------*'
130 '*  Description    : Sets the various bits in the BIOS keyboard    *'
140 '*                    flag, causing the LED's on the AT keyboard    *'
150 '*                    to flash.                                     *'
160 '*  Author         : MICHAEL TISCHER                                *'
170 '*  developed on   : 09/10/1988                                     *'
180 '*  last update    : 09/10/1988                                     *'
190 '*******************************************************************'
200 '
210 CLS : KEY OFF
220 PRINT "NOTE: This program can be run only if GWBASIC was started from"
230 PRINT "the DOS level with the command <GWBASIC /m:600000> and the"
240 PRINT "computer is an AT."
250 PRINT
260 PRINT "If this is not the case, please enter <s> for STOP."
270 PRINT "Otherwise press any other key...";
300 A$ = INKEY$ : IF A$ = "s" THEN END
310 IF A$ = "" THEN 300
320 CLS
330 GOSUB 60000                 'install routine for the interrupt call
340 PRINT "LEDB - (c) 1988 by MICHAEL TISCHER"
350 PRINT : PRINT "Watch the LEDs on your keyboard!"
360 SCRL% = 16                                       'the SCROLL LOCK flag
370 NUML% = 32                                          'the NUM LOCK flag
380 CAPL% = 64                                         'the CAPS LOCK flag
390 FOR X% = 1 TO 10                          'run through the loop 10 times
400   FLAGS% = CAPL% : GOSUB 50000                            'set CAPS LOCK
410   FOR Y% = 1 TO 100 : NEXT                                   'delay loop
420   GOSUB 51000                                       'CAPS LOCK off again
430   FLAGS% = NUML% : GOSUB 50000                             'set NUM LOCK
440   FOR Y% = 1 TO 100 : NEXT                                   'delay loop
450   GOSUB 51000                                        'NUM LOCK off again
460   FLAGS% = SCRL% : GOSUB 50000                          'set SCROLL LOCK
470   FOR Y% = 1 TO 100 : NEXT                                   'delay loop
480   GOSUB 51000                                     'SCROLL LOCK off again
490 NEXT
500 FLAGS% = SCRL% OR NUML% OR CAPL%          'manipulate all three flags
510 FOR X% = 1 TO 10                             'run through loop 10 times
520   GOSUB 50000                                       'set all three flags
530   FOR Y% = 1 TO 400 : NEXT                                   'delay loop
540   GOSUB 51000                                      'clear all flags again
550   FOR Y% = 1 TO 400 : NEXT                                   'delay loop
560 NEXT
570 PRINT "That's all."
580 END
590 '
50000 '*****************************************************************'
50010 '* set one or more of the flags in the BIOS keyboard status      *'
50020 '*---------------------------------------------------------------*'
50030 '* Input   : FLAGS% = the flags to be set                         *'
50040 '* Output  : none                                                 *'
50050 '* Info    : the variable Z% is used as a dummy variable          *'
50060 '*****************************************************************'
50070 '
50080 DEF SEG = &H40                           'set BIOS variable segment
50090 POKE &H17, PEEK(&H17) OR FLAGS%                        'set the flags
50100 INTR% = &H16                          'call BIOS keyboard interrupt
50110 AH% = 1                              'function 1: character ready?
50120 DEF SEG                            'switch back to the GW segment
50130 CALL IA(INTR%,AH%,Z%,Z%,Z%,Z%,Z%,Z%,Z%,Z%,Z%,Z%,Z%)
50140 RETURN                                          'back to the caller
50150 '
51000 '*****************************************************************'
51010 '* clear one or more the flags in the BIOS keyboard status       *'
51020 '*---------------------------------------------------------------*'
```

```
51030 '* Input   : FLAGS% = the flags to be cleared                       *'
51040 '* Output  : none                                                   *'
51050 '* Info    : the variable Z% is used as a dummy variable            *'
51060 '*******************************************************************'
51070 '
51080 DEF SEG = &H40                             'set BIOS variable segment
51090 POKE &H17, PEEK(&H17) AND NOT(FLAGS%)                 'clear the flags
51100 INTR% = &H16                        'call the BIOS keyboard interrupt
51110 AH% = 1                                  'function 1: character ready?
51120 DEF SEG                                 'switch back to the GW segment
51130 CALL IA(INTR%,AH%,Z%,Z%,Z%,Z%,Z%,Z%,Z%,Z%,Z%,Z%,Z%)
51140 RETURN                                             'back to the caller
51150 '
60000 '*******************************************************************'
60010 '* initialize the routine for the interrupt call                    *'
60020 '*-----------------------------------------------------------------*'
60030 '* Input   : none                                                   *'
60040 '* Output  : IA is the start address of the interupt routine        *'
60050 '*******************************************************************'
60060 '
60070 IA=60000!       'start address of the routine in the BASIC segment
60080 DEF SEG                                            'set BASIC segment
60090 RESTORE 60130
60100 FOR I% = 0 TO 160 : READ X% : POKE IA+I%,X% : NEXT   'poke routine
60110 RETURN                                             'back to the caller
60120 '
60130 DATA  85,139,236, 30,  6,139,118, 30,139,  4,232,140,  0,139,118
60140 DATA  12,139, 60,139,118,  8,139,  4, 61,255,255,117,  2,140,216
60150 DATA 142,192,139,118, 28,138, 36,139,118, 26,138,  4,139,118, 24
60160 DATA 138, 60,139,118, 22,138, 28,139,118, 20,138, 44,139,118, 18
60170 DATA 138, 12,139,118, 16,138, 52,139,118, 14,138, 20,139,118, 10
60180 DATA 139, 52, 85,205, 33, 93, 86,156,139,118, 12,137, 60,139,118
60190 DATA  28,136, 36,139,118, 26,136,  4,139,118, 24,136, 60,139,118
60200 DATA  22,136, 28,139,118, 20,136, 44,139,118, 18,136, 12,139,118
60210 DATA  16,136, 52,139,118, 14,136, 20,139,118,  8,140,192,137,  4
60220 DATA  88,139,118,  6,137,  4, 88,139,118, 10,137,  4,  7, 31, 93
60230 DATA 202, 26,  0, 91, 46,136, 71, 66,233,108,255
```

Pascal listing: LEDP.PAS

```
{*********************************************************************}
{*                            L E D P                                *}
{*-------------------------------------------------------------------*}
{*    Description    : sets the various bits in the BIOS keyboard    *}
{*                     status byte causing the LEDs on the AT        *}
{*                     keyboard to turn on.                          *}
{*-------------------------------------------------------------------*}
{*    Author         : MICHAEL TISCHER                               *}
{*    developed on   : 08/16/1988                                    *}
{*    last update    : 08/17/1988                                    *}
{*********************************************************************}

program LEDP;

uses CRT,                                   { bind in the CRT unit }
     DOS;                                   { bind in the DOS unit }

const SCRL =  16;                              { Scroll Lock bit }
      NUML =  32;                                 { Num Lock bit }
      CAPL =  64;                                { Caps Lock bit }
      INS  = 128;                                   { Insert bit }

{*********************************************************************}
{* SETFLAG: sets one the flags in the BIOS keyboard status byte      *}
{* Input  : the flag to be set (see constants)                       *}
{* Output : none                                                     *}
{*********************************************************************}

procedure SetFlag(Flag : byte);
```

```
var BiosTSByte : byte absolute $0040:$0017;{ BIOS keyboard status byte }
    Regs       : Registers;   { processor registers for interrupt call }

begin
  BiosTSByte := BiosTSByte or Flag;   { mask out the corresponding bit }
  Regs.AH := 1;                     {   function no.: character ready? }
  intr($16, Regs);                     { call BIOS keyboard interrupt }
end;

{**********************************************************************}
{* CLRFLAG: clears one of the flags in the BIOS keyboard status byte   *}
{* Input  : the flag to be cleared (see constants)                     *}
{* Output : none                                                       *}
{**********************************************************************}

procedure ClrFlag(Flag : byte);

var BiosTSByte : byte absolute $0040:$0017;    { BIOS keyb. status byte }
    Regs       : Registers;   { processor registers for interrupt call }

begin
  BiosTSByte := BiosTSByte and ( not Flag );              { mask out bit }
  Regs.AH := 1;                        { function no.: character ready? }
  intr($16, Regs);                      { call BIOS keyboard interrupt  }
end;

{**********************************************************************}
{**                          MAIN PROGRAM                            **}
{**********************************************************************}

var counter : integer;

begin
  writeln('LEDP  -  (c) 1988 by Michael Tischer');
  writeln(#13,#10, 'Watch the LEDs on your keyboard!');

  for counter:=1 to 10 do             { run through the loop 10 times }
    begin
      SetFlag( CAPL);                                  { turn on CAPS }
      Delay( 100 );                          { wait 100 milliseconds }
      ClrFlag( CAPL );                         { turn CAPS off again }
      SetFlag( NUML);                                   { turn on NUM }
      Delay( 100 );                          { wait 100 milliseconds }
      ClrFlag( NUML );                          { turn NUM off again }
      SetFlag( SCRL);                         { turn SCROLL LOCK off }
      Delay( 100 );                          { wait 100 milliseconds }
      ClrFlag( SCRL );                   { turn SCROLL LOCK off again }
    end;

  for counter:=1 to 10 do                 { run through loop 10 times }
    begin
      SetFlag(CAPL or SCRL or NUML);             { all three flags on }
      Delay( 200 );                          { wait 200 milliseconds }
      ClrFlag(CAPL or SCRL or NUML);            { all flags off again }
      Delay( 200 );                          { wait 200 milliseconds }
    end;
end.
```

C listing: LEDC.C

```
/***********************************************************************/
/*                              L E D C                                */
/*---------------------------------------------------------------------*/
/*    Description    : Sets the various bits in the BIOS keyboard      */
/*                     flag, causing the LEDs on the AT keyboard to    */
/*                     flash.                                          */
/*---------------------------------------------------------------------*/
/*    Author         : MICHAEL TISCHER                                 */
/*    developed on   : 22.08.1988                                      */
/*    last update    : 22.08.1988                                      */
/*---------------------------------------------------------------------*/
/*    (MICROSOFT C)                                                    */
/*    creation       : CL /AS LEDC.C                                   */
/*    call           : LEDC                                            */
/*---------------------------------------------------------------------*/
/*    (BORLAND TURBO C)                                                */
/*    creation       : via the command COMPILE / MAKE                  */
/***********************************************************************/

/*== Include files ====================================================*/

#include <dos.h>

/*== Macros ===========================================================*/

#ifndef MK_FP                              /* was MK_FP already defined? */
#define MK_FP(seg, ofs) ((void far *) ((unsigned long) (seg)<<16|(ofs)))
#endif

/*== Constants ========================================================*/

#define SCRL  16                                      /* Scroll Lock bit */
#define NUML  32                                         /* Num Lock bit */
#define CAPL  64                                        /* Caps Lock bit */
#define INS  128                                           /* Insert bit */

/*-- BIOS_KBF creates a pointer to the BIOS keyboard flag ------------*/

#define BIOS_KBF ((unsigned far *) MK_FP(0x40, 0x17))

/***********************************************************************
*  Function          : D E L A Y                                       *
**---------------------------------------------------------------------**
*  Description       : Waits a certain length of time.                 *
*  Input parameters  : PAUSE = the number of milliseconds to wait.     *
*  Return value      : none                                            *
*  Info              : Since this function uses the BIOS timer for time *
*                      measurement, the accuracy is limited to about   *
*                      1/60 of a second.                               *
***********************************************************************/

void delay( unsigned pause )
{
 long timer;                  /* stores the timer value to be reached */
 union REGS inregs,                  /* stores the processor registers */
            outregs;    /* INREGS before, OUTREGS after the intr call */

 inregs.h.ah = 0;                               /* ftn. no.: read timer */
 int86(0x1a, &inregs, &outregs);           /* call BIOS timer interrupt */

 /*- calculate the target time value  and check to see if this     ----*/
 /*- value has been reached.                                       ----*/

 timer = outregs.x.dx + ((long) outregs.x.cx << 16) +
        (pause * 18 + ((pause << 1) / 10)) / 1000;
 do                                                    /* polling loop */
  int86(0x1a, &inregs, &outregs);                 /* read timer again */
```

```
 while ((outregs.x.dx + ((long) outregs.x.cx << 16)) <= timer);
}
/***********************************************************************
* Function          : S E T _ F L A G                                 *
**-------------------------------------------------------------------**
* Description       : Sets individual bits or flags in the BIOS       *
*                     keyboard flag.                                  *
* Input parameters : FLAG = the bits or flags to be set              *
* Return value      : none                                            *
***********************************************************************/

void set_flag( unsigned flag )
{
 union REGS regs;                    /* stores the processor registers */

 *BIOS_KBF |= flag;    /* set the specified bits in the keyboard flag */
 regs.h.ah = 1;                        /* ftn. no.: character present? */
 int86(0x16, &regs, &regs);            /* call BIOS keyboard interrupt */
}
/***********************************************************************
* Function          : C L R _ F L A G                                 *
**-------------------------------------------------------------------**
* Description       : Clears individual bits or flags in the BIOS     *
*                     keyboard flag.                                  *
* Input parameters : FLAG = the bits or flags to be cleared          *
* Return value      : none                                            *
***********************************************************************/

void clr_flag( unsigned flag )
{
 union REGS regs;                    /* stores the processor registers */

 *BIOS_KBF &= ~flag;          /* mask out bits in the BIOS keyb. flag */
 regs.h.ah = 1;                        /* ftn. no.: character present? */
 int86(0x16, &regs, &regs);            /* call BIOS keyboard interrupt */
}

/**********************************************************************/
/**                           MAIN PROGRAM                           **/
/**********************************************************************/
void main()
{
 unsigned i;                                          /* loop counter*/

 printf("LEDP  -  (c) 1988 by Michael Tischer\n\n");
 printf("Watch the LEDs on your keyboard!\n");



 for (i=0; i<10; ++i)                /* run through the loop 10 times */
  {
   set_flag( CAPL );                                  /* turn CAPS on */
   delay( 100 );                              /* wait 100 milliseconds */
   clr_flag( CAPL );                            /* turn CAPS off again */
   set_flag( NUML);                                   /* turn on NUM */
   delay( 100 );                              /* wait 100 milliseconds */
   clr_flag( NUML );                             /* turn NUM off again */
   set_flag( SCRL);                             /* turn on SCROLL LOCK */
   delay( 100 );                              /* wait 100 milliseconds */
   clr_flag( SCRL );                     /* turn SCROLL LOCK off again */
  }

 for (i=0; i<10; ++i)                /* run through the loop 10 times */
  {
   set_flag(CAPL | SCRL | NUML);                 /* all three flags on */
   delay( 200 );                              /* wait 200 milliseconds */
   clr_flag(CAPL | SCRL | NUML);                /* all flags off again */
   delay( 200 );                              /* wait 200 milliseconds */
  }
}
```

Chapter 13

Expanded Memory Specification

When the IBM PC was being developed in 1980 its capabilities were quite advanced for its time. This was also true of the size of its main memory. The maximum size of 640K seemed so large at the time that no one could imagine what a user would do with so much memory. Thus the first PCs were equipped with 64K, then 128K, and later 256K of memory. But today memory requirements are much greater and the standard amount of RAM for PCs, and especially ATs, has grown to the full 640K.

As we enter the age of the 80386 microprocessor, with the introduction of graphic user interfaces and multitasking operating systems (Windows®, OS/2®), 640K will soon no longer be enough to make full use of the capabilities of the PC. But we have reached a boundary that cannot be crossed by just adding more memory chips to the computer. A normal PC or XT is limited to 640K and an AT to 16 megabytes. The 16 meg is only available in the protected mode of the 80286 processor, and is inaccessible to normal DOS applications.

Adding memory

To provide a way around this problem, some leading PC firms got together several years ago and devised a way to add more memory to PCs, XTs and ATs that could also be accessed under DOS. These companies were Lotus (the developers of Lotus 1-2-3), Intel (manufacturer of PC processors) and Microsoft (developers of MS-DOS and OS/2). They developed a standard known as the LIM standard, after the first letters of the company names.

This standard allows up to 8 megabytes to be added to a PC on an expansion card. Only 64K of this 8 megabytes is visible in the 1 megabyte address range of the 8088 processor, in a window called the page frame. Memory installed in this manner is called *expanded memory*, and should not be confused with the extended memory which ranges beyond 1 megabyte on an AT. The whole system is referred to as the expanded memory system, or EMS for short.

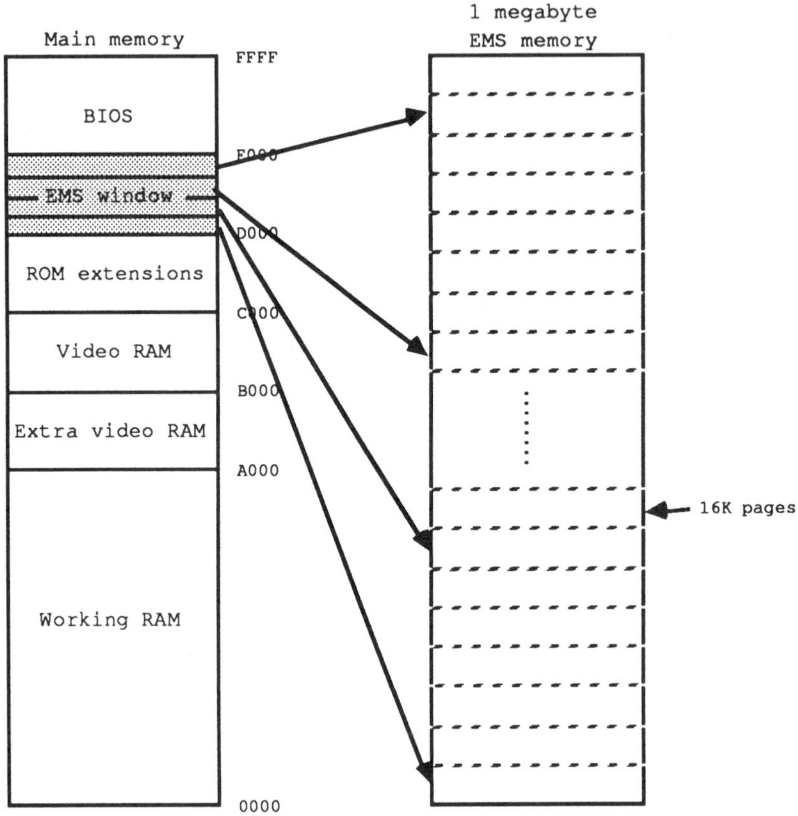

EMS memory access (LIM standard) using a window

There is always at least 64K in the 1 megabyte address space of the PC which is not used for main memory, BIOS, video RAM, or other system expansions, so the EMS developers decided to use this as a window into the EMS memory. Usually this window is at segment address D000H, but the EMS hardware allows it to be changed.

Since this window is under the 1 megabyte memory limit, it can be accessed with normal assembly language instructions, similar to the way the video RAM is accessed. Both read and write accesses are possible. We will look at concrete examples of these accesses later on in this chapter.

Page frame division

The whole procedure is somewhat refined by the fact that the page frame is further divided into 16K pages. This allows the programmer to access four completely different, and perhaps widely separated, pages from the EMS memory.

The registers on the EMS card allow the programmer to set which pages of the EMS memory will be visible in the page frame. The address lines on the EMS card are programmed so that the EMS pages are mapped into the page frame and appear in the 8088's address space. This process is known as bank-switching.

In addition to the hardware, the EMS also includes a software interface which handles programming the EMS registers and other memory management tasks. It is called the EMM (Expanded Memory Manager) and gives you a standard interface which you can use to access the EMS cards of different manufacturers. This also applies for the extended EMS standard (EEMS) developed by AST Research, Quadram, and Ashton-Tate, which goes far beyond the LIM standard.

The EMM

Similar to the DOS interrupt 21H, which provides a standard interface to the operating system functions, the EMM functions can be called through interrupt 67H. Before a program tries to use EMS memory and the corresponding EMM, it should first check to make sure that an EMS is installed. If it does not do this and there is no EMM, the results of a call to interrupt 67H are completely unpredictable. Maybe it just won't work; maybe the system will crash.

To prevent this, a program which uses the EMS should first check to make sure it exists. To do this we can use the fact that the EMM is bound into the system as a normal device driver when the computer is booted. As such, it naturally has a driver header which precedes it in memory and defines its structure for DOS. The name of the driver is found at address 10 in the driver header. The LIM standard prescribes that this name must be EMMXXXX0. The example programs at the end of this chapter test for this name by first determining the segment address of the interrupt handler for interrupt 67H. If the EMM is installed, the segment address points to the segment into which the EMMXXXX0 device driver was loaded. Since the driver header is at offset address 0 relative to the start of this segment, we just compare the memory locations starting at 10 with the name EMMXXXX0 to see if the EMS memory and the corresponding EMM are installed.

Once this is verified, access to this memory requires just three steps:

1.) Just as conventional memory must be allocated with a DOS function, a program must first allocate a certain number of EMS pages for itself from the EMM. The number of pages to be allocated depends on both the memory requirements of the program and how much EMS memory is available.

2.) If the desired number of pages were successfully allocated, the specified pages must first be loaded into one of the four pages of the page frame so that data can be written into them or read from them. This results in a mapping between one of the allocated pages and one of the four physical pages within the page frame.

3.) When the program is ended or it is done using the EMS storage, the allocated pages should be released again. If this is not done, the allocated pages will still be owned by the program (even after it ends) and cannot be given to other programs.

As with DOS interrupt 21H, the function number of an EMM call must be loaded into the AH register before the interrupt call. In contrast to the DOS functions, the function number does not correspond directly to the value in the AH register and you must add 3FH to the function number. Thus for a call to function 2H you would have to load the value 3FH + 2H or 41H into the AH register. After the function call this register contains the error status of the function. The value 0 signals that the function was executed successfully, while values greater than or equal to 80H indicate an error.

About errors

You can get the error codes from the error descriptions in the Appendices, but you should be aware of one particular error. If the value 84H is in the AH register after a call to EMM interrupt 67H, it means that an invalid function number was passed in the AH register.

The following functions are required for a transient program to access the EMS memory:

Function	Task
01H	Get EMM status
02H	Get segment address of the page frame
03H	Get number of pages
04H	Allocate EMS pages
05H	Set mapping
06H	Release EMS pages

To guarantee proper operation of the EMS hardware and the EMM, you should check the EMM status before allocating EMS memory. This is done with function 01H, which requires no parameters beside the function number in the AH register. If it returns the value 0 in the AH register, then everything is OK and you can start working with the EMS memory.

Limits to EMS allocation

Naturally the number of allocatable EMS pages is limited by the number of free pages. Thus you should ensure that the memory requirements of the program do not exceed the available memory. Here we can use function 03H, which returns the number of free EMS pages. This function requires no parameters beside the function number and returns the number of unallocated pages in the BX register. It also returns the total number of installed EMS pages in the DX register.

If enough EMS memory exists for our program, or if the memory requirements are adapted to the available memory, we can then allocate the memory. Function 04H must be passed the number of pages to be allocated in the BX register. If the requested number of pages were successfully allocated (AH register contains 0 after the function call), the caller will find a handle to the allocated pages in the BX register. This handle must be used to access the allocated pages and identifies the caller to the EMM. This handle must be saved by the caller and losing it means not only that the allocated pages cannot be accessed, they can also no longer be released. This function can be called multiple times by a program to allocate multiple logical page blocks.

Once we have the page handle we can start accessing the pages. The handle is passed to the appropriate functions in the DX register. This also applies to function 05H, which maps a logical page to one of the four physical pages of the page frame. The number of the logical page is passed in the BX register and the physical page number in the AL register. Note that both specifications start at zero. If you have allocated 15 pages, then the numbers of the logical pages run from zero to 14.

Once the appropriate page is in the page frame, it can be accessed just like normal memory. The offset address of the start-of-page is calculated from the physical page number, but the corresponding segment address must be determined with an EMM function. Since this address does not change while working with the EMS memory, you can read it once at the beginning of the program and then save it in a variable. Function 02H returns the segment address of the page frame in the BX register.

When you are done using the EMS, be sure to return the allocated pages to the EMM. All you have to do is pass the page handle to function 06H.

In addition to these six functions, which a normal program can use to access EMS memory, there are six more functions which can be useful under certain circumstances. These are the following:

Function	Task
07H	Get EMM version number
08H	Save current mapping
09H	Reset saved mapping
0CH	Get number of EMM handles
0DH	Get the number of pages allocated to a handle
0EH	Get all handles and numbers of allocated pages

Version numbers

Reading the EMM version number is of interest because the LIM standard has changed somewhat since it was introduced. Some functions are no longer supported and new functions have been added. The functions presented here are from Version 3.2, which has now been superseded by version 4.0. Version 3.2 represents a good compromise not only because is it very widely used, but because it is also completely compatible with Version 4.0. If you don't want to support earlier or later EMS versions in your program, you should check the version number at the start of the program. The version number will be returned in the AL register after a call to function 07H. It is encoded as a BCD number.

Functions 08H and 09H are important for TSR programs which want to use the EMS memory for their own purposes. When a TSR program interrupts a transient program and places itself in the foreground, it must take into account the fact that the interrupted program may have been using EMS memory and had created a certain mapping. Since this mapping must not be changed when returning to the interrupted program, it must be saved when the TSR is activated and then restored when the TSR exits. Function 08H saves the current EMM mapping and function 09H resets the saved status. Both functions must be passed the handle of the function. In this case it is the handle of the TSR program, not the handle of the interrupted program.

The last three functions are only important for the memory manager and will not be discussed here. More information can be found in the appendix in the EMM function descriptions.

Demonstration programs

The following pages contain two programs, one written in Pascal and one in C, which illustrate how to use EMS memory. There is no assembly language program since, in principle, calls to the EMM functions involve just loading variables and constants into registers and calling the EMM interrupt 67H. Using the information in the Appendices, it should be easy to write an assembly language program which uses the EMS. There is no BASIC program because EMS memory is intended to be used with complex and memory-intensive applications for which BASIC (or at least GW-BASIC) is not suited.

The two programs are almost identical, so we will limit ourselves to a discussion of the basic program structure. The programs offer a number of functions and procedures which can be used to access the various EMM functions. Both programs also contain a function called EMS_INST (or EmsInst) which determines if an EMM is installed. In Pascal we have a problem because a pointer has to be loaded with an address which consists of separate segment and offset addresses. Since this is not possible in Pascal, there is an INLINE procedure called MK_FP which (like the C macro of the same name) combines a segment and an offset address into a (FAR) pointer. The fact that this is a FAR pointer is important because the page frame is not in the program's data segment and thus cannot be addressed via the DS register. This is not a problem in Turbo Pascal because the code is generated to work with FAR data pointers. In C we have to make sure that the program is compiled in a memory model which uses FAR pointers for data. This occurs in compact, large, and huge models.

The main program firsts tests to see if EMM is present and then uses various functions to obtain status information about the EMS memory, which it displays on the screen. Then a page is allocated and mapped to the first page (page 0) of the page frame. The current contents of the video RAM are copied into this page and the video RAM is then erased.

After the copy procedure, a message is displayed for the user and the program waits for a key to be pressed. Then it copies the old screen contents back to video RAM from page 0 of the page frame and the program ends.

This program shows that the contents of a page in the page frame can be treated just like ordinary data. After you have created a pointer to the corresponding page you can manipulate the data on this page, including complex objects like structures and arrays, just like any other data. It is important to make sure that your objects fit on one page or that you do not forget to change pages or load a new page into the page frame to access larger objects.

C listing: EMMC.C

```
/*********************************************************************/
/*                            E M M C                                */
/*-------------------------------------------------------------------*/
/*    Description    : a collection of functions for using EMS       */
/*                     storage (expanded memory).                    */
/*-------------------------------------------------------------------*/
/*    Author         : MICHAEL TISCHER                               */
/*    developed on   : 08/30/1988                                    */
/*    last update    : 08/30/1988                                    */
/*-------------------------------------------------------------------*/
/*    (MICROSOFT C)                                                  */
/*    creation       : CL /AC EMMC.C                                 */
/*    call           : EMMC                                          */
/*-------------------------------------------------------------------*/
/*    (BORLAND TURBO C)                                              */
/*    creation       : via the RUN command in the menu line          */
/*                     (no project file)                             */
/*    Info           : Note that the Compact memory model must be    */
/*                     selected via the compiler model menu option.  */
/*********************************************************************/

/*== Include files ==================================================*/

#include <dos.h>
#include <stdlib.h>
#include <string.h>

/*== Typedefs =======================================================*/

typedef unsigned char BYTE;                /* build ourselves a byte */
typedef unsigned int WORD;
typedef BYTE BOOL;                         /* like BOOLEAN in Pascal */

/*== Macros =========================================================*/
```

```
/*-- MK_FP creates a FAR pointer out of segment and offset addresses -*/

#ifndef MK_FP                              /* is MK_FP defined yet? */
#define MK_FP(seg, ofs) ((void far *) ((unsigned long) (seg)<<16|(ofs)))
#endif

/*-- PAGE_ADR returns a pointer to the physical page X within the ----*/
/*-- page frame of the EMS memory.                              ----*/

#define PAGE_ADR(x) ((void *) MK_FP(ems_frame_seg() + ((x) << 10), 0))

/*== Constants =======================================================*/

#define TRUE  1                      /* constants for working with BOOL */
#define FALSE 0

#define EMS_INT 0x67          /* interrupt number for access to the EMM */
#define EMS_ERR -1                                /* returned on error */

/*== Global variables ================================================*/

BYTE emm_ec;                      /* the EMM error codes are placed here */

/**********************************************************************
*  Function          : E M S _ I N S T                                *
**------------------------------------------------------------------**
*  Description       : Determines if EMS memory and the associated    *
*                      EMS driver (EMM) are installed.                *
*  Input parameters : none                                           *
*  Return value      : TRUE, if EMS memory installed, else FALSE      *
**********************************************************************/

BOOL ems_inst()
 {
  static char emm_name[] = { 'E', 'M', 'M', 'X', 'X', 'X', 'X', '0' };
  union REGS regs;            /* processor registers for interrupt call */
  struct SREGS sregs;       /* segment registers for the interrupt call */
  BYTE i;                                             /* loop counter */
  char *emm_inspect;  /* pointer to the name in the interrupt handler */

  /*-- construct pointer to name in the header of a switch driver ----*/

  regs.x.ax = 0x3567;           /* ftn. no.: get interrupt vector 0x67 */
  intdosx(&regs, &regs, &sregs);             /* call DOS interrupt 0x21 */
  emm_inspect = (char *) MK_FP(sregs.es, 10);     /* construct pointer */

  /*-- search for the name of the EMS driver ------------------------*/

  for(i=0; i<sizeof emm_name && *(emm_inspect++)==emm_name[i++]; )
   ;
  return( i == sizeof emm_name );              /* TRUE if name found */
 }

/**********************************************************************
*  Function          : E M S _ N U M _ P A G E                        *
**------------------------------------------------------------------**
*  Output            : Determines the total number of EMS pages       *
*  Input parameters : none                                           *
*  Return value      : EMS_ERR on error, else the number of EMS pages *
**********************************************************************/

int ems_num_page()
 {
  union REGS regs;            /* processor registers for interrupt call */

  regs.h.ah = 0x42;                  /* ftn. no.: get number of pages */
  int86(EMS_INT, &regs, &regs);                            /* call EMM */
  if (emm_ec = regs.h.ah)                       /* did an error occur? */
   return(EMS_ERR);                              /* yes, display error */
  else                                                     /* no error */
```

```
  return( regs.x.dx );              /* return total number of pages */
 }

/***********************************************************************
* Function          : E M S _ F R E E _ P A G E                        *
**--------------------------------------------------------------------**
* Description       : Returns the number of free EMS pages.            *
* Input parameters  : none                                             *
* Return value      : EMS_ERR on error, else the number of free EMS    *
*                     pages.                                           *
***********************************************************************/

int ems_free_page()
 {
  union REGS regs;          /* processor registers for interrupt call */

  regs.h.ah = 0x42;                 /* ftn. no.: get number of pages */
  int86(EMS_INT, &regs, &regs);                           /* call EMM */
  if (emm_ec = regs.h.ah)                      /* did an error occur? */
   return(EMS_ERR);                             /* yes, display error */
  else                                                   /* no error */
   return( regs.x.bx );              /* return number of free pages */
 }

/***********************************************************************
* Function          : E M S _ F R A M E _ S E G                        *
**--------------------------------------------------------------------**
* Description       : Determines the segment address of the EMS page   *
*                     frames.                                          *
* Input parameters  : none                                             *
* Return value      : EMS_ERR on error, else the segment address of    *
*                     the page frame.                                  *
***********************************************************************/

WORD ems_frame_seg()
 {
  union REGS regs;          /* processor registers for interrupt call */

  regs.h.ah = 0x41;         /* ftn. no.: get segment addr page frame */
  int86(EMS_INT, &regs, &regs);                           /* call EMM */
  if (emm_ec = regs.h.ah)                      /* did an error occur? */
   return(EMS_ERR);                             /* yes, display error */
  else                                                   /* no error */
   return( regs.x.bx );                   /* return segtment address */
 }

/***********************************************************************
* Function          : E M S _ A L L O C                                *
**--------------------------------------------------------------------**
* Description       : Allocates the specified number of pages and      *
*                     returns a handle for accessing these pages.      *
* Input parameters  : PAGES : the number of pages to be allocated      *
*                             (each 16 KByte)                          *
* Return-Wert       : EMS_ERR on error, else the EMS handle.           *
***********************************************************************/

int ems_alloc(int pages)
 {
  union REGS regs;          /* processor registers for interrupt call */

  regs.h.ah = 0x43;                     /* ftn. no.: allocate pages */
  regs.x.bx = pages;           /* set number of pages to be allocated */
  int86(EMS_INT, &regs, &regs);                           /* call EMM */
  if (emm_ec = regs.h.ah)                      /* did an error occur? */
   return(EMS_ERR);                             /* yes, display error */
  else                                                   /* no error */
   return( regs.x.dx );                          /* return EMS handle */
 }

/***********************************************************************
```

```
* Function          : E M S _ M A P                                    *
**--------------------------------------------------------------------**
* Description       : Maps one of the allocated pages specified        *
*                     by the given handle onto a physical page in the  *
*                     page frame.                                      *
* Input parameters  : HANDLE: the handle returned by EMS_ALLOC         *
*                     LOGP  : the logical page (0 to n-1)              *
*                     PHYSP : the physical page (0 to 3)               *
* Return-Wert       : FALSE on error, else TRUE.                       *
************************************************************************/

BOOL ems_map(int handle, int logp, BYTE physp)
 {
  union REGS regs;          /* processor registers for interrupt call */

  regs.h.ah = 0x44;                          /* ftn. no.: set mapping */
  regs.h.al = physp;                            /* set physical page */
  regs.x.bx = logp;                              /* set logical page */
  regs.x.dx = handle;                              /* set EMS handle */
  int86(EMS_INT, &regs, &regs);                          /* call EMM */
  return (!(emm_ec = regs.h.ah));
 }

/***********************************************************************
* Function          : E M S _ F R E E                                  *
**--------------------------------------------------------------------**
* Description       : Releases the memory specified by the handle.     *
* Input parameters  : HANDLE: the handle returned by EMS_ALLOC         *
* Return value      : FALSE on error, else TRUE.                       *
************************************************************************/

BOOL ems_free(int handle)
 {
  union REGS regs;          /* processor registers for interrupt call */

  regs.h.ah = 0x45;                       /* ftn. no.: release pages */
  regs.x.dx = handle;                              /* set EMS handle */
  int86(EMS_INT, &regs, &regs);                          /* call EMM */
  return (!(emm_ec = regs.h.ah));/* if AH contains 0, everything's OK */
 }

/***********************************************************************
* Function          : E M S _ V E R S I O N                            *
**--------------------------------------------------------------------**
* Description       : Determines the EMM version number.               *
* Input parameters  : none                                             *
* Return value      : EMS_ERR on error, else the EMM version number    *
* Info              : In the version number, 10 stands for 1.0, 11 for *
*                     1.1, 34 for 3.4, etc.                            *
************************************************************************/

BYTE ems_version()
 {
  union REGS regs;          /* processor registers for interrupt call */

  regs.h.ah = 0x46;                /* ftn. no.: get EMM version num. */
  int86(EMS_INT, &regs, &regs);                          /* call EMM */
  if (emm_ec = regs.h.ah)                       /* did an error occur? */
   return(EMS_ERR);                          /* yes, display error */
  else         /* no error, calculate version number from BCD number */
   return( (regs.h.al & 15) + (regs.h.al >> 4) * 10);
 }

/***********************************************************************
* Function          : E M S _ S A V E _ M A P                          *
**--------------------------------------------------------------------**
* Description       : Saves the mapping between the logical and        *
*                     physical pages.                                  *
* Input parameters  : HANDLE: the handle returned by EMS_ALLOC.        *
* Return value      : FALSE on error, else TRUE.                       *
```

```
***************************************************************************/

BOOL ems_save_map(int handle)
 {
  union REGS regs;          /* processor registers for interrupt call */

  regs.h.ah = 0x47;                          /* ftn. no.: save mapping */
  regs.x.dx = handle;                                /* set EMS handle */
  int86(EMS_INT, &regs, &regs);                            /* call EMM */
  return (!(emm_ec = regs.h.ah));/* if AH contains 0, everything's OK */
 }

/***************************************************************************
*  Function          : E M S _ R E S T O R E _ M A P                      *
**------------------------------------------------------------------------**
*  Description       : Restores a mapping between logical and physical    *
*                      pages saved with EMS_SAVE_MAP.                     *
*  Input parameters : HANDLE: the handle returned by EMS_ALLOC           *
*  Return value      : FALSE on error, else TRUE.                         *
***************************************************************************/
BOOL ems_restore_map(int handle)
 {
  union REGS regs;          /* processor registers for interrupt call */

  regs.h.ah = 0x48;                       /* ftn. no.: restore mapping */
  regs.x.dx = handle;                                /* set EMS handle */
  int86(EMS_INT, &regs, &regs);                            /* call EMM */
  return (!(emm_ec = regs.h.ah));/* if AH contains 0, wverything's OK */
 }

/***************************************************************************
*  Function          : P R I N T _ E R R                                  *
**------------------------------------------------------------------------**
*  Description       : Prints an EMS error message on the screen and      *
*                      ends the program.                                  *
*  Input parameters : none                                               *
*  Return value      : none                                               *
*  Info              : This function may only be called if an error       *
*                      occurred on a prior call to the EMM.               *
***************************************************************************/

void print_err()
 {
  static char nid[] = "unidentifiable";
  static char *err_vec[] =
   { "Error in the EMS driver (EMM destroyed)",              /* 0x80 */
      "Error in the EMS hardware",                            /* 0x81 */
      nid,                                                    /* 0x82 */
      "Illegal EMM handle",                                   /* 0x83 */
      "EMS function called does not exist",                   /* 0x84 */
      "No more EMS handles available",                        /* 0x85 */
      "Error while saving or restoring the mapping",          /* 0x86 */
      "More pages requested than physically present",         /* 0x87 */
      "More pages requested than are still free",             /* 0x88 */
      "Zero pages requested",                                 /* 0x89 */
      "Logical page does not belong to handle",               /* 0x8A */
      "Illegal physical page number",                         /* 0x8B */
      "Mapping storage is full",                              /* 0x8C */
      "The mapping has already been saved",                   /* 0x8D */
      "Restored mapping without saving first"
   };

  printf("\nError in access to EMS memory!\n");
  printf("         ... %s\n", (emm_ec<0x80 || emm_ec>0x8E) ?
                               nid : err_vec[emm_ec-0x80]);
  exit( 1 );                        /* End program with error code */
 }

/***************************************************************************
*  Function          : V R _ A D R                                        *
```

```
**--------------------------------------------------------------------**
*  Description      : Returns a pointer to the video RAM.              *
*  Input parameters : none                                             *
*  Return value     : VOID pointer to the video RAM.                   *
***********************************************************************/

void *vr_adr()
 {
  union REGS regs;          /* processor registers for interrupt call */

  regs.h.ah = 0x0f;                        /* ftn. no.: get video mode */
  int86(0x10, &regs, &regs);             /* call BIOS video interrupt */
  return ( MK_FP((regs.h.al==7) ? 0xb000 : 0xb800, 0) );
 }

/***********************************************************************/
/**                           MAIN PROGRAM                           **/
/***********************************************************************/

void main()
{
 int  numpage,                                 /* number of EMS pages */
      handle,                    /* handle to access to the EMS memory */
      i;                                              /* loop counter */
 WORD pageseg ;                  /* segment address of the page frame */
 BYTE emmver;                                   /* EMM version number */

 printf("EMMC  -  (c) 1988 by MICHAEL TISCHER\n\n");
 if ( ems_inst() )                         /* is EMS memory installed? */
  {                                                             /* yes */
   /*-- output information about the EMS memory ----------------------*/

   if ( (emmver = ems_version()) == EMS_ERR)       /* get version num. */
    print_err();        /* error: output error message and end program */
   else                                                    /* no error */
    printf("EMM version number              : %d.%d\n",
           emmver/10, emmver%10);

   if ( (numpage = ems_num_page()) == EMS_ERR) /* get number of pages */
    print_err();        /* error: output error message and end program */
   printf("Number of EMS pages             : %d (%d KByte)\n",
          numpage, numpage << 4);

   if ( (numpage = ems_free_page()) == EMS_ERR)
    print_err();        /* Error: output error message and end program */
   printf("...         free               : %d (%d KByte)\n",
          numpage, numpage << 4);

   if ( (int) (pageseg = ems_frame_seg()) == EMS_ERR)
    print_err();        /* Error: output error message and end program */
   printf("Segment address of the page frame: %X\n", pageseg);

   printf("\nNow a page will be allocated from the EMS memory and\n");
   printf("the screen contents will be copied from the video RAM\n");
   printf("to this page.\n");
   printf("                                     ... press any key\n");
   getch();                                          /* wait for a key */

   /*-- allocate a page and map it to the first logical page in    ---*/
   /*-- page frame.                                                ---*/
   if ( (handle = ems_alloc(1)) == EMS_ERR)
    print_err();        /* Error: output error message and end program */
   if ( !ems_map(handle, 0, 0) )                         /* set mapping */
    print_err();        /* Error: output error message and end program */

   /*-- copy 4000 bytes from the video RAM to the EMS memory ---------*/

   memcpy(PAGE_ADR(0), vr_adr(), 4000);
```

```
    for (i=0; i<24; ++i)                          /* clear the screen */
     printf("\n");

    printf("The old screen contents will now be cleared and will be\n");
    printf("lost. But since it was stored in the EMS memory, they\n");
    printf("can be copied from there back into the video RAM.\n");
    printf("                                   ... press any key\n");
    getch();                                          /* wait for a key */

    /*-- copy the contents of the video RAM from the EMS memory     ----*/
    /*-- and release the allocated EMS memory again.                ----*/

    memcpy(vr_adr(), PAGE_ADR(0), 4000);              /* copy VRAM back */
    if ( !ems_free(handle) )                        /* release memory */
     print_err();       /* Error: output error message and end program */
    printf("END");
  }
 else                               /* the EMS driver was not detected */
  printf("No EMS memory installed.\n");
}
```

Pascal listing: EMMP.PAS

```
{**********************************************************************}
{*                              E M M P                               *}
{*--------------------------------------------------------------------*}
{*    Task              : Implement certain functions to demonstrate   *}
{*                        access to EMS memory using EMM.             *}
{*--------------------------------------------------------------------*}
{*    Author            : MICHAEL TISCHER                             *}
{*    Developed on      : 08/30/1988                                  *}
{*    Last update       : 06/21/1989                                  *}
{**********************************************************************}

program EMMP;

Uses Dos, CRT;                                 { Add DOS and CRT units }

type  ByteBuf = array[0..1000] of byte;     { One memory range as bytes }
      CharBuf = array[0..1000] of char;     { One memory range as chars }
      BytePtr = ^ByteBuf;                     { Pointer to a byte range }
      CharPtr = ^CharBuf;                     { Pointer to a char range }

const EMS_INT   = $67;                { Interrupt # for access to EMM }
      EMS_ERR   = -1;                             { Error if this occurs }
      W_EMS_ERR = $FFFF;                      { Error code in WORD form }
      EmmName   : array[0..7] of char = 'EMMXXXX0';        { Name of EMM }

var   EmmEC,                           { Allocation of EMM error codes }
      i         : byte;                                  { Loop counter }
      Handle,                        { Handle for access to EMS memory }
      EmmVer    : integer;                     { Version number of EMM }
      NumPage,                                    { Number of EMS pages }
      PageSeg   : word;                 { Segment address of page frame }
      Keypress    : char;

{**********************************************************************}
{* MK_FP: Creates a byte pointer from the given segment and offset    *}
{*        addresses.                                                  *}
{* Input   : - Seg = Segment to which the pointer should point        *}
{*           - Ofs = Offset addr. to which the pointer should point   *}
{* Output  : Entire pointer                                           *}
{* Info    : The returned pointer can be recast toward any other      *}
{*           pointer.                                                 *}
{**********************************************************************}

{$F+}               { This routine is intended for a FAR model, and    }
                    { should therefore be treated as one UNIT          }
```

```
function MK_FP( Seg, Ofs : word ) : BytePtr;

begin
  inline ( $8B / $46 / $08 /   { mov ax,[bp+8] (Get segment address)     }
           $89 / $46 / $FE /   { mov [bp-2],ax (and place in pointer)    }
           $8B / $46 / $06 /   { mov ax,[bp+6] (Get offset address)      }
           $89 / $46 / $FC );  { mov [bp-4],ax (and place in pointer)    }
end;

{$F-}                                        { Re-enable NEAR routines }

{************************************************************************}
{* EmsInst: Determines the existence of EMS and corresponding EMM     *}
{* Input    : none                                                     *}
{* Output   : TRUE if EMS is available, otherwise FALSE                *}
{************************************************************************}

function EmsInst : boolean;

var Regs : Registers;       { Processor register for the interrupt call }
    Name : CharPtr;                    { Pointer to the EMM names }
    i    : integer;                                  { Loop counter }

begin
  {*-- Move pointer to name in device driver header ------------------*}

  Regs.ax := $3567;             { Function #: Get interrupt vector $67}
  MsDos( Regs );                          { Call DOS interrupt $21 }
  Name := CharPtr(MK_FP(Regs.es, 10));                { Move pointer }

  {*-------- Search for EMS driver ---*}
  i := 0;                      { Start comparison with first character }
  while ((i<sizeof(EmmName)) and (Name^[i]=EmmName[i])) do
    Inc( i );                              { Increment loop counter }
  EmsInst := (i = sizeof(EmmName));         { TRUE if name is found }
end;

{************************************************************************}
{* EmsNumPage: Determines the total number of EMS pages               *}
{* Input    : none                                                     *}
{* Output   : EMS_ERR if error occurs, otherwise  number of EMS pages  *}
{************************************************************************}

function EmsNumPage : integer;

var Regs : Registers;       { Processor register for the interrupt call }

begin
  Regs.ah := $42;              { Function #: Determine number of pages }
  Intr(EMS_INT, Regs);                                   { Call EMM }
  if (Regs.ah <>0 ) then                         { Error occurred? }
    begin                                                  { YES }
      EmmEC := Regs.ah;                            { Get error code }
      EmsNumPage := EMS_ERR;                        { Display error }
    end
  else                                                { No error }
    EmsNumPage := Regs.dx;           { Return total number of pages }
end;

{************************************************************************}
{* EmsFreePage: Determines the number of free EMS pages               *}
{* Input    : none                                                     *}
{* Output   : EMS_ERR if error occurs, otherwise the number of un-    *}
{*            used EMS pages                                           *}
{************************************************************************}

function EmsFreePage : integer;

var Regs : Registers;       { Processor register for the interrupt call }
```

```
begin
  Regs.ah := $42;                  { Function #: Determine no. of pages }
  Intr(EMS_INT, Regs);                                      { Call EMM }
  if (Regs.ah <>0 ) then                              { Error occurred? }
    begin                                                       { YES }
      EmmEC := Regs.ah;                               { Mark error code }
      EmsFreePage := EMS_ERR;                           { Display error }
    end
  else                                                     { No error }
    EmsFreePage := Regs.bx;           { Return number of free pages }
end;

{***********************************************************************}
{* EmsFrameSeg: Determines the segment address of the page frame      *}
{* Input   : none                                                     *}
{* Output  : EMS_ERR if error occurs, otherwise the segment address   *}
{***********************************************************************}

function EmsFrameSeg : word;

var Regs : Registers;      { Processor register for the interrupt call }

begin
  Regs.ah := $41;          { Function #: Get segment addr. page frame }
  Intr(EMS_INT, Regs);                                      { Call EMM }
  if (Regs.ah <>0 ) then                              { Error occurred? }
    begin                                                       { YES }
      EmmEC := Regs.ah;                               { Mark error code }
      EmsFrameSeg := W_EMS_ERR;                         { Display error }
    end
  else                                                     { No error }
    EmsFrameSeg := Regs.bx;       { Return segment addr. of page frame }
end;

{***********************************************************************}
{* EmsAlloc: Allocates the specified number of pages and returns a    *}
{*           handle for access to these pages                         *}
{* Input   : PAGES: Number of allocated pages                         *}
{* Output  : EMS_ERR returns error, otherwise the handle              *}
{***********************************************************************}

function EmsAlloc( Pages : integer ) : integer;

var Regs : Registers;      { Processor register for the interrupt call}

begin
  Regs.ah := $43;                          { Function #: Alocate pages }
  Regs.bx := Pages;                     { Set number of allocated pages }
  Intr(EMS_INT, Regs);                                      { Call EMM }
  if (Regs.ah <>0 ) then                              { Error occurred? }
    begin                                                       { YES }
      EmmEC := Regs.ah;                               { Mark error code }
      EmsAlloc := EMS_ERR;                              { Display error }
    end
  else                                                     { No error }
    EmsAlloc := Regs.dx;                                { Return handle }
end;

{***********************************************************************}
{* EmsMap  : Creates an allocated logical page from a physical page in*}
{*           the page frame                                           *}
{* Input   : HANDLE: Handle received from EmsAlloc                    *}
{*           LOGP  : Logical page about to be created                 *}
{*           PHYSP : The physical page in page frame                  *}
{* Output  : FALSE if error, otherwise TRUE                          *}
{***********************************************************************}

function EmsMap(Handle, LogP : integer; PhysP : byte) : boolean;

var Regs : Registers;      { Processor register for the interrupt call }
```

```
begin
  Regs.ah := $44;                           { Function #: Set mapping }
  Regs.al := PhysP;                              { Set physical page }
  Regs.bx := LogP;                                { Set logical page }
  Regs.dx := Handle;                                { Set EMS handle }
  Intr(EMS_INT, Regs);                                    { Call EMM }
  EmmEC := Regs.ah;                                { Mark error code }
  EmsMap := (Regs.ah = 0)               { TRUE is returned if no error }
end;

{*********************************************************************}
{* EmsFree : Frees memory when given with an allocated handle       *}
{* Input   : HANDLE: Handle received by AllocEms                    *}
{* Output  : FALSE if an error, otherwise TRUE                      *}
{*********************************************************************}

function EmsFree(Handle : integer) : boolean;

var Regs : Registers;       { Processor register for the interrupt call }

begin
  Regs.ah := $45;                           { Function #: Release page }
  Regs.dx := handle;                                { Set EMS handle }
  Intr(EMS_INT, Regs);                                    { Call EMM }
  EmmEC := Regs.ah;                                { Mark error code }
  EmsFree := (Regs.ah = 0)              { TRUE is returned if no error }
end;

{*********************************************************************}
{* EmsVersion: Determines the version number of EMM                 *}
{* Input   : none                                                   *}
{* Output  : EMS_ERR if error occurs, otherwise the version number  *}
{*           (11=1.1, 40=4.0, etc.)                                  *}
{*********************************************************************}

function EmsVersion : integer;

var Regs : Registers;       { Processor register for the interrupt call }

begin
  Regs.ah := $46;                   { Function #: Determine EMM version }
  Intr(EMS_INT, Regs);                                    { Call EMM }
  if (Regs.ah <>0 ) then                          { Error occurred? }
    begin                                                     { YES }
      EmmEC := Regs.ah;                            { Mark error code }
      EmsVersion := EMS_ERR;                         { Display error }
    end
  else               { No error, compute version number from BCD number }
   EmsVersion := (Regs.al and 15) + (Regs.al shr 4) * 10;
end;

{*********************************************************************}
{* EmsSaveMap: Saves dispay between logical and physical pages of the *}
{*             given handle                                         *}
{* Input   : HANDLE: Handle assigned by EmsAlloc                     *}
{* Output  : FALSE if error occurs, otherwise TRUE                  *}
{*********************************************************************}

function EmsSaveMap( Handle : integer ) : boolean;

var Regs : Registers;       { Processor register for the interrupt call }

begin
  Regs.ah := $47;                               { Function #: Map save }
  Regs.dx := handle;                                { Set EMS handle }
  Intr(EMS_INT, Regs);                                    { Call EMM }
  EmmEC := Regs.ah;                                { Mark error code }
  EmsSaveMap := (Regs.ah = 0)              { Return TRUE if no error }
end;
```

```
{***********************************************************************}
{* EmsRestoreMap: Returns display between logical and physical pages, *}
{*                from the page saved by EmsSaveMap                   *}
{* Input    : HANDLE: Handle assigned by EmsAlloc                     *}
{* Output   : FALSE if an error occurs, otherwise TRUE                *}
{***********************************************************************}

function EmsRestoreMap( Handle : integer ) : boolean;

var Regs : Registers;       { Processor register for the interrupt call }

begin
  Regs.ah := $48;                          { Function #: Restore map }
  Regs.dx := handle;                                { Set EMS handle }
  Intr(EMS_INT, Regs);                                    { Call EMM }
  EmmEC := Regs.ah;                                { Mark error code }
  EmsRestoreMap := (Regs.ah = 0)          { TRUE returned if no error }
end;

{***********************************************************************}
{* PrintErr: Displays an error message and ends the program           *}
{* Input    : none                                                    *}
{* Output   : none                                                    *}
{* Info     : This function is called only if an error occurs during a *}
{*            function call within this module                        *}
{***********************************************************************}

procedure PrintErr;

begin
  writeln('ATTENTION! Error during EMS memory access');
  write('     ... ');
  if ((EmmEC<$80) or (EmmEc>$8E) or (EmmEc=$82)) then
    writeln('Unidentifiable error')
  else
    case EmmEC of
      $80 : writeln('EMS driver error (EMM trouble)');
      $81 : writeln('EMS hardware error');
      $83 : writeln('Illegal EMM handle');
      $84 : writeln('Called EMS function does not exist');
      $85 : writeln('No more free EMS handles available');
      $86 : writeln('Error while saving or restoring mapping ');
      $87 : writeln('More pages requested than are actually ',
                    'available');
      $88 : writeln('More pages requested than are free');
      $89 : writeln('No pages requested');
      $8A : writeln('Logical page does not belong to handle');
      $8B : writeln('Illegal physical page number');
      $8C : writeln('Mapping memory range is full');
      $8D : writeln('Map save has already been done');
      $8E : writeln('Mapping must be saved before it can',
                    'be restored');
    end;
  Halt;                                               { Program end }
end;

{***********************************************************************}
{* VrAdr: Returns a pointer to video RAM                              *}
{* Input    : none                                                    *}
{* Output   : Pointer to video RAM                                    *}
{***********************************************************************}

function VrAdr : BytePtr;

var Regs : Registers;       { Processor register for the interrupt call }

begin
  Regs.ah := $0f;                  { Function #: Determine video mode }
  Intr($10, Regs);                        { Call BIOS video interrupt }
```

```
  if (Regs.al = 7) then                         { Monochrome video card? }
    VrAdr := MK_FP($B000, 0)               { YES, video RAM at B000:0000 }
  else                                          { Color, EGA or VGA card }
    VrAdr := MK_FP($B800, 0);                   { Video RAM at B800:0000 }
end;

{************************************************************************}
{* PageAdr: Returns address of a physical page in page frame           *}
{* Input   : PAGE: Physical page number (0-3)                           *}
{* Output  : Pointer to the physical page                               *}
{************************************************************************}

function PageAdr( Page : integer ) : BytePtr;

begin
  PageAdr := MK_FP( EmsFrameSeg + (Page shl 10), 0 );
end;

{************************************************************************}
{**                          MAIN  PROGRAM                            **}
{************************************************************************}

begin
  ClrScr;                                                { Clear screen }
  writeln('EMMP  -  (c) 1988 by MICHAEL TISCHER',#13#10);
  if EmsInst then                            { Is EMS memory installed? }
    begin                                                         { YES }
                  {*-- Display EMS memory information --------------*}

      EmmVer := EmsVersion;               { Determine EMM version number }
      if EmmVer = EMS_ERR then                        { Error occurred? }
        PrintErr;           { YES, Display error message and end program }
      writeln('EMM Version number            : ',EmmVer div 10, '.',
              EmmVer mod 10);

      NumPage := EmsNumPage;          { Determine total number of pages }
      if NumPage = EMS_ERR then                       { Error occurred? }
        PrintErr;           { YES, Display error message and end program }
      writeln('Number of EMS Pages           : ', NumPage, ' (',
               NumPage shl 4, ' KByte)');

      NumPage := EmsFreePage;          { Determine number of free pages }
      if NumPage = EMS_ERR then                       { Error occurred? }
        PrintErr;           { YES, Display error message and end program }
      writeln('... free EMS pages remaining : ', NumPage, ' (',
               NumPage shl 4, ' KByte)');

      PageSeg := EmsFrameSeg;            { Segment address of page frame }
      if PageSeg = W_EMS_ERR then                     { Error occurred? }
        PrintErr;           { YES, Display error message and end program }
      writeln('Segment address of page frame: ', PAgeSeg);

      writeln;
      writeln('Now a page from EMS memory can be allocated,  and the');
      writeln('screen contents can be copied from video RAM into this');
      writeln('page.');
      writeln('                                   ... Please press a key');
      Keypress := ReadKey;                          { Wait for a keypress }

      {*-- Page is allocated, and the data is passed to the first-----*}
      {*-- logical page in the page frame                        -----*}

      Handle := EmsAlloc( 1 );                        { Allocate one page }
      if Handle = EMS_ERR then                        { Error occurred? }
        PrintErr;           { YES, Display error message and end program }
      if not(EmsMap(Handle, 0, 0)) then                    { Set mapping }
        PrintErr;         { Error: Display error message and end program }

                {*-- Copy 4000 bytes from video RAM into EMS memory --*}
```

```
      Move(VrAdr^, PageAdr(0)^, 4000);

      ClrScr;                                     { Clear screen }
      while KeyPressed do                 { Read keyboard buffer }
        Keypress := ReadKey;
      writeln('Old screen contents are cleared.  However, the  data ');
      writeln('from the screen is in EMS, and can be re-copied onto ');
      writeln('the screen.                                          ');
      writeln('                                ... Please press a key');
      Keypress := ReadKey;                   { Wait for a keypress }

      {*-- Copy contents of video RAM from EMS memory and release   --*}
      {*-- the allocated EMS memory                                  --*}

      Move(PageAdr(0)^, VrAdr^, 4000);       { Copy over video RAM }
      if not(EmsFree(Handle)) then                { Release memory }
        PrintErr;       { Error: Display error message and end program }
      GotoXY(1, 15);
      writeln('END')
    end
  else                                   { EMS driver not available }
    writeln('ATTENTION! No EMS memory installed.');
end.
```

Chapter 14

Mouse Programming

A few years ago mice were considered luxuries for PC applications. Today most PCs have mice connected to them. Part of the mouse's popularity stems from the development of new and more powerful video standards such as EGA and VGA. These graphic cards helped advance the graphic user interfaces such as GEM® and Microsoft Windows®, which are almost unusable without a mouse.

Applications and operating systems alike benefit from mouse support. Ventura Publisher® and Microsoft Works® both make intensive use of the mouse. In addition, DOS Version 4.0 accepts mouse as well as keyboard input.

A software interface acts as the connection between a program and the mouse. Microsoft Corporation designed this interface for its own mice, but other mouse manufacturers accept this interface as a standard. The interface was made available to the industry as a minimum standard to retain compatibility with the Microsoft mouse.

This function interface is usually installed either through a device driver which is loaded during system boot, or through a terminate and stay resident (TSR) program such as MOUSE.COM, included with the Microsoft mouse package.

Mouse functions

Mouse functions may be accessed in the same way as DOS and BIOS functions (you may wish to review the techniques used for addressing DOS and BIOS functions—see Chapters 6 and 7 for more information). The individual functions can be called through interrupt 33H. The identification number of the function must be passed to the AX register. The other processor registers are used in various combinations for passing information to a function.

A total of 34 different functions can be called in this manner, but most applications use only a few of these functions. Before we examine each function, let's look at the concepts behind the mouse interface. This will help you to understand the way individual functions work. We deliberately concentrated here on text oriented mouse control. Pixel oriented applications should use a graphic interface such as Windows or GEM from the start, because they provide friendlier functions for mouse input than the programming interface offered in this chapter.

About mouse buttons

Unlike the keyboard, which has many keys and keyboard codes for each key, a PC mouse usually has two or even three mouse buttons. These mouse buttons permit the user to select data in an application program. Another important piece of information is the actual position of the mouse's *pointer* (cursor) on the screen. The word pointer stems from the pointer's usual shape: an arrow or a pointing finger.

The mouse driver software always interprets the pointer's location on the screen relative to a virtual graphic screen. This virtual screen's resolution depends on the video mode and video card currently in use. Since this virtual graphic display screen is also used within the text modes to determine the mouse's position and forms the basis for communication with the mouse interface, a conversion occurs between the graphic coordinates and the mouse pointer's line/column position. Since every column or line corresponds to eight pixels, the graphic coordinates must be either divided by eight or left shifted by three places in binary mode, which mathematically produces the same result. The processor executes the shifting much faster than it can execute the actual division.

More about the mouse pointer

The pointer shows the mouse's relative location on the screen. Its shape can vary from application to application, and it can even change appearance within an application. Word processors often display the mouse pointer as a block, similar to the text cursor. In text mode the application can only determine the starting and ending line of the pointer. The pointer's size depends on the current character matrix and video mode. The options for creating a software pointer are more complex, since two 16-bit values called the *screen mask* and *cursor mask* govern the pointer's appearance.

The mouse driver must determine the appearance of the pointer every time the pointer changes position on the screen. The cursor mask and screen mask values are linked with the two bytes which describe the character code and the character color within video RAM. This linkage occurs in two steps. First the character code and the attribute byte are linked with screen mask through a binary AND. The result of this connection is then linked with the cursor mask through an exclusive OR. The result then appears on the screen.

This type of linkage allows a number of options for changing the pointer's appearance. Four of the most common pointer options are:

- Pointer appears as one specific character in one specific color
- Pointer appears as one specific character, but color changes when the pointer overlaps a character (e.g., inverse video)
- Pointer appears as one specific character, but the character color changes when the pointer overlaps a character
- Pointer appears as one specific character, but character color changes to a variant of the character color when the pointer overlaps a character

The standard measurement unit in the mouse interface is the *mickey*, named after Mickey Mouse® (1 mickey = 1/200"). The mouse hardware measures all distances in multiples of mickeys. We will use this as the measurement standard throughout the rest of this chapter.

Function 00H: Reset mouse driver

A program should call the function 00H before calling any of the mouse functions. This resets the mouse driver. It can also determine whether a mouse and mouse driver exist, by examining the content of the AX register after the function call. If the AX register contains the value 0000H after the function call, no mouse driver was installed. Even if a mouse is connected, the mouse driver no longer exists. If a mouse driver and mouse exist, function 00H returns the value FFFFH in the AX register. The BX register contains the number of buttons on the mouse. As mentioned above, PC mice usually have two mouse buttons, although some mice have three buttons. Since very few applications need or use three buttons, two buttons will be all you'll need in most cases.

Function 00H resets the numerous mouse parameters to their default values. The mouse pointer moves to the center of the screen. The cursor mask and screen mask are defined in such a manner that the cursor appears as an inverse video rectangle. Video page 0 is selected as the default page on which the pointer appears. The pointer disappears from the screen immediately.

Function 01H: Display mouse pointer

Function 01H displays the pointer on the screen. Load the function number into the AX register; no other parameters are needed. Since the mouse driver follows the movement of the mouse even when the mouse pointer has been disabled, it may not necessarily reappear at the position where it was when it disappeared.

Function 02H: Remove mouse pointer

Function 02H removes the mouse pointer from the screen. Load the function number into the AX register; no other parameters are needed. The calls between functions 01H and 02H must be called in proper proportions to be effective. For example, calling function 02H twice in succession means that you must also call function 01H twice in succession to return the pointer to the screen.

Functions 01H and 02H aren't used very much. Often, all you'll need to do is call function 00H and function 01H at the beginning of a program, and call function 02H at the end of the program. These functions come into play more frequently if the application program writes characters directly into video RAM, bypassing the slow DOS and BIOS display routines. Avoid writing characters over the mouse pointer, or two things will happen:

1) The mouse pointer disappears if overwritten by another character.

2) The mouse driver produces the wrong character on the screen when the user moves the mouse pointer. Before the pointer appears at a certain position on the screen, it records the character which occupied this position until now. This character is restored to the old position as soon as the pointer moves to another position on the screen. During a direct write access to video RAM, the driver does not record that a new character was output at the position of the pointer. Therefore, the old (and incorrect) character is displayed on the screen during the movement of the pointer.

You can avoid this potential source of errors by removing the pointer before character output, and returning the old character to the screen. The new character will be stored when the pointer is restored to the screen. This action should not be done for every character output, since it slows the system down and negates the advantages of direct access to video RAM. We recommend that you remove the pointer once from the screen before extensive output such as construction of a screen window. After the operation the pointer can be restored on the screen.

Even though the DOS and BIOS character output functions write their output directly to video RAM, you shouldn't worry about programming the pointer when working with these functions The reason is that during installation, the mouse driver moved interrupt vector 10H, which handles BIOS and DOS screen output, to its own routine. The driver can then display or disable the pointer as needed.

Function 04H: Move mouse pointer

Function 04H allows movement of the pointer to a specific location on the screen, without moving the mouse. Pass the function number to the AX register, the new horizontal coordinate (column) to the CX register, and the new vertical coordinate (line) to the DX register. Please note that these coordinates, like all other functions, must be relative to the virtual screen. Text coordinates must be multiplied by eight (or shifted left three binary places) before they can be passed to function 04H. The coordinates must be located inside a screen area designated as the mouse's range of movement.

Function 00H sets the complete range of the mouse's movement to the entire screen area. Functions 07H and 08H limit this range to a smaller area.

Function 07H & 08H: Set range of movement

Function 07H specifies the horizontal range of movement. Pass the function number to the AX register, the minimum X-coordinate to the CX register and the maximum X-coordinate to the DX register.

Function 08H specifies the vertical range of movement. Pass the function number to the AX register, the minimum Y-coordinate to the CX register and the maximum Y-coordinate to the DX register.

After calling these functions the mouse driver automatically moves the pointer within the range, unless it is already within the indicated borders. The user cannot move the pointer outside this range.

Function 10H: Exclusion area

In addition to the area of movement allotted to the pointer, the mouse driver also supplies an exclusion area. This exclusion area is a section of the screen which renders the mouse pointer invisible when the user moves the pointer into this section. The mouse pointer becomes visible again as soon as the user moves the pointer away from the exclusion area. This area is undefined after the call of function 00H. It can be defined at any time by calling function 10H, but the mouse driver can control only one exclusion area at a time. The coordinates of the exclusion area are passed to function 10H in the CX:DX and SI:DI register pairs. These register pairs specify the upper left corner and lower right corner respectively. CX and SI accept the X-coordinate, DX and DI the Y-coordinate.

The exclusion area and function 02H play special roles during direct access to video RAM. Although function 02H removes the pointer from the screen, this can occur in conjunction with function 10H only if the pointer is already within the exclusion area, or if the user moves the pointer within the exclusion area. This makes function 10H practical for situations involving the creation of a larger display area (e.g., a window). This allows the pointer to remain on the screen as long as it is not within this exclusion area.

The exclusion area can be removed by calling function 01H or function 00H. Function 01H makes the pointer visible automatically if it is already within the exclusion area.

Function 1DH: Set display page

Function 1DH sets the display page on which the pointer appears. This function is required only if the program switches a display page other than the current one to the foreground through direct video card programming. Pass the number of the display page to the BX register. When BIOS interrupt 10H activates a display page, this function can be omitted, since the mouse driver will automatically adapt to the change.

Function 0FH: Set pointer speed

Two parameters determine the speed at which the mouse pointer moves on the display screen. They specify the relationship between the distance of a pointer movement and the pixels traversed in the virtual mouse display screen. Function 0FH allows the user to set these parameters for horizontal and vertical movement. The parameters are passed in the CX and DX registers (horizontal and vertical, respectively). These numbers indicate the number of mickeys, which correspond to eight pixels in the virtual mouse display screen. These eight pixels correspond to one line or column in the text mode display screen.

The default values after calling function 00H are 8 horizontal mickeys and 16 vertical mickeys. In text mode the pointer moves one column after the pointer is moved 8 mickeys (about .04") horizontally. A jump to the next line occurs only after the pointer is moved 16 mickeys (about .08") vertically.

These settings normally can be set at default values, since they work well with all resolutions in text mode. This function allows changes if you want faster or slower pointer movement.

Function 0AH: Set pointer shape

Function 0AH determines the appearance of the pointer in text mode. The cursor mask and screen mask mentioned above are determining factors of the pointer's appearance in text mode. Pass 0AH to the AX register and the value determining the cursor's shape to the BX register.

Software-specific pointer

If the BX register contains the value 0, the mouse driver selects the pointer as specified by the software. The screen mask number must be loaded into the CX register, and the cursor mask number must be loaded into the DX register. These numbers indicate the addresses from which the mouse driver can access pointer shape parameters.

Hardware-specific pointer

If the BX register contains the value 1, the mouse driver selects the pointer as specified by the hardware. Starting line of the hardware pointer must be loaded into to the CX register, and the ending line must be loaded into the DX register.

Video mode and pointer size

Remember that the allowable values for starting line and ending line depends on the video mode currently in use:

- The monochrome display adapter allows values from 0 to 13.
- The color graphics adapter only allows values from 0 to 7.
- EGA and VGA cards accept values from 0 to 7. The EGA/VGA BIOS automatically adapts the number selected to the size of the character matrix currently in use.

The functions listed up until now set the various parameters which control the mouse driver. The mouse driver also supports a group of functions which read the mouse's position as well as the status of the mouse buttons. These functions can be divided into two categories for reading external devices such as the mouse, keyboard, printer or disk drives. These categories are the *polling method* and the *interrupt method*. The mouse driver supports both methods.

Polling method

The polling method constantly reads a device within a loop. This loop terminates only when the desired event occurs. Since the execution of this loop requires the full capabilities of the CPU, no time normally remains to perform other tasks.

Interrupt method

The interrupt method has an advantage over the polling method, since the interrupt system allows the CPU to execute other tasks until the desired event occurs. Once this happens, the mouse driver calls an interrupt routine which reacts to the event and executes further instructions.

Function 03H: Get pointer position/button status

The polling method offers four functions which operate in conjunction with the mouse interface. These functions can be accessed through function 03H, which return the current pointer position and mouse button status. Function 03H passes the horizontal pointer position to the CX register and the vertical pointer position to the DX register. Since these coordinates also refer to the virtual mouse screen, they must be converted to the text screen's coordinate system by dividing the components by eight, or by shifting the bits right by three binary places.

The following table shows how the mouse button status is returned to the BX register. Only the three lowest bits represent the status of one of the two or three mouse buttons. The bit for the corresponding mouse button contains the value 1 when the user presses that mouse button during the function call.

Mouse button status returned in the BX register after calling function 03H																
5	4	3	2	1	0	9	8	7	6	5	4	3	2	1	0	⇐ Bits
X	X	X	X	X	X	X	X	X	X	X	X	X				⇐ Disregard these bits
															1	= left mouse button activated
														1		= right mouse button activated
													1			= center mouse button activated

Function 0CH: Set event handler

Function 0CH sets the address of a mouse *event handler* (interrupt routine). The function number must be passed to the AX register. The segment and offset address of the event handler must be passed to the ES:DX register pair. The event mask must be passed to the CX register. The individual bits of this flag determine the conditions under which the event handler should be called. The following table shows the CX register coding:

Event mask coding in CX register during function 0CH call																
5	4	3	2	1	0	9	8	7	6	5	4	3	2	1	0	⇐ Bits
X	X	X	X	X	X	X	X	X								⇐ Disregard these bits
															1	= Mouse movement
														1		= Left mouse button activated
													1			= Left mouse button released
												1				= Right mouse button activated
											1					= Right mouse button released
										1						= Center mouse button activated
									1							= Center mouse button released

The mouse driver calls the event handler after executing the function, as soon as at least one of the specified events occurs. The call is made using the FAR call, rather than the INT instruction. This difference is important to remember when developing an event handler, since the handler must be ended with a FAR RET instruction rather than an IRET instruction. Similar to an interrupt routine, none of the various processor registers can be changed when they are returned to the caller. For this reason the registers must be stored on the stack immediately after the call, and the register contents must be restored at the end of the routine.

Information is passed to the event handler from the mouse driver through individual processor registers. The information concerning the event can be found in the AX register, where each bit has the same significance as in the event mask during the call of function 0CH (see above table). Individual bits may be set which have no meaning for the event handler. For example, if the event handler should only be called when the left mouse button is activated (bit 1), bits 0 and 4 may also be set during the event handler call, because the mouse was moved and the right mouse button had been released at the same time.

The event handler can obtain the current button status from the contents of the CX register. The coding is identical during the call to the function 03H. Bits 0 to 2 represent the different mouse buttons. The current pointer position can be found in the CX and DX registers, representing the horizontal and vertical positions, respectively. The position can only be set after conversion to the text screen's coordinate system.

During the development of an event handler, the DS register should point to the data segment of the mouse driver during the handler call, instead of the interrupted program. If the event handler accesses its own data segment, it must first load its address into the DS register.

Function 18H: Install alternate event handler

Function 18H allows the installation of an event handler which reacts to limited-range keyboard events as well as mouse events. This function signals an event if the <Ctrl>, <Alt> or <Shift> keys are pressed when a mouse button is pressed or released.

This function is almost identical in register assignments as function 0CH. The event mask in the CX register has been extended by the three events, as shown in the following table:

Event mask coding in CX register during function 18H call																
5	4	3	2	1	0	9	8	7	6	5	4	3	2	1	0	⇐ Bits
X	X	X	X	X	X	X	X									⇐ Disregard these bits
															1	= Mouse movement
														1		= Left mouse button activated
													1			= Left mouse button released
												1				= Right mouse button activated
											1					= Right mouse button released
										1						= Shift key pressed during mouse button event
									1							= Ctrl key pressed during mouse button event
								1								= Alt key pressed during mouse button event

Even during the call of such an alternative event handler, little changes in comparison with the event handlers which were installed by calling function 0CH. Only the content of the AX register must be interpreted a little differently, since its construction corresponds to the event mask shown above.

Up to three alternative event handlers can be installed by calling function 18H. During the function 0CH call, the event handler indicated replaces the previously installed handler. Three different event handlers can be installed by calling function 18H three times. This is only valid if the three event handlers are equipped with different event masks. If an event mask passes to function 18H which is already equipped with a handler, the new handler replaces the existing handler.

Demonstration programs

This chapter lists programs in C and Turbo Pascal which demonstrate mouse access functions. These programs show the techniques of developing and installing an event handler, which is the most complicated part of mouse reading. Both programs include functions or procedures which call various mouse functions. These routines require little programming—they load the processor registers with the necessary values, then call interrupt 33H. Since the event handler needs the most programming, the text here will focus on that subject.

Installing an event handler in a higher level language program is somewhat difficult, since it must meet certain requirements. These requirements are normally beyond the control of a programmer in a higher level language. The requirements are as follows:

- The event handler must be a FAR procedure, and must be terminated with a FAR RET instruction.
- The event handler must store the various processor registers during the call and restore them before completion.
- The event handler must load the segment address of the higher level language data segment into the DS register to provide access to global variables of the program.

These requirements can be met in some versions of Turbo Pascal, Turbo C and Microsoft C, although some very complex programming would be required. The traditional solution (write a routine in assembly language) is easier and faster to implement. Therefore, we wrote the event handler itself in assembler, assembled the program and linked the resulting object module to the higher level language program.

This assembler routine is named AssmHand. It stores the various processor registers on the stack after the call, then calls a C function or Pascal procedure named MouEventHandler. The AssmHand routine passes arguments provided by the mouse driver to the MouEventHandler routine. These arguments include:

- The event flag, which describes the event that caused the handler call.
- The current mouse button status.
- The current position of the mouse pointer.

This information is converted from virtual graphic screen coordinates into text screen coordinates (25 lines x 80 columns).

The stack handles parameter passing. The C version of AssmHand must pass the arguments onto the stack in the reverse order of their declaration. After loading the DS register and calling the higher level language routine, these arguments must be taken from the stack again by incrementing the stack pointer by the memory requirements of the arguments (8 bytes). This is only required for the C version of the routine. The Turbo Pascal version performs this task on its own.

After calling this routine, the AssmHand routine returns the processor registers to the stack and passes control to the caller using a FAR RET instruction.

The AssmHand instructions execute very quickly, but the handler itself may require more execution time than expected. This introduces the problem of recursion, since an event in connection with the mouse may recur during the handler execution. The AssmHand driver then must be recalled before the previous call terminated.

To avoid this situation and the complications which can occur, AssmHand maintains a variable named active in its code segment. During execution this variable contains the value 1. Before setting this variable, the program tests if active already contains the value 1. This indicates that the last call was not yet completed. If this situation occurs, the handler execution terminates immediately, thus avoiding recursion.

Even if this method avoids recursion problems, remember that it can produce its own problems. The suppression of the higher level language handler does not take note of the event, because the handler was not called by the mouse driver. Although we offer the recursion trap as an option, we recommend that you program the higher level language handler as efficiently as possible to avoid using processor time. This will keep call suppression to a minimum.

AssmHand must first be installed through function 0CH, using the MouISetEventHandler procedure/function. MouISetEventHandler is called by the MouInit procedure/function, which initializes the mouse module. This should be called by any application program as the first procedure/function of this module. The number of lines and columns of the display screen must be passed to it as arguments, to determine the size of an internal buffer needed for the various procedure/functions within the module.

This buffer allows division of the screen into individual mouse ranges, each equipped with its own code, cursor mask and screen mask. These mouse regions are very important in mouse access. They permit the definition of objects such as sliders, O.K. buttons or menu items. As soon as the user moves the pointer to and object and presses a mouse button, the object executes a particular step in the program.

MouDefRange defines these regions. The registration of these regions occurs through the procedure/function MouDefRange, which must receive a pointer to a vector or array, and the number of elements stored there. These elements of the type RANGE describe a screen area and the cursor or screen mask assigned to the pointer as soon as it reaches this area. An area can comprise a single character or the total screen. The user can define the array with individual area descriptors. The area code depends on the position of the descriptor within the array, and is provided automatically by the procedure/function MouDefRange. The first area has the value 0, the second the value 1, etc. The screen areas not covered by an area descriptor are assigned the code NO_RANGE.

During the creation of this array, especially during the definition of the cursor and screenmask in the PtrMask array, the C implementation provides helpful macros and constants. The Pascal program has functions and constants available for this purpose. The creation of a variable of the type PTRVIEW, stored in the PtrMask field within an area descriptor, is handled by the macro or function MouPtrMask. The cursor and screen mask for the character must be passed to MouPtrMask to define the pointer's appearance on the screen.

If PtrSameChar is indicated, the pointer appears as the character which it covers. If another pointer is desired, the pointer can be defined with PtrDifChar. When the call occurs, enter the ASCII code of the desired character for PtrDifChar.

As a second parameter MouPtrMask gets the pointer's color from the cursor mask and screen mask. Many options for color are possible:

- PtrSameCol ensures that the pointer assumes the color of the character currently overlapped by the pointer.
- PtrSameColB creates a pointer which assumes the color of the character currently overlapped. However, bit 7 of the attribute byte is set to 1 so that the character either blinks or appears with a high-intensity background color.
- PtrInvCol makes the pointer appear in the inverse color of the character currently overlapped by the pointer.
- PtrDifCol displays the pointer on the screen in the color indicated by the code following PtrDifCol.

In addition to the different mouse areas specified through MouDefRange, a pointer can be assigned to the remaining screen, which is the area carrying the code NO_RANGE. A program can use MouSetDefaultPtr to obtain the cursor and screen mask of the pointer as a parameter of type PTRVIEW. The constants and macros or functions described above can be used to create this parameter.

The MouEventHandler changes the cursor and screen mask for each area. Since it is called for every mouse event (including mouse movement), it can determine the mouse area where the pointer is currently located. To make this happen as fast as possible, it tests if the mouse area contains the position of the pointer.

MouEventHandler uses the internal region buffer which was created by MouInit during the call. It reflects exactly the video RAM structure, and contains one byte for every screen position. Each byte contains the code of the area to which the screen position was assigned. The event handler can use the current position of the pointer as an index to this area buffer. A single memory access is enough to determine the mouse area in which the pointer is located. The area code found is stored in the global variable MouRng, and is used as an index to the array of the mouse descriptor from which it determines the cursor and screen mask for this area.

The higher level language event handler has another assignment which may be even more important. It controls the variable MouEvent, in which the current mouse events are stored. This task cannot be performed by simply copying the mouse events which were passed through AssmHand from the mouse driver. This only shows the current event, but no preceding events. If the user presses and holds the left mouse button, then presses the right mouse button, this results in two event handler calls. This signals each case of an active mouse button. The preceding call (the active left mouse button) is no longer recognized by the call, since it reports only the current event (the depressed right mouse button).

The event handler must isolate the various events which are reflected in the EvFlags variable, and accept only new events in the MouEvent variable. This variable reflects the current status of the mouse buttons, and the pointer's current movement or position. MouEvent can handle the most important mouse sensing tasks, waiting for the occurrence of a certain event (usually a pressed mouse button).

MouEventWait waits for the occurrence of an event which was specified by the bitmask that was passed earlier. This bitmask can be defined through the logical OR function with the following constants:

EV_MOU_MOVE	Mouse movement
EV_LEFT_PRESS	Left mouse button pressed
EV_LEFT_REL	Left mouse button released
EV_RIGHT_PRESS	Right mouse button pressed
EV_RIGHT_REL	Right mouse button released

The procedure/function can be instructed to wait for one or more of these events to occur. The AND or OR correspond to the logical comparisons of the same names. Which events occur can be sensed through the results of a bitmask in which the individual bits represent the various events, and through which the constants described above can be sensed.

Pascal listing: MOUSEP.PAS

```
{**********************************************************************}
{*                        M O U S E P . P A S                        *}
{*--------------------------------------------------------------------*}
{*    Task          : Demonstrate the different functions available  *}
{*                    in mouse programming                            *}
{*--------------------------------------------------------------------*}
{*    Author        : MICHAEL TISCHER                                 *}
{*    Developed on  : 04/21/1989                                      *}
{*    Last update   : 06/01/1989                                      *}
{**********************************************************************}

uses Dos;                                              { Add DOS unit }

{$L c:\tp\mousepa}                            { Link assembler module }
                                     { adjust path to your system needs }
{== Declaration of external functions ================================}

{$F+}                                                 { FAR function }
procedure AssmHand ; external ;             { Assembler event handler }
{$F-}                                { FAR functions no longer accessible }

{== Constants ========================================================}

const

{-- Event-Codes ------------------------------------------------------}

      EV_MOU_MOVE    =  1;                          { Mouse movement }
      EV_LEFT_PRESS  =  2;                { Left mouse button pressed }
      EV_LEFT_REL    =  4;               { Left mouse button released }
      EV_RIGHT_PRESS =  8;               { Right mouse button pressed }
      EV_RIGHT_REL   = 16;              { Right mouse button released }
      EV_MOU_ALL     = 31;                         { All mouse events }

      LBITS          =  6;         { EV_LEFT_PRESS or EV_LEFT_REL    }
      RBITS          = 24;         { EV_RIGHT_PRESS or EV_RIGHT_REL }

      NO_RANGE     = 255;        { Mouse pointer not in xy range }

      PtrSameChar     = $00ff;          { Same character              }
      PtrSameCol      = $00ff;          { Same color                  }
      PtrInvCol       = $7777;          { Inverse color               }
      PtrSameColB     = $807f;          { Same color, blinking        }
      PtrInvColB      = $F777;          { Inverse color, blinking     }

      EAND            = 0;          { Event comparisons for MouEventWait }
      EVOR            = 1;

      CRLF              = #13#10;                              { CR/LF }

{== Type declarations ================================================}

type  FNCTPTR   = longint;                { Address of a FAR function }
      PTRVIEW  = longint;                  { Mask for mouse pointer }
      RANGE  = record                       {  Describes a mouse range }
                 x1,                           { Upper left and lower }
                 y1,                         { right coordinates for the }
                 x2,                                  { specified range }
                 y2      : byte;
                 PtrMask : PTRVIEW;             { Mask for mouse pointer }
               end;
      RNGARRAY = array [0..100] of RANGE;
      RNGPTR   = ^RNGARRAY;
      PTRREC   = record                          { Allows access to any }
                   Ofs : word;                   { mouse pointer record }
                   Seg : word;                               { existing }
                 end;
```

```
     PTRVREC  = record                                { Allows access to }
                  ScreenMask : word;                          { PTRVIEW }
                  CursorMask : word;
                end;
     RNGBUF   = array [0..10000] of byte;                { Range buffer }
     BBPTR    = ^RNGBUF;                       { Pointer to a range buffer }

{== global variables ===============================================}

var  NumRanges,                                      { Number of ranges }
     TLine,                                      { Number of text lines }
     TCol      : byte;                         { Number of text columns }
     MouAvail  : boolean;                   { TRUE if mouse is available }
     OldPtr,                             { Old mouse pointer appearances }
     StdPtr    : PTRVIEW;              { Mask for standard mouse pointer }
     BufPtr    : BBPTR;            { Pointer to range recognition buffer }
     ActRngPtr: RNGPTR;               { Pointer to current range vector }
     BLen      : integer;                { Range buffer length in bytes }
     ExitOld   : pointer;               { Pointer to old exit procedure }

{-- Variables which are loaded into mouse handler on every call --}

     MouRng,                                       { Current mouse range }
     MouCol,                                { Mouse column (text screen) }
     MouRow    : byte;                       { Mouse line (text screen) }
     MouEvent  : integer;                                   { Event mask }

{-- Variables which load with any occurrence of expected events -}

     EvRng,                      { Range in which the mouse can be found }
     EvCol,                                               { Mouse column }
     EvRow : byte;                                          { Mouse line }

{******************************************************************}
{*  MouPtrMask: Executes Cursor-Mask and Screen-Mask from a bitmap    *}
{*              containing character and color                       *}
{**--------------------------------------------------------------**}
{*  Input  : Chars = Bitmask of character as found in Cursor-Mask    *}
{*                   and Screen-Mask                                 *}
{*           Color  = Bitmask of character color as found in         *}
{*                   Cursor-Mask and Screen-Mask                     *}
{*  Output : Cursor-Mask and Screen-Mask as a value of typ PtrView   *}
{*  Info:    The constants PtrSameChar, PtrSameCol, PtrSameColB,     *}
{*           PtrInvCol, PtrInvColB, and the results of the PtrDifChar *}
{*           and PtrDifCol functions also control character & color  *}
{******************************************************************}

function MouPtrMask( Chars, Color  : word ) : PTRVIEW;

var Mask : PTRVIEW;          { For creating Cursor-Mask and Screen-Mask }

begin
  PTRVREC( Mask ).ScreenMask := ( ( Color and $ff ) shl 8 ) +
                                ( Chars and $ff );
  PTRVREC( Mask ).CursorMask := ( Color and $ff00 ) + ( Chars shr 8 );
  MouPtrMask := Mask;                           { Return mask to caller }
end;

{******************************************************************}
{*  PtrDifChar: Defines character structure of cursor and screen    *}
{*              mask in conjunction with character                  *}
{**--------------------------------------------------------------**}
{*  Input  : ASCII code of the character on which pointer is based  *}
{*  Output : Cursor and screen mask for this cursor                 *}
{*  Info:    Function result should be computed with the help of the *}
{*           MouPtrMask function                                    *}
{******************************************************************}

function PtrDifChar( Chars : byte ) : word;
```

```
begin
  PtrDifChar := Chars shl 8;
end;

{***********************************************************************}
{* PtrDifCol: Creates the character segment of the cursor and screen *}
{*             mask in conjunction with the mouse pointer color       *}
{**-------------------------------------------------------------------**}
{* Input  : Character color on which the mouse pointer will be based *}
{* Output : cursor and screen mask for this color                     *}
{* Info:    The function's result should be computed with the help    *}
{*          of the MouPtrMask function                                *}
{***********************************************************************}

function PtrDifCol( Color : byte ) : word;

begin
  PtrDifCol := Color shl 8;
end;

{***********************************************************************}
{* MouDefinePtr: Assigns the mouse driver the cursor mask and         *}
{*               screen mask, from which the driver can create the    *}
{*               mouse pointer                                        *}
{**-------------------------------------------------------------------**}
{* Input  : Mask = The cursor and screen mask as a parameter of       *}
{*                 type PTRVIEW                                       *}
{* Info:    - The mask parameter should be created with the help of  *}
{*            the MouPtrMask function                                 *}
{*          - The most significant 16 bits represent the screen mask,*}
{*            the least significant 16 bits represent cursor mask    *}
{***********************************************************************}

procedure MouDefinePtr( Mask : PTRVIEW );

var Regs : Registers;             { Processor regs for interrupt call }

begin
  if OldPtr <> Mask then                 { Mask change since last call? }
    begin                                                        { YES }
      Regs.AX := $000a;        { Funct. no. for "Set text pointer type" }
      Regs.BX := 0;                            { Create software pointer }
      Regs.CX := PTRVREC( Mask ).ScreenMask;     { Low-word is AND mask }
      Regs.DX := PTRVREC( Mask ).CursorMask;   { High-word ist XOR mask }
      Intr( $33, Regs);                             { Call mouse driver }
      OldPtr := Mask;                             { Reserve new bitmask }
    end;
end;

{***********************************************************************}
{* MouEventHandler: Called by the assembler routine AssmHand as soon *}
{*                  as a mouse event occurs                           *}
{**-------------------------------------------------------------------**}
{* Input  : EvFlags  = The event mask                                 *}
{*          ButState = Current mouse button status                    *}
{*          X, Y     = Current coordinates of the mouse pointer on    *}
{*                     the text screen                                *}
{***********************************************************************}

procedure MouEventHandler( EvFlags, ButState, x, y : integer );

var NewRng : byte;                                { Number of new range }

begin

  MouEvent := MouEvent and not(1);                    { Bit 0 excluded }
  MouEvent := MouEvent or ( EvFlags and 1 );            { Bit 0 copied }

  if ( EvFlags and LBITS ) <> 0 then { Lft button released or pressed? }
    begin                                                        { YES }
```

```
      MouEvent := MouEvent and not( LBITS );  { Remove previous status }
      MouEvent := MouEvent or ( EvFlags and LBITS );      { Add status }
    end;
  if ( EvFlags and RBITS ) <> 0 then  { Rgt button released or pressed?}
    begin                                                       { YES }
      MouEvent := MouEvent and not( RBITS );  { Remove previous status }
      MouEvent := MouEvent or ( EvFlags and RBITS );      { Add status }
    end;

  MouCol := x;                          { Convert columns to text columns }
  MouRow := y;                              { Convert lines to text lines }

  {-- Determine range in which the mouse should be found and        ----}
  {-- determine whether range has changes since the previous call  ----}
  {-- of the handler. If so, the cursor image must be redefined.   ----}

  NewRng := BufPtr^[ MouRow * TCol + MouCol ];              { Get range }
  if NewRng <> MouRng then                                 { New range? }
    begin                                                       { YES }
      if NewRng = NO_RANGE then                    { Outside of a range? }
        MouDefinePtr( StdPtr )                  { YES, standard pointer }
      else                                       { NO, range recognized }
        MouDefinePtr( ActRngPtr^[ NewRng ].PtrMask );
    end;
  MouRng := NewRng;           { Reserve range number in global variable }
end;

{*********************************************************************}
{*  MouIBufFill: Store the code for a mouse range within the         *}
{*               modulare range memory                               *}
{**-----------------------------------------------------------------**}
{*  Input   : x1, y1 = Upper left corner of the mouse range          *}
{*            x2, y2 = Lower right corner of the mouse range         *}
{*            Code   = Range code                                    *}
{*********************************************************************}

procedure MouIBufFill( x1, y1, x2, y2, Code : byte );

var Index   : integer;                               { Points to array }
    Column,                                            { Loop counter }
    Line    : byte;

begin
  for Line:=y1 to y2 do                       { Count individual lines }
    begin
      Index := Line  * TCol + x1;                  { First line index }
      for Column:=x1 to x2 do    { Go through the columns in this line }
        begin
          BufPtr^[ Index ] := Code;                         { Save code }
          inc( Index );                      { Set index to next array }
        end;
    end;
end;

{*********************************************************************}
{*  MouDefRange:   Allows the registration of different screen ranges,*}
{*                 which the mouse recognizes as different ranges.   *}
{*                 The mouse pointer's appearance changes when it    *}
{*                 senses each range                                 *}
{**-----------------------------------------------------------------**}
{*  Input  : Number = Number of screen ranges                        *}
{*           BPtr   = Pointer to the array in which the individual   *}
{*                    ranges are written as a structure of type      *}
{*                    RANGE                                          *}
{*  Info:    - The free areas of the screen are assigned the code    *}
{*             NO_RANGE                                              *}
{*           - When the mouse pointer enters one of the ranges,      *}
{*             the mouse range calls the event handler               *}
{*********************************************************************}
```

```
procedure MouDefRange( Number : byte; BPtr : RNGPTR );

var ActRng,                            { Number of the current range }
    Range : byte;                                    { Loop counter }

begin
  ActRngPtr := BPtr;                   { Reserve pointer to vector  }
  NumRanges := Number;                      { and number of ranges }
  FillChar( BufPtr^, BLen, NO_RANGE );     { All elements=NO_RANGE }
  for Range:=0 to Number-1 do          { Check out different ranges }
   with BPtr^[ Range ] do
     MouIBufFill( x1, y1, x2, y2, Range );

  {-- Redefine mouse pointer ------------------------------------------}
  ActRng := BufPtr^[ MouRow * TCol + MouCol ];             { Get range }
  if ActRng = NO_RANGE then                     { Outside a range? }
    MouDefinePtr( StdPtr )                   { YES, standard pointer }
  else                                        { NO, range recognized }
    MouDefinePtr( BPtr^[ ActRng ].PtrMask );
end;

{***********************************************************************}
{* MouEventWait: Waits for a specific mouse event                     *}
{**------------------------------------------------------------------**}
{*  Input  : TYP        = Type of comparison between different events *}
{*           WAIT_EVENT = Bitmask which specifies the awaited event   *}
{*  Output : Bitmask of the occurring event                           *}
{*  Info:    - WAIT_EVENT can be used in conjunction with OR for other*}
{*             constants like EV_MOU_MOVE, EV_LEFT_PRESS etc.         *}
{*           - Comparison types can be given as AND or OR. If AND is  *}
{*             selected, the function returns to the caller if all   *}
{*             anticipated events occur. OR returns the function to   *}
{*             the caller if at least one of the events occurs.       *}
{***********************************************************************}

function MouEventWait( Typ : BYTE; WaitEvent : integer ) : integer;

var ActEvent : integer;
    Line,
    Column   : byte;
    CEnd     : boolean;

begin
   Column := MouCol;                { Reserve current mouse position }
   Line := MouRow;
   CEnd := false;

  repeat
    {-- Wait for one of the events to occur ---------------------------}

    if Typ = EAND then                             { AND comparison? }
      repeat                             { YES, all events must occur }
        ActEvent := MouEvent;                     { Get current event }
      until ActEvent = WaitEvent
    else                                             { OR comparison }
      repeat                          { At least one event must occur }
        ActEvent := MouEvent;                     { Get current event }
      until ( ActEvent and WaitEvent ) <> 0;

    ActEvent := ActEvent and WaitEvent;         { Check event bits only }

    {-- While waiting for mouse movement, the event is accepted     -- }
    {-- nonly if the mouse pointer moves to another line and/or     -- }
    {-- column in the text screen                                    - }

    if ( ( (WaitEvent and EV_MOU_MOVE) <> 0 )  and
          ( Column = MouCol ) and  ( Line = MouRow ) ) then
      begin       { Mouse moved, but still at the same screen position }
        ActEvent := ActEvent and not( EV_MOU_MOVE );     { Move bit out }
        CEnd := ( ActEvent <> 0);              { Still waiting for events? }
```

```
      end
    else                                                { Event occurs }
      CEnd := TRUE;
  until CEnd;

  EvCol := MouCol;                     { Determine current mouse position }
  EvRow := MouRow;                                { and range in global }
  EvRng := MouRng;                                        { variables }

  MouEventWait := ActEvent;
end;

{***********************************************************************}
{*  MouISetEventHandler: Installs an event handler which is called     *}
{*                       when a particular mouse event occurs.         *}
{**-------------------------------------------------------------------**}
{*  Input  : EVENT = Bitmask which describes the event, called         *}
{*                   through an event handler                          *}
{*           FPTR  = Pointer to the event handler of type FNCTPTR      *}
{*  Info:    - EVENT can be used through OR comparisons in conjunc-    *}
{*             tion with constants like EV_MOU_MOVE, EV_LEFT_PRESS etc*}
{*           - The event handler must be a FAR procedure, and change   *}
{*             none of the given processor registers                   *}
{***********************************************************************}

procedure MouISetEventHandler( Event : integer; FPtr : FNCTPTR );

var Regs : Registers;              { Processor regs for interrupt call }

begin
  Regs.AX := $000C;               { Funct. no. for "Set Mouse Handler" }
  Regs.CX := event;                                  { Load event mask }
  Regs.DX := PTRREC( FPtr ).Ofs;            { Offset address of handler }
  Regs.ES  := PTRREC( FPtr ).Seg;          { Segment address of handler }
  Intr( $33,  Regs );                              { Call mouse driver }
end;

{***********************************************************************}
{*  MouIGetX: Returns the text column in which the mouse pointer can   *}
{*            be found                                                 *}
{**-------------------------------------------------------------------**}
{*  Output : Mouse column converted to text screen                     *}
{***********************************************************************}

function MouIGetX : byte;

var Regs : Registers;              { Processor regs for interrupt call }

begin
  Regs.AX := $0003;              { Funct. no. for "Get mouse position" }
  Intr( $33,  Regs );                              { Call mouse driver }
  MouIGetX := Regs.CX shr 3;     { Convert column and return new value }
end;

{***********************************************************************}
{*  MouIGetY: Returns the text line in which the mouse pointer can     *}
{*            be found                                                 *}
{**-------------------------------------------------------------------**}
{*  Output : Mouse line converted to text screen                       *}
{***********************************************************************}

function MouIGetY : byte;

var Regs : Registers;              { Processor regs for interrupt call }

begin
  Regs.AX := $0003;              { Funct. no. for "Get mouse position" }
  Intr( $33, Regs );                               { Call mouse driver }
  MouIGetY := Regs.DX shr 3;       { Convert line and return new value }
end;
```

```
{**********************************************************************}
{*  MouShowMouse: Show mouse pointer on the screen                    *}
{**------------------------------------------------------------------**}
{*  Info: Calls between MouShowMouse and MouHideMouse must be evenly  *}
{*        balanced                                                    *}
{**********************************************************************}

procedure MouShowMouse;

var Regs : Registers;              { Processor regs for interrupt call }

begin
  Regs.AX := $0001;                       { Funct. no. for "Show Mouse" }
  Intr( $33, Regs );                               { Call mouse driver }
end;

{**********************************************************************}
{*  MouHideMouse: Hide mouse pointer from the screen                  *}
{**------------------------------------------------------------------**}
{*  Info: Calls between MouShowMouse and MouHideMouse must be evenly  *}
{*        balanced                                                    *}
{**********************************************************************}

procedure MouHideMouse;

var Regs : Registers;              { Processor regs for interrupt call }

begin
  Regs.AX := $0002;                       { Funct. no. for "Hide Mouse" }
  Intr( $33, Regs);                                { Call mouse driver }
end;

{**********************************************************************}
{*  MouSetMoveArea: Specify movement range for mouse pointer          *}
{**------------------------------------------------------------------**}
{*  Input  :  x1, y1 = Coordinates of range's upper left corner       *}
{*            x2, y2 = Coordinates of range's lower right corner      *}
{*  Info:    - The coordinates indicate the text screen coordinates,  *}
{*             and not the virtual graphic screen used by the mouse   *}
{*             driver                                                 *}
{**********************************************************************}

procedure MouSetMoveArea( x1, y1, x2, y2 : byte );

var Regs : Registers;              { Processor regs for interrupt call }

begin
  Regs.AX := $0008;             { Funct. no. for "Set vertical limits" }
  Regs.CX := integer( y1 ) shl 3;          { Conversion to virtual     }
  Regs.DX := integer( y2 ) shl 3;          { mouse screen              }
  Intr( $33, Regs );                          { Call mouse driver      }
  Regs.AX := $0007;           { Funct. no. for "Set horizontal limits" }
  Regs.CX := integer( x1 ) shl 3;          { Conversion to virtual     }
  Regs.DX := integer( x2 ) shl 3;          { mouse screen              }
  Intr( $33, Regs );                          { Call mouse driver      }
end;

{**********************************************************************}
{*  MouSetSpeed: Configures movement speed of mouse pointer           *}
{**------------------------------------------------------------------**}
{*  Input  : XSpeed = Speed in X-direction                            *}
{*           YSpeed = Speed in Y-direction                            *}
{*  Info:    - Parameters are measured in units of                    *}
{*             mickeys (8 per pixel)                                  *}
{**********************************************************************}

procedure MouSetSpeed( XSpeed, YSpeed : integer );

var Regs : Registers;              { Processor regs for interrupt call }
```

```
begin
  Regs.AX := $000f;       { Funct. no. for "Set mickeys to pixel ratio" }
  Regs.CX := XSpeed;
  Regs.DX := YSpeed;
  Intr( $33, Regs);                          { Call mouse driver }
end;

{***********************************************************************}
{*  MouMovePtr: Moves mouse pointer to a specific position on the     *}
{*              screen                                                 *}
{**-------------------------------------------------------------------**}
{*  Input  : COL = New screen column for mouse pointer                *}
{*           ROW = New screen line for mouse pointer                  *}
{*  Info:    - The coordinates indicate the text screen, and not the  *}
{*             virtual graphic screen used by the mouse driver        *}
{***********************************************************************}

procedure MouMovePtr( Col, Row : byte );

var Regs   : Registers;            { Processor regs for interrupt call }
    NewRng : byte;               { Range into which the mouse is moved }

begin
  Regs.AX := $0004;       { Funct. no. for "Set mouse pointer position" }
  MouCol := col;                             { Store coordinates in }
  MouRow := row;                                 { global variables }
  Regs.CX := integer( col ) shl 3;      { Convert coordinates and store }
  Regs.DX := integer( row ) shl 3;              { in global variables }
  Intr( $33, Regs );                              { Call mouse driver }

  NewRng := BufPtr^[ Row * TCol + Col ];                  { Get range }
  if NewRng <> MouRng then                               { New range? }
    begin                                                      { YES }
      if NewRng = NO_RANGE then                 { Outside of a range? }
        MouDefinePtr( StdPtr )                { YES, standard pointer }
      else                                    { NO, range recognized }
        MouDefinePtr( ActRngPtr^[ NewRng ].PtrMask );
    end;
  MouRng := NewRng;             { Place range number in global variable }
end;

{***********************************************************************}
{*  MouSetDefaultPtr: Defines default pointer appearance for screen   *}
{*                    ranges not assigned as special ranges           *}
{**-------------------------------------------------------------------**}
{*  Input  : Standard = Cursor and screen mask for mouse pointer      *}
{*  Info:    - The parameters should be created with the help of the  *}
{*             MouPtrMask function                                    *}
{***********************************************************************}

procedure MouSetDefaultPtr( Standard : PTRVIEW );

begin
  StdPtr := Standard;              { Reserve bitmask in global variable }

  {-- If the pointer isn't currently in a range, convert to default ---}

  if MouRng = NO_RANGE then                              { No range? }
   MouDefinePtr( Standard );                                    { NO }
end;

{***********************************************************************}
{*  MouEnd: End the mouse module functions and procedures             *}
{**-------------------------------------------------------------------**}
{*  Info:    - This procedure doesn't have to be called direct from the*}
{*             application, since the MouInit function defines this  *}
{*             as the exit procedure                                  *}
{***********************************************************************}
```

```
{$F+}                    { must be FAR to allow call as exit procedure }

procedure  MouEnd;

var Regs : Registers;               { Processor regs for interrupt call }

begin
  MouHideMouse;                                 { Hide mouse from screen }
  Regs.AX := 0;                                     { Reset mouse driver }
  Intr( $33, Regs);                                  { Call mouse driver }

  FreeMem( BufPtr, BLen );                   { Release allocated memory }

  ExitProc := ExitOld;                     { Restore old exit procedure }
end;

{$F-}                                           { No more FAR procedures }

{***********************************************************************}
{* MouInit: Initializes mouse functions and procedures as well as    *}
{*          variables                                                 *}
{**------------------------------------------------------------------**}
{* Input  : Columns = Number of screen columns                        *}
{*          Lines   = Number of screen lines                          *}
{* Output : TRUE if a mouse driver is installed, else FALSE           *}
{* Info:    - This function must be the first called from an          *}
{*            application program, before other procedures and        *}
{*            functions can be called                                 *}
{***********************************************************************}

function MouInit( Columns, Lines : byte ) : boolean;

var Regs : Registers;               { Processor regs for interrupt call }

begin
  TLine := Lines;                           { Store number of lines and }
  TCol  := Columns;                       { columns in global variables }

  ExitOld := ExitProc;                    { Set address of exit procedure }
  ExitProc := @MouEnd;                { Define MouEnd as exit procedure }

  {-- Allocate and fill mouse range ----------------------------------}

  BLen := TLine * TCol;                { Number of characters in screen }
  GetMem( BufPtr, BLen );              { Allocate internal range buffer }
  MouIBufFill( 0, 0, TCol-1, TLine-1, NO_RANGE );

  Regs.AX := 0;                                { Initialize mouse driver }
  Intr( $33, Regs );                                 { Call mouse driver }
  MouInit := ( Regs.AX <> 0 );               { Mouse driver installed? }

  MouSetMoveArea( 0, 0, TCol-1, TLine-1 );               { Set move area }

  MouCol   := MouIGetX;                  { Load current mouse position }
  MouRow   := MouIGetY;                         { into global variables }
  MouRng   := NO_RANGE;                       { Pointer in no set range }
  MouEvent := EV_LEFT_REL or EV_RIGHT_REL;    { No mouse button pressed }
  StdPtr   := MouPtrMask( PTRSAMECHAR, PTRINVCOL );        { Std. pointer }
  OldPtr   := PTRVIEW( 0 );

 {-- Install assembler event handler "AssmHand" ------------------------}
 MouISetEventHandler( EV_MOU_ALL, FNCTPTR(@AssmHand) );

end;

{***********************************************************************
*                          M A I N    P R O G R A M                    *
***********************************************************************}

const Ranges : array[0..4] of RANGE =                  { The mouse range }
```

```
  (
   ( x1:  0; y1:  0; x2: 79; y2:  0 ),           { Top line          }
   ( x1:  0; y1:  1; x2:  0; y2: 23 ),           { Left column       }
   ( x1:  0; y1: 24; x2: 78; y2: 24 ),           { Bottom line       }
   ( x1: 79; y1:  1; x2: 79; y2: 23 ),           { Right column      }
   ( x1: 79; y1: 24; x2: 79; y2: 24 )            { Lower right corner }
  );

var Dummy : integer;                     { Get result from MouEventWait }

begin
  {-- Configure mouse pointer for the different mouse ranges ----------}
  Ranges[ 0 ].PtrMask := MouPtrMask( PtrDifChar($18), PtrInvCol);
  Ranges[ 1 ].PtrMask := MouPtrMask( PtrDifChar($1b), PtrInvCol);
  Ranges[ 2 ].PtrMask := MouPtrMask( PtrDifChar($19), PtrInvCol);
  Ranges[ 3 ].PtrMask := MouPtrMask( PtrDifChar($1a), PtrInvCol);
  Ranges[ 4 ].PtrMask := MouPtrMask( PtrDifChar($58), PtrDifCol($40));

  writeln(#13#10,'MOUSEP - (c) 1989 by MICHAEL TISCHER'#13#10);
  if MouInit( 80, 25 ) then                  { Initialize mouse module }
   begin                      { OK, there's an installed mouse driver }
    writeln('Move the mouse pointer around the screen. As you move ',CRLF,
            'it around the edge of the screen, you will see the mouse',CRLF,
            'pointer change its appearance. The pointer shape changes ',CRLF,
            'as you move the mouse from edge to edge.       ',CRLF,CRLF,
            'To end this program, move the mouse pointer to the    ',CRLF,
            'lower right corner of the screen, and press both the  ',CRLF,
            'left and right mouse buttons at the same time.        ');

    MouSetDefaultPtr( MouPtrMask( PtrDifChar( $DB ), PtrDifCol( 3 ) ) );
    MouDefRange( 5, @Ranges );                       { Range definition }
    MouShowMouse;                   { Display mouse pointer on the screen }

    {-- Wait until the user presses both the left and right mouse  -----}
    {-- buttons simultaneously while the pointer is in range 4     -----}

    repeat                                                { Read loop }
     Dummy := MouEventWait( EAND, EV_LEFT_PRESS or EV_RIGHT_PRESS );
    until EvRng = 4;
   end
  else                  { No mouse installed OR no mouse driver installed }
    writeln('Sorry, no mouse driver currently installed.');
end.
```

Assembler listing: MOUSEPA.ASM

```
;***********************************************************************;
;*                          M O U S E P A                               *;
;*---------------------------------------------------------------------*;
;*    Task            : Create mouse called event handler for use with *;
;*                      a Turbo Pascal program.                         *;
;*---------------------------------------------------------------------*;
;*    Author          : MICHAEL TISCHER                                 *;
;*    Developed on    : 04/24/1989                                      *;
;*    Last update     : 04/24/1989                                      *;
;*---------------------------------------------------------------------*;
;*    assembly        : MASM /MX MOUSEPA;    or                         *;
;*                      TASM -MX MOUSEPA;                               *;
;*                      ... add to MOUSEP program code                  *;
;***********************************************************************;

;== Data segment =======================================================

DATA   segment word public
DATA   ends                          ;note--no variables in this program

;== Program ============================================================

CODE   segment byte public           ;Program segment
```

```
        assume CS:CODE            ;CS points to the code segment whose
                                  ;contents are unknown to DS, SS & ES

public     AssmHand               ;Allows the TP program to read
                                  ;the address of the assembler handlers

extrn     MouEventHandler : near  ;TP event handler to be called

active     db  0                  ;points to whether a call can occur

;-------------------------------------------------------------------
;-- AssmHand : The event handler which first calls the mouse driver, then
;--           calls the TP MouEventHandler procedure
;--           Direct call from TP not allowed

AssmHand    proc far

          ;-- First save all processor registers on stack ---

          cmp  active,0           ;Call done yet?
          jne  ende               ;NO --> Don't exit call

          mov  active,1           ;No more calls, please

          push ax
          push bx
          push cx
          push dx
          push di
          push si
          push bp
          push es
          push ds

          ;-- Push arguments for TP function call onto stack -------
          ;-- Call:
          ;--   MouEventHandler (EvFlags, ButStatus, x , y : integer );

          push ax                 ;Push event flags onto stack
          push bx                 ;Push mouse button status onto stack

          mov  di,cx              ;Move horizontal ordinate onto DI
          mov  cl,3               ;Counter for coordinate number

          shr  di,cl              ;Divide DI (horizontal ord.) by 8 and
          push di                 ;push onto stack

          shr  dx,cl              ;Divide DX (vertical ord.) by 8 and
          push dx                 ;push onto stack

          mov  ax,DATA            ;Segment address of data segment AX
          mov  ds,ax              ;Move data from AX to DS register

          call  MouEventHandler   ;Call TP procedure

          ;-- Get reserved registers from stack ----------------------

          pop  ds
          pop  es
          pop  bp
          pop  si
          pop  di
          pop  dx
          pop  cx
          pop  bx
          pop  ax

          mov  active,0           ;Re-enable call
```

```
ende:      ret                  ;Return to mouse driver

AssmHand    endp

;----------------------------------------------------------------------

CODE       ends                 ;End of code segment
           end                  ;End of program
```

C listing: MOUSEC.C

```
/**********************************************************************/
/*                           M O U S E C . C                          */
/*--------------------------------------------------------------------*/
/*    Task           : Demonstrates mouse access from the C language  */
/*--------------------------------------------------------------------*/
/*    Author         : MICHAEL TISCHER                                */
/*    Developed on   : 04/20/1989                                     */
/*    Last update    : 06/14/1989                                     */
/*--------------------------------------------------------------------*/
/*    Microsoft C                                                     */
/*    Creation       : CL /AS MOUSEC.C MOUSECA.OBJ                    */
/*    Call           : MOUSEC                                         */
/*--------------------------------------------------------------------*/
/*    Turbo C (integrated system)                                     */
/*    Creation       : Create a project file containing the following:*/
/*                       MOUSEC                                       */
/*                       MOUSECA.OBJ                                  */
/*                     Make sure that memory model is set to small.   */
/*                     If you didn't assemble the MOUSECA.ASM file    */
/*                     using the /MX option in MASM, make sure that   */
/*                     Case-Sensitive Link on Linker options is OFF.  */
/*                     Disable stack checking before compilation.     */
/*                     >>NOTE: One warning will occur (about the      */
/*                     ButState in the MouEventHandler function).     */
/*                     The program will run. Do   N O T   remove      */
/*                     the ButState declaration - the AssmHand routine*/
/*                     needs it<<                                     */
/*    Call           : MOUSEC                                         */
/**********************************************************************/

/*== Add include files ===============================================*/

#include <dos.h>
#include <stdlib.h>

extern void far AssmHand( void );          /* External declaration   */
                                           /* of assembler handler   */
/*== Typedefs ========================================================*/

typedef unsigned char BYTE;                          /* Create a byte */
typedef unsigned long PTRVIEW;                 /* Mouse pointer mask */
typedef struct {                             /* Describe a mouse range */
                BYTE x1,              /* Upper left coordinates of the */
                     y1,              /* specified range               */
                     x2,                  /* Lower right corner of the */
                     y2;                  /* specified range           */
                PTRVIEW ptr_mask;                /* Mouse pointer mask */
               } RANGE;
typedef void (far * MOUHAPTR)( void );     /* Pointer to event handler */

/*== Constants =======================================================*/

#define TRUE  ( 1 == 1 )
#define FALSE ( 1 == 0 )

/*-- Event codes -----------------------------------------------------*/

#define EV_MOU_MOVE      1                              /* Move mouse */
```

```
#define EV_LEFT_PRESS    2             /* Left mouse button pressed */
#define EV_LEFT_REL      4            /* Left mouse button released */
#define EV_RIGHT_PRESS   8            /* Right mouse button pressed */
#define EV_RIGHT_REL    16           /* Right mouse button released */
#define EV_MOU_ALL      31                     /* all mouse events */

#define NO_RANGE 255               /* mouse pointer not in range xy */

/*-- Macros -------------------------------------------------------*/

#define MouGetCol()          (ev_col)       /* Return mouse position & */
#define MouGetRow()          (ev_row)          /* range the moment the */
#define MouGetRange()        (ev_rng)          /* event occurs         */
#define MouAvail()           ( mavail )      /* Available mouse = TRUE */
#define MouGetCurCol()       ( moucol )       /* Returns current mouse */
#define MouGetCurRow()       ( mourow )       /* position and current  */
#define MouGetCurRng()       ( mourng )       /* mouse range           */
#define MouIsLeftPress()     ( mouevent & EV_LEFT_PRESS )
#define MouIsLeftRel()       ( mouevent & EV_LEFT_REL )
#define MouIsRightPress()    ( mouevent & EV_RIGHT_PRESS )
#define MouIsRightRel()      ( mouevent & EV_RIGHT_REL )
#define MouSetMoveAreaAll() MouSetMoveArea( 0, 0, tcol-1, tline-1 );

#define ELVEC(x)  ( sizeof(x) / sizeof(x[0]) ) /* No. of elements in X */

/*-- Bitmask creation macros defining mouse pointer's appearance.  ---*/
/*-- Syntax for calling MouPtrMask (sample):                        ---*/
/*--    MouPtrMask( PTRDIFCHAR( 'x' ), PTRINVCOL )                  ---*/
/*-- When the pointer is represented as a lowercase x, the inverse ---*/
/*-- character color takes effect.                                  ---*/

#define MouPtrMask( z, f )\
  ( (( (PTRVIEW) f) >> 8 << 24) + ((( PTRVIEW) z) >> 8 << 16) +\
    (((f) & 255) << 8) + ((z) & 255) )

#define PTRSAMECHAR    ( 0x00ff )       /* Same cahracter             */
#define PTRDIFCHAR(z)  ( (z) << 8 )     /* Other characters           */
#define PTRSAMECOL     ( 0x00ff )       /* Same color                 */
#define PTRINVCOL      ( 0x7777 )       /* Inverse color              */
#define PTRSAMECOLB    ( 0x807f )       /* Same color (blinking)      */
#define PTRINVCOLB     ( 0xF777 )       /* Inverse color (blinking)   */
#define PTRDIFCOL(f)   ( (f) << 8 )     /* Other color                */
#define PTRDIFCOLB(f)  (((f)|0x80) << 8) /* Other color (blinking)    */

#define EAND  0                /* Event comparisons for MouEventWait() */
#define EVOR 1

#define MOUINT(rin, rout) int86(0x33, &rin, &rout)
#define MOUINTX(rin, rout, sr) int86x(0x33, &rin, &rout, &sr)

/*-- Macros for converting mouse coordinates between virtual mouse    */
/*-- screen and text screen                                        ----*/

#define XTOCOL(x)  ( (x) >> 3 )                             /* X v 8 */
#define YTOROW(y)  ( (y) >> 3 )                           /* Row v 8 */
#define COLTOX(c)  ( (c) << 3 )                             /* C x 8 */
#define ROWTOY(r)  ( (r) << 3 )                           /* Row x 8 */

/*== global variables ===============================================*/

BYTE tline,                                      /* No. of text lines */
     tcol,                                     /* No. of text columns */
     mavail = FALSE;                     /* TRUE when mouse is available */

/*-- Mask for standard mouse pointer ---------------------------------*/

PTRVIEW stdptr = MouPtrMask( PTRSAMECHAR, PTRINVCOL );

BYTE     * bbuf,                    /* Ptr to range recognition buffer */
         num_range = 0;                  /* No range defined until now */
```

```
RANGE * cur_range;                /* Pointer to current range vector */
int     blen;                               /* Length of BBUF in bytes */

/*-- Variables which load every time the mouse handler is called -----*/

BYTE mourng = NO_RANGE,                        /* Current mouse range */
     moucol,                             /* Mouse column (text screen) */
     mourow;                                /* Mouse row (text screen) */
int  mouevent = EV_LEFT_REL + EV_RIGHT_REL;               /* Event mask */

/*-- Variables which load every time an event anticipated by the   ---*/
/*-- mouse handler occurs                                          ---*/

BYTE ev_rng,                  /* Range in which the mouse can be found */
     ev_col,                                          /* Mouse column */
     ev_row;                                             /* Mouse row */

/***********************************************************************
*  Function           : M o u D e f i n e P t r                        *
**-------------------------------------------------------------------**
*  Task               : Defines the cursor mask and screen mask which   *
*                       determines the mouse pointer's appearance       *
*  Input parameters : MASK = Both bitmasks, made into a 32-bit value    *
*                             of type UNSIGNED LONG                     *
*  Return value       : None                                            *
*  Info               :  Most significant 16 bits of MASK = screen mask *
*                        least significant 16 bits of mask = cursor mask *
**********************************************************************/

#pragma check_stack(off)                     /* No stack checking here */

void MouDefinePtr( PTRVIEW mask )
{
 static PTRVIEW oldercursor = (PTRVIEW) 0;      /* Last value for MASK */
 union REGS regs;                 /* Processor regs for interrupt call */

 if ( oldercursor != mask )                /* Changes since last call? */
  {                                                              /* YES */
   regs.x.ax = 0x000a;         /* Funct. no. for "Set text pointer type" */
   regs.x.bx = 0;                            /* Create software pointer */
   regs.x.cx = mask;                            /* Low word is AND-mask */
   regs.x.dx = mask >> 16;                     /* High word is XOR-mask */
   MOUINT(regs, regs);                             /* Call mouse driver */
   oldercursor = mask;                               /* Note old bitmask */
  }
}

/***********************************************************************
*  Function           : M o u E v e n t H a n d l e r                  *
**-------------------------------------------------------------------**
*  Task               : Calls AssmHand routine from mouse driver, when  *
*                       a mouse related event occurs.                   *
*  Input parameters : EvFlags   = Event's event mask                    *
*                       ButState = Mouse button status                  *
*                       X, Y     = Current pointer position, converted  *
*                                  into text screen coordinates         *
*  Return value       : None                                            *
*  Info               : - This function ise only operational through a  *
*                         mouse driver call, and shouldn't be called    *
*                         from another function.                        *
**********************************************************************/

void MouEventHandler( int EvFlags, int ButState, int x, int y )
{
 #define LBITS ( EV_LEFT_PRESS | EV_LEFT_REL )
 #define RBITS ( EV_RIGHT_PRESS | EV_RIGHT_REL )

 unsigned newrng;                                   /* New range number */
```

```
 mouevent &= ~1;                                          /* Clear bit 0 */
 mouevent |= ( EvFlags & 1 );                    /* Copy EvFlags to bit 0 */

 if ( EvFlags & LBITS )     /* Left mouse button pressed or released? */
  {                                                           /* YES */
   mouevent &= ~LBITS;                         /* Clear previous status */
   mouevent |= ( EvFlags & LBITS );                   /* Add new status */
  }

 if ( EvFlags & RBITS )    /* Right mouse button pressed or released? */
  {                                        /* YES, Clear and set bits */
   mouevent &= ~RBITS;                         /* Clear previous status */
   mouevent |= ( EvFlags & RBITS );                   /* Add new status */
  }

 moucol = x;                     /* Convert columns into text columns */
 mourow = y;                            /* Convert rows into text rows */

 /*-- Check range in which mouse is currently located, and compare  --*/
 /*-- to range since last call. If a change occurs, the pointer's  ---*/
 /*-- appearance will have to be changed.                          ---*/

 newrng = *(bbuf + mourow * tcol + moucol);              /* Get range */
 if ( newrng != mourng )                                 /* New range? */
  MouDefinePtr((newrng==NO_RANGE) ? stdptr :
                                   (cur_range+newrng)->ptr_mask);
 mourng = newrng;          /* Place range number in global variables */
}

#pragma check_stack               /* Re-enable stack checking and old  */
#pragma check_stack               /* status                            */

/***********************************************************************
*  Function          : M o u I B u f F i l l                           *
**-------------------------------------------------------------------**
*  Task              : Stores a specific screen range code within     *
*                      screen memory affecting the module             *
*  Input parameters : x1, y1 = Upper left corner of the screen        *
*                      x2, y2 = Lower right corner of the screen      *
*                      CODE   = Range code                            *
*  Return value      : None                                           *
*  Info              : This functions should only be called from within *
*                      this module.                                   *
***********************************************************************/

static void MouIBufFill( BYTE x1, BYTE y1,
                         BYTE x2, BYTE y2, BYTE code )
{
 register BYTE * lptr;            /* Floating pointer to range mem. */
 BYTE i, j;                                          /* Loop counter */

 lptr = bbuf + y1 * tcol + x1;               /* Pointer to first line */

 /*-- Go through individual lines ------------------------------------*/
 for (j=x2 - x1 + 1 ; y1 <= y2; ++y1, lptr+=tcol )
  memset( lptr, code, j );                                /* Set code */
}

/***********************************************************************
*  Function          : M o u D e f R a n g e                           *
**-------------------------------------------------------------------**
*  Task              : Allows the definition of different screen ranges *
*                      which configure a different code for the mouse  *
*                      pointer, depending on the pointer's location.   *
*  Input parameters : - NUMBER = Number of screen ranges               *
*                      - PTR    = Pointer to screen description vector *
*                                 (type RANGE)                          *
*  Return value      : None                                             *
*  Info              : - Free screen ranges receive the code NO_RANGE.  *
*                      - When entering the specified screen range, the *
```

```
*                     mouse handler automatically changes the mouse  *
*                     pointer's appearance to correspond with that   *
*                     range.                                         *
*                   - Since the specified pointer is stored, but the *
*                     specified vector isn't copied to  a separate   *
*                     buffer, the contencs of the vecros should not  *
*                     be changed on the next call of this function.  *
**********************************************************************/

void MouDefRange( BYTE number, RANGE * ptr )
{
 register BYTE i,                                  /* Loop counter */
               range;                               /* Mouse range */

 cur_range = ptr;                     /* Reserve pointer to vector  */
 num_range = number;                  /* and number of ranges       */
 memset( bbuf, NO_RANGE, blen );
 for (i=0 ; i<number ; ++ptr )
  MouIBufFill( ptr->x1, ptr->y1, ptr->x2, ptr->y2, i++);

 /*-- Redefine mouse pointer -----------------------------------------*/

 range = *(bbuf + mourow * tcol + moucol);     /* Current mouse range */
 MouDefinePtr( ( range == NO_RANGE ) ? stdptr
               : (cur_range+range)->ptr_mask );
}

/**********************************************************************
*  Function          : M o u E v e n t W a i t                        *
**------------------------------------------------------------------**
*  Task              : Waits for a specific event from the keyboard.  *
*  Input parameters : TYP         = Establishes comparison between    *
*                                   different events.                 *
*                     WAIT_EVENT = Bitmask which specifies wait event. *
*  Return value      : Bitmask which describes this or another event.  *
*  Info              : - WAIT_EVENT can be used with other constants   *
*                        such as EV_MOU_MOVE or EV_LEFT_PRESS when used *
*                        in conjunction with EVOR.                    *
*                      - EAND  & EVOR are allowable types. EAND has the *
*                        ability to return to the caller once ALL events*
*                        have occurred; EVOR returns to the caller when *
*                        at least one event occurs.                   *
**********************************************************************/

int MouEventWait( BYTE typ, int wait_event )
{
 int cur_event;                               /* Current event mask */
 register BYTE column = moucol,              /* Last mouse position */
               line   = mourow;
 BYTE ende = FALSE;                      /* TRUE if an event occurs */

 while ( !ende )                       /* Repeat until event occurs */
  {
   /*-- Wait until one of the events occurs -------------------------*/

   if ( typ == EAND )                 /* EAND: All events must occur */
     while ( (cur_event = mouevent) != wait_event)
      ;
   else                         /* EVOR: At least one event must occur */
     while ( ( (cur_event = mouevent) & wait_event) == 0)
      ;

   cur_event &= wait_event;                 /* Check event bits only */

   /*-- When moving the mouse, the event is only accepted if the    --*/
   /*-- pointer moves to another row or column on the text screen   --*/

   if ((wait_event & EV_MOU_MOVE) && column==moucol && line==mourow)
    {                      /* Mouse moves, but in same screen position */
     cur_event &= (~EV_MOU_MOVE);                 /* Examine move bit */
```

```
      ende = (cur_event != 0);                    /* Are events pending? */
     }
    else                                              /* Event occurred */
     ende = TRUE;
   }
  ev_col = moucol;                       /* Set current mouse position */
  ev_row = mourow;                       /* and mouse range; place in  */
  ev_rng = mourng;                       /* global variables           */
  return( cur_event );                          /* Return event mask */
 }

/***********************************************************************
*  Function          : M o u I S e t E v e n t H a n d l e r          *
**-------------------------------------------------------------------**
*  Task              : Installs an event handler which handles events   *
*                      called from the mouse driver.                    *
*  Input parameters  : EVENT = Bitmask which specifies the event which  *
*                              calls the event handler.                 *
*                      PTR   = Pointer to the mouse handler             *
*  Return value      : None                                             *
*  Info              : - EVENT can be used in conjunction with the EVOR *
*                        comparison on constants such as EV_MOU_MOVE,   *
*                        EV_LEFT_PRESS                                  *
***********************************************************************/

static void MouISetEventHandler( unsigned event, MOUHAPTR ptr )
{
 union REGS regs;               /* Processor regs for interrupt call */
 struct SREGS sregs;          /* Segment register for interrupt call */

 regs.x.ax = 0x000C;          /* Funct. no. for "Set Mouse Handler" */
 regs.x.cx = event;                               /* Load event mask */
 regs.x.dx = FP_OFF( ptr );              /* Offset address of handler */
 sregs.es  = FP_SEG( ptr );             /* Segment address of handler */
 MOUINTX( regs, regs, sregs );                   /* Call mouse driver */
}

/***********************************************************************
*  Function          : M o u I G e t X                                  *
**-------------------------------------------------------------------**
*  Task              : Determines text column in which pointer lies.    *
*  Input parameters  : None                                             *
*  Return value      : Mouse pointer column, relative to text screen    *
***********************************************************************/

static BYTE MouIGetX( void )
{
 union REGS regs;               /* Processor regs for interrupt call */

 regs.x.ax= 0x0003;          /* Funct. no. for "Get mouse position" */
 MOUINT( regs, regs );                          /* Call mouse driver */
 return XTOCOL( regs.x.cx );             /* Convert and return column */
}

/***********************************************************************
*  Function          : M o u I G e t Y                                  *
**-------------------------------------------------------------------**
*  Task              : Determines text row in which pointer lies.       *
*  Input parameters  : None                                             *
*  Return value      : Mouse pointer row, relative to the text screen   *
***********************************************************************/

static BYTE MouIGetY( void )
{
 union REGS regs;               /* Processor regs for interrupt call */

 regs.x.ax= 0x0003;          /* Funct. no. for "Get mouse position" */
 MOUINT(regs, regs);                            /* Call mouse driver */
 return YTOROW(regs.x.dx);                  /* Convert and return row */
}
```

```
/***********************************************************************
*  Function          : M o u S h o w M o u s e                          *
**--------------------------------------------------------------------**
*  Task              : Display mouse pointer on the screen.             *
*  Input parameters : None                                              *
*  Return value      : None                                             *
*  Info              : Calls of MouHidemMouse() and MouShowMouse() must *
*                      be kept balanced.                                *
***********************************************************************/

void MouShowMouse( void )
{
 union REGS regs;             /* Processor regs for interrupt call */

 regs.x.ax = 0x0001;                  /* Funct. no. for "Show Mouse" */
 MOUINT(regs, regs);                           /* Call mouse driver */
}

/***********************************************************************
*  Function          : M o u H i d e M o u s e                          *
**--------------------------------------------------------------------**
*  Task              : Hide mouse pointer from screen.                  *
*  Input parameters : None                                              *
*  Return value      : None                                             *
*  Info              : Calls of MouHidemMouse() and MouShowMouse() must *
*                      be kept balanced.                                *
***********************************************************************/

void MouHideMouse( void )
{
 union REGS regs;             /* Processor regs for interrupt call */

 regs.x.ax = 0x0002;                  /* Funct. no. for "Hide Mouse" */
 MOUINT(regs, regs);                           /* Call mouse driver */
}

/***********************************************************************
*  Function          : M o u S e t M o v e A r e a                      *
**--------------------------------------------------------------------**
*  Task              : Defines a screen range within which the mouse    *
*                      pointer may be moved.                            *
*  Input parameters : x1, y1 = Coordinates of upper left corner         *
*                      x2, y2 = Coordinates of lower right corner       *
*  Return value      : None                                             *
*  Info              : - Both parameters apply to text screen, NOT the  *
*                        mouse driver's virtual graphic screen    -     *
***********************************************************************/

void MouSetMoveArea( BYTE x1, BYTE y1, BYTE x2, BYTE y2 )
{
 union REGS regs;             /* Processor regs for interrupt call */

 regs.x.ax = 0x0008;        /* Funct. no. for "Set vertical Limits" */
 regs.x.cx = ROWTOY( y1 );                /* Conversion to virtual */
 regs.x.dx = ROWTOY( y2 );                /* mouse screen          */
 MOUINT(regs, regs);                           /* Call mouse driver */
 regs.x.ax = 0x0007;      /* Funct. no. for "Set horizontal Limits" */
 regs.x.cx = COLTOX( x1 );                /* Conversion to virtual */
 regs.x.dx = COLTOX( x2 );                /* mouse screen          */
 MOUINT(regs, regs);                           /* Call mouse driver */
}

/***********************************************************************
*  Function          : M o u S e t S p e e d                            *
**--------------------------------------------------------------------**
*  Task              : Determines the difference between mouse movement *
*                      speed and the resulting pointer speed on the     *
*                      screen.                                          *
*  Input parameters : - XSPEED = Horizontal speed                       *
```

```
*                       - YSPEED = Vertical speed                       *
*  Return value       : None                                            *
*  Info               : - Both parameters are based on mickeys          *
*                           (mickey / 8 pixel).                         *
************************************************************************/

void MouSetSpeed( int xspeed, int yspeed )
{
 union REGS regs;                 /* Processor regs for interrupt call */

 regs.x.ax = 0x000f;   /* Funct. no. for "Set mickeys to pixel ratio" */
 regs.x.cx = xspeed;
 regs.x.dx = yspeed;
 MOUINT(regs, regs);                             /* Call mouse driver */
}

/************************************************************************
*  Function           : M o u M o v e P t r                             *
**---------------------------------------------------------------------**
*  Task               : Moves the mouse pointer to a specific position  *
*                       on the screen.                                  *
*  Input parameters : - COL = new screen column                         *
*                       - ROW = new screen row                          *
*  Return value       : None                                            *
*  Info               : - Both parameters apply to the text screen, NOT *
*                           to the mouse driver's virtual graphic screen *
************************************************************************/

void MouMovePtr( int col, int row )
{
 union REGS regs;                 /* Processor regs for interrupt call */
 unsigned newrng;                 /* Range in which the mouse can move */

 regs.x.ax = 0x0004;   /* Funct. no. for "Set mouse pointer position" */
 regs.x.cx = COLTOX( moucol = col ); /* Convert coordinates and store */
 regs.x.dx = ROWTOY( mourow = row ); /* in global variables            */
 MOUINT(regs, regs);                             /* Call mouse driver */

 newrng = *(bbuf + mourow * tcol + moucol);             /* Get range */
 if ( newrng != mourng )                                /* New range? */
  MouDefinePtr((newrng==NO_RANGE) ? stdptr :
                              (cur_range+newrng)->ptr_mask);
 mourng = newrng;            /* Place range number in global variables */
}

/************************************************************************
*  Function           : M o u S e t D e f a u l t P t r                 *
**---------------------------------------------------------------------**
*  Task               : Defines mouse pointer for screen ranges without *
*                       the help of MouDefRange.                        *
*  Input parameters : STANDARD = Bitmask for standard mouse pointer     *
*  Return value       : None                                            *
************************************************************************/

void MouSetDefaultPtr( PTRVIEW standard )
{
 stdptr = standard;              /* Place bitmask in global variables */

 /*-- If mouse is currently in no range, go direct to conversion   ---*/
 /*-- to new pointer appearance                                     ---*/

 if ( MouGetRange() == NO_RANGE )                /* Not in any range? */
  MouDefinePtr( standard );                                   /* NO */
}

/************************************************************************
*  Function           : M o u E n d                                     *
**---------------------------------------------------------------------**
*  Task               : Ends mouseC module functions.                   *
*  Input parameters : None                                              *
```

```
*  Return value     : None                                             *
*  Info             : Function is called automatically when program    *
*                     ends, as long as MouInstall is called first.     *
***********************************************************************/

void MouEnd( void )
{
 union REGS regs;              /* Processor regs for interrupt call */

 MouHideMouse();                  /* Hide mouse pointer from screen */
 regs.x.ax = 0;                               /* Reset mouse driver */
 MOUINT(regs, regs);                           /* Call mouse driver */

 free( bbuf );                          /* Release allocated memory */
}

/***********************************************************************
*  Function         : M o u I n i t                                    *
**--------------------------------------------------------------------**
*  Task             : Initializes variables and mousec module          *
*  Input parameters : Columns, = Text screen resolution                *
*                     Lines                                            *
*  Return value     : TRUE if a mouse is installed, else FALSE         *
*  Info             : This function must be called as the first one in *
*                     the module.                                      *
***********************************************************************/

BYTE MouInit( BYTE columns, BYTE lines )
{
 union REGS regs;              /* Processor regs for interrupt call */

 tline = lines;                 /* Store no. of lines and cols   */
 tcol  = columns;               /* in global variables           */

 atexit( MouEnd );              /* Call MouEnd at end of program */

 /*-- Allocate and fill mouse range buffer --------------------------*/

 bbuf = (BYTE *) malloc( blen = tline * tcol );
 MouIBufFill( 0, 0, tcol-1, tline-1, NO_RANGE );

 regs.x.ax = 0;                          /* Initialize mouse driver */
 MOUINT(regs, regs);                           /* Call mouse driver */
 if ( regs.x.ax != 0xffff )              /* Mouse driver installed? */
  return FALSE;                                             /* NO */

 MouSetMoveAreaAll();                     /* Set range of movement */

 moucol = MouIGetX();                /* Load current mouse pos.  */
 mourow = MouIGetY();                /* into global variables    */

 /*-- Install assembler event handler "AssmHand" ---------------------*/
 MouISetEventHandler( EV_MOU_ALL, (MOUHAPTR) AssmHand );

 return mavail = TRUE;                      /* Mouse is installed */
}

/***********************************************************************
*                      M A I N         P R O G R A M                   *
***********************************************************************/

int main( void )
{
 static RANGE ranges[] =                            /* Mouse ranges */
  {
   {  0,  0, 79,  0, MouPtrMask( PTRDIFCHAR(0x18), PTRINVCOL)   },
   {  0,  1,  0, 23, MouPtrMask( PTRDIFCHAR(0x1b), PTRINVCOL)   },
   {  0, 24, 78, 24, MouPtrMask( PTRDIFCHAR(0x19), PTRINVCOL)   },
   { 79,  1, 79, 23, MouPtrMask( PTRDIFCHAR(0x1a), PTRINVCOL)   },
   { 79, 24, 79, 24, MouPtrMask( PTRDIFCHAR('X'),  PTRDIFCOLB(0x40) ) },
```

```
 };

printf("\nMOUSEC - (c) 1989 by MICHAEL TISCHER\n\n");
if ( MouInit( 80, 25 ) )                        /* Initialize mouse module */
 {                                  /* OK, there is an installed mouse driver */
  printf("Move the mouse pointer around on the screen. When you move\n"\
         "the mouse  pointer  to  the  border  of  the  screen,  the\n"\
         "mouse pointer changes in appearance,  depending  upon  its\n"\
         "Current position.\n\n"
         "Move  the mouse pointer  to the lower right corner  of the\n"\
         "screen,  and press both  the left  and right mouse buttons\n"\
         "to end this demo program.\n" );

  MouSetDefaultPtr( MouPtrMask( PTRDIFCHAR( '[' ), PTRDIFCOL( 3 ) ) );
  MouDefRange( ELVEC( ranges ), ranges );         /* Range definition */
  MouShowMouse();                /* Display mouse pointer on the screen */

  /*-- Wait until the user presses the left and right mouse        --*/
  /*-- buttons simultaneously, AND the mouse pointer lies int       --*/
  /*-- range 4                                                      --*/

  do                                                     /* Read loop */
   MouEventWait( EAND, EV_LEFT_PRESS | EV_RIGHT_PRESS );
  while ( MouGetRange() != 4 );

  return 0;                                /* Return OK code to DOS */
 }
else                              /* No mouse OR mouse driver installed */
 {
  printf("Sorry, no mouse driver installed.\n");
  return 1;                              /* Return error code to DOS */
 }
}
```

Assembler listing: MOUSECA.ASM

```
;***********************************************************************;
;*                             M O U S E C A                           *;
;*---------------------------------------------------------------------*;
;*    Task            : Mouse driver event handler intended for         *;
;*                      linking to a C program compiled as a SMALL     *;
;*                      memory model.                                  *;
;*---------------------------------------------------------------------*;
;*    Author          : MICHAEL TISCHER                                *;
;*    Developed on    : 04/20/1989                                     *;
;*    Last update     : 06/14/1989                                     *;
;*---------------------------------------------------------------------*;
;*    assembly        : MASM /MX MOUSECA;                              *;
;*                      ... link to program MOUSEC                     *;
;***********************************************************************;

;== Segment declarations for the C program ============================

IGROUP group _text                 ;Inclusion for program segment
DGROUP group const,_bss,  _data    ;Inclusion for data segment
       assume CS:IGROUP, DS:DGROUP, ES:DGROUP, SS:DGROUP

CONST  segment word public 'CONST';This segment includes all read-only
CONST  ends                        ;constants

_BSS   segment word public 'BSS'   ;This segment includes all un-
_BSS   ends                        ;initialized static variables

_DATA  segment word public 'DATA'  ;This segment includes all initialized
                                   ;global and static variables
_DATA  ends

;== Program ===========================================================
```

```
_TEXT  segment byte public 'CODE' ;Program segment

public      _AssmHand              ;Gives the C program the ability to
                                   ;access assembler handler addresses

extrn       _MouEventHandler : near ;Event handler to be called

active      db  0                  ;Indicates whether a call is under
                                   ;execution

;-----------------------------------------------------------------------
;-- _AssmHand : The event handler called by the mouse driver, then
;--            called by the MouEventHandler() function
;-- Call from C: not allowed!

_AssmHand   proc far

            ;-- Place all processor registers on the stack ---

            cmp  active,0           ;Call still not finished?
            jne  ende              ;NO --> Do not exit call

            mov  active,1           ;No more calls

            push ax
            push bx
            push cx
            push dx
            push di
            push si
            push bp
            push es
            push ds

            ;-- Place all arguments for calling C_FCT on the stack ---
            ;-- Call: MouEventHandler( int EvFlags, int ButStatus,
            ;--                        int x,       int y );

            mov  di,cx             ;Place horizontal coordinate in DI
            mov  cl,3              ;Counter for coordinate number
            shr  dx,cl             ;Divide DX (vertical coord.) by 8
            push dx                ;and place on the stack

            shr  di,cl             ;Divide DI (horizontal coord.) by 8
            push di                ;and place on the stack

            push bx                ;Push mouse button status onto stack
            push ax                ;Push event flag onto stack

            mov  ax,DGROUP         ;Move segment address of DGROUP to AX
            mov  ds,ax             ;Move AX to DS register

            call _MouEventHandler  ;C function call

            add  sp,8              ;Get arguments from stack

            ;-- Pop register contents off of stack ---------

            pop  ds
            pop  es
            pop  bp
            pop  si
            pop  di
            pop  dx
            pop  cx
            pop  bx
            pop  ax

            mov  active,0           ;Re-enable call
```

```
ende:      ret                      ;Return to mouse driver

_AssmHand   endp

;------------------------------------------------------------------------

_text      ends                     ;End of code segment
           end                      ;End of program
```

Chapter 15

Determining Processor Types

There are number of utility programs on the market today which can tell you about the configuration of a PC. This information can include the amount of available RAM, the running DOS version and the type of processor the PC has.

This information can be very useful for developing programs in high level languages, since code generation can be adapted to the particular processor. For example, both Microsoft C and Turbo C allow special code generation for the 8088, the 80286 and the 80386, which makes full use of the capabilities of the particular processor and instruction set. This can dramatically improve performance for programs which work with large groups of data. One way to take advantage of this would be to compile the program once for each of the three processor types. Then a program could be developed to serve as the boot for the actual program. This boot program would determine the type of processor being used and load the main program version most compatible with the processor.

Which processor is which?

This raises the question of how to determine which type of processor is being used, since unlike other configuration information, we cannot find this out by making a BIOS or DOS call. Unfortunately, there is no machine language instruction which instructs the processor to reveal its identity, so we have to use a trick. This trick relies on a condition which, according to a few hardware manufacturers, is totally impossible.

This is a test which involves the different ways the various processors execute certain machine language instructions. Although processors from the 8086 to the 80386 are upwardly software compatible, the development of this processor series brought small changes in the logic of certain instructions. Since these changes are only noticeable in rare situations, a program developed for the 8088 processor will also run correctly on all other processors in the Intel 80x86 series. But if we deliberately put a processor into such a situation, we can determine its identity from its behavior.

These differences are only noticeable at the assembly language level, so our test program must be written in assembly language. We have included listings at the end of this chapter which allow the test routine to be included in Pascal, C and BASIC programs as well.

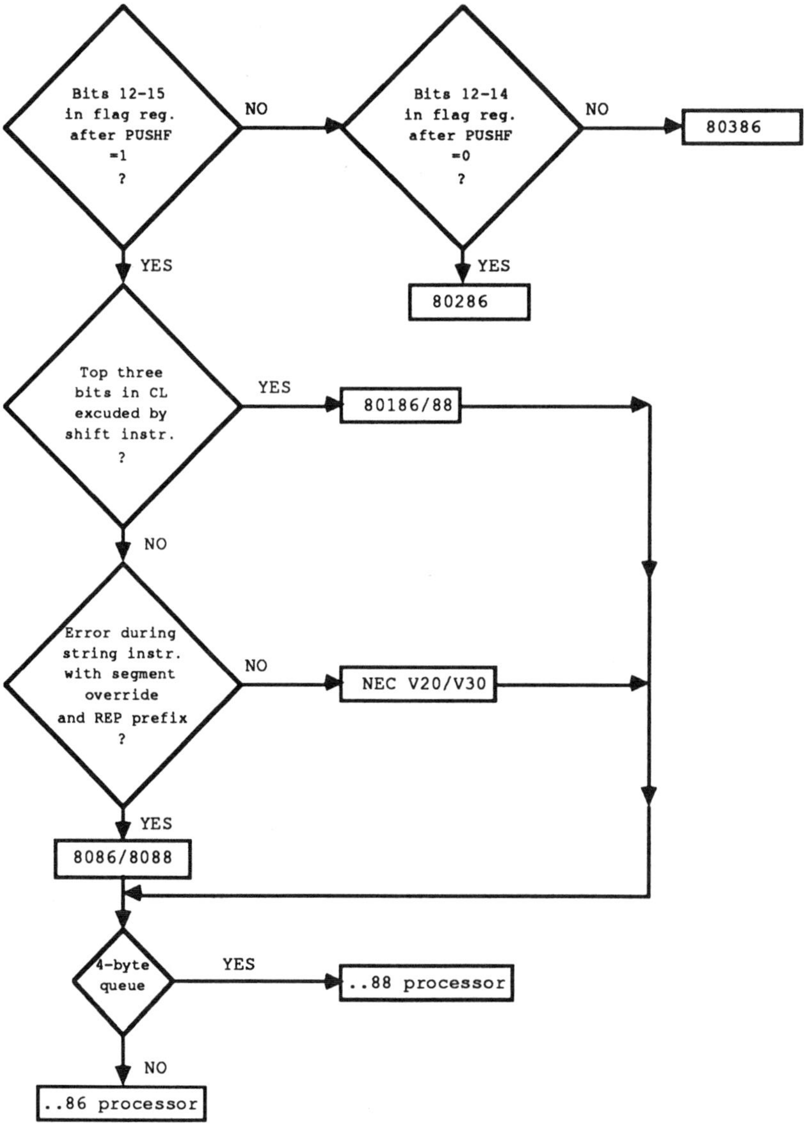

Determining processor type on a PC

As the flowchart above shows, the routine consists of several tests which can distinguish various processor types from one another. The next test executes only when the current test returns a negative response.

Flag register test

The first test concerns the different layout of the flag register in the different processors. The meaning of bits 0 to 11 is the same in all processors, but bits 12-15 are also defined in processors from 80286 up (through the introduction of the protected mode). This can be noticed in the instructions PUSHF (push the contents of the flag register onto the stack) and POPF (fetch the contents of the flag register from the stack). On processors through the 80188 these instructions always set bits 12-15 of the flag register to 1, but this doesn't occur in the 80286 and 80386 processors. The first test in the routine takes advantage of this fact, in which it places the value 0 on the stack and then loads it into the flag register with the POPF instruction. Since there is no instruction for comparing the contents of bits 12 to 15, the flag register is pushed back onto the stack with a PUSHF instruction. This is so we can get the contents into the AX register with POP AX, where we can test bits 12 to 15.

If all four bits are set, then the processor cannot be an 80286 or an 80386, and the next test is performed. However, if not all four bits are set, then we have reduced the set of possible processors to the 80826 and the 80386. Since POPF also operates differently between these two processors, it is easy to tell them apart. We simply repeat the whole process, this time by placing the value 07000H on the stack instead of 0. When the flag register is loaded with the POPF instruction, bits 12 to 14 of the flag register will be set to 1. If these bits are no longer 1 when the contents of the flag register are fetched from the stack, then the processor must be an 80286, which, in contrast to the 80386, sets these three bits back to 0. The test is then concluded for these two processors.

Narrowing down the field

If the processor did not pass the first test, the following test will show if it is an 80188 or 80186. With the introduction of these two processors, the shift instructions (like SHL and SHR) were changed in the way they use the CL register as a shift counter. While in previous processors the number of shifts could be between 0 and 255, the upper three bits of the CL register are now cleared before the instructions starts, limiting the number of shift operations. This makes sense since a word will contain all zeros anyway after at most 16 shifts (17, if the carry flag is shifted). Additional shifts will cost valuable processor time and will not change the value of the argument at all.

The second test makes use of this behavior by shifting the value 0FFH in the AL register 21H positions to the right with the SHR instruction. If the processor executing the instruction is an 80188 or later type, the upper three bits of the shift counter will first be cleared, and only one shift is performed instead of 21H shifts.

```
  021H (00100001(b))  number of shifts
& 01fH (00011111(b))  mask out the upper three bits
----------------------------------------------------
  001H (00000001(b))  actual number of shifts
```

Unlike its predecessors, which would actually shift the value 0FFH to the right 021H times and return the value 0, the 80188 and 80186 will return the value 07FH. By checking the contents of the AL register after the shift we can easy tell if the processor is an 80188 or 80186 (AL not zero), or not (AL equal to 0). If the processor also fails this test, then we know it is an 8088/8086 or V20/30.

V20 and V30 processors

The V20 and V30 processors are 8088/8086 "clones" which use the same instruction set as their Intel cousins, but which operate considerably faster due to the optimization of internal logic and improved manufacturing. This speed also results in a higher cost, so some PC manufacturers avoid using these processors.

In addition to the faster execution of instructions, these processors also corrected a small error which occurs in the 8088 and 8086 processors. If a hardware interrupt is generated during the execution of a string instruction (such as LODS) in connection with the REP(eat) prefix and a segment override, the execution of this instruction will not resume after the interrupt has been processed. This can easily be determined because the CX register, which functions as the loop counter in this instruction, will not contain a 0 as expected after the instruction.

We make use of this behavior in the test program by loading the CX register with the value 0FFFFH, and then executing a string instruction 65535 times with the REP prefix and segment override. Since even a fast processor needs some time to do this, a hardware interrupt will be generated during one of the 65535 executions of this instruction. In the case of the 8088 or 8086, the instruction will not be resumed after the interrupt, and the remaining "loop passes" will not execute. The test program verifies this from the CX register after the instruction has been executed.

Data bus test

Once we have distinguished between the 8088/8086 and the V20/30, one last test is performed for all processors (except the 80286 and 80386). In this test we determine if the processor is using an 8-bit or a 16-bit data bus. This allows us to tell the difference between the 8088 and 8086, the V20 and V30, or the 80188 and the 80186. We cannot determine the width of the data bus with assembly language commands, but the data bus width is related to the length of the instruction queue within the processor.

Queue

The queue stores the instructions following the instruction currently being executed. Since these instructions are taken from the queue and not from memory, this improves execution speed. This queue is six bytes long on processors with a 16-bit data bus, but only four bytes long on processors with an 8-bit data bus.

The last test is based on this difference in length. The string instruction STOSB (store string byte) used in connection with the REP prefix modifies three bytes in the code segment immediately following the STOSB instruction. These bytes are placed so that they are found within the queue on a processor with a six-byte queue; the processor won't even notice the change. On a processor with a four-byte queue, these instructions are still outside the queue, so the modified versions of the instructions are loaded into the queue. The program makes use of this by modifying the instruction INC DX, which increments the contents of the DX register which contains the processor code in the routine. This instruction is executed only when the processor has a six-byte queue, and the instruction was already in the queue by the time the modification was performed.

On a processor with a four-byte queue, this instruction is replaced by the STI instruction, which doesn't affect the contents of the DX register (or the processor code). STI sets the interrupt bit in the processor flag register. Since this procedure always increments the processor code by one for 16-bit processors, the processor codes in the routine are chosen so that the code for the 16-bit version of a processor always follows the code for the 8-bit version of the same processor.

The following BASIC and Pascal programs use DATA or inline statements instead of assembly language. However, we included the assembly language versions of these statements here so that you can follow the program logic. The C implementation requires direct linking of C and the assembly language routine.

BASIC listing: PROCB.BAS

```
100 '**********************************************************************'
110 '*                              P R O C B                              *'
120 '*--------------------------------------------------------------------*'
130 '*  Task            : Examines the main processor and tells the       *'
140 '*                    user the processor type                         *'
150 '*  Author          : MICHAEL TISCHER                                 *'
160 '*  Developed on    : 09/06/1988                                      *'
170 '*  Last update     : 05/23/1989                                      *'
180 '**********************************************************************'
190 '
200 CLS : KEY OFF
210 PRINT"ATTENTION: This program should only be run when GW-BASIC is loaded from"
220 PRINT"the DOS prompt using the command  <GWBASIC  /m:60000>."
230 PRINT : PRINT"If this isn't the case, press the <s> key to stop."
240 PRINT"Otherwise, press any other key to continue...        ";
250 A$ = INKEY$ : IF A$ = "s" THEN END
260 IF A$ = "" THEN 250
270 CLS                                                    'Clear screen
280 GOSUB 60000                                'Install assembler routine
290 CALL PT(PTYP%)                              'Determine processor type
300 RESTORE 1000              'Read DATA statements starting at line 1000
310 FOR I% = 0 TO PTYP% : READ P$ : NEXT               'Get processor name
320 PRINT "PROCB  -  (c) 1988 by MICHAEL TISCHER"
330 PRINT "Your PC contains a(n) ";P$;" processor."
340 END
350 '
1000 DATA "INTEL 8088", "INTEL 8086", "NEC V20", "NEC V30"
1010 DATA "INTEL 80186", "INTEL 80188", "INTEL 80286", "INTEL 80386"
```

```
1020 '
60000 '*******************************************************************'
60010 '* Routine for determining onboard processor type                  *'
60020 '*-----------------------------------------------------------------*'
60030 '* Input   : none                                                  *'
60040 '* Output : PT is the starting address of the assembler routine *'
60050 '* Call to the routine:CALL PT(PTYP%)                              *'
60060 '*******************************************************************'
60070 '
60080 PT=60000!                   'Starting address of BASIC segment routine
60090 DEF SEG                                        'Define BASIC segment
60100 RESTORE 60140
60110 FOR I% = 0 TO 105 : READ X% : POKE PT+I%,X% : NEXT   'POKE routine
60120 RETURN                                               'Return to caller
60130 '
60140 DATA  85,139,236,156,  6, 51,192, 80,157,156, 88, 37,  0,240, 61
60150 DATA   0,240,116, 19,178,  6,184,  0,112, 80,157,156, 88, 37,  0
60160 DATA 112,116, 54,254,194,235, 50,144,178,  4,176,255,177, 33,210
60170 DATA 232,117, 18,178,  2,251,190,  0,  0,185,255,255,243, 38,172
60180 DATA  11,201,116,  2,178,  0, 14,  7,253,176,251,185,  3,  0,232
60190 DATA  23,  0,250,243,170,252,144,144,144, 66,144,251, 50,246,139
60200 DATA 126,  6,137, 21,  7,157, 93,202,  2,  0, 95,131,199,  9,235
60210 DATA 227
```

Assembler listing: PROCBA.ASM

```
;**********************************************************************;
;*                            P R O C B A                             *;
;*--------------------------------------------------------------------*;
;*    Task:            : Determines the type of processor installed in *;
;*                       a PC                                         *;
;*                       This BASIC version of the program converts   *;
;*                       DATA statements into machine language, and   *;
;*                       executes this code in the BASIC program      *;
;*--------------------------------------------------------------------*;
;*    Author           : MICHAEL TISCHER                              *;
;*    Developed on     : 09/05/1988                                   *;
;*    Last update      : 05/24/1989                                   *;
;*--------------------------------------------------------------------*;
;*    assembly         : MASM PROCBA;                                 *;
;*                       LINK PROCBA;                                 *;
;*                       EXE2BIN PROCBA PROCBA.BIN                    *;
;*                           convert to DATA statements and add to    *;
;*                           a BASIC program                          *;
;**********************************************************************;

;== Constants =========================================================

p_80386    equu   7               ;Codes for different processor
p_80286    equ    6               ;types
p_80186    equ    5
p_80188    equ    4
p_v30      equ    3
p_v20      equ    2
p_8086     equ    1
p_8088     equ    0

;== Code ==============================================================

code       segment para 'CODE'    ;Definition of CODE segment

           org  100h

           assume cs:code, ds:code, ss:code, es:code

getproc    proc far               ;GW-BASIC waits for CALL FAR procedure


           push bp                ;Push BP onto stack
           mov  bp,sp             ;Move SP after BP
```

```
          pushf                    ;Save contents of flag registers
          push es                  ;Mark ES

          ;-- test for 80386/80286 - -----------------------------------

          xor  ax,ax               ;Set AX to 0 and
          push ax                  ;push onto stack
          popf                     ;Get as flag register from stack
          pushf                    ;Put on stack again and
          pop  ax                  ;return to AX
          and  ax,0f000h           ;Don't clear the top 4 bits
          cmp  ax,0f000h           ;Are bits 12-15 all equal to 1?
          je   not_a_386           ;YES-> Not an 80386 or 80286

          ;-- Test to see if it should be handled as 80386 or 80286 ----

          mov  dl,p_80286          ;This narrows it down to one of the
          mov  ax,07000h           ;two processors
          push ax                  ;Push value 07000H onto the stack
          popf                     ;Return as flag register
          pushf                    ;and push back onto stack
          pop  ax                  ;Pop off and return to AX register
          and  ax,07000h           ;Do not mask bits 12-14
          je   pende               ;Are bits 12-14 equal to 0?
                                   ;YES-> Treat it as an 80286

          inc  dl                  ;NO-> Treat it as an 80386
          jmp  pend                ;Test ended

          ;-- Test for 80186 or 80188 ----------------------------------

not_a_386 label near

          mov  dl,p_80188          ;Load code for 80188
          mov  al,0ffh             ;Set all bits in AL register to
          mov  cl,021h             ;Number of shift operations after CL
          shr  al,cl               ;Shift AL CL times to the right
          jne  t88_86              ;If AL<>0 then it must be handled as
                                   ;80188 or 80186

          ;-- Test for NEC V20 or V30 --- ------------------------------

          mov  dl,p_v20            ;Load code for NEC V20
          sti                      ;Interrupts should be enabled starting
          mov  si,0                ;with the first byte in ES
          mov  cx,0ffffh           ;Read a complete segment
          rep  lods byte ptr es:[si]      ;REP with segment override
                                   ;works only with NEC V20/V30 chips
          or   cx,cx               ;Has the complete segment been read?
          je   t88_86              ;YES--> it's a V20 or V30

          mov  dl,p_8088           ;NO--> must be an 8088 or 8086

          ;-- Test for ...88 or ...86 / V20 or V30 ---------------------

t88_86    label near

          push cs                  ;Push CS onto the stack
          pop  es                  ;and pop off to ES
          std                      ;Using string inst. count backwards
          mov  al,0fbh             ;Code for "STI"
          mov  cx,3                ;Execute string instruction 3 times
          call get_di              ;Call starting address DI
t86_1:    cli                      ;Suppress interrupts
          rep  stosb
          cld                      ;Using string inst. ocunt backwards
          nop                      ;Fill queue with dummy command
          nop
          nop
```

```
         inc  dx                  ;Increment processor code
         nop
q_end:   sti                      ;Re-enable interrupts

         ;------------------------------------------------------------

pend     label near               ;End processor test

         xor  dh,dh               ;Set high byte or processor code to 0
         mov  di,[bp+6]           ;Get addr. of processor code variables
         mov  [di],dx             ;Place processor code in this variable
         pop  es                  ;Pop off stack and place in ES
         popf                     ;Pop flag register off of stack and
         pop  bp                  ;Return BP
         ret  2                   ;FAR return takes us back to GW-BASIC
                                  ;Remove parameters from stack

getproc  endp                     ;End of PROG procedure

;-- GET_DI Check with DI for 88/86 Test -------------------------------

get_di   proc near

         pop  di                  ;Pop return address off of stack
         add  di,9                ;Remove starting 9 bytes from it
         jmp  t86_1               ;Return to the test routine

get_di   endp

;== End ================================================================

code     ends                     ;End of CODE segment
         end  getproc
```

Pascal listing: PROCP.PAS

```
{**********************************************************************}
{*                             P R O C P                              *}
{*--------------------------------------------------------------------*}
{*    Task            : Examines the processor type in the PC and     *}
{*                      tells the user the processor type             *}
{*--------------------------------------------------------------------*}
{*    Author          : MICHAEL TISCHER                               *}
{*    Developed on    : 08/16/1988                                    *}
{*    Last update     : 05/23/1989                                    *}
{**********************************************************************}

program PROCP;

type  ProNames = array[0..7] of string[11]; { Array of processor names }

const ProcName : ProNames = ( 'INTEL 8088',                { Code 0 }
                              'INTEL 8086',                { Code 1 }
                              'NEC V20',                   { Code 2 }
                              'NEC V30',                   { Code 3 }
                              'INTEL 80188',               { Code 4 }
                              'INTEL 80186',               { Code 5 }
                              'INTEL 80286',               { Code 6 }
                              'INTEL 80386' );             { Code 7 }

{**********************************************************************}
{* GETPROC: Determines processor type in PC                           *}
{* Input   : none                                                     *}
{* Output  : Processor code (see CONST)                               *}
{* Info    : This function can be used in a program when added as     *}
{*           a UNIT                                                   *}
{**********************************************************************}

function getproc : byte;

begin            { Machine code routine for determining processor type }
```

```
 inline(
        $9C/$51/$52/$57/$56/$06/$33/$C0/$50/$9D/$9C/$58/$25/$00/
        $F0/$3D/$00/$F0/$74/$13/$B2/$06/$B8/$00/$70/$50/$9D/$9C/
        $58/$25/$00/$70/$74/$36/$FE/$C2/$EB/$32/$90/$B2/$04/$B0/
        $FF/$B1/$21/$D2/$E8/$75/$12/$B2/$02/$FB/$BE/$00/$00/$B9/
        $FF/$FF/$F3/$26/$AC/$0B/$C9/$74/$02/$B2/$00/$0E/$07/$FD/
        $B0/$FB/$B9/$03/$00/$E8/$16/$00/$FA/$F3/$AA/$FC/$90/$90/
        $90/$42/$90/$FB/$88/$56/$FF/$07/$5E/$5F/$5A/$59/$9D/$EB/
        $07/$90/$5F/$83/$C7/$09/$EB/$E4
       );
end;

{***********************************************************************}
{**                          MAIN PROGRAM                             **}
{***********************************************************************}

begin
  writeln('PROCP  -  (c) 1988 by MICHAEL TISCHER');
  writeln(#13#10, 'Your PC contains a(n) ', ProcName[getproc],
              ' processor.');
  writeln(#13#10);
end.
```

Assembler listing: PROCPA.ASM

```
;**********************************************************************;
;*                             P R O C P A                            *;
;*--------------------------------------------------------------------*;
;*     Task            : Determines the type of processor installed in *;
;*                       a PC.                                         *;
;*                       This version is converted by INLINE statements *;
;*                       and then used by a Pascal program.            *;
;*--------------------------------------------------------------------*;
;*     Author          : MICHAEL TISCHER                               *;
;*     Developed on    : 08/22/1988                                    *;
;*     Last update     : 05/24/1989                                    *;
;*--------------------------------------------------------------------*;
;*     assembly        : MASM PROCPA;                                  *;
;*                       LINK PROCPA;                                  *;
;*                       EXE2BIN PROCPA PROCPA.BIN                     *;
;*                       ... convert to INLINE statements and add to   *;
;*                           Pascal programs                           *;
;**********************************************************************;


;== Constants =========================================================

p_80386   equu   7              ;Codes for different types of
p_80286   equ   6               ;processors
p_80186   equ   5
p_80188   equ   4
p_v30     equ   3
p_v20     equ   2
p_8086    equ   1
p_8088    equ   0

;== Code ==============================================================

code      segment para 'CODE'     ;Definition of CODE segment

          org  100h

          assume cs:code, ds:code, ss:code, es:code

getproc   proc near               ;This program is the essential main
                                  ;program

          pushf                   ;Get contents of flag registers
          push cx                 ;Get contents of all altered registers
          push dx                 ;and push them onto stack
          push di
```

```
            push si
            push es

            ;-- Test for 80386/80286 ------------------------------------

            xor  ax,ax              ;Set AX to 0
            push ax                 ;and push onto stack
            popf                    ;Pop into flag register from stack
            pushf                   ;Return to stack
            pop  ax                 ;And pop back into AX
            and  ax,0f000h          ;Avoid clearing the to 4 bits
            cmp  ax,0f000h          ;Are bits 12-15 all equal to 1?
            je   not_a_386          ;YES->Not an 80386 or an 80286

            ;-- Test whether to handle it as an 80386 or 80286 -----------

            mov  dl,p_80286         ;This narrows it down to one of
            mov  ax,07000h          ;the two processors
            push ax                 ;Push value 7000H onto the stack
            popf                    ;Pop off as flag register
            pushf                   ;and push it back onto the stack
            pop  ax                 ;Pop off and return to AX register
            and  ax,07000h          ;Avoid masking bits 12-14
            je   pende              ;Are bits 12-14 all equal to 0?
                                    ;YES->Handle it as an 80286

            inc  dl                 ;NO->Handle it as an 80386
            jmp  pende              ;End of test

            ;-- Test for 80186 or 80188 ---------------------------------

not_a_386 label near

            mov  dl,p_80188         ;Load code for 80188
            mov  al,0ffh            ;Set all bits in AL register to 1
            mov  cl,021h            ;Number of shift operations after CL
            shr  al,cl              ;Shift AL CL times to the right
            jne  t88_86             ;If AL is unequal to 0 it must be
                                    ;handled as an 80188 or 80186

            ;-- Test for NEC V20 or V30 ---------------------------------

            mov  dl,p_v20           ;Load code for NEC V20
            sti                     ;Interrupts should be enabled starting
            mov  si,0               ;with the first byte in ES
            mov  cx,0ffffh          ;Read a complete segment
            rep  lods byte ptr es:[si]      ;REP w/ segment override only
                                    ;works with NEC V20 and V30 processors
            or   cx,cx              ;Has complete segment been read?
            je   t88_86             ;YES-> V20 or V30

            mov  dl,p_8088          ;NO-> Must be an 8088 or 8086

            ;-- Test for 8088 or 8086/V20 or V30 ------------------------

t88_86      label near

            push cs                 ;Push CS onto stack
            pop  es                 ;Pop off to ES
            std                     ;Using string inst. count backwards
            mov  al,0fbh            ;Instruction code for "STI"
            mov  cx,3               ;Execute string instruction 3 times
            call get_di             ;Get starting address of DI
t86_1:      cli                     ;Suppress interrupts
            rep  stosb
            cld                     ;Using string inst. count backwards
            nop                     ;Fill queue with dummy instruction
            nop
            nop
```

```
        inc  dx                  ;Increment processor code
        nop
q_end:  sti                      ;Re-enable interrupts

        ;------------------------------------------------------------

pende   label near               ;End testing

        mov  [bp-1],dl           ;Place processor code in return var.
        pop  es                  ;Pop saved registers from
        pop  si                  ;stack
        pop  di
        pop  dx
        pop  cx
        popf                     ;Pop flag register from stack and
        jmp  endit               ;Return to calling program

getproc endp                     ;End of PROG procedure

;-- GET_DI examines DI for 88/86 test ---------------------------------

get_di  proc near

        pop  di                  ;Pop return address off of stack
        add  di,9                ;Take first 9 bytes from there
        jmp  t86_1               ;Return to the testing routine

endit   label near

get_di  endp

;== End ================================================================

code    ends                     ;End of CODE segment
        end  getproc
```

C listing: PROCC.C

```
/***********************************************************************/
/*                              P R O C C                              */
/*---------------------------------------------------------------------*/
/*    Task              : Determines the processor type in a PC        */
/*---------------------------------------------------------------------*/
/*    Author            : MICHAEL TISCHER                              */
/*    Developed on      : 08/14/1988                                   */
/*    Last update       : 06/22/1989                                   */
/*---------------------------------------------------------------------*/
/*    (MICROSOFT C)                                                    */
/*    Creation          : CL /AS /c PROCC.C                            */
/*                        LINK PROCC PROCCA                            */
/*    Call              : PROCC                                        */
/*---------------------------------------------------------------------*/
/*    (BORLAND TURBO C)                                                */
/*    Creation          : Create a project file containing these lines: */
/*                        PROCC                                        */
/*                        PROCCA.OBJ                                   */
/***********************************************************************/

extern int getproc()     ;          /* Includes the assembler routine */

/***********************************************************************/
/**                          main  program                            **/
/***********************************************************************/

void main()

{
 static char * procname[] = {    /* Vector w/ pointers to proc. names */
                          "Intel 8088",                  /* Code 0 */
                          "Intel 8086",                  /* Code 1 */
                          "NEC V20",                     /* Code 2 */
```

```
                                    "NEC V30",                  /* Code 3 */
                                    "Intel 80188",              /* Code 4 */
                                    "Intel 80186",              /* Code 5 */
                                    "Intel 80286",              /* Code 6 */
                                    "Intel 80386"               /* Code 7 */
                                   };

 printf("\nPROCC (c) 1988 by Michael Tischer\n\n");
 printf("This PC contains a(n) %s processor\n",
        procname[ getproc() ] );
}
```

Assembler listing: PROCCA.ASM

```
;**********************************************************************;
;*                              P R O C C A                           *;
;*--------------------------------------------------------------------*;
;*    Task            : Make a function available to a C program which *;
;*                      examines the type of processor installed in a  *;
;*                      PC and informs the calling program of this     *;
;*                      information.                                   *;
;*--------------------------------------------------------------------*;
;*    Author          : MICHAEL TISCHER                                *;
;*    Developed on    : 08/15/1988                                     *;
;*    Last update     : 05/24/1989                                     *;
;*--------------------------------------------------------------------*;
;*    assembly        : MASM PROCCA;                                   *;
;*                      ... link to a C program                        *;
;**********************************************************************;

IGROUP group _text                  ;Include program segment
DGROUP group const,_bss,  _data     ;Include data segment
       assume CS:IGROUP, DS:DGROUP, ES:DGROUP, SS:DGROUP

CONST  segment word public 'CONST';This segment includes all read-only
CONST  ends                         ;constants

_BSS   segment word public 'BSS'  ;This segment includes al un-initial-
_BSS   ends                         ;ized static variables

_DATA  segment word public 'DATA' ;This segment includes all initialized
                                    ;gobal and static variables

_DATA  ends

;== Constants ===========================================================

p_80386    equu  7                  ;Codes for different processor tpyes
p_80286    equ   6
p_80186    equ   5
p_80188    equ   4
p_v30      equ   3
p_v20      equ   2
p_8086     equ   1
p_8088     equ   0

;== Program =============================================================

_TEXT  segment byte public 'CODE' ;Program segment

public    _getproc                  ;Function made available for other
                                    ;programs

;-- GETPROC: Determines the type of processor in the current PC --------
;-- Call from C : int getproc( void );
;-- Output      : The processor type's number (see constants above)

_getproc  proc near

          pushf                     ;Secure flag register contents
```

```
        ;-- Test for 80386/80286 -----------------------------------

        xor  ax,ax              ;Set AX to 0
        push ax                 ;and push onto stack
        popf                    ;Pop flag register off of stack
        pushf                   ;Push back onto stack
        pop  ax                 ;and pop off of AX
        and  ax,0f000h          ;Do not clear the upper 4 bits
        cmp  ax,0f000h          ;Are bits 12-15 al equal to 1?
        je   not_a_386          ;YES --> Not an 80386 or 80286

        ;-- Test for handling as an 80386 or 80286 ------------------

        mov  dl,p_80286         ;In any case, this routine checks for
        mov  ax,07000h          ;one of the two processors
        push ax                 ;Push 07000h onto stack
        popf                    ;Pop flag register off
        pushf                   ;and push back onto the stack
        pop  ax                 ;Pop into AX register
        and  ax,07000h          ;Bits 12-14 not included
        je   pende              ;Are bits 12-14 all equal to 0?
                                ;YES--> Handle it as an 80286

        inc  dl                 ;NO --> Handle it as an 80386
        jmp  pende              ;End test

        ;-- Test for 80186 or 80188 ---------------------------------

not_a_386 label near

        mov  dl,p_80188         ;Load code for 80188
        mov  al,0ffh            ;Set all bits in AL register to 1
        mov  cl,021h            ;Move number of shift operations to CL
        shr  al,cl              ;AL CL shift to the right
        jne  t88_86             ;If AL <> 0, handle is as an
                                ;80188 or 80186

        ;-- Test for NEC V20 or V30 ---------------------------------

        mov  dl,p_v20           ;Load code for NEC V20
        sti                     ;Enable interrupts
        push si                 ;Mark contents of SI register
        mov  si,0               ;Starting with first byte in ES, read
        mov  cx,0ffffh          ;a complete segment
        rep  lods byte ptr es:[si]  ;REP with a segment override
                                    ;(works ony with NEC V20, V30)
        pop  si                 ;Pop SI off of stack
        or   cx,cx              ;Has entire segment been read?
        je   t88_86             ;YES--> V20 or V30

        mov  dl,p_8088          ;NO --> Must be 8088 or 8086

        ;-- Test for 88/86 or V20/V30 -------------------------------

t88_86  label near

        push cs                 ;Push CS onto stack
        pop  es                 ;and pop ES off
        std                     ;Increment on string instructions
        mov  di,offset q_end    ;
        mov  al,0fbh            ;Instruction code for "STI"
        mov  cx,3               ;Execute string instruction 3 times
        cli                     ;Suppress interrupts
        rep  stosb
        cld                     ;Increment on string instructions
        nop                     ;Fill queue with dummy instructions
        nop
        nop

        inc  dx                 ;Increment processor code
```

```
        nop
q_end:  sti                         ;Re-enable interrupts

        ;-------------------------------------------------------------

pende   label near                  ;End testing

        popf                        ;Pop flag register off of stack
        xor  dh,dh                  ;Set high byte of proc. code to 0
        mov  ax,dx                  ;Processor code=return value of funct.
        ret                         ;Back to caller

_getproc  endp                      ;End of procedure

;== End ===============================================================

_text   ends                        ;End of program segment
        end                         ;End of assembler source
```

Chapter 16

PC Hardware Interrupts

Now that you're more familiar with the DOS and BIOS interrupts that are triggered by software, let's look at hardware interrupts. As the term suggests, these interrupts operate mainly through calls from PC hardware.

We'll begin with the interrupts which are called directly by the processor. These eight interrupts can also be triggered by software through the use of the INT instruction.

Interrupt 00H: Division by zero

The 8088 has two assembly language instructions (DIV and IDIV) which permit division of a 16-bit or 32-bit whole number by an 8-bit or a 16-bit whole number. According to the general rules of mathematics, division by zero is illegal. This means that you cannot perform the equation 485/0. The equation has no result. Because of this, the 8088 prohibits any divisions using a denominator of 0. If a division by zero occurs, the processor triggers interrupt 0. The vector assigned to it is pointed to by DOS during its initialization to its own routine. During the call of this interrupt, the DOS routine call executes. Most versions of DOS display a "Division by Zero" message. The program then continues with the instruction following the division that caused the error.

Interrupt 01H: Single step

The CPU calls this interrupt when the TRAP bit in the flag register of the CPU is set to 1. The interrupt then receives a call after every execution of a machine language instruction. This interrupt allows the user to trace the execution of every instruction in a assembly language program to determine changes in register contents or the instructions executed.

Constant re-execution of interrupt 1 during an execution of interrupt 1 could cause infinite recursion, and an eventual stack overflow. To prevent this, the processor resets the TRAP bit during entry into the interrupt routine. It stores the complete flag register and the TRAP bit on the stack.

If an IRET instruction ends this interrupt routine, it automatically sets the TRAP bit to the old value by restoring the complete flag register from the stack. After completion of the next instruction, interrupt 1 is recalled. Once the programmer has obtained all desired information about the program, the TRAP bit can be disabled. However, the program being examined doesn't know it's being run in single-step mode, and has no instruction to reset the TRAP bit in the flag register.

Resetting the TRAP bit

The key to this problem lies in interrupt 1's routine. This is where the TRAP bit must be reset. Even this is somewhat complicated, since the bit was reset during the call of this routine, then later reset as part of the flag register from the stack. The only option of resetting the TRAP bit is taking the flag register from the stack from within the interrupt routine, resetting the TRAP bit and return the complete flag register to its original position on the stack. If an IRET instruction then terminates the interrupt routine, the CPU restores the flag register from the stack. Since the TRAP bit is no longer set, no additional calls of interrupt routine result, and the program executes undisturbed.

Interrupt 1 is rarely executed in application programs. Because of this, DOS sets the vector of interrupt 1 to an IRET instruction. If a program accidentally sets the TRAP bit, nothing happens aside from slower execution, since interrupt 1 executes after every instruction. Interrupt 1 is most useful in utility programs (e.g., the DEBUG program) which permit program execution in *trace mode*, i.e., execution of every machine language instruction at slow speed.

Interrupt 02H: NMI

This *non-maskable interrupt* (NMI) is so designated because it cannot be masked (i.e., you cannot prevent this interrupt's execution). You can suppress the execution of all interrupts using the CLI instruction, except this one. NMI alerts the user of any errors in RAM. These errors can be caused by defects in one of the system's RAM chips. Since a defective RAM chip can cause serious damage and data problems in the system, this interrupt receives top priority over all others.

During the system boot, DOS points the vector to its own routine. If a RAM error does occur, this calls the proper BIOS routine which displays a message on the screen and stops the system.

Interrupt 03H: Breakpoint

This interrupt is also used in utility programs. Unlike the other interrupts, which are called by two-byte-long assembly language instructions (byte 1=CDH, byte 2=interrupt number), interrupt 3 can be called with a single-byte assembly language instruction (CCH). This interrupt is very useful for testing programs up to a certain point in the code. Interrupt 3 halts a running program, and allows the user to examine the current contents of the registers.

Applying interrupt 3

Using a specific utility program for reference (e.g., DEBUG), you place a call for interrupt 3 in the program in process where you want execution to stop. When the processor reaches this location during program execution, it calls interrupt 3. The testing program contains a routine which displays the current register contents and other data. Then this routine replaces the interrupt 3 call with the instruction which formerly occupied its location.

You could argue that instead of the call for interrupt 3, any other interrupt could be called to interrupt the program, if a suitable interrupt routine had been installed to display register contents, etc. Interrupt 3 offers some advantages over this. It can be called with a single-byte instruction.

Imagine a program in which a RET instruction occurs at some location. This instruction is one byte long and normally ends a subroutine. Another subroutine follows which starts with an assembly language instruction. The user wants to examine the register contents at the end of the first subroutine. He would place a breakpoint (the call for interrupt 3) at the same location as the RET instruction.

The single-byte instruction to call interrupt 3 has an advantage here. If this instruction was two or more bytes long, it would overwrite the RET instruction, and part or all of the first instruction in the following subroutine. If this program call occurred in the course of execution, the program code would change and a crash could happen. This doesn't happen since the instruction for calling interrupt 3 is only one byte. At worst it would overwrite only one instruction.

This interrupt has no application other than use with a testing/debugging utility. Otherwise, DOS points to a routine which contains an IRET (Interrupt RETurn) instruction, which immediately returns the system to the interrupted program.

Interrupt 04H: Overflow error

This interrupt can be called by a instruction which is based on a condition. It's the INTO (INTerrupt on Overflow) assembly language instruction which only calls interrupt 04H when a set overflow bit occurs in the flag register during execution. This can happen after math operations (e.g., multiplication using the MUL instruction), if the result of this operation cannot be represented within a set number of bits. This interrupt can also be called using the normal INT instruction, but this instruction doesn't read the status of the overflow bit. Since this interrupt is seldom used, DOS sets it to an IRET instruction.

Interrupt 05H: Hardcopy

Interrupt 05H belongs with the BIOS interrupts, even though it is technically a hardware interrupt. Pressing the <Prt Sc> key calls this interrupt through BIOS. This key has labels which differ from one manufacturer to another. The Tandy 1000 HD version is labeled <PRINT>, but most others have <PrtSc> labels. This key sends the current contents of the screen to a printer interfaced to the PC. This printout is called *hardcopy*.

DOS initializes the vector of this interrupt in the vector table. Both assembly language programs and programs written in high level languages can access this interrupt using the INT instruction.

Interrupts 06H—07H: Unused

At the time of this writing, interrupts 06H and 07H are unused. They are reserved for later use, but can be used now for other applications.

Interrupts 08H—0FH

Interrupts 08H to 0FH are generated by the 8259 interrupt controller. This chip receives all interrupt demands within the system first. It determines the *priority* in which multiple interrupt requests must be executed. The interrupt given highest priority passes through the INTR line to the CPU. Up to eight interrupt sources (devices) can be connected to the 8259, with each device assigned a different priority. With the help of the interrupt bits in the flag register, the CPU can suppress all interrupt calls from the 8259 (except NMI interrupt 2—see above).

Interrupt generation from special equipment can be prevented. For this the interrupt mask register of the 8259 must be accessed through port 21H. The eighth bit of this register is connected to the maximum of eight devices which create interrupts. Bit 0 represents device 0, bit 7 the device with the number 7. If a bit has the value 0, the CPU receives the interrupt calls generated by the device assigned to it from the 8259. If it contains the value 1, the interrupt calls are suppressed. If several interrupt calls occur at the same time, the device which is connected to bit 0 gets the highest priority and bit 7 the lowest priority. If the highest priority interrupt has been processed, theoretically the interrupt with the next priority down can be transmitted from the 8259 to the CPU.

Interrupt instruction register

The 8259 knows about the completion of an interrupt call through its interrupt instruction register at port address 20H. This register enables communication between a program and the 8259. When an interrupt initiated by a device attached to the 8259 finishes processing, it must send an OUT assembly language instruction which transmits the value 20H (an EOI = End Of Interrupt) to this port. This tells the 8259 that interrupt processing is done, and the next interrupt can be called.

The bit assignment in the interrupt mask registers (i.e., device assignments and priorities) differ between individual members of the PC family. You can usually assume that the device connected to bit 0 of the interrupt mask register triggers interrupt 08H. The device connected to bit 1 triggers interrupt 09H, etc. Interrupt 0FH (the last interrupt called by the 8259) is triggered by the device attached to bit 7 of the interrupt mask register. Generally these eight interrupts have designations of IRQ0, etc. up to IRQ7. IRQ stands for *Interrupt ReQuest.*

AT interrupt controllers

The AT has two 8259 interrupt controllers, so it can control up to 16 interrupt sources. The interrupts in the second controller have designations ranging from IRQ8 to IRQ15. If an interrupt request is made from one of the eight interrupt sources of the second interrupt controller, it simulates the request from a device connected to bit 2 of the first interrupt controllers. Because of this, all interrupt requests from the second interrupt controller have a higher priority than those from devices 4 to 7 of the first interrupt controllers. If several devices demand attention from the second interrupt controller, it services the interrupt source with the highest priority, which is the one connected to the lowest bit in the interrupt mask register.

Interrupt requests from the devices on the second interrupt controller can be suppressed by manipulating the corresponding bits in the interrupt mask register. This register is located at port address A1H, not at 21H like the first interrupt controller. The interrupt instruction register of the second interrupt controller, to which the EOI instruction must be sent after the completion of the interrupt from this controller, is at address A0H instead of 20H. In addition to the EOI instruction to the second interrupt controller, an EOI instruction must be sent to the first interrupt controller on port 20H at the end of the interrupt routine. This results from the interconnection between these two controllers, since every interrupt request to the second interrupt controller triggers an interrupt request on the first interrupt controller.

The following figures show the interrupt request devices and their priorities.

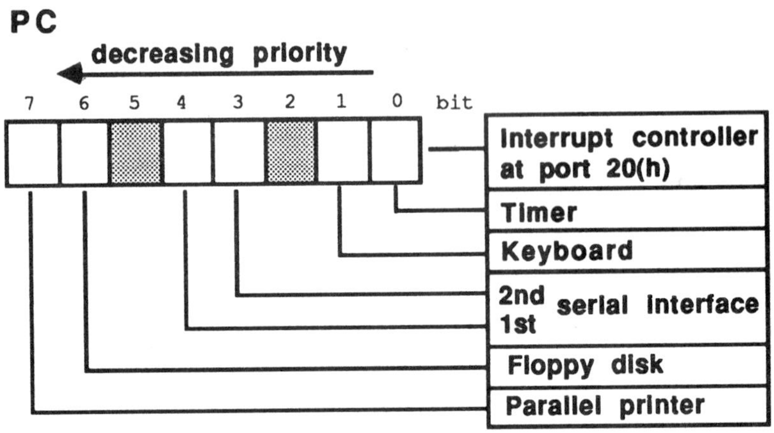

Interrupt requests and priorities (PC)

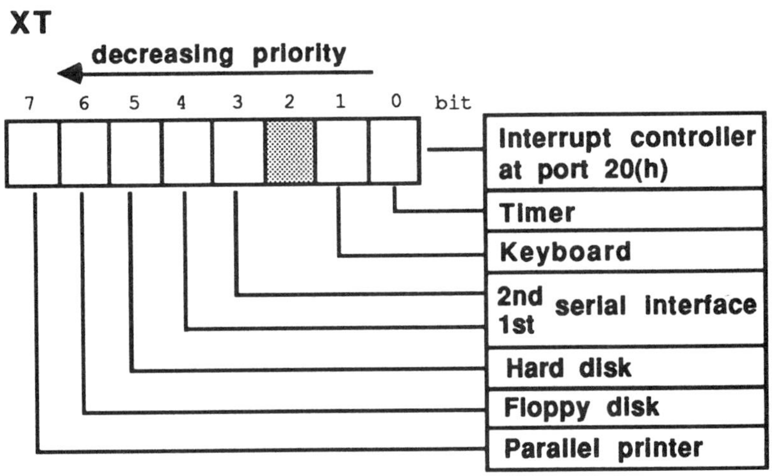

Interrupt requests and priorities (XT)

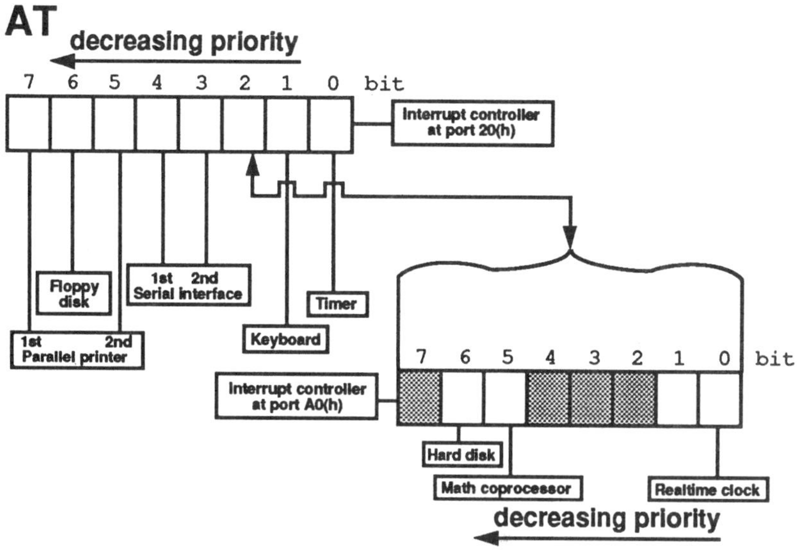

Interrupt requests and priorities (AT)

Interrupt 08H: Timer

The PC's 8253 timer chip oscillates at 1,193,180 cycles per second. It receives its signal from the 8284A clock generator chip. After 65,536 of these signals (about 18.2 cycles per second), it calls interrupt 08H, which the 8259 transmits to the CPU. Since the occurrence of these interrupt calls is independent of the clock frequency, this interrupt works well for time measurement. After 18.2 calls means that a second has elapsed. BIOS points the interrupt vector of this interrupt to its own routine, which is called 18.2 times per second. The routine increments the time counter at every call and switches off the disk motor if no access to the disk has occurred within a certain span of time. After this task has been completed, the routine calls interrupt 1CH. It can be accessed by the user for routines which depend upon a continuous signal.

Interrupt 09H: Keyboard

The keyboard has either an Intel 8048 processor (for PC/XT) or an 8042 processor (for AT). It controls the keyboard and registers if a key was pressed, released or pressed and held. The keyboard chip sends a signal to the 8259, which causes the CPU to call interrupt 09H (unless an interrupt request with a higher priority is present). The CPU calls a BIOS routine which reads the character from the keyboard and stores it in the keyboard buffer.

Interrupts 0AH—0CH: Various

These interrupts vary with the hardware connected to the computer. Check your technical manuals and hardware manuals for more information, and experiment.

Interrupt 0DH: Hard disk

The system calls interrupt 0DH if a hard disk is connected to the computer. This occurs when a read or write operation ends and BIOS must be informed of this fact.

Interrupt 0EH: Disk

The disk controller(s) calls this interrupt in conjunction with the 8259 when the controller needs the attention of the CPU. A BIOS routine following this interrupt communicates on the lowest level with the controller. During the call of this interrupt, the controller passes certain information to inform BIOS that a read or write operation was completed, or an error occurred.

Interrupt 0FH: Printer

A parallel printer calls this interrupt in conjunction with the 8259 when the controller needs the attention of the CPU.

AT interrupts

Because of the second interrupt controller in the AT, it has more hardware interrupts than the PC or XT. This second interrupt controller can call interrupts 70H to 77H. These interrupts were available to older PCs for application programs. Recently manufactured PCs and XTs cannot use these interrupts. Similar to the first interrupt controller, the device connected with bit 0 of the second interrupt controller's interrupt mask triggers interrupt 70H. The device on bit 1 calls interrupt 71H, bit 2 calls interrupt 72H, etc.

Only interrupts 70H and 75H are called by the interrupt controller because devices are only connected to bits 0 and 5 of the interrupt mask register. However, the interrupt vectors of interrupts 71H to 74H and 76H and 77H should not be redirected.

Interrupt 70H: Realtime clock

Interrupt 70H can stop a program because of alarm time, the current time and date, or just an interrupt call repeated within a certain time span. The interrupt is normally serviced by a BIOS routine which detects the reason for the interrupt then responds accordingly.

Interrupt 75H: Math coprocessor

Interrupt 75H informs the AT's CPU that a mathematical coprocessor (80287) attached to the system requires attention (e.g., because it has completed a certain calculation).

Interrupt 76H: AT hard disk

The AT hard disk controller calls this interrupt after completing a hard disk access.

Demonstration programs

The two sample programs below demonstrate some of the hardware interrupts described in this chapter. Both programs are resident interrupt drivers which are installed and deactivated using the same principles as demonstrated by programs earlier in this book.

The first program displays the current time in the upper right corner of the display screen. The second program sends the contents of a screen to a file instead of a printer.

Clock timing

Before discussing each program's structure, you should know about the basic principles of the clock. Interrupt 1CH implements the clock. Timer interrupt 8H calls interrupt 1CH 18.2 times per second.

When this routine counts the number of calls that occur, it knows that exactly one second elapses after 18.2 calls, and that it must display the time on the screen once every second. This is great, except that the clock can count one, two, even 18 calls—but not 18.2 calls.

One solution would be to have the clock update the screen display after 18 interrupt calls. This would result in the clock running fifteen minutes fast every day. You can solve this problem using a trick that we use in everyday living. Our year doesn't have exactly 365 days. Every four years the calender has a leap year, which keeps our dates on schedule with Earth's realtime clock.

The PERMCLK program does something similar with the clock. After 18 calls of the timer interrupt routine, the clock advances one second and the new time appears on the screen. Therefore, the time advances by five seconds after 5x18 (90) calls. Five seconds in reality equals 5x18.2 (91) calls. To compensate for the missing call, the program adds a sixth second after 19 calls. This makes the time measurement more accurate. Since a second actually corresponds to 18.20648193 calls, the clock will still be fast by a few seconds after a day passes. To compensate for this, an additional second is introduced after 20 calls. This makes the clock only about a second fast within a 24-hour period. That's fairly accurate, especially when you consider that the average PC doesn't remain switched on for more than eight hours at a time.

```
;**********************************************************************;
;*                            P E R M C L K                           *;
;*--------------------------------------------------------------------*;
;*    Task          : displays the current time on the                *;
;*                    display Screen                                  *;
;*--------------------------------------------------------------------*;
;*    Author        : MICHAEL TISCHER                                 *;
;*    developed on  : 8.10.87                                         *;
;*    last Update   : 9.21.87                                         *;
;*--------------------------------------------------------------------*;
;*    assembly      : MASM PERMCLK;                                   *;
;*                    LINK PERMCLK;                                   *;
;*                    EXE2BIN PERMCLK PERMCLK.COM                     *;
;*--------------------------------------------------------------------*;
;*    Call          : PERMCLK                                         *;
;**********************************************************************;

;== Constants ==========================================================

    CLKCOLUMN = 72                 ;line and column in which the time
    CLKLINE   = 0                  ;is displayed
    CLKNUM    = 6                  ;after how many 1/18 S. is the clock displayed
    CLKCOLOR  = 70h                ;color of the clock: inverted

;== here starts the actual Program ==============================

code      segment para 'CODE'      ;Definition of the CODE-segment

          org 100h

          assume cs:code, ds:code, es:code, ss:code

start:    jmp  perminit            ;Call of the initialization routine

;== Data (remain in memory ) ========================================

alterint  equ this dword           ;old interrupt vector 1CH
intaltofs dw (?)                   ;offset address interrupt vector 1CH
intaltseg dw (?)                   ;segment address interrupt vector 1CH

time      equ this byte            ;accepts the current time
tenhours  db (?)                   ;10 hours as ASCII
onehour   db (?)                   ;one hours as ASCII
          db ":"
tenmint   db (?)                   ;ten minutes as ASCII
onemin    db (?)                   ;one minutes as ASCII
          db ":"
tensecs   db (?)                   ;ten seconds as ASCII
onesec     db (?)                  ;one seconds as ASCII

tcount    db 18                    ;decremented on every timer-call
numcount  db CLKNUM                ;display counter for clock
count1    db 5                     ;correction counter 1
count2    db 31                    ;correction counter 2


;== this is the new keyboard-interrupt (remains in memory ) ==========

newint    proc far

          jmp  short newtimer

          db "JS"                  ;Identification of the program

newtimer: push ax                  ;record all registers which are changed
```

```
          push bx                   ;by the program
          push cx
          push dx
          push di
          push si
          push es
          push ds

          push cs                   ;store CS on the stack
          pop  ds                   ;return as DS


          dec  numcount             ;decrement counter for display
          jne  nonum                ;not yet zero

          mov  numcount,CLKNUM      ;set to original value

nonum:    dec tcount                ;already called 18 times ?
           je  nextsec              ;YES --> one Second passed
          cmp numcount,255          ;display clock now ?
          jne stl                   ;NO --> output
          jmp restore               ;YES --> back

nextsec:  mov tcount,18             ;set Call-counter new
          dec count1                ;correction-counter1 dec. 5 times ?
          jne settime               ;NO --> increment ASCII-time
          mov count1,5              ;YES --> set to 5 again
          inc tcount                ;increment Call-counter
          dec count2                 ;correction-counter2
                                    ;decremented 31 times?
          jne settime               ;NO --> increment ASCII-time
          mov count2,31             ;YES --> set again to 31
          inc tcount                ;increment Call-counter

settime:  inc onesec                ;increment one second (ASCII)
           cmp onesec,":"           ;one second = 10?
stl:      jne output                ;NO --> output time
           mov onesec,"0"           ;set one second to zero
          inc tensecs               ;increment ten second (ASCII)
          cmp tensecs,"6"           ;ten second = 6 (60 Seconds)?
          jne output                ;NO --> output time
          mov tensecs,"0"           ;set ten seconds to zero
          inc onemin                ;increment one minute (ASCII)
          cmp onemin,":"            ;one minute = 10?
          jne output                ;NO --> output time
          mov onemin,"0"            ;set one minute to zero
          inc tenmint               ;increment ten minute (ASCII)
          cmp tenmint,"6"           ;ten minute = 6 (60 Minutes)
          jne output                ;NO --> output time
          mov tenmint,"0"           ;set ten minute to zero
          inc onehour               ;increment one hour (ASCII)
          cmp onehour,":"           ;one hour = 10?
          jne test24                ;NO --> test 24 hour
          mov onehour,"0"           ;YES --> set one hour to zero
          inc tenhours              ;increment ten hour (ASCII)
          jmp short output

test24:   cmp onehour,"4"           ;one hour = 4?
          jne output                ;NO --> output time
           cmp tenhours,"2"         ;YES --> ten hour = 2?
          jne output                ;NO --> output time
          mov tenhours,"0"          ;a new day started
          mov onehour,"0"

output:  mov  ah,15                 ;read current display page
          int  10h                  ;call BIOS video-interrupt
          mov  ah,3                 ;read current cursor-position
          int  10h                  ;call BIOS video-interrupt
          push dx                   ;store on stack
```

```
          mov  si,offset time    ;offset address of the time-string
          mov  cx,1              ;write each character once
          mov  dx,CLKLINE shl 8 + CLKCOLUMN ;cursor-position for time
          mov  bl,CLKCOLOR       ;color of the clock
          mov  di,8              ;8 characters are output
pritime:  mov  ah,2              ;set cursor-position
          int  10h               ;call BIOS video-interrupt
          mov  dh,CLKLINE shl 8  ;repeat line
          inc  dl                ;increase column for next character
          mov  ah,9              ;output a character
          lodsb                  ;get character from the string
          int  10h               ;call BIOS video-interrupt
          dec  di                ;all characters processed ?
          jne pritime            ;NO --> output next character

          pop  dx                ;get old cursor-position
          mov  ah,2              ;and set again
          int  10h               ;call BIOS video-interrupt

restore:  pop  ds                ;restore all recorded registers
          pop  es                ;again
          pop  si
          pop  di
          pop  dx
          pop  cx
          pop  bx
          pop  ax
          jmp  cs:[alterint]     ;jump to old timer-Interrupt

newint    endp

instend   equ this byte          ;if SHOWCL is installed, memory
                                 ;can be released from here on

;== Data (can be overwritten by DOS =======================

installm  db 13,10,"PERMCLK (c) 1987 by Michael Tischer",13,10,13,10
          db "PERMCLK was installed and can be deactivated ",13,10
          db "through a new Call",13,10,"$"

deactmsg  db "PERMCLK was deactivated ",13,10,"$"

;== Program (can be overwritten by DOS) ====================

;-- Start and Initialization Routine -----------------------------

perminit  proc near

          mov  ax,351Ch          ;get content of interrupt vector 1C
          int  21h               ;call DOS-function
          cmp  word ptr es:[bx+2],"SJ" ;test if PERMCLK
          jne  install           ;not yet installed  --> install

          ;-- PERMCLK deactivated again ---------------------------

          mov  dx,es:intaltofs   ;offset address of interrupt 1CH
          mov  ax,es:intaltseg   ;segment address of interrupt 1CH
          mov  ds,ax             ;to DS
          mov  ax,251Ch          ;return content of the interrupt
          int  21h               ;vector 1CH to old routine

          mov  ah,49h            ;release the storage of old
          int  21h               ;PERMCLK again

          push cs                ;store CS on the stack
          pop  ds                ;return as DS

          mov  dx,offset deactmsg ;message: program removed
          mov  ah,9              ;output function number for string
          int  21h               ;call DOS function
```

```
          mov  ax,4C00h         ;code for program executed correctly
          int  21h              ;end program with end-code

          ;-- Install PERMCLK -----------------------------------

install:  mov  intaltseg,es     ;segment and offset address of the
          mov  intaltofs,bx     ;interrupt vector 1CH

          mov ah,02Ch           ;read function number for time
          int 021h              ;call DOS interrupt 21H
          mov al,cl             ;transmit minute to AL
          mov di,offset tenmint ;ASCII result to TENMINT
          call binascii         ;convert 2 numbers to ASCII
          mov al,ch             ;transmit hour to AL
          mov di,offset tenhours ;ASCII result to TENHOURS
          call binascii         ;convert 2 numbers to ASCII
          mov al,dh             ;transmit seconds to AL
          mov di,offset tensecs ;ASCII result to TENSECS
          call binascii         ;convert 2 numbers to ASCII

          mov  dx,offset newint ;offset address new interrupt-routine
          mov  ax,251Ch         ;point content of the interrupt
          int  21h              ;vector 1C to user routine

          mov  dx,offset installm ;message: program installed
          mov  ah,9             ;output function number for string
          int  21h              ;call DOS-function

          ;-- only the PSP, the new interrupt-routine and the --------
          ;-- Data for it, must remain resident

          mov  dx,offset instend ;calculate the number of
          mov  cl,4             ;paragraphs (each 16 Bytes) which
          shr  dx,cl            ;the program has available
          inc  dx
          mov  ax,3100h         ;end program with end-code 0 (o.k)
          int  21h              ;but remain resident

perminit  endp

;-- BINASCII : convert binary-value into 2-digit ASCII ----------------
;-- Input    : AL = the binary-value to be converted
;--            DI = the offset address for the 2 ASCII numbers
;-- Output   : none
;-- Register : AX, CL and FLAGS are changed

binascii  proc near

          xor ah,ah             ;HI-Byte for division = 0
          mov cl,10             ;decimal system is used
          div cl                ;divide value by 10
          or  ax,03030H         ;convert result into ASCII
          mov [di],ax           ;and store
          ret                   ;back to caller

binascii endp

;== End ===============================================================

code      ends                  ;end of the CODE-segment
          end  start
```

Installation and reinstallation has similarities to the resident interrupt driver already discussed. It installs itself during its first call and deactivates itself on the following call.

The code following the INSTALL label initializes all the program's variables. First the DOS function 2CH reads in the current time, converts the time into ASCII code and places the data in the variables TENHOURS, TENMINT and TENSECS. These variables, which are part of an ASCII string, act as buffers for the time display and are updated once every second. After these variables have been initialized, the program installation takes place.

Let's look at the clock itself, the new interrupt routine of interrupt 1CH. It begins in the listing at the label NEWINT. It jumps to the label NEWTIMER to bypass the identification code. All registers changed by the following commands are stored on the stack. Then the counter (the variable) NUMCOUNT is decremented. NUMCOUNT has nothing to do with time measurement; it determines how often to display the time on the screen. Normally the clock must be redisplayed when the time has changed (every second). Since the screen scrolls in some applications (e.g., DOS), the clock would quickly disappear from the display. To display a clock that looks stationary, it must be redisplayed more often than once a second.

When NUMCOUNT reaches the value 0, this means that the clock display reappears with the following commands, even if a new second hasn't occurred. After NUMCOUNT reaches zero, it resets to its original value so that it can be decremented again the next time the routine is called. The constant CLOCKNUM contains the original value (6), which displays the clock after 6/18 second (one-third of a second). You may preset other values to display the clock more or less often.

At the label NONUM the counter TCOUNT decrements. It contains the number of remaining calls until a second has elapsed. If the number is equal to zero, a second has elapsed and a jump occurs to the label NEXTSEC where it resets to 18 so that the next second can be displayed after 18 calls.

If a second hasn't elapsed, the program tests for whether the variable NUMCOUNT reached zero and resets to its starting value during this call of the timer interrupt. If this was the case, the time appears on the screen and the interrupt ends. If the time isn't displayed, the interrupt can be ended directly.

After NEXTSEC resets TCOUNT to 18, the first correction counter decrements. If it is equal to zero, it means that five seconds have elapsed and that the next second can only be initiated after 19 calls. The TCOUNT counter increases from 18 to 19 and the first correction counter resets to five. Then the second correction counter decrements. If it then contains the value zero, then 31x5 seconds have passed and the next second can only be initiated after 20 calls.

At the label SETTIME, incrementing the least significant digit of seconds (one) in the variable ONEMIN sets the new time. A test is made for the start of a new minute, a new hour or a new day; the time changes accordingly.

The label OUTPUT begins the actual time display. OUTPUT reads the current display page and cursor position. This data passes to the stack so it can be restored after the time is displayed on the screen. The cursor moves into position and the program displays the clock, character by character.

In the final step, the previously stored current cursor position is removed from the stack and set. This occurs through a function of the BIOS video interrupt.

This concludes the work of the timer routine. It restores the registers from the stack, passing them unchanged to the interrupted program. It finally ends with a jump to the old timer routine.

The HC2FILE program

The second sample program in this chapter reroutes hardcopy data to a file instead of a printer. The program requires the entry of the program name and the path and name of the hardcopy file. This name can contain a device and path designation, but must have a three digit number as an extension (e.g., 000 or 153). A sample call would look like this from the DOS prompt:

```
C>hc2file a:hc.001
```

You would then press <Shift><Prt Sc> as you would for a printed screen hardcopy. To capture hardcopies in sequence, the number in the file extension automatically increments after the creation of every hardcopy file. For example, the first hardcopy goes to a file named HC.001 and a second hardcopy would go to a file named HC.002. During output the individual characters are read from the current display page, but their colors (an attribute) are not stored. The screen lines in the file write to disk in sequence (no carriage returns separate lines). You can view this file on the screen using the DOS TYPE command.

The program expects a filename during the first call from the DOS level. If you omit the filename, the HC2FILE program will not be installed. If you call the program again after its installation without passing a filename, it deactivates the installed hardcopy program and releases the memory it occupied. If the program is called again with a filename after a successful installation, the installed hardcopy program remains active, and the new name for the hardcopy file takes effect.

Perhaps the new hardcopy interrupt routine may be of interest. You call it after installation by pressing <Shift> <Prt Sc>.

First it determines the number of the current display page and the current cursor position using a function of the BIOS video interrupt. It stores these on the stack, returning them to BIOS after the output of the hard copy. Then it opens the file which is to receive the hard copy. An error message is output if the attempt fails. In the next step the display screen content is read line for line into a buffer (starting at the beginning of the PSP) and is written from there to a file. Here also an error message is output through DOS if an error is reported and the file is erased.

If the hardcopy could be output successfully, the file is closed and the extension of the filename (the number of the hardcopy) is incremented. Once the number 1,000 is reached, the numbering restarts at 0.

Warning:

An important restriction during the use of this program must be observed. It can only be called when no access is made simultaneously by DOS to the disk or hard disk. If the new hardcopy is called during the DOS access, most systems will crash because DOS is not capable of controlling several file or disk accesses simultaneously. DOS is not re-entrant. Remember this limitation when using this routine, because it cannot be bypassed.

```
;**********************************************************************;
;*                            H C 2 F I L E                           *;
;*--------------------------------------------------------------------*;
;*    Task              : Outputs the Hardcopy of an 80-column-text   *;
;*                        screen in a file instead of the printer.    *;
;*                        The file must have a three digit number     *;
;*                        as extension which is incremented after     *;
;*                        the output of the hard copy so that several *;
;*                        hard copy files can be created in succession*;
;*--------------------------------------------------------------------*;
;*    WARNING           : after installation of this program          *;
;*                        no hard copy may be called during           *;
;*                        a disk or hard disk access.                 *;
;*                        The system will crash since DOS is not      *;
;*                        reentrant!                                  *;
;*--------------------------------------------------------------------*;
;*    Author            : MICHAEL TISCHER                             *;
;*    developed on      : 8.11.87                                     *;
;*    last Update       : 9.21.87                                     *;
;*--------------------------------------------------------------------*;
;*    assembly          : MASM HC2FILE;                               *;
;*                        LINK HC2FILE;                               *;
;*                        EXE2BIN HC2FILE HC2FILE.COM                 *;
;*--------------------------------------------------------------------*;
;*    Call              : HC2FILE [(Dr:)(Path)Filename.zzz]           *;
;**********************************************************************;

;== here starts the actual Program =============================

code      segment para 'CODE'     ;definition of the CODE-segment

          org 100h

          assume cs:code, ds:code, es:code, ss:code

start:    jmp  hcinit             ;Call of the initialization-routine

;== Data (remain in storage) ========================================

alterint  equ this dword          ;old Interrupt vector 05H
intaltofs dw (?)                  ;offset address Interrupt vector 05H
intaltseg dw (?)                  ;segment address Interrupt vector 05H

print     db 0                    ;indicates if printing is in progress
handle    dw (?)                  ;key for access to File

hcerr     db "HC2FILE: Error on output of the hard copy",13,10,"$"
```

```
;== this is the new hard copy interrupt (remains in memory ) ==========

newint    proc far

          jmp  short newhc

          db "RL"               ;Identification of the program

newhc:    sti                   ;interrupts are again permitted
          cmp cs:print,0        ;printing in progress?
          je  dohc              ;NO --> print out
          jmp newhcend          ;YES --> do not output hard copy

dohc:     mov  cs:print,1       ;print now
          push ax               ;save all registers which are changed
          push bx
          push cx
          push dx
          push di
          push si
          push es
          push ds

          mov  ax,cs            ;bring CS to AX
          mov  ds,ax            ;and then set DS and ES
          mov  es,ax
          cld                   ;on string commands count up

          mov  ah,15            ;read current display page
          int  10h              ;call BIOS video-interrupt
          mov  ah,3             ;read current cursor-position
          int  10h              ;call BIOS video-interrupt
          push dx               ;store on the stack

          mov  ah,3Ch           ;create function number for file
          xor  cx,cx            ;should become normal file
          mov  dx,130           ;filename at DS:130
          int  21h              ;call DOS-interrupt 21H
          jc   error            ;carry-flag set --> Error

          mov  handle,ax        ;save handle of the file

          mov  bl,-1            ;begin with line 0
nextline: inc  bl               ;increment line number
          cmp  bl,25            ;all lines printed ?
          je   datclose         ;YES --> close file
          call hcline           ;NO --> output a line
          jnc  nextline         ;no error --> next line

          mov  ah,3Eh           ;close function nr. for file
          mov  bx,handle        ;access-key
          int  21h              ;call DOS-interrupt 21H
          mov  ah,41h           ;erase function nr. for file
          mov  dx,130           ;filename at DS:130
          int  21h              ;call DOS-interrupt 21H

error:    mov  dx,offset hcerr  ;error message offset address
          mov  ah,9             ;output function nr. for string
          int  21h              ;call DOS-interrupt 21H
          jmp  short restore

          ;-- all lines output successfully ----------------------

datclose: mov  ah,3Eh           ;close function nr. for file
          mov  bx,handle        ;access-key
          int  21h              ;call DOS-interrupt 21H
          jc   error            ;not closed --> Error

          mov  bx,128           ;address of number of command line
```

```
          mov  bl,[bx]              ;number of characters in command line
          add  bl,128               ;calculate character end address
          xor  bh,bh                ;Hi-Byte of the address is 0
          inc  byte ptr [bx]        ;increment last number
          cmp  byte ptr [bx],":"    ;reached ten ?
          jne  restore              ;NO --> RESTORE
          mov  byte ptr [bx],"0"    ;set one number back to 0
          inc  byte ptr [bx-1]      ;increment ten number
          cmp  byte ptr [bx-1],":";has hundred been reached?
          jne  restore              ;NO --> RESTORE
          mov  byte ptr [bx-1],"0";ten numbers set back to 0
          inc  byte ptr [bx-2]      ;increment  number
          cmp  byte ptr [bx-2],":";has one thousand been reached?
          jne  restore              ;NO --> RESTORE
          mov  byte ptr [bx-2],"0";whole number is again 0

restore:  pop  dx                   ;get old cursor-position
          mov  ah,2                 ;and set again
          int  10h                  ;call BIOS video-interrupt

          mov  print,0              ;hard copy output finished
          pop  ds                   ;restore all stored registers
          pop  es
          pop  si
          pop  di
          pop  dx
          pop  cx
          pop  bx
          pop  ax
newhcend: iret                      ;back to keyboard routine

newint    endp

;-- HCLINE   : Write a display line into the file ----------------
;-- Input    : BL = the number of the line
;--            BH = the number of the display page
;-- Output   : Carry-flag = 1 : Error
;-- Register : AX, CX, DX, SI, DI and FLAGS are changed

hcline    proc near

          push bx                   ;store BX on the stack

          xor  di,di                ;copy at start of PSP
          xor  dl,dl                ;start with column 0
          mov  si,80                ;process 80 columns

getc:     mov  ah,2                 ;set function number for cursor
          mov  dh,bl                ;display line to DH
          int  10h                  ;call BIOS video-interrupt
          mov  ah,8                 ;read function number for character
          int  10h                  ;call BIOS video-interrupt
          stosb                     ;store character in the buffer
          inc  dl                   ;increment column
          dec  si                   ;all column processed?
          jne  getc                 ;NO --> get next character

          mov  ah,40h               ;function nr. for writing
          mov  bx,handle            ;access key
          mov  cx,80                ;every line has 80 bytes
          xor  dx,dx                ;offset address of the buffer is 0
          int  21h                  ;call DOS-interrupt 21H

          pop  bx                   ;restore BX
          ret                       ;back to caller

hcline    endp


instend   equ this byte             ;if HC2FILE is installed, the memory
```

```
                                  ;can be released starting here

;== Data (can be overwritten by DOS) =====================

installm  db 13,10,"HC2FILE (c) 1987 by Michael Tischer",13,10,10
          db "HC2FILE was installed and can be ",13,10
          db "deactivated with a new call (without parameter) ",13,10
          db "A new call with parameters changes the ",13,10
          db "Name of the file to which hardcopy is output.",13,10,"$"
deactmsg  db "HC2FILE was deactivated",13,10,"$"
ninstall  db "HC2FILE was not yet installed",13,10,"$"
newnam    db "HC2FILE was already installed, only filename "
          db "was changed",13,10,"$"

;== Program (can be overwritten by DOS) ==================

;-- Start and Initialization-Routine --------------------------------

hcinit    proc near

          mov  si,128             ;address of the command line in PSP
          cmp  byte ptr [si],0    ;was parameter passed
          mov  ax,3505h           ;get content of interrupt vector 5
          int  21h                ;call DOS-function (flags remain)
          jne  install            ;NO --> install program

          ;-- HC2FILE deactivate again ------------------------------

          cmp  word ptr es:[bx+2],"LR" ;test if HC2FILE
          je   away               ;YES --> remove again

          mov  dx,offset ninstall ;was not yet installed
          mov  al,1               ;end-code: error
          jmp  short hcfend1      ;terminate program

away:     mov  dx,es:intaltofs    ;offset address of interrupt 5
          mov  ax,es:intaltseg    ;segment address of interrupt 5
          mov  ds,ax              ;to DS
          mov  ax,2505h           ;set content of the interrupt
          int  21h                ;vector 5 to old routine again

          mov  ah,49h             ;release the memory of old
          int  21h                ;HC2FILE again

          push cs                 ;store CS on the stack
          pop  ds                 ;restore DS
          mov  dx,offset deactmsg ;message: program removed
hcfend:   xor  al,al              ;end-code: everything o.k.
hcfend1:  mov  ah,9               ;output function number for string
          int  21h                ;call DOS-function
          mov  ah,4Ch             ;function nr. for prg.termination
          int  21h                ;end program with end-code

          ;-- install HC2FILE  -------------------------------------

install:  cmp  word ptr es:[bx+2],"LR" ;test if HC2FILE
          jne  newinst            ;NO --> first installation

          ;-- was already installed, change only filename -------------

          mov  cl,[si]            ;number of characters in command line
          inc  cl                 ;also the number of characters
          xor  ch,ch              ;erase HI-Byte
          mov  di,128             ;also ES:DI, but in old HC2FILE
          cld                     ;on string commands count up
          rep  movsb              ;copy filename in PSP
                                  ;of the old HC2FILE
          xor  al,al              ;NUL terminates the filename
          stosb                   ;store in PSP of the old HC2FILE
          mov  dx,offset newnam   ;offset address of the message
```

```
         jmp  short hcfend       ;terminate program

newinst: mov  intaltseg,es       ;store segment and offset
         mov  intaltofs,bx       ;address of interrupt vector 05H

         mov  bl,[si]            ;number of characters in command line
         add  bl,129             ;calculate end addr. of character
         xor  bh,bh              ;Hi-Byte of the address is 0
         mov  byte ptr [bx],0    ;set NUL behind the file name

         mov  dx,offset newint   ;offset address new interrupt-routine
         mov  ax,2505h           ;deflect content of the interrupt
         int  21h                ;vector 5 to user routine

         mov  dx,offset installm ;message: program installed
         mov  ah,9               ;output function number for string
         int  21h                ;call DOS-function

         ;-- only the PSP, the new interrupt-routine and the ---------
         ;-- Data pertaining to it must remain resident.

         mov  dx,offset instend  ;calculate number of paragraphs
         mov  cl,4               ;(each 16 Bytes) available to
         shr  dx,cl              ;the Program
         inc  dx
         mov  ax,3100h           ;end program with end-code 0 (o.k)
         int  21h                ;but remain resident

hcinit   endp

;== End ==============================================================

code     ends                    ;End of the CODE-segment
         end  start
```

Chapter 17

Hard Disk Partitioning

FDISK is the hard disk partitioning program available in MS-DOS. You probably used the FDISK command if you installed your own hard drive, or if you've enhanced a PC with an operating system such as XENIX, CP/M-86 or OS/2. FDISK is the key to operating high capacity hard disks and to installing multiple operating systems on one computer.

FDISK represents only one step of a three step formatting process. This process formats and partitions a hard disk drive, preparing it for one or more operating systems.

Low level formatting

The first step, called *low level formatting*, divides the hard disk into *cylinders* (tracks) and sectors. This division writes corresponding address markers on the hard disk. Low level formatting is required, since many hard disk units come from the manufacturer unformatted, like floppy disks.

Some XT-compatible PCs had to be low level formatted using the DEBUG program. DEBUG called the low level format routine from the hard disk controller's ROM-BIOS. Most hard disk manufacturers now provide programs which make the low level formatting process much simpler.

Partitioning

The next step in formatting the hard disk is *partitioning*. As the name suggests, this process divides the hard disk into definite regions. The original purpose of partitioning was to divide hard disks into areas which could be occupied by different operating systems, without the operating systems conflicting with one another.

The drop in hardware prices in the late 1980s provided another reason for partitioning. Hard disks became available at low prices with capacities of 40 megabytes and more.

This posed a problem. Versions of DOS below Version 3.3 could only support a maximum of 32 megabytes per hard disk. In addition, earlier versions of DOS couldn't partition hard disks into several units.

DOS version 3.3

Version 3.3 of DOS still limited hard disk access to a maximum of 32 megabytes, but offered some alternatives to the user. DOS 3.3 allowed the configuration of a primary partition in the first 32 megabytes of the hard disk, as well as 23 additional extended partitions using drive specifiers of D to Z. Since every extended partition can have up to 32 megabytes, this partitioning increased the maximum hard disk capacity to 768 megabytes. FDISK names these partitions PRI DOS and EXT DOS.

DOS version 4.0

DOS version 4.0 permits mass storage device support up to 2 gigabytes, thanks to revised device drivers. However, many users still prefer partitioning their hard disk unit into logical hard disks (smaller drives), since file management is easier on the logical drives than having hundreds of files on one drive.

FDISK creates a special sector called the partition sector which it places on the first hard disk sector (head 0, cylinder 0, sector 1). BIOS loads this partition sector into memory address 0000:7C00, unless the user has placed a disk in drive A: before power-up or reset. If the computer finds the code sequence 55H, AAH in the last two bytes of this 512-byte sector, it treats this sector as executable and starts program execution with the first byte of the sector. Otherwise, BIOS displays an error message and either starts an infinite loop or starts ROM BASIC, depending on the manufacturer and version of the system.

Hard disk partition sector layout		
Addr.	Content	Type
+000H	Partition code	
+1BEH	1st entry in the partition table	16 bytes
+1CEH	2nd entry in the partition table	16 bytes
+1DEH	3rd entry in the partition table	16 bytes
+1EEH	4th entry in the partition table	16 bytes
+1FEH	Partition sector recognition code (AA55H)	2 bytes
Length: 200H (512) bytes		

The program code in the boot sector recognizes the active partition and the operating system to be started. The boot sector and the required operating system code loads and executes. Since this program code by definition must also be at memory address 0000:7C00, the partition code moves to memory address 0000:0600 and releases the memory for the boot sector.

The routine obtains the location of the boot sector to be loaded from the hard disk, and the boot sector's corresponding partition. The partition table located in the partition sector at address 1BEH contains this information.

Partition table entry layout		
Addr.	Content	Type
+00H	Partition status 00H = inactive 80H = boot partition	1 byte
+01H	Read/write head where partition starts	1 byte
+02H	Sector and cylinder where partition starts	1 word
+04H	Partition type 00H = entry not occupied 01H = DOS with 12-bit FAT (primary partition) 02H = XENIX 03H = XENIX 04H = DOS with 16-bit FAT (primary partition) 05H = extended DOS-Partition (after DOS 3.3) 06H = DOS-4.0 partition with more than 32 meg DBH = Concurrent DOS Other codes possible in conjunction with other operating systems or special driver software	1 byte
+05H	Read/write head at end of partition	1 byte
+06H	Sector and cylinder at end of partition	1 word
+08H	Distance of first sector of the partition (boot sector) from partition sector (measured in sectors)	1 dword
+0CH	Number of sectors in this partition	1 dword
Length: 10H (16) bytes		

Every partition is described within this table through a 16-byte structure. Since the table is almost at the end of the partition sector, there is only room available for four entries. This limits the number of partitions to four. To provide more partitions on a hard disk, some manufacturers offer a special configuration program which moves the table ahead within the partition sector and installs new partition code which accesses the reconfigured table. The basic format of the table remains unchanged. Remember that individual partition entries do not always start with the first table entry. The partition of a hard disk can be described through the first, second, third or even fourth table entry.

The boot partition can be recognized through the first field of the partition structure. The value 00H stands for "inactive," while the value 80H indicates the partition for booting. If the partition code detects no bootable partition, more than one partition, or even unknown code during the table check, the booting process terminates and the system goes into an endless loop. The only alternative is to reset the system.

If the partition code recognizes the partition to be booted, it can determine the position of this partition on the hard disk through the two following bits. The sector and cylinder number are coded in the form compatible with BIOS interrupt

13H (disk/hard disk). Bits 6 and 7 of the sector number represent bits 8 and 9 of the cylinder number. Interrupt 13H and its functions are the only means of accessing the hard drive. DOS functions are unavailable until after the system boots DOS.

Even though this information is enough to load the boot sector of the starting partition, the partition table contains some additional information which is important for later changes and additions. The position of the boot sector is followed by a field which describes the type of operating system hidden behind the partition.

Besides the starting sector, the ending sector of the partition is indicated in the partition sector. The position of this sector is again described through an indication of the head, cylinder and sector numbers. The last two fields of a table entry contain the number of sectors within the partition, the distance of the boot sector of the partition from the partition sector, as counted in sectors.

When the partition table is checked, it usually determines that the first partition starts with sector one, track zero of the second read/write head, instead of immediately following the partition sector. This wastes almost all of track one of the first read/write head, almost the complete first track of the first head is wasted, not counting the partition sector in the first sector of this track.

The extended DOS partitions suffer from some inconsistencies. First of all, DOS Version 3.3 allows only one extended partition on a hard disk, other than the primary partition. FDISK provides the extended partition with a partition sector containing a partition table instead of program code. This table consists of two entries:

1.) A description of the extended partition proper, along with a partition type value of either 1 (DOS partition with 12-bit FAT) or 4 (DOS partition with 16-bit FAT)

2.) A description of the next extended DOS partition, if one is present.

Any additional extended partitions are preceded by partition sectors, as described above. This creates a chained list which ends only when the partition type field within the partition sector contains the value 0.

The following programs in Pascal and C display the contents of the partition sector, and follow the partition sectors of any extended partitions.

Pascal program: FIXPARTP.PAS

```
{**********************************************************************}
{*                       F I X P A R T P . P A S                      *}
{*--------------------------------------------------------------------*}
{*    Task           : Display hard disk partitioning                 *}
{*--------------------------------------------------------------------*}
{*    Author         : MICHAEL TISCHER                                *}
{*    Developed on   : 04/26/1989                                     *}
{*    Last update    : 06/22/1989                                     *}
{*--------------------------------------------------------------------*}
{*    Call           : FIXPARTP [ Drive number ]                      *}
{*                       Default is drive 0 (drive C:)                *}
{**********************************************************************}

uses Dos;                                          { Add DOS unit }

{== Type declaration ==================================================}

type  SecPos     = record           { Describes the position of a sector }
                     Head : byte;                     { Read/write head }
                     SecCyl : word;         { Sector and cylinder number }
                   end;

      PartEntry = record                 { Entry in the partition table }
                     Status    : byte;                { Partition status }
                     StartSec  : SecPos;                  { First sector }
                     PartTyp   : byte;                  { Partition type }
                     EndSec    : SecPos;                   { Last sector }
                     SecOfs    : longint;      { Offset of the boot sector }
                     SecNum    : longint;            { Number of sectors }
                   end;

      PartSec    = record              { Describes the partition sector }
                     BootCode  : array [0..$1BD] of byte;
                     PartTable : array [1..4] of PartEntry;
                     IdCode    : word;                           { $AA55 }
                   end;

{**********************************************************************}
{*  ReadPartSec : Read a partition sector from the hard disk and      *}
{*                place in a buffer                                   *}
{**------------------------------------------------------------------**}
{*  Input   : - HrdDrive : BIOS code of the drive ($80, $81 etc.)     *}
{*            - Head     : Read/write head number                     *}
{*            - SecCyl   : Sector and cylinder number in BIOS format  *}
{*            - Buf      : Buffer into which sector should be loaded  *}
{**********************************************************************}

function ReadPartSec( HrdDrive, Head : byte;
                      SecCyl        : word;
                      var Buf       : PartSec ) : boolean;

var Regs : Registers;              { Processor regs for interrupt call }

begin
  Regs.AX := $0201;               { Function no. for "Read", 1 sector }
  Regs.DL := HrdDrive;                       { Load additional         }
  Regs.DH := Head;                           { parameters into the     }
  Regs.CX := SecCyl;                         { different registers     }
  Regs.ES := seg( Buf );
  Regs.BX := ofs( Buf );
  Intr( $13, Regs);                       { Call hard disk interrupt }
  ReadPartSec := ( Regs.Flags and 1 ) = 0;  {Carry flag indicates error}
end;

{**********************************************************************}
{*  GetSecCyl: Determines the combined sector/cylinder coding of BIOS *}
{*             sector and cylinder number                             *}
{**------------------------------------------------------------------**}
{*  Input   : SecCyl   : Value to be decoded                          *}
```

```
{*           Sector   : Reference to the sector variable              *}
{*           Cylinder : Reference to the cylinder variable            *}
{**********************************************************************}

procedure GetSecCyl( SecCyl : word; var Sector, Cylinder : integer );

begin
  Sector   := SecCyl and 63;                    { Exclude bits 6 and 7 }
  Cylinder := hi( SecCyl ) + ( lo( SecCyl) and 192 ) shl 2;
end;

{**********************************************************************}
{*  ShowPartition: Displays hard disk partitioning on the screen      *}
{**------------------------------------------------------------------**}
{*  Input  : DR : Number of the corresponding hard disk drive         *}
{*               (0, 1, 2 etc.)                                       *}
{**********************************************************************}

procedure ShowPartition( DR : byte );

var Head     : byte;                          { Head of current partition }
    SecCyl   : byte;           { Sector and cylinder of current partition }
    ParSec   : PartSec;                      { Current partition sector }
    Entry    : byte;                                     { Loop counter }
    Sector,                                          { Get sector and   }
    Cylinder : integer;                              { cylinder numbers }
    Regs     : Registers;            { Processor regs for interrupt call }

begin
  writeln;
  DR := DR + $80;                        { Prepare drive number for BIOS }
  if ReadPartSec( DR, 0, 1, ParSec ) then      { Read partition sector }
    begin                                         { Sector is readable }
      Regs.AH := 8;                                  { Read drive data }
      Regs.DL := DR;
      Intr( $13, Regs);                     { Call hard disk interrupt }
      GetSecCyl( Regs.CX, Sector, Cylinder );
      writeln('╔═══════════════════════════════════════════'+
              '══════════════════════════════╗');
                  { Upper left corner can be typed using <Alt><201> }
                  { Top horiz. line can be typed using <Alt><205>   }
                  { Upper right corner can be typed using <Alt><187>}
      writeln('║ Drive    ', DR-$80, ':    ', Regs.DH+1:2,
              ' Heads with       ', Cylinder:5, ' cylinders and ',
              Sector:3, ' sectors     ║');
                        { Vert. lines can be typed using <Alt><186> }
      writeln('║ Partition table  in  partition sector     '+
              '                          ║');
                        { Vert. lines can be typed using <Alt><186> }
      writeln('╠═╤══╤═══════════════╤═════════════╤'+
              '════════════╤══════╤══════╣');
                            { Left T can be typed using <Alt><204>   }
                            { Top T can be typed using <Alt><209>    }
                            { Right T can be typed using <Alt><185>  }
      writeln('║ │  │               │     Start     │'+
              '     End     │Dis.fr.│        ║');
          { First and last vert. lines can be typed using <Alt><186> }
              { Remaining vert. lines can be typed using <Alt><179> }
      writeln('║#.│Boot│Type              │Head Cyl. Sec.│'+
              'Head Cyl. Sec.│Bootsec│Number ║');
          { First and last vert. lines can be typed using <Alt><186> }
              { Remaining vert. lines can be typed using <Alt><179> }
      writeln('╠═╪══╪═══════════════╪═════════════╪'+
              '════════════╪══════╪══════╣');
                            { left T can be typed using <Alt><204>   }
                            { crosses can be typed using <Alt><216>  }
                            { Right T can be typed using <Alt><185>  }
```

```
 for Entry:=1 to 4 do                          { Execute table entries }
       with ParSec.PartTable[ Entry ] do
         begin
         write('| ', Entry, '|');
          { Type first line using <Alt><186>, second using <Alt><179> }
         if Status = $80 then write ('YES ')
                              else write (' NO ');
         write('|');
                              { Type thin vert. line using <Alt><179> }
         case PartTyp of                     { Display partition type }
           $00        : write('Not occupied       ');
           $01        : write('DOS, 12-bit FAT    ');
           $02        : write('XENIX              ');
           $03        : write('XENIX              ');
           $04        : write('DOS, 16-bit FAT    ');
           $05        : write('DOS, extd.partition');
           $DB        : write('Concurrent DOS     ');
           else         write('Unknown    (',PartTyp:3,')     ');
         end;
         GetSecCyl( StartSec.SecCyl, Sector, Cylinder );
         write('|', StartSec.Head:2,' ',Cylinder:5,'  ',Sector:3 );
         GetSecCyl( EndSec.SecCyl, Sector, Cylinder );
                                    {Enter vert. line using <Alt><179> }
         write(' |', EndSec.Head:2,' ',Cylinder:5,'  ',Sector:3 );
                                    {Enter vert. line using <Alt><179> }
         writeln(' |', SecOfs:7,'|', SecNum:7,'|');
               { Enter first and second vert. lines using <Alt><179>, }
               { third line using <Alt><186>                          }
end;
      writeln('╚═╧═══╧══════════════════╧═══════════╧'+
              '══════════╧═══════╧═══════╝'#13#10);
                         { Left angle can be typed using <Alt><200>   }
                         { Horiz. lines can be types using <Alt><205> }
                         { Bottom Ts can be typed using <Alt><207>    }
                         { Right angle can be typed using <Alt><188>  }
    end
  else
    writeln('Error during boot sector access!');
end;

{**********************************************************************
*                         M A I N    P R O G R A M                   *
**********************************************************************}

var HrdDrive,                                { Variables for converting }
    DError    : integer;                     { given arguments          }

begin
  writeln( #13#10'--------------------------------- FIXPARTP - (c)',
          ' 1989 by MICHAEL TISCHER ---' );
  HrdDrive := 0;                            { Default is first hard disk }
  if ParamCount = 1 then                  { Other drive specifier given? }
    begin                                                          { YES }
      val( ParamStr(1), HrdDrive, DError );                { ASCII/decimal }
      if DError <> 0 then                          { Conversion error? }
        begin                                                      { YES }
          writeln(#13#10'Illegal drive specifier!');
          exit;                                             { End program }
        end;
    end;
  ShowPartition( HrdDrive );                  { Display partition sector }
end.
```

C program: FIXPARTC.C

```
/***********************************************************************/
/*                        F I X P A R T C . C                          */
/*---------------------------------------------------------------------*/
/*    Task            : Displays hard disk partitioning                */
/*---------------------------------------------------------------------*/
/*    Author          : MICHAEL TISCHER                                */
/*    Developed on    : 04/26/1989                                     */
/*    Last update     : 06/22/1989                                     */
/*---------------------------------------------------------------------*/
/*    Call            : FIXPARTC [ Drive_number ]                      */
/*                        Default is drive 0 (Drive C:)                */
/***********************************************************************/

#include <dos.h>
#include <string.h>
#include <stdlib.h>

/*== Constants ========================================================*/

#define TRUE  ( 1 == 1 )
#define FALSE ( 1== 0 )

/*== Macros ===========================================================*/

#define HI(x) ( *((BYTE *) (&x)+1) )   /* Returns high byte of a word */
#define LO(x) ( *((BYTE *) &x) )        /* Returns low byte of a word */

/*== Type declarations ================================================*/

typedef unsigned char BYTE;
typedef unsigned int WORD;

typedef struct {                  /* Describes the position of a sector */
                BYTE Head;                          /* Read/write head */
                WORD SecCyl;                /* Sector and cylinder number */
               } SECPOS;

typedef struct {                        /* Entry in the partition table */
                BYTE          Status;               /* Partition status */
                SECPOS        StartSec;                 /* First sector */
                BYTE          PartTyp;                /* Partition type */
                SECPOS        EndSec;                    /* Last sector */
                unsigned long SecOfs;            /* Offset of boot sector */
                unsigned long SecNum;              /* Number of sectors */
               } PARTENTRY;

typedef struct {                       /* Describes the partition sector */
                BYTE      BootCode[ 0x1BE ];
                PARTENTRY PartTable[ 4 ];
                WORD      IdCode;                              /* 0xAA55 */
               } PARTSEC;

typedef PARTSEC far *PARSPTR; /* Pointer > partition sector in memory */

/***********************************************************************/
/*  ReadPartSec : Reads a partition sector from the hard disk into a   */
/*                buffer                                               */
/*  Input   : - HrdDrive : BIOS code of the drive  (0x80, 0x81 etc.)   */
/*            - Head     : Number of read/write heads                  */
/*            - SecCyl   : Sector and cylinder number in BIOS format   */
/*            - Buf      : Buffer into which sector should be loaded   */
/*  Output : TRUE if sector is read without error, otherwise FALSE     */
/***********************************************************************/

BYTE ReadPartSec( BYTE HrdDrive, BYTE Head, WORD SecCyl, PARSPTR Buf )
```

```
 union REGS   Regs;            /* Processor regs for interrupt call */
 struct SREGS SRegs;

 Regs.x.ax = 0x0201;              /* Funct.no. for "Read", 1 Sector */
 Regs.h.dl = HrdDrive;                   /* Load parameters into */
 Regs.h.dh = Head;                      /* different registers as */
 Regs.x.cx = SecCyl;                    /* needed                 */
 Regs.x.bx = FP_OFF( Buf );
 SRegs.es  = FP_SEG( Buf );

 int86x( 0x13, &Regs, &Regs, &SRegs );    /* Call hard disk interrupt */
 return !Regs.x.cflag;
}

/***********************************************************************/
/*  GetSecCyl: Determines the combined sector/cylinder coding from     */
/*             BIOS sector/cylinder number                             */
/*  Input  : SecCyl   : Value to be decoded                            */
/*           Sector   : Reference to the sector variable               */
/*           Cylinder : Reference to the cylinder variable             */
/*  Output: none                                                       */
/***********************************************************************/

void GetSecCyl( WORD SecCyl, int *Sector, int *Cylinder )

{
 *Sector   = SecCyl & 63;                  /* Exclude bits 6 and 7 */
 *Cylinder = HI(SecCyl) + ( ( (WORD) LO(SecCyl) & 192 ) << 2 );
}

/***********************************************************************/
/*  ShowPartition: Displays hard disk partitioning on the screen       */
/*  Input: LW : Number of the hard disk (0, 1, 2, etc.)                */
/*  Output: none                                                       */
/***********************************************************************/

void ShowPartition( BYTE LW )
{
 #define AP ParSec.PartTable[ Entry ]

 BYTE       Head,                    /* Head for current partition */
            Entry,                                 /* Loop counter */
            SecCyl;       /* Sector and cylinder of current partition */
 PARTSEC    ParSec;                   /* Current partition sector */
 int        Sector,                 /* Get sector and cylinder     */
            Cylinder;               /* number                      */
 union REGS Regs;              /* Processor regs for interrupt call */

 printf("\n");
 LW |= 0x80;                     /* Prepare drive number for BIOS */
 if ( ReadPartSec( LW, 0, 1, &ParSec ) )     /* Read partition sector */
  {                                         /* Sector can be read */
   Regs.h.ah = 8;                              /* Read disk data */
   Regs.h.dl = LW;
   int86( 0x13, &Regs, &Regs );          /* Call hard disk interrupt */
   GetSecCyl( Regs.x.cx, &Sector, &Cylinder );
   printf( "╔═══════════════════════════════════════════════════"
           "═══════════════════════════╗\n");
             /* Upper left corner can be typed using <Alt><201>  */
             /* Horizontal line can be typed using <Alt><205>    */
             /* Upper right corner can be typed using <Alt><187> */
   printf( "║ Drive    %2d:    %2d heads with        %4d"
           " cylinders,     %3d sectors    ║\n",
           LW-0x80, Regs.h.dh+1, Cylinder, Sector );
 /* Vertical lines at beginning and end can be typed using <Alt><186> */
   printf( "║ Partition table in partition sector         "
           "                              ║\n");
 /* Vertical lines at beginning and end can be typed using <Alt><186> */
```

```
printf( "╟═╤══╤═════════════════╤═══════════╤"
        "═══════════╤═══════╤══════╣\n");
            /* Left T can be typed using <Alt><199>           */
            /* Horiz. lines can be typed using <Alt><205>     */
            /* Ts in middle of line can be typed using <Alt><209> */
            /* Right T can be typed using <Alt><185>          */
printf( "║ │  │                │   Start   │"
        "   End     │Dis.fr.│      ║\n");
        /* First and last vertical lines in the above line        */
        /* can be typed using <Alt><186>                          */
        /* Remaining vertical lines can be typed using <Alt><179> */
printf( "║#.│Boot│Type            │Head Cyl. Sec.│"
        "Head Cyl. Sec.│BootSec│Number ║\n");
        /* First and last vertical lines in the above line        */
        /* can be typed using <Alt><186>                          */
        /* Remaining vertical lines can be typed using <Alt><179> */
        printf( "╠═╫══╫════════════════╫═══════════╫"
        "═══════════╫═══════╫══════╣\n");
               /* Left T can be typed using <Alt><204>           */
               /* Horizontal lines can be typed using <Alt><205> */
               /* Crosses can be typed using <Alt><215>          */
               /* Right T can be typed using <Alt><185>          */
/*-- Check partition table ---------------------------------------*/
for ( Entry=0; Entry < 4; ++Entry )
 {
  printf( "║ %d│", Entry );
            /* First vertical line can be typed using <Alt><186>  */
            /* Second vertical line can be typed using <Alt><179> */
  if ( AP.Status == 0x80 )                  /* Partition active? */
   printf("Yes ");
  else
   printf ("No  ");
  printf("│");
                 /* Vertical line can be typed using <Alt><179> */
  switch( AP.PartTyp )                 /* Display partition types */
   {
    case 0x00 : printf( "Not occupied        " );
                break;
    case 0x01 : printf( "DOS, 12-Bit FAT     " );
                break;
    case 0x02 : printf( "XENIX               " );
                break;
    case 0x03 : printf( "XENIX               " );
                break;
    case 0x04 : printf( "DOS, 16-Bit FAT     " );
                break;
    case 0x05 : printf( "DOS, extended part." );
                break;
    case 0xDB : printf( "Concurrent DOS      " );
                break;
    default   : printf( "Unknown    (%3d)    ",
                        ParSec.PartTable[ Entry ].PartTyp );
   }

  /*-- Display physical and logical parameters --------------------*/
  GetSecCyl( AP.StartSec.SecCyl, &Sector, &Cylinder );
  printf( "│%2d %5d  %3d ", AP.StartSec.Head, Cylinder, Sector );
/* Vertical line can be typed using <Alt><179> */
 GetSecCyl( AP.EndSec.SecCyl, &Sector, &Cylinder );
  printf( "│%2d %5d  %3d ", AP.EndSec.Head, Cylinder, Sector );
/* Vertical line can be typed using <Alt><179> */
  printf( "│%6lu │%6lu ║\n", AP.SecOfs, AP.SecNum );
 }
  /* First and second vertical lines can be typed using <Alt><179> */
  /* Third vertical line can be typed using <Alt><186>             */
printf( "╚═╧══╧════════════════╧═══════════╧"
```

```
            "═══════════╧══════╧══════╝\n" );
                    /* Left angle can be typed using <Alt><200>       */
                    /* Horizontal lines can be typed using <Alt><205> */
                    /* Ts can be typed using <Alt><207>               */
                    /* Right angle can be typed using <Alt><188>      */
  }
 else
  printf("Error during boot sector access!\n");
}

/***********************************************************************
*                         M A I N    P R O G R A M                     *
***********************************************************************/

int main( int argc, char *argv[] )
{
 int HrdDrive;

 printf( "\n------------------------------ FIXPARTC - (c)"
        " 1989 by MICHAEL TISCHER ---\n" );
 HrdDrive = 0;                          /* Default is first hard disk */
 if ( argc == 2 )                          /* Other drive specified? */
  {                                                         /* YES */
   HrdDrive = atoi ( argv[1] );
   if ( HrdDrive == 0 && *argv[1] != '0' )
    {
     printf("\nIllegal drive specifier!");
     return( 1 );                                   /* End program */
    }
  }
 ShowPartition( HrdDrive );             /* Display partition sector */
 return( 0 );
}
```

Chapter 18

The PC Ports

Chapter 2 of this book described a series of CPU support chips which help the CPU control the system. These chips stay in constant contact with the CPU, which delegates tasks to and obtains information from the support chips.

Ports

The *ports* represent the interfaces between the CPU and the other system hardware. A port can be viewed as an 8-bit-wide data input or output connected to a particular piece of hardware. A port has an assigned address with values ranging from 0 to 65,535. The CPU uses the *data bus* and *address bus* to communicate with the ports. If the CPU needs access to a port, it transmits a *port control signal*. This signal instructs the other hardware that the CPU wants to access a port instead of RAM. Ports have addresses which are also assigned to memory locations in RAM, but these addresses have nothing to do with those memory locations. The port address is placed on the lowest 16 bits of the address bus. This instructs the system to transfer the eight bits of information following on the data bus to the proper port. The hardware connected with this port receives the data and responds accordingly.

The 80(x)xx processor series has two instructions that control this process from within a program. The IN instruction inputs data from a port to the CPU; the OUT instruction outputs data from the CPU to a port.

The system can set the port address of a certain hardware device—this address is not a constant value. For this reason, there are many similarities in port addressing between the PC, XT and AT. There are few differences between the PC and XT, but many differences exist between the PC and AT.

The following table shows the port addresses of individual chips in each system.

Component	PC/XT	AT
DMA controller (8237A-5)	000-00F	000-01F
Interrupt controller (8259A)	020-021	020-03F
timer	040-043	040-05F
Programmable Peripheral Interface (PPI 8255A-5)	060-063	none
Keyboard (8042)	none	060-06F
Realtime clock (MC146818)	none	070-07F
DMA page register	080-083	080-09F
Interrupt controller 2 (8259A)	none	0A0-0BF
DMA controller 2 (8237A-5)	none	0C0-0DF
Math coprocessor	none	0F0-0F1
Math coprocessor	none	0F8-0FF
Hard disk controller	320-32F	1F0-1F8
Game port	200-20F	200-207
Expansion unit	210-217	none
Interface for second parallel printer	none	278-27F
Second serial interface	2F8-2FF	2F8-2FF
Prototype card	300-31F	300-31F
Network card	none	360-36F
Interface for first parallel printer	378-37F	378-37F
Monochrome Display Adapter and parallel printer connection	B0-3BF	3B0-3BF
Color/Graphics Adapter	3D0-3DF	3D0-3DF
Disk controller	3F0-3F7	3F0-3F7
First serial interface	3F8-3FF	3F8-3FF

Chapter 19

Interaction between Keyboard, BIOS and DOS

The preceding chapters of this book described three levels of PC system architecture:

- DOS
- BIOS
- hardware

We've examined each level separately throughout this book. This chapter investigates the interaction between the three levels. We'll use the keyboard as an example, because it best illustrates the connection between the three levels. We'll start with the lowest level (the hardware itself) and progress to the highest level (an application program which communicates with the user through the keyboard).

Hardware level

The hardware level consists of the keyboard itself, which connects to the CPU through a cable. This keyboard contains either an Intel 8048 (PC/XT) or 8042 (AT) processor. The processor's task monitors the keyboard to determine whether a key was depressed or released. If a user depresses a key for longer than half a second, the 8048 enables key repeat at a rate of 10 characters per second. While the 8048 can only repeat at this frequency, the 8042's repeat frequency can be changed to other values. This repetition continues until the user releases the key. The keyboard processor assigns each key a number, instead of a character or ASCII code. It views control keys such as <Shift> and <Ctrl> like any other key. In the 83-key standard PC keyboard, the processor assigns numbers to the keys ranging from 1 to 83 decimal.

BIOS level

When you press a key, this key code passes to the CPU as a byte. When you release the key the processor passes the code to the CPU again, along with an added 128. This is the same as setting bit 7 in the byte. The keyboard instructs the 8259 interrupt controller that the CPU should trigger interrupt 9H. If the CPU responds we reach the next level, because a BIOS routine is controlled through interrupt 9H. While this routine is being called, the keyboard processor sends the key code to port 60H of the main circuit board using the asynchronous transmission protocol. The BIOS routine checks this port and obtains the number of the depressed or released key. This routine then generates an ASCII code from this key code.

This task is more complex than first appears, since the BIOS routine must test for a control key such as <Shift> or <Alt>. Depending on the key or combination of keys, either a normal ASCII code or an extended keyboard code may be required. The extended key codes include any keys which don't necessarily input characters (e.g., cursor keys).

Once BIOS determines the correct code, this code passes to the 16-byte BIOS keyboard buffer. If it is full, the routine produces a beep which informs the user of an overflow in the keyboard buffer. The processor returns to the other tasks which were in progress before the call to interrupt 9.

The next level, BIOS interrupt 16H, reads the character in the keyboard buffer and makes it available to a program. This interrupt includes three BIOS routines for reading characters from the keyboard buffer, as well as the keyboard status (e.g., which control keys were pressed). These three routines can be called with an INT assembly language instruction from an application program.

DOS level

The keyboard's device driver routines represent the DOS level. These DOS routines read a character from the keyboard and store the character in a buffer, using the BIOS functions from interrupt 16H. In some cases, the DOS routines may clear the BIOS keyboard buffer. If the system uses the extended keyboard driver ANSI.SYS, ANSI.SYS can translate certain codes (e.g., function key 1) into other codes or strings. For example, it's possible to program the <F10> key to display the DIR command on the screen. You can theoretically call device driver functions from within an application program, but in practice DOS functions usually address these functions.

DOS is the highest level you can go. Here you'll find the keyboard access functions in DOS interrupt 21H. These functions call the driver functions, transmit the results and perform many other tasks. For example, characters and strings can be read and displayed directly on the screen until the user presses the <Return> key. These strings are called by an application program and form the end of this chain of events.

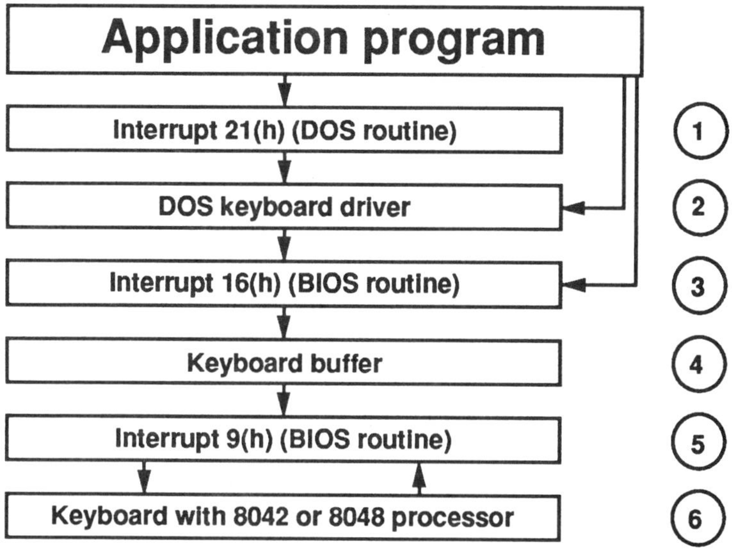

Levels of keyboard access

The keyboard access levels are as follows:

(1) Enables functions available for keyboard access

(2) Reads a character with the functions of interrupt 16H and converts it into other characters or character strings as needed

(3) Reads keyboard status or a character from the keyboard buffer and transfers it to the calling program

(4) Accepts the character entered

(5) Receives codes from the keyboard, converts them into ASCII or extended keyboard codes and adds them to the keyboard buffer

(6) Calls interrupt 9 when the key is depressed or released

When you consider the many levels through which a key code has to travel before reaching an application program, you might be thinking that direct keyboard access would be much faster. In principle that's true, but the process as described above offers several advantages. One advantage is that the system offers complex functions which reduce programming work, such as simultaneously displaying a line on the screen as you enter it from the keyboard. Also, using higher level functions make programs hardware independent, so that they'll run on PCs that may not be hardware-compatible with the IBM PC but still use DOS as the operating system.

The program which concludes this chapter demonstrates a method of changing the system levels. The challenge is to increase the size of the BIOS keyboard buffer. The keyboard buffer usually holds up to 16 characters before emitting beeps to tell the user that the buffer is full.

The assembler program which follows increases the size of the keyboard buffer to 128 characters (256 bytes). It generates extended interrupt handlers for hardware keyboard interrupt 09H and BIOS keyboard interrupt 16H.

```
;**********************************************************************;
;*                          K E Y B U F                               *;
;*--------------------------------------------------------------------*;
;*   Task            : Installs extended keyboard reading interrupt   *;
;*                     routines and implements a virtual keyboard     *:
;*                     buffer of up to 256 bytes (128 characters).    *;
;*                     An initial call installs the program, while a  *:
;*                     second call disables the program.              *;
;*--------------------------------------------------------------------*;
;*   Author          : MICHAEL TISCHER                                *;
;*   Developed on    : 08/24/1988                                     *;
;*   Last update     : 06/23/1989                                     *;
;*--------------------------------------------------------------------*;
;*   Assembly        : MASM KEYBUF;                                   *;
;*                     LINK KEYBUF;                                   *;
;*                     EXE2BIN KEYBUF KEYBUF.COM                      *;
;*--------------------------------------------------------------------*;
;*   Call            : KEYBUF                                         *;
;**********************************************************************;

;== BIOS variable segment ==========================================

bios      segment at 40h          ;Segment begins at 0040:0000

          org 1ah

          ;-- BIOS pointer points to the keyboard ring buffer ----------

b_next    dw  (?)                 ;Pointer to next character
b_last    dw  (?)                 ;Pointer to last character

bios      ends

;== Constants ======================================================

KB_LEN    equ 128                 ;Keyboard buffer length must be a
                                  ;power of 2 (change this constant to
                                  ;change the size of the keyboard buffer
                                  ;e.g., 2, 4, 8, 16, 32, etc.)

;== Start of program ===============================================

code      segment para 'CODE'     ;Definition of CODE segment

          org 100h

          assume cs:code, ds:code, es:code, ss:code

start:    jmp kb_ini              ;First executable instruction

;== Data (stays in memory) =========================================

keybuf_id dw "CS"                 ;Identifies the program

env_seg   dw (?)                  ;Segment address of environment

int9      equ this dword          ;Old interrupt vector 09H
```

```
int9_ofs  dw (?)                ;Offset address interrupt vector 09H
int9_seg  dw (?)                ;Segment address interrupt vector 09H

int16     equ this dword        ;Old interrupt vector 16H
int16_ofs dw (?)                ;Offset address interrupt vector 16H
int16_seg dw (?)                ;Segment address interrupt vector 16H

;-- Virtual keyboard buffer is placed in the PSP of this program, ------
;-- making the program resident until a second  call  disables it ------

nextkey   dw 0                  ;Offset address of next key
curkey    dw KB_LEN - 2         ;Offset address of current key

;== New interrupt hander ==============================================

new_int9  proc far              ;New INT 9H handler

          assume ds:bios        ;Assign DS the BIOS variable segment

          pushf                 ;Simulate interrupt call to old INT
          call cs:int9          ;9H handler

          ;-- Get character from BIOS keyboard buffer -----------------

          cli
          push es               ;Push all registers which will be
          push ds               ;changed by this new interrupt
          push di               ;handler onto the stack
          push bx
          push ax

          mov  ax,bios          ;Get segment address of BIOS variable
          mov  ds,ax            ;segment to DS
          mov  di,cs:nextkey    ;Move DI to next character in KEYBUF
          mov  bx,b_next        ;BIOS: Get address of next character

ni9_0:    cmp  bx,b_last        ;Still a character in BIOS kbd buffer?
          je   ni9_end          ;No more characters --> END

          ;-- Still a character in the BIOS keyboard buffer --

          mov  ax,[bx]          ;Get character from BIOS kbd. buffer
          add  bx,2             ;Set pointer to next character
          cmp  bx,3eh           ;Reached end of keyboard buffer?
          jne  ni9_1            ;NO --> NI9_1

          mov  bx,1eh           ;YES --> Set start of kbd. buffer

ni9_1:    cmp  di,cs:curkey     ;Virtual keyboard buffer full yet?
          je   ni9_0            ;YES --> Don't store any more chars
          mov  cs:[di],ax       ;Characters in virtual kbd. buffer
          add  di,2             ;Set pointer to next character
          and  di,KB_LEN-1      ;Wrap-around
          jmp  ni9_0            ;Get next character

ni9_end:  mov  cs:nextkey,di    ;Mark position for next character
          mov  b_next,bx        ;Set BIOS pointer to next character
          pop  ax               ;Pop registers off of stack
          pop  bx
          pop  di
          pop  ds
          pop  es

          iret                  ;Return to interrupt caller

          assume ds:code        ;DS indicates code segment
new_int9  endp

;-- New handler for BIOS keyboard interrupt 16H ----------------------
```

```
new_int16 proc far                ;New interrupt 16H handler

          sti                     ;Enable interrupt
          cmp  ah,1               ;Read keyboard status?
          ja   status             ;YES --> Status

          ;-- Update keyboard LEDs when function 1 of the old keyboard -
          ;-- handler is called

          push  ax                ;Push function code on the stack

          pushf                   ;Push flags onto stack
          mov  ah,1               ;Funct.no.: Key ready?
          call cs:[int16]         ;Call old handler

          pop  ax                 ;Pop function code off of stack
          push bx                 ;Push BX onto stack

ni16_0:   mov  bx,cs:curkey       ;Get pointer to current key
          add  bx,2               ;Set to next word
          and  bx,KB_LEN-1        ;Wrap-around
          or   ah,ah              ;Read character?
          je   ni16_2             ;YES --> Get character from buffer

          ;-- Function 1: Help caller determine whether a character is -
          ;-- available                                                -

          cmp  bx,cs:nextkey      ;Found a character in KEYBUF?
          je   ni16_1             ;NO --> NI16_1

          mov  ax,cs:[bx]         ;YES, Get character from KEYBUF
ni16_1:   pop  bx                 ;Pop BX off of stack
          ret  2                  ;Return to caller but DO NOT remove
                                  ;flags from stack

          ;-- Function 0: Read character from the keyboard buffer ------

ni16_2:   cmp  bx,cs:nextkey      ;Character found in KEYBUF?
          je   ni16_0             ;NO --> NI16_0

          mov  ax,cs:[bx]         ;YES -- > Get character from KEYBUF
          mov  cs:curkey,bx       ;Store position for current character
          pop  bx                 ;Pop BX off of stack
          iret                    ;Return to caller

status:   jmp  cs:[int16]         ;Jump to old handler

new_int16 endp

;-------------------------------------------------------------------

instend   equ this byte           ;Everything must remain resident up
                                  ;to this memory location

;== Data (cann be overwritten from DOS) ============================

installm  db 13,10,"--- KEYBUF (c) 1988 by Michael Tischer ---",13,10,13,10
          db "KEYBUF now enabled. Entering KEYBUF a second time",13,10
          db "from the  DOS prompt disables the KEYBUF program.",13,10,"$"

removeit  db 13,10,"--- KEYBUF (c) 1988 by Michael Tischer ---",13,10
          db "KEYBUF program now disabled.",13,10,"$"

;== Program (can be overwritten from DOS) ==========================

;-- Start and nitialization routine ---------------------------------

kb_ini    label near

          mov  ax,3509h           ;Get contents of interrupt vector 9H
```

```
          int  21h                ;Cal DOS function
          cmp  es:keybuf_id,"CS"  ;Program already installed?
          jne  install            ;NO --> Install

          ;-- If KEYBUF is already installed, remove it ---------------

          cli                     ;Disable interrupts
          lds  dx,es:int9         ;DS:DS = old handler address int9H
          mov  ax,2509h           ;Return interrupt vector for int 9H
          int  21h                ;to old interrupt handler

          lds  dx,es:int16        ;DS:DS = Old handler address int16H
          mov  ax,2516h           ;Return interrupt vector 16H to old
          int  21h                ;interrupt handler
          sti                     ;Enable interrupt

          mov  bx,es              ;Move segment address of program
          mov  es,es:env_seg      ;Get segment address of environment
          mov  ah,49h             ;from code segment and
          int  21h                ;release memory

          mov  es,bx              ;Release memory of
          mov  ah,49h             ;old KEYBUF using
          int  21h                ;DOS interrupt 49H

          push cs                 ;Push CS onto stack
          pop  ds                 ;Pop DS off of stack

          mov  dx,offset removeit ;Message: Program disabled
          mov  ah,9               ;Write function number for string
          int  21h                ;Call DOS function

          mov  ax,4C00h           ;Funct. no.: End program
          int  21h                ;Call DOS interrupt --> END

          ;-- Install KEYBUF ------------------------------------------

install   label near

          ;-- In order  to configure  new keyboard buffer  within the --
          ;-- PSP, the segment address must first be moved to the end --
          ;-- of the PSP, where it cannot be overwritten              --

          mov  ax,[2Ch]           ;Load segment address of environment
          mov  env_seg,ax         ;and place in code segment

          mov  ax,3509h           ;Get contents of interrupt vector 9H
          int  21h                ;Call DOS function
          mov  int9_seg,es        ;Mark segment and offset address of
          mov  int9_ofs,bx        ;interrupt vector 9H

          mov  ax,3516h           ;get contents of interrupt vector 16H
          int  21h                ;Call DOS function
          mov  int16_seg,es       ;Mark segment and offset address of
          mov  int16_ofs,bx       ;interrupt vector 16H

          cli                     ;Disable interrupt
          mov  ax,2509h           ;Funct. no.: Set interrupt vector 9H
          mov  dx,offset new_int9 ;Offset addr. of new int. 9H handler
          int  21h                ;Call DOS interrupt

          mov  ax,2516h           ;Funct. no.: Set interrupt vector 16H
          mov  dx,offset new_int16;Offset addr. of new int. 16H handler
          int  21h                ;Call DOS interrupt
          sti                     ;Enable interrupts

          mov  dx,offset installm ;Message: Install program
          mov  ah,9               ;Function number for string display
          int  21h                ;Call DOS function
```

```
        ;-- Just PSP, new interrupt routine and corresponding --------
        ;-- data must be resident                             --------

        mov  dx,offset instend  ;Get offset address of last byte
        add  dx,15              ;Make paragraph "full"
        mov  cl,4               ;Compute number of resident
        shr  dx,cl              ;paragraphs
        mov  ax,3100h           ;Terminate but keep resident program
        int  21h                ;with end code of (0)

;== Ende ==============================================================

code    ends                    ;End of code segment
        end  start
```

Appendices

Appendices A to F contain descriptions of each interrupt.

These descriptions include documentation of the interrupt, any sub-functions (if applicable) and a listing of input and output registers (if applicable). Each interrupt title has the following format:

Interrupt hex_numberH **Interrupt_type (i/o_register)**
Interrupt_name

Every processor register important to the called function is mentioned. Registers that aren't included in this list don't apply to the called function, and can contain any value during the call of the interrupt.

The output listing identifies the register that contains information returned by the function after the call is completed. The register assignment depends on whether or not the function call is successfully executed. If a specific value is supposed to be in the AX register after a successful execution, but the function doesn't execute properly, then the value in this register won't have any meaning. Problems in each function will be addressed as needed.

In addition to the description of the input and output registers, details about the function may also be included. For example, the function may be used in conjunction with another function. There may also be information about any changes in register contents caused by the function call. This is very important to the assembly language programmer who wants to keep data in a register after the function call. This programmer wants to avoid any changes in the contents of the registers.

Appendix A

Important Hardware Interrupts

Interrupt 00H **Hardware (CPU)**
Division by zero

The CPU calls this interrupt when it encounters a divisor of 0 during one of the two assembly language division instructions (DIV or IDIV). According to the rules of mathematics, dividing a number by 0 is illegal. During the booting process, this interrupt points to a routine that, when called, displays the "Division by Zero" error message (or a similar message) on the screen. The interrupt continues with the execution of the current program.

Interrupt 01H **Hardware (CPU)**
Single step

The CPU calls this interrupt when the TRAP bit in the flag register of the CPU has been set to 1. Then the interrupt is called after the execution of each assembly language instruction. This allows the user to follow these instructions, determine the changes in register contents and determine which instructions are executed. To prevent the call of the interrupt after the execution of every instruction in the trap routine (which would create an endless loop and a stack overflow), the processor resets the TRAP bit upon entry to the trap routine. If the trap routine ends with the IRET instruction, it automatically resets the TRAP bit to its old value by restoring the complete flag register from the stack. Because of this, the execution of the next instruction calls interrupt 1 again. Once the programmer has obtained the necessary information about a program from single step mode, the TRAP mode (or TRAP bit) can be disabled.

Interrupt 02H **Hardware (CPU)**
NMI

The hardware calls this interrupt when an error is discovered in the RAM chips. The system calls the non-maskable interrupt because this type of error impairs the capabilities of the system, and can lead to a crash. The NMI has the highest priority of all interrupts and therefore is executed faster than other interrupts. The NMI usually calls a BIOS routine which informs the user of a memory error, lists the number of defective memory chips and stops the system.

If the NMI detects an error, the math coprocessor included in some PCs can also trigger the NMI. Even though NMI usually cannot be suppressed, the PC allows an exception to this rule. Some PC/XT and AT models have a special port (port A0H on PCs and XTs, port 70H on ATs). If a 0 value is written to one of these ports, the NMI interrupt is disabled . If the ports return the value 80H, the NMI interrupt is enabled.

Interrupt 03H **Hardware (CPU)**
Breakpoint

While the other interrupts can be called with a two-byte assembly language instruction (first byte CDH, second byte the number of the interrupt), interrupt 3 is called by the single-byte instruction CCH. This interrupt can be used to test programs when you want to execute the program up to a certain instruction, then stop and display the current register contents. Utilities designed for program testing like DEBUG implement this by placing calls for interrupt 3 where the break should occur. When the program is executed and the processor reaches the instruction, it calls interrupt 3. The program testing utility contains a routine which displays the register contents and other information.

Interrupt 04H **Hardware (CPU)**
Overflow

This interrupt can be called by the INTO (INTerrupt on Overflow) conditional assembly language instruction. The call occurs when the overflow bit in the flag register is set during the execution of the INTO instruction. This can happen following math operations (e.g., multiplication with the MUL instruction) that produce a result which cannot be represented within a specified number of bits. This interrupt can also be called with the normal INT instruction, but this instruction isn't controlled by the status of the set overflow bit. Since it is seldom used, DOS points this interrupt to an IRET instruction.

Interrupt 05H **BIOS**
Hardcopy

BIOS calls this interrupt when the user presses the <Prt Sc> key. The system then makes a hardcopy by sending the current screen contents to a printer. BIOS initializes the interrupt vector from the vector table and points to the BIOS hardcopy routine in ROM-BIOS. Assembly language and programs written in higher level languages can use this interrupt with the INT instruction to get a hardcopy during program execution.

Interrupt 08H **Hardware (8259 interrupt controller)**
Timer

In the PC, the 8259 timer chip receives 1,193,180 signals per second from the heart of the system, which is an oscillating quartz crystal. After 65,536 of these signals (1 second), it triggers a call of interrupt 8, which the 8259 transmits to the CPU. Since the frequency of the call of this interrupt is independent of the system clock frequency, interrupt 8 works well for timekeeping. The PC also uses the interrupt for timekeeping. BIOS points the interrupt vector of this interrupt to its own routine, which is called 18.2 times per second. A time counter increments every second and disables the disk drive motor if disk access hasn't occurred within a certain time period.

Interrupt 09H **Hardware (8259 interrupt controller)**
Keyboard

PC keyboards contain an independent processor. This Intel processor carries either the number 8048 (PC/XT) or 8042 (AT). This processor monitors the keyboard and registers whether a key was depressed or released. When either of these actions occur, this processor must inform the CPU so that the code of the activated key can be sent to the system and processed. The keyboard instructs the interrupt controller to call interrupt 9. This interrupt calls a BIOS routine that reads the character from the keyboard and places it into the keyboard buffer.

Appendix B

BIOS Interrupts and Functions

Interrupt 10H, function 00H — BIOS
Video: Set video mode

Selects and initializes a video mode and clears the screen. This function is a fast method of clearing the screen while maintaining the current video mode.

Input: AH = 00H
AL = Video mode

0:	40x25 text mode, monochrome	(color card)
1:	40x25 text mode, color	(color card)
2:	80x25 text mode, monochrome	(mono card)
3:	80x25 text mode, color	(color card)
4:	320x200 4-color graphics	(color card)
5:	320x200 4-color graphics (colors displayed in monochrome)	(color card)
6:	640x200 2-color graphics	(color card)
7:	Internal mode	(mono card)

Output: No output

Remarks: The colors for modes 4, 5 and 6 can be set with function 11.

The contents of the BX, CX, DX registers and the SS, CS and DS segment registers are not affected by this function. The contents of all other registers may change, especially the SI and DI registers.

Interrupt 10H, function 01H — BIOS
Video: Define cursor type

Defines the starting and ending lines of the cursor. This cursor exists independently of the current display page.

Input: AH = 01H
CH = Starting line of the cursor
CL = Ending line of the cursor

Output: No output

Remarks: The values allowed for the cursor's starting and ending line depend on the installed video card. The following values are permitted:

Monochrome display cards:	0–13
Color display cards:	0–7

BIOS defaults to the following values:

Monochrome display cards:	11–12
Color display cards:	6–7

You can use this function to set the cursor only within the permitted ranges. Setting cursor lines outside these parameters may result in an invisible cursor or system problems.

The contents of the BX, CX, DX registers and the segment registers SS, CS and DS are not affected by this function. The contents of all the other registers may change, especially the SI and DI registers.

Interrupt 10H, function 02H — BIOS
Video: Position cursor

Repositions the cursor, which determines the screen position for character output by using one of the BIOS functions.

Input:
AH = 02H
BH = Display page number
DH = Screen line
DL = Screen column

Output: No output

Remarks: The blinking cursor moves through this function when the addressed display page is the current display page.

Values for the screen line parameter range from 0 to 24.

Values for the screen column parameter range from 0 to 79 (for an 80-column display) or from 0 to 39 (for a 40-column display), depending on the selected video mode.

You can make the cursor disappear by moving it to a nonexistent screen position (e.g., column 0, line 25).

The number of the display page parameter depends on how many display pages are available to the video card.

The contents of the BX, CX, DX registers and the SS, CS and DS segment registers are not affected by this function. The contents of all other registers may change, especially the SI and DI registers.

Interrupt 10H, function 03H — BIOS
Video: Read cursor position

Senses the text cursor's position, starting line and ending line in a display page.

Input:
AH = 03H
BH = Display page number

Output:
DH = Screen line in which the cursor is located
DL = Screen column in which the cursor is located
CH = Starting line of the blinking cursor
CL = Ending line of the blinking cursor

Remarks:
The number of the display page parameter depends on how many display pages are available to the video card.

Line and column coordinates are related to the text coordinate system.

The contents of the BX register and the SS, CS and DS segment registers are not affected by this function. The contents of all the other registers may change, especially the SI and DI registers.

Interrupt 10H, function 04H — BIOS
Video: Read lightpen position

Senses the position of the lightpen on the screen if applicable.

Input:
AH = 04H

Output:
AH = Lightpen position reading status
- 0: Lightpen position unreadable
- 1: Lightpen position readable

DH = Screen line of the lightpen (text mode)
DL = Screen column of the lightpen (text mode)
CH = Screen line of the lightpen (graphic mode)
BX = Screen column of the lightpen (graphic mode)

Remarks:
This function call must be repeated until 1 is returned in the AH register, because only then can coordinates be read from the other registers.

Coordinates indicated represent the current video mode's resolution.

Usually the coordinates of the light pen cannot be accurately sensed in the graphic mode. The Y-coordinate (line) is always a multiple of 2, so it isn't possible to determine whether the lightpen is in line 8 or 9. The X-coordinate (column) is always a multiple of 4 in 320x200 graphic mode and a multiple of 8 in the 640x200 bitmap mode.

The contents of the CL register and the SS, CS and DS segment registers are not affected by this function. The contents of all the other registers may change, especially the SI and DI registers.

Interrupt 10H, function 05H **BIOS**
Video: Select current display page

Selects the current display page (text mode only) which should be displayed.

Input: AH = 05H
AL = Display page number

Output: No output

Remarks: The number of the display page depends on the number of display pages available to the video card.

On switching to a new display page, the screen cursor points to the position of the text cursor in this page.

Switching between various display pages does not affect their contents (the individual characters).

You can write characters to an inactive display page.

The contents of the BX, CX, DX registers and the SS, CS and DS segment registers are not affected by this function. The contents of the other registers, such as the SI and DI registers, may change.

Interrupt 10H, function 06H **BIOS**
Video: Initialize window/scroll text upward

Clears window or scrolls a portion of the current display page up by one or more lines, depending on the input.

Input: AH = 06H
AL = Number of window lines to be scrolled upward (0=clear window)
CH = Screen line of the upper left corner of the window
CL = Screen column of the upper left corner of the window
DH = Screen line of the lower right corner of the window
DL = Screen column of the lower right corner of the window
BH = Color (attribute) for blank line(s)

Output: No output

Remarks: Initializing a window (placing a 0 in the AL register) fills the window with blank spaces (ASCII code 32).

The contents of the lines scrolled out of the window are lost and cannot be restored.

Function 0 of this interrupt is better for clearing the entire screen.

The contents of the BX, CX, DX registers and the SS, CS and DS segment registers are not affected by this function. The contents of all other registers may change, especially the SI and DI registers.

Interrupt 10H, function 07H — BIOS
Video: Initialize window/scroll text downward

Clears window or scrolls a portion of the current display page up by one or more lines, depending on the input.

Input:
AH = 07H
AL = Number of window lines to be scrolled downward (0=clear window)
CH = Screen line of the upper left corner of the window
CL = Screen column of the upper left corner of the window
DH = Screen line of the lower right corner of the window
DL = Screen column of the lower right corner of the window
BH = Color (attribute) for blank line(s)

Output:
No output

Remarks:
This function only affects the current display page.

Initializing a window (placing a 0 in the AL register) fills the window with blank spaces (ASCII code 32).

The contents of the lines scrolled out of the window are lost and cannot be restored.

Function 0 of this interrupt is better for clearing the entire screen.

The contents of the BX, CX, DX registers and the SS, CS and DS segment registers are not affected by this function. The contents of all other registers may change, especially the SI and DI registers.

Interrupt 10H, function 08H — BIOS
Video: Read character/attribute

Reads the ASCII code of the character at the current cursor position and its color (attribute).

Input:
AH = 08H
BH = Display page number

Output:
AL = ASCII code of the character
AH = Color (attribute)

Remarks: The number of the display page depends on the number of display pages made available to the video card.

This function can also be called in graphic mode. The function compares the bit pattern of the character on the screen with the bit pattern of the character in character ROM of the video card and with the character patterns stored in a RAM table whose addresses appear in interrupt 1FH. If the character cannot be identified, the AL register contains the value 0 after the function call.

The contents of the BX, CX, DX registers and the SS, CS and DS segment registers are not affected by this function. The contents of the other registers may change, especially the SI and DI registers.

Interrupt 10H, function 09H **BIOS**
Video: Write character/attribute

Writes a character with a certain color (attribute) to the current cursor position in a predefined display page.

Input:
AH = 09H
BH = Display page number
CX = Number of times to write the character
AL = ASCII code of the character
BL = Attribute

Output: No output

Remarks: If the character should be displayed several times (the value of the CX register is greater than 1), all characters must fit into the current screen line in the graphic mode.

The control codes (e.g., bell, carriage return) appear as normal ASCII codes.

This function can display characters in graphic mode. The patterns of the characters, with the codes from 0 to 127, are determined by a table in ROM. The patterns of the characters with the codes from 128 to 255 are determined by a RAM table that was previously installed by DOS the GRAFTABL command.

In text mode, the contents of the BL register define the attribute byte of the character. In graphic mode this register determines the color of the character. The 640x200 bitmap mode only allows the values 0 and 1 for selecting colors from the color palette. The 320x200 bitmap mode only allows the values 0 to 3 for selecting colors from the color palette.

If the graphic mode is active during character output and bit 7 of the BL register is set, an exclusive OR is performed on the character pattern and the graphic pixels behind the character pattern.

After character output, the cursor remains in the same position as the character.

The contents of the BX, CX, DX registers and the SS, CS and DS segment registers are not affected by this function. The contents of all other registers may change, especially the SI and DI registers.

Interrupt 10H, function 0AH BIOS
Video: Write character

Writes a character to the current cursor position in a predefined display page by using the color of the character previously at this position.

Input:
AH = 0AH
BH = Display page number
CX = Number of times to write the character
AL = ASCII code of the character

Output: No output

Remarks:
If the character should be displayed several times (the value of the CX register is greater than 1), all characters must fit into the current screen line in the graphic mode.

The control codes (e.g., bell, carriage return) appear as normal ASCII codes.

This function can display characters in graphic mode. The patterns of the characters with the codes from 0 to 127 are determined by a table in ROM and the patterns of the characters with the codes from 128 to 255 are determined by a RAM table previously installed by the GRAFTABL command.

In text mode, the contents of the BL register define the attribute byte of the character. In graphic mode this register determines the color of the character. The 640x200 bitmap mode only allows the values 0 and 1 for selecting colors from the color palette. The 320x200 bitmap mode only allows the values 0 to 3 for selecting colors from the color palette.

If the graphic mode is active during character output and bit 7 of the BL register is set, an exclusive OR is performed on the character pattern and the graphic pixels behind the character pattern.

The cursor remains in the same position after character output.

The contents of the BX, CX, DX registers and the SS, CS and DS segment registers are not affected by this function. The contents of all other registers may change, especially the SI and DI registers.

Interrupt 10H, function 0BH, sub-function 0 BIOS
Video: Select palette

Selects the border and background color for graphic or text mode.

Input:
AH = 0BH
BH = 0
BL = Border/background color

Output:
No output

Remarks:
In graphic mode, the color value passed defines the color of both the border and background. In text mode, the background color of each character is defined individually, so the passed color value only defines the color of the screen border.

Values for the color passed can range from 0 to 15.

The contents of the BX, CX, DX registers and the SS, CS and DS segment registers are not affected by this function. The contents of all other registers may change, especially the SI and DI registers.

Interrupt 10H, function 0BH, sub-function 1 BIOS
Video: Select color palette

Selects one of the two color palettes for the 320x200 bitmapped graphic mode.

Input:
AH = 0BH
BH = 1
BL = Color palette number

Output:
No output

Remarks:
Two color palettes are available. They have the numbers 0 and 1 and contain the following colors:

Palette 0: Green, red, yellow
Palette 1: Cyan, magenta, white

The contents of the BX, CX, DX registers and the SS, CS and DS segment registers are not affected by this function. The contents of all other registers may change, especially the SI and DI registers.

Interrupt 10H, function 0CH — BIOS
Video: Write graphic pixel

Draws a color pixel at the specified coordinates in graphic mode.

Input:
AH = 0CH
AL = Pixel color value (see below)
BH = Graphics page
CX = Screen column
DX = Screen line

Output:
No output

Remarks:
The pixel value color parameter depends on the current graphic mode. 640x200 bitmapped mode only permits the values 0 and 1. In the 320x200 bitmapped mode, the values 0 to 3 are permitted, which generates a certain color according to the chosen color palette. 0 represents the selected background color; 1 represents the first color of the selected color palette; 2 represents the second color of the color palette, etc.

The contents of the BX, CX, DX registers and the SS, CS and DS segment registers are not affected by this function. The contents of all other registers may change, especially the SI and DI registers.

Interrupt 10H, function 0DH — BIOS
Video: Read graphic pixel

Reads the color value of a pixel at the specified coordinates in the current graphic mode.

Input:
AH = 0DH
DX = Screen line
CX = Screen column

Output:
AL = Pixel color value

Remarks:
The pixel color value parameter depends on the current graphic mode. 640x200 bitmapped mode permits the values 0 and 1 only. In the 320x200 bitmapped mode, the values 0 to 3 are permitted, which generates a certain color according to the color palette chosen. 0 represents the selected background color; 1 represents the first color of the selected color palette; 2 represents the second color of the color palette, etc.

The contents of the BX, CX, DX registers and the SS, CS and DS segment registers are not affected by this function. The contents of all other registers may change, especially the SI and DI registers.

Interrupt 10H, function 0EH — BIOS
Video: Write character

Writes a character at the current cursor position in the current display page. The new character uses the color of the character that was previously in this position on the screen.

Input:
AH = 0EH
AL = ASCII code of the character
BL = Foreground color of the character (graphic mode only)

Output:
No output

Remarks:
This function executes control codes (e.g., bell, carriage return) instead of reading them as ASCII codes. For example, the function sounds a beep instead of printing the bell character.

After this function displays a character, the cursor position increments so that the next character appears at the next position on the screen. If the function reaches the last display position, the display scrolls up one line and output continues in the first column of the last screen line.

The foreground color parameter depends on the current graphic mode. 640x200 bitmapped mode only permits the values 0 and 1. In the 320x200 bitmapped mode, the values 0 to 3 are permitted, which generates a certain color according to the chosen color palette. 0 represents the selected background color; 1 represents the first color of the selected color palette; 2 represents the second color of the color palette, etc.

The contents of the BX, CX, DX registers and the SS, CS and DS segment registers are not affected by this function. The contents of all other registers may change, especially the SI and DI registers.

Interrupt 10H, function 0FH **BIOS**
Video: Read display mode

Reads the number of the current video mode, the number of characters per line and the number of the current display page.

Input: AH = 0FH

Output: AL = Video mode

0:	40x25 text mode, monochrome	(color card)
1:	40x25 text mode, color	(color card)
2:	80x25 text mode, monochrome	(mono card)
3:	80x25 text mode, color	(color card)
4:	320x200 4-color graphics	(color card)
5:	320x200 4-color graphics (colors represented in monochrome)	(color card)
6:	640x200 2-color graphics	(color card)
7:	Internal mode	(mono card)

AH = Number of characters per line
BH = Current display page number

Remarks: The contents of the BX, CX, DX registers and the SS, CS and DS segment registers are not affected by this function. The contents of all other registers may change, especially the SI and DI registers.

Interrupt 10H, function 13H **BIOS (AT only)**
Video: Write character string

Displays a character string on the screen, starting at a specified screen position on a specified display page. The characters are taken from a buffer whose address passes to the function.

Input: AH = 13H
AL = Output mode (0–3)
0: Attribute in BL, retain cursor position
1: Attribute in BL, update cursor position
2: Attribute in the buffer, retain cursor position
3: Attribute in the buffer, update cursor position
BH = Display page number
BL = Attribute byte of the character (modes 0 and 1 only)
BP = Offset address of the buffer
CX = Number of characters to be displayed
DH = display line
DL = display column
ES = segment address of the buffer

Output: No output

Remarks: Modes 1 and 3 set the cursor position following the last character of the character string. On the next call of a BIOS function for character output, the next string of characters appears following the original character string. This does not occur in the modes 0 and 2.

In modes 0 and 1, the buffer contains only the ASCII codes of the characters to be displayed. The BL register contains the color of the character string. However, in modes 2 and 3 each character has its own attribute byte when the character is stored in the buffer. The BL register doesn't have to be loaded in this mode. Even though the character string is twice as long in these modes as the number of the characters to be displayed, the CX register requires only the number of ASCII characters in the string and not the total length of the character string.

Control codes (e.g., bell) are interpreted as control codes only, and not as characters.

When the string reaches the last position on the screen, the display scrolls upward by one line and output continues in the first column of the last screen line.

The contents of the BX, CX, DX registers and the SS, CS and DS segment registers are not affected by this function. The contents of all other registers may change, especially the SI and DI registers.

Interrupt 11H **BIOS**
Determine configuration

Reads the configuration of the system as recorded during the booting process.

Input: No input

Output: AX = Configuration

PC and XT:

Bit 0: 1 if the system has one or more disk drives
Bit 1: Unused
Bits 2-3: RAM available on main circuit board
- 00: 16K
- 01: 32K
- 10: 48K
- 11: 64K

Bits 4-5: Video mode after system boot
- 00: Unused
- 01: 40x25, color card
- 02: 80x25, color card
- 03: 80x25, mono card

Bits 6-7: Number of disk drives in the system if bit 0 is equal to 1
- 00: 1 disk drive
- 01: 2 disk drives
- 10: 3 disk drives
- 11: 4 disk drives

	Bit 8:	0 when a DMA chip is present
	Bits 9-11:	Number of RS-232 cards connected
	Bit 12:	1 when system has a joystick attached
	Bit 13:	Unused
	Bits 14-15:	Indicates the number of printers available
AT:	Bit 0:	1 if the system has one or more disk drives
	Bit 1:	1 when a math coprocessor exists in the system
	Bit 2-3:	Unused
	Bit 4-5:	Video mode during system boot
	00:	Unused
	01:	40x25, color card
	02:	80x25, color card
	03:	80x25, mono card
	Bits 6-7:	Number of disk drives in the system if bit 0 is equal to 1
	00:	1 disk drive
	01:	2 disk drives
	10:	3 disk drives
	11:	4 disk drives
	Bit 8:	Unused
	Bits 9-11:	Number of RS-232 cards connected
	Bit 12-13:	Unused
	Bits 14-15:	Indicates the number of printers available

Remarks: The type of PC must be known (PC, XT or AT) in order to properly interpret the meanings of the individual bits of the configuration word.

The memory size indicated in bits 2 and 3 of the PC/XT configuration word refers only to the main circuit board. Interrupt 12H lets you determine the total amount of available memory.

The video mode recorded in bits 4 and 5 is the mode that was activated when the system was switched on. To determine the current video mode use function 15 of interrupt 10H.

The contents of the AX register are affected by this function.

Interrupt 12H — BIOS
Determine memory size

Input: No input

Output: AX = Memory size in kilobytes

Remarks: The PC and the XT can accept a maximum of 640K of RAM. The AT accepts up to 14 megabytes of RAM memory beyond the 1 megabyte limit. The memory size returned by this function ignores this extended memory. To determine the memory size beyond the 1 megabyte limit, use function 88H of interrupt 15H (available only on the AT).

The contents of the AX register are affected by this function.

Interrupt 13H, function 00H — BIOS
Disk: Reset

Resets the disk controller and any connected disk drives. A reset should be executed after each disk operation during which an error occurred.

Input: AH = 00H
DL = 0 or 1

Output: Carry flag=0: Operation completed (AH=0)
Carry flag=1: Error (AH=error code)

Remarks: The value in the DL register is unnecessary since all the disk drives execute a reset. XT and AT models use this register to determine whether a reset should be performed on the disk drives or the hard disk.

The following error codes can occur:

01H:	Function number not permitted
02H:	Address not found
03H:	Write attempt on write protected disk
04H:	Sector not found
08H:	DMA overflow
09H:	Data transmission beyond segment border
10H:	Read error
20H:	Error in disk controller
40H:	Track not found
80H:	Time out error, unit not responding

The contents of the BX, CX, DX, SI, DI, PB registers and the segment registers are not affected by this function. The contents of all other registers may change.

Interrupt 13H, function 01H — BIOS
Disk: Read status

Reads the status of the disk drive since the last disk operation.

Input: AH = 01H
DL = 0 or 1

Output: Carry flag=0: Operation completed (AH=0)
Carry flag=1: Error (AH=error code)

Remarks: The value in the DL register is unnecessary, since disk drives constantly return their status. XT and AT models use this register to determine whether the status of the hard disk should be checked.

The following error codes can occur:

01H:	Function number not permitted
02H:	Address not found
03H:	Write attempt on write protected disk
04H:	Sector not found
08H:	DMA overflow
09H:	Data transmission beyond segment border
10H:	Read error
20H:	Error in disk controller
40H:	Track not found
80H:	Time out error, unit not responding

The contents of the BX, CX, DX, SI, DI, PB registers and the segment registers are not affected by this function. The contents of all other registers may change.

Interrupt 13H, function 02H **BIOS**
Disk: Read disk

Reads one or more disk sectors into a buffer.

Input:
AH = 02H
AL = Number of sectors to be read
BX = Offset address of buffer
CH = Track number
CL = Sector number
DH = Disk side number (0 or 1)
DL = Disk drive number
ES = Buffer segment address

Output:
Carry flag=0: Operation completed (AH=0)
Carry flag=1: Error (AH=error code)

Remark:
The number of sectors to be read into the AL register is limited to sectors which logically follow each other on a track on one side of the disk.

The following error codes can occur:

01H:	Function number not permitted
02H:	Address not found
03H:	Write attempt on a write protected disk
04H:	Sector not found
08H:	DMA overflow
09H:	Data transmission over segment border
10H:	Read error
20H:	Error in disk controller
40H:	Track not found
80H:	Time out error, drive not responding

The contents of the BX, CX, DX, SI, DI, BP registers and the segment registers are not affected by this function. The contents of all the other registers may change.

Interrupt 13H, function 03H **BIOS**
Disk: Write to disk

Writes one or more sectors to a disk. The data to be transmitted are taken from a buffer.

Input:
AH = 03H
AL = Number of sectors to be written
BX = Offset address of buffer
CH = Track number
CL = Sector number
DH = Disk side number (0 or 1)
DL = Disk drive number
ES = Buffer segment address

Output:
Carry flag=0: Operation completed (AH=0)
Carry flag=1: Error (AH=error code)

Remark:
The number of sectors that can be written in the AL register is limited to sectors which logically follow each other on a track on one side of the disk.

The following error codes can occur:

01H:	Function number not permitted
02H:	Address not found
03H:	Write attempt on a write protected disk
04H:	Sector not found

08H:	DMA overflow
09H:	Data transmission over segment border
10H:	Read error
20H:	Error in disk controller
40H:	Track not found
80H:	Time out error, drive not responding

The contents of the BX, CX, DX, SI, DI, BP registers and the segment registers are not affected by this function. The contents of all other registers may change.

Interrupt 13H, function 04H **BIOS**
Disk: Verify disk sectors

Compares one or more sectors on disk with the data stored in a buffer. This can be used to verify that the data was properly saved to disk.

Input:
AH = 04H
AL = Number of sectors to be verified
BX = Offset address of buffer
CH = Track number
CL = Sector number
DH = Disk side number (0 or 1)
DL = Disk drive number
ES = Buffer segment address

Output:
Carry flag=0: Operation completed (AH=0)
Carry flag=1: Error (AH=error code)

Remarks:
The number of sectors to be verified in the AL register is limited to sectors which logically follow each other on a track on one side of the disk.

The following error codes can occur:

01H:	Function number not permitted
02H:	Address not found
03H:	Write attempt on a write protected disk
04H:	Sector not found
08H:	DMA overflow
09H:	Data transmission over segment border
10H:	Read error
20H:	Error in disk controller
40H:	Track not found
80H:	Time out error, drive not responding

The contents of the BX, CX, DX, SI, DI, BP registers and the segment registers are not affected by this function. The contents of all other registers may change.

Interrupt 13H, function 05H **BIOS**
Disk: Format track

Formats a complete track on one side of a disk. A buffer which contains information about the sectors to be formatted must be passed to the function.

Input:
AH = 05H
AL = Number of sectors to be formatted
BX = Offset address of buffer
CH = Track number
DH = Disk side number (0 or 1)
DL = Disk drive number
ES = Buffer segment address

Output:
Carry flag=0: Operation completed (AH=0)
Carry flag=1: Error (AH=error code)

Remark:
The number of sectors to be formatted is limited to sectors which logically follow each other on a track on one side of the disk.

The buffer passed in ES:BX contains an entry consisting of four consecutive bytes for every sector to be formatted.

1: Track number
2: Page number
3: Logical sector number
4: Number of bytes in this sector:
  0: 128 bytes
  1: 256 bytes
  2: 512 bytes (PC standard)
  3: 1,024 bytes

The logical sector number increments continuously, but may not be the same as the physical sector number.

The following error codes can occur:

01H: Function number not permitted
02H: Address not found
03H: Write attempt on a write protected disk
04H: Sector not found
08H: DMA overflow
09H: Data transmission over segment border
10H: Read error
20H: Error in disk controller
40H: Track not found
80H: Time out error, drive not responding

The contents of the BX, CX, DX, SI, DI, BP registers and the segment registers are not affected by this function. The contents of all the other registers may change.

Interrupt 13H, function 15H — BIOS (AT only)
Disk: Determine drive type

Senses disk change and drive type. The AT supports both the standard 320/360K drives and the 1.2 megabyte drives.

Input: AH = 15H
DL = Disk drive number (0 or 1)

Output: Carry flag=0: Operation completed (AH=unit type)
AH=0: Device not present
AH=1: Unit does not recognize disk change
AH=2: Unit recognizes disk change
AH=3: Hard disk (see remarks below)
Carry flag=1: Error

Remark: The AT has a controller which selectively controls 2 disk drives and a hard disk, or one disk drive and 2 hard disks. In the latter case, the first hard disk has the number 1 and can be accessed with this function.

The contents of the BX, CX, DX, SI, DI, BP registers and the segment registers are not affected by this function. The contents of all other registers may change.

Interrupt 13H, function 16H — BIOS (AT only)
Disk: Media change

Senses a disk change. The AT supports both the standard 320/360K drives and the 1.2 megabyte drives. This function reads any disk change that may have occurred since the last disk access.

Input: AH = 16H
DL = Disk drive number (0 or 1)

Output: AH=0: No disk change
AH=6: Disk changed since last disk access

Remarks: The contents of the BX, CX, DX, SI, DI, BP registers and the segment registers are not affected by this function. The contents of all other registers may change.

Interrupt 13H, function 17H **BIOS (AT only)**
Disk: Determine disk format

Determines the format of a disk. The AT's 1.2 megabyte disk drive can read both 320/360K disks and 1.2 megabyte disks. While the BIOS can determine disk format during a read or write access, it first must be informed of the format. Function 23 must be called on the AT before you can call function 5 (format).

Input: AH = 17H
AL = Format
AL=1: 320/360K format on 320/360K drive
AL=2: 320/360K format on 1.2 megabyte drive
AL=3: 1.2 megabyte format on 1.2 megabyte drive

Output: Carry flag=0: Operation completed
Carry flag=1: Error

Remark: The following error codes can occur:

01H:	Function number not permitted
02H:	Address not found
03H:	Write attempt on a write protected disk
04H:	Sector not found
08H:	DMA overflow
09H:	Data transmission over segment border
10H:	Read error
20H:	Error in disk controller
40H:	Track not found
80H:	Time out error, drive not responding

The contents of the BX, CX, DX, SI, DI, BP registers and the segment registers are not affected by this function. The contents of all other registers may change.

Interrupt 13H, function 00H **BIOS (XT and AT only)**
Hard disk: Reset

Resets the hard disk controller and any interfaced hard disk drives. A reset should be executed after every hard disk operation during which an error was reported.

Input: AH = 00H
DL = 80H or 81H

Output: Carry flag=0: Operation completed (AH=0)
Carry flag=1: Error (AH=error code)

Remarks: The first hard disk drive is assigned the number 80H, the second is assigned the number 81H.

The value in the DL register is unnecessary since all the hard disk drives execute a reset. XT and AT models use this register to determine whether a reset should be performed on the disk drives or on the hard disk.

The following error codes can occur:

01H:	Addressed function or unit not available
02H:	Address not found
04H:	Sector not found
05H:	Error on controller reset
07H:	Error during controller initialization
09H:	DMA transmission error: Segment border exceeded
0AH:	Defective sector
10H:	Read error
11H:	Read error corrected by ECC
20H:	Controller defect
40H:	Search operation failed
80H:	Time out, unit not responding
AAH:	Unit not ready
CCH:	Write error

The contents of the BX, CX, DX, SI, DI, BP registers and the segment registers are not affected by this function. The contents of all other registers may change.

Interrupt 13H, function 01H **BIOS (XT and AT only)**
Hard disk: Read disk status

Reads the status of the hard disk since the last hard disk operation.

Input: AH = 01H
DL = 80H or 81H

Output: Carry flag=0: Operation completed (AH=0)
Carry flag=1: Error (AH=error code)

Remarks: The first hard disk drive is assigned the number 80H, the second is assigned the number 81H.

The value in the DL register is unnecessary since the status is consistently returned for each disk drive. XT and AT models use this register to determine whether the status of the disk drives or hard disk should be checked.

The following error codes can occur:

01H:	Addressed function or unit not available
02H:	Address not found
04H:	Sector not found
05H:	Error on controller reset
07H:	Error during controller initialization
09H:	DMA transmission error: Segment border exceeded
0AH:	Defective sector
10H:	Read error
11H:	Read error corrected by ECC
20H:	Controller defect
40H:	Search operation failed
80H:	Time out, unit not responding
AAH:	Unit not ready
CCH:	Write error

The contents of the BX, CX, DX, SI, DI, BP registers and the segment registers are not affected by this function. The contents of the other registers may change.

Interrupt 13H, function 02H **BIOS (XT and AT only)**
Hard disk: Read disk

Reads one or more hard disk sectors into a buffer.

Input:
AH = 02H
AL = Number of sectors to be read (1-128)
BX = Offset address of buffer
CH = Cylinder number
CL = Sector number
DH = Read/write head number
DL = Hard disk number (80H or 81H)
ES = Buffer segment address

Output:
Carry flag=0: Operation completed (AH=0)
Carry flag=1: Error (AH=error code)

Remarks: The first hard disk drive is assigned the number 80H, the second is assigned the number 81H.

Since the eight bits of the CH register can address only 256 cylinders at a time, bits 6 and 7 of the CL register (sector number) form bits 8 and 9 of the cylinder number, which enables the addressing of up to 1,023 cylinders at a time.

If several sectors are being read and the system reaches the last sector of a cylinder, reading continues at the first sector of the next cylinder of the next read/write head. If the system reaches the last read/write head, reading continues on the first sector of the following cylinder on the first read/write head.

The following error codes can occur:

01H:	Addressed function or unit not available
02H:	Address not found
04H:	Sector not found
05H:	Error on controller reset
07H:	Error during controller initialization
09H:	DMA transmission error: Segment border exceeded
0AH:	Defective sector
10H:	Read error
11H:	Read error corrected by ECC
20H:	Controller defect
40H:	Search operation failed
80H:	Time out, unit not responding
AAH:	Unit not ready
CCH:	Write error

The contents of the BX, CX, DX, SI, DI, BP registers and the segment registers are not affected by this function. The contents of all other registers may change.

Interrupt 13H, function 03H **BIOS (XT and AT only)**
Hard disk: Write to disk

Writes one or more sectors to the hard disk. The data to be transmitted are taken from a buffer in the calling program.

Input:

AH = 03H
AL = Number of sectors to be written (1-128)
BX = Offset address of buffer
CH = Cylinder number
CL = Sector number
DH = Read/write head number
DL = Hard disk number (80H or 81H)
ES = Buffer segment address

Output: Carry flag=0: Operation completed (AH=0)
Carry flag=1: Error (AH=error code)

Remarks: The first hard disk drive is assigned the number 80H, the second is assigned the number 81H.

Since the eight bits of the CH register can address only 256 cylinders at a time, bits 6 and 7 of the CL register (sector number) form bits 8 and 9 of the cylinder number, enabling the addressing of up to 1,023 cylinders at a time.

If several sectors are being written and the system reaches the last sector of a cylinder, writing continues at the first sector of the next cylinder of the next read/write head. If the system reaches the last read/write head, writing continues on the first sector of the following cylinder on the first read/write head.

The following error codes can occur:

01H:	Addressed function or unit not available
02H:	Address not found
04H:	Sector not found
05H:	Error on controller reset
07H:	Error during controller initialization
09H:	DMA transmission error: Segment border exceeded
0AH:	Defective sector
10H:	Read error
11H:	Read error corrected by ECC
20H:	Controller defect
40H:	Search operation failed
80H:	Time out, unit not responding
AAH:	Unit not ready
CCH:	Write error

The contents of the BX, CX, DX, SI, DI, BP registers and the segment registers are not affected by this function. The contents of all other registers may change.

Interrupt 13H, function 04H **BIOS (XT and AT only)**
Hard disk: Verify disk sector

Verifies one or more sectors of a hard disk. Unlike the corresponding floppy disk function, the data on the hard disk are not compared with the data in memory. During data storage, four check bytes are stored for every sector; these check bytes verify the contents of a sector.

Input:
AH = 04H
AL = Number of sectors to be verified (1-128)
BX = Offset address of buffer
CH = Cylinder number
CL = Sector number
DH = Read/write head number
DL = Hard disk number (80H or 81H)
ES = Buffer segment address

Output:
Carry flag=0: Operation completed (AH=0)
Carry flag=1: Error (AH=error code)

Remarks:
The first hard disk drive is assigned the number 80H, the second is assigned the number 81H.

Since the eight bits of the CH register can only address 256 cylinders at a time, bits 6 and 7 of the CL register (sector number) form bits 8 and 9 of the cylinder number, which enables the addressing of up to 1,023 cylinders at a time.

If several sectors are being verified and the system reaches the last sector of a cylinder, verification continues at the first sector of the next cylinder of the next read/write head. If the system reaches the last read/write head, verification continues on the first sector of the following cylinder on the first read/write head.

The following error codes can occur:

01H: Addressed function or unit not available
02H: Address not found
04H: Sector not found
05H: Error on controller reset
07H: Error during controller initialization
09H: DMA transmission error: Segment border exceeded
0AH: Defective sector
10H: Read error
11H: Read error corrected by ECC
20H: Controller defect
40H: Search operation failed
80H: Time out, unit not responding
AAH: Unit not ready
CCH: Write error

The contents of the BX, CX, DX, SI, DI, BP registers and the segment registers are not affected by this function. The contents of all other registers may change.

Interrupt 13H, function 05H **BIOS (XT and AT only)**
Hard disk: Format cylinder

Formats a complete cylinder (17 sectors) of a hard disk. A buffer, which contains information about the sectors to be formatted, must be passed to the function.

Input:
AH = 05H
AL = 17
BX = Offset address of buffer
CH = Cylinder number
CL = 1
DH = Read/write head number
DL = Hard disk number (80H or 81H)
ES = Buffer segment address

Output:
Carry flag=0: Operation completed (AH=0)
Carry flag=1: Error (AH=error code)

Remarks:
The first hard disk drive is assigned the number 80H, the second is assigned the number 81H.

Since the eight bits of the CH register can only address 256 cylinders at a time, bits 6 and 7 of the CL register (sector number) form bits 8 and 9 of the cylinder number, which enables the addressing of up to 1,023 cylinders at a time.

Since a complete cylinder is always formatted, the first sector to be formatted in the CL register is always sector 1. For the same reason the number of sectors to be formatted in the AL register is always 17, since the average hard disk operates with 17 sectors per cylinder.

The buffer, whose address is passed in ES:BX, must always be at least 512 bytes long. Only the first 34 bytes of this buffer are used for formatting the 17 sectors of a cylinder. Two succeeding bytes contain information about the corresponding physical sector. Before the function call, the first byte isn't significant. After the function call the first byte indicates whether or not the sector could be formatted (00H) or (80H). The second byte returns the logical sector number of the physical sector and must be placed in the buffer by calling the program before the function call.

The following error codes can occur:

01H:	Addressed function or unit not available
02H:	Address not found
04H:	Sector not found
05H:	Error on controller reset
07H:	Error during controller initialization
09H:	DMA transmission error: Segment border exceeded
0AH:	Defective sector
10H:	Read error
11H:	Read error corrected by ECC
20H:	Controller defect
40H:	Search operation failed
80H:	Time out, unit not responding
AAH:	Unit not ready
CCH:	Write error

The contents of the BX, CX, DX, SI, DI, BP registers and the segment registers are not affected by this function. The contents of all other registers may change.

Interrupt 13H, function 08H **BIOS (XT and AT only)**
Hard disk: Check format

Conveys the formatting information found on the hard disk.

Input:
AH = 08H
CH = Cylinder number
CL = Sector number
DH = Read/write head number (0=first head)
DL = Hard disk number

Output:
Carry flag=0: Operation completed (AH=0)
Carry flag=1: Error (AH=error code)

Remarks:
The first hard disk drive is assigned the number 80H, the second is assigned the number 81H.

Since the eight bits of the CH register can address only 256 cylinders at a time, bits 6 and 7 of the CL register (sector number) form bits 8 and 9 of the cylinder number, enabling the addressing of up to 1,023 cylinders at a time.

The total capacity of the hard disk unit in bytes can be calculated with the following formula:

```
Capacity = Heads * Cylinders * Sectors * 512
```

The following error codes can occur:

01H:	Addressed function or unit not available
02H:	Address not found
04H:	Sector not found
05H:	Error on controller reset
07H:	Error during controller initialization
09H:	DMA transmission error: Segment border exceeded
0AH:	Defective sector
10H:	Read error
11H:	Read error corrected by ECC
20H:	Controller defect
40H:	Search operation failed
80H:	Time out, unit not responding
AAH:	Unit not ready
CCH:	Write error

The contents of the BX, CX, DX, SI, DI, BP registers and the segment registers are not affected by this function. The contents of all other registers may change.

Interrupt 13H, function 09H **BIOS (XT and AT only)**
Hard disk: Adapt to foreign drives

Interfaces other hard disk drives for access through BIOS functions.

Input: AH = 09H
DL = Number of hard disk to be interfaced (80H or 81H)

Output: Carry flag=0: Operation completed (AH=0)
Carry flag=1: Error (AH=error code)

Remarks: The first hard disk drive is assigned the number 80H, the second is assigned the number 81H.

BIOS takes the information about the hard disk drive to be interfaced (number of units, read/write heads, etc.) from a table. The address of this table for the hard disk unit numbered 80H is stored in interrupt vector 41H, and the unit numbered 81H is stored in interrupt 46H.

The following error codes can occur:

01H:	Addressed function or unit not available
02H:	Address not found
04H:	Sector not found
05H:	Error on controller reset
07H:	Error during controller initialization
09H:	DMA transmission error: Segment border exceeded
0AH:	Defective sector
10H:	Read error
11H:	Read error corrected by ECC

20H:	Controller defect
40H:	Search operation failed
80H:	Time out, unit not responding
AAH:	Unit not ready
CCH:	Write error

The contents of the BX, CX, DX, SI, DI, BP registers and the segment registers are not affected by this function. The contents of all other registers may change.

Interrupt 13H, function 0AH **BIOS (XT and AT only)**
Hard disk: Extended read

Reads one or more sectors from the hard disk drive into a buffer. Besides the actual 512 bytes stored in the sector, the function also reads the four check bytes (ECC).

Input:
AH = 0AH
AL = Number of sectors to be read (1–127)
BX = Offset address of buffer
CH = Cylinder number
CL = Sector number
DH = Read/write head number
DL = Hard disk number (80H or 81H)
ES = Buffer segment address

Output:
Carry flag=0: Operation completed (AH=0)
Carry flag=1: Error (AH=error code)

Remarks:
The first hard disk drive is assigned the number 80H, the second is assigned the number 81H.

Normally the controller computes the four check bytes. Here the buffer reads the information direct.

Since the eight bits of the CH register can only address 256 cylinders at a time, bits 6 and 7 of the CL register (sector number) form bits 8 and 9 of the cylinder number, enabling the addressing of up to 1,023 cylinders at a time.

If several sectors are being read and the system reaches the last sector of a cylinder, reading continues at the first sector of the next cylinder of the next read/write head. If the system reaches the last read/write head, reading continues on the first sector of the following cylinder on the first read/write head.

The following error codes can occur:

01H:	Addressed function or unit not available
02H:	Address not found
04H:	Sector not found
05H:	Error on controller reset

07H:	Error during controller initialization
09H:	DMA transmission error: Segment border exceeded
0AH:	Defective sector
10H:	Read error
11H:	Read error corrected by ECC
20H:	Controller defect
40H:	Search operation failed
80H:	Time out, unit not responding
AAH:	Unit not ready
CCH:	Write error

The contents of the BX, CX, DX, SI, DI, BP registers and the segment registers are not affected by this function. The contents of all other registers may change.

Interrupt 13H, function 0BH **BIOS (XT and AT only)**
Hard disk: Extended write

Writes one or more sectors to the hard disk drive. Besides the actual 512 bytes stored in a sector, four check bytes (ECC) stored at the end of every sector are transmitted from the buffer.

Input:
AH = 0BH
AL = Number of sectors to be read (1–127)
BX = Offset address of buffer
CH = Cylinder number
CL = Sector number
DH = Read/write head number
DL = Hard disk number (80H or 81H)
ES = Buffer segment address

Output:
Carry flag=0: Operation completed (AH=0)
Carry flag=1: Error (AH=error code)

Remarks:
The first hard disk drive is assigned the number 80H, the second is assigned the number 81H.

Normally the controller calculates the four check bytes. Here the system reads them direct from the buffer.

Since the eight bits of the CH register can only address 256 cylinders at a time, bits 6 and 7 of the CL register (sector number) form bits 8 and 9 of the cylinder number, enabling the addressing of up to 1,023 cylinders at a time.

If several sectors are being written and the system reaches the last sector of a cylinder, writing continues at the first sector of the next cylinder of the next read/write head. If the system reaches the last read/write head, writing continues on the first sector of the following cylinder on the first read/write head.

The following error codes can occur:

01H: Addressed function or unit not available
02H: Address not found
04H: Sector not found
05H: Error on controller reset
07H: Error during controller initialization
09H: DMA transmission error: Segment border exceeded
0AH: Defective sector
10H: Read error
11H: Read error corrected by ECC
20H: Controller defect
40H: Search operation failed
80H: Time out, unit not responding
AAH: Unit not ready
CCH: Write error

The contents of the BX, CX, DX, SI, DI, BP registers and the segment registers are not affected by this function. The contents of all other registers may change.

Interrupt 13H, function 0DH **BIOS (XT and AT only)**
Hard disk: Reset

Resets the hard disk controller and any interfaced hard disk drives. A reset should be executed after every hard disk operation during which an error was reported.

Input: AH = 0DH
DL = Hard disk drive number (80H or 81H)

Output: Carry flag=0: Operation completed (AH=0)
Carry flag=1: Error (AH=error code)

Remarks: The value in the DL register is unnecessary since all the hard disk drives execute a reset. XT and AT models use this register to determine whether a reset should be performed on the disk drives or on the hard disk.

This function is identical to function 0 listed above.

The first hard disk drive is assigned the number 80H, the second is assigned the number 81H.

The following error codes can occur:

01H: Addressed function or unit not available
02H: Address not found
04H: Sector not found
05H: Error on controller reset
07H: Error during controller initialization
09H: DMA transmission error: Segment border exceeded
0AH: Defective sector

20H:	Controller defect
40H:	Search operation failed
80H:	Time out, unit not responding
AAH:	Unit not ready
CCH:	Write error

The contents of the BX, CX, DX, SI, DI, BP registers and the segment registers are not affected by this function. The contents of all other registers may change.

Interrupt 13H, function 10H **BIOS (XT and AT only)**
Hard disk: Drive ready?

Determines if the drive is ready (i.e., the last operation has been completed and the drive can perform the next task).

Input: AH = 10H
DL = Hard disk drive number (80H or 81H)

Output: Carry flag=0: Drive ready (AH=0)
Carry flag=1: Error (AH=error code)

Remarks: The first hard disk drive is assigned the number 80H, the second is assigned the number 81H.

The following error codes can occur:

01H:	Addressed function or unit not available
02H:	Address not found
04H:	Sector not found
05H:	Error on controller reset
07H:	Error during controller initialization
09H:	DMA transmission error: Segment border exceeded
0AH:	Defective sector
10H:	Read error
11H:	Read error corrected by ECC
20H:	Controller defect
40H:	Search operation failed
80H:	Time out, unit not responding
AAH:	Unit not ready
CCH:	Write error

The contents of the BX, CX, DX, SI, DI, BP registers and the segment registers are not affected by this function. The contents of all other registers may change.

Interrupt 13H, function 11H **BIOS (XT and AT only)**
Hard disk: Recalibrate drive

Recalibrates hard disk after an error occurs, especially after a read or write error.

Input: AH = 11H
DL = Hard disk drive number (80H or 81H)

Output: Carry flag=0: Operation completed (AH=0)
Carry flag=1: Error (AH=error code)

Remarks: The first hard disk drive is assigned the number 80H, the second is assigned the number 81H.

The following error codes can occur:

01H: Addressed function or unit not available
02H: Address not found
04H: Sector not found
05H: Error on controller reset
07H: Error during controller initialization
09H: DMA transmission error: Segment border exceeded
0AH: Defective sector
10H: Read error
11H: Read error corrected by ECC
20H: Controller defect
40H: Search operation failed
80H: Time out, unit not responding
AAH: Unit not ready
CCH: Write error

The contents of the BX, CX, DX, SI, DI, BP registers and the segment registers are not affected by this function. The contents of all other registers may change.

Interrupt 13H, function 14H **BIOS (XT and AT only)**
Hard disk: Controller diagnostic

Initializes an internal diagnostic test of the hard disk controller.

Input: AH = 14H
DL = Hard disk drive number (80H or 81H)

Output: Carry flag=0: Operation completed (AH=0)
Carry flag=1: Error (AH=error code)

Remarks: The first hard disk drive is assigned the number 80H, the second is assigned the number 81H.

The following error codes can occur:

01H:	Addressed function or unit not available
02H:	Address not found
04H:	Sector not found
05H:	Error on controller reset
07H:	Error during controller initialization
09H:	DMA transmission error: Segment border exceeded
0AH:	Defective sector
10H:	Read error
11H:	Read error corrected by ECC
20H:	Controller defect
40H:	Search operation failed
80H:	Time out, unit not responding
AAH:	Unit not ready
CCH:	Write error

The contents of the BX, CX, DX, SI, DI, BP registers and the segment registers are not affected by this function. The contents of all other registers may change.

Interrupt 13H, function 15H **BIOS (AT only)**
Hard disk: Determine drive type

Determines whether or not the computer hardware assigned numbers 80H and 81H are hard disk drives. The AT contains a controller capable of controlling both hard disks and disk drives. This controller can manage either two disk drives and one hard disk, or one disk drive and two hard disks.

Input: AH = 15H
DL = Hard disk drive number (80H or 81H)

Output: Carry flag=0: Operation completed (AH=drive type)
0: Equipment not available
1: Drive does not recognize disk change
2: Drive recognizes disk change
3: Hard disk unit
Carry flag=1: Error (AH=error code)

Remarks: The first hard disk drive is assigned the number 80H, the second is assigned the number 81H.

The contents of the BX, CX, DX, SI, DI, BP registers and the segment registers are not affected by this function. The contents of all other registers may change.

Interrupt 14H, function 00H — BIOS
Serial port: Initialize

Initializes and configures a serial port. This configuration includes parameters for word length, baud rate, parity and stop bits.

Input:

AH = 00H
DX = Number of serial port (0=first serial port, 1=second serial port)
AL = Configuration parameters

- Bits 0-1: Word length
  - 10(b) = 7 bits
  - 11(b) = 8 bits
- Bit 2: Number of stop bits
  - 00(b) = 1 stop bit
  - 01(b) = 2 stop bits
- Bits 3-4: Parity
  - 00(b) = none
  - 01(b) = odd
  - 11(b) = even
- Bits 5-7: Baud rate
  - 000(b) = 110 baud
  - 001(b) = 150 baud
  - 010(b) = 300 baud
  - 011(b) = 600 baud
  - 100(b) = 1200 baud
  - 101(b) = 2400 baud
  - 110(b) = 4800 baud
  - 111(b) = 9600 baud

Output:

AH = Serial port status
- Bit 0: Data ready
- Bit 1: Overrun error
- Bit 2: Parity error
- Bit 3: Framing error
- Bit 4: Break discovered
- Bit 5: Transmission hold register empty
- Bit 6: Transmission shift register empty
- Bit 7: Time out

AL = Modem status
- Bit 0: Modem ready to send status change
- Bit 1: Modem on status change
- Bit 2: Telephone ringing status change
- Bit 3: Connection to receiver status change
- Bit 4: Modem ready to send
- Bit 5: Modem on
- Bit 6: Telephone ringing
- Bit 7: Connection to receiver modem

Remarks: The contents of the BX, CX, DX, SI, DI, BP registers and the segment registers are not affected by this function. The contents of all the other registers may change.

Interrupt 14H, function 01H **BIOS**
Serial port: Send character

Sends a character to the serial port.

Input:
AH = 01H
DX = Number of serial port (0=first serial port, 1=second serial port)
AL = Character code to be sent

Output:
AH: Bit 7 = 0: Character transmitted
Bit 7 = 1: Error
Bit 0-6: Serial port status
- Bit 0: Data ready
- Bit 1: Overrun error
- Bit 2: Parity error
- Bit 3: Framing error
- Bit 4: Break discovered
- Bit 5: Transmission hold register empty
- Bit 6: Transmission shift register empty

Remarks: The contents of the BX, CX, DX, SI, DI, BP registers and the segment registers are not affected by this function. The contents of all other registers may change.

Interrupt 14H, function 02H **BIOS**
Serial port: Read character

Receives a character from the serial port.

Input:
AH = 02H
DX = Number of serial port (0=first serial port, 1=second serial port)

Output:
AH: Bit 7 = 0: Character received:
AL = Character received
Bit 7 = 1: Error:
Bit 0-6: Serial port status:
- Bit 0: Data ready
- Bit 1: Overrun error
- Bit 2: Parity error
- Bit 3: Framing error
- Bit 4: Break discovered
- Bit 5: Transmission hold register empty
- Bit 6: Transmission shift register empty

Remarks: This function should only be called if function 3 has determined that a character is ready for reception.

The contents of the BX, CX, DX, SI, DI, BP registers and the segment registers are not affected by this function. The contents of all other registers may change.

Interrupt 14H, function 03H — BIOS
Serial port: Read status

Reads the status of the serial port.

Input:
AH = 03H
DX = Number of the serial port (the first serial port has the number 0)

Output:
AH = Serial port status
- Bit 0: Data ready
- Bit 1: Overrun error
- Bit 2: Parity error
- Bit 3: Framing error
- Bit 4: Break discovered
- Bit 5: Transmission hold register empty
- Bit 6: Transmission shift register empty

AL = Modem status:
- Bit 0: Modem ready to send status change
- Bit 1: Modem on status change
- Bit 2: Telephone ringing status change
- Bit 3: Connection to receiver status change
- Bit 4: Modem ready to send
- Bit 5: Modem on
- Bit 6: Telephone ringing
- Bit 7: Connection to receiver modem

Remarks:
This function should always be called before calling function 2 (read character).

The contents of the BX, CX, DX, SI, DI, BP registers and the segment registers are not affected by this function. The contents of all other registers may change.

Interrupt 15H, function 83H — BIOS (AT only)
Cassette interrupt: Set flag after time interval

Sets bit 7 of a flag to 1 after a certain amount of time in microseconds elapses.

Input:
AH = 83H
ES = Segment address of the flag
BX = Offset address of the flag
CX = High word of elapsed time in microseconds
DX = Low word of elapsed time in microseconds

Output:
No output

Remarks:
A microsecond is a millionth of a second.

The contents of the BX, SI, DI, BP registers and the segment registers are not affected by this function. The contents of all other registers may change.

Interrupt 15H, function 84H, sub-function 0 BIOS (AT only)
Cassette interrupt: Read joystick switch settings

Reads the status of switches on joysticks interfaced to a PC, if game ports and joysticks are present.

Input: AH = 84H
DX = 0

Output: Carry flag=1: No game port connected
Carry flag=0: Game port present:
AL = Switch settings:
Bit 7=1: First joystick's first switch enabled
Bit 6=1: First joystick's second switch enabled
Bit 5=1: Second joystick's first switch enabled
Bit 4=1: Second joystick's second switch enabled

Remarks: Sub-function 1 reads the joystick position(s).

The contents of the BX, CX, SI, DI, BP registers and the segment registers are not affected by this function. The contents of all other registers may change.

Interrupt 15H, function 84H, sub-function 1 BIOS (AT only)
Cassette interrupt: Read joystick position

Reads the positions of joysticks interfaced to a PC if game ports and joysticks are present.

Input: AH = 84H
DX = 1

Output: Carry flag=1: No game port connected
Carry flag=0: Game port present:
AX = X-position of first joystick
BX = Y-position of first joystick
CX = X-position of second joystick
DX = Y-position of second joystick

Remarks: Sub-function 0 reads the joystick switch status.

The contents of the SI, DI, BP registers and the segment registers are not affected by this function. The contents of all other registers may change.

Interrupt 15H, function 85H **BIOS (AT only)**
Cassette interrupt: <Sys Req> key activated

Responds to pressure or release of the <Sys Req> key. The keyboard routine calls this function.

Input: AH = 85H
AL = 0: <Sys Req> key depressed
AL = 1: <Sys Req> key released

Output: No output

Remarks: This function acts as an intermediary for application programs, so that the application program will respond appropriately when the user presses the <Sys Req> key.

Interrupt 15H, function 86H **BIOS (AT only)**
Cassette interrupt: Wait

Returns control to the calling program after a certain amount of time has elapsed.

Input: AH = 86H
CX = High word of pause time in microseconds
DX = Low word of pause time in microseconds

Output: No output

Remarks: A microsecond is a millionth of a second.

The contents of the BX, SI, DI, BP registers and the segment registers are not affected by this function. The contents of all other registers may change.

Interrupt 15H, function 87H **BIOS (AT only)**
Cassette interrupt: Move memory areas

Moves areas of RAM from below the 1 megabyte limit to the range above the 1 megabyte limit, and from above the 1 megabyte limit to below the 1 megabyte limit.

Input: AH = 87H
CX = Number of words to move
ES = Segment address of global descriptor table
SI = Offset address of global descriptor table

Output: Carry flag=0: No error
Carry flag=1: Error:
AH=1: RAM parity error
AH=2: Incorrect GDT on function call
AH=3: Protected mode could not be initialized

Remarks: See Section 7.10.1 for more information about the global descriptor table (GDT).

Only words can be transferred; individual bytes cannot be transferred.

Maximum amount of memory allowed in a transfer is 64K. The value in the CX register cannot exceed 8000H.

All interrupts are disabled during the memory block move.

The contents of the BX, CX, DX, SI, DI, BP registers and the segment registers are not affected by this function. The contents of all other registers may change.

Interrupt 15H, function 88H **BIOS (AT only)**
Cassette interrupt: Determine memory size beyond 1 megabyte

Determines the amount of memory installed beyond the 1 megabyte limit.

Input: AH = 88H

Output: AX = Memory size

Remarks: The value in the AX register represents memory in kilobytes (K).

Memory size below the 1 megabyte limit can be determined using interrupt 12H.

The contents of the BX, CX, DX, SI, DI, BP registers and the segment registers are not affected by this function. The contents of all other registers may change.

Interrupt 15H, function 89H **BIOS (AT only)**
Cassette interrupt: Switch to virtual mode

Switches the 80286 processor to virtual mode.

Input: AH = 89H

Output: No output

Remarks: This function should be called only if you know how virtual mode operates. Improper use of this function can easily lead to a system crash.

Interrupt 16H, function 00H BIOS
Keyboard: Read character

Reads a character from the keyboard buffer. If the buffer doesn't contain a character, the function waits until a character is entered. Then the character is read and removed from the keyboard buffer.

Input: AH = 00H

Output: AL = 0: Extended key code:
AH = Extended key code
AL>1: Normal key activated:
AL = ASCII code of key
AH = Scan code of key

Remarks: ASCII code definition occurs independent of the keyboard. Scan codes apply only to the type of keyboard attached to the PC. See Appendix J for a list of ASCII codes and Section 7.11 for a list of extended key codes.

The contents of the BX, CX, DX, SI, DI, BP registers and the segment registers are not affected by this function. The contents of all other registers may change.

Interrupt 16H, function 01H BIOS
Keyboard: Read keyboard for character

Reads the keyboard buffer for a character ready to be entered. If a character is available, the function passes the character to the calling function. The character remains in the keyboard buffer and can be re-read when a program calls either function 0 (see above) or function 1. The function returns to the calling program immediately after the call.

Input: AH = 01H

Output: Zero flag = 1: No character in the keyboard buffer
Zero flag = 0: Character available in keyboard buffer:
AL = 0: Extended key code:
AH = Extended key code
AL>1: Normal key:
AL = ASCII code of the key
AH = Scan code of the key

Remarks: ASCII code definition occurs independent of the keyboard. Scan codes only apply to the type of keyboard attached to the PC. See Appendix J for a list of ASCII codes and Section 7.11 for a list of extended key codes.

The contents of the CX, DX, SI, DI, BP registers and the segment registers are not affected by this function. The contents of all other registers may change.

Interrupt 16H, function 02H **BIOS**
Keyboard: Read keyboard status

Reads and returns the status of certain control keys and various keyboard modes.

Input: AH = 02H

Output: AL = Keyboard status

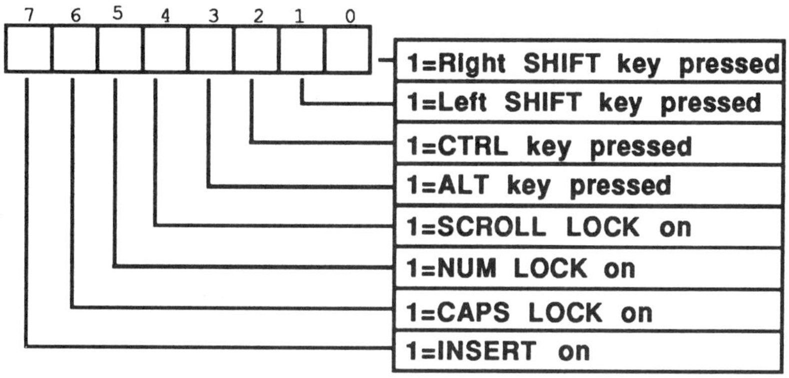

Keyboard status

Remarks: The contents of the BX, CX, DX, SI, DI, BP registers and the segment registers are not affected by this function. The contents of all other registers may change.

Interrupt 17H, function 00H **BIOS**
Printer: Write character

Writes a character to one of the printers interfaced to the PC.

Input: AH = 00H
AL = Character code to be printed
DX = Printer number

Output: AH = Printer status:
Bit 0=1: Time out error
Bit 1: Unused
Bit 2: Unused
Bit 3=1: Transfer error
Bit 4=0: Printer offline
Bit 4=1: Printer online
Bit 5=1: Printer out of paper
Bit 6=1: Receive mode selected
Bit 7=0: Printer busy

Remarks: Parallel port LPT1 is assigned the number 0, parallel port LPT2 is assigned the number 1 and parallel port LPT3 is assigned the number 2.

The contents of the BX, CX, DX, SI, DI, BP registers and the segment registers are not affected by this function. The contents of all other registers may change.

Interrupt 17H, function 01H **BIOS**
Printer: Initialize printer

Initializes the printer interfaced to the PC. This function should be executed before executing function 0 (see above).

Input: AH = 01H
DX = Printer number

Output: AH = Printer status

Remarks: Parallel port LPT1 is assigned the number 0, parallel port LPT2 is assigned the number 1 and parallel port LPT3 is assigned the number 2.

The contents of the BX, CX, DX, SI, DI, BP registers and the segment registers are not affected by this function. The contents of all other registers may change.

Interrupt 17H, function 02H **BIOS**
Printer: Read printer status

Returns the status of the printer interfaced to the PC.

Input: AH = 02H
DX = Printer number

Output: AH = Printer status

Remarks: Parallel port LPT1 is assigned the number 0, parallel port LPT2 is assigned the number 1 and parallel port LPT3 is assigned the number 2.

The contents of the BX, CX, DX, SI, DI, BP registers and the segment registers are not affected by this function. The contents of all other registers may change.

Interrupt 18H **BIOS**
Call ROM BASIC

Accesses BASIC in ROM if a system disk cannot be found during the system bootstrap process.

Input: No input

Output: No output

Remarks: Very few PCs or compatibles have built-in ROM BASIC (this is a throwback from the early days of the PC). If a PC doesn't have ROM BASIC, interrupt 18H returns the system to the calling program. However, if the PC does has ROM BASIC, interrupt 18H calls BASIC. In most cases, the only way to return to DOS is by warm-starting the computer (pressing the <Ctrl><Alt><Delete> keys) or turning the computer off and on again. Some versions of ROM BASIC allow an exit to DOS by entering the SYSTEM command from BASIC.

Interrupt 19H **BIOS**
Boot process

Boots the computer.

Input: No input

Output: No output

Remarks: Pressing the <Ctrl><Alt><Delete> keys invokes this interrupt from the keyboard.

Interrupt 1AH, function 00H **BIOS**
Date and time: Read clock count

Reads the current clock count. The clock count increments 18.2 times per second. This calculates the time elapsed since the computer was switched on.

Input: AH = 00H

Output: CX = High word of the clock count
DX = Low word of the clock count
AL = 0: Less than 24 hours have elapsed since the last reading
AL<>0: More than 24 hours have elapsed since the last reading

Remarks: The AT, which has a battery powered realtime clock, sets the clock count to the current time when the computer boots. PCs (which don't have realtime clocks) set the counter to 0 during booting.

The contents of the BX, CX, DX, SI, DI, BP registers and the segment registers are not affected by this function. The contents of all other registers may change.

Interrupt 1AH, function 01H **BIOS**
Date and time: Set clock count

Sets the contents of the current clock count, which increments 18.2 times per second. This calculates the time elapsed since the computer was switched on and sets the current time through this function.

Input: AH = 01H
CX = High word of clock count
DX = Low word of clock count

Output: No output

Remarks: The AT, which has a battery powered realtime clock, sets the clock count to the current time when the computer boots. PCs (which don't have realtime clocks) set the counter to 0 during booting. PC owners should use this function to set the current time.

The contents of the AX, BX, CX, DX, SI, DI, BP registers and the segment registers are not affected by this function. The contents of all other registers may change.

Interrupt 1AH, function 02H **BIOS (AT only)**
Date and time: Read realtime clock

Reads the time from the realtime clock.

Input: AH = 02H

Output: Carry flag = 0: O.K.:
CH = Hours
CL = Minutes
DH = Seconds
Carry flag = 1: Dead clock battery

Remarks: All time readings appear in BCD format.

The contents of the BX, SI, DI, BP registers and the segment registers are not affected by this function. The contents of all other registers may change.

Interrupt 1AH, function 03H **BIOS (AT only)**
Date and time: Set realtime clock

Sets the time on the realtime clock.

Input:
AH = 03H
CH = Hours
CL = Minutes
DH = Seconds
DL = 1: Daylight Saving Time
DL = 0: Standard Time

Output: No output

Remarks: All time settings must be in BCD format.

The contents of the BX, SI, DI, BP registers and the segment registers are not affected by this function. The contents of all other registers may change.

Interrupt 1AH, function 04H **BIOS (AT only)**
Date and time: Read date from realtime clock

Reads the current date from the realtime clock.

Input: AH = 04H

Output:
Carry flag = 0: O.K.:
CH = Century (19 or 20)
CL = Year
DH = Month
DL = Day
Carry flag = 1: Dead clock battery

Remarks: All date readings appear in BCD format.

The contents of the BX, SI, DI, BP registers and the segment registers are not affected by this function. The contents of all other registers may change.

Interrupt 1AH, function 05H **BIOS (AT only)**
Date and time: Set date in realtime clock

Sets the current date in the realtime clock.

Input: AH = 05H
CH = Century (19 or 20)
CL = Year
DH = Month
DL = Day

Output: No output

Remarks: All date settings must be in BCD format.

The contents of the BX, CX, SI, DI, BP registers and the segment registers are not affected by this function. The contents of all other registers may change.

Interrupt 1AH, function 06H **BIOS (AT only)**
Date and time: Set alarm time

Sets alarm time for the current day. The alarm time triggers interrupt 4AH.

Input: AH = 06H
CH = Hours
CL = Minutes
DH = Seconds

Output: Carry flag=0: O.K.
Carry flag=1: Dead clock battery or programmed alarm time.

Remarks: All alarm settings must be in BCD format.

During booting, interrupt 4AH points to an IRET command. If this interrupt doesn't point to a particular routine responding to the alarm, nothing will happen once the alarm time is reached.

Only one alarm time can be active at a time. If another alarm setting already exists, you must first delete it by using interrupt 26–1AH, function 7 (see below).

The contents of the BX, CX, SI, DI, BP registers and the segment registers are not affected by this function. The contents of all other registers may change.

Interrupt 1AH, function 07H **BIOS (AT only)**
Date and time: Reset alarm time

Clears an existing alarm setting created by using function 06H above.

Input: AH = 07H

Output: No output

Remarks: This function must be called when you want to change an alarm setting. Reset the alarm, then use function 06H to set the new alarm time.

The contents of the BX, CX, SI, DI, BP registers and the segment registers are not affected by this function. The contents of all other registers may change.

Interrupt 1BH **BIOS/DOS**
Keyboard: <Break> key pressed

Records the occurrence of a <Ctrl><Break> key combination and triggers interrupt 1BH. During the system boot, BIOS sets interrupt 1BH to an IRET command in order to prevent any reaction.

This routine sets a flag to indicate that the user has pressed <Ctrl><Break>. Following the execution of one of the DOS functions, this flag is tested for character input or output. If the system encounters <Ctrl><Break>, the current program stops. In addition, when a batch file is in process, the program asks whether the batch file should be continued or terminated.

Pressing <Ctrl><C> doesn't activate the interrupt. This key combination forces DOS to end the currently executing program. However, the DOS functions for character input/output search for this key combination.

To prevent termination of an application program, this interrupt can also be pointed to a user routine by pressing <Break> or <Ctrl><Break>.

Input: No input

Output: No output

Remarks: Before returning control to the calling program, this interrupt must restore all registers to their previous values.

Interrupt 1CH **BIOS**
Periodic interrupt

The timer IC calls interrupt 8H approximately 18.2 times per second. After ending its task, it calls interrupt 1CH in order to allow an application program access to the signals from the timer IC. During booting, BIOS initializes the interrupt vector of interrupt 1CH so that it points to an IRET command, which prevents any response if the interrupt is called. For example, this interrupt can be pointed to a user routine to create a constant display clock on the screen.

Input: No input

Output: No output

Remarks: This interrupt must restore all registers to their previous values before returning control to the calling program.

Interrupt 1DH **BIOS**
Video table

Sets a pointer to a table. The vector of this interrupt in the vector table, starting at address 0000:0074, stores the offset and segment address of this table. The table itself contains a collection of parameters used by BIOS for initializing a certain video mode. This involves the 16 memory locations on the video card, whose heart is a 6845 video processor. For this reason the table to which the vector points and which is part of the ROM-BIOS, consists of 16 consecutive bytes that indicate the contents of individual registers for a certain video mode. The first of these 16 bytes is copied into the first register of the 6845, the second byte into the second register, etc. The table in ROM contains a total of four 16-byte entries: 40x25 color mode, 80x25 color mode, 80x25 monochrome mode and one entry for the various color graphics modes.

Do not call this interrupt. If you do, the system will attempt to read the video table as executable code and will crash.

Input: No input

Output: No output

Interrupt 1EH **BIOS/DOS**
Drive table

Sets a pointer to a table. The vector of this interrupt in the vector table starting at address 0000:0078 stores the offset and segment address of this table. The table itself contains a collection of parameters used by BIOS in disk drive access. BIOS has a table in ROM, but deviates the interrupt vector of interrupt 30 to its own table which allows faster disk access than the BIOS table (see Section 7.7 for more information about this table).

Do not call this interrupt. If you do call it, the system will attempt to read the drive table as executable code and will crash.

Input: No input

Output: No output

Interrupt 1FH **BIOS/DOS**
Character table

Sets a pointer to a table. The vector of this interrupt in the vector table, starting at address 0000:007C, stores the offset and segment address of this table. The table itself contains character patterns for the characters possessing ASCII codes 128 to 255. BIOS needs this table in order to display the graphic mode characters on the screen. These characters are displayed by placing the character patterns, which are stored in this table, on the screen as individual pixels.

Since the character patterns for codes 0 to 127 are already stored in a table in ROM-BIOS, this table contains only the character patterns for codes 128 to 255. The DOS GRAFTABL command loads a table for codes 127 to 255 into RAM and points the interrupt vector of interrupt 31 to this table. A user table can be added to display on the screen, in graphic mode, certain characters that are not part of the normal PC character set. The construction of the table requires that eight consecutive bytes define the appearance of the character. The first eight bytes of the table define the appearance of ASCII code 128, the next eight bytes define ASCII code 129, etc. Each set of eight bytes represent the eight lines which denote a character in graphic mode. The eight bits of each byte indicate the eight columns of pixels for each line.

Do not call this interrupt. If you do call it, the system will attempt to read the character table as executable code and will crash.

Input: No input

Output: No output

Appendix C

DOS Interrupts and Functions

Subdirectory access

RAM control

Device driver access

Time and date

DTA

Search directory

File access (FCB)

File access (handle)

Interrupt vectors

Disk/hard disk access

PSP access

DOS flag access

File information access

Country-specific functions

Other functions

Interrupt 20H **DOS**
Terminate program **(Version 1 and up)**

Restores the three interrupt vectors whose contents were stored in the PSP before the program call, terminates the currently running program and returns control to MS-DOS. If the program redirected the vectors to its own routine, these vectors cannot be overwritten by another program. However, the terminating program releases the RAM it had occupied. Before turning control over to the calling program, this memory releases and all data buffers clear.

Input: CS = Segment address of the PSP

Output: No output

Remarks: COM programs automatically store the segment address of the PSP in the CS register. EXE programs require additional programming to load the segment address of the PSP into the CS register. Since the code and the PSP are stored in two separate segments, the address of the PSP must be loaded into the CS register. The code executes from another segment, which makes it impossible to call interrupt 32. To help overcome this problem, the value 0 and then the segment address of the PSP are pushed onto the stack. If a FAR RETURN command then executes, the program execution continues in the PSP segment at offset address 0. There a call for interrupt terminates the program.

For the first version of DOS, this interrupt is the usual method for ending a program. To terminate a program in DOS Version 2 and up, functions 31H or 4CH of DOS interrupt 21 H should be called instead.

Interrupt 21H, function 00H **DOS**
Terminate program **(Version 1 and up)**

Terminates execution of the currently running program and returns control to the calling program. Before this happens, the three interrupt vectors, whose contents had been stored in the PSP before the call of the program, are restored. If the program redirects these vectors to its own routine, they cannot be overwritten by another program. However, the terminating program does release the RAM it had occupied. Before turning control over to the calling program, the function releases this memory and clears all buffers.

Input: AH = 00H
CS = segment address of the PSP

Output: No output

Remarks: COM programs automatically store, in the CS register, the segment address of the PSP. Since the code and the PSP are stored in two separate segments, you cannot execute this function from an EXE program.

Instead of this function, use either function 31H or 4CH of interrupt 21H for terminating a program.

Interrupt 21H, function 01H **DOS**
Character input with echo **(Version 1 and up)**

Reads a character from the standard input device and displays it on the standard output device. When the function is called but a character doesn't exist, the function waits until a character is available. Since standard input and output can be redirected, this function is able to read a character from an input device other than the keyboard and send it to an output device other than the screen. The characters that are read may originate from other devices or from a file. If the character comes from a file, the input doesn't redirect to the keyboard once it reaches the end of the file. So, the function continues to try to read data from the file after it passes the end.

Input: AH = 01H

Output: AL = Character read

Remarks: If extended key codes are read, the function passes code 0 to the AL register. The function must be called again to read the actual code.

If the function encounters a <Ctrl><C> character (ASCII code 3), it calls interrupt 23H.

The contents of the AH, BX, CX, DX, SI, DI, BP, CS, DS, SS, ES and the flag registers are not affected by this function.

Interrupt 21H, function 02H **DOS**
Character output **(Version 1 and up)**

Displays a character on the standard output device. Since this device can be redirected, the character can be displayed on another output device or sent to a file. This function doesn't test whether or not the storage medium (disk or hard disk) is already full. Therefore, it will continue to try to write characters to this file.

Input: AH = 02H
DL = code of the character to be output

Output: No output

Remarks: Control codes such as backspace, carriage return and linefeed are executed when the function sends characters to the screen. If the output is redirected to a file, control codes are stored as normal ASCII codes.

If the function encounters a <Ctrl><C> character (ASCII code 3), it calls interrupt 23H.

The contents of the processor registers and the flag registers are not affected by this function.

Interrupt 21H, function 03H **DOS**
Read character auxiliary input **(Version 1 and up)**

Reads a character from the serial port. Access defaults to the device with the designation COM1, unless a MODE command previously redirected serial access.

Input: AH = 03H

Output: AL = Character received

Remarks: Since the serial port has no internal buffer, it can receive characters faster than it can read them. The unread characters are then ignored.

Before calling this function, communication parameters (baud rate, number of stop bits, etc.) must be set using the MODE command. Otherwise DOS defaults to 2400 baud, one stop bit, no parity and a word length of 8 bits.

The BIOS functions called from interrupt 14H are a more efficient way to access the serial port. Since they also allow reading of the serial port status, these functions offer more flexibility than the DOS functions.

If the function encounters a <Ctrl><C> character (ASCII code 3), it calls interrupt 23H.

The contents of the AH, BX, CX, DX, SI, DI, BP, CS, DS, SS, ES and the flag registers are not affected by this function.

Interrupt 21H, function 04H **DOS**
Auxiliary output **(Version 1 and up)**

Sends a character to the serial port. Unless a MODE command previously redirected serial access, access defaults to the device with the designation COM1.

Input: AH = 04H
DL = Character set for output

Output: No output

Remarks: As soon as the receiving device sends a signal to the function indicating that it is ready to receive it, the function transmits the character. Control then returns to the calling program.

Before calling this function, communication parameters (baud rate, number of stop bits, etc.) must be set using the MODE command.

Otherwise DOS defaults to 2400 baud, one stop bit, no parity and a word length of 8 bits.

The BIOS functions called from interrupt 14H are a more efficient way to access the serial port. Since they also allow reading of the serial port status, they offer more flexibility than the DOS functions.

If the function encounters a <Ctrl><C> character (ASCII code 3), it calls interrupt 23H.

The contents of the processor registers and the flag registers are not affected by this function.

Interrupt 21H, function 05H **DOS**
Character output to printer **(Version 1 and up)**

Sends a character to the printer. Access defaults to the device with the designation LPT1 (identical to PRN), unless a MODE command previously redirected printer access.

Input: AH = 05H
DL = Character code to be printed

Output: No output

Remarks: The function transmits the character only when the printer signals that it is ready to receive it. Then control returns to the calling program.

If the function encounters a <Ctrl><C> character (ASCII code 3), it calls interrupt 23H.

The BIOS functions called from interrupt 17H are more efficient for printer access. They offer more flexibility than the DOS printer functions for character output.

The contents of the processor registers and the flag registers are not affected by this function.

Interrupt 21H, function 06H **DOS**
Direct console I/O **(Version 1 and up)**

Reads characters from the standard input device and displays them on the standard output device. The read or written character isn't tested by the operating system (e.g., <Ctrl><C> has no effect on the program). Since standard input and output can be redirected, this function can read a character from an input device other than the keyboard and sends it to an output device other than the screen. The characters read may originate from other devices or from a file. When writing characters, this function doesn't test whether or not the storage medium (disk or hard disk) is already full. Also, the calling program cannot determine whether all the characters have been read from an input file.

During character input, the function doesn't wait until a character is available. Instead, the function returns control to the calling program.

Input: AH = 06H
DL = 0–254: Send character code
DL = 255: Read a character

Output: Character output: No output
Character input: Zero flag=1: No character ready
Zero flag=0: Character read is in the AL register

Remarks: If extended key codes are read, the function passes code 0 to the AL register. The function must be called again to read the actual code.

ASCII code 255 (blank) cannot be displayed with this function because the function interprets ASCII code 255 as a command to input a character.

The contents of the AH, BX, CX, DX, SI, DI, BP, CS, DS, SS and ES registers are not affected by this function.

Interrupt 21H, function 07H **DOS**
Unfiltered character input without echo **(Version 1 and up)**

Reads a character from the standard input device without displaying the character on the standard output device. If a character doesn't exist when the function is called, the function waits until a character is available. The read character is not tested by the operating system (e.g., <Ctrl><C> has no effect on the program). Since standard input and output can be redirected, this function can read a character from an input device other than the keyboard. The characters that are read may originate from other devices or from a file. If the characters come from a file, the input doesn't redirect to the keyboard once it reaches the end of file. This causes the function to continue to try reading data from the file after it passes the end of file.

Input: AH = 07H

Output: AL = Character read

Remarks: If extended key codes are read, the function passes code 0 to the AL register. The function must be called again to read the actual code.

The contents of the AH, BX, CX, DX, SI, DI, BP, CS, DS, SS, ES and the flag registers are not affected by this function.

Interrupt 21H, function 08H — DOS
Character input without echo — (Version 1 and up)

Reads a character from the standard input device without displaying the character on the standard output device. If no character exists when the function is called, the function waits until a character is available.

Since standard input can be redirected, this function can read a character from an input device other than the keyboard. The characters read may originate from other devices or from a file. If the characters come from a file, the input doesn't redirect to the keyboard on reaching the end of file, so the function continues to try reading data from the file after it passes the end of file.

Input: AH = 08H

Output: AL = Character read

Remarks: If extended key codes are read, the function passes code 0 to the AL register. The function must be called again to read the actual code.

If the function encounters a <Ctrl><C> character (ASCII code 3), it calls interrupt 23H.

The contents of the AH, BX, CX, DX, SI, DI, BP, CS, DS, SS, ES and the flag registers are not affected by this function.

Interrupt 21H, function 09H — DOS
Output character string — (Version 1 and up)

Displays a character string on the standard output device. Since this device can be redirected, the character may be displayed on another output device or sent to a file. This function doesn't test whether or not the storage medium (disk or hard disk) is already full, and will continue to try to write the string to a file.

Input: AH = 09H
DS = String segment address
DX = String offset address

Output: No output

Remarks: The string must be stored in memory as a series of bytes which contain the ASCII codes of the characters to be output. A dollar sign character "$" (ASCII code 36) indicates, to DOS, the end of the string.

Control codes, such as backspace, carriage return and linefeed, are executed within the string.

The contents of the processor registers and the flag registers are not affected by this function.

Interrupt 21H, function 0AH **DOS**
Buffered input **(Version 1 and up)**

Reads a number of characters from the standard input device and transmits the characters to a buffer. The input ends when the user presses the <Return> key. The ASCII code of this key (13) is then placed in the buffer as the last character of the string.

Since standard input can be redirected, this function can read a character from an input device other than the keyboard. The characters read may originate either from other devices or from a file. If the characters come from a file, the input doesn't redirect to the keyboard on reaching the end of file, so the function continues to try reading data from the file after it passes the end.

Input: AH = 0AH
DS = Buffer segment address
DX = Buffer offset address

Output: No output

Remarks: The first byte of the buffer accepts the maximum number of characters (including the carriage return which ends the input) which can be read into the buffer, starting at memory location 2. In order to inform the function of the maximum number of characters it may read, this information must be entered, by the calling program, into the buffer before the function call.

After completion of the input, DOS places the number of characters read (excluding the carriage return) in memory location 1.

The buffer must be the number of the characters to be read plus 2 bytes.

When the input reaches the second to last memory location in the buffer, the computer beeps if you attempt to enter any character other than the <Return> key (end of input).

Extended key codes occupy two bytes in the buffer. The first byte contains the code 0, and the second byte contains the extended key code.

If the function encounters a <Ctrl><C> character (ASCII code 3), it calls interrupt 23H.

The <Backspace> and cursor keys let you edit the input without storing these keys in the buffer.

The contents of the processor registers and the flag registers are not affected by this function.

Interrupt 21H, function 0BH — DOS
Get input status — (Version 1 and up)

Determines whether a character is available for reading from the standard input device.

Input: AH = 0BH

Output: AL = 0: No character available
AL = 255: One or more characters available for reading

Remarks: If the function encounters a <Ctrl><C> character (ASCII code 3), it calls interrupt 23H.

The contents of the AH, BX, CX, DX, SI, DI, BP, CS, DS, SS, ES and the flag registers are not affected by this function.

Interrupt 21H, function 0CH — DOS
Reset input buffer and then input — (Version 1 and up)

Clears the input buffer then calls one of the character input functions. Since all the character input functions get their characters from the standard input device and standard input may redirected, this function only operates when the keyboard is the standard input device. In this case the characters could be entered before the function call but not read by a function. These existing characters are erased to ensure that the function call only reads characters which were inputted after its call.

Input: AH = 0CH
AL = Function to be called during call of function 10
DS = Input buffer segment address
DX = Input buffer offset address

Output: Functions 1, 6, 7 and 8: AL = Character to be read
Function 10: No output

Remarks: Functions 1, 6, 7, 8 and 10 can be passed to the function as calling functions.

The contents of the AH, BX, CX, DX, SI, DI, BP, CS, DS, SS, ES and the flag registers are not affected by this function.

Interrupt 21H, function 0DH — DOS
Disk reset — (Version 1 and up)

Sends all data stored in an internal DOS buffer to a block driver device (e.g., disk drive, hard disk). The open files (handles or FCBs) remain open.

Input: AH = 0DH

Output: No output

Remarks: Despite this function call, all open files must be closed in an orderly manner. Otherwise the current directory entry of the file may not update properly, which prevents access to new file data.

The contents of the processor registers and the flag registers are not affected by this function.

Interrupt 21H, function 0EH — DOS
Select default disk drive — (Version 1 and up)

Defines the the current default disk drive. Its designation appears as a prompt on the screen when the command interpreter expects input from the user. The drive indicated here will be used for all file access in which no special device was specified.

Input: AH = 0EH
DL = Drive number

Output: AL = Number of installed drives or volumes

Remarks: Drive A: has code number of 0, drive B: code number 1, etc.

Even if the PC has only one disk drive and one hard disk, the number of volumes in the AL register can be greater than two because the hard disk can be divided into multiple volumes. In addition, the PC can have one or more RAM disks as part of its configuration. For a PC with a single disk drive, you can only have two volumes because drive A: also simulates drive B:.

Unlike DOS Version 2, which permits 63 different device codes, DOS Version 3 permits 26 different devices (the letters A to Z). To keep compatibility between versions, limit your device access to a maximum of 26 devices.

BIOS interrupt 11H does a better job of reading the number of disk drives than this function.

The contents of the AH, BX, CX, DX, SI, DI, BP, CS, DS, SS, ES and the flag registers are not affected by this function.

Interrupt 21H, function 0FH — DOS
Open file (FCB) — (Version 1 and up)

Opens a file if one is available. After this function call executes successfully, the file can be read or written.

Input:
AH = 0FH
DS = FCB segment address of the file
DX = FCB offset address of the file

Output:
AL = 0: File found and opened
AL = 255: File not found

Remarks:
Both normal and extended FCBs can be used.

If the file was found, DOS enters, into the FCB, the file size, the date and the time of its creation or last modification.

DOS sets the record length at 128 bytes. This record length can be changed in the FCB before opening a file. If you need a longer record length, the DTA must be moved (the original DTA is only 128 bytes long).

If random file access is performed, the random record field in the FCB must be set after the file opens successfully.

The file pointer points to the first byte of the file after the file opens.

The contents of the AH, BX, CX, DX, SI, DI, BP, CS, DS, SS, ES and the flag registers are not affected by this function.

Interrupt 21H, function 10H — DOS
Close file (FCB) — (Version 1 and up)

Writes all data currently in the DOS buffer to the file and closes the file. In addition, the directory entry changes to reflect the new file size and the date and time of the most recent modification to the file.

Input:
AH = 10H
DS = FCB segment address of the file
DX = FCB offset address of the file

Output:
AL = 0: File closed and directory entry revised
AL = 255: File not found in directory

Remarks:
Only open files can be closed.

For disk files, the disk which was in the drive when the function call occurred must also be the disk that contains the file. Otherwise, the function call writes an incorrect FAT and an incorrect directory to the disk, which makes the data that is already on the disk useless.

The contents of the AH, BX, CX, DX, SI, DI, BP, CS, DS, SS, ES and the flag registers are not affected by this function.

Interrupt 21H, function 11H **DOS**
Search for first match (FCB) **(Version 1 and up)**

Searches for the first occurrence in the disk directory of the filename indicated in the FCB.

Input:
AH = 11H
DS = FCB segment address
DX = FCB offset address

Output:
AL = 0: File found
AL = 255: File not found

Remarks:
The FCB passed to the function contains the drive specifier and the filename for which the function should search.

The filename can contain the wildcard "?" to search for a group of files.

The search is made only in the current directory of the indicated device.

If the function searches for a normal file, a normal FCB can pass the information to the function. However, if you wish to search for a file with special attributes (volume name, subdirectories, hidden files, etc.), extended FCBs must be used.

If a file was found, the DTA contains an FCB of the same type as the FCBs. This FCB in the DTA contains the found filename. For this reason, the DTA must always be large enough to accept either a normal or an extended FCB.

The DTA can be switched to its own buffer using function 1AH, to ensure that it is large enough to accept the FCB.

The contents of the AH, BX, CX, DX, SI, DI, BP, CS, DS, SS, ES and the flag registers are not affected by this function.

Interrupt 21H, function 12H **DOS**
Search for next match (FCB) **(Version 1 and up)**

Searches for additional occurrences in the disk directory of the filename indicated in the FCB, after the file was found by function 17 (see above).

Input: AH = 12H
DS = FCB segment address
DX = FCB offset address

Output: AL = 0: File found
AL = 255: File not found (no other files available)

Remarks: This function can only be called after calling function 11H.

The FCB passed to the function contains the drive specifier and the filename for which the function should search.

If another filename was found its name is recorded in the FCB at the beginning of the DTA.

The DTA can be switched with function 1AH to its own buffer to ensure that it is large enough to accept the FCB.

The contents of the AH, BX, CX, DX, SI, DI, BP, CS, DS, SS, ES and the flag registers are not affected by this function.

Interrupt 21H, function 13H **DOS**
Delete file (FCB) **(Version 1 and up)**

Erases one or more files in the current directory of the specified device.

Input: AH = 13H
DS = FCB segment address
DX = FCB offset address

Output: AL = 0: file(s) erased
AL = 255: No file(s) found, or file(s) assigned Read Only attribute (undeletable)

Remarks: The FCB passed to the function contains both the device on which the files to be erased are located and the name of the file.

The filename can contain the wildcard "?" to erase a group of files.

Only files in the current directory of the indicated device may be erased.

If the function is used to delete a normal file, a normal FCB can pass the information to the function. However, if you want to delete a file with special attributes (volume name, subdirectories, hidden files, etc.), extended FCBs must be used.

Volumes may be deleted with this function; subdirectories may not.

The contents of the AH, BX, CX, DX, SI, DI, BP, CS, DS, SS, ES and the flag registers are not affected by this function.

Interrupt 21H, function 14H — DOS
Sequential read (FCB) — (Version 1 and up)

Reads the next sequential data block from a file.

Input:
AH = 14H
DS = FCB segment address
DX = FCB offset address

Output:
AL = 0: Block read
AL = 1: End of file reached
AL = 2: Segment wrap
AL = 3: Partial record read

Remarks:
The function can only be called after the file was opened by the indicated FCB.

The DTA reads the block. If the DTA is not large enough, function 1AH must move the DTA into its own buffer.

The FCB records the size of the block and the corresponding number of bytes read.

Error 2 occurs when the DTA reaches the end of a segment and the block being read extends beyond the end of the segment.

Error 3 occurs when a partial block appears at the end of the file. The block is read in anyway and blank spaces bring the block up to the allocated block size.

After reading a block, the file pointer resets to the beginning of the next block so that the next function call automatically reads the next block.

The contents of the AH, BX, CX, DX, SI, DI, BP, CS, DS, SS, ES and the flag registers are not affected by this function.

Interrupt 21H, function 15H — DOS
Sequential write (FCB) — (Version 1 and up)

Writes a sequential block to a file.

Input:
AH = 15H
DS = FCB segment address
DX = FCB offset address

Output:
AL = 0: Block written
AL = 1: Medium (disk/hard disk) full
AL = 2: Segment overflow

Remarks:
The function can only be called after the file was opened by the indicated FCB.

The DTA writes the block it contains to the file. If the DTA is not large enough to hold the file, function 1AH must be used to move the DTA into its own buffer.

The FCB records the size of the block and the corresponding number of bytes written.

Error 2 occurs if the DTA reaches the end of a segment and the block being written extends beyond the end of the segment.

After writing a block, the file pointer resets to the beginning of the next block, so that the next function call automatically writes the next block.

The contents of the AH, BX, CX, DX, SI, DI, BP, CS, DS, SS, ES and the flag registers are not affected by this function.

Interrupt 21H, function 16H — DOS
Create or truncate file (FCB) — (Version 1 and up)

Creates a new file, or dumps the contents of an existing file (file size=0 bytes). This function call allows other functions to read or write to the open file.

Input:
AH = 16H
DS = FCB segment address
DX = FCB offset address

Output:
AL = 0: File created or cleared
AL = 255: File could not be created (e.g., directory full)

Remarks:
The contents of an existing file called by this function are lost.

After calling this function, the file is already open; you don't need to open the file using function 0FH (see above).

If you open the file using an extended FCB, you can assign certain attributes to the file (e.g., volume name, hidden file, etc.).

You cannot create a subdirectory using this function.

After opening the file, the file pointer moves to the first byte of the file.

The contents of the AH, BX, CX, DX, SI, DI, BP, CS, DS, SS, ES and the flag registers are not affected by this function.

Interrupt 21H, function 17H **DOS**
Rename file (FCB) **(Version 1 and up)**

Renames one or more files in the current directory of the specified device.

Input:
AH = 17H
DS = FCB segment address
DX = FCB offset address

Output:
AL = 0: File(s) renamed
AL = 255: No file found, or new filename matches old filename

Remarks:
The FCB here is a special FCB, based on a normal FCB. The first 12 bytes contain the drive specifier and the name of the file to be renamed. However, this type of FCB has the new drive specifier and the new filename stored starting at memory location 10H. The drive specifier must be identical for both filenames.

The name of the file to be renamed can contain the wildcard "?", which renames several files. If the new filename contains the wildcard "?", the places in the filename and extension where a question mark appears in this parameter remain unchanged.

The contents of the AH, BX, CX, DX, SI, DI, BP, CS, DS, SS, ES and the flag registers are not affected by this function.

Interrupt 21H, function 19H **DOS**
Get default disk drive **(Version 1 and up)**

Returns the drive specifier of the default (current) disk drive.

Input: AH = 19H

Output: AL = Drive specifier

Remarks: This function identifies drive A as code 0, drive B as code 1, etc.

The contents of the AH, BX, CX, DX, SI, DI, BP, CS, DS, SS, ES and the flag registers are not affected by this function.

Interrupt 21H, function 1AH **DOS**
Set DTA address **(Version 1 and up)**

Transfers the DTA (Disk Transfer Area) to another area of memory. The DTA acts as buffer memory for all FCB supported file accesses.

Input: AH = 1AH
DS = New DTA segment address
DX = New DTA offset address

Output: No output

Remarks: This function must be called if the existing DTA has insufficient memory to handle the transmitted data.

When the program starts, MS-DOS places the DTA at address 128 in the PSP. Since the program starts after address 255 of the PSP, it is 128 bytes long.

DOS does not test the length of the DTA. Instead it assumes that the DTA is large enough to accept the transmitted data. If this is not the case, a DOS function can overwrite the excess data.

DOS recognizes an error during various functions if the DTA is at the end of a segment and the data to be transmitted exceeds the end of the segment.

The contents of the processor registers and the flag registers are not affected by this function.

Interrupt 21H, function 1BH — DOS
Get allocation information for default drive — (Version 1 and up)

Returns information about the format of the default drive.

Input: AH = 1BH

Output:
AL = Number of sectors per cluster
DS = Media descriptor segment address
BX = Media descriptor offset address
DX = Number of clusters

Remarks: The media descriptor can return the following codes:

F8H: Hard disk
F9H: Disk drive: double-sided, 15 sectors per track (AT only)
FCH: Disk drive: single-sided, 9 sectors per track
FDH: Disk drive: double-sided, 9 sectors per track
FEH: Disk drive: single-sided, 8 sectors per track
FFH: Disk drive: double-sided, 8 sectors per track

The contents of the AH, BX, CX, DX, SI, DI, BP, CS, DS, SS, ES and the flag registers are not affected by this function.

Interrupt 21H, function 1CH — DOS
Get allocation information for specified drive — (Version 1 and up)

Returns information about the format of the specified drive.

Input:
AH = 1CH
DL = Drive specifier

Output:
AL = Number of sectors per cluster
DS = Media descriptor segment address
BX = Media descriptor offset address
DX = Number of clusters

Remarks: This function identifies drive A as code 0, drive B as code 1, etc.

The media descriptor can return the following codes:

F8H: Hard disk
F9H: Disk drive: double-sided, 15 sectors per track (AT only)
FCH: Disk drive: single-sided, 9 sectors per track
FDH: Disk drive: double-sided, 9 sectors per track
FEH: Disk drive: single-sided, 8 sectors per track
FFH: Disk drive: double-sided, 8 sectors per track

The contents of the AH, BX, CX, DX, SI, DI, BP, CS, DS, SS, ES and the flag registers are not affected by this function.

Interrupt 21(h), function 1DH **DOS**
Reserved **(Version 1 and up)**

Interrupt 21(h), function 1EH **DOS**
Reserved **(Version 1 and up)**

Interrupt 21(h), function 1FH **DOS**
Reserved **(Version 1 and up)**

Interrupt 21(h), function 20H **DOS**
Reserved **(Version 1 and up)**

Interrupt 21H, function 21H **DOS**
Random read (FCB) **(Version 1 and up)**

Reads a specified file record into the DTA.

Input:
AH = 21H
DS = FCB segment address
DX = FCB offset address

Output:
AL = 0: Record read
AL = 1: End of file reached
AL = 2: Segment overflow
AL = 3: Partial record read

Remarks:
The function can only be called after the file was opened by the indicated FCB.

The record whose address is stored in the FCB starting at location 21H is read.

The DTA reads the record. If the DTA is not large enough, function 1AH must be called to move the DTA into its own buffer.

The FCB records the size of the record and the corresponding number of bytes read.

During the function call, the file pointer moves to the beginning of the record being read so that a subsequent call of a sequential read (function 14H—see above) reads the same record sequentially.

The record number does not increment following the function call, so a new call of this function would read the same record.

Error 2 occurs when the DTA reaches the end of a segment and the record being read extends beyond the end of the segment.

Error 3 occurs when a partial record appears at the end of the file. The record is read in anyway and blank spaces bring the record up to the allocated record size.

The contents of the AH, BX, CX, DX, SI, DI, BP, CS, DS, SS, ES and the flag registers are not affected by this function.

Interrupt 21H, function 22H **DOS**
Random write (FCB) **(Version 1 and up)**

Writes data from memory to the specified record in a file.

Input:
AH = 22H
DS = FCB segment address
DX = FCB offset address

Output:
AL = 0: record was written
AL = 1: Medium (disk/hard disk) full
AL = 2: segment overflow

Remarks:
The function can only be called after the file was opened by the indicated FCB.

The record whose address is stored in the FCB starting at location 21H is read.

The record is written from the DTA to the file. If the DTA is not large enough, function 1AH must move the DTA into its own buffer.

The FCB records the size of the record and the number of bytes read.

During the function call, the file pointer moves to the beginning of the record being read. This instructs subsequent calls of a sequential read (function 14H—see above) to read the same record sequentially.

The record number does not increment following the function call, so a new call of this function would read the same record.

Error 2 occurs when the DTA reaches the end of a segment and the record being written extends beyond the end of the segment.

The contents of the AH, BX, CX, DX, SI, DI, BP, CS, DS, SS, ES and the flag registers are not affected by this function.

Interrupt 21H, function 23H — DOS
Get file size in records (FCB) — (Version 1 and up)

Determines the size of a file based on the number of records in that file.

Input: AH = 23H
DS = FCB segment address
DX = FCB offset address

Output: AL = 0: Number of records found starting at FCB address 21H
AL = 255: File not found

Remarks: The FCB passed contains the drive specifier as well as the name and extension of the file to be examined.

Unlike the other FCB supported file accesses, the FCB requires the record size before the application can call this function.

A record size of 1 returns the size of the file in bytes.

The contents of the AH, BX, CX, DX, SI, DI, BP, CS, DS, SS, ES and the flag registers are not affected by this function.

Interrupt 21H, function 24H — DOS
Set random record number — (Version 1 and up)

Sets the record number in the FCB to the current position of the file pointer. Random access may begin at the point at which earlier sequential accesses left off.

Input: AH = 24H
DS = FCB segment address
DX = FCB offset address

Output: No output

Remarks: The function can only be called after the file was opened by the indicated FCB.

The contents of the processor registers and the flag registers are not affected by this function.

Interrupt 21H, function 25H **DOS**
Set interrupt vector **(Version 1 and up)**

Sets any interrupt vector to another routine.

Input: AH = 25H
AL = Interrupt number
DS = New interrupt routine segment address
DX = New interrupt routine offset address

Output: No output

Remarks: Before calling this function, the old contents of the interrupt vector to be changed should be read and stored using function 35H. After the program terminates, the old contents of the interrupt vector should be restored.

The contents of the processor registers and the flag registers are not affected by this function.

Interrupt 21H, function 26H **DOS**
Create PSP **(Version 1 and up)**

Copies the PSP (program segment prefix) of the executing program to a specified address in memory.

Input: AH = 26H
DX = New PSP segment address

Output: No output

Remarks: The new PSP offset address is 0.

DOS Version 1 uses this function to execute other programs by creating a PSP, loading the program after this PSP and executing it.

For DOS Version 2 up, use the EXEC function 4BH to load and execute additional programs instead of this function.

The contents of the processor registers and the flag registers are not affected by this function.

Interrupt 21H, function 27H **DOS**
Random block read (FCB) **(Version 1 and up)**

Reads one or more sequentially stored records into memory.

Input:
AH = 27H
CX = Number of records to be read
DS = FCB segment address
DX = FCB offset address

Output:
AL = 0: Record read
AL = 1: End of file reached
AL = 2: Segment overflow
AL = 3: Partial record read
CX = Number of records read

Remarks:
The function can only be called after the file was opened by the indicated FCB.

The starting record is the record whose address is stored in the FCB, starting at location 21H.

The record data passes to the DTA. If the DTA is not large enough, function 1AH must move the DTA into its own buffer.

The FCB records the size of the record and the corresponding number of bytes read.

After the function call, the file pointer moves to the end of the last record that was read so that it points to the next record (following the last record read).

Error 2 occurs when the DTA reaches the end of a segment and the record being read extends beyond the end of the segment.

Error 3 occurs when a partial record appears at the end of the file. The record is read in anyway and blank spaces bring the record up to the allocated record size.

The contents of the AH, BX, CX, DX, SI, DI, BP, CS, DS, SS, ES and the flag registers are not affected by this function.

Interrupt 21H, function 28H — DOS
Random block write (FCB) — (Version 1 and up)

Writes one or more records in sequence to the specified file.

Input:
AH = 28H
CX = Number of records to be written
DS = FCB segment address
DX = FCB offset address

Output:
AL = 0: Record written
AL = 1: Medium (disk/hard disk) full
AL = 2: Segment overflow
CX = Number of records written

Remarks:
The function can only be called after the file was opened by the indicated FCB.

The starting record is the record whose address is stored in the FCB starting at location 21H.

The FCB records the size of the record and the corresponding number of bytes read.

The data is written from the DTA to the file. If the DTA is not large enough, function 1AH must move the DTA into its own buffer.

After the function call, the file pointer moves to the end of the last record written so that it points to the next record, which follows the last record written. The record number increments by the number of records written.

Error 2 occurs when the DTA reaches the end of a segment and the record being written extends beyond the end of the segment.

The contents of the AH, BX, CX, DX, SI, DI, BP, CS, DS, SS, ES and the flag registers are not affected by this function.

Interrupt 21H, function 29H — DOS
Parse filename to FCB — (Version 1 and up)

Transfers an ASCII format filename into the proper fields of an FCB. The filename can include a drive specifier, filename and file extension.

Input:
AH = 29H
DS = Segment address of filename in memory
SI = Offset address of filename in memory
ES = FCB segment address
DI = FCB offset address

AL = Transmission parameters:

Bit 1 = 1: The drive specifier in the FCB changes only if the filename passed contains a drive specifier

0: The drive specifier changes anyway. If the filename passed contains no drive specifier, the the FCB defaults to 0 (current drive)

Bit 2 = 1: The filename in the FCB changes only if the filename parameter passed contains a filename

0: The filename changes. If the filename passed does not contain a filename, the filename in the FCB fills with spaces (ASCII code 32)

Bit 3 = 1: The file extension in FCB changes only if the filename passed contains an extension

0: The file extension in the FCB changes. If the filename passed has no extension, the extension field is padded with spaces (ASCII code 32)

Bits 4–8: Should contain the value 0

Output:

AL = 0: The filename passed contains no wildcards
AL = 1: The filename passed contains wildcards
AL = 255: Invalid drive specifier
DS = Segment address of the first character after parsed filename
SI = Offset address of the first character after parsed filename
ES = FCB segment address
DI = FCB offset address

Remarks:

The filename must end with an end character (ASCII code 0).

If the filename contains the wildcard "*", all corresponding fields in the FCB fill with the wildcard "?".

The contents of the AH, BX, CX, DX, SI, DI, BP, CS, DS, SS, ES and the flag registers are not affected by this function.

Interrupt 21H, function 2AH — DOS
Get system date — (Version 1 and up)

Reads the current system date.

Input:

AH = 2AH

Output:

AL = Day of the week (0=Sunday, 1=Monday, etc.)
CX = Year
DH = Month
DL = Day

Remarks:

DOS calls the clock driver to read the date.

The contents of the AH, BX, CX, DX, SI, DI, BP, CS, DS, SS, ES and the flag registers are not affected by this function.

Interrupt 21H, function 2BH **DOS**
Set system date **(Version 1 and up)**

Sets the current system date as returned by function 2AH (see above).

Input: AH = 2BH
CX = Year
DH = Month
DL = Day

Output: AL = 0: O.K.
AL = 255: Date incorrect

Remarks: The date passes to the clock driver.

If the PC does not have a realtime clock, the date remains in effect until the PC is switched off or rebooted.

If the date entry is incorrect, the PC retains the old date.

The contents of the AH, BX, CX, DX, SI, DI, BP, CS, DS, SS, ES and the flag registers are not affected by this function.

Interrupt 21H, function 2CH **DOS**
Get system time **(Version 1 and up)**

Gets the current system time.

Input: AH = 2CH

Output: CH = Hours
CL = Minutes
DH = Seconds
DL = Hundredths of a second

Remarks: DOS calls the clock driver to read the time.

The contents of the AH, BX, CX, DX, SI, DI, BP, CS, DS, SS, ES and the flag registers are not affected by this function.

Interrupt 21H, function 2DH **DOS**
Set system time **(Version 1 and up)**

Sets the current system time.

Input: AH = 2DH
CH = Hours
CL = Minutes
DH = Seconds
DL = hundredths of a second

Output: AL = 0: O.K.
AL = 255: Incorrect time

Remarks: The time passes to the clock driver.

If the PC does not have a realtime clock, the time remains in effect until the PC is switched off or rebooted.

If the time entry is incorrect, the PC retains the old time.

The contents of the AH, BX, CX, DX, SI, DI, BP, CS, DS, SS, ES and the flag registers are not affected by this function.

Interrupt 21H, function 2EH **DOS**
Set verify flag **(Version 1 and up)**

Sets the verify flag. This flag determines whether data should be verified after a write operation to a block driver for proper transmission.

Input: AH = 2EH
DL = 0
AL = 0: Don't verify data
AL = 1: Verify data

Output: No output

Remarks: This flag can be controlled at the user level with the VERIFY ON and VERIFY OFF commands.

The contents of the processor registers and the flag registers are not affected by this function.

Interrupt 21H, function 2FH **DOS**
Get DTA address **(Version 2 and up)**

Returns the address of the DTA (Data Transmission Area), which serves as a data buffer for all FCB supported file accesses.

Input: AH = 2FH

Output: ES = DTA segment address
BX = DTA offset address

Remarks: This function determines the address of the DTA, but not the DTA's size.

After the start of a program, the DTA starts at memory location 128 of the PSP and has a length of 128 bytes.

The contents of the AH, BX, CX, DX, SI, DI, BP, CS, DS, SS, ES and the flag registers are not affected by this function.

Interrupt 21H, function 30H — DOS
Get MS-DOS version number — (Version 2 and up)

Returns the DOS version number.

Input: AH = 30H

Output: AL = Major version number (e.g., version 2.01=2)
AH = Minor version number (e.g., version 3.01=01)

Remarks: The major (whole) version number represents the number preceding the decimal point. For example, the version number 3.3 returns the major version number 3.

The minor (fractional) version number represents the number following the decimal point. It is always given as two digits. For example, Version 2.1 returns the minor version number 10 (0AH).

If the AL register contains a value of 0, the program runs under DOS Version 1. DOS Version 1.0 cannot use this function.

The contents of the DX, SI, DI, BP, CS, DS, SS, ES and the flag registers are not affected by this function.

Interrupt 21H, function 31H — DOS
Terminate and stay resident — (Version 2 and up)

Terminates the currently executing program and returns control to the calling program. The current program remains in memory for later recall.

Input: AH = 31H
AL = Return code
DX = Number of paragraphs to be reserved

Output: No output

Remarks: The return code in the AL register indicates whether or not the program called by it correctly executes. The calling program can read this number by calling function 77 (4DH). This value can be tested from within a batch file using the ERRORLEVEL and IF commands.

The number of 16-byte paragraphs to be reserved indicates how many bytes, beginning with the PSP, cannot be released for other uses.

Memory blocks reserved by function 48H are not affected by the value in the DX register because they can only be released by calling function 49H.

Interrupt 21H, function 33H, sub-function 0 — DOS
Get <Ctrl><Break> flag — (Version 2 and up)

Reads the <Ctrl><Break> flag. This determines whether DOS should test for active <Ctrl><C> or <Ctrl><Break> keys on each function call, or on character input/output calls. <Ctrl><C> and <Ctrl><Break> trigger interrupt 23H.

Input: AH = 33H
AL = 0

Output: DL = 0: Test only during character input/output
DL = 1: Test on every function call

Remarks: Since the <Ctrl><Break> flag is not part of the environment block of a program, it affects all programs which call the DOS character functions that test for <Ctrl><C> or the <Break> key.

The contents of the AH, BX, CX, DX, SI, DI, BP, CS, DS, SS, ES and the flag registers are not affected by this function.

Interrupt 21H, function 33H, sub-function 1 — DOS
Set <Ctrl><Break> flag — (Version 2 and up)

Sets and unsets the <Ctrl><Break> flag. This determines whether DOS should test for the activation of the <Ctrl><C> or <Ctrl><Break> keys on each DOS function call or character input/output calls. <Ctrl><C> and <Ctrl><Break> trigger interrupt 23H.

Input: AH = 33H
AL = 1
DL = 0: Test only during character input/output
DL = 1: Test on every function call

Output: No output

Remarks: Since the <Ctrl><Break> flag is not part of the environment block of a program, it affects all programs which call the DOS character functions that test for <Ctrl><C> or the <Break> key.

The contents of the processor registers and the flag registers are not affected by this function.

Interrupt 21H, function 35H **DOS**
Get interrupt vector **(Version 2 and up)**

Returns the current contents of an interrupt vector and the address of the interrupt routine that belongs to it.

Input: AH = 35H
AL = Interrupt number

Output: ES = Interrupt routine segment address
BX = Interrupt routine offset address

Remarks: To ensure compatibility with future versions of DOS, instead of reading the vector's contents directly from the interrupt vector table, call this function for reading an interrupt vector.

The contents of the AH, BX, CX, DX, SI, DI, BP, CS, DS, SS, ES and the flag registers are not affected by this function.

Interrupt 21H, function 36H **DOS**
Get free disk space **(Version 2 and up)**

Returns information about the device (the block driver) from which the available memory space can be calculated.

Input: AH = 36H
DL = Device code

Output: AX = 65535: Device unavailable
AX< 65535: Number of sectors per cluster
BX = Number of available clusters
CX = Number of bytes per sector
DX = Total number of clusters on the device

Remarks: This function identifies drive A as code 0, drive B as code 1, etc.

The remaining memory on the medium can be computed from the number of bytes per sector multiplied by the number of sectors per cluster, multiplied by the number of free clusters.

The contents of the SI, DI, BP, CS, DS, SS, ES and the flag registers are not affected by this function.

Interrupt 21H, function 38H **DOS**
Get country **(Version 2 and up)**

Determines country-specific parameters, which are set in the CONFIG.SYS file using the DOS COUNTRY command.

Input: AH = 38H
AL = 0
DS = Buffer segment address
DX = Buffer offset address

Output: No output

Remarks: Before the function call, function 30H should be used to determine the DOS version. This can help the programmer compensate for differences between DOS versions during the call and return of this function.

The buffer must have at least 32 bytes allocated for recording the various country-specific parameters.

Following the function call, the individual bytes of this buffer contain the following information :

Bytes 0–1: Date format
0 = USA: Month-day-year
1 = Europe: day-month-year
2 = Japan: Year-month-day
Byte 2: ASCII code of the currency symbol
Byte 3: 0
Byte 4: ASCII code of the thousand character (comma/period)
Byte 5: 0
Byte 6: ASCII code of decimal character (period/comma)
Byte 7: 0
Bytes 8–31: reserved

The contents of the processor registers and the flag registers are not affected by this function.

Interrupt 21H, function 38H, sub-function 0 **DOS**
Get country **(Version 3 and up)**

Gets the country-specific parameters that are currently set.

Input: AH = 38H
DS = Buffer segment address
DX = Buffer offset address
AL = 0: read current country parameters
AL = 1–254: Country code parameters to be read
AL = 255: Country code parameters to be read placed in the BX register

Output: Carry flag=0: O.K.
Carry flag=1: Invalid country code

Remarks: Before the function call, function 30H should be used to determine the DOS version. This can help the programmer compensate for differences between DOS versions during the call and return of this function.

The buffer must have at least 32 bytes allocated for recording the various country specific parameters.

Following the function call, the individual bytes of this buffer contain the following information:

Bytes 0–1: Date format
- 0 = USA: Month-day-year
- 1 = Europe: Day-month-year
- 2 = Japan: Year-month-day

Bytes 2–6: Currency indicator (string terminated by an end character)
Byte 7: ASCII code of the thousand character (comma/period)
Byte 8: 0
Byte 9: ASCII code of decimal character (period/comma)
Byte 10: 0
Byte 11: ASCII code of the date separation character
Byte 12: 0
Byte 13: ASCII code of the time separation character
Byte 14: 0
Byte 15: Currency format
- bit 0 = 0: Currency symbol before the value
- bit 0 = 1: Currency symbol after the value
- bit 1 = 0: No spaces between value and currency symbol
- bit 1 = 1: Space between value and currency symbol

Byte 16: Precision (number of decimal places)
Byte 17: Time format
- bit 0 = 0: 12-hour clock
- bit 0 = 1: 24-hour clock

Bytes 18-21: Address of character conversion routine (see below)
Bytes 22-33: reserved

Addresses 18 to 21 are the offset and segment addresses of a FAR procedure, which is used for accessing the country specific characters from the character set of the PC. The routine views the AL register's contents as the ASCII code of a lower case letter that should be converted to a capital letter. If a capital letter exists, it is retained in the AL register after the call. If the letter doesn't exist, the contents of the AL register remain unchanged. For example, the routine could be used to convert a lower case "a" into a capital "A".

The contents of the AH, BX, CX, DX, SI, DI, BP, CS, DS, SS, ES and the flag registers are not affected by this function.

Interrupt 21H, function 38H, sub-function 1 — DOS
Set country — (Version 3 and up)

Sets the current country-specific parameters. These parameters can be read using function 38H, sub-function 0. Previous versions of DOS required country-specific settings fromthe CONFIG.SYS file using the COUNTRY command. This function allows the user to set and change these parameters after booting.

Input:
AH = 38H
DX = 65535
AL = 1–254: Number of the country
AL > 254: Look in BX for country number
BX = Number of the country (if AL > 254)

Output:
Carry flag=0: O.K.
Carry flag=1: Invalid country code

Remarks:
Before the function call, function 30H should be used to determine that this command exists.

This function only allows setting of the country code, for which DOS has preset parameters. These parameters cannot be changed from this function.

The contents of the AH, BX, CX, DX, SI, DI, BP, CS, DS, SS and ES registers are not affected by this function.

Interrupt 21H, function 39H — DOS
Create subdirectory — (Version 2 and up)

Creates a new subdirectory on the specified device.

Input:
AH = 39H
DS = Subdirectory path segment address
DX = Subdirectory path offset address

Output:
Carry flag=0: Subdirectory created
Carry flag=1: Error (AX = error code)
AX=3: Path not found
AX=5: Access denied

Remarks:
The subdirectory path passed is an ASCII string which is terminated by an end character (ASCII code 0).

If the subdirectory path contains a drive specifier, the indicated device is accessed. Otherwise DOS creates the subdirectory on the current device.

An error can occur if any element of the path designation doesn't exist, a subdirectory already exists by that name, or the directory to be made is a subdirectory of the root directory and it is already filled.

The contents of the BX, CX, DX, SI, DI, BP, CS, DS, SS and ES registers are not affected by this function.

Interrupt 21H, function 3AH — Delete subdirectory
DOS (Version 2 and up)

Deletes a subdirectory from the specified drive.

Input:
AH = 3AH
DS = Subdirectory path segment address
DX = Subdirectory path offset address

Output:
Carry flag=0: Subdirectory deleted
Carry flag=1: Error (AX = error code)
AX=3: Path not found
AX=5: Access denied
AX=6: Directory to be deleted is the current directory

Remarks:
The subdirectory path passed is an ASCII string which is terminated by an end character (ASCII code 0).

If the subdirectory path contains a drive specifier, the indicated device is accessed. Otherwise DOS deletes the subdirectory from the current device.

An error can occur if any element of the path designation doesn't exist, the subdirectory is the current directory, or the directory to be deleted still contains files.

The contents of the BX, CX, DX, SI, DI, BP, CS, DS, SS and ES registers are not affected by this function.

Interrupt 21H, function 3BH — Set current directory
DOS (Version 2 and up)

Sets the current subdirectory for the device indicated.

Input:
AH = 3BH
DS = Subdirectory path segment address
DX = Subdirectory path offset address

Output:
Carry flag=0: Subdirectory set
Carry flag=1: Error (AX = error code)
AX=3: Path not found

Remarks:
The subdirectory path passed is an ASCII string which is terminated by an end character (ASCII code 0).

If the subdirectory path contains a drive specifier, the indicated device is accessed. Otherwise DOS deletes the subdirectory from the current device.

An error can occur if any element of the path designation doesn't exist.

The contents of the BX, CX, DX, SI, DI, BP, CS, DS, SS and ES registers are not affected by this function.

Interrupt 21H, function 3CH **DOS**
Create or truncate file (handle) **(Version 2 and up)**

Creates a new file, or dumps the contents of an existing file (file size=0 bytes). This function call allows other functions to read or write to the open file.

Input:
AH = 3CH
CX = File attribute
Bit 0 = 1: File is read only
Bit 1 = 1: Hidden file
Bit 2 = 1: System file
DS = Filename segment address
DX = Filename offset address

Output:
Carry flag=0: O.K. (AX = file handle)
Carry flag=1: Error (AX = error code)
AX=3: Path not found
AX=4: No available handle
AX=5: Access denied

Remarks:
The various bits of the file attribute can be combined with each other.

The filename must be available as an ASCII string terminated by an end character (ASCII code 0). The filename parameter can contain a driver specifier, path, filename and extension. No wildcards are allowed. If you omit the drive specifier or path, DOS accesses the current drive or current directory.

An error can occur if any element of the path designation doesn't exist, if the file must be created in the root directory which is already full, or if a file with the same name already exists but cannot be cleared because it is write protected (bit 0 in the file attribute byte = 1).

If the function call executed successfully, all other handle functions can be called with this handle once the file opens.

The file pointer is set to the first byte of the file.

The contents of the BX, CX, DX, SI, DI, BP, CS, DS, SS and ES registers are not affected by this function.

Interrupt 21H, function 3DH **DOS**
Open file (handle) **(Version 2 and up)**

Opens an existing file for access by other functions.

Input:
AH = 3DH
AL = Access mode
Bits 0–2: Read/write access
000(b) = File is read only
001(b) = File can only be written
010(b) = File can be read and written
Bit 3: 0(b)
Bits 4–6: File sharing mode
000(b) = Only current program can access the file (FCB mode)
001(b) = Only the current program can access the file
010(b) = Another program can read but not write the file
011(b) = Another program can write but not read the file
100(b) = Another program can read and write the file
Bit 7: Handle flag
0 = Child program of the current program can access file handle
1 = Current program can access file handle only
DS = Filename segment address
DX = Filename offset address

Output:
Carry flag=0: O.K. (AX = file handle)
Carry flag=1: Error (AX = error code)
AX=1:Missing file sharing software
AX=2: File not found
AX=3: Path not found or file doesn't exist
AX=4: No handle available
AX=5: Access denied
AX=12: Access mode not permitted

Remarks:
The filename must be available as an ASCII string terminated by an end character (ASCII code 0). The filename parameter can contain a driver specifier, path, filename and extension. No wildcards are allowed. If you omit the drive specifier or path, DOS accesses the current drive or current directory.

If the function call executes successfully, all other handle functions can be called with this handle once the file opens.

The file pointer is set to the first byte of the file.

DOS Version 2 uses only bits 0 to 2 of the access mode. All other bits, even under Version 3, should be 0 to ensure proper execution of the call.

DOS Version 3 uses the file sharing mode in bits 4 to 6 of the access mode only if the file is on a mass storage device which is part of a network. These three bits decide if and how the file, while it is open using the current call, may be accessed by other programs from other PCs on the network.

Error 12 can occur only under DOS Version 3 and only within a network when the file is already opened by another program and if no other program can gain access to that file.

The contents of the BX, CX, DX, SI, DI, BP, CS, DS, SS and ES registers are not affected by this function.

Interrupt 21H, function 3EH **DOS**
Close file (handle) **(Version 2 and up)**

Writes any data in the DOS buffers to a currently open file, then closes the file. If changes occur to the file, the new file size and the last date and time of modification are added to the directory.

Input: AH = 3EH
BX = Handle to be closed

Output: Carry flag=0: O.K.
Carry flag=1: Error (AX = error code)
AX=6: Unauthorized handle or file not opened

Remarks: Do not accidentally call this function with the numbers of the previous handle (the numbers 0 to 4) because the standard input device or standard output device may close. This would leave you unable to enter characters from the keyboard or display characters on the screen.

The contents of the BX, CX, DX, SI, DI, BP, CS, DS, SS and ES registers are not affected by this function.

Interrupt 21H, function 3FH **DOS**
Read file or device (handle) **(Version 2 and up)**

Reads a certain number of characters by using a handle from a previously opened file or device and passes the characters to a buffer. The read operation starts at the current file pointer position.

Input: AH = 3FH
BX = File or device handle
CX = Number of bytes to be read
DS = Buffer segment address
DX = Buffer offset address

Output: Carry flag=0: O.K. (AX = number of bytes read)
Carry flag=1: Error (AX = error code)
AX=5: Access denied
AX=6: Illegal handle or file not open

Remarks: Characters can be read from a file or from a device (e.g., the standard input device [keyboard], which has the handle 0).

When the carry flag resets after the function call but the AX register has the value 0, this means that the file pointer has already reached the end of the file before the function call. So, no files could be read.

When the carry flag resets after the function call but the contents of the AX register are smaller than the contents of the CX register before the function call, this means that the desired number of bytes wasn't read because the end of the file was reached.

After the function call, the file pointer follows the last byte read.

The contents of the BX, CX, DX, SI, DI, BP, CS, DS, SS and ES registers are not affected by this function.

Interrupt 21H, function 40H **DOS**
Write to file or device (handle) **(Version 2 and up)**

Writes a certain number of characters from a buffer to an open file or device by using a handle. The write operation begins at the file pointer's current position.

Input:
AH = 40H
BX = File or device handle
CX = Number of bytes to be written
DS = Buffer segment address
DX = Buffer offset address

Output:
Carry flag=0: O.K. (AX = number of bytes written)
Carry flag=1: Error (AX = error code)
AX=5: Access denied
AX=6: Illegal handle or file not open

Remarks: Characters can be written to a file or to a device (e.g., the standard output device [screen], which has the handle 1).

When the carry flag resets after the function call but the AX register has the value 0, this means that the file pointer has already reached the end of the file before the function call. Therefore no files could be written.

When the carry flag resets after the function call but the contents of the AX register are smaller than the contents of the CX register before the function call, this means that the desired number of bytes were not written because the end of file was reached.

After the function call, the file pointer follows the last byte written.

The contents of the BX, CX, DX, SI, DI, BP, CS, DS, SS and ES registers are not affected by this function.

Interrupt 21H, function 41H **DOS**
Delete file (handle) **(Version 2 and up)**

Deletes the filename passed to the function. Through the call of this function, a file is erased and its name is passed to the function.

Input:
AH = 41H
DS = Filename segment address
DX = Filename offset address

Output:
Carry flag=0: O.K.
Carry flag=1: Error (AX = error code)
AX=2: File not found
AX=5: Access denied

Remarks:
The filename must be available as an ASCII string terminated by an end character (ASCII code 0). The filename parameter can contain a drive specifier, path, filename and extension. No wildcards are allowed. If you omit the drive specifier or path, DOS accesses the current drive or current directory.

An error occurs when any element of the path designation doesn't exist or when the file has the attribute Read Only and therefore can not be written to or deleted. This attribute can be changed by using function 43H.

You cannot delete subdirectories or volume names with this function.

The contents of the BX, CX, DX, SI, DI, BP, CS, DS, SS and ES registers are not affected by this function.

Interrupt 21H, function 42H **DOS**
Move file pointer (handle) **(Version 2 and up)**

Moves the file pointer of a previously opened file by using its handle. This allows random access because the individual records don't have to be read in sequence. The new file pointer position is given as an offset from the current position, either from the beginning of the file or from the end of the file. The offset itself is indicated as a 32-bit number.

Input:
AH = 42H
AL = Offset code
AL=0: Offset is relative to the beginning of the file
AL=1: Offset is relative to the current position of the file pointer
AL=2: Offset is relative to the end of the file
BX = Handle
CX = High word of the offset

DX = Low word of the offset

Output: Carry flag=0: O.K.
DX = High word of the file pointer
AX = Low word of the file pointer
Carry flag=1: Error (AX = error code)
AX=1: Illegal offset code
AX=6: Illegal handle or File not open

Remarks: If offset codes 1 and 2 are accessed, negative offsets may be used to move the file pointer backwards or to place the pointer at the beginning of the file. It's possible to set the file pointer before the end of the file, which causes an error during the next read or write access to the file.

The position of the file pointer passed after the function call is always relative to the beginning of the file. The offset code used during the function call is independent of this file pointer position.

Passing offset code 2 and offset 0 returns the size of the file. This action moves the file pointer to the last byte of the file and the pointer's position returns to the calling program after the function call.

The contents of the BX, CX, , SI, DI, BP, CS, DS, SS and ES registers are not affected by this function.

Interrupt 21H, function 43H, sub-function 0 **DOS**
Get file attributes **(Version 2 and up)**

Determines file attributes.

Input: AH = 43H
AL = 0
DS = Filename segment address
DX = Filename offset address

Output: Carry flag = 0: O.K. (CX = file attribute)
Bit 0=1: File can be read but not written
Bit 1=1: File hidden (not displayed on DIR)
Bit 2=1: File is a system file
Bit 3=1: File is the volume name
Bit 4=1: File is a subdirectory
Bit 5=1: File was changed since the last date/time
Carry flag = 1: Error (AX = error code)
AX=1: Unknown function code
AX=2: File not found
AX=3: Path not found

Remarks: The filename must be available as an ASCII string terminated by an end character (ASCII code 0). The filename parameter can contain a driver specifier, path, filename and extension. No wildcards are allowed. If you omit the drive specifier or path, DOS accesses the current drive or current directory.

An error occurs when any element of the path designation or the file does not exist.

The contents of the BX, CX, , SI, DI, BP, CS, DS, SS and ES registers are not affected by this function.

Interrupt 21H, function 43H, sub-function 1 **DOS**
Set file attributes **(Version 2 and up)**

Sets the file attributes.

Input:

AH = 43H
AL = 1
CX = File attributes
Bit 0 = 1: File can be read but not written
Bit 1 = 1: File hidden (not displayed on DIR)
Bit 2 = 1: File is a system file
Bit 3 = 0
Bit 4 = 0
Bit 5 = 1: File was changed since the last date/time
DS = Filename segment address
DX = Filename offset address

Output:

Carry flag=0: O.K.
Carry flag=1: Error (AX = error code)
AX=1: Unknown function code
AX=2: File not found
AX=3: Path not found
AX=5: Attribute cannot be changed

Remarks:

The filename must be available as an ASCII string terminated by an end character (ASCII code 0). The filename parameter can contain a driver specifier, path, filename and extension. No wildcards are allowed. If you omit the drive specifier or path, DOS accesses the current drive or current directory.

An error occurs when any element of the path designation or the file does not exist.

Neither subdirectories nor volume names can be accessed with this function. For this reason bits 3 and 4 of the file attribute must be 0 during the function call. If you attempt to access a subdirectory or a volume name anyway, the function returns error code 5.

The contents of the BX, CX, DX, SI, DI, BP, CS, DS, SS and ES registers are not affected by this function.

Interrupt 21H, function 44H, sub-function 0 — DOS
IOCTL: Get device information — (Version 2 and up)

Permits access of a character driver's device attribute.

Input:
AH = 44H
AL = 0
BX = Handle

Output:
Carry flag=0: O.K. (DX = device attribute)
Bit 14 = 1: Processes control characters through IOCTL
Bit 7 = 1: Character driver
Bit 5 = 0: Cooked mode operation
1: Raw mode operation
Bit 3 = 1: Clock driver operation
Bit 2 = 1: NUL driver operation
Bit 1 = 1: Console output driver (screen)
Bit 0 = 1: Console input driver (keyboard)
Carry flag=1: Error (AX = error code)
AX=1: Unknown function code
AX=6: Handle not opened or does not exist

Remarks:
A handle is passed (not the name of the addressed character driver which must be connected with this driver). This can be one of the five pre-assigned handles (0 to 4). A handle could have been previously opened for a certain device with the help of the Open function (function 3DH), and then passed to the function. For example, since the standard input and output devices (handles 0 and 1) can be redirected, this method assures that the indicated device is accessed.

If bit 7 in the device attribute is unequal to 1, the driver addressed is not a character driver and the significance of the individual bits in the device attribute disagrees with those of the device driver.

The contents of the BX, CX, DX, SI, DI, BP, CS, DS, SS and ES registers are not affected by this function.

Interrupt 21H, function 44H, sub-function 1 — DOS
IOCTL: Set device information — (Version 2 and up)

Sets the character device attributes.

Input:
AH = 44H
AL = 1
BX = Handle
CX = Number of bytes written
DX = Device attributes
Bit 14 = 1: Processes control characters through IOCTL using sub-functions 2 and 3
Bit 7 = 1: Character driver

Bit 5 = 0: Cooked mode operation
Bit 5 = 1: Raw mode operation
Bit 3 = 1: Clock driver operation
Bit 2 = 1: NUL driver operation
Bit 1 = 1: Console output driver (screen)
Bit 0 = 1: Console input driver (keyboard)

Output: Carry flag=0: O.K.
Carry flag=1: Error (AX = Error code)
AX=1: Unknown function code
AX=6: handle not opened or handle does not exist

Remarks: A handle is passed but it is not the name of the addressed character device, which must be connected with this device. This can be one of the five pre-assigned handles (0 to 4). A handle could have previously been opened, with the Open function, for a certain device and then passed to the function. For example, since the standard input and output devices (handles 0 and 1) can be redirected, this method assures that the indicated device is accessed.

To change various device attribute bits with this function, use sub-function 0 to read the device attributes first. Then this sub-function can reset the device attribute bits in the device driver.

If bit 7 in the device attribute is unequal to 1, the driver addressed is not a character driver. The meanings of the individual bits in the device attribute disagree with those in the device driver.

This function is especially useful for switching between cooked mode and raw mode within a character driver (bit 5).

The contents of the BX, CX, DX, SI, DI, BP, CS, DS, SS and ES registers are not affected by this function.

Interrupt 21H, function 44H, sub-function 2 **DOS**
IOCTL: Read data from character device **(Version 2 and up)**

Reads data from a character device. This function defines the number of bytes of data to read from the buffer, which contains the data taken from the character device.

Input: AH = 44H
AL = 2
BX = Handle
CX = Number of bytes to be read
DS = Buffer segment address
DX = Buffer offset address

Output: Carry flag=0: O.K. (AX = Number of bytes sent)
Carry flag=1: Error (AX = Error code)
AX=1: Unknown function code
AX=6: Handle not opened or does not exist

Remarks: A handle is passed, but it is not the name of the addressed character device which must be connected with this device. This can be one of the five pre-assigned handles (0 to 4). A handle could have previously been opened with the Open function (function number 3DH) for a certain device, then passed to the function. For example, since the standard input and output devices (handles 0 and 1) can be redirected, this method assures that the indicated device is accessed.

An error always occurs if the handle passed is connected with a block driver instead of a character driver.

The driver defines the data type and structure.

The contents of the BX, CX, DX, SI, DI, BP, CS, DS, SS and ES registers are not affected by this function.

Interrupt 21H, function 44H, sub-function 3 **DOS**
IOCTL: Send data to character device **(Version 2 and up)**

Sends data from an application program directly to a character device. The calling function defines the number of bytes to be transferred from a buffer to the device.

Input: AH = 44H
AL = 3
BX = Handle
CX = Number of bytes to be transmitted
DS = Buffer segment address
DX = Buffer offset address

Output: Carry flag=0: O.K.
AX = Number of bytes sent
Carry flag=1: Error (AX = Error code)
AX=1: Unknown function code
AX=6: Handle not opened or does not exist

Remarks: A handle is passed, but it is not the name of the addressed character device which must be connected with this device. This can be one of the five pre-assigned handles (0 to 4). A handle could have previously been opened with the Open function (function number 61) for a certain device, then passed to the function. For example, since the standard input and output devices (handles 0 and 1) can be redirected, this method assures that the indicated device is accessed.

An error always occurs if the handle passed is connected with a block driver instead of a character driver.

The driver defines the data type and structure.

The contents of the BX, CX, DX, SI, DI, BP, CS, DS, SS and ES registers are not affected by this function.

Interrupt 21H, function 44H, sub-function 4 **DOS**
IOCTL: Read data from block device **(Version 2 and up)**

Reads data for an application directly from a block device. The calling function defines the number of bytes to be copied by the device into a buffer.

Input:
AH = 44H
AL = 4
BX = Device designation
CX = Number of bytes to be read
DS = Buffer segment address
DX = Buffer offset address

Output:
Carry flag=0: O.K.
AX = Number of bytes sent
Carry flag=1: Error (AX = Error code)
AX=1: Unknown function code
AX=15: Unknown device

Remarks: Instead of defining the device driver, the device designation parameter defines the device from which data will be received. Code 0 represents device A:, 1 represents device B:, etc.

The driver defines the data type and structure.

The contents of the BX, CX, DX, SI, DI, BP, CS, DS, SS and ES registers are not affected by this function.

Interrupt 21H, function 44H, sub-function 5 **DOS**
IOCTL: Send data to block device **(Version 2 and up)**

Sends data from an application program directly to a character device. The calling function defines the number of bytes to be transferred from a buffer to the device.

Input:
AH = 44H
AL = 5
BX = Device designation
CX = Number of bytes to be sent
DS = Buffer segment address
DX = Buffer offset address

Output:
Carry flag=0: O.K.
AX = Number of bytes sent
Carry flag=1: Error (AX = Error code)
AX=1: Unknown function code

AX=15: Unknown device

Remarks: Instead of defining the device driver, the device designation parameter defines the device from which data will be received. Code 0 represents device A:, 1 represents device B:, etc.

The driver defines the data type and structure.

The contents of the BX, CX, DX, SI, DI, BP, CS, DS, SS and ES registers are not affected by this function.

Interrupt 21H, function 44H, sub-function 6 — DOS
IOCTL: Read input status — (Version 2 and up)

Determines whether a device driver can transmit data to an application program.

Input:
AH = 44H
AL = 6
BX = Handle

Output:
Carry flag=0: O.K. (AX = Input status)
  AX=0: Driver not ready
  AX=255: Driver ready
Carry flag=1: Error (AX = Error code)
  AX=1: Unknown function code
  AX=5: Access denied

Remarks: The handle passed can refer to either a character driver or a file.

The contents of the BX, CX, DX, SI, DI, BP, CS, DS, SS and ES registers are not affected by this function.

Interrupt 21H, function 44H, sub-function 7 — DOS
IOCTL: Read output status — (Version 2 and up)

Determines whether a device driver can receive data from an application program.

Input:
AH = 44H
AL = 7
BX = Handle

Output:
Carry flag=0: O.K. (AX = Output status)
  AX=0: Driver is not ready
  AX=255: Driver is ready
Carry flag=1: Error (AX = Error code)
  AX=1: Invalid function number
  AX=5: Access denied

Remarks: The handle passed can refer to either a character driver or a file.

If the handle refers to a file, the block device driver signals its readiness to receive data, even if the medium containing the file is full and no additional data can be appended to the end of the file.

The contents of the BX, CX, DX, SI, DI, BP, CS, DS, SS and ES registers are not affected by this function.

Interrupt 21H, function 44H, sub-function 8 — DOS
IOCTL: Test for changeable block device — (Version 3 and up)

Determines whether the block device medium (e.g., disk, hard disk, etc.) can be changed.

Input:
AH = 44H
AL = 8
BL = Device designation

Output:
Carry flag=0: O.K. (AX=status code)
  AX = 0: Medium changeable
  AX = 1: Medium unchangeable
Carry flag=1: Error (AX = Error code)
  AX=1: Invalid function number
  AX=15: Invalid drive number

Remarks: The device designation parameter defines the device being addressed instead of the device driver. Code 0 represents device A:, 1 represents device B:, etc.

The contents of the BX, CX, DX, SI, DI, BP, CS, DS, SS and ES registers are not affected by this function.

Interrupt 21H, function 44H, sub-function 9 — DOS
IOCTL: Test for local or remote drive — (Version 3.1 and up)

Determines whether a drive (block device) is local (part of the PC making the inquiry) or remote (part of another PC in a network).

Input:
AH = 44H
AL = 9
BL = Device designation

Output:
Carry flag=0: O.K.
DX = device attribute
Bit 12 = 0: Local
Bit 12 = 1: Remote
Carry flag=1: Error (AX = Error code)
  AX=1: Invalid function number
  AX=15: Invalid drive specification

Remarks: You can access this sub-function only if networking software has previously been installed.

The contents of the BX, CX, DX, SI, DI, BP, CS, DS, SS and ES registers are not affected by this function.

Interrupt 21H, function 44H, sub-function 0AH **DOS**
IOCTL: Test for local or remote handle **(Version 3.1 and up)**

Determines whether a file associated with this handle is local (part of the PC making the inquiry) or remote (part of another PC in a network).

Input:
AH = 44H
AL = 0AH
BX = Handle

Output:
DX = IOCTL code
Bit 15 = 0: Local
Bit 15 = 1: Remote
Carry flag=1: Error (AX = Error code)
AX=1: Invalid function number
AX=6: Handle not opened or does not exist

Remarks: You can access this sub-function only if networking software has previously been installed.

The contents of the BX, CX, DX, SI, DI, BP, CS, DS, SS and ES registers are not affected by this function.

Interrupt 21H, function 44H, sub-function 0BH **DOS**
IOCTL: Change retry count **(Version 3 and up)**

Sets the variables that specify the number of attempts at file access. One PC within a network may try to access a file that is already being accessed by another PC. The PC attempting access repeats the file access procedure the number of times and the number of waiting periods defined by these variables.

Input:
AH = 44H
AL = 0BH
BX = Number of attempts
CX = Waiting time between attempts

Output:
Carry flag=0: O.K.
Carry flag=1: Error (AX = Error code)
AX=1: Invalid function number

Remarks: You can only access this sub-function if networking software has previously been installed.

The contents of the BX, CX, DX, SI, DI, BP, CS, DS, SS and ES registers are not affected by this function.

Interrupt 21H, function 45H **DOS**
Duplicate handle **(Version 2 and up)**

Creates a duplicate of the handle passed. This duplicate handle interfaces with the same file or device as the first handle. If the first handle refers to a file, the value of the first handler's file pointer joins with the file pointer of the duplicate handle.

Input:
AH = 45H
BX = Handle

Output:
Carry flag=0: O.K. (AX = the new handle
Carry flag=1: Error (AX = Error code)
AX=4: No additional handle available
AX=6: Handle not opened or does not exist

Remarks:
Without having to close the file, this function updates a file directory entry after its modification. A file can be closed using function 62 (3EH).

If the file pointer of one of the two handles changes position due to the call of a read or write function, the other file pointer also changes automatically.

The contents of the BX, CX, DX, SI, DI, BP, CS, DS, SS and ES registers are not affected by this function.

Interrupt 21H, function 46H **DOS**
Force duplicate of handle **(Version 2 and up)**

Refers a second file handle to the save device or file as the first file handle. The second handle's file pointer also contains the same value as the first handle's file pointer.

Input:
AH = 46H
BX = First handle
CX = Second handle

Output:
Carry flag=0: O.K.
Carry flag=1: Error (AX = Error code)
AX=4: No additional handle available
AX=6: Handle not opened or does not exist

Remarks:
If the function call connects the second handle to an open file, the file closes before the forced duplication.

If the file pointer of one of the handles changes position due to the call of a read or write function, the other file pointer also changes automatically.

The contents of the BX, CX, DX, SI, DI, BP, CS, DS, SS and ES registers are not affected by this function.

Interrupt 21H, function 47H **DOS**
Get current directory **(Version 2 and up)**

Gets an ASCII string listing the complete path designation of the current directory of the indicated device. This string passes to the specified buffer.

Input:
AH = 47H
DL = Device designation
DS = Buffer segment address
SI = Buffer offset address

Output:
Carry flag=0: O.K.
Carry flag=1: Error (AX=Error code)
AX=15: Invalid drive specification

Remarks:
The device designation parameter defines the device being addressed instead of the device driver. Code 0 represents the current device, 1 represents device A:, etc.

The path description in the buffer terminates with an end character (ASCII code 0). This description has no drive specifier or \ character (root directory specifier). If the root directory is the current directory, the end character becomes the first character in the buffer.

The contents of the BX, CX, DX, SI, DI, BP, CS, DS, SS and ES registers are not affected by this function.

Interrupt 21H, function 48H **DOS**
Allocate memory **(Version 2 and up)**

Reserves an area of memory for program use.

Input:
AH = 48H
BX = Number of paragraphs to be reserved

Output:
Carry flag=0: O.K.
AX=Memory area segment address)
Carry flag=1: Error (AX = Error code)
AX=7: Memory control block destroyed
AX=8: Insufficient memory
BX = Number of paragraphs available

Remarks:
A paragraph consists of 16 bytes.

If memory allocation was successfully executed, the allocated range begins at address AX:0000.

This function always fails when executed from within a COM program because the PC assigns the total amount of free memory to a COM program when it executes.

The contents of the CX, DX, SI, DI, BP, CS, DS, SS and ES registers are not affected by this function.

Interrupt 21H, function 49H — DOS
Release memory — (Version 2 and up)

Releases memory previously allocated by function 72 (49H—see above) for any purpose.

Input:
AH = 49H
ES = Memory area segment address

Output:
Carry flag=0: O.K.
Carry flag=1: Error (AX = Error code)
AX=7: Memory control block destroyed
AX=9: Incorrect memory area passed in ES

Remarks:
Since DOS knows the size of the memory area to be released, no parameter exists for passing memory size.

If the wrong segment address appears in the ES register during the function call, memory assigned to another program can be released. This can lead to a system crash or other consequences.

The contents of the BX, CX, DX, SI, DI, BP, CS, DS, SS and ES registers are not affected by this function.

Interrupt 21H, function 4AH — DOS
Modify memory allocation — (Version 2 and up)

Changes the size of a memory area previously reserved using function 72 (3FH—see above).

Input:
AH = 4AH
BX = New memory area size in paragraphs
ES = Memory area segment address

Output:
Carry flag=0: O.K.
Carry flag=1: Error (AX = Error code)
AX=7: Memory control block destroyed
AX=8: Insufficient memory
BX = Number of paragraphs available

Remarks: A paragraph has 16 bytes.

If the wrong segment address appears in the ES register during the function call, memory assigned to another program can be released. This can lead to a system crash or other consequences.

Since the PC assigns the total amount of free memory to a COM program when it executes, this function call always fails when executed from within a COM program.

COM programs should use this function to release all unnecessary memory since all RAM becomes part of a COM program. This is especially important before calling the EXEC function (function number 75 (4BH).

The contents of the CX, DX, SI, DI, BP, CS, DS, SS and ES registers are not affected by this function.

Interrupt 21H, function 4BH, sub-function 0 — DOS
Execute program — (Version 2 and up)

Executes another program from within a program and continues execution of the original program after the called program finishes its run. The function requires the name of the program to be executed and the address of a parameter block, which contains information that is important to the function.

Input:
AH = 4BH
AL = 0
ES = Parameter block segment address
BX = Parameter block offset address
DS = Program name segment address
DX = Program name offset address

Output:
Carry flag=0: O.K.
Carry flag=1: Error (AX = Error code)
 AX=1: Invalid function number
 AX=2: Path or program not found
 AX=5: Access denied
 AX=8: Insufficient memory
 AX=10: Wrong environment block
 AX=11: Incorrect format

Remarks: The directory name passed is an ASCII string which is terminated by an end character (ASCII code 0). It can contain a path designation and drive specifier. No wildcards are allowed. If no drive specifier or path designation exists, the function accesses the current drive or directory.

Only EXE or COM programs can be executed. To execute a batch file, the command processor (COMMAND.COM) must be called using the /c parameter followed by the name of the batch file.

The parameter block must have the following format:

Bytes 0–1: Environment block segment address
Bytes 2–3: Command parameter offset address
Bytes 4–5: Command parameter segment address
Bytes 6–7: First FCB offset address
Bytes 8–9: First FCB segment address
Bytes 10–11: Second FCB offset address
Bytes 12–13: Second FCB segment address

If the segment address of the environment block is a 0, the called program has the same environment block as the calling program.

The command parameters must be stored so that the parameter string begins with a byte representing the number of characters in the command line. Next follow the individual ASCII characters, which are terminated by a carriage return (ASCII code 13) (this carriage return is not counted as a character).

The first FCB passed is copied to the PSP of the called program starting at address 5CH. The second FCB passed is copied to the PSP of the called program starting at address 6CH. If the called program does not obtain information from the two FCBs, any desired value can be entered into the FCB fields at the parameter block.

After the call of this function, all registers are destroyed except the CS and IP registers. For later recall, save their contents before the function call.

The program called should have all the handles available to the calling program.

Interrupt 21H, function 4BH, sub-function 3 **DOS**
Execute overlay **(Version 2 and up)**

Loads a second program into memory as an overlay without automatically executing the second program.

Input:
AH = 4BH
AL = 3
ES = Parameter block segment address
BX = Parameter block offset address
DS = Program name segment address
DX = Program name offset address

Output:
Carry flag=0: O.K.
Carry flag=1: Error (AX = Error code)
AX=1: Invalid function number
AX=2: Path or program not found
AX=5: Access denied
AX=8: Insufficient memory

AX=10: Wrong environment block
AX=11: Incorrect format

Remarks: The directory name passed is an ASCII string which is terminated by an end character (ASCII code 0). It can contain a path designation and drive specifier. No wildcards are allowed. If no drive specifier or path designation exists, the function accesses the current drive or directory.

Only EXE or COM programs can be executed. To execute a batch file, the command processor (COMMAND.COM) must be called using the /c parameter followed by the name of the batch file.

The parameter block must have the following format:

Byte 0–1:	Segment address where the overlay will be stored (offset address=0)
Byte 2–3:	Relocation factor

The relocation factor requires the value 0 for COM programs. Use the segment address at which the program should load when accessing EXE programs.

The contents of the BX, CX, DX, SI, DI, BP, CS, DS, SS and ES registers are not affected by this function.

Interrupt 21H, function 4CH — DOS
Terminate with return code — (Version 2 and up)

Terminates a program and passes an end code for which function 77 (4DH-see below) searches. This function releases the memory previously occupied by the terminated program.

Input: AH = 4CH
AL = Return code

Output: No output

Remarks: This function may be used for program termination instead of the other functions listed earlier.

This function call restores the contents of the three interrupt vectors that were stored in the PSP when the program started execution.

Before passing control to the calling program, all handles opened by this program close, along with the corresponding files. This is not applicable to files accessed using FCBs.

A batch file can test for the return code using the ERRORLEVEL and IF batch commands.

Interrupt 21H, function 4DH — DOS
Get return code — (Version 2 and up)

Checks a program, called from another program by the EXEC function, for the return code passed by the called program when it terminates.

Input: AH = 4DH

Output: AH = Type of program termination
- AH=0: Normal end
- AH=1: End through <Ctrl><C> or <Break>
- AH=2: Device access error
- AH=3: Call of function 49 (31H)

AL = Return code

Remarks: This function reads the return code of the called program only once.

The contents of the AX, BX, CX, DX, SI, DI, BP, CS, DS, SS, ES and flag registers are not affected by this function. The contents of all other registers may change.

Interrupt 21H, function 4EH — DOS
Search for first match — (Version 2 and up)

Searches for the first occurrence of the filename listed. The file can have certain attributes, so a search can be made through subdirectories and volume names.

Input:
AH = 4EH
CX = File attribute
DS = Filename segment address
DX = Filename offset address

Output:
Carry flag=0: O.K.
Carry flag=1: Error (AX = Error code)
- AX=2: Path not found
- AX=18: No file with the attribute found

Remarks: The directory name passed is an ASCII string which is terminated by an end character (ASCII code 0). It can contain a path designation and drive specifier. No wildcards are allowed. If no drive specifier or path designation exists, the function accesses the current drive or directory.

The search defaults to normal files (attribute 0). Any set attribute bits extends the search to normal files and any other file types.

If a matching file occurs, the first 43 bytes of the DTA contain the following information about this file:

Bytes 0–20:	Reserved
Byte 21:	File attribute
Bytes 22–23:	Time of last modification to file

Bytes 24–25: Date of last modification to file
Bytes 26–27: Low word of file size
Bytes 28–29: High word of file size
Bytes 30–42: ASCII filename and extension terminated by an end character (ASCII code 0)

This function may only be called to search for the first occurrence of a file. If you want to search for a group of files using wildcards, function 4FH (see below) must be called.

The contents of the BX, CX, DX, SI, DI, BP, CS, DS, SS and ES registers are not affected by this function.

Interrupt 21H, function 4FH **DOS**
Search for next match (handle) **(Version 2 and up)**

Searches for subsequent occurrences of the filename listed after function 78 (above) executed successfully.

Input: AH = 4FH

Output: Carry flag=0: O.K.
Carry flag=1: Error (AX=Error code)
AX=18: No other files found with this attribute

Remarks: If a matching file occurs, the first 43 bytes of the DTA contain the following information about this file:

Bytes 0–20: Reserved
Byte 21: File attribute
Bytes 22–23: Time of last modification to file
Bytes 24–25: Date of last modification to file
Bytes 26–27: Low word of file size
Bytes 28–29: High word of file size
Bytes 30–42: ASCII filename and extension terminated by an end character (ASCII code 0)

This function can only be called if function 4EH has been called once and if the DTA remains unchanged.

The contents of the BX, CX, DX, SI, DI, BP, CS, DS, SS and ES registers are not affected by this function.

Interrupt 21H, function 54H **DOS**
Get verify flag **(Version 2 and up)**

Gets the current status of the verify flag. This flag determines whether or not data transmitted to a medium (floppy disk or hard disk) should be verified after the transmission.

Input: AH = 54H

Output: AL = Verify flag
AL=0: Verify off
AL=1: Verify on

Remarks: Function 2EH (see above) controls the status of the verify flag.

The contents of the AH, BX, CX, DX, SI, DI, BP, CS, DS, SS, ES and flag registers are not affected by this function.

Interrupt 21H, function 56H **DOS**
Rename file (handle) **(Version 2 and up)**

Renames a file or moves the file to another directory of a block device. Moving is possible only within the different directories of one particular device (i.e., you can't move a file from a hard disk directory to a floppy disk directory).

Input: AH = 56H
DS = Old filename segment address
DX = Old filename offset address
ES = New filename segment address
DI = New filename offset address

Output: Carry flag=0: O.K.
Carry flag=1: Error (AX = Error code)
AX=2: File not found
AX=3: Path not found
AX=5: Access denied
AX=11: Not the same device

Remarks: The directory name passed is an ASCII string which is terminated by an end character (ASCII code 0). It can contain a path designation and drive specifier. No wildcards are allowed. If no drive specifier or path designation exists, the function accesses the current drive or directory.

An error occurs if you attempt to move the file to a filled root directory.

This function cannot access subdirectories or volume names.

The contents of the BX, CX, DX, SI, DI, BP, CS, DS, SS and ES registers are not affected by this function.

Interrupt 21H, function 57H, sub-function 0 **DOS**
Get file date and time **(Version 2 and up)**

Gets the date and time of the creation or last modification of a file.

Input: AH = 57H
AL = 0
BX = Handle

Output: Carry flag=0: O.K.
CX=Time
DX=Date
Carry flag=1: Error (AX = Error code)
AX=1: Invalid function
AX=6: Invalid handle

Remarks: In order for it to be accessed with a handle, the file must have been previously opened or created using one of the handle functions.

The time appears in the CX register in the following format:

Bits 0–4: Seconds in 2-second increments
Bits 5–10: Minutes
Bits 11–15: Hours

The date appears in the DX register in the following format:

Bits 0–4: Day of the month
Bits 5–8: Month
Bit 9–15: Year (relative to 1980)

The contents of the BX, CX, DX, SI, DI, BP, CS, DS, SS and ES registers are not affected by this function.

Interrupt 21H, function 57H, sub-function 1 **DOS**
Set file date and time **(Version 2 and up)**

Stores the date and time of the creation or last modification of a file in the corresponding file and device.

Input: AH = 57H
AL = 1
BX = Handle
CX = Time
DX = Date

Output: Carry flag=0: O.K.
Carry flag=1: Error (AX = Error code)
AX=1: Invalid function
AX=6: Invalid handle

Remarks: In order to be accessed with a handle, the file must have been previously opened or created using one of the handle functions.

The time appears in the CX register in the following format:

Bits 0–4:	Seconds in 2-second increments
Bits 5–10:	Minutes
Bits 11–15:	Hours

The date appears in the DX register in the following format:

Bits 0–4:	Day of the month
Bits 5–8:	Month
Bit 9–15:	Year (relative to 1980)

The contents of the BX, CX, DX, SI, DI, BP, CS, DS, SS and ES registers are not affected by this function.

Interrupt 21H, function 58H, sub-function 0 **DOS**
Get allocation strategy **(Version 3 and up)**

Determines the method currently in use by MS-DOS for allocating blocks of memory. If a program allocates memory using function 48H, different programs in memory may already have memory blocks assigned to them. Since these requested memory blocks vary in size, DOS has three methods of allocating memory to a program:

- First fit: DOS starts searching at the start of memory and allocates the first memory block it finds of the requested size;
- Best fit: DOS searches all available memory blocks and allocates the smallest suitable memory block it finds (the most efficient method);
- Last fit: DOS starts searching at the end of memory and allocates the first memory block it finds of the requested size.

Input: AH = 58H
AL = 0

Output: Carry flag=0: O.K.
AX=0: First fit (start from beginning of memory)
AX=1: Best fit (search for best-fitting memory block)
AX=2: Last fit (start from end of memory)
Carry flag=1: Error (AX = Error code)
AX=1: Invalid function number

Remarks: The allocation strategy applies to all programs.

The contents of the BX, CX, DX, SI, DI, BP, CS, DS, SS and ES registers are not affected by this function.

Interrupt 21H, function 58H, sub-function 1 — DOS
Set allocation strategy — (Version 3 and up)

Defines the method currently in use by MS-DOS for allocating blocks of memory. If a program allocates memory using function 48H, different programs in memory may already have memory blocks assigned to them. Since these requested memory blocks vary in size, DOS has three methods of allocating memory to a program:

- First fit: DOS starts searching at the start of memory and allocates the first memory block it finds of the requested size;
- Best fit: DOS searches all available memory blocks and allocates the smallest suitable memory block it finds (the most efficient method);
- Last fit: DOS starts searching at the end of memory and allocates the first memory block it finds of the requested size.

Input:

AH = 58H
AL = 1
BX = Allocation strategy
  BX=0: First fit (start from beginning of memory)
  BX=1: Best fit (search for best-fitting memory block)
  BX=2: Last fit (start from end of memory)

Output:

Carry flag=0: O.K.
Carry flag=1: Error (AX = Error code)
  AX=1: Invalid function number

Remarks:

The allocation strategy applies to all programs.

The contents of the BX, CX, DX, SI, DI, BP, CS, DS, SS and ES registers are not affected by this function.

Interrupt 21H, function 59H — DOS
Get extended error information — (Version 3 and up)

Gets information about errors that occur during the call of one of the functions of either interrupt 21H or interrupt 24H. This information includes detailed information about the error, its origin and the action the user should take to alleviate the error.

Input: AH = 59H
BX = 0

Output: AX = Description of error
BH = Cause of error
BL = Recommended action
CH = Source of error

Remarks: The following codes describe the error:

Code	Error
0:	No error
1:	Invalid function number
2:	File not found
3:	Path not found
4:	Too many files open at once
5:	Access denied
6:	Invalid handle
7:	Memory control block destroyed
8:	Insufficient memory
9:	Invalid memory address
10:	Invalid environment
11:	Invalid format
12:	Invalid access code
13:	Invalid data
14:	Reserved
15:	Invalid drive
16:	Current directory cannot be removed
17:	Different device
18:	No additional files
19:	Medium write protected
20:	Unknown device
21:	Device not ready
22:	Unknown command
23:	CRC error
24:	Bad request structure length
25:	Seek error

Code	Error
26:	Unknown medium type
27:	Sector not found
28:	Printer out of paper
29:	Write error
30:	Read error
31:	General failure
32:	Sharing violation
33:	Lock violation
34:	Unauthorized disk change
35:	FCB not available
80:	File already exists
81:	Reserved
82:	Directory cannot be created
83:	Terminate after call of interrupt 24H

The following codes describe the cause of the error:

Code	Error
1:	No memory available on the medium
2:	Temporary access problem–may end soon
3:	Access unauthorized
4:	Internal error in system software
5:	Hardware error
6:	Software failure not caused by running application program
7:	Application program error
8:	File not found
9:	Invalid file format/type
10:	File locked
11:	Wrong medium in drive, bad disk or medium problem
12:	Other error

The following codes describe the action needed to fix the error:

Code	Error
1:	Repeat process several times, then ask user to abort/ignore
2:	Repeat process several times pausing each time, then ask user to abort/ignore
3:	Ask user for correct information (e.g., filename)
4:	Terminate program as completely as possible
5:	Terminate program NOW (no file closing, etc.)
6:	Ignore error
7:	Ask user to remove error source and repeat process

The following codes describe the source of the error:

Code	Error
1:	Unknown
2:	Block device (disk drive, hard disk, etc.)
3:	Network
4:	Serial device
5:	RAM

The contents of the CS, DS, SS and ES registers are not affected by this function. All other register contents are destroyed.

Interrupt 21H, function 5AH **DOS**
Create temporary file (handle) **(Version 3 and up)**

Creates a temporary file in memory for storage during program execution. The filename doesn't matter because the access occurs through the assigned handle. Since this function allows several files open at the same time, DOS creates filenames from the current date and time. Every temporary file is ensured its own particular name because the function cannot be called more than once at a time.

Input:
AH = 5AH
CX = File attribute
DS = Directory segment address
DX = Directory offset address

Output:
Carry flag=0: O.K.
AX=Handle
DS=Complete filename segment address
DX=Complete filename offset address
Carry flag=1: Error (AX = Error code)
AX=3: Path not found
AX=5: Access denied

Remarks: The directory name passed is an ASCII string which is terminated by an end character (ASCII code 0). It can contain a path designation and drive specifier. No wildcards are allowed. If no drive specifier or path designation exists, the function accesses the current drive or directory.

The bits of the file attribute have the following meanings:

Bit 0 = 1: Read only file
Bit 1 = 1: Hidden file
Bit 2 = 1: System file

Temporary files are not automatically deleted after program execution. The file must be closed using function 3EH, then the temporary file must be deleted using function 41H.

The contents of the BX, CX, DX, SI, DI, BP, CS, DS, SS and ES registers are not affected by this function.

Interrupt 21H, function 5BH — **DOS**
Create new file (handle) — **(Version 3 and up)**

Creates a file in the specified directory based upon an ASCII file format. If no drive specifier or path is provided, the file opens in the default (current) directory.

Input:

AH = 5BH
CX = File attributes:
  CX=00: Normal file
  CX=01: Read-only file
  CX=02: Hidden file
  CX=04: System file
DS = ASCII file specification segment address
DX = ASCII file specification offset address

Output:

Carry flag=0 (AX= file handle)
Carry flag=1 (AX = Error code)
  AX=3: Path not found
  AX=4: No handle available
  AX=5: Access denied
  AX=80 (50H): File already exists

Remarks:

An error occurs when any element of the path designation doesn't exist, when the filename already exists in the specified directory, or when an attempt is made to create the file in an already full root directory.

The file defaults to the normal read/write attribute, which allows both read and write operations. This attribute can be changed by using function 43H.

Interrupt 21H, function 5CH — **DOS**
Control record access — **(Version 3 and up)**

Locks or unlocks a particular section of a file. This function operates on multitasking and networking systems.

Input:

AH = 5CH
AL = Function code
  AL=00: Lock file section
  AL=01: Unlock file section
BX = File handle
CX = High word of section offset
DX = Low word of section offset
SI = High word of section length
DI = Low word of section length

Output:
Carry flag=0: Successful lock/unlock
Carry flag=1: Error (AX = Error code)
AX=1: Invalid function code
AX=6: Invalid handle
AX=33 (21H): All or part of section already locked

Remarks:
This function can only be used on files already opened or created using functions 3CH, 3DH, 5AH or 5BH.

The corresponding call to unlock a file region must contain the identical file offset and file region length.

Interrupt 21H, function 5EH, sub-function 0 **DOS**
Get machine name **(Version 3.1 and up)**

Returns the address of an ASCII string which defines the local computer type within a network.

Input:
AH = 5EH
AL = 00
DS = User buffer segment address
DX = User buffer offset address

Output:
Carry flag=0: Successful execution
CH = 00: Name undefined
CH > 00: Name defined
CL = NETBIOS name number (when CH<>00)
DS = Identifier segment address (when CH<>00)
DX = Identifier offset address (when CH<>00)
Carry flag=1: Error (AX = Error code)
AX=1: Invalid function code

Remarks:
The computer type is a 15-byte-long string terminated by an end character (ASCII code 0).

Interrupt 21H, function 5EH, sub-function 2 **DOS**
Set printer setup **(Version 3.1 and up)**

Specifies a string which precedes all output to a particular printer used by a network. This string allows network users to assign their own individual printing parameters to the shared printer.

Input:
AH = 5EH
AL = 02
BX = Redirection list index (see Remarks below)
CX = Printer setup string length
DS = Printer setup string segment address
SI = Printer setup string offset address

Output: Carry flag=0: Successful execution
Carry flag=1: Error (AX = Error code)
AX=1: Invalid function code

Remarks: The contents of register BX (redirection list index) come from function 94 5EH, sub-function 2. Function 5EH, sub-function 3 (see below) can supply the current printer setup string.

Interrupt 21H, function 5EH, sub-function 3 — DOS
Get printer setup — (Version 3.1 and up)

Gets the printer setup string assigned to a particular network printer by using function 5EH, sub-function 2 (see above).

Input:
AH = 5EH
AL = 03
BX = Redirection list index)
DS = Setup string receiving buffer segment address
SI = Setup string receiving buffer offset address

Output: Carry flag=0: Successful execution
CX=Printer setup string length
ES=Segment address of buffer retaining setup string
DI=Offset address of buffer retaining setup string
Carry flag=1: Error (AX = Error code)
AX=1: Invalid function code

Remarks: The contents of register BX (redirection list index) come from function 5EH, sub-function 2. Function 5EH, sub-function 3 can supply the current printer setup string.

Interrupt 21H, function 5FH, sub-function 2 — DOS
Get redirection list entry — (Version 3.1 and up)

Gets the system redirection list. This list assigns local names to network printers, files or directories.

Input:
AH = 5FH
AL = 02
BX = Redirection list index (see Remarks below)
DS = Device name buffer segment address (16 bytes)
SI = Device name buffer offset address (16 bytes)
ES = Network name buffer segment address (128 bytes)
DI = Network name buffer offset address (128 bytes)

Output:

Carry flag=0: Successful execution
BH = Status flag
 0: Valid device
 1: Invalid device
BL = Device type
 3: Printer
 4: Drive
BP = Destroyed
CX = Parameter value in memory
DX = Destroyed
DS = ASCII format local device name segment address
SI = ASCII format local device name offset address
ES = ASCII format network name segment address
DI = ASCII format network name offset address
Carry flag=1: Error (AX = Error code)
 AX=1: Invalid function code
 AX=18: No more files available

Remarks:

The contents of register CX come from function 5FH, sub-function 3 (see below).

Interrupt 21H, function 5FH, sub-function 3 **DOS**
Redirect device **(Version 3 and up)**

Redirects device access in a network, assigning a network name to a local device.

Input:

AH = 5FH
AL = 03
BL = Device type
 BL=3: Printer
 BL=4: Drive
CX = Parameter value in memory
DS = ASCII format local device name segment address
SI = ASCII format local device name offset address
ES = ASCII format network name and password segment address
DI = ASCII format network name and password offset address

Output:

Carry flag=0: Successful execution
Carry flag=1: Error (AX = Error code)
 AX=1: Invalid function code; string format incorrect; device redirected
 AX=3: Path not found
 AX=5: Access denied
 AX=8: Insufficient memory

Remarks:

The contents of register CX are supplied from function 5FH, sub-function 3.

Device names can be drive specifiers (e.g., A:), printer names (i.e., LPT1, PRN, LPT2 or LPT3) or null strings. If you enter a null string and password as the device name, DOS tries to open access to the network using the password.

Interrupt 21H, function 5FH, sub-function 4 — DOS
Cancel redirection — (Version 3 and up)

Disables the current redirection by removing local name assignments to network printers, files or directories.

Input:
AH = 5FH
AL = 04
BX = Redirection list index (see Remarks below)
DS = ASCII format local device name segment address
SI = ASCII format local device name offset address

Output:
Carry flag=0: Successful execution
Carry flag=1: Error (AX = Error code)
AX=1: Invalid function code; device name not on network
AX=15: Redirection halted

Remarks:
Device names can be drive specifiers (e.g., A:), printer names (i.e., LPT1, PRN, LPT2 or LPT3) or strings beginning with double backslashes (i.e., \\). A string preceded by two backslashes terminates communications between the local computer and the network.

Interrupt 21H, function 62H — DOS
Get PSP address — (Version 3 and up)

Gets the segment address of the PSP from the currently executing program.

Input:
AH = 62H

Output:
BX = PSP segment address

Remarks:
The PSP starts at address BX:0000.

The contents of the AX, CX, DX, SI, DI, BP, CS, DS, SS, ES registers and the flag registers are not affected by this function.

Interrupt 21H, function 63H, sub-function 0 **DOS**
Get lead byte table **(Version 2.25 only)**

Gets the address of the system table which defines the byte ranges for the PC's extended character sets.

Input: AH = 9963H
AL = 00: Get address of system lead byte table

Output: DS = Table segment address
SI = Table offset address

Remarks: This function is available only in DOS Version 2.25.

Interrupt 21H, function 63H, sub-function 1 **DOS**
Set or clear interim console flag **(Version 2.25 only)**

Clears the interim console flag.

Input: AH = 63H
AL = 01: Clear or set interim console flag
DL = Interim console flag setting
DL=01: Set interim console flag
DL=00: Clear interim console flag

Output: No output

Remarks: This function is available only in DOS Version 2.25.

Interrupt 21H, function 63H, sub-function 2 **DOS**
Get interim console flag **(Version 2.25 only)**

Gets the interim console flag.

Input: AH = 63H
AL = 02: Get interim console flag value

Output: DL = Flag value

Remarks: This function is available only in DOS Version 2.25.

Interrupt 21H, function 64H **DOS**
Reserved **(Version 3 and up)**

Interrupt 21H, function 65H **DOS**
Get extended country information **(Version 3.3 and up)**

Gets information about the specific country/code page.

Input: AH = 65H
AL = sub-function:
AL = 1: Get international information

AL = 2: Get uppercase pointer table
AL = 4: Get pointer to uppercase pointer table (filename)
AL = 6: Get pointer to collation table
BX = Code page:
BX = -1: active CON device
CX = Length of buffer allocated to receive information
DX = Country ID number
DX = -1: Default
ES:DI = Address of buffer allocated to receive information

Output: Carry flag=0: Successful execution
Carry flag=1: Error (AX = Error code)

Remarks: The information this function returns is an extended version of the information returned by int 21H, function 38H.

An error may occur if the country code in DX is invalid, or if the code page number is different from the country code, or if the buffer length specified in the CX register is less than five bytes. If the buffer is not long enough to receive all the information, the function accepts as much information as the buffer will accept. This buffer contains the following information after the call:

Byte 0: ID code for information
Bytes 1-2: Length of buffer
Bytes 3-4: Country ID
Bytes 5-6: Code page
Bytes 7-8: Date format
0 = USA: Month-day-year
1 = Europe: Day-month-year
2 = Japan: Year-month-day
Bytes 9-13: Currency indicator
Bytes 14-15: ASCII code of the thousand character (comma/period)
Bytes 16-17: ASCII code of the decimal character (period/comma)
Bytes 18-19: ASCII code of the date separation character
Bytes 20-21: ASCII code of the time separation character
Byte 22: Currency format
bit 0 = 0: Currency symbol before the value
bit 0 = 1: Currency symbol after the value
bit 1 = 0: No spaces between value and currency symbol
bit 1 = 1: Space between value and currency symbol
Byte 23: Precision (number of decimal places)
Byte 24: Time format
bit 0 = 0: 12-hour clock
bit 0 = 1: 24-hour clock
Bytes 25-28: Address of character conversion routine
Bytes 29-30: ASCII data separator
Bytes 31-40: Reserved

Interrupt 21H, function 66H **DOS**
Get or set code page **(Version 3.3. and up)**

Gets or sets the current code page.

Input:
AH = 66H
AL = sub-function:
AL = 1: Get code page
AL = 2: Select code page
BX = Selected code page (if AL = 2)

Output:
Carry flag=0: Successful execution
If AL =1 used for input:
BX = active code page
DX = default code page
Carry flag=1: Error (AX = Error code)

Remarks:
If sub-function 2 is used, COUNTRY.SYS supplies the code page number.

The DEVICE... (CONFIG.SYS), NLSFUNC and MODE CP PREPARE commands (AUTOEXEC.BAT) must have already configured the system for code page switching before this function may be called.

Interrupt 21H, function 67H **DOS**
Set handle count **(Version 3.3 and up)**

Sets the maximum number of accessible files and devices that may be currently opened using handles.

Input:
AH = 67H
BX = Number of handles desired

Output:
Carry flag=0: Successful execution
Carry flag=1: Error (AX = Error code)

Remarks:
The PSP's default table reserved for the process can control 20 handles.

An error occurs if the content of the BX register is greater than 20, or if insufficient memory exists to allocate a block for the extended table.

If the number in the BX register is greater than the number of entries assigned by the FILES entry in the CONFIG.SYS file, no error occurs. However, attempts at opening a file or device fail if all file entries are in use, even if file handles are still available.

Interrupt 21H, function 68H **DOS**
Commit file **(Version 3.3 and up)**

Writes all DOS buffers associated to a specific handle to the specified device. If the handle points to a file, the file's contents, date and size are updated.

Input: AH = 68H
BX = File handle

Output: Carry flag=0: Successful execution
Carry flag=1: Error (AX = Error code)

Remarks: This function performs the same task as closing and reopening a file or duplicate handle, even without handles. If this function accesses a character device's handle, the carry flag returns 0 but nothing else happens.

Multiprocessing and networking applciations maintain control of the file.

Interrupt 22H **DOS**
Terminate address **(Version 1 and up)**

Contains the address of a routine which terminates a program. Control returns to the program that called for termination. You should never call this routine directly.

DOS stores the contents of this interrupt vector in the PSP of the program to be executed before passing control to the program. This prevents program changes to the vector, which could prevent DOS from calling the termination routine.

Interrupt 23H **DOS**
<Ctrl><C> handler address **(Version 1 and up)**

Contains the address of a routine which executes when the user presses <Ctrl><C> or <Ctrl><Break>. You should never directly call this routine.

DOS stores the contents of this interrupt vector in the PSP of the program to be executed before passing control to the program. This prevents program changes to the vector, which could prevent DOS from calling the termination routine.

Interrupt 24H **DOS**
Critical error handler address **(Version 1 and up)**

Represents a routine called during hardware access (e.g., disk drive) when a critical error occurs. You should never directly call this routine.

When an application routine is called during a critical error, bit 7 of the AH register indicates the type of failure (0 = disk/hard disk error, 1= other errors). A disk/hard disk error will only be reported after several attempted accesses. During the call, the DI register receives one of the following codes:

0: Disk write protected
1: Access on unknown device
2: Drive not ready
3: Invalid command
4: CRC error
5: Bad request structure length
6: Seek error
7: Unknown device type

8:	Sector not found
9:	Printer out of paper
10:	Write error
11:	Read error
12:	General failure

The error routine restores the SS, SP, DS, ES, BX, CX and DX registers to the same values that they contained during the call. During execution it can only access functions 1 to 0CH of interrupt 21H. It should be terminated by an IRET instruction and pass one of the following codes to the AL register:

0:	Ignore error
1:	Repeat the operation
2:	Terminate program using interrupt 23H
3:	Fail system call (Version 3 and up only)

If a program changes the content of this interrupt vector, the program can terminate without restoring the memory contents. Since RAM can be released and used by other programs, the critical error routine can be overwritten by another program in memory. When this occurs, a critical error could cause a system crash because a completely different code now exists at the location of the old error handler routine.

Before passing control to the program, DOS stores the contents of this interrupt vector in the PSP of the program to be executed. This prevents program changes to the vector, which could prevent DOS from calling the termination routine. During program termination, the contents of the interrupt vector pass from the PSP to the vector; then the system calls the routine.

Interrupt 25H — DOS
Absolute disk read — (Version 1 and up)

Reads one or more consecutive sectors from a disk or hard disk.

Input:
- AL = Drive specifier
- CX= Number of sectors to read
- DX= First sector to read
- DS= Buffer segment address
- BX= Buffer offset address

Output:
- Carry flag=0: O.K.
- Carry flag=1: Error (AX = Error code)
  - AX=1: Bad command
  - AX=2: Bad address
  - AX=4: Sector not found
  - AX=8: DMA error
  - AX=16: CRC error
  - AX=32: Disk controller error
  - AX=64: Seek error
  - AX=128: Device does not respond

Remarks: In the AL register 0 represents drive A:, 1 represents drive B:, etc.

All the sectors of the medium can be accessed. DOS itself uses this interrupt to read the root directory and the FAT of a medium. The data are read from the medium into the buffer of the calling program. After the function call, the contents of all registers, except the segment register, may change.

After the interrupt call, the stack pointer changes position because two bytes stored on the stack during the call are removed and not returned. These bytes represent the flag register, which can be read from the stack using the POPF instruction. The old value of the stack pointer can be set by adding 2 to its contents. If you omit the stack pointer correction, the stack could overflow. Because of this, you cannot call this interrupt from higher level languages. You must call it from assembly language.

The contents of the BX, CX, DX, SI, DI, BP, CS, DS, SS and ES registers are not affected by this function. The contents of all other registers may change.

Interrupt 26H **DOS**
Absolute disk write **(Version 1 and up)**

Writes one or more consecutive sectors to a disk or hard disk.

Input:
AL = Device designation
CX = Number of sectors to be written
DX = First sector to be written
DS = Buffer segment address
BX = Buffer offset address

Output:
Carry flag=0: O.K.
Carry flag=1: Error (AX = Error code)
- AX=1: Bad command
- AX=2: Bad address
- AX=3: Medium write protected
- AX=4: Sector not found
- AX=8: DMA error
- AX=16: CRC error
- AX=32: Disk controller error
- AX=64: Seek error
- AX=128: Device does not respond

Remarks: In the drive specifier 0 represents drive A:, 1 represents drive B:, etc.

All the sectors of the medium can be accessed. DOS itself uses this interrupt to write the root directory and the FAT to a medium. The data are written from the buffer of the calling program to the medium. After the function call, the contents of all registers, except the segment register, may change.

After the interrupt call, the stack pointer changes position because two bytes stored on the stack during the call are removed and not returned. These bytes represent the flag register, which can be read from the stack using the POPF instruction. The old value of the stack pointer can be set by adding 2 to its contents. If you omit the stack pointer correction, the stack could overflow. Because of this, you cannot call this interrupt from higher level languages. You must call it from assembly language.

The contents of the BX, CX, DX, SI, DI, BP, CS, DS, SS and ES registers are not affected by this function. The contents of all other registers may change.

Interrupt 27H **DOS**
Terminate and stay resident **(Version 1 and up)**

Terminates the currently executing program and returns control to the program that called the current program. Unlike other functions used for program termination, the memory used by the current program keeps the program code for later recall.

Input: CS = PSP segment address
DX = Number of bytes + 1 to be reserved

Output: No output

Remarks: This function is only suitable for calling COM programs.

The number of bytes to be reserved relates to the beginning of the PSP.

The value in the DX register has no effect on memory blocks reserved by function 48H of interrupt 21H.

An error occurs during the call of this interrupt if the value in the DX register ranges from FFF1H to FFFFH.

This interrupt does not close open files.

Interrupt 2FH, sub-function 0 **DOS**
Get print spool install status **(Version 3 and up)**

Gets current installation status of the print spooler.

Input: AH = 2FH
AL = 0

Output: Carry flag=0: Successful execution
AL = 0: O.K. to install
AL = 1: Don't install
AL = 255: Already installed
Carry flag=1: Error (AX = Error code)
AX=1: Invalid function
AX=2: File not found
AX=3: Path not found

AX=4: Too many files currently open
AX=5: Access denied
AX=8: Print queue full
AX=9: Print spooler busy
AX=12: Name too long
AX=15: Invalid drive

Interrupt 2FH, sub-function 1 **DOS**
Send file to print spooler **(Version 3 and up)**

Passes a file to the print spooler.

Input:
AH = 2FH
AL = 1
DS = Print packet (see below) segment address
DX = Print packet (see below) offset address

Output:
Carry flag=0: Successful execution
Carry flag=1: Error (AX = Error code)
AX=1: Invalid function
AX=2: File not found
AX=3: Path not found
AX=4: Too many files currently open
AX=5: Access denied
AX=8: Print queue full
AX=9: Print spooler busy
AX=12: Name too long
AX=15: Invalid drive

Remarks: The five-byte print packet contains print spooler information. The first byte indicates the DOS version (0=Versions 3.1 to 3.3); the remaining bytes indicate the segment and offset addresses of the file specification.

Interrupt 2FH, sub-function 2 **DOS**
Remove file from print queue **(Version 3 and up)**

Deletes a file from the print spooler queue.

Input:
AH = 2FH
AL = 2
DS = ASCII-format file segment address
DX = ASCII-format file offset address

Output:
Carry flag=0: Successful execution
Carry flag=1: Error (AX = Error code)
AX=1: Invalid function
AX=2: File not found
AX=3: Path not found
AX=4: Too many files currently open
AX=5: Access denied
AX=8: Print queue full

AX=9: Print spooler busy
AX=12: Name too long
AX=15: Invalid drive

Remarks: This sub-function allows wildcards (? and *) in file specifications, allowing you to delete more than one file at a time from the print queue.

Interrupt 2FH, sub-function 3 **DOS**
Cancel all files in print queue **(Version 3 and up)**

Cancels all files waiting in the print spooler queue for printing.

Input: AH = 2FH
AL = 3

Output: Carry flag=0: Successful execution
Carry flag=1: Error (AX = Error code)
AX=1: Invalid function
AX=2: File not found
AX=3: Path not found
AX=4: Too many files currently open
AX=5: Access denied
AX=8: Print queue full
AX=9: Print spooler busy
AX=12: Name too long
AX=15: Invalid drive

Interrupt 2FH, sub-function 4 **DOS**
Hold print jobs for status check **(Version 3 and up)**

Halts all print jobs while testing for spooler status.

Input: AH = 2FH
AL = 4

Output: Carry flag=0: Successful execution
Carry flag=1: Error
DX = Number of errors
DS = Print queue segment address
SI = Print queue offset address

Remarks: The print queue segment and offset addresses point to a set of 64-byte filenames in the queue. Each entry contains an ASCII file specification.

The first filename in the queue is the file currently printing in the print spooler. The last filename in the queue has a zero in the first byte of the specification.

Appendix D

EMM Functions

Interrupt 67H, function 1H **LIM/EMS**
Extended memory: Get status

Returns the error status of the EMM after calling any EMS functions.

Input: AH = 40H

Output: AH = EMM status
AH=00H: O.K.
AH=80H: Internal error, EMM possibly destroyed
AH=81H: EMS hardware error

Remarks: Do not call this function unless you know that EMS memory and a corresponding EMM are installed (see Chapter 13 for more information). This function should be the first EMM call a program makes, to ensure that the hardware and software are functioning properly.

Interrupt 67H, function 2H **LIM/EMS**
Extended memory: Get segment address of the page frame

Determines the segment address of the page frame.

Input: AH = 41H

Output: AH = 0: O.K.
BX = Page frame segment address
AH > 0: Error
AH=80H: Internal error, EMM possibly destroyed
AH=81H: EMS hardware error

Remarks: Do not call this function unless you know that EMS memory and a corresponding EMM are installed (see Chapter 13 for more information). The addresses of the four physical pages can be calculated from this segment address, whereby the first page starts at address PAGE_FRAME:0000. The three other pages follow at 16K intervals.

Interrupt 67H, function 3H — LIM/EMS
Extended memory: Get number of EMS pages

Informs the calling program how many 16K EMS pages are installed, and how many EMS pages are still available or unallocated.

Input: AH = 42H

Output:
AH = 0: O.K.
BX = Number of free (unallocated) pages
DX = Total number of EMS pages
AH > 0: Error
AH=80H: Internal error, EMM possibly destroyed
AH=81H: EMS hardware error

Remarks: Do not call this function unless you know that EMS memory and a corresponding EMM are installed (see Chapter 13 for more information).

The number of kilobytes of free EMS memory can be calculated by multiplying the number of free pages by 16.

Interrupt 67H, function 4H — LIM/EMS
Extended memory: Allocate EMS memory

Allocates a given number of 16K EMS pages for later access.

Input:
AH = 43H
BX = Number of logical (16K) pages to be allocated

Output:
AH = 0: O.K.
DX = Handle for accessing allocated memory
AH > 9: Error
AH=80H: Internal error, EMM possibly destroyed
AH=81H: EMS hardware error
AH=85H: No more handles available
AH=87H: Not enough pages free
AH=88H: No pages were requested

Remarks: Do not call this function unless you know that EMS memory and a corresponding EMM are installed (see Chapter 13 for more information).

The handle returned can be used for future access and for releasing the allocated memory. If this handle is "lost", the handle cannot be recovered, nor can memory be released or used by other programs.

A call to this function may fail because there are not enough pages free or because the EMM has been called so often that no more handles are available.

The handles normally have the numbers FF00H, FE01H, FD02H, FC03H, etc.

Interrupt 67H, function 5H **LIM/EMS**
Extended memory: Set mapping

Places one of the pages previously allocated by function 4H in one of the four physical pages within the page frame.

Input:
AH = 44H
AL = Physical page number (0 to 3)
BX = Logical page number
DX = Handle

Output:
AH = Error status
AH=00H: O.K.
AH=80H: Internal error, EMM possibly destroyed
AH=81H: EMS hardware error
AH=83H: Invalid handle
AH=8AH: Invalid logical page
AH=8BH: Invalid physical page

Remarks:
Do not call this function unless you know that EMS memory and a corresponding EMM are installed (see Chapter 13 for more information).

The handle used when calling this function must have been returned by a previous call to EMM function 4H.

The logical pages are numbered from 0 on, so that the value 0 must be passed to access the first logical page. The largest value allowed is the number of allocated pages minus one.

Before accessing the physical page, the segment address of the page frame must be determined with function 2H.

Interrupt 67H, function 6H **LIM/EMS**
Extended memory: Release pages

Releases pages allocated with function 4H to the EMM. This makes these pages available to other applications.

Input:
AH = 45H
DX = Handle

Output:
AH = Error status:
AH=00H: O.K.
AH=80H: Internal error, EMM possibly destroyed
AH=81H: EMS hardware error
AH=83H: Invalid handle
AH=85H: Error while saving and restoring mapping

Remarks: Do not call this function unless you know that EMS memory and a corresponding EMM are installed (see Chapter 13 for more information).

The handle used when calling this function must have been returned by a previous call to EMM function 4H.

All of the pages allocated to this handle are released by this function. It is impossible to release individual pages.

After a successful call to this function the handle is no longer valid and cannot be used for accessing EMS memory.

If the function returns an error, you should repeat the call at least three times or the pages will remain allocated and will not be available for other programs.

Interrupt 67H, function 7H **LIM/EMS**
Extended memory: Get EMM version

Determines the version number of the EMM (Expanded Memory Manager).

Input: AH = 46H

Output: AH = 0: O.K.
AL = EMM version number
AH > 0: Error
AH=80H: Internal error, EMM possibly destroyed
AH=81H: EMS hardware error

Remarks: Do not call this function unless you know that EMS memory and a corresponding EMM are installed (see Chapter 13 for more information).

The EMM version number is stored in the AL register as a BCD number, in which the upper four bits represent the version number preceding the decimal point and the lower four bits represent the version number following the decimal point. See also the demonstration programs in Chapter 13.

Interrupt 67H, function 8H **LIM/EMS**
Extended memory: Save mapping

Saves current mapping between the four physical pages in the page frame and the associated logical pages.

Input: AH = 47H
DX = Handle

Output: AH = Error status
AH=00H: O.K.
AH=80H: Internal error, EMM possibly destroyed
AH=81H: EMS hardware error
AH=83H: Invalid handle
AH=8CH: Mapping memory full
AH=8DH: Mapping for handle already stored, not restored using function 9H

Remarks: Do not call this function unless you know that EMS memory and a corresponding EMM are installed (see Chapter 13 for more information).

The handle used when calling this function must have been returned by a previous call to EMM function 4H.

This function is intended for use within a TSR program or by the operating system in a multitasking environment, but can be used by any program.

Interrupt 67H, function 9H **LIM/EMS**
Extended memory: Restore mapping

Restores mapping between the logical and physical pages saved by function 8H.

Input: AH = 48H
DX = Handle

Output: AH = Error status:
AH=00H: O.K.
AH=80H: Internal error, EMM possibly destroyed
AH=81H: EMS hardware error
AH=83H: Invalid handle
AH=8EH: Mapping storage contains no entry for this handle

Remarks: Do not call this function unless you know that EMS memory and a corresponding EMM are installed (see Chapter 13 for more information).

The handle used when calling this function must have been returned by a previous call to EMM function 4H.

Calling this function fails whenever the mapping for this handle has not been saved with function 8H, or the mapping has already been restored by a previous call to function 9H.

This function is intended for use within a TSR program or by the operating system in a multitasking environment, but can be used by any program.

Interrupt 67H, function 0CH — LIM/EMS
Extended memory: Get number of handles

Returns the number of memory blocks and the number of handles allocated by function 4H.

Input: AH = 4BH

Output:
AH = 0: O.K.
BX = Number of allocated handles
AH > 0: Error
  AH=80H: Internal error, EMM possibly destroyed
  AH=81H: EMS hardware error

Remarks: Do not call this function unless you know that EMS memory and a corresponding EMM are installed (see Chapter 13 for more information).

The number of allocated handles is not the same as the number of programs which are currently accessing the EMS memory. Each program can request an arbitrary number of EMS memory blocks/handles with function 4H.

Interrupt 67H, function 0DH — LIM/EMS
Extended memory: Get number of allocated pages

Returns the number of pages which have been allocated to the specified handle.

Input:
AH = 4CH
DX = Handle

Output:
AH = 0: O.K.
BX = Number of allocated pages
AH > 0: Error
  AH=80H: Internal error, EMM possibly destroyed
  AH=81H: EMS hardware error
  AH=83H: Invalid handle

Remarks: Do not call this function unless you know that EMS memory and a corresponding EMM are installed (see Chapter 13 for more information).

The number of allocated pages must range from 1 to 512.

Interrupt 67H, function 0EH **LIM/EMS**
Extended memory: Get all handles

Loads the numbers of all active handles and the number of pages allocated to each into an array.

Input: AH = 48H
ES = Segment address of array
DI = Offset address of array

Output: AH = 0: O.K.
BX = Number of allocated logical pages
AH > 0: Error
AH=80H: Internal error, EMM possibly destroyed
AH=81H: EMS hardware error

Remarks: Do not call this function unless you know that EMS memory and a corresponding EMM are installed (see Chapter 13 for more information).

If the function returns successfully, the memory area to which the ES:DI register pair points will contain two words for each active handle. The first word contains the handle itself and the second word contains the number of pages allocated to the handle. The number of these entries is returned in the BX register.

Since the EMM can manage a maximum of 256 handles, the array will never occupy more than 1024 bytes (1K).

Appendix E

EGA/VGA BIOS Functions

Interrupt 10H, function 00H **EGA/VGA**
Screen: Set video mode

Sets and initializes the video mode.

Input: AH = 00H
AL = EGA video mode
0: 40x25-character text, 16 colors (EGA/VGA - color monitor)
1: 40x25-character text, 16 colors (EGA/VGA - color monitor)
2: 80x25-character text, 16 colors (EGA/VGA - color monitor)
3: 80x25-character text, 16 colors (EGA/VGA - color monitor)
4: 320x200 pixel graphics, 4 colors (EGA/VGA - color monitor)
5: 320x200 pixel graphics, 4 colors (EGA/VGA - color monitor)
6: 640x200 pixel graphics, 2 colors (EGA/VGA - color monitor)
7: 80x25-character text, mono (EGA/VGA - mono monitor)
13: 320x200 pixel graphics, 16 colors (EGA/VGA - color monitor)
14: 640x200 pixel graphics, 16 colors (EGA/VGA - color monitor)
15: 640x350 pixel graphics, mono (EGA/VGA - mono monitor)
16: 640x350 pixel graphics, 4 colors (64K EGA-hi-res monitor)
640x350 pixel graphics, 16 colors (128K EGA/VGA-hi-res monitor)
17: 640x480 pixel graphics, 2 colors (VGA only)
18: 640x480 pixel graphics, 16 colors (VGA only)
19: 320x200 pixel graphics, 256 colors (VGA only)

Output: No output

Remarks: Modes 0 and 1, 2 and 3, 4 and 5 differ in the output of the color signal that is suppressed in the first mode. This isn't possible on an EGA/VGA card so the modes are identical. If bit 7 of the AL register is set when this function is called, the contents of the video RAM will not be erased when the new mode is enabled. The task is to program the video controller and define a color palette. The contents of registers BX, CX, DX, SI, DI, BP and the segment registers are not affected by this function.

Interrupt 10H, function 01H — EGA/VGA
Screen: Define cursor appearance

Defines the starting and ending lines of the screen cursor. This function is independent of the display page being displayed.

Input:
AH = 01H
CH = Starting line of the cursor
CL = Ending line of the cursor

Output:
No output

Remarks:
Since the possible values depend on the size of the current video mode's character matrix, the values in the CH and CL registers always refer to an eight-line character matrix. The values should thus be between zero and seven. The EGA/VGA BIOS adapts these values to the current size of its own character matrix.

The contents of registers BX, CX, DX, SI, DI, BP and the segment registers are not affected by this function.

Interrupt 10H, function 02H — EGA/VGA
Screen: Position cursor

Moves the cursor into position on the screen.

Input:
AH = 02H
BH = Video page number
DH = Screen line
DL = Screen column

Output:
No output

Remarks:
The cursor moves only if the specified display page is the current page.

The values for the screen line and column are based on the resolution of the current display mode.

Assigning the DH and DL registers values for a non-existent screen position (e.g., column 0, line 255) makes the cursor disappear from the screen.

The number of the display page is based on how many display pages the card has available.

The contents of registers BX, CX, DX, SI, DI, BP and the segment registers are not affected by this function.

Interrupt 10H, function 03H **EGA/VGA**
Screen: Read cursor position

Reads the position of the text cursor on the screen and the starting and ending lines of the screen cursor.

Input: AH = 03H
BH = Video page number

Output: DH = Screen line in which cursor is located
DL = Screen column in which cursor is located
CH = Starting line of screen cursor
CL = Ending line of screen cursor

Remarks: The screen line and screen column parameters refer to the text coordinate system, even if a graphic mode is active.

The starting and ending lines of the cursor are returned correctly only in the text modes. They have no meanings in graphic modes.

The contents of registers BX, SI, DI, BP and the segment registers are not affected by this function.

Interrupt 10H, function 05H **EGA/VGA**
Screen: Select current display page

Selects the current display page, and thereby the page which appears on the screen (text mode only).

Input: AH = 05H
AL = Display page number

Output: No output

Remarks: The number of available display pages depends on the amount of video RAM installed on the EGA/VGA card.

When a new page is selected the screen cursor will be moved to the position of the text cursor on this page.

Switching between different pages does not change the contents of these pages.

The contents of registers BX, CX, DX, SI, DI, BP and the segment registers are not affected by this function.

Interrupt 10H, function 06H **EGA/VGA**
Screen: Scroll text lines up

Scrolls part of the current display page up by one or more lines.

Input:
AH = 06H
AL = Number of lines to be scrolled up
AL=0: Clear window
CH = Screen line of upper left corner of window
CL = Screen column of upper left corner of window
DH = Screen line of lower right corner of window
DL = Screen column of lower right corner of window
BH = Color (attribute) for blank line(s)

Output: No output

Remarks: Normally the contents of the current display page are scrolled, but in the 320x200 four-color graphic mode this function only affects display page 0.

Clearing the screen window (number of lines = 0) is the same as filling it with spaces (ASCII code 32).

The contents of the lines scrolled out of the window are lost and cannot be recovered.

Use function 0 of this interrupt to clear the screen.

The interpretation of the attribute byte in the BL register depends on the current video mode. In text mode it is interpreted as any other attribute byte in video RAM. In 640x200 two-color mode this byte represents the color value for eight successive pixels. In 320x200 four-color mode this byte represents the color value of four successive pixels. In all other graphic modes it represents the color of all of the pixels in the cleared screen area.

The contents of registers BX, CX, DX, SI, DI, BP and the segment registers are not affected by this function.

Interrupt 10H, function 07H **EGA/VGA**
Screen: Scroll text lines down

Scrolls part of the current display page down one or more lines.

Input:
AH = 07H
AL = Number of lines to be scrolled down
AL=0: Clear window
CH = Screen line of upper left corner of window
CL = Screen column of upper left corner of window
DH = Screen line of lower right corner of window

DL = Screen column of lower right corner of window
BH = Color (attribute) for blank line(s)

Output: No output

Remarks: Normally the contents of the current display page are scrolled, but in 320x200 four-color graphic mode this function only affects display page 0.

Clearing the screen window (number of lines = 0) is the same as filling it with spaces (ASCII code 32).

The contents of the lines scrolled out of the window are lost and cannot be recovered.

To clear the entire screen, use function 0 of this interrupt instead.

The interpretation of the attribute byte in the BL register depends on the current display mode. In the text mode it is interpreted like any other attribute byte in the video RAM. In the 640x200 two-color mode this byte represents the color value for eight successive pixels. In the 320x200 four-color mode it represents the color value of four successive pixels. In all other graphic modes it represents the color of all of the pixels in the cleared screen area.

The contents of registers BX, CX, DX, SI, DI, BP and the segment registers are not affected by this function.

Interrupt 10H, function 08H **EGA/VGA**
Screen: Read character/color

Reads and returns the ASCII code and color (attribute) of the character at the current cursor position.

Input: AH = 08H
BH = Video page number

Output: AL = ASCII code of character
AH = Color (attribute)

Remarks: This function can also be called in the graphic mode, whereby the bit pattern of the character on the screen will be compared with the bit patterns of the characters. If the character cannot be identified, the AL register will contain the value zero after the call.

In the 320x200 four-color graphic mode this function only affects display page 0.

The contents of registers BX, CX, DX, SI, DI, BP and the segment registers are not affected by this function.

Interrupt 10H, function 09H **EGA/VGA**
Screen: Write character/color

Writes character with the specified color at the current cursor position (in a specified display page).

Input:
AH = 09H
BH = Video page number
CX = Repeat factor
AL = ASCII code of character
BL = Attribute

Output: No output

Remarks: If the graphic mode is active and the specified character is to be printed more than once (the value of the CX register is greater than 1), all of the characters must fit on the current screen line.

In the 320x200 four-color graphic mode this function correctly works only on display page 0.

Within a graphic mode the attribute in the BL register specifies the foreground color of the character, whereby the background color is zero. If bit seven is set, the character will be XORed with the bitmap at the output position.

The controls codes for bell, carriage return, etc. are not recognized as control codes, and are displayed as normal ASCII characters.

This function can also be used to output characters in the graphic mode, in which case the character patterns are taken from one of the EGA character tables.

This function does not move the cursor to the next screen position.

The contents of registers BX, CX, DX, SI, DI, BP and the segment registers are not affected by this function.

Interrupt 10H, function 0AH **EGA/VGA**
Screen: Write character

A character will be written to the current screen position on the specified display page and the color of the old character at this position will be retained.

Input:
AH = 0AH
AL = ASCII code of the character
BH = Video page number
BL = Foreground color of character for graphic modes
CX = Repeat factor

Output: No output

Remarks: If the graphic mode is active and the specified character is to be printed more than once (the value of the CX register is greater than 1), all of the characters must fit on the current screen line.

The controls codes for bell, carriage return, etc. are not recognized as such and are displayed as normal ASCII characters.

This function can also be used to output characters in the graphic mode, in which case the character patterns are taken from one of the EGA character tables.

Within a graphic mode the attribute in the BL register specifies the foreground color of the character, whereby the background color is zero. If bit seven is set, the character will be XORed with the bitmap at the output position.

This function does not move the cursor to the next screen position.

The contents of registers BX, CX, DX, SI, DI, BP and the segment registers are not affected by this function.

Interrupt 10H, function 0BH, sub-function 0 **EGA/VGA**
Screen: Select border/background color

Selects the border and background color for the graphic or text mode.

Input:
AH = 0BH
BH = 0
BL = Border/background color

Output: No output

Remarks: This function should be called only when the EGA/VGA card is in the 320x200 or 640x200 graphic mode. Use function 10H for all other modes.

Bits zero to three of the BL register set the background and border color. Setting bit four will enable high-intensity colors.

The contents of registers BX, CX, DX, SI, DI, BP and the segment registers are not affected by this function.

Interrupt 10H, function 0BH, sub-function 1 **EGA/VGA**
Screen: Select color palette

Selects one of the two color palettes for the 320x200 graphic mode.

Input:
AH = 0BH
BH = 1
BL = Color palette number

Output: No output

Remarks: This function should be called only when the EGA/VGA card is in the 320x200 or 640x200 graphic mode. Use function 10H for all other modes.

The EGA/VGA BIOS emulates the two CGA color palettes with the numbers 0 and 1. They contain the following colors:

Palette 0: green, red, yellow
Palette 1: cyan, magenta, white

The contents of registers BX, CX, DX, SI, DI, BP and the segment registers are not affected by this function.

Interrupt 10H, function 0CH — EGA/VGA
Screen: Write pixel

Sets the color value of a screen pixel in the graphic mode.

Input:
AH = 0CH
BH = Video page
DX = Screen line
CX = Screen column
AL = Color value

Output: No output

Remarks: The color value depends on the colors available in the current display mode.

If bit seven of the AL register is set, the color value will be XORed with the previous color value of the pixel.

The display page is ignored in the 320x200 four-color graphic mode.

The contents of registers BX, CX, DX, SI, DI, BP and the segment registers are not affected by this function.

Interrupt 10H, function 0DH — EGA/VGA
Screen: Read pixel

The color value of a pixel in the graphic mode is returned.

Input:
AH = 0DH
BH = Video page
DX = Screen line
CX = Screen column

Output: AL = Color value

Remarks: The color value depends on the colors available in the current display mode.

The display page is ignored in the 320x200 four-color graphic mode.

The contents of registers BX, CX, DX, SI, DI, BP and the segment registers are not affected by this function.

Interrupt 10H, function 0EH **EGA/VGA**
Screen: Write character

Writes a character to the current cursor position on the current display page. The color of the old character at this position will be retained.

Input: AH = 0EH
AL = ASCII character code
BL = Foreground color of character

Output: No output

Remarks: This function does not treat the various control codes like bell and carriage as normal characters, and implements them as the control characters they represent.

After displaying a character with this function, the cursor position is incremented so that the next character will be printed at the following screen position. If the last screen position has been reached, the screen will be scrolled up one line and the output will continue in the first column of the last screen line.

If bit seven of the BL register is set, the color value will be XORed with the previous color value of the pixels. The background color is zero.

Characters can be displayed in the graphic mode with this function. The character patterns are taken from one of the EGA character tables.

The contents of registers BX, CX, DX, SI, DI, BP and the segment registers are not affected by this function.

Interrupt 10H, function 0FH **EGA/VGA**
Screen: Returns current display mode

Reads the number of the current display mode, the number of characters per line, and the number of the current display page.

Input: AH = 0FH

Output: AL = Video mode:
0: 40x25-character text, 16 colors (EGA/VGA - color monitor)
1: 40x25-character text, 16 colors (EGA/VGA - color monitor)

2: 80x25-character text, 16 colors (EGA/VGA - color monitor)
3: 80x25-character text, 16 colors (EGA/VGA - color monitor)
4: 320x200 pixel graphics, 4 colors (EGA/VGA - color monitor)
5: 320x200 pixel graphics, 4 colors (EGA/VGA - color monitor)
6: 640x200 pixel graphics, 2 colors (EGA/VGA - color monitor)
7: 80x25-character text, mono (EGA/VGA - mono monitor)
13: 320x200 pixel graphics, 16 colors (EGA/VGA - color monitor)
14: 640x200 pixel graphics, 16 colors (EGA/VGA - color monitor)
15: 640x350 pixel graphics, mono (EGA/VGA - mono monitor)
16: 640x350 pixel graphics, 4 colors (64K EGA - high-resolution monitor)
640x350 pixel graphics, 16 colors (128K EGA/VGA - high-resolution monitor)
17: 640x480 pixel graphics, 2 colors (VGA only)
18: 640x480 pixel graphics, 16 colors (VGA only)
19: 320x200 pixel graphics, 256 colors (VGA only)
AH = Number of characters per line
BH = Number of current display page

Remark: The contents of registers BX, CX, DX, SI, DI, BP and the segment registers are not affected by this function.

Interrupt 10H, function 10H, sub-function 00H **EGA/VGA**
Screen: Set palette registers

Sets the contents of a palette register in the attribute controller of the EGA/VGA card.

Input:
AH = 10H
AL = 00H
BL = Color value
BH = Register to be addressed

Output: No output

Remarks: Since the register number is not checked by the BIOS, you can also program the other registers in the attribute controller. These include the mode control register, overscan register and others.

The contents of registers BX, CX, DX, SI, DI, BP, and the segment registers are not affected by this function.

Interrupt 10H, function 10H, sub-function 01H **EGA/VGA**
Screen: Set screen border color

Copies resulting value into the overscan register of the EGA attribute controller.

Input:
AH = 10H
AL = 01H
BH = Border color

Output: No output

Remark: The contents of registers BX, CX, DX, SI, DI, BP and the segment registers are not affected by this function.

Interrupt 10H, function 10H, sub-function 02H **EGA/VGA**
Screen: Set all palette registers

Configures all 16 palette registers and the overscan register.

Input:
AH = 10H
AL = 02H
ES = Segment address of color table
DX = Offset address of color table

Output: No output

Remarks: The ES:BX register pair points to a 17-byte table. The first 16 bytes will be transferred to the 16 palette registers of the attribute controller and the 17th byte will be copied into the overscan register.

The contents of registers BX, CX, DX, SI, DI, BP and the segment registers are not affected by this function.

Interrupt 10H, function 10H, sub-function 03H **EGA/VGA**
Screen: Set blinking attribute

Determines whether bit 7 in the attribute byte of a character in the text mode will enable character blinking, or display characters on a high-intensity background.

Input:
AH = 10H
AL = 00H
BL = Blinking attribute
BL=0: high-intensity background
BL=1: blinking

Output: No output

Remark: The contents of registers BX, CX, DX, SI, DI, BP and the segment registers are not affected by this function.

Interrupt 10H, function 10H, sub-function 07H **VGA**
Screen: Read out palette register

Reads the contents of one of the attribute controller's palette registers.

Input:
AH = 10H
AL = 07H
BH = Number of palette register

Output: BL = Contents of addressed palette register

Remarks: Since the BIOS doesn't verify the number of the palette register read, this function can read all the registers of the attribute controller.

The contents of registers BL, CX, DX, SI, DI, BP and all segment registers are not affected by this function.

Interrupt 10H, function 10H, sub-function 08H **VGA**
Screen: Read contents of overscan register

Returns the contents of the overscan register containing the screen's border color.

Input: AH = 10H
AL = 08H

Output: BH = Contents of the overscan register

Remarks: The contents of registers BL, CX, DX, SI, DI, BP and all segment registers are not affected by this function.

Interrupt 10H, function 10H, sub-function 09H **VGA**
Screen: Read contents of all palette registers and the overscan register

Copies the contents of the 16 palette registers and overscan register into a buffer.

Input: AH = 10H
AL = 09H
ES = Segment address of the buffer
DX = Offset address of the buffer

Output: No output

Remarks: The buffer must be a minimum of 17 bytes long to allow room for all the palette registers (bytes 0-15) plus the overscan register (byte 16).

The contents of registers BL, CX, DX, SI, DI, BP and all segment registers are not affected by this function.

Interrupt 10H, function 10H, sub-function 10H **VGA**
Screen: Define a DAC color register

Allows the definition of one of the 256 available DAC color registers.

Input: AH = 10H
BX = Number of the DAC color register (0-255)
CH = Green value
CL = Blue value
DH = Red value

Output: No output

Remarks: Only bits 0 to 5 in the CH, CL and DH registers are of importance to this function. All other bits are ignored.

The contents of registers BL, CX, DX, SI, DI, BP and all segment registers are not affected by this function.

Interrupt 10H, function 10H, sub-function 12H **VGA**
Screen: Load multiple DAC color registers

Allows the definition of multiple DAC color registers.

Input:
AH = 10H
AL = 12H
BX = Number of the first DAC color register (0-255)
CX = Number of registers to be loaded
ES = Segment address of the buffer
DX = Offset address of the buffer

Output: No output

Remarks: The assigned buffer must be able to hold a group of three consecutive bytes for each DAC color register. The first byte contains the red value; the second byte contains the green value; and the third byte contains the blue value. These first three bytes correspond to the first DAC color register being accessed, the next three for the bytes to the next DAC color register.

Only bits 0 to 5 in the CH, CL and DH registers are of importance to this function. All other bits are ignored.

If the sum of BX and CX is greater than 255, the first DAC color register is reloaded after the last register is loaded.

The contents of registers BL, CX, DX, SI, DI, BP and all segment registers are unchanged by this function.

Interrupt 10H, function 10H, sub-function 13H **VGA**
Screen: Select color register or select a DAC register group

Manipulates bit 7 of the mode control registers.

Input:
AH = 10H
AL = 13H
BL = 00H or 01H (see below)
BH = see below

Output: No output

Remarks: This sub-function performs as two different sub-functions, depending on the value contained in the BL register. Sub-function 00H allows color selection, while sub-function 01H allows the selection of the active DAC register group.

Sub-function 00H copies bit 0 in the BH register into bit 7 of the mode control register, thus providing a method of color selection. If bit 0 in the BH register contains a value of 0, then the 256 DAC color registers are divided into four groups of 64 registers. Color selection involves bits 0-5 in the corresponding palette register, as well as bits 2-3 of the color select register. These eight bits act as the index for the DAC color register. If bit 0 in the BH register contains a 1, the DAC color registers are divided into 16 groups of 16 registers. Then color selection involves the lowest 4 bits of the palette register and the lowest 4 bits of the color select register, acting as the 8-bit index to the DAC color table.

Sub-function 01H loads the color select register, whose contents are specified by the active group of DAC color registers. The contents of the BH register are copied to the color select register.

The contents of registers BL, CX, DX, SI, DI, BP and all segment registers are not affected by this function.

Interrupt 10H, function 10H, sub-function 15H **VGA**
Screen: Read a DAC color register

Returns the contents of one of the 256 DAC color registers.

Input:
AH = 10H
AL = 15H
BX = Number of the DAC color registers

Output:
CH = Green value
CL = Blue value
DH = Red value

Remarks: Only bits 0 to 5 in the CH, CL and DH registers are of importance to this function. All other bits are ignored.

The contents of registers BX, DL, SI, DI, BP and all segment registers are not affected by this function.

Interrupt 10H, function 10H, sub-function 17H **VGA**
Screen: Load contents of multiple DAC color registers

Loads several DAC color registers at a time.

Input:
AH = 10H
AL = 17H
BX = Number of the first DAC color register to be loaded (0-255)
CX = Number of registers to be loaded
ES = Segment address of buffer
DX = Offset address of buffer

Output: No output

Remarks: The contents of each DAC color register are represented within a buffer by three consecutive bytes. The red value is loaded into the first of these registers; the green value is loaded into the second of these registers; and the blue value is loaded into the third register. The first group of three bytes corresponds to the first DAC color register addressed, the second group to the next DAC color register, etc.

Only bits 0 to 5 in the CH, CL and DH registers are of importance to this function. All other bits are ignored.

If the sum of BX and CX is greater than 255, the first DAC color register is reloaded after the last register is loaded (wrap-around occurs).

The contents of registers BX, CX, DX, SI, DI, BP and all segment registers are not affected by this function.

Interrupt 10H, function 10H, sub-function 18H **VGA**
Screen: Load DAC mask register

Loads the specified value into the DAC mask register.

Input:
AH = 10H
AL = 18H
BL = Value of DAC mask register

Output: No output

Remarks: The contents of the DAC mask register play an important role in color selection. An AND instruction adds it to the index access to the DAC color table.

The contents of registers BH, CX, DX, SI, DI, BP and all segment registers are not affected by this function.

Interrupt 10H, function 10H, sub-function 19H — VGA
Screen: Read out contents of the DAC mask register

Reads the current contents of the DAC mask register.

Input: AH = 10H
AL = 19H

Output: BL = Contents of the DAC mask register

Remarks: The contents of the DAC mask register play an important role in color selection. An AND instruction adds it to the index access to the DAC color table.

The contents of registers BH, CX, DX, SI, DI, BP and all segment registers are not affected by this function.

Interrupt 10H, function 10H, sub-function 1AH — VGA
Screen: Returns method of color selection and color select register

Returns the method of color selection, contained in the contents of bit 7 of the mode control register. It also returns the contents of the color select register chosen by the active group of DAC color registers.

Input: AH = 10H
AL = 1AH

Output: BL = Bit 7 of mode control register
BH = Contents of color select registers

Remarks: The contents of registers BX, CX, DX, SI, DI, BP and all segment registers are not affected by this function.

Interrupt 10H, function 10H, sub-function 1BH — VGA
Screen: Convert DAC color register into gray scales

Converts a specified range within a DAC color table into gray scales.

Input: AH = 10H
AL = 1BH
BX = Number of first DAC color register to be converted
CX = Total number of DAC color registers to be converted

Output: No output

Remarks: Conversion into grays results from changes to the red, green and blue values, as well as the intensity of these values. The default factor for red is 0.3, the default factor for green is 0.59, and the default for blue 0.11.

The contents of registers BX, CX, DX, SI, DI, BP and all segment registers are not affected by this function.

Interrupt 10H, function 11H, sub-function 00H **EGA/VGA**
Screen: Load user-defined character set

Loads a user-defined character set from RAM into one of the two EGA character tables.

Input:
AH = 11H
AL = 00H
BH = Lines per character (also bytes per character)
BL = Character table (0 or 1)
CX = Number of characters in table
DX = ASCII code of first character in table
ES = Segment address of character table in RAM
BP = Offset address of character table in RAM

Output: No output

Remarks: A maximum of 512 characters can be loaded per character table.

The loaded character set is not activated, nor are the CRTC registers programmed to the size of the characters. The changes will not be visible on the screen unless the character definitions are loaded into the active character table.

The contents of registers BX, CX, DX, SI, DI, BP and the segment registers are not affected by this function.

Interrupt 10H, function 11H, sub-function 01H **EGA/VGA**
Screen: Load 8x14 character set

Loads the entire 8x14-pixel character set from EGA/VGA ROM-BIOS into one of the two character set tables.

Input:
AH = 11H
AL = 01H
BL = Character table (0 or 1)

Output: No output

Remarks: The loaded character set is not activated, nor are the CRTC registers programmed to the size of the characters. The changes will not be visible on the screen unless the character definitions are loaded into the active character table.

The contents of registers BX, CX, DX, SI, DI, BP and the segment registers are not affected by this function.

Interrupt 10H, function 11H, sub-function 02H **EGA/VGA**
Screen: Load 8x8 character set

Loads the entire 8x8-pixel character set from EGA/VGA ROM-BIOS into one of the two character set tables.

Input:
AH = 11H
AL = 02H
BL = Character table (0 or 1)

Output: No output

Remarks: The loaded character set is not activated, nor are the CRTC registers programmed to the size of the characters. The changes will not be visible on the screen unless the character definitions are loaded into the active character table. The EGA card displays 43 lines on the screen, while the VGA card displays 50 lines.

The contents of registers BX, CX, DX, SI, DI, BP and the segment registers are not affected by this function.

Interrupt 10H, function 11H, sub-function 03H **EGA/VGA**
Screen: Activate character set

Activates one (or two) of the four 256-character character sets.

Input:
AH = 11H
AL = 03H
BL = Number of the character set to activate

Output: No output

Remarks: Bits zero and one of the BL register specify the number of the character set to be accessed when bit three of the attribute byte of the character is zero.

Bits two and three of the BL register specify the number of the character set to be accessed when bit three of the attribute byte of the character is one.

If the contents of bits zero and one are identical to the contents of bits two and three of the BL register, then bit three of the character attribute byte has no effect on the character displayed. Only 256 different characters can then be displayed on the screen.

The contents of registers BX, CX, DX, SI, DI, BP and the segment registers are not affected by this function.

Interrupt 10H, function 11H, sub-function 04H — VGA
Screen: Load 8x16 character set

Loads the entire 8x16-pixel character set from the VGA BIOS into one of the two character set tables.

Input:
AH = 11H
AL = 04H
BL = Corresponding character set table (0 or 1)

Output: No output

Remarks: The loaded character set is not activated, nor are the CRTC registers programmed to the size of the characters. The changes will not be visible on the screen unless the character definitions are loaded into the active character table. The VGA card displays 25 text lines on the screen.

The contents of registers BX, CX, DX, SI, DI, BP and the segment registers are not affected by this function.

Interrupt 10H, function 11H, sub-function 10H — EGA/VGA
Screen: Load and activate user-defined character set

Loads a user-defined character set from RAM into one of the two EGA character tables and activates it by programming the CRTC registers.

Input:
AH = 11H
AL = 10H
BH = Lines per character (also bytes per character)
BL = Character table (0 or 1)
CX = Number of characters in table
DX = ASCII code of first character in table
ES = Segment address of character table in RAM
BP = Offset address of character table in RAM

Output: No output

Remarks: A maximum of 512 characters can be loaded per character table.

The number of text lines displayed on the screen results from the height of the individual characters. It is calculated by dividing the number of screen lines (350) by the character height.

The starting and ending lines of the screen cursor are automatically adapted to the height of the new character matrix.

The contents of registers BX, CX, DX, SI, DI, BP and the segment registers are not affected by this function.

Interrupt 10H, function 11H, sub-function 11H — EGA/VGA
Screen: Load and activate 8x14 character set

Loads the entire 8x14-pixel character set from EGA/VGA ROM-BIOS into one of the two character set tables, and activates it by programming the CRTC registers.

Input:
AH = 10H
AL = 11H
BL = Character table (0 or 1)

Output: No output

Remarks: The function sets the EGA screen to display 25 lines of text, or sets the VGA screen to display 28 lines of text.

The starting and ending lines of the screen cursor are automatically adapted to the height of the new character matrix.

The contents of registers BX, CX, DX, SI, DI, BP and the segment registers are not affected by this function.

Interrupt 10H, function 11H, sub-function 12H — EGA/VGA
Screen: Load and activate 8x8 character set

Loads the entire 8x8-pixel character set from the ROM-BIOS of the EGA/VGA card into one of the two character set tables, and activates it by programming the CRTC registers.

Input:
AH = 10H
AL = 12H
BL = Character table (0 or 1)

Output: No output

Remarks: The function sets the screen to display 43 lines of text (EGA) or 50 lines of text (VGA).

The starting and ending lines of the screen cursor are automatically adapted to the height of the new character matrix.

The contents of registers BX, CX, DX, SI, DI, BP and the segment registers are not affected by this function.

Interrupt 10H, function 11H, sub-function 14H **VGA**
Screen: Load 8x16 character set

Loads a complete 8x16 character set from the VGA card BIOS into one of the two character set tables, and activates it through CRTC register programming.

Input:
AH = 10H
AL = 14H
BL = Character table (0 or 1)

Output: No output

Remarks: When this function is called, the VGA card displays 25 lines of text on the screen.

The starting and ending lines of the screen cursor automatically change to match the height of the new character matrix.

The contents of registers BX, CX, DX, SI, DI, BP and all segment registers are not affected by this function.

Interrupt 10H, function 11H, sub-function 30H **EGA/VGA**
Screen: Get information about the character generator

Returns various information about the current status of the character generator.

Input:
AH = 11H
AL = 03H
BH = Type of information desired
- BH=0: contents of interrupt vector 1FH
- BH=1: contents of interrupt vector 43H
- BH=2: address of the ROM 8x14 character table
- BH=3: address of the ROM 8x8 character table
- BH=4: address of the second half of the 8x8 character table
- BH=5: address of the alternative ROM 9x14 character table
- BH=6: Address of the alternative ROM 8x16 character table
- BH=7: Address of the alternative ROM 9x16 character table

Output:
CX = Height of current character matrix
DL = Number of columns per line - 1
ES = Segment address of the pointer
BP = Offset address of the pointer

Remarks: The contents of registers BX, CX, DX, SI, DI, BP and the segment registers CS, DS and SS are not affected by this function.

Interrupt 10H, function 12H, sub-function 10H **EGA/VGA**
Screen: Determine EGA/VGA configuration

Reads the configuration of the EGA/VGA card.

Input: AH = 12H
BL = 10H

Output: BH = Monitor connected
BH=0: color or high-resolution monitor
BH=1: monochrome monitor
BL = EGA/VGA RAM capacity
BL=0: 64K
BL=1: 128K
BL=2: 192K
BL=3: 256K

Remarks: The contents of registers DX, SI, DI, BP and the segment registers are not affected by this function.

Interrupt 10H, function 12H, sub-function 20H **EGA/VGA**
Screen: Activate alternate hardcopy routine

Installs an alternative hardcopy routine which prints as many lines as are displayed on the screen. The hardcopy routine of the normal ROM-BIOS always prints 25 lines and is not suited for creating a hardcopy of the EGA/VGA modes, which display more than 25 lines on the screen.

Input: AH = 12H
BL = 20H

Output: No output

Remark: The contents of registers BX, CX, DX, SI, DI, BP and the segment registers are not affected by this function.

Interrupt 10H, function 12H, sub-function 30H **EGA/VGA**
Screen: Specify number of scan lines

Selects the number of scan lines on the screen.

Input: AH = 12H
BL = 30H
AL = Scan line status
AL=0 : 200 scan lines (EGA and VGA)
AL=1 : 350 scan lines (EGA and VGA)
AL=2 : 400 scan lines (VGA only)

Output: No output

Remarks: The selected number of scan lines can only be displayed when the appropriate video card and monitor are in use. For example, a CGA monitor can only display 200 scan lines, even if the video card can operate in a higher resolution.

The contents of registers BX, CX, DX, SI, DI and BP and all segment registers are not affected by this function.

Interrupt 10H, function 12H, sub-function 31H **VGA**
Screen: Toggle palette register loading

Toggles the automatic loading of palette registers in VGA BIOS. The system either loads alternate display modes when function 00H is invoked, or loads default values.

Input:
AH = 12H
BL = 31H
AL = Automatic palette register loading
AL=0: Yes
AL=1: No

Output: No output

Remarks: The contents of registers BX, CX, DX, SI, DI, BP and all segment registers are not affected by this function.

Interrupt 10H, function 12H, sub-function 32H **EGA/VGA**
Screen: Enable/disable CPU access to video RAM

Enables or disables direct CPU access to video RAM and its different I/O ports.

Input:
AH = 12H
BL = 32H
AL = Access status
AL=0: Access enabled
AL=1: Access denied

Output: No output

Remarks: The EGA BIOS doesn't recognize this function, but you can still suppress video card access directly using bit 1 of the output register (port address 3C2H).

The contents of registers BX, CX, DX, SI, DI, BP and all segment registers are not affected by this function.

Interrupt 10H, function 12H, sub-function 33H **VGA**
Screen: Enable/disable automatic gray scaling in DAC color registers

Toggles automatic gray scaling in VGA BIOS. This is different from function 10H, sub-function 1BH, which enables selective gray scaling in DAC color registers.

Input:
AH = 12H
BL = 33H
AL = DAC color register gray scaling
AL=0 : On
AL=1 : Off

Output:
No output

The contents of registers BX, CX, DX, SI, DI, BP and all segment registers are not affected by this function.

Interrupt 10H, function 12H, sub-function 34H **VGA**
Screen: Enable/disable text cursor emulation

Toggles text cursor emulation mode. Calling function 01H (for defining the starting and ending lines of the cursor) doesn't compensate for character matrices in different resolutions. This function controls that change when in VGA mode.

Input:
AH = 12H
BL = 34H
AL = Cursor emulation mode
AL=0: On
AL=1: Off

Output:
No output

Remarks:
The contents of registers BX, CX, DX, SI, DI, BP and all segment registers are not affected by this function.

Interrupt 10H, function 12H, sub-function 36H **VGA**
Screen: Suppress screen refresh

Temporarily suppresses screen refresh. Disabling refresh relieves video RAM of many system level tasks, especially those involving complex screen graphics.

Input:
AH = 12H
BL = 36H
AL = Screen refresh
AL=0: On
AL=1: Off

Output:
No output

Remarks: The contents of registers BX, CX, DX, SI, DI, BP and all segment registers are not affected by this function.

Interrupt 10H, function 13H **EGA/VGA**
Screen: Display a string

Displays a string at a specified position on the screen, in a specific display page. The characters are taken from a buffer whose address is passed to the function.

Input:
AH = 13H
AL = Output mode (0-3)
  AL=0: Attribute in BL, reserve cursor position
  AL=1: Attribute in BL, update cursor position
  AL=2: Attributes in buffer, reserve cursor position
  AL=3: Attributes in buffer, update cursor position
BL = Attribute byte of characters (modes 0 and 1 only)
CX = Number of characters to be printed
DH = Screen line
DL = Screen column
BH = Video page
ES = Segment address of the buffer
BP = Offset address of the buffer

Output: No output

Remarks: In modes 1 and 3 the cursor position is placed after the last character of the string so that BIOS output will continue at the character after the string. This does not happen in modes 0 and 2.

In modes 0 and 1 the buffer contains only the ASCII codes of the characters to be printed. The color of all of the characters in the string is specified by the BL register. In modes 2 and 3, each character in the buffer is followed by the corresponding attribute byte, so that each character has its own attribute. The BL register does not have to be loaded in these modes. Although the string must be twice as long as the number of characters to be printed in these modes, the CX register contains just the number of ASCII characters to be printed, not the string buffer's length.

Control codes such as bell and carriage return are interpreted as control codes and not as normal ASCII codes. An error occurs when carriage return and linefeed are printed on a display page other than zero, however. These characters may be printed on display page 0, regardless of the display page specified in BH.

When the last screen position is reached the screen will move up one line and the output will continue with the first column of the last screen line.

When printing in the graphic mode the contents of the BL register determine the foreground color of the character (the background is zero). If bit seven of the BL register is set, the color value will be XORed with the old color value.

This function can also be used to print characters in the graphic mode, in which case the character patterns will be taken from one of the EGA/VGA character tables.

The contents of registers BX, CX, DX, SI, DI, BP and the segment registers are not affected by this function.

Interrupt 10H, function 1AH **VGA**
Screen: Determine video card type

Determines the existence of the active video card.

Input: AH = 13H
AL = 0

Output: AL = 1AH
BL = Device code for active video card
BH = Device code for inactive video card

Remarks: If the value 1AH is not loaded into the AL register, then the video card in operation is not a VGA card (the 1AH indicates a VGA BIOS). The function can return the following device codes:

FFH = Unknown video card
00H = No video card
01H = MDA with monochrome display
02H = CGA with CGA monitor
04H = EGA with EGA or multisync monitor
05H = EGA - monochrome display
07H = VGA - analog monochrome display
08H = VGA - analog color display (VGA, multisync)

The contents of registers CX, DX, SI, DI, BP and all segment registers are not affected by this function.

Appendix F

Mouse Driver Interrupts

Interrupt 33H, function 00H **Mouse**
Reset mouse driver

Resets (initializes) the mouse driver.

Input: AX = 0000H

Output: AX = Mouse installation status
AX=FFFFH: Mouse driver installed
AX=0000H: Error, no mouse driver installed
BX = Number of mouse buttons

Remarks: The reset process executes the following tasks:

Moves the mouse pointer to the center of the screen and clears the pointer from the screen. When enabled, the default pointer appears as an inverse video square. The representation is always in display page 0, independent of the current display mode. The entire screen area becomes the total range of mouse movement.

Installs the event handler is installed by a program (default is disabled).

Installs lightpen emulation (default is disabled).

Specifies mouse pointer's speed. Default relative speed is 8 mickeys per 8 horizontal pixels and 16 mickeys per 16 vertical pixels.

Specifies maximum mouse speed (default is 64 mickeys per second).

Interrupt 33H, function 01H **Mouse**
Display mouse pointer

Displays the mouse pointer on the screen. This pointer follows any movement the user makes with the mouse device.

Input AX = 0001H

Output: No output

Remarks: This function increments an internal counter which determines whether the mouse pointer should be displayed on the screen. When the mouse driver is initialized using function 00H, this pointer contains the value -1 (i.e., the mouse pointer does not appear). If this counter contains the value 0 after calling function 01H, the mouse pointer appears on the screen.

The mouse driver follows the mouse movement even when the mouse pointer is not displayed on the screen. After calling this function, the mouse pointer may not appear at the same location as it was when the pointer was previously removed by calling function 00H or function 02H.

Interrupt 33H, function 02H **Mouse**
Remove mouse pointer

Removes the mouse pointer from the screen.

Input AX = 0002H

Output: No output

Remarks: This function decrements an internal counter which determines whether the mouse pointer should appear on the screen. If the counter contains the value 0, the mouse pointer is displayed on the screen, while the value -1 removes the mouse pointer from the screen.

The mouse driver follows the mouse movement even when the mouse pointer is not displayed on the screen.

After calling this function, the mouse pointer may not appear at the same location as it was when the pointer was previously removed by calling function 00H or function 02H.

Interrupt 33H, function 03H **Mouse**
Get pointer position/button status

Returns the current position of the mouse pointer and the current status of the mouse buttons.

Input AX = 0003H

Output BX = Mouse button status
Bit 0=1: Left mouse button activated
Bit 1=1: Right mouse button activated
Bit 2=1: Center mouse button activated
Bits 3-15: Unused
CX = X coordinate (horizontal mouse position)
DX = Y coordinate (vertical mouse position)

Remarks: The coordinates returned in the CX and DX registers refer to the pixel positions in the virtual mouse display screen rather than physical positions on the actual display screen.

If the mouse is equipped with only two mouse buttons, the information about the central mouse button does not have significance.

Interrupt 33H, function 04H **Mouse**
Move mouse pointer

Moves the active mouse pointer to a certain position on the screen.

Input AX = 0004H
CX = X coordinate (horizontal mouse position)
DX = Y coordinate (vertical mouse position)

Output: No output

Remarks: The coordinates returned in the CX and DX registers refer to the pixel positions in the virtual mouse display screen rather than physical positions on the actual display screen.

If the position indicated is outside the range of movement specified by functions 07H and 08H, the function adjusts coordinates so that the mouse pointer remains within this range of movement.

The mouse pointer moves to the new position, even if the mouse is not currently visible. Once re-enabled, the mouse pointer appears at this new position.

Interrupt 33H, function 05H **Mouse**
Determine number of times mouse button was activated

Informs the calling program of how often a mouse button has been pressed since the last call of function 05H. Function 05H also informs the calling program of the pointer's location on the screen when the button was last activated.

Input
AX = 0005H
BX = Mouse button activated
BX=0: Left mouse button
BX=1: Right mouse button
BX=2: Center mouse button

Output:
BX = Status of all mouse buttons:
Bit 0=1: Left mouse button activated
Bit 1=1: Right mouse button activated
Bit 2=1: Center mouse button activated
Bits 3-15: Unused
BX = Mouse buttons activated since last function call
CX = Horizontal mouse position during the last activation
DX = Vertical mouse position during the last activation

Remarks:
The coordinates returned in the CX and DX registers refer to the pixel positions in the virtual mouse display screen rather than physical positions on the actual display screen. The activation counter for the mouse button addressed is reset to 0 when this function is called.

Interrupt 33H, function 06H **Mouse**
Determine number of times mouse button was released

Informs the calling program of how often a mouse button has been released since the last call of function 06H. Function 06H also informs the calling program of the pointer's location on the screen when the button was last activated.

Input
AX = 0006H
BX = mouse button addressed
BX=0: Left mouse button
BX=1: Right mouse button
BX=2: Center mouse button

Output:
BX = Status of all mouse buttons
Bit 0=1: Left mouse button activated
Bit 1=1: Right mouse button activated
Bit 2=1: Center mouse button activated
Bits 3-15: Unused
BX = Mouse buttons activated since last function call
CX = Horizontal mouse position during the last activation
DX = Vertical mouse position during the last activation

Remarks: The coordinates returned in the CX and DX registers refer to the pixel positions in the virtual mouse display screen rather than physical positions on the actual display screen.

The activation counter for the mouse button addressed is reset to 0 when this function is called.

Interrupt 33H, function 07H **Mouse**
Set horizontal range of movement

Defines the horizontal range of movement for the mouse pointer. Once set, the user cannot move the mouse pointer out of this range.

Input AX = 0007H
CX = Minimal horizontal pointer position
DX = Maximum horizontal pointer position

Output: No output

Remarks: The coordinates passed in the CX and DX registers refer to the pixel positions in the virtual mouse display screen rather than physical positions on the actual display screen.

If the mouse pointer is outside of this range when function 07H is called, the mouse driver automatically moves the mouse pointer within the limits of the range of movement. If the value in the DX register is less than the value in the CX registers, the two parameters are exchanged.

Interrupt 33H, function 08H **Mouse**
Set vertical range of movement

Defines the vertical range of movement for the mouse pointer. Once set, the user cannot move the mouse pointer out of this range.

Input AX = 0008H
CX = Minimum vertical pointer position
DX = Maximum vertical pointer position

Output: No output

Remarks: The coordinates passed in the CX and DX registers refer to the pixel positions in the virtual mouse display screen rather than physical positions on the actual display screen.

If the mouse pointer is outside of this range when function 07H is called, the mouse driver automatically moves the mouse pointer within the limits of the range of movement.

If the value in the DX register is less than the value in the CX registers, the two parameters are exchanged.

Interrupt 33H, function 09H **Mouse**
Set mouse pointer (graphic mode)

Defines the appearance of the mouse pointer in graphic mode, as well as the bitfield which compensates for the pixels around the mouse pointer.

Input
AX = 0009H
BX = Pointer width starting at left border of bitfield
CX = Pointer height starting at top border of bitfield
ES = Segment address of bitfield
DX = Offset address of bitfield

Output: No output

Remarks: The bitfield consists of 64 bytes, of which the first 32 are an AND comparison, and the remaining 32 are an OR combination. Both sets of bytes are based upon the current pixel pattern.

Interrupt 33H, function 0AH **Mouse**
Set mouse pointer (text mode)

Defines the bitmask which specifies the appearance of the mouse pointer in text mode.

Input
AX = 000AH
BX = Pointer type
BX=0: Software pointer
BX=1: Hardware pointer
CX = AND mask (software pointer) or starting line (hardware pointer)
DX = XOR mask (software pointer) or ending line (hardware pointer)

Output: No output

Remarks: If the software pointer is selected, the code of the character beneath the mouse pointer and its attribute byte are combined logically with the mask in the CX register through a binary AND, and then with the value in the DX register through an exclusive OR (XOR). The attribute byte is combined with the most significant byte (CH and DH). The character code is combined with the least significant byte (CL and DL).

The hardware pointer is the same shape as the normal text mode cursor. Monochrome mode values for the starting and ending lines range from 0 to 13. Color mode values for the starting and ending lines range from 0 to 7.

Interrupt 33H, function 0BH **Mouse**
Determine movement values

Determines the distance between the current mouse position and the mouse position during the last call of function 0BH.

Input AX = 000BH

Output: CX = Horizontal distance from last point in mickeys
DX = Vertical distance from last point in mickeys

Remarks: These values must be interpreted as signed numbers. Positive values indicate movement toward the bottom or right border of the screen, while negative values indicate movement toward the top or left border of the screen.

These values are given in mickeys.(1 mickey=1/200 inch) rather than in pixels.

Interrupt 33H, function 0CH **Mouse**
Set event handler

Sets the address of an event handler called by the mouse driver when a particular mouse event occurs.

Input AX = 000CH
CX = Events which trigger the call of the event handler (event mask)
Bit 0: Mouse movement
Bit 1: Left mouse button activated
Bit 2: Left mouse button released
Bit 3: Right mouse button activated
Bit 4: Right mouse button released
Bit 5: Center mouse button activated
Bit 6: Center mouse button released
Bits 7-15: Unused
ES = Segment address of handler
DX = Offset address of handler

Output: No output

Remarks: The event handler is called by the mouse driver through a FAR call assembler instruction, and therefore must be terminated with a FAR RET instruction. None of the various processor registers may be returned to the caller with a changed content.

The mouse driver passes the following information to the event handler through the processor registers during the call:

AX = event mask. The bits correspond to the various events as indicated in the CX register during the installation of the event handler. In addition, other bits can be set, since the value reflects the current status of the mouse driver, and is not limited to the selected events.

BX = mouse button status:

Bit 0 = Left mouse button activated
Bit 1 = Right mouse button activated
Bit 2 = Center mouse button activated

CX = horizontal mouse position.

DX = vertical mouse position.

SI = length of last horizontal mouse movement.

DI = length of the last vertical mouse movement.

DS = data segment of the mouse driver.

The coordinates returned in the CX and DX registers refer to the pixel positions in the virtual mouse display screen rather than physical positions on the actual display screen.

The values in the SI and DI registers refer to mickeys (one mickey = 1/200 inch).

These mickey values must be interpreted as signed numbers. Positive values indicate movement toward the bottom or right border of the screen, while negative values indicate movement toward the top or left border of the screen.

Interrupt 33H, function 0DH **Mouse**
Enable lightpen emulation

Enables emulation of the lightpen, and simulates a lightpen which if none is present.

Input AX = 000DH

Output: No output

Remarks: Lightpen emulation only makes sense when used with an application which supports the lightpen, or makes lightpen reading routines available (e.g., the PEN command in PC-BASIC).

The lightpen and mouse are closely related in programming: The position of the mouse pointer is directly related to the lightpen's position on the screen, and pressing the left and right mouse button has the same result as pressing the button on the lightpen.

Interrupt 33H, function 0EH **Mouse**
Disable lightpen emulation

Disables the lightpen emulation enabled by a previous call to function 0DH.

Input AX = 000EH

Output: No output

Remarks: Lightpen emulation only makes sense when used with an application which supports the lightpen, or makes lightpen reading routines available (e.g., the PEN command in PC-BASIC).

The lightpen and mouse are closely related in programming: The position of the mouse pointer is directly related to the lightpen's position on the screen, and pressing the left and right mouse button has the same result as pressing the button on the lightpen.

Interrupt 33H, function 0FH **Mouse**
Set pointer speed

Defines the relationship between mickeys and screen pixels. This specifies the sensitivity of the mouse and the speed at which the mouse pointer moves across the screen.

Input AX = 000FH
CX = Number of horizontal mickeys
DX = Number of vertical mickeys

Output: No output

Remarks: Values in the CX and DX registers can range from 1 to 32767.

The default setting is 8 horizontal mickeys and 16 vertical mickeys. This causes the mouse pointer to move twice as fast horizontally as it moves vertically.

Calling function 00H (Reset mouse driver) changes any previously set values to the default values.

Interrupt 33H, function 10H **Mouse**
Exclusion area

Designates any area of the screen as an exclusion area. The mouse pointer disappears if moved into the exclusion area.

Input AX = 0010H
CX = X-coordinate, upper left corner of exclusion area
DX = Y-coordinate, upper left corner of exclusion area
SI = X-coordinate, lower right corner of exclusion area
DI = Y-coordinate, lower right corner of exclusion area

Output: No output

Remarks: The coordinates passed in the CX, DX, DI and SI registers refer to the pixel positions in the virtual mouse display screen rather than physical positions on the actual display screen.

Calling function 00H (Reset mouse driver) or function 01H (Display mouse pointer) deletes the exclusion area coordinates.

Interrupt 33H, function 13H **Mouse**
Set maximum for mouse speed doubling

Sets the maximum limit for doubling mouse speed. If the speed of the mouse movement exceeds a certain limit, the mouse driver doubles the mouse pointer speed by doubling the movement's relationship between points and mickeys.

Input AX = 0013H
DX = Limit in mickeys per second

Output: No output

Remarks: 1 mickey=1/200 inches.

To prevent doubling of the mouse speed, the limit can be set higher.

Speeds in excess of 5,000 mickeys per second cannot be achieved by practical means.

Interrupt 33H, function 14H — Mouse
Exchange event handlers

Installs a new event handler for certain mouse events, but also retains the address of the old event handler.

Input

AX = 0014H
CX = Events which should trigger event handler call
Bit 0: Mouse movement
Bit 1: Left mouse button activated
Bit 2: Left mouse button released
Bit 3: Right mouse button activated
Bit 4: Right mouse button released
Bit 5: Center mouse button activated
Bit 6: Center mouse button released
Bit 7-15: Unused

ES = Segment address of new event handler
DX = Offset address of new event handler

Output:

CX = Event mask of the previously installed event handler
ES = Segment address of previously installed event handler
DX = Offset address of previously installed event handler

Remarks:

The event handler is called by the mouse driver through a FAR call assembler instruction, and therefore must be terminated with a FAR RET instruction. None of the various processor registers may be returned to the caller with a changed content.

The mouse driver passes the following information to the event handler through the processor registers during the call:

AX = event mask. The bits correspond to the various events as indicated in the CX register during the installation of the event handler. In addition, other bits can be set, since the value reflects the current status of the mouse driver, and is not limited to the selected events.

BX = mouse button status:

Bit 0 = Left mouse button activated
Bit 1 = Right mouse button activated
Bit 2 = Center mouse button activated

CX = horizontal mouse position.

DX = vertical mouse position.

SI = length of last horizontal mouse movement.

DI = length of the last vertical mouse movement.

DS = data segment of the mouse driver.

The coordinates returned in the CX and DX registers refer to the pixel positions in the virtual mouse display screen rather than physical positions on the actual display screen.

The values in the SI and DI registers refer to mickeys (one mickey = 1/200 inch).

These mickey values must be interpreted as signed numbers. Positive values indicate movement toward the bottom or right border of the screen, while negative values indicate movement toward the top or left border of the screen.

Interrupt 33H, function 15H **Mouse**
Determine mouse status buffer size

Returns the size of the mouse status buffer, in which a program can store the complete status of the mouse driver.

Input AX = 0015H

Output: BX = Mouse status buffer size in bytes

Remarks: Function 16H (Store mouse status) stores the mouse status in the buffer.

Interrupt 33H, function 16H **Mouse**
Store mouse status

Stores mouse status information in a buffer.

Input AX = 0016H
ES = Segment address of mouse status buffer
DX = Offset address of mouse status buffer

Output: No output

Remarks: The caller is responsible for creating a buffer large enough to contain all the status information. Before calling this function, call function 15H (Determine mouse status buffer size) to determine the size of the mouse status buffer.

This function works well when called before executing a program using the EXEC function. This allows the mouse status to be saved in memory, then restored from within the called program.

Interrupt 33H, function 17H **Mouse**
Restore mouse status

Reads all mouse parameters from a buffer where they had been stored by function 16H.

Input
AX = 0017H
ES = Segment address of mouse status buffer
DX = Offset address of mouse status buffer

Output:
No output

Interrupt 33H, function 18H **Mouse**
Install alternate event handler

This function permits a program to install a limited range event handler. This handler can be called by the mouse driver when certain mouse events occur in conjunction with the keyboard.

Input
AX = 0018H
CX = Events which should trigger the call of the event handler
Bit 0: Mouse movement
Bit 1: Left mouse button activated
Bit 2: Left mouse button released
Bit 3: Right mouse button activated
Bit 4: Right mouse button released
Bit 5: Shift key pressed during mouse button event
Bit 6: Ctrl key pressed during mouse button event
Bit 7: Alt key pressed during mouse button event
Bits 8-15: Unused
ES = Segment address of event handler
DX = Offset address of event handler

Output:
AX = Installation status
AX=0018H: Event handler installed
AX=FFFFH: Event handler could not be installed

Remarks:
At least one of bits 5 to 7 must be set in the event mask of the CX register to ensure that the event reacts to at least one of the control keys. If the programmer prefers not to read the Shift, Ctrl or Alt keys along with mouse buttons, use functions 0CH or 14H instead.

An error can occur if three alternate event handlers were previously installed, or if an event handler with the same event mask already exists.

Remarks: The event handler is called by the mouse driver through a FAR call assembler instruction, and therefore must be terminated with a FAR RET instruction. None of the various processor registers may be returned to the caller with a changed content.

The mouse driver passes the following information to the event handler through the processor registers during the call:

AX = event mask. The bits correspond to the various events as indicated in the CX register during the installation of the event handler. In addition, other bits can be set, since the value reflects the current status of the mouse driver, and is not limited to the selected events.

BX = mouse button status:

Bit 0 = Left mouse button activated
Bit 1 = Right mouse button activated
Bit 2 = Center mouse button activated

CX = horizontal mouse position.

DX = vertical mouse position.

SI = length of last horizontal mouse movement.

DI = length of the last vertical mouse movement.

DS = data segment of the mouse driver.

The coordinates returned in the CX and DX registers refer to the pixel positions in the virtual mouse display screen rather than physical positions on the actual display screen.

The values in the SI and DI registers refer to mickeys (one mickey = 1/200 inch).

These mickey values must be interpreted as signed numbers. Positive values indicate movement toward the bottom or right border of the screen, while negative values indicate movement toward the top or left border of the screen.

Interrupt 33H, function 19H — Mouse
Determine address of alternate event handler

Returns the address of an alternate event handler to the caller.

Input
AX = 0019H
CX = Event handler event mask

Output:
CX = 0000H: Error
ES = Segment address of event handler
DX = Offset address of event handler

Remarks:
See the description of function 18H above for additional information about the meanings of each bit in the event mask.

The function call fails if no alternate event handler with the indicated event mask was previously installed.

Interrupt 33H, function 1AH — Mouse
Set mouse sensitivity

Defines the relationship between physical mouse movement and mouse pointer movement. Also defines the maximum for doubling mouse speed.

Input
AX = 001AH
BX = Number of horizontal mickeys
CX = Number of vertical mickeys
DX = Maximum limit for doubling the mouse speed

Output:
No output

Remarks:
Values in the CX and DX registers can range from 1 to 32767.

The default setting is 8 horizontal mickeys and 16 vertical mickeys. This causes the mouse pointer to move twice as fast horizontally as it moves vertically.

To prevent doubling of the mouse speed, the limit can be set higher.

Speeds in excess of 5,000 mickeys per second cannot be achieved by practical means.

Calling function 00H (Reset mouse driver) changes any previously set values to the default values.

Interrupt 33H, function 1BH **Mouse**
Determine mouse sensitivity

Returns the parameters previously set by calling function 1AH or functions 0FH and 13H.

Input AX = 001BH

Output: BX = Number of horizontal mickeys
CX = Number of vertical mickeys
DX = Maximum limit for doubling the mouse speed

Interrupt 33H, function 1CH **Mouse**
Set mouse hardware interrupt rate

Determines the frequency at which the mouse hardware reads the current mouse position and mouse button status.

Input AX = 001CH
BX = Interrupt rate
Bit 0: No interrupts
Bit 1: 30 interrupts per second
Bit 2: 50 interrupts per second
Bit 3: 100 interrupts per second
Bit 4: 200 interrupts per second
Bits 5-15: Unused

Output: No output

Remarks: This function is only available for the Inport mouse.

If more than one bit is set in the BX register, only the least significant bit which is set counts.

The mouse's resolution increases with the number of interrupts. The increased number of mouse interrupts decreases the speed of the foreground program.

Interrupt 33H, function 1DH **Mouse**
Set display page

Specifies the display page on which the mouse pointer appears.

Input AX = 001DH
BX = Number of the display page

Output: No output

Remarks: Default value is display page 0.

Calling this function only makes sense if the application program works with several display pages, as available on CGA, EGA and VGA cards.

Interrupt 33H, function 1EH **Mouse**
Determine display page

Determines the display page on which the mouse pointer appears.

Input AX = 001EH

Output: BX = Number of the display page

Interrupt 33H, function 1FH **Mouse**
Deactivate mouse driver

Deactivates the current mouse driver and returns the address of the previous interrupt handlers for interrupt 33H.

Input AX = 001FH

Output: AX = Error status
AX=FFFFH: Error
AX=001FH: O.K.
ES = Segment address of previous event handler
BX = Offset address of previous event handler

Remarks: This call releases any previously installed and active mouse driver interrupt routines. The exception to this is the handler for interrupt 33H, but the caller can reload this interrupt vector with its original value since this address is returned in the ES:BX register pair.

Interrupt 33H, function 20H **Mouse**
Activate mouse driver

Activates a mouse driver previously deactivated by function 1FH.

Input AX = 0020H

Output: No output

Interrupt 33H, function 21H — Mouse
Reset mouse driver

Resets the mouse driver, disables the mouse pointer and disables the currently installed event handler.

Input AX = 0021H

Output: AX = Error status
AX=FFFFH: Error
AX=0021H: O.K.
BX = Number of mouse buttons

Remarks: Unlike function 00H, this function does not perform a total mouse hardware reset.

Interrupt 33H, function 24H — Mouse
Determine mouse type

Determines the type of mouse installed and the version number of the mouse driver.

Input AX = 0024H

Output: BH = Whole number of the version number
BL = Fraction of the version number
CH = Mouse type
CH=1: Bus mouse
CH=2: Serial mouse
CH=3: Inport mouse
CH=4: PS/2 mouse
CH=5: HP mouse
CL = IRQ number
CL=0: PS/2
CL=2, 3, 4, 5 or 7: IRQ number in the PC

Remarks: If the version number of the mouse driver is for example 6.24, the value 6 is returned in the BH register and the value 24 is returned in the BL register.

Appendix G

Introduction to Number Systems

Throughout this book we talked about numbers notated in the *binary* and *hexadecimal systems* instead of the normal decimal system. This Appendix presents a brief introduction to these number systems.

Decimal system

Before explaining the new number systems, you should know the basic concepts of the decimal system. The decimal number 1989 can also be written as 1*1000+9*100+8*10+9*1. This shows that if you number the digits from right to left, the first number represents a column of ones, the second number represents a column of tens, the third number represents a column of hundreds and the fourth number represents a column of thousands. The numbers increase from right to left in powers of 10.

The first digit of any number system has the value 1. The factor by which the value increases from one column to the next differs among the number systems. This factor corresponds to the numbers with which the number system works. The factor is 10 with the decimal system because ten different numbers are available for each digit (0 to 9).

This principle of powers for each column also applies to the binary and hexadecimal systems.

Binary system

Since a computer recognizes the numbers 0 and 1 on its lowest functional level, the binary system is essential to computing. The value of the numbers double from column to column because the binary system only uses powers of two for each column (i.e., the numbers 0 and 1 instead of the numbers 0 to 9).

Now let's count the binary places starting from right to left as we did in the decimal example described above. The first (right hand) position counts as one, the second as two, the third as four and the fourth as eight. The places then follow as 16, 32, 64, 128, etc.

For example, 11001 binary converts to 25 decimal, or the equation 1*16+1*8+0*4+0*2+1*1.

Hexadecimal system

Unlike the binary system, the hexadecimal system operates with more basic numbers than the decimal system. This system counts single digits from 0 to F. Since only the ten numbers of the decimal system are able to represent a number, the numbers from 10 to 15 in hexadecimal use the letters A to F in addition to the numbers 0 to 9. AH stands for 10, BH for 11, CH for 12, DH for 13, EH for 14 and FH for 15.

By using 16 numbers or letters for each position, the value by which each position increments is 16.

The first position has the value 1, the second 16, the third 256 and the fourth 4,096.

For example, the hexadecimal number FB3H converts into 4,019 decimal, or 15*256+11*16+3*1.

Hex and binary

The hexadecimal system and the binary system are easily converted back and forth. For example, one four-digit binary number converts to a single-digit hexadecimal number. Because of this, the hexadecimal system is an important part of assembly language programming. It's much simpler to convey a byte (an eight-bit number) using two hexadecimal digits than it is for the developer to compute a 16-bit binary equivalent.

This book denotes all binary numbers by the letter (b), and all hexadecimal numbers by the letter H.

The following illustrations should help explain number systems more clearly.

Places	5	4	3	2	1
Decimal	10000	1000	100	10	1
Binary	16	8	4	2	1
Hexadecimal	65536	4096	256	16	1

Number positions in each number system

Decimal	Binary	Hexadecimal
0	0(b)	0H
1	1(b)	1H
2	10(b)	2H
3	11(b)	3H
4	100(b)	4H
5	101(b)	5H
6	110(b)	6H
7	111(b)	7H
8	1000(b)	8H
9	1001(b)	9H
10	1010(b)	AH
11	1011(b)	BH
12	1100(b)	CH
128	10000000(b)	80H
129	10000001(b)	81H
256	100000000(b)	100H
1024	10000000000(b)	400H
4096	1000000000000(b)	1000H
65535	1111111111111111(b)	FFFFH

Comparing selected numbers in each number system

Appendix H

Glossary of Terms

8086, 8088, 80186, 80286, 80386

Microprocessors manufactured by the Intel Corporation. They are upwardly compatible, which means that the 80836 can execute any program developed for an 8086, 8088, 80186 or 80286 microprocessor. However, the 8088 can't always execute an application developed for one of the later microprocessors. The processors of this family act as main processors for different types of PCs.

Address

The Intel-80xx family of microprocessors form an address from one of the four segment registers, in conjunction with another register or a constant. The contents of the segment register becomes the segment address, and the other register or constant becomes the offset address. Both addresses are logical addresses that are related to a physical address (the actual number of a memory location). This physical address can be determined by multiplying the segment register by 16 and adding the offset address.

Address area

The number of memory locations addressable by a microprocessor.

Address bus

A line connecting the CPU with memory (RAM and ROM). If the CPU wants to address a memory location, it must first place its address on the address bus in order to set the "switches" for access to this memory location.

Arena header

The data structure which precedes the memory area of the TPA assigned to a program. DOS uses this area to store the memory area's size and other information.

ASCII

Abbreviation for **American Standard Code for Information Interchange.** ASCII is a standardized assignment of numbers from 0 to 255 that represents characters (e.g., letters, numbers). The ASCII codes from 0 to 127 comprise the *standard ASCII character set*, while the codes from 128 to 255 comprise the *extended ASCII character set.*

Assembly language

A small number of simple instructions that the processor can understand. Every higher level language program is finally translated into these instructions for processing by the CPU.

Asynchronous data transfer

Also known as *serial transfer*. Bytes are transmitted and/or received bit by bit according to a predetermined transfer protocol.

AT

Abbreviation for **Advanced Technology**. AT computers have an 80286 processor.

Attribute

A byte following each character that defines the character's color and appearance for display on the screen.

AUTOEXEC.BAT

Filename for the automatically executing batch file for which DOS searches during the booting process. After DOS is loaded and started, it searches the root directory of the device from which it booted for a file named AUTOEXEC.BAT. During the booting process, this *batch file* executes programs and parameters through the command processor.

Batch files

Text files saved with the file extension .BAT. These files contain DOS commands or command sequences. Batch file execution treats these commands as if the user had entered the commands from the keyboard.

Baud

A measurement of data transfer speed. One baud roughly equals one data bit per second.

BCD

Abbreviation for **Binary Coded Decimal**. This number represents a two-digit decimal number encoded in one byte. The upper four bits represent the most significant digit and the lower four bits represent the least significant digit.

Binary system

The number system understandable by a computer at its lowest level. Binary notation counts from 0 to 1. The first position of a binary number has the value 1, the second has the value 2, the third has the value 4, the fourth has the value 8, etc.

BIOS

Abbreviation for **Basic Input/Output System.** It contains the device drivers which perform access to the peripheral devices such as the keyboard, monitor, disk drives, etc. The BIOS is located in addresses F000:E000—F000:FFFF.

BIOS interrupts

Interrupts 10H to 17H and interrupt 1AH, through which the many functions of the ROM-BIOS can be called.

BIOS version

Release date of the BIOS as stored in the eight bytes starting at memory location F000:FFF5. This version appears in the form Month/Day/Year.

Block driver

The *device drivers* which control access to devices that process data in data blocks (disk drives and hard disks). Block drivers are addressed through a letter (drive specifier) which enables one block driver to control several devices with different letters. The disk driver has the drive specifiers A: and B:, while the hard disk driver can be addressed with the specifier C:.

Boot sector

Contained on every mass storage medium from which DOS can be booted. Sector 0 contains certain information and a short program which loads a DOS boot routine, then initializes DOS.

Booting

The process that starts after the user has switched on the computer. BIOS tests and initializes the various circuit chips in the system, then loads the operating system.

BPB

Abbreviation for **BIOS Parameter Block.** The BPB defines the format and design of a mass storage device (disk drive and hard disk) for DOS. It is available in the boot sector of every mass storage device, but must be passed to DOS by the initialization routine of a block device driver.

CALL

Assembly language instruction that triggers the execution of a subroutine. After the routine ends, a RET instruction executes, which is followed by the instruction following the initial CALL.

Carry flag

Bit 0 in the processor's flag register. Many operating system functions use it to tell the calling program whether the called function executed correctly, or if an error occurred. In the latter case, the carry flag is set (1) after the function call.

Character driver

A device driver which controls access to devices that process characters as bytes. The screen, keyboard and printer are device drivers. Character drivers have their own names, such as CON, PRN and AUX.

Child program

A program which is called by another program. For example, if the FORMAT command is called from the DOS level, the parent program is the command processor.

CLI

Clear interrupts instruction. This instruction instructs the CPU to ignore all subsequent interrupt requests until the STI (STart Interrupts) instruction re-enables interrupt response (the NMI [Non-Maskable Interrupt] is exempt from this instruction).

Clock driver

A character device responsible for getting the time and date from DOS, incrementing the time and date and passing the incremented amounts back to DOS.

Clock generator

Produces several million pulses per second and synchronizes various components of the system with each other.

Cluster

Multiple sectors of a mass storage device. Files and subdirectories can be stored in different clusters. The number of sectors per cluster varies from one device to another.

COM files

Executable programs which must be stored within a 64K memory segment. COM files combine program code, data and stack in this 64K area.

COMMAND.COM

The file containing the MS-DOS command processor.

Command line

A line from which program or batch file calls can be entered into the command processor.

Command parameters

The name for all characters passed in the *command line*, following the program or batch file calls. The EXEC function copies these parameters into the PSP of the loaded program.

Command processor

Also called *shell*. The command processor is a part of the operating system which accepts and processes user input. Its main function is to load and start application programs and batch files.

CON

Abbreviation for **CONsole driver**, the two device drivers which control the keyboard and the screen.

CONFIG.SYS

The DOS configuration file. It contains certain commands for configuring DOS, as well as additional device drivers. CONFIG.SYS loads and executes only once (during the booting process).

Control characters

ASCII characters which represent certain non-alphanumeric characters. This applies to all ASCII codes less than 32. The PC only uses ASCII codes 0, 7, 8, 9, 10, 11, 12 and 13 as control characters.

Cooked mode

Character mode that checks for certain unusual characters, which are either converted to other characters or completely filtered out. Character drivers operate either in *raw mode* or *cooked mode*.

CP/M-80

Early operating system, the predecessor of MS-DOS. CP/M is used by computers that are based upon Z-80 microprocessors.

CPU

Abbreviation for **Central Processing Unit**. The microprocessor which forms the "brain" of a computer.

CRC

Abbreviation for **Cyclical Redundancy Check**. The CRC tests for errors during data transfer to and from a disk.

CRT

Abbreviation for **Cathode Ray Tube.** A CRT generates a screen display with the help of an electron beam which sends electrical impulses to a glass screen at the end of the CRT.

DASD

Abbreviation for **Direct Access Storage Device.** In DOS and BIOS terminology this concept is used for disk drives and hard disks.

Data bus

A data line which connects the CPU with memory (RAM and ROM). Data can be transmitted between the CPU and memory over this line.

Device driver

Driver systems which interface DOS and hardware by making basic functions available for communicating with the hardware. Device driver functions can be called by the higher level DOS functions. DOS differentiates between character drivers and block drivers.

Disks

Flat plastic materials containing magnetic media for storing data. Formatted disks are partitioned into tracks and sectors.

Disk controller

Regulates the activities of the disk drive.

Disk status

Lists the status of the last disk operation. It indicates if and when an error occurred during this disk access.

Disk formats

The PC market supports several disk formats. PC and XT disk drives use 5-1/4" disks that are formatted on one or two sides. Each side contains 40 tracks with eight or nine sectors per track (each sector stores 512 bytes). The capacity of these disks is between 160K (single-sided) and 360K (double-sided). The AT uses 5-1/4" disks with two formatted sides, each side containing 80 tracks with 15 sectors per track (each sector stores 512 bytes). The total capacity of these disks is 1.2 megabytes.

The newest disk formats on the market allow the use of 3-1/2" micro floppy disks.

Display page

Also called *screen page* and *video page*. Some video cards can control one or more display pages. Only one of these pages can be displayed on the screen at one time.

DMA

Abbreviation for **Direct Memory Access.** Transmits data from the circuit chips of a peripheral device directly into memory, without making a detour through the CPU.

DMA controller

A chip capable of transferring large amounts of data directly into memory without passing through the CPU. A good example is the access to a disk drive or hard disk drive.

DOS

Abbreviation for **Disk Operating System.** DOS sets up basic file handling tasks for communicating between computer and disk drive(s).

DTA

Abbreviation for **Disk Transfer Area.** File and directory accesses use the DTA for disk data transmission. Its size depends upon the current operation, where the calling program must ensure that enough memory exists to accept the transmitted data. After the start of a program, DOS places the beginning of the DTA into memory location 128 of the PSP, which makes 128 bytes available.

ECC

Abbreviation for **Error Correction Code.** ECC is used when data is stored on a hard disk. Unlike the CRC, the ECC permits the recognition of errors as well as their correction within certain parameters.

EGA

Abbreviation for **Enhanced Graphic Adapter.** This is a special, high resolution variation on the Color/Graphics Adapter (CGA).

EMM

Abbreviation for Expanded Memory Manager. Allows access to EMS memory.

EMS

Abbreviation for Expanded Memory System. This section of RAM goes beyond the 1 megabyte limit set by PCs and XTs. EMS is only accessible through the EMM.

End character

Also called *return code*. The end character is ASCII code 0, which is sometimes assigned the name NUL. It usually indicates the last character in a character string.

Environment block

Every program has an assigned environment block whose address is stored in the PSP of the current program. The environment block itself consists of a series of ASCII strings which contain certain information, such as the search path for files (PATH).

EOI

Abbreviation for **End Of Interrupt.** This instruction indicates.the completion of a hardware triggered interrupt to the interrupt handler.

Extended key code

Keys and key combinations that can be entered with a PC keyboard but have no direct relation to the ASCII character set. They are often entered by pressing and holding the <Alt> key, then entering a three-digit number on the numeric keypad.

EXE files

Executable programs which can be of any length and can store their code, data and stack in different memory segments (see also *COM files*).

EXEC

DOS function for loading and executing programs. The command processor also uses this function to execute applications programs and batch files.

FAR instructions

Machine language instructions that contain an address of a variable or a subroutine with a segment address and an offset address. They can address variables or subroutines located in another memory segment (farther away than 64K).

FAT

Abbreviation for **File Allocation Table**. This is a table located on every external storage medium (disk and hard disk). It informs DOS which areas of a storage medium are available, which areas are already occupied with data, and which areas are useless because of defects. The FAT also links together the different parts of a file.

FCB

Abbreviation for **File Control Block**. DOS controls file access to RAM using FCBs.

Fixed disk

Another term for *hard disk.*

Filter

A program that reads characters from the standard input device, manipulates them in some desired way, and then displays them on the standard output device.

Flag register

A 16-bit register in which several of these bits indicate certain aspects of the processor's status.

Function

A routine that can be called with a DOS or BIOS interrupt.

Garbage collection

A routine that removes variables which are no longer required from the variable memory of a BASIC program. Every BASIC interpreter has garbage collection.

GDT

Abbreviation for **Global Descriptor Table**. The GDT describes the individual memory segments when the processor is in protected mode.

General registers

The processors of the Intel-80xx family have the following general registers: AX, BX, CX, DX, DI, SI and BP. They are all 16 bits wide. The AX, BX, CX and DX registers can be separated into two 8-bit registers. These two half registers are designated as AH, AL, BH, BL, CH, CL, DH and DL.

Handle

A numerical value that acts as a key for access to files and devices. It is passed by DOS to a program which calls one of the functions for opening or creating a file or device.

Hard disk

A mass storage unit consisting of several magnetic media stacked on top of one another. Unlike disks, hard disks are divided into cylinders and sectors. Each of these disks can store data on both their top and bottom sides.

Hard disk format

The PC hard disk format consists of 17 sectors per cylinder and 512 bytes per sector. The number of disks and the number of cylinders per disk may vary.

Hardware interrupt

An interrupt or interrupt request, called by PC hardware, to attract the attention of the CPU to a device (e.g., the keyboard). Certain devices only call certain interrupts.

Hexadecimal system

A number system distantly related to the binary system. The basic numbering of this system goes from 0 to 15, instead of from 0 to 9 (the numbers 10 to 15 are represented by the letters A, B, C, D, E and F). The first position of a hexadecimal number has the value 1, the second 16, the third 256, the fourth 4,096, etc.

IN

Assembly language instruction to read data from a port into the CPU.

Internal commands

All commands whose code is stored in the transient portion of the command processor, and, therefore, don't have to be loaded from a storage medium (e.g., DIR, COPY and VER).

Interrupt

An interruption of a program through an interrupt call, the execution of an interrupt routine and, finally, the resumption of the interrupted program. The processors of the Intel-80xx family can process 256 different interrupts which are divided into hardware and software interrupts.

Interrupt controller

Monitors the various interrupt requests within the system and decides which interrupts to process first.

Interrupt routine

The program called during the appearance of an interrupt. Each interrupt has its own interrupt routine, whose address is stored in the interrupt vector table. The interrupt routine must be terminated with a machine language IRET instruction.

Interrupt vector table

A table containing the addresses of the interrupt routines, which are called when a particular interrupt appears. Each entry in this table consists of two words. The first word contains the offset address and the following word contains the segment address of the interrupt routine. The table starts at memory location 0000:0000, where the address of the interrupt routine for interrupt 0 is stored. The four following memory locations contain the address of the interrupt routine for interrupt 1, etc.

IRET

The Interrupt RETurn assembly language instruction. IRET terminates the execution of an interrupt routine and then continues the execution of the program at the location following the interruption of the program.

Keyboard status

Indicates whether the user has pressed the <Shift>, <Ctrl> or <Alt> keys, and whether the <Insert>, <CapsLock>, <NumLock> or <ScrollLock> modes are active.

Kilobyte

Abbreviated as **K**. Equals 2^{10} or 1,024 bytes.

Math coprocessor

Relieves the CPU of the processing of complicated floating-point mathematical formulas. It also accelerates the processing of worksheets within a spreadsheet program.

Megabyte

Often abbreviated as **meg**. Equal to 2^{10} kilobytes or 1,048,576 bytes.

Media descriptor byte

A byte within the File Allocation Table (FAT), which identifies the mass storage device's current format. DOS can manipulate the various formats of the mass storage which it supports and also checks the media descriptor byte for the current format.

Memory allocation

In all PCs the lower 640K is assigned to RAM. The video RAM follows, and then the ROM, which extends to the 1 megabyte memory limit. ATs may have up to 15 megabytes of additional RAM.

Microprocessor

The brain of a computer. Its main task is to execute assembly language instructions.

Model identification

The type of PC used, as coded into address F000:FFFE. FCH stands for AT, FEH often stands for XT and FFH often stands for PC.

MS-DOS

Abbreviation for **MicroSoft Disk Operating System**. MS-DOS is the primary PC operating system.

Multiprocessing

The simultaneous execution of several programs (not supported by DOS at the time of this writing).

NEAR instructions

Assembly language instructions that contain the offset address of only a variable or a subroutine (no segment address). These instructions can address variables or subroutines located only within the current 64K memory segment.

Nibble

Also spelled *nybble*. Bytes can be subdivided into two nibbles. The low nibble occupies bits 0 to 3 of a byte, while the high nibble occupies bits 4 to 7 of a byte.

NMI

Abbreviation for **Non-Maskable Interrupt.** The NMI remains constantly active. It is the only interrupt not affected by the CLI assembly language instruction.

OUT

An assembly language instruction which sends data to a port.

Overlay

A program loaded into memory allocated for it by another program. The calling program calls certain routines within this overlay as needed.

Paragraph

A group of 16 bytes in the 8088 which starts at a memory location divisible by 16 (e.g., 0, 16, 32, 48, etc.).

Parent program

A program that can execute another program (see *child program*) and continue its own processing after the child program's execution. For example, if a FORMAT command is called from DOS level, the command processor is the parent program.

Parity

A process used to detect errors during serial data transmission. Either even or odd parity can be used.

PC

Abbreviation for **Personal Computer** (i.e., all computers equipped with a 8088 or 8086 processor).

Peripheral interface

Connects the CPU to various peripheral devices (e.g., speaker).

Ports

The connections between the CPU and various other circuit chips within the system. Each chip has one or more assigned ports, which have a specific address. The CPU addresses the individual chips by writing values into the proper port or by reading values from the proper port.

Printer status byte

Describes the current status of the printer. It can indicate whether the printer is out of paper, is switched ONLINE or has not responded (time-out).

PRN

The device designation of the printer.

Program counter

Also called IP (Instruction Pointer). The program counter and the CS segment register combined form the memory address from which the processor will read the next command to be executed.

Protected mode

Allows multiprocessing, more than 1 megabyte of memory and control over virtual memory on computers possessing the 80286 and 80386 processors.

PSP

Abbreviation for **Program Segment Prefix**. The PSP is a 256 byte long data structure, which is placed in front of every program to be executed but not stored with the file on disk or hard disk. The program itself or program data start after this data structure.

RAM

Abbreviation for **Random Access Memory**. This is the memory that the user can read from and write to.

Raw mode

Character mode that transmits all characters from a device to the calling program without any changes (see *cooked mode*).

Real mode

Forces 80286 and 80386 processors to emulate dual high-speed 8088 processors incapable of multiprocessing or control of more than 1 megabyte of memory.

Register

Memory locations inside the processor that provide faster access than memory locations in RAM.

Reset

A resetting and reboot of the system. You can trigger a reset by pressing the <Alt><Ctrl><Delete> key combination.

Resident

Programs that remain in memory after execution without being overwritten by other programs or data. Resident programs can be recalled later.

ROM

Abbreviation for **Read Only Memory.** ROM can only be read, not written.

ROM BASIC

A small BASIC interpreter, placed in the ROMs of older PCs starting at address F000:6000. ROM BASIC is called by the system when BIOS fails to load the operating system.

RS-232

An interface that permits the computer to communicate with other devices over only one line. The individual data is transmitted serially (i.e., bit by bit).

RTC

Abbreviation for **RealTime Clock.** The battery backed clock on the AT.

Scan code

A code passed to the CPU by the keyboard processor when a key is pressed or released. It indicates the number assigned to the key within the keyboard. For this reason, the scan codes of the various PC keyboards differ from each other.

Sector

The smallest data division of a disk or hard disk. A sector contains 512 bytes.

Segment descriptor

Describes the location and size of the segment in addition to other information. It is used in protected mode on the 80286 and 80386 processors. All segment descriptors are gathered in the global descriptor table (GDT).

Segment register

The processors of the Intel-80xx family have four 16-bit segments that define the beginning of a 64K memory segment. They are named DS, ES, CS and SS.

Software interrupts

An interrupt or interrupt request called by a program using the INT instruction. Each of the 256 existing interrupts can be called using this instruction.

Standard input device

The keyboard. The standard input can be redirected to another device or a file using the < character.

Standard output device

The monitor screen. The standard output can be redirected to another device or a file using the > character.

STI

The **STart Interrupts** assembly language instruction. This instruction disables any previous CLI command and re-enables all inactive interrupts.

Time-out

Occurs during communication between the CPU and a device when the CPU sends data to the device and, after a certain amount of time, the device offers no response.

Timer

Similar to the clock. The timer generates a cyclical signal used to measure time.

TPA

Abbreviation for **Transient Program Area**. This is the part of RAM below the 1 megabyte limit not occupied by DOS that is used for storing programs and data.

UART

Abbreviation for **Universal Asynchronous Receiver Transmitter**. A chip that acts as the controller for the serial interface.

Video controller

Displays a picture on the screen by sending the proper signals to the monitor.

Video RAM

RAM, which is used for storing characters or graphics for display on the screen, made available by a video card. It can be addressed like normal RAM.

Virtual memory

Permits program access to memory, which it assumes to be RAM but is actually a mass storage device. Virtual memory must first be loaded into RAM for access.

Volume

Part of a mass storage device that has files, its own FAT, its own root directory and its own subdirectories. Each volume can have its own volume name. While disks can store only one volume under DOS, hard disks can be divided into several volumes to accommodate several operating systems.

Appendix I

Scan Codes

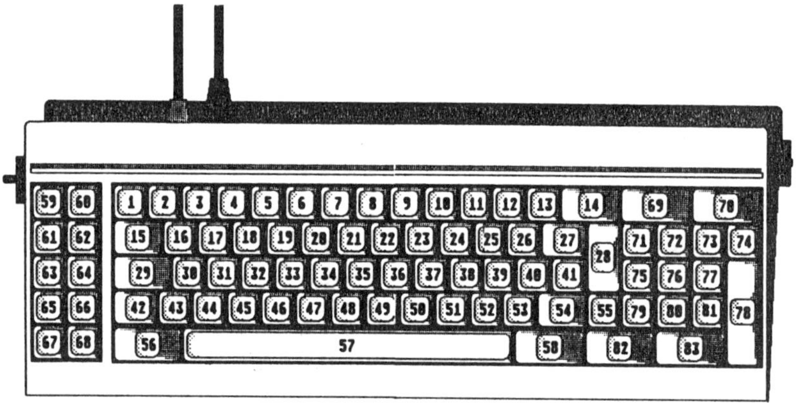

PC/XT keyboard scan codes

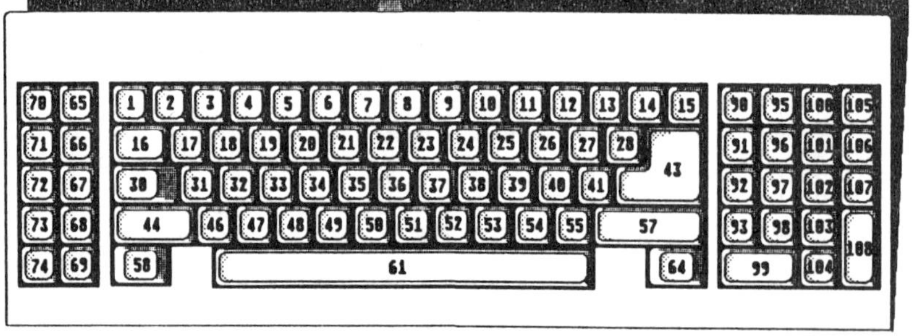

AT keyboard scan codes

Appendix J

ASCII Character Set

Dec.	Hex	Chr.	Dec.	Hex	Chr.	Dec.	Hex	Chr.	Dec.	Hex	Chr.
0	00		32	20		64	40	@	96	60	`
1	01	☺	33	21	!	65	41	A	97	61	a
2	02	●	34	22	"	66	42	B	98	62	b
3	03	♥	35	23	#	67	43	C	99	63	c
4	04	♦	36	24	$	68	44	D	100	64	d
5	05	♣	37	25	%	69	45	E	101	65	e
6	06	♠	38	26	&	70	46	F	102	66	f
7	07	•	39	27	'	71	47	G	103	67	g
8	08	◘	40	28	(	72	48	H	104	68	h
9	09	○	41	29	)	73	49	I	105	69	i
10	0A	◙	42	2A	*	74	4A	J	106	6A	j
11	0B	♂	43	2B	+	75	4B	K	107	6B	k
12	0C	♀	44	2C	,	76	4C	L	108	6C	l
13	0D	♪	45	2D	-	77	4D	M	109	6D	m
14	0E	♫	46	2E	.	78	4E	N	110	6E	n
15	0F	☼	47	2F	/	79	4F	O	111	6F	o
16	10	►	48	30	0	80	50	P	112	70	p
17	11	◄	49	31	1	81	51	Q	113	71	q
18	12	↕	50	32	2	82	52	R	114	72	r
19	13	‼	51	33	3	83	53	S	115	73	s
20	14	¶	52	34	4	84	54	T	116	74	t
21	15	§	53	35	5	85	55	U	117	75	u
22	16	▬	54	36	6	86	56	V	118	76	v
23	17	↨	55	37	7	87	57	W	119	77	w
24	18	↑	56	38	8	88	58	X	120	78	x
25	19	↓	57	39	9	89	59	Y	121	79	y
26	1A	→	58	3A	:	90	5A	Z	122	7A	z
27	1B	←	59	3B	;	91	5B	[	123	7B	{
28	1C	∟	60	3C	<	92	5C	\	124	7C	¦
29	1D	↔	61	3D	=	93	5D	]	125	7D	}
30	1E	▲	62	3E	>	94	5E	^	126	7E	~
31	1F	▼	63	3F	?	95	5F	_	127	7F	▓

Dec.	Hex	Chr.	Dec.	Hex	Chr.	Dec.	Hex	Chr.	Dec.	Hex	Chr.
128	80	Ç	160	A0	á	192	C0	└	224	E0	α
129	81	ü	161	A1	í	193	C1	┴	225	E1	ß
130	82	é	162	A2	ó	194	C2	┬	226	E2	Γ
131	83	â	163	A3	ú	195	C3	├	227	E3	π
132	84	ä	164	A4	ñ	196	C4	─	228	E4	Σ
133	85	à	165	A5	Ñ	197	C5	┼	229	E5	σ
134	86	å	166	A6	ª	198	C6	╞	230	E6	μ
135	87	ç	167	A7	º	199	C7	╟	231	E7	τ
136	88	ê	168	A8	¿	200	C8	╚	232	E8	Φ
137	89	ë	169	A9	⌐	201	C9	╔	233	E9	Θ
138	8A	è	170	AA	¬	202	CA	╩	234	EA	Ω
139	8B	ï	171	AB	½	203	CB	╦	235	EB	δ
140	8C	î	172	AC	¼	204	CC	╠	236	EC	∞
141	8D	ì	173	AD	¡	205	CD	═	237	ED	φ
142	8E	Ä	174	AE	«	206	CE	╬	238	EE	ε
143	8F	Å	175	AF	»	207	CF	╧	239	EF	∩
144	90	É	176	B0	░	208	D0	╨	240	F0	≡
145	91	æ	177	B1	▒	209	D1	╤	241	F1	±
146	92	Æ	178	B2	▓	210	D2	╥	242	F2	≥
147	93	ô	179	B3	│	211	D3	╙	243	F3	≤
148	94	ö	180	B4	┤	212	D4	╘	244	F4	⌠
149	95	ò	181	B5	╡	213	D5	╒	245	F5	⌡
150	96	û	182	B6	╢	214	D6	╓	246	F6	÷
151	97	ù	183	B7	╖	215	D7	╫	247	F7	≈
152	98	ÿ	184	B8	╕	216	D8	╪	248	F8	°
153	99	Ö	185	B9	╣	217	D9	┘	249	F9	•
154	9A	Ü	186	BA	║	218	DA	┌	250	FA	·
155	9B	¢	187	BB	╗	219	DB	█	251	FB	√
156	9C	£	188	BC	╝	220	DC	▄	252	FC	η
157	9D	¥	189	BD	╜	221	DD	▌	253	FD	^{2}
158	9E	₧	190	BE	╛	222	DE	▐	254	FE	■
159	9F	ƒ	191	BF	┐	223	DF	▀	255	FF	

Index

Abacus pc catalog

Order Toll Free 1-800-451-4319

5370 52nd Street SE • Grand Rapids, MI 49512
Phone: (616) 698-0330 • Fax: (616) 698-0325

Beginners Books for new PC Users

Beginners Series books remove the confusing jargon and get you up and running quickly with your PC.

COBOL for Beginners* - Teaches this popular language using MBP, MicroFocus and Microsoft COBOL. Includes quizzes, explanations and demonstrations.
ISBN 1-55755-070-0 $18.95
Canada: 53904 $22.95

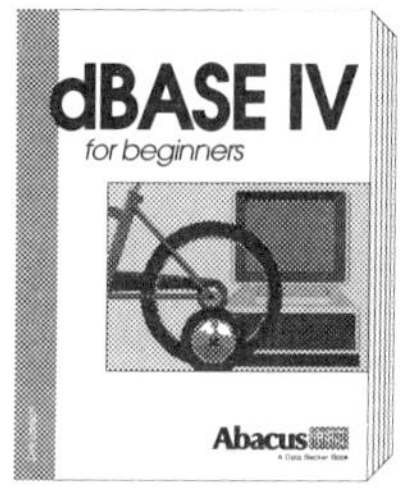

dBASE IV for Beginners - Simply and easily explains the fundamentals of dBASE. Learn to operate this package quickly and use its powerful commands and functions.
ISBN 1-55755-069-7 $18.95
Canada: 52066 $22.95

QuickBASIC for Beginners - Learn QuickBASIC quickly and easily. Begins by teaching you to write small and simple applications to simplify your everyday tasks.Complete descriptions of all QuickBASIC commands.
ISBN 1-55755-111-1. $18.95
Canada: $22.95

DOS 5.0 for Beginners - Gets the new user up and running quickly using Microsoft's latest DOS 5.0. You'll find clear explanations and plenty of "hands on" examples here. Describes the most important DOS commands clearly and understandably.
ISBN 1-55755-112-X. $18.95
Canada: $22.95

WordPerfect for Beginners - Contains all the important information about WordPerfect.Learn the essentials of WordPerfect's command set through practical examples - from writing a letter to composing longer documents.
ISBN 1-55755-117-0. $18.95
Canada: $22.95

*Companion Disk available for $14.95 each ($19.95 CDN)

To order direct call Toll Free 1-800-451-4319

In US and Canada add $5.00 shipping and handling. Foreign orders add $13.00 per item.
Michigan residents add 4% sales tax.

Windows System Programming

Learn to program Windows applications faster and easier.

Programming applications for Windows is said to be complex. This in-depth guide shows you how to speed up your Windows programming projects.

This bible for Windows programmers includes the tools you need to improve your programming techniques. Contains several sample applications with exhaustive documentation and background information, saving you time and effort in developing your own applications. Numerous programming examples in the popular C language lead you step-by-step through the creation process.

Topics include:

- Introduction to the Windows programming
- Using GDI for graphic and text output
- Bitmaps and the color palette manager
- Managing both static and dynamic dialog boxes
- The MDI (Multiple Document Interface)
- Data exchange between applications using DDE
- Parallel and serial interface access
- Windows memory management
- Fine tuning Windows applications
- The DLL (Dynamic Link Libraries) concept

Includes a companion diskette containing both source codes and EXE files of sample applications. The source codes can be compiled using Microsoft C Version 5.1 and higher (not included with this package) and the Microsoft Software Development Kit (SDK - not included with this package).

Windows System Programming.
Authors: Peter Wilken, Dirk Honekamp
Item #B116. ISBN 1-55755-116-2.
Suggested retail price $39.95 with companion disk. Available August.

To order direct call Toll Free 1-800-451-4319

In US and Canada add $5.00 shipping and handling. Foreign orders add $13.00 per item.
Michigan residents add 4% sales tax.

QuickBASIC Toolbox
is for all QuickBASIC programmers who want professional results with minimum effort. It's packed with powerful, ready-to-use programs and routines you can use in your own programs to get professional results quickly.

Some of the topics include:

- Complete routines for SAA, interfacing mouse support, pull-down menus, windows, dialog boxes and file requestors.
- Descriptions of QuickBASIC routines.
- A BASIC Scanner program for printing completed project listings and more.

This book/disk combination will teach you how to write even better QuickBASIC code.
330 page book with companion disk.
ISBN 1-55755-104-9 $34.95
Canada: 57911 $45.95

Assembly Language Step by Step
For lightning execution speed, no computer language beats assembly language. This book teaches you PC assembly and machine language the right way - one step at a time. The companion diskette contains a unique simulator which shows you how each instruction functions as the PC executes it. Includes companion diskette containing assembly language simulator.
ISBN 1-55755-096-4. $34.95
Canada: 53927 $45.95

To order direct call Toll Free 1-800-451-4319

In US and Canada add $5.00 shipping and handling. Foreign orders add $13.00 per item.
Michigan residents add 4% sales tax.

PC Assembly Language Step by Step

For lightning execution speed, no computer language beats assembly language. This book teaches you PC assembly and machine language the right way - one step at a time. The companion diskette contains a unique simulator which shows you how each instruction looks as the PC executes it. Includes companion diskette containing assembly language simulator.

ISBN 1-55755-096-4. $34.95

Canada: 53927 $45.95

Upgrading & Maintaining your PC

Your PC represents a major investment. This book shows you how to turn your PC into a high performance computing machine. It describes what you'll see when you open the "hood" and how all of the parts work together. Whether you want to add a hard drive, increase your memory, upgrade to a higher resolution monitor, or turn your XT into a fast AT or 386 screamer, you'll see how to do it easily and economically, without having to be an electronics wizard.

ISBN 1-55755-092-1. $24.95

Canada: 53926 $33.95

New BeckerTools 2.0 for Windows:
Indispensable utilities for every Windows user

If you're a Windows user you'll appreciate **BeckerTools Version 2** for Windows. **BeckerTools** will dramatically speed-up your file and data management chores and increase your productivity. Where Windows' File Manager functions end, **BeckerTools** features begin by giving you powerful, yet flexible features you need to get the job done quickly. **BeckerTools** has the same consistent user interface found in Windows so there's no need to learn 'foreign' commands or functions. Manipulating your disks and files are as easy as pointing and shooting with the mouse. You'll breeze through flexible file and data functions and features that are friendly enough for a PC novice yet powerful enough for the advanced user. You won't find yourself 'dropping out' of Windows to perform powerful and essential DOS functions like undeleting a file or waiting for a diskette to be formatted. **BeckerTools** has the enhanced applications available with the click of a mouse button. Item #S110 ISBN 1-55755-110-3. With 3 1/2" and 5 1/4" diskettes. Suggested retail price $129.95.

BeckerTools Version 2 is as easy as pointing and shooting with the mouse. **BeckerTools** takes advantage of Windows' multitasking capabilities and **BeckerTools** keeps you informed of it's progress as it works.

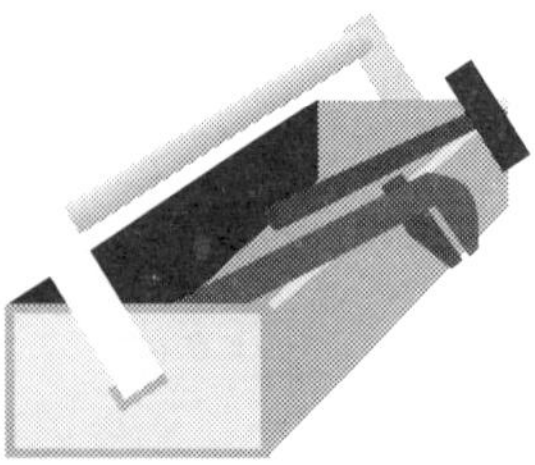

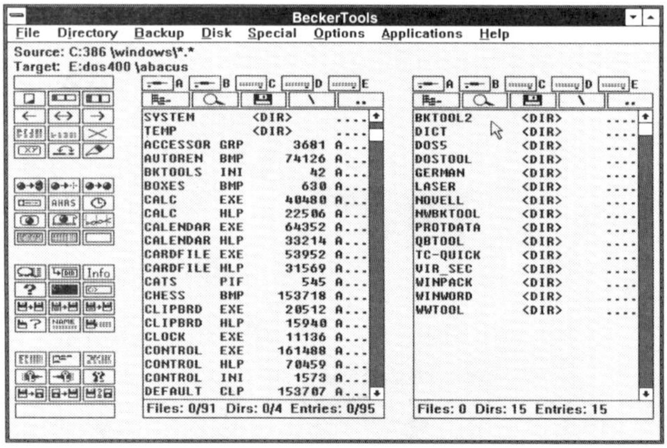

Here are some of the things that <u>you can easily do</u> with **BeckerTools Version 2:**

- Launch applications - directly from **BeckerTools**
- Associate files - logically connects applications with their file types
- Backup (pack files) hard disk - saves 50% to 80% disk space - with password protection
- User levels - 3 levels for beginning, intermediate and advanced users
- Undelete - recover deleted files
- Undelete directories - recover directories in addition to individual files
- Delete files - single, groups of files or directories, including read-only files
- Duplicate diskettes - read diskette once, make multiple copies
- Edit text - built-in editor with search and replace
- Format diskettes - in any capacity supported by your drive and disk type
- Compare diskettes - in single pass
- Wipe diskette - for maximum security
- Screen blanker - prevent CRT "burnout"
- File grouping - perform operations on files as a group
- Create a bootable system diskette
- Reliability checking - check for physical errors on disk media
- Edit files - new hex editor to edit virtually and type of file
- Dozens of other indispensable features

To order direct call Toll Free 1-800-451-4319

In US and Canada add $4.00 shipping and handling. Foreign orders add $12.00 per item.
Michigan residents add 4% sales tax.